THE
Concert Companion

A COMPREHENSIVE GUIDE
TO SYMPHONIC MUSIC

by

Robert Bagar and Louis Biancolli

with an introduction by DEEMS TAYLOR

Whittlesey House

McGRAW-HILL BOOK COMPANY, INC.

New York : London

THE CONCERT COMPANION

Copyright, 1947, by The Philharmonic-Symphony Society of New York

PUBLISHED BY WHITTLESEY HOUSE
A DIVISION OF THE MCGRAW-HILL BOOK COMPANY, INC.

PRINTED IN THE UNITED STATES OF AMERICA BY
KINGSPORT PRESS, INC., KINGSPORT, TENNESSEE

INTRODUCTION

by DEEMS TAYLOR

THERE ARE other books of program notes, of course; but most of them present difficulties for the average reader. Some run to many volumes and are so erudite that they are likely to be heavy going for the nonprofessional; others cover only a limited field; still others stick to cold facts with no trimmings; and too many are written in such a high rhapsodic vein that the music they describe comes rather as an anticlimax. This book manages to avoid all these pitfalls.

Its origin might interest you. Early in 1941 Pitts Sanborn died. He had been, among other things, the program annotator for the concerts of the New York Philharmonic-Symphony Orchestra, and his sudden passing made it imperative to find a successor who would write the notes for the remaining concerts of the 1940-1941 season. The Philharmonic-Symphony's board of directors found, not one, but two. They were the young and comparatively unknown music critics of the *New York World-Telegram*. They took over Sanborn's job so effectively that they are now not quite so young and are definitely far from unknown. This book is a compendium of what they wrote over a period of a little less than seven years.

I know of no similar book that covers such a wide and catholic field. The oldest composer discussed is Tomás Luis De Victoria, who would be celebrating his four hundred and seventh birthday if he were alive. The youngest, Lukas Foss, is three hundred and eighty-two years his junior.

For the book's extraordinary range the authors undoubtedly have to thank the Philharmonic-Symphony's fondness for guest-conductors. The guest-conductor makes for a varied repertoire. The one-man orchestra, unless its conductor has a high degree of curiosity and tolerance, tends to find itself, season after season, playing programs made up of the maestro's favorites, plus a few cautious novelties that are played once and then dropped. On the other hand, the orchestra that goes in for guest-conductors—and the Philharmonic-Symphony has had its ample share—lives in a state of excited polyandry, with each newcomer bringing *his* favorites and introducing *his* pet novelties.

Thus in addition to the acknowledged masters, the three B's and the like, you find here many names that seldom appear on symphony programs—Benjamin, Fernandez, Khrennikoff, Pfitzner, Revueltas, to name a few. Also, you will find works discussed which, while seldom played—Mahler's Ninth for instance—have a definite historical significance. If Shakespeare survives, he owes some of his permanence to Marlowe and Jonson.

The unique feature of this book is its hospitality to American composers. Of the one hundred and sixty-three composers listed, forty-three are Americans. Here again are many names that are undeniably important but which, for one reason or another, are seldom found in existing reference books.

The Concert Companion has more than quantity to recommend it. The thematic analyses are sound, simple enough to be intelligible to the layman, and blessedly brief. If there must be thematic analyses—and some flagellant souls demand them—the Bagar-Biancolli brand is the least soporific. Happily, the authors give more space to biographical material and anecdota, which I think is an excellent idea. As a reader of program notes I derive more pleasure from learning that So-and-So composed his third symphony while under the influence of hashish than from being told that the first theme is announced by two tubas and a viola d'amore; and while you will search in vain, through the pages that follow, for that particular titbit, you will, I can promise you, find many others equally arresting and possibly more accurate.

CONTENTS

vii

PREFACE

The Concert Companion is offered as a combined guide and reader in the hope that concert-goers of widely differing tastes will find what they need in a comprehensive survey of over one hundred and sixty composers and their music.

For the music lover interested solely in technique and form, brief analyses of old and new scores have in most cases been provided. Where the authors felt that instrumentation would help, that too has been included. In those instances where technical analysis has been furnished, relevant facts about scores have been stressed and an attempt has been made to describe and locate themes in a clear and helpful way. The only musical training prescribed here is careful listening. The average ear and memory will accomplish more than any amount of detailed analysis.

The Concert Companion also attempts to present the man behind the music. As a general rule, the setting of the birth of each masterpiece is given; a frame has been put around the music. Stories surrounding a classic have been told to evoke the distant day and scene of composition. Details of drama or tragedy have been so narrated as to suggest possible parallels in the music.

Thus, in preparing these background vignettes, the authors have purposely used material designed to sharpen interest in the composer and his music. Any anecdote of human appeal, they felt, would make the music friendlier by bringing its composer closer to the listener. Several years of service as the annotators of the New York Philharmonic-Symphony Society have convinced the authors of the widespread interest in the personal drama behind the music, the revealing glimpse of a composer at work, some intimate story of pain and struggle mysteriously enshrined in the symphony or concerto, a hint, perhaps, of the romantic circumstances out of which some great love music grew. For the Bachs, the Beethovens, and the Brahmses were human—all too human, indeed—and their music is there as a testament of their moods of despair and their moments of exaltation.

The authors believe that readers will find *The Concert Companion* a quick and handy source of information for radio and phonograph listening as well. Composers are presented in alphabetical order, each introduced by a quotation reflecting some striking aspect of his music or personality. Only essential facts

of date and place of birth and death are given under each name. It was felt that
the biographical and historical details woven into each "program note" would
suffice. Compositions have been grouped in orderly sequence according to their
form—symphony, concerto, overture, suite, and so forth. In general, analyses
and instrumentation, where given, are reserved for the end of the note. A few
technical analyses used in this volume were the work of our predecessor, the
late Pitts Sanborn. The authors, both of whom were Mr. Sanborn's associates
on the music staff of the *New York World-Telegram,* often assisted him in the
preparation of much of this material. These particular analyses have been
differentiated from the others by appearing within quotation marks.

While "comprehensive," the volume necessarily omits many compositions
that occasionally occur on concert programs. No effort has been made—or could
be made—to cover the whole field in one volume. For one reason or another,
several worth-while "classics" were regretfully denied admittance; and of the
living composers, especially the Americans, it is fervently hoped that the
omission of some names will not be misunderstood. We have tried to make the
list as representative as possible. That it is far from exhaustive we are the first
to admit. We are even prepared to venture that several names now omitted
will become far more significant and more widely publicized in years to come.

This problem of selection was one of the most difficult to solve categorically.
The authors obviously could not restrict themselves to the Philharmonic-
Symphony repertory of the last seven years. Many eligible works would thus
have been ignored. Accordingly several gaps were filled to make the selection
as "standard" as possible. A few compositions like Liszt's *Les Préludes* and
Grieg's *Peer Gynt* music, which are no longer conspicuous in the subscription
seasons of the major American orchestras, were included because of their
abiding popularity with a large mass of music lovers.

As a rule, selection has been based on the frequency of performance by our
leading orchestras and in the growing repertories of radio and records. In many
instances, however, works have been included because of their significance in
modern trends and what is regarded in professional circles as their assured
future. Here again there is a wide margin for prophetic error. The history of
music provides warning enough that he is indeed a bold prophet who would
dare predict the fate of any new composition ten years hence. Given the scope
of this volume, the authors have sought to allot special emphasis to modern
scores—foreign as well as American. This emphasis, however, has entailed no
sacrifice to the "standard" repertory. Whatever his favorite symphony, or overture, or concerto, it is earnestly hoped that the reader will find it in these pages.

Another difficulty encountered by the authors in assembling this material was the risk of duplication. That is, in a few cases pretty much the same background material might be used for two or more works by the same composer. An instance is the twin inspiration of Berlioz' *Fantastic* and *Romeo and Juliet* symphonies. Another is the similar background of Chopin's two piano concertos. The writers circumvented this risk by dividing the assignment and approaching the individual scores from slightly different angles. However, in the overwhelming majority of "program notes" the material is as independent as the particular context allows. It is suggested that in consulting the book for a specific composition, notes about other music preceding and following it in date of writing might be referred to for additional information about the personal background.

No music book of this kind could be complete without the expression of a deep-felt sense of gratitude to several American annotators who early raised the program note to the level of a new literary genre. High among these one unhesitatingly places William Foster Apthorp and Philip Hale, both of the Boston Symphony Orchestra. To them, and to their scholarly successor John N. Burk, to Felix Borowski of the Chicago Symphony Orchestra as well as to our immediate predecessors of the Philharmonic-Symphony, the late Lawrence Gilman and Pitts Sanborn, the authors owe not only many analytical clues, but also several quoted fragments of judgment and translation. A special word of thanks must go to Arthur Judson and Bruno Zirato, managers of the Philharmonic-Symphony Society, for their constant support and cooperation; and to them and to the entire Board of Directors for the privilege of using this material in book form.

ROBERT BAGAR and LOUIS BIANCOLLI

Isaac Albéniz

BORN: CAMPRODÓN, CATALONIA, SPAIN, MAY 29, 1860. DIED: CAMBO-LES-BAINS, BASSES-PYRÉNÉES, FRANCE, MAY 18, 1909.

His lofty and extraordinary intuition might be compared to a wine skin, holding a fragrant vintage, gilded by a Mediterranean sun. From it Albéniz filled his goblet until it brimmed; he handled it with the generosity of a wasteful child, and one was overcome and intoxicated by this fullness and fragrance and light.—FELIPE PEDRELL.

"Fête-Dieu à Séville" from the Suite *Iberia*

[*Transcribed for orchestra by E. Fernandez Arbós*]

A PROLIFIC WRITER of piano music, Albéniz composed in Paris (between 1893 and the year of his death) the Suite *Iberia,* which consists of twelve pieces, each depicting some place or scene in Spain. These, as Professor J. B. Trend says in an essay written for Grove's *Dictionary of Music and Musicians,* are "inspired by the rhythms, harmonies, and turns of phrase for Spanish popular music; particularly the songs and dances of Andalusia."

Blanche Selva first performed the Suite at a Paris recital and soon other pianists, including Joaquin Malats and the composer himself, helped the cause along. Nowadays few are the pianists—from under to postgraduate—who are not intimately acquainted with this music, as well as other keyboard compositions of Albéniz.

It was Albéniz's friend and colleague E. Fernandez Arbós who exhorted the composer to orchestrate the Suite. Pursuing the suggestion with a kind of waning enthusiasm, Albéniz finally gave up the task, after obtaining poor results with the first two sections "Evocation" and "El Puerto," and, rather imperiously, he imposed it on Arbós. Whereupon the latter began at the beginning with "Evocation," transcribing six numbers of the Suite.

H. R. Burke, program annotator for the St. Louis Symphony, has said of the Suite *Iberia* that it is "a gallery of paintings in tone. Not 'illustrations.' Not 'sketches.' Not 'impressions.' They tell no story. They are no surface outlines. They are not sensory evocations of the moment. . . . With the spirit of Spain they are interpenetrant."

Debussy held that *Iberia* represented Albéniz's best, and Dukas characterized the Spaniard as a "landscape painter with a rich palette, as generous with his colors as with his money, the sort, who for fear five cents on a letter was not enough would put ten."

As the French title "Fête-Dieu à Séville" indicates, the music is concerned with the observance of the festival of *Corpus Christi,* a feast of the Catholic Church, which occurs on the Thursday following Trinity Sunday, in Seville (and, undoubtedly, other Andalusian places). An ecclesiastical procession is headed by a priest carrying aloft, under a shading, richly brocaded canopy, the Host, or Blessed Sacrament. Bearers of incense and banners and lights attend the Host, while worshippers throng the line of march in the streets and others crowd the overlying balconies. Flowers in profusion are strewn before the procession and, as its progress is halted now and then, a *saeta* is improvised by the spectators. This spontaeous and unaccompanied song is hurled back and forth by the votaries, and sometimes it reaches great emotional heights. The music of "Fête-Dieu à Séville" begins with a marchlike melody, which is shot through with brusque accents. The sound rises, and presently the saeta enters and runs against a counterpoint of the march theme. The march subsides to a low rumble, the saeta takes the initiative, modulating from key to key with, every so often, a break in its course. Saeta and march take turns with the lead and suddenly the saeta bursts through fortissimo, as the march, hurried into a dance-like tempo, finally ends on a crash. Now the saeta is heard again, very serene, and then gently it fades away, bringing the piece to its conclusion.

R. C. B.

Anton Stepanovich Arensky

BORN: NOVGOROD, RUSSIA, AUG. 11, 1861. DIED: TERIJOKI, FINLAND, FEB. 25, 1906.

By the nature of his talent and his tastes as composer he was the closest approximation to Anton Rubinstein. . . . In his youth Arensky had not entirely escaped my own influence, later he fell under Tschaikowsky's.—RIMSKY-KORSAKOFF.

"Variations on a Theme by Tschaikowsky" (for String Orchestra), Op. 35 A

WHEN TSCHAIKOWSKY died, several Russian composers—associates and former pupils—wrote commemorative pieces. Anton Arensky, who early came under Tschaikowsky's influence, incorporated his tribute in a string quartet. Among Tschaikowsky's lyric works were *Sixteen Children's Songs,* with piano accompaniment, grouped as Op. 54. From them Arensky chose the fifth, a "Legend" about the Infant Christ, using it as theme for a set of seven variations, dedicated "to the memory of Peter Ilyitch Tschaikowsky." In the final variation the melody, seemingly a new theme, appears in reverse. Arensky is supposed to have alluded here to the practice of holding guns upside down at military funerals. After the theme is announced, moderato, by the first violins, to pizzicato support, the seven variations and coda follow:

Variation I: (Un poco più mosso) the theme goes from minor to major, and back to minor.

Variation II: (Allegro non troppo), violas and cellos take up the theme against repeated sixths, mostly in the high violins.

Variation III: (Andantino tranquillo) the melody is given out serenely in the major.

Variation IV: (Vivace) bristles with telling pizzicato effects.

Variation V: (Andante) while cellos and basses discourse the theme, violas and violins chant a different melodic pattern. Later the roles are reversed.

Variation VI: (Allegro con spirito) arpeggios and tremolos almost conceal the theme in places.

Variation VII: (Andante con moto) the first violins reverse the melody. Apart from the basses, largely heard in pizzicato, all strings are muted. The coda reverts to the moderato marking of the opening.

Rimsky-Korsakoff and others give sharp pen portraits of Arensky as gambler, drunkard, and roué, who dissipated himself into consumption and an early death. Riesemann adds that he was lazy, hot-tempered, and abusive. His pupil Scriabin hated him cordially.

"Drinking bouts—card playing—galloping consumption—a period of dying in Nice—and then death in Finland," runs Rimsky-Korsakoff's terse obituary of a former pupil.

L. B.

Carl Philipp Emanuel Bach

BORN: WEIMAR, MAR. 8, 1714. DIED: HAMBURG, DEC. 15, 1788.

Hamburg is not at present possessed of any musical professor of great eminence except M. Carl Philipp Emanuel Bach; but he is a legion!—
Dr. Charles Burney, 1773.

Concerto for Stringed Instruments in D major

[*Transcribed for orchestra by Maximilian Steinberg*]

I. Allegro moderato. II. Andante lento molto. III. Allegro.

WHILE IN Paris in the early twenties Serge Koussevitzky heard C. P. E. Bach's D major Concerto at a concert of the Society of Ancient Instruments. The instruments being used were a violon, a quinton, a viol d'amour, a viola da gamba, and a bass viol. Mr. Koussevitzky resolved then and there to make an orchestral arrangement of this music himself, but later he changed his mind and delegated the job to Maximilian Steinberg. The latter scored it for flute, two oboes, bassoon, horn, and strings. Mr. Koussevitzky first led the work in America at a Boston Symphony Orchestra concert in Boston on Oct. 24, 1924.

Carl Philipp Emanuel Bach—variously known as the "Berlin Bach" and "Hamburg Bach," was Johann Sebastian Bach's third son. With the idea of becoming a lawyer he first studied philosophy at the Thomas Schule in Leipzig, later attending the Leipzig and Frankfort-on-the-Oder universities. However, he soon established a reputation as composer and clavecin player. In Frankfort he founded and directed a chorus, and when he moved on to Berlin in 1738 Frederick the Great engaged him as court clavecinist. Frederick was an expert flute player, and one of young Bach's duties was accompanying him whenever the imperial mood prompted. In 1767 he replaced Telemann as music director of a Hamburg church, remaining there to his death. Probably the greatest compliment ever paid Johann Sebastian's gifted son was that of the Danish poet Gerstenberg, who, writing from Copenhagen in 1767, called him *"Ein Raffael durch Töne"* which may be freely rendered as "A Raphael of music."

The D major concerto for chamber ensemble was probably written during Bach's Hamburg period. It was while there in 1772 that Dr. Charles Burney, the English music chronicler, paid him a visit, recording his impressions in "The Present State of Music in Germany, the Netherlands and United Provinces," published the following year in London. Dr. Burney writes:

When I went to his house, I found with him three or four rational and well-bred persons, his friends, besides his own family, consisting of Mrs. Bach, his eldest son, who practices the law, and his daughter. The instant I entered he conducted me upstairs into a large and elegant music room furnished with pictures, drawings and prints of more than 150 eminent musicians, among them many Englishmen, and original portraits in oil of his father and grandfather.

After I had looked at these, M. Bach was so obliging as to sit down at his Silbermann clavichord . . . upon which he played three or four of his choicest and most difficult compositions with the delicacy, precision, and spirit for which he is so justly celebrated among his countrymen. In the pathetic and slow movements, whenever he had a long note to express, he absolutely contrived to produce from his instrument a cry of sorrow and complaint such as can only be effected upon the clavichord and perhaps by himself.

After dinner, which was elegantly served and cheerfully eaten, I prevailed upon him to sit down again at the clavichord, and he played with little intermission till nearly 11 o'clock at night. During this time he grew so animated and possessed that he not only played but looked like one inspired. His eyes were fixed, his underlip fell, and drops of effervescence [!] distilled from his countenance. He said, if he were to be set to work frequently in this manner, he should grow young again. He is now fifty-nine, rather short in stature, with black hair and eyes, and brown complexion, has a very animated countenance, and he is of a cheerful and lively disposition.

Dr. Burney went on to describe C. P. E. Bach as "one of the greatest composers who ever existed" and was apparently so bowled over by his host's erudition that he risked subsequent ridicule by affirming, "he is learned even beyond his father." Still, he modified the assertion with the words, "I think."

The staggering catalogue of C. P. E. Bach's works includes some 210 separate clavecin solos, 52 concertos with orchestral accompaniment, 47 trios of all kinds, 18 symphonies, 12 clavecin sonatas (accompanied), 19 other solo pieces, 3 clavecin quartets, a *Magnificat,* 22 sets of music for the "Passion," 3 oratorios, and at least 100 different songs and choruses, besides other church music. He also left a valuable record of contemporary playing in a *Versuch über die wahre Art das Clavier zu spielen* (*A Test of the True Way to Play the Clavier*), published 1753-1762.

The statement, "It appears to me that it is the special province of music to move the heart," has been given by biographers as C. P. E. Bach's oft expressed artistic credo.

L. B.

Johann Sebastian Bach

BORN: EISENACH, MAR. 21, 1685. DIED: LEIPZIG, JULY 28, 1750.

Music owes almost as much to Bach as Christianity does to its founder.
—SCHUMANN.

"Passacaglia in C minor"

[*Transcribed for orchestra by Ottorino Respighi*]

BY A COINCIDENCE not altogether surprising in the case of Bach, two orchestral versions of the great *Passacaglia* were premiered in America during the early months of 1930. At about the time that Arturo Toscanini requested Ottorino Respighi to make a transcription of the organ classic for a Philharmonic-Symphony concert, the late Frederick Stock embarked on one of his own for the Chicago Symphony Orchestra, dedicating it to Horace S. Oakley, vice-president of the Orchestral Association, who had died at sea on Dec. 15, 1929. The Chicago version was played on Jan. 3, 1930, the Philharmonic on Apr. 16. Among other transcribers of the *Passacaglia* have been Heinrich Esser, Alexander F. Goedicke, and Leopold Stokowski.

Respighi had no intention of making the orchestra sound like an organ in his rendering. Guardedly, he called his version an *interpretazione orchestrale*. Employed in the "interpretation" are three flutes, piccolo, three oboes, English horn, three clarinets, bass clarinet, three bassoons, double bassoon, six horns, four trumpets, three trombones, bass tuba, tympani, organ pedal, and strings.

In Respighi's transcription Bach's eight-bar theme—borrowed in part from a *Trio en Passacaille* by the eighteenth-century André Raison—is announced forte by bassoons, double bassoon, trombones, tuba, organ, cellos and string basses. (Stock, in his version, announces the theme in the cellos and double basses alone. In the Bach organ original the stately theme is given out by the pedals). The twenty variations then follow, Respighi assigning the first to the strings. The set reaches its peak in a brilliant orchestral tutti. There is a pause. Then the double fugue sets in, built on the first part of the passacaglia theme, plus a countertheme in eighth notes.

Though one of the great organ classics, the *C minor Passacaglia* was not originally written for that instrument. Curiously enough, Bach first composed it for the double-manual harpsichord, later rewriting it for organ, probably while at Weimar. Albert Schweitzer, the staunch Bach paladin and scholar, rightly observed of the *Passacaglia*: "Its polyphonic structure is so thoroughly suited to the organ that we can hardly understand nowadays how anyone could

7

have ventured to play it on a stringed instrument." Someone might retort th:
of course Bach was not just "anyone," but a law unto himself.

The fact that the theme is announced and retained solely in the basses
supposed to distinguish the passacaglia form from that of the chaconne, closel
allied to it in origin. In the latter the theme, while proclaimed in the basse.
may move upward in the variations. Bach, however, started a mild but linger
ing controversy among lexicographers by allowing the theme to slip away twic
from its moorings in the basses. Sticklers for definition still insist the *Passacagli*
should be termed the *C minor Chaconne!* Both the passacaglia and chaconn
(or ciacona) were old Spanish or Italian dances in triple time. While there i
no certainty, the passacaglia was probably originally Spanish, since the word
derives from *pasacalle*. Pronounced in Castillian, it sounds almost the same a
the Italian variant. The Spanish term, meaning "pass along the street," i
applied to the ancient dance as well as to a variety of music played on guitar
and other instruments in the streets. The French equivalent *passe-rue* means :
street song.

The noblest symphonic use of the classic passacaglia form is the finale o
Brahms's Fourth Symphony, which, again, is founded on a majestic eight-ba
theme in triple time.

L. B.

"Chaconne"

[*Transcribed for orchestra by A. Walter Kramer*]

ONE OF the most transcribed compositions of the most transcribed composer in
history, the Bach *Chaconne* is derived from the unaccompanied D minor
Partita (or suite or sonata), of which it is the last movement. It is regarded as
the classic of classics in the violin-recital repertory, and through transcriptions
—many critics consider Ferrucio Busoni's the best—has won an almost equal
status in the solo-piano repertory. Transcriptions for other instruments, including some for guitar and accordion, are on record, and Joachim Raff, Alfredo
Casella, and A. Walter Kramer are only three of a legion of arrangers for
orchestra.

Mr. Kramer's version is scored for woodwinds in pairs, four horns, two
trumpets, trombone, tuba, tympani, harp, and strings. It has been performed
by the Cincinnati Symphony, the Minneapolis Symphony, the Cleveland Orchestra, the Seattle Symphony, the New York Orchestra, and the Musicians
Symphony Orchestra.

"A triumph of spirit over matter" is the way Philipp Spitta sums up the Bach
Chaconne. "The spirit of the master urges the instrument to incredible utterance," declares Bach's great biographer. "At the end of the major section it
sounds like an organ, and sometimes a whole band of violins might seem to be

playing." To the French Bach scholar, Albert Schweitzer, the piece "conjures up a whole world—we seem to hear sorrow contending with pain, till at last they blend in a mood of profound resignation." Schweitzer calls attention to the way the *Chaconne* intersperses monophonic writing amid the rich fabric, "so as to give the hearer relief and to heighten the effect of the polyphony."

Yet, despite its noble style, melodic invention, supreme balance, and richness of expression—even because of these qualities,—musicians like Casella have complained that except in the hands of great violin virtuosi, performance of the *Chaconne* "always leaves a sense of unfulfilment sometimes even painful." In the preface to his own rendering, the modern Italian composer points to the "disproportion between the natural resources of the violin, limited by its four strings, and the amplitude of the piece in sonority, polyphony, and orchestral implications."

In differentiating the chaconne and passacaglia forms, Schweitzer emphasizes that the latter is "in reality a chaconne," both being old dance forms (the chaconne of assumed Andalusian origin) "connected by the fact that they are developed out of a recurring theme of eight bars in 3/4 time. In the chaconne the theme may appear in all the parts; in the passacaglia it is confined to the bass."

The chaconne was one of the dance forms employed in the ballet music woven into eighteenth-century opera scores, others being the gavotte, minuet, bourrée, and gigue. According to a variously reported story, the so-called "god of the dance," Gaetan Vestris, complained at rehearsal one day that Gluck had omitted a chaconne from the opera *Iphigénie en Aulide*—an unheard-of liberty! Vestris' son, Auguste, was to dance in the Paris production. "Chaconne!" Gluck is supposed to have shrieked: "When did the Greeks ever dance a chaconne?"

Vestris countered: "Didn't they? Well, so much the worse for the Greeks! You must write a chaconne! Don't forget, I am the god of the dance!" "Then go and dance in heaven!" Gluck fired back. Marie Antoinette is said to have interceded and patched things up between the irate dancer and rebel composer. (P.S. Vestris got his chaconne.)

We owe the oldest autograph of Bach's six extended works for solo violin, of which the D minor Partita is one, to Pölchau, an early nineteenth-century music manuscript hunter who equaled the famous Renaissance collector and scholar Poggio Bracciolini in rummaging ardor. The manuscript, dating from the 1720's, bears Pölchau's scrawled remark: "I found this excellent work, in Bach's own handwriting, in Petersburg in 1814, among a lot of old papers, destined for the butter shop, that had belonged to Palschau, the pianist."

Pölchau, whose collected "finds" later went into the safe-deposit vaults of the Berlin Royal Library, was wrong about the handwriting. It was not Bach's, but that of his second wife, Anna Magdalena, who besides bearing the Leipzig master thirteen children, managing house, taking care of four other children by his first wife, and imbibing daily musical instruction from him, loyally copied out many of his works. The six "sonatas"—three of them are usually labeled "partitas" or "suites"—were first written out in Cöthen, where they were composed in the service of Prince Leopold. Anna Magdalena made a second copy in the early 1730's during her husband's Leipzig period, binding them into one volume with an equal number of "sonatas" for solo violoncello. In the first part of the title—a curious mélange of Latin, Italian, and French—the diligent lady states, *"composée par Sr. J. S. Bach,"* appending, with becoming pride, the words, *"écrite par Madame Bach. Son épouse."*

Simrock of Bonn first printed the violin sonatas in 1802. Robert Schumann's edition for Breitkopf and Härtel, brought out in 1854, included a piano accompaniment, Mendelssohn having already provided the chaconne of the second Partita with similar support in 1847. The three Partitas in the group are largely sequences of dance forms and alternate with the "sonatas" proper, the usual pattern of which is a slow movement followed by a fugue, then an andante or siciliano, capped by a fleet and sprightly finale.

Considered from any point of view—musical, technical, esthetic—the six works in question have long been a boon to violinists and a source of wonder to the student of balance, breadth, and proportion in music. The finest wielders of the bow admit indebtedness to them not only as a key to broader artistic vistas and imaginative depth, but in grasp of form and design. To the fiddler willing to meet Bach in technical combat they also serve to strengthen and add independence to the fingers of the left hand and broaden the bowing. In the words of Jeffrey Pulver, writing in *The Strad,* "the violinist can do without them only to his detriment." Purely violinistic passages abound in these works, though the influence of the organ, Bach's mightiest instrumental medium, is strong, and at times there is, in the words of Albert Schweitzer, "some justification for the question whether Bach . . . has not overstepped the bounds of artistic possibility."

The organ and clavier tend to overshadow the violin in the solo hierarchy of Bach. Yet, as in all other fields, Bach was superbly equipped for a full evaluation of the violin's resources. It had been his first instrument. The very first music he heard probably came from his father's violin. He served with true professional status as master violinist in the ducal orchestra at Weimar, rising to the post of Konzertmeister in 1714. As to whether Bach was a great violinist and what his style was like, there is no way of determining apart from the written record of a supreme thoroughness in all things.

L. B.

Prelude and Fugue in B minor for Organ

[Transcribed for orchestra by Dimitri Mitropoulos]

LONG REGARDED as the last of Bach's works in this form, the Prelude and Fugue in B minor belongs with the Leipzig set of organ compositions along with the great *St. Anne's Fugue* in E flat. It is prevailingly elegiac in a way that sets it apart from all of Bach's other organ music.

The prelude section moves along broad lines in richly developed style. Boldly planned in a mood of marked solemnity, the Fugue mounts in structural power to a truly sublime climax. To Sir Hubert Parry it suggested "a deep temperamental meditation on the remorselessness of destiny and the helplessness of man in the face of it."

Schweitzer, alluding to its architectural splendor, regarded the work as epitomizing Gothic in music. "As in that medieval form of architecture," he pointed out, "the luxuriant detail of the work only works to unify and vitalize the simple boldly flung lines, and to exhibit a power in its utmost flexibility."

The contemplative intensity of feeling marking the Leipzig group of Bach's organ classics helps distinguish it from earlier works for this instrument, many written at Weimar and Cöthen.

Mr. Mitropoulos's transcription is scored for two flutes, piccolo, two oboes, two clarinets, bass clarinet, two bassoons, contrabassoon, four horns, four trumpets, three trombones, tuba, tympani, and strings.

L. B.

Chorale-Prelude, "Credo" ("Wir glauben all' an einen Gott")

[Transcribed for orchestra by Leopold Stokowski]

THE CREED hymn of Bach's many chorale-preludes for organ is found in the third section of the four-part *Clavierübung* (meaning "keyboard practice"), an exhaustive manual of organ and clavier music published between the years 1731 and 1742. The hymn is Martin Luther's free rendering of the Nicene Creed. With the anonymous melody it first appeared in "Johann Walther's Hymn-Book" at Wittenberg, in 1524. A year later it was selected for singing at the funeral of Friedrich the Wise of Saxony, who had been Luther's patron, thus setting a precedent long observed at a later period. In church practice during the Reformation the hymn followed the sermon. Bach's chorale-prelude versions of the so-called "catechism" hymns cover the chief points of the Lutheran faith.

Bach scholars have labeled this organ prelude the "Giant Fugue," a referenc to the mounting stride-by-stride figure for the pedals, which suggested t Professor Terry "the impregnable foundation on which rests the faith of th Church." This figure he likened to the pedal device on which Bach construct the *Credo in Unum Deum* and *Confiteor* of the great B minor Mass. Of th two hundred and more separate organ works of Bach, the chorale-prelude number 143, of which twenty-one are "Catechism Preludes." W. R. Anderso has said that "no one gets to the real heart of Bach who does not know th chorale-preludes."

The present transcription of Bach's organ creed dates from Mar. 28, 1924 when Leopold Stokowski conducted it on a program of the Philadelphi Orchestra in Philadelphia. The following Apr. 1, Mr. Stokowski introduced i to New York during one of the orchestra's regular visits to Carnegie Hall.

Another recent transcription of the same chorale-prelude is that of Hermann Boessenroth, for many years librarian and trumpet player of the Minneapoli Symphony Orchestra. This version was listed simply as "Credo" when the Minneapolis unit, under Dimitri Mitropoulos's direction, played it on Feb. 28 1941, in memory of its tympanist, William Faetkenheuer, who had died three days before after serving the orchestra steadily since its inaugural concert on Nov. 5, 1903.

L. B.

Three Chorale-Preludes: "Nun komm', der Heiden Heiland," "Meine Seele erhebt den Herren," "Wachet auf, ruft uns die Stimme"

[*Transcribed for orchestra by Ottorino Respighi*]

AMONG THE earliest works of Bach were organ movements founded on chorale melodies. It has been said that his very first essay in composition may well have been some treatment or other of such a chorale melody. Bach's writing for the organ was a lifetime addiction—with excursions into other fields, from time to time. And, as a matter of fact, his career ended with the dictation of a chorale-prelude, as he lay on his deathbed.

The chorale-preludes have been called "miniature symphonic poems" utilizing the original hymns associated with the chorale melodies as a "poetic basis."

Respighi transcribed for orchestra three of the chorale preludes, *Nun komm', der Heiden Heiland, Meine Seele erhebt den Herren* and *Wachet auf, ruft uns die Stimme*. In the Italian composer's version they were performed for the first time (from manuscript) by the Philharmonic-Symphony under the direction of Arturo Toscanini on Nov. 13, 1930.

The melody of *Nun komm', der Heiden Heiland* was set for organ five times
y Bach, besides being used in his Cantatas No. 36, 61, and 62. It is alleged that
ne melody is associated with Luther's Advent or Christmas Hymn of the same
ame, which was a simplification of the Latin air for *Veni Redemptor Gen-
um*. Respighi's version is founded on the first of three chorales contained in
ne Achtzen Chorale, whose original key was G minor.

Respighi, however, transposed the key to C minor, and he scored it for
rst and second violins, violas in two parts, cellos in three parts, double basses,
nd a bassoon which is in unison with the third cellos.

Meine Seele erhebt den Herren, fourth in the set of six Chorale-Preludes
ublished by Schübler between 1746 and Bach's death, is in itself a transcription
or organ stemming from the Cantata No. 10, which was composed for the
east of the Visitation of Mary, *circa* 1740. This work is also known as the
German Magnificat."

Respighi has scored the piece for two oboes, one clarinet, one bassoon, one
muted trumpet, first violins, violas, cellos, and basses.

The transcription of *Wachet auf, ruft uns die Stimme* is based on an organ
prelude, which is in turn an adaptation of a chorus from the Church Cantata
No. 140, composed in Leipzig in 1731, or thereabouts, for the twenty-seventh
Sunday after Trinity. The original melody, however, comes from Philipp
Nicolai's hymn, which was published in 1599. Bach's organ work is the first
in the set of six Chorale-Preludes brought out by Schübler.

The score calls for two clarinets, two bassoons, double-bassoon, four horns,
three trumpets, three trombones, first and second violins, violas, cellos, and
double basses.

R. C. B.

Brandenburg Concerto in F major, No. 2, for Solo Flute, Oboe, Trumpet, Violin, and Orchestra

I. Allegro moderato. II. Andante. III. Allegro.

CHRISTIAN LUDWIG, Margrave of Brandenburg, a lavish amateur of music,
commissioned Bach to compose a set of six concertos for him. Hence the name
by which they are known.

It has been assumed that Bach and the Margrave met either in Carlsbad or
Meiningen in 1718 or 1720 while Bach was still in the service of Prince Leopold
of Anhalt-Cöthen. In any case, the concertos were completed on Mar. 24, 1721,
and delivered to the Margrave in Berlin with a letter of dedication in French
couched in the servile and effusive style of the period. Professor Terry has
translated the document as follows:

Monseigneur:

Two years ago, when I had the honor of playing before your Royal Highness
I experienced your condescending interest in the insignificant musical talents with
which heaven has gifted me, and understood your Royal Highness's gracious willingness to accept some pieces of my composition. In accordance with that condescending command, I take the liberty to present my most humble duty to your Royal
Highness in these Concerti for various instruments, begging your Highness not to
judge them by the standards of your own refined and delicate taste, but to seek in
them rather the expression of my profound respect and obedience.

In conclusion, Monseigneur, I most respectfully beg your Royal Highness to
continue your gracious favor toward me, and to be assured that there is nothing I
so much desire as to employ myself more worthily in your service.

With the utmost fervor, Monseigneur, I subscribe myself,

Your Royal Highness's most humble and most obedient servant,

Jean Sebastian Bach.

The autograph score of the second *Brandenburg Concerto,* which like the
first is in F major, carries the following title: *"Concerto 2do a Tromba,
1 Flauto, 1 Hautbois, 1 Violino concertati, e 2 Violini, 1 Viola e Violone in
Ripieno col Violoncello e Basso per il Cembalo."*

Though in other respects a true concerto grosso, the second *Brandenburg
Concerto* is unorthodox in that the solo group—the so-called "concertino"—
comprises four instruments. The four movements are I. Allegro moderato,
F major, 4/4; II. Andante, D minor, 3/4; III. Allegro assai, F major, 2/4 time,
in which a fugue is discoursed by the "concertino" foursome. Of the separate
movements Philipp Spitta wrote:

"The marvelously beautiful Andante is soft and tenderly simple, while the
first and last movements rush and riot with all the freshness and vigor of
youth."

How the eighteenth-century concerto grosso worked out in general practice
may be gathered from a picture in the British Museum. There Handel, a great
master of this form, is shown with his instrumental ensemble. The seating
plan makes clear the relation of the two groups. Handel is surrounded, rather
than merely confronted, by the musicians. He is seated at a double-keyboard
clavicembalo. To his right, directly under his eye, is grouped the "concertino,"
the solo players. Behind him, out of sight, are the supporting players—the
"concerto grosso"—and *ripienisti.* The "concertino" group, accordingly, were
within direct range of the "conductor's" signals. This group relayed his wishes
to the others.

The word "concerto" was probably first applied to music for a solo instrument and accompaniment by Scipio Bargaglia in a manual published in Venice
in 1587. A century later Giuseppe Torelli adopted the term "concerto grosso"
to cover a "concerto" with a greater number of instruments. Yet in 1691,

eventeen years before Torelli's death, Michelletti published his "Sinfonie et
oncerti a quatro," and in 1698 a sheaf of "Concerti musicali." The term
concerto" recurs in seventeenth-century tracts. However, it was this same
Torelli who determined the form of the grand solo for violin and, as Philip
Hale observed, "opened the way to Arcangelo Corelli, the father of modern
violinists, composers, or virtuosos."   L. B.

Suite No. 3, in D major

I. Overture. II. Air. III. Gavottes 1 and 2. IV. Bourrée. V. Gigue.

IF THERE is one melody that has carried the name of Bach into every music-
lover's heart it is the one known as the *Air for the G String*. Its original resting
place is the Suite No. 3, in D major. In this work the "air," in two-part form
(4/4), occupies second place as a Lento for strings. Most listeners know the
melody through Wilhelmj's arrangement for violin solo. The German virtuoso,
of course, transposed the "air" from D major to C major, keeping it on the
one string.

The Suite in question contains five other sections: Overture, Gavottes 1 and
2, Bourrée, and Gigue. The Overture consists of a slow section (Grave, D
major, 4/4), a brisk fugue (Vivace), in the same key and time, and a return
of the first part. Following the style of the old concerto grosso, many passages
are assigned to violin solo in the fugue section.

Both the slow introduction and the fugue feature oboes and violins in unison.
Employed in the entire Suite are two oboes, three trumpets, kettledrums, and
strings.

Bach left four such suites in all, one in C major, one in B minor, and two in
D major, each calling for a different array of instruments. The popular B
minor Suite is for flute and strings only. The scheme was supplemented of
course, by a continuo, the name given the figured instrumental bass part, in
Bach's day generally played at a harpsichord by the conductor.

What circumstantial evidence there is points to the Suite's having been
composed by Bach at Cöthen (1717-1723), where he was in the service of Prince
Leopold, a highly cultivated musician. The Prince put an orchestra of eighteen
at Bach's disposal and on occasion participated himself. The ensemble probably
rehearsed in Bach's rooms at the castle, and one can picture the great man
seated at his harpsichord in one corner of the apartment getting his little
orchestra in shape for the next musical soiree.

The suites were not called that by Bach, but "ouvertures." That was the
practice of the time, the overture being a sequence of dance movements, with
the introductory section modeled on the French overture form established by

Lully. Strictly speaking, the first number listed on this program is the overtur
to an overture. After Bach's death the suites lapsed into virtual oblivion fc
almost a century, to be rescued by Mendelssohn at the Leipzig Gewandhau
concerts in 1838. It was Mendelssohn, too, who first performed the Third Suit
in London in 1844 and, as early as 1830, played the opening section on th
piano for Goethe. "The opening is so pompous and dignified," the Germar
poet observed, "that one can really see a file of important people going down
great staircase."

L. B.

Toccata and Fugue in C major

[Transcribed for orchestra by Theodore Bloomfield]

No record exists as to the exact or approximate date of composition of the
C major Toccata. Close scrutiny of its organ style, however, has convinced
most Bach specialists that it belongs with the music of Bach's Weimar period
which extended from 1708 to 1717. That Bach composed it for both local use
and recital tours seems probable. One venturesome scholar has gone so far as
to suggest that Bach wrote it in 1714 for a trip to Cassel, where his playing
earned him the gift of a costly ring from the Prince of Hesse. But this is pure
guesswork. Internal evidence is all we have, and this clearly proves that Bach
was no longer the sedulous pupil of older masters like Buxtehude. The strict
formalism had yielded to a freer, more supple technic, in part the influence of
Vivaldi and Corelli, in part the outgrowth of Bach's maturer genius.

Three distinct movements make up the Toccata: a Prelude, with an elaborately florid passage for manual, followed by a brilliant pedal solo; an Adagio
of thoughtful songlike beauty; and a brisk Fugue in 6/8 time. In all, Bach
wrote five toccatas. Albert Schweitzer traced the toccata form back to Claudio
Merulo (1532-1604) of Venice. The word "toccata" comes from the Italian
verb, *toccare,* to touch or feel. Hence a toccata is literally a "touching" or "tap,"
and by expansion a keyboard composition offering wide scope for showy
execution.

Completed in 1943, Mr. Bloomfield's version of Bach's C Major Toccata and
Fugue was first performed by the San Francisco Symphony Orchestra on
Feb. 21, 1946. Pierre Monteux conducted. The scoring calls for two flutes,
piccolo, three oboes, three clarinets, two bassoons, contra-bassoon, four horns,
three trumpets, three trombones, tuba, tympani, bass drum, and strings.

In orchestrating the great organ classic, Mr. Bloomfield was faced with the
dilemma of all transcribers of Bach: whether to transcribe freely and invite a
volley of brickbats from the purists, or to hew to Bach's line religiously and
risk detailed comparison with the original. Mr. Bloomfield finally solved the
problem with a compromise: *By attempting to score the Toccata as Bach*

himself might have done had he been able to avail himself of the orchestral resources of today. He had given the authors the following information:

I have not tried to imitate the organ throughout, although in some places there has been a definite attempt at the organ sonority. For example, the extended pedal solo in the introduction of the first movement has been scored for cellos and basses— half arco and half pizzicato—and bassoon, this being the sound most closely approximating that of the organ pedals. The tutti at the close of the second movement (modulating back to C major) will also be found to resemble the organ sonority.

This Toccata lends itself particularly well to orchestration, as the broad theme of the first movement proper sounds effective in its alternate statements by the string and wood-wind choirs, the serene intermezzo in A minor will be beautiful on almost any medium (and is in fact frequently played by itself as a solo on violin and cello programs), and the marcato fugue subject is equally well adapted to the string, wood-wind, and brass sections.

The Fugue has been scored in such a way as to require a slower, more robust tempo; here again I have been guided by the organ conception, there being a certain speed beyond which the semiquaver figures cannot be played on the pedals. The fugue also contains certain virtuosic passages for the instruments, notably the staccato figuration of the wood winds in the E minor section. In the last two measures I have added ascending chords above descending bass line, this being perhaps the most noticeable departure from Bach's original.

L. B.

Toccata and Fugue in D minor
[*Symphonic transcription by Leopold Stokowski*]

MR. STOKOWSKI has furnished the authors with the following statement regarding the Toccata and Fugue in D minor, which he has transcribed:

Of all the music of Bach this Toccata and Fugue is among the freest in form and expression. Bach was in the habit of improvising on the organ and clavichord, and this Toccata probably began as an improvisation in the church of St. Thomas in Leipzig. It has a power and majestic intensity that is cosmic in scope. One of its main characteristics is immense freedom of rhythm and plasticity of melodic outline. In the sequence of harmonies it is bold and path breaking. Its tonal architecture is irregular and asymmetric. Of all the creations of Bach this is one of the most original. Its inspiration flows unendingly. In spirit it is universal, so that it will always be contemporary and have a direct message for all men.

Mily Alexeievitch Balakireff

BORN: NIJNY-NOVGOROD, RUSSIA, JAN. 2, 1837. DIED: ST. PETERSBURG, MAY 29, 1910.

It was in no spirit of calculated nationalism that he brought to maturity the Russian (and Russian-Oriental) idiom which had begun to take form in Glinka's music: this idiom was the natural and necessary vehicle of his thinking.—M. D. CALVOCORESSI.

"Islamey," Oriental Fantasy

[Transcribed for orchestra by Alfredo Casella]

THE SHADOWS of Franz Liszt and the Caucasus hover jointly over Balakireff's brilliant fantasy for piano. When published in 1869, *Islamey* promptly caught the fancy of the great virtuoso. Its ebullient style and idiom seemed tailor-made for his prodigious powers. Liszt performed it widely and long coached it into the repertory of his most gifted pupils. Among these was Alexander Siloti, to whom Alfredo Casella was later to dedicate his orchestral version, "in token of admiration and affection." What actually inspired Balakireff to write the fantasy was a trip through the wildly picturesque highlands of the Caucasus.

Written in 1908, Casella's version was published in both Russia and France. Scored for large orchestra, it requires four flutes, piccolo, two oboes, English horn, two clarinets, clarinetto piccolo, three bassoons, double bassoon, four horns, four trumpets, three trombones, tuba, four kettledrums, bass drum, three cymbals, side drum, tambourine, triangle, glockenspiel, gong, small bell (in A flat), two harps, and strings. Built freely around three themes, the fantasy employs a markedly Oriental melody immediately introduced in an Allegro agitato, D flat major, 12/16. English horn and cellos chant a second subject (Un poco meno mosso). Following the return of the first subject, the English horn discourses the theme of the trio (Andantino espressivo, A major, 6/8). Cello, violin, and viola extend this in respective solos. After a brilliant review of earlier themes, the coda sets in (Presto furioso, 2/4).

Casella's arrangement was first performed by The Theodore Thomas Orchestra in Orchestra Hall, Chicago, on Nov. 19, 1909.

L. B.

Samuel Barber

BORN: WEST CHESTER, PA., MAR. 9, 1910.

His music reveals not only imaginative sympathy and technical address, but a respect for brevity which is the soul of more than wit. When he has said his say, he has the good sense to stop.—PITTS SANBORN.

"Symphony in One Movement"

SAMUEL BARBER wrote this Symphony during the winter of 1935-1936. It was given its premiere by the Augusteo Orchestra, Rome, Italy, under the direction of Bernardino Molinari in December, 1936. Its American premiere occurred at a concert of the Cleveland Orchestra, conducted by Artur Rodzinski, in January, 1937. A special honor was accorded it when Mr. Rodzinski elected to perform it at the Salzburg Festival in the summer of 1937, making it the only American symphonic work in the calendar. In 1942, the composer revised the symphony, and in the new form it was first played by the Philadelphia Orchestra, under Bruno Walter, on Feb. 18, 1944. The Philharmonic-Symphony introduced it to New York, under Mr. Walter's direction on Mar. 8 of that year.

Mr. Barber's own explanation of the Symphony follows:

The form of my *Symphony in One Movement* is a synthetic treatment of the four-movement classical symphony. It is based on three themes of the initial Allegro non troppo, which retain throughout the work their fundamental character. The Allegro opens with the usual exposition of a main theme, a more lyrical second theme, and a closing theme. After a brief development of the three themes, instead of the customary recapitulation, the first theme, in diminution, forms the basis of a scherzo section (Vivace). The second theme (oboe over muted strings) then appears in augmentation, in an extended Andante tranquillo. An intense crescendo introduces the finale, which is a short passacaglia based on the first theme (introduced by the violoncelli and contrabassi), over which, together with figures from other themes, the closing theme is woven, thus serving as a recapitulation for the entire symphony.

Samuel Barber wrote his first music at the age of seven. He entered the Curtis Institute of Music when he was thirteen, studying piano with Isabella Vengerova, voice with Emilio de Gogorza, and composition with Rosario Scalero. In 1932 he was graduated, and three years later he was awarded the Prix de Rome, whereupon he put in two years as a student at the American

Academy in the Italian capital. His next honors included two successi
awards of the Pulitzer Prize for Music, a distinction equaled up to then by
other musician. He has composed prolifically, and his output includes song
choral pieces, chamber music, and orchestral compositions.

Mr. Barber's orchestral works have been listed in the programs of t
Augusteo Orchestra in Rome, the Vienna Philharmonic, the BBC in Londo
and those of all the major American orchestras.

Among the pieces in larger forms are the *Essay for Orchestra, Adagio f
Strings,* the Overture to *The School for Scandal, Music for a Scene fro
Shelley,* a Violin Concerto and two symphonies. His chamber music cor
prises a String Quartet in B Minor, a Serenade for String Quartet, *Dov
Beach* for voice and string quartet, and a Sonata for Cello and Piano. In add
tion to these, Mr. Barber has written a considerable number of songs. H
choral works are *The Virgin Martyrs* and *A Stopwatch and an Ordnance Ma
(for men's chorus and kettledrums).

R. C. B.

Adagio for String Orchestra, Op. 11

This piece was composed in 1936 as the slow movement of a string quart
in B minor, and in the course of the same year was played in Rome by t
Pro Arte String Quartet.

The first performance by string orchestra occurred on Nov. 5, 1938. Th
occasion was a broadcast of the NBC Symphony, under the direction
Arturo Toscanini. The work bears this dedication: "To my aunt and uncl
Louise and Sidney Homer."

"Molto adagio espr. cantando" is the instruction at the beginning of th
score. The key is B flat minor. Although 4/2 indicates the time at the oper
ing, there are measures marked 5/2, 6/2, 3/2.

The Adagio is based on a single lyric subject, given out immediately b
the first violins. The violas take it up, and there is canonic treatment. Th
theme appears in the other voices, eventually rising in the high strings to
fortissimo climax. A pause is followed by a tranquil close.

The *Adagio for Strings* was the recipient of a signal honor in that Mr
Toscanini played it during a South American tour, it being the only compo
sition by an American to be so favored.

"Second Essay"

In 1937, Samuel Barber composed his *Essay for Orchestra,* which was firs
performed by Arturo Toscanini and the NBC Symphony in 1938. It was the

described as having been suggested by the literary form; the themes concise and developed within the limits of the so called "essay" form.

The *Second Essay* follows along the same lines, but is for larger orchestra and somewhat broader in scope. The main theme is announced at once by solo flute, a second theme by violas, and a third figure by the brass. A fugal section follows, beginning in the wood winds and developed in the full orchestra with the intertwining of the first two themes. After a stretto and a fortissimo statement of the first theme, a coda, built on the ostinato third figure, brings the work to a broad conclusion.

Béla Bartók

BORN: NAGYSZENTMIKLÓS, HUNGARY, MAR. 25, 1881. DIED: NEW YORK, SEPT. 26, 1945.

Béla Bartók is perhaps the only man who has achieved a synthesis of the primitive and artistic languages of music.—ALFRED EINSTEIN.

Concerto for Two Pianos with Orchestral Accompaniment

I. Allegro molto. II. Lento ma non troppo. III. Allegro non troppo.

THE PRESENT work started as a Sonata for Two Pianos and Percussion, and grew up to a Concerto for Two Pianos with Orchestral Accompaniment. Bartók originally wrote it for the Basle (Switzerland) section of the International Society for Contemporary Music. As a piece of chamber music for two pianos and two percussion groups it was first performed there in January, 1938.

In that form, the work was later played in London (International Society for Contemporary Music), Brussels, Amsterdam, Paris, Zürich, Luxembourg, Budapest, and Venice. Its single American performance took place at a session of the New Friends of Music in the Town Hall, New York, on Nov. 3, 1940. The soloists were the composer and his pupil and wife, Ditta Pasztory Bartók, with Saul Goodman and Henry Denecke, Jr., assisting as percussionists.

The score then called for two pianos, three tympani, cymbals, triangle, two side drums, bass drum, tam-tam, and xylophone. Immediately after the American premiere, Mr. Bartók decided to amplify the "sonata," completing the new version the following month. He wrote,

It seemed advisable, for certain technical reasons, to add orchestral accompaniment to the work, though, as a matter of fact, it gives only color to certain portions of the work. The two-piano and percussion parts remain practically unchanged, except for some of the climactic parts which are now taken over from the two pianos as tuttis by the orchestra.

In the new version the scoring includes, besides pianos and percussion, two flutes, piccolo, two oboes, English horn, two clarinets, two bassoons, contrabassoon, four horns, two trumpets, three trombones, celesta, and strings. Fritz Reiner led the New York Philharmonic-Symphony in the premiere of this version on Jan. 4, 1943. Mr. and Mrs. Bartók were again the soloists.

The three-movement work opens with a brooding slow passage leading to the main section (Allegro molto) in rhythmically barbaric and energetic style. The second theme of this movement appears in many contrapuntal combinations. The middle movement is a Lento ma non troppo, with an A-B-A sectional division. In the rondo-like finale (Allegro non troppo, 2/4) the xylophone gives out the relatively extended chief theme. Throughout the composition, percussion instruments often play solo roles. There is wide rhythmic variety and striking counterpoint, besides daring effects of grouping and color. Also apparent is Mr. Bartók's well-known flair for utilizing short themes, especially in his piano music. These are handled with typical contrapuntal boldness. However, one or two longer themes crop up, notably in the finale, in which the xylophone states a sustained melody. The primitive and folkish quality felt in Mr. Bartók's earlier music marks much of this work too.

At ten Béla Bartók was already playing the piano in public and composing. At thirteen he began studying with Laszlo Erkel in Pressburg. A few years later he entered the Academy of Budapest. After graduating in 1903, he earned his living as teacher, pianist, organist, and arranger. He was appointed professor of piano at the Academy in 1907. While still a student he became the close friend and associate of Zoltan Kodály. Together they did research in Hungarian folk songs that was later to color their own music and esthetics. Among early influences, too, were Richard Strauss and Liszt, later Debussy. Between 1905 and 1914, Mr. Bartók spent almost as much time collecting Hungarian folk music as teaching and composing. The blunt, earthy, at times wildly passionate qualities of this material crept increasingly into his music.

As composer Bartók first aroused wide popular response through two stage works, a ballet and an opera pantomime. Otto Gombosi, the Hungarian writer, has tried to show how the basic rhythmic trait of Bartók's music adapts it readily to kinetic spectacle. He states:

In its deepest fundamentals, Bartók's music is of an elemental strength. . . . Rhythm of extreme potency is one of its most characteristic features. This rhythm gives his music that Dionysian strain that produces its elemental effect, besides also giving it the strong backbone of the vision of sound. This is the reason for the pantomimic aptitude of this music, which found its strongest expression in Bartók's few stage works.

Though Bartók had frequently toured Europe as pianist-composer, he first visited America in 1927. He returned here from Budapest late in 1940, accompanied by his wife, Ditta Pasztory, who had never been to America before. They appeared in the premiere of the Sonata for Two Pianos and Percussion less than a week after their arrival. For more than a year Mr. Bartók worked at Columbia University on the Milman Parry collection of Yugoslav folk music.   L. B.

Concerto for Orchestra

I. Andante non troppo; allegro vivace. II. Allegro scherzando. III. Elegy: Andante non troppo. IV. Intermezzo interrotto: Allegretto. V. Finale: Presto.

THE Concerto for Orchestra was composed in October, 1943, for the Koussevitzky Musical Foundation, as a memorial tribute to Natalie Koussevitzky. It was first performed by the Boston Symphony Orchestra at an afternoon concert in Boston, Dec. 1, 1944, Serge Koussevitzky conducting. The same band was responsible also for its New York premiere in Carnegie Hall on Jan. 10, 1945.

It is scored for three flutes, piccolo, three oboes, English horn, three clarinets, bass clarinet, three bassoons, contra-bassoon, four horns, three trumpets, three trombones, tuba, tympani, tambourine, bass drum, cymbals, triangle, tam-tam, two harps, and strings.

According to the composer, "The general mood of the work represents, apart from the jesting second movement, a gradual transition from the sternness of the first movement and the lugubrious death song of the third, to the life assertion of the last one."

Grimly ironic is the fact that Bartók composed the piece during his convalescence from a grave illness, only to succumb to it a little over a year later.

In any case, Bartók gave an explanation for calling this a concerto, instead of a symphony:

The title of this symphony-like orchestral work is explained by its tendency to treat of single instruments or instrument groups in a "concertant" or soloistic manner. The "virtuoso" treatment appears, for instance, in the fugato sections of the development of the first movement (brass instruments), or in the "perpetuum mobile"-like passage of the principal theme in the last movement (strings), and, especially, in the second movement, in which pairs of instruments consecutively appear with brilliant passages.

As for the structure of the work, the first and fifth movements are written in a more or less regular sonata form. The development of the first fugato contains sections for brass; the exposition in the Finale is somewhat extended, and its development consists of a fugue built on the last theme of the exposition. Less traditional forms are found in the second and third movements. The main part of the second consists of a chain of independent short sections, by wind instruments consecutively introduced in five pairs (bassoons, oboes, clarinets, flutes, and muted trumpets). Thematically, the five sections have nothing in common. A kind of trio —a short chorale for brass instruments and side drum—follows, after which the five sections are recapitulated in a more elaborate instrumentation. The structure of the fourth movement is also chainlike; three themes appear successively. These constitute the core of the movement, which is enframed by a misty texture of rudimentary motifs. Most of the thematic material of this movement derives from the "introduction" to the first movement. The form of the fourth movement—intermezzo interrotto [interrupted intermezzo]—could be rendered by the letter symbols ABA—Interruption—BA.

R. C. B.

Ludwig van Beethoven

BORN: BONN, DEC. 16, 1770. DIED: VIENNA, MAR. 26, 1827.

Keep your eye on him; he will make the world talk about him some day.—MOZART, *in a letter to his father,* 1787.

Symphony in C major, No. 1, Op. 21

I. Adagio molto; Allegro con brio. II. Andante cantabile con moto. III. Menuetto: Allegro molto e vivace; Trio. IV. Adagio; Allegro molto e vivace.

CONFUSED EXPLOSIONS of the outrageous effrontery of a young man."

"It is believed that a prodigal use of the most barbaric dissonances and a noisy use of all the orchestral instruments will make an effect. Alas, the ear is stabbed, but there is no appeal to the heart."

The above quotations might be taken as the bitter reactions of a critic or subscriber to a wild-eyed young composer's latest detonation in Carnegie Hall. One envisions a modern orchestra gone berserk in a slashing criss-cross of atonal shrieks.

They are nothing of the sort. The first statement alludes to an eruption in the Leipzig Gewandhaus on Nov. 26, 1801; the second to another at the Paris Conservatory early in 1810. The "outrageous effrontery" was a symphony in C major. The "young man" was Ludwig van Beethoven, age thirty.

Beethoven wrote his First Symphony on the threshold of the nineteenth century. He had previously composed only two works for orchestra, both piano concertos. Over him, as guides and warnings, hovered Haydn and Mozart, whose combined output of symphonies exceeded 150. Before him stretched a new world of expressive art, and he already glimpsed its contours.

Echoes of the "old order" of Haydn and Mozart abound in the score. The accepted patterns and conventions were too strong to break overnight. But there was enough in the symphony to stamp it Beethoven's and proclaim a fresh outlook and aim. Minor audacities of key and discord jarred on orthodox ears. There are little innovations in the use of the basses, in the scoring for winds, in developing crescendos that point to the future. Enough, apparently, to have alarmed the sentinels of the older regime into pronouncing the symphony "a danger to musical art."

Most of all, there was the third movement, innocuously labeled "Menuetto." That looked traditional enough, at least in print. Haydn had inserted a minuet in all 118 of his symphonies, and then there was Mozart. But

Beethoven's third movement carried a joker, the qualifying words: Allegro molto e vivace. That joker was literally a "joke," a "scherzo," a bright bubbling piece of badinage built on a simple ascending scale in G major, that "flashed across the musical heavens in a dazzling arc of new light." Despite the title, a concession to the past, Beethoven had brought the "scherzo" into the symphony, and there it remained.

In the words of W. J. Henderson,

Beethoven's innovation was in the thought rather than in the form. In the minuet of the First Symphony the form is untouched, but the conception is revolutionary. It altered the course of all modern symphonic composition quite as manifestly as the composer's passage without pause from the scherzo to the finale of the fifth. There are many learned pages about the Mozart and Haydn influence in the First Symphony, but the minuet is the leap of Beethoven's genius over the boundaries of tradition.

The symphony was premiered in Vienna on one of the most staggering programs in history. Beethoven gave the concert, first announced in the *Wiener Zeitung* on Mar. 26, 1800, for his own benefit. On the scheduled day, the program fairly sagged under the catalogue of numbers. It read:

Today, Wednesday, April 2d, 1800, Herr Ludwig van Beethoven will have the honor to give a grand concerto for his benefit in the Royal Imperial Court Theater beside the Burg. The pieces which will be performed are the following:

1. A grand symphony by the late Chapelmaster Mozart.
2. An aria from *The Creation* by the Princely Chapelmaster Herr Haydn, sung by Mlle. Saal.
3. A grand concerto for the Pianoforte, played and composed by Herr Ludwig van Beethoven.
4. A Septet, most humbly and obediently dedicated to Her Majesty the Empress, and composed by Herr Ludwig van Beethoven, for stringed and three wind instruments, played by Messrs. Schuppanzigh, Schreiber, Schindlecker, Bär, Nickel, Matauschek, and Dietzel.
5. A Duet from Haydn's *Creation*.
6. Herr Ludwig van Beethoven will improvise on the Pianoforte.
7. A new grand symphony with complete orchestra, composed by Herr Ludwig van Beethoven.

Tickets for boxes and stalls are to be had of Herr Beethoven at his lodgings in the Tiefen Graben, No. 241, third story, and of box-keeper.

Prices of admission are as usual. ·
The beginning is at half-past six o'clock.

History does not record at what time the concert ended. One commentator, writing it up six months later in the *Allgemeine Musikalische Zeitung,* pointed out the beauties of the Concerto, without specifying which one

Beethoven played. He applauded the "taste and sentiment" of the Septet, which became highly popular. He found Beethoven's improvising, which even astonished Mozart years before, to his liking. Although he praised the new symphony for containing "much art" and "abundant and original" ideas, he found that the wind instruments "were used far too much; so that the music is more for a band of wind instruments than an orchestra."

The conductor, Paul Wranitzky, and his orchestra almost succeeded in wrecking the concert. The men hated Herr Wranitzky and were prejudiced against Beethoven's music. There had been only a partial rehearsal, and during the performance they ignored conductor and soloist alike. The playing was described as "shameful" in a Leipzig paper. However, the work gained steadily in public favor.

Beethoven later offered the Symphony, the Septet, the Piano Concerto, Op. 19, and the Piano Sonata, Op. 22, to the publisher Hofmeister for the lump sum of seventy ducats, or $140. For the symphony alone he asked the fabulous figure of $50.

"You will perhaps be astonished," he wrote, "that I make no difference between a sonata, a septet, and a symphony. But I make none, because I think a symphony will not sell as well as a sonata, although it should surely be worth more."

*   *   *

"The Symphony is in the customary four sections, or movements. The key is C major. Yet it does not begin in that key, but with a discord in F major that shocked some pedants at the time. The slow introduction of twelve measures leads to the first movement proper (Allegro con brio). Its pages have spirit, gaiety, elegance, for this Symphony has well been termed a 'symphony of comedy,' though here and there a cloud may for the moment obscure its sunny brightness. The eighteenth century was not over when Beethoven composed it, and he was still looking at music through the eyes of Haydn and Mozart, in spite of the fact that the student may readily discover Beethovenish characteristics that are not derived from either Haydn or Mozart and distinct intimations of the moods and manners of the nineteenth century to come. However, comedy itself is not all compact of sunshine and, as the German proverb has it, laughter and weeping dwell in the same bag.

"This brisk Allegro is followed in the then prevailing order by the slow movement (Andante cantabile con moto, in F major, and consequently not too slow). It is mainly built up on a tricky tune that no less an authority than Professor Tovey described as 'kittenish.' The attentive listener should observe in this movement the recurrent passage of dotted notes for drums on G and then on C, the drums being tuned not in the tonic, but in the dominant. Yet bold though this device might have seemed, it was not wholly original. Mozart had anticipated Beethoven in his *Linz Symphony*.

"The third movement in name is the minuet usual in symphonies of the eighteenth century (Menuetto: Allegro molto e vivace, in C major), but in reality Beethoven was already looking forward toward the scherzo, with which he was presently to replace the minuet. This movement, then, is much less the stately dance in triple rhythm than a scherzo of generous proportions, rich in modulations and glowing color. The scherzo, like the minuet, always includes a trio section. Listen in this trio to the delicious dialogue between wind instruments and strings and to the rousing crescendo that ends it just before the repetition of the minuet.

"The finale, in C major, opens with seven measures of adagio devoted to a playful scale passage ascending in the violins. The music then plunges into an Allegro molto e vivace, beginning with a sprightly theme for strings, which races along to the conclusion in a whirl of merriment and humorous sallies."

L. B.

Symphony in D major, No. 2, Op. 36

I. Adagio molto; allegro con brio. II. Larghetto. III. Scherzo. IV. Allegro molto.

THERE MAY be possible only a few one-word descriptions of Beethoven's Second Symphony, but "joyous" would surely be one of them. It is difficult to see eye to eye with the savant who declared that "pleasing badinage" comes pelting down from it. However, a certain Spazier, known to have been a cultivated musician and a person of "sound judgment," found completely strange things to say about the work's finale. To him that segment represented a "gross monster, a pierced dragon which will not die, and even in losing its blood, wild with rage, still deals vain but furious blows with his tail, stiffened by the last agony."

Compare this with an expression of Hector Berlioz's regarding the same section: "It is a second scherzo in two time, and its playfulness has perhaps something still more delicate, more piquant."

One may be permitted, one trusts, a confused state of mind, thanks to the above. In fact, an amazing picture presents itself, that of *a gross monster which deals vain but furious blows with its pleasing tail, losing blood and badinage in its playfulness, the while.*

Seriously, one inclines toward Berlioz' views. There is joy in the Symphony, but the surprising thing about the whole matter is that Beethoven could have written it at all in the depressing circumstances surrounding him at the time. Its youthful gaiety is as far removed from the composer's immediate troubles as a polar bear from the Equator, adding one more refutation to the argument that a composer's work mirrors his mental state—among other things—at the time of creation.

To begin with, his deafness, which had recently come upon him with a great "roaring in the ears," was increasing. Besides which, he was a victim of colic. Typical of a man at a loss to understand—or, perhaps, a man like Beethoven, to brook—his ills, he consulted many a physician with little success. He went through fantastic therapeutic and untherapeutic ordeals, trying hot baths, cold baths, all sorts of pills and herbs, nostrums, panaceas, and no one knows what else. One of his medical advisers suggested rest in the country, so Beethoven hied himself to Heiligenstadt, then a quiet little village not far from Vienna, which looked across verdant meadows to the Danube and beyond to the distant Carpathian Mountains. A legend about the locality had it that the ancient Emperor Protus had planted there the first vines of Noricum and also that the bubbling waters of a mineral spring had been blessed by St. Severinus, thus giving them marvelous curative properties.

Only to add to Beethoven's trials came the crushing news that Giulietta Guicciardi had married a Count Gallenberg. This "little minx" of 17, together with her cousins, the Countess Josephine and Therese von Brunswick, had been his pupil, and she had won his heart during the process. The composer had asked her hand in marriage, and it is said that one of her parents looked with tolerance on the idea, the other not at all. This, as can be readily imagined, was "the most unkindest cut of all," so that his thought of putting an end to himself seemed a logical outgrowth of accumulated despairs. He wrote to his brothers a letter, known as "Beethoven's Will," which is an amazing example of documented melancholy.

The Beethoven of that period, the winter of 1802-1803, is, strangely enough, the Beethoven of the Second Symphony with its carefree, tripping lightness. Marion M. Scott (Master Musicians Series) remarks eloquently on that theme:

There was in Beethoven something that transcended the ethics of Aeschylus and Sophocles—something that set him beside blind Homer and Virgil, whose high thoughts reflected "the radiance of some mysterious and unrisen day." Like them he could pass through tragedy to the greater knowledge beyond, where birth and death, joy and sorrow, are but different sides of the same gold coin of life minted by God in eternity.

Beethoven had walked the meadows of Heiligenstadt and his mind had roamed the Elysian Fields of music before he passed into the valley of the shadow of death. But just before the path had gone down, he had seen, as sometimes happens in mountain regions, across the near gulf and intervening ranges, a radiant vision of distant mountains on the horizon—he had seen Joy. He has left us that vision in the passages of his D Major Symphony which prefigures the *Choral Symphony* that was to come. He saw that vision because "he always held his head high even when in pain."

*   *   *

"As in the case of the First Symphony, the Second has a slow introduction (Adagio molto), but this introduction is much longer and, though based in style on Haydn's symphonic introductions, is instinct with the new romantic freedom and contains a surprising prediction of the Ninth Symphony in a descending octave passage.

"The Allegro con brio that follows starts off with a buoyant theme that sets the pace for an energetic and generally cheerful movement. It is in the ensuing Larghetto in A major that we hear in full proclamation the individual voice of Beethoven, as we have not heard it before. This has been aptly called one of the most luxurious slow movements in the world, and its richness in melodies has been described as 'reckless.'

The next movement, again in D major, is this time called frankly a Scherzo, not a menuetto. This concise Allegro is particularly noteworthy for the prophecy in its trio of the trio of the scherzo of the Ninth Symphony.

"The finale, Allegro molto in D, is a forthright, humorous rondo. In view of the tragedy of that summer, this Symphony might, perhaps, best be looked upon as an escape."

R. C. B.

Symphony in E flat major, No. 3 ("Eroica"), Op. 55

I. Allegro con brio. II. Marcia funebre: Adagio assai. III. Scherzo: Allegro vivace; Trio. IV. Finale: Allegro molto.

THE TALE has been told often of this symphony's original dedication to "Buonaparte" and of the subsequent shift on a new title-page to *Sinfonia Eroica—Composta per festeggiare il sovvenire d'un grand' uomo* (Heroic Symphony—Composed to celebrate the memory of a great man) when Beethoven discovered that Napoleon had proclaimed himself Emperor. The details require no enumeration. However, much as some of us might enjoy evading the fact of its first purpose, the symphony was already completed when Beethoven suffered a democrat's change of heart, and like it or not, the piece is a kind of program music, written in admiration of Bonaparte. In support of that contention we have what are alleged to be Beethoven's own words spoken at the announcement of Napoleon's death, "Did I not foresee the catastrophe when I wrote the funeral march in the *Eroica?*"

Since Beethoven left no actual program other than the title-page maneuvers, it is interesting to study the strive and heave of attempted explanations that have been perpetrated. Czerny, among others, envisioned the first Allegro as a sea fight, the Funeral March as a memorial to Nelson, yet both suggestions seem oblivious of the "Buonaparte" dedication.

No less a personage than Berlioz advanced the theory that "the Scherzo and the Finale picture funeral games given in honor of the dead hero, such as Homer describes in his *Iliad*." Marx, on the other hand, comes forward with the following solution of the entire work, "I. An ideal battle as the *Einbegriff* [purport] of an heroic life; II. A nocturnal inspection of the battlefield; III. Merrymaking in camp; IV. Celebration of peace."

Lenz supplies this account, "I. Life and death of a hero; II. Funeral; III. Truce at the grave; IV. Funeral feast and heroic ballad." Oulibicheff argued that the Scherzo connoted an armistice, the soldiers on pleasure bent. The Finale, he admitted, had him guessing, since he could not seem to relate it to the preceding sections. An ingenious view by Ambros of the variations has them "following one upon the other like a procession of many generations of men marching up to the Cyclopean monument erected to the hero and crowning it with wreath and flowers."

Richard Wagner, last but not least, felt that the Funeral March portrays the "deeply, stoutly suffering man," the Scherzo the "gladly, blithely doing man," and the Finale "man entire, harmoniously at one with self, in those emotions where the memory of sorrow becomes itself the shaping force of noble deeds."

The musicologist, the historian, and the fictionist may be permitted their interpretations, but the music remains as a monument to a great and powerfully expressive mind, whose thoughts and imaginings, whatever they may have been, became crystallized into the brilliant, overwhelming pattern of a timeless creation.

The Symphony was written in the years 1803-1804. It obtained a private performance or, possibly, a general rehearsal, in the palace of Prince Lobkowitz in December, 1804. The first public performance occurred in the Theater an der Wien on Apr. 7, 1805, at a concert sponsored by the violinist Franz Clement. And here, we are surprised to learn, the work, according to the printed program, is dedicated to the Prince!

At its premiere the Symphony occasioned one piece of impromptu criticism from the gallery, says Czerny, when a listener shouted down, "I'd give another kreuzer if they would stop."

Some other declarations—from more serious and reflective sources, however —were not altogether favorable to the work, one authority characterizing it as "virtually a daring and wild fantasia, of inordinate length and extreme difficulty of execution. There is no lack," he continued, "of striking and beautiful passages in which the force and talent of the composer are obvious; but . . . the work seems to lose itself in utter confusion."

Another expert suggested shortening the symphony, because, "it would gain immensely." And so it went!

Perhaps, it is best to go to the composer himself for an opinion on his own work, an opinion given when he had already done eight of the nine symphonies. In the summer of 1817, Beethoven and the poet Christian Kuffner, who is allegedly responsible for the text of the Choral Fantasia, Op. 80, were at dinner in the tavern Zur Rose, Nussdorf. Kuffner asked his celebrated companion which of his symphonies was his favorite.

"Eh! Eh!" Beethoven, in excellent spirits, replied, "Why, the *Eroica*."

The poet remarked, "I should have guessed the C Minor."

"No," Beethoven insisted, "the *Eroica*."

R. C. B.

Symphony in B flat major, No. 4, Op. 60

I. Adagio; Allegro vivace. II. Adagio. III. Allegro vivace. Trio. Un poco meno allegro. IV. Finale: Allegro ma non troppo.

BIOGRAPHERS AND annotators cannot be blamed for waxing lyrical over this symphony. Few can resist reading a romance in its pages. A "symphony of love" one has boldly dubbed it. Others, with Beethoven's famous undated and unaddressed letter to the "Immortal Beloved" in mind, regard the Fourth as a similar testament of passion.

Romain Rolland is certain the symphony is secretly addressed to the Countess Theresa von Brunswick, whom Beethoven wooed and won ... for a while. "A pure, fragrant flower," says the Frenchman of the symphony, "which treasures up the perfume of those days." Another French scholar, Vincent d'Indy, appears to prefer Theresa's cousin, Countess Giulietta Guicciardi, as the symphony's heroine.

There is no known way of determining whether Theresa or Giulietta inspired the symphony, though the facts and circumstances favor Theresa. Actually, it is pure supposition to attribute the Fourth to romantic pressure at all. What is beyond question is that the spring and summer of 1806, when the symphony was presumably written, were one of the happiest and serenest breathing spells in Beethoven's stormy career. The spring had been almost purely a holiday, spent in Hungary on the estate of Count Brunswick. There he had reveled in the beautiful natural surroundings of the place and courted the Count's sister Theresa. And, there, in May, he apparently became engaged to her. Anyway, we have Theresa's word for it. As customary in Beethoven's love life, the affair came to nothing. One biographer explains Beethoven's failure ever to marry as a conflict between the real and the ideal. "He idealized women," says Peter Latham; "idealized them romantically without any reference to realities; and one after another the girls on whom he cast his eyes were discarded because they failed to live up to his impossible standards."

The assumed circumstances of Beethoven's stay on the Brunswick estate at Martonvasar have led the Theresa theorists to date the mysterious epistle to the "Immortal Beloved" as of that enchanted spring. Toward the summer, Beethoven's visit with the Brunswicks came to an end. He had accepted an invitation to spend the summer and autumn with his friend and patron Prince Lichnowsky at the Castle Grätz in Silesia. In October, he was back in Vienna. Accompanying him to the Austrian capital were the G major Piano Concerto, the *Rasoumowsky Quartets,* Op. 59, and the C minor Variations. Also, the Symphony in B flat major, No. 4, Op. 60, with its romantic confidences, if any.

The dedication of the Symphony to a Count Franz von Oppersdorf ties in with Beethoven's sojourn at the Castle Grätz. One day Beethoven and Prince Lichnowsky visited the Count, who occupied a castle in near-by Oberglogau. Beethoven's Second Symphony was among the numbers played by the Count's excellent private orchestra. Beethoven was naturally delighted. Later, when the Count commissioned him to write a symphony, he accepted eagerly. Beethoven pocketed the advanced five hundred florins.

He intended the great C minor Symphony for the Count. The contract included six months' performing rights. But Beethoven changed his mind, disposed otherwise of the Fifth Symphony, apologized humbly to his titled client, and sent along the Fourth, instead. Hence the dedication. The Count, quite humanly, was anything but mollified. He said nothing, but no further commissions came from Oberglogau. Doubtless what nettled Count Oppersdorf most was the fact that the Fourth, when delivered, had already been sold and premiered. The first performance had occurred at a special subscription concert organized for Beethoven's benefit and held at the house of another of Beethoven's titled clients, Prince Lobkowitz, in March, 1807.

Robert Schumann's famous remark about the Fourth Symphony—"a slender Greek maiden between two Norse giants"—was, of course, no allusion to either of the named Austrian countesses. Whether Schumann, in his own romantic and buoyant way, regarded it in any strict sense as a "symphony of love" is not known. What he sought to emphasize was the striking contrast between the softer moods of the Fourth and the epic sweep of the Third and Fifth.

Certainly Beethoven has climbed down from the panoramic peaks of the *Eroica,* and some fierce psychological crisis looms grimly between the Fourth and the Fifth. Supreme hero worship inspired the *Eroica,* and supreme victory over blackest despair the Fifth. The Fourth lives in its own serener element. "Beethoven must have been inspired by the very genius of happiness when he conceived and worked out the many beautiful themes of this joyous composition," says Grove. Of course, the Fourth also sounds a note of passion and mystery. No composition of Beethoven's is ever sweetness and light alone.

* * *

"Mystery and romance breathe through the elaborate introduction (Adagio, B flat major, 4/4) which this Symphony, like the Second, possesses, but the mood turns to merriment when the theme of the Allegro vivace (also B flat major, 4/4) makes its skipping entrance. The second movement (Adagio, E flat major, 3/4) is akin in its luxuriance of inspiration and melodic richness to the Larghetto of the Second Symphony, establishing another bond between the Second and the Fourth. Here we must listen to Hector Berlioz, who has written of the first half of this Symphony with a unique eloquence:

The character of this score is generally lively, nimble, joyous, or of a heavenly sweetness. If we except the meditative Adagio, which serves as an introduction, the first movement is almost entirely given up to joyfulness. The motive in detached notes with which the Allegro begins is only a canvas on which the composer spreads other and more substantial melodies, which thus render the apparently chief idea of the beginning an accessory. This artifice, though it is fertile in curious and interesting results, had already been employed by Mozart and Haydn with equal success. But we find in the second section of this same Allegro an idea that is truly new, the first measures of which captivate the attention; this idea, after leading the hearer's mind through mysterious developments, astonishes it by its unexpected ending. . . .

This astonishing crescendo is one of the most skilfully contrived things we know of in music: you will hardly find its equal except in that which ends the famous Scherzo of the Symphony in C minor. And this latter, in spite of its immense effectiveness, is conceived on a less vast scale, for it sets out from piano to arrive at the final explosion without departing from the principal key, while the one whose march we have just described starts from mezzoforte, is lost for a moment in a pianissimo beneath which are harmonies with vague and undecided coloring, then reappears with chords of a more determined tonality, and bursts out only at the moment when the cloud that veiled this modulation is completely dissipated. You might compare it to a river whose calm waters suddenly disappear and only leave the subterranean bed to plunge with a roar in a foaming waterfall.

As for the Adagio—it escapes analysis. It is so pure in form, the melodic expression is so angelic and of such irresistible tenderness, that the prodigious art of the workmanship disappears completely. You are seized, from the first measures, by an emotion which at the end becomes overwhelming in its intensity; and it is only in the works of one of the giants of poetry that we can find a point of comparison with this sublime page of the giant of music. Nothing, indeed, more resembles the impression produced by this Adagio than that which we experience when we read the touching episode of Francesca da Rimini in the *Divina Commedia,* the recital of which Virgil cannot hear 'without weeping in sobs' and which, at the last verse, makes Dante fall as a dead body falls. This movement seems to have been sighed by the Archangel Michael one day when, seized by an access of melancholy, he stood upon the threshold of the empyrean and contemplated the worlds.

"The third movement (Allegro vivace, B flat major, 3/4), sometimes called a minuet, sometimes a scherzo, is planned on a large scale and is further remarkable for the fact that, as in the Scherzo of the Seventh Symphony, the delicious trio (Un poco meno mosso) is played twice, the minuet or scherzo proper being repeated each time.

"In the exuberant Finale (Allegro ma non troppo, B flat major, 2/4) perpetual motion in tone, flashing and glittering with tunefulness and fun, holds sway. The movement opens with a suggestion of Bach, and presently we are aware that Beethoven has assimilated the spirit of Mozart and Haydn as at an earlier time he had paid them the compliment of imitation."

The score calls for one flute, two oboes, two clarinets, two bassoons, two horns, two trumpets, kettledrums, and the usual strings.

L. B.

Symphony in C minor, No. 5, Op. 67

I. Allegro con brio. II. Andante con moto. III. Allegro. IV. Finale: Allegro.

SINCE CONFLICT and struggle are elements readily translated into art and promptly grasped as such, the adoption as a rallying victory cry of the fournote rhythmic figure that blazes like a streak of lightning through the first movement of Beethoven's C minor Symphony was logically apt. Implicit in Beethoven's tense fabric is a titanic clash of wills. On the one hand, Fate. Not the cold, impersonal law of things indifferent to Man, but an active enemy. On the other, Man, drawing on his deepest resources to rise victor in deadly combat with the foe. If the chroniclers have not lied, Beethoven conceived the rhythmic motto as symbolic of "Fate knocking on the door," thus supplying a key to the ensuing drama. Even without this clue, a study of Beethoven's temperament and high ethical purposes, together with a normal esthetic reaction to the music itself, would suffice to establish the drama as an epic struggle on a moral plane.

Accordingly, unlike the Seventh Symphony, which has released "roaring cataracts of nonsense" along various lines of interpretation, the Fifth is clearly patterned on a moral program capable of a single broad analysis. Expounders of this "program" have been legion, from Berlioz down. Each has defined its message according to his own style and taste. Each has termed the "enemy" according to his own philosophical bent, from "monster," "fiend," "forces of evil" to a "malign Providence." But all have viewed the contest as moving from abject despair and helplessness through prayerful truce to savage defiance and victory. Commentators have even sensed in the C minor's raging pages a stern grapple with the thought of suicide, and Beethoven's harsh accesses of anguish might well bear them out. Unquestionably the Fifth Symphony enshrines some fierce encounter with conscience raised to cosmic

tterance. So long as man is prey to moral and mental torture, the C minor
ill hymn his torment and release.

That is one way of viewing the Fifth Symphony. Another is to examine it
long strictly esthetic lines. The absolute logic of composition has struck all
udents. Massive and compact, the symphony follows the relentless course of
s ideas. Nothing alien or irrelevant to Beethoven's scheme crops up. Every-
ing is irrevocably right. Nothing lingers unduly, nothing disappears too
on. One instinctively expects the return of a theme in its new guise. Art and
uman nature blend in a single entity, until the symphony becomes the echo
f our own shrieking inner selves. Perhaps only in Dante do we find such
erce admission of human pain and ecstasy rendered in such condensed and
oncentrated speech.

Beethoven allowed the germinal ideas of the C minor Symphony to simmer
ong in his mind. Motives for three movements were sketched as early as
800 and 1801, though the finishing touches were not applied to the sym-
hony until March, 1808, at Heiligenstadt, his favorite country haunt outside
ienna. In the interim the ideas underwent constant rejection and revision.
By his own admission, the creative process was always an arduous one of
rial and error that droned on in his head. Years would go by before he jotted
lown an idea that had taken root and vegetated in his brain. Acutely con-
cious of what he wanted, he waited for a theme to develop as if out of its
wn inherited traits. "Then begins in my head the working out in breadth,
eight, and depth," he once wrote. "Since I am aware of what I want, the
undamental idea never leaves me. It mounts, it grows. I see before my
nind the picture in its whole extent, as if in a single grasp." Often Beethoven
vrote out the trend of an idea in words, interpolating random notes. Some-
imes in the midst of a conversation or during a walk he would mutter or howl
trange sequences of sound in an effort to seize and fix a stray idea.

We can thus visualize the probable course of the C minor from emo-
ional inception to full development. Some experience or group of experiences had shaken Beethoven severely. Certainly bitter memories of Giulietta
Guicciardi and Therese von Brunswick enter the C minor's confessional.
Beethoven's deafness was steadily growing worse. In the Heiligenstadt Will
ne reviewed his "blighted hopes" and in his wretchedness shrieked to high
neaven for one more day of "pure joy." Thoughts of suicide and early
death probably assailed him. Then themes began to filter through his mind,
colored by these thoughts and seizures of grief, until the plan of a great moral
drama took shape. He would fight destiny to victory and achieve reconciliation with the world. Around this decision musical and emotional patterns
slowly formed. With the musician and man so closely coordinated in thought
and feeling, the process of shifting from emotional to artistic planes was
complete and true. After stern and unsparing scrutiny of each detail, the

struggle finally took finished form as the C minor Symphony. The poet Wordsworth believed that art was the calm remembrance of emotional states Beethoven's great symphony was thus a monument to an ordeal shaped in the quiet sessions of creative genius.

The work was first performed on Dec. 22, 1808, at the Theater an der Wien, Vienna, on an all-Beethoven program. It formed part of the first program of the New York Philharmonic Society on Dec. 7, 1842.

*   *   *

"Among the satisfactions that an audience has in listening to Beethoven's Fifth Symphony is the pleasure of recognition. The work begins immediately with the full orchestra sounding three eighth-note G's, followed by a descent of a major third to a long-held E flat. From these four notes so combined the entire first movement is derived, and the same rhythmic figure crops up repeatedly in the succeeding movements.

"Although the figure in question is rhythmic rather than melodic, it is so compelling that the hearer catches it at once and is haunted by it forever after. Concertgoers are as familiar with 'Fate knocking at the door' as with the music of 'The Star-Spangled Banner' or 'Home, Sweet Home.' But if the Fifth Symphony has its theme tattoo, it has also its theme song—the principal subject of the second movement. This bravely ingratiating melody, given out at once by violas and cellos in unison, everybody is certain to remember. And if the subsidiary themes of the first and the second movements and the principal subject of the scherzo are a trifle less definitely striking as tunes, they too are not the sort of thing that goes in one ear and out of the other.

"The uncanny scherzo (Allegro, C minor, 3/4), introduced by the common chord of C minor in arpeggio, is the musical embodiment of the terror that walketh by night. Berlioz says of the opening: 'It is as fascinating as the gaze of a mesmerizer.' A famous bridge passage, a supreme example of musical suspense, leads from the nightmare of the scherzo, pianissimo at first and then in a sweeping crescendo, to the triumphant proclamation of the C major finale (Allegro maestoso, 4/4)."

The effect produced by this Symphony on a contemporary composer is indicated in the frenetic outburst of the veteran Lesueur to the youthful Berlioz: "Ouf! Let me get out; I must have air. It is unbelievable! Marvellous! It has so upset and bewildered me that when I wanted to put on my hat, *I could not find my head!*"

The Symphony is dedicated to Prince von Lobkowitz and Count Rasumowsky. The score calls for flutes, oboes, clarinets, bassoons, horns, trumpets in pairs, kettledrums, and the usual strings, plus, in the finale, piccolo, double-bassoon, and three trombones.

L. B.

Symphony in F major, No. 6 ("Pastoral"), Op. 68

I. Cheerful impressions awakened by arrival in the country (Allegro ma non troppo). II. Scene by the brook (Andante molto moto). III. Merry gathering of country folk (Allegro). IV. Thunderstorm: tempest (Allegro). V. Shepherd's Song; glad and grateful feelings after the storm (Allegretto).

THE FIRST performance of this Symphony took place at the Theater an der Wien, Vienna, on Dec. 22, 1808. All the pieces performed on that occasion were by Beethoven. The composer had inserted an advertisement in the *Wiener Zeitung,* a week before the event, but only a few persons attended. The present work was listed in the printed program at the concert as "A Symphony entitled *Recollections of Life in the Country,* in F major, No. 5"— (obviously the *Pastoral* with the wrong numbering). Also included were an aria, "Ah, perfido," which was sung by Josephine Kilitzky; Hymn with Latin text written in church style, with chorus and solo; the G major Piano Concerto, played by Beethoven; a "Grand Symphony in C minor No. 6"—(again wrong numbering); the *Sanctus* from the Mass in C major; Fantasie for Pianoforte Solo, and the Fantasie for Pianoforte, "into which the full orchestra enters little by little, and at the end the chorus joins in the Finale."

Beethoven, not unusual for him, had experienced some bad moments with the orchestra at rehearsals and, as might have been expected, he flayed some of its members cruelly. Furthermore, his attitude at the concert was rather curious, teetering between friendliness and irony. When Prince Wielhorsky took his seat in the theater, Beethoven nodded to him in sardonic manner, and some have advanced the theory this was owing to the fact that of the many invited notabilities the Prince alone showed up.

Adding more fuel to the general conflagration, the clarinets apparently made an unfortunate error during the performance of the Fantasie for Piano, Chorus, and Orchestra. Beethoven, who was at the piano, jumped up and in stentorian tones said, "Silence! Silence! That is all wrong. Once more, once more!" It developed that Beethoven himself had been guilty of a slip when he absent-mindedly played a repeat which he had previously decided to cut. Naturally, the orchestra members rebelled at their public humiliation, and several threatened to depart forthwith. Nevertheless, the concert was gone through somehow. It began at half-past six and ended four hours later!

At the little country place of Heiligenstadt, the Sixth Symphony was completed in the middle of the year 1808.

In his very first sketches of the Symphony, Beethoven wrote the instruction that "The hearer should be permitted to discover the situations for him-

self," adding, almost as an afterthought, "He who has ever conceived an ide
of country life ought to be able, without many indications, to think of th
author's meaning." Still later the composer did some reconsidering, an
prefixed each movement with a special title, at the same time inserting
"More an expression of feeling than of painting," a legend which appeare
in the program at the Symphony's first hearing.

Beethoven was passionately fond of Nature for herself, besides findin
solace in communion with her from the assorted ills that beset him. His lov
of her was simplicity itself. He could admire her through listening to th
song of a bird at dawn, through gazing upon the gentle slope of some grass
meadow or the graceful curve of leaf-laden branches over a bubbling stream
"She was also a friend with whom he took pleasures in familiar talk, th
only intercourse to which his deafness presented no obstacle," wrote Vincen
d'Indy.

Although the Symphony was inspired by the rural beauties of Heiligenstad
and its environs, its general scheme follows too closely the plan of a worl
by Justin Heinrich Knecht for it to have been an accident. This, too, is .
symphony, and it had been described by its composer as "A Musical Por
trait of Nature: Grand Symphony for two violins, viola and bass, two flutes
two oboes, bassoons, horns, trumpets, and drums *ad lib.,* in which are ex
pressed in sounds . . ." then followed an explanation of its five movements
thus:

I. A beautiful country where the sun is shining, brooks traverse the vale, th
birds twitter, a waterfall tumbles from the mountain, the shepherd plays his pipe
the lambs gambol around, and there the sweet voice of the shepherdess is heard

II. Suddenly the sky is overcast, an oppressive closeness pervades the air, black
clouds pile up, the wind rises, thunder is heard from afar, and the storm
approaches.

III. The tempest bursts in all its fury. The wind howls, and the rain beats
down. The trees groan, and the waters of the streams rush furiously.

IV. The storm gradually subsides, the clouds disperse, and the sky becomes
clear.

V. Nature raises its joyful voice to heaven in song of gratitude to the Creator.

The curious thing about the whole matter is that the Knecht Symphony
was published by a firm that brought out simultaneously the set of three early
piano sonatas, composed by Beethoven around 1783. And still more curious
is the fact that on the back cover of the sonatas the publisher had placed an
advertisement of the Knecht Symphony, movements, description, and all!
It seems logical to assume that Beethoven took more than one peek at that
advertisement. However, in rebuttal it must be said that "storm" music was
no novelty in Beethoven's time. There was one such example in Steibelt's
Concerto for Piano, provocatively labeled, "The Storm; Preceded by a Pastoral

ondo." Another item, which used to get frequent hearings at the Abbé
ogler's organ concerts, carried the title, "The Shepherd's Pleasure, Inter-
upted by a Storm."

The *Pastoral Symphony* is scored for two flutes, piccolo, two oboes, two
larinets, two bassoons, two horns, two trumpets, two trombones, kettledrums,
nd strings.

R. C. B.

Symphony in A major, No. 7, Op. 92

I. Poco sostenuto. Vivace. II. Allegretto. III. Presto. Presto meno assai.
IV. Finale: Allegro con brio.

ᏒICHARD WAGNER, rather given to lofty phrase making, once called this
ymphony "the apotheosis of the dance," and through his mystic, super-
atural imaginings, he went on to say that it "belongs to the Night Spirit and
is crew, and if anyone plays it, tables and benches, cans and cups, the grand-
other, the blind and the lame, aye, the children in the cradle, fall to danc-
ng." All this, of course, is pre-Walt Disney fantasy.

Vincent d'Indy, less obstreperous, perhaps, refers to it as "nothing else than
pastoral symphony. The rhythm of the piece has truly nothing of the dance
bout it; it would seem, rather, to come from the song of a bird."

Thus, we have two completely opposing views from two eminent musi-
ians, and the followers of both have been legion. Many other impressions
f the composition, you can be sure, have been set down in the stark, staring
oldness of print, but it would serve no purpose to go about enumerating
hem, save that of confusion, before which the Messrs. Wagner and D'Indy,
ll unwittingly, have genuflected nobly.

According to Thayer, Beethoven started work on the symphony in the
pring of 1812. There are some differences of opinion as to that date, Pro-
l'homme advancing the theory that initiatory sketches were struck in the
vinter of 1811-1812. In any case, a letter of Beethoven's, written on May 8,
812, carried the significant message that a new symphony was in process of
onstruction. Another letter, penned on July 19, stated simply, "A new sym-
hony is now ready."

Among the pieces composed by Beethoven in that year were the Eighth
ymphony, a Piano Trio in B flat major, Three Equali for Four Trombones,
he G major Sonata for Violin and Piano, and other items. The Seventh
ymphony was dedicated to Count Moritz von Fries, and it was published in
816. The piano edition of the number Beethoven dedicated to the Tsarina
Elizabeth Alexiewna.

On Dec. 8, 1813, the Seventh Symphony had a remarkable success at its
vorld premiere in the large hall of the University of Vienna. Spohr reports

the performance as giving "extraordinary pleasure . . . in spite of the ofte
ridiculous conducting of Beethoven." He hints further that at the rehearsal
Beethoven's directing took on all the qualities of podial gymnastics; h
would call for a diminuendo by crouching low and for the correspondin
crescendo by straightening up. Yet tragedy stalked all through the event, fc
Beethoven, whose deafness prevented him from hearing all but the loud tone
of the orchestra, made a pathetic blunder at one point—during a very so
passage.

The program at the premiere of the Seventh offered besides, two Marche
one each by Dussek and Pleyel, "played by Mälzel's automatic trumpeter wit
full orchestral accompaniment," and *Wellington's Sieg, oder die Schlacht be
Vittoria.* (The "automatic trumpeter," one of the strange contraptions c
Johann Nepomuk Mälzel, celebrated maker of automata, need scarcely b
pointed to as the forerunner of present-day innovations in musical instr
ments, as, for instance, on one delirious occasion in our own Carnegie Hal
an airplane propeller!)

Beethoven had completed *Wellington's Sieg* in October of 1813, in honc
of the Duke of Wellington's victory over the French in Spain on June 21 c
the same year.

Mälzel had engineered the whole idea of that concert, which was to b
"for the benefit of Austrian and Bavarian soldiers disabled at the battle c
Hanau." So successful was it that a second was given on Dec. 12, the admissio
prices being ten and five florins, and the "gate" at both events amounting t
4,006 gulden—which is a lot of gulden. The composer's pleasure knew n
bounds, naturally. In fact, he so bubbled over with joy that he made gratefu
avowal, by way of a public letter, to all who had participated in the ver
tures. To Mälzel, however, went the major part of his penned tribute wit
the words:

It is Mälzel, especially, who deserves all our thanks. He was the first to co
ceive the idea of the concert, and it was he that busied himself with the organiz
tion and the ensemble in all the details. I owe him special thanks for having give
me the opportunity of offering my compositions to the public use and thus fu
filling the ardent vow made by me long ago of putting the fruits of my labor o
the altar of the country.

The Symphony was played again in Vienna on Feb. 27, 1814. The follow
ing Nov. 29, it was given, together with a new cantata, *Der glorreiche Augen
blick,* dedicated to the Congress at Vienna, and *Wellington's Sieg.* In the hug
gathering were the Empress of Austria, the Tsarina of Russia, and the Quee
of Prussia. The same program was repeated at a concert for Beethoven's bene
fit on Dec. 2, but a small audience attended. Important first performances c

ie work occurred at Leipzig, on Dec. 12, 1816; London, June 9, 1817; Paris,
Mar. 1, 1829; New York, Nov. 18, 1843 (Philharmonic Society).

Beethoven's Seventh Symphony has not lacked distinguished choreog-
aphers, since the celebrated Isadora Duncan danced all but the first movement at a performance in the Metropolitan Opera House on Nov. 6, 1908,
with the Symphony Orchestra of New York under Walter Damrosch's direc-
ion, and the Ballet Russe de Monte Carlo has presented a choreographic ver-
ion of the entire work.

The Symphony is scored for two flutes, two oboes, two clarinets, two bas-
oons, two horns, two trumpets, tympani, and the usual strings.

* * *

"The Seventh Symphony begins in its title key of A major with a long
introduction (Poco sostenuto), which has almost the importance of a sepa-
ate movement. The second theme of this introduction, a capricious, tripping
melody, first given out by a solo oboe, is not only one of the most captivating
hat Beethoven ever invented, but might by the unprejudiced witness be very
well taken for either an invitation to the dance or the caroling of a bird.
The principal theme of the main body of the movement (Vivace, A major),
irst announced by the flute, dominates the whole movement with its dotted
dactylic rhythm. D'Indy to the contrary notwithstanding, this theme might
in its turn be taken just as well by the same listener for a further invitation
io the dance as again for the piping of a bird.

"The second movement, an Allegretto opening in A minor on a long-held,
mysterious 6-4 chord of the tonic, is one of the most remarkable pages in all
Beethoven. Here, if the dance simile is to be preserved, it must be a solemn,
ritual dance. Thus, the movement has been likened to a procession in the
catacombs. But it has been likened as well to the love dream of an odalisque!

"The third movement is in reality a brilliant scherzo, though marked only
Presto (in F major). Twice it is interrupted by the strains of the somewhat
less rapid trio (Assai meno presto, D major), enshrining the melody which
d'Indy says was taken from the pilgrims' hymn of Lower Austria.

"The Finale is an Allegro of enormous energy and rhythmic incisiveness,
whose tumultuous measures have been specifically compared with widely
diverse dances. Some, like d'Indy, have heard here the rough jollity of merrymaking peasants, a 'Bauertanz' or 'Peasant Dance,' while to others this
Finale is nothing less than the ceremonial dance of those priests of Cybele,
the Corybants, round the cradle of the infant Zeus."

R. C. B.

Symphony in F major, No. 8, Op. 93

> I. Allegro vivace e con brio. II. Allegretto scherzando. III. Tempo d
> minuetto. IV. Allegro vivace.

THE EIGHTH SYMPHONY's first performance was a private one at the hous
of the Archduke Rudolph in Vienna, on Apr. 20, 1813. It was not given
public hearing until the following year, at Vienna's Redoutensaal, Feb. 2?
1814. The audience reacted indifferently, and the next day one reviewe
attributed that to the presence on the same program of the very popula
Seventh, whose Allegretto had been encored. Beethoven, who called th
Eighth his "little symphony in F" (as distinguished from his "great" sym
phony in A, the Seventh) was irritated by the public's coldness, remarking
peevishly that the Eighth was "much better" than the Seventh, and under th
circumstances one can sympathize with the curious turnabout. It took time fo
the Eighth to make any impression on audiences, although attempts were mad
to that end by performing along with it the Allegretto of the Seventh!

The Eighth has not escaped the attention of commentators who woul
provide it with a specific program. Thus, it has been described as a "militar
trilogy," for reasons best known to the phrase maker. Vincent d'Indy, probabl
under the influence of the *Pastoral*, spoke of the effect of Nature on Beethoven'
soul. He supports his theory with the suggestion that a peasant band is bur
lesqued in the trio of the Minuetto. For him the Hungarian theme used in th
Finale connotes the presence of gypsy musicians amid the rustic festivitie

Pitts Sanborn's less programmatic viewpoint defines this as the

symphony of laughter—not the laughter of childlike glee or of a reckless and de
spairing levity. Rather it is the "vast and inextinguishable laughter" Shelley speak
of in *Prometheus Unbound*. It is the laughter of a man who has lived and suf
fered and, scaling the heights, achieved the summit. . . . Only here and ther
does a note of rebellion momentarily obtrude itself; and here and there, in brie
lyrical repose, we have, remembering Sir Thomas Browne, an intimation o
Divinity more than the ear discovers.

*   *   *

"The first movement (Allegro vivace e con brio, F major, 3/4) opens with a
bright tune that sets the joyous mood and temper of the work. A second subjec
of the 'rollicking movement is one of Beethoven's most delicious inspirations.

"The second movement (Allegretto scherzando, B flat major, 2/4) has a
persistent and staccato ticking. This gave rise to the legend that it was based
on a canon or round, 'Ta, ta, lieber Mälzel,' written by Beethoven as a tribute
to the inventor of the metronome. Although historians have not taken the

gend to their bosoms, the ticking goes on metronomically all the same. Of
is section Berlioz once remarked, 'It is one of those productions for which
either model nor pendant can be found. This sort of thing falls entire from
eaven into the composer's brain. He writes it at a single sitting, and we are
nazed at hearing it.' What Berlioz did not know, obviously, was that the
iovement's spontaneous quality was obtained at the expense of much labor,
; Beethoven's sketches indicate.

"The third movement presents, instead of a scherzo, a 'stately minuet'
Tempo di minuetto, F major, 3/4). It is not the symphonic minuet that we
ieet with in the First Symphony, but one more typical of the eighteenth-
entury dance with its court formality. Yet, according to dependable sources,
ie music is 'not untinged with irony, for all its courtly melodiousness.'

"Incidentally, while Beethoven's intentions regarding this minuet are not
iysterious, dispute has come up about the tempo at which to play it. In his
eatise *On Conducting,* Richard Wagner said of it:

I have, myself, only once been present at a rehearsal of one of Beethoven's
ymphonies, when Mendelssohn conducted. The rehearsal took place at Berlin,
nd the symphony was No. 8 (in F major). . . . This incomparably bright sym-
hony was rendered in a remarkably smooth and genial manner. Mendelssohn
imself once remarked to me, with regard to conducting, that he thought most
arm was done by taking a tempo too slow, and that, on the contrary, he always
ecommended quick tempi, as being less detrimental. Really good execution, he
iought, was at all times a rare thing, but shortcomings might be disguised if care
vas taken that they should not appear very prominent; and the best way to do
iis was 'to get over the ground quickly.' . . . Beethoven, as is not uncommon
vith him, meant to write a true minuet in his F major Symphony. He places it
etween the two main Allegro movements, as a sort of complementary antithesis
› an Allegro scherzando which precedes it; and, to remove any doubt as to his
ntention regarding tempo, he designates it *not* as a minuetto, but as Tempo di
iinuetto. This novel and unconventional characterization of the two middle
iovements of a symphony was almost entirely overlooked. The Allegretto scher-
ando was taken to represent the usual andante, the Tempo di minuetto the
amiliar scherzo; and, as the two movements thus interpreted seem rather paltry,
nd none of the usual effects could be got out of them, our musicians came to
egard this symphony as a sort of accidental hors d'oeuvre of Beethoven's muse,
vho, after the exertions of the A major Symphony, 'had chosen to take things
ather easily.' Accordingly, after the Allegretto scherzando, the time of which is
nvariably dragged somewhat, the Tempo di minuetto is universally served up as a
efreshing *Ländler,* which passes the ear without leaving any distinct impression.
Vow the late Kappelmeister Reissiger, of Dresden, once conducted this symphony
here, and I happened to be present at the performance, together with Mendels-
ohn. We talked about the dilemma just described and its proper solution, con-
erning which I told Mendelssohn that I believed I had convinced Reissiger, who

had promised that he would take the tempo slower than usual. Mendelssoh.
perfectly agreed with me. We listened. The third movement began, and I wa
terrified on hearing precisely the old Ländler tempo, but, before I could give wa
to my annoyance, Mendelssohn smiled and pleasantly nodded his head, as if t
say, 'Now it's all right! Bravo!' So my terror changed to astonishment. . .
Mendelssohn's indifference to this queer, artistic contretemps raised doubts in m
mind whether he saw any distinction and difference in the case at all. I fancie
myself standing before an abyss of superficiality, a veritable void.

"In the finale (Allegro vivace, F major, 4/4) 'joy is truly unconfined and th
music roars and billows with the impact of Olympian laughter.'"

R. C. B.

Symphony in D minor, No. 9, with Final Chorus or Schiller's "Ode to Joy," Op. 125

I. Allegro ma non troppo, un poco maestoso. II. Molto vivace. Presto. III
Adagio molto e cantabile. Andante moderato. IV. Allegro assai. Quarte
and Chorus.

THOUGH THE controversy has quieted down considerably, Beethoven's grea
choral symphony was long a storm center of esthetic wrangling. Was the chora
finale a mistake or a supreme stroke of genius? Did Beethoven conceive th
broad outlines of the D minor Symphony with the sung text in mind as ar
integral part? Are the first three movements strictly "absolute," i.e., withou
program, or do they unfold some moral and intellectual drama reaching ar
inevitable denouement in Schiller's "Ode to Joy"?

The safest and easiest answer, one implying utter faith in the Master, is tha
Beethoven knew what he was about, that the choral movement, far from being
an accident or a gigantic artistic blunder, was the one and only solution of the
emotional and symphonic issues raised by the first three movements. We know
that he cast aside a tentatively sketched instrumental finale, later utilizing the
discarded material in the A minor Quartet, Op. 132. We also know that Czerny
affirmed bluntly that Beethoven expressed dissatisfaction with the choral device
after the premiere and resolved to substitute a purely orchestral finale. But
Beethoven was forever discarding and rejecting and revising. The rejection of
a sketch proves little. And as for Czerny's statement, Schindler flatly and
conclusively refuted it.

The scholarly alignment over the crucial issue of the finale has been formidable. As recently as Mar. 29, 1929, Philip Hale left Symphony Hall in
Boston a confirmed dissenter. "Better to leave the hall with the memory of the

Adagio," he wrote, "than to depart with the vocal hurry-scurry and shouting of the finale measures assailing ears and nerves."

Beethoven had so pitilessly handicapped the singers, Hale avowed, that they sounded like "an irritated kennel." Assuredly it was no sacrilege, he went on, to view the finale as a let-down from the sublimities of the earlier sections. There is more frenzied joy in the Scherzo; greater world-embracing humanity, loftier, nobler spirit in the Adagio," he declared. Besides, the Theme of Joy itself was "not one of Beethoven's most fortunate inventions." It might be pointed out here that this particular "invention" of Beethoven cost him over two hundred trial sketches before he hit upon the melodic sequence that would best suit his purpose, his aim being a self-developing idea of exultant joy capable of ramifying to sublime breadth and power. Tovey, Grove, and Wagner agree in recognizing it as a great theme, Grove stating that a "nobler and more enduring tune does not exist" and Wagner going into raptures over its "pure and lasting humanity" as Beethoven treats it.

Professor Tovey solved the problem of whether to regard the finale as the "crime or crown" of the whole symphony, by the simple logic of deduction: "There is no part of Beethoven's Choral Symphony which does not become the clearer to us for assuming that the choral finale is right; and there is hardly a point that does not become difficult and obscure as soon as we fall into the habit which assumes that the choral finale is wrong."

Proceeding on this premise, then, it is erroneous (1) to regard the finale as a blunder and detach it from the other three movements; (2) to accept the finale as an accident, sublime in itself, but alien to the work as a whole, in short, to consider the Ninth Symphony as music's supreme hybrid and not be unduly upset over the fact; and (3) to conclude that an instrumental finale would have fitted Beethoven's scheme better.

Assuming, accordingly, that the choral finale is right, does it signify a programmatic content in the other three movements? Grove thought not, taking the position that the symphony has no meaning other than its musical one. The train of thought and feeling developed in the "Ode to Joy" could be followed, he believed, without any attempt to reconcile it with the emotional trend of the Allegro, Scherzo, and Adagio.

Lawrence Gilman was stung to vehement rebuttal by this "shocking exhibition of esthetic irresponsibility." With true esthetic valor, he flouted the blithe assumption that a supposedly organic work of art could be built of irreconcilable parts as an "amazingly frivolous thesis." Gilman flatly rejected the idea of a symphonic mongrel, "three-fourths absolute music and one-fourth cantata." Like Wagner and Tovey, he sought a unifying poetic line, a "spiritual cord, which threads it, in Shankara's phrase, like the string in a chain of pearls." Briefly, a vision of life. In this vision, "fatefulness and transport, wild humor,

and superterrestrial beauty, mystery and exaltation, tragical despair and shou
ing among the stars" blended powerfully.

A more concrete program than that has been assigned to the symphony, c
which Marion M. Scott's version is the tersest: the first movement is Destin
and the "inexorable order of the universe"; the second, physical exuberance an
energy; the third, Love; the fourth, Joy, which was to Beethoven what Charit
was to St. Paul, "the one thing without which all else was incomplete."

This would bear out Professor Tovey's thesis that the Ninth Symphon
considered as a dramatic unit, is virtually "a search for a theme on which th
mind could rest as a final solution of typical human doubts and difficulties.
This theme was that of the choral "Ode to Joy." The transition from the instru
mental to the choral is dramatic, though the shift is by no means abrup
Beethoven employs a bridge passage that is the essence of drama. He survey
the past and eyes the magnificent future. Scott says (Master Musician Series)

With fiercely clamoring cellos and basses, Beethoven reviews and dismisses eac
movement in turn; then comes the earliest glimpse of the new order, a for
shadowing of the great tune which is to be the theme of the finale. This first reveal
itself in the cellos and basses, then gradually shines out in full beauty in th
orchestra; the realization, when it comes, is a moment to live for.

The weird and restless clamor returns and is silenced only by the baritone'
rebuke: "O, friends, friends, not these sounds! Let us sing something mor
pleasant, more full of gladness." And the chorus swings into action with the firs
three verses from Schiller's Ode. The baritone has certainly given a clue to th
nature of the emotional transition that would be revealing if the music itself di
not fully convey the change. The introductory words are not Schiller's. Beethove
intended the dramatic contrast to strike home at once. Surely, the need fo
words in the finale argues a "content" in the earlier movements, lending itsel
to programmatic analysis. Wagner, always a daring pioneer in exploring th
uncharted programs of great symphonic music, felt it did and arrived at
highly plausible reading of Beethoven's "vision of life." It follows:

I. A struggle, conceived in the greatest grandeur, of the soul contending fo
happiness against the oppression of that inimical power which places itself betwee
us and the joys of earth, appears to be the basis of the first movement. The grea
principal theme, which at the very beginning, issues forth bare and mighty, as i
were, from a mysteriously hiding veil, might be transcribed, not altogether in
appropriately to the meaning of the whole tone poem, in Goethe's words: "Re
nounce, thou must—renounce!"

II. Wild delight seizes us at once with the first rhythms of this second move
ment. It is a new world which we enter, one in which we are carried away to dizz
intoxication. With the abrupt entrance of the middle part there is suddenly dis
closed to us a scene of worldly joy and happy contentment. A certain sturdy chee
fulness seems to address itself to us in the simple, oft-repeated theme.

III. How differently these tones speak to our hearts! How pure, how celes-
lly soothing they are as they melt the defiance, the wild impulse of the soul
rassed by despair into a soft, melancholy feeling! It is as if memory awoke within
—the memory of an early enjoyed, purest happiness. With this recollection a
eet longing, too, comes over us, which is expressed so beautifully in the second
eme of the movement.

IV. A harsh outcry begins the transition from the third to the fourth move-
ents, a cry of disappointment at not attaining the contentment so earnestly
ught. Then, with the beginning of the Ode, we hear clearly expressed what
ust appear to the anxious seeker for happiness as the highest lasting pleasure.

Schiller's Ode had long dominated Beethoven's thoughts, both as expressing
s own ideas of human brotherhood and as a suitable text for musical setting.
t various times during a period of roughly thirty years, he entertained the idea
rendering the exultant verses into music. The history of Beethoven's contact
ith this hymn, together with a study of its full import, is a further guide to
understanding of the Ninth Symphony, though biographers like Thayer
smiss as "fantastic" the theory that Beethoven conceived the work *ab initio*
a celebration of joy."

As early as 1793 we find a record of Beethoven's having announced plans to
t Schiller's poem. It occurs in a letter written to Charlotte von Schiller by
ischenich, a worthy burgher of Bonn, Beethoven's birthplace. "I am enclosing
ith this a setting of the 'Feuerfarbe,'" he writes, "on which I should like to
ave your opinion. It is by a young man of this place whose musical talents are
niversally praised and whom the elector has sent to Haydn in Vienna. He
roposes also to compose Schiller's 'Freude,' and indeed strophe by strophe."
aydn's new pupil was the twenty-three-year-old Beethoven. It took him three
ecades to carry out the plan he had divulged to his fellow townsman regarding
chiller's poem, and then by no means "strophe by strophe." His sketchbooks
ow occasional tinkering with the idea in 1798 and 1811. For a while he
ought of setting the verses as a concert aria and even of introducing the words
sung interludes in an overture. In 1822, while developing some already begun
etches of the D minor Symphony, he made a free outline of the choral
ovement, using Schiller's Ode as text.

In devising the choral finale as the logical outgrowth of his symphony,
eethoven was naturally confronted with an artistic problem all the more
aggering because utterly unprecedented—that of making such a movement
t one of the longest and most elaborate symphonic spans in music. Schindler
rites:.

When he reached the development of the fourth movement, there began a
ruggle such as is seldom seen. The object was to find a proper manner of intro-

ducing Schiller's Ode. One day on entering the room he exclaimed, "I have i
I have it!" With that he showed me the sketchbook bearing the words "Let v
sing the song of the immortal Schiller, 'An die Freude.' "

Reasons of unity and time forced Beethoven to employ in all only one-thir
of the ninety-six lines making up Schiller's "An die Freude" poem, and thos
in freely rearranged order. Grove was sure Beethoven had omitted some of th
lines because of their "bad taste," though Schiller's indiscretion amounts t
nothing more *gauche* than a few lines about wine drinking. Since Beethove
knew the whole ode by heart and it had come to have a poetic and spiritu:
influence upon him as an unbroken unit, it may help to outline the poer
stanza by stanza as the romantic German poet wrote it. Incidentally, Schille
was twenty-five when he wrote it as a kind of tribute to his friendship wit
Christian Gottfried Körner. The ode was designed to be sung by frienc
"around the festive board," the chorus, in the style of Greek drama, repeatin
and commenting upon the sentiments expressed.

Each of the eight twelve-line stanzas contains a four-line chorus. Stanza
shows how joy makes all men brothers; Stanza II invites all those capable c
love and friendship to join the circle; Stanza III states that all living creature
are capable of joy; Stanza IV describes joy as the controlling force in th
universe, not merely in a material way, but in the intellectual, moral, an
religious sense too, as taken up in Stanza V. The remainder of the poer
reviews the effects of joy, proving in Stanza VI that by making men generou
helpful, and forgiving it makes them gods, in Stanza VII that it lifts soci:
intercourse to higher levels, where our thoughts confront the "Good Spirit,
and in Stanza VIII that joy makes for noble feeling and action. Finally, th
chorus swears, "by this golden wine," to live by this definition of joy.

By one of those puzzling reversals so typical of Beethoven's career, the I
minor, though bought and paid for a London Philharmonic premiere, was firs
produced in Vienna where it was tumultuously received. The place was th
Kärnthnerthortheater; the date May 7, 1824. The Gesselschaft der Musikfreund
when offered the work, had turned it down as too great a financial risl
Beethoven then thought of Berlin as a suitable locale for the premiere. Bu
Viennese patrons and friends prevailed on his civic pride to bestow the hono
on his own beloved Vienna, their main argument being that shame an
humiliation would reflect on one and all if the premiere occurred elsewher

When the work was given in London the following year, mention was dul
made of the original commission. In fact, the manuscript copy owned by th
London Philharmonic Society makes no bones about its having been "compose
for the Philharmonic Society in London." Actually, the score bears a dedicatio

to Friedrich Wilhelm III of Prussia, who acknowledged receipt of it by sending Beethoven an alleged diamond ring that was found to encase not a diamond but a cheap "reddish stone" which Beethoven wrathfully disposed of at the nearest jeweler. Efforts have been made to clear the Prussian ruler of practical joking, on the suspicion that the gems were surreptitiously changed en route.

The choral text follows, accompanied by Natalie Macfarren's translation (Novello & Co.):

BARITONE:—O Freunde, nicht diese Töne! Sondern lasst uns angenehmere anstimmen, und freudenvollere. (O friends, no more these sounds continue! Let us raise a song of sympathy, of gladness. O joy, let us praise thee!)

[BARITONE SOLO, QUARTET, AND CHORUS]

Freude, schöner Götterfunken,	Praise to Joy, the God-descended
Tochter aus Elysium,	Daughter of Elysium!
Wir betreten feuer-trunken,	Ray of mirth and rapture blended,
Himmlische, dein Heiligthum!	Goddess, to thy shrine we come.
Deine Zauber binden wieder,	By thy magic is united
Was die Mode streng getheilt;	What stern Custom parted wide,
Alle Menschen werden Brüder,	All mankind are brothers plighted
Wo dein sanfter Flügel weilt.	Where thy gentle wings abide.
Wem der grosse Wurf gelungen,	Ye to whom the boon is measured,
Eines Freundes Freund zu sein,	Friend to be of faithful friend,
Wer ein holdes Weib errungen,	Who a wife has won and treasured,
Mische seinen Jubel ein!	To our strain your voices lend!
Ja, wer auch nur eine Seele	Yea, if any hold in keeping
Sein nennt auf dem Erdenrund!	Only one heart all his own,
Und wer's nie gekonnt, der stehle	Let him join us, or else weeping,
Weinend such aus diesem Bund!	Steal from out our midst, unknown.
Freude trinken alle Wesen	Draughts of joy, from cup o'erflowing,
An den Brüsten der Natur;	Bounteous Nature freely gives
Alle Guten, alle Bösen	Grace to just and unjust showing,
Folgen ihrer Rosenspur.	Blessing everything that lives.
Küsse gab sie uns und Reben,	Wine she gave to us and kisses,
Einen Freund, geprüft im Tod;	Loyal friend on life's steep road,
Wollust ward dem Wurm gegeben,	E'en the worm can feel life's blisses,
Und der Cherub steht vor Gott.	And the Seraph dwells with God.

[TENOR SOLO AND CHORUS]

Froh, wie seine Sonnen fliegen	Glad as the suns His will sent plying
Durch des Himmels prächt'gen Plan,	Through the vast abyss of space,
Laufet, Brüder, eure Bahn,	Brothers, run your joyous race,
Freudig, wie ein Held zum Siegen.	Hero-like to conquest flying.
Freude, schöner Götterfunken,	Praise to Joy, the God-descended
Tochter aus Elysium,	Daughter of Elysium!
Wir betreten feuer-trunken,	Ray of mirth and rapture blended,
Himmlische, dein Heiligthum!	Goddess, to thy shrine we come.
Deine Zauber binden wieder,	By thy magic is united
Was die Mode streng getheilt;	What stern Custom parted wide,
Alle Menschen werden Brüder,	All mankind are brothers plighted
Wo dein sanfter Flügel weilt.	Where thy gentle wings abide.

[Chorus]

Seid umschlungen Millionen!
  Diesen Kuss der ganzen Welt!
  Brüder über'm Sternenzelt
Muss ein lieber Vater wohnen.
Ihr stürzt nieder, Millionen?
  Ahnest du den Schöpfer, Welt?
  Such' ihn über'm Sternenzelt!
Über Sternen muss er wohnen.

O ye millions, I embrace ye,
  With a kiss for all the world!
  Brothers, o'er yon starry sphere
Surely dwells a loving Father.
O ye millions, kneel before Him,
  World, dost feel thy Maker near?
  Seek Him o'er yon starry sphere,
O'er the stars enthroned, adore Him!

[Chorus]

"Freude, schöner Götterfunken,
  Tochter aus Elysium," etc.
    [and]
"Seid umschlungen, Millionen!
  Diesen Kuss der ganzen Welt," etc.
Ihr stürzt nieder, Millionen,
  Ahnest du den Schöpfer, Welt?
  Such' ihn über'm Sternenzelt!
Brüder! Brüder!
Über'm Sternenzelt
Muss ein lieber Vater wohnen.

"Praise to Joy, the God-descended
  Daughter of Elysium," etc.
    [and]
"O ye millions, I embrace ye!
  With a kiss for all the world!" etc.
O ye millions, kneel before Him,
  World, dost feel thy Maker near?
  Seek Him o'er yon starry sphere,
Brothers! Brothers!
O'er the stars enthroned, adore Him!

[Chorus]

Freude, Tochter aus Elysium,
  Deine Zauber binden wieder,
Was die Mode streng getheilt;
  Alle Menschen werden Brüder,
Wo dein sanfter Flügel weilt.

Joy, thou daughter of Elysium,
  By thy magic is united
What stern Custom parted wide.
  All mankind are brothers plighted
Where thy gentle wings abide.

[Quartet and Chorus]

"Seid umschlungen, Millionen!" etc.

"O ye millions, I embrace ye!" etc.

L. B.

Concerto for Piano and Orchestra in C major, No. 1 Op. 15

I. Allegro con brio. II. Largo. III. Rondo: Allegro scherzando.

Altogether, Beethoven composed seven piano concertos, or, perhaps, six an
a third, since only the first movement of one such work survives. Five of then
however, are in the active repertory, though the second is infrequently playec

The C major, No. 1, was written, it is said, in 1797, some two years after th
B flat major, which is commonly known as the second. An error in th
publication of the two concertos brought about the inconsistent numberin;
The C major was first performed, according to Bekker, in Vienna, on Apr.
1800, when Beethoven also introduced the First Symphony.

Before either of these two concertos, though, Beethoven had delivered himse
of another, in E flat, at the tender age of fourteen. The manuscript, thirty-tw
pages long, shows a complete solo part with the orchestral introduction, as we

interludes, in piano transcription. Thayer is of the opinion that Beethoven ored the work originally for small orchestra, consisting of strings, flutes, and rns. For a long time it remained unknown. In 1865 Thayer, quoting the emes, included it in his catalogue of Beethoven's works, and Guido Adler fered an edition of the music, which was published in 1888.

The other attempt at the form, which immediately precedes any of the five tablished concertos, is that in the key of D, and here we call again on Thayer, ho advances the theory that it was composed between Beethoven's eighteenth d twenty-third year. Of this, only the first movement exists.

The C major Concerto opens with a brilliant orchestral utterance, offering e first two themes on which it dwells for some time, prior to the entrance of e solo instrument. Written in the period of Beethoven's Mozart-Haydn con-iousness, it shows strongly the influence of both men. Yet in the middle of the ovement a new power asserts itself, that of Beethoven, who appears to be aring himself loose from the old moorings.

The second movement again bows in the general direction of Mozart with s graceful melody, given principally to the piano. A clarinet takes the lead casionally, and the piano part weaves about it in delicate ornamentation.

The third movement is a Rondo, leaning to the Haydnesque, not only as to 10ice of form, but also with respect to the joyous spirit of the music.

R. C. B.

The B flat Piano Concerto, No. 2, Op. 19, actually the first in date of omposition, was probably completed in March, 1795. It was revised for the erformance in Prague of 1798. Beethoven, however, was never satisfied with it. Vith refreshing candor he wrote to the publisher Hofmeister in 1801: "I value 1e concerto at only ten ducats, because, as I have already written, I do not give out as one of my best." Though many might haggle over the price, analysts nd concert pianists have agreed with him. "Beethoven was perfectly right," 1e English biographer Marion M. Scott commented dryly, "the Concerto, 1ough elegant, is indeterminate. Its best touches are never made fully effective —as, for example, the transition from C major ff to D flat pp at bars 39 to 43 n the first movement."

Concerto for Piano and Orchestra in C minor, No. 3, Op. 37

I. Allegro con brio. II. Largo. III. Rondo: Allegro.

APRIL 5, 1803, was a hectic day for a young man in Vienna named Ludwig an Beethoven. A concert of his music was scheduled for that evening at the Theater an der Wien. Among the works billed were a First and Second

Symphony, an Oratorio, and a Piano Concerto in C minor. The soloist was
be himself. Parts of the Concerto and Oratorio were still unwritten. Mar
passages looked like hieroglyphic symbols. A rehearsal was to begin at eigl
and continue till long past noon. So that the Gargantuan program might en
before midnight, the concert was to start at six. Prices had been doubled an
tripled, and grumblings were already heard from the Viennese public.

It is not known whether Beethoven slept on the night of Apr. 4. At five th
following morning his friend and pupil, Ferdinand Ries, found him in be
writing out the trombone parts of the Oratorio. The solo passages of the Cor
certo were indicated by empty spaces or strange scrawlings. Beethoven mac
some speedy additions to the scores and left with Ries for the rehearsal. "It wa
terrible," says Ries. So terrible that Beethoven despaired of the concert's goin
through without mishap. In the midst of the arduous rehearsing the men grev
hungry and sullen. Prince Charles Lichnowsky, who was present, saved the da
by sending out for bread, cold meat, and wine, and inviting the musicians t
partake. They did, avidly, and their mood brightened. The rest of the rehearsa
went better. At 2:30, after six and a half grueling hours, they adjourned ti
early evening.

At the concert the Ritter (Knight) von Seyfried turned the pages fo
Beethoven in the Concerto. It was then and long remained a practice for concer
pianists to play with the music before them. But Beethoven's manuscript wa
almost bare of notes. The few markings were signs recognizable to Beethover
alone. The titled page turner has left an account of his plight:

I saw almost nothing but empty leaves; at the most here and there a fev
Egyptian hieroglyphics, wholly unintelligible to me, scribbled down to serve a
clues for him. He played nearly all the solo part from memory. As was often th
case, he had not had time to put it all on paper. Whenever he reached the end o
an "invisible" passage, he gave me a secret nod. My evident anxiety not to mis
the decisive moment amused him greatly.

Whatever the cause, the public was far from impressed by the new concerto
Even the Oratorio *Christus in Oelberg* was coolly received. But just as the
rehearsal was saved from a fiasco by the timely appearance of food, the concer
and its irritations were promptly forgotten at a late supper described by the
Ritter von Seyfried as "jovial." If Beethoven could "laugh heartily" at the
memory of the Ritter's distress while turning empty pages, he was taking the
whole dismal affair like a sport. No doubt the 1,800 gulden he netted from the
concert helped cheer him up when the niggardly notices appeared. The Vien
nese press either dismissed the concert lightly or groused about the raised
admission prices.

Ries was the soloist at the Concerto's second performance, which occurred a
the Augarten in Vienna late in July the following year. Beethoven conducted

s wrote out a cadenza which met with the composer's approval; but while earsing, muffed some notes in a knotty passage. Beethoven urged him to ite an easier one. Ries did, though he was thoroughly peeved about it. At the icert Beethoven sat down just as his friend was about to begin the cadenza. es tells what happened next:

'I could not prevail on myself to choose the easier passage, and when I boldly gan the harder one Beethoven gave a tremendous jerk with his chair. owever, it all went well, and delighted him so that he cried 'Bravo' loudly. is pleased the audience, and gave me at once a position as an artist." When nposer and soloist met after the concert Beethoven again congratulated Ries, to was a star pupil of his. But he added sternly: "How obstinate you are! you had failed in that passage, I would never have given you a lesson again." The C minor Concerto marks a stage in Beethoven's development midway tween a style broadly influenced by Mozart and one more distinctly his own. he opening theme of the first movement (Allegro con brio, C minor, 4/4), st announced by unison strings, is strictly Beethovenish. The second subject flat major), appearing first in clarinets and first violins, bears a strong ozartean flavor. Unlike Beethoven's later concertos, the slow movement argo, E major, 3/8) does not flow into the finale without a break. The rich velopment of the broad melody which is its base is without parallel in ncerto literature. The finale, in masterly rondo form (Allegro, C minor 2/4), ntains an enharmonic change in the solo writing that foreshadows the style a much later Beethoven.

In all, three noblemen, two of them princes, are variously associated with the minor Concerto: Prince Lichnowsky, who fed the orchestra at rehearsal, the itter von Seyfried, who turned pages of "invisible" writing, and Prince Louis erdinand of Prussia, to whom the work is dedicated.

L. B.

Concerto for Piano and Orchestra in G major, No. 4, Op. 58

I. Allegro moderato. II. Andante con moto. III. Rondo: Vivace.

DEDICATED TO the Archduke Rudolph of Austria, this Concerto had its first ublic performance in the Theater an der Wien, Vienna, on Dec. 22, 1808. he program on that memorable—in more ways than one—occasion was all-eethoven. The list offered, besides the Concerto, "A symphony entitled Recollections of Life in the Country, in F major, No. 5"—(obviously the astoral with the wrong numbering); an Aria, "Ah, perfido," delivered by osephine Kilitzky; Hymn with soloists and chorus; Grand Symphony in C ninor, No. 6—(again wrong numbering); the Sanctus from the Mass in C

major; Fantasia for Pianoforte Solo; Fantasia for Pianoforte "into which th
full orchestra enters little by little, and at the end the chorus joins in the Finale

The Josephine Kilitzky mentioned as singer of "Ah, perfido," by the wa
got her opportunity after two others had rejected the engagement—Ann
Pauline Milder, because Beethoven had referred to her betrothed as "a stup
ass," and Antonia Campi, because her husband resented the fact that she ha
not been approached first. Mme. Campi, we are told, was an extremely capab
artist with a beautiful voice and seventeen children, among them one set o
triplets and four pairs of twins!

The Kilitzky girl, scared stiff, could barely sing a note. As one auditor put i
"That the beautiful child trembled more than she sang was to be laid to th
terrible cold; for we shivered in the boxes, although wrapped in furs an
cloaks." However, subsequent reports on her capabilities are all to the compli
mentary. She sang for many years, and often and well, no matter—one surmise
—whether the mercury was up or down.

The opinion of early nineteenth-century critics is divided on the subject o
Beethoven's powers as pianist. J. B. Cramer, an eminent performer himsel
said of him, "All in all, Beethoven was, if not the greatest, certainly one of th
greatest and most admirable pianists I have ever heard." But Ludwig Spoh
balanced the scale after hearing Beethoven play. He said:

It was by no means an enjoyment, for, in the first place, the piano was woefull
out of tune, which, however, troubled Beethoven little, for he could hear nothin
of it; and, secondly, of the former so much admired excellence of the virtuos
scarcely anything was left, in consequence of his total deafness. In the forte th
poor deaf man hammered in such a way upon the keys that entire groups of note
were inaudible, so that one lost entire intelligence of the subject, unless the ey
followed the score at the same time. I felt moved with the deepest sorrow at s
hard a destiny.

Yet Reichardt, who was present at the first hearing of the G major Concerto
wrote, "He played . . . with astounding cleverness and in the fastest possibl
tempi. The Adagio, a masterly movement of beautifully developed song, h
sang on his instrument with a profound melancholy that thrilled me." It ma
be pointed out that certain others found Beethoven's playing good only in th
slower movements and that he was otherwise considered a violent performer

The G major Concerto lay neglected for a considerable period, while it
mates the C minor, No. 3, and the *Emperor* took all the honors. It wa
Mendelssohn who saved it, possibly, from oblivion, and his revival of the work
at the Leipzig Gewandhaus in 1836, stirred Schumann into writing, "I have
received a pleasure from it such as I have never enjoyed, and I sat in my plac
without moving a muscle or even breathing—afraid of making the least noise."

Beethoven wrote three cadenzas for this Concerto, two for the first movement d another for the Rondo. Over the one with the difficult double trills (first movement) he wrote "Cadenza (*ma senza cadere*)."

At the beginning of the first movement (Allegro moderato, G major, 4/4) Beethoven flies in the face of tradition by giving the opening phrase to the piano alone, whereupon the orchestra enters. For the rest of the movement the procedure is orthodox enough.

The second movement (Andante con moto, E minor, 2/4) is one of the most famous in the literature of the concerto. Its instrumental dialogue has been thus described by William Foster Apthorp:

The strings of the orchestra keep repeating a forbidding figure of strongly marked rhythm in staccato octaves; this figure continues at intervals in stern, unchanging forte through about half the movement and then gradually dies away. In the intervals of this harsh theme the pianoforte, as it were, improvises little snaps of the tenderest, sweetest harmony and melody, rising for a moment into the wildest frenzied exultation after its enemy, the orchestra, has been silenced by its soft pleading, then falling back into hushed sadness as the orchestra comes in once more with a whispered recollection of its once so cruel phrase, saying as plainly as an orchestra can say it, "The rest is silence!"

This Andante has been compared to Orpheus taming the wild beasts with his music. Says Tovey:

The orchestra does not imitate wild beasts, and the pianoforte does not imitate a lyre or a singer. But the orchestra (consisting of the strings alone) is entirely in octaves, without a vestige of harmony, so long as it remains stubborn and rough in its share of the dialogue with the quiet, veiled tones of the solo.

The finale (Rondo: Vivace, G major, 2/4), succeeding the Andante without pause, opens pianissimo, its lively first theme given out by the strings. The second subject is announced in due course by the piano. This movement is especially noteworthy for the scale of its "enormous coda."

R. C. B.

Concerto for Piano and Orchestra in E flat major, No. 5 ("Emperor"), Op. 73

I. Allegro. II. Adagio un poco moto. III. Rondo: Allegro.

THERE IS slight irony in the fact that Beethoven's fifth piano concerto bears the title *Emperor*. Beethoven wrote it in Vienna in 1809 while the city was occupied by Napoleon's troops. Along with other Viennese he suffered the usual restrictions imposed by an army of occupation. His resentment against the self-elevated despot mounted. He probably remembered how his early admiration prompted him to dedicate his *Eroica Symphony* to Napoleon. And how he had

angrily ripped the dedication page from the score when the ambitious "man
the people" had proclaimed himself "Emperor" in 1804. "This man will tramp
the rights of men underfoot to indulge his ambition and become a great
tyrant than any other," he raged to his young friend and pupil, Ferdinand Ri

But the title *Emperor Concerto* was not Beethoven's, just as *Jupiter Sympho*
was not Mozart's idea. Unquestionably, Beethoven would have strongly
sented the title, if only out of personal bitterness at the imperial upstart w
had betrayed his republican beginnings. The way he felt may be gathered fro
a story told about him during the occupation. He was seated in his favor
coffee house one day as a French officer passed by. "If I as a general knew
much about strategy as I the composer know about counterpoint," he shout
at the officer, shaking his fist, "I would give you something to do!" The wide
accepted theory regarding the origin of the title is that an early publisher
pianist thought it an appropriate term to convey the concerto's "grand dime
sions and intrinsic splendor." Of course, the dedication on the score publish
in February, 1811, reads *"Grand Concerto pour le pianoforte avec accompagn
ment de l'orchestre composé et dédié à Son Altesse Impériale Roudolp
Archi-Duc d'Autriche, par L. v. Beethoven Oeuv. 73."* So the early enthusi
who so dubbed the concerto may have had an actual "Emperor" in mind, n
merely a high-sounding term of praise. Yet, Beethoven never called it th
any more than he christened his Sonata in C sharp minor the *Moonlight Sona*

Though completed in 1809, the Concerto apparently collected dust for tw
years before anyone played it. Late in 1811, Friedrich Schneider was soloist
the supposed premiere of the work at a concert in Leipzig directed by Johar
Philipp Christian Schulz. The *Allgemeine Musik Zeitung* of January, 181
carried the following remarks about the new concerto:

It is without doubt one of the most original, imaginative, most effective but al
one of the most difficult of all existing concertos. Herr Musikdirector Schneid
played it with such mastery as could scarcely have been believed possible, an
this not only in the attention given to facility, clarity, technical certainty, an
delicacy, but with insight into the spirit and feeling of the work.

The orchestra, too, with unmistakable respect and love for the composer, fu
filled every desire in its playing of the work for the solo performer. So it coul
not have been otherwise than that the crowded audience was soon put into such
state of enthusiasm that it could hardly content itself with the ordinary expression
of recognition and enjoyment.

Its first performance in Vienna on Feb. 12, 1812, with Karl Czerny as soloist
somehow failed to work the audience up to "such a state of enthusiasm" tha
it had to resort to exceptional "expressions of recognition and enjoyment.
But then the whole occasion was slightly on the eccentric side. A Charitab
Society of Noble Ladies had put on a combined concert and art exhibi

'Represented" were three pictures, after Raphael, Poussin, and Toryes, "as Goethe describes them in his *Elective Affinities*." A vast array of sopranos, tenors, violinists, and pianists, was listed. Thayer, in his biography of Beethoven, haughtily dismisses "the trills of Miss Sessi and Mr. Siboni" as "appropriate to the occasion and the audience."

Theodor Körner, then visiting Vienna, makes the remark in a letter written home on Feb. 15 that "a new concerto by Beethoven for the pianoforte did not succeed." The *Thalia* attributed the failure to the refusal of the "proud and overconfident" Beethoven to write down to the crowd. "He can be understood and appreciated only by connoisseurs," it declared, "and one cannot reckon on their being in a majority at such an affair." The majority evidently was more interested in the trio of tableaux "as described in Goethe's *Elective Affinities*." The set consisted of "The Queen of Sheba Doing Homage to King Solomon," "Esther Fainting before King Ahasuerus," and "The Arrest of Haman by Command of Ahasuerus in the Presence of Esther." The edifying spectacle caused such a flurry among the members of the Charitable Society of Noble Ladies that each of the tableaux had to be repeated. The *Emperor Concerto* must have seemed pretty tame stuff by comparison!

The *Emperor Concerto* opens with the full orchestra vigorously sounding a tonic chord of E flat. There follows a cadenza for the solo instrument in rhapsodic vein, broken into by fortissimo chords. A short transitional passage introduces the first violins in the chief theme, later taken up by clarinets. A pianissimo section, in E flat minor, brings in the second theme, also on the strings, which pass it on to the horns several measures later.

The piano reenters the scheme with an extended treatment of the first and second subjects. When the piano takes up the second theme it is in B minor, with pizzicato supports from the strings. The orchestra then intones the theme, forte. There is development, largely centering in the first theme, and a mighty crescendo leads to the pause and cadenza. Here Beethoven breaks with the custom of the time, expressly forbidding any impromptu virtuosity on the part of the soloist. *"Non si fa una cadenza,"* he enjoins, *"ma s'attacca subito il sequente"* ("Don't make a cadenza here, but attack what follows immediately.") The orchestra accompanies the latter section of Beethoven's cadenza.

The main part of the second movement (Adagio un poco moto, B major, 4/4) is a sequence of "quasi-variations" (as Sir George Grove described them) on the hymnlike melody first announced by the strings, with the violins muted. A second subject, in pensive mood, is brought in softly by the piano. With the piano first throwing out a thematic hint of the chief subject of the Rondo to come, the Adagio movement bridges over into the finale (Allegro, E flat major, 6/8) without a break. Both themes of the Rondo are stated and fully expounded by the solo instrument. The movement has been called the "most spacious and triumphant of concerto rondos." Toward the end of the coda

occurs a famous passage in which the kettledrums, marking the rhythm of t
first subject pianissimo, accompany the piano's diminuendo chords in a lo
descent.

L. B.

Concerto for Violin and Orchestra in D major, Op. 61

I. Allegro ma non troppo. II. Larghetto. III. Finale: Rondo.

DATING FROM a particularly productive period in Beethoven's career, t
Concerto was written for Franz Clement, who introduced it at the Theater
der Wien, Vienna, on Dec. 23, 1806. Also produced in that period were t
opera *Fidelio,* the *Leonore Overtures,* the three *Rasoumowsky Quartets,* t
G major Piano Concerto, and the Fourth and Fifth Symphonies. It may
interesting to note that the Concerto was far from completed when Cleme
called his rehearsal, so the violinist played it at sight at the concert.

Franz Clement was a magnificent violinist, according to ear witnesses. H
possessed a virtuoso technic, besides "great refinement and elegance" (in h
playing, one presumes). Yet he was not averse to occasional little sallies in
boastful display. At the same concert he performed a work—either a fantas
or a set of variations, the authorities are not exactly sure which—with the viol
upside down!

Be that as it may, the Concerto was enthusiastically received, as the saying i
and a good deal of the applause surely went to Clement's performance of i
It is generally believed that the work, as we know it today, differs materiall
from the version played at its premiere. The manuscript is now in the possessio
of the Vienna Library—or it was, up to advices just pre-Anschluss—and
shows a great number of corrections in ink, in pencil, and in red chalk, all i
Beethoven's hand. A few of them may have been suggested by Clement afte
his memorable performance. The present work, corrections and all, was pub
lished in 1809, with a dedication "*à son Ami Monsieur de Breuning, Secretair
Aulique au Service de sa Majesté l'Empereur d'Autriche par Louis va
Beethoven.*"

As has been pointed out above, the audience did like the work, but ther
were several conservatives present who did a mite of carping, as conservative
will. For example, Johann Nepomuk Möser wrote of it:

The judgment of connoisseurs is unanimous; its many beauties must be con
ceded, but it must also be acknowledged that the continuity is often completel
broken and that the endless repetitions of certain commonplace passages ma
easily become tedious to the listener. It is to be said that Beethoven might emplo
his indubitable [no less!] talents more fittingly by giving us such works as th
first symphonies in C and D, the charming Septet in E flat, the ingenious Quinte

D major, and more of his earlier compositions, which will always place him the front rank of composers. It is to be feared, at the same time, that if eethoven continues upon this path he and the public will fare badly.

There were other malcontents at that introductory performance. Some of em were bothered no end with Beethoven's use of the kettledrum and one it quipped, so slyly: "A Concerto for the Kettledrum."

Conversely, Paul Bekker regarded the work as eminently suited to the violin. e says of the Larghetto:

As in the G major Pianoforte Concerto, Beethoven makes the slow movement his Violin Concerto a kind of imaginative dialogue in the manner of improvition. . . . The climax is reached in a violin melody of enchanting beauty and ɔirituality, whence the orchestra suddenly brings us back to earth and to the eerful, somewhat lengthy, but forceful closing Rondo.

It is a matter of history that Beethoven had a work for violin and orchestra i mind as early as 1788, when he partially wrote a *Concertstück in C*. The ɪanuscript eventually landed in the library of the Gesellschaft der Musik-eunde, Vienna. The single movement was finished by Joseph Hellmsberger nd published in 1876. Juan Manén made another version, he touched up the ɪchestration, added a cadenza and performed it at Barcelona in 1930.

That Beethoven had intentions to produce still another concerto is suggested y the fact that the title page of the piano arrangement of the D major carries ɪe line "his first concerto for violin by Louis van Beethoven."

Paul Bekker wrote as follows:

The Violin Concerto opens with a broadly designed orchestral prelude from vhich the solo part is later gradually differentiated. Before this occurs, the rich ɪought material underlying the work is displayed and its course indicated. Bee-hoven must have written the work lovingly and in a moment of very happy nspiration. The Allegro begins with a nobly pathetic march, a tense knocking notive for the kettledrum, continued through the whole movement, now energetic nd menacing, now tender and persuasive.

Bekker goes on to assure us that the themes are absolutely suited to the haracter of the violin as Beethoven understood it; the tuneful lyrical quality is mphasized, virtuosity wisely suppressed.

Comparing this use of the violin for lyrical expression with the earlier violin omances, Bekker declares that Beethoven gives the violin its true function as ɪ solo instrument.

The main theme is sometimes dreamy, sometimes majestic and brilliant, rising ɪt the close to the perfection of melody. As in the G major Pianoforte Concerto, Beethoven makes the slow movement of his Violin Concerto a kind of imagina-ive dialogue in the manner of improvisation. . . . The climax is reached in a

violin melody of enchanting beauty and spirituality, whence the orchestra sud
denly brings us back to earth and to the cheerful, somewhat lengthy, but forcefu
closing Rondo.

R. C. B.

Concerto for Piano, Violin, Violoncello, and Orchestra in C major, Op. 56

I. Allegro. II. Largo. III. Finale: Rondo alla Polacca.

ALLEGEDLY INTENDED as a "renovation" of the concerto-grosso style of Bach'
day, the triple concerto has suffered a relatively harsh fate, as Beethoven's com
positions go. The solo demands are such that three first-class artists are required
one and, occasionally, two soloists, being, of course, the normal concerto re
quirement. That, together with the work's seeming "dryness" of style, ha
militated against its becoming a repertory staple. No "request" program ever
lists it, and whenever it comes up for a hearing many look upon it as a freak
and the performance as a stunt. In a way, it is the black sheep of Beethoven'
larger orchestral works. Premiered in 1807, it enjoyed no further performance
in Beethoven's lifetime.

As for the Concerto's merits and demerits, partisanship has been strong on
both sides. The most adulatory biographers will turn on it ruthlessly. For
instance, Marion M. Scott levels the threefold charge that it "rouses expecta
tions of great music it never fulfils," that it "deals out platitudinous craftsmanship," that it is "animated by duty, not inspiration." The late Paul Bekker, in
one of his two or three lapses from starry-eyed worship, regretfully avowed that
the triple concerto was "one of very few examples in which it is clear that
technical effort actually outweighs inspiration." Somehow, he felt, Beethoven's
usually unsparing critical faculty had allowed an "inferior conception to pass
muster." In short, even the gods nodded!

Sir Donald Francis Tovey, leaping indignantly to the work's defence,
belabored all critics and concertgoers who imputed "dullness" and "dryness"
to it. "Beethoven cannot be thus lightly dismissed," he retorted. "If it were not
by Beethoven, but by some mysterious composer who had written nothing else
and who had the romantic good fortune to die before it came to performance,
the very people who blame Beethoven for writing below his full powers would
be the first to acclaim it as the work of a still greater composer." His position
was that judging the triple concerto by any other standards but its own was
futile and unrevealing. "Let us take it on its own terms," he counseled.

Taking the Concerto, accordingly, "on its own terms" involves the major
premise that Beethoven knew what he wanted in writing a triple concerto and
only forwarded it to his publisher with the full approval of his own "critical

faculty." Tovey, moreover, is convinced that without the triple concerto Beethoven "could not have achieved" the Piano Concertos in G and E flat and the Violin Concerto. In this sense Op. 56 may even be viewed as "a study for these works." As proof Tovey gives the sombrely reserved melody of the Adagio, first given with muted violins, as foreshadowing the E flat Concerto in mood and tone color.

Concerning the charge of "dullness," the British savant admitted the "severe" simplicity of the thematic and ornamental material used in the Concerto, but shows them to be necessary to Beethoven's scheme. He felt that the vast architectural plan adopted by Beethoven could not effectively be "combined with a severe study in pure color" if the themes were such "as to attract attention to themselves." In other words, the themes should be considered purely as formulas in an abstract scheme. "In no case of this type will any sensible person suppose that the composer's invention is at fault."

In Tovey's opinion the triple concerto in many ways satisfies the Greek ideal of combining simplicity and subtlety as the highest quality in art. He conceded its "extraordinary" severity. What is required of performers and listeners alike is the "fullest recognition of the grand manner in every detail."

It is thought that Beethoven composed the triple concerto with the Archduke Rudolph in mind for the solo piano part. There is only circumstantial evidence to support this theory. What makes it plausible is that Rudolph, about sixteen at the time, had just become a pupil of Beethoven. The work was sketched in the spring of 1805, though reference to it is made in Beethoven's letter of Aug. 26, 1804, to Breitkopf and Härtel. There he offers it as one of three large works, for the munificent sum of 2,000 florins, less than $1,000, with three "new solo sonatas" thrown in, apparently, for good measure. The first of the large works was the *Mount of Olives Oratorio*. The second was "a new Grand Symphony." It is given the title of "Bonaparte" in the course of the letter and, of course, is none other than the *Eroica*. The third large work is mentioned as a "concertante for piano, violin, and violoncello and full orchestra."

Possibly to make the offer as attractive as possible Beethoven points out one or two novel features in the "Bonaparte" symphony and the "concertante." After stating that the symphony will contain "three obbligato horns," he remarks with astonishing casualness, "I think it will interest the musical public." As for the triple concerto, Breitkopf and Härtel no doubt readily agreed that "a concertante with three such concerting parts is indeed also something new." Presently the Titan discusses terms, and a less casual note of worldly shrewdness creeps into the letter.

If, as I expect, you agree to the conditions stated for these works, as regards their publication, I would give them to you for a fee of 2,000 florins. I assure you, on my honor, that, with regard to certain works, such, for instance, as sonatas, I am a loser, since I get almost sixty ducats for a single solo sonata.

Pray, do not think that I boast. Far be it from me to do anything of the sor
But in order the quicker to arrange for an edition of my works, I am ready to be
loser to some extent.

The Concerto was published in 1807, the year that also saw the publicatio
of the *Appassionata Sonata* and the Thirty-two Variations in C minor, thoug
little else of Beethoven's. Its premiere occurred that summer at the Augarten i
Vienna. No other performance is recorded until 1830, when Bocklet, Maysede
and Merk, respectively, pianist, violinist, and cellist, joined in a revival of it i
the Austrian capital.

For the opening movement of the work, Beethoven adopts the accepted devic
of double exposition, the solo instruments following the orchestra in stating th
themes. Cellos and basses announce the main Allegro theme (C major, 4/4)
after which the first violins bring in the flowing second subject, in G. The sol
voices then discourse the chief theme. The cello takes it up first, followed b
the violin, and then both suavely make way for the piano.

In the second movement, marked Largo (A flat major, 3/8), the solo cell
launches into the cantabile theme after its partial statement by muted violin
The piano weaves some embroidery around the theme, while clarinets an
bassoons restate it. Solo violin and cello promptly join in, and the movemen
soon leads into the Finale (Rondo alla Polacca, C major, 3/4).

This is based on an unpretentious tune in polonaise style. The solo cell
tackles it first, then the violin, after which soloists and orchestra enlarge on th
theme at some length. A rondo in polonaise style was no innovation i
Beethoven's time. Others had used it, though it was Chopin of course who gav
the polonaise tremendous concert appeal through his piano renderings. Beetho
ven uses the polonaise three times in all: in the Serenade Trio, Op. 8, in
piano piece (Op. 89), and in the triple concerto. Tovey sets them apart from
other polonaises as "eminently aristocratic and charmingly feminine."

What has especially intrigued those who accept the Concerto wholeheartedl
is Beethoven's adroit way of relating the ingenious trio-writing to the orchestra
support. Of course, the old concerto-grosso plan promptly suggests itself. Th
American writer Krehbiel went so far as to say that the triple concerto i
interesting "if for no other reason than that it is a comparatively moder
exfoliation of the concerto grosso of the Bach period."

L. B.

Overture to "Prometheus," Op. 43

SOMETIME IN 1800 Beethoven began to compose the music for a "heroic and
allegorical ballet," *Die Geschöpfe des Prometheus* (*The Creatures of Prome
theus*). It was completed early in the following year and, all told, it consisted

of sixteen numbers, preceded by an overture. Salvatore Vigano, an Italian dancer and choreographer, had provided Beethoven with the scenario and dance action. Vigano's travels once brought him to Madrid where he met and married the beautiful Spanish dancer, Maria Medina. A personable chap, Vigano was also a bit of a musician, a leaning he may have inherited from Boccherini, who was his uncle. When necessary he could also compose the music for a *divertissement*.

Vigano and wife arrived in Vienna in 1793, and it took only a short time for them both to become immensely popular with the art, culture, and court crowd. Mme. Medina, in particular, excited much admiration, as might have been expected, since the Viennese have ever responded nobly to female pulchritude. She must have been truly outstanding, for it is said the Empress of Austria herself felt a pang or two of jealousy at the frequent visits made by Francis II to the Hoftheater where the dancer appeared.

In any case, the ballet was given its first showing at the Hoftheater on Mar. 28, 1801. Curtain time was at 6:30 P.M., and the curtain raiser was a singspiel, *Der Dorfbarbier* (*The Village Barber*), by Johann Schenk, Haydn's teacher. This work had already made an auspicious debut in Vienna some five years previously.

The program of the event carried the following "argument" of the ballet:

The basis of this allegorical ballet is the fable of Prometheus. The Greek philosophers, by whom he was known, allude to him as a lofty soul who drove the people of his time from ignorance, refined them by means of science and the arts, and gave them manners, customs, and morals. As a result of that conception, two statues which have been brought to life are introduced into this ballet, and these, through the power of harmony, are made sensitive to the passions of human existence. Prometheus leads them to Parnassus, in order that Apollo, the god of the arts, may enlighten them. Apollo gives them as teachers Amphion, Arion, and Orpheus to instruct them in music, Melpomene to teach them tragedy; Thalia, comedy; Terpsichore and Pan, the shepherd's dance, and Bacchus, the heroic dance, of which he was the originator.

A laconic statement by Beethoven concerning Vigano's part in the proceedings reveals that he may have expected too much of the choreographer. He wrote to the Leipzig publisher Hofmeister on Apr. 22, 1801, "I have written a ballet, in which, however, the ballet master has not made the best of his part." At any rate, the piano score for *Die Geschöpfe des Prometheus* was published by Artaria, of Vienna, in June, 1801, with a dedication to Prince Lichnowsky. The orchestral version of the Overture was brought out by Hofmeister and Kühnel in 1804.

Oddly enough, the music for the finale contains two themes that Beethoven utilized in other compositions of his. One of these, in E flat major, appears in a *Contretanz*. It was also employed as chief subject in the Fiftee Variations and Fugue, composed in 1802, and in a similar capacity for th Finale of the *Eroica Symphony*, completed in 1804.

R. C. B.

Overture to "Coriolanus," Op. 62

ALTHOUGH BEETHOVEN was familiar with Shakespeare's tragedy, *Coriolanu* and had read Plutarch's *Lives*, his overture was directly inspired by a Germa work *Coriolan*, written in 1802 by an Austrian official and playwrigh Heinrich Joseph von Collin. This fact is not highly important. Both Collin an Beethoven knew their Shakespeare and Plutarch. Plutarch, in turn, knew hi Livy. Substantially, the crux of the Coriolanus story is the same in all accounts The pride and obstinacy of the Roman patrician finally yield to the wife's an mother's pleas. Coriolanus may have died in exile, may have committed sui cide, may have been treacherously slain by the Volscian general Aufidius Plutarch, Livy, and von Collin differ on the subject. It is even possible Corio lanus never existed; or if he did, the stories of the Greek Themistocles an Alcibiades, who also went over to the enemy, somehow got tangled up wit his own. History has shrouded the facts in legend. Art alone—Plutarch's, Livy's Shakespeare's, Beethoven's—has given the epic figure of Rome's banished her a living reality.

Gaius Marcius Coriolanus was said to have derived the surname he bor from his conquest of the Volscian city Corioli in 493 B.C. A proud aristocrat he fought and denounced the popular tribunes of Rome. The tribunes wer the spokesmen of the plebeian classes. Coriolanus proposed that before distrib uting the corn supplies from Sicily to the people, the system of tribunes shoul be abolished. He was charged with disloyalty and sent into exile.

The Volscians received him with open arms. Coriolanus mustered a huge army and, after a series of victories, marched on Rome. Reaching the gates of his native city, he paused before launching the final onslaught. Deputations of patricians and priests came out to plead with him. Coriolanus would not budge. For having banished him, Rome must pay with her utter ruin. The Romans now played their trump card. They sent his wife Virgilia, his mother Volumnia, and his son Marcus. Coriolanus, contemptuous and unshakable at first, finally gave in. At this point Shakespeare followed Plutarch in having Coriolanus murdered by the Volscian Aufidius. In Collin's play, Coriolanus takes his own life.

Wagner, in one of his best prose essays, advises listeners to forget all about the Collin play and concentrate on the denouement of Shakespeare's tragedy as the true dramatic counterpart of Beethoven's overture. The reference is to the third scene of Act V, where Coriolanus is confronted by his family in the

olscian camp on the outskirts of Rome. Thus the opening section, with its
ortissimo C's, resounding chords, and dramatic first theme, would depict the
efiant renegade in his mad resolve to level Rome. In keeping with this
nalysis, the poignantly lyrical second theme, announced in the first violins
1 E flat, presents the contrasting voice of Volumnia imploring her son to
esist. Wagner says:

We shall see one solitary shape loom forth, the defiant Coriolanus in conflict
ith his inmost voice, that voice which only speaks the more unsilenceably when
ssuing from his mother's mouth. And of the dramatic development there will
emain but that voice's victory over pride, the breaking of the stubbornness of a
ature strong beyond all bonds.

Reichard was convinced that Beethoven intended the *Coriolanus Overture*
s a self-portrait, that the music reveals more to us of Beethoven's character
han of Coriolanus'.

L. B.

Overture to "Leonore," No. 2, Op. 72

Few operas have aroused such controversy as Beethoven's single contribution
o the stage, *Fidelio,* first entitled *Leonore.* At one end are those belittling the
core as purely "symphonic" rather than "operatic"; at the other, the Bee-
hoven devotees, among them highly respected conductors and singers, rank-
ng it at the very top of the repertory. Between extremes are as many varieties
of opinion as there are approaches to dramatic art. But there is no denying
Fidelio's pulsing humanity and emotional power. Beethoven's sincerity as
rtist and man rings out from every phrase. It is not fantastic to regard
Fidelio as a companion portrait to the *Eroica.* In the symphony, Beethoven
nshrines an ideal hero, in the opera, an ideal heroine—the fearless and devoted
Leonore.

If the opera itself has stirred up esthetic strife, what shall be said of the
angle of conflict and confusion caused by *Fidelio's* four overtures? The
chronology and appropriateness of all four have been freely argued over,
and a fat volume could be made of the scholarly pros and cons. In 1924, Josef
Braunstein's keen analysis of the overtures appeared to clinch the issue of
chronological order. The numbering of the *Leonore* overtures is now accepted
as correct in its given sequence; *i.e.,* No. 1 really came first (actually a discarded attempt), No. 2 second, and No. 3 third. Internal evidence of style
confirms this. The fourth overture, entitled *Fidelio,* came last.

The second overture to *Leonore* was first heard at the world premiere of
Fidelio, on Nov. 20, 1805, in Vienna's Theater an der Wien, and thus boasts
a special distinction apart from its intrinsic worth. Dr. Henry Reeve, attending the third performance of Beethoven's opera, left a description of the com-

poser: "Beethoven presided at the pianoforte and directed the performance himself. He is a small, dark, young-looking man, and wears spectacles." The opera was cordially received, and at the end of the performance copies of complimentary verses "showered down from the gallery," according to the observant doctor. Later the opera was withdrawn and revised. When it reappeared in Vienna in March, 1806, it was provided with a remodeled version of the earlier overture, which explains *Leonore No. 3.* A final revision of the opera in 1814 accounts for version No. 4, called the *Fidelio Overture,* and the one now regularly doing duty as curtain raiser.

The story of *Fidelio* hinges on an episode of political tyranny. Florestan is imprisoned in a Spanish dungeon by his ruthless enemy Pizarro. He is slowly starving to death. His wife Leonore, intent on freeing him, disguises herself as a man and secures a job as assistant to the jailor Rocco. She gives her name as Fidelio. Pizarro decides to slay Florestan before the expected arrival of Don Fernando, the state minister. He orders a grave dug.

Rocco gets Leonore to help him dig the grave. When Pizarro at length tries to stab Florestan, Leonore rushes to shield him. "First kill his wife!" she shouts. Pizarro, furious, tries to slay them both, but Leonore whips out a pistol. "One word more and you die!" she cries. Suddenly a trumpet call sounds. Don Fernando has arrived. Florestan and Leonore are saved and reunited.

The introductory part of the overture consists of an Adagio based on Florestan's despairing aria, "In des Lebens Frühlingstagen" ("In the Springtime of Life"). There follows a brilliant Allegro, unfolding at some length. With dramatic suddenness the off-stage trumpet calls, announcing deliverance for Florestan and Leonore, are heard. Florestan's aria returns, again adagio, and soon the violins discourse a fresh theme before the stirring Coda begins.

Clearly the opening Adagio and middle Allegro section are of such broad scope that no classic recapitulation of material was possible, and the coda, as pointed out, "is not big enough to compensate for its absence." In the third *Leonore Overture,* Beethoven altered the formal design to bring the music into stricter conformity with sonata structure. The reprise of the Allegro section sets it markedly apart from its predecessor. Moreover, to make room for both the Allegro reprise and the more fully developed coda, much of the Adagio and Allegro material of the earlier overture had to be omitted in the third.

Because of its more brilliant exposition and incisive Presto finale, the *Leonore No. 3* ranks first in popularity, though the No. 2 has been regarded as a more masterly "tone poem" in mirroring the opera's action. Paul Bekker even thought the second superior in "grandeur of conception and imaginative originality."

On the subject of preferences, Romain Rolland's advice should be heeded: "Let us prefer them both!" As for which of the four overtures best serves to introduce Beethoven's great opera, opinion is again divergent, though all would agree that the fourth, and shortest, is the most convenient. Perhaps Olin Downes said the final word on that point when he stated flatly that the ideal *Fidelio* overture "will never be heard, and never was written." In any case, *Leonore* overtures Nos. 2 and 3, whatever their disqualifications as operatic overtures, are certainly self-sustaining dramas.

L. B.

Overture to "Egmont," Op. 84

ONE OF the first things Josef Härtl did, after taking over the management of the Vienna Court Theaters in 1808, was to put into process a revival of plays by Goethe and Schiller with specially composed music. Beethoven, coming prominently into the scheme, did the music for Goethe's *Egmont,* supplying an overture, four entr'actes, two songs for the heroine, Clärchen, the music for Clärchen's death, a "melodrama" and, for finale, a *Triumph Symphony*. The last named is the Overture's coda. The music completed and the play rehearsed and in readiness, the production took place at the Hofburg Theater, Vienna, on May 24, 1810.

There were several interesting sidelights to the musical aspects of the venture. Beethoven, for one thing, had indicated a preference for one of Schiller's plays, specifically, *William Tell*. The usual intrigues—rampant in Beethoven's times as in ours—circumvented that, for the assignment went to one Adalbert Gyrowetz, a Bohemian composer. Then, the fact that Beethoven could choose Schiller over Goethe is in itself a rather startling thing when we recall what Romain Rolland has had to say of the Beethoven-Goethe mutual admiration society.

Others have been prompted to remark on the strong spiritual bonds—alleged or otherwise—between the two men. Rochlitz, for instance, quoted the composer as saying once, "I would have gone to my death, yes, ten times to my death for Goethe. Then, when I was at the height of my enthusiasm, I thought out my *Egmont* music. Goethe—he lives and wants us all to live with him. It is for that reason that he can be composed. Nobody is so easily composed as he."

Goethe, on the other hand, though reputedly not a Beethoven fan, wrote in a letter, shortly after his meeting with the composer, a brief analysis of Beethoven the man:

I made the acquaintance of Beethoven at Teplitz. His talent astonished me prodigiously, but he is, unfortunately, a wholly untamed person. It is true that he is not utterly wrong when he finds the world detestable, but this will not make it more enjoyable for himself and for others. Yet he is to be excused and much pitied, for he has lost his hearing, which is, perhaps, of less injury to his art than to his social relations. Already laconic by nature, he will be doubly so by reason of the infirmity.

Evening the score, as it were, Beethoven also did some character reading, for he told Härtl on one occasion, "Goethe is too fond of the atmosphere of the court; fonder than becomes a poet. There is little room for sport over the absurdities of the virtuosi when poets, who ought to be looked upon as the foremost teachers of the nation, can forget everything else in the enjoyment of court glitter."

The foregoing proves rather confusing as to the actual relationship between Goethe and Beethoven, but, at least, we have the *Egmont* music, for which we are either indebted to Härtl, as liaison agent, or to out-and-out intrigue, which sometimes serves a noble purpose.

The hero of Goethe's tragedy, Count Egmont (1522-1568), took an important part in the early upheavals in the Low Countries, which later resulted in their liberation from the Spanish rule. At first he was a captain in the military retinue of Charles V, the Spanish Emperor, in the campaign against the French. However, his success against the Maréchal de Thermes, in 1558, earned for him the enmity of the Duke of Alba. His countrymen, nevertheless, gave him the adoration due an emancipator, since he had rescued Flanders from the French yoke.

Philip II, who succeeded Charles V, made a bold stroke in attempting to turn Flanders into a Spanish dependency, and Egmont, among others, protested, though not to the point of open rebellion. His days were numbered with that gesture, for when the Duke of Alba went to the Netherlands in 1567, to quell uprisings, Egmont was imprisoned and finally put to death for high treason at Brussels, on June 4, 1568. With his execution he became immediately a symbol of martyrdom, such was his hold on the popular imagination.

In the construction of the play, Goethe did some dramaturgical handsprings, inventing the heroine Clärchen and blithely, as dramatists will, overlooking certain other issues. The author said of his work, "Had I been willing to make Egmont, as history informs us, the father of a dozen children, his flippant actions would have seemed too ridiculous, and so it was necessary for me to have another Egmont, one that would harmonize better with the scenes in which he took part and my poetic purpose." And he asks, reasonably enough, "For what, then, are poets, if they only wish to repeat the account of a historian?"

The Overture begins in the key of F minor, offering a theme that might be likened to an ancient and stately Spanish dance, bolstered with staccato chords. Its central section could be descriptive of an epic struggle. There is a startling pause at its zenith, and eight triple-piano measures give the impression of a "brief requiem," which is, in effect, a modulatory passage to the coda's "Triumph Symphony" (F major).

R. C. B.

Grand Fugue in B flat major, Op. 133
[Transcribed for orchestra by Felix Weingartner]

ORIGINALLY THIS fugue was the concluding section of the String Quartet in B flat major, No. 13, Op. 130. The work, completed in 1825, was so admired by Holz that he declared to the composer, "This is the greatest of your quartets." Beethoven answered, "Each in its way. Art demands of us that we shall not stand still. You will find a new manner of voice treatment (part writing) and, thank God, there is less lack of fancy than ever before."

The Fugue was deemed unplayable for a long time. It became the innocent target of such choice descriptive terms as "grotesque, uncouth, and cacophonous," as Eric Blom tells us. However, it was finally published separately, and Beethoven wrote a new finale for his quartet in 1826.

The Grand Fugue, *tantôt libre, tantôt recherchée,* is a colossal structure, teeming with ideas and of unbelievable scope. It opens with an introduction, which brings forward the motto subject, its various transformations foreshadowing the character of the three parts of its later development. As the fugue itself begins, a new subject makes its entrance, a rhythmic theme of widely leaping intervals, and the motto assumes the position of countersubject. Beethoven works all this into a first section, which is in itself a complete fugue. The second section is briefer and utilizes the motto theme as principal subject. The third section brings both themes into a rich counterplay, almost a contention, it would seem, with the motto theme emerging winner, the other runner-up. To conclude, the composer, with the greatest skill, welds the two musical ideas into a solidly knit pattern.

The B flat major Quartet, as originally conceived, consisted of six movements which were not directly related and devoid of anything like progressive development. Rather did the first five, each a complete unit, each differing in mood from the others, possess a close spiritual kinship with the last, the Grand Fugue, which came as a most natural and eloquent culmination. Blom makes the observation that the Grand Fugue, removed from its moorings to the B flat major Quartet, is deprived of the "antecedents" which made its conclusions logical. Yet he felt that the Quartet had lost much more.

R. C. B.

"Romance" ("Romanze") in G major, for Violin and Orchestra, Op. 40

BEETHOVEN WROTE two "Romances" for violin and orchestra—one in G major (Op. 40) marked Andante, the other in F major (Op. 50) marked Adagio cantabile. Despite the opus numbering, they both date from 1803. The earlier one was published that year, the later in 1805. Both have been arranged for violin and piano, solo violin and string quartet, and even for piano alone. They are very similar in form and mood. As their title would indicate, they are songlike in spirit, "romance" or "Romanze" being a song. It will be recalled that Mozart occasionally borrowed this term from vocal music, applying it to middle movements of some of his best piano concertos. Where it is used, the purpose is to show in advance that melodic invention and lyric feeling predominate.

In both of these "Romances" the solo violin introduces the principal theme—with orchestral accompaniment in the F major, and without it in the G major. The double-stop passage opening the Romance in G is a sample and a warning of the kind of technical challenge awaiting the violinist. Much of the composition should sound like "a tender dialogue," said Leopold Auer, "and in keeping with this colloquial style should be played with unaffected beauty of tone and expression."

One or two German biographers of Beethoven speak of the "sweetness" and "rich feeling" of the "Romance in G." They warn against mistaking these qualities for weakness and sentimentality. However, the English biographer, Marion M. Scott, confessed being puzzled by these violin pieces. "They are beautiful in their way," he writes in the Master Musicians Series, "not easy as to technique, very difficult to interpret satisfactorily. . . . Their music leaves one where it found one. I suspect Beethoven had no strong poetic idea when he composed them."

The original accompaniment calls for one flute, two oboes, two bassoons, two horns, and strings.

L. B.

"Marcia alla turca" ("Turkish March"), from "The Ruins of Athens," Op. 113

WHEN BEETHOVEN once referred to his "little operas," he was not thinking of *Fidelio* as one of them. "Little"—even in jest—is hardly the word to describe that massive music drama which many regard as the summit of operatic writing. Besides, Beethoven wrote only one opera, despite the jubilant vow of the British doctor who exclaimed after a performance of *Fidelio*: "I shall go to every opera he wrote!" Unfortunately the "little operas" were merely sheaves of incidental music for two melodramas by a fashionable German playwright of the time, August Friedrich Ferdinand von Kotzebue (1761-1819). One of these plays was *King Stephan—Hungary's First Benefactor,* the other *The Ruins of Athens* (*Die Ruinen von Athen*). The music for both these stage works was commissioned and written in 1811, and the story goes that Beethoven completed the combined assignment in one month.

The plays and the overtures and incidental music were all warmly received when they opened the new theater at Pesth on Feb. 9, 1812. Quite different, however, was the response to the overtures in England. Charles Neate, the English pianist and sometime agent, had been entrusted with several recent scores of Beethoven, among them the Seventh Symphony and the two overtures. Philharmonic patrons were so disappointed by the overtures that Neate was sternly rebuked: "For God's sake don't buy anything more of Beethoven!" Beethoven was somewhat nettled when he learned of the British reaction from his friend and pupil Ries. "I by no means reckon them among my best works," he said, referring to the overtures, "which, however, I can boldly say of the Symphony in A." Some years later, Kotzebue's *Ruins of Athens* was revised for the opening of the Josephstadt Theater on Oct. 3, 1822, and now retitled, *The Consecration of the House*. For that occasion Beethoven wrote a new overture, discarding the original one.

Besides the overture, the music for *The Ruins of Athens* comprises three choruses, one duet, a recitative and aria, an off-stage interlude, a march with chorus, and the famous "Marcia alla turca." Though there is some doubt on this point, it has long been supposed that the overture to *The Ruins of Athens* once served as overture to the revised version of *Fidelio* in 1814, when Beethoven was frantically weighing the pros and cons of each of the overtures composed for this opera. It is certain, in any case, that the overture to *The Creatures of Prometheus,* was so employed at one performance.

Another little irony connected with the music to *The Ruins of Athens* is the suspicion that the theme was of Russian origin! Whatever its nationality, the quaintly martial melody is already foreshadowed in Beethoven's Six Variations for Piano in D major (1809) dedicated "to my friend Franz Oliva." In listening to this march it is perhaps helpful to remember the historical context of Kotzebue's play. The Greeks, long smarting under the Turkish yoke, were preparing to make a valiant bid for independence. Kotzebue's so-called "Nachspiel" reflects this struggle in the fervid mood of the time. As the march opens, we may visualize the approach of Turkish troops from afar. The music is soft and distant, gradually rising in volume and intensity. The troops come closer, and as the columns sweep by the orchestra rises to a resounding fortissimo. Then the process is reversed, the volume diminishing with the receding troops till soldiers and music both disappear in the distance.

L. B.

Arthur Benjamin

BORN: SYDNEY, AUSTRALIA, SEPT. 18, 1893.

Benjamin has evolved no personal idiom, but is content to use common chromatic parlance for the expression of ideas which are his own. If these ideas are not very profound nor strongly individualized, neither are they, on the other hand, derivative, and his conspicuous skill in presenting them so as to appeal to his hearers makes him one of the more approachable of postwar English composers.—FRANK S. HOWES.

"Overture to an Italian Comedy"

ONE OF a group of roving British musicians, Arthur Benjamin has helped preserve the solidarity of the Empire in music. Trained first at the Brisbane school in Australia, he went to London in 1911 to study at the Royal College of Music, fought in France in the infantry and the R.A.F., and went home to teach piano at the Sydney Conservatory. In a few years he had returned to London and joined the staff of the Royal College of Music as professor of composition. In 1938 he moved on to Canada, and has since made his home in Vancouver, where he composes, teaches, and leads the Vancouver Symphony Orchestra.

Mr. Benjamin's career as composer was launched with a string quartet in 1924, which won the Carnegie Award. Later came *Three Impressions* for voice and string quartet, a sonatina for violin and piano, two works for the stage— one the farce *The Devil Take Her!* (produced at Columbia University) —a Violin Concerto, and a *Romantic Fantasy* for violin, viola, and orchestra, besides music for the screen. His *Prelude to a Holiday* was performed by the Indianapolis Symphony Orchestra, Fabien Sevitzky conducting.

The *Overture to an Italian Comedy* was first performed in 1937 at the Royal College of Music, with Malcolm Sargent directing. There were twenty performances in the next two years throughout England. After the premiere the *Daily Telegraph* reviewer remarked: "Mr. Benjamin has done what so many modern composers are unwilling to do—he has written music that is frankly and unashamedly jolly."

The composer had no specific comedy in mind to which his Overture could be affixed, though he evidently sought to depict the characteristics of an Italian dramatic genre bustling with gay intrigue and prankish merriment. However, a Neapolitan folk song and snatches of Neapolitan dances narrow

74

its locale to Naples, and even a tarantella breaks into Mr. Benjamin's festive orchestral web. The prevailing mood is one of carnival gaiety.

The work lasts about six minutes and is scored for two flutes, one piccolo, two oboes, two clarinets in B flat, two bassoons, four horns, two trumpets in C, three trombones, percussion, glockenspiel, harp, and the usual strings.

L. B.

"Cotillon"

THE ORCHESTRAL suite *Cotillon* is based on original melodies drawn from *The Dancing School,* a medley compiled by W. Pearson and Young in London in 1719. Many of the airs and ballads gathered were the reigning "hits" of the day. What the composer strove to do was to dress them in fresh harmonies and instrumentation without sacrificing the mood and feeling of the early eighteenth century. The standard cotillon of the period, involving a sequence of country dances as crowning events in an evening's entertainment, often ran to twenty-four separate "figures" of contrasting style and has been regarded as precursor of the Victorian lancers.

A brief introduction built around an episode from the first dance ushers in the nine short figures, entitled as follows: "Lord Hereford's Delight" (full orchestra), "Daphne's Delight" (wood winds and strings), "Marlborough's Victory" (full orchestra), "Love's Triumph" (strings), "Jigg It E Foot" (full orchestra), "The Charmer" (small orchestra), "Nymph Divine" (small orchestra with harp solo), "The Tattler" (full orchestra), "Argyll" (full orchestra). The concluding figure enlarges into a coda.

L. B.

Robert Russell Bennett

BORN: KANSAS CITY, JUNE 15, 1894.

Taking anything from a whistled melody to a piano sketch from its author to the lighted orchestra pit of a theatrical production demands a great many things besides theatrical training, but if I were asked what the greatest asset one can have in this work is, I should have to answer, "Counterpoint."—ROBERT RUSSELL BENNETT.

"A Symphony in D for the Dodgers"

I. Allegro con brio: "Brooklyn Wins." II. Andante lamentoso: "Brooklyn Loses." III. Scherzo. IV. Finale: "The Giants Come to Town."

ROBERT RUSSELL BENNETT is an ardent supporter of the New York Giants baseball club, therefore he writes a musical ode to their bitterest rivals, the Brooklyn Dodgers. Played for the first time over Radio Station WOR on May 16, 1941, the work is in four movements and, as the composer says, "in fairly strict form." In the summer of that year it obtained its concert premiere at the Lewisohn Stadium by the Philharmonic-Symphony orchestra, Wilhelm Steinberg conducting and "Red" Barber acting as narrator.

Despite his loyalty to the Giants, Mr. Bennett's sense of fair play was beautifully stimulated by the fighting, peppery, cocky group of men who performed feats of derring-do for the sake of Brooklyn and Leo Durocher, not to omit their own economic interests. He, therefore, penned this symphony as a "sincere tribute to a brilliant and colorful baseball team."

Mr. Bennett's own description of his symphony follows:

The Allegro con brio is in sonata form and has the subtitle "Brooklyn Wins." It means to picture the ecstatic joy of the town after the home team wins a game.

The second movement is the slow movement. It is an Andante lamentoso, with gloom and tears—and even fury. It is called "Brooklyn Loses." Somebody has suggested that the movement be called "Brooklyn Loses—but not very often."

The third movement is the Scherzo. . . . The Scherzo pictures the popular and energetic president of the club, Mr. Larry MacPhail [now indissolubly attached to the New York Yankees], going a-hunting for a star pitcher. We hear the horns' bay call—then we hear him in Cleveland, Ohio, trying to trade for the great pitcher Bob Feller. He offers Prospect Park and the Brooklyn Bridge as an even trade, but the Cleveland management says "No" in the form of a big E flat minor chord. After repeated attempts we hear the hunting horns again, as he resumes the hunt in other fields.

The Finale of the *Symphony in D for the Dodgers,* like that of Beethoven's Ninth, is a choral movement. The text, again like Beethoven's Ninth Symphony, is an ode to joy. It is purely fictitious, this text, but it speaks for itself. The subtitle of this Finale is "The Giants Come to Town."

Mr. Bennett began the study of the piano with his mother. His father, a band and orchestra conductor, taught him to play many other instruments. He got work in New York as a copyist and arranger. Then he did a year of service in the United States Army, during the First World War, at the conclusion of which he returned to Broadway and launched upon a highly profitable career of arranging for Broadway musicals. He visited France and while there won a coveted Guggenheim Fellowship. It was renewed for one more year, and in that period he completed a host of works, which include a symphony; a suite for orchestra *Paysage;* a one-act opera *An Hour of Delusion;* an "operetta-ballet à l'antique" *Endymion;* a number of songs, choruses, and chamber music items.

There have been other compositions, all of which brought him important attention, but he has devoted most of his time to film music, composing, arranging, and conducting being a part of his daily program. In April, 1935, his opera *Maria Malibran,* with a libretto by Robert A. Simon, music critic of *The New Yorker,* was given its premiere in a production by the Juilliard School of Music.

Of his *Symphony in D for the Dodgers,* Mr. Bennett says that it is primarily a piece of music, that the hearer is at liberty to put such program meanings to it as may occur to him, and that his intentions, as composer, are extremely general.

R. C. B.

Hector Berlioz

BORN: LA CÔTE SAINT-ANDRÉ, DEC. 11, 1803. DIED: PARIS, MAR. 8, 1869.

*All modern programmists have built upon him—Liszt, Richard Strauss, and Tschaikowsky. Wagner felt his influence, though he belittled it. His own words, "I have taken up music where Beethoven left it," indicate his position. He is the real beginner of that interpenetration of music and the poetic idea which has transformed modern art.—*ERNEST NEWMAN.

"Symphonie Fantastique," Op. 14 A

I. Dreams, Passions. II. A Ball. III. Scene in the Meadows. IV. March to the Scaffold. V. Dream of a Witches' Sabbath.

UNDER THE title *Episode in the Life of an Artist,* two works were composed by Berlioz, the *Symphonie Fantastique* and *Leilo, or the Return to Life,* a lyric monodrama. The symphony was completed in 1830, and it obtained its first performance at the Paris Conservatoire on Dec. 5, of that year. America's first experience with it came at a concert of the Philharmonic Society in New York, on Jan. 27, 1866.

By the composer's own admission Goethe's *Faust* inspired this symphony, and, as Berlioz averred, the source provided him with subject matter for his *Huit Scènes de Faust* (which he afterward denied) and a projected *Faust* ballet. But a stronger inspiration was his overwhelming love for the Irish actress Henrietta Smithson. Overwhelming, however, is scarcely the word for the soul-searing, terrifying passion he felt for this woman. A letter he wrote to his friend Humbert Ferrand on Feb. 6, 1830, contains the following torch song:

I am again plunged in the anguish of an interminable and inextinguishable passion, without motive, without cause. She is always in London, and yet I think I feel her near me: all my remembrances awake and unite to wound me; I hear my heart beating, and its pulsations shake me as the piston strokes of a steam engine. Each muscle of my body shudders with pain. In vain! 'Tis terrible! Oh, unhappy one! If she could for one moment conceive all the poetry, all the infinity of a like love, she would fly to my arms, were she to die through my embrace. I was on the point of beginning my great symphony (*Episode in the Life of an Artist*), in which the development of my infernal passion is to be portrayed; I have it all in my head, but I cannot write anything. Let us wait.

Berlioz could go on in that manner without having exchanged so much as a word with his beloved. He had not even met her, knowing her merely through her performances of Ophelia and Juliet and in a language completely alien to him. Realizing the futility of drawing her attention to him, young and unknown as he then was, he yet literally shelled her with violently ardent missives. The lady read them, though they frightened her at first. Finally she refused to bother with any more of them. She left Paris, some time later, and Berlioz, still aflame, wrote his symphony. But he had, apparently, heard disquieting rumors concerning his *idéale,* for in another letter to Ferrand he forwarded a program of the work, in which he presented her as a courtesan in the "Dream of a Witches' Sabbath." He said, "I do not wish to avenge myself. I pity her and I despise her. She is an ordinary woman, endowed with an instinctive genius for expressing lacerations of the human soul, but she has never felt them, and she is incapable of conceiving an immense and noble sentiment, as that with which I honored her."

On discovering that the rumors were false, Berlioz, with characteristic suddenness, struck all reference of courtensanship out of his program. Just for the record and without going into the attendant sensationalism, be it reported that the composer's extraordinary love, which had burned for three years almost without abatement, culminated in his marriage to Miss Smithson. It was a very unsuccessful union, which ended some years later in a separation. Mme. Berlioz died in poverty at a humble lodging in Montmartre in March, 1854. Her husband married again the following October.

In the *Symphonie Fantastique* Berlioz presents an *idée fixe,* a quasi-pathological fixation, which *possesses* the music as it *possesses* the thoughts of the *artist* of the program. It emerges in a variety of aspects, fervent, beatific, distant and ignoble, "according to the nature of the changing scene."

This "immense symphony," as Berlioz termed it, crashed into a musical cosmos still ringing with the echoes of Beethoven's voice. The *Pastoral* and the *Leonore* Overtures had not been superseded as program music, Wagner was a stripling of seventeen, Liszt's *Symphonic Poem* was to come twenty years later. With this strangely forceful music, new in spirit as in construction and compellingly programmatic, Berlioz achieved his first impressive and first enduring composition.

Berlioz's own account of his work is given in the full score of the symphony, as published by Breitkopf and Härtel, together with an English translation by Harry Brett. The Brett version follows:

PROGRAM OF THE SYMPHONY

A young musician of unhealthily sensitive nature and endowed with vivid imagination has poisoned himself with opium in a paroxysm of lovesick despair.

The narcotic dose he had taken was too weak to cause death, but it has thrown him into a long sleep accompanied by the most extraordinary visions. In this condition his sensations, his feelings, and his memories find utterance in his sick brain in the form of musical imagery. Even the Beloved One takes the form of a melody in his mind, like a fixed idea which is ever returning and which he hears everywhere. [This recurring melody, or *idée fixe,* which typifies the Beloved One, is first heard in the Allegro, in C major.]

FIRST MOVEMENT

DREAMS, PASSIONS
(*Largo, C minor, 4/4; Allegro agitato e appassionato assai, C major, 4/4*)

At first he thinks of the uneasy and nervous condition of his mind, of somber longings, of depression and joyous elation without any recognizable cause, which he experienced before the Beloved One had appeared to him. Then he remembers the ardent love with which she suddenly inspired him; he thinks of his almost insane anxiety of mind, of his raging jealousy, of his reawakening love, of his religious consolation.

SECOND MOVEMENT

A BALL
(*Allegro non troppo, A major, 3/8*)

In a ballroom, amidst the confusion of a brilliant festival, he finds the Beloved One again.

THIRD MOVEMENT

SCENE IN THE MEADOWS
(*Adagio, F major, 6/7*)

It is a summer evening. He is in the country, musing, when he hears two shepherd lads who play, in alternation, the *ranz des vaches* (the tune used by the Swiss shepherds to call their flocks). This pastoral duet, the quiet scene, the soft whisperings of the trees stirred by the zephyr wind, some prospects of hope recently made known to him, all these sensations unite to impart a long unknown repose to his heart and to lend a smiling color to his imagination. And then She appears once more. His heart stops beating, painful forebodings fill his soul. "Should she prove false to him!" One of the shepherds resumes the melody, but the other answers him no more. . . . Sunset . . . distant rolling of thunder . . . loneliness . . . silence. . . .

FOURTH MOVEMENT

MARCH TO THE SCAFFOLD
(*Allegretto non troppo, G minor and B flat major, 4/4*)

He dreams that he murdered his Beloved, that he has been condemned to death and is being led to execution. A march that is alternately somber and wild, brilliant and solemn, accompanies the procession. . . . The tumultuous outbursts are

followed without modulation by measured steps. At last the fixed idea returns,
for a moment a last thought of love is revived—which is cut short by the death
blow.

FIFTH MOVEMENT

DREAM OF A WITCHES' SABBATH

(Larghetto, C major, 4/4; and Allegro, E flat major,
C minor, and C major, 6/8)

He dreams that he is present at a witches' revel, surrounded by horrible
spirits, amidst sorcerers and monsters in many fearful forms, who have come together for his funeral. Strange sounds, groans, shrill laughter, distant yells, which
other cries seem to answer. The Beloved melody is heard again, but it has lost its
shy and noble character; it has become a vulgar, trivial, grotesque dance tune.
She it is who comes to attend the witches' meeting. Riotous howls and shouts
greet her arrival. . . . She joins the infernal orgy . . . bells toll for the dead . . .
a burlesque parody of the *Dies irae* . . . the Witches' round dance. . . . The
dance and the *Dies irae* are heard together.

R. C. B.

Orchestral Excerpts from the Dramatic Symphony "Romeo and Juliet," Op. 17

(*a*) Festivities at the House of Capulet. (*b*) Love Scene. (*c*) Scherzo,
"Queen Mab."

I WILL MARRY Juliet and write my greatest symphony on the play!" These
words were attributed to Hector Berlioz by the critic of the *Illustrated London
News*. In his memoirs, Berlioz blandly admits the fact but denies making the
statement. "I did both, but I never said anything of the kind. I was in far too
much perturbation to entertain such ambitious dreams. Only through much
tribulation were both ends gained."

By "perturbation" and "tribulation" Berlioz, of course, meant Henrietta
(*née* Harriet Constance) Smithson. The Irish actress, later memorialized in
that fevered stream of consciousness, the *Fantastic Symphony*, came down to
Paris in 1827 with an English company for a Shakespeare season at the Odéon.
Berlioz attended the first performance, *Hamlet*. Henrietta was the Ophelia.
The combined magic of Henrietta and Shakespeare was too much for the
susceptible youth. He fell madly in love.

As a cure he resolved to stay away from Shakespeare and Smithson. But
the announcement of *Romeo and Juliet* broke down his resistance. He went
to the Odéon. The effect beggars analysis. Henrietta now became the Juliet
of his dreams. His passion became a torture and a nightmare. Once, the sight
of Henrietta in a stage lover's arms sent him screaming insanely out of the

theater. Repeatedly rebuffed by his idol, Berlioz went into a prolonged fit of wild, wandering gloom. He walked the streets in a daze. He whined and whimpered through the countryside. He was haunted day and night by a composite image of Ophelia, Juliet, and Henrietta. Who could blame the Irish girl for being startled out of her wits? There was no precedent for Berlioz's behavior. Even Shakespeare had never chronicled so violent a campaign. Wildly written and hoarsely shouted pleas proved unavailing. Out of the pit of gnarled self-torture grew the *Fantastic Symphony*.

Henrietta held out for six years. Finally she gave in. Her own career now lay in ruins. But her volcanic suitor was fast rising to power and prestige. Juliet became Mrs. Hector Berlioz. A Parisian critic, after listening to the premiere of the *Romeo and Juliet Symphony* some years later, charged Berlioz with not understanding Shakespeare. He should have known better.

Although twelve years separate Berlioz's soul-searing experiences and the composition of the *Romeo and Juliet Symphony,* the work derives emotionally from those hectic Shakespeare nights at the Odéon. The surcharged emotional atmosphere of the early period is vividly recalled in Berlioz's memoirs. In one place he speaks of going from *Hamlet* to *Romeo and Juliet*. He writes:

Ah, what a change from the dull gray skies and icy winds of Denmark to the burning sun, the perfumed nights of Italy! From the melancholy, the cruel irony, the tears, the mourning, the lowering destiny of Hamlet, what a transition to the impetuous youthful love, the long-drawn kisses, the vengeance, the despairing fatal conflict of love and death in those hapless lovers! By the third act, half suffocated by my emotion, with the grip of an iron hand upon my heart, I cried out to myself: "I am lost! I am lost!"

As Henrietta Smithson soon found out, Berlioz was not understating it.

Ironically, Berlioz set to work on his symphony in the midst of a fresh crisis in his relations with Henrietta. The roles were reversed. As Madame Berlioz, Henrietta was now fanatically jealous. She was against his going on foreign tours. She reviled his friends. Her theatrical appeal was a thing of the romantic past, and so was her beauty. She finally took to drink. In short, Shakespeare had become drab, domesticated routine. Henrietta leveled recurring charges of infidelity at her erratic spouse. These accusations "became so intolerable" that Berlioz "determined to justify them," as J. H. Elliot cynically observes. In Berlioz's Shakespearean world of make-believe, Juliet was now a wedded but untamed Katherine. The idol had stepped down to become a shrew. Whatever the truth of Henrietta's charges, Berlioz was at least faithful to the memory of that first great flush of literary and romantic passion caused by the historic Shakespeare season at the Odéon in 1827. In all fairness, the tender *Romeo and Juliet Symphony* is as justly the work of Henrietta Smithson as the *Fantastic Symphony* which anathematizes her.

The dramatic symphony for solo voices, chorus, and orchestra was composed between January and September, 1839. The great violin virtuoso Niccolo Paganini has been credited with the 20,000-franc grant made to Berlioz at this time. Whether the money came from the pocket of the notoriously tight-fisted Italian or some unnamed benefactor, at least it was Paganini who brought the sum in person. Berlioz, assuming Paganini to be the donor, asked him to name the subject of his, Berlioz's, next composition. "I cannot advise you," said Paganini. "You know best what suits you best." Berlioz later records that after long deliberation, he "fixed on a choral symphony on Shakespeare's *Romeo and Juliet,* and wrote the prose words for the choral section, which Emile Deschamps . . . put into verse for me." How the Bard of Avon fired his imagination can be gathered from a passage in his recollections in which he describes himself as "floating on the halcyon sea of poetry, wafted onward by the sweet, soft breeze of imagination; warmed by the golden sun of love unveiled by Shakespeare." Dedicated to Paganini, the symphony was performed at the Conservatory in November, 1839. Its success was immediate. Berlioz himself conducted an orchestra numbering 160 and a chorus of 98. Two further performances followed in December. The one disagreeable feature was the already noted remark of a critic, that Berlioz had failed to understand Shakespeare. Least of all, was the critic's contention, did Berlioz grasp the love scenes! The same reviewer went one step further by declaring that the "Queen Mab" scherzo reminded him of the "operations of an imperfectly oiled squirt and the tinkling of glasses in a tavern."

One of the names on Berlioz's free ticket list for that concert was Richard Wagner. The penniless young German composer, his mind then teeming with huge plans, admitted being enthralled by the "puissance of an orchestral virtuosity" he had never even dreamed of. "The reckless boldness and severe precision . . . took me by storm," he recounted in later tranquillity, "and impetuously fanned the flame of my personal feeling for music and poetry." Yet, Wagner once expressed the opinion that the *Romeo and Juliet Symphony* consisted of "piles of rubbish heaped up among the most brilliant inventions." He conceded, however, that Berlioz was "devilishly smart." Anyway, Wagner thought highly enough of his French colleague to send him an engraved copy of the orchestral score of *Tristan and Isolde.* Berlioz, a frank critic at all times, confessed "he could not understand any of it."

Wagner's well-known bent for assimilating others' ideas—consciously or not —is revealed in the "Pilgrims' Chorus" from *Tannhauser* and the prelude to the third act of *Lohengrin.* Both show the influence of Berlioz's score, particularly the final ensemble of reconciliation between the feuding families. Especially is this so in mood and orchestration.

Berlioz divided the symphony into three sections, each having subsections, the whole actually divisible into twelve separate numbers. And the subdivision can be carried still further. The music depicting the festivities at the house of the Capulets follows immediately upon that conveying Romeo's rapturous musings in the garden. There is a sudden transition to festive excitement as a dance theme is worked up to sparkling gaiety. Yet, a sinister note of strife creeps into the whirling music. The following "Love Scene" was regarded by Berlioz as "the best piece of writing I have done." Wagner and many others have agreed with him. "Over the whole of the music, with its soft enchanting melodies, there lies a delicate bloom," says the English biographer Elliot. "It is music of a love untouched by eroticism; it wounds the heart as any contemplation of the pure and undefiled always must. . . ." After the "Love Scene" comes the "Queen Mab" scherzo, where Berlioz's genius for orchestration reveals itself in a dazzling, gossamer-spun web of dreamy enchantment.

Walter Damrosch has stressed the innovation that Berlioz made in the symphonic form by reproducing the dialogue between Romeo and Juliet in the balcony love scene so vividly that you can almost understand the words, "Romeo by passionate phrases of violas and cellos in unison, and Juliet's responses in the agitated but gentle phrases of oboes, flutes, and clarinets." Incidentally, his father, Dr. Leopold Damrosch, met Berlioz in 1863 at a Festival given in his honor by Prince Loewenberg in his palace at Silesia and was later the first to conduct the *Romeo and Juliet Symphony* in America.

L. B.

Excerpts from the Dramatic Legend "The Damnation of Faust," Op. 24

I. Ballet of the Sylphs. II. Minuet of the Will-o'-the-Wisps. III. Rakoczy March.

WHEN GÉRARD DE NERVAL's sensitive French translation of Goethe's *Faust* appeared in November, 1827, it was eagerly welcomed, among others, by two stalwart romantics, the seventy-eight-year-old author of the original and a twenty-four-year-old musical sans-culotte named Hector Berlioz.

"I cannot read *Faust* any more in German," said the aged German poet. "But in this translation into French everything is again fresh, new, and ingenious."

Berlioz recorded his own reaction thus:

The marvellous book fascinated me at once: I could not put it down; I read it constantly, at my meals, in the theater, in the street, everywhere. This translation in prose contained some versified fragments, songs, hymns, etc. I yielded to the temptation of setting music to them. Hardly had I finished this difficult task—when I committed the folly of having the score printed at my expense.

His relations with *Faust,* extending over twenty years, were to cost him a tidy fortune all told.

The job of setting eight scenes from *Faust* was completed during the autumn of 1828. The following April, he sent a copy of the score to Humbert Ferrand, a close friend and confidant. The printer was still unpaid, so Berlioz, inveterately short of funds, requested the loan of "another hundred francs" to defray expenses. Ferrand, doubtless hard pressed himself, delayed complying till June. By that time Berlioz had found a pupil with money, and his self-styled act of folly was expiated in full. But the "Faust" jinx was still to be reckoned with.

Berlioz was at this time in the midst of his frantic courtship of Henrietta Smithson, the Irish actress whose Ophelia and Juliet at the Odéon had brought him to a condition approaching nervous collapse. In his abnormally emotional state the Nerval translation of *Faust* took on graver and more romantic significance. "The love of Ophelia has increased my abilities a hundredfold," he proclaimed as he brought his *Huit scènes de Faust* to completion.

Characteristically, a copy of the *Faust* settings was sent to Goethe himself. Berlioz shrank from nothing. Had Virgil been alive, a copy of the stage work *Les Troyens* would no doubt have been mailed to Rome promptly on publication, just as the morning's post at Stratford-on-Avon would similarly have brought Shakespeare the freshly printed score of Berlioz's *Romeo and Juliet Symphony,* had history and circumstance made contemporaries of the two. In an accompanying letter the composer humbly offered Goethe the "obscure homage" of his *Eight Scenes,* imploring indulgence if the great man, addressed as *Monseigneur,* found the tribute wanting. He had been bowled over by a poetic masterpiece. *Voilà!* Goethe should forgive a young composer's presumptuous imagination.

As it happened, Goethe consulted his friend Carl Zelter about the score. In due course the poet received a scurrilously worded report comparing the music to a "fragment of an abortion resulting from a hideous incest." The Berlioz-Goethe correspondence accordingly came to an abrupt end.

Since much of this music was incorporated into the "concert opera," or "operatorio," *La damnation de Faust,* appearing some seventeen years later, it is important to note the titles of the set of "scenes": "Song of the Easter Festival," "Peasants under the Lime Trees," "Concerts of Sylphs," "Story of a Rat," "Song of Mephistopheles: Story of a Flea," "The King of Thule," "Marguerite's Romanza and Chorus of Soldiers," and "Serenade of Mephistopheles." Though sometimes stated, Berlioz did not bring the sections unaltered into the later scheme. The first three underwent particularly drastic revision. The orchestral excerpts usually grouped on concert programs were the work of a wiser and maturer Berlioz.

The cold reception accorded the *Huit scènes de Faust* probably explains Berlioz's protracted delay in returning to the subject. The plan of a "Faust" cantata was long in his mind, though it was not till early in 1846, while touring in Eastern Europe, that his project was put on paper. Sections were written in Austria, Hungary, Bohemia, and Silesia. Resolved to write most of the text himself (the Nerval verses took up only one-sixth of the planned book in Berlioz's estimate), he started confecting verses for his music as he rolled along in an old German postchaise. He recounts in his memoirs:

I began with Faust's invocation to Nature, not trying either to translate or even imitate, but only to use it as an inspiration, and extract all its musical substance. My attempt gave me hopes of being able to continue.

> Nature immense, impénétrable et fière!
> Toi seule donnes trêve a mon ennui sans fin!

Once launched, I wrote the rest by degrees, as my musical ideas came to me, and composed the score with a facility I never experienced with any of my other works. I wrote when I could and where I could; in the coach, on the railroad, in steamboats, and even in towns. . . . Thus I wrote the introduction, "Le vieil hiver a fait place au printemps," in an inn at Passau. At Vienna I did the Elbe scene, Mephistopheles' song, "Voici des roses," and the sylphs' ballet.

He records that while lost one night in Budapest he wrote the choral refrain of the "Ronde des Paysans" by gaslight in a shop. In Prague an inspiration seized him in his sleep. So that the idea would not elude him the following morning he jumped out of bed and jotted down the theme for the angels' chorus in Marguerite's apotheosis, "Remonte au ciel, âme naïve, que l'amour égara." The words and music of the students' Latin song "Jam nox stellata velamina pandit," we owe to a visit to Breslau. Returning to France, Berlioz composed the trio "Ange adoré dont la céleste image" while visiting the Baron de Montville, near Rouen. With the exception of the "Rákóczy March," the remainder of *The Damnation of Faust* was written in Paris— "always improvised," says Berlioz, "either at my own house, or at the café, or in the Tuileries Gardens, and even on a stone in the Boulevard du Temple."

In the course of this "Faust" Odyssey he insisted that he never sought ideas. "I let them come to me," he affirmed blandly; "and they presented themselves in a most unforeseen manner." After thoroughly revising the score, deleting passages, adding others, and rewriting most of it, he set to work knitting the sections together "with all the patience and determination of which I am capable."

The mere presence of the "Rákóczy March" in *The Damnation of Faust*
a story in itself. Most historians have taken Berlioz to task for transporting
aust to Hungary for the sole ostensible purpose of making the stirringly
ored Hungarian battle song a tolerable intrusion. Berlioz wrote the march in
ienna early in 1846 before leaving for Budapest, on the suggestion of a musi-
l dilettante that the French composer could best curry favor with the Hun-
arians by orchestrating one of their national airs. Shown a collection of
Iungarian melodies, Berlioz selected the "Rákóczy" and, if he is to be trusted,
ashed off the rousing composition "in one night." When premiered in
udapest on Feb. 15, the piece was stormily received. Its overpowering effect
n the audience encouraged Berlioz to find a spot for the march in his
Damnation of Faust. The accommodation was effected with typical resource-
ilness. Faust promptly materialized in Hungary and was made to witness the
harge of the Hungarian army across a plain where he was walking deep in
hought. Quite expectedly the French composer was charged by nettled Ger-
nan critics with committing mayhem on Goethe's sancrosanct text. Berlioz
nswers the accusation in his memoirs:

A German critic found it exceedingly strange that I had made Faust travel to
ich a place. I do not see why I should not, and I should not have hesitated the
east in the world to take him anywhere else if it would have helped my score.
had not bound myself to follow Goethe's plan, and the most eccentric travels
aay be attributed to a character like Faust without any shock to probability.
Other critics took up this singular thesis later and attacked me with still greater
iolence for the changes I made in Goethe's plan! As if there were no other
Fausts" than Goethe's! . . . I have often wondered why those same critics never
eproached me for the libretto of my *Romeo and Juliet Symphony,* which is little
ke the immortal tragedy. No doubt because *Shakespeare is not a German.* Patriot-
m! Fetishism! Cretinism!

The world premiere of *The Damnation of Faust* in oratorio form at the
'aris Opéra Comique on Dec. 6, 1846, was a heart-breaking failure. This,
lespite Théophile Gautier's widely circulated dictum, while the work was
till in rehearsal, that Berlioz, with Hugo and Delacroix, now constituted
the trinity of romantic art." Other "Berliozites" worked day and night to boost
heir idol's prestige. The event was glowingly publicized as certain to bring
ogether "the elite of the worlds of art and elegance." On the day of the per-
ormance the theater was half empty. Bad weather and political disturbances
vere said to account for the poor attendance.
Berlioz saw at once that all was lost, that his new work was "about to expire
or want of a public." The biographer Boschot reviews the composer's feelings
hus: "there will be excellent articles, but for what purpose? His genius is
mothered in isolation. Berlioz without a public spells one thing only, ruin.
n short, Paris has again rejected him." The "ruin," in practical terms,

amounted to some 10,000 francs in debts, and of the comments in the pre
none was more virulent than the quip that "the audience was more com
posed than the music." Which is a sad commentary on any audience hearin
the "Rákóczy March" for the first time.

As an opera, *The Damnation of Faust* was first staged in Monte Carlo o
Feb. 18, 1903, the same version reaching the Metropolitan Opera House o
Dec. 7, 1906, with Geraldine Farrar, Charles Rousselière, and Pol Plançon i
the chief roles.

L. B.

Overture to the Opera "Benvenuto Cellini," Op. 23

LIKE THE better known *Le Carnaval romain,* the *Benvenuto Cellini* overtur
was written for Berlioz's opera about the adventurous Italian sculptor an
goldsmith who has been called half scalawag and half genius. That Berlio
should have composed two overtures for one opera is not surprising. Beethove
wrote four for the opera *Fidelio.* Rossini was different. Often, lacking an ove
ture for a new opera, he would borrow one from an earlier opera. One famou
overture began life as prelude to a serious opera long before it found its righ
ful place at the head of that comic masterpiece *The Barber of Seville.*

The opera *Benvenuto Cellini* was begun in 1834, but it was not until 183
that we find the poet Heinrich Heine writing: "From Berlioz we shall soo
have an opera. The subject is an episode from the life of Benvenuto Cellin
the casting of his Perseus statue. Something extraordinary is expected, sinc
this composer has already achieved the extraordinary." Excited over Cellini
swashbuckling memoirs and a short story "Salvator Rosa," by the Germa
E. T. A. Hoffmann, Berlioz had appealed to the French poet Alfred de Vign
for a Cellini libretto. De Vigny, deep in other matters, referred the appeal t
Léon de Wailly. The latter agreed to supply the text, but only after August
Barbier consented to collaborate with him. De Vigny supervised the proces
freely criticizing and revising. Whatever the reason—perhaps a plethora c
poetic gifts—the result was far from brilliant. "Audiences and critics almo:
to a man have found it ineffective, a bore," wrote Pitts Sanborn. The co
laborators evidently felt that only the wildest flights of fancy would do for s
fabulous a figure as Cellini. Enmeshed in the clumsy network of Roma
intrigue are conspiracies, masquerades, stabbings, and escapes, besides the ir
credible casting of the statue of Perseus—allegedly the work of an hour! An(
finally, "the crowning of the hero's love for Teresa, the papal Treasurer'
daughter, with a marriage blessed by Cardinal Salviati."

No opera could breathe with so weighty a millstone about its neck. Th
novelty, produced at the Paris Opéra on Sept. 10, 1838, was accordingly
fiasco. Caricaturists flailed Berlioz as the composer of "Malvenuto Cellini.

et, though the opera was "hissed with admirable energy and unanimity," Berlioz philosophically records, the overture made out better. In fact, the Parisians received it with "exaggerated applause." Berlioz naturally attributed the failure to a bad performance. In his *Mémoires* he notes that *Benvenuto* was "massacred at the Opéra." He never lost faith in the worth and vitality of his opera. Subsequent revivals of *Benvenuto Cellini* have not borne him out. Another dismal failure awaited the work when it was produced at Covent Garden in 1855. But the two overtures have maintained an independent life of their own in the concert repertory.

Cellini's ebullient character is given out in an Allegro deciso con impeto (G major, 2/2), containing the main motive of the overture. There is an abrupt pause. A contrasting slow section (Larghetto, G major, 3/4) based on the Cardinal's stately monologue, "A tous péchés pleine indulgence," follows. To this is added part of the "Ariette d'Arlequin" from the opera. The buoyant Allegro returns, altered and amplified. Then a fresh lyric theme in D major, 2/2, deriving from a love duet between Cellini and Teresa.

L. B.

Overture, "Le Carnaval romain" ("The Roman Carnival"), Op. 9

SOME YEARS later Berlioz composed a second overture to *Benvenuto Cellini,* not as a substitute for the original, but as a prelude to the second act. This he called *Le Carnaval romain* (*The Roman Carnival*). The rollicking saltarello used in that part of the opera as the grand carnival dance, dominates the second overture. From the first act of the opera Berlioz borrowed Benvenuto's aria "O Teresa, vous que j'aime," assigning it first to the English horn (Andante sostenuto, C major, 3/4), and later letting the bassoons echo it against the saltarello figure in the second violins. Toward the end the brisk carnival motive gains full sway over the orchestra.

The beautiful English horn solo first appearing as the tenor aria can be traced even further back in origin than the operatic score. Berlioz first employed the theme in his cantata *La Mort de Cléopatre,* written for the Prix de Rome early in 1829 and rejected by the awards jury in July. Berlioz uses the suave and swaying theme to illustrate the words, "the bosom of the sea," occurring in the text. As J. H. Elliot points out, such "transfers of thematic material," more or less modified, repeatedly crop up in Berlioz's music.

When first performed in the Salle Herz, Paris, on Feb. 3, 1844, with Berlioz conducting, the *Roman Carnival Overture* was so warmly received that it had to be repeated on the spot.

Berlioz was an uncompromising stickler for the correct saltarello tempo During the rehearsal of *Benvenuto Cellini* at the Opéra the fiery-tempered young genius had clashed hotly with the conductor François Antoine Habeneck over the proper timing. In the second-act carnival scene the dancers, unable to fall in step with Habeneck's sluggish pace, appealed to Berlioz, who was present. "Faster! faster! Stir them up!" screamed the composer. In the excitement Habeneck broke a violin bow. "If you were to break fifty bows," bellowed Berlioz, "that would not prevent your time being too slow by half!" Habeneck, who was only human, dismissed the orchestra with the words: "Since I am not fortunate enough to please Monsieur Berlioz, we will leave off for today. You can go."

Years later at the Salle Herz premiere of the *Roman Carnival Overture* Berlioz, glowing with the triumph of having his work encored, spotted Habeneck in the audience. Revenge was short and sweet. The conductor had come to gloat over an expected Berlioz fiasco. After the encore he looked glum and beaten. "Now you can see how it ought to go!" Berlioz snapped. Habeneck, he notes down gleefully, "took care to make no reply."

L. B.

Leonard Bernstein

BORN: LAWRENCE, MASS., AUG. 25, 1918.

It is impossible for me to make an exclusive choice among the various activities of conducting, symphonic composition, writing for the theater, or playing the piano. What seems right for me at any given moment is what I must do, at the expense of pigeon-holing or otherwise limiting my services to music. I will not compose a note while my heart is engaged in a conducting season; nor will I give up writing so much as a popular song, while it is there to be expressed, in order to conduct Beethoven's Ninth. There is a particular order involved in this, which is admittedly difficult to plan; but the order must be adhered to most strictly. For the ends are music itself, not the conventions of the music business; and the means are my own personal problem.—LEONARD BERNSTEIN.

Symphony, "Jeremiah"

I. Prophecy. II. Profanation. III. Lamentation.

ON JAN. 28, 1944, this work was given its world premiere by the Pittsburgh Symphony Orchestra under the direction of the composer. On that occasion Mr. Bernstein supplied the program annotator, William E. Benswanger, with the following information:

In the summer of 1939 I made a sketch for a Lamentation for Soprano and Orchestra. This sketch lay forgotten for two years, until in the spring of 1942 I began a first movement of a symphony. I then realized that this new movement, and the scherzo that I planned to follow it, made logical concomitants with the Lamentation. Thus the Symphony came into being, with the Lamentation greatly changed, and the soprano supplanted by a mezzo-soprano. The work was finished on Dec. 31, 1942, and is dedicated to my father.

The Symphony does not make use to any great extent of actual Hebrew thematic material. The first theme of the scherzo is paraphrased from a traditional Hebrew chant, and the opening phrase of the vocal part in the Lamentation is based on a liturgical cadence still sung today in commemoration of the destruction of Jerusalem by Babylon. Other resemblances to Hebrew liturgical music are a matter of emotional quality rather than of notes themselves.

As for programmatic meanings, the intention is again not one of literalness, but of emotional quality. Thus the first movement ("Prophecy") aims only to parallel in feeling the intensity of the prophet's pleas with his people; and the scherzo ("Profanation") to give a general sense of the destruction and chao brought on by the pagan corruption within the priesthood and the people. Th third movement ("Lamentation"), being a setting of poetic text, is naturally a more literary conception. It is the cry of Jeremiah, as he mourns his beloved Jeru salem, ruined, pillaged, and dishonored after his desperate efforts to save it.

The text is from the Book of Lamentations I, i, ii, iii, iv; IV, xiv and xv V, xx and xxi. An approximate translation follows:

How she sits desolate—
The city once so full of people—
She is become as a widow!
So great among nations,
Princess among her provinces,
She has become a tributary!
She weeps, she weeps in the night,
And her tears are upon her cheeks;

There is no comfort among all her lovers;
All her friends have betrayed her,
They have become her enemies,
Judah is exiled through affliction
And great servitude;
She dwells among the nations,
She finds no rest;
All her pursuers have overtaken her
In the narrow passes.

Jerusalem has sinned, sinned greatly. . . .

They [the sinful priests and prophets] wandered
Like blind men in the streets,
Polluted with blood,
So that their garments could not be touched
"Depart, unclean," men cried to them
"Depart, depart, touch us not!"

Lord, wilt Thou forget us forever?
How long more wilt Thou forsake us?
Turn us unto Thee, O Lord. . . .

Mr. Bernstein led the New York Philharmonic-Symphony in a New York premiere of the work on Mar. 29, 1944. Jennie Tourel was the soloist.

The Symphony is scored for two flutes, piccolo, two oboes, English horn, two clarinets, E flat clarinet and bass clarinet, two bassoons, contra-bassoon, four horns, three trumpets, three trombones, tuba, tympani, snare drum, bass drum, cymbals, triangle, maracas, piano, and strings.

Leonard Bernstein majored in music at Harvard College, studying composition with Edward Burlingame Hill, A. Tillman Merritt, and Walter Piston. He received his piano instruction from Helen Coates and Heinrich Gebhard. He spent two years at the Curtis Institute of Music, Philadelphia, studying conducting with Fritz Reiner, orchestration with Randall Thompson, and piano with Isabella Vengerova.

He was a pupil of Serge Koussevitzky in conducting during the first two sessions of the Berkshire Music Center, in Tanglewood, becoming his assistant in the school's third session in 1942. Mr. Bernstein conducted various concerts in Boston and Cambridge, Mass., and during the season 1944-1945 served as assistant conductor of the New York Philharmonic-Symphony Society.

Besides the Symphony, Mr. Bernstein has composed several works in other forms, including a Clarinet Sonata and a song cycle, "Five Kid Songs, I Hate Music." Also he has done an exhilarating score for the ballet, *Fancy Free,* commissioned by the Ballet Theater, a string quartet, and six anti-Fascist songs, for which he provided his own texts.

In addition to these he is responsible for the clever score to the successful musical comedy *On The Town*. He was appointed conductor of the New York City Symphony in 1945.

R. C. B.

Suite from the Ballet "Fancy Free"

THE BALLET *Fancy Free,* with choreography by Jerome Robbins, has been one of the most successful productions in the repertory of the Ballet Theater. From its engaging score Mr. Bernstein extracted the present music and made it into the form of a suite containing, in all, six sections. They are: (1) "Dance of the Three Sailors"; (2) "Scene at the Bar"; (3) "Pas de Deux"; (4) "Pantomime" (Competition); (5) "Three Variations" (Gallop, Waltz, Danzon); (6) "Finale."

When the Suite was given its first performance by the Pittsburgh Symphony, Mr. Bernstein conducting, on Jan. 14, 1945, the composer wrote the following explanation for the concert program:

From the moment the action begins, with the sound of a juke box wailing behind the curtain, the ballet is strictly Young America of 1944. The curtain rises on a street corner, with a lamppost, a side-street bar, and New York skyscrapers tricked out with a crazy pattern of lights, making a dizzying backdrop. Three sailors explode onto the stage; they are on shore leave in the city and on the prowl for girls.

The tale of how they meet first one girl, then a second, and how they fight over them, lose them, and in the end take off after still a third, is the story of the ballet.

Georges Bizet

BORN: PARIS, OCT. 25, 1838. DIED: BOUGIVAL, JUNE 3, 1875.

The miracle of Bizet's music lies in the fact that it appeals to the musically illiterate and to the most fastidious technicians. Such a thing is rare in our history. It is very difficult for a musician to discourse on what all may understand in a style sufficiently refined to interest the most exacting of his hearers.—EMILE VUILLERMOZ.

Symphony in C major

I. Allegro vivo. II. Adagio. III. Allegro vivace; Trio. IV. Allegro vivace.

THIS SYMPHONY was written in 1885, when Bizet was seventeen years of age. He tried his hand at another such work in 1860, a "fantasie symphonique," which he wrote during his stay in Italy as a holder of the Prix de Rome. It was revised several times, given its first performance at a Pasdeloup Concert in Paris in 1869 and published in 1880 under the title *Roma.*

There are two versions of the discovery of the present work. In an article in the French periodical *Le Ménestrel* of Nov. 11, 1938, Paul Bertrand says the C major Symphony was "discovered some years ago by our friend Jean Chantavoine [French musicologist and for many years General Secretary of the Paris Conservatory]." However, the score that was brought out in Vienna in September, 1935, by Universal Edition offers an explanatory preface in German, French, and English. The English version reads:

begun Oct. 29, 1855; finished November, 1855. . . . The symphony by Georges Bizet has, it is strange to say, fallen into oblivion. The Glasgow music writer, D. C. Parker, has called the attention of General Music Director Felix von Weingartner upon the autograph of the work, which is preserved in the library of the Paris Conservatoire, whereupon Mr. Weingartner conducted the world premiere of the work in Basel on Feb. 26, 1935.

Weingartner later conducted the Symphony in Vienna. Paris first heard it in June, 1936, under Charles Münch. It was played there again in October, 1938, as part of the program commemorating the hundredth anniversary of Bizet's birth. Eugène Bigot was the conductor. Sir Hamilton Harty conducted its initial performance in England at a concert of the London Symphony Orchestra. It was added to the Philharmonic-Symphony's repertory by John Barbirolli on Oct. 17, 1940.

It has been pointed out that Bizet, although not showing a great deal of originality in this work, still gave evidence to a startling ability to follow the best models. The first movement's two subjects have been likened in spirit, if not more, to Beethoven and Mozart, respectively, although the orchestration already foreshadows the glittering Bizet of *Carmen*.

The slow movement with its mournful oboe theme, against a pizzicato in the violas, brings Rossini to the memory of one observer. The movement, as a whole, has a maturity not ordinarily found in the works of seventeen-year-olds.

The First Allegro vivace is a fast minuet, in which the dance is the thing, with alternating passages of song to provide contrast. The trio, employing the same material, is also dancelike, except that this time it is a sort of peasant dance. Afterward, the minuet returns in all its lightness and grace.

A march episode in the last section recalls the later music of the little boys in *Carmen*. In general, the beginning of the movement is a *perpetuum mobile* for the first violins. Then the march theme is played against string figures, following which a plain and unaffected song acts as a middle part of the exposition. The material then is developed, and a climax leads into the recapitulation. A cheery coda finishes the work.

R. C. B.

"L'Arlésienne" Suites Nos. 1 and 2

ALPHONSE DAUDET's tragedy of the French Midi *L'Arlésienne* (*The Woman of Arles*) is remembered today because Georges Bizet wrote the incidental music for the original production. The play was staged at the Théâtre du Vaudeville in Paris on Oct. 1, 1872. Up to that time, Bizet had been gaining increasing attention as an opera composer. Already to his credit were *Les Pêcheurs de perles, La jolie fille de Perthe,* and *Djamileh.* However, the opera that was to make him world-famous—*Carmen*—belonged to the near future.

In Daudet's play a curious thing happens—or does not happen: the Woman of Arles, who motivates the tragic action, never appears, except, to be sure, as an enveloping mood of evil fascination. "The fatal Woman of Arles," wrote Pitts Sanborn, "for love of whom the youthful hero takes his life, illumines the whole action with her malignant flame, but only the report of her envenoming beauty comes like an incantation to Rose Mamai's farm from the unseen city on the Rhone." It is this Rose Mamai, the anguished mother of the fatally smitten boy, who emerges as the play's actual central figure. Camille Bellaigue, the French critic, wrote with shrewd insight of the role of Bizet's music in this tragic setting:

Everything is alive; even inanimate objects have a voice and tears. At night, the burning plain, before it falls asleep, responds to the cry of the shepherds calling home their flocks. A lament arises from the pool of Vaccares and hangs

over the waters. Finally, at the nocturnal hour when the youth, mad with lov
carries out his terrible suicide, the belated guests at his tragic wedding feast g
their way singing. They sing that old Provençal air, the "March of the Kings,
in a lugubrious key—already it has an almost funereal sound—and the shado
and deathlike stillness seem to engulf it like a last sigh, a last gleam of life.

Bizet composed twenty-seven separate pieces for Daudet's Provençal dram
which was withdrawn after its fifteenth performance. From this music h
selected enough to make a tidy concert suite consisting of four number
I. Prelude; II. Minuetto; III. Adagietto; and IV. Carillon, which contains
chimelike figure persisting for fifty-six measures. This last number depicts th
peasants' jubilant celebration of the feast of St. Eloi.

After Bizet's death Guiraud compiled a second suite from the remainin
material. This included I. Pastorale; II. Intermezzo; III. Minuetto (No. 2); an
IV. Farandole, in which Bizet brings in the famous Provençal dance, said to b
of Greek origin. In dancing it the couples move in a procession headed b
musicians playing the galoubet and tambourin, native instruments of Provenc
and the Languedoc. The man in the first row signals the couples behind hir
with a flag, handkerchief, or ribbon.

L. B.

Marc Blitzstein

BORN: PHILADELPHIA, MAR. 2, 1905.

No matter what one may think of Blitzstein's political views, it is only fair to say that whatever the effect of his music on politics, the effect of political beliefs on his music has been to give it a conviction and a direction which it had hitherto seemed to lack.—JOHN TASKER HOWARD.

Symphonic Poem, "Freedom Morning"

THIS WORK was premiered in the Royal Albert Hall, London, on Sept. 28, 1943, at an Anglo-American concert sponsored jointly by the United States Army and Lord Beaverbrook's *Daily Express*. Taking part in the program were the London Symphony Orchestra, led by the Technical Sergeant Hugo Weisgall; Roland Hayes, Negro tenor, a Negro chorus, composed of 200 members of aviation engineering units stationed in England. Mr. Blitzstein, who penned the score for that concert, later wrote *The New York Times* a letter, in which he traced the growth of *Freedom Morning* and told of his work with the Negro choristers:

When back in 1937, Orson Welles and John Houseman produced my musical play, *The Cradle Will Rock,* I discovered for the first time the immense versatility and adaptability of Negro singers and actors. During the past few weeks I have had the opportunity to find out more about their talents. I have been living with the United States Army Negro Chorus stationed somewhere in England. I have coached them in Earl Robinson's "Ballad for Americans" and their own spirituals, while at the same time composing an orchestral work, *Freedom Morning,* dedicated to them.

My orchestra work was composed in a super-sized Nissen hut used for the showing of movies and for Chaplain William Perkins' Sunday services. Ordinarily I'm crochety about the conditions under which I write music; I must be hermetically sealed from the outside. I can bear no disturbing sounds—certainly not someone else's music! There, to my great surprise, I worked steadily and swiftly on *Freedom Morning* with a dozen G.I.'s almost crawling over me, relaxing, working, snoring (a foot from my ear), booming out their tunes, peering over my shoulder as I wrote and played. At one point in the music, a passage close to their own rhythms, one man in fatigues produced a pair of drumsticks, and tapped out on his lap a beat which I straightway incorporated into the score.

The speed and ease of writing may have been partly due to the fact that I hadn't written a concert work in a long time and was hungry to do one. It also was influenced by the ease and flow of the men themselves, and the contagion of their spirit. This was their piece I was writing, and here they were.

Freedom Morning is dedicated to "all Negro troops in the service of the United States." Traditional Negro folk themes are woven into Mr. Blitzstein's tribute, besides some swing sequences and the two spirituals, "My Lord's Goin' to Rain Down Fire" and "When the Stars Begin to Fall."

The work was given its American premiere by the Philadelphia Orchestra, Saul Caston conducting, at the Academy of Music, Philadelphia, on Friday afternoon, Apr. 14, 1944, and repeated Saturday evening, Apr. 15.

Film Suite, "Native Land"

THE SUITE is part of a score for the full-length documentary "Native Land," made in 1941 by Frontier Films, Inc. It was composed during the fall and winter 1940-1941, in a cutting room in the very heart of New York's Broadway district.

Mr. Blitzstein writes:

The subject matter of the film was taken from the files of the so-called "LaFollette Civil Liberties" investigation, and is part fictional, part actual. Paul Robeson is the narrator (although one never sees him in the film itself); and so I found myself writing songs for him as well as incidental music.

I think of *Native Land* as my most ambitious film score to date. There are about fifty minutes of music, of which about twenty-five are used in the Suite. The numbers are as follows: "The Fathers"; "Mulberry Street"; "Dusty Sun" (for baritone and orchestra); "American Day" (for baritone and orchestra); "Parade; Hooded Legion"; "Memorial Day"; "Funeral"; "Finale."

The music is scored for flute, piccolo, oboe, English horn, two clarinets, tenor saxophone, bassoon, two trumpets, trombone, piano, percussion, and strings.

Three excerpts of the Suite were performed privately by Howard Hanson and members of the N. Y. Philharmonic-Symphony on May 17, 1946, when Mr. Blitzstein was awarded a grant of $1,000 by the American Academy of Arts and Letters. The full concert Suite was first publicly performed on a Philharmonic-Symphony program led by Laszlo Halasz at the Lewisohn Stadium on July 10, 1946.

Among Mr. Blitzstein's other works are the operas *The Cradle Will Rock* and *No for an Answer;* incidental music for plays; scores for films ("Hands," "Surf and Seaweed," "Valley Town," "Night Shift," "Spanish Earth").

The Airborne, a symphony for Speaker, Baritone, Tenor, Male Chorus, and Orchestra, was performed on Apr. 1, 1946, by the New York City Symphony at the City Center. Leonard Bernstein conducted.

Ernest Bloch

BORN: GENEVA, SWITZERLAND, JULY 24, 1880.

*In this age of the gradual materialization of art, Ernest Bloch is as a
voice crying in the wilderness. The voice is that of a Hebrew prophet.*
—MARION BAUER.

Symphony, "Israel," for Soprano, Contralto, Baritone, Women's Chorus, and Orchestra

COMPOSED IN Europe between 1912 and 1916, the *Israel Symphony* was premiered on an all-Bloch program given by Arthur Bodanzky and the Society of
the Friends of Music in Carnegie Hall on May 3, 1917. Mr. Bloch, who shared
the podium with Mr. Bodanzky at that concert, conducted the symphony. Later
he dedicated the published score to Mrs. J. F. D. Lanier, president and founder
of the Society. It was then announced that the composer's original intention
had been to supplement the score with a contrasting section. This was to
express rejoicing over the "redemption of the Jews." The section already
written was designed, in part, as a meditation on the "sorrows of the Jews."
It was pointed out that Mr. Bloch had the traditional Hebrew service of Yom
Kippur (The Day of Atonement) in mind.

Later Block decided to give up the idea of writing a sequel. Questioned on
this point, Mrs. Lanier divulged the following facts:

Bloch considered only the first part had been written. . . . After the war was
over and the real horrors, the moral degradation of the world, were exposed to
humanity seeking solace from the heartbreaking effects of the terrible holocaust,
Bloch's whole nature revolted at the hypocrisy, greed, and mental degradation
from which the veil had been torn by relentless hands, and the second part,
expressing joy in the redemption of the Jewish people, has never been written, he
tells me, and never will be.

Later Mr. Bloch wrote the Philharmonic-Symphony that he had undergone
no change of heart in his world view of an ethical problem.

When I composed this work, the world was about in the same predicament as at
present. *Plus ça change, plus c'est la même chose.* Humanity does not change very
much, indeed. A few more additions to so-called "progress," more speed, more
inventions, new bombers, robot bombs, more devilish weapons, it is true, and,
morally, more regression also. The same hypocrisy prevails, the same fallacies
and, probably, the same vain hopes for a "better world." But this refers more to
Schelomo—The Ecclesiastes: *Vanity of vanities, all is vanity*—than to *Israel.*

OKALOOSA - WALTON JUNIOR COLLEGE

Mr. Bloch further communicated:

I intended first to call this work "Fêtes Juives," but I hesitated, and it was Romain Rolland who suggested *Israel*. Of course, what I meant by "Fêtes Juives" was rather the *symbolic meaning* of these festivities. The first movement, "Yom Kippur," the Day of Atonement, a *retour sur soi-même,* qualms of conscience. . . . It seems to me that nowadays more than ever Man may atone for his follies. The second part of the work is more contemplative, serene, a kind of prayer, in the desert, perhaps.

As for the "musical idiom," I was never much preoccupied by the prevalent styles of the moment, the accredited theories or fads, and I wrote my music just as I *felt* it. Oscar Wilde said: "It is only the *modern* that ever becomes old-fashioned; nothing is so dangerous as being too modern; one is apt to grow old-fashioned quite suddenly." Let us hope that this may apply to *Israel* also.

I heard this work only three times, since it was composed: when I conducted it myself in New York and Philadelphia [1917-1918] and later in Turin, Italy, 1932. I have not opened my score since.

Though a single unit, the Symphony falls into three sections: a slow introduction marked Lent et solennel, evoking a dirgelike mood of meditation, the theme given out by solo horn, oboe, and viola; an Allegro agitato (D minor, 3/4), in which the main theme—of bold, barbaric character—is first announced by the flutes, English horn, clarinet, and high strings; and an Andante moderato 4/4, which follows a fierce climax and brings in the voices. Called a "fresco of Hebrew struggle," the Allegro agitato has been described as follows:

Its agitation and pulsation fill the auditor's mind with a profusion of vivid impressions. . . . Moses' acceptance of the law of mankind. . . . The heresy at the foot of Mt. Sinai. . . . The reign of the Kings. . . . The feasts of joy. . . . The skirmishes with hostile neighbors. . . . The destruction of the Temple.

Suddenly this excitement subsides. A prayerlike plaint is sounded by the bassoon, echoed by the English horn, clarinet, first violin, harp and solo viola. One is haunted as by an appeal for life—as if a voice were gasping, strangled. The energetic first theme returns, bringing an enigma of wild unrestraint. Elation, gaiety, and other vanities appear on the threshold.

The music moves through a heaving sea of celebration, until the early meditative mood returns in a transitional passage marked Calme. What follows is a formal reprise, clearly reviewing the original material. There is a cyclic return of the theme of the introduction, preparing the way for the final supplication to God.

This huge climax is enhanced by Bloch's use of the human voice. The voices are placed in such a position as to create an effect of prayer coming from otherworldly regions. The everlasting cry of the Jew is iterated by woodwinds and French horn as the symphony ends.

The following text is used:

Sopranos and Altos:	Adonai, my Elohim,
	O my Elohim!
	Allelouyah! O my Elohim!
Sopranos:	Hear Thou my voice, my Elohim.
	Hear my prayer.
Alto solo:	O I implore Thee, O my Elohim,
	Thou art my refuge.
Soprano:	I implore Thee,
	In Thee I trust,
	I am steadfast, O my Elohim!
Sopranos and Altos:	Hm [with closed lips]
	Allelouyah!
Bass:	Adonai, my Elohim!
	O my Elohim, Thou art my refuge.
	Hear Thou my prayer, O hear my crying.
Alto and Bass:	In Thee I trust, O my Elohim!
	I am steadfast.

The score calls for four flutes (two interchangeable with piccolos), three oboes, English horn, three clarinets, bass clarinet, three bassoons, contra-bassoon, six horns, four trumpets, three trombones, tuba, three or four tympani, bass drum, cymbals, side drum, two harps, celesta, triangle, low tam-tam, and strings (with at least four double basses sounding low C), besides four women's voices (two sopranos and two altos), and solo bass. Bloch instructs that the voices be "placed among the instruments, or at the rear of the platform."

As an "orchestral drama," the *Israel Symphony* was produced by Alice and Irene Lewisohn and their Neighborhood Playhouse group at the Manhattan Opera House early in May, 1928. Nikolai Sokoloff and the Cleveland Orchestra rendered the music while mimes enacted a dramatized version of the traditional Jewish ceremony. The stage set showed the Wailing Wall at Jerusalem. An assembly of grieving believers finally receive the revelation of the Atonement, as a divine light falls on the sacred scroll of the Torah. Writing of the *Israel Symphony* at that time, Olin Downes, of *The New York Times,* mentioned "the mystic and rhapsodic spirit of the composition; its passion and fury, its wild denunciations, the haunting beauty of certain pages, the barbaric defiance of others." For Bloch, he went on, "does not always write of an Israel repentant and in ashes. Sometimes he prophesies war."

David Ewen, in his book *Modern Composers,* writes:

Something of the ecstasy of the Hebraic prophet has molded the artistic career of Ernest Bloch. No Biblical Jeremiah consecrated himself to the pronouncement of prophetic truths with more passionate idealism and self-abnegation than Bloch to the composition of music. To Bloch, the creation of music in general—and Hebrew music in particular—has been a sacrosanct mission.

It has been recorded that as a child Bloch wrote upon a slip of paper a vow that he would devote his life to music. This slip of paper he placed under a mound of rocks over which he burned a ritual fire. Bloch's career, thus launched, assumed in his eyes the aspect of religious consecration. And a consecration it has remained to the present day.

The *Israel Symphony* comes midway in the Jewish Cycle of Bloch's compositions. In the first of them, *Three Jewish Poems,* the composer admits a certain restraint in the orchestral writing: "I held myself back." More representative of his whole personality were the *Psalms, Schelomo,* and *Israel.* These, he feels, stemmed from "the passion and the violence that I believe to be characteristics of my nature." Generally regarded as the crowning work of the Cycle, the *Avodath Haḳodesh* (Sacred Service), composed in 1932-1934, has been termed by Marion Bauer "the quintessence of Bloch's life experience as man and artist." In it Bloch hoped to create "A song of Faith for all humanity." Though intensely Jewish in its roots, its message seemed to him "a gift of Israel to the whole of mankind, embodying a philosophy acceptable to all men."

Said Mr. Downes, "the implications of the work far transcend those of liturgical observance"—a statement Bloch would doubtless endorse for the whole Jewish Cycle, for his artistic creed has embraced all life, experience, and aspiration.

L. B.

"Three Jewish Poems"

Dance. Rite. Funeral Procession.

THIS MUSIC, consisting of three sections, Dance, Ritual and Funeral Procession, was composed between August and September, 1913, at Satigy, near Geneva. However, it did not obtain its premiere until Mar. 23, 1917, when the composer himself conducted it at a concert of the Boston Symphony Orchestra in Boston. It is dedicated to the memory of the composer's father.

The score calls for two flutes, piccolo, two oboes, English horn, two clarinets, two bassoons, contra-bassoon, four horns, three trumpets, three trombones and tuba, tympani, snare drum, bass drum, cymbals, deep drum, triangle, tam-tam, glockenspiel, chimes, harp, celesta, and strings.

The composer has detailed his program for the music as follows:

DANCE

Night. Round multicolored fires, members of the tribe are squatting; the musicians improvise. A woman, half-dressed, suggests the movements of a dance.

Suddenly she stops, hesitating . . . as though listening to an inner voice . . . and then in silence she begins her real dance, at once languorous and mysterious, then somber and ardent, as though performing a rite. . . .

Has she perceived the profound sources of Life? And does she seek to reveal them by her gestures? . . . More and more agitated, she seems to struggle against this inner demon; little by little she yields to it, with more passionate ardor, and lets herself be possessed by it, and, intoxicated, overwhelmed, she sinks down, swooning.

Her companions approach . . . and try to revive her.

The dance resumes. . . . It is almost like a ceremony for Astarte and Baal, which the crowd, excited in its turn, now frantically joins.

RITE

A procession of priests advances serenely to the strains of a broad melody. They arrive before the altar; the priestly trumpets announce the sacrifice, at first mysteriously, then little by little more ardently, fanatically: a solemn rite is to be performed, and Jehovah is about to manifest himself in His terrible grandeur. Suddenly, with a peal of thunder, a column of fire kindles the altar. The crowd, terrified, prostrates itself, covering their faces, before the Presence, august and mysterious. . . .

Then calm returns. . . . A very sweet and ecstatic melody mingles with the blue fumes of the sacrifice. . . . A profound mystery spreads over everything. . . .

The priests resume their march. . . . But, after this communion with God, the human soul is purified, ennobled. It is suffused by divine love; a great calm and sweet peace reign and the deep faith of the soul expands in a song of gratitude.

FUNERAL PROCESSION

1. *The Poem of Death.*—A procession, cold, icy, and mournful; then sinister, implacable accents, and the desperate resistance of Man to the idea of death. . . .

The terrifying summons of the trombones: It is Death itself, which claims its due, its prey. . . . Man tries to tear himself from his cruel destiny, but his sorrow, his lamentations, are in vain . . . the irrevocable summons cries out to him: "It must be . . . it must be. . . ."

2. A mystic song arises, a consolation; perhaps a wish to accept, for the sorrow remains latent—one *wishes* to believe, one *tries* to hope—but the heart remains heavy and full of tears.

But this struggling, desperate anguish ends by overcoming everything. The summons of Death sounds again implacably. . . . A last supplicating gesture . . . the horror of facing reality . . . this is the bitter, unbounded sorrow of seeing those whom we have loved disappear forever . . . "Nevermore . . . nevermore. . . ."

Their bodies are taken away. Every trace of the corporeal is effaced, and Man remains alone, lost, haggard. . . . He groans . . . he sinks to the ground, overwhelmed by sorrow, without resistance. . . .

Then a song of ineffable sweetness arises, calm, serene, mystic. . . . Well beyond human suffering. . . . Is it hope? Consolation, . . . the song does not speak to us of another Life . . . nor does it deny one. It tells us perhaps that none of our efforts, of our struggles, are lost. . . . The smile, the goodness, the tenderness of our dead survive . . . they are still with us . . . they still seem to lean towards us . . . we feel their gaze, the warmth of the hands that are no more. . . .

In the distance . . . the "Dance" is heard . . . as if Life were resuming—as if under a veil—as if it were hardly possible . . . and once more the motive of the mystic procession. . . .

And it is Acceptance. Man no longer resists, no longer suffers. He yields. And the procession becomes incorporeal, no longer seems hostile or cruel. . . . It is the LAW. . . .

And it is also Peace, which descends upon us. . . .

R. C. B.

"Schelomo" ("Solomon"): Hebrew Rhapsody, for Cello and Orchestra

COMPOSED DURING January and February, 1916, at Geneva, *Schelomo* is one of several works of Bloch's "peculiarly Hebraic in character." As he himself wrote:

It is not my purpose, not my desire, to attempt a "reconstitution" of Jewish music, or to base my works on melodies more or less authentic. I am not an archaeologist. I hold it of first importance to write good, genuine music, my music. It is the Jewish soul that interests me, the complex, glowing, agitated soul, that I feel vibrating throughout the Bible; the freshness and naïveté of the Patriarchs; the violence that is evident in the prophetic books; the Jew's savage love of justice; the despair of the Preacher in Jerusalem; the sorrow and immensity of the Book of Job; the sensuality of the Song of Songs. All this is in us; all this is in me, and it is the better part of me. It is all that I endeavor to hear in myself and to transcribe in my music: the venerable emotion of the race that slumbers way down in our soul.

Just before he came to this country, the composer met the cellist Alexander Barjansky. In the latter's home, in Switzerland, he saw a wax sculpture of King Solomon, made by the cellist's wife Catherine. That sculpture was the inspiration for this orchestral rhapsody, which Bloch then wrote in a few weeks and dedicated to Barjansky.

Schelomo was given its first performance by the Society of the Friends of Music, with Hans Kindler as the soloist, on May 3, 1917, at Carnegie Hall. The Philharmonic-Symphony added the piece to its repertory with the performance given, also in Carnegie Hall, on Feb. 19, 1931, when Alfred Wallenstein played the solo part and Bernardino Molinari conducted.

R. C. B.

Luigi Boccherini

BORN: LUCCA, ITALY, FEB. 19, 1743. DIED: MADRID, MAY 28, 1805.

In all probability Boccherini's name will long live by reason of a minuet from a string quartet.—PHILIP HALE.

Symphony in A major

I. Allegro assai. II. Menuetto: Allegro. III. Andante. IV. Finale: Allegro ma non troppo presto.

ALTHOUGH LUIGI BOCCHERINI wrote over 500 works, he is known today chiefly as the composer of a cello concerto and a minuet. Five hundred, however, is scarcely a patch on the huge output of Christoph Graupner, who was a contemporary of Bach's, for that worthy delivered himself of more than 1,300 church works, 116 symphonies, 80 overtures, 50 concertos, and just too many others. "Beside fecundity such as this," says Lawrence Gilman, "Haydn is a dawdler." And Hadow, remarking on assembly-line production by the early symphonists, observes that "The manner in which symphonies were poured out, in sets of six and otherwise, by numerous composers during the eighteenth century puts utterly out of question the loftiness of aim and purpose which has become a necessity since the early years of the nineteenth century."

Hadow, of course, refers to the multitude of forgotten men, whose music is never nowadays—and who knows whether it will ever be—played. Boccherini, for all his prolificness was a most serious musician and an acclaimed virtuoso of the cello.

In 1768, or thereabouts, the Spanish Ambassador at Paris, who was a gifted and very industrious musical amateur, urged Boccherini to try his fortunes in Madrid where, the dignitary promised enthusiastically, there would be a cordial welcome awaiting him from the Prince of the Asturias (who later became Charles IV).

The Ambassador had overcalculated, for on the Italian composer's arrival in Madrid (he was accompanied by the violinist Filippo Manfredi) he looked in vain for either princely or kingly reception. However, it was the Infante Don Luis, brother of the King of Spain, who became his patron. To him Boccherini dedicated his Symphony in C major, as well as six quartets (Op. 6) on whose title page he described himself as *"Compositore e virtuoso di camera di S.A.R. Don Luigi Infante d'Ispagna."* He held that high position until the death of the Infante, in 1785, and later found another patron in the Marquis Benavante. When, in 1787, he dedicated a work to Friedrich Wilhelm II of

Prussia, he earned the monarch's favor and obtained, as a result, the title of *Kammer Komponist,* together with an annual pension, which stopped only with the King's death, ten years later.

All the wealth and success that attended him were a direct contrast to the manner in which he ended his days. Except for a brief subvention from Lucien Bonaparte, Boccherini's last few years were years of neglect and misery, and his death in Madrid came amid extreme poverty.

In what must have been a pretty busy lifetime he wrote 20 symphonies, an opera, an orchestral suite, 4 cello concertos, much sacred music, 2 octets, 16 sextets, 125 string quintets, 12 piano quintets, 18 quintets for strings and either flute or oboe, 91 string quartets, 54 string trios, 42 trios, several sonatas and duets for violin, and other works.

The present Symphony, dating from 1787 (the German period), is in four movements. The first, Allegro assai, opens with a theme for full orchestra. It is repeated softly, and a vigorous passage leads to the second theme, which is given to flute and first violins, again very softly. The working out introduces a variant of the second theme for flute. It is taken up by the oboe, followed by a series of chords, which lead to the development of the first theme by strings and wood winds in quick modulations. The recapitulation is led to by a very quiet passage for flute and strings.

The second movement is an Allegro. The minuet flows gently out of the strings. The rhythm becomes more decisive, and the first part closes with a measure of lilting quality. This part is made longer in its repetition, after which there is a trio, a kind of leaping, skipping dance for flute solo and again for flute and first violins. At its conclusion the minuet returns.

The third movement, Andante, opens with a melodious song for oboe and solo viola, accompanied by the strings. Full orchestral chords are interposed between this and a succeeding passage in which the first violins take up the melody. A middle section is in the minor. The main tune again takes its place with the oboe and solo viola.

The fourth movement, Allegro ma non troppo presto, starts with a rondolike melody for violins. It spreads suddenly to all corners of the orchestra, with no lessening of the melodic character in this larger form. A second theme for strings is in imitation, and the development section starts with it in bassoons and violins. The first subject is sweetly developed, followed by the recapitulation. The movement closes, after a few soft violin measures, with three sonorous chords.

R. C. B.

Alexander Borodin

BORN: ST. PETERSBURG, NOV. 12, 1833. DIED: ST. PETERSBURG, FEB. 28, 1887.

We old sinners, as always, are in the whirlwind of life—professional duty, science, art. We hurry on and do not reach the goal. Time flies like an express train. The beard grows gray, wrinkles make deeper hollows. We begin a hundred different things. Shall we ever finish any of them?—ALEXANDER BORODIN.

Symphony in B minor, No. 2, Op. 5

I. Allegro. II. Prestissimo. III. Andante. IV. Allegro.

AMONG THE astonishing facts about the B minor Symphony is that it was, virtually, the work of a musical amateur—of a man who by profession and even preference was one of Russia's foremost experimental chemists. Borodin was also a noted surgeon and founder of the first Russian School of Medicine for Women, besides being a brilliant lecturer and writer on chemistry. When he said to a friend, "I love my profession," Dr. Borodin was not alluding to music. But he cherished his hobby fondly. Even during laboratory hours he did not forget that he was also a musician. At intervals he would hum or sing fresh themes to himself. While writing a treatise on chemical groupings, he might jot down a symphonic idea. During the summer months he would indulge his avocation freely, though he never abandoned chemical research for long. In winter he composed mainly when sick. Musical friends were urged never to say, "I hope you are well," but "I hope you are ill." Illness meant so much extra time for his hobby.

About this versatile genius, equally adept in two widely separated fields, Rimsky-Korsakoff once wrote: "It broke my heart to see how completely his life was filled with self-denial owing to his own *inertia*." Despite Borodin's relatively modest output in music, *inertia* seems hardly the word. A full-time surgeon-consultant and chemist who could also turn out a massive, though unfinished, opera (*Prince Igor*), a brilliant symphonic poem (*On the Steppes of Central Asia*), two symphonies, plus two movements of a third, besides composing chamber music and the words and music of several songs, would seem to have been anything but *inert*.

Thus, it is easy to see why the B minor Symphony came into being only after six long years of intermittent toil. A performance was promised by the St. Petersburg Musical Society for early in January, 1876. What might have been expected in Borodin's double life happened. In the hectic whirl of lectures, consultations, research, and illness, Borodin lost the manuscript of the first and last movements. There were still some days to go. So, the diligent doctor buckled down to the dismal work of reorchestration. As a crowning touch of irony Borodin took sick, ran up a high temperature, and suffered one of his frightful sieges of headache. We have a self-portrait of the ailing man feverishly penciling the two movements in bed. Borodin was being factual, not facetious, when he exclaimed: "Never has a professor of the Academy of Medicine and Surgery been found in such a position!"

Despite his thorough early training and a strong creative urge, Borodin's musical career, hampered as it was, might have remained purely potential had it not been for outside influence and prodding. Linked with the B minor Symphony, for instance, are several great names, beginning with that of Balakireff. By prompting Borodin to write a symphony, Balakireff boasted of having cured him of "considering himself an amateur and not putting much faith in the importance of his compositions." Next, Stassoff, the critic, helped arouse Borodin's nationalist fervor by acquainting him with the "Prince Igor" literature. From that reading sprang not only the opera, but also the B minor, which Stassoff dubbed "the Paladin Symphony." Borodin later told Stassoff that the ruggedly barbaric first movement pictured the gathering of ancient Russian princes; that the Andante harked back to the songs of the early Slav minstrels (bayans); and that the Finale was intended to evoke a banquet of legendary heroes, held amid the rejoicing populace. By thus exciting his interest in the balladry of medieval Russia, Stassoff fostered Borodin's development as a main exponent of the "nationalist" Russian school of program music.

Still another name in the evolution of the B minor Symphony is that of Rimsky-Korsakoff. In his autobiography, Rimsky blandly advances the claim that the much revised B minor Symphony "was reduced to its final form by the composer principally under the influence of our talks about orchestration." Rimsky, while commenting on some "heaviness" in the orchestration, especially in an earlier version, speaks warmly of the "bold handling of the brass." What "heaviness" there was in the version first played by Napravnik prompted the critic Ivanov to write: "Hearing this music, you are reminded of the ancient Russian knights in all their awkwardness," adding, however, "and also in all their greatness." Borodin "considerably lightened" the Scherzo for the revision later used at one of Rimsky's own concerts. Rimsky, incidentally, agreed with Stassoff in calling the B minor a "Paladin Symphony," hence a "program" symphony, though he was unable to relate the "Scherzo"—with the exception of the Trio—to the scheme and spirit of the rest.

The cycle of celebrities closes with the name of Franz Liszt. Borodin visited Liszt in Weimar in the summer of 1877. The great man was then eagerly following the rise of musical nationalism in Russia. Together they played a piano arrangement of the B minor Symphony. Liszt was enchanted, insisting at Borodin alter nothing, no matter what he heard against the score. While e dwelt at length on its "perfect logic of construction," what most struck him as its unabashed daring. "It is vain to say that there is nothing new under he sun; *this* is quite new," he told the speechless Borodin. "You would not nd *this,* or *this,* in any other composer," he went on, indicating certain passages. "Yesterday a German came to call on me. He brought me his third ymphony. Showing him your work, I said: 'We Germans are still a long way rom this.'"

Waxing more and more fervid, Liszt then exclaimed: "No! You Russians re indispensable to us! Without you I am powerless. You have a quick and ital spring within you; the future belongs to you." Thanks partly to Liszt, the ymphony soon made the rounds of European concert centers. The earliest American performance seems to have been one in Cincinnati during the season of 1898-1899. "If there is any symphony that can be called preeminently virile nd Russian," wrote Paul Rosenfeld in 1920, "it is assuredly Borodin's Second" —a judgment few would care to dispute even in 1944.

L. B.

Excerpts from "Prince Igor"

I. March. II. Dance of the Young Maidens. III. Polovtzian Dances.

IRONICALLY BORODIN did not complete *Prince Igor* himself, though he had devoted years of research into the history, customs, and vagaries of the Polovtsians, a people of Central Asia around whom the dramatic subject evolves. It was completed by Rimsky-Korsakoff and Glazounoff, both of whom labored long and lovingly on the remaining unorchestrated portions, as well as on the development of certain sketches made by Borodin.

The idea for the piece was suggested to Borodin by the Russian critic Vladimir Stassoff. That was in 1869. Twenty-one years later, on Nov. 4, 1890, *Prince Igor* was given its premiere performance at St. Petersburg. Borrowing a good deal of the thematic material for the dances and choruses from actual melodies of tribes, Borodin placed them in the second act of his work.

Borodin and Stassoff collaborated on the libretto, which is mostly derived from the *Epic of the Army of Igor,* an apocryphal early Russian poem which appeared in 1800 and was regarded by many Russian scholars as a literary fraud.

The action of the opera takes place in twelfth-century Russia. Prince Igor Severski, setting out on a campaign against the Polovtsians, leaves his wife Jaroslavna in the care of his brother-in-law, Prince Galitzky. Igor's son Vladimir accompanies him on the expedition. During their absence Galitzky, together with two deserters, concocts a plot for the overthrow of the government, and when Jaroslavna hears of it she denounces him. Almost at the same time the news arrives announcing Igor's defeat.

Igor and his son, in the meantime, are being regally entertained by their conqueror, the Khan Konchak. And Ovlour, a Polovtsian convert to Christianity, even offers Igor and Vladimir an avenue of escape. But the prisoners refuse, at first, being too honorable for such underhanded devices. Not the least important reason, however, is the fact that Vladimir has fallen in love with Konchakovna, the Khan's daughter.

When some Polovtsian warriors return from Igor's capital city Poutivle with many prisoners and much booty the royal captives change their minds and make the break for freedom in the company of Ovlour. But Little Konchakovna, who is informed of the attempt, turns them in, loving Vladimir as much as she does. Vladimir is captured, but Igor and Ovlour get away. The last scene shows the return of Igor to his wife, "who is weeping amid the ruins of her palace."

The dances, which are so well known in the concert hall, take place in the opera during the festivities in honor of Igor and Vladimir at the Polovtsian camp.

R. C. B.

Orchestral Sketch, "On the Steppes of Central Asia"

Prefacing the score of this "orchestral sketch" is the following description of the picture Borodin sought to evoke:

Out of the silence of the sandy steppes of Central Asia come the sounds of a peaceful Russian song. Along with them are heard the melancholy strains of Oriental melodies, then the stamping of approaching horses and camels. A caravan, accompanied by Russian soldiers, traverses the measureless waste. With full trust in its protective escort, it continues its long journey in carefree mood. Onward the caravan moves. The Songs of the Russians and those of the Asiatic natives mingle in common harmony. The refrains curl over the desert and then die away in the distance.

We have Borodin's own word for it that whatever European prestige he enjoyed as composer he owed to this tone picture of the Asiatic plain. To his friend Gavrouschkiewitch he wrote in May, 1886:

The most popular of my works abroad is my symphonic sketch *Dans les steppes de l'Asie central*. It has made the rounds of Europe from Christiania to Monaco. In spite of its patriotic program—the success of Russian arms in Asia—the work has been encored almost everywhere and often repeated by request, as at the Strauss concerts in Vienna and the Lamoureux concerts in Paris.

Borodin wrote the "sketch" in 1880 for the twenty-fifth anniversary of the reign of Czar Alexander II, which explains the reference to "patriotic program." Among the imperial festivities was an exhibition of *tableaux vivants,* "living pictures," drawn from episodes in Russian history. Central Asia, with its teeming legend and brooding expanse, long fascinated Borodin. His opera *Prince Igor* is a tribute to the exotic mystery and mingled culture of the region. In much of Borodin's music we sense the ominous stillness of the vast waste, with its wandering tribes and plodding camels, and remember Shelley's line, "the lone and desert sands stretch far away."

A year after composing *On the Steppes of Central Asia,* Borodin paid his second visit to Liszt at Weimar. Thoroughly enchanted with the work, Liszt persuaded Borodin to make a four-piano arrangement before he tackled anything else. The dedication of the "orchestral sketch" is to "Dr. F. Liszt." The scoring calls for two flutes, oboe, English horn, two clarinets, two bassoons, four horns, two trumpets, three trombones, tympani, and strings.

L. B.

Johannes Brahms

BORN: HAMBURG, MAY 7, 1833. DIED: VIENNA, APR. 3, 1897.

*Many new and remarkable talents have made their appearance, and a fresh musical power seemed about to reveal itself among the many aspiring artists of the day, even though their compositions were known only to the few. I thought to follow with interest the pathway of these elect; there would, there must, after such promise, suddenly appear one who should utter the highest ideal expression of his time, who should claim the Mastership by no gradual development, but burst upon us fully equipped, as Minerva sprang from the brain of Jupiter. And he has come, this chosen youth, over whose cradle the Graces and Heroes seem to have kept watch. His name is Johannes Brahms.—*SCHUMANN, *in the Neue Zeitschrift für Musik, Oct. 28, 1853.*

Symphony in C minor, No. 1, Op. 68

I. Un poco sostenuto; Allegro. II. Andante sostenuto. III. Un poco allegretto e grazioso. IV. Adagio; Più andante; Allegro non troppo, ma con brio; Più allegro.

WHY BRAHMS delayed giving the world a symphony till he was forty-three might well puzzle students of the history of music. At that age Beethoven had already composed eight of his Immortal Nine, having launched the first in his thirtieth year. The incredible Mozart had scarcely reached his tenth birthday when the ink dried on his initial venture. Mendelssohn was a ripe fifteen at his symphonic debut, though the boy had twelve other symphonies to his unofficial credit. Schubert's First dates from his sixteenth year. Before he reached his majority, he had added five more to his symphonic score card.

Schumann was only thirty-one when his Fourth Symphony was performed, and, of course, Haydn, living in the fantastic eighteenth century, ran up a total of at least half a hundred before he was forty-three. Tschaikowsky's record was four symphonies before his thirty-eighth year, the first dating from his late twenties. A later countryman, Dmitri Shostakovich, wrote his first symphony at nineteen, at thirty-five completed his seventh in a besieged city, and at thirty-seven gave the world his eighth.

What made Brahms wait? Established and widely hailed as heir to the German tradition, he had long been expected to put his signature to a symphony. Vast technic and inventive resource were his to give. Friends prodded him repeatedly. Schumann impatiently awaited a fresh outburst of romanticism from him, tempered, of course, by Brahms's own classic reserve. If only he would make a beginning, counseled the older composer and sponsor, "the end would come of itself." Brahms did make several "beginnings." As a young man Beethoven's Ninth Symphony and Schumann's *Manfred* stirred him to symphonic writing. But the three movements of an abortive work ended as parts of the D minor piano concerto and *A German Requiem*.

Fresh sketches were made in the late fifties, and soon it was common talk in musical circles that Brahms had finally made the plunge and was writing a symphony. Friends even reported that Brahms carried the completed manuscript about with him for years before the premiere in 1876. Albert Dietrich saw an early version of the first movement in 1862. Later Clara Schumann made none too glowing allusions to the manuscript in her secret diary. The symphony shaped up slowly. Something was holding it back.

To begin with, Brahms was always a prey to sharp self-criticism. Loss of confidence recurringly assailed him. Frequently he thought himself no composer at all. Whether seriously or jestingly, he often dismissed compositions of his own with flippant phrases. It was probably a way of inviting needed praise and encouragement. That he brought true humility to his work there can be no question. He toiled ceaselessly over a score to achieve technical perfection. He deleted, rejected, and rewrote unsparingly. Thus, the C minor Symphony underwent a long process of change and correction. False leads and forced developments called for fresh starts. Constant renewal of ideas was necessary. After all, Brahms was rather on the spot. A recognized master of form and standard bearer of a rising neoclassical camp, he could not betray his ideals with a specimen of feeble and shoddy workmanship. Nothing short of a compact and finished product would satisfy him or the waiting world.

Then, Brahms's views on musical esthetics were maturing to a fixed classical outlook. In that long period since the fifties, Mendelssohn and Schumann had ceased to exert marked influence on his methods. The chasm between himself and the ebullient romantics had widened. Bach and Beethoven now bulked larger than ever in his artistic cosmos. Classicism was molding a brave new world in his consciousness. The romantic in Brahms remained, subject to a stern discipline. But the polyphonist and architect, eschewing liberties of color and "expression," steadily gained firmer sway. Brahms could afford to wait until his symphony blossomed into full-fledged growth as the new manifesto of an older creed. He owed it to himself and the Great Tradition. "Composing a symphony is no laughing matter," he confessed succinctly.

Over his labors hovered another huge shadow—Beethoven. As an epic figure in the German lineage and a bridge to Bach, the Bonn master loomed as a guide and a warning. Brahms was drawn to the fierce, pulsing vigor, and rock-bottom classic force of his predecessor. But Beethoven, too, had written a C minor Symphony. The risk was great. Brahms was courting disaster. Enemies would charge arrogance and overweening ambition. Malicious comparisons would be made, and his own puny merits would be measured with a Titan's gauge. "You have no idea how it feels to hear behind you the tramp of a giant like Beethoven," he complained.

Brahms was right, but so were those who believed in him. The expected happened. The Wagnerites and supporters of the Weber-Berlioz-Liszt school of unfettered romanticism pounced on the work as an ultimatum. Enmities deepened, and alignments were more sharply marked. Von Bülow's dictum that this was the Tenth Symphony—an allusion to Beethoven's Nine—aroused the foe to stinging rebuttal. Even Hanslick, Viennese high priest of the Brahms cult, made reservations. Brahms was attacked for his cold, hollow formalism, for resisting the main currents of the new music. In a word, he was a reactionary, harking back to the closed system of classicism.

But others knew that something else had come to pass. They recognized the grandeur and lyric surge of Brahms, his flair for simple melody, his warm humanity and manly strength. They saw, too, that far from reaction the C minor marked a fresh stage in the development of the sonata form and a valid application of the full resources of counterpoint. If Brahms avoided the lush personal colorism of others and concentrated on an "absolute" ideal, he showed, on the other hand, even more rhythmic and harmonic ingenuity than they within his chosen classic frame. In the use of cross-accents, syncopation, rhythm combination, and novel turn of melodic phrase, Brahms had already outdistanced the daring innovators of his time.

He never stooped to theatrical effects. Development and climax were immense and inevitable in Brahms's symphonic scheme. Themes expanded and changed in answer to a logic of their own. No composer since Beethoven had shown such intellectual grasp of sheer design. This was music of strength, molded in the great line, and noble and moving in its own way. That it could ever have been flouted by critics as morbid, strained, unnatural, and forbidding is hard to believe today. Its musing tenderness and epic sweep have locked it securely in the hearts of concertgoers.

"A portentous introduction (Un poco sostenuto, C minor, 6/8) prefaces the first movement (Allegro, C minor, 6/8). The first theme is given out by the violins in the fifth measure. The second theme (E flat major) appears in the wood winds. The character of the movement is austere and epic.

"The second movement (Andante sostenuto, E major, 3/4) is imbued with a profound lyricism, which flowers into some of the loveliest pages in all Brahms.

"Instead of a scherzo, there follows a movement marked Un poco allegretto e grazioso (A flat major, 2/4), which Grove aptly characterizes as 'a sort of national tune or Volkslied of simple sweetness and grace.' The opening

ubject is sung first by the clarinet. The place of a trio is delightfully filled by a
ontrasting middle section (B major, 6/8).

"The stupendous finale begins with an introductory section (Adagio, C
ninor, 4/4) that touches briefly on thematic material to be developed later."

L. B.

Symphony in D major, No. 2, Op. 73

I. Allegro non troppo. II. Adagio non troppo. III. Allegretto grazioso,
quasi andantino. IV. Allegro con spirito.

ALTHOUGH IT took Brahms some fifteen years of planning and replanning,
ecurring delays and spells of misgiving, before he launched his first symphony,
he second, in D major, came within a year of his initial effort. The earlier
vork marked a great step forward in art, workmanship, and self-confidence.
Iaving taken it, Brahms plunged eagerly into his second attempt.

By the end of September, 1877, he was playing the new work with Ignaz
Brüll in a four-hand piano version to an informal gathering of musical savants
n a room at Friedrich Ehrbar's piano warehouse in Vienna. On Dec. 30,
Hans Richter led the Vienna Philharmonic in its official world premiere. The
udience, reacting lukewarmly at first, waxed steadily more enthusiastic, and
ven compelled Richter to repeat the Allegretto grazioso.

Unquestionably, this Symphony, with its sunnier moods, made a readier
ppeal than had the C minor. However, this obvious turn to a lyrical and
astoral vein disappointed some doctrinaire Brahmsians,. who were expecting
nother massive utterance in epic form, like the First.

The Leipzig critic Dörffel, normally a Brahms advocate, fairly raged in his
lisappointment. "The Viennese are much more easily satisfied than we," he
umed. "We make quite different demands on Brahms and require from him
nusic which is something more than pretty . . . when he comes before us as a
ymphonist."

The allusion to the Viennese was not far-fetched. Many have sensed a frank
pirit of Viennese *gemütlichkeit* in the D major. The work has even been
lubbed Brahms's "Vienna Symphony," reflecting, allegedly, "the fresh,
iealthy life to be found in beautiful Vienna."

The idyllic moods of the Second Symphony, contrasting sharply with the
ustere sublimities of the C minor, again prompted comparison with Beethoven.
Both had written C minor symphonies. The Bonn master had followed the
C minor with a *Pastoral Symphony,* and so, presumably, had Brahms. Others
ound a closer analogy in Beethoven's Third and Fourth Symphonies, the
·enial following the heroic.

Richard Specht even describes the work as a "serenade" rather than a symphony, "suffused with the sunshine and the warm winds playing on the water." What gives color to Mr. Specht's impression is the fact that Brahms actually composed the symphony in the lake country around Pörtschach-am See in the summer of 1877.

Yet, despite its lyric suavity and freedom from the passionate stress of the First Symphony, Brahms at first alluded to the newly completed work as gloomy and awesome when queried by friends. Always evasive, flippant, and disparaging in remarks concerning his own music, he went to all lengths in mystifying his friends about the symphony.

To emphasize its alleged grim character, he spoke of it as in the key of F minor, instead of D major. The day before the Vienna premiere he informed Elisabet von Herzogenberg that the orchestra would play the new symphony with crepe bands on their sleeves, "because of its dirgelike effect." When printed, he added, the score would have a black border.

In another puckish moment earlier in November he had assured Frau von Herzogenberg that the new composition amounted to very little indeed. "The new symphony is merely a '*Sinfonie*,' and I shall not need to play it to you beforehand," he wrote. "You have only to sit down at the piano, put your small feet on the two pedals in turn, and strike the chord of F minor several times in succession, first in the treble, then in the bass, fortissimo and pianissimo, and you will gradually gain a vivid impression of my 'latest.'"

In September, Brahms gave a hint of the nature of his new symphony in a letter to Dr. Billroth, a famous Viennese surgeon and patron of music. "I do not know whether I have a pretty symphony: I must enquire of skilled persons."

Brahms may have doubted the success of his effort to express sunlit cheer and geniality in his new work. But, if by "pretty" he meant a beguiling lyricism and bright badinage, rhythmic caprice, and fresh spontaneity, the "skilled persons" could only have answered in the affirmative.

"Pretty," of course, is hardly the word for the tragic undertones and broad humanity readily sensed in page after page of the symphony. Its idyllic suavity and pastoral freshness are dominant moods, but a graver note of somber poetry recurs throughout, especially in the Adagio.

Walter Niemann no doubt goes too far in glimpsing ghostly traceries in the Second, "glimmering in a supernatural, uncanny way." Yet, while the Symphony's keynote is anything but granitic gloom, there is discernible a sober depth of feeling either minimized or overlooked by Brahms's contemporaries because of the striking contrast with the C minor. Time has somehow softened the rugged contours of the First and enriched and deepened the Second.

Surely nobody would now regard the C minor as "a scientific treatise full of philosophic thought." So, few listeners are likely to be satisfied with the description of the D major as "a glimpse of Nature, a spring day amid soft mosses, springing woods, birds' notes, and the bloom of flowers."

"The opening movement (Allegro non troppo, D major, 3/4) is remarkable for the lyricism of its themes. After the so-called fundamental motive of the first measure (cellos and double basses), the melodious chief theme is given out by horns and woodwind. A graceful subsidiary theme is heard in the violins. The second subject, nostalgic in its wistfulness, appears in the violas and cellos. A horn solo in the coda evokes the mystery of forest deeps from an old and bardic time.

"The second movement (Adagio non troppo, B major, 4/4) is of a profoundly romantic and yet somewhat elusive character. Not a scherzo, but rather the old-time minuet, is hinted at in the third movement (Allegretto grazioso, quasi andantino, G major, 3/4). The engaging melody is sung immediately by the oboes over chords in the clarinets and bassoons and pizzicato arpeggios in the cellos. Each of the two trios that the movement boasts is a variation on this theme. An acute critic has said of the Allegretto: 'Like many well-known things, it is not always remembered in its full variety and range, or we should hear less of its being too small for its place in a big symphony.'

"The finale (Allegro con spirito, D major, 2/2) is in sonata form. Thematically it is both rich in invention and reminiscent of passages in the earlier movements. A kinship to the finale of Haydn's last *London Symphony* has also been remarked. Of the four movements this Allegro con spirito is the most vigorous and vivacious, concluding, after pages of Olympian struggle, in a victorious coda of overwhelming brilliance."

L. B.

Symphony in F major, No. 3, Op. 90

I. Allegro con brio. II. Andante. III. Poco allegretto. IV. Allegro.

BRAHMS's FAITHFUL sloganeers were ready when the Third Symphony appeared. They had established a parallel, at least to their own satisfaction, between the C minor Symphonies of the Master and Beethoven. They had promptly recognized Brahms's Second as a "Pastoral"—did not Beethoven's *Pastoral* follow the C minor, and did not the idyllic moods of the Second invite analogy with Beethoven's great nature study?

The votaries found Brahms's Third Symphony even easier to christen. Its dominant mood was heroic. In a flash Hans Richter named it the "Eroica." No true Brahmsian could resist the temptation. The symphonies bore the same number. The moods were alike. It was not fair of Brahms to use a different key and omit a funeral march.

Richter's felicitous title was hurriedly endorsed by Eduard Hanslick. "Truly," said Brahms's staunchest paladin of the press, "if the first symphony in C minor is characterized as the 'Pathetic' or the 'Appassionata,' and the second in D major as the 'Pastoral,' the new symphony in F major may be appropriately called Brahms's 'Eroica.'" Still, Hanslick saw fit to limit the designation of "heroic" to the opening and final movements, pointing out that the symphony led to no tragic action, such as the Funeral March in Beethoven's Third. Besides, there were passages in Brahms's score "quivering with the romantic twilight of Schumann and Mendelssohn."

Clara Schumann evidently disagreed with the Richter-Hanslick thesis. She knew what Brahms's Third Symphony was—a forest idyl! Another friend, Joseph Joachim, differed even more sharply. The Hungarian violinist heard the finale as a symphonic rendering of the Greek legend of Hero and Leander! Max Kalbeck's own theory was simpler: the symphony owed its origin to a statue, that of Germania at Rüdesheim. Brahms had admired the statue, *ergo* the symphony. It is just possible that Brahms himself had no clear-cut idea of program or inspiration regarding his symphony. Gustav Mahler used to preach that if a composer could say what he had to say in words, he should not bother trying to say it in music.

There is irony in Hugo Riemann's belief that Brahms intended a tribute to Wagner in the first movement by way of some string harmonies suggesting a passage for women's chorus in the Venusberg scene in *Tannhäuser*. Riemann pointed out that Wagner died while Brahms was working on his Third Symphony. What more natural than a *beau geste* to a deceased rival! Sad to relate, embattled Wagnerians still regarded Brahms as Public Enemy No. 1. The more militant and unscrupulous formed cabals to wreck Brahms performances. If the Wagnerian goon squads gathered at the premiere in Vienna on Dec. 2, 1883, detected the *Tannhäuser* echo in the first movement, it probably only made matters worse. They were in no mood to scent appeasement in the enemy camp.

Well, the Wagnerians remained true to their dead master. They hissed vigorously after the first movement. To no avail. There was no doubt about the general reaction. The audience liked the symphony, in fact hailed it rousingly. The hissing continued after each movement, but progressively feebler. At the end the hostile barrage was completely obliterated by the applause. The premiere almost led to a duel between members of the opposing factions. The staunch Brahmsian, Arthur Faber, infuriated by a hisser sitting behind him, was prepared to settle matters on the field of honor, but magnanimously relented at a supper party given in Brahms's honor after the premiere.

The Third Symphony promptly strikes a heroic note with the announcement of a "motto" theme to be heard recurringly. It is given out in three powerful ascending chords for horns, trumpets, and woodwind. The highest voice, consisting of F, A flat, F, is said to stand for *Frei aber froh* (free but happy), Brahms having adopted that as a personal slogan. Parenthetically, it might be pointed out that Brahms never married. One analyst discerned 'occult dramatic signification" in the way Brahms uses the "motto" device at one point.

The three challenging chords serve to introduce the majestic first subject, chanted by the violins with viola and cello support. The passage resembling the one in the *Tannhäuser* Venusberg Scene occurs in a transition section leading to the next theme. This second subject consists of a repeated phrase in pastoral mood first allotted to clarinet and bassoon. At one point the solo oboe is heard uttering the three "motto" notes. In the development section horn and oboe join in another return of the *"Frei aber froh"* motive. The three introductory chords usher in a restatement of earlier material.

Clarinets and bassoon give out the gentle hymnlike opening theme of the Andante movement (C major, 4/4). A resemblance has been noted between this melody and a prayerlike episode in both the overture and finale of Herold's opera *Zampa*. The theme is then freely varied.

The third movement (Poco allegretto, C minor, 3/8) replaces the usual scherzo and is more in the style of a romanza in melancholy vein. The movement contains a tender and contemplative melody first assigned to the cellos.

The impassioned and heroic finale (F minor, 2/2) opens with a spectral theme rustling through the strings, "with all the haste of a vision in a dream." Horns and cellos later chant a sturdy song of brighter cast. There follows what amounts to a clash between opposing moods of gloom and jubilation. The gloom vanishes. Presently echoes of the "motto" theme are heard and the strings bring back, in tremolo, what Apthorp called the "ghost" of the chief theme of the first movement.

L. B.

Symphony in E minor, No. 4, Op. 98

I. Allegro non troppo. II. Andante moderato. III. Allegro giocoso.
IV. Allegro energico e passionato.

A SYMPHONY IN E minor! The strong anti-Brahms bloc found much to carp about in the choice of that key for a symphony. And all that to-do concerning what must appear today to be an inconsequential detail! At its first performance (Meinengen, Oct. 25, 1885, Brahms conducting) the epigrams, pro and con, went thick and fast. It has been suggested that Brahms chose the key of E minor because of its "pale, wan character, to express the deepest melancholy." In support is Haydn's use of that key for one of his symphonies, termed the *Symphony of Mourning.* Raff had also written an E minor Symphony, though that work, titled *In Summer,* scarcely belongs in the department of melancholy and desolation.

Nevertheless, the tug of war went on. Even in Vienna, the composer's habitat, the symphony occasioned the same sort of reaction. Hugo Wolf, then writing musical criticism, hurled a venomous screed against the piece, lashing out particularly against the key. Brahms's adherents persisted doggedly in their exaltation of the symphony, perhaps with more enthusiasm than conviction. "There is no God but E minor," they virtually said, "and the Fourth of Brahms is his prophet." Yet some penetrating observers have felt that the inordinate praise was given merely to hide disappointment in the music.

Be that as it may, the Symphony took time to come into general favor. Brahms himself felt uncertain about this creation of his. In his usual cryptic fashion he had referred to it in a letter to Bülow as "a couple of entr'actes." Another luscious bit of phrase making on his part envisioned the Symphony as a "choral work without text." Eager to obtain opinions, he played it in four-hand piano version with Ignaz Brüll for Hanslick, Billroth, Richter, and Kalbeck. To the latter he posed the question, "If persons like Billroth, Hanslick and you do not like my music, whom will it please?" Yet Kalbeck could later say that the symphony relates the tragedy of human life. The Andante to him is comparable to a field laid waste, like the Campagna near Rome; the scherzo to a Carnival at Milan; and the finale to a passage in Sophocles' *Oedipus Coloneus,* which reads, "Not to have been born at all is superior to every other view of the question."

Of the Andante, Elisabet von Herzogenberg wrote to Brahms that it "has the freshness and distinction of character with which only you could endow it, and even you have had to recourse for the first time to certain locked chambers of your soul."

The E Minor Symphony was the last of his own works that Brahms heard performed in public. This was at a Philharmonic Concert in Vienna on Mar. 7, 1897, not quite a month before his death. In her *Life of Johannes Brahms,* Florence May gives a graphic picture of the occasion:

The Fourth Symphony had never become a favorite work in Vienna. Received with reserve on its first performance, it had not since gained much more from the general public of the city than the respect sure to be accorded there to an important work by Brahms. Today, however, a storm of applause broke out at the end of the first movement, not to be quieted until the composer, coming to the front of the artists' box in which he was seated, showed himself to the audience. The demonstration was renewed after the second and the third movements, and an extraordinary scene followed the conclusion of the work.

The applauding, shouting house, its gaze riveted on the figure standing in the balcony, so familiar and yet in present aspect so strange, seemed unable to let him go. Tears ran down his cheeks as he stood there, shrunken in form, with lined countenance, strained expression, white hair hanging lank; and through the audience there was a feeling as of a stifled sob, for each knew that they were saying farewell. Another outburst of applause and yet another; one more acknowledgment from the master; and Brahms and his Vienna had parted forever.

The E minor has been called an "elegiac" and a "character symphony." In this work the composer—perhaps, the hero—draws into himself in meditative contemplation. The vigor and daring and defiance implicit in the first movement of the Third Symphony have been transformed here into something nobler, more sweeping, more majestic in scope. Niemann finds this work an expression of Brahms's "own tragic recognition . . . that, as a tragic composer, his place is not at the side of Beethoven."

Brahms's use of the passacaglia or chaconne form for his finale gave his intimates much concern lest the average listener be completely deaf to its architectural magnitude. His manipulation of all the forces involved, the strict adherence to the very soul of the form, the richly contrasting orchestral colors, the subtlety of his treatment—and often disguising—of the theme point to a giant craftsmanship. Yet, despite the innumerable elements entering into its construction, the movement seethes with eloquent statement and, at the same time, flows with a perfect symphonic unity. Brahms had done a pioneering job in making the last section of a symphony a passacaglia (Percy Goetschius calls it a chaconne and gives plausible reasons for it), and he had by no means let his listeners down.

R. C. B.

Concerto for Piano and Orchestra in D minor, No. 1, Op. 15

I. Maestoso. II. Adagio. III. Rondo: Allegro non troppo.

A HEAVY RESPONSIBILITY fell on the shoulders of Johannes Brahms when he was barely twenty. Impressed by his great gifts, friends were already publicizing him as the great new hope of German music.

In a famous manifesto called "New Paths" Robert Schumann greeted him as the one composer uttering "the highest ideal expression of his time." The young genius had "burst upon us, fully equipped, like Minerva from the brain of Jupiter." Over his cradle, said Schumann, "the Graces and Heroes seem to have kept watch." The violinist Joseph Joachim had already told the world that Brahms was "the most considerable musician of his age," and Albert Dietrich, the conductor, was now writing his friend Nauman that "genius was written on Brahms's brow and shines forth from his clear blue eyes."

Intentionally or not, Brahms's friends were putting him on the spot. The gibe of a music critic of the time long rang in his ears: "We wish him a speedy deliverance from his overenthusiastic friends!" Quite naturally, Schumann's adulatory prose poem aroused distrust in some quarters, resentment in others. Many high-ranking musicians were frankly skeptical. Von Bülow, later to become a staunch Brahmsian, told Liszt that Schumann's pronouncement, "does not in the least disturb the tranquillity of my slumbers. It is fifteen years since Schumann spoke similarly of the *genius* of W. Sterndale Bennett."

With battle lines thus forming, Brahms felt impelled to justify the faith of his following. If he were truly "the spiritual son of Robert Schumann" and the standard bearer of a new trend, he could prove it best in a symphony. So he buckled down to a project that began as a symphony, became a sonata, and ended as the D minor Piano Concerto.

By January, 1854, he could write to Schumann: "I have been trying my hand at a symphony, have even orchestrated the first movement, and have composed the second and third." But something was wrong. Brahms, no doubt obsessed by the fear of letting his rhapsodic friends down, wrote to Joachim: "You have regarded the movement of my symphony through rose-colored glasses. I must alter and improve it all. A good deal is wrong in the composition."

As for the orchestration, Brahms attributed, "the best part of it" to his scholarly friend, Julius Otto Grimm. The "young eagle," as Schumann dubbed Brahms, was far from satisfied. The score never got beyond the third movement. Actually, it took Brahms another twenty years to work up enough courage to turn out a completed symphony.

But that was only the first stage of the early project. What there was of a symphony was speedily converted into a sonata for two pianos, completed in the spring of 1854, and first played by Clara Schumann and young Brahms at Klems on May 24. "I tried over the three movements of his sonata," reads Frau Schumann's diary. "They appeared to me quite powerful, quite original, noble and clearer than any of his earlier works. We played them twice, and on Sunday I shall play them with Dietrich."

Alas, there was still something wrong! Brahms was not quite sure what. Grimm, who followed Brahms and Dietrich as Frau Schumann's partner in playing the sonata, was certain he had detected the trouble. The contents of the sonata, he told Brahms, deserved "more dignified form." A concerto was just the thing. Brahms agreed.

The sonata's first two movements became once and for all the Maestoso and Adagio movements of the D minor Piano Concerto. The third movement was shelved for years, eventually emerging as the "Behold All Flesh" chorus of Brahms's *German Requiem,* where it remained. While the symphony sonata underwent its latest transformation, Joachim was frequently consulted on some technical points. "Here is the first movement. I have simplified and lightened it," we find Brahms writing his friend in April, 1856.

After a fresh revision in 1858, both Joachim and Frau Schumann expressed unqualified approval. "The whole thing seems to me to be almost too rich. But that is a good fault!" writes the violinist. "All my hopes of obtaining something new and beautiful in music rest with my dear friend!" At a rehearsal in Hanover, Frau Schumann found parts of the work "more beautiful than even Johannes himself imagined or expected." The whole concerto was "wonderful, so rich, so full of feeling, and at the same time so well proportioned." She notes that "Johannes" was very happy and "played the last movement prestissimo out of sheer delight."

Despite the encomiums of friends, a jinx was still on the much-transformed music. At the premiere in the Royal Theater, of Hanover, on Jan. 22, 1859, "the public was wearied and the musicians puzzled." A local critic found the concerto "difficult to understand, even dry, and in parts eminently fatiguing." After the Leipzig premiere, five days later, the *Signale* correspondent dismissed the concerto as "a symphony with piano obbligato, in which the solo part is as ungrateful as possible, and the orchestral part a series of lacerating chords."

The response of public and press convinced Brahms that something was still amiss in the concerto. In a letter to Joachim he speaks of the Leipzig premiere as "a brilliant and decisive failure," despite the excellent playing. "The first and second movements," he writes candidly, "were listened to without a sign. At the conclusion three pairs of hands were brought together very slowly, whereupon a perfectly audible hissing from all sides forbade any such demonstration." Always sharply critical of his own work, Brahms goes on to say that "this is the best thing that could happen to one; it forces one to pull his thoughts together and stimulates his courage." Joachim will understand. "After all, I am only experimenting and feeling my way as yet." Then he asks, quite humanly: "But the hissing was too much, wasn't it?"

Anyway, Brahms set to work on further revision. "When I have improved its form, the concerto will meet with approval," he declared. The *Neue Zeitschrift,* which had earlier carried Schumann's epoch-making tribute, again stood by him. "In the face of disparaging criticism from certain sections of the public and press, we feel it our duty to point out the admirable features of this work, as well as to protest the none too honorable way in which judgment was pronounced against it." Stress was put on the concerto's poetic essence as the "one unmistakable sign of significant and original creative power."

There was no word, of course, from the man who had given Brahms the great send-off six years before. Schumann, who had built such great hopes on his "spiritual son," was dead. Hopelessly insane, he had lingered on for two years in Dr. Richarz's private asylum in Endenich, near Bonn. An attempt at suicide by diving into the Rhine at Düsseldorf had climaxed the gathering signs of trouble. Brahms himself was involved in one of the earlier incidents. One day Schumann bellowed wildly at him: "Why do you play so fast, Johannes? I beg of you, be moderate!" A glance at Schumann confirmed Brahms's suspicions. The younger man wept.

Brahms's association with Schumann's widow is one of the famous friendships of music. After Schumann's death, Brahms helped straighten out his tangled professional affairs. Biographers differ widely on the kind of intimacy that grew up between the protégé and widow. Though Frau Schumann was thirteen years older than Brahms, some believe the relationship, at least for a time, was more than "strictly platonic." Filial devotion no doubt entered Brahms's attachment to the widow. In later years the situation took on an ironic twist, duly noted by Eduard Hanslick. "Brahms is cultivating a patriarchal beard with the hope of passing for her father," observed the Viennese critic in 1880.

Brahms is said to have paid direct homage to Schumann in at least two movements of the D minor Concerto. Joachim long maintained that Schumann's tragic plunge into the Rhine directly inspired the opening movement. Max Kalbeck went a step further in his biography of Brahms. In the manuscript score the motto over the Adagio movement reads: *Benedictus qui venit in nomine Domini* (Blessed is he who comes in the name of the Lord). Kalbeck said the inscription referred to Schumann. The theory is plausible. Brahms often addressed the senior composer as "Mynheer Domine."

In the first movement (Maestoso, D minor, 6/8) a long orchestral passage, in which the strings state the main theme over a roll of tympani, prefaces the entrance of the piano. After discoursing the theme, the piano brings in a second subject in F major, soon taken up by the strings. The piano now embroiders figures against it. There is elaborate development, with a return of this material, and the piano again gives out both themes, the second one now appearing in D major. The coda unreels brilliantly at some length. The romanzalike slow movement (Adagio, D major, 6/4) is based on a poetic theme taken up by the piano after strings and bassoons announce it. A contrasting middle section features two clarinets in a subsidiary theme. The finale is a fully expounded rondo (Allegro non troppo, D minor, 2/4), ending with another long and brilliant coda, after the piano has offered a cadenza. Besides the piano, the score calls for two flutes, two oboes, two clarinets, two bassoons, four horns, two trumpets, tympani, and strings.

Public and critics had reacted so unfavorably to the Hanover and Leipzig premieres of the D minor Concerto that the house of Breitkopf and Härtel actually turned it down when Brahms submitted it for publication. Rieter-

Biedermann were its first publishers in 1861. The concerto had to make its way into public favor slowly. As Pitts Sanborn pointed out, it was not until the turn of the century, for instance, that "it began to win full recognition in this country."

L. B.

Concerto for Piano and Orchestra in B flat major, No. 2, Op. 83

I. Allegro non troppo. II. Allegro appassionato. III. Andante. IV. Allegretto grazioso.

THAT EMINENT thorn in the side of Wagner and bright *boutonnière* in the coat of Brahms, Eduard Hanslick labeled this work a "symphony with piano obbligato." However, it might have been closer to the truth to regard it as a symphony for piano and orchestra, because the term, "with piano obbligato," does seem to give it an undeserved parlor petiteness.

The Concerto was first performed in the Redouten Saal, Budapest, on Nov. 9, 1881. On that occasion the program offered also the Cherubini Overture to *Medea* and Brahms's C minor Symphony. The composer appeared as soloist in the Concerto (conducted by Alexander Erkel), and he conducted the other pieces.

Some two decades previously, Brahms had written a First Concerto, which had never known real popularity. The second essay in the form came at a most opportune time, for Brahms, doing a good deal of concert playing, felt the need for such a work. So, established as he had become, thanks to the First and Second Symphonies, he approached the task of composing it with considerable enthusiasm and, it is safe to say, seriously aware of the capriciousness of public favor.

It met with success all over, save in Leipzig where, despite the local intelligentsia's growing respect of Brahms, Mendelssohn was still considered the *ne plus ultra* of piano-concerto composers. Nevertheless, Leipzig did somersaults in capitulating to the piece when Brahms made his last public appearance as a conductor at the Gewandhaus years later (Jan. 31, 1895). So much so that the listeners responded with unbridled enthusiasm to both concertos, played by Eugen d'Albert.

The first movement (Allegro non troppo, B flat major, 4/4) begins with the initial statement of the first subject in dialogue for horn, piano, and woodwind. A cadenza for the piano leads to a tutti, in which both the first and the second subjects are given full play. The development section is long and elaborate.

The fiery scherzo (Allegro appassionato, F major, 3/4) Max Kalbeck believed had been written for the violin concerto and then discarded. The piano gives out the first theme fortissimo. The strings sing the second theme tranquillo e dolce. After a trio in D major, the first part is repeated, but much altered.

The third movement (Andante, B flat major, 6/4) opens with an expressive melody, given first to a solo cello (an instrument that has a particularly important part in this movement), which resembles Brahms's song "Immer leiser wird mein Schlummer," not written, however, till 1886. A second melody, introduced by piano and clarinet in F sharp, recalls another song by Brahms, "Todessehnen," written in 1878. The first melody comes back in the cello and dominates the coda, against trills and arpeggios in the piano.

The finale (Allegretto grazioso, B flat major, 2/4) is a rondo on a grand scale, based on three themes.

R. C. B.

Concerto for Violin and Orchestra in D major, Op. 77

I. Allegro ma non troppo. II. Adagio. III. Allegro giocoso, ma non troppo vivace.

THE NAME of Joseph Joachim, the great violin virtuoso, is closely linked with the Brahms concerto. To begin with, the dedication is to him. Then, the Hungarian violinist was the soloist (and Brahms the conductor) at the New Year's Day premiere at a Gewandhaus concert in Leipzig in 1879. A Brahms biographer, the English Fuller-Maitland, goes so far as to read a second dedication to Joachim in the markedly Hungarian flavor of the finale.

Most important of all, Joachim was brought in as consultant while Brahms toiled over the violin passages. Composer and interpreter-to-be argued the merits and demerits of certain passages from the practical standpoint. Joachim even furnished a cadenza. The fingering and bowing indications are Joachim's, not Brahms's. And before publication in October, 1879, after the concerto had made the rounds for several months, Joachim caused further alterations. Brahms yielded to the expert. Eduard Hanslick was not overstating it when he termed the concerto "the ripe fruit of the friendship between Joachim and Brahms."

Brahms was ultimately so satisfied with the work that he wrote his publisher Simrock, "it is well to be doubted whether I could write a better concerto." Whether he could or not no one will ever know. Like Beethoven and Mendelssohn he wrote only one.

A scherzo movement was evidently included in Brahms's original draft of the concerto. That would have extended the work to four movements. After removing it from the concerto—"for reasons of style" according to Richard Specht—Brahms incorporated the scherzo into the B flat major Piano Concerto, No. 2. At least so Max Kalbeck, Brahms's most voluminous biographer, affirms. Kalbeck's story of its final resting place, whatever the actual facts, has some circumstantial evidence to back it up. Brahms began the B flat Piano Concerto the same year as the Violin Concerto. Moreover the place of origin was the same—Pörtschach-am-See, a beautiful spot on the Wörthersee near the Italian frontier, where Brahms spent three summers.

The place so enchanted Brahms that he wrote to Hanslick the very air bristled with melodies and one had "to be careful not to tread on them." The G major Sonata for Piano also stems from the Pörtschach-am-See sojourns.

Two of Brahms's standard biographers vary widely in chronicling the Gewandhaus premiere. Florence May, in her two-volume work, quotes the Leipzig critic Dörffel, whose review appeared in the *Leipziger Nachrichten:* "Joachim played with a love and devotion which brought home to us in every bar the direct or indirect share he has had in the work. As to the reception, the first movement was too new to be distinctly appreciated by the audience, the second made considerable way, the last aroused great enthusiasm."

Our old friend Kalbeck harked back to the occasion in gloomier vein: "The work was heard respectfully, but it did not awaken a particle of enthusiasm. It seemed that Joachim had not sufficiently [!] studied the concerto or he was severely indisposed. Brahms conducted with visible excitement."

Brahms's "visible excitement" may also have been either the cause or the effect of a "comical incident" related by Kalbeck. The composer apparently hurried to the concert hall from a social visit. Faux pas No. 1: he appeared on the podium in gray street trousers. Faux pas No. 2: the absent-minded composer had forgotten to fasten his suspenders. Faux pas No. 3 (*Q. E. D.*): his shirt showed. "These laugh-provoking trifles," Kalbeck solemnly observes, "were not calculated to elevate one's mood."

The Violin Concerto was again the bond of collaboration between Brahms and Joachim the following May at the unveiling of a memorial to their mutual friend Robert Schumann in the city of Bonn. They worked together in planning the commemorative program largely devoted to Schumann's music, and each conducted separate numbers at the concert. The Brahms Concerto was the one work on the program not by Schumann, with Joachim again the soloist and the composer directing. The choice of the Concerto was appropriate. In a sense it enshrined the friendship of all three, since Joachim had been instrumental in bringing Schumann and Brahms together.

Constructed mainly along classical lines followed by Mozart and Beethoven in their concertos, the Brahms D major is also closely linked to the Mendelssohn and Bruch concertos in romantic feeling. "Latent heat behind formal exterior" was a phrase once applied to Brahms's music. The Concerto is typically Brahmsian in its supreme blend of reflective breadth and warm humanity of mood and melody. Nobody today would join the early wag in describing the work as "written not *for* but *against* the violin." And any critic who now dared call it "clumsy and devoid of flexibility," as a contemporary of Brahms did, would be laughed out of court.

An idyllic subject, in reverielike mood, serves as chief theme of the opening movement (Allegro ma non troppo, D major, 3/4). Violas, cellos, bassoons, and horns first announce it. What is regarded as the high point of the movement occurs in the merging of a long solo cadenza with the serene return of this theme in the coda section.

It has been pointed out that Brahms reverted to the older tradition of concerto form in having the orchestra expound the basic material of the first movement at some length before bringing the solo violin in. "When the violin does come in," says Fuller-Maitland, "it is with a kind of breathless passage." A passage, incidentally, that caused several hours of discussion and consultation between Brahms and Joachim.

The oboe first chants the soothing chief melody of the slow movement (Adagio, F major, 2/4), which may be compared with a serenade or romanza. Brahms allegedly based this theme on an old Bohemian folksong. In taking it up, the solo violin modifies it and then announces an ornamental second subject. The first melody returns after a development section.

In bold, jocund rhythms, the finale (Allegro giocoso, ma non troppo vivace, D major, 2/4) is really a compact rondo on three themes, the first given out in thirds by the violin. Studded with intricate and brilliant passagework, the movement has been called a virtuoso's paradise. Its gypsylike flavor and folkish rhythms strongly hint at Brahms's intent to pay his Hungarian friend more than a dedicatory tribute.

L. B.

Double Concerto for Violin, Cello, and Orchestra in A minor, Op. 102

I. Allegro. II. Andante. III. Vivace non troppo.

IN THE summer of 1887, Brahms wrote this Concerto, besides the *Gypsy Songs* Op. 103, while vacationing at Thun, Switzerland. Ever the disparager of his own works—not too seriously, you can be sure—Brahms wrote to his friend Elizabet von Herzogenberg about it in a letter from Thun, dated July 20, 1887:

"I can give you nothing worth calling information about the undersigned musician," he said. "True, he is now writing down a thing which does not yet figure in his catalogue—but neither does it figure in other people's! I leave you to guess the particular form of the idiocy!"

The composer also observed that the writing of such a work might better have been left "to someone who understands fiddles better than I do," that it was a "strange notion," that it could be considered his "latest piece of folly." All this, of course, from a man who had already put to his credit four magnificent symphonies, and as magnificent a violin concerto, among other magnificent compositions.

Brahms had in mind the early concerto grosso when he penned this piece. In those works of the seventeenth and eighteenth centuries the solo instrument is actually a collective entity, comprising several instruments, technically known as the concertino, and set against the orchestral tutti for contrast. It would be expected that Brahms should modernize the form somewhat, following in the tradition of—yet going beyond—the Beethoven Triple Concerto in C major for Piano, Violin, Cello, and Orchestra.

The combination of solo instruments employed proved mystifying and unnatural to many of Brahms's rabid enthusiasts. In their flutter and ado over his selection of violin and cello for the solo group, however, they had surely missed the major point. Brahms would have been the last composer in the world to utilize an unusual combination for the sake of haphazard pleasure or mere display. He had strong musical ideas to express, ideas that, as he saw it, wanted just such a medium as this for their proper statement.

A good deal of the unreasoning attitude toward the Concerto has become dissipated by now. Regrettably, it is not performed frequently enough. Walter Niemann thinks that is owing to the extraordinary demands of the work, requiring "two players of consummate technic and sure mastery, so thoroughly accustomed to playing together as can hardly happen, except with members of the same family."

The Double Concerto, soon after its completion, was performed for the first time at a private concert in the Louis-Quinze Room of the Baden-Baden Kurhaus. Brahms was the conductor. The official world premiere took place at Cologne, on Oct. 18, 1887, with Joachim and Hausmann appearing as soloists and Brahms again as conductor. (All three had taken part at the private hearing.) The work was published in 1888, and Brahms's dedication of it to Joachim reads, "To him for whom it was written."

The first movement (Allegro, A minor, 4/4) opens with an introductory passage in which the orchestra alludes to the chief subject and the cello follows with a rhapsodic recitative. The woodwinds give out in A major the initial phrase of the second subject. Both subjects are heard in the first tutti. A rising syncopated theme in F major is also to be carefully noted.

The slow movement (Andante, D major, 3/4) is described by Niemann as "most lovely . . . a great ballade, steeped in the rich, mysterious tone of a northern evening atmosphere." Four notes for the horns and woodwind bring on the flowing chief melody broadly sung by the solo instruments in octaves.

The finale (Vivace non troppo, A minor, 4/4), which has been called the "clearest of rondo types," abounds in thematic material. The first subject announced by the cello and repeated by the violin, has the gypsy flavor so dear to Brahms. It can be detected in another melody assigned to the clarinets and bassoons against rising arpeggios by the solo instruments, which is prominent in the development. The coda, tender at first and then exuberantly joyous, concludes the double concerto, and at the same time the composer's employment of the orchestra, in a triumphant A major.

R. C. B.

"Academic Festival Overture," Op. 80

ON THE façade of a house at Ischl in Upper Austria there is a plaque which carries an inscription informing passers-by that "the great tone poet Dr. Johannes Brahms" once lived there. Actually, Brahms spent twelve summers at the famous spa. His attachment to the town was strong, though as a rule he avoided the fashionable gathering places. During the summer of 1880, Brahms wrote two overtures in the house at Ischl. These were the *Tragic* and the *Academic Festival*.

The title of the latter is almost self-explanatory. It is a tribute to university life, specifically the University of Breslau. On May 11, 1879, that institution had conferred an honorary doctor's degree on the man so signally heralded years before by Schumann as the great new voice of German music. Brahms himself was not a university man. Yet, once, in 1853, he had visited Joachim at Göttingen. While there he acquainted himself with the favorite songs of the university students. And now, almost thirty years later, Brahms remembered them as he showed his gratitude to Breslau for the doctoral honor.

Naturally, the first performance occurred under the highest academic auspices. On Jan. 4, 1881, before a gathering of Breslau's learned officialdom, the new doctor of philosophy conducted his *Academic Festival Overture*. To Max Kalbeck, Brahms, in one of his elfin moments of self-derogation, referred to the overture as "a very jolly potpourri of students' songs à la Suppé." Kalbeck, jolted by what he regarded as a grave lapse from dignity, taunted Brahms about his "potpourri." No doubt, he asked bitingly, the new Herr Doktor had even employed "The Fox Song," a freshman ditty. "Yes, indeed!" Brahms replied unabashed.

"Minus an introduction, the overture (Allegro, C minor, 2/2) begins immediately with the principal subject given out by the first violins. A quieter section follows, the melody in the violas. The first of the students' songs 'Wir hatten gebauet ein stättliches Haus' ('We had built a stately house') is impressively intoned by the three trumpets (C major, 4/4).

"The second students' song 'Der Landesvater' ('The Father of the Country') appears in E major in the second violins. The mood changes now to one of frank jollity with the ragging of the freshmen. The 'Fox Song,' 'Was kommt dort von der Höh'' ('What Comes There from on High'), is introduced in G major by the two bassoons to an accompaniment of violas and cellos. The fourth and last students' song 'Gaudeamus Igitur,' famous the world over wherever there are students (Maestoso, C major, 3/4), is proclaimed by all the wind against rushing scales in the upper strings, ending the overture brilliantly."

The scoring calls for two flutes, piccolo, two oboes, two clarinets, two bassoons, double bassoon, four horns, three trumpets, three trombones, bass tuba, a set of three kettledrums, bass drum, cymbals, triangle, and strings as usual.

L. B.

"Tragic Overture," Op. 81

THE TRAGIC *Overture* was first performed at a concert of the Vienna Philharmonic under the direction of Hans Richter.

Brahms gave no indication of his meaning when he gave his work the title *Tragic* and, as might be expected, explanations of the "tragedy" have been supplied *post facto* by the barrel. Some of the comments have been ultrareserved, others not.

"The overture opens (Allegro ma non troppo, D minor, 2/2) with two fortissimo chords, constituting one of the principal figures of the themes, after which the strings announce the commanding first subject. There is impassioned development, followed by a sustained passage indicative of complete dejection. The trombones intone a message of comfort. The quieter second subject emerges in the violins. A proud climax mounts to a defiant culmination.

"The recapitulation brings back the two fortissimo chords and the first subject, in the strings as before, but now abbreviated. A more moderate section, in part new and in part derived from earlier material, suggested to Grove a funeral march. Further working out prepares for the coda, which, in the words of Tovey, 'gathers up the remaining threads of the story in a catastrophe clearly represented by the solemn emphasis with which the trombones bring in the "decisive close to the first subject."'

"The work is scored for piccolo, two flutes, two oboes, two clarinets, two bassoons, four horns, two trumpets, three trombones, tuba, and strings."

Variations on a Theme by Joseph Haydn in B flat major, Op. 56A

THESE VARIATIONS exist in two forms, for symphony orchestra and for two pianos. Which of the versions came first has long puzzled biographers. The orchestral work precedes the other in the Brahms catalogue, but the two-piano version was published first, in November, 1873. The previous August, Brahms and Clara Schumann played the set on two pianos at a friendly gathering in Bonn. The orchestral Variations were first performed at a Vienna Philharmonic concert on Nov. 2, 1873. Otto Dessoff conducted.

Brahms first saw the Theme three years earlier, in the autumn of 1870, when Karl Ferdinand Pohl brought him some Haydn manuscript music to examine. It was part of a Divertimento for two oboes, two horns, three bassoons, and "serpent," bearing the title *Divertimento mit dem Chorale St. Antoni*. It seems likely that Haydn wrote it for open-air performance in 1782 or 1783. Whether the *St. Anthony Chorale* was Haydn's own invention or a theme of anonymous origin has never been settled. Brahms went on the assumption that it was Haydn's. The Variations were first played in America at a Brooklyn concert by Theodore Thomas' Orchestra on Apr. 11, 1874.

In the Haydn original, as in the Brahms version, the Theme is given out in B flat major, Andante 2/4. Brahms even preserves most of the Haydn scoring in stating the Theme, except that the "serpent" and third bassoon are replaced by a double bassoon, and the string bass is reinforced. The eight Variations follow: I. Poco più animato; II. Più vivace; III. Con moto; IV. Andante con moto; V. Vivace; VI. Vivace; VII. Grazioso; and VIII. Presto non troppo, capped by a finale in passacaglia form (Andante, B flat major, 2/2).

L. B.

"Hungarian Dances"

I OFFER THEM as genuine gypsy children which I did not beget, but merely brought up with bread and milk," Brahms wrote to his publisher Simrock. The "gypsy children" referred to were a group of four-hand piano arrangements of Hungarian Dances. Maybe they were "genuine," and maybe they were brought up on "milk and bread." The fact is these adopted waifs caused Brahms more irritation than any of his own "begotten" musical children.

No sooner did the first two books appear in 1869 than a storm of abuse broke over his head. Charges of plagiarism were leveled at him. Newspapers accused him of stealing melodies intact from Budapest composers. Others went further: even the arrangements were pilfered! The Hungarian violinist Remenyi, who had earlier accompanied Brahms on a Hungarian tour, claimed ost of the tunes as his very own. "I was in the habit of composing melodies the inns where we stopped," he maintained later, "Brahms saw some of em. In order to practice an innocent deception, I gave several of them the ames of national songs without betraying their authorship."

Remenyi conveniently ignored the fact that the melodies in question had ppeared in popular Hungarian collections long before the Remenyi-Brahms ur. As for the other charges of plagiarism and theft, they were malicious es prompted by spite and jealousy. Nobody took the trouble to read the title age of the "Hungarian Dances." Brahms made no claim of originality here. The dances were merely "arranged for piano." Simrock, not Brahms, as responsible for the ambiguity that crept in later when the words were ltered to "set [*gesetzt*] for piano." Brahms retorted angrily by signing a let-er to Simrock, "Yours, *beside himself* [*gesetzt*], J. Brahms."

Another significant fact is that the collection carried no opus number. rahms, totally incapable of shady dealings, was not attempting to palm off ne Magyar-gypsy melodies as his. Still further proof is that he first offered ne set at an absurdly low fee to the Budapest publisher Roszavolgyi. The Iungarian, however, turned the arrangements down as an unsound invest-nent. Simrock was wiser. He gave Brahms the stipulated 80 Friedrichdors nd proceeded to make a huge fortune on the arrangements. Brahms never egretted the bargain. He was notoriously indifferent to money. Incidentally, imrock gave an ironic twist to the plagiarism issue by himself beginning a aw suit against a "plagiarist" of the Brahms arrangements!

Though Remenyi had sharpened his interest in the material, Brahms had lways been drawn to the wild and passionate music of Hungary. At the 'rater in Vienna, gypsy fiddlers would improvise fiery strains for him. While n tour with Remenyi he culled tunes from the teeming repertories of native ands. Remenyi himself is said to have played native airs and dances "with a ire and abandon," exciting audiences to wild acclaim. Besides the popular Budapest tunes of individual authorship, Brahms noted down one or two tra-litional themes. At least three of the combined set of twenty-one Hungarian Dances are regarded as Brahms originals. When Remenyi was in America in 879 he complained to a reporter of the *New York Herald* that Brahms had given the world an utterly false impression of these Hungarian melodies. "I :an no longer play them," he lamented. "People now think I play them wrong."

Books I (Nos. 1 to 5) and II (Nos. 6 to 10) of the four-hand piano arrange-nents had appeared in 1869. It was not till 1880 that Brahms issued Books III and IV, the former containing Hungarian Dances Nos. 11 to 16, the latter Nos. 17 to 21. Brahms also arranged the set in Book I for two hands. Joseph Joachim, with Brahms's permission, set the dances for violin and piano. Numbers 5 and 6 were also arranged for two voices and piano by the great

singer Pauline Viardot. As for the orchestral versions, Brahms himself
responsible only for Nos. 1 and 3 of Book I and No. 10 of Book II. Anto
Dvorak transcribed Nos. 17 to 21. Andreas Hallen transcribed Nos. 2, 4, and 2
and Albert Parlow the remainder.

In 1874 the *Allgemeine Musikalische Zeitung* printed a list of the composer
of most of the tunes used in Brahms's first ten arrangements. The origina
titles of the dances were also given. Number 5, for example, was attribute
to Keler-Bela, the Budapest bandmaster. Its title was "Bartfai-emlek" ("Re
membrance of Bartfa"). The composer of No. 6 was Adolf Nittinger. It
title was "Rozsa Bokor" ("Rose Bush"). Number 7 merely carried the word
"Volksthümlich" ("in folk style"). Its composer was unknown.

When first shown Brahms's arrangements, Elisabet von Herzogenberg, hi
friend and confidante, exclaimed: "You have said the last word about thes
melodies! You have taken material which concealed beauty within itself and
raised it to a level of the purest art, without sacrificing any of its wildness and
elemental power."

The Hungarian influence was a strong and recurring factor in Brahms'
music. The finales of both the Violin Concerto and Second Piano Concerto
show it markedly, as does the finale of the Piano Quartet, Op. 26. Among
other works, it is present in the B minor Capriccio, Op. 76; the waltzes for
piano duet; the Piano Trio, Op. 87; and the String Quartet, Op. 111. The
Piano Variations on a Hungarian Air and the "Zigeunerlieder" for vocal quar
tet and piano explain themselves. The "Ungarische Tänze" are right at home
in the Brahms treasure house of music.

L. B.

Benjamin Britten

BORN: LOWESTOFT, SUFFOLK, ENGLAND, NOV. 22, 1913.

Certainly his copious resource, quick wit, and unquestionable virtuosity constitute a valuable endowment which can hardly fail to bear fruit.—FRANK S. HOWES.

"Sinfonia da Requiem," Op. 20

I. Lacrymosa. II. Dies Irae. III. Requiem Aeternam.

A BRILLIANT Violin Concerto, bristling with tart wit and novel effects, brought Benjamin Britten into the Philharmonic-Symphony fold of composers on Mar. 28, 1940. A few days later, England's *enfant terrible* of music was already at work on a composition of totally different purpose—a *Sinfonia da Requiem,* intended as an act of devotion to the memory of his father and mother. The score, completed that spring in Amityville, Long Island, is thus inscribed.

The Latin titles, indicating the mood and scheme of the work, derive from the Catholic Requiem Mass, though the relation of the Sinfonia to the Catholic ceremony, avowedly, is emotional rather than liturgical. Mr. Britten has remarked that though "short for a symphony," his composition was "conceived on festival proportions," and the scoring—for large orchestra, including triple woodwind, saxophone, six horns, piano, and a vast battery of percussion—bears him out. An analysis from the composer's own pen is given below.

I. "Lacrymosa" (Andante ben misurato). A slow marching lament in a persistent 6/8 rhythm with a strong tonal center on D. There are three main motives: (1) a syncopated, sequential theme announced by the cellos and answered by a solo bassoon; (2) a broad theme, based on the interval of a major seventh; (3) alternating chords on flute and trombones, outlined by the piano and harps. The first section of the movement is quietly pulsating; the second a long crescendo leading to a climax based on the first cello theme. There is no pause before

II. "Dies Irae" (Allegro con fuoco). A form of Dance of Death, with occasional moments of quiet marching rhythm. The dominating motif of this movement is announced at the start by the flutes and includes an important tremolando figure. Other motives are: a triplet repeated (note figure in the trumpets), a slow smooth tune on the saxophone, and a livelier syncopated one on the brass. The scheme of the movement is a series of climaxes of which the last is the most powerful, causing the music to disintegrate and to lead directly to

III. "Requiem Aeternam" (Andante piacevole). Very quietly over a background of solo strings and harps; the flutes announce the quiet D major tune, which **is** the principle motif of the movement. There is a middle section in which the strings play a flowing melody. This grows to a short climax, but the opening tune is soon resumed and the work ends quietly in a long sustained clarinet note.

John Barbirolli led the premiere of this score at a New York Philharmonic Symphony concert on Mar. 29, 1941.

Benjamin Britten was only twelve when he went to study with Frank Bridge, the English composer, who remained a close friend and adviser. Later at the Royal College of Music in London, John Ireland and Arthur Benjamin became his teachers in composition and piano, respectively. As early as 1934 his works were appearing on the programs of the Florentine festivals of Contemporary Music. In fact, before he was twenty-four, young Britten was something of a festival stand-by. The Florentine festival sought him out in 1934, the Barcelona in 1936, the London in 1938, the Norwich in 1936, and the Salzburg in 1937.

He writes at terrific speed, if the quantity and variety of his output are any clue. Music for the stage, radio plays, and films figures amply among his published compositions. On the list of instrumental works alone are a Sinfonietta for chamber orchestra, a Phantasy for oboe, violin, viola, and cello; a *Simple Symphony* for string orchestra; a piano suite, *Holiday Tales;* a suite for violin and piano; a suite for orchestra, *Soirées Musicales (After Rossini)*, a piano concerto, and a set of Variations for Strings on a Theme of Frank Bridge. "Peter Grimes," first produced in America at the Berkshire Festival of 1946, proved Mr. Britten's marked originality as operatic composer.

Mr. Britten early attracted the notice of a group of English critics, among them Edward Evans, who wrote as follows:

After Britten had first made his name with works like the choral variation *A Boy Was Born,* revealing fertility in ideas and the requisite technical fluency to express them, there arose for a time the danger that he might become the bright young thing of the musical world.

His facility was astonishing, and everything he wrote came off. But he did not always resist the temptation to squander his gifts on mere smartness. That danger, however, passed quickly. Young as he is, his recent works show the concentration upon essentials that heralds maturity.

L. B.

Max Bruch

BORN: COLOGNE, JAN. 6, 1838. DIED: FRIEDENAU, OCT. 2, 1920.

The Bruch concertos occupy a position of honor in the violin repertory. . . . From the standpoint of the violinist who plays in public they are artistic Declarations of Independence; they are the eloquent and inspiring documents which supply the proof that Bruch freed himself from all mechanical fetters.—LEOPOLD AUER.

Concerto for Violin and Orchestra in G minor, No. 1, Op. 26

I. Allegro moderato. II. Adagio. III. Allegro energico.

OVER TEN years elapsed between the first sketches and the completion of this Concerto. Bruch began jotting down ideas in 1857. However, it was not till 1865 that he gave them serious consideration. The Concerto received its finishing touches at Coblenz and Sondershausen. On Apr. 24, 1866, it obtained its first performance at the last winter concert of the Music Institute at Coblenz, under the composer's direction.

Two postponements of the work had been occasioned by the illness of Johann Naret-Koning, concertmaster of the Mannheim Symphony, the violinist scheduled to play its premiere. When the first performance was finally given, a last-minute replacement played the solo violin part, one Otto von Königslöw, concertmaster of Gürzenich Orchestra and violin teacher at the Conservatory of Cologne.

Following the premiere, Bruch took his work to the repair shop and did a complete job of overhauling it. In the summer of 1866 he sent it on to Joseph Joachim with a request for his advice and criticism, and in the same note he advanced the theory that the work was less a concerto than a "fantasie." Anyway, he left it to Joachim to decide that question.

The celebrated violinist returned the manuscript together with numerous suggestions for revision. He reassured the apprehensive Bruch, however, with the declaration, "I find that the title 'concerto' is fully justified; for a fantasie, the last two movements are too completely and symmetrically developed. The different sections are brought together in beautiful relationship, and yet—this is the principal thing—there is sufficient contrast." He then pointed out that Spohr had called his *Gesangscene* a concerto.

When the suggested changes were made, plus others contemplated by Bruch himself, the Concerto was given its first performance in the revised version at an informal and nonpublic rehearsal in the Royal Theater, Hanover, on October, 1867. Joachim was the soloist and Bruch the conductor. The formal premiere of the new version took place at Bremen, on Jan. 7, 1868, under the direction of Karl Reinthaler, who was the head of the Singakademie in that city. Some time later in the same year the Concerto was published with a dedication to Joachim, to whom Bruch dedicated also his Third Concerto, Op. 58.

The Concerto in G minor, No. 1, Op. 26, begins with an introduction, or prelude, which is not related to any other part of the first movement. The first theme is brought in by the violin, against a tremolo accompaniment. The second theme is also introduced by the solo violin, and on the heels of a long passage of development the prelude returns, following which some intermediary measures bring forth the slow movement.

Three main themes are the formal basis of the Adagio, and one of these has been called "a melodic glory of the nineteenth century." It is heard a good deal throughout the movement as its chief feature, while the two other themes function mainly as contrasting entities.

The finale, after a brief prelude, launches into a theme of steady, marchlike rhythm, via the solo violin. A lyrical second theme enters by way of the orchestra, and with a considerable development of the material the Concerto comes to a brilliant coda, with which it ends.

R. C. B.

Anton Bruckner

BORN: ANSFELDEN, UPPER AUSTRIA, SEPT. 4, 1824. DIED: VIENNA, OCT. 11, 1896.

> *For a few, he was and is, at rare intervals, a seer and a prophet—one who knew the secret of a strangely exalted discourse, grazing the sublime, though his speech was often both halting and prolix. He stammered, and he knew not when to stop. But sometimes, rapt and transfigured, he saw visions and dreamed dreams as colossal, as grandiose, as aweful in lonely splendor, as those of William Blake. We know that for Bruckner, too, some ineffable beauty flamed and sank and flamed again across the night.—*LAWRENCE GILMAN.

Symphony in E flat major, No. 4 ("Romantic")

I. Allegro molto moderato. II. Andante. III. Scherzo. IV. Finale.

THOUGH THIS Symphony was completed on Nov. 22, 1874, it was not given the subtitle *Romantic* until two years later. It is believed that the composer tacked subtitle, as well as a "program," on it under the influence of Wagner. The latter, be it remembered, had gone so far as to concoct an elaborate literary interpretation of the Beethoven Ninth. Bruckner knew Wagner. In fact, he had dedicated—with the latter's permission—his Third Symphony to him. He trembled with adulatory excitement at the mere thought of Wagner. If Wagner, therefore, could invent a "program" for the Beethoven piece, was there anything wrong in Bruckner's doing a like service for his own—belatedly?

The beginning of the *Romantic Symphony* Bruckner described as follows: "A citadel of the Middle Ages. Daybreak. Reveille is sounded from the tower. The gates open. Knights on proud chargers leap forth. The magic of nature surrounds them."

Gabriel Engel, in his biography of Bruckner, declares:

That the composer did not regard the "program" seriously is evident from his remark concerning the Finale: "And in the last movement I've forgotten completely what picture I had in mind. . . . The work possesses, however, an unmistakable unity hitherto without precedent in absolute music, for all four parts spring from the main theme, in the first movement. So logical and masterly is the development of this theme in the course of the work that the climax is not reached until the closing portion of the Finale.

The Fourth Symphony underwent two revisions, the first occurring in 1878, and the second during 1879-1880, when the Finale was rewritten.

Seven years after its completion, on Feb. 20, 1881, it was given its premiere at a Philharmonic concert in Vienna. Hans Richter was the conductor. Richter had invited Bruckner to one of the rehearsals. During the playing of one passage, Richter stopped the orchestra, puzzled. He turned to the composer asking, "What note is this?" Bruckner, ever aiming to please, answered, "Any you choose. Quite as you like." When the rehearsal was over Bruckner presented the conductor with a thaler (a three-mark piece).

Richter later said:

The thaler is the memento of a day when I wept. For the first time I conducted a Bruckner symphony, at rehearsal. Bruckner was an old man then. His works were hardly performed anywhere. When the Symphony was over Bruckner came to me. He was radiant with enthusiasm and happiness. I felt him put something in my hand. "Take it, and drink a mug of beer to my health." It was a thaler.

The conductor kept the coin, not wishing to offend the aging composer. He finally fixed it to his watch chain.

In any case, at the performance the public approved of the Symphony whole-heartedly. Bruckner was called to the stage for bows after each movement.

Another number in that program was a piece by Bülow. It was a symphonic poem going under the trenchant title of *The Singer's Curse*. It was not received favorably. Bülow, quite jealous of Bruckner's success, asked (referring to the Symphony), "Is that German music?" The answer has not been recorded.

The *Romantic Symphony* is dedicated to the Prince Constantin Hohenlohe-Schillingfürst, who was the Lord Marshal to the Emperor of Austria. It was given its initial performance in the United States at New York on March 16, 1888, under the direction of Anton Seidl.

Werner Wolff's biography of Bruckner says of the work,

The word "Romantic" has been used for this symphony in its most popular sense, meaning imaginative, unrestrained, nebulous and mysterious. Nostalgic reverie is also called "romantic" at times and this meaning, too, has been applied to the Fourth.

Gabriel Engel clearly proves how differently this music can be felt. He wrote [in *Chord and Discord,* January, 1940]: "The long chain of dark-tinged compositions preceding the Fourth makes the radiant sunrise which begins that symphony all the more amazing." Again and again he stressed "joyful upheaval."

The first movement (Allegro molto moderato, E flat major, 2/2) begins with a string tremolo in E flat, and soon a horn call is heard against that. The wood winds imitate the call, out of which the initial part of the first theme is constructed. Its second part consists of what has been called the "typical Bruckner rhythm," two even quarter notes followed by a triplet of three quarter notes. This fragment is given a good deal of development, and presently there is a modulation to the key of D flat. The violas announce the second

eme proper, a subject of "cantabile nature." The cellos take it up, playing it
ainst a contrapuntal imitation in the violins. The first section of the move-
ent ends with a development of the second part of the opening theme.
'ithout repeat, another call-like phrase, this time in the brass, ushers in a sort
free fantasia. The recapitulation comes next, proceeding along well-estab-
hed lines of form, and the second theme is heard now in the key of B major.
here follows a coda, whose chief structural feature is the prominence
ven to the first fragment of the first theme. The movement concludes very
norously.

The second movement (Andante, C minor, 4/4) corresponds to a romanza
nstructed on three subjects. The cellos bring in the first, the violins the
cond, and the strings and wood winds the third.

The third movement (Scherzo, B flat major, 2/4) is built on a series of
nting-horn calls. There is a free development and a subsequent trio in G flat
ajor entails the development of a theme in 3/4, whose spirit is almost that of
minuet. After the trio, the scherzo is repeated.

The fourth movement (mässig bewegt E flat major, 2/2) opens with softly
toned horn phrases which grow into another theme for trumpets. The full
chestra announces this theme in unison and fortissimo. A second theme, of
livelier nature, is first stated by the strings and later by the whole orchestra.
here follows a free development and the movement takes up its various
bjects in an elaborate counterpoint. It closes with a "sonorous apotheosis."

The Fourth Symphony is scored for three flutes (one interchangeable with
ccolo), two oboes, two clarinets, two bassoons, four horns, three trumpets,
ree trombones, bass tuba, three kettledrums, and strings. The Finale calls for
pair of cymbals.

R. C. B.

Symphony in E major, No. 7

I. Allegro moderato. II. Adagio: Sehr feierlich und langsam (Very solemn
and slow). III. Scherzo: Allegro. Trio: etwas langsamer (Somewhat
slower). IV. Finale: Bewegt doch nicht schnell (With movement, but not
fast).

ACCORDING TO one version of the story, Bruckner was working on the Adagio
ovement of his Seventh Symphony when news of Richard Wagner's death in
'enice reached him. The date of the Adagio's completion is given as Apr. 21,
883, in this account. Wagner, Bruckner's idol and inspiration, died on Feb. 13.
was thus a matter of simple inference to regard the Adagio as a disciple's
ment over a Master's demise. If the story is straight, the coincidence is one of
ie neatest and most convenient in musical annals.

However, according to a second version, equally if not better substantiate by the record, Bruckner completed the Adagio in October, 1882, or four month before Wagner's death. This version offers three possibilities regarding th Adagio. (1) It is not a dirge. (2) If it is a dirge, then the commemoration Wagner was an afterthought. (3) Granted it is a dirge and granted it is memory of Wagner, then the explanation holds that is often made of th funeral march in the *Eroica Symphony; i.e.,* like Beethoven, Bruckner mu have been looking a bit ahead and speculating on his own and the worl grief over the dreaded loss.

In support of the third possibility we have abundant evidence. There is th written record, in words and music, of Bruckner's love and reverence for th master. More specifically, there are excerpts from two letters written to h devoted pupil Felix Mottl. In one, first printed in the *Schwäbischer Merkur* February, 1900, Bruckner states: "One day I came home and felt very sad. It impossible, I thought, that the Master should live much longer. And then th C sharp minor Adagio came to me." In the other, written while Mottl w preparing the premiere at Carlsruhe, Bruckner makes the plea: "Please take very slow and solemn tempo. At the close, in the Dirge [In Memory of th death of the Master], think of our Ideal."

Moreover, ten years earlier Bruckner had dedicated his third symphon "To the Master, Richard Wagner, in deepest reverence." He might well hav dedicated all his symphonies to the Bayreuth genius, so complete was h devotion. Instead, the names of Franz Liszt, the King of Bavaria, and th Emperor of Austria adorn other dedication pages. The common belief is tha in his unfinished Ninth Symphony, Bruckner reached out beyond royalty an empire, even beyond Richard Wagner, and dedicated it to God!

The matter of Bruckner's intentions regarding the Adagio has puzzled an annoyed commentators. Biographers are divided on the subject, and equall positive. A faint suspicion creeps into some of the writings that Bruckner wa induced by certain Wagnerites and Brucknerites to accommodate himself to slight juggling of chronology. If not that, then some well-meaning member the cult has tampered with the record. In any case, this much is certain: if th Adagio followed Wagner's death, it enshrines his memory in elegiac form If it did not, well, Wagner is there anyway, in some other form.

In fact, Wagner, at least in the spirit, was always there with Bruckner. Th simple, awkward, unassuming organist and school teacher from the north, th pious villager of peasant stock described as half yokel and half seer, had e countered the music of Wagner and lost his head and heart to it. To adapt th Master's theories to absolute music and to find a place for them in the sy phony became a fixed goal. For better or for worse, Bruckner had formed lifelong attachment. In some ways he paid dearly for it. Vienna was an arme camp. In the press Wagnerites and anti-Wagnerites fumed venomously at eac

ther. To those who trooped after Richard of Bayreuth, Eduard Hanslick was
kind of devil incarnate. For the perfect Wagnerite to be seen in affable con-
ersation with the critic of the *Neue freie Presse* amounted to artistic suicide.
His reviews bristled with acid gibes at the Wagner cult. And when the Bruck-
erites set up their idol as a kind of alter ego of the Bayreuth master, Bruckner's
oom was sealed. The Hanslick faction pursued the new quarry like Greek
uries. They saw him deliberately pitted against their own standard-bearer,
Brahms, and raged still more.

Disciples of Bruckner affirmed that Hanslick lay awake nights "plotting his
estruction," that he tried to have him ejected from the Vienna Conservatory,
hat he intrigued to prevent performances of his work. Hanslick no doubt went
ll lengths to demolish Bruckner as a composer. That he schemed to discredit
im as a teacher is going a bit too far. Hanslick had his own ideas about music.
Brahms's largely coincided with them. Wagner's did not. For Hanslick it was
ad enough to have Wagnerism wreck opera, as he saw it. To find it poaching
n symphonic grounds under another's name was adding insult to injury. That
vas his temperament. To the very end he refused to accept Wagner and
Bruckner, and he went to his grave a byword and a monster to their camp
ollowers.

When the Seventh Symphony, after triumphing in Leipzig, Munich, and
Graz, finally reached Vienna in a performance by the Philharmonic under
Hans Richter's direction, the anti-Brucknerites were ready for it. They espe-
ially resented the action of a sturdy Bruckner wing among the subscribers in
ecalling the composer four or five times after each movement. Hanslick,
dmitting quite frankly that he found himself unable to judge Bruckner's
nusic dispassionately, nevertheless proceeded to blast away at it as "unnatural,"
inflated," "sickly," and "decayed." Max Kalbeck, writing in the *Presse,*
onfected a wild jingle from well-known lyrics to illustrate Bruckner's style of
omposition. "We believe as little in the future of the Bruckner symphony,"
e went on, "as in the victory of chaos over cosmos." He observed of the chief
heme of the first movement, "No one knows where it comes from or where
t is going; or rather, it comes from the Nibelungs and goes to the devil." To
Kalbeck the theme of the Scherzo was a "mixture of swagger and beggarli-
ess." G. Dömpke of the *Wiener Allgemeine Zeitung* could do nothing better,
n his rage, than scream out: "Bruckner composes like a drunkard!"

The Emperor Franz Joseph is said to have asked Bruckner once to name a
vish and it would be granted. Whether facetiously or not, Bruckner is supposed
o have requested him to stop Eduard Hanslick from insulting him in print.
Composers have their own way of shaking off the accumulated quills of a
ifetime. Bruckner reserved final judgment on Hanslick until late in his career,
vhen his pupil Carl Hruby credited him with the statement: "I guess Hanslick
nderstands as little about Brahms as about Wagner, me, and others. And the

Doctor Hanslick knows as much about counterpoint as a chimney sweep about astronomy."

One of the strangest phenomena of nineteenth-century European music was that Bruckner, a simple, naïve, lonely, and sensitive man, with thoughts fixed on God and eternity, should have been one of the most cordially hated composers of his time. The adoring band of followers partly made up for it in loyalty and fighting spirit, and the Viennese public soon came to recognize his worth. But in the enemy camp his very appearance was cause for ridicule. Hanslick even taunted him on his "Emperor Claudius head," and the trium-virate—Dömpke, Kalbeck, Hanslick—reveled in descriptions of the comical, ill-dressed figure forever bowing acknowledgments to his embattled flock. Some felt, too, that there was no place in gay Vienna for this boorish ascetic from the provinces, with his sheltered, unromantic life and his funny home-spun dialect. To Hanslick there was always something ludicrous in the spectacle of this pious man, steeped in textbook counterpoint and churchly lore, swept off his feet by the new current and going over, body and soul, to Wagnerism. He saw Bruckner as leading a double life. In one he was the formidable contrapuntist Albrechtsberger returned to life. In the other he was Wagner. And Hanslick thought he had dealt the fatal blow with the line: "Behold Albrechtsberger walking arm in arm with Wagner!"

Some of the finest words ever written about Bruckner came from Felix Weingartner not long after the Austrian composer's death. They make bracing reading after the oafish blasts of the Hanslick-Dömpke-Kalbeck battery.

Think of this schoolmaster and organist, risen from the poorest surroundings and totally lacking in education, but steadily composing symphonies of dimensions hitherto unheard of, crowded with difficulties and solecisms of all kinds which were the horror of conductors, performers, listeners, and critics, because they interfered sadly with their comfort.

Think of him thus going unswervingly along his way toward the goal he had set himself, in the most absolute certainty of not being noticed and of attaining nothing but failure—and then compare him with our fashionable composers borne on by daily success and advertisement, who puzzle out their trifles with the utmost *raffinerie*. And then bow in homage to this man, great and pathetic in his naïveté and his honesty. I confess that scarcely anything in the new symphonic music can weave itself about me with such wonderful magic as can a single theme or a few measures of Bruckner. . . .

The Seventh Symphony is dedicated "To His Majesty the King, Ludwig II of Bavaria, in deepest reverence." Besides the usual strings, the score calls for flutes, oboes, clarinets and bassoons in pairs, four horns, three trumpets, three trombones, four tubas, one double-bass tuba, three kettledrums, triangle, and cymbals.

In the first movement (Allegro moderato, E major, 2/2), the chief theme is
given out by the cellos and repeated by the violins and wood winds. The
second theme is stated by oboe and clarinet. The Adagio (Sehr feierlich und
langsam, C sharp minor, 4/4) is the most famous movement in any of Bruckner's symphonies. After his death this magnificent lamentation was performed
in many German cities as a tribute to his memory. The Scherzo (Sehr schnell,
A minor, 3/4) is based on two themes, the second of a tempestuous nature.
The trio (Etwas langsamer, F major) is of a contrasting character. After it the
Scherzo is repeated. The Finale (Bewegt, doch nicht schnell, E major, 2/2)
is a rondo beginning with a subject of noteworthy brilliance. It ends with a
coda imposing in its power.

Arthur Nikisch introduced the work on Dec. 30, 1884, at a concert in
Leipzig given, according to one record, for the purpose of raising money for
a Wagner monument. Theodore Thomas led the American premiere in
Chicago on July 29, 1886.

L. B.

Symphony in D minor, No. 9

I. Feierlich (Solemnly). II. Scherzo, Bewegt lebhaft (Mosso vivace).
III. Adagio, sehr langsam, feierlich (Very slowly, solemnly).

A SYMPHONY DEDICATED to God! Such, at any rate, is the legend handed down
about Bruckner's farewell symphony. According to the story, Bruckner, who
died while working on the final bars of the Adagio, intended to inscribe the
symphony "to the dear Lord."

"I have done my duty on earth," said Bruckner to a caller shortly after his
seventieth birthday. "I have accomplished what I could, and my only wish is
to be allowed to finish my Ninth Symphony. Three movements are almost
complete. The Adagio is nearly finished. There remains only the Finale. I
trust Death will not deprive me of my pen." He prayed nightly to God for
time to complete it. "If He refuses, then He must take the responsibility for
its incompleteness," he remarked.

Despite attacks of dropsy and a dangerous heart condition, Bruckner worked
feverishly at his symphony. But he died without finishing it. For some years
it was thought Bruckner left sections of the work in an imperfect state. However, the publication of the ninth volume of a critical edition of Bruckner's
works in the early thirties proved that the three movements of the Ninth
Symphony, as the composer left them, "must be unconditionally regarded and
respected as his final intention."

Moreover, it developed that Bruckner had also been engaged for some time
on sketches of an Allegro-Finale. Professor Orel, who edited the ninth volume
of the Bruckner's works, included a sketch of this unfinished Finale which

revealed Bruckner's main outlines of form and structure up to the beginning
of the coda. Unfortunately, there is no hint anywhere of how the symphony
was to end. In the words of Willi Reich: "That portion always treated by
Bruckner as a grand summation and, hence, probably the most important
passage in the symphony, must remain an eternal mystery."

Reich, in an article appearing in *Chord and Discord*—the magazine of The
Bruckner Society of America—now assailed the frequent practice of using
Bruckner's *Te Deum* as a choral finale to the Ninth Symphony. "One glance
at this mighty torso of a Finale," he stated, "is enough to convince us that the
practice . . . corresponds in no respect to the composer's true intention, for
this final choral work shows no relationship to the thematic world unfor-
gettably established in the three completed movements of the symphony."

This conclusion coincided with Professor Orel's own contention in the first
published version of Bruckner's original score: "Bruckner's clear intent to
conclude the Ninth Symphony with a gigantic instrumental Finale proves the
utter futility of any attempt to establish a spiritual connection between it and
the *Te Deum*—an attempt so frequently made by conductors, despite the
insuperable period of a decade separating the conception of the two works in
the mind of the composer. Furthermore, the Adagio of the Symphony . . .
attains symbolic significance through the realization that the inexorable grip of
Fate wrested the pen from the aged master's hand almost at the very moment
in which he would have sealed the work with a completed, formal Allegro-
Finale."

The appearance of this authentic edition of Bruckner's Ninth caused something of a stir in musical circles because of the so-called "Loewe Version" long
in use. For years it had been supposed that Bruckner's manuscript had been
left in a highly unsatisfactory state, that thanks to Bruckner's faithful disciple
Ferdinand Loewe a rough garbled manuscript had been rendered playable
through a polished arrangement. There had been a sensational premiere of
Loewe's version on Feb. 11, 1903, in Vienna, under his own direction. Many
Brucknerites, who had not even suspected the existence of this posthumous
work, were astounded by the revelation. This, incidentally, occurred seven
years after the master's death. In 1904, Loewe published the edited score. Some
years after the Vienna premiere, doubts began to arise among Bruckner scholars
about Loewe's emendations. Drastic, uncalled-for changes of orchestration were
suspected, and glaring instances of un-Bruckner-like transitions were noted.

Max Auer wrote as follows in the *Zeitschrift für Musik* (later quoted by
Chord and Discord):

Listeners began to notice frequent details in the music which seemed inexplicable in the light of Bruckner's frank and sturdy symphonic character.
When the Scherzo leaped lightly forth, all-aglitter with typically French *esprit*
the audience was reminded of the scintillating manner of Berlioz's instrumentation

the minds of many there arose some such questions as these: Where are those abrupt, Bruckneresque transitions between the passages? Why do the various phrases end in gentle expirations? In short, whence comes this odd finesse, this smooth polish, into the work of a composer universally noted for his rugged individuality?

The answer was provided by two important events. One was the *Kritische Gesamtausgabe* of Bruckner's music, sponsored by the Bruckner Gesellschaft. The other was a semiprivate performance—also sponsored by the Bruckner Gesellschaft—at the Tonhalle in Munich on Apr. 2, 1932, of both the "Loewe version" and the original. The conclusion was unanimous: "So far from being unplayable, the original version far surpassed the 'Loewe Version' by the splendor of its orchestral coloring and the power of its dynamic contrasts. The two versions differed so vastly in spirit that they might be said to belong to different worlds." Thus Bruckner's Ninth Symphony became available to the world in two widely opposed versions. It should be pointed out that Professor Orel arrived at his thesis of Bruckner's own "definitive" version only after an arduous study of all the detailed revisions made by the composer. He established that three movements of the Ninth Symphony were the final stage in a long process of evolution. As evidence, Professor Orel traced the Symphony's slow growth through six separate versions!

There was never any question of Loewe's good intentions in all this. Actually, it was regarded by the less embattled Brucknerites as a case of misplaced zeal. Professor Orel himself stressed this in a subsequent lecture at the University of Vienna. Loewe, he affirmed, had been actuated solely by the desire of a devoted friend and disciple "to render more acceptable to the ears of his contemporaries the general tonal ruggedness of this symphony as left by the master" (Willi Reich). Ironically, it was probably modesty that restrained Loewe from divulging the changes he had made in Bruckner's orchestration. He regarded the task as a labor of love. And despite growing critical suspicion, his version stood for thirty years as a standard repertory score. Such as it was, he had rendered a service somewhat parallel to Rimsky-Korsakoff's in editing *Boris Godounoff*.

When Otto Klemperer and the New York Philharmonic-Symphony Society offered the American premiere of the restored original version in Carnegie Hall on Oct. 11, 1934, Lawrence Gilman called it a "consecrational disclosure." With several others he then concluded that the Loewe version, with which the music world had been familiar, was an "astonishing perversion and distortion of Bruckner's intentions." He now spoke of Loewe's edition as "unauthorized, injudicious, and impertinent." Students who followed the performance with the old score, he ventured, "must have noticed the instances in which not only Loewe the tonal chiseller, but Loewe the superfluous decorator, was put to rout, and something native and strong and unmistakably Brucknerian restored to the structure of the score."

Continuing, Mr. Gilman wrote:

They must have noticed here the omission of an excrescent wood-wind phra. or kettledrum solo, there the restoration of significant chord passages, or th felicitous substitution of violas for bassoon, or the assumption by tubas, wit magical effect, of a passage given inexplicably to muted cellos and violas, or th alteration of dynamics and tempo marks. Above all, they must have listene incredulously to the climax of the Adagio as Bruckner actually wrote it, a passag exalted from banality to greatness merely by the simple and honest process letting it sound as its creator intended.

This point about the Adagio was dwelt on at greater length in Gilman Sunday article in the *New York Herald Tribune* two days later:

If the student will turn to page 136, bar 3, of Loewe's edition of the orchestr score in the Universal Ed. (page 186, bar 1, of the Eulenburg miniature score) h will find that Bruckner apparently builds the climax of the movement at th point upon a fortissimo proclamation of the main theme by the trombones, tub string basses, and bassoons under a simple chord of E major sustained and reite ated by woodwinds, horns, tubas, and a repeated figure of the violins—a sonorou but hardly distinguished treatment of the subject.

But one has only to examine Bruckner's original score (page 180, bar 1) to se at once that what Bruckner said and clearly intended to say at this point was som thing utterly different from what Loewe has represented him as saying. A Bruckner wrote the passage, the mighty theme in the basses, with its upward lea of a tenth, is heard against an audacious and magnificent dissonance formed by th simultaneous sounding and reiteration (in the woodwind, violins, and upper brass of the notes E, F sharp, G sharp, A, B, and C. The effect is unforgettable—a inspiration of sheer genius that, at a stroke, alters the passage from rather empt rhetoric to poignant eloquence.

But Loewe seems to have been shocked by it. He preferred something smoothe and more decorous. So he sandpapered Bruckner's superb dissonance, remove offending notes from the chord, and turned it into an orthodox E major, retainin only the passing and innocuous F sharp in the violin figure. Thus manicured an made harmoniously presentable, the passage might have been composed b Mendelssohn himself in one of his more daring moments.

Another example of Loewe's tampering with the original occurs in the fir movement, page 41, bars 4 to 5. There Bruckner pauses on a seventh chor The orchestra is silent for a bar and a half. Like nature, Loewe apparentl abhorred a vacuum, the result being that the silence was filled with a phras of his own for oboe and clarinet. As a rule Loewe's changes were in the instr mentation, but these bristle on every page of the score. Loewe, it was suggeste was evidently resolved to translate Bruckner's economy into Wagner's luxur For Bruckner's scoring almost foreshadows modern technic in expressi instrumentation. In one place Bruckner achieves a contrast by dividing a them between strings and wood winds. Loewe joined the instruments in a combined statement of the theme, thus destroying the intended color effect.

Theodore Thomas conducted the American premiere of Bruckner's Ninth Symphony at a concert of the Chicago Orchestra on Feb. 20, 1904, only a year after the Viennese premiere. Karl Muck first directed it in Boston on Nov. 1, 1907, bringing it to New York a few days later, on Nov. 7. There has naturally been speculation as to whether Bruckner deliberately chose the key of D minor with Beethoven's own Ninth Symphony in mind. Bruckner anticipated this. "It grieves me," he once remarked to his friend August Goellerich, "to have conceived the theme of the Ninth in D minor. People will say: 'Obviously Bruckner's Ninth *must* be in the same key as Beethoven's Ninth.' But I cannot discard or transpose the theme because it appeals to me just the way it is, and it looks well in D minor." The former practice of adding the *Te Deum* as a choral finale only strengthened the analogy in people's minds.

The three movements are marked as follows: I. Feierlich (Solemnly), D minor, 2/2; II. Scherzo, Bewegt lebhaft (Mosso vivace), D minor, 3/4; III. Adagio, Sehr langsam, feierlich, E major, 4/4.

The First Movement is unorthodox in structure. Each of the four major themes is built up to a resounding outburst. After some prefatory material, the spacious first theme rings out boldly in D minor from the top of a crescendo. The second theme, slower and more lyrical, is brought in by the first and second violins in A major, ending in a C major phrase. Violins and violas presently take up the third theme, and then expound a fourth theme, which is an extension of the third. There is a crescendo, mounting to a shattering climax, and soon the second main section of the movement—free fantasia and review—begins. The chief theme dominates the coda. There a motive from the introduction is heard too.

The second movement, substantially a classical scherzo with trio, is broadly worked out. The main theme first appears pizzicato among the strings. This is freely elaborated at some length, after which the trio (F sharp major, 3/8), faster than other interludes of this kind, begins. Two themes, one for strings, spiccato, the other, etwas ruhiger (somewhat quieter), for strings and oboes, are developed in the trio, and the scherzo proper returns.

The Adagio is substantially in sonata form. The first theme is given out by the violins. "This deeply earnest theme," said Gilman, "with its upward step of a minor ninth, is characteristically Brucknerian, though the wraiths of Liszt and Wagner do unmistakably peer out at us through the bars." Later the second theme is introduced in broad style by the first and second violins. Its key is A flat major. There is detailed development of both themes. The pace sharpens as a last Bruckner crescendo gets under way. The orchestra recalls the first theme fortissimo, and there is sudden peace, ghostly and elegiac. "The flickering violins and the dark-tinged tubas," wrote Werner Wolff, "convey the picture of the deeply absorbed composer writing the last pages with a trembling hand. This time Bruckner tells us a story—the story of his end."

L. B.

Overture in G minor

In 1862, at the age of thirty-seven, Bruckner, dissatisfied with the dull and academic instruction of the Viennese Simon Sechter, switched to Otto Kitzler, who was conducting opera at Linz. Kitzler, an arch-modernist of the time, coached him in theory and composition and introduced him to the magic world of Richard Wagner, who remained Bruckner's musical deity to the end.

An early symphony, in F minor, lacking a scherzo, dates from the Kitzler regime, but shows the influence of Mendelssohn, rather than of Wagner. The G minor Overture, more directly inspired by Kitzler's worship of Wagner, also belongs to this period, its composition dating from January, 1863. Kitzler himself thought well of the work, though he grouped it with two or three other pieces, among them a march, under the benevolent label of *Schularbeiten*.

Wagnerian traces are unmistakable in the harmonic scheme, and the finale suggests Wagner's Magic Fire motive, though the resemblance is doubtless pure accident. Contrasting with a strict classicism, Bruckner's own romantic flair asserts itself sturdily. A theme for strings in the body of the overture foreshadows in melodic structure the chief theme of the first movement of the Eighth Symphony, and the very last pages bear a similarity to the finale of the Fourth Symphony. Bruckner's contrapuntal skill is clearly manifested, and a recurrent cello phrase of querying nostalgic mood is enough to stamp the overture Bruckner's.

The work was buried away with other early Bruckneriana until Felix Weingartner put it on a Vienna Philharmonic program in October, 1921. The manuscript is now in the Vienna State Library.

L. B.

Ferruccio Busoni

BORN: EMPOLI, NEAR FLORENCE, ITALY, APR. 1, 1866. DIED: BERLIN, JULY 27, 1924.

He reminds one strongly of Balthazar Claes, the old alchemist in "La Recherche de l'absolu" of Balzac, seeking endlessly, insatiably, indefatigably for some artistic philosopher's stone; some formula which will inevitably produce the "magnum opus" of which he dreams. It seems always within reach, and yet constantly eludes him.
—CECIL GRAY.

Second Orchestral Suite, "Geharnischte" ("Armor"), Op. 34A

THE *Geharnischte Suite,* with its obvious northern flavor, belongs to a period in Busoni's writing when his treatment of themes, color, and structure was still influenced by the romantic school. It is only with the *Comedy Overture* of 1897 that he strikes out on paths leading to "a new classicism," so-called. Often referred to as *The Finnish Suite,* the *Geharnischte* commemorates a set of friendships formed in Helsingfors, where Busoni had spent a year, 1889-1890, teaching at the Conservatory and where he had met and married Gerda Sjöstrand.

The suite—composed in 1895, revised in 1903, and published in 1905—is dedicated to "den Leskowiten (1889)," which suffices to establish the Finnish connection. Lesko, incidentally, was the name of the Newfoundland dog that Busoni took with him to Helsingfors. Each of the four movements is dedicated to one of Busoni's friends in Helsingfors. The first, the "Vorspiel" or "Introduction," bears the name of Jean Sibelius. The second, "Kriegstanz" or "Danza Guerresca" ("War Dance"), is dedicated to Adolf Paul. The third, "Grabdenkmal" or "Monumento funebre" ("Funeral monument"), an andante grave, 4/4, is dedicated to the conductor and composer, Armas Jaernefelt. The fourth— "Ansturm" or "Assalto" ("Onslaught")—an allegro impetuoso in D minor, 6/4, is dedicated to Eero Jaernefelt. A picture of an armored knight on horseback appears on the score cover, bearing out the title *geharnischte* and indicating the martial and chivalric character of the music. The word, as Philip Hale once suggested, conveys not only the ideas of armor and harness, but defiance as well, since a *geharnischte Antwort* signifies a "defiant reply."

Hugo Leichtentritt discerns "recollections from northern shores in the spirit which breathes in these martial sounds, these rhythms full of obstinate northern energy, these austere plastic melodies." Resemblances to Sibelius' symphonic works have been pointed out, especially in the way of building up climaxes. The hints of northern color and feeling are especially strong in the third movement, which mounts to a brilliant climax in the middle and then tapers off gradually to a hush. In the final section a fiery and stormy energy contrasts with a soft passage suggesting "a faint echo of far-off fighting."

L. B.

"Indian Fantasy" for Piano and Orchestra, Op. 44

In August, 1891, Busoni and his wife set sail for America. He had accepted a post, thanks to the urgings of friends, at the New England Conservatory in Boston. However, Busoni was anything but an inconsiderate son, so that the thought of properly caring for his parents had also a good deal to do with the trip. America, even then, was a land of hope and promise and valid dollars! The first couple of weeks in Boston were enough to discourage him; conditions at the Conservatory were scarcely idyllic, and the financial framework of the institution teetered dangerously. He was not very happy. He withstood a year of it and resigned, his colleagues praising him for his courage, though they declared, "you are strong enough to stand on your own feet."

Nevertheless, there was compensation for his stay in Boston: (1) a son was born to him, and (2) he hobnobbed with the celebrated Arthur Nikisch, who was flourishing there in the role of conductor. Moving with his family to New York he launched out on the life of a "traveling virtuoso," which was, to him, infinitely preferable. But he missed Europe. "In America," he once wrote, "the *average* is better than elsewhere, but along with that there is much more *average* than elsewhere, and, as far as I can see, it will soon be *all average!*" In the spring of 1894, he decided to go back—to "elsewhere."

He returned, strange as it seems, in 1910. This time he found conditions more bearable. He undertook several concert tours, and even visits to "dear old Boston" proved less irritating than previously. A former New York pupil of his, Natalie Curtis, brought to his attention the music of the Indians, and he reacted to it with characteristic *élan*. Not till the next year, on another concert tour of America, was he to go slightly beyond the toying-with-the-idea stage. But, he thought, he must not be ridiculous, he must not ape Dvorak and create a work on Indian tunes in the Leipzig tradition. It occurred to him that some simple plan, following a "mother-son-bride-war-peace" idea might prove effective. There the matter rested till 1915, when he made a new visit to America. He was received royally at his New York recital, his audience including such stellar pianists as Josef Hofmann, Raphael Joseffy, Mark Hambourg, Carl Friedberg, Harold Bauer, and Percy Grainger.

His tour proved only of fair financial success, but his time had not been wasted altogether, for he completed, among other works, the *Indian Fantasy,* on which he had devoted much toil, though intermittently, since his earlier sojourn. Its progress had been labored, but now it was finished.

He played the work for the first time in public at a concert of the Zurich Municipal Orchestra, Volkmar Andreae conducting, in January, 1916, and performed it often after that. His pupil, intimate friend, and collaborator (for the edition of the *Well-Tempered Clavier*) Egon Petri has also played it frequently.

R. C. B.

"Sarabande" and "Cortège," Studies for *Doctor Faust,* Op. 51

BUSONI'S ACKNOWLEDGED masterpiece, *Doctor Faust,* is regarded by his biographers Edward J. Dent and Gisella Selden-Roth as a kind of summing up of his whole career as creative musician and esthetic theorist. Goethe's works had long been a second Bible to Busoni, and the Faust legend had assumed for him a great symbolic spectacle of art and life. Dent professes to see Busoni himself in much of the role of Faust. The cry of Faust, "Give me Genius, with all its sufferings," is said to echo Busoni's own tragic plea for expressive power, and Faust's constant delving into the riddles and mysteries of art and thought is taken as mirroring Busoni's own bent. Indeed, Busoni has even been regarded as a composite Faust and Mephistopheles, combining, philosophically, the seeker after truth and the eternal sceptic.

His theory of the theater, as applied to *Doctor Faust,* appears in the second stanza of the Prologue: "The Stage exhibits the gestures of life, but it bears plainly the mark of unreality. If it is not to become a distorting mirror, it must act fairly and truly as a magic mirror. Grant that the stage only lowers the values of what is true, it can then do full justice to the incredible, and though you may laugh at drama judging it as reality, it will compel you to seriousness if you regard it as mere play." Busoni insisted on calling his opera a "puppet play," though probably only in an oblique and abstract sense. As Dent points out, Busoni cannot seriously have planned his *Faust* for puppet performance, since it could be given only in "a large opera house with every modern technical appliance, not to speak of its vast choral and instrumental requirements."

Rather is the puppet-play idea an indication of the opera's "remoteness from everyday sentiment and sentimentality" (in keeping with Busoni's basic theory of art). The opera may lack "humanity," but in its approach to the ideal of the puppet show, it "gains in austerity and dignity." The idea is further enforced by the sketch of a puppet theater appearing on an inner curtain, showing an array of the opera's characters.

When the work was presented in London by the B.B.C. in March, 1937, F. Bonavia pointed out that its unusual character precluded "all possibility of its being measured by common standards." He called it "a singular epic of disillusion and disenchantment," and stressed the hardships involved in staging Busoni's magnum opus, mentioning, too, the recurring tours de force devised for the cast of twenty singers. In the opera, Busoni's human "puppets" appear, disappear, and alter shapes in startling sequence, at times suggesting the topsy-turvy wonderland of Salvador Dali's surrealism in their symbolic transformations.

The *Sarabande* and *Cortège* were published as "studies" in 1921. In her book on Busoni, Gisella Selden-Roth, speaks of them as a temporary "goal" set up and reached by Busoni while slowly evolving the whole plan of *Doctor Faust*. The *Sarabande*—described by Pannain as "a symphonic intermezzo of intense lyrical life, where the fundamental situation of the Faust-Busoni drama finds its being"—is closely associated with Faust's last entrance and is designed to introduce and foreshadow his death. The *Cortège,* a weirdly fantastic interlude, was later incorporated with Busoni's *Tanzwalzer* into the music accompanying the procession of guests at the wedding festivities of the Duke and Duchess of Parma. The scene leads to the entrance of "the famous Doctor Faust," who proceeds to evoke Solomon and the Queen of Sheba, Samson and Delilah, and Salome and John the Baptist for the Duchess's entertainment. Both pieces were first played in Berlin on Jan. 13, 1921, at the second of three concerts of Busoni's music organized by the newly founded magazine *Der Anbruch.* Also on that program was the *Tanzwalzer,* later similarly utilized in *Doctor Faust.*

Busoni was still at work on *Doctor Faust* when he died. The job of completing it went to Philipp Jarnach, and the premiere followed soon thereafter, on May 21, 1925, in Dresden. His earlier operas, *Die Brautwahl* and *Arlecchino* had been produced, respectively, in Hamburg in 1912 and in Zurich in 1918.

L. B.

John Alden Carpenter

BORN: PARK RIDGE, ILL., FEB. 28, 1876.

Carpenter's music is characterized by certain easily discernible traits, chief of which are a whimsical fancy, a delicate, even poetic, humor and tender sentiments. . . . He is a composer who produces music with manifest enjoyment and whose quick impulses are governed by good taste.—W. J. HENDERSON.

Symphony No. 2

I. Moderato: Allegro. II. Andante. III. Allegro.

In 1936, John Alden Carpenter retired from the position of vice-president of the family concern of George B. Carpenter and Company, dealers in mill, railway, and ship supplies. His had been the career of the successful business executive, but together with that he had managed to devote full-time activity to composition. His musical leanings were first discovered by his mother, an amateur singer, who gave him his earliest lessons. Educated at Harvard where he also took all the music courses offered, he received further musical training from Edward Elgar and Bernard Ziehn.

Carpenter has been able to follow his bright, particular muse with a special freedom, thanks to economic independence. This is exemplified in the un-academic progress of his works, which form a line that runs a full gamut of experimentation and inquisitive thinking. In "Green River," a song dating from 1909, and in other early pieces, "we find whole-tone progressions and an apparent desire to exploit the upper reaches of the overtone series; and these things were written by a man who at that time had not yet heard one note of Debussy!"

A Violin Sonata (1911), while akin to certain aspects of the César Franck style, proceeds under its own steam most of the way, stamping the composer as one "who is not afraid of showing influences," as John Tasker Howard reports in his book, *Our Contemporary Composers,* "yet who is not content to be an imitator." Carpenter's first real bid for important attention came with his composition of *Adventures in a Perambulator* (1914). This is a piece of pro-gram music for orchestra, given to light fun making and whimsy. In the Concertino for Piano and Orchestra (1915) he again avoids the heavier moods, focusing on novelty devices that foreshadow a jazz rhythm persuasion.

The Birthday of the Infanta, composed for a ballet production of the Chicago Opera Company in 1919, surveys the Hispanic accents with a subject that moves through a wide variety of colorful scenes. In 1921 he penned the score for another ballet, *Krazy Kat,* based on a comic-strip character. Here he first employed the shimmering meters of jazz. The music, far from being a slapstick commentary, intensifies the dramatic, human side of the ballet's subject—without preachment, that is.

Skyscrapers, still another ballet, was produced at the Metropolitan Opera House in 1926. The composer had completed it two years previously. Simple as is the theme of the choreography, the music avoids the obvious imitation of sounds. It endeavors to get beyond the "external features of this life," as presented by "a series of moving decorations," and to remark on the more serious matter of human frailty.

A String Quartet of Carpenter's was performed at the Library of Congress Festival of 1928. *Song of Faith,* written at the invitation of the United States George Washington Bicentennial Commission, obtained its premiere performance in 1932. Then came a work for orchestra with piano obbligato entitled *Patterns,* which was introduced by the Boston Symphony Orchestra in the autumn of 1932. *Sea Drift,* taking inspiration from Walt Whitman's poems (which had functioned in like capacity for the Delius composition of the same title, as well as the Vaughan Williams *Sea Symphony*), was given a first hearing by the Philharmonic-Symphony Society under the direction of Werner Janssen in November, 1934.

A Quintet for Piano and Strings; a symphonic *Danza;* a Violin Concerto, premiered by Zlatko Balakovic and the Chicago Symphony Orchestra in 1937; the Symphony No. 1, written for the fiftieth anniversary of the same orchestra (1940); and *Song of Freedom* (1941), for unison chorus and orchestra comprise other major works, besides the present one.

The composer's own account of the Symphony No. 2 follows:

This work . . . derives some of its basic thematic material from a piano quintet which I composed in 1934 during a stay in Algiers. Some of the native tunes heard there "rubbed off" to some extent in the coloring of the last movement of my work, which is otherwise devoid of programmatic intent.

First Movement. A short, introductory passage leads to the first statement, by the tympani, of one of the recurring rhythmic patterns of the movement, followed by the principal subject, divided among horns, clarinets, and strings. A secondary subject is later developed on the same rhythmic pattern.

Second Movement. In this section also the tympani establish at the outset the basic rhythmic structure. There is a principal theme for strings and a secondary subject, announced tutti.

Third Movement. The finale is based, for the most part, on two themes, in various forms. The movement is brought to a climax with a final broad statement on the second theme of the middle movement.

Bruno Walter led the premiere of this score at a New York Philharmonic-Symphony concert on Oct. 22, 1942.

R. C. B.

"Skyscrapers, A Ballet of American Life"

ALTHOUGH INTENDED originally for Serge Diaghileff's Ballets Russes and planned for production at Monte Carlo in March, 1925, *Skyscrapers* was first staged at the Metropolitan Opera House on Feb. 16, 1926. Negotiations between Carpenter and the Russian impresario had already reached a deadlock when Giulio Gatti-Casazza, general manager of the opera company, placed his bid for the ballet novelty. Robert Edmond Jones was appointed collaborator. Samuel Lee, a Broadway producer, was also called in to assist. Later the noted scenic designer related how he and the composer conducted their teamwork. Mr. Jones wrote:

Carpenter would play the music, giving me an impression of the changing orchestration. He played each passage over and over again for hours. This would give me certain ideas of movement, for which I drew tentative designs, to be discussed with him. Countless series of patterns were made during six months of grueling, unremitting labor. From these we selected the final succession of designs, one growing from the other, parallel with the program of the music.

The piano version of *Skyscrapers* carries the following résumé of the ballet:

Skyscrapers is a ballet that seeks to reflect some of the many rhythmic movements and sounds of modern American life. It has no story in the usually accepted sense, but proceeds on the simple fact that American life reduces itself essentially to violent alterations of work and play, each with its own peculiar and distinctive rhythmic character. The action of the ballet is merely a series of moving decorations reflecting some of the obvious external features of this life, as follows:

Scene 1: Symbols of restlessness.
Scene 2: An abstraction of the skyscraper and of the work that produces it—and the interminable crowd that passes by.
Scene 3: The transition from work to play.
Scene 4: Any "Coney Island," and a reflection of a few of its manifold activities —interrupted presently by a "throw-back," in the movie sense, to the idea of work, and reverting with equal suddenness to play.
Scene 5: The return from play to work.
Scene 6: Skyscrapers.

Reviewing the Metropolitan novelty for the magazine *Musical America,* of which he later became editor, Oscar Thompson thus described the action:

With the parting of the curtains for *Skyscrapers,* blinking red lights are revealed at either side of the stage, that are at once understood to represent traffic signals. These, as the program makes clear, are "symbols of restlessness." A fantastic "drop" is lifted, and reveals "an abstraction of the skyscraper" and "the work that produces it—and the interminable crowd that passes by." Girders in angular confusion are etched against vacancy, men in the semblance of overalls go through the motions of violent labor, while shadows in human shape move listlessly, meaninglessly by.

The whistles blow, the workers emerge, each steps into the arms of a short-skirted, bare-legged partner, and there is a dancing exodus for the resorts of pleasure. The stage picture that follows is one of striking illusion, representative of "any Coney Island," with its ferris wheels, its scenic railways, its street shows, its heedless, fun-mad, dance-addled crowds, swirling through rhythmic gestures and formations, glorifying the American girls' nether extremities, with no particular thought as to whether she has either brain or heart.

There is a "throw-back," as movie parlance has it, to the idea of work, with a sudden cessation of the dancing, and a return, in the midst of the Coney Island revelry, to the men in overalls swinging their sledges and crouched about their riveting fires. This is followed by an equally violent reversion to play, in which flappers, sailors, minstrel show end men, comic policemen, and characters of a midway plaisance are manipulated in colorful, but on the whole, orderly succession of dances.

The fifth scene brings the transition from play to work, as the men in overalls surrender their dance partners to return to the labors of the skyscraper. Gigantic shadows, suggesting a Herculean power behind the building of a great city's business edifices, are cast upward against the girders as the ballet ends.

The Negro chorus, recruited from Harlem, has a curious place in the Coney Island scene. White-Wings, blackface street sweeper, goes to sleep, propped against a traffic sign. Shadowy figures emerge, as in a dream, and sing in melancholy mood, until with a sudden snapping of the strain, they begin dancing, one by one. Then White-Wings wakes up and takes up the same jerky, jazzy steps.

Of the music itself, Mr. Thompson had the following to say:

More often it is of a semijazz, than of a real jazz character; sometimes, as in the episode of the singing Negroes, it is even remote from the spirit of jazz. His jazz and semijazz are not bald incorporations of cabaret tunes. He has created his own musical ideas, save for a few incorporated phrases of "Massa's in the Cold, Cold Ground," and a fleeting suggestion or two of "Yankee Doodle," "Dem Goo-Goo Eyes," and various vaguely remembered "Blues." The work was written for a symphonic orchestra, not for jazz band. Saxophones and a banjo have parts, but rather minor ones. This is not literal jazz, but jazz as it has filtered through the mind of a musician who thinks in terms of art, and whose purpose was to write an art work, not merely to add to America's store of popular music.

A few days before the performance at the Metropolitan Mr. Carpenter had cleared up some points regarding his alleged use of out-and-out jazz idiom in a statement to the *New York Herald Tribune:*

In *Skyscrapers,* photographic effects have not been sought. The effect might better be described as a reflection, with all the exaggeration and distortion a reflection is likely to have. It must be understood that the music is not jazz, as jazz is generally heard and understood. It would be impossible to give jazz through the medium of a symphony orchestra.

Therefore *Skyscrapers* may be called jazz filtered through an orchestra of that sort. It is jazz once removed. Jazz itself depends on the sonority of the jazz band. To get something of this sonorous jazz effect we have used the saxophones and a banjo. . . .

Jazz opera is a big job. It must be remembered that opera is a very old form; jazz is modern, and can hardly be made to fit. For opera we must choose something poetic and remote. Jazz is very near and real. It would be absurd to hear people trying to "talk" to each other in jazz. The modern composers, Stravinsky and the rest, it will be noticed, are not using the opera form. They do not feel at home in it, apparently. Instead, they write ballets. The ballet is flexible; you can do what you want with it—but not opera.

In the cast of the Metropolitan production were Albert Troy (The Strutter), Rita de Leporte (Herself), Roger Dodge (White-Wings). Louis Hasselmans conducted.

L. B.

Mario Castelnuovo-Tedesco

BORN: FLORENCE, ITALY, APR. 3, 1895.

He is essentially an exponent of emotionalism, so much so that he is
sometimes to be classed as a romantic . . . though with a natural gift
for a clear and rhythmic musical form which is never allowed to fall
into a state of anarchy such as is to be found in the work of the late
German and Italian romanticists.—GASTONE ROSSI-DARIA.

Overture, "King John"

SHAKESPEARE IS by no means a new inspirational font for Mr. Castelnuovo-
Tedesco, for he has composed several overtures based on plays, and thirty-three
settings—at the last count—of the celebrated bard's verses. The present work is
dedicated to John Barbirolli and was written expressly for the Philharmonic-
Symphony Society's Centennial season of 1941-1942. The premiere occurred on
Mar. 15, 1942, in Carnegie Hall, New York.

In a letter to the Society, Mr. Castelnuovo-Tedesco wrote of this Overture,
as follows:

It is the seventh of my *Shakespeare Overtures* (the first six being *The Taming
of the Shrew, Twelfth Night, Julius Caesar, A Winter's Tale, Midsummer Night's
Dream,* and *The Merchant of Venice*) and is entitled *King John.* (What could be
better than to dedicate *King John* to John?)

King John is one of the "minor" Shakespeare historical dramas, but it has,
as always, some beautiful scenes and, although I didn't try to follow the plot of
the drama, I found, just at the end, the following lines which seemed prophetic
and which really inspired me. This is the quotation:

> "This England never did nor never shall
> Lie at the proud foot of a conqueror,
> But when it first did help to wound itself.
> Now these, her princes, are come home again,
> Come the three corners of the world in arms,
> And we shall shock them: nought shall make us rue
> If England to itself do rest but true."

I have nothing to add. I believe the quotation is eloquent for itself; and it is
too early to speak of the music (besides, I don't like to speak of my music).

Mario Castelnuovo-Tedesco began the study of piano with Del Valle in his
native Florence. After receiving a diploma in 1914 he became a pupil of

Ildebrando Pizzetti in composition, and later he was graduated from the Royal Conservatory of Music Luigi Cherubini in Florence. Mr. Castelnuovo-Tedesco has been a most prolific composer, boasting a considerable number of piano pieces, songs, chamber-music works, three compositions for violin and orchestra, two piano concertos, a cello concerto, a concertino for harp and chamber orchestra, a musical comedy, a chamber opera, a ballet, and music incidental to plays.

He has made numerous appearances as a concert pianist, and he has not been at all inactive as a conductor. Mr. Castelnuovo-Tedesco's creative career has not been a bed of roses from its inception, for his music suffered the barbs and sneers of an unsympathetic public in his own Italy for a spell.

Gastone-Rossi-Daria has discovered the composer's music to be something of a "redemption from the empty and inane sentimentalism based on sobs and fainting fits which ruled during our 'veristic' crisis of the 1890-1910 period." And he suggests, further, that it comes as a natural reaction to the "inorganic condition and academism" of the style of Mascagni and Bossi.

R. C. B.

Emmanuel Chabrier

BORN: AMBERT (PUY-DE-DÔME), FRANCE, JAN. 18, 1841. DIED: PARIS, SEPT. 13, 1894.

*I am virtually self-taught, I belong to no school. I have more tempera-
ment than talent. There are many things which one must learn in
youth which I shall never reach; but I live and breathe in music, I
write as I feel, with more temperament than technique, but what is
the difference—I think I am an honest and sincere artist.*—CHABRIER.

"España," Rhapsody for Orchestra

CHABRIER'S *España* is a tone picture to the life of a land of dazzling color and
entrancing rhythms. On his gorgeously hued canvas the French composer
caught the irresistible spirit of the Spain that fascinated him. Others had heard
Spain with the ears of Russians and Frenchmen, like Rimsky-Korsakoff and
Bizet. Debussy had reveled subjectively in a whirl of studied impressions, and
Ravel had captured the surface glitter. But it was Chabrier who "mixed with
the dancers; drank the manzanilla and looked into the eyes of the gypsy girls;
who clapped hands as the Andalusians twisted their hips and in his ecstasy
shouted, *Olle, Olle!*"

Chabrier was a thorough man during his travels in Spain in the spring of
1883. Songs and dances that intrigued him he promptly jotted down for future
reference in his music. The work of gathering them together in a web of vivid
tone thrilled him, and the excitement may be felt in the rhapsody *España*,
which brought him world renown. The score was first performed at a
Lamoureux concert in the Château d'Eau, Paris, on Nov. 4, 1883, and speedily
embarked on its path of glory through the concert halls of Europe.

Embedded in Chabrier's symphonic travelogue is a sheaf of Spanish dances.
Chief among them are the Jota and the Malagueña, a popular dance in triple
time closely related to the Fandango, and accompanied with castanets, or
tambourine, and guitar. The Jota, equally famous as a national dance, is in
rapid 3/8 time. Chabrier added a theme of his own to the scheme, the striking
melody announced by the trombones.

Written in F major, the rhapsody calls for two flutes, piccolo, two oboes,
two clarinets, four bassoons, four horns, two trumpets, two cornets, three
trombones, tuba, tympani, bass drum, cymbals, triangle, tambourine, two harps,
and strings.

The composer Cécile Chaminade once recalled,

Chabrier was the very incarnation of the everyday Parisian—caustic, full of animal spirits, brusque, and a "good fellow." My salon was at that time ornamented with a picture of Gounod, and I shall always retain a vivid mental picture of poor Chabrier, with hand upraised, striding across the room, and addressing the portrait with a volume of furious invective. It took us a world of trouble to calm him down.

L. B.

George Whitefield Chadwick

BORN: LOWELL, MASS., NOV. 13, 1854. DIED: BOSTON, APR. 4, 1941.

*It is impossible to think of a more honest and accomplished musician,
or one who, without pretense or megalomania, accomplished as much
for the development of his native art.*—OLIN DOWNES.

Symphonic Sketch, "Jubilee"

PUBLISHED IN 1907 with a dedication to Frederick S. Converse, Chadwick's
orchestral suite *Symphonic Sketches* consists of four sections, of which
"Jubilee," composed in 1895, is the first. The others are entitled "Noël,"
"Hobgoblin," and "A Vagrom Ballad." Though intending the four "sketches"
to be played as a unit, Chadwick states on the flyleaf of the score that they
could be played independently, "if more expedient." As an epitome of the mood
and spirit of the "Jubilee" Sketch the composer had the following poem printed
over the score:

> No cool gray tones for me!
>   Give me the warmest red and green,
>   A cornet and a tambourine,
> To paint *my* jubilee!
>   For when the flutes and oboes play,
>   To sadness I become a prey;
>   Give me the violets and the May,
> But no gray skies for me!

The symphonic sketch (marked allegro molto vivace, A major, 6/4)
promptly justifies its title with a jovial carnival-like theme given out fortissimo
by the whole orchestra. After the material is fully expounded, a bold 4/4
theme is announced in unison by bass clarinet, bassoons, violas, and cellos,
with pizzicato violins as partial accompaniment. The horns presently utter a
C major phrase, continued by the strings. The jubilant opening motive returns
and soon a lyric episode (lento espressivo) for wood winds and horns appears.
The first violins review earlier material and "Jubilee" ends sonorously with a
coda (presto) built on the first subject.

The C major phrase for horns was referred to as a "patting Juba horn call"
by Philip Hale. "Juba" was a dance or "breakdown" used in Negro celebrations
on southern plantations. The "patting" referred to the knee and thigh slapping
accompanying the dancing, with the word "Juba" shouted repeatedly as a

efrain. To illustrate its use Hale quoted a "Stein Song" appearing in Richard Hovey's *More Songs from Vagabondia* published in Boston in 1896:

> When the wind comes up from Cuba
> And the birds are on the wing,
> And our hearts are patting Juba
> To the banjo of the spring. . . .

Chadwick's orchestral suite was once described as "the farcical glorification of the life of the American tramp" probably from the verses accompanying the "Vagrom Ballad"—A tale of tramps and railway ties, Of old clay pipes and rum, Of broken heads and blackened eyes And the 'thirty days' to come." An early critic even spoke of the sketches as "an American counterpart of Till Eulenspiegel, Villon, and "La Bohème." Both "Jubilee" and "A Vagrom Ballad" were deemed by others an ingenious expression of "the frankness, swagger and recklessness that Europeans commonly associate with Americans."

Of the so-called "Boston classicists" or "New England Academicians" Chadwick probably had the broadest sense of humor. The spirit of fun recurs in his music, reaching best utterance in "Jubilee" and the symphonic ballad *Tam o'Shanter*. As John Tasker Howard points out, he is the one composer of the old school who "makes us chuckle." The note of laughing impertinence flashes through Chadwick's music, a "certain jaunty irreverence," according to Hale, "a snapping of the fingers at Fate and the Universe." Critics and commentators welcomed this typically "American" trait, the general opinion being that "none but a Yankee can say such things and get away with it." No doubt, modern concertgoers, exposed to repeated volleys of a more daring "swagger" and "irreverence," can take Chadwick's milder brand without flinching.

Shortly before Chadwick's death, Howard, in his book on American music, spoke of the "steadiness" and "freshness" that gave enduring vitality to his music. "After all," he contended, "modernity is youth, and of youthfulness Chadwick has had his full share. The man himself is far older than his music."

A week after Chadwick's death on Apr. 4, 1931, the *New York Times* carried Olin Downes's sound appraisal of the part played in American music by the distinguished composer, teacher, and conductor:

Chadwick, of old New England stock, imbued with the American traditions and ideals of New England, embraced a whole period of musical development in the course of his career and the number and character of his works. When all is said and done, he more than any other one man gives his creative period its stamp and character and represents most completely the body of serious American music. . . . He was a creative musician of rich and exceptional gifts, and he endeavored, and succeeded in his endeavor, to be a composer thoroughly master of his business.

The *Symphonic Sketches* were first performed as a sequence by the Boston Symphony Orchestra on Feb. 7 and 8, 1908. Dr. Karl Muck conducted. Chadwick himself directed the whole suite with the Chicago Symphony on Jan. 20 and 21, 1910. Performances of single sections had been heard several years before publication of the Suite.

L. B.

Ernest Chausson

BORN: PARIS, JAN. 21, 1855. DIED: LIMAY, NEAR MANTES, JUNE 10, 1899.

Chausson's creative activity falls within a difficult period in French music. Schumann was only a remembered enthusiasm among the French, and Debussy had not yet arrived. In the interim Saint-Saëns provided sustenance too insubstantial for an alert mind; and from both the teachings of César Franck and the Wagnerian tide which washed over French music, Chausson shaped the elements of his timid and highly personal style.—ABRAHAM VEINUS.

Symphony in B flat major, Op. 20

I. Lent; Allegro vivo. II. Très lent. III. Animé; très animé.

FRENCH MUSIC suffered a sharp loss in the untimely death of Ernest Chausson. Riding a bicycle on his estate at Limay, the forty-four-year-old composer lost control and crashed headlong into a stone wall. Critics and musicians agreed that a rare, sensitive gift had been snuffed out prematurely. As an avowed disciple and champion of César Franck, Chausson has fostered a new trend. But his aims were only partially realized. His creative output was small, and his own diffidence stood in the way of his accomplishing more. Some of his Conservatory friends thought that he had pursued ideals beyond his powers of fulfillment. As in the case of the Russian Liadoff, indecision and timidity further hampered Chausson's work. He was a man of impeccable standards in life and art, and he numbered among his devoted friends Gabriel Fauré, Henri Duparc, Vincent d'Indy, Pierre de Bréville, and Charles Bordes. These men were said to have banded together in the fight for "musical righteousness as they saw it."

Chausson left only a few compositions, and of these few only two have gained a secure repertory status, at least outside of France. One is the B flat major Symphony. The other is the *Poème* (Op. 25) for violin and orchestra. This latter work is not only a favorite of recital and concert programs, but has even entered the ballet repertory as the music of Antony Tudor's *Jardin aux Lilas* (*Lilac Garden*). Two other compositions of Chausson's are occasionally heard: the symphonic poem *Viviane* (Op. 5) and the Concerto for Violin, Piano, and String Quartet (Op. 21), besides several sensitive songs.

Chausson's only symphony was finished in 1890 and first played at a concert of the Société Nationale in Paris on Apr. 18, 1891. It is said that the Symphony did not seize the imagination of the Parisian public till Arthur Nikisch con-

ducted it at a concert of the Berlin Philharmonic Orchestra in the Cirque
d'Hiver. That performance occurred on May 13, 1897. In a curiously parallel
set of circumstances, the Boston Symphony Orchestra performed the American
premiere of Chausson's symphony during a visit to Philadelphia on Dec. 4,
1905. The eminent French composer, Vincent d'Indy, appearing as "conductor
by invitation," directed the performance.

The first movement of the symphony begins with an introductory section
(Lent, B flat major, 4/4), featuring a theme given to violas, cellos, double
basses, clarinet, and first horn. This theme reappears forcefully in the finale.
Horn and bassoon offer the chief motive of the main body of the opening
movement (Allegro vivo, B flat major, 3/4). A passage ending in a staccato
phrase among the wood winds serves as transition to the second theme, which
is given out by cellos and clarinet. After elaborate development and recapitulation, the coda, built around the main theme, sets in (Presto, 4/4).

The second movement begins solemnly with a passage for strings, clarinet,
bassoon, and two horns (Très lent, D minor, 4/4). A haunting phrase for
English horn and clarinet, set against soft-spun figures in the violas and cellos,
is heard. The first theme returns, somewhat altered in the horns. The pace
sharpens, as the cellos join the English horn in an expressive discourse over
string arpeggios. This builds up to a striking climax, and the first theme is
back among the strings, fortissimo.

In the third and last movement, there is again an introductory passage
(Animé, B flat minor, 4/4). Here trumpet and wood winds sketch the first
theme of the main body of the movement, which is marked Très animé. The
basses then unfold the vigorous theme fully, and the violins take it up over a
pulsing woodwind figure. In broad chorale style the second theme enters in
D flat, announced by the orchestra, and extended by the oboe. This choralelike
theme figures prominently in the development section. Motives from the first
movement are also recalled toward the end, among them the main subject of
the introduction, now intoned majestically by the basses.

The score calls for three flutes (one interchangeable with piccolo), two oboes,
English horn, two clarinets, bass clarinet, three bassoons, four horns, four
trumpets, three trombones, bass tuba, three kettledrums, two harps, and strings.
The symphony is dedicated to Chausson's brother-in-law the painter Henry
Lerolle, a devotee of music.

Pierre de Bréville, in a tribute which appeared in the *Mercure de France* not
long after his friend's death, wrote:

Chausson, like César Franck, was unknown during his lifetime. He did not
occupy the public place to which he had a right. Directors of concerts thought
little about him, managers of theaters were not curious about his opera, and the
newspapers were as a rule unkind or silent. . . . He was interested in the music

f his colleagues; their success brought him joy. He was ingenious in his methods
f bringing young talent before the public; he was always ready to render them
ny service in a delicate manner. If he met with ingratitude, he did not mind it,
or kindness was natural to him, and he was generous because he was in love with
enerosity.

L. B.

Carlos Chávez

BORN: NEAR MEXICO CITY, JUNE 13, 1899.

We cannot, like Chávez, borrow from a rich, melodic source or lose ourselves in an ancient civilization, but we can be stimulated and instructed by his example. For Chávez it may already be said that his work presents itself as one of the first authentic signs of a new world with its own new music.—AARON COPLAND.

Concerto for Piano and Orchestra, No. 1

I. Allegro agitato. II. Molto lento. III. Allegro.

THE COMPOSER's intention was to make this work a "virtuoso concerto," with orchestra and piano sharing the virtuosity, rather than emphasizing the solo part and reducing the rest to a subsidiary role of accompaniment. When Chávez first showed the composition to Dimitri Mitropoulos, the latter suggested "Concerto Sinfonico" as a more appropriate title than "concerto." The work falls into the usual three divisions, with a slow movement (Molto lento), in sustained lyric vein, contrasting with an opening Allegro agitato of impetuous, energetic drive, and a scherzolike Allegro finale.

Chávez drew up his plans for the concerto in the spring of 1938 while residing in the country district of Ixtapan de la Sal, Mexico. Detailed work on it did not begin until that fall, when he returned to Mexico City and was made recipient of a Guggenheim Fellowship. After making some progress on it, Chávez was obliged to shelve it because of sundry other activities, including tours, teaching, writing, and whatever else demanded the time and attention of Mexico's leading musical nationalist. Two years later, in October, 1940, again in Mexico City, he resumed work on the concerto, completing it two months later on New Year's Eve.

Dimitri Mitropoulos led the premiere of the Concerto at a New York Philharmonic-Symphony concert on Jan. 1, 1942. Eugene List was the soloist.

In a broad sense Carlos Chávez is to Mexican music what Enesco is to Rumanian, Béla Bartók to Hungarian, and Villa-Lobos to Brazilian music, with allowances made for obvious differences in personal temperament, technic, and national heritage. Like the others, Chávez early became absorbed in his country's folk lore and went to native sources for fresh inspiration. For years he has striven to make Mexicans and foreigners alike conscious of the wealth of source material embedded in Mexico's Indo-Spanish traditions. At the same time he has sought to link this heritage with modern reality, so that his music in one breath may express a kind of primitive barbarism and in the next a machine-age impetus. Accordingly, we find him composing, on the one hand, an Indian symphony and two ballets founded on Aztec themes, and, on the other, a ballet symphony *H. P.* (*Horse Power*), a *Proletarian Symphony,* and a study in dynamic force called *Energia,* scored for nine instruments. In an *Antigone Symphony* he further showed his bent for archaic idioms by attempting to bring its spare, laconic style into conformity with supposed Greek theories of music.

In his treatment of native Mexican material Chávez began by incorporating folk tunes bodily into his compositions. Later he evolved a style of his own, utilizing the spirit and idiom of native themes and enriching them with fresh nuances of his own. It is said that "singlehanded" he created a style, part Indian, part Spanish, and part modernist, that "no future Mexican composer can afford to ignore."

In a preliminary study of the late Silvestre Revueltas' music for a work to be entitled *Panorama de la Musica Mexicana—Desde la Independencia hasta la Actualidad* (*Panorama of Mexican Music, from the Independence to the Present*), the Mexican scholar Otto Mayer-Serra paused to evaluate the role of Carlos Chávez in fusing the nationalist spirit and the technical innovations of modern European music into a new entity. He said (*Musical Quarterly,* April, 1941):

Mexico was not without a musician who could understand the urgency of incorporating Mexican musical nationalism with the main trends of modern style. Before long Mexican music was to assimilate the new technical contributions of European music, from those of French impressionism to those of the most advanced schools of Central Europe. To have grasped the need for this and to have attempted such a combination of the most recent modernism with the ancestral musical values of his country are the historical merits of Carlos Chávez.

Revueltas and Chávez turned equally to folk sources for unexploited raw materials, though by temperament and conviction they represent different phases of Mexican nationalism. Revueltas was more engrossed in the songs and feasts and teeming life around him, Chávez delving constantly into primitive Mexican roots, and reviving archaic scales, instruments, and ritualistic devices. In the music of Revueltas the beat and throb of the immediate scene predominate; in that of Chávez—at least that consciously deriving from early Indian sources—there is a constant striving "to reconstruct musically this atmosphere of primitive purity, in the conviction that he is thus giving expression to the 'true' Mexican character."

Chávez himself, however, has viewed the problem of "Mexican music" in somewhat less restricted terms than some observers have led others to believe.

To him the term "Mexican music" involves three distinct elements. (1) The Indian music of ancient Mexico, the purest form of which is not the Aztec, as often supposed, but that of the nomadic Yaquis, Series, and Huicholes tribes. (2) European music, especially Spanish, brought in through colonization. (Chávez points out that another important, though less predominant, factor was the infiltration of Negro slave music along the whole coast of the Gulf of Mexico.) (3) The new Mexican product arising from a blend of both elements. The first two elements, besides differing radically in character, followed two lines of development, or, rather, the Indian music, from the Conquest, remained static, whereas the other evolved periodically into new forms. The proportion of the two elements has long been a controversial issue among students of Mexican music. Chávez said:

Mexican music is largely the product of a mixture of influences, that is, of cross-breeding. This mixed ancestry, chiefly Indo-Spanish, is never found to be in exact proportions of half and half. In the majority of cases, one basic element is altered by the other in a proportion much smaller than fifty per cent. . . . We do not depreciate European music, or music of any other nation. We admire the genuine expression of any people. Nor is our desire to recover the Mexican tradition one merely for the sake of recovering it. Mexico is as rich, as personal, as strong in music as in painting and in architecture.

Apart from this tireless delving into primitive culture and the unremitting work of arousing Mexicans to a national musical consciousness, Chávez has devoted time and energy to bringing his country into line with the educational and concert-giving traditions of other lands. In 1928 he founded and still conducts the Symphony Orchestra of Mexico, the programs of which have grown in frequency and novelty. As its conductor he took care, too, that the works of younger Mexican composers, still unknown to the public, would get a hearing. An appointment to direct the National Conservatory of Music came to him the same year. He held the post till 1933, initiating government-sponsored researches into folk lore and ancient instruments. One of the results of this renaissance of Indian culture was the founding in Mexico City of a small orchestra using archaic Aztec and Nahua instruments, such as the *teponaxtles* (percussion), *sonaja* (rattles), *vihuela* (guitars), and instruments made of clay

Chávez was also made head of the Mexican Department of Fine Arts of the Secretariat of Education, in 1934 writing a score for orchestra and chorus entitled *Llamadas* (*Calls*), for the dedication of the Palace of Fine Arts *Llamadas* was based on the same theme employed by the painter Diego Rivera in the hall's murals, described by Luis Sandi as "an invitation to rebellion and a chant of hope for the oppressed classes."

L. B.

Luigi Cherubini

BORN: FLORENCE, ITALY, SEPT. 14, 1760. DIED: PARIS, MAR. 15, 1842.

*As a composer Cherubini was no pseudo-classic but a really great
artist, whose purity of style, except at rare moments, just failed to
express the ideals he never lost sight of, because in his love of those
ideals there was too much fear.*—DONALD FRANCIS TOVEY.

Overture to the Ballet Opera "Anacreon"

'N ONE of the few occasions when Napoleon Bonaparte assumed the role of
usic critic, he remarked to Luigi Cherubini: "You have great talent, Citoyen
1erubini, but your music is too loud; let us talk of Paisiello's, which lulls me
ntly." Cherubini replied blandly: "I understand perfectly, Citoyen Consul—
u prefer music that does not prevent you from dreaming of affairs of state."
apoleon made him pay for the taunt. While in power, he prevented Cherubini
om rising to his rightful position in Parisian music and society. Discouraged,
1erubini stopped composing for a while and found relief in painting pictures
his country place. He never forgave Napoleon. During the Hundred Days
llowing Napoleon's escape from Elba, Cherubini lived in London. When
ey brought him news of Waterloo he nodded grimly. At last he could square
counts with the imperial upstart. At his next concert in London he conducted
e *Anacreon* overture.

If revenge was sweet for Cherubini, other memories evoked by the *Anacreon*
erture were less so. Eleven years earlier the premiere of the ballet opera,
nacréon, ou l'Amour fugitif, had been a scandalous fiasco. A pitiless audience
1d laughed itself sick over an inept libretto about the bibulous Greek poet
ho had choked to death on a raisin seed. Hissing mingled with guffaws as
nacreon uttered solemn platitudes about wine and women. At one point the
anagement feared the performance would have to be halted. That was when
nacreon addressed an attendant, whom he was offering a drink, as *mon
clave intéressant* (my interesting slave). It was sometime before the uproar
bsided. The evening, however, had begun promisingly—the overture was a
eat success and remained one. For, like dozens of similar compositions in
e concert repertory, the *Anacreon* is an overture that long ago discarded
opera.

Though tinged with the romanticism of the period, the *Anacreon* overture is
1iefly remarkable for its purity and nobility of classic line. The stately chords
the opening have been likened to Doric temple columns in solidity and

dignity. Pages of the overture remind one of Gluck's *Iphigenia in Aulis* overture as well as the finale of Mozart's Symphony in E flat. Noel Straus once pointed out the striking similarity between the main theme of the Overture and the opening theme of another work composed the same year—Beethoven's *Eroica Symphony*. Rossini later utilized a device strikingly developed by Cherubini in this overture, *i.e.*, the extended and gradually built up crescendo. This occurs in the main section (Allegro, D major, 4/4), following a long, murmurous passage. Perhaps the best example of Rossini's own use of the device is found in the *Semiramide* overture. A slow introduction (Largo assai, D major, 2/2), leading to a poetic colloquy between horns and wood wind, and ending in a fortissimo tutti, precedes the Allegro section of Cherubini's overture. Woven into the fabric are several themes from the opera. The scoring calls for two flutes, two oboes, two clarinets, two bassoons, four horns, two trumpets, three trombones, tympani, and strings.

History has been rather unkind to the composer of *Anacreon,* whose full name was Maria Luigi Carlo Zenobio Salvatore Cherubini. Niggardly notice is taken of him today, yet during his lifetime serious musicians ranked him with Mozart and Beethoven. To the public his fame even surpassed theirs. Composers like Mendelssohn, Weber, Spohr sang his praises. His influence was felt by Schumann and Brahms. The operas of Weber, Spontini, and Meyerbeer show traces of Cherubini's best style. A Viennese writer daringly predicted in 1806 that Beethoven's *Fidelio* would some day rank beside Cherubini's *Faniska!* Critics ridiculed him. "As a contrapuntist," said a recent writer, "he was worthy to walk arm in arm with Bach." Today a seasoned concert-goer could be forgiven for asking: "Who was Cherubini?" Someone might even reply, "The gruff, diehard classicist who once threw Hector Berlioz out of the Paris Conservatory."

L. B.

Overture to "The Water Carrier"

PRODUCED AT the Théâtre de la Rue Feydeau, Paris, on Jan. 16, 1800, the three-act opéra comique, *Les Deux Journées* (*The Two Days,* though known in English as *The Water Carrier*) made its Italian-born composer famous. Both Beethoven and Goethe later wrote warmly of the work. Nor was Bouilly, the librettist, without his day of glory. In the opera, Count Armand, President of the French Parliament, and his wife Constance escape Cardinal Mazarin's persecution by hiding in a cart belonging to a Savoyard water carrier named Mikeli. Sometime after the premiere of the opera, a delegation of Parisian water carriers visited Bouilly. They offered the librettist a year's supply of water free of charge! Though the plot is set in the reign of Louis XIII, the veiled allusions to the recent Reign of Terror were not lost on the Parisian

dience. Bouilly supposedly based the story on an actual hairbreadth escape
ring the revolutionary upheaval.

Divided into two sections, the overture (E major, 4/4) opens with an
ndante (molto sostenuto), serving as introduction to the body of the over-
re—an Allegro constructed on two themes. One analyst sensed "forebodings
evil, dreamy prophecies of impending woe" in the grave Andante opening.
he first theme of the Allegro, announced by strings and picked up fortissimo
the full orchestra, is supposed to depict Count Armand, the escaping official.
he mellower second theme, given out first by bassoons and violas, is thought
express the wife's tender devotion and anxiety.

The overture is scored for two flutes, two oboes, two clarinets, two bassoons,
ree horns, bass trombone, tympani, and strings.

L. B.

Frédéric Chopin

BORN: ZELAZOWA-WOLA, POLAND, FEB. 22, 1810. DIED: PARIS, OCT. 17, 1849.

The piano bard, the piano rhapsodist, the piano mind, the piano soul is Chopin. Tragic, romantic, lyric, heroic, dramatic, fantastic, soulful, sweet, dreamy, brilliant, grand, simple: all possible expressions are found in his compositions, and all are sung by him upon his instrument.—ANTON RUBINSTEIN.

Concerto for Piano and Orchestra in E minor, No. Op. 11

I. Allegro maestoso. II. Romanze. III. Rondo.

CHOPIN WROTE two piano concertos, the present one in E minor and a previo one in F minor. The reason for the reversed numbering is owing to the f that the E minor was published first. This work is dedicated to "M. Fr. Ka brenner," a pianist and composer some twenty years older than Chopin. It w given its first performance in a Warsaw theater on Oct. 11, 1830, at a conce which offered, besides, a symphony by C. Gorner, an aria by Carlo Eva Silva, which was sung by Anna Wolkow, the overture to Rossini's *Willia Tell,* a cavatina from that composer's *La Donna Del Lago,* delivered Constantia Gladkowska, a young artist who happened to be, at that time, t object of Chopin's affections, and a fantasia on Polish airs, composed a performed by Chopin. He played his own Concerto on that occasion.

Chopin scored the E minor Concerto for two flutes, two oboes, two clarine two bassoons, four horns, two trumpets, trombone, three kettledrums, strin and solo piano. Since the composer's powers of orchestration were not t brilliant, the orchestral score has undergone revision by several editors.

The first movement follows a traditional plan, such as Mozart or Beethov might have employed. The orchestra announces the principal theme in tv sections—the first giving the melody to the violins forte, the second doi likewise though piano. A second subject comes through also in the strings a leads into its exposition by the solo piano. There follows a pianistic developme of the material, involving much bravura and technical coloration. All throu; the movement piano and orchestra lines interweave. The piano closes t movement with glittering passage work.

The second movement, aptly named Romanze, is whimsically described l Chopin himself in a letter written May 25, 1830:

The adagio is in E major, and of a romantic, calm, and partly melancholy character. It is intended to convey the impression which one receives when the eye rests on a beloved landscape that calls up in one's soul beautiful memories—for instance, on a fine moonlit spring night. I have written for violins with mutes an accompaniment to it. I wonder if that will have a good effect? Well, time will show.

The concluding Rondo has a sixteen-bar introduction by the orchestra, following which the piano brings out the main theme scherzando. After some measures of working out, the solo instrument announces a new subject risoluto. Considerable passage work follows; after that the second subject, in different guise, is played by the piano over a delicate string accompaniment. More bravura passages, a recapitulation, and a rousing coda conclude the Concerto.

A curious custom prevailed in those days, which dictated that the movements of concertos or symphonies sandwich somewhere between them contrasting divertissements, thus, the Allegro of the Concerto was separated from the ensuing Romanze by Soliva's aria. The Concerto met with instantaneous favor, its Allegro being vociferously applauded.

The day after the premiere performance, Chopin wrote to his close friend Titus Wojciechowski, "Yesterday's concert was a success; I hasten to let you know. I inform your Lordship that I was not a bit, not a bit, nervous and played the way I play when I am alone, and it went well. Full hall."

The Constantia Gladkowska previously referred to was a singer who made her operatic debut in a work by Fernando Paer entitled *Agnese* in 1830. Chopin could utter winged words concerning her art, but he lacked the courage to tell her of his love. He asked his friend, John Matuszynski, to intercede for him once when he learned the lady was indisposed, "God forbid," he wrote, "that she should suffer in any way on my account. Set her mind at rest and tell her that as long as my heart beats I shall not cease to adore her. Tell her even that after my death my ashes shall be strewn under her feet." Why the lady should suffer on his account, in the first place, is not known. But be that as it may, Miss Gladkowska was married to a Warsaw merchant the following year, a situation that Chopin survived rather handsomely. Some years later he even found the courage to propose marriage to a daughter of Count Wodzinski, but papa frowned "No" on the proposed union, and that was that. The composer finally took as his blushing mate a lady named George Sand, who smoked cigars and liked to wear trousers.

R. C. B.

Concerto for Piano and Orchestra in F minor, No. 2 Op. 21

I. Maestoso. II. Larghetto. III. Allegro vivace.

CHOPIN WROTE to his friend Titus Wojciechowski in 1829: "While my thoughts were with her, I composed the Adagio of my concerto." The thoughts of the nineteen-year-old composer, of course, were again with Constantia Gladkowska: For it is the memory of this richly gifted singer that lies embedded in the Adagio—actually a larghetto—of Chopin's Second Piano Concerto.

Chopin's thoughts were warm, but dreamy and soothing, too, for a change. As a rule they were wild and menacing when they dwelt on Constantia: "I could tear out my hair," he once swore to Titus, "when I think that I could be forgotten by her!" Constantia, alas, did not find it hard to forget the pining young genius!

To Titus, Chopin also confided that in Constantia he had found his ideal; that he worshipped her "faithfully and sincerely," adding, with almost grotesque casualness, that for the past six months he had not exchanged a single syllable with the aloof beauty "of whom I dream every night." Once in Vienna he dined with a Mrs. Beyer merely because the lady bore the name of Constantia, and he confessed tingling with pleasure whenever a pocket handkerchief or napkin marked "Constantia" came into his hands. Writing to a friend about his idol, he stopped abruptly after the syllable "Con-," remarking, "No, I cannot complete her name, my hand is too unworthy." We have the more sober authority of Franz Liszt that the girl was "sweet and beautiful." Like many others, Chopin greatly admired Constantia's voice. In his letters he even speaks highly of her "pure intonation and genuine warmth of feeling." After hearing her sing an aria at a concert, Zielinski told Chopin that "her low B alone was worth a thousand ducats."

Despite the "inspirational" part played by Constantia Gladkowska in the composition of the Concerto, the dedication is to the Countess Delphine Potocka, a rich and cultivated singer who maintained a lavish salon in Paris. She was a loyal friend and proved herself worthy of the dedication. She hurried back to Paris from Nice to be at Chopin's bedside when she heard of his fatal illness. Gallant to the end, Chopin exclaimed as she entered the room: "Now I know why God has delayed so long in calling me to Him. He wanted me to have the pleasure of seeing you once more." Urged by the dying man, the Countess sang. What she sang has been a matter of dispute, some biographers claiming a hymn by Stradella, some a psalm by Marcello, some an air by Pergolesi, and some an aria by Bellini. Anyway, she sang—and Chopin was grateful.

The F minor Concerto was first heard at Chopin's concert debut in Warsaw
Mar. 17, 1830. All available seats were sold long in advance, and the rising
genius enjoyed a great success in the double role of composer pianist. Following
quaint practice of the time, the opening Allegro was separated on the pro-
ram from the Larghetto and Rondo. Sandwiched between them was a
Divertissement for the French Horn, composed and played by Görner," to
quote from the printed program. Listed as concluding number was a medley
National Airs, "composed and played by Chopin." We have the composer's
own report on the concert:

The first Allegro of the F minor Concerto (not intelligible to all) received the
award of a "Bravo." But I believe this was given because the public wished to
how that it understands and knows how to appreciate serious music. There are
people enough in all countries, who like to assume the air of connoisseurs! The
adagio [Larghetto] and Rondo produced a very great effect. After these the
applause and the "Bravos" came really from the heart. But the potpourri on
Polish airs missed fire completely. There was some applause, to be sure, but evi-
ently only to show the player that the audience had not been bored.

In the opening movement (Maestoso, F minor, 4/4) Chopin follows classic
precedent by having first the orchestra, then the solo instrument, expound the
material. The strings give out the chief subject, the oboe, followed by first
violins, then taking up the second theme, this time in A flat major. After some
prefatory measures, the piano discourses the leading theme and prolongs it.
Brilliant passage work now leads to the second subject, again in A flat major.
The piano next brings in fresh material, in C minor. There is development,
limited to the first theme, the orchestra sounds a tutti, and piano and orchestra
review the material. In the second movement (Larghetto, A flat major, 4/4)
Chopin's designation of Adagio in his letters is misleading, since he merely
meant "slow movement" by the term), the piano unfolds the poetic theme with
great delicacy and then embroiders on it. The strings support the piano as it
enters a declamatory phase. Finally, the Larghetto subject returns in the piano
with added embroidery, followed by a brief coda. Weakest in structure is the
third movement (Allegro vivace, F minor, 3/4), opening with an announcement of the chief theme by the piano. After an orchestral passage, followed by
the theme's return in more striking guise, the piano goes on from a descending
sequence to a brilliant passage in triplets. Comment on the chief theme by the
strings is cut short by the return of the piano in a secondary A flat major
subject, with the strings giving mild support. The piano and orchestra work
over the material, and a horn solo ushers in the final section, featuring more
piano triplets.

L. B.

Muzio Clementi

BORN: ROME, ITALY, 1752. DIED: EVESHAM, WORCESTERSHIRE, ENGLAND, MAR. 10, 1832

A fundamentally classic spirit, severely trained, and the possessor of a truly exceptional constructive and polyphonic technique, Clementi in these symphonies aims visibly to renew the great classic heredity with with the new aspirations of the century.—ALFRED CASELLA.

Symphony in D major, No. 2
[Revised by Alfredo Casella]

I. Andante sostenuto; Allegro vivace. II. Larghetto cantabile. III. Minuett pastorale. IV. Finale: Allegro molto vivace.

UNTIL 1917, musicians had repeatedly asked the question, "Where are th symphonies of Muzio Clementi?" Though remembered chiefly as teacher pianist, composer of elegant sonatas and sonatinas, author of a famous key board manual *"Gradus ad Parnassum,"* publisher and manufacturer, the grea Clementi was also known to have experimented in orchestral compositior Surviving records showed that more than twenty of his symphonies had bee performed in London alone between 1785 and 1832. Paris and the Germa cities had also heard them. Contemporary comments were highly favorabl And Clementi himself had spoken of the symphonies as his "testament t posterity." Yet only two of Clementi's symphonies were ever printed, in 178 What had become of the others?

The one known fact was that Clementi had bequeathed his huge estat including the manuscripts, to his widow. Then, in 1871, the British Museur acquired some Clementi papers. These included the first movement of Symphony in D. There was still no clue to the whereabouts of the bulk Clementi's "testament." A suspicion gained ground that the dying Clemen considering them defective, had ordered the symphonies destroyed.

The theory of their irretrievable loss did not satisfy the French schola Wyzewa and Saint-Foix, who had been doing research in their specialty, t life and music of Mozart. They examined the Clementi music at the Briti Museum early in 1914. So stunned were they by its beauty, they promptly too up the cry, "Where are the symphonies of Clementi?" They urged a hu; manuscript hunt on the British music public. "We feel certain," they declare "that the discovery of these works would be of the greatest importance for t history of European music and especially for the history of music in Englanc 'heir "hunch" was right; but for three years there was silence in England—and so a war.

Then, in 1917, a British musicologist, Dr. William H. Cummings, died. tuffed in a chest in the attic of his house was a jumble of dusty old music heets. Closer scrutiny revealed them to be Clementi manuscripts. Here were hole movements of at least four symphonies—in all 154 sheets. The Cummings estate put them up for auction at Sothebys. And there, on the incentive f Dr. Carl Engel, they were purchased for the Library of Congress in Vashington, D. C. How the Clementi manuscripts fell into Dr. Cummings' ossession remains one of the few gaps in the mystery still to be filled.

In any case, Saint-Foix came to Washington in 1924 and summarized his ndings in the *Revue de Musicologie*. Though parts were missing, there were our symphonies to be pieced together from the heap of manuscript. "Unclassied, often undecipherable, full of erasures, deletions, and changes," was his eport on the state of the long-lost treasure. Clementi had apparently never ested in his work of revision. Even after constant performance, he had evidently continued the grim work of improving his symphonies. Heinrich Simon, riting for the *Musical Quarterly* in 1942, describes how shocked he was while aspecting the manuscript. "Most of the sheets looked as if rats had set themelves to gnawing at them without mercy," he wrote, in many instances noticing ne absence of anything resembling a margin. (Clementi, who was notoriously rifty, is said to have felt very strongly on the subject of paper wastage.)

Where margins do exist in the manuscript, Clementi did not overlook their se for making personal memoranda. One such note, appearing on a page of ne D major Symphony, reads: "Lent to Emma 50+5—10 sh. 110+50 5+4.55." Emma was Clementi's English wife, possibly addicted to exceeding her budget. Other jottings include two Latin inscriptions: *Non cuiumque datum est habere nasum* (it is not given to everyone to possess a nose) nd *Risu inepto res ineptior nulla est* (nothing is more inept than inept aughter). Scholars have not yet established just what bearing they had on ne domestic situation, though one cannot help speculating.

After Saint-Foix a still more practical visitor to the Library of Congress vas Alfredo Casella. Long a devotee of Clementi's music, the Italian comoser resolved to restore the symphonies to working shape. Accordingly, it is Casella who writes the closing chapter of this lost-and-found mystery. After pending a week over the manuscript in October, 1934, he declared all four ymphonies "capable of restitution." The first symphony gave most trouble, he pieces were so scattered. Less problematic was the second, in D major, or the Library of Congress possessed all but the introduction and the opening bars of the first Allegro. Casella then made an exciting discovery. Some f the fragments in the British Museum were the very parts missing from he D major Symphony! There was some protest from Saint-Foix, whe viewed the joining of these parts as an esthetic mesalliance. Casella bluntly retorted: "The manuscript of this symphony is complete to the last detail, and entirely ready for performance." Thus reconstructed, the D major Symphony, No. 2, was heard in Italy, a century after its "disappearance" early in 1936 on a broadcast of the Augusteo Orchestra in Rome. Casella conducted. The music correspondent of the *New York Times* then reported that the Clementi symphonies

revealed Muzio Clementi as one of the great masters of the modern symphony in a vital transitional period between the eighteenth and early nineteenth centuries, when circumstances and over-hasty criticism robbed Italy of the honor of having contributed to the development of symphonic art. A serious gap in the history of Italian symphony is now filled. Built on the classic eighteenth-century model, they still contain elements betokening the birth of a new art epoch.

The D major Symphony, No. 2, as restored by Casella, was introduced to America on Dec. 4, 1936, at a concert of the Boston Symphony Orchestra conducted by Serge Koussevitzky. On that occasion Mr. Koussevitzky predicted that the work was "bound to become an indispensable part of the standard repertory." During the intermission a message was read expressing the "good wishes" of Mrs. Cecilia Clementi Pitman, of Bronxville, N. Y., who described herself as "a great granddaughter of Muzio Clementi." Mr. Rodzinski introduced the symphony to Philharmonic-Symphony audiences at the concerts of Nov. 16 and 17, 1944.

All four of Clementi's rehabilitated symphonies are scored for wood winds in twos, two horns, two trumpets, three trombones, tympani, and strings.

L. B.

Frederick Shepherd Converse

BORN: NEWTON, MASS., JAN. 5, 1871. DIED: WESTWOOD, MASS., JUNE 8, 1940.

*I am through with the extravagant elements of modern music. No
more experimentation of that sort for me. It is already old-fashioned.
What we need is deeper spiritual and emotional significance in our
music. Given that, all the rest will take care of itself.*—FREDERICK
SHEPHERD CONVERSE, *in* 1938.

"Flivver Ten Million": A Joyous Epic Inspired by the Familiar Legend "The Ten-millionth Ford Is Now Serving Its Owner"

THE WIDELY advertised achievement of the Ford plant, "The Ten-millionth
Ford Is Now Serving Its Owner," flashed on billboards and windows in the
mid-twenties, stirred Frederick Shepherd Converse to symphonic action. He
found magic in the line, a magic worthy, as he confessed, "of celebration in
music and verse." What other product of this age had so entwined itself
around the lives of our people, he asked in a note to Philip Hale, annotator of
the Boston Symphony Orchestra. He goes on to say:

The marvel of its success seemed far to outshine the wonders of Aladdin's
lamp, or the golden touch of Midas. Here was epic poetry right at hand; and as I
thought of it, it seemed that the things about us are more vital to us than anything
else. The ancients had their Scylla and Charybdis; we have our semaphore and
"traffic cop," all equally perilous to pass: and I believe that the moon shines as
tenderly on the roadside in Westwood as ever it did on the banks of Euphrates.
Hearing and admiring *Pacific 231*, I said to myself, "I too must try something
of this kind for the *Flivver*."

I set about it purely for my amusement, and not too seriously; for he who wishes
to express American life or experience must include the saving grace of humor.
I wondered what Mark Twain would have done with such a theme if he had been
a musician. The piece turned out to be quite frankly program music, and this is
the story as it came to me:

Dawn in Detroit. Chanticleer announces the dawn—the city stirs—sunrise.
The Call to Labor. Bells—distant factory whistles.
The Din of the Builders. Fugal factory noises.
The Birth of the Hero. From the welter emerges the hero, full-fledged, ready
for service. He tries his metal. He wanders off into the great world in search of
adventure.

May Night by the Roadside. America's Romance.
The Joy Riders. America's Frolic.
The Collision. America's Tragedy.
Phoenix Americanus. The hero, righted and shaken, proceeds on his way wit redoubled energy, typical of the indomitable spirit of America.

The form is entirely free. The above episodes are rather short and are containe in one movement. There are some chief motives which serve for thematic deve opment, like that of "The Builders" and many subsidiary ones.

The instruments used in *Flivver Ten Million* comprise three flutes an piccolo, two oboes, English horn, two clarinets, bass clarinet, two bassoon contra-bassoon, four horns, three trumpets, three trombones, tuba, a set o three tympani, bass drum, snare drum, tambourine, cymbals, bell, tam-tam Ford automobile horn, slapstick, rattle, xylophone, anvil, wind machine, celesta two harps, organ, and strings.

The first "road test" of Converse's orchestral motor car occurred at a con cert of the Boston Symphony Orchestra on Apr. 20, 1927. That summe Willem van Hoogstraten wheeled the new vehicle into the New York aren at a Philharmonic concert in the Lewisohn Stadium.

George Gershwin used a finished product of the *genus auto* in his sym phonic travelogue *An American in Paris*. Of course, it is not a Ford; or, a any rate, Gershwin did not specify the make. But we are made aware of Parisian cousin of the four-wheeled "hero" in several warning blares of ar automobile horn. So much for surface locomotion. In the conquest of space there have been at least two symphonic odes to mechanical flight, beside the many dedicated to Phaeton's mythical climb to the sun. In 1920, Emersor Whithorne wrote *The Aeroplane, a Tonal Impression of Flight,* and in 1946 Marc Blitzstein waxed rhapsodic over man's winged victory in a choral sym phony *The Airborne*. In the broadly mechanical line, Mossoloff the Russiar turned his orchestra into a realistic *Iron Foundry*. The Machine Age in music obviously did not end—or begin—with Honegger's *Pacific* 231.

Converse abandoned a business career to give all his time to music. Though he had prepared himself at Harvard for banking and finance, he had also studied music with John K. Paine. Later he supplemented his studies with Carl Baermann and George Whitfield Chadwick and attended and gradu ated from the Royal Academy of Music in Munich. After instructing for two years at the New England Conservatory, Converse returned to Harvard to teach composition, but resigned in 1907, after three years, to devote his full energies to writing music. Some years later, however, he returned to the New England Conservatory, becoming Dean of the Faculty in 1931.

Among Converse's numerous works—many still in manuscript—are sym phonies, overtures, symphonic poems, concertos, chamber music, a cantata, an ratorio, incidental music to plays, and several operas. The Metropolitan Opera Company singled out his one-act romantic opera *The Pipe of Desire* for production on Mar. 18, 1910, thus establishing a precedent for the performance here of operas by American composers.

L. B.

Aaron Copland

BORN: BROOKLYN, N. Y., NOV. 14, 1900.

It seems to me that we American composers have become more self-reliant. Speaking for myself, I know that I no longer feel the need of seeking out conscious Americanisms. Because we live here and work here, we can be certain that when our music is mature it will also be American in quality. American individuals will produce an American music, without any help from conscious Americanisms. There doesn't seem to me to be any short-cut to that end.—AARON COPLAND.

"Statements for Orchestra"

I. Militant. II. Cryptic. III. Dogmatic. IV. Subjective. V. Jingo. VI. Prophetic.

COMMISSIONED BY the League of Composers for performance by the Minneapolis Symphony Orchestra, this work consists of six brief sections. The composer spent the summer of 1934 at Lake Bemidji, Minnesota, where he sketched several of the movements. The others had been planned as early as 1933, at Friend's Lake, New York. The orchestration was completed in New York City, June, 1935. However, only the fifth and sixth sections were played by the Minneapolis Symphony under Eugene Ormandy's direction over an NBC broadcast on Jan. 9, 1936.

The title *Statements* was chosen to indicate short, terse, orchestral movements of a well-defined character, each lasting three minutes. The separate movements were given suggestive titles as an aid to the public in understanding what the composer had in mind when writing these pieces.

The "Militant" statement is based on a single theme, announced unisono, at the beginning by three flutes, two oboes, bassoon, and strings. The "Cryptic" statement is orchestrated for brass and flute alone with an occasional use of bass clarinet and bassoon. The "Dogmatic" statement is in tri-partite form; the middle section quotes the theme of the composer's *Piano Variations*. The "Subjective" statement is scored for strings alone, without double basses. The "Jingo" statement utilizes the full orchestra. It is built in rondo form on a chromatic melody with occasional bows to a well-known tune. The final section, a "Prophetic" statement, is rhapsodic in form and centers about a chorale-like melody sung by the solo trumpet. *Statements for Orchestra* is dedicated to Mary Senior Churchill. Dimitri Mitropoulos led the premiere of this score at a New York Philharmonic-Symphony concert in Carnegie Hall on Jan. 7, 1942.

Soon after his graduation from Boys' High School, Brooklyn, Mr. Copland began the study of harmony and composition with Rubin Goldmark. That was in 1917. Four years later he became enrolled in the American school at Fontainebleau, subsequently working with Nadia Boulanger. He returned to this country in 1924, and, almost unbrokenly, since then his time has been divided between composing and lecturing. Mr. Copland can point with pride to the fact that he was the first composer to receive a Guggenheim Fellowship (1925-1927). He has been active as a lecturer at the New School for Social Research, and his interest in contemporary music is evidenced by his sponsoring, in association with Roger Sessions, the Copland-Sessions Concerts, offering programs of music by budding American composers. He founded the American Festivals of Contemporary Music, held at Yaddo, Saratoga Springs, N. Y. Mr. Copland is a member of the faculty at the Boston Symphony Orchestra's Berkshire Music Center, at Tanglewood, Lenox, Mass. He has written numerous articles for musical periodicals, as well as several books.

In his lucidly written book *Our New Music,* Mr. Copland discusses, among other pertinent subjects, the necessity for the composer to become acquainted with the problems and possibilities facing him today. He says:

Our concert halls are little more than musical museums where the same music and the same composers are on permanent display day by day, year after year. In such surroundings every new piece and every new composer takes on the air of an intruder.

Composers during the past ten years have gradually begun to realize that an entirely new public is listening to music. This is not a concertgoing public but a public that gets its music through the radio, the phonograph, or even the movies. It seems to me that the introduction of these new means for reproducing music is comparable in importance to the invention of the printing press. The spread of good music among millions of new listeners is certain to have as profound an effect on composers as the spread of literacy had upon writers. For the first time democracy has entered the realm of serious music. This is a thrilling fact, which eventually will change every phase of our musical life. . . .

The question is: Can we composers write a music that will be of interest to these hitherto untouched millions of listeners, and if so, what manner of music shall it be?

Probably no two composers would agree on an answer to this question. But one thing is certain: the new musical audiences will have to have music that they can comprehend. That is axiomatic. It must therefore be simple and direct. But there is no reason why it should not be a music that exploits all those new devices discovered during the first years of the twentieth century.

It is not a time for poignantly subjective Lieder but a time for large mass singing. We are the men who must embody the new communal ideals in a new communal music.

R. C. B.

"A Lincoln Portrait"

THIS COMPOSITION grew out of a suggestion made by the conductor André
Kostelanetz shortly after America entered the war. What Mr. Kostelanetz
had in mind was the use of music as a medium for conveying the "magnificent spirit of our country." He discussed the idea with three American composers. From that discussion resulted a panel of three portraits—*A Lincoln
Portrait* by Aaron Copland, a *Portrait for Orchestra* of Mark Twain by Jerome
Kern, and a *Portrait of Mayor Fiorello H. LaGuardia* by Virgil Thomson.

"The greatness of a nation is expressed through its people, and those people
who have achieved greatness are the logical subjects for a series of musical
portraits," Mr. Kostelanetz explained. "The qualities of courage, dignity,
strength, simplicity, and humor which are so characteristic of the American
people are well represented in these three outstanding Americans."

Mr. Kostelanetz, to whom the score is dedicated, conducted the premiere
of *A Lincoln Portrait* at a Pension Fund Concert of the Cincinnati Symphony
Orchestra in Cincinnati on May 14, 1942. The work was first performed in
Boston by the Boston Symphony on Mar. 26, 1943, and in New York by the
same orchestra the following Apr. 1. Since then *A Lincoln Portrait* has been
played by most of the major American orchestras. There have been numer-
ous performances of this work in London, Zurich, and Buenos Aires. Mr.
Copland was informed that the work, rendered with a Spanish translation of
Lincoln's fervid utterances, caused a "political demonstration" at its Buenos
Aires premiere.

For the Boston premiere, Mr. Copland informed the annotator John N.
Burk that his first impulse had been to do a portrait of Walt Whitman, "the
patron poet of all American composers." Mr. Kostelanetz, however, convinced
him that a political figure of world stature would be a wiser choice. "From
that moment," Mr. Copland wrote, "the choice of Lincoln as my subject
seemed inevitable."

In discussing my choice with Virgil Thomson, he amiably pointed out that
no composer could possibly hope to match in musical terms the stature of so
eminent a figure as that of Lincoln. Of course, he was quite right. But secretly
I was hoping to avoid the difficulty by doing a portrait in which the sitter himself might speak. With the voice of Lincoln to help me I was ready to risk the
impossible.

The letters and speeches of Lincoln supplied the text. It was a comparatively
simple matter to choose a few excerpts that seemed particularly apposite to our
own situation today. I avoided the temptation to use only well-known passages,
permitting myself the luxury of quoting only once from a world-famous speech.
The order and arrangement of the selections are my own.

The first sketches were made in February and the portrait was finished on April sixteenth. The orchestration was completed a few weeks later. I worked with musical materials of my own, with the exception of two songs of the period: the famous "Camptown Races" and a ballad that was first published in 1840 under the title "The Pesky Sarpent" but is better known today as "Springfield Mountain." In neither case is the treatment a literal one. The tunes are used freely, in the manner of my use of cowboy songs in *Billy the Kid*.

The composition is roughly divided into three main sections. In the opening section I wanted to suggest something of the mysterious sense of fatality that surrounds Lincoln's personality. Also, near the end of that section, something of his gentleness and simplicity of spirit. The quick middle section briefly sketches in the background of the times he lived. This merges into the concluding section where my sole purpose was to draw a simple but impressive frame about the words of Lincoln himself.

THE TEXT

"Fellow citizens, we cannot escape history."

That is what he said,

That is what Abraham Lincoln said:

"Fellow citizens, we cannot escape history. We of this Congress and this administration will be remembered in spite of ourselves. No personal significance or insignificance can spare one or another of us. The fiery trial through which we pass will light us down, in honor or dishonor, to the latest generation. We —even we here—hold the power and bear the responsibility."

He was born in Kentucky, raised in Indiana, and lived in Illinois.

And this is what he said:

"The dogmas of the quiet past are inadequate to the stormy present. The occasion is piled high with difficulty, and we must rise with the occasion. As our case is new, so we must think anew and act anew. We must disenthrall ourselves, and then we shall save our country."

When standing erect he was six feet four inches tall.

And this is what he said:

He said:

"It is the eternal struggle between two principles—right and wrong throughout the world . . . It is the same spirit that says, 'You toil and work and earn bread and I'll eat it.' No matter in what shape it comes, whether from the mouth of a king who seeks to bestride the people of his own nation and live by the fruit of their labor, or from one race of men as an apology for enslaving another race, it is the same tyrannical principle."

Lincoln was a quiet man.

Abe Lincoln was a quiet and melancholy man.

But when he spoke of democracy,

This is what he said:

He said:

"As I would not be a slave, so I would not be a master. This expresses my idea of democracy. Whatever differs from this, to the extent of the difference, is no democracy."

Abraham Lincoln, sixteenth President of these United States, is everlasting in the memory of his countrymen,

For on the battleground at Gettysburg, this is what he said:

This is what Abe Lincoln said:

". . . that from these honored dead we take increased devotion to that cause for which they gave the last full measure of devotion: that we here highly resolve that these dead shall not have died in vain; that this nation, under God, shall have a new birth of freedom; and that government of the people, by the people, and for the people, shall not perish from the earth."

The scoring is for wood winds in pairs, four horns, three trumpets, three trombones, tuba, percussion, harp, and strings.

L. B.

Orchestral Suite from the Ballet "Appalachian Spring"

IN ITS original scoring for thirteen instruments this music was first heard in New York on May 14, 1945, when Martha Graham and her company presented the new ballet *Appalachian Spring,* at the National Theatre. Mr. Copland promptly set to work on an arrangement for symphony orchestra. Printed at the head of the published score is the following information:

Appalachian Spring was composed in 1943-1944 as a ballet for Miss Martha Graham on a commission from the Elizabeth Sprague Coolidge Foundation. It was first performed by Miss Graham and her company at the Coolidge Festival in the Library of Congress in Washington, D. C., on Oct. 30, 1944.

The original scoring called for a chamber ensemble of thirteen instruments. The present arrangement for symphony orchestra was made by the composer in the spring of 1945. It is a condensed version of the ballet, retaining all essential features, but omitting those sections in which the interest is primarily choreographic.

The action of the ballet concerns "a pioneer celebration in spring around a newly built farmhouse in the Pennsylvania hills in the early part of the last century. The bride-to-be and the young farmer husband enact the emotions, joyful and apprehensive, their new domestic partnership invites. An older neighbor suggests now and then the rocky confidence of experience. A revivalist and his followers remind the new householders of the strange and terrible aspects of human fate. At the end the couple are left quiet and strong in their new house." [As described by Edwin Denby in the *New York Herald Tribune,* May 15, 1945. On the same day John Martin, of the *New York Times,* wrote: "It is completely simple, homely, dedicated, and a lovelier work you would have to go far to find."]

In May, 1945, *Appalachian Spring* received both the Pulitzer Prize for music and the Award of the Music Critics Circle of New York for the outstanding theatrical composition of the season 1944-1945. Artur Rodzinski introduced the concert suite on Oct. 4, 1945, at the opening concert of the New York Philharmonic-Symphony season.

Mr. Copland gave the authors the following information:

The music of the ballet takes as its point of departure the personality of Martha Graham. I have long been an admirer of Miss Graham's work. She, in turn, must have felt a certain affinity for my music because in 1931 she chose my Piano Variations as background for a dance composition entitled *Dithyramb*. I remember my astonishment, after playing the Variations for the first time at a concert of the League of Composers, when Miss Graham told me she intended to use the composition for dance treatment. Surely only an artist with a close affinity for my work could have visualized dance material in so rhythmically complex and esthetically abstruse a composition. I might add, as further testimony, that Miss Graham's *Dithyramb* was considered by public and critics to be just as complex and abstruse as my music.

Ever since then, at long intervals, Miss Graham and I planned to collaborate on a stage work. Nothing might have come of our intentions if it were not for the lucky chance that brought Mrs. Elizabeth Sprague Coolidge to a Graham performance for the first time early in 1942. With typical energy, Mrs. Coolidge translated her enthusiasm into action. She invited Martha Graham to create three new ballets for the 1943 annual fall Festival of the Coolidge Foundation in Washington, and commissioned three composers—Paul Hindemith, Darius Milhaud, and myself—to compose scores especially for the occasion.

After considerable delay Miss Graham sent me an untitled script. I suggested certain changes to which she made no serious objections. I began work on the music of the ballet in Hollywood in June, 1943, but didn't complete it until a year later in June, 1944, at Cambridge, Mass.

The premiere took place in Washington a year later than originally planned —in October, 1944. The principal roles were danced by Miss Graham, Erick Hawkins, Merce Cunningham, and May O'Donnell. Isamu Noguchi designed the architectural setting, Edith Guilfond supplied the costumes, Louis Horst conducted. Needless to say Mrs. Coolidge sat in her customary seat in the first row, an unusually interested spectator. (She was celebrating her eightieth birthday that night.)

The title *Appalachian Spring* was chosen by Miss Graham. She borrowed it from the heading of one of Hart Crane's poems, though the ballet bears no relation to the text of the poem itself.

The Suite arranged from the ballet contains the following sections, played without interruption:

1. Very slowly. Introduction of the characters, one by one, in a suffused light.

2. Fast. Sudden burst of unison strings in A major arpeggios starts the action. A sentiment both elated and religious gives the keynote to this scene.

3. Moderate. Duo for the Bride and her Intended—scene of tenderness and passion.

4. Quite fast. The Revivalist and his flock. Folksy feelings—suggestions of square dances and country fiddlers.

5. Still faster. Solo dance of the Bride—presentiment of motherhood. Extremes of joy and fear and wonder.

6. Very slowly (as at first). Transition scene to music reminiscent of the introduction.

7. Calm and flowing. Scenes of daily activity for the Bride and her Farmer-husband. There are five variations on a Shaker theme. The theme, sung by a solo clarinet, was taken from a collection of Shaker melodies compiled by Edward D. Andrews, and published under the title *The Gift To Be Simple*. The melody I borrowed and used almost literally, is called "Simple Gifts." It has this text:

> 'Tis the gift to be simple,
> 'Tis the gift to be free,
> 'Tis the gift to come down
> Where we ought to be.
> And when we find ourselves
> In the place just right,
> 'Twill be in the valley
> Of love and delight.
> When true simplicity is gain'd,
> To bow and to bend we shan't be asham'd.
> To turn, turn will be our delight,
> 'Til by turning, turning we come round right.

8. Moderate. Coda. The Bride takes her place among her neighbors. At the end the couple are left "quiet and strong in their new house." Muted strings intone a hushed, prayerlike passage. The close is reminiscent of the opening music.

The concert arrangement of *Appalachian Spring* calls for an orchestra of modest proportions: woodwinds by twos; horns, trumpets, and trombones by twos; piano, harp, percussion, and the usual strings. The score is dedicated to Mrs. Elizabeth Sprague Coolidge.

In addition to *Appalachian Spring* Mr. Copland has composed four other ballets:

Grohg (1922-1925). Not produced. An orchestral *Dance Symphony* is derived from this ballet.

Hear Ye! Hear Ye! (1934). Choreography by Ruth Page. First produced at the Chicago Opera House, Rudolph Ganz conducting, Nov. 30, 1934.

Billy the Kid (1938). Choreography by Eugene Loring. First produced by the Ballet Caravan in Chicago, October, 1938.

Rodeo (1942). Choreography by Agnes de Mille. First produced by the Ballet Russe de Monte Carlo, Franz Allers conducting, at the Metropolitan Opera House, Oct. 16, 1942.

L. B.

"Quiet City," for Trumpet, English Horn, and String Orchestra

Scored originally as incidental music to the Group Theatre's production in 1939 of Irwin Shaw's play of the same name, *Quiet City* was later premiered as a one-movement orchestral piece by the Saidenburg Little Symphony in the Town Hall, New York. Critics and public received it warmly. To one writer it evoked visions of "silent streets, the slogging gait of a dispossessed man, and some of the feeling of mournful beauty that comes from loneliness." Another sensed hints of "the opening of an Alfred Hitchcock thriller," and a third "bleak brooding spreading suggestively over the mirrored metropolis."

Mr. Shaw's play, an experimental fantasy delving into the "night thoughts of many different kinds of people in a great city," had used a trumpet player as author's mouthpiece, the recurring trumpeting being designed to "arouse the conscience of his fellow players and of the audience." After two tryout performances on successive Sunday nights in April, 1939, the play was "withdrawn for revisions." In preparing the accompanying score, Mr. Copland had in mind music that would be "evocative of the nostalgia and inner distress of a society profoundly aware of its own insecurity."

Urged by friends to make use of some of the thematic material as the basis for an orchestral piece, Mr. Copland set to work that summer after completing his duties at the Berkshire Music Center, where he served on the faculty. When the piece was played by the Boston Symphony Orchestra, Serge Koussevitzky conducting, he explained that he had "borrowed the name, the trumpet, and some themes from the original play."

In the stage version Mr. Copland was limited in the scoring to clarinet, saxophone, and piano, besides the trumpet. The addition of English horn and string orchestra and the form of the composition as a whole "was the result of work in a barn studio two miles down the road from Tanglewood," he then wrote.

The orchestration was completed in September, 1939, and the score dedicated to Ralph Hawkes, junior member of the London firm of Boosey and Hawkes, who subsequently published the music. *Quiet City* has since been played by more than forty orchestras in the United States, Canada, Great Britain, Australia, South Africa, and South America.

The composition was heard on a New York Philharmonic-Symphony program in the Lewisohn Stadium concert series on Aug. 8, 1941.

L. B.

Suite from "Billy the Kid"

AT THE suggestion of Lincoln Kirstein, director of the Ballet Caravan, Aaron Copland set to work on a score for a native American ballet, whose subject was to be the young desperado of the Wild West, Billy the Kid. Mr. Copland had doubts, at first, concerning his own qualifications as a "cowboy composer," but insistence on the part of Mr. Kirstein brushed aside all misgivings. The resultant work has proved one of the most popular in the Ballet Caravan's repertory.

Mr. Copland admits that he was torn between the use and nonuse of cowboy songs as a foundation for his music. He found certain obstacles to overcome, the major ones having to do with making an orchestral speech of the simple unaffected tunes, and another none-too-negligible obstacle being his own distaste for cowboy music as such.

Mr. Kirstein, in the meantime, assured the composer that it made no difference whether or not the songs were employed, but, even as he said so, he tucked a sheaf of them under Mr. Copland's arm. In Paris, the following summer, the composer began working on the outline of the scenario, and, *mirabile dictu,* he found that his attitude toward cowboy songs had changed considerably, so much so, in fact, that the completed score carries, in full or in part, such eminent examples of musical cowboyiana as "Great Granddad," "Git Along Little Dogies," "The Old Chisholm Trail," "Old Paint," "The Dying Cowboy" and others. Mr. Copland did not interpolate "Home on the Range," for, as he puts it, "I had to draw the line some place."

The Suite consists of six episodes from Mr. Copland's music for *Billy The Kid,* sandwiched between the initial section, "The Open Prairie," and its repetition.

R. C. B.

"El Sálon México"

THE FIRST performance of this work was given by the Mexico Symphony Orchestra under the direction of Carlos Chávez on Aug. 27, 1937. Since then it has become quite a programmatic fixture with orchestras in the United States. *El Sálon México* is scored for two flutes, piccolo, two oboes, English horn, two clarinets, E flat clarinet, bass clarinet, two bassoons, contra-bassoon, four horns, three trumpets, three trombones, tuba, tympani, military drum, tambour de Provence, bass drum, cymbals, Chinese blocks, wood block, gourd, and xylophone. The composition is dedicated to Victor Kraft.

Mr. Copland's own explanation of *El Sálon México* follows:

During my first visit to Mexico, in the fall of 1932, I conceived the idea of writing a piece based on Mexican themes. I suppose there is nothing strange in such an idea. Any composer who goes outside his native land wants to return bearing musical souvenirs. In this case my musical souvenirs must have been very memorable, since it wasn't until 1933 that I began to assemble them into the form of an orchestral work.

From the very beginning the idea of writing a work based on popular Mexican melodies was connected in my mind with a popular dance hall in Mexico City called Sálon México. No doubt I realized, even then, that it would be foolish for me to attempt to translate into musical sounds the more profound side of Mexico; the Mexico of the ancient civilization or the revolutionary Mexico of today. In order to do that one must really know a country. All that I could hope to do was to reflect the Mexico of the tourists, and that is why I thought of the Sálon México. Because in that "hot spot" one felt, in a very natural and unaffected way, a close contact with the Mexican people. It wasn't the music I heard, but the spirit that I felt there, which attracted me. Something of that spirit is what I hope to have put into my music.

I followed no general rule in the use of the themes that I treated. Almost all of them come from the *Cancionero Mexicano* by Frances Toor, or from the erudite work of Ruben M. Campos, *El folk-lore y la Musica Mexicana*. To both authors I owe thanks. Probably the most direct quotation of a complete melody is that of *El Mosco* (No. 84 in the book by Campos), which is presented twice, immediately after the introductory measures (in which may be found fragments of *El Palo Verde* and *La Jesusita*).

R. C. B.

Arcangelo Corelli

BORN: FUSIGNANO, NEAR IMOLA, ITALY, FEB. 17, 1653. DIED: ROME, JAN. 8, 1713.

His merit was not depth of learning like that of Alessandro Scarlatti, nor great fancy or rich invention in melody or harmony, but a nice ear and most delicate taste which led him to select the most pleasing harmonies and melodies and to construct the parts so as to produce the most delightful effect upon the ear.—GEMINIANI.

"Christmas Concerto," Concerto Grosso, No. 8, in G minor ("Fatto per la Notte di Natale"), Op. 6

I. Vivace; Grave; Allegro. II. Adagio; Allegro. III. Vivace. IV. Allegro; Pastorale.

LIKE HANDEL, Corelli wrote twelve concerti grossi. And the parallel goes further. Each composer had them published as a set, and each set is numbered Opus 6! Corelli's twelve appeared in 1712 in Rome, Handel's in 1730 in London. Moreover, Handel did not hesitate to use the Roman dozen as a model for the London set. Corelli and Vivaldi had become cherished models in instrumental writing of this kind. Of course, Handel and Bach stamped their own genius on the concerto-grosso form.

Further resemblance between the Corelli and Handel concerts is seen in the allotment of instruments. Like Handel's concertos, Corelli's *Christmas Concerto* is scored for two solo violins and solo cello (comprising the so-called "concertino obbligato") and two violins, viola, and bass (comprising the "concerto grosso"). Corelli adds the words: *Ad arbitrio che si potranno radoppiare, i.e.,* "with the option of doubling" the instruments. Supplementary musicians thus engaged were called *ripienisti,* which may be freely translated from the Italian as "fillers-in."

How the eighteenth-century concerto grosso worked out in general practice may be gathered from a picture in the British Museum. There Handel is shown with his instrumental ensemble. The seating plan makes clear the relation of the two groups. Handel is surrounded, rather than merely confronted, by the musicians. He is seated at a double-keyboard clavicembalo. To his right, directly under his eye, is grouped the "concertino," the solo players. Behind him, out of sight, are the supporting players—the "concerto grosso"—and *ripienisti.* The "concertino" group, accordingly, were within direct range of the "conductor's" signals. This group relayed his wishes to the others. "The different bodies of the Handelian orchestra governed one another with elasticity," Romain Rolland points out in his book on Handel, "and it was the incisive rhythm of the little cembalo which put the whole mass into motion."

The word "concerto" was probably first applied to music for a solo instrument and accompaniment by Scipio Bargaglia in a manual published in Venice in 1587. A century later, Giuseppe Torelli adopted the term "concerto grosso" to cover a "concerto" with a greater number of instruments. Yet in 1691, seventeen years before Torelli's death, Michelletti published his "Sinfonie et concerti a quatro," and in 1698 a sheaf of "Concerti musicali." The term "concerto" recurs in seventeenth-century tracts. However, it was this same Torelli who determined the form of the grand solo for violin and, as Philip Hale observed, "opened the way to Arcangelo Corelli, the father of modern violinists, composers, or virtuosos."

The noted violinist Francesco Geminiani was only one of the numerous pupils of this sire of virtuosos. Others were Pietro Locatelli—whose effects of changed accordature were later imitated by Paganini—and Pietro Castrucci, who for a time was first violinist in Handel's opera orchestra. Corelli's own violin teacher was not Giovanni Battista Bassani, as was long assumed, but Giovanni Benvenuti of Bologna. Matteo Simonelli taught him counterpoint. Corelli spent three years in Germany, from 1679 to 1681, largely in Munich, in the employ of the Elector of Bavaria, though there is evidence of his appearing in Heidelberg and Hanover, where the Elector George, later George I of England, kept an orchestra. A supposed visit in 1672 to Paris, where Corelli allegedly aroused Lully's jealousy, is apocryphal.

In 1682, having attracted wide attention through his skill on the violin and the publication of a set of sonatas for two violins, cello, and basso continuo, Corelli, now in Rome, was invited by Cardinal Pietro Ottoboni to make his beautiful palace his home. Corelli accepted and gave concerts there every Monday, at the same time steadily adding to his pupil enrollment.

Corelli had a passion for painting. Handel, who met him during his tour of Italy, observed that Corelli "liked nothing better than seeing pictures without paying for it, and saving money." Some of the stories about Corelli's parsimony seem well founded. He is said to have dressed shabbily and walked when he could easily have paid for a carriage. When he died he left Cardinal Ottoboni some great paintings he had collected, besides the equivalent of $300,000. The cardinal kept the pictures but distributed his thrifty friend's savings to Corelli's needy relations.

The contemporary picture of Corelli is that of a modest, amiable soul, "simple in his ways of life." He was eulogized for his "nice ear and most delicate taste." George Mattheson called him "the prince of all musicians." An Italian colleague of Corelli's went even further, dubbing him *"Il virtuo-*

sissimo di violin e vero Orfeo di nostri tempi" ("the virtuoso of violin virtu
osos and the true Orpheus of our time").

Corelli's importance in musical history is based alike on his work as com
poser, especially in his treatment of instruments, and his development o
violin technic and style. Evidently not a dazzling technician himself, to judg
from the more reliable reports of one or two pupils, he cultivated instead, a
broad, polished style of expressive nobility.

In *The Oxford History of Music,* Sir Hubert Parry points out that Corell
was almost the first composer to show "a consistent instinct for style, and
this marks one of the most important attainments in the development o
instrumental music." Before Corelli, "composers had hardly any idea of adapt
ing their thoughts to the idiosyncrasies of their instruments, and for the mos
part wrote mere voice parts for them; but Corelli at last attained to the poin
of writing music to which only the instruments for which he wrote could
adequately give effect."

According to Dr. Burney, it was thanks to Corelli that the violin was "ren
dered respectable," the eighteenth-century musical historian even predicting
that it would remain so, "as long as the present system of music shall con
tinue to delight the ears of mankind."

L. B.

Suite for String Orchestra

[*Arranged for string orchestra by Ettore Pinelli*]

I. Sarabande. II. Gigue. III. Badinerie.

ETTORE PINELLI, an Italian violinist, conductor, and teacher (1843-1915),
drew the material for his arrangement from a set of twelve sonatas for violin
with basso continuo, constituting Arcangelo Corelli's Opus 5. The widely
played violin favorite *La Folia* also derives from one of these sonatas, the
twelfth. When first published in folio in Rome in 1700, the Corelli score bore
the title: XII *suonate a violino e violone o cembalo*. At least six editions of
the work were issued by 1799. Apparently the first "arrangement"—for two
flutes and bass—was that later published in London and Amsterdam. Francesco
Geminiani, a pupil of Corelli, made them into a set of Concerti Grossi, also
published in London.

The Pinelli suite, consisting of a "Sarabande," a "Gigue," and a "Bad
inerie," was introduced to America on Dec. 29, 1927, by Bernardino Molinari
on the occasion of his American debut as guest conductor of the St. Loui
Symphony Orchestra. Bach used the French word *badinerie* as title for the
last movement of his B minor Suite for Flute and Strings. Philip Hal

noted Cottgrave's *French and English Dictionary* of 1673 as defining the
word thus: "foolery, foppery, toying, tumbling, juggling, any kind of apish
umbolling."

L. B.

"La Folia," for Violin and Orchestra

LIKE so many other dances later used in instrumental music—the chaconne
and saraband among them—the "folia" was of early Spanish origin. A few
scholars have identified it as Portuguese, rather than Spanish. In any case,
before it crossed the Iberian border into France and Italy the "folia" was a
slow and stately dance in 3/4 time. To the Italians it became known as
follia di spagna, and to the French, in the plural form, as *folies d'Espagne.*
The title was later used for a species of air with variations of which Corelli's
La Folia is the most famous example. Samples of the old Spanish dance were
given by Francesco Salinas (1513-1590) in his *De Musica,* printed in Salamanca
in 1577. Writing variations on the "folia" theme became quite a sport with
subsequent composers. Vivaldi, Frescobaldi, Lully, Pergolesi, Bach, Cherubini, and Liszt, to mention only the better known names, all let their fancy
play with the graceful melody.

Corelli used the highly adaptable theme at the end of his twelve "Suonati
a violino e violone e cembalo, Op. 5." From this finale, the French violinist
Hubert Leonard (1819-1900), prepared the arrangement for violin and orchestra which has long been familiar on concert programs. The theme is
announced in D minor (Adagio, 3/4) by the violin, which then passes it to
the massed violins. A second melody is brought in by the flute. As the pace
quickens, the main theme returns to the solo instrument for its first variation,
and the violin then exchanges embroidery with several accompanying instruments. Another variation follows (Andante, 4/4) and the violin soon fades
down for a pianissimo version of the theme. The tempo again quickens, and
the violin is soon toying with the theme with pizzicato support from the
other strings. After some playful traceries, the violin once more discourses
a slow variation, and a cadenzalike passage sets in. The orchestra takes over
the theme, before giving way to the violin for a calm and tender farewell
of the "folia" theme.

L. B.

François Couperin

BORN: PARIS, NOV. 10, 1668. DIED: PARIS, SEPT. 12, 1733.

He is the courtly composer par excellence, who found court atmos-
phere as congenial as the convent is to the mystic and the ascetic.
—F. BONAVIA.

"Prelude and Allegro"

[*Transcribed for orchestra by Darius Milhaud*]

THE *Prelude and Allegro* derive from *La Sultane,* a "Sonade en Quatuor"
for strings and clavecin continuo by François Couperin, long known a
"Couperin Le Grand," as a token of esteem and to set him apart from othe
members of the gifted French family. Milhaud scored the two opening sec
tions for modern orchestra at the request of Vladimir Golschmann, who foun
the "quartet" in Volume X of Maurice Cauchie's twelve-volume edition c
Couperin's works (1932-1933), sponsored by Mrs. Louise B. Dyer, Australia
patroness of music. The St. Louis Symphony conductor discussed it with th
French composer while vacationing in California in the summer of 194(
(Milhaud was teaching at Mills College in Oakland.) The arrangement wa
then commissioned for the St. Louis season of 1940-1941. Completed by th
middle of November, the *Prelude and Allegro* were premiered by M
Golschmann's orchestra on Jan. 17, 1941. The pieces entered the Philharmoni
Symphony repertory on Mar. 10, 1943, at a concert conducted by Efren
Kurtz.

The *Prelude* opens with a grave section scored for strings and trombone
Wood winds soon join in, the mood continuing solemn and stately. Ther
follow alternations of choirs, the winds first, then the strings (in subdue
style), low strings and horns, finally the full orchestra. The *Allegro* follow
gay and spirited, but with a marked feeling and accent of Couperin's day
After a series of episodes for flutes, oboes, and violins, the fabric broadens an
develops to a vigorous climax.

Couperin was long regarded as the court composer par excellence. On
associates fastidious taste and refinement with his name, as well as a certai
artificiality. Admirers speak of his "charming artlessness," "gentle melodies,
and "airy grace." He was famous as harpsichordist and organist. His harpsi
chord manual *L'Art de toucher le clavecin,* which influenced Bach, was ded
cated to Louis XIV, who gave him the title of *Ordinaire de la musique de l*
chambre du roi. Music owes him a debt for many services, other than hi

velve-volume legacy of composition. "He reduced harmony to a system,"
ys F. Bonavia; "he taught performers to use their thumbs on the keyboard;
e was the first to write chamber music for three players; he made of the
uite' something more than a collection of oddly assorted fantasias." In ideals
id outlook he wrote for an aristocratic class "with an etiquette, a mode of
fe, and an art all of its own, as far removed from the world of men and
vely passions as a company of Trappists." Couperin, incidentally, favored
omen's hands for "tender, sentimental" passages on the harpsichord. "[They]
e generally better," he wrote. "I have already said that muscular suppleness
ontributes much more than strength to good playing." He even favored the
istaff side in choosing titles for compositions: *La Dangereuse, La Manon,
a Superbe, La Diane, La Voluptueuse, La Diligente*. As a rule the music
ives little hint of the provocative content promised. Who *La Sultane* was and
hy Couperin gave the name to a string quartet is a lost secret, if it ever was
itended as one.

L. B.

Henry Cowell

BORN: MENLO PARK, CALIF., MAR. 11, 1897.

Perhaps my method can be made clear by saying what I do not do in producing my music. I do not compose according to any set scheme. I do not compose while either in an emotional or intellectual fever. I do not follow any formula, nor do I give myself to an improvisational, unformed wandering. I do not try to follow the style of any other composer, old or new.—HENRY COWELL.

"Tales of Our Countryside"

THE FOUR sections comprising this work were written separately and at wide intervals as piano pieces. As such, the composer introduced them himsel In putting them together for the present number, Mr. Cowell made co siderable changes in their harmonic structures, besides lengthening the appreciably. He now conceives of *Tales of Our Countryside* as a compositic for piano and orchestra.

An interesting side to the creation of the piano pieces is that each was con posed in a different state of the Union, a matter that lends geographic validi to the title of the reconstructed works: "Deep Tides" was completed in Cal fornia, in 1923; "Exultation" in New York, 1928; "Harp of Life" in Iow 1925, and "Lilt of the Reel" in Kansas, 1925.

The flavor of the four sections is modal, the first, third, and fourth, of Iris character, occupying a place between the Aeolian and major modes, and th second favoring the Mixolydian. All the melodies are deliberately simple an in folk style and all original. Mr. Cowell, in other words, has chosen the pat of imitation and reference, instead of incorporating actual tunes. There is n attempt at development whatever, the themes coming in for simple exposi tion all through, a situation, the composer asserts, which prevents the con position from being a piano concerto.

Tales of Our Countryside, finished in 1940, had its world premiere in Atlan tic City at a concert of the All-American Youth Orchestra under the directic of Leopold Stokowski.

Henry Cowell attracted much attention early in his creative career for h theory of "tone clusters" (the performance of note groups on the piano b means of the fist or forearm). He has toured Europe and America, recita and concert bent, finding the time, also, to put to paper many a new compo

ion. To date his achievements as composer are numerous. He has done a
...llet (1918), a symphony, other orchestral works—in addition to *Tales of
...ur Countryside*—notably, *Synchrony* (1930), *Reel* (1933), and *Old Ameri-
...n Country Set* (1938).

R. C. B.

Paul Creston

BORN: NEW YORK, OCT. 10, 1906.

Freshness in ideas, clever colors, and a certain healthy brightness seem to prove that Creston does not write merely because he has technic, but chiefly because he feels creative urge.—LEONARD LIEBLING.

Symphony No. 2, Op. 35

I. Introduction and Song. II. Interlude and Dance.

SYMPHONY No. 2 was completed in June, 1944. It is in two movements: (1) "Introduction and Song," and (2) "Interlude and Dance," and was conceived as an "apotheosis" of the two foundations of all music: song and dance. Mr Creston has furnished the authors with the following analysis of the score

In the opening of the Introduction are presented four themes as a cumulative ground bass, *i.e.,* successively superimposed. Theme 1, played by cellos, and Theme 2, played by violas, are the main basis of the entire symphony. Whatever new thematic material emerges is either a ramification or a development of these two themes.

The Song is largely built on a variation of Theme 1, tender and simple in character, presented first by the flute and then by the horn. After a minor climax, the inversion of Theme 1 is presented by violins and is followed by Theme 2, with the mood gradually increasing in intensity. A short, agitated episode leads to the varied Theme 1 with the whole orchestra participating and played with great breadth and majesty. The movement closes quietly with the original flute theme this time played by the oboe, slightly varied rhythmically but equally tender and simple in feeling.

The Interlude opens with a completely transformed Theme 1, quite aggressive and defiant, leading to a rather quiet section, but soon returning to the aggressive character. This last merges into the Dance without pause, which after a rhythmic introduction begins with another variation of Theme 1 (muted trumpet). Each appearance of this variation of Theme 1 alters further the rhythm and contour of the melody. As the excitement mounts, Theme 2 soars above the ever-recurrent rhythmic pulses, developing to a climax and into the next section of the Dance In the second section, based on a variation of Theme 1 inverted, the rhythmic pattern has changed and there is a greater sense of driving forward. This theme variant goes through several metamorphoses as the section builds to the major climax and then subsides to an altered version of the original cumulative ground bass. Above three concurrent rhythms which were presented separately earlier in

he Dance, the flute theme of the Song (now played by violins) becoming more and
nore intense, brings the composition to a close.

Symphony No. 2 is dedicated "in profound gratitude" to Dr. William
Filler, family friend and physician. Artur Rodzinski led the premiere at a
New York Philharmonic-Symphony concert on Feb. 15, 1945.

Entirely self-taught in theory and composition, Paul Creston studied piano
with Randegger and Déthier and organ with Pietro Yon before being appointed, in 1934, organist and choirmaster of St. Malachy's Church, New
York. A Guggenheim Fellowship was awarded him in 1938 and 1939. Among
his works are a Prelude and Dance, a Partita for Flute, Violin, and Strings,
chamber music, and a tone poem, *Threnody,* besides a Symphony, Op. 20, a
Suite for Saxophone (or Clarinet) and Piano, and a Concertino for Marimba
and Orchestra, the first such work to ennoble the instrument to serious concert status. He has also conducted experiments and research in acoustics,
esthetics, and musical therapy.

In 1943, Mr. Creston garnered three awards: a Citation of Merit from
he National Association for American Composers and Conductors, a $1,000
grant by the American Academy of Arts and Letters, and the New York
Music Critics' Circle Award for his First Symphony.

Mr. Creston has been associated with the Blue Network, composing and
directing several programs. Recently he was awarded a $1,000 grant by the
Alice M. Ditson Fund.

Mr. Creston avowedly follows abstract and absolute trends in his music,
rather than fixed programs. *Threnody* marks only a partial departure from a
strictly formal and impersonal style. Generally he hews to purely formal
lines and works out conceptions entirely in musical terms, rather than at-
empting to evoke pictures or tell stories. "I regard music as a language that
begins where vocal language ends," he told the authors.

L. B.

Scherzo from Symphony, Op. 20

A DOMINANT RHYTHMIC element recurs in Mr. Creston's music. Melodic, harmonic, and formal elements, he feels, have long been explored to the neglect
of further adventures in rhythm, though admittedly he strives to give equal
stress to all factors. Thus, the first movement of his Symphony, Op. 20,
couched in sonata style, emphasizes form. The second, the Scherzo, stresses
rhythm. The third, the Andante, exploits the resources of tone color. In the
Finale, Mr. Creston seeks to synthesize all elements, with the rhythmic
predominant. He writes:

The Scherzo is a contrast to both the vigorously majestic first movement and the
serenely calm movement following it. It is in 3/4 meter. Rhythm is the reigning

element, with overlapping and subdivisional patterns abounding throughout. The middle section is cast in lyric vein, but the rhythmic aspect of the movement is maintained in the alternating figure played by the cellos and basses. Fragments of the original theme are interspersed gradually, and finally the theme itself emerge and is developed to its conclusion.

Completed in January, 1940, the symphony was premiered by the New York City Symphony, Fritz Mahler conducting, in February, 1941. Reviewing the novelty, Virgil Thomson hailed its "gusto and buoyancy," observing that Mr. Creston's "musical facility and technical command are more like what we import from Europe than like what we currently grow here." Mr. Stokowski's All American Youth Orchestra played the Scherzo several times on tour.

L. B.

Tone Poem, "Threnody"

WITH FRITZ REINER conducting, *Threnody* had its world premiere at a concert of the Pittsburgh Symphony on Dec. 2, 1938. Eugene Goossens added the work to the Cincinnati Symphony's repertory on Jan. 3 and 4, 1941, conducting it again on July 1 at a concert of the New York Philharmonic-Symphony at the Lewisohn Stadium. Mr. Creston began work on it in February, 1938, completing it two months later. Although avowedly autobiographical insofar as it grew out of a personal experience, *Threnody* should be considered on its merits as abstract music, according to the composer. The following analysis is from Mr. Creston's pen:

The introductory theme, played by muted strings alone at first and soon developed into a minor climax with the addition of other instruments is the "spiritual" theme. It is in the style of harmonized Gregorian chant; its modality is quite free. After a short fermata, the second, or "human," theme is presented by the violas, with flutes and sustained horns in the background.

The melodic interval of a fourth, which characterizes this theme, becomes extended to a fifth, a sixth, and finally a seventh, as the intensity of the emotion increases, ultimately leading to a third section, a violent outburst, and the main climax of the composition.

A gradual calming down leads to the second theme once more, this time played by violins and cellos, and so altered that only the general feeling of it is present. A short choral-like episode played by the brass choir alternating with the wood winds, brings back the first theme, also varied slightly from its original appearance. The composition comes to a quiet close with a solo flute and muted strings.

L. B.

Concerto for Saxophone (E flat alto) and Orchestra

I. Energetic. II. Meditative. III. Rhythmic.

THIS WORK was commissioned by Cecil Leeson, for whom the composer had already written a Suite and a Sonata. Like the preceding works for that instrument, it is designed to demonstrate the capabilities of the E flat alto saxophone as a solo instrument. Wilhelm Steinberg led the premiere of this concerto at a New York Philharmonic-Symphony concert on Jan. 27, 1944. Vincent J. Abato was the saxophone soloist.

The Concerto is in three movements: I. Energetic; II. Meditative; III. Rhythmic. The first movement opens with a vigorous orchestral introduction against short, interspersed, brilliant passages by the saxophone, leading to a lyric presentation of this first main theme by the orchestra, the saxophone playing an embellished version of it. The second theme is lightly rhythmic in character with a subdivisional rhythm in the accompaniment. These two themes are developed at some length, and the movement comes to an end with the main theme in augmentation played by the orchestra with brilliant scale passages by the saxophone.

The second movement utilizes the accompanying figure of the second theme in the preceding movements, as an introductory section and also as the accompanying figure throughout the entire movement. A little beyond the middle, logically though unexpectedly, a cadenza makes its appearance: a cadenza based on both the main theme and the accompanying figure of this movement . . . which leads to a quiet, meditative conclusion.

The final movement is in 4/4 meter, somewhat marchlike in tempo and scherzolike in feeling. As the second movement glorifies the tone of the saxophone, this movement stresses the staccato (tonguing) and dramatic capabilities of the instrument. True to its title "Rhythmic," the reigning element is rhythm in many phases: cross rhythms, subdivisional and overlapping rhythms, all within the 4/4 meter. The form is a modified rondo form.

L. B.

"Pastorale and Tarantella"

THIS COMPOSITION is in the form of a prelude and dance. The *Pastorale* is based on a rhythmic figure presented by bassoons and clarinets in the first measure, on which are superimposed during the movement, various aspects of a single theme first announced by three flutes in parallel triads. No new themes are introduced at any time, and the movement is really a continuous development of this single idea.

The *Tarantella* is in large ternary (A-B-A) form, with a short introduction (writes Mr. Creston). The A section is built on a ten-measure ground bass first played by the contrabasses alone, on which are piled themes and instrumental colors, developing to a presentation of it chordally in the brass choir and finally rhythmically in the tympani alone. A bridge passage leads to the B section, light in character in contrast to the dramatic quality of the first section. The repetition of the A section is slightly shortened, and the piece is brought to a vigorous conclusion..

Two of the theories as to the origin of the *Tarantella* are (1) that the dance movements were caused by the bite of the tarantula; (2) that the movements were a means of eliminating the poison injected by this type of spider. In either case, it is certain that the dance must have been a violent one . . and this is the conception the composer has adhered to. The present-day social form of the *Tarantella* is a gay and light dance of marathonic length, usually becoming a test of endurance between dancers and musicians.

Pastorale and Tarantella was completed in November, 1941, and was first performed by the NYA Symphony Orchestra under Dean Dixon, and later by the NBC Symphony Orchestra also under Dean Dixon.

                                                                    L. B.

Claude Debussy

ORN: SAINT-GERMAIN-EN-LAYE, NEAR PARIS, AUG. 22, 1862. DIED: PARIS, MAR. 25, 1918.

> *"Rien de trop"*: that is the artist's motto. Instead of amalgamating the instruments for mass effects, he throws into relief their individuality or delicately grafts one timbre on to another, without anything of their true nature being spoiled. Like the Impressionist painters of those times, he paints with pure colors, with that delicate sobriety that spurns all harshness and ugliness.—ROMAIN ROLLAND.

Prelude to "The Afternoon of a Faun"

DEBUSSY'S WAS essentially a spirit of revolt, and he manifested such tendencies early in life. Thus at the age of sixteen he is found differing with his superiors at the Paris Conservatory on doctrinal matters. Yet he proved a brilliant enough pupil to merit the Prix de Rome six years later with the cantata *L'Enfant prodigue*. Alfred Bruneau could say a scant two decades later, "One will search vainly in the academic cantata *L'Enfant prodigue,* of which the gentle Guiraud, his [Debussy's] master, was so proud, for a trace of the tendencies which now ravish some and shock others." The rebel, it seems, could hew to the line of tradition and authority when he was so moved.

He never completed his course at the Villa Medici in Rome, returning to Paris, which, like the rest of the musical world, was then at the feet of Richard Wagner. But Debussy capitulated to the siren beckonings of a group of painters known as the "Impressionists," also rebels who strained at the leash of dogma. They were headed by Edouard Manet, whose researches pursued the theory of the effect on color by light and atmosphere. To a mind and an imagination as sensitive as Debussy's, these were provocative advancements. He consorted with the proponents of the theories, and he became intimately conversant with their work. Then, turning to the writers and poets Stéphane Mallarmé, Pierre Louys, Paul Verlaine, and André Gide, the "Symbolists," he found further stimulation. The barely recognizable ideas began to take shape. It was during his spiritual apprenticeship with the Symbolists that he composed his *Ariettes Oubliées,* and here was revealed for the first time the Debussy of the later years.

Is it any wonder, then, that he was drawn to Mallarmé's "The Afternoon of a Faun," a brief pastoral poem, whose sensuous, "ingenious couplings of syllables and subtle associations of timbres" provided a quasi-music in the very sounds of the lines? He began the task of changing into music thi "euphonic putting together of words" and finished it in 1894.

The Prelude to *The Afternoon of a Faun* obtained its initial performanc on Dec. 23, 1894, under the auspices of the National Society of Music, Pari. Gustave Doret conducted. A second performance was given at a Colonn Concert, also in Paris, on Oct. 20, 1895. The piece made its American bow i Boston on Apr. 1, 1902. Walter Damrosch and the New York Symphon Orchestra introduced it to local audiences on Nov. 12, 1905.

The idea for the ballet based on the Mallarmé-Debussy collaboration ha been ascribed variously to Serge Diaghileff, Leon Bakst, and Vaslav Nijinsky However, Romola Nijinsky claims prior right for her husband. Nevertheles: it was given first at the Théâtre du Châtelet, Paris, on May 29, 1912, with choreography by Nijinsky and scenery and costumes by Bakst. Diaghileff, o course, was the producer, and the Faun was embodied by the world-renowne dancer. The premiere proved a *succès de scandale,* owing chiefly to th "Faun's amorous behavior with the scarf." Audiences at subsequent perform ances, though, showed that they could take that bright particular bit of th choreography in stride. Today the ballet is one of the most popular in th repertory, and America, too, has succumbed completely to its fascination.

R. C. B.

"La Mer" ("The Sea"): Three Symphonic Sketches

THE THREE movements of *La Mer* were originally entitled, I. "Mer belle au Îles Sanguinaires" ("Fair sea at Îles Sanguinaires"), II. "Jeux de vagues ("Play of the waves"), and III. "Le vent fait danser la mer" ("The win makes the sea dance"). Debussy later changed the first to "De l'aube à mid sur la mer" ("From dawn to noon at sea") and the third to "Dialogue du ven et de la mer" ("Dialogue of the wind and the sea"). An interesting sideligh on the change of the first section's title is the fact that the Îles Sanguinaire: little islands in the gulf of Ajaccio, had never been seen by Debussy, logicall enough, since he had never been to Corsica.

What is reputed to be Debussy's first mention of this composition appeare in a letter to Durand, dated Sept. 12, 1903. On the same day he wrote to Andr Messager:

You may not know that I was destined for a sailor's life and that it was onl quite by chance that fate led me in another direction. But I have always held passionate love for her [the sea]. You will say that the ocean does not exactl wash the Burgundian hillsides—and my seascapes might be studio landscapes; bu I have an endless store of memories and, to my mind, they are worth more tha the reality, whose beauty often deadens thought.

Debussy remembered those days as a boy of seven which he spent at Cannes. There he fell victim to the spell of the Mediterranean. During later years he often went to ocean resorts, and he expressed time and again his sentiments concerning his "old friend, the sea, always innumerable and beautiful." His marine voyages consisted, however, of two crossings of the English Channel.

Because he claimed that "the sight of the sea itself fascinated him to such a degree that it paralyzed his creative faculties"—according to one report—Debussy composed most of *La Mer* away from the seashore. Actually, most of it was done in Paris, though he finished it at Eastbourne, England, a smart watering place. *La Mer* was given its first performance at the Concerts Lamoureux in Paris, on Oct. 15, 1905, Camille Chevillard conducting.

The summer of 1904 had proved an eventful period in his life. He left his wife Lily for Emma Bardac, wife of a noted financier and former mistress of Gabriel Fauré. One of the results of this maneuver was Lily's attempted suicide. She wounded herself seriously in the region of the heart, and immediately Paris raged with the scandal. He had been bought, it was said, by a rich woman. But Debussy had known her intimately almost from the day of his marriage to Lily. More than once he had given thought to breaking relations with his wife and becoming united to this woman of the world, who was also a brilliant conversationalist and a gifted singer. The sound of Lily's voice had "made his blood run cold." The comforts which were Mme. Bardac's to give could prove the thawing influence.

Nevertheless these events had not been forgotten when the new work obtained its world premiere the following year. Laloy wrote, "Prudish indignation had not yet been appeased, and on all sides people were ready to make the artist pay dearly for the wrongs that were imputed to the man." The press offered, as the press will, widely divergent opinions concerning *La Mer,* though some of the scholars, journalistic and otherwise, could make allowances for Chevillard's heavy conducting. But the controversy flourished, even after performances conducted by Debussy himself. At one of the Concerts Colonne under the composer's direction, the friends and enemies went to it full tilt. There were cries of "bravo" and cries of contempt. The end of the number was the signal for a demonstration that lasted for ten minutes. Hostilities broke out again during Jacques Thibaud's performance of the Bach *Chaconne,* which followed *La Mer.* The noted violinist was forced to stop in the middle of his interpretation and to wait for the armistice, which, one supposes, eventually came.

Some of the expressions recorded in the press of the time are worth noting. Pierre Lalo, son of the composer Edouard Lalo, observed acidulously in *Le Temps,* "I neither hear, nor see, nor feel the sea." And Gaston Carraud wrote in *La Liberté,* "It is certainly genuine Debussy—that is to say, the most individual, the most precious, and the most subtle expression of our art—but it almost suggests the possibility that some day we may have an Americanized Debussy."

The unqualified praise came from such quarters as Louis Laloy and M. D. Calvocoressi. The former said, "Without in any way abandoning this delicate sensitiveness (creating delightful impressionistic pictures out of atmospheric vibrations) which is perhaps unequaled in the world of art, his style has today become concise, decided, positive, complete, in a word, classical." The latter greeted "a new phase in M. Debussy's evolution; the inspiration is more robust, the colors are stronger, the lines more definite."

Debussy's program for his richly imaginative, exotically colored, and delicately nuanced creation consists of no more than the titles for the three sections. In this, as in other works of his, he shuns the well-worn paths of traditional form, devising, instead, forms and architectures of his own. Yet *La Mer* possesses certain aspects of the cyclic scheme in that it carries fragments of themes heard in the first section into the concluding pages of the third.

R. C. B.

Two Nocturnes: "Nuages" ("Clouds"), "Fêtes" ("Festivals")

THE NOCTURNES consist, properly, of three sections, "Nuages," "Fêtes," and "Sirènes." In the last, the orchestra is complemented by a chorus of women's voices. The Nocturnes were mostly written during 1898, and they were published in the following year. Camille Chevillard conducted the premiere of "Nuages" and "Fêtes" at a Paris Lamoureux concert on Dec. 9, 1900. The complete set obtained its premiere at another Lamoureux concert on Oct. 27, 1901.

Debussy himself wrote an explanation of the triptych:

The title *Nocturnes* is to be interpreted here in a general and, more particularly, in a decorative sense. Therefore, it is not meant to designate the usual form of a nocturne, but rather all the impressions and the special effects of light that the word suggests.

"Nuages" renders the immutable aspect of the sky and the slow, solemn motion of the clouds, fading away in gray tones slightly tinged with white.

"Fêtes" gives us the vibrating, dancing rhythm of the atmosphere with sudden flashes of light. There is also the episode of the procession (a dazzling fantastic vision) which passes through the festive scene and becomes merged in it. But the background remains persistently the same: the festival with its blending of music and luminous dust participating in the rhythm.

"Nuages" is scored for two flutes, two oboes, English horn, two clarinets, three bassoons, four horns, kettledrums, harp, and strings. "Fêtes" calls for three flutes, two oboes, English horn, two clarinets, three bassoons, four horns, three trumpets, three trombones, bass tuba, two harps, a set of three kettledrums, cymbals, snare drum (in the distance), and strings.

R. C. B.

"Ibéria": "Images pour Orchestre," No. 2

I. "Par les rues et par les chemins" ("In the Streets and Byways"). II. "Les parfums de la nuit" ("The Fragrance of the Night"). III. "Le matin d'un jour de fête" ("The Morning of a Festival Day").

DEBUSSY's SET of *Images for Orchestra* are an impressionist's three-power pact, with England represented by *Gigues* (No. 1), Spain by *Ibéria* (No. 2), and France by *Rondes de printemps* (No. 3). The story of their composition follows a zigzag line from 1905 to 1911. In a letter to his publisher Jacques Durand, Debussy plainly indicates the *Images* were originally planned for two pianos. But the material expanded, impressions multiplied, and Debussy soon found the intended medium inadequate for his wider vision. The pieces were to be ready by July 1, 1906, but the final touches were not applied till 1911. A rough draft of the *Ibéria* score bears the date Dec. 25, 1908.

The delay is partly explained by Debussy in a letter containing a surprising fling at users of the word "impressionism," a term inextricably linked with his fame: "I am trying to achieve something *different*—an effect of *reality*—what some imbeciles call *impressionism,* a term that is utterly misapplied, especially by the critics." From Puys, near Dieppe, on Aug. 8, 1906, he wrote that he was plagued by the problem of deciding which of three equally effective finales he should adopt for *Ibéria.* "Shall I toss up a coin," he muses, "or shall I await a fourth solution?"

Curiously enough, though seeking an "effect of reality" in depicting Spain, Debussy had spent no more than a few hours in the country, having once crossed the border to attend a bullfight in San Sebastián. Beyond that he knew Spain the way most of us do, from books, hearsay, pictures, and music. Yet, no less an authority than Manuel de Falla, to whom the country was an open songbook, promptly praised the authentic ring of *Ibéria,* and the critic Boutarel flatly stated that the audience was actually "in Spain" while the music unfolded. Debussy could carry his listeners over the frontier on the magic carpet of his imagination. What he did not hear or see or smell he divined.

To de Falla this music evoking "the intoxicating spell of Andalusian nights," picturing jubilant crowds dancing to guitars and badurras, and mirroring

Spain's rich contrasts of sunlight and shadow, was a glowing manifesto to native Spanish composers infinitely closer to their country's flashing hues and rhythms. *Ibéria,* he felt, ideally exemplified the art of utilizing "merely the fundamental elements of popular music, instead of following the usual method of employing authentic folk songs." Debussy's was "better and truer" Spanish music, he conceded, than that of many Spanish contemporaries. He went so far as to credit Debussy with an influence on Albéniz' own Iberian tone picture. But there his chronology is faulty, for the record shows that the influence, if it existed at all, operated the other way. Léon Vallas points out that Debussy was familiar with at least the first section of his Spanish colleague's *Ibéria,* published in 1906, while working on one of his own. The French composer enjoyed playing Albéniz' brilliant pictures of Spanish life on the piano and singled them out for special praise in his written criticism. Vallas accepted de Falla's theory as "very flattering to Debussy" but regretfully concluded that "it was Debussy who came under the influence of Albéniz."

Ibéria was first performed in Paris on Feb. 20, 1910, at the third of four Concerts de Musique Française organized by Durand. Gabriel Pierné conducted. Pierné had earlier complained about the hardship Debussy's score imposed on orchestra and conductor alike. "I have seen Pierné," Debussy wrote "I think he exaggerates the difficulties of a performance of *Ibéria.*"

To the program annotator who sought material for the premiere note he remarked impatiently: "It is useless to ask me for anecdotes about this work there is no story attached to it, and I depend on the music alone to arouse the interest of the public." Yet, when the *Rondes de Printemps* section of *Image* was performed on Mar. 2, the annotator, Charles Malherbe, allegedly a Debussy's suggestion, stated significantly, "These are real pictures in which the composer has endeavored to convey, aurally, impressions received by the eye He attempts to blend the two forms of sensation, in order to intensify them." Naturally the "impressions received by the eye" applied here to the French countryside. In the case of *Ibéria* any such optical stimuli would have been limited to brief glimpses of the Plaza de Toros at San Sebastián.

At its world premiere, *Ibéria* aroused marked enthusiasm. Debussy devotee stormily demanded an immediate repetition. Pierné was on the point of complying, when the opposing camp set up a howl of protest. *Ibéria* was not encored. Critical reaction varied. Some writers, among them Jean Chantavoine felt Debussy had let his constituents down after the high hopes inspired by *Pelléas et Mélisande.* M. Chantavoine, writing in the *Revue Hebdomadaire* phrased his disappointment obliquely: "It was high time for M. Debussy to give those who admire his talents or genius an opportunity of agreeing with those who do not." Others charged Debussy with imitating his imitators Gaston Carraud, critic of *Liberté,* for example, reproached Debussy for "taking back out of the hands of his successors his own processes after they have de graded them." Like them, he complained, Debussy was putting more brains than emotion in his music!

To Alfred Bruneau, composer of *L'Attaque du Moulin,* went the distinction of penning the notice that has become the general verdict of subsequent writers and concertgoers:

These delicate Spanish sketches bear no resemblance to the bold canvases of Albéniz and Chabrier. One recognizes M. Debussy's personality in the smallest details. They contain no trace of violence or roughness, in spite of the lively gaiety that animates the first and last sections. They are delightfully poetic, exquisite in coloring, full of fascinating charm and marvellous artistry.

L. B.

"Fantaisie for Piano and Orchestra"

I. Andante ma non troppo. Allegro giusto. II. Lento e molto espressivo. Allegro molto.

WRITTEN DURING 1889-1890, as part of the composer's work in connection with his Prix de Rome duties, the *Fantaisie for Piano and Orchestra* was never performed during Debussy's lifetime—by his express order. It was published, as a matter of fact, two years after his death.

Debussy, then a young man of twenty-nine or thirty, might have been expected to cheer over a performance of the piece that had been scheduled by the Société Nationale. However, he found many faults with it and one fine day, after a rehearsal, he calmly went from music stand to music stand, collecting the parts. He then notified the authorities that he had withdrawn his work, giving the excuse that certain sections of it required revising.

Alfred Cortot, writing about this particular composition, has had this to say:

While admitting Debussy's reserve with regard to certain weaknesses of orchestral realisation—and that not only in the finale—in regretting, even, a defect of proportion which cuts short the last, as well as the recapitulation and the coda of the first movement, there remains, all the same, the fact that the *Fantaisie* is a work containing more than the promise of a student. . . . The freshness and simplicity of the ideas of the first movement, the dreamy and tender melancholy of the slow movement, the mysterious transition which links it to the finale and the decision of character, which, in this movement, underlies the rhythmic modifications of the initial theme, all this belongs to a musician sure of himself, in possession of his personal expression, if not yet absolute master of his business.

The *Fantaisie* is dedicated to René Chansarel. It consists of two main parts: I. Andante ma non troppo, which ushers in an Allegro giusto; and II. Lento molto espressivo, which leads into an Allegro molto. The orchestral score calls for three flutes (third interchangeable with piccolo), two oboes, English horn, two clarinets, two bassoons, four horns, three trumpets, kettledrums, cymbals, two harps, and strings.

Debussy's abbreviated stay at the Villa Medici, in Rome, was anything but a happy experience for him. In the first place, he found it difficult to meet the Prix de Rome requirements, though he was more than eager to prove his interest and application by working hard at his tasks. He sent the first of the "required" compositions, *Zuleïma,* a fragment of a lyric drama, set to a text by Georges Boyer, who had based it on Heine's *Almanzor.*

The Académie's answer was no less than a stern rebuke, expressing complete displeasure with the composition. The official report went, "M. Debussy seems today to be tormented with a desire to be bizarre, incomprehensible, unperformable."

The second "required" offering, the symphonic suite *Printemps,* inspired by Botticelli's painting *Primavera,* also earned the Académie's hearty disapproval. It was described as having "a pronounced tendency—too pronounced—to exploit that which is strange." The composer was admonished to steer away from "the vague impressionism that is one of the most dangerous enemies of truth in art."

The other pieces he submitted—completing his Prix de Rome assignment— were *La Demoiselle élue,* and the *Fantaisie,* neither of which, however, was written in Rome, for by the time Debussy came around to those, he had already taken French leave from Italian soil. They were composed in Paris.

R. C. B.

"Sarabande"

[Transcribed for orchestra by Maurice Ravel]

EARLY IN 1923, Ravel orchestrated two of Debussy's piano pieces for Serge Koussevitzky, who introduced them at a concert in Paris in May. One of them, *Danse,* composed in 1890, stemmed from Debussy's youth, before his impressionist style had begun to mature.

The second, *Sarabande,* composed in 1901, marked a long stride forward in expressive mastery and belonged to the period of *Pelléas et Mélisande* and *The Afternoon of a Faun.* It was one of three pieces published that year under the title, *Pour le piano.* In the same archaic frame the remaining two were called *Prélude* and *Toccata.* Together they represented a conscious effort at blending classical form and modernist nuance. Suggestions of Bach filter through the *Prélude.* The *Toccata* hints strongly of Domenico Scarlatti. In the *Sarabande* Debussy recalls the French suite, and if any names are evoked they are Rameau and Couperin, though his own is implicit in the whole scheme. Using free harmonization, Debussy modified the outmoded forms, tinging them with his own growing ideas of color. Analogies with Erik Satie's *Sarabandes,* which also reshape classic contours to new expressive ends, have been noted. It is interesting to learn that Ravel scandalized fellow students in Pessard's harmony class at the Conservatory by playing Satie's *Sarabandes* and *Gymnopédies* during the instructor's absence one day.

Like Debussy and Satie before him, Ravel delighted in utilizing older forms. He strove to infuse fresh life into them and welcomed co-workers in the field. One has only to recall such titles as *Prélude, Menuet, Rigaudon,* and *Pavane* among his works. The difference between the two men is that Ravel constantly returned to the eighteenth century for refreshment in clarity and precision, whereas for Debussy it was only a stage along his path to subtler vistas of expression.

They had much in common in exploring the resources of the piano and seeking novel devices. They used similar titles and often the same unusual scales. They both found inspiration in Spain and the Orient, and both were pagan in outlook. But Debussy's idiom remained personal, intense, sensuous, and atmospheric, while Ravel's dazzled through icy glitter and fierce logic, with frequent flashes of keen satire and irony. Impressionism with Debussy was a way of thinking and feeling. The medium went hand in hand with the need. For Ravel it was one of many mediums to scrutinize coolly and cultivate at leisure. That these two styles, divergent in aim, could best unite over a Sarabande was but natural. It is worth recalling that before their respective styles drew them apart, they had been close colleagues and often played Mozart's piano music for four hands together.

Ricardo Viñes, widely recognized as an authentic Debussy interpreter, first played *Pour le piano* at the Société Nationale, Paris, on Jan. 11, 1902. The set won instant acclaim, and the *Toccata* was encored. Oscar Thompson points out in his book on Debussy that when *Sarabande* originally appeared in slightly different form in the magazine *Grand Journal de Lundi,* the indication read, "rather like an old picture, or a memory of the Louvre."

Sarabande uses sevenths and ninths in what was a daring succession for the time, Mr. Thompson remarks, "though the effect for modern ears is both grave and slightly archaic." The melody he describes as one of Debussy's "most serene" and, because of the effect achieved by the reproduction of a chord on different degrees of the scale, calls the piece "one of the works that have come to be styled 'impressionistic.'"

Marked *"Avec une élégance grave et lente"* (C sharp minor, 3/4), *Sarabande* is scored, in Ravel's transcription, for two flutes, oboe, English horn, two clarinets, two bassoons, two horns, one trumpet, cymbals, tam-tam, harp, and strings.

L. B.

Frederick Delius

BORN: BRADFORD, ENGLAND, JAN. 29, 1862. DIED: GREZ-SUR-LOING, FRANCE, JUNE 10, 1934

> *As Beethoven is the morning and Wagner the high noon, so Delius*
> *is the sunset of that great period of music which is called Romantic.*
> —PHILIP HESELTINE.

Intermezzo "The Walk to the Paradise Garden," from the Opera "A Village Romeo and Juliet"

BASED ON Gottfried Keller's poignant story, *Romeo und Julia auf dem Dorfe*
Delius' "music drama" in a prologue and three acts, was premiered at the
Berlin Komische Oper in 1907. A previous opera *Koanga* was also first produced in Germany in 1904, and as early as 1897 an overture fantasy *Over the
Hills and Far Away* was conducted by Dr. Haym at Elberfeld. Three years
after its German premiere, *A Village Romeo and Juliet* was produced at Covent
Garden, London, though it was not until 1920 that a revival in the same theatre
brought a more appreciative response from a public previously cool to Delius'
operatic style.

The setting of the Keller-Delius tragedy is a German village in the nineteenth
century. A deadly feud, in the Shakespearean tradition of the Montagues and
Capulets, exists between two families, further embittered by the boy Sali's
falling in love with Vrenchen, daughter of his father's enemy. Unable to cope
with the situation, the lovers elope. On the road they meet a symbolic figure,
the Dark Fiddler, who tries to lure them into a life of sin and gathers a band
of revelers about him. Sali and Vrenchen resist and resolve to end their woe
in a suicide pact. Sali leads Vrenchen to a river barge. As they board it Sali
pulls a plug out of the barge, and the river soon closes over them.

The Intermezzo depicts the reverielike mood of the young lovers in the
"Paradise Garden" of a village fair, where they stop first in their elopement.
A dreamy melody, prefaced by soft harmonies, is ushered in by the cellos and
taken up by the oboe. The tranquil atmosphere continues through a development section, climaxed by a powerful outburst from the whole orchestra, after
which the music calms down again and sinks quietly to rest.

Delius was a long time coming into his own in England, but by 1929
Sir Thomas Beecham was directing a Delius Festival in which no less than
six full-length programs were devoted to his music. In his *Survey of Contemporary Music,* Cecil Gray, one of England's leading spokesmen for new music,
writes eloquently of the vein of melancholy and nostalgia in his countryman's
work:

Although Delius' outlook is always intensely personal, his art is never in any way autobiographic like that of most romantic artists. . . . The tender melancholy of so much of his music conveys a sense of detachment; it is the emotion which is felt by the spectator rather than by the actor in the tragedy. . . . He seems always to stand outside and above his own creation, like the chorus in Greek tragedy—sympathetic, understanding, but always aloof and impersonal.

The music of Delius belongs essentially to the same phase of romanticism as the art of Flaubert, Gauguin, Verlaine, and Baudelaire. They are all alike possessed by the nostalgia of the infinite and the unappeasable longing for an impossible bliss.

L. B.

"Paris, A Night Piece" ("The Song of a Great City")

Delius' symphonic tribute grew out of a long sojourn in Paris, where he occupied an apartment in the Latin Quarter, wrote prolifically, and lived probably the serenest and happiest period of his life. His stay ended in 1896, so his *Song of a Great City,* composed in 1899, was something of a flashback to those happy days. One has only to recall the hardships of his early career and the recurring physical pain and total blindness of the last years to realize what the quiet Parisian interlude must have meant to this intensely subjective artist.

Delius left no clue to the emotional or dramatic sequence of the sketch, apart from his own impressionist technic and idiom, which ought to suffice. However, three writers long associated with him rendered explanatory notes. R. A. Streatfield, a close friend and devotee, wrote:

Paris is a musical picture of the composer's impressions of the great city by night. It is no mere exercise in musical realism, though it displays a keen sense of pictorial effect. Rather it is a personal record of the feelings engendered by the contemplation of the sleeping city. It is a study of effects rather than of causes, and in this is a peculiarly characteristic example of Delius' attitude toward music, and of his employment of its resources.

In strictly rhapsodic vein is the German effusion of Max Chop, who illuminated *Paris* in a series of monographs on contemporary composers, published in Leipzig in 1907:

Enigmatic city! thou that slumberest when busy people press forward toward work and happiness, and awakest when the soft twilight colors all things with mystery. City of joy, of strange feelings, of loud music and of women, beautiful and rouged. City of mysteries! Unveiled only to him who, shunning the day, turns homeward only when the wan blue light of dawn appears, and who smiles in slumberland when the streets are awakened by the gray lights of morn.

Herr Chop's glowing apostrophe would seem to apply more to Charpentier's vision of street life in the opera *Louise.* As for Charpentier, Philip Heseltine, in 1923, gratuitously thwacks the French composer as a "vulgarian" in contrasting his tone picture with that of his friend. He says:

> There is no program to the work, nor is there any portrayal—scarcely indeed more than a suggestion of external things. For Delius, Paris is not so much the capital city of France as a corner of his own soul, a chapter of his own Memoirs. The superficialities of *La Vie Parisienne* have been dealt with by Offenbach the trifler and Charpentier the vulgarian, with whom Delius would disdain competition.

Freely constructed, the work shifts repeatedly in tempo and mood. It begins with an Adagio passage in D major, 6/8, featuring a solo theme for oboe, and ends quietly, after a prestissimo, with the oboe recalling the same melody. Embedded in the scheme are several Parisian street cries. Charpentier, incidentally, worked several of these Parisian motifs into the symphonic fabric of *Louise*. Delius, however, did not hear the opera till after he had penned his own impressions, so the idea was not borrowed.

Dedicated to Dr. Hans Haym, who conducted the world premiere with the Municipal Orchestral of Elberfeld, Germany, in 1900, *Paris* was first performed in America at a concert of the Boston Symphony Orchestra on Nov. 26, 1906. Max Fiedler conducted.

L. B.

"A Song of Summer"

THE SONG OF SUMMER belongs with a group of seven works written by Delius during the total blindness and partial paralysis that set in late in 1924. No music came from his pen for at least four years. He lived in his beautiful villa at Grez-sur-Loing, near Fontainebleau, devotedly nursed by his wife, and visited from time to time by friends and devotees.

The music world expected no further activity from him. Then, in 1928, the silence was broken. Delius' creative muse was busy again. In the few years remaining he extended his already huge output with a *Fantastic Dance* (orchestra), the *Irmelin* prelude (orchestra), A Caprice and Elegy (cello and chamber orchestra), a violin and piano sonata, *Songs of Farewell* (double choir and orchestra), and *Idyll* (soprano, baritone, and orchestra).

Delius and English music owed it all to a gifted young composer and organist from Yorkshire named Eric Fenby. An admirer of Delius' music, the twenty-three-year-old musician wrote to Grez offering the composer his services as musical and literary secretary. Fenby felt sure a system of dictation could be devised whereby Delius could continue composing without undue strain. Delius agreed to try it out, though he long regarded the plan as futile.

Fenby was duly installed at Grez in October, 1928, and remained with the composer to the end. After some discouraging trials, the blind man and his amanuensis developed a working system of composition that brought results. Delius even managed to dictate some important articles, among them one on "Romanticism in Music."

A Song of Summer was the first product of this method. Its genesis traces back to an earlier work of Delius', *A Poem of Love and Life,* the manuscript of which was long regarded as lost. Actually Delius had discarded it as of negligible worth, though it remained in its filing cabinet for future revision.

As a first experiment he asked Fenby one day to transcribe the piece for two pianos, explaining that he wanted to hear whether anything in it was worth preserving. His friend Balfour Gardiner had already done some work on it. Fenby read through the score and was "hopelessly disappointed," as he tells in his book *Delius As I Knew Him.*

"I trembled to think what I would say should he ask me for my opinion on that symphonic poem!" Fenby writes.

The secretary discussed it first with Mrs. Delius, who advised him to be perfectly frank with the master. "You must forget your youth," she said, "and stand up to him. I will always stand by you!"

As a rule Delius resented adverse opinions of his music and had been known to flail back pitilessly at carping critics. Fenby did not know this and admits he never would have worked up enough courage had he been so warned. Well, the Yorkshire youth criticized the work "fearlessly," as he says, and, surprisingly, Delius, after wincing a bit, took it in good part.

"Look here, Fenby," he said, "I've got an idea. Select all the good material, develop it, and make a piece out of it yourself. Now take your time; never hurry your work, whatever you do."

Fenby finished the job in short order and played some of it for Delius. "Good, good, good, Fenby," said the composer.

"I can work with you. You are a natural musician. You've got the sense of my ideas in the most wonderful way. It seems almost uncanny. You have awakened my interest again, and now that you have shown me what you can do, it has set my mind working to see what I can make of it."

A few weeks later Delius began remolding the "good" material salvaged from *A Poem of Love and Life* for a new composition. This eventually became *A Song of Summer,* premiered on Sept. 17, 1931, by Sir Henry Wood in the BBC season of Promenade Concerts.

Fenby narrates how Delius one day decided to write an entirely new opening for the orchestral work. Delius was sitting in his carriage under an elder tree waiting for his secretarial "notator" to take it down.

"Eric, is that you?" asked Delius, when he heard footsteps on the garden path.

"Bring your score paper and sit beside me." Fenby did so.

"I want you to imagine that we are sitting on the cliffs in the heather looking out over the sea," said Delius.

"The sustained chords in the high strings suggest the clear sky and the stillness and calmness of the scene, 7/4 in a bar (four and three); divided strings, chord of D major—A, D, F sharp, doubled at the octave, lowest note in the A string of the violas.

"Dovetail the violin parts (F sharp and D), (A and F sharp), and mark the score lento molto and each voice pianissimo. Hold the chords two bars. . . ."

At another point Delius inquired: "You remember that figure that comes in the violins when the music becomes more animated?" The sightless composer sang it to Fenby. "I'm introducing it here to suggest the gentle rise and fall of the waves."

Again, Delius, with sung illustration: "The ti, er figure, is the same value as the one that comes in that solo oboe passage later on."

Fenby: "Is that ti, er in the flute G natural, Delius?"

Delius: "Yes, that flute suggests a seagull gliding by. Now put a horn call on the fourth beat of the last bar."

Delius was anything but calm and collected during this creative groping in the dark, according to Fenby.

"He could not keep still," he says, "but would wriggle about in his armchair, gesticulate wildly with his hands . . . until, bathed in perspiration, he could go on no longer. Then he would be carried away exhausted."

One day Delius woke up from an afternoon nap and screamed out to his wife: "Jelka, I can see my hands!" It was only an illusion.

L. B.

Norman Dello Joio

BORN: NEW YORK, JAN. 24, 1913.

Music is in a state of decline. This state reflects the world's confusion which has no recognizable future. As a composer, I believe that the creative arts as well as all branches of learning should serve as an instrument for a moral and spiritual renascence. Unless this challenge is met now, man's hope for freedom and liberation from fear shall always be an illusion.—NORMAN DELLO JOIO.

Ricercari for Piano and Orchestra

I. Allegretto giocoso. II. Adagio. III. Allegro vivo.

THE RICERCARI for Piano and Orchestra do not follow the traditional fugal form of the type of composition developed in the sixteenth and seventeenth centuries and known by that name. They preserve, however, one very characteristic trait, *viz.*, the development of a germinal idea in fantasia form. Although each of the three movements (Allegretto giocoso, Adagio, and Allegro vivo) develops in all directions, *i.e.*, harmonically, melodically, and rhythmically, it is a harmonic feature (the chord F sharp, G, B natural, D) that provides the musical stimulus for the first movement. The second evolves on a melodic idea (a seven-measure period played by a solo clarinet). The last movement exploits a rhythmical pattern.

The role of the piano throughout is that of a very definite solo instrument which is intimately associated with the development of the work. A cadenza-like passage for the piano in the first movement behaves as a liaison agency for the return to the main idea.

Mr. Dello Joio had in mind, while working on this composition, a sort of twentieth-century Scarlatti style, one not overly complex in its contrapuntal texture. The Ricercari for Piano and Orchestra are dedicated to Felix Greissle.

The score calls for two flutes, piccolo, two oboes, two clarinets, two bassoons, four horns, three trumpets, three trombones, tuba, tympani, cymbals, and strings. George Szell conducted the premiere of the Ricercari at a Philharmonic-Symphony concert in Carnegie Hall on Dec. 19, 1946. The composer was the soloist.

Norman Dello Joio stems from a long line of Italian musicians. His father Casimir, an organist and composer, was his first teacher. Mr. Dello Joio continued his musical training with his godfather Pietro Yon, then organist at St. Patrick's Cathedral in New York.

At the age of nineteen, Mr. Dello Joio entered the Institute of Musical Art in New York where he studied piano and organ with Gaston Dethier. While there he found that his greatest interest lay in composition. This talent was recognized almost immediately, and he was awarded the Elizabeth Sprague Coolidge Award for his Piano Trio. He was later given a fellowship to the Juilliard Graduate School where he studied composition with Barnard Wagenaar. In the summers of 1940 and 1941 he entered the Berkshire Music Center where he studied with Paul Hindemith. During the intervening winter he continued with Hindemith at the Yale School of Music.

In 1942 Mr. Dello Joio won the Town Hall Composition Award for his orchestral work *Magnificat* and has since won two successive Guggenheim Fellowships (1944-1945, 1945-1946). In 1946 he received a $1,000 grant from the American Academy of Arts and Letters.

Mr. Dello Joio started his professional career assisting his father as church organist. He soon held positions in his own right as organist and choirmaster in many New York churches. From 1941 to 1943, he was Musical Director of the ballet company "Dance Players." At the present time he is teaching composition at Sarah Lawrence College in Bronxville, N. Y.

His major orchestral works include Symphony for Voices and Orchestra (set to "Western Star" by Stephen Vincent Benét); *Concert Music* (tone poem for full orchestra); *Magnificat,* for Orchestra; Concerto for Two Pianos and Orchestra; Concerto for Harp and Orchestra; Concertino for Flute and String Orchestra; Concertino for Piano and Orchestra.

Among his many works for chorus are *The Mystic Trumpeter, A Jubilant Song,* and *Madrigals.* He wrote the score to the ballet *On Stage!,* performed extensively in the United States and abroad. He has also done numerous pieces in the field of chamber music and piano solo.

R. C. B.

David Diamond

BORN: ROCHESTER, N. Y., JULY 9, 1915.

My emotional life and reactions to certain events and situations have worked hand in hand with purely abstract musical conception and manipulation of material, and it was always the material that remained foremostly important to me in my working stages.—DAVID DIAMOND.

Symphony No. 2

I. Adagio funebre. II. Allegro vivo. III. Andante espressivo, quasi adagio.
IV. Allegro vigoroso.

BEGUN EARLY in 1942, this symphony was completed in February, 1943, and performed for the first time anywhere by the Boston Symphony Orchestra, in Boston, on Oct. 13, 1944. Serge Koussevitzky conducted. Leonard Bernstein led the New York premiere of the work at a concert of the New York City Symphony at the City Center on Feb. 4, 1946. In submitting an analysis of the score to John N. Burk, program annotator of the Boston Symphony, Mr. Diamond disavowed any specific "program." He wrote:

Naturally enough, this work was composed during days of tense world unrest, and I am quite sure that a certain amount of exterior emotional influence has affected the quality of the symphony, though I cannot guarantee the *raison d'être* for its inspiration. Indeed, I have one or two friends who, when I played sketches for them or described some of the material, immediately pounced upon all sorts of vague and ridiculous analogies of the kind one associates with analyses of the recent Shostakovich symphonies. It was in no way my intention to have the musical substance represent specific emotional reactions or to conjure up programmatic fantasies. I have a horror of anything as prosaic as that, and since I have never known that method of musical conception, I can only say that the opposite is true.

The composer's own analysis of the Second Symphony follows:

I. Adagio funebre. A lyric movement of elegiac character consisting of two subjects: a long melody for the violins in unison (heard immediately after a short introduction by violas and cellos divisi) and accompanied by an ostinato figure in cello and basses; and a plangent melody for oboe solo accompanied by trilling violas—heard midway during the movement. The structure of the entire movement may be considered as a sonata-allegro movement in slow tempo, utilizing all the formal and technical features of development and recapitulation.

II. Allegro vivo. The scherzo movement, which has for its basic material a rhythmic figure mockingly tossed back and forth between cellos and basses and one bassoon. The rhythmic figure out of which this movement is built is derived from the second subject in the first movement. There is no trio section by itself. The contrasting triolike sections exist within the movement itself, most prominent being the section for brass in octaves accompanied by solo tympani and in later form by strings in unison accompanied by tympani.

III. Andante espressivo, quasi adagio. This movement makes use of rhythmic, harmonic, and melodic elements heard in the first movement. After a short introduction utilizing the dirgelike motif (heard at the outset of the first movement in basses and tympani) in the first movement, there grows a short theme for muted violas (later to be developed in the fugato section). A clarinet solo follows leading directly into a choralelike section for strings, which, for the main part, is played in unison by the first violins unaccompanied. The clarinet solo heard in the opening is eventually heard in the second half of the movement as the fugato subject played by horns and strings in unison. As contrast, there are several wistful episodes for strings alternating with passages of strong emotional contrast. The movement is extensively worked out in restatement and development of all the elements heretofore heard.

IV. Allegro vigoroso. The function of this movement is definitely that of the lively rondo-finale. The movement opens with a vigorous marchlike subject for unison strings. Several of the episodes have important thematic functions; especially so the lyric folk-song-like "B" section and the pizzicato C episodes for strings alone. The form is easily followed as: A-B-A (modified)-B-A-C-A (modified-C-A-B-A-C (modified)-A-coda.

The scoring calls for three flutes, piccolo, two oboes, English horn, two clarinets, bass clarinet, two bassoons, contra-bassoon, four horns, three trumpets, three trombones, tuba, tympani, bass drum, snare drum, triangle, cymbals, large gong, glockenspiel, xylophone, and strings.

Mr. Diamond studied with André de Ribaupierre at the Cleveland Institute of Music, Bernard Rogers at the Eastman School of Music, Roger Sessions and Paul Boepple at the Dalcroze Institute, as well as privately in New York City and with Nadia Boulanger at Fountainebleau and Paris. He has won numerous awards, and in 1937 he was commissioned by the League of Composers to write a chamber-music work (the Quintet for Flute, String Trio, and Piano). Already many orchestral works have been put to his credit, besides a cello concerto.

Mr. Diamond has also composed music for chamber orchestra, a number of string quartets, songs, and piano pieces. His compositions have been performed by the Philadelphia Orchestra, the Philharmonic-Symphony, the St. Louis Symphony, the Rochester Philharmonic, the National Orchestral Association, the Columbia Broadcasting Symphony, the NBC Symphony, the Coolidge Quartet, and the Barrère-Britt Ensemble.

"Rounds for String Orchestra"

Cᴏᴍᴍɪꜱꜱɪᴏɴᴇᴅ ʙʏ Dimitri Mitropoulos, *Rounds for String Orchestra* was completed in July, 1944. Mr. Mitropoulos and the Minneapolis Symphony performed the work for the first time on Nov. 24, of the same year. The following analysis is from the composer's own pen:

The different string choirs enter in strict canonic fashion as an introduction to the main subject, which is played by the violas and soon restated by the cellos and basses. The Adagio is an expressive lyric movement, acting as a resting point between the two fast movements. The last movement again makes use of characteristic canonic devices, though it may more specifically be analyzed as a kind of fugal countersubject for the principal thematic ideas, so helping to "round" out the entire work and unify the entire formal structure.

William Barclay Squire (Grove's *Dictionary of Music and Musicians*) describes a round as

A species of canon in the unison, so called because the performers begin the melody at regular rhythmical periods, and return from its conclusion to its beginning, so that it continually passes round and round from one to another of them. Rounds and catches, the most characteristic forms of English music, differ from canons in only being sung at the unison or octave, and also in being rhythmical in form.

In 1843, Enoch Hawkins, an expert in this form of entertainment, founded a Round, Catch, and Canon Club, whose members—and they were quite a few—passed the time singing their new compositions till the wee small hours.

Ernst von Dohnányi

BORN: PRESSBURG, HUNGARY, JULY 27, 1877.

*His compositions show a strong feeling for classic forms, great orig-
inality of ideas, and treatment that is always interesting and felicitous
in the extreme.*—J. A. FULLER-MAITLAND.

"Variations on a Nursery Air," for Orchestra with Piano Obbligato, Op. 25

THE NURSERY air employed by the composer in this work is the familiar "Ah,
vous dirai-je, Maman," which we have long known as the setting, so to speak,
of the alphabet. The same tune was used by Mozart as the subject of his
Twelve Variations for Clavier in C major (K. 265). The Dohnányi Variations
number eleven, linked to a concluding fugato. And the tonality, as in the
Mozart, is C major.

At an all-Dohnányi concert given by the short-lived State Symphony Orchestra in Carnegie Hall, Feb. 17, 1925, the composer conducted all the pieces
programmed, excepting the present composition, where he appeared as soloist.
Ignatz Waghalter was the batonist in his place. A program note printed at the
time spoke of the music as being

a humorous work, but it is humor in which satire lurks. It begins with a consciously pompous Introduction (Maestoso), serious and self-important, after which
the theme is heard (Allegro)—music of the utmost naïveté and transparency. The
work swings from serious to comic, and back again over the same path. It includes
such essays in scholastic form as a passacaglia and a fugato, the latter heard at the
end.

Ernst (or, as in Hungarian, Erno) Dohnányi obtained his first lessons in
music from his father, who was professor of mathematics at the Gymnasium
in Pressburg. Later on he studied piano with Carl Forstner, organist of the
Pressburg cathedral, who subsequently taught him harmony. In 1894, the young
man matriculated at the Royal Hungarian Academy of Music in Budapest,
becoming there a pupil of Stephan Thomán in piano and Hans Kössler in
composition.

His composing dates from early Pressburg days, when he delivered himself
of several pieces in the larger forms, *viz.*, a string sextet, three string quartets
and piano sonatas, songs, and other music. A Symphony in F, written while
he was at Budapest, was awarded the King's prize and given its first per-

formance in 1897. In that year, too, he received piano lessons from the famous Eugen d'Albert, and shortly thereafter made his first appearances in Berlin and Vienna, where he was acclaimed as an "artist of the highest rank."

He continued his successes throughout Europe, then making his first American tour in the spring of 1900. Some years later he became a professor of piano at the Royal Academy of Music, Berlin, and in 1919 was made director of the Budapest Conservatory, also assuming conductorship of the Philharmonic Orchestra of that city.

Dohnányi's many compositions embrace instrumental, as well as vocal forms, including two symphonies, a piano concerto, a violin concerto, a suite for orchestra (not omitting the present Variations), several essays in chamber music, numerous piano solos, the ballet *Der Schleier der Pierrette,* the one-act opera *Tante Simona,* a later (and more important) operatic venture *The Tower of Voivod,* in addition to songs. *The Tower of Voivod,* derived from a Hungaro-Szekeler folk ballad, made an immediate success at its initial hearing in Budapest, Mar. 18, 1922.

R. C. B.

Paul Dukas

BORN: PARIS, OCT. I, 1865. DIED: PARIS, MAY 18, 1935.

He is the master of his emotion and knows how to keep it from noisy futility. That is why he never indulges in those parasitic developments which so often disfigure the most beautiful effects.—CLAUDE DEBUSSY.

Scherzo, "L'Apprenti sorcier" ("The Sorcerer's Apprentice")

COMPOSED IN 1897, this music claims as program inspiration the fanciful tale in Goethe's *Der Zauberlehrling,* which in turn stems from the 1800-year-old work of Lucian *The Lie Fancier.* In that ancient account Eucrates relates some of his experiences as an apprentice to the "spindle-shanked" Pancrates, who had lived in a cave for twenty-three years, while taking instruction in magic from Isis.

Eucrates' story (englished by William Tooke, London, 1820) is as follows:

When we came to an inn he [Pancrates] would take the wooden bar of the door, or a broom, or the pestle of a wooden mortar, put clothes upon it, and speak a couple of magic words to it. Immediately the broom, or whatever else it was, was taken by all the people for a man like themselves; he went out, drew water, ordered our victuals, and waited upon us in every respect as handily as the completest domestic. When his attendance was no longer necessary, my companion spoke a couple of other words and the broom was again a broom, the pestle again a pestle, as before. This art, with all I could do, I was never able to learn from him; it was the only secret he would not impart to me; though in other respects he was the most obliging man in the world. At last, however, I found an opportunity to hide me in an obscure corner, and overheard his charm, which I snapped up immediately, as it consisted of only three syllables. After giving his necessary orders to the pestle without observing me, he went out to market. The following day, when he was gone out about business, I took the pestle, clothed it, pronounced the three syllables, and bid it fetch me some water. He directly brought me a large pitcherful. Good, said I, I want no more water; be again a pestle. He did not, however, mind what I said; but went on fetching water, and continued bringing it, till at length the room was overflowed. Not knowing what to do, for I was afraid lest Pancrates, at his return, should be angry (as indeed was the case), and having no alternative, I took an ax and split the pestle in two, but this made bad worse; for now each of the halves snatched up a pitcher and fetched water; so that for one water carrier I now had two. Meanwhile in came Pancrates; and understanding what had

appened, turned them into their pristine form: he, however, privately took himself
way and I have not set eyes on him since.

R. A. Barnett has paraphrased Goethe's long ballad into the following
ramatic monologue:

hey call him "the great magician!" "Great?" Bah!
, too, am great—as great as he, for I, too, can call up imps and sprites to do
    whatever I bid!
Now will I call some uncanny sprite to fetch me water from the pool.
he broom! Come, broom! thou worn-out battered thing—
.e a sprite! Stand up! 'Tis well! Two elfin legs now I give thee!
iood! What's more a head! There! Now, broom!
ake thou a pail and fetch me water from the pool!
.io quickly and draw water for me, for me, your Master!
.rave! Thou faithful broom! Thou bustling broom!
Vhat! Back again? And—again?
.nd yet—*again?* Stop!
his pailful completes thy work; the bath is filled!
top! Stop! I say. *I command!*
'hou diabolic, damned thing, stop!
.e a broom once more! What? Wilt not obey?
) thou cub of Hell!
.hen, will I with my hatchet, cut thee in two!
'here!
'e demons! Now thou art *two* and double thy hellish work!
'he flood increases—the water engulfs me—Master!
.Aaster of Masters! Come! I am a poor helpless creature, the sprite I called will not
    obey!
.he Master came and said:
'Broom! To thy corner as of old!
.ee! I make sprites do as they are told!"

The glittering fame of such contemporaries as Debussy and Ravel and of at
.east two of the celebrated "Six" unwarrantedly eclipsed the less striking,
hough certainly not negligible, efforts of Paul Dukas. His career, like that of
nany a French musician of his time, was taken up with the duties of teacher,
.ritic, and composer. A student at the Paris Conservatory—where he later
.aught—he twice earned the Prix de Rome, came under the influence of the
mpressionists and utilized some of their harmonic and orchestral innovations,
.t the same time holding firmly to classical and Romantic concepts.
Early works of his were the two overtures, *King Lear* and *Götz von Ber-
ichingen*. These were followed by melodies, choruses, symphonic and dramatic
ketches, all or most of which remain unpublished. The opera *Ariane et Barbe-
Bleue* (1907), set to a text by Maurice Maeterlinck, is unquestionably his

masterpiece. His compositions include an "imposing Sonata in E flat Mino which carries a hint of Beethoven" (1901); the Variations, Interlude and Fina for Piano on a Theme of Rameau (1903); pieces of chamber music, a pianist homage to the memory of his friend Debussy, *La Plainte au loin du faun* (1921), and numerous other works. However, it remained for *The Sorcerer Apprentice* to bring him a lasting international reputation.

While still in his forties and still composing, Dukas ceased giving manuscrip to publishers. And before he died he burned most of his later works, of whicl it is said, there were many.

R. C. B.

Anton Dvorak

BORN: MÜHLHAUSEN, BOHEMIA, SEPT. 8, 1841. DIED: PRAGUE, MAY 1, 1904.

*He is one of the phenomena of the nineteenth century—a child of
nature, who did not stop to think, and said on paper anything which
came into his head.*—SIR CHARLES STANFORD.

Symphony in D minor, No. 2, Op. 70

I. Allegro maestoso. II. Poco adagio. III. Scherzo: Vivace; Poco meno
mosso. IV. Finale: Allegro.

HE LONDON Philharmonic Society conferred an honorary membership on
Anton Dvorak in June, 1884, at the same time commissioning him to do a new
symphony. Work was begun on it in December of that year, and the piece was
completed by the end of March, 1885. The composer wrote to his publisher
Simrock on Mar. 25, "Whatever may happen to the symphony, it is, thank God,
completed. It will be played in London for the first time on Apr. 22, and I am
curious as to the result." He conducted the premiere himself on that occasion,
following which he notified Simrock that "It had an exceptionally brilliant
success."

He did not exaggerate one iota, for press and public enthused over it as they
had over the earlier *Stabat Mater*. Some observers, riding verbally high, wide,
and handsome, compared it with the Schubert C major—to Dvorak's advantage—and still others even went so far as to place it above the compositions of
Brahms. Since "figures don't lie," it may be interesting to note that Brahms
was allegedly paid 40,000 marks by Simrock for his Fourth Symphony. That
amounted to $10,000 in 1885. All that Simrock would offer Dvorak for his
second Symphony was 3,000 marks, though he finally handed over 6,000,
Dvorak's own valuation of his work. Ergo, 6,000 marks were the equivalent of
$1,500 in the same year and, from a financial standpoint, a Brahms symphony
would rate six and two-thirds times higher than one by Dvorak, all of which
may prove anything or nothing.

In any case, Sir Arthur Sullivan conducted the rest of the program at the
concert which introduced the Dvorak Second. The other numbers were the
overtures to Spohr's *Faust,* to Mozart's *Don Giovanni,* and the Beethoven
Leonore No. 1.

The first movement (Allegro maestoso, D minor 6/8) opens with the soft
playing of the first theme by the violas and cellos in unison over a tonic organ
point in the basses, horns, and kettledrums. Clarinets take up the phrase a

fifth higher, with a slight variation, while the strings play a diminished seventh
A more vigorous subsidiary theme follows, which is developed at length by th
orchestra until a fortissimo climax is attained with the return of the first theme
At this point the first horn launches out with a phrase by itself, which soo
diminishes to a single G flat, whereupon the wood wind enters pianissimo wit
a contrasting phrase of chromatic make-up, taken by the strings. After a retar
the second theme comes through in B flat major by way of the woodwin
supported by the strings. The development of this theme takes some time, an
there follows a concluding theme in the same key, starting among the string
against a background of trills and arpeggios in the wood winds, then fadin
out in the latter choir. The first part of the movement is not repeated, the musi
flowing at once into the free fantasia, which is of a rather forceful character
The third section of the movement opens with the principal subject given ou
softly by the clarinets in thirds in the key of B flat minor, and there is a
immediate response by the bassoons and basses in A flat minor, then in I
minor, against forceful harmonies in the other choirs, save trumpets an
trombones. The full orchestra bursts out with a double forte in the tonic I
minor. An elaborate coda concludes the movement.

The second movement (Poco adagio, F major, 4/4) introduces an ecclesi
astical-sounding theme by means of the wood winds, as the strings accompan
pizzicato. Subsidiary passage work in the wood winds, to string and horn
accompaniment, heads finally into a second theme given out by the first violin
and cellos in octaves. The movement develops on its own, that is to say, withou
benefit of traditional rules and regulations. However, the formal amenities ar
observed through the balancing effect produced by the reentrance of the firs
theme in the cellos against arpeggios for the flutes, and oboe and furthe
enhanced by the return of the second theme. It is interesting to note that th
whole section teems with melody, with detailed ornamentation and is re
markable for the richness of its orchestration.

The third movement (Scherzo: Vivace, D minor 6/4) produces a "piquan
effect . . . by the almost constant juxtaposition of two contrasted themes or
rather, theme and countertheme, the one coming in the wind and the other i
the strings, or vice versa. Here, also, Dvorak gives full play to that piquanc
of rhythm which is so dear to his Czech heart." A Poco meno mosso in G majo
of an idyllic type forms the trio of the movement.

The fourth movement (Finale: Allegro, D minor 2/2) depends almos
entirely on the opening phrase of its first theme. "This stern figure, in whic
all the inherent chromatic quality of the (so-called) harmonic minor scale i
thrown into bold relief, keeps reappearing in *very various* forms even in th
major mode throughout the movement, which is worked out with infinit
energy and dramatic force." Though the strong concluding chord possesses a
major third, the minor mode prevails in the movement.

R. C. B.

Symphony in G major, No. 4, Op. 88

I. Allegro con brio. II. Adagio. III. Allegretto grazioso; molto vivace.
IV. Allegro ma non troppo.

REFERENCES TO Dvorak's Fourth Symphony as "the English Symphony" are largely traceable to the fact that it was first published by the English firm of Novello. It was wrongly assumed that the London Philharmonic performance of Apr. 14, 1890, was its world premiere. True, Dvorak led that performance himself, but he had already directed an earlier one in Prague, in February. If any of Dvorak's symphonies warrants the "English" label, it is the D minor Symphony, commissioned and premiered by the London society several years before. Moreover, the G major was written as a token of gratitude for the composer's election to the Prague Academy. In the manuscript Dvorak's dedication reads: "To the Bohemian Academy of Emperor Franz Josef for the Encouragement of Art and Literature, in thanks for my election." So much for "the English Symphony." External fact and intrinsic quality would seem to suggest "Bohemian Symphony" as a more appropriate title. Only one symphony of Dvorak carries, in title and content, any allusion to a truly foreign inspiration. That is, of course, the *New World Symphony,* in which thoughts of his native Bohemia mingle with impressions of America.

How the house of Novello came by the publication of the G major is a little story in itself. Relations between Dvorak and his German publisher Simrock had become strained. Simrock was complaining that Dvorak's longer works brought him little revenue, and that the shorter pieces were not best sellers either. The correspondence grew heated. Simrock finally offered 1,000 marks for the symphony, meanwhile clamoring for more of the "shorter pieces." Dvorak refused. Simrock's taunts about his more ambitious scores were too much for him. He replied that he had a "lot of ideas for big works in mind," and Simrock's negative attitude was only making it hard for him to place symphonies with other publishers. If Simrock wanted piano pieces and songs it was just too bad. The mood for such compositions was not on him. He had bigger plans: "I shall simply do what God imparts me to do," he concludes. "That will certainly be the best thing." The crafty publisher promptly changed his tune. "Simrock, at once alarmed, replied that their contract of 1879 was still valid, and thereby, Dvorak must first offer to him every new work he composed," says Paul Stefan in his book on Dvorak. "Dvorak did not reply. Novello acquired the Symphony, and Dvorak wrote for him the four-hand piano score."

Novello published the work in 1892. Dvorak had begun it in August, 1889, after complaining to his friend Göbl that "his head was so full of ideas" it was a pity it took so much time jotting them down. Acceding to an oft-expressed wish of Simrock's, he had just composed his E flat major Piano Quartet, Op. 87. By Nov. 8, three months after starting work on it, the symphony in G major was ready for the printer. Dvorak led the premiere the following February. When Hans Richter wanted to follow suit, Simrock blocked him. The watchful publisher "insisted that he must first acquire the work," says Stefan, "and therefore, would, of course, receive the royalty from Richter's performance." Then began the diplomatic exchange of notes with the composer.

Dvorak was on his sixth trip to England when he conducted the London premiere of the Symphony in April. During that visit Cambridge University bestowed on him the honorary degree of Doctor of Music, thus stealing a march on the rule-bound Austrian authorities. Earlier that year the University of Prague had made him a Doctor of Music, or thought it had. Baron Gautsch, the Austrian Minister of Education, speedily ruled out the bestowal: There was no Doctorate of Music in Austrian Universities! Then Cambridge acted and, presto! Vienna fished out a doctor's degree, too.

The simple, carefree mood of the G major Symphony long ago endeared it to concertgoers. Compositions often arouse widely contrasted feelings in listeners. The G major is not one of them. English critics in 1890 spoke of it as "pastoral," teeming with "rural sights and sounds," and stressed its freshness and charm. To an American critic writing in 1941, the score was "redolent of the Bohemian countryside" and marked by "decided charm and allure." The word "idyllic" occurs so often in references to the symphony that if a title were needed "Idyllic Symphony" would serve as well as any. The term "Pastoral Symphony" for the G major was outlawed by Kretschmar, who had already affixed it to Dvorak's F major Symphony. But the strong outdoor atmosphere is readily sensed in the G major. In fact, few critics have failed to note its power as a growth of the soil.

After the London premiere, *The Musical Times* reported that the new work was "generally speaking, of a pastoral character, having been written, like the 'Pastoral' symphony, under the influence of rural sights and sounds. . . . All is fresh and charming." The reviewer scented a story in the Adagio movement which the composer, unluckily, never divulged. "Wanting the story," he wrote, "one must be content with picturesque utterances, a great deal of absolute beauty, and the fresh aroma which the whole work gives forth." To a New York colleague of fifty-one years later, the music was "idyllic, close to the soil, and permeated with the folk spirit of a once so happy land."

The botanical note is stressed in the analysis of the biographer Hoffmeister, who spoke of Dvorak's thoughts as "breaking into flower, not like little blossoms lodged in the stony crevices of an architectural structure, but as the Czech meadows flower, in luxuriant garlands of varied charm and color." Hoffmeister, with whom the "bright, idyllic" mood of the symphony begins with the very

ey of G major, speaks of it as "simple straightforward music, without any
retence at scholasticism." To him the work "rejoices freely in its existence."
hen comes the floral simile, after which it is not surprising to learn that the
rst movement "is planned in a delicious idyllic mood."

On Mar. 11, 1892, shortly after Novello published the Symphony in London,
e New York Philharmonic Society introduced it to America at a concert in
e Metropolitan Opera House. Anton Seidl, who conducted, again brought
ut the work in the season of 1895-1896, and Emil Paur led it during the
ason of 1899-1900. The symphony also figured in the repertory for four
asons of Josef Stransky's regime—1914-1915, 1915-1916, 1916-1917, and 1918-
19. It was then shelved by the society until 1932, when Sir Thomas Beecham
vived it during his guest conductorship. In December, 1938, another British
onductor, John Barbirolli, restored the miscalled "English Symphony" to the
hilharmonic repertory. Incidentally, Hans Richter, after being deterred by
imrock in 1890, enjoyed great success with the work when he played it in
ondon and Vienna. By then Simrock had learned his lesson. After the G
najor Symphony, Dvorak, disregarding Simrock, wrote another large-scale
ork, the *Requiem*. This, too, won him highly flattering notices in England
nd Austria. Novello was again the publisher.

After that, with one or two exceptions, the name Simrock appears on all
Dvorak's published scores. One exception is the cantata *The American Flag,*
et to a text by J. R. Drake in 1892, and published by G. Schirmer of New York.
n 1912, the same Berlin house that once alleged Dvorak's "larger works did
ot earn it anything," published two posthumous symphonies, without number,
ne in E flat major, the other in D minor, originally listed as Op. 10 and 13.
he two works, dating, respectively, from 1873 and 1874, bring Dvorak's total
umber of symphonies to seven. Five, ending with the *New World,* were
ublished during his lifetime. A remarkable feature of the two unnumbered
mphonies is the influence of Wagner, whom Dvorak was shortly to forswear
or the camp of Brahms and Hanslick.

In his early analysis, Kretschmar maintained that the G major Symphony
elonged in a class with the Symphonic Poems and Slavonic Rhapsodies. He
enied its symphonic character, noting, for instance, the lack of normal de-
elopment of themes in the opening movement. Stefan, on the other hand,
eels the symphony grips the imagination because of the "wholly subjective"
ay of solving the problems it poses. And while the national coloring is
narked, as he says, it goes beyond a purely Czech range, in the same way as the
cond series of Slavonic Dances.

In the introduction to the opening movement (Allegro con brio, 4/4, G
najor) a lovely song of melancholy tinge, in G minor, is uttered by cellos and
orns. With the final chord the mode changes to major and the flute brings
a bright theme which has been likened to the "chirping of a bird." A

cadenza then leads to the first chief subject in the cellos. The strings chant part of the second theme, then taken up by clarinets and flutes. The wood wind now usher in a delicate motif pianissimo, the whole orchestra soon shouting it fortissimo. The first theme returns and fades away to phrases from the oboes and flutes which suggested "the tinkling of bells" to the Philharmonic annotator of 1892.

After bringing back the introduction, Dvorak reviews his material, altering themes and melodic fragments with fascinating shifts in color and rhythm. Abrupt transitions of mood occur. Or, as our early colleague expressed it, "outbursts of violent energy alternate in bewildering rapidity with moments of tranquillity." The movement is remarkable for its wealth of full-fledged themes, which are set off in contrast rather than fully developed.

The second movement (Adagio, 2/4, C minor and major) begins with a somber phrase reiterated by the strings. This prefatory passage contains the melodic and rhythmic material of the first section. Clarinets then discourse in a minor-and-major exchange frequent in Dvorak's music. In the second section of the movement the strings and winds take turns at a staccato figure accompanying the main melody. The figure is used in building up a striking climax. After repetition, with changes in harmony, a brief coda ends the movement. Hoffmeister saw an amusing contrast in the emergence of a "quiet religious melody side by side with a series of coquettish passages." Stefan was reminded of one of the Piano Mood Pictures, "In the Old Castle," by the Adagio, as well as of the choral theme of the *Hussite Overture*.

An odd device in the third movement (Allegretto grazioso, 3/8, G minor and major), as Stefan points out, is the "counterpoint of oboe and bassoon, in a virtual Cossack dance, to the theme of the coda, which changes from triple time to duple time." With rapid staccati in the winds and counterthemes in the strings contrastingly marked, the effect was thought to be "thoroughly comical" in 1892. What would normally be the trio of a scherzo is taken up with a charmingly simple melody in folk style. It recalls like passages in Schubert's music.

A fanfare of trumpets ushers in the last movement (Allegro non troppo, 2/4, G major) as if heralding a brisk whirl of Bohemian folk dancing. Instead, the strings announce a stately subject in two eight-measure parts, which goes through four variations. Two new themes now appear, one a flute solo, the other for clarinets, against a drolly rumbling bass. The tempo speeds up with the return of the first subject. Echoes of the chief subject of the opening movement filter through as the finale mounts to a brilliant climax.

"This symphony is not profound," says a Czech biographer. "It awakens no echo of conflict or passion. It is a simple lyric singing of the beauty of our country for the artist's consolation. It is a lovable expression of a genius who can rejoice with the idyllicism of his own forebears."

L. B.

Symphony in E minor, No. 5 ("From the New World"), Op. 95

I. Adagio; Allegro molto. II. Largo. III. Scherzo. IV. Allegro con fuoco.

WHEN ANTON DVORAK died in his beloved Prague, America mourned him as it might a native son. Editorials hymned his merits as composer and man. National figures delivered glowing tributes. Organizations sang and played his praises. Obituaries ran long and fervent, and friends and associates of the Bohemian composer during his American sojourn filled magazines and press with reminiscences.

Dvorak had come to America late in 1892. Apart from a visit to his homeland, he remained here for almost three years as head of the National Conservatory of Music in New York. In that time he taught, led concerts, composed, and absorbed American folk ways. America broadened his outlook and gave him financial security for the rest of his days. When he finally gathered his family about him and departed in 1895, he had made a noble bequest. Into a great symphony Dvorak had poured an alien's homage. The title, *From the New World,* clearly denoted its derivation. The words were superfluous. Few could ever mistake its place of origin. The staunch Czech nationalist had frankly borrowed the spirit, if not the letter, of American folk melodies. America had a stake in this man's finest achievement. The symphony has ranked high in popular favor, and the Largo long ago became a household word. Hence, the observance in 1941 of the centenary of the birth of this fiercely democratic Czech, who also wrote a cantata on the American flag and once planned to compose a new national anthem for America, was peculiarly an American duty and privilege at a time when so much that he held dear was silenced in his native land.

New Yorkers may justly regard this symphony with even greater pride, for the writing of it occurred in the five-room apartment occupied by Dvorak and his family at 327 East 17th Street. On the same street, west of the brownstone dwelling, loomed the Conservatory building. There the bearded, rugged Bohemian imparted higher musical learning to American youth. In its auditorium he rehearsed and conducted school musicales. At home, surrounded by his children and ceaselessly chattering birds, he composed. Less than three months after his arrival he had jotted down sketchily the first notes of his new symphony. It is said Mrs. Jeannette Thurber, who founded the school and engaged Dvorak, had noted his sudden interest in Negro and Indian folk music and urged him to express his reactions to America in a symphony. The "sudden interest" was prompted by three people, the critic James G. Huneker, Mrs. Thurber herself, and H. T. Burleigh, the Negro baritone and arranger,

who was enrolled in the school as student. Quantities of Negro melodies wer
shown Dvorak, who pored over them avidly. Burleigh was invited to the hous
repeatedly to sing them for him. Often Dvorak would stop him midway in
song and ask, "Do the Negroes really sing them that way?" Among th
melodies he was especially struck by was "Swing Low, Sweet Chariot." Anyor
with an ear for tune detection can readily identify part of the song in th
G major theme introduced by the flute in the opening movement of th
Symphony.

There was nothing surprising in Dvorak's instant sympathy for Negro musi
The folk element always fascinated him, and much of his music is steeped i
the brisk rhythms and melodic turns of Bohemian and Moravian folk song
He constantly counseled composers to explore native sources for fresh stimulu
Even the street cries of city dwellers were important in learning to give artisti
voice to a people's temper. Only thus, he felt, could a truly national musi
evolve. But Dvorak never advised using folk songs bodily. Composers migh
master their traits and let the music echo and reflect them without direc
citation. The other way lay hack arrangement and slavish quotation.

Harry Rowe Shelley, another Conservatory student of Dvorak's, in a maga
zine article written many years after Dvorak's death, recalled how he wa
present the day the Czech applied the finishing touches to the Largo, probabl
the most widely known symphonic movement after the Allegro moderato o
Schubert's *Unfinished Symphony*. Dvorak was seated at a piano in his shir
sleeves. Birds twittered from cages all over the apartment. Suddenly he "san
out the great theme with passion and fervor," his neck veins taut, his eye
bulging. "His whole body vibrated," wrote Shelley. When it was finished th
composer turned excitedly to the listener. "Is it not beautiful music?" h
exclaimed.

Anton Seidl, who later led the New York Philharmonic orchestra in th
world premiere on Dec. 15, 1893, used to say, "It is not a good name, *New
World Symphony!* It is homesickness, home longing." Like others, Seidl wa
struck by the unmistakable nostalgia of the Largo. William Fisher, still anothe
Conservatory student of the Bohemian composer, later made a popular chora
arrangement to frankly nostalgic words. In fact, many non-concertgoers
unfamiliar with the Largo as a symphonic movement, mistakenly suppos·
"Goin' Home" to be a Negro melody arranged for chorus.

Most astonishing of all, of course, is the theory, fully endorsed by biographers
that Dvorak in composing the Largo had in mind the story of Hiawatha i
Longfellow's poem. Here again analytical readings varied. Some construed th·
mood as Hiawatha's wooing, others as the Indian hero's lament at the grav·
of Minnehaha. To his pupil Shelley, Dvorak explained a transitional passage in
the Largo, marked Un poco più mosso, as the Indian girl's sobbing as she bid·
Hiawatha farewell. An English analyst once interpreted the plaintive chie·

eme as "a lovely night on the margin of a forest." How the swing band
aders who blare it nightly view it is their secret.

Dvorak orchestrated large parts of the symphony in Spillville, Iowa, where
: spent his summers in a large Czech colony. There he joked and chatted with
ompatriots and was freed from the constant need of using English, which he
ever fully mastered. As a hobby he indulged a flair for pigeon raising. He was
simple man of sturdy peasant stock, with little formal education and neither
ne nor taste for literature. Living with his countrymen sharpened his hunger
r home. He had come to love and admire America. Everybody was friendly
d helpful and his pupils worshipped him. His pay at the Conservatory was
bulous for him—$15,000 a year, or 30,000 gulden. (In Prague, his yearly pay
d been 1,200 gulden.) But he missed his country. He turned down the offer
a renewed contract and in the spring of 1895 sailed for home.

As for the controversy stirred up by the symphony and its bruited use of
merican folk material, opinion divided roughly into two schools. One group,
pported by the German annotator Kretschmar, accepted the work as a sort
: rhapsody on American Negro and Indian motives. The other attacked the
eory violently, emphasizing the strong Czech flavor of its pages and barely
lmitting random echoes of American folk music. Dvorak himself settled the
sue later when he flatly denied incorporating folk songs verbatim in his
mphony. "Omit the nonsense about my having made use of 'Indian' and
merican' motives," he wrote to the Berlin conductor, Oscar Nedbal, en-
osing Kretschmar's analysis. "That is a lie. I tried to write only in the spirit
: those national American melodies."

Shortly before the Philharmonic performance, Dvorak released a statement
which he laid down the then startling dictum that future American music
ould have to be founded on Negro melodies. "These beautiful and varied
emes are the product of the soil," he said. "They are American. They are the
lk songs of America, and your composers must turn to them. In the Negro
elodies of America I discover all that is needed for a great and noble school
f music."

When the *New World Symphony* raised the issue of Dvorak's use of Negro
aterial, his words aided in inciting a great hunt for suspected originals.

"Each of the four movements of the 'New World' Symphony is prefaced by
n introduction. In the case of the first movement, this is an Adagio in E minor,
/8, in which the horns and lower strings foreshadow the chief theme of the
nsuing Allegro molto (E minor, 2/4). The second theme, announced by the
ute and then taken up by the violins, soon chants its kinship to 'Swing Low,
weet Chariot.'

"The second movement is the celebrated Largo (D flat major, 4/4). The
rincipal theme is a haunting melody for English horn. There is an episode in
vhich the oboe gives out a new theme, in C sharp minor, over an organ point

in the cellos. This episode, according to Dvorak himself, is intended to sugges the gradual awakening of animal life on the prairie. Striking use is made c trills bandied back and forth among the instrumental choirs, as if they were th voices of the night or early morning in conversation.

"The animated Scherzo (Molto vivace, E minor, 3/4) has been likened t an Indian dance with chanting. There are two trios, one in E major, one i C major.

"The finale (Allegro con fuoco, E minor, 4/4), after the usual introductio begins with the first subject blared forth by horns and trumpets against fo tissimo chords for full orchestra. A jiglike melody in triplets is heard. Th clarinet intones the second theme against a tremolo in the strings. Themes fror the earlier movements appear, providing this final movement with a ric pattern of important motives from the entire symphony. A tremendous clima is built up near the end."

The work is scored for piccolo, two flutes, two oboes, English horn, tw clarinets, two bassoons, four horns, two trumpets, three trombones, bass tub, kettledrums, triangle, cymbals, and the usual strings.

L. B.

Concerto for Piano and Orchestra in G minor, Op. 33

I. Allegro agitato. II. Andante sostenuto. III. Allegro con fuoco.
(Piano part in the edition of Vilem Kurz)

Composed in the summer of 1876, this Concerto was given its first performanc at Prague on Mar. 24, 1878, with Slavkovsky to play the solo part. Its comple tion came between the writing of the Moravian Duets and the Stabat Mater and certain observers have noted resemblances between it and the two work which sandwich it.

Harriet Cohen, distinguished English pianist, has said of the piece,

The only Piano Concerto which Dvorak wrote is not typical of his work, as ar the violin or cello concertos. The themes of this Concerto are delightful and cha acteristic. The principal subject in the first movement is reminiscent of Beethove at his best in its direct simplicity. But this Concerto has never had the recognitio to which it is entitled, principally because of the unsuitability of most of the pian writing, and perhaps the weakness in the working out of the development section Not only are some of the technical passages ungainly, but the composer almos continuously throughout the work wrote the same passages for the left and righ hand. This sort of piano writing is all very well now and again, but, as can b imagined, there are moments of appalling difficulty, because a passage that migh suit the right hand working from the thumb to the little finger may be practicall impossible for the left hand, in this case working from little finger to thumb. Thi doubling of technical passages has also an extraordinary laborious effect, and it often means that a large part of the keyboard is being used continuously, thereby proving very fatiguing to the listener. It is significant that although he did not think it one of his major works, he was particularly fond of the themes in the first and last movements: it is important to note that he recognized the impracticability of many of its passages for the pianoforte [Miss Cohen, of course, refers to the original].

The pianistic deficiencies of the Concerto, therefore, were known to Dvorak himself, and he had said time and again that he would rewrite much of the passage work, but he never got to it. Vilem Kurz did the rewriting, however, and with Dvorak's authorization. In this version little of the original was altered. What the reviser did was to clarify the piano part, wherever possible, without changing its melodic or harmonic content or its essential structure.

The first movement of the Concerto is thematically rich, as well as unusually free in the quality of its modulations. With respect to the latter it proceeds quite unconventionally (for its time) before the entrance of the second subject, in B flat. The movement generally conforms to precedent, and one notes that it opens with the tutti of classical custom. The mood is elegiac, almost religious, which accounts for its comparison to the *Stabat Mater,* a work composed in the same year as the Concerto.

A brighter, romantic atmosphere pervades the second movement, which recalled to Otokar Sourek, the *Moravian Duets.*

The third movement has three subjects, the first of which appears frequently, while the remaining two are utilized as "first and second subjects, respectively, in F sharp minor and B minor, to be finally reconciled in G major. In the B minor theme the 'oriental' interval of the augmented second is used melodically, a rare occurrence in Dvorak's music." The folk tune "Nepujdu domu" ("I'm not going home") is heard fragmentarily in the third movement and at one point (in the stretto) the tune is played almost in toto.

R. C. B.

Concerto for Violin and Orchestra in A minor, Op. 53

I. Allegro ma non troppo. II. Adagio ma non troppo. III. Finale: Allegro giocoso, ma non troppo.

JOSEPH JOACHIM was the godfather of this Concerto, giving it the benefit of his spiritual and editorial care—who knows just how much? In any case Dvorak completed his first version of the work in 1879. He revised it during the following year and sent it to the great violinist for his approval. In a letter to the publisher Simrock, written on Sept. 16, 1882, Dvorak says,

Here I am again in Berlin. I have played over the Violin Concerto twice with Joachim. It pleased him, and Mr. Keller [Simrock's agent], who was also there, was very much delighted. As for me, I am glad that at last the whole business is finished. The revision has been in Joachim's hands for at least two years. He was so kind as to make over the solo part, and only in the Finale have I to make a few alterations and in some places to lighten the instrumentation. I must go again to Berlin at the beginning of November; by that time everything should be ready, and Joachim can make a rehearsal in the Hochschule.

At that rehearsal, however, Keller interpolated many a word of advice concerning improvements—to his mind—here, there, and everywhere else and to Dvorak's complete annoyance, needless to say. The composer, after a few irate letters between himself and Keller, made some cuts in the Finale, but under no circumstances would he touch the other movements. The Concerto, bearing the inscription, "Composed and dedicated to the great Master Joseph Joachim with deepest respect," obtained its first performance at Vienna, on Dec. 3, 1883, by the Philharmonic Orchestra with Franz Ondricek to play the solo part.

The initial performance in this country occurred in Chicago, on Oct. 31, 1891. Max Bendix and the Chicago Symphony Orchestra under the direction of Theodore Thomas were the artists concerned. New York heard it first under New York Symphony auspices on Jan. 5, 1894. Henri Marteau was the violinist, Walter Damrosch the conductor. Maud Powell played it at its first appearance in the Philharmonic repertory on Apr. 6, 1894. The Concerto has been called "violinistic," which would seem to be in its favor, and another observer has praised it for its "skillful workmanship and admirable style."

As is more or less customary with concertos, the work is in three movements. The first movement (Allegro ma non troppo, A minor) is fundamentally in sonata form, although the composer has taken occasional turns to the left and to the right of the straight path in the endeavor to "transcend the classic model." There is first an orchestral flourish, which serves to usher in the principal theme, announced by the solo violin. Lyrical and, at the same time, vigorous in character, the theme concludes with several arpeggios. With the utterance of the subject in a different key the orchestra now heads into a sequence of development, and the violins mention a new theme in octaves against a counterpoint in the wood winds. For a considerable period the material already offered is developed and, next, the solo instrument takes up a third theme. This is given the benefit of elaboration, and during the ensuing development subtle echoings of the first theme enter the picture. The echoes and the subtlety presently lead to a full realization of this subject in the orchestra, the violins, specifically, restating it in octaves. On the heels of a crescendo the orchestra subsides, to lead, without pause, into the next section.

The second movement (Adagio ma non troppo, F major, 3/8) is entered into by means of the principal subject. Simplicity is the word for the construc-

ion. Dvorak often drew from the substantial store of Czech melodies and no
ess so in this case. The solo instrument sings a romanza, or air, against a
background played by the woodwind. For a time the violin is engaged with
florid passages, soon returning to the simple tune of the initial theme. Then in
he tonality of F minor the solo instrument brings forward another phase of
the movement, a Poco più mosso, and later works its way in figures of various
kinds around a third subject. This, given out by the strings in C major,
Un poco tranquillo, quasi Tempo I, is rather related to the first theme.
At this point the solo violin launches into a rhapsodic mood, and it is maintained for some time. The second subject is brought back in an orchestral tutti.
Later the wood winds reassert the principal theme with the solo violin engaging
in a series of figures around it. The flutes and oboes now head into some
measures of syncopation. There is a return of the third theme, first heard in the
orchestra, then in the solo instrument. In conclusion two horns offer the first
theme, while the solo violin traces an ornamental line around it.

The third movement (Finale: Allegro giocoso, ma non troppo, A major, 3/8)
is a lively rondo, in which three themes arise, all announced first by the solo
instrument. There is much dash and *élan* to the section, the themes are folkish
and bright. These, together with other materials, are woven into a vivid
example of the rondo form, and the Concerto ends brilliantly.

R. C. B.

Concerto for Cello and Orchestra in B minor, Op. 104

I. Allegro. II. Adagio ma non troppo. III. Allegro moderato.

THOUGH COMPLETED in Prague during the summer of 1895, the B minor Cello
Concerto belongs with a substantial group of works, topped by the *New World
Symphony,* originating from Dvorak's American period. They include a
quartet, written in three days, a quintet, a piano suite, a sonatina for piano and
viola, and *Ten Biblical Songs.* The world-famous *Humoresque* was also
written on American soil. As further tribute to the New World, Dvorak
composed a cantata on the American flag, planned a *Hiawatha* opera, and
toyed with the idea of replacing "The Star-Spangled Banner" with a new
anthem. Add a weekly routine of teaching, coaching, and conducting, plus the
job of running a music conservatory in New York, and it can be seen that
Dvorak's American stay was no frolic.

Dvorak had begun work on his Cello Concerto in his East Seventeenth Street
apartment in New York the previous November. The inspiration is said to
have come earlier that year from hearing Victor Herbert, later to blossom out
as America's foremost operetta composer, play the solo part in the Philharmonic

Society's premiere of his own second cello concerto. Dvorak expressed grea
admiration for the music of Herbert, then mainly known as a highly skillec
cellist who had played with the Metropolitan Opera orchestra under Anto
Seidl and in concerts directed by Theodore Thomas.

Others believe the suggestion to write a cello concerto was made to Dvoral
by Professor Hans Wihan, a friend and colleague in Prague. Professor Wihan
himself a cellist, wanted the work for his own public use. In any case the dedi
cation is to him. Wihan was one of two cellists who had an editorial finger ir
the Concerto pie. The other was Alwin Schroeder, consulted by Dvorak ir
New York about certain passage writing. The Wihan role is a little more
complicated than Schroeder's.

In June, 1895, Dvorak informed his publisher Simrock that the "principa
part with fingering and bowing indications has been made by Professor Wihar
himself." Wihan apparently wanted to go much further in the collaboratior
and argued heatedly with Dvorak as to what should and should not go intc
the Concerto. Fearing the stubborn professor might prevail on Simrock tc
incorporate his notions into the scoring, Dvorak wrote the publisher on Oct. 3

My friend Wihan and I have differed as to certain things. Many of the passage
do not please me, and I must insist that my work be printed as I have written it
In certain places the passages may, indeed, be printed in two versions—a com
paratively easy and a more difficult one.
The Finale closes gradually diminuendo—like a breath—with reminiscences o
the first and second movements; the solo dies away to a pianissimo, then there is a
crescendo, and the last measures are taken up by the orchestra, ending stormily.
That was my idea, and from it I cannot recede.

Just how much of Schroeder and Wihan survived disputes and consultation
in the passage writing, there is no way of determining. Dvorak was not the first
and certainly not the last, composer to consult an expert on at least the practica
side of the solo work. Some of the most gripping soliloquies in concerto litera
ture owe their origin, at least in part, to half-forgotten musicians who knew
their violin or cello or piano as their composer friends could never hope tc
know them. Of course a Paganini does not consult a fiddler about a violir
concerto and a Pablo Casals can get along nicely without calling in the
Schroeders and Wihans. With them the solo writing begins at home. In othe
cases, calling in the specialist has saved the composer many later headaches.

The world premiere occurred in London on Mar. 16, 1896, with Leo Sterr
as soloist, at a concert of the Philharmonic Society, led by Dvorak himself
The Society had invited him over for one concert the previous November, bu
he had delayed four months before finally appearing in the English capital
His Symphony in G and the *Biblical Songs* were also on the program. Publishec
that year by Simrock, the Concerto brought the composer 6,000 marks.

After the London premiere, Leo Stern reappeared as soloist in the work in Breslau and Leipzig. Later he came to America and played the Concerto with the Chicago Orchestra in January, 1897, and two months later with the New York Philharmonic. Schroeder, entering the picture first as consultant, reentered as soloist in the Concerto's first hearing in Boston on Dec. 19, 1896.

Besides solo cello, the B minor Concerto is scored for two flutes, two oboes, two clarinets, two bassoons, four horns, two trumpets, three trombones, tuba, tympani, triangle, and strings. The three movements are marked I. Allegro (B minor, 4/4); II. Adagio ma non troppo (G major, 3/4); III. Allegro moderato (B minor, 2/4). One of the striking features of this work is indicated in Dvorak's letter to Simrock, *i.e.,* the "reminiscences of the first and second movements" contained in the finale. This applies especially to the main theme of the Allegro, first stated in B minor by the clarinet and bassoons and later picked up by the solo cello in E minor. This opening theme is heard in varying guises throughout the work. In the rondo finale it returns as a rhythmic variant. Whatever influence Victor Herbert's cello music in particular and the American milieu in general may have exerted on Dvorak's concerto, there is no escaping the Slavic folk flavor of many pages. Dvorak was steeped in the melodic and rhythmic ways of the Czech countryside. The nostalgia that chants through the Concerto was a genuine and deep-rooted homesickness that colored much of the music of his American period.

L. B.

"Ein Heldenlied" ("A Hero's Song")

AFTER RETURNING from America to his own country in the spring of 1895, Dvorak settled down to a period of rest at his countryplace in Vysoka. In the fall he returned to the Prague Conservatory of Music as director and professor of composition. Shortly thereafter the composing urge seized him and he added two string quartets, in G major (Op. 105) and in A flat major (Op. 106), to his huge output. Then Dvorak's thoughts unexpectedly turned to "program" music. Apart from pictorial and narrative details in the earlier overtures, the field was virtually new to him. Up to then his symphonic work had been largely in classical sonata mold; his music had adhered to "pure" and formal ideals. Now, as if to show the world that he too could play the "program" game of Berlioz, Liszt, Smetana, Richard Strauss, and the Russians, he plunged into a series of "symphonic poems," completing five separate examples in less than two years.

The direct literary stimulus for the first four came from a reading of the tragic folk ballads of the Czech poet K. J. Erben. Each is based on a legend, part fairy tale, part grim, ghastly fantasy, recounted by the poet. Their translated titles are *The Water Sprite* (Op. 107), *The Noon Witch* (Op. 108), *The*

Golden Spinning-Wheel (Op. 109), and *The Forest Dove* (Op. 110), which was finished at Vysoka toward the end of 1896.

A Hero's Song (in Czech, *Pizen bohatyrska*), the last in the series, forming Op. 110, does not tie in with the fantastic and legendary scope of the cycle. Instead its relation to the other "poems" is ethical and philosophical. Allegedly the motivating idea of the series is moral conflict and providential control of human destiny. The folkish flavor also proclaims its kinship with the other four. The "hero" of the title is no warrior, but an idealist crusading for "lofty" thoughts. The thematic scheme covers "strength, determination, disappointment, protest, revived hope, struggle, and finally triumph of the idea," in the view of Otakar Sourek and Paul Stefan, Dvorak's biographers. Sometime later it invited unfair comparison with Richard Strauss's *Ein Heldenleben*, which followed it in six months, especially since it was assumed that Dvorak, too, intended the *Hero's Song* as autobiography. Sourek and Stefan find a parallel in the "hero's final triumph" and Dvorak's own career through the recognition and security that had come to him after the early years of struggle and uncertainty.

Jan Lowenbach speaks of the work's thematic unity and four-part symphonic plan as showing how Dvorak adjusted his classical preferences to free dramatic exposition.

A swift opening section, Allegro con fuoco, is followed by a slow movement, Poco adagio lacrimoso. After a brief recall of the introductory theme, there follows a scherzo section, then a recapitulation of the opening part, with a brilliant climax leading to the finale. The main motives dominating the scheme alter and develop according to Dvorak's philosophical plan of struggle toward victory, with new contrasts constantly enriching the development.

Sourek and Stefan have labeled the three themes, "Determination" (with eight variations), "Disappointment," and "Solace and Hope," the third appearing first in the middle part of the Adagio section.

Gustav Mahler, who had been conducting the Vienna Philharmonic since Sept. 24, 1898, wrote Dvorak that autumn for permission to conduct his latest score, whatever it might be. Dvorak replied by forwarding his two latest compositions, *The Forest Dove* and *A Hero's Song*. Mahler wrote back that he was "overjoyed" with both, and thus the premiere of Dvorak's last symphonic work occurred in the Austrian capital on Dec. 4, 1898. Prague did not hear it until June, 1899, when Oscar Nedbal directed it. According to Mr. Lowenbach, the "symphonic poem" took nineteen days to sketch out in full, from Aug. 4 to 2, 1897, at Vysoka. Although the score was ready for performance on Oct. 2, it lay in Dvorak's desk drawer a year before Mahler received his appointment and made his request.

The lapse of several months of creative inactivity between *The Water Spri*

and *A Hero's Song* has been attributed to Dvorak's grief over the death of
Brahms, his friend and revered master. Dvorak attended the burial on Apr. 6,
1897, and was moved to tears by Richard von Perger's funeral oration. The loss
apparently left him powerless to work. He laid aside sketches for new compositions, and the publisher Simrock's reminder that he had promised Brahms
to arrange some of his last piano ·pieces was unavailing. At length Dvorak
resumed work on a revision of his opera *The Jacobins,* and soon the impulse
came to round out his cycle of *symphonische Dichtungen* with a fifth, *A Hero's
Song.*

L. B.

"Carneval," Overture for Grand Orchestra, Op. 92

DVORAK CONCEIVED the *Carneval Overture* as the middle unit of a "triple
overture" designed to convey feelings aroused in him by "three great creative
forces of the Universe—Nature, Life, and Love," the first and third embodied
in the companion pieces *In der Natur* and *Othello.*

A melodic theme, recurring in all three overtures, is supposed to reflect the
composer's awe before the "unchangeable laws of the Universe."

In *Carneval,* Dvorak is said to have imagined "a lonely, contemplative
wanderer" reaching a city at nightfall while a street carnival is in full swing.
Instruments clang on all sides, mingling with the gay laughter of the revelers,
who join in a brisk dance. The violins set up a wild cry as the wanderer is
whirled "into the Bohemian revel."

As the hubbub subsides the listener is expected to follow "a pair of straying
lovers." A solo violin chants a soft theme, with the English horn and flutes
chiming in suavely, and a pastoral theme brings "recollection of tranquil scenes
of nature."

The peaceful mood is shattered by a return of the merrymakers, as the
brusque Slavic dance of the opening section returns. All three themes, "the
humorous, the pathetic, and the pastoral," merge, with the first dominant, and
the overture ends in the first key, A major.

The "triple overture" served Dvorak as a "farewell" token when he left
Prague for America in the spring of 1892 and as a gesture of greeting to the
New World when he led his first concert here, at the Music Hall (now Carnegie
Hall), New York, on Oct. 21, 1892. The first occasion was its world premiere,
the second its American.

L. B.

"Slavonic Dances," Op. 46 and Op. 72

DVORAK'S FIRST set of *Slavonic Dances,* issued in 1878, carried his name across
national boundaries to distant parts. "Like Byron he awoke to find himself

famous," wrote W. H. Hadow, "and to look back upon the times of darknes
and disappointment as a man looks back upon his dreams."

Indirectly Dvorak had Brahms to thank for the sudden climb to fame
Brahms had spoken highly of Dvorak's music to the publisher Simrock. Both
were enchanted with the folkish charm of the earlier *Moravian Duets,* and
Simrock commissioned the Bohemian composer to write a set of *Slavonic
Dances* in the style of Brahms's *Hungarian Dances.* Dvorak had barely com
pleted the first of his three *Slavonic Rhapsodies* when he promptly set to work
on the series. In his previous music, he had continually employed the Polka
Furiant, and Sousedska, but these represented his first extended use of authentic
Czech dance forms. The first of them was ready on Mar. 18, 1878, the others
following in short order. Of the set Nos. 1 and 8 are Furiants, No. 6 a Polka
Nos. 3 and 4 Sousedskas, No. 2 a Dumka, and Nos. 5 and 7 (Allegro vivace
and Allegro assai) Skocnas, or "Spring Dances."

Sourek and Stefan point out in their biography that Dvorak "idealizes the
folk dance here," appropriating only the rhythmic base. "Melody and harmony
are his personal property," they write, whereas Brahms uses gypsy melodies
bodily. On their appearance Louis Ehlert, writing in the *Berliner National-
zeitung,* predicted that the *Slavonic Dances* "would make the rounds of the
whole world" because of the "heavenly naturalness surging through them."
He hailed the "real, naturally real talent" of their composer and the fine workmanship of the dances. "This is no pastiche pieced together haphazardly from
national echoes," he remarked. Composed first for piano for two hands, they
were immediately arranged for orchestra by Dvorak. Simrock paid him 300
marks for the set and then proceeded to make a fortune through an unprecedented sale. Eight years later, when a second sheaf was issued as Op. 72, the
house paid Dvorak ten times as much. In the interim, Dvorak's market value
had gone up, roughly, one thousand per cent!

In explaining the quick and unexpected popularity of the dances, Hoffmeister
mentions that at the time "nationalism in music was beginning to be appreciated and the *Slavonic Dances* came as a distinct revelation. They were, it was
felt, authentic, springing directly from the soul of the people. Something of the
Slavic character speaks in every phrase of them—the stormy high-spirited mood
of the Furiants; the whimsical merriment, the charm, the touch of coquetry,
the ardent tenderness of the lyrical passages."

It has been pointed out that the first set, comprising dances native to
Bohemia, is almost strictly Czech in style, while the second is Slavonic in a
wider sense, with the feeling predominantly Yugoslav or Little Russian.

                                                                    L. B.

Edward Elgar

BORN: BROADHEATH, NEAR WORCESTER, ENGLAND, JUNE 2, 1857. DIED: WORCESTER, FEB. 23, 1934.

*From the point of view of one person or another I understand all my music has been a crime: "Cockaigne," the "Coronation Ode," and the "Imperial March." Yes, I believe there are a good many people who have objected to them. But I like to look on the composer's vocation as the old troubadours or bards did. In those days it was no disgrace for a man to be turned on to step in front of an army and inspire them with a song. For my part, I know that there are a lot of people who like to celebrate events with music. To these people I have given tunes. Is that wrong? Why should I write a fugue or something that won't appeal to any one, when the people yearn for things which can stir them?—*EDWARD ELGAR.

Variations on an Original Theme ("Enigma"), Op. 36

FOR A NUMBER of years following the first performance of this work in London, June, 1899, musical sleuths—from tyro to Tovey and back—conducted exhaustive research, shall we say?, in the matter of identifying the characters professed by each of the Variations. Elgar had made cryptic utterances regarding the hidden personalities in the score, which only served to accelerate the hunt. "In this music," he once said, "I have sketched, for their amusement and mine, the idiosyncrasies of fourteen of my friends, not necessarily musicians; but this is a personal matter and need not have been mentioned publicly. The Variations should stand simply as a 'piece' of music. The *Enigma* I will not explain—its 'dark saying' must be left unguessed."

Nevertheless, the feverish activity of the "sleuths" was partially rewarded, and the rest of the mystery was finally cleared up when Sir Ivor Atkins, a very close friend of Elgar's, aired the entire facts in the London *Musical Times* after the composer's death.

The fourteen Variations were marked with initials, pseudonyms, or asterisks. The first is a tonal portrait of the composer's wife. The second represents the pianist H. D. Stuart-Powell. The third connotes Richard Baxter Townshend. The fourth describes, so to speak, William M. Baker, a country squire.

Richard Arnold, son of the poet and essayist Matthew Arnold, is the subject of the fifth. Isabel Fitton, a viola player, is the "Ysobel" of the sixth. The seventh Variation, "Troyte," refers to the aggressive and vehement Arthur

Troyte Griffith. The eighth pays an elegant tribute to Winifred Norbury, a patrician lady of the preceding generation.

A. A. Jaeger was the inspiration for the ninth, which carries the designation "Nimrod." Of this Variation Elgar said, "It is a record of a long summer evening talk when my friend Jaeger grew nobly eloquent—as only he could—on the grandeur of Beethoven and especially of his slow movements."

Dora Penny, an intimate friend, answers "present" to the tenth Variation. The eleventh, which was productive of much amusement to Elgar, depicts not only George Robertson Sinclair, organist of Hereford Cathedral, but the latter's bulldog Dan, as well. The cellist Basil G. Nevinson is the topic of the twelfth. The next discusses Lady Mary Lygon, and the clarinet's quoting of a phrase from the Mendelssohn overture *Sea-calm and Prosperous Voyage* is related to the fact that she was on her way to Australia when Elgar composed the thirteenth Variation. The fourteenth, and final one, is the composer's self-portrait.

R. C. B.

Overture, "Cockaigne (in London Town)," Op. 40

WHEN THIS overture was first played at a Philharmonic Society concert in Queen's Hall, London, on June 20, 1901, it gave rise to endless discussion, because it unashamedly tried to portray London in tone, and in sonata form, no less. "London, as represented by its parks and open spaces, the bands marching from Knightsbridge to Buckingham Palace, Westminster with its dignified associations of Church and State, is mirrored in glowing orchestral colors," Grove said of it.

However, the mere fact that a composer had employed sonata form for the expression of a definite program, of known images, static and kinetic, proved a source of irritation to many minds of a puristic turn.

Sir Donald F. Tovey, brilliant essayist, has written in defense of this overture,

British music is emerging from various forms of darkness before dawn; and of these forms perhaps the darkest is that which a now almost too popular psychology calls "the inferiority complex." When, at the turn of the century, Elgar expressed his love of London in an overture neither more nor less vulgar than Dickens, the principal impression made on the musical criticism of those ancient days was one of reverential dread at the audacity of the English composer who handles the resources of the sonata form as if he had the presumption to understand them.

Tovey goes on to say that orchestration had not previously been a particular gift of English composers, yet Elgar had succeeded in breaking that tradition quite suddenly by his use of "sonata form stated in terms of consummate orchestration."

Further, he admits to finding no "vulgarity in Elgar's Brass Band as it comes blaring down B flat street. . . . The *Cockaigne Overture* is true to nature and says its say straightforwardly in terms of the highest art."

The overture is scored for double-bassoon, four horns, two trumpets, three or five trombones, kettledrums, bass and tenor drums, organ, and the usual strings and wood winds.

The first American performance of the piece took place in Boston at a concert of the Boston Symphony Orchestra under the direction of Wilhelm Gericke on Nov. 29, 1901. On Nov. 8, 1914, Walter Damrosch and the Symphony Society of New York offered it in Carnegie Hall.

R. C. B.

"Falstaff": A Symphonic Study for Orchestra

WRITTEN FOR the Leeds Festival of October, 1913, Elgar's *Falstaff* obtained its American premiere by the New York Symphony Orchestra on Dec. 12, 1913. It is an out-and-out piece of program music, whose subject is not the hero of *The Merry Wives of Windsor,* but the Falstaff of *Henry IV* (1 and 2) and *Henry V.*

This study—or, as it has also been named, symphonic poem—is in one movement with two interludes. Recognizably, there are four principal divisions to the music, as is also implied in the carefully contrived subtitles of Elgar, though none of these divisions is shown in the score. He has named the sections:

I. Falstaff and Prince Henry
II. Eastcheap—Gadshill—The Boar's Head, Revelry and Sleep
III. Falstaff's March—The Return through Gloucestershire—The New King —The Hurried Ride to London
IV. King Henry V's Progress—The Repudiation of Falstaff and His Death.

Elgar's hero is by no means the character of Morgann's description, "made up by Shakespeare wholly of incongruities—a man at once young and old, enterprising and fat, a dupe and a wit, harmless and wicked, weak in principle and resolute by constitution, cowardly in appearance and brave in reality; a knave without malice; a lyar without deceit; and a knight, a gentleman and a soldier, without either (*sic*) dignity, decency, or honour."

The composer flouts the image of Falstaff evoked in *The Merry Wives of Windsor,* that "caricature, which, unluckily, is better known to English playgoers than the real Falstaff." He prefers to clothe him with the virtues implicit in three words,—knight, gentleman, and soldier—all contained in the last clause of Morgann's statement.

Another musical interpreter of Falstaff, Giuseppe Verdi, saw the character as a "rogue who commits every kind of rascally action, but in an amusing way."

Yet the opera libretto by Arrigo Boito has its roots also in the nobler presentation to be found in *Henry IV,* with particular reference to the considerable monologue on Honor.

It is quite obvious, from Elgar's words, that he himself needed no ideological support of his hero from sources outside his own imagination and understanding. And though his discussion is abundantly interspersed with quotations from many writers, the listener may look upon them as additional aids to the comprehension of Elgar's *Falstaff.*

One such is taken from Hazlitt: "The true spirit of humanity, the thorough knowledge of the stuff we are made of, the practical wisdom with the seeming fooleries, have no parallel anywhere else. . . . In one point of view they are laughable in the extreme, in another they are equally affecting—if it is affecting to show what a little thing is human life."

According to the composer, Falstaff is represented here by five themes, four in the first section, the fifth in the second. The principal one, which opens the piece, depicts the fat knight, "in a green old age, mellow, frank, gay . . . loose, unprincipled, and luxurious." The three other themes in the first part are, "One for clarinet, a chord for horns and answering chord for strings; one for high wood winds, which the composer has related to the line, 'I am not only witty in myself, but the cause that wit is in other men,' " and another, consisting of an upward crescendo for the cellos, which is connected with the line, "Sweet wag, when thou art king."

The fifth "personal" Falstaff theme appears as a "boastful and vociferous" expression, associated with Shakespeare's words, "I am a rogue, if I were not at half swords with a dozen of them two hours together."

The score for this music calls for two flutes, piccolo, two clarinets, bass clarinet, two oboes, English horn, two bassoons, contra-bassoon, four horns, three trumpets, three trombones, tuba, tympani, drums, two harps, and strings.

R. C. B.

March, "Pomp and Circumstance," in D major, Op. 39

Premiered on Oct. 19, 1901, in Liverpool, England, at the season's opening concert of the Liverpool Orchestral Society, this composition was the first in a planned series of Six Military Marches grouped under the "generic name," as Elgar called it, of *Pomp and Circumstance.* The second march, in A minor, was given on the same occasion. Elgar subsequently wrote three others, but he died before rounding off the set with a final march. Since the project was to include a "soldier's funeral march," the poignant choral tribute, "For The Fallen," has been suggested as a fitting substitute for the missing sixth. When critics taunted Elgar with writing "a plain, honest tune which the man in the street could sing or whistle," he retorted:

Why should I write a fugue or something that won't appeal to any one, when the people yearn for things which can stir them? With regard to the *Pomp and Circumstance* marches, I did not see why the ordinary quick march should not be treated on a large scale in the way that the waltz, the old-fashioned slow march, and even the polka have been treated by the great composers; yet all marches on the symphonic scale are so slow that people can't march to them. I have some of the soldier instinct in me, and so I have written two marches of which, so far from being ashamed, I am proud.

As further rejoinder, he asked: "Why should a composer always write in an exacting spirit? Why not relax the bow occasionally?"

Elgar's D major march follows a simple A-B-A-B pattern, with the rugged introductory theme representing A (Allegro, con molto fuoco) and a majestic trio theme (Largamente) representing B. After the trio subject is repeated, a resounding coda sets in. Shortly after composing the march, Elgar used the trio melody as the final chorus of his *Coronation Ode,* with words by Arthur Christopher Benson. So stirring was the effect of the finale at the premiere of the *Ode* in Queen's Hall, London, that the composer was brought back to the stage five times. One enthusiastic patron shouted down from the balcony: "Let's have the last part again!" The original trio tune, with Benson's words, is now widely known as "Land of Hope and Glory," the refrain of which runs as follows:

> Land of Hope and Glory, Mother of the Free,
> How shall we extol thee, who are born of thee?
> Wider still and wider shall thy bounds be set;
> God who made thee mighty, make thee mightier yet.

L. B.

Georges Enesco

BORN: DOROHOIÛ, RUMANIA, AUG. 19, 1881.

*People have been puzzled and annoyed because they have been unable
to catalogue and classify me in the usual way. They could not decide
exactly what type of music mine was. It was not French after the
manner of Debussy, it was not exactly German, they declared. In
short, while it did not sound outlandish, it did not closely resemble
anything familiar, and people are annoyed when they cannot readily
classify one.*—GEORGES ENESCO.

"Rumanian Rhapsody in A major," Op. 11, No. 1

GEORGES ENESCO himself conducted the world premieres of his first and second
Rumanian Rhapsodies at one of Pablo Casals' concerts in the Salle Gaveau,
Paris, on Feb. 7, 1908. By then it had become clear that a new voice had joined
the swelling chorus of European music, a voice from a hitherto quiet corner of
the music world. Creatively, the history of Rumanian music almost coincides
with the career of Georges Enesco. Before that there had been good schooling
and good performance and a great deal of folk singing and dancing. But in the
art circles of Europe, Rumania had been conspicuous by her absence.

And in Enesco, Rumania presented a spokesman who combined two great
virtues. As a technician he could match the best other countries could offer.
He was a pianist, a violinist, a cellist, an organist, and conductor, and had won
acclaim in the Vienna and Paris conservatories. Composers like Fauré and
Massenet had early recognized his gifts and encouraged him to go on. Then,
Enesco was a staunch nationalist, steeped in the folklore and tradition of his
land, and eager to make his music a channel for this legacy. Very early Enesco
began to write music around his country's popular songs and dances. There
was a *Poème Roumain,* a *Pastorale Fantasie,* and then came the *Rumanian
Rhapsodies.* Of course, there was more to Georges Enesco than folklore and
rhapsody. There was music strictly his own, with traces of French and German
influences, to be sure, but music of a sensuous character that reflected personal
esthetics rather than national moods. Essentially, however, he was and remains
a Rumanian in music.

In the *First Rumanian Rhapsody,* Enesco is, of course, the nationalist. These
are genuine folk motives that appear and reappear in the pulsing web. There
are dances colored in the rustic ways of the peasantry and themes of a marked
gypsy flavor, all a-throb in a heaving carrousel of rhythm. "There is no hyper-

refinement, no devitalizing or polishing up of the original tunes," wrote Olin Downes in his review of the Boston premiere in 1912. "They fly by in rotation, faster and faster, wilder and wilder, with capricious changes of rhythm, sudden pianissimos and mad bursts of tone, and whirling figures that set off the flight of the main melodies."

And what were these melodies like? Did the Rumanian folk tune have a quality of its own? Yes and no. Enesco himself has said Rumanian music shows traces of Indian and Egyptian folk songs, brought in by nomad captives of the ancient Romans. This may account for the Oriental sensuousness. Then there are hints of Magyar and Slavic influences and the warmth and animation of Latin sources. So that Rumanian folk music is almost a unique amalgam of multiple racial elements. Chief among the types of Rumanian melody are the *doinas* (laments) and the dances Sirba and Hora, of which Dinicu's *Hora Staccato* is a now famous example.

In the rhapsodic scheme of the A major, the main role is played by a widely popular drinking song *"Am un leu si vrau sa* ("I have a coin and I want a drink"). It emerges at the very beginning in fragments given out by the clarinet, answered by the oboe, and before long it is dancing merrily among the strings. Four other melodies appear in the course of the *Rhapsody*. They succeed each other in a span of growing intensity. Though one or two themes are developed slightly, the changes are rather shifts in pace and orchestral color. The transitions are such as to give the impression of gathering momentum toward an exciting goal. There are moments of deceiving repose, sudden headlong sweeps like chromatic descents among the wood winds, and toward the end a maddening accelerando that seems to catch the frenzy of a dance carnival at its climax of whirling revelry.

L. B.

Manuel de Falla

BORN: CADIZ, SPAIN, NOV. 23, 1876.

Falla's music is completely Spanish in feeling and expression. All the characteristic features of Spanish popular music are to be found in his works. So authentic is his reconstruction of the native idioms that many critics have classified a work like "El Amor Brujo" as a pure folklore product. But this ballet contains not a single folk tune, though it is directly inspired by the gypsy folklore of Andalusia. The process by which Falla achieves this authentic yet personal reconstruction is one of assimilation rather than imitation.—GILBERT CHASE.

Three Dances from the Ballet "The Three-cornered Hat" ("El sombrero de tres picos")

(a) The Neighbors. (b) The Miller's Dance. (c) Final Dance.

PEDRO DE ALARCON's racy novelette *El sombrero de tres picos* was the source of Manuel de Falla's picturesque ballet. The story of the amorous corregidor and the miller's wife had come to the attention of Serge de Diaghileff, while the Russian Ballet was touring Spain. It seems that de Falla had already written a score for a "pantomime" adapted from Alarcon's tale by the playwright Martinez Sierra. As such, the work had been warmly acclaimed at the Eslava Theater in Madrid. It then bore the title *El corregidor y la molinera*. After de Falla had played parts of the score for Diaghileff, the noted ballet impresario urged the composer to rearrange the music for the dance. In the "pantomime" the story, as Cyril W. Beaumont points out, "was so minutely expressed as to leave little or nothing to the art of the choreographer." De Falla revised the score, also adding the Farucca and Jota. Leonide Massine, enchanted with Andalusian song and dance, set to work on the choreography.

For atmosphere Diaghileff, de Falla, and Massine visited colorful out-of-the-way places in Andalusia. "One night," writes Beaumont, "as they walked in the streets, they encountered a blind man, chanting a melody to the accompaniment of a broken guitar." The same melody is used by de Falla in his score. The ballet *El sombrero de tres picos,* with choreography by Massine and décor by Pablo Picasso, was first produced at the Alhambra Theater, London, on July 22, 1919. Massine danced the Miller, Thamar Karsavina the Miller's Wife, and Leon Woizikowsky the corregidor. Two days later the *Daily Telegraph* said of the new ballet:

Over the whole brisk action is the spirit of frivolous comedy of a kind by no means common only to Spain of the eighteenth century. A young miller and his wife are the protagonists, and if their existence be idyllic in theory, it is extraordinarily strenuous in practice—choreographically. But that is only another way of saying that M. Massine and Madame Karsavina, who enact the couple, are hardly ever off the stage, and that both of them work with an energy and exuberance that almost leave one breathless at moments. The miller and his wife between them, however, would scarcely suffice even for a slender ballet plot. So we have as well an amorous Corregidor (or Governor), who orders the miller's arrest so that the way may be cleared for a pleasant little flirtation—if nothing more serious—with the captivating wife. Behold the latter fooling him with a seductive dance, and then evading her admirer with such agility that, in his pursuit of her, he tumbles over a bridge into the mill stream. But, as this is comedy, and not melodrama, the would-be lover experiences nothing worse than a wetting, and the laugh, which is turned against him, is renewed when, having taken off some of his clothes to dry them, and gone to rest on the miller's bed, his presence is discovered by the miller himself, who, in revenge, goes off in the intruder's garments after scratching a message on the wall to the effect that "Your wife is no less beautiful than mine!"

In the concert suite drawn from the ballet score, the first dance is entitled "The Neighbors," the second "The Miller's Dance," the third "Final Dance." The first (Allegro ma non troppo, D major, 3/4) evokes a scene in festive mood as the neighbors gather outside the miller's house on St. John's Eve. The second (Moderato assai, molto ritmico e pesante, C major, 3/4), typically Andalusian in its contrast of strong rhythms and languorous melody, depicts the Miller's rough, forthright nature, with its tinge of melancholy. To Joaquin Turina this dance "was like an affirmation of Southern art." The third dance (Allegro ritmico) is a Jota in triple time, shifting in mood and rhythm and mounting to a brilliant finale, which accompanies the Falstaff-like drubbing of the amorous magistrate.

L. B.

Suite from the Ballet Pantomime El amor brujo ("Love the Sorcerer")

GREGORIO MARTINEZ SIERRA based his libretto for this "ballet with voice and orchestra" on an Andalusian gypsy tale. J. B. Trend observes that the story derives "from the folk tale, found from Cornwall to Czechoslovakia, in which the ghost of the dead lover always appears at the moment when a new lover tries to take his place. . . . Falla's ballad shows how 'love lays the specter' . . . and the method employed is, as might be imagined, dancing." El amor brujo was given its premiere at the Teatro de Lara, Madrid, Apr. 15, 1915, with Pastora Imperio as the soloist. Later a concert version was performed at

Madrid, during the 1915-1916 season, at one of the events scheduled by the Sociedad de Musica, E. Fernandez-Arbos conducting. Arturo Toscanini led performances of the complete work at concerts of the Philharmonic Society, Mar. 1 and 2, 1928, Sophie Braslau appearing as the assisting artist, and again on Apr. 19 and 20, 1934, during his conductorship of the Philharmonic-Symphony.

Jean-Aubrey declares that the thematic material of *El amor brujo* is "built on rhythms, modes, cadences, or forms inspired but never directly borrowed from Andalusian folk song. . . . We should be wrong to see in Falla nothing but an 'evoker' of picturesque Spain. He is rather a poet of Spanish emotion."

The score calls for two flutes, piccolo, oboe, two clarinets, bassoon, two horns, two trumpets, tympani, piano, bells, and strings.

The various episodes of the Suite, together with an English translation of the text, follow:

I. Introduction and Scene (Allegro furioso, ma non troppo vivo, 3/4). Featured in this section is a decisively rhythmic figure, which becomes developed in another part.

II. "The Gypsies—Evening" (Tranquillo e misterioso, 3/4). There are thirty-three measures of prelude, following which a solo by the oboe ushers in the first of the songs.

III. "Chanson du chagrin d'amour" (Allegro, 3/4, 6/8).

> Ay, I do not know what I feel, nor what passes over me,
> When this cursed gypsy is far away;
> My blood burns from jealousy as fire burns in Hell,
> When the river calls, ay, what does it want to say?
> What does it mean to say? Ay!
> For love of another he forgets me, ay!
> My pain tortures me,
> My love poisons me,
> My pain kills me—ay!

IV. "The Homecomer" (Vivo, ma non troppo, 2/4). A muted trumpet plays a solo, followed by fast scales and glissandos in wood wind, strings and piano.

V. "Dance of Terror" (Allegro ritmico, 2/4). The oboe and a muted trumpet succeed each other with solos over accompaniment by piano, tympani, horns and strings pizzicato. There is a furious climax and the sound makes sudden shifts from pianissimo to fortissimo.

VI. "The Magic Circle" (Andante molto tranquillo, 3/4). A mysterious sequence —piano, muted strings, and muted trumpets. The flutes echo the opening phrase, and the strings close the section.

The clock strikes twelve (Lento e lontano), as Candelas prepares to dispel evil spirits with her dance.

VII. "Ritual Dance of Fire" (Allegro, ma non troppo, e pesante 2/4). A prelude of twenty-three measures, the oboe then states the main theme. Subsequently the irst violins and both horns (unison) bring on a second theme. Finally first and econd violins, together with a flute, announce the third.

VIII. "Scene" (Poco moderato—Allegro—Tempo primo, 3/4). Following a solo y the oboe, the strings—fortissimo—reminisce on the theme of the Introduction. olos for flute and oboe, and then a fermata.

IX. "Song of the Will-o-the-Wisp" (Vivo, 3/8).

> Oh, this love's a Jack-o'-lantern,
> Jack-o'-lantern is his way!
> Then, alas, those black eyes flaming,
> They saw Jack-o'-lantern play!
> > Oh, this love . . . etc., etc.
> Alas for the heart that's sorrowful
> And burns in that flame alway.
> > Oh, this love . . . etc., etc.

X. "Pantomime" (Allegro, 3/4). The theme of the Introduction is developed by he full orchestra. A pause, and then begins a poetic nocturne in G major (Andan-:ino tranquillo, 7/8).

A solo cello sings a tender song over a whispered accompaniment by flutes, strings and piano. And later the first violins and violas take up the lyrical strain. While the strings play a soft series of chords, the oboe floats above them (molto tranquillo, poco rubato). Now the cello's song is sweetly recalled by a solo violin; and solos for horn and trumpet end the section.

XI. "Dance of the Game of Love" (Allegretto mosso, 3/8, 3/4).

> You are that wicked gypsy that a gypsy loved.
> The love she gave you, you did not deserve.
> Who could have said that you would betray her for another?

* * *

> I am the voice of your destiny,
> I am the fire in which you burn,
> I am the wind in which you sigh,
> I am the sea in which you drown.

XII. Finale—"Morning Chimes" (Allegretto tranquillo, 4/4).

> And now the day is dawning.
> Ring out, O bells, ring out!
> For the glory of my love returns.

R. C. B.

Gabriel Fauré

BORN: PAMIERS, FRANCE, MAY 12, 1845. DIED: PARIS, NOV. 4, 1924.

*It is not difficult to see why Fauré's example was inspiring to a gen-
eration of composers who were quickly tiring of impressionism.
They easily overlooked the fact that Fauré had his roots in the
romantic movement, because his was a pre-Wagnerian brand of
romanticism—delicate, reserved, and aristocratic. Moreover, no matter
what its derivation may have been, it possessed all the earmarks of
the French temperament: harmonic sensitivity, impeccable taste,
classic restraint, and a love of clear lines and well-made proportions.*
—AARON COPLAND.

Ballade for Piano and Orchestra in F sharp major, Op. 19

ORIGINALLY WRITTEN for piano solo in 1881, the Ballade was later made into the
present orchestral version. Alfred Cortot, celebrated French pianist and champion of French music, discusses the work in his book *La Musique française
de piano:*

M. Fauré's individuality is recognizable at once in the completely novel conception of a form that seemed to have been fated, by Romanticism, to the exclusive
expression of passionate and heady emotion. To the contrary, the work is calm and
controlled in an atmosphere of quiet happiness, which emphasizes an instrumental
technique, deliberately light and pellucid. . . .

The grace of the orchestral version, where the added instruments assume part
of the original harmonic framework, seems to me greater than that for the piano.
The variety of timbres accentuates, yet without allowing it to predominate, the play
of translucent, quicksilver virtuosity, the swirl of arpeggios, the rushing flight of
scales, the mad ripple of trills, and from this point of view holds several attractive
modifications.

Though he composed a number of large works, such as the D minor
Symphony, Op. 40, the present work, the Violin Concerto, Op. 14, the *Requiem*
and some others, Fauré is best known for his chamber music and songs. Among
his other compositions are his only opera *Penelope* (produced at Monte Carlo,
Mar. 4, 1913) and also incidental music for quite a few dramatic productions,
notably Alexandre Dumas' *Caligula,* Edmond Haracourt's *Shylock,* after
Shakespeare, and *Julius Caesar,* by the last-named.

The distinguished American composer, Aaron Copland, has written of
Fauré in his book *Our New Music:*

It is true, of course, that Fauré's influence was confined almost exclusively to
France. Nevertheless, as he was head of the Paris Conservatory for fifteen years and

the teacher of Ravel, Florent Schmitt, Roger Ducasse, Nadia Boulanger, and many other leading figures in French musical life, his artistic principles gained broad circulation.

"It was during the last twenty-five years of his life, when Fauré had already passed the half-century mark—from about 1898 to 1923—that he really found himself as a composer. This means that Fauré's best work was written at a time when impressionism held the center of the stage in France. It follows, therefore, that interest in his work was quite overshadowed by the more spectacular achievements of Debussy. Nevertheless, if he was able to steer a course all his own, completely free of impressionist influence, it was because of the strongly personal character of his musical nature.

R. C. B.

"Pavane" and "Fileuse"

FAURÉ's PAVANE is often compared with Ravel's *Pavane pour une Infante défunte,* and even confused with it. Yet, despite the elegiac mood dominating both, they differ widely in melodic and harmonic treatment. Besides, a chorus is optional in the Fauré score, the full title of which reads, *Pavane pour orchestre, avec chœur ad libitum.* The piece dates from 1887 and was premiered in Paris a year later. The score calls for wood winds and horns in pairs, besides strings. Like the Ravel *Pavane,* the work is built around a single basic theme, announced by solo flute (Andante molto moderato) at the second measure against pizzicato figures in the second violins and violas.

The delicately woven interlude *Fileuse* is taken from Fauré's incidental music to an English version of Maurice Maeterlinck's tragic stage fable *Pelléas et Mélisande.* The translation was made for Mrs. Patrick Campbell, who first appeared in it at the Prince of Wales Theater, London, on June 21, 1898. America first heard the Fauré score as part of that production during Mrs. Campbell's tour in 1902. As an orchestral suite the music was first heard at a Lamoureux concert in Paris on Feb. 3, 1901, and then consisted of three pieces: *Prelude, Fileuse,* and *Death of Melisande.* It was thus published by J. Hamelle in Paris in 1901. A *Sicilienne* was subsequently added to the suite.

The French word *fileuse* means "spinner." The music (Andantino, quasi allegretto, G major, 3/4), constituting the play's second entr'acte, sets the mood for the opening scene of Act III, the stage directions for which read: "A room in the castle. Pelléas and Mélisande are discovered. Mélisande is at the back of the room, spinning." Musically, Maeterlinck's play evokes the name of Debussy, rather than that of Fauré. Debussy's famous lyric drama *Pelléas et Mélisande* was staged for the first time at the Opéra Comique in Paris, in 1902, with Mary Garden as the wistful woodland waif. The "revolutionary" score stirred up a sharp controversy. Fauré's, antedating it by four years and less unorthodox in idiom, made its way peacefully into the concert repertory.

L. B.

Oscar Lorenzo Fernandez

BORN: RIO DE JANEIRO, BRAZIL, NOV. 4, 1897.

A Brazilian music critic has called Fernandez "brasileirissimo" in appreciation of his devotion to the spirit of native folklore. Fernandez uses both the method of actual quotation of popular songs and the invention of original melodies in the native vein.—NICOLAS SLONIMSKY.

"Batuque" from the Suite "Reisado do Pastoreio"

COMPOSED IN 1930, "Batuque"—subtitled "Danza di negri"—is part of an orchestral suite, *Reisado do Pastoreio*. It was first performed in Rio de Janeiro on Aug. 29 of that year by the National Music School orchestra, with Francisco Braga conducting. The American premiere of "Batuque" occurred in Boston on Apr. 4, 1937, at a concert of the State Symphony Orchestra, with the Brazilian Burle Marx conducting. It was also performed at the World's Fair Music Festival on May 4, 1939, with the same conductor, and at the Lewisohn Stadium on July 16, 1942, when Efrem Kurtz directed the New York Philharmonic-Symphony. Mr. Kurtz led the first performance by the Society in Carnegie Hall on Mar. 21, 1943. The NBC Symphony has also played it.

The three-part Suite consists of a "Reisado" (song and dance of the Magi), "Toada" ("Tune"), and "Batuque" ("Danza di negri"). Said to have been brought to Brazil by African slaves, the "batuque" is defined as "a style of dance of the Negroes," with the Portuguese verb *batucar* meaning to dance the batuque. Nicolas Slonimsky was quoted by John N. Burk, annotator of the Boston Symphony Orchestra, in describing the "batuque" as a Negro dance usually marked by "strong, insistent rhythms, against the background of an ostinato figure, which would, when translated into Western terms, classify it with the passacaglia."

In writing "Batuque," Fernandez had in mind some "mysterious Negro ritual" of the Brazilian jungle. On the first page of the score appear the words: "Deep night. From the forest comes a somber rhythm of dancing. It is the savage Batuque of the Negroes. A fierce crescendo carries it to the point of paroxysm." The scoring is for one flute, two piccolos, two oboes, English horn, two clarinets, bass clarinet, two bassoons and contra-bassoon, four horns, three trumpets, three trombones, tuba, tympani, snare drum, bass drum, cymbals, tam-tam, piano, and strings.

The *Revista Brasileira de Musica* of June, 1938, observed that if Fernandez's name disguised his Brazilian origin, "Batuque" alone would certify it. "It is utterly Brazilian," it insisted, "with no trace of any element not stemming from the native soil." According to the writer, "the strongly dissonant harmonies prepare the ear and spirit for the Negro mystery; the basses announce the tense and barbarous atmosphere in which the tragedy of the race will be enacted." Fernandez makes marked use in the "Batuque" of the Mixolydian mode dominant in Negro Brazilian folk music. A theme of "African cantilena" first chanted by the horn, runs through the work as "an ineffable lament." Over the persistent rhythm of the basses, the "lament" grows in color and vigor against varying counterpoint. The scheme is boldly polytonal, notably where the "ritual" is supposed to grow frenzied and "the assembly is seized with an almost paranoic delirium."

Fernandez has still another symphonic "Batuque" to his credit, deriving from his folk opera *Malazarte,* based on a Brazilian legend. It won the New Music prize at the Bogota Festival in 1938. In all his music, Fernandez strives to apply modern technical resources to the full exploitation of native rhythms and melodies. He does not hesitate to quote freely from popular sources where necessary for color and atmosphere.

Fernandez has been called "brasileirissimo," second only to Heitor Villa-Lobos in national esteem. He studied at the Institute Nacional de Musica in his native Rio, becoming professor of harmony there is 1925. His *Trio Brasileiro,* largely based on folk themes, won first prize in an International Composers' Contest in Rio in 1924. Fernandez founded the magazine *Illustracao Musical* in 1930, and in 1936 was appointed director of the Brazilian conservatory. As conductor he has toured South America and Cuba.

L. B.

Arthur Foote

BORN: SALEM, MASS., MAR. 5, 1853. DIED: BOSTON, APR. 8, 1937.

He knew what he wanted to say and how he wanted to say it. Thus his music was distinguished by clarity and directness, good taste and craftsmanship. To say that it is not great music is not to belittle its importance in its day.—JOHN TASKER HOWARD.

Suite for String Orchestra in E major, Op. 63

THE SUITE was written in 1907. All told there are three sections to the composition, a Pizzicato replacing an earlier second movement. The work was given its first performance at a Boston Symphony concert in Boston on Apr. 16, 1909, under Max Fiedler's direction. It was published the same year and dedicated to Fiedler. The composer's own description of the complete score follows:

The Prelude (E major, 2/2) is brief and is based throughout on the first phrase of eight notes; it is of a flowing melodic character with much imitation among the several voices.

The Pizzicato (A minor, 6/8) is continuously so; it is interrupted by an Adagietto (F major, 3/4) which is played with the bow (arco), the instruments being muted.

The Fugue is in E minor, 4/4, and is pretty thoroughly planned out, with a long pedal point just at the last return of the theme; there are no inversions or augmentations, etc. The first four notes of the theme are heard often by themselves, and, if those notes are observed by the listener at their first entrances, the Fugue will be very clear at the first hearing.

Arthur Foote, a music pupil of John Knowles Paine at Harvard College, later studied organ and piano with B. J. Lang. He was organist of the First Unitarian Church, Boston, from 1878 to 1910. He made many appearances also as pianist, though composition was his major love. He wrote many works, including orchestral pieces, items for chorus and orchestra, many chamber compositions, and some 150 songs.

R. C. B.

Lukas Foss

BORN: BERLIN, AUG. 15, 1922.

The artist who feels that his art is not an escape from the world, but a direct expression of it, this artist always has the urge to come to grips with the problems of his time and seeks their solution in his particular field of expression. Time can thus become a great incentive.—LUKAS FOSS.

"The Prairie," a Cantata for Mixed Chorus, Four Solo Voices, and Orchestra

THIS CANTATA is a setting of Carl Sandburg's poem "Prairie" (from the collection *Cornhuskers*), as adapted by the composer. It obtained its first performance—by the Collegiate Chorale, Robert Shaw, director—in the Town Hall on May 15, 1944. On that occasion the printed program contained this statement by Mr. Foss:

The attempt to develop an oratorio style based on the American soil and spirit is not new, but Sandburg's epic poem, it seems to me, offers new possibilities in its earthy and almost religious approach. It is a new expression of an old faith drawn from the native soil. The protagonist, simply, is the prairie, but through this poem the prairie grows until it becomes the symbol for the all-embracing principle of *growth* itself.

Mr. Foss's own explanation of his work follows:

The opening movement, which has the nature of a prologue, speaks of the prairie, as we are accustomed to visualize it. The author, in a pastoral tenor solo, sings of open valleys and far horizons, and the music breathes fresh air. After this pastoral introduction, a fugue is heard in the orchestra, above which the chorus takes up a new theme in the manner of a chorale. This is the voice of the prairie: "I am here when the cities are gone. I am here before the cities come. . . . I am dust of men. . . . I who have seen the red births and the red deaths of sons and daughters, I take peace or war, I say nothing and wait."

As a complete contrast, a folklike movement follows, but the melodies remain original throughout the work, no native tunes having been used. With the reentry of the chorus, the prairie becomes "mother of men, waiting." Then the author reaches far back into the past and we see the cities rising on the prairie, out of the prairie, while the chorus chants of the years when the red and the white man met. A male voice calls out: "To a man across a thousand years I offer a handshake; I say to him: *Brother, make the story short, for the stretch of a thousand years is short."* In rugged 5/4 and 7/4 rhythms follows what may be styled the industrial section, ending with a fugue for male voices on the words: "What brothers these i the dark of a thousand years." A lyrical intermezzo brings us back to the prairie This consists of a short a capella chorus "Cool Prayers," a soprano song, "O Prairi Girl," and a scherzando duet, "Songs Hidden in Eggs." These are held togethe by a dreamy little shepherd's lay, a nostalgic wood-wind refrain of the prairie. Th tenor's voice introduces the seventh and last section, and everyone joins in the fin hymn to the future, expressing the healthy and sunny optimism unique to thi country: "I speak of new cities and new people. I tell you the past is a bucket c ashes. . . . I tell you there is nothing in the world, only an ocean of tomorrows. Thus, having opened to us the past and the present, the prairie announces th future, "Tomorrow is a day."

Under Artur Rodzinski's direction *The Prairie* was given its first Phil harmonic-Symphony performance on Jan. 18, 1945.

Although Lukas Foss is of foreign birth, he prefers to be—and generally is— considered an American composer. Arriving in the United States at the age o fifteen, with four years' attendance at the Paris Conservatory already to hi credit, he was exposed, during his most formative years to the American idea Moreover, he reached his majority in this country, duly becoming a citizer and he confesses to a feeling and appreciation of it equal to those of a devote native son. He entered the Curtis Institute of Music in Philadelphia, where b studied composition with Rosario Scalerio, conducting with Fritz Reiner, an piano with Isabelle Vengerova. He was graduated with honors three years late He became a member of Serge Koussevitzky's conducting classes at the thre summer sessions of the Berkshire Music Center and, while there, he also too Paul Hindemith's courses in composition. Subsequently, he worked with th distinguished composer at Yale University.

Mr. Foss has composed a number of works, most of which have obtaine performance. He wrote incidental music to Shakespeare's *The Tempest* o commission from the King-Coit School for a Theater Guild production of th play. The score was a Pulitzer Prize winner in 1942. The League of Composer has presented his Sonata for Violin and Piano, a trio of pieces for two piano and a Duo for Cello and Piano, all of which have also been given radio pe formances. An Allegro Concertante, several piano, two-piano and violin work and other items are included in the list. On Oct. 15, 1943, the Boston Symphon under the direction of Serge Koussevitzky, offered the premiere of a purel orchestral composition by Mr. Foss. Its title, too, is *The Prairie.* Yet the r semblance ends almost there, for the only relationship between it and thi Cantata lies in the fact that the composer built his orchestral score on theme from the latter.

R. C. B.

César Franck

BORN: LIÉGE, BELGIUM, DEC. 10, 1822. DIED: PARIS, NOV. 8, 1890.

All true creators must be in advance of their time and must of necessity be misunderstood by their contemporaries. César Franck was no more of an exception to this rule than other great musicians have been; like them, he was misunderstood.—GUY ROPARTZ.

Symphony in D minor

I. Lento; Allegro non troppo. II. Allegretto. III. Allegro non troppo.

MILD-MANNERED and serene, an angel in piety, César Franck was the last man on earth designed by nature and God to become a storm center. But the pious and humble organist of Sainte Clothilde, the Conservatory teacher who had made daily rounds of instruction for a few extra francs, had found the key to a new art. And promptly believers hailed him as a musical Messiah. Just as readily flocked the disbelievers to deride and silence him. Partisanship clashed noisily about his head. To his disciples he was the *maître* of *maîtres,* the angel of a new Annunciation. To his detractors he had betrayed French music to German academicism. To the composers who clustered lucratively about the opera houses he was enigma and anathema both. Rabid nationalists concerned with keeping the tradition of French verve and gaiety brushed the new music aside as the work of an alien, a Belgian, a Walloon. What had Paris to do with deep, sober thought in music and the chanting of celestial choirs?

Definitely something new was to sweep like a tide over French music, and his modest and serene soul, steeped in the Catholic faith and a classicist at heart, was responsible. For a vision had come to Père Franck, and men who have visions have followers. And their followers must arm against infidels. In the deep recesses of his soul Franck had viewed divinity. Like many before him he gave his vision glowing utterance. Painters, poets, and prophets before him had gloried in the unveiled mysteries of the Beyond. They were called mystics. César Franck belonged in their company, and a new word entered the teeming glossary of music—mysticism. d'Indy, Chausson, Ropartz, among others, were to propound the new gospel. And their testament was the D minor Symphony.

To express this fervent message, Franck employed the full resources of classical form, but his idiom was romantic—fiery and personal. His methods and technic were modern. He viewed design with the discipline of an eighteenth-century composer, and he was launching an epochal device of composi-

tion, one never fully exploited before, the cyclical form. He organized hi
material with superb singleness of aim. The plan of his symphony, fully
expounded, was a marvel of logic and evolution. And this, too, incensed the
champions of freedom in French art. In short, Franck had couched his vision
in solidly grounded terms. Knowing the man, his goodness and honesty, his
disciples did not misplace their faith.

For Franck regarded his work in music as a mission. For it he sacrificed
prospects of worldly gain. Fame never entered his scheme of things. The glory
came after him. He considered his art as a sacred trust and himself a mere
witness of the Light. Sincerity was the keynote of his creed. Sham, pretence
and bombast were alien to it. Accordingly, the D minor Symphony, whatever
its structural faults, is the work of a supreme artist intent on absolute truth in
revealing himself and his faith through an expressive medium. Few musical
works come as close to saintliness. In shaping his rapture, technic and form
merged and dissolved. The result was pure vision in terms of music. In the last
analysis, art becomes as irrelevant to the artist as religion to the saint.

Debussyites and Franckists have often come to grips over the respective
claims of their founding fathers. Mysticism and impressionism would seem to
be poles apart, the one a sudden grasp of divine truth, the other a keen discipline
of the senses, at best symbolism. Yet Debussy's tinctured skies and seas and
Franck's angelic whirrings have much in common. Both report flashes of quick
insight. Intuition is their open sesame to fresh sources of knowledge. Both dwell
in a starlit cosmos of imagination, and the world is the richer for their per-
ceptions. Given the sincerity of the artist and a valid medium of expression, the
stimulus can be a darting gold fish or an inner glow of fierce faith. What the
artist does with the material makes the difference.

Not since Bach had music reentered Gothic cathedrals so piously clad. Like
the organ works of the Leipzig master, the D minor Symphony evokes images
of naves and vaults. A kind of winged ecstasy mounts to the topmost spires.
One hears the eerie chants of unseen choirs. A smell of incense filters in. Within
this temple of his art, Franck knelt and turned his gaze upward. All his doubts
and yearnings came forth. Compassion and comfort softened his pleas. Presently the curtains parted. The devout man was answered. Triumph and
rejoicing rang from above in a blazing Hallelujah.

César Franck was sixty-seven years old when the Paris Conservatory orchestra
rather reluctantly premiered the D minor Symphony. He was indifferent to
acclaim. His previous compositions had reached a small public, in spite of a
tireless clique of well-wishers. His work was done. He had one more year to
live. Never doubting that he had left an enduring hymn of faith for posterity,
he turned a deaf ear to the raw contention set off by his Symphony. At the
premiere everything went against it. The musicians were apathetic. The public
was puzzled. The enemy cabals were bitterly derisive. The professors raised

their hands in horror over the use of the English horn in a symphony. Charles Gounod, the darling of the opera, flailed the work with a ready dictum: "The affirmation of incompetence pushed to dogmatic lengths."

When Franck arrived home after the concert his family huddled about him eager for news of the performance. Did the public like the symphony? What did they say? Who was there? Was there a great ovation? How did it go? To it all Franck replied simply: "Oh, it sounded well; just as I thought it would."

L. B.

The symphony is dedicated to Henri Duparc. It is scored for two flutes, two oboes, one English horn, two clarinets, one bass clarinet, two bassoons, four horns, two trumpets, two cornets-à-piston, three trombones, bass tuba, a set of three kettledrums, harp, and strings.

Opening with a Lento (D minor, 4/4) the symphony offers first a phrase which is the foundation for the movement's first theme, given to the cellos and basses. Some thirty measures of development lead to an Allegro non troppo (D minor, 2/2). Here the theme is allotted to all the strings, and it attains a development. After a repetition of the opening passage a new theme enters into the plan, molto cantabile, F major, for the strings. A third theme of vigorous quality follows; developed, it prefaces a free fantasia. The introductory theme reappears in canonic imitation among the brasses. There is a resumption of the Allegro non troppo subject, which leads to the end of the movement.

In the second movement (Allegretto, B flat minor, 3/4), pizzicato chords for strings and harp serve as introduction for the main motive, a doleful one, played by the English horn. Clarinet, horn, and flute take up the material, followed by the violins which give out another theme, dolce cantabile, B flat major. The English horn and other wind instruments discuss the main theme in the key of B flat minor. A section of a more animated nature comes next, in which the lively subject is first given to the violins, pianissimo. Against this the clarinets utter a second subject in the section, which is developed in modulatory fashion up to the return of the main theme of the movement. A combination of themes brings the movement to a close.

The finale (Allegro non troppo, 2/2) begins with some measures of introduction. A chief subject makes its appearance, dolce cantabile, in the cellos and the bassoons. Following a sixty-measure period, the brasses supply a phrase in B major, to which the strings respond. The cellos and basses now advance a melancholy motive. At this point the opening theme of the second movement is announced by the English horn to a triplet accompaniment. There is a retard in the tempo. Excerpts of themes from the second and third movements run an alternate course. The original tempo returns. There is a crescendo and a restatement of the first D major theme, fortissimo. The main subject of the second movement is also played with immense sonority. With the subsiding of the music there appears again the third theme of the first movement, leading to a coda, whose pattern is dependent on the chief themes of the first movement together with the first theme of the finale.

R. C. B.

George Gershwin

BORN: BROOKLYN, N. Y., SEPT. 26, 1898. DIED: HOLLYWOOD, CALIF., JULY 11, 1937.

> *Gershwin proved in his own achievements what Paul Whiteman and*
> *I had always believed when we were first associated in his band: that*
> *the better elements of jazz could be incorporated into art music and*
> *be the basis of a series of symphonic creations typically expressive of*
> *our nation.*—FERDE GROFE.

"An American in Paris"

A TYPICAL YOUNGSTER of the big city, one who could "take care of himself," whatever the occasion, George Gershwin took up music quite suddenly. He heard a schoolmate, Max Rosen, play some little number like *Humoresque* in the assembly hall, one day. Right there and then he decided to look into "this music stuff." Making the acquaintance of Rosen, he began to ply him with questions, and before long he was practicing the piano (instead of the violin) at the house of another friend.

He became so proficient that when the family bought a piano he amazed everyone with his expert performance of the current popular tunes. Music lessons now were a matter of course. Some time later he even took instruction in harmony.

When Gershwin was sixteen years of age he obtained a position with the music publishing house of J. H. Remick & Company. He functioned as a "song plugger," a calling in which pianistic gifts were—and probably still are—secondary to the ability to "spot" the songs of the publishers' catalogue with prominent artists. He was a salesman, in other words, trying to persuade singers, dancers, etc., to use his employers' songs in their acts. That, of course, was preradio exploitation.

In 1916, a piece of his *When You Want 'Em You Can't Get 'Em, When You've Got 'Em You Don't Want 'Em* was accepted for publication. Shortly thereafter another was published. In all, he earned the round sum of twelve dollars for those two early essays. He continued with the writing for a time and, finally, completely discouraged, began to look for something more tangible, something that promised a weekly pay envelope.

The position of rehearsal pianist for a Dillingham-Ziegfeld production, *Miss 1917*, was offered to him. He took it gladly. In the meantime, he was making a good deal of headway among the cognoscenti, because of his clever piano playing. Through a series of circumstances he was given the opportunity to write his first score for a revue, *La La, Lucille,* which was produced in 1919.

A song, "Swanee," written in that year, became such a sensation that it was interpolated in a show *Sinbad,* which starred Al Jolson. Then came a long string of scores for the Broadway stage, including those for *George White's Scandals; Lady, Be Good; Oh, Kay; Strike up the Band; Funny Face; Girl Crazy; Of Thee I Sing* and others, in addition to a galaxy of scores for the movies.

When, early in 1924, Paul Whiteman, the "King of Jazz," decided to go symphonic in grand style he approached Gershwin, suggesting that he write a concert work for his famous orchestra. The composer, who had not been without his higher ambitions, accepted with alacrity, and in three weeks the score of the *Rhapsody in Blue* was ready. Whiteman's own pianist and arranger, Ferde Grofe, did the editing—the mystery is how much?—and the orchestration of the piece.

It was given its first performance by the Whiteman Orchestra, with Gershwin as soloist, in the old Aeolian Hall on Feb. 12, 1924. The composition met with instantaneous success. Since then it has been played with something like regularity in many parts of the world. Other orchestral works followed, among them the Concerto in F, the Second Rhapsody, and *An American in Paris.*

An American in Paris was commissioned by Dr. Walter Damrosch for performance by the Philharmonic-Symphony Society. It obtained its premiere on Dec. 13, 1928.

Of this music Gershwin's friend and colleague Deems Taylor wrote an enlightening essay, which was utilized in the program notes of the Society when the work was first given. It is herewith reprinted:

By its composer's own confession, *An American in Paris* is an attempted reconciliation between two opposing schools of musical thought—a *Pax Romana,* as it were, imposed upon two customarily warring camps. It is program music in that it engages to tell an emotional narrative; to convey, in terms of sound, the successive emotional reactions experienced by a Yankee tourist (perhaps from Broadway) adrift in the City of Light. It is absolute music as well, in that its structure is determined by considerations musical rather than literary or dramatic. The piece, while not in strict sonata form, resembles an extended symphonic movement in that it announces, develops, combines, and recapitulates definite themes. Only, whereas the ordinary symphonic movement is based upon two principal themes, *An American in Paris* manipulates five.

While Mr. Gershwin has been heard to hope—and probably not in vain—that his new work can be absorbed and enjoyed purely as a piece of orchestral music, he admits that *An American in Paris* (which, oddly enough, was largely written in Paris) follows a fairly explicit story. What follows is based upon Mr. Gershwin's own version of the succession of events, augmented by a few details supplied by the helpful commentator and—as yet—unrepudiated by the composer.

You are to imagine, then, an American, visiting Paris, swinging down the Champs-Elysées on a mild, sunny morning in May or June. Being what he is, he starts without preliminaries, and is off at full speed at once, to the tune of The First Walking Theme, a straightforward diatonic air, designed to convey an impression of Gallic freedom and gaiety.

Our American's ears being open, as well as his eyes, he notes with pleasure the sounds of the city. French taxicabs seem to amuse him particularly, a fact that the orchestra points out in brief episodes introducing four real Paris taxi horns (imported at great expense for the occasion). These have a special theme allotted to them (the driver, possibly?), which is announced by the strings whenever they appear in the score.

Having safely eluded the taxis, our American apparently passes the open door of café where, if one is to believe the trombones, La Maxixe is still popular. Exhilarated by this reminder of the gay nineteen-hundreds, he resumes his stroll through the medium of the Second Walking Theme, which is announced by the clarinet in French with a strong American accent.

Both themes are now discussed at some length by the instruments, until our tourist happens to pass—something. The composer thought it might be a church, while the commentator held out for the Grand Palais—where the Salon holds forth. At all events, our hero does not go in. Instead, as revealed by the English horn, he respectfully slackens his pace until he is safely past.

At this point, the American's itinerary becomes somewhat obscured. It may be that he continues down the Champs-Elysées; it may be that he has turned off—the composer retains an open mind on the subject. However, since what immediately ensues is technically known as a bridge passage, one is reasonably justified in assuming that the Gershwin pen, guided by an unseen hand, has perpetrated a musical pun, and that when the Third Walking Theme makes its eventual appearance our American has crossed the Seine, and is somewhere on the Left Bank. Certainly it is distinctly less Gallic than its predecessors, speaking American with a French intonation, as befits that region of the city where so many Americans foregather. "Walking" may be a misnomer, for despite its vitality the theme is slightly sedentary in character, and becomes progressively more so. Indeed, the end of this section of the work is couched in terms so unmistakably, albeit, pleasantly, blurred, as to suggest that the American is on the terrasse of a café, exploring the mysteries of an Anise de Lozo.

And now the orchestra introduces an unhallowed episode. Suffice it to say that a solo violin approaches our hero (in the soprano register) and addresses him in the most charming broken English; and his response being inaudible—or at least unintelligible—repeats the remark. This one-sided conversation continues for some little time.

Of course, one hastens to add, it is possible that a grave injustice is being done to both author and protagonist, and that the whole episode is simply a musical transition. The latter interpretation may well be true, for otherwise it is difficult to believe what ensues: our hero becomes homesick. He has the blues; and if the behavior of the orchestra be any criterion, he has them very thoroughly. He realizes suddenly,

overwhelmingly, that he does not belong to this place, that he is that most wretche
creature in all the world, a foreigner. The cool, blue Paris sky, the distant upwar
sweep of the Eiffel Tower, the bookstalls on the quay, the pattern of horse-chestnu
leaves on the white, sun-flecked street—what avails all this alien beauty? He is n
Baudelaire, longing to be "anywhere out of the world." The world is just what h
longs for, the world that he knows best; a world less lovely—sentimental and a littl
vulgar perhaps—but for all that, home.

However, nostalgia is not a fatal disease—nor, in this instance, of overlong
duration. Just in the nick of time the compassionate orchestra rushes another them
to the rescue, two trumpets performing the ceremony of introduction. It is apparen
that our hero must have met a compatriot; for this last theme is a noisy, cheerfu
self-confident Charleston, without a drop of Gallic blood in its veins.

For the moment, Paris is no more; and a voluble, gusty, wise-cracking orchestr
proceeds to demonstrate at some length that it's always fair weather when tw
Americans get together, no matter where. Walking Theme number two enters soo
thereafter, enthusiastically abetted by number three. Paris isn't such a bad plac
after all: as a matter of fact, it's a grand place! Nice weather, nothing to do ti
tomorrow, nice girls—and by the way, whatever became of that lad Volstead? Th
blues return, but mitigated by the Second Walking Theme—a happy reminiscenc
rather than a homesick yearning—and the orchestra, in a riotous finale, decides t
make a night of it. It will be great to get home; but meanwhile, this is Paris!

An American in Paris is scored for strings, flutes, piccolo, two oboe
English horn, two clarinets, bass clarinet, three saxophones, two bassoon
contra-bassoon, four horns, three trumpets, three trombones, tuba, tympan
snare drum, bass drum, cymbals, rattle, triangle, two tom-toms, four auto
mobile horns, xylophone, wire brush, wood block, glockenspiel, and celest

R. C. B.

Concerto for Piano and Orchestra in F major

I. Allegro. II. Andante. III. Allegro agitato.

AT THE invitation of the Symphony Society of New York and its conducto
Walter Damrosch, this Concerto was given its premiere at Carnegie Hall o
Dec. 3, 1925. The composer himself played the solo part. Of the work D
Damrosch said:

Various composers have been walking around jazz like a cat around a plate o
hot soup, waiting for it to cool off, so that they could enjoy it without burning thei
tongues, hitherto accustomed only to the more tepid liquid distilled by cooks of th
classical school. Lady Jazz, adorned with her intriguing rhythms, has danced he
way around the world, even as far as the Eskimos of the North and the Polynesian
of the South Sea Isles. But for all her travels and her sweeping popularity, she ha
encountered no knight who could lift her to a level that would enable her to b
received as a respectable member of the musical circles.

George Gershwin seems to have accomplished this miracle. He has done it boldly by dressing this extremely independent and up-to-date young lady in the classic garb of a concerto. Yet he has not detracted one whit from her fascinating personality. He is the Prince who has taken Cinderella by the hand and openly proclaimed her a princess to the astonished world, no doubt to the fury of her envious sisters.

Gershwin, making no bones about his lack of technical knowledge, said of the work's first movement, "It's in sonata form—but," which should give the listener an idea anyway. The second movement is a sustained Andante in three-part song form. And the Finale is, by intent, a rondo.

The score calls for two flutes, piccolo, English horn, two oboes, two clarinets, bass clarinet, two bassoons, four horns, three trumpets, three trombones, tuba, kettledrums, bass drum, snare drum (played with wire brush), cymbals, a "Charleston stick" (something between a slapstick and a wood block), a xylophone, bells, and strings.

R. C. B.

Selections from "Porgy and Bess"

THE NEGRO folk opera *Porgy and Bess* represented George Gershwin's last major work. Based on the Du Bose and Dorothy Heyward play *Porgy,* it was produced by the New York Theater Guild at the Alvin Theatre on Oct. 10, 1935, where it ran for 124 performances.

The drama critic of the *New York Times,* Brooks Atkinson, remarked on the following day:

These comments are written by a reviewer so inured to the theater that he regards operatic form as cumbersome. Why commonplace remarks that carry no emotion have to be made in a chanting monotone is a problem in art he cannot fathom. Even the hermit thrush drops into conversational tones when he is not singing from the topmost spray in a tree. Turning *Porgy* into an opera has resulted in a deluge of casual remarks that have to be thoughtfully intoned and that amazingly impede the action. Why do composers vex it so? "Sister, you goin' to the picnic?" "No, I guess not." Now why in heaven's name must two characters in an opera clear their throats before they can exchange that sort of information? . . . To the ears of a theater critic there are intimations in *Porgy and Bess* that Mr. Gershwin is still easiest in mind when he is writing songs with choruses. He, and his present reviewer, are on familiar ground when he is writing a droll tune like "A Woman Is a Sometime Thing" or a lazy darkie solo like "I Got Plenty o' Nuttin'," or made-to-order spirituals like "Oh, de Lawd Shake de Heaven," or Sportin' Life's hot-time number entitled "There's a Boat That's Leavin' Soon for New York." If Mr. Gershwin does not enjoy his task most in moments like this, his audience does. In sheer quality of character they are worth an hour of formal musical transitions.

However, in the *New York Herald Tribune* of the same date, Lawrence Gilman wrote in his music column:

Perhaps it is needlessly Draconian to begrudge Mr. Gershwin the song hits which he has scattered through his score and which will doubtless enhance his fame and popularity. Yet they mar it. They are its cardinal weakness. They are a blemish upon its musical integrity . . . it is not Gershwin, the apt and accommodating lyricist, who is most conspicuously present in *Porgy and Bess,* but Gershwin the musical dramatist, who has, in certain fortunate moments of this score, been moved to compassionate and valid utterance by the wildness and the pathos and the tragic fervor that can so strangely agitate the souls of men. These pages will abide, and honor the composer, long after the musical comedy treacle which drips from other pages has ceased to gladden even those whose favor is scarcely worth the price.

"Rhapsody in Blue"

GEORGE GERSHWIN's pretensions about serious composition date from the history-making *Rhapsody in Blue.* It had a successful premiere, although a grudging attitude on the part of some writers was not altogether missing. And later observers, assessing the work perhaps less subjectively, did comment on its "total lack of resemblance to real jazz" and, further, noted that it was "Tschaikowsky, in its melodic E major episode, rather than New Orleans, or even Harlem." While Tschaikowsky is "a Steppe or two removed from that particular section," as one punster put it, "there is his influence in the long line of the melody, which—without the rhythmic triplet figure that accompanies it —is, at least, of the boiling romantic school, but certainly not jazz."

The piano part of the *Rhapsody,* which Gershwin played so well at the premiere of the composition—and, subsequently, even better—moved one watcher of the musical skies to say, "It is the kind of writing, in its invention and technical figurations, that a very competent pianist-composer might dream up. . . . George Gershwin, it seems all too obvious, could now be a concert pianist to reckon with, had he set his course in that direction."

                                                                    R. C. B.

Henry F. Gilbert

BORN: SOMERVILLE, MASS., SEPT. 26, 1868. DIED: CAMBRIDGE, MASS., MAY 19, 1928.

The music of Henry F. Gilbert is so racy of the soil that it stamps its composer as one of our first nationalists.—JOHN TASKER HOWARD.

"Comedy Overture on Negro Themes"

BEST KNOWN of Gilbert's concert works, this Overture is only one among many of his compositions attesting a predilection for American Negro music. There are, for example, the *Negro Rhapsody* and a ballet pantomime *The Dance in Place Congo*. The latter work was produced for the first time at the Metropolitan Opera House on Mar. 23, 1918.

Composed in 1906, the *Comedy Overture on Negro Themes* was revised three years later. In the altered form it was performed in New York on Aug. 17, 1910, at a municipal concert on the Central Park Mall, conducted by Franz Kaltenborn. Two months later, when the fall symphonic season got under way, the Overture moved indoors at a concert in Pittsburgh led by Modest Altschuler. For the Boston Symphony premiere of Apr. 13, 1911, Gilbert furnished the following information:

This overture was originally intended as the prelude to an opera, the plot of which is based upon the Uncle Remus stories of Joel Chandler Harris. The libretto of this opera is by Charles Johnson (Bengal Civil Service, retired) and the music by myself. Circumstances have unfortunately compelled us to abandon this work before its completion. I have, however, saved the overture from the wreck and have both rewritten and reorchestrated it.

My scheme in the opera was to base the music on motives from traditional Negro songs and dances even as the Uncle Remus stories are based upon traditional Negro folklore. I have therefore used as thematic material for the overture certain piquant and expressive bits of melody which I have gathered from various collections of Negro folk music. There are three motives of four measures each and one theme eight measures in length. Upon the material contained in these twenty measures the whole piece is built.

The overture has five well-defined sections. The first movement is light and humorous, the theme being made from two four-measure phrases taken from Charles L. Edwards' book *Bahama Songs and Stories*..... This is followed by a broader and somewhat slower phrase. I have here used the only complete Negro tune which occurs in the piece. This tune is unusually wild and romantic in character and withal of considerable nobility. This tune, and many like it, were formerly used as working songs by the roustabouts and stevedores on the Mississippi River steamboats in the old days. The original words were as follows:

I'se gwine to Alabammy, Oh . . .
For to see ma Mammy, Ah . . .

Next comes a fugue. The theme of this fugue consists of the first four measures of the Negro spiritual "Old Ship of Zion" as noted by Jeanette Robinson Murphy in *Southern Thoughts for Northern Thinkers*. (This theme is introduced early in the overture and given to bassoons, bass trombone, violoncellos, and double basses). The peroration of the fugue is built up from the theme, in augmentation.

It is given out by the brass instruments and interspersed with phrases from the roustabouts' song, also somewhat developed and treated in a new manner harmonically. After this a short phrase of sixteen measures serves to reintroduce the comic element. There is a repetition of the first theme and considerable recapitulation, which leads finally to the development of a new ending or coda, and the piece ends in an orgy of jollity and ragtime.

The overture is scored for three flutes (one interchangeable with piccolo), two oboes, two clarinets, two bassoons, four horns, two trumpets, three trombones, bass tuba, kettledrums, glockenspiel, and the usual strings.

Alexander Glazounoff

BORN: ST. PETERSBURG, AUG. 10, 1865. DIED: PARIS, MAR. 21, 1936.

Glazounoff's music is melodious, although his melody is not remarkable for richness or variety. It is usually most characteristic in moods of restrained melancholy. His harmony is far more distinctive than original, and frequently full of picturesque suggestion.—ROSA NEWMARCH.

Symphony in C minor, No. 6, Op. 58

I. Adagio; Allegro passionato. II. Andante variatioro. III. Intermezzo: Allegretto. IV. Andante maestoso; Scherzando.

GLAZOUNOFF HAS been called the "Janus of Russian music," Janus being the two-faced Roman god who looked simultaneously in opposite directions. Rooted in native classicism and on the threshold of new trends, Glazounoff was regarded as standing midway in the symphonic current of his day. Hence his works are a kind of halfway house in the vast metropolis of Russian music.

The Sixth Symphony dates from 1896, the premiere occurring in St. Petersburg on Feb. 21, 1897, at a concert of the Young Russian School founded by the publisher and patron saint of new talent, Belaiev, who personally incurred the expense of much of the series. The work is in the usual four movements, the second being a theme with seven variations.

A preferatory Adagio in C minor, with cellos and double basses giving out a theme pianissimo misterioso and the brasses later sustaining syncopated harmonies over quivering strings, leads to the first movement proper, an Allegro passionato, as the strings discourse the opening theme in altered rhythms. The violins, followed by the wood winds, unfold a new theme, against which appear fragments of the first. There is free development. The winds now repeat the second theme in A flat major, and a vigorous coda sets in after a brief review of the opening section.

The violins give out the subject of the second movement, Tema con variazioni, and the seven variations follow in this order: I. Più mosso: Allegro moderato; II. Allegretto; III. Scherzino, allegro; IV. Fugato: Andante mistico (Gregorian Phrygian mode); V. Notturno; VI. Allegro moderato; VII. Finale: Moderato maestoso.

A theme for wood winds announced against cello pizzicati opens the third movement "Intermezzo" (Allegretto). This leads to a trio section (Più mosso), followed in turn by a second theme given out by flute and pizzicato violins.

The opening section returns and the "Intermezzo," actually a scherzo, ends with the trio freely suggested.

Two themes, melodically similar, are set off against each other throughout the concluding movement in a series of changing tempos and rhythms, the whole in the spirit of a Russian dance.

L. B.

Concerto for Violin and Orchestra in A minor, Op. 82

I. Moderato. II. Andante. III. Allegro.

BEGUN IN 1904, this Concerto was completed in the following year, receiving its first performance on Oct. 17, 1905, at Queen's Hall, London, with Mischa Elman as the soloist. Henry J. Wood conducted. The score calls for two flutes, piccolo, two oboes, two clarinets, two bassoons, four horns, two trumpets, three trombones, kettledrums, campanelle, triangle, cymbals, harp, and strings, in addition to the solo violin.

In a report of the premiere the reviewer for the *London Musical Times* said that the concerto was

dedicated to M. Leopold Auer, who at the composer's request, had undertaken to play it for the first time, but M. Glazounoff, visiting the professor while he was giving Elman a lesson, was so impressed by his extraordinary ability that the composer asked M. Auer, if he would allow Elman to give the first performance of the work, a request to which the distinguished violinist willingly assented.

America first heard this music at a concert of the Russian Symphony Orchestra, Mar. 3, 1910. Again Mischa Elman was the soloist, and the performance was conducted by Modest Altschuler.

In the first movement (Moderato, A minor, 4/4), a lyrical theme for the solo violin appears at the beginning, accompanied softly by clarinets and bassoons. This particular theme is heard often throughout the work. A second lyrical theme is also introduced by the solo violin.

The second movement (Andante, D flat major, 3/4) opens as an aria on the G string of the solo violin. Presently the mood changes and an agitato appears, teeming with complicated passage work for the solo instrument. After the reentrance of the main subject of the movement by way of the wood winds, the music returns to the important subject of the previous movement.

The third movement (Allegro, A major, 6/8) is reached with a bridging cadenza of ornate design for the solo violin. A sort of dialogue ensues between trumpet and violin on the notes of the principal theme. This is later given a fortissimo emphasis by the entire orchestra. Still other melodic material comes in, contributing to a "general musical merrymaking."

R. C. B.

Reinhold Moritzovich Glière

BORN: KIEV, JAN. 11, 1875.

Rich flexibility, not too daring romantic harmony, rounded lyricism,
a broad melodic vein originating partly in the Russian song, partly
in Russian Orientalism, partly in the cantilena of French opera, and
avoidance of eccentricity and the grotesque.—SERGEI ALEXEIVICH
BUGOSLAVSKY.

Symphony in B minor, No. 3 ("Ilya Mourometz"), Op. 42

I. Wandering of the Pilgrims: Ilya Mourometz and Sviatogor. II. Solovei
the Brigand. III. At the Palace of Prince Vladimir. IV. The Feats of Valor
and the Petrification of Ilya Mourometz.

CELEBRATED FOR his prodigious stature and strength, Ilya Mourometz figures as
a favorite hero in the epic ballads of old Russia. These early tales, called *bilini,*
literally "things which have been," are part legend and part history, mingling
Christian and pagan elements. They form several cycles, beginning with a
group centering in mythical heroes endowed with superhuman powers.
Mourometz belongs to the cycle of the Prince of Vladimir, the last of the
Scandinavian princes of Kiev, who was baptized in 988 and is credited with
bringing Christianity into Russia.

In the *bilini,* Vladimir, like King Arthur, dominates a kind of Round Table
(called *druzhina,* or friendly following), with Mourometz one of his doughtiest
knights. While the fabulous note is weaker in this cycle than in the earlier one,
the accounts of Ilya Mourometz combine elements of both cycles. The giant
Sviatogor and the Herculean brigand Solovei also belong to the greater marvels
of the first *bilini*.

An actual Ilya Mourometz seems to have lived about the time of Vladimir,
since there is early evidence of him as "a great chief and mighty warrior" in
resisting the early Tartar invaders of Russia. In the seventh century Ilya's
portrait appeared with those of the saints of Kiev. The inscription even carried
the legend that Ilya the *bogatyr,* or hero, was finally turned into stone.

Dedicated to Alexander Glazounoff, the *Ilya Mourometz Symphony* was
written between 1908 and 1911 and first performed in Moscow in 1912, by the
Imperial Russian Musical Society, under the direction of Emil Cooper. Its
American premiere occurred at a concert of the Chicago Symphony Orchestra
during the season of 1917-1918. Glière inserted the following extracts from the
Mourometz *bilini* in the score, which have been rendered as follows:

I

In olden times, in the days of the gracious Prince Vladimir, lived Ilya Mourometz (Ilya of Mourom), a peasant's son. For thirty long years he had remained seated and motionless.

One day two wandering pilgrims appeared (gods of old were they) and cried to him, "Arise! Go forth! Thou shalt a puissant bogatyr [hero] become."

And Ilya Mourometz arose and went forth into the limpid land. Procuring a bogatyr's steed, he set out to find the noble bogatyr Sviatogor.

The humid earth could scarcely bear the weight of Sviatogor. He was not allowed to go to Holy Russia, but he was permitted to roam over the lofty summits of the Sviaty Gory [Holy Mountains].

Ilya approached him, saluting him with respect. They leaped astride two fleet steeds, and rode a long, long time over the Holy Mountains, diverting themselves with heroic games. They discovered an immense coffin, into which Sviatogor laid himself, and from whose profound depths he could not be raised. Before he died he gave much sage counsel to Ilya. Then his body became covered with rivulets of sweat, and he expired. . . .

The heroic force was transmitted to Ilya, who traveled the straight road to the superb capital, Kiev. His courser galloped as the falcon flies, bestrode lakes and streams, while his tail swept away cities.

II

In a dense forest seven oaks sheltered Solovei, the Brigand. The right road is slippery, the right road is barred. Whistling like a nightingale, sending forth ferocious cries, Solovei, the Brigand, bows to earth thick forests, and all the men, if any there be in the forests, lie dead.

Cherished by Solovéi, the Brigand, three maidens live in the forest. They own piles of gold, heaps of silver and of beautifully rounded pearls. With precious gifts they entice the passers-by.

Solovei, the Brigand, hears the powerful gait of the bogatyr. He whistles, this brigand, like a nightingale, he sends forth ferocious cries. Ilya bends his giant bow and shoots an arrow of glowing iron. The arrow pierces the right eye of Solovéi, the Brigand; it stretches him out on the humid earth. Ilya ties the brigand to his damasked stirrup and drags him towards the palace of Vladimir, the Great Sun.

III

Vladimir is holding a noble feast, to which have gathered in numbers the princes, the boyars and the bogatyrs of invincible strength. Arriving at the principal gate of the palace, Ilya commands the brigand to send forth his nightingale call and his ferocious cries. Then trembles the roof of the palace, then fall all the great bogatyrs, the princes so proud, the famous boyars. All fall. Prince Vladimir alone, though enfeebled, stands.

Ilya slices off the head of the turbulent Solovéi. Vladimir, in recompense, gives Ilya the place of honor at his table, and all the puissant bogatyrs acknowledge him their distinguished brother.

IV

Batygha, the Wicked, and his pagan army arose in Orda, the land of gold. The smoky breath of their horses obscured the gleam of the sun, and from them arose the Tatar odor that suffocated every Christian.

Ilya Mourometz advanced at the head of his twelve bogatyrs. For twelve days they battled, defying the entire army of miscreants.

Those are not two mountains that meet. They are, in the limpid land, two bogatyrs who draw near, Ilya and Oudalaya Polyenitsa [giant warrior]. At the first shock they exchange blows, but neither is wounded. Each seizes by the mane the mount of the other, but without advantage. They dismount and grip each other vigorously. They struggle and strain until evening, and from evening until midnight, and from midnight until dawn. Ilya falls on the humid earth, and by this contact his strength is doubled. He strikes the white breast of the warrior with a blow so formidable that it sends him above the great trees of the forest. Soon he puts out the shining eyes, detaches the rebel head from its shoulders, fixes it on a Tàtar lance, and carries it back in acclamation to the camp of his heroic friends.

Seven bogatyrs advance with Ilya Mourometz in the limpid land. "Where is the Heavenly Army that we, the bogatyrs, have annihilated?" They had scarcely pronounced the mad words when there sprang out two warriors, who shouted, "Come then, bogatyrs, measure your strength with ours." One bogatyr stood forth. Suddenly the two warriors became four. Ilya sabered them—and they were eight, unhurt. All the bogatyrs threw themselves upon the Heavenly Host, charging and sabering; but they multiplied again and again, and charged upon the bogatyrs. The bogatyrs fled to the rocky mountains, toward the somber caverns. One flees—he is changed into stone. Another, and he, too, is petrified. Ilya Mourometz runs toward the mountains, and he, even he, is suddenly changed into stone.

And since that day have the bogatyrs disappeared from Holy Russia.

Glière is familiar to the outside world largely through three compositions— the third symphony (*Ilya Mourometz*), the symphonic poem *The Sirens,* and the *Red Poppy* ballet music. He was one of the first Russian composers of widely recognized standing to identify himself with the new Soviet order. With Serge Vasilenko he became closely associated with the early trend known as "military communism." His contributions to strictly "occasional" revolutionary currents include two works for wind ensemble, a *March of the Red Army* and a piece written for the "Comintern Festival."

Glière attended school and first studied music in his native Kiev. In 1894 he went to Moscow and enrolled at the conservatory. There he studied violin with Johann Hrimaly and composition with Arensky, Conus, Taneieff, and Ippolitoff-Ivanoff. On graduating he was awarded the gold medal in composition. He continued his harmony studies in the Gnessin School. After spending two years abroad, mostly in Berlin, he returned to Moscow, where he divided his time between composition and teaching. In 1913, Glière was appointed professor of composition at the Kiev Conservatory, becoming director the following year. He held the post till 1920, when he joined the faculty of the Moscow Conservatory. Through his work, the Kiev Conservatory moved to front rank.

In the early years of the Soviet Republic, Glière took part in educational campaigns looking to the founding of concert series throughout the country. He also spent the years 1920-1925 in folk-music research with the Society for Proletarian Culture, and for a time was connected with the Eastern Workers' University. His interest in folklore led to a government commission to collect Turkish folk music. Some of the material thus gathered found its way into his Turkish folk opera *Schach-Senem*.

Glière's extensive output consists of some two hundred works in all forms, including chamber music, songs, operas, symphonic poems, three symphonies, and at least four ballets. The best known of the ballets is *Krasni Mak* (*Red Poppy*). It has been a repertory stand-by in Soviet theaters since its premiere in 1927, and a selection from it—the *Russian Sailors' Dance*—has become a familiar concert brevity in America.

Apart from folk music, particularly that of Oriental Russia, Glière's work was early influenced by Borodin, Rimsky-Korsakoff, Glazounoff, Tschaikowsky, some of the late nineteenth-century French masters, and Scriabin. In recent years his style has been increasingly colored by native Russian material and the realities of socialist society.

Sergei Alexeivich Bugoslavsky issued a brochure on Glière in Moscow in 1927. In it he stressed the point that in his music Glière has scrupulously avoided the "nonmusical, the philosophical, the theoretical, the esthetic, the abstract." The emotional keynote of Glière's music Bugoslavsky found in a "clear and life-affirming *Weltanschauung*."

L. B.

"Marche Heroique," Op. 71

THE MARCHE HEROIQUE evidently grew out of Glière's interest in eastern Russia. Geographically, the setting of the march, which is actually a symphonic poem, seems to be Buriat and Mongolia, though the score gives no indication that it was written for any special occasion. Asiatic echoes filter through the scheme, especially in an evocative theme assigned to flute and English horn. March rhythms in percussion and wood winds are first heard against a folkish theme announced by the low strings, before the "heroic" march motive, markedly Russian in character, is introduced by the brasses and promptly amplified by the whole orchestra. The martial mood continues, new march rhythms enter. The episode for flute and English horn uncoils in Asiatic style. The *Marche Heroique*—wherever the marching and whatever the goal—rises with frequent outcries from the brasses to a triumphant close.

L. B.

Michail Ivanovitch Glinka

BORN: NOVOPASSKOI, RUSSIA, JUNE 2, 1803. DIED: BERLIN, FEB. 15, 1857.

Glinka was the founder of an entirely new school of orchestration, an orchestration (characterized by bright, pure, transparent coloring) which has since been employed by almost every Russian composer of note, modified only in later years by Lisztian and Wagnerian influences.—GERALD ABRAHAM.

Overture to "Russlan and Ludmilla"

ON THE sound principle that in union there is strength, several Russian intellects conspired to produce the strange concoction that is the libretto of Glinka's *Russlan and Ludmilla*. A charming poetic tale in the Pushkin original, the story underwent an early experiment in collectivism. Pushkin, approached by Glinka in 1837, was prepared to modify the poem to suit it for operatic use. But Pushkin was slain in a duel before he set to work. Glinka then turned to his friends. Before the libretto returned to him, it bore distinct traces of five additional personalities—K. Bahktourin, Nestor Koukolnik, Michael Guedeonoff, N. Markowich, and an army man, Captain Chirkoff. To round out the process of alteration, Glinka applied some touches of his own and the libretto was finished—finished in both senses!

The premiere in St. Petersburg on Dec. 10, 1842, was a fiasco. Many reasons have been advanced for the failure of *Russlan and Ludmilla* to stir that first-night audience. Six years earlier Glinka had given St. Petersburg the work ordinarily named as marking the birth of Russian national opera, *i.e., A Life for the Czar*. Its success was instantaneous. The music was of irresistible charm, with its melodic warmth and rich folk flavor. Added to that was the strong patriotic appeal of the story of Ivan Sussanin's heroic self-sacrifice in preventing Czar Michael Romanoff from falling into the hands of the Polish invaders in the seventeenth century. Despite aristocratic gibes that this was "coachmen's music," unlike the more polished products imported from Western Europe, *A Life for the Czar* triumphed. Even the emperor was pleased, probably as much by the edifying spectacle of Sussanin's valor as by the lavishly colored score. So pleased, in fact, that Glinka was rewarded with a ring valued at 4,000 rubles and the lucrative post of choirmaster of the Czar's Chapel. But *Russlan and Ludmilla* was a grievous let-down. For one thing, the audience was left cold by the rambling fantasy of Tartar sorcerers, malign dwarfs, and magically evoked storms and darknesses during which beauteous princesses disappeared mysteriously. Fairy tale was one thing on the Russian stage. There was always room in opera and ballet and theater for vividly enacted legends of old Slavic wizardry. But here all was rambling and incoherent.

In the first act Ludmilla vanishes eerily in the midst of festivities at the court of her father the Grand Duke of Kiev. In the next act Russlan, her lover, is in the cave of a friendly wizard, from whom he learns that Ludmilla has been abducted by the dwarf Tchernomor. Meanwhile Naina, an evil sprite, is siding with Farlaf, a Varangian chieftain who wants Ludmilla for himself. At one moment, Russlan finds himself on a field shrouded in mist. As the mist lifts, he observes a monstrous head on the ground. Its mere breathing causes a tempest to rise! Siegfried-like, he stabs the monster and promptly discovers a way to overcome Ludmilla's gnomish abductor—with a magic sword! Then Russlan becomes a kind of Odysseus. In the wicked domain of Naina, he successfully resists the blandishments of a bevy of sirens, though only with the help of his sorcerer friend. In the end Russlan defeats Tchernomor with his trusty sword. But Ludmilla is plunged in enchanted slumbers! Russlan vainly tries to arouse her. And now Farlaf, the Varangian, decides to turn kidnapper himself. In a prankish mood, he seizes the sleeping princess and carries her back to her father in Kiev. Russlan finally awakens her with a magic ring given him by the sorcerer.

The patchwork libretto was a double affront to the Russian public. First it insulted their intelligence; then, it profaned the sacred memory of their beloved poet Pushkin, who had made a fascinating little fable in verse of the legend of Russlan and Ludmilla. Moreover, the music itself was disturbing. In *A Life for the Czar* listeners had reveled in the smooth flow of nationally colored tunes. But the new score was not as easy to take. There were daring devices of harmony and rhythm. There were sounds that were strange, exotic, Oriental. Some of the music was harsh and barbaric. Emphatically, the audience did not relish this discordant modernism! How could it know that *Russlan and Ludmilla* would be a rich source book for future Russian composers. For here, in its naked force and fresh novelty, was the newborn child of Russian symphonic and operatic idiom. "Partly from hints taken from Russian and Oriental folk music," declare Wallace Brockway and Herbert Weinstock in their book *The Opera,* "partly from his own knack for exotic combination, Glinka had evolved that unmistakable, highly colored idiom that obviously differentiates Russian from other types of music."

An extreme example of the reaction to Glinka's hodge-podge opera was that of the Grand Duke Michail Pavlovich, who told Franz Liszt that he had devised a new form of punishment for offending members of his military entourage. "I condemn them to hear a performance of *Russlan and Ludmilla,*" he confided. Dostoievsky, on the other hand, never missed a performance of Glinka's fairy-tale opera. Most of all, he enjoyed the plot! Given to mysticism and symbolic delving, he sensed deep connotations in the involved libretto.

As Messrs. Brockway and Weinstock point out, "In it he saw an elaborate political allegory—a kind of Slavic *Zauberflöte.*" In short, a few, if not all, of Glinka's many librettists may have slyly injected revolutionary propaganda into Pushkin's whimsical fairy tale of a sleeping beauty in the dim long-ago of legendary Russia.

Outside Russia, Glinka's *Russlan and Ludmilla* is known only through its overture, though a few record enthusiasts treasure Feodor Chaliapin's rendering of Farlaf's Rondo, a kind of "patter song." Modeled on the classical overture, the music starts with a tutti of fortissimo chords, after which violins, violas, and flute give out the chief theme (*Presto,* D major, 2/2). There is a brisk passage for wood winds against pizzicati in the strings, before violas and cellos and bassoon introduce the second subject, a folklike melody of lilting grace and friendliness. This theme appears in F major. After that, the orchestra repeats it fortissimo. There is a final theme taken from one of Russlan's arias. Then the material is developed and repeated, and the overture ends in a rousing coda. An early use of the whole-tone scale may be detected in a descending bass passage of the coda, a device employed in the opera as a sort of pre-Wagnerian leitmotif to suggest the dark, gnomish machinations of the dwarf Tchernomor. Incidentally, this appearance of the whole-tone scale antedates Debussy's assimilation of it by fifty years.

L. B.

"Jota Aragonese," Caprice Brilliant

THE FIRST of many Russian masters to turn to Spanish folk sources for symphonic material, Glinka was originally drawn to this popular heritage by what he felt was its kinship to Russian folk music, Oriental elements being strong in both.

Besides, he wanted to devise a new orchestral form, the *fantaisie pittoresque,* that would reach a wider public than the concert-hall connoisseurs inured to the standard symphonic forms. In all, four examples of the new *fantaisie,* two based on Russian themes, *Kamarinskaia* and *Capriccio,* and two on Spanish themes, *Nuit d'été à Madrid* and *Jota Aragonese,* came from his pen.

Together with Liszt's symphonic poems, they served as models for Balakireff, Rimsky-Korsakoff, and Borodin. The Spanish pieces even blazed the trail for native Spanish composers in exploiting their country's melodic treasures.

In the spring of 1844, Glinka, disgusted with the ridicule heaped upon his opera *Russlan and Ludmilla* by hostile critics, left St. Petersburg for a European concert tour. His delicate health also called for a change of climate. Moreover, he looked forward eagerly to fresh stimulus from the national music of France and Spain. In Paris, Hector Berlioz raved in print about the "novel accents and charming strangeness" of his music.

In February, 1845, Glinka wrote his mother of a new project to study Spanish melodies, "which are analogous to Russian melodies," and apply himself to a "great new work."

He went still further in a letter to his friend Konkolnik:

I have decided to enrich my repertory with some orchestral concert pieces under the name of *fantaisies pittoresques*. . . . It strikes me as a way of reconciling the exigencies of art and the time and of availing oneself of the progress in instruments and execution to write pieces accessible alike to connoisseurs and the general public. . . .

I shall compose these *fantaisies* in Spain. Original local melodies will supply me with excellent source material, the more so since this field has not been previously exploited. And, besides, a given theme will help keep my unbridled imagination within bounds.

Glinka arrived in Spain early in June, 1845. At Valladolid, where he decided to spend the summer, he was quickly fascinated by popular songs and dances. For the first time he heard a Spanish guitarist, Castilla, strum the national Jota, with variations, and the idea promptly struck him of an orchestral fantasy based on the theme. The following winter he sketched out the work in Madrid.

Both *fantaisies pittoresques* on Spanish melodies are drenched in local color and brim over with the vitality of the *Russlan and Ludmilla* overture. Glinka knew how to mold folk material to good symphonic purpose.

Regarding the authenticity of Spanish music as treated by non-Spaniards, what goes for so much of this genre in the music of Rimsky-Korsakoff, Chabrier, Debussy, Ravel, etc., goes for Glinka's *fantaisies, viz.,* that the material is basically Spanish but the treatment French or Russian. In music, as in all art, the true artist is rooted in his national origins.

L. B.

Christoph Willibald Gluck

BORN: WEIDENWANG, JULY 2, 1714. DIED: VIENNA, NOV. 15, 1798.

A great triumph, my dear Christine! On the 19th we had the first performance of "Iphigénie." I was carried away by it, and people can no longer talk of anything else. All heads are fermenting as a result of this event, as much as could possibly be imagined—it is incredible, there are dissensions and quarrels, as though it were a matter of some religious dispute; at court, although I publicly expressed myself in favor of this inspired work, there are partisanships and debates of a particular liveliness; and in town it seems to be worse still.—MARIE ANTOINETTE, *in a letter to her sister Marie Christine Josepha, April,* 1774.

Overture to "Iphigenia in Aulis"

IN ITS original form this Overture lacked an ending to make it a complete concert unit, *i.e.,* as performed at the opera it continued without a break into the opening scene. Mozart was allegedly the first to contrive a finale for it. Later, Wagner, dissatisfied with Mozart's coda, provided one of his own. It is his version, which includes other alterations, that is regularly used today. The Overture is typically eighteenth century in its main pattern, beginning with a slow section (Andante) and continuing with a brisker section (Allegro). Much given to emotional analysis, Wagner labeled each of the four themes appearing in Gluck's overture. The first he called "a motive of appeal from painful, gnawing heart sorrow"; the second, "a motive of violence, of commanding, overbearing demand"; the third, "a motive of grace, of maidenly tenderness"; and the fourth, "a motive of painful, tormenting pity."

Gluck composed his opera to a libretto by Bailli du Roullet, who based it on Racine's *Iphigénie,* in turn based on the play of Euripides. It was performed for the first time at the Paris Opera on Apr. 19, 1774. We have the testimony of Marie Antoinette herself of the sensation it caused in the French capital. Iphigenia was long a favorite heroine of literature and music. Countless operas were written about Agamemnon's tragic dilemma in sacrificing his beloved daughter for having killed a sacred stag. Despite Achilles' efforts to rescue the young victim, Iphigenia is claimed by the offended goddess Diana and forced to serve as her priestess in Tauris. Thus was the immobilized Greek fleet permitted to sail for Troy. Gluck and his librettist, however, averted the tragedy by allowing Diana to be mollified without sacrifice. Iphigenia becomes the wife of Achilles, and the Trojan War resumes without further appeasement of the outraged goddess. Nietzsche maliciously asked how the saintly Parsifal ever became the father of Lohengrin. "One might as well have asked Gluck," wrote Alfred Einstein, "how Iphigenia, the wife of Achilles, managed to get to Tauris as high priestess." Gluck later wrote of Iphigenia's subsequent duties as priestess in the opera *Iphigenia in Tauris*.

Dr. Burney, the ubiquitous eighteenth-century chronicler of music, was among the privileged few to hear the music of *Iphigenia in Aulis* before it was written. He paid Gluck a visit in Paris in 1769. The composer played excerpts from many of his operas for the distinguished English visitor and then ran off the music of a new and still unscored work—*Iphigenia*.

"Though he had not as yet committed a note of it to paper," reported Dr. Burney, "[it] was so well digested in his head, and his retention was so wonderful, that he sang it nearly from the beginning to the end, with as much readiness as if he had a fair score before him."

L. B.

Overture to the Opera "Alceste"

An epoch-making document attaches to Gluck's *Alceste*. It appears in the score as a dedicatory epistle to the Grand Duke of Tuscany, later the Emperor Leopold II. Expressing Gluck's views on operatic reform, and outlining the purpose of *Alceste,* it reads as a challenge to opera tastes and styles dominant at the time. It amounts to a powerful plea for simplicity and directness in opera writing. The score was published with this manifesto in 1769, two years after the Viennese premiere of *Alceste* in its first form. The second, or French, version was not premiered in Paris till 1776, seven years after the opening shot of the new campaign in opera had been fired.

In marvelously direct speech the manifesto calls for an end to superfluous and purely decorative devices in opera. The following quotation renders the lengthy preface in somewhat condensed form. The paragraphing has been altered for more convenient reading. The original is in Italian and was actually the work of Gluck's librettist Ranieri Calzabigi. But Gluck signed it, having first expounded to Calzabigi just what his aims were and how he wanted them expressed.

I resolved to divest *Alceste* entirely of all those abuses which have so long disfigured Italian opera and made of the most splendid and most beautiful of spectacles the most ridiculous and wearisome.

I have striven to restrict music to its true office of serving poetry by means of expression and by following the situations of the story.

I did not wish to halt an actor in the greatest heat of dialogue in order to wait for

tiresome ritornello, nor to hold him up in the middle of a word on a vowel
favorable to his voice.

I have sought to abolish all the abuses against which good sense and reason have
long cried out in vain.

*I have felt that the overture ought to apprise the spectators of the nature of the
action that is to be represented and to form, so to speak, its argument;* that the
concerted instruments should be introduced in proportion to the interest and the
intensity of the words.

I believed that my greatest labor should be devoted to seeking a beautiful simplicity.

I have avoided making displays of difficulty at the expense of clearness.

I did not judge it desirable to invent novelties if they were not naturally suggested
by the situation and the expression.

I have thought it right to set aside any rule for the sake of an intended effect.

Simplicity, truth, and naturalness are the great principles of beauty in all artistic
manifestations.

In the hyperbolic style of his day, Gluck ends his appeal to reason by
soliciting "the most powerful patronage of Your Royal Highness, whose
August Name I beg you may have the grace to prefix to this my opera, a name
which with so much justice enjoys the suffrages of an enlightened Europe."

The libretto of *Alceste* is based on Euripides' play, where the emphasis, as
Alfred Einstein has shown, is on hospitality, rather than wifely devotion as in
Calzabigi's libretto. In Euripides' version Admetus, a Thessalonian king, is
told he is about to die. Apollo, who has been feted by Admetus after being
exiled from heaven, asks the Fates to spare his friend. They agree, on one condition. Someone else must die in his place. Admetus' wife Alcestis volunteers
and dies. The great hero Hercules then steps in as *deus ex machina*. In gay
mood, he visits his friend Admetus. He inquires about the mourning. Not to
dampen the strong man's spirits, Admetus lies. "A stranger has died here,
someone you do not know." Hercules feasts at Admetus' table and is soon
drunk and rowdy. An angry attendant then tells him the truth about Alcestis.
The news promptly sobers him up. He hastens to the funeral monument and
recovers Alcestis from Thanatos, the Greek personification of Death.

In the Italian version brought out at Vienna, Hercules is dropped entirely.
Instead, Apollo himself restores Alcestis to Admetus, out of gratitude. Calzabigi
rightly felt that the Greek hero's tipsy cavorting in a house in mourning would
jar on eighteenth-century taste. However, Guillard, who adapted the script for
Paris, brings the hero back into the story, though in a less objectionable state.
In the new version Alcestis never actually dies. As she dons the veil and prepares to depart, Hercules drives away the ministers of Death with his club.
Apollo thereupon assures him of immortality for his deed. The Gluck opera
stresses Alcestis' poignant situation as wife and mother more than Euripides'

play. The theme of sacrifice and separation is treated more touchingly. And, of course, the music of Gluck weaves a web of tragic pathos over the action making it doubly moving as personal drama.

It is readily apparent in the overture that Gluck means to abide by the principles laid down in his famous dedication. The action is simply and eloquently foreshadowed in the mingled themes of unrelenting fate and plaintive pleading. Gluck called the overture an *intrada,* since it merges into the opening scene. "It is the first truly tragic introduction to an opera," says Alfred Einstein in the Master Musicians Series. "The tutti are darkly colored by the trio of trombones, the form not in the least sonatalike and 'dramatic,' but heavily charged, neutral, purely a prologue to a gloomy action, and especially disconsolate where it becomes gentle and supplicating. But fate is inexorable, like the sustained A in the basses. This piece in D minor is the ancestor of an illustrious line, from the overture to *Don Giovanni* to the *Tragic Overture* of Brahms."

There can be no doubt in any listener's mind about the prevailing mood of *Alceste.* Few operas are so plainly tragic in atmosphere. Some unjustly called it "The dismal Alceste," and there is the recorded gibe of a member of the anti-Gluck faction, made at the Paris premiere in 1776: "For nine days the theater has been closed, and on the tenth it opens with a Requiem."

Unless records to the contrary turn up, the honor of presenting *Alceste* for the first time in America goes to Wellesley College, where Gluck's opera was given twice in March, 1938. The Metropolitan Opera House waited till Jan. 24, 1941, before producing it. A successful earlier revival of Gluck's *Orfeo* had encouraged the management to hazard a production of the 174-year-old novelty. Ettore Panizza conducted, and Marjorie Lawrence and René Maison headed the cast. Of course, all music lovers were already acquainted with Alceste's dramatic address to the ministers of death, "Divinités du Styx," occurring in the first act of the *tragédie-opéra.* Significantly, Gluck also called his opera, a *tragedia in musica.*

L. B.

Karl Goldmark

BORN: KESZTHELY, HUNGARY, MAY 18, 1830. DIED: VIENNA, JAN. 2, 1915.

If he has never sounded the deepest notes of human emotion, or given the world any passage of real sublimity, his works have given great pleasure to many classes of musicians.—J. A. FULLER-MAITLAND.

Concerto for Violin and Orchestra in A minor, Op. 28

I. Allegro moderato. II. Air: Andante. III. Moderato; Allegretto.

THE CASPER MILQUETOAST of the composing fraternity may well have been Karl Goldmark, if we are to accept fully W. Beatty-Kingston's description of him in *Music and Manners*. The English writer's pen sketch is repetitious and also studiedly figurative—reflecting, perhaps, the journalistic style of his period —but it is vivid and sympathetic, none the less, and it is worth including here. He says:

A meek little man of thirty-four, slightly bent and grizzled, timid and retiring in manner, of apologetic address, shabby appearance and humble bearing. Before Hellmesberger took him up and made his works known to the musical public of the Austrian capital, Goldmark had undergone many trials and disappointments, as well as no little actual privation. Although his chamber music and songs made a decided hit shortly after I came to know him, it was not until nine years later—and then only through his steadfast friends' influence with the intendant of the Imperial theaters—that his grand opera *Die Königin von Saba,* a work teeming with gorgeous Oriental color, was brought out at the Hoftheater. Goldmark's was one of those gentle natures that are intensely grateful for the least encouragement.

A word or two of judicious praise anent any work of his composition would at any moment dispel the settled sadness of his expression and cause his dark features to brighten with lively pleasure. I have often watched him during rehearsals of his Quartet and Quintet, sitting quiet in a corner and not venturing to make a suggestion when anything went wrong, though his eyes would flash joyously enough when the performers happened to hit off the exact manner in which he wished his meaning to be interpreted. A less talkative person, for a musical composer, it would be difficult to discover.

Even when he was among his professional brethren, who were, for the most part, extremely kind to him, he would nervously shrink from mixing in conversation and open his lips to no one but his cigar for hours at a stretch. If abruptly addressed, he was wont to cast a deprecatory glance at his interlocutor, as though he would mildly exclaim: "Don't strike me, pray; but you may if you will!" That being the sort of man he was, it is not surprising that I failed to become very intimate with Karl

Goldmark, although I heartily admired some of his compositions and was for a long time ready at any moment to develop a strong liking for him. But it is easier to shake hands with a sensitive plant and elicit a warm, responsive grip from that invariably retiring vegetable than to gain the friendship of a man afflicted with unconquerable diffidence. So, after several futile attempts to break down Goldmark's barriers of reserve, by which I am afraid I made him extremely uncomfortable, resolved to confine my attention to his music, which, for the most part, is well worth studying and highly satisfactory to the cultivated musician's ear.

It is interesting to note that the composer numbered Brahms among his many intimates. The picture of the "meek" and "timid" and "apologetic" Goldmark loses some of its most prominent features in view of the fact that Brahms's devastatingly blunt criticism of his confrere's music could alter their relationship but little. A real mouse might have gone scurrying to his corner in the face of such assaults. Of course, Beatty-Kingston does not tell us just what method of attack he employed in trying to "break down the barriers of Goldmark's reserve." After all, even an "invariably *un*retiring vegetable" might be sparing of its "warm, responsive grip," if proffered a mailed fist to shake. The foregoing, possibly, contains implications unfair to Beatty-Kingston, who, to give him his due, sounds like a genuinely hurt man in his unsuccessful attempts to win over Goldmark's friendship.

The Violin Concerto in A minor was given its first performance at a concert of the Privat Musikverein, Nuremburg, Oct. 28, 1878. On that occasion the soloist was Johann Lauterbach, one of the most noted violinists of the nineteenth century. The rest of the program at that premiere included, besides Lassen's *Beethoven Overture,* the Sixth Symphony of Beethoven, and a number of songs delivered by a Miss C. Gradel. Lauterbach performed, probably as an encore, a concert etude of his own composition. The violinist played the Goldmark Concerto again at a Gesellschaft concert in Vienna four nights later. Other works in that program consisted of Bach's cantata, *Herr Gott dich loben wir,* Mendelssohn's setting of Psalm 114, both numbers done with chorus, naturally, and Bizet's *L'Arlésienne Suite,* which made its bow in the Austrian capital.

Not the most frequently played of violin concertos, the Goldmark A minor is in the usual three movements. They are marked, I. Allegro moderato, A minor, 4/4; II. Air, which is an Andante in G major, 3/4; and III. Allegretto, 3/4, which is preceded by a short introductory section marked Moderato, A minor, 4/4.

R. C. B.

Morton Gould

BORN: RICHMOND HILL, LONG ISLAND, N. Y., DEC. 10, 1913.

Morton Gould is one of those who has approached jazz "from above." . . . That is, he did not come to serious music as an alumnus of Tin Pan Alley, but rather the other way around. . . . Gould has not let his work in the popular field swamp his serious activities, and he has tried to maintain a fruitful connection between the two. He has little use for the "art-for-art's sake boys."—JOHN TASKER HOWARD.

"American Symphonette," No. 2

I. Moderately fast, with vigor. II. Pavane. III. Racy.

THUS FAR Morton Gould has written four of what he terms *Symphonettes*. In each of these he has tried to "fuse the elements of our popular American idioms with the classical form and structure." The composer suggests that the works have been written as entertainment music "in the better sense of the term."

The first three *Symphonettes* are based on jazz and swing idioms, whereas the fourth makes use of the melodic and rhythmic principles common to popular Latin-American music.

The *American Symphonette* No. 2 has been performed frequently by noted orchestras. Its second movement Pavane has made special progress, having made the circuit of dance, as well as concert groups. It is a special favorite of school orchestras.

Mr. Gould began to compose at the age of four when he also demonstrated a marked ability for the piano. A pupil of Abby Whiteside and Vincent Jones, he later took musical courses at the Juilliard School of Music and at New York University.

He has played the piano often in public, displaying a particular aptitude for the fist, forearm, and elbow technique, which is an important adjunct of the musical ideology of *tone clusters*. A staff member of the Radio City Music Hall for a time, Mr. Gould subsequently moved his lares and penates to radio, where he has been eminently successful, and to the movies, where the same holds true.

A considerable number of Mr. Gould's compositions show clearly his predilection for combining native idiom with standard form. He has written for orchestra a *Chorale and Fugue in Jazz;* a Piano Concerto; *Foster Gallery*, based on melodies of Stephen Foster; a Symphony, an *American Suite, Lincoln*

Legend, and *Spirituals,* besides three sonatas and a sonatina for piano. His latest works include the score for the ballet *Interplay* and that for the musical comedy *Billion Dollar Baby.*

R. C. B.

"Spirituals for String Choir and Orchestra"

1. Proclamation. 2. Sermon. 3. A Little Bit of Sin. 4. Protest. 5. Jubilee.

IN WRITING the suite Mr. Gould sought to convey the mood and idiom of White and Negro spirituals, without resorting to literal exposition of specific tunes. Admittedly, fragments of actual spirituals were woven into certain passages. As a rule, Mr. Gould's aim was to "utilize the idiomatic elements in conjunction with much original material." Mr. Gould told the authors:

I have tried to write music the way one speaks. I tried to make it as direct and simple as possible. Part of the "Jubilee" section is in boogie-woogie pattern. Of course, many contemporary jazz effects coincide with certain rhythmic patterns in our Spirituals. The White and Negro spirituals make a tremendous body of folk material. One group ties into the other. That is, our White songs are influenced by our Negro songs, and the other way around. What I tried to do was to synthesize some of these features.

My starting premise was that our spirituals develop a wide gamut of emotions, musically. These emotions are specifically American. The songs range from strictly spiritual ones that are escapist in feeling, or light and gay, to those having tremendous depth and tragic impact.

My idea was to get five moods, widely contrasted in feeling. The titles are self-explanatory. Although most of the work is original as far as thematic material goes, I have used fragments of folk tunes here and there.

I like them called *Spirituals for String Choir and Orchestra,* because my plan was to use the strings as if they were a vocal choir. The second movement, "Sermon," is only for strings. The analogous idea would be a group of people singing folk songs with antiphonal responses.

Edvard Grieg

BORN: BERGEN, NORWAY, JUNE 15, 1843. DIED: BERGEN, SEPT. 4, 1907.

Anyone with a sense of tune will realize the charm of Grieg's music, and anyone who knows Norway will recognize its special character. Grieg is Norway. His music is synonymous with Norwegian temper and nature, lore, light, and landscape. But he is more than that. It so happened that the very national idiom in which he expressed himself was also his own personal idiom. The more he sang about his land, the more truly he spoke of himself. The more local his endeavor, the more universal his appeal. That is why his music has greatness and originality as well.—CHRISTEN JUL.

Concerto for Piano and Orchestra in A minor, Op. 16

I. Allegro molto moderato. II. Adagio. III. Allegro moderato molto e marcato.

EFFORTS HAVE been made to read a strictly autobiographical program into the A minor Concerto of Grieg. That it is a burst of youthful ardor in some great flush of excitement no one can doubt. The love of nature courses through it, and a soaring emotionalism. There is a strange hymnlike intimacy in the Adagio, and Norwegian folk echoes abound, reflecting Grieg's constant preoccupation with the homeland. In any case, the facts surrounding its composition would suggest the idyllic.

It was the summer of 1868. Grieg was only twenty-five. The year before he had married Nina Hagerup, whom he met in Christiana, where he led the Philharmonic and taught. A daughter was born to them, and the Griegs planned a vacation in Denmark. Grieg's health was never too robust, and here was a chance to drop a taxing routine, rest, and compose only when he felt the urge. Husband, wife, and baby daughter arrived in Copenhagen early in June. The child was left behind with grandparents in the Danish capital, and the Griegs set out for Sölleröd, an hour's journey, where a cozy two-room gardener's cottage, rented by friends, awaited them. They spent a healthy, leisurely summer. Grieg slept late, ate heartily, took long walks, and enjoyed the lovely countryside. At night he met friends in an inn near by and chatted over a glass. Several hours a day he was left alone to compose (he could never bear anyone within earshot while at work with the piano). And the A minor Concerto was born. No wonder Gerard Schjelderup, stunned by its "natural impressions," saw "all Norway in its infinite variety and unity" before his eyes, comparing the Adagio to a "lonely mountain-girt tarn which lies dreaming of infinity."

Grieg's German biographer Richard H. Stein heard a "joy of life, amorous longing, and youthful fire" in the Concerto, contrasting it with the tragic Violin Sonata, Op. 45. "Apparently Grieg mirrored himself here," he wrote of the first movement. In the final surge of tone he even sensed Grieg's joy in his growing artistic powers. In the Adagio the piano wove about the suave theme "sounds learned from nature herself" and carried the hymn "out of church into the free fields of God." He felt certain the Adagio had deep significance as a personal creed. A reverielike passage in D in the finale represented the "image of the beloved appearing to Grieg and giving reality to his dreams of longing." Later, this same love theme, expanded, rose jubilantly to a "love of all humanity"—the "Seid umschlagen Millionen!" of Schiller's "Ode to Joy."

As for the sober facts, the Concerto was dedicated to the pianist Edmund Neupart (b. 1842, Christiana, d. 1888, New York), who first played it in Copenhagen on Apr. 3, 1869, and in Christiana the following year. There was a performance by Erika Lie at a Gewandhaus concert in Leipzig in February 1872, and seven years later Grieg played it himself with the same organization. On that occasion a writer in the *Neue Zeitschrift für Musik* spoke of "its great color, Nordic flashes, original details, and charming mixture of major and minor," besides its echoes of "Gade, Mendelssohn, and Willmers, with something of Weber and much of Liszt."

Neupart wrote to Grieg from Copenhagen after the world premiere:

On Saturday your divine Concerto resounded in the great hall of the Casino. The triumph I achieved was tremendous. Even as early as the cadenza in the first movement the public broke into a real storm. The three dangerous critics, Gade, Rubinstein, and Hartmann, sat in the stalls and applauded with all their might. I am to send you greetings from Rubinstein and say that he is astounded to have heard a composition of such genius. He would like to make your acquaintance.

That other keyboard idol of the time, Franz Liszt, had already made the acquaintance of the young man from the north. Liszt wrote to him glowingly of an early violin sonata that had come to his notice. In it he discerned a "strong, creative, inventive, and well-disciplined talent which has only to follow its natural bent to reach even higher levels." He urged Grieg to visit him so that they might "know each other better." Liszt's intercession with the Norwegian government brought Grieg a grant permitting him to visit the great man in his monastery home in Rome. Grieg relates the episode in his letters home. Liszt promptly asked for the piano concerto, which had just arrived in manuscript from Liepzig. The gathering included a "Chevalier de Concilium," Winding, Sgambati, and "a German Lisztite, who goes so far in aping his idol at he even wears the gown of an abbé." Some young ladies were present, of the kind that would like to eat Liszt, skin, hair, and all; their adulation is mply comical."

He and Winding were eager to see if Liszt would play the concerto at sight, rieg considering it impossible. But the incredible Abbé did, and Grieg even ought the difficult cadenza went best of all, though the first movement was oo fast" and "helter-skelter." Liszt stopped at one place, left the piano and ith upraised arms strode across the huge cloister floor, "literally roaring out ιe theme." When he got to a particular G in the score, "he stretched out his rms imperiously and exclaimed: 'G! G! not G sharp! Splendid!" At the end e said to Grieg warmly: *"Fahren Sie fort . . . und lassen Sie sich nicht bschrecken!"* (Keep it up, and don't be intimidated!) Liszt made suggestions ›out amplifying the orchestration which Grieg adopted but later modified in revised version.

The pianist Oscar Meyer, reminiscing in the *Neue Musikzeitung,* Stuttgart, 910, adds another detail to the monastic tableau:

It happened that in turning the pages Liszt missed a modulation and played n orchestral fortissimo with great pomp in the major instead of in the minor. Vhen Grieg pointed out the error, Liszt stared at him indignantly, took a red rayon from the desk and made some vigorous marks in the notes. After repeated idelong scowls at the composer, he went on with his playing.

The A minor Concerto abounds in fresh and striking themes handled with ramatic contrast. In the opening movement (Allegro molto moderato, A ninor, 4/4), after a prefatory roll of drums against a sustained pianissimo in he horns and tuba and a brief cadenza for piano, the wood winds and horns nnounce the marchlike subject later taken up by the piano in development gainst string accompaniment. The piano toys with subsidiary themes, one Animato e molto leggiero, the other more flowing, with flute and clarinet ntering in imitation. The trumpet gives out the second theme (Tempo lento, ›iù tranquillo), which is picked up by the piano, developed, and accelerated. The orchestra then weaves an elaborate passage against arpeggios in the piano. The first theme is back on the piano, and the strings take notice. A brilliant adenza leads to a brief coda.

Muted strings, soon joined by wood winds and horns, discourse the theme of he Adagio (D flat major, 3/8), the piano trailing after with ornamental ›assage work and the strings busy sustaining harmonies. Then the theme wells p full-throated from piano and orchestra.

The finale (Allegro moderato molto e marcato, A minor, 2/4), following he Adagio without a break, is a rondo on five themes. The first, in A minor, ›f marked Norwegian flavor, is extensively worked out by the piano to string ιccompaniment. The second (also in A minor) begins with bravura writing for the piano and ends in lyrical chromatics. A brisk march figure in C majo[r] furnishes the third theme, sounded first by the piano, while piano and orchestr[a] combined announce the fourth. A flowing last theme is adopted by the pian[o] to cello accompaniment after flute and clarinet have first sung it to tremulou[s] strings. There is a long repetition, then the coda, and the fifth theme surge[s] up maestoso from trumpets and trombones against piano and orchestra.

L. B.

"Peer Gynt," Suite No. 1, Op. 46, and Suite No. 2, Op. 5[5]

GRIEG'S FIRST impulse was to turn down Ibsen's invitation to write the incidenta[l] music for his poetic satire *Peer Gynt*. This was in January, 1874. Ibsen offere[d] to share equally the "400 specie dollars" he proposed to ask for the play[.] Needing the money desperately, Grieg accepted. Yet he felt his temperamen[t] unsuited to the task. *Peer Gynt* was philosophical fantasy, pillorying Norwe[-] gians for their apathy and vacillation. Grieg also believed that the nature of th[e] play, though soon to be hailed as a poetic glory of Norwegian literature, did no[t] invite music. Moreover, he smarted over Ibsen's thrusts at his own people[.] Ironically, it was this very assignment, so reluctantly taken on, that establishe[d] Grieg's fame the world over.

After Ibsen's death, Grieg confessed to a friend that he had finally come t[o] agree with Peer Gynt's central thesis. He wrote:

Many Norwegians formerly believed, as I myself did, that Peer Gynt repre[-] sents only an exceptional type. Unhappily it has been shown in the last years how shockingly true to the life the poet sketched that national character. Ibsen expose[d] a dangerous side of our whole people mercilessly. For that reason it is that h[e] stands in such bad odor in our country politically.

Drastically cut and revised, Ibsen's satiric drama was produced at the Christiania Theater, in what is now Oslo, on Feb. 24, 1876—two long year[s] after Grieg had been approached to compose the music for it. And how the conscientious Grieg had worked at the score! There were thirty-six perform[-] ances that year, all with Grieg's music. John Macy called *Peer Gynt* a "fantasti[c] satire not only on the nation, but upon universal human nature. It is a classi[c] that belongs to the world."

Peer Gynt was the third of a trilogy of satirico-lyric dramas written by Ibsen[.] The others were *Love's Comedy* and *Brand*. The play is written in octosyllabi[c] rhymed verse and shows the poet in Ibsen at the peak of his metrical mastery[.] Despite the poetic atmosphere, there is slashing satire throughout, and Nor[-] wegians must have squirmed in their seats as the pitiless exposé of nationa[l] traits struck home. "A poem of which any literature might be proud," wrote

Edmund Gosse of *Peer Gynt*. And from which any people might learn! The following is Grieg's own summary of the action, inserted as a preface to the published score of the Second Suite:

Peer Gynt, the only son of poor peasants, is drawn by the poet as a character of a morbidly developed fancy and a prey to megalomania. In his youth he has many wild adventures—comes, for instance, to a peasants' wedding where he carries off the bride up to the mountain peaks. Here he leaves her to roam about with wild cowherd girls. He then enters the kingdom of the mountain king, whose daughter falls in love with him and dances to him. But he laughs at the dance and the troll music, whereupon the enraged mountain folk wish to kill him. But he succeeds in escaping and wanders to foreign countries, among others to Morocco, where he appears as a prophet and is greeted by Arab girls. After many wonderful guidings of Fate he at last returns as an old man, after suffering shipwreck on his way to his home as poor as he left it. Here the sweetheart of his youth, Solvejg, who has stayed true to him all these years, meets him, and his weary head at last finds rest in her lap.

Aase, whose name appears in the second section of Suite No. 1, is Peer Gynt's mother, distracted and alarmed by her son's wild talk and ruffianly conduct. She is something of a symbolic figure, like almost everyone else in the play, and her death was said to signify, according to Henry T. Finck, "the dying of nature in the autumn, far up in the North—the disappearance of the sun for months, leaving this globe in a ruddy darkness."

Anitra, whose dance makes up the third section of Suite No. 1, is the seductive daughter of a Bedouin chief. Peer Gynt elopes with her on horseback. But Anitra gallops back home after regaining some jewels Peer had stolen. During "Anitra's Dance" in the tent of the Arab chief, Peer, garbed as an Arab, soliloquizes sardonically. "What is beauty?" he asks, as he sips black coffee and smokes a long pipe; "a mere convention, a coin made current by time and place." Grieg cautioned that the music of "Anitra's Dance" is conceived as accompaniment to Peer Gynt's monologue, and should therefore be played behind the scene pianissimo."

Suite No. 1 consists of I. "Morning Mood" (Allegro pastorale, E major, 6/8); II. "Aase's Death" (Andante doloroso, B minor, 4/4); III. "Anitra's Dance" (Tempo di mazurka, A minor, 3/4); and IV. "In the Hall of the Mountain King" (Alla marcia e molto marcato, B minor, 4/4).

Suite No. 2 failed to achieve the popularity of Suite No. 1, perhaps because the material and mood of the earlier were such as to preclude the need for a second helping of *Peer Gynt*. The Second Suite originally consisted of I. "The Abduction of the Bride"; II. "Arabian Dance"; III. "Peer Gynt's Homecoming"; IV. "Solvejg's Song"; and V. "Dance of the Daughter of the Mountain King." Later Grieg discarded the fifth section and counseled others to follow his practice.

L. B.

"Symphonic Dance No. 2"

THE SYMPHONIC DANCE No. 2 is from a group of four such arrangement published by Grieg as Op. 64 in 1898. It is marked Allegretto grazioso, major, 2/2. The melodies used in all four are Norwegian folk songs and dance Grieg was a staunch nationalist in cherishing his musical country's folklore yet, except where he openly employed native themes in piano or orchestra treatments, as in Op. 64, he made up his own tunes. A very small fraction o his works contain literal quotations from folk sources, and only two othe works (Op. 30 and Op. 35), besides the *Four Symphonic Dances,* frankl incorporate Norwegian melodies.

L. B.

Charles Tomlinson Griffes

BORN: ELMIRA, N. Y., SEPT. 17, 1884. DIED: NEW YORK, APR. 8, 1920.

The man Charles Tomlinson Griffes died April 8, 1920, in his thirty-sixth year. Griffes the musician is today a vital part of the American tradition, and lives in the memory of his friends and in the musical experience of a wide public.—MARION BAUER.

"The White Peacock," Op. 7, No. 1

THE DEATH in 1920 of Charles Tomlinson Griffes brought to an untimely end one of the most promising careers in American music. Though he wrote only a few works, which some musicologists have grouped as belonging to three distinct periods, they speak of an impressive talent and great versatility.

In the first group are pieces, according to John Tasker Howard, written during his

student period, when he was definitely under the influence of his German teachers, Rüfer and Humperdinck. It was then that he wrote German songs. In his second style Griffes leaned toward the French Impressionists, and also showed his fondness for the Russian Orientalism that was to appear as the mysticism of his later works, "The Lake at Evening," from the three tone-pictures for piano, and "The White Peacock," from the *Roman Sketches* for piano, show him in this period and demonstrate his power of impressionistic description. . . .

The third period shows an advanced trend; a grasping of something less rigid than the tempered scale, a medium to sound the overtones he wanted us to hear. It was in this period that Griffes composed his Piano Sonata and his larger orchestral works. The Sonata has the intellectual consistency of a Schönberg, a pursuit of tonal logic without the sacrifice of poetic conception.

Familiar to concert audiences are *The Pleasure-dome of Kubla Khan,* the *Poem* for flute and orchestra, and other compositions.

The orchestral version of "The White Peacock" calls for strings, wood winds, four horns, celesta, tam-tam, and two harps. It was first played by the Philadelphia Orchestra, in Philadelphia, Dec. 19, 1919. Hans Lange and the Philharmonic-Symphony performed it in Carnegie Hall at the concerts of Feb. 6, 7, 8, and 9, 1936.

"The White Peacock" and its three companions in the set *Roman Sketches* take inspiration from poems of William Sharp.

R. C. B.

"The Pleasure-dome of Kubla Khan"

In 1912 Griffes, inspired by Coleridge's famous poem, composed *The Pleasure-dome of Kubla Khan*. Four years later he revised the score. The work was brought out in Boston at a concert of the Boston Symphony Orchestra, Pierre Monteux conducting, on Nov. 28, 1919. At that time Griffes supplied the program book with the following note:

The instruments called for are three flutes (one interchangeable with piccolo), two oboes, English horn, two clarinets, bass clarinet, three bassoons, four horns, three trumpets, three trombones, bass tuba, kettledrums, bass drum, cymbals, tambourine, tam-tam, celesta, pianoforte, two harps, strings.

I have taken as a basis for my work those lines of Coleridge's poem describing the "stately pleasure-dome," the "sunny pleasure-dome with caves of ice," the "miracle of rare device." Therefore I call the work *The Pleasure-dome of Kubla Khan* rather than "Kubla Khan." These lines include 1 to 11 and lines 32 to 38. It might be well to quote some of the lines—at least the last six:

> "In Xanadu did Kubla Khan
>   A stately pleasure-dome decree;
> Where Alph, the sacred river, ran
> Through caverns measureless to man
>   Down to a sunless sea.
> So twice five miles of fertile ground
> With walls and towers were girdled round.
> And here were gardens bright with sinuous rills
>   Where blossomed many an incense-bearing tree;
> And here were forests ancient as the hills,
> Enfolding sunny spots of greenery.

* * *

> "The shadow of the dome of pleasure
>   Floated midway on the waves;
> Where was heard the mingled measure
>   From the fountain and the caves.
> It was a miracle of rare device,
> A sunny pleasure-dome with caves of ice!"

As to argument, I have given my imagination free rein in the description of this strange palace, as well as of purely imaginary revelry which might take place there. The vague, foggy beginning suggests the sacred river, running "through caverns measureless to man down to a sunless sea." Then gradually rise the outlines of the palace, "with walls and towers girdled round." The gardens with fountains and "sunny spots of greenery" are next suggested. From inside come sounds of dancing and revelry, which increase to a wild climax and then suddenly break off. There is a return to the original mood suggesting the sacred river and "the caves of ice."

Louis Gruenberg

BORN: BREST LITOVSK, RUSSIA, AUG. 3, 1884.

I reject, as emphatically as I am able, ALL systems that tend to cramp the emotional sweep of one's impression.—LOUIS GRUENBERG.

Concerto for Violin and Orchestra, Op. 47

I. Rhapsodie. II. With simplicity and warmth. III. Lively and with good humor.

COMMISSIONED BY Jascha Heifetz, this Concerto was given its world premiere a concert of the Philadelphia Orchestra, in Philadelphia, on Dec. 1, 1944. Mr. Heifetz was the soloist, and Eugene Ormandy conducted. Requested by Louise Beck, the annotator, to supply information about the new score, Mr. Gruenberg replied with a refreshingly candid statement on program notes and composition in general and his Concerto in particular. The following are excerpts from Mr. Gruenberg's reply:

You ask me to send you some notes concerning my new concerto. . . . I have often wondered why a composer should be asked to invent (mostly) episodes in words after he has perspired and prayed over a composition for a seemingly everlasting period, when the work itself is its own illuminating commentary.

Oh, if only we could really hide faults and shortcomings with words! Can I say that the concerto is beautiful, profound, and terribly important as I sometimes thought in highly optimistic moments, or, shall I say that it has turned out only fairly satisfactory as I have in pessimistic moods?

What *can* a composer say concerning something he has slaved over after sending it out in the world except to hope, to hope, and hope again? What else should be expected from a composer except music? And if he delivers beautiful melodies supported by beautiful harmonies and orderly construction, that is, to sum it up in two words, passion and order, surely, if he delivers this there is no need for words. But, if he doesn't, well, there is even greater need for silence on his part.

However, the composition is the result of a commission by Heifetz who desired to add an American concerto to his already stupendous repertory, and this was, of course, nothing less than a challenge. It raised up that question of questions again as to what was really American music. To my mind, American music consists of all human emotions. Nothing less!

In order to add spice to the work, I have used several bars of two Negro Spirituals in the second movement besides endeavoring to imitate a hillbilly fiddler and a small-town religious revival meeting in the third. The composition was composed in three weeks, polished, orchestrated and completed months later, last May.

Miss Beck was also informed that Mr. Heifetz's counsel was sought certain technical matters. When the solo writing struck the violinist as ov intricate, Mr. Gruenberg blandly rejoined: "You're Heifetz, aren't you?" T composer later confessed that while writing the Concerto he "got rid of all l violin inhibitions."

Mr. Gruenberg's words about the Negro Spirituals in the second moveme refer mainly to a solo passage in which the violin discourses sections of "C Holy Lord" and "Master Jesus." The "hillbilly fiddler" is heard scraping aw at the "Arkansas Traveler" in the third movement, which follows the seco movement without a break. To heighten the local color, Mr. Gruenberg ad harmonica, clappers, tambourine, and gong to his ample scoring at this poir

In recent years Mr. Gruenberg has gained prominence as a composer f films. Earlier he had won recognition through his operas *Jack and the Bea stalk* and *Emperor Jones*. Concerning subsequent compositions Mr. Gruenbe has informed the authors as follows:

These orchestral compositions have been written since 1940 and have be voluntarily withheld from performance for further examination: Op. 41, Seco Piano Concerto; Op. 42, Second Symphony; Op. 44, Third Symphony; Op. 4 *Music to an Imaginary Ballet;* Op. 48, *Americana;* Op. 46, *Music to an Imagina Legend;* Op. 49, *Dance Rhapsody;* Op. 50, Fourth Symphony.

The picture scores have been "Fight for Life," "Commandos Strike at Dawr "Counterattack," "American Romance," and "So Ends Our Night."

L. B.

Henry Hadley

BORN: SOMERVILLE, MASS., DEC. 20, 1871. DIED: NEW YORK, N. Y., SEPT. 6, 1937.

*He lived mentally with every new development in tone, and inter-
estedly watched the revolutionary experiments of the advanced school,
but he felt in them nothing that answered to his own fundamental
approach to music, and so he remained true to the ideas and ideals of
the masters whom he revered most deeply.*—LEONARD LIEBLING.

Overture "In Bohemia," Op. 28

CALLED, WITH all due respect, "the Henry Ford of American music," Henry
Hadley probably produced more music than any other native composer. Though
prolific, he wrote with immense care and skill. The facility rarely, if ever,
became slipshod haste. He evidently composed in all forms with equal ease.
He was a widely acclaimed conductor, too, as guest, associate, and regular
director, and he early identified himself with the practical needs and endeavors of America composers. Out of this interest in the problems of his
colleagues grew the National Association for American Composers and Conductors. Europe knew Hadley as conductor and composer. In 1920 the Metropolitan Opera Company took cognizance of his gifts by producing one of his
five operas—*Cleopatra's Night.*

The overture *In Bohemia* was written at Garden City, Long Island, in 1900
and intended for performance at the annual "High Jinks" meeting of the
Bohemian Club in the Bohemian Grove, California. Hadley was to conduct.
However, European commitments made it impossible for him to appear, so
the overture was first played—with great success—in Europe. Later Victor
Herbert conducted it in Pittsburgh for the first time in America. It is to
America's beloved operetta king that the overture is dedicated, the inscription
reading "To my good friend Victor Herbert." There is a second dedication,
however, at the head of the first page of the score: "To the Bohemian Club of
San Francisco."

The work is built around a buoyant and vigorous theme announced fortissimo by the entire orchestra (Allegro con brio, E flat major, 6/4 against a
cross rhythm of 6/2). This recurs in vividly changing guise through the overture and finally looms majestically in the coda. There are freshness and strength
in the writing, mingled with suave melody, suggesting—as the *London
Standard* critic noted when Hadley was guest of the London Symphony

Orchestra in Queen's Hall on May 23, 1913—"that the artist's life is a mixture of stern endeavor and dreamy pleasure."

Realizing that many listeners might be misled by the title of his overture Hadley explained to Felix Borowski of the Chicago Symphony that the reference was to the free fellowship of art. "The title *In Bohemia*, in this instance, has no national meaning, but refers only to that Elysium where true artists dwell."

L. B.

George Frederick Handel

BORN: HALLE, FEB. 23, 1685. DIED: LONDON, APR. 14, 1759.

I should be sorry, my lord, if I have only succeeded in entertaining them; I wished to make them better.—HANDEL *to Lord Kinnoul, after the first London performance of* The Messiah, Covent Garden, *Mar. 23, 1743.*

"Water Music" Suite

[*Arranged by Sir Hamilton Harty*]

I. Allegro. II. Air. III. Bourrée. IV. Hornpipe. V. Andante. VI. Allegro deciso.

IF NEWMAN FLOWER had not come along to explode the legend, Handel's *Water Music* suite would still rank as one of the great peace offerings in the history of art.

According to the long-accepted story, Handel planned the work in 1715 as a gesture of appeasement to George I. Handel had been George's Kapellmeister when he was still Elector of Hanover. In 1712, Handel obtained permission from his ruler to visit England. The visit proved highly lucrative, and Handel failed to return to his Hanoverian post. Finally Mahomet went to the mountain. Queen Anne died in 1714, and Handel's former employer found himself proclaimed King of England. The King was supposedly incensed over Handel's playing truant.

Lord Burlington and Baron Kielmansegg, the Master of the King's Horse, thought up a plan of reconciliation, which was carried out. During a "royal water party" on the Thames, the King's barge was followed by another bearing Handel and a group of musicians. The King was enchanted by the music and naturally asked its composer's name. When told it was Handel, the two were promptly reconciled.

The story would be all right except for the date. Documents unearthed by Mr. Flower revealed the barge episode as occurring in 1717, almost two years after the records show Handel and the King to have become friends again. Moreover, it is just possible that the King never took Handel's truancy too hard. Handel accompanied him on a trip to Hanover in 1716, and later George fixed an annuity for life of £200 on him. Queen Anne had earlier put him on her pension list.

The *Daily Courant* of July 19, 1717, describes the incident as taking place two days earlier. The King's barge moved from Lambeth down to Chelsea during what was then termed "a state progress." The river was fairly blanketed with barges, among them one conveying the musicians. The London sheet reported:

Many other barges with persons of quality attended, and so great a number of boats that the whole river in a manner was covered. A City Company's barge was employed for the music, wherein were fifty instruments of all sorts, who played all the way from Lambeth, while the barges drove with the tide without rowing as far as Chelsea, the finest symphonies, composed expressly for this occasion by Mr. Handel, which His Majesty liked so well that he caused it to be played over three times in going and returning.

At eleven His Majesty went ashore at Chelsea, where a supper was prepared, and then there was another very fine concert of music which lasted till two, after which His Majesty came again into his barge and returned the same way, the music continuing to play until he landed.

A report made to the Duke of Brandenburg on July 19 by his envoy Frederic Bonnet gives further details of the expedition down the Thames besides one or two surrounding circumstances.

Some weeks ago, the King expressed a wish to Baron von Kilmanseck to have a concert on the river, by subscription. . . . The baron addressed himself therefore to Heidegger, a Swiss by nationality, but [sic] the most intelligent agent the nobility could have for their pleasures. Heidegger answered that much as he was eager to oblige His Majesty he must reserve the subscription for the big enterprises, to wit, the masquerades, each of which was worth from 300 to 400 guineas to him.

Baron Kilmanseck, seeing that H. M. was vexed about these difficulties, resolved to give the concert on the river at his own expense, and so this concert took place the day before yesterday.

Bonnet added that the musicians' barge kept close to the side of the King's float and that the men "played all kinds of instruments, *viz.,* trumpets, hunting horns, oboes, bassoons, German flute, French flutes-à-bec, violins, and basses, but without voices." Evidently a more observant reporter than the *Daily Courant* man, he even contributes the information that the music "took an hour for each performance."

John Walsh first published the *Water Music* in 1720, and later, because of its growing popularity, he brought out a harpsichord edition of *Handel's Celebrated Water Musick Compleat*. Hamilton Harty chose six of the twenty pieces comprising the original *Water Music* and arranged them for modern orchestra in an edition published in 1922.

                                                                    L. B.

Concerto Grosso for String Orchestra in B flat major, Op. 6, No. 7

I. Largo. II. Allegro. III. Largo, e piano. IV. Andante. V. Hornpipe.

A PICTURE IN the British Museum reveals clearly how Handel's instrumental ensembles were distributed and the place occupied by the tutti, or concerto grosso, in the seating plan. For the term has a double meaning, signifying a group of players as well as an orchestral work with two or more solo instruments.

The picture shows Handel surrounded, rather than solely faced, by the musicians. He is seated at a double-keyboard clavicembalo. To his right, directly under his eye, is grouped the concertino, consisting of the solo players. Behind him, out of sight, are the supporting players, the concerto grosso, and supplementary musicians known as *ripienists,* which may be freely translated from the Italian as "fillers-in."

The concertino group, accordingly, lies within direct range of Handel's signals and relays his wishes to the others. "The different bodies of the Handelian orchestra governed one another with elasticity," Romain Rolland observes in his book on Handel; "and it was the incisive rhythm of the little cembalo which put the whole mass into motion." Mechanical stiffness in performance was thus avoided, according to M. Rolland. On the other hand, a split-second closeness of thought between Handel and his subconductors in the concertino and concerto grosso was absolutely essential.

Like Bach, whose *Brandenburg Concertos* appeared twenty years before his own, Handel found valuable models for his instrumental style in the Italian school of Corelli and Vivaldi, though, naturally, the Anglo-German composer, like the Leipzig master before him, stamped his own indelible genius on the form. The concerto grosso in Handel's treatment is usually a dialogue, bandying echoes and contrasts, between the solo instruments and the tutti. The seventh, however, lacks the concertino.

Handel composed his Twelve Grand Concertos in thirty-two days, roughly one every third day. This is not astonishing in Handel's case. *Rinaldo* was completed in fourteen days and *The Messiah* in twenty-eight. His facility was breathtaking, and contrapuntal patterns came to him almost spontaneously. Speed did not detract from workmanship, however. A mind so snugly geared to creative activity and so richly stocked with criteria of form could think normally in terms of perfection.

On Oct. 29, 1729, the *London Daily Post* carried an announcement to the effect that "this day are published proposals for printing by subscription, with His Majesty's royal license and protection, Twelve Grand Concertos, in Seven

Parts, for Four Violins, a Tenor, a Violoncello, with a thorough-bass for the Harpsichord. Composed by Mr. Handel. Price to subscribers, two guineas. Ready to be delivered by April next. Subscriptions are taken by the author, at his house in Brook Street, Hanover Square, and by Walsh."

Walsh, the publisher, further announced on Nov. 22 that "two of the above concertos will be performed this evening at the Theatre Royal, Lincoln's Inn," and later, on Apr. 21, 1740, that the concertos "now are played in most public places with the greatest applause." Many other works of Handel just as rapidly became public property in his lifetime. It is well to keep this in mind when we read the catalogue of his pilferings from the works of others. Warranted or not in putting the ingenuities of others to noble purpose on his own premises, Handel fully redeemed himself in the largesse of his art. He gave unremittingly of his genius, and unremittingly others profited. Of the organ concertos alone Dr. Burney wrote that "public players on keyed instruments, as well as private totally subsisted on these concertos for nearly thirty years."

Notable in the seventh of the twelve concerti grossi is the soaring lyricism of the third movement, regarded as foreshadowing Beethoven; also, the sprightly hornpipe of the finale, in which Handel makes use of the Scotch snap or catch (a short note followed by a long). Popular as a dance in sixteenth-century England, the hornpipe still flourished in Lancashire and Derbyshire after its decline elsewhere. Though in triple time in Handel's day, it gave way to common time and other alterations about 1760, when prominent dancers began to bring it into the theater.

L. B.

Concerto for Orchestra and Organ in D major

[*Transcribed by Sir Hamilton Harty*]

I. Adagio. Allegro moderato. II. Adagio. Allegro con brio.

Arranged by Sir Hamilton Harty early in 1933, the D major Concerto was premiered in the new version by the London Symphony Orchestra at Queens Hall, London, on Oct. 9 of that year. The transcriber conducted. On the following Jan. 9, Frederick Stock led the Chicago Symphony Orchestra in the American premiere of Sir Hamilton's transcription.

The original Concerto is to be found in volume No. 47 of the Handel Gesellschaft edition begun in 1856 under the general supervision of the German musicologist and biographer Friedrich Chrysander. Included in the volume are three orchestral concertos, the *Fire Works Music,* the *Water Music,* and two double concertos. Sir Hamilton also arranged the *Fire Works* music for current use.

Handel's manuscript allows for improvisation on the organ, though nothing more than a framework part is indicated. Handel, a widely acclaimed organist, gave himself wide latitude for a prodigious show of technic in impromptu playing. Sometimes not even the bare outline is given in the scoring, the *ad libitum* giving the organist complete freedom of improvisation.

Besides the organ, Sir Hamilton's transcription calls for two oboes, two clarinets, two bassoons, four horns, three trumpets, kettledrums, and strings.

On the subject of improvisation, Romain Rolland once remarked that Handel's instrumental music seemed constantly that way. "When you have studied with minute care each detail," he said, "obtained from your orchestra an irreproachable precision, tonal purity, and finish, you will have done nothing unless you have made the face of the improvising genius rise from the work."

In short, this was music "to be served piping hot to an audience."

L. B.

Suite from the Opera "Il Pastor Fido" ("The Faithful Shepherd")
[*Arranged by Sir Thomas Beecham*]

(a) Introduction and Fugue. (b) Adagio. (c) Gavotte. (d) Finale.

WHILE ON a visit to London in 1712, Handel submitted the score of *Il Pastor Fido* to Owen MacSwiney, then managing the opera season at the King's Theatre. It is supposed that Handel had written most of the music before leaving Hanover late in the autumn. The work went into rehearsal early in November and was produced on the twenty-sixth. As C. F. Abdy Williams points out, the price scale was "as usual," running from 2s. 6d. for balcony seats to 8s. for boxes. Although the illustrious Cavaliere Valeriano Pellegrini, delicately described by Williams as "an artificial soprano," took part, the opera was dropped in February after six performances. It went better when revived on May 18, 1734, then attaining fourteen performances. But the new version was vastly different. To begin with, it was "intermixed with choruses," and the scenery was modified "after a particular manner." Then, a danced Prologue, entitled "Terpsichore" and described as a "play for dancing or a ballet with singing," was affixed to the opera.

The modest work was much in the style of the pastoral genres common to the literature and music of the time. Giacomo Rossi furnished Handel with an Italian libretto based on an involved network of intrigue. The scene, of course, is Arcadia. The interlocked sequence of requited and unrequited love begins with Mirtillo's love for Amarillis. Though secretly in love with Mirtillo, Amarillis is promised to Silvio. To even matters, Dorinda is in love with Silvio. Also nursing a heartache is Eurilla, a confidante of Amarillis, secretly in love with Mirtillo. The situation is saved by the threatened death of Mirtillo and the high priest Tirenio's stern rebuke *"Non e più tempo di vendette, o d'ira, ma di grazia ed amore"* ("this is no longer a time for vengeance and anger, but for grace and love"). After which Amarillis marries Mirtillo and Dorinda Silvio, followed by a choral outburst and a *ballo generale.*

Long interested in salvaging Handel dances from oblivion, Sir Thomas Beecham arranged a suite from *Il Pastor Fido* consisting of seven separate numbers. Premiered in 1939 at a concert of the London Philharmonic Orchestra led by Sir Thomas, the Suite was first played in America by the St. Louis Symphony Orchestra, Vladimir Golschmann conducting, on Dec. 13, 1940. Sir Thomas had earlier made an arrangement of dances from Handel operas for Serge Diaghileff's Russian Ballet. Consisting of eleven numbers, the Suite was used in the ballet *The Gods Go A-begging,* first produced in London on July 16, 1928.

L. B.

Howard Hanson

BORN: WAHOO, NEB., OCT. 28, 1896.

Hanson's style is best classified by the much-used term "conservatively modern." He believes in the constant expansion of harmonic, melodic, and rhythmic idioms, but his innovations have their roots firmly planted in the classics.—JOHN TASKER HOWARD.

"Nordic" Symphony

I. Andante solenne; Allegro con fuoco. II. Andante teneramente con simplicità. III. Allegro con fuoco. Finale.

EARLIEST OF Mr. Hanson's larger works, the *Nordic Symphony* was composed when he was only twenty-two and premiered under his direction by the Augusteo Orchestra in Rome. Most of the major American orchestras have since given it a hearing. The lines "To him that overcometh will I give to eat of the tree of life, which is in the midst of the paradise of God" appear on the flyleaf of the score.

Developed in free classical style and cyclical in form, the symphony is divided into three movements: Andante solenne: Allegro con fuoco; Andante teneramente con semplicità; Allegro con fuoco leading into the finale. In the first movement appears the thematic material around which the "cyclical" pattern revolves. In Mr. Hanson's own words, this opening section "sings of the solemnity, austerity, and grandeur of the North, of its restless surging and strife, of its somberness and melancholy."

The slow movement, sharply contrasting with the first, is inscribed "to my mother" and characterized by "a feeling of wistful sadness." The third movement, rugged and fiery in spirit, is dedicated "to my father." In it Mr. Hanson gives concrete expression to his love of Swedish folk songs in themes of folklike flavor. In the finale, following the third movement without interruption, the symphony's initial subject is repeated and serves as a coda.

The *Nordic Symphony* as a whole is dedicated to Major Felix Lamond, founder and head of the music department of the American Academy in Rome. Because of its highly melodious and romantic character, it was for many years the most popular of Mr. Hanson's symphonic compositions.

L. B.

Symphony No. 2 ("Romantic")

I. Adagio; Allegro moderato. II. Andante con tenerezza. III. Allegro con brio.

ONE OF the two most frequently performed of Howard Hanson's symphonies (the other being the *Nordic*), the *Romantic* was commissioned by Serge Koussevitzky for the fiftieth anniversary of the Boston Symphony Orchestra. Its first performance occurred in Boston on Nov. 28, 1930, with Mr. Koussevitzky conducting. In October, 1939, Mr. Hanson's symphony figured on two special programs of the Boston Symphony arranged by Mr. Koussevitzky "in honor of the American composer." Arturo Toscanini led the first performances of the *Romantic* in New York with the Philharmonic-Symphony on Mar. 1, 3, and 6, 1933.

The score of the *Romantic Symphony* calls for two flutes, piccolo, two oboes, English horn, two clarinets, two bassoons, contra-bassoon, four horns, three trumpets, three trombones, tuba, tympani, snare drum, cymbals, and strings. Mr. Hanson's own analysis of the symphony, written for the Boston premiere, follows:

The work is in three movements: The first (Adagio; Allegro moderato) begins with an atmospheric indication in the wood winds, joined first by the horns, then the strings, and finally the brass choir, and then subsiding. The principal theme is announced Allegro moderato, by four horns, with an accompaniment of strings and wood winds, and is imitated in turns by the trumpets, wood winds, and strings. An episodic theme appears quietly in the oboe and then in the solo horn. A transition leads into the subordinate theme, Lento, with the theme itself in the strings and a countersubject in the solo horn.

The development section now follows, with the principal theme announced in a changed mood by the English horn and developed through the orchestra. The episodic theme, influenced by the principal theme, also takes an important part in this section. The climax of the development section leads directly to the return of the principal theme in the original key by the trumpets. This is followed in turn by the episodic theme, now in the clarinets, and then in the first horn, with canonic imitation in the oboe. The subordinate theme then follows, and the movement concludes quietly in a short coda.

The second movement (Andante con tenerezza) begins with its principal theme, announced by the wood winds, with a sustained string accompaniment. The interlude in the brass, taken from the introduction of the first movement and interrupted by florid passages in the wood winds, develops into the subordinate theme which is taken from the horn solo in the first movement. A transition, again interrupted by a florid wood-wind passage, leads into a restatement of the principal theme of the movement.

The third movement (Allegro con brio) begins with a vigorous accompaniment figure in strings and wood winds, the principal theme of the movement—reminiscent of the first movement—entering in the four horns and later repeated in the basses. The subordinate theme, Molto meno mosso, is announced first by the cellos and then taken up by the English horn, the development of which leads into the middle section Più mosso.

This section begins with a pizzicato accompaniment in the violas, cellos, and basses, over which is announced a horn call. This call is taken up by the trombones and leads into a fanfare first in the trumpets, then in the horns and wood winds, and then again in the trumpets and the wood winds. The climax of this fanfare comes with the announcement of the principal theme of the first movement by the trumpets, against the fanfare rhythm in the wood winds. The development of this theme leads into a final statement of the subordinate theme of the first movement, fortissimo. A brief coda of this material leads to a final fanfare and the end of the symphony.

At the time of the Boston premiere of the Second Symphony, Mr. Hanson made some controversial remarks that were widely quoted and discussed. They concerned the conflict in modern music between realism and romanticism. Mr. Hanson stated:

The symphony represents for me my escape from the rather bitter type of modern musical realism which occupies so large a place in contemporary thought. Much contemporary music seems to me to be showing a tendency to become entirely too cerebral. I do not believe that music is primarily a matter of the intellect, but rather a manifestation of the emotions. I have, therefore, aimed in this symphony to create a work that was young in spirit, lyrical and romantic in temperament, and simple and direct in expression.

In a later communication to the Philharmonic-Symphony, Mr. Hanson reverted to the earlier declaration.

That statement launched a musical bomb at the time, for, as you will recall, the Nineteen Twenties marked the heyday of the atonalists and any composer under seventy-five who wrote an undisguised triad was considered a traitor to the cause. By my little manifesto I also added to my worries the job of explaining a few thousand times what I meant by "romantic." My guess is that I didn't quite know what I did mean, except that it was a convenient red-flag word at that time. My explanation today would be somewhat simpler. I believe that there are essentially two types of music, warm-blooded music and cold-blooded music, and every possible admixture of the two. The *Romantic* is definitely warm-blooded music. Whatever else may be said of it, it has certainly proved to be my most popular work with the general public.

Besides being played by most symphony orchestras in America, the *Romantic Symphony* also became one of the better known American scores in Europe. The principal melody of the slow movement was used, in jazz form, as the theme of the United States Army Dance Band on its extensive tour of Europe during the war. Army radio stations broadcast the popular version repeatedly. Moreover, the romantic slow subject of the first movement was adopted as band theme by the students of the National High School Orchestra in Interlochen. For several years this theme served to open the annual series of broadcasts from Interlochen. A jazz version of the same melody later appeared in an arrangement by Syl Novelli, with lyrics by Sylvia Dee, author of the lyrics of "Chickery Chick!"

To date Howard Hanson has written four symphonies, all of them obtaining their concert premieres on programs of the Boston Symphony Orchestra. The first, the *Nordic,* dates from 1929, and is one of the best known of his numerous scores. During the composition of his Third Symphony in 1937, Mr. Hanson made another significant reference to his Second Symphony: "Like my *Romantic* symphony, the Third one, too, stands as an avowal against a certain coldly abstract, would-be sentimental music professed by certain composers of high gifts." Mr. Hanson's Fourth Symphony won the Pulitzer Prize for 1944.

An articulate and influential figure in American music, Mr. Hanson studied at Luther College of Wahoo, Neb., and later in the School of Music of the University of Nebraska. There were also intervals of study at the Institute of Musical Art in New York (with Percy Goetschius in composition) and at the Northwestern University School of Music at Evanston, Ill. At twenty, Mr. Hanson became professor of theory at the College of the Pacific in San José, Calif. At twenty-three he was appointed dean of the Conservatory of Fine Arts of the same college, and at twenty-five he was awarded the Prix de Rome, bringing him a three-year fellowship in composition at the American Academy in Rome. When he returned to America in 1924, Mr. Hanson was made Director of the Eastman School of Music, Rochester, N. Y., where he has been serving in the triple role of administrator, instructor, and conductor. Among his numerous compositions are three symphonic poems, choral works, and chamber music. An opera, *Merrymount,* with a libretto by Richard Stokes, was staged by the Metropolitan Opera Company in 1932. John Tasker Howard, in *Our Contemporary Composers* writes:

Hanson's importance to American music does not rest on any single work, nor indeed on any one phase of his activity. If he has a particular artistic creed, it is a belief in the necessity for absolute freedom of creative expression, each composer writing out of the depths of his own soul that which seems to him to be good. When such a creed is generally held by composers, critics, and music lovers, academic questions concerning degrees of newness will give way, he says, to the more essential problem of assaying each new work for the precious metal of vital beauty, without which no work can live.

                                                                      L. B.

Roy Harris

BORN: LINCOLN COUNTY, OKLA., FEB. 12, 1898.

*He comes from the West and, as a sort of musical Walt Whitman, is
filled with a sense of destiny.*—DOUGLAS MOORE.

Symphony No. 3 (In One Movement)

AFTER THE Boston Symphony premiere of Mr. Harris's Third Symphony in
February, 1939, a young student at Harvard wrote a review for the March-April
number of *Modern Music*. In it he spoke of the new work as "mature in every
sense, beautifully proportioned, eloquent, restrained, and affecting." The budding critic confessed "experiencing a strong desire to hear the Harris again,
because it greatly excited me." This laudable desire he later satisfied in
a very practical way—by conducting the symphony himself. The Harvard
student's name was Leonard Bernstein.

Of the same symphony Oscar Thompson expressed what is now a widespread
opinion:

Without exalting it to a place beside the symphonies that are the recognized
masterpieces of other eras, there is good reason to look upon the Harris Third
Symphony as a work which is as representative of our times as are the best works of
Shostakovich and Prokofieff, of Hindemith and Bartok, or of any of those Europeans who do not, like Strauss, Sibelius, and Rachmaninoff, belong essentially to
another generation.

Mr. Harris wrote this symphony late in 1938. The printer had the score the
following January. One month later, on Feb. 24, Serge Koussevitzky directed
its world premiere with the Boston Symphony Orchestra. Mr. Koussevitzky
repeated it in Boston on Oct. 6, 1939; at the Berkshire Festival on Aug. 3, 1940;
and again in Boston, on Dec. 26 and 27, 1941. Other major orchestras have
included the work in their repertories. By 1945, some fifty performances had
already been given of this symphony, which Mr. Koussevitzky is quoted as
having called "the first truly great orchestral work to be produced in America."
For the Boston premiere, Mr. Harris supplied the program annotator John N.
Burk with a structural outline, instead of the customary detailed analysis, of
the One-movement Symphony. The composer's plan follows:

Section   I. Tragic—low string sonorities
Section II. Lyric—strings, horns, wood winds
Section III. Pastoral—emphasizing wood-wind color

Section IV. Fugue—dramatic
      A. Brass—percussion predominating
      B. Canonic development of Section II material constituting background for further development of fugue
      C. Brass climax. Rhythmic motif derived from fugue subject
Materials: 1. Melodic contours—diatonic—polytonal
          2. Harmonic textures—consonance—polytonal

The symphony is scored for three flutes, piccolo, two oboes, English horn, two clarinets, bass clarinet, two bassoons, four horns, three trumpets, three trombones, tuba, tympani, vibraphone, cymbals, triangle, and strings.

Described as the "most frequently performed serious American composer," Roy Harris was first educated in California. There he studied music with Arthur Farwell. In 1926 he went to Paris, where his teacher was Nadia Boulanger. He was twice awarded a Guggenheim Fellowship. In 1930 Mr. Harris obtained a Creative Fellowship from the Pasadena Music and Arts Association. Later he became head of the composition department of the Westminster Choir School of Princeton, N. J., before being appointed Composer in Residence at Cornell University.

Among his major compositions are five symphonies, an Andantino for Orchestra, a Chorale for String Orchestra, a Prelude and Fugue for String Orchestra, a *Time Suite,* a Violin Concerto, a Piano Concerto, two string quartets, a string sextet, a quintet for piano and wind instruments, and a large work for chorus and orchestra entitled *Folk Song Symphony*. Mr. Harris defines as a "prominent characteristic" of his music the "organic development of the melodic line in avoidance of symmetrical and particularly of sequential pattern."

Wrote Mr. Thompson:

Harris is in intention a melodist. Harmonically he is not, for his times, an extremist. The problems that seem most to have occupied him are those of form. He has been a practical proponent of the twentieth-century view of content determining form. Closely allied are the composer's concepts of melodic form. Aiming at long-drawn or continuous melody, he may be said to have shaped the structure to fit the melody, rather than forcing the melodic substance into the regular segments of a fixed form. . . . Harris's music is always clear.

                                      L. B.

Joseph Haydn

BORN: ROHRAU, LOWER AUSTRIA, MAR. 31, 1732. DIED: VIENNA, MAY 31, 1809.

*I know that God has bestowed a talent upon me, and I thank Him
for it. I think I have done my duty and been of use in my generation
by my works. Let others do the same.*—HAYDN.

Symphony in D major (Breitkopf & Härtel No. 13)

I. Allegro molto. II. Adagio cantabile. III. Menuetto. IV. Finale: Allegro
molto.

THIS SYMPHONY enjoys the dubious distinction of being variously numbered in
different catalogues of Haydn's works. Breitkopf and Härtel's *Complete Critical
Edition of Haydn's Symphonies* lists it as No. 13; Haydn's own record of his
compositions designates it as No. 14; Zulehner's *Verzeichniss der Symphonien
von Joseph Haydn* adds to the confusion by numbering it 69, and Pohl's
Manuscript Catalogue does a like service by giving it No. 89.

The multi-ambiguity involved here is too obvious for comment. It would be
following a safe course, however, to title the work as at the head of this note,
keeping in mind, of course, the Breitkopf and Härtel *Complete Critical Edition
of Haydn's Symphonies*.

At the age of thirty-two and with two years' experience in the employ of the
Esterhazy family already to boast about, Haydn wrote this symphony. It contains a minuet, a musical form over which conductors of the period were none
too enthusiastic. In those days, the minuet could be played or not, depending
on some conductorial caprice, and if it was not played there were no upheavals
in the musical cosmos.

The symphony opens with an Allegro molto, D major, 4/4, the unison violins
announcing at once an animated theme forte. As was his custom at this stage
of his career, Haydn employs a single theme, set in an atmosphere of what
might be termed subsidiary material. Little of the nature of development, as it
became later understood, is discernible here. The whole movement flows
spontaneously and with a youthful cheerfulness.

The following Adagio cantabile, G major, 2/2, is a melodious solo for the
cello, the other strings supplying the accompaniment.

The Menuetto, D major, 3/4, has an engaging trio in G major for solo flute
and strings.

The theme of the Finale (Allegro molto, D major, 2/4) bears a resemblance
to the principal subject of the Finale of Mozart's *Jupiter Symphony*. It is given

first in the unison violins, and later it plies its way through both winds and strings, with contrasting material interrelated.

The score calls for two flutes, two oboes, four horns, tympani, and the usual strings.

R. C. B.

Symphony in F minor, No. 49 ("La Passione")

I. Adagio. II. Allegro di molto. III. Menuetto. IV. Finale: presto.

ON MAY 1, 1761, Haydn entered the service of the Esterhazy family in the capacity of Vice-Kappellmeister, an agreement, formal, long, and strict and one which in our time, perhaps, might be viewed as barely skirting chattelism, having been duly signed by the interested parties. That Haydn was able in some thirty years of association with the Esterhazys to compose a fantastic number of works in almost all the branches of music may read like death to libertarian theorizing. In relation to that period, however, the terms of the contract must be recognized as being of the utmost advantage to Haydn. What opportunities for development he might have had in other circumstances can scarcely be determined now. Suffice it to say that his genius flourished under the conditions, and we are indebted to that segment of his career for "nearly all his operas, most of his arias and songs, the music for the marionette theater —of which he was particularly fond—and the greater part of his orchestral and chamber works."

Except for the trio of the Minuet, which is in F major, this Symphony adheres to the tonality of F minor, and it bears a relationship to Symphonies Nos. 22, 23, and 24, in the order of the movements. The opening Adagio is in sonata form, melancholy in character. The following Allegro is a section of teeming excitement. One expects the entrance of a great chorus at any moment, so powerful seem to be the music's vocal characteristics. The Minuet is stately and dignified, and the closing movement is vigorous and, with reference to the long interval leaps and the steadily increasing syncopation, extremely bold. The work, as a whole, is in the big manner, dramatic—oratorical, even—and strongly emotional. The symphony is scored for strings, oboes, and horns.

R. C. B.

Symphony in D major, No. 10 (B. & H. No. 86)

I. Adagio; Allegro spiritoso. II. Capriccio: Largo. III. Minuetto. IV. Finale.

THIS SYMPHONY is one of six that were composed for Paris between 1784 and 1789. It is believed that it was given its first performance at a Concert de la

Loge Olympique in 1789. The score calls for flute, two oboes, two bassoons, two horns, two trumpets, tympani, and strings.

That thriving musical center Paris first became aware of one Joseph Haydn when his *Stabat Mater* appeared in a program of the Concerts Spirituel, in 1781. Yet instrumental music had scarcely made the headway it was soon to make, choral and operatic pieces then being the rage.

Haydn's symphonies, however, found many ready takers at the Spirituel concerts. In fact, his symphonic music was received quite enthusiastically. It is not surprising, therefore, that the rival organization Concerts de la Loge Olympique should approach Haydn with the suggestion that he write a series of symphonies for it.

The composer accepted the commission with alacrity, and the Symphony in D major, which Breitkopf and Härtel list as 86, was the fifth of the set.

The musical events sponsored by the Concert de la Loge Olympique were flossily fashionable. The organization had its associations with freemasonry. The subscribers obtained admission to the concerts through the payment of a subscription fee of two *louis d'or* a year, besides having to wear a special badge which featured a silver lyre on a sky-blue background.

The life of the Loge Olympique and its concerts ran from 1786 to 1789, ending with the coming of the Revolution. The attendance comprised a most exclusive society. Queen Marie Antoinette and the lords and ladies of her court were frequent visitors. The extreme flourish and fashion were carried to the garb of the musicians, who were constrained to wear brocaded coats, lace ruffles, swords, and plumed hats (which, gratifyingly, they could remove while performing).

The Symphony in D major begins with an introduction which courses through twenty-one measures in a rising crescendo to a fortissimo. A bright theme is carried forward by the violins against sonorous chords in the rest of the orchestra. A second theme, which is in effect a melodic foil of the first, is repeated frequently, though it is not developed.

The slow movement, which Haydn called a Capriccio, boasts a theme which is the pivotal feature of the section in that there is a constant return to it, but each time evoking new impressions, such was the composer's fertility of thought. There are, however, instances of the freedom implied in the word "capriccio" through unexpected modulations and unusual turns of the music.

The Minuetto offers an interesting contrast of mood between its two parts, a sprightly first one and a fluidly moving trio.

The Finale, presenting a staccato main theme, adheres more or less to the demands of the sonata form.

R. C. B.

Symphony in G major (B. & H. No. 88)

I. Adagio; Allegro. II. Largo. III. Menuetto; Trio. IV. Finale: Allegro con spirito.

THE PRESENT symphony was performed in Paris in 1787. The score calls for one flute, two oboes, two bassoons, two horns, two trumpets, tympani, and strings.

After a slow introduction (Adagio, G major, 3/4) the main part of the first movement begins with an opening theme which is first announced softly by all the strings, save the basses, and later repeated by the full orchestra, forte, with the addition of a new figure in the bass. Two more themes appear, each a variant of the first. A contrapuntally ornate free fantasia comes next. The movement closes with a coda based on the original theme.

The second movement (Largo, D major, 3/4) introduces a melody of a grave character by means of the oboe and cellos, while violas, basses, bassoon, and horn supply an accompaniment. The melody is repeated, but this time not only is the accompaniment more sumptuous, but the violins converge on a counter figure. A transitional passage follows. It is played by a larger orchestra, the subject appearing first in the leading violins and flute and subsequently in the oboe and cello. There are a development and an ensuing coda which is rather brief.

The third movement (Menuetto, Allegretto, G major, 3/4) is a simple minuet.

The last movement (Allegro con spirito, G major, 2/4) amounts to a fully developed rondo based on a peasant-dance theme. In his later symphonies Haydn was partial to the rondo form for his final movements. Michel Brenet wrote:

In some finales of his last symphonies, he gave freer rein to his fancy and modified with greater independence the form of his first allegros; but his fancy, always prudent and moderate, is more like the clear, precise arguments of a great orator than the headlong inspiration of a poet. Moderation is one of the characteristics of Haydn's genius; moderation in the dimensions, in the sonority, in the melodic shape; the liveliness of his melodic thought never seems extravagant, its melancholy never induces sadness.

R. C. B.

Symphony in G major, No. 92 ("Oxford")

I. Adagio; Allegro spiritoso. II. Adagio. III. Menuetto. IV. Presto.

TRADITIONALLY THE *Oxford Symphony* commemorates the fact that the University of Oxford made Joseph Haydn a Doctor of Music in July, 1791. The decision to confer the doctorate was prompted by the recommendation of Dr. Charles Burney, the great musical historian, during the Austrian composer's first visit to London. Yet, though the symphony formed part of the three-day festivities held in Haydn's honor in the academic haunts and though the words, "expressly intended for this concert" appeared in the announcement, the work was actually written in Paris three years earlier. The story goes that Haydn did have a brand-new symphony in his portfolio when he journey up to the university town early in July. But there was little time for proper rehearsal, so the G major was substituted. At any rate, the records show no previous performance of the conveniently styled *Oxford Symphony*.

Haydn accepted the honorary degree with alacrity, quite unlike Handel before him. His outspoken predecessor had declined the exalted offer with a contemptuous reference to the costs involved, a reference couched, incidentally, in his choicest Hanoverian English: "What the devil I throw my money away for that the blockhead wish?" History does not reveal Haydn and Handel as wanton squanderers. But W. S. Rockstro, in mitigating Handel's oafish rebuff, points out that the honorary doctorate would have entailed fees amounting to the equivalent of $500. Quite possibly Haydn gave some thrifty thought to the financial angle, too, since he records in his carefully kept notebook of expenditures that the trip cost him six guineas. "I had to pay one and a half guineas for the bell peals at Oxforth [*sic*], and half a guinea for the robe," he further notes.

The "robe" in question was a dazzling ensemble of cherry and cream-colored silk. Later he wrote that he wore this gorgeous academic vestment for three days. "I only wish my Vienna friends could have seen me," he remarks. After the solemnities making him *doctor musicae* he shouted in English: "I thank you." The G major Symphony figured on the second of the three programs, with Haydn himself directing. On July 11, the *Morning Chronicle* reported that "a more wonderful composition never was heard. The applause given to Haydn, who conducted this admirable effort of his genius, was enthusiastic; but the merit of the work, in the opinion of all the musicians present, exceeded all praise."

Haydn had arrived in London early in January, in the company of the ebullient Johann Peter Salomon. The English impresario and one-time concert-master and ensemble player had pictured such an inviting prospect of British acclaim and affluence that Haydn was lured away from his pensioned comfort in Vienna. Earlier attempts by Salomon and his agents had proved futile. What helped clinch the negotiations was the death in 1790 of Prince Nicolaus Esterhazy, his patron employer, freeing Haydn from routine duties. Salomon promised productions of six Haydn symphonies in London, to be conducted by the composer. The terms were quite fabulous. The impresario, for his part, was in desperate need of a celebrity of Haydn's standing, having organized a series of subscription concerts at the Hanover Square Rooms. Haydn was his trump card in London's growing managerial rivalry.

Surely enough, wherever the illustrious visitor went, he was lionized. People of high rank paid him flattering attention. The best houses offered their hospitality. Ambassadors called on him, and the delegates of music societies outdid one another in bestowing honors upon him. Haydn, who never overlooked the dividends of fame, proudly wrote home to Austria: "I could dine out every night." It was a day of poetic tributes. Dr. Burney, at whose suggestion the Oxford authorities had conferred the degree on Haydn, gave further vent to his feelings in verse which need not detract from his standing as a musical scholar:

> Welcome, great master, to our favored isle,
> Already partial to thy name and style;
> Long may thy fountain of invention run
> In streams as rapid as it first begun;
> While skill for each fantastic whim provides,
> And certain science ev'ry current guides.

There is strong evidence, too, of Haydn's having formed at least one romantic attachment in London. The lady was the widow Schroeter. Haydn told his biographer Dies that she was sixty years old, though many are inclined to doubt Haydn's word. Anyway, "she was still lovely and amiable," the widely feted composer confessed, "and I should in all likelihood have married her if I had been single." In Vienna Frau Haydn patiently awaited Joseph's return. The widow's address is faithfully recorded in Haydn's notebook: "Mistress Schroeter, No. 6 James Street, Buckingham Gate." All in all, Haydn had every reason to repeat the visit in 1794. England had been good to him.

Typical of London's response to Haydn's two visits is the following excerpt from a newspaper account:

It is truly wonderful what sublime and august thoughts this master weaves into his works. Passages often occur which it is impossible to listen to without becoming excited—we are carried away by admiration and are forced to applaud with hand and mouth. The Frenchmen here cannot restrain their transports in soft adagios. [*sic!*]

It is not unlikely that these Gallic seizures were witnessed by the observant London critic during the Adagio of the G major Symphony.

A slow introduction (Adagio, G major, 3/4), twenty measures in length, leads to the main section of the opening movement (Allegro spiritoso, G major, 3/4), with the strings announcing the first subject. The strings also usher in the second theme piano, this time in D major. The development leads to a long coda. The three-part slow movement (Adagio, D major, 2/4) is mostly in Haydn's gracefully lyric vein, with a sharply contrasting middle episode in D minor. The freely rhythmic Menuetto (Allegretto, G major, 3/4) enshrines an ingenious trio (also G major, 3/4), brought in by bassoons and horns against pizzicato strings. The chief theme of the finale (in sonata form, Presto, G major, 2/4), again given out by the strings, belongs with Haydn's best melodic flights. The scoring is for flute, two oboes, two bassoons, two horns, two trumpets, kettledrums, and strings.

L. B.

Symphony in D major, No. 93 (Salomon No. 2)

I. Adagio; Allegro. II. Andante. III. Menuetto: Allegro. IV. Finale: Allegro spiritoso.

HAYDN WROTE twelve symphonies for Salomon, six for each visit. The impresario musician himself played first violin in the forty-piece orchestra at Haydn's disposal. Following the practice of the time, the composer sat at a harpsichord, from time to time playing chords to keep the ensemble together. J. Cuthbert Hadden, writing in the Master Musicians Series, relays an anecdote first told by Haydn's friend Albert Dies. The episode occurred during the rehearsal of the D major Symphony—Haydn's first encounter with the Salomon orchestra. "The symphony began with three single notes, which the orchestra played much too loudly. Haydn called for less tone a second and a third time, and still was dissatisfied. He was growing impatient. At this point he overheard a German player whisper to a neighbor in his own language: 'If the first three notes don't please him, how shall we get through all the rest?' Thereupon, calling for the loan of a violin, he illustrated his meaning to such purpose that the band answered to his requirements in the first attempt."

W. H. Hadow, in *The Oxford History of Music,* wrote:

The twelve symphonies which he wrote for Salomon are not only the greatest of his orchestral works, but those also in which we can most clearly trace the effect of his intercourse with Mozart. Dr. Pohl especially notes the influence of the *Jupiter Symphony* both in the richer orchestration and in the freer use of episode and incident.

The minuets, far different from Mozart's courtly dance measures, have all his old rustic drollery and humor, the rhythms have all his old incisiveness of touch, the folk tunes that he loved grow thick along the wayside. The melodies of his own sowing are unmistakable in hue and shapeliness. And the music is all suffused with the sense of mellowness and maturity, of long experience and an old age honorably won; it is too serene for passion, too wise for sadness, too single-hearted for regret, it has learned the lesson of life and will question its fate no further.

Sir Donald Tovey combines this symphony, the D major, No. 102, and the String Quartet in F major, Op. 77, No. 2, into what he considers Haydn's "greatest instrumental works." He adds, "Nothing in Haydn is difficult to follow, but almost everything is unexpected if you listen closely, and without preconceptions."

The D major Symphony is typical of Haydn's scrupulously lucid form and orchestration, beside boasting unusual subtlety and expressive power. To Tovey it was "arguably the greatest of Haydn's instrumental works." While there are moments in the Symphony of soft tenderness where the mood borders on the wistful, its predominant note is gay and spirited.

In the first movement a nobly spun Adagio (D minor, 4/4) prefaces the main Allegro section (D major, 2/2). Haydn shows his mastery of economic and compact form in constructing the movement almost entirely from one theme, a cheerful melody announced by the violins. This same melody appears in slightly altered guise when it modulates to A major. But the movement is actually monothematic, like so many others in Haydn's symphonies.

The second movement (Andante) is in three parts, the third a return and expansion of the first. A fetching melody is given out in G major, at first simply, then with increasing subtlety. This section is followed by a contrastingly vigorous interlude in G minor. Then the first part is repeated in the major, enriched and varied, among the novel features being a long cadenzalike passage for wood winds.

The third movement Menuetto (Allegro, D major, 3/4) opens boldly, with a robust and sharply accented theme "more suggestive of wooden shoes in the kitchen than of powdered wigs in the ballroom." The dainty trio returns us to courtlier surroundings. Violins and oboe take up the melody with the grace and punctilio of the salon.

The Finale (Allegro spiritoso, D major, 2/2) is perhaps the finest of the four movements in its harmonic and contrapuntal richness. The folklike first theme is announced by the first violins over a pedal D in the cellos and horns. Toward the end there is again some charming writing for wood winds.

L. B.

Symphony in C major (B. & H. No. 97) (Salomon No. 1)

I. Adagio; Vivace. II. Adagio ma non troppo. III. Menuetto: Allegretto; Trio Finale. IV. Presto assai.

THE ABOVE numbering of Haydn's C major Symphony represents a compromise and a simplification. Few composers have had as little luck with the actual arithmetic of their output as Haydn. In the new Breitkopf and Härtel edition the Symphony is No. 97. In the old it was No. 7. Peters Edition carries it as No. 5. In the respective reckonings of Messrs. Pohl, Wotquenne, and Zulehner it is No. 15, No. 138, and No. 20. Haydn listed it as No. 108 in his own catalogue.

Even the *Salomon* listing is misleading. Actually, it was the D major Symphony—now listed as No. 2 of the twelve Haydn wrote for London—that was played first at the Salomon concerts in London. But the London Philharmonic catalogue lists the Symphony as No. 1. To add to the confusion, there is even divided opinion about its date of composition and performance. The years 1791 and 1792 are equally possible. In any case, the first Salomon concert occurred in the Hanover Square Rooms on Mar. 11, 1791, and Haydn did not leave London till the end of June, 1792.

The symphony is scored for flutes, oboes, bassoons, horns and trumpets in pairs, tympani, and strings. An introductory Adagio (C major, 3/4) is given to wood winds and strings, followed by a fortissimo statement by the full orchestra of the main theme of the movement proper (Vivace, C major, 3/4). Strings and wood winds then play with the theme. There is a bold flourish by the strings, and the second theme, gentle and lilting, is brought in by the first violins in G major, with strings and bassoons supporting. Both themes are reviewed and developed, leading to a coda, at the end of which the first theme is vigorously recalled.

The second movement (Adagio ma non troppo, F major, 4/4) is built on a serene and soothing melody announced by the strings. This theme is put through two variations. A section in F minor, introduced by a crisp triplet figure in the strings, comes midway in the movement.

The third movement (Menuetto: Allegretto, 3/4), returning to C major, opens with a forte announcement by the full orchestra of a theme typical of Haydn at his courtliest. A delicately spun trio, entrusted to first violins, oboe, and bassoon, intervenes before the return of the main minuet subject.

The finale (Presto assai, C major, 2/4) is a brisk and chattery rondo, with principal theme and two subsidiaries. In the course of it strings and wood winds set up a lively exchange of phrase and rhythm. The movement has its daring little touches and makes one of Haydn's brightest and most animated colloquies in symphonic speech.   **L. B.**

"Toy" Symphony

I. Allegro. II. Minuet. III. Finale.

It is hardly likely that the Bavarian town of Berchtesgaden will go down in history as the place where Joseph Haydn purchased some toy instruments in 1788. Of course, the accounts of Haydn's purchase are somewhat conflicting. According to one version, the instruments were bought in a well-known toy-shop in Berchtesgaden. According to another, Haydn purchased them at a toy fair in Vienna. In any case, when he returned to the Esterhazy estate, Haydn had with him a new *Kindersinfonie*—toys and all. The story goes that the Esterhazy musicians chuckled so much over the music that, in spite of its simplicity, they failed to keep time.

In early editions this *Toy Symphony* is entitled either *Kindersinfonie* or *Symphonie Burlesque*. The toys used have varied somewhat, depending on caprice and ingenuity. Besides first and second violins and basses, the instruments used are a tambourine, a triangle, a bass-drum, cymbals, a ratchet, a toy drum, a toy trumpet, a "cuckoo," a "quail," and a "bobwhite." The three miniature movements are Allegro, Minuet, and Finale, the last given at a faster tempo with each repetition.

Naturally, the *Toy Symphony* is little more than a *jeu d'esprit*, as J. Cuthbert Hadden states in his biography—a bagatelle "not requiring serious notice, especially in the case of Haydn, to whom humor in music was a very different matter from the handling of rattles and penny trumpets and toy drums."

Haydn probably dashed off the symphonic trifle in one of his impish moments of practical joking. Of these periodic seizures Hadden writes sympathetically:

A leading trait in his character was his humor and love of fun. As he remarked to Albert Dies, "A mischievous fit comes over me sometimes that is perfectly beyond control." The incident of the removal of the fellow chorister's pigtail will at once recur to the memory. The *Surprise Symphony* is another illustration, to say nothing of the *Toy Symphony* and *Jacob's Dream*.

Mozart often experienced spells of a similar kind. One such impulse materialized as a *Musical Joke,* in which the instruments not only remain blithely out of tune, but begin and stop playing when least expected.   **L. B.**

Concerto for Harpsichord and Orchestra in D major

I. Vivace. II. Larghetto. III. Rondo, all'Ongherese.

WHEN MME. LANDOWSKA first played this Concerto with the Philharmonic-Symphony (Feb. 22, 1945) she supplied the authors of this book with the following explanation (from her essay *Musique Galante*) of the work:

Whereas Haydn's cello concerto became an integral part of every cellist's repertoire, the ones composed for keyboard all but disappeared into oblivion. I knew, however, that Haydn had written at least twenty concertos for the keyboard. So I started forthwith on the quest for the material. It was impossible to discover the autograph of the score or any part of the Haydn Concerto. The keyboard sonatas by Haydn possessed such an unbelievable wealth of invention that I could hardly wait to find what Haydn had done in the field of the concerto. I finally came upon the separate parts of the D major Concerto in an eighteenth-century manuscript copy and in a contemporary edition of Haydn.

It was thus in Paris that I gave the first performance of the D major Concerto. I played it all over Europe and, as the work met in every instance with such a spontaneous response, it was not surprising that many publishers were eager to publish such a sure-fire work.

This Concerto, concise and coruscating, contains within itself all the elements of Haydn's genius. The larghetto is a marvel of suavity and gentleness, and at certain moments in its development it reminds us strangely of Beethoven.

The old edition of Haydn's time by Artaria bears the following title: "*Concerto par il Clavicembalo o Forte Piano con l'accompagnamento Di Due Violini, Viola, Due Oboe, Due Corni E Basso composto dal Sig. Giuseppe Haydn Maestro di Capella di S. A. il Principe d'Esterhazy.*" Let us not be surprised by the mention of cembalo or forte piano. During the time of Haydn, Mozart, and Philippe Emmanuel Bach, the harpsichord was still in wide use, while the forte piano was first beginning to come into popularity and all the works of this period, whether in manuscripts or print, bear the inscription "For harpsichord or forte piano."

Concerto for Cello and Orchestra in D major

I. Allegro moderato. II. Adagio. III. Allegro.

IN ALL, Haydn wrote six complete concertos for the cello, and there is some proof that the solo part of a seventh also exists. He was as prolific of concertos as he was of symphonies, having written some half-hundred or so for various instruments.

This work was finished in 1784 and first performed by Anton Kraft, a gifted cellist who was a member of Haydn's Esterhazy orchestra. Kraft was a native of Bohemia. He joined the orchestra in 1778, remaining with it until Haydn's retirement in 1790. He later played in the orchestras of Prince Graffalkowitsch and Prince Lobkowitz, and he was still a member of the latter when he died in 1820. Incidentally, the cello part in Beethoven's triple concerto was written for Kraft.

The cellist was also a sort of composer. He took lessons from Haydn for a time, but the latter, noting that his pupil was giving more and more time to composition—while his cello playing suffered for it—stopped the lessons abruptly. He notified Kraft that he had learned "all that he needed for his purposes." There is no way of telling, of course, whether or not Haydn stifled a great creative talent.

The D major Concerto has been described as "a small-scale work, like Haydn's other concertos of the period, resembling a vocal scena with the cello as a prima donna of the virtuoso type." It was originally scored for two oboes, two horns, and strings. François Auguste Gevaert, the noted Belgian musician, subsequently revised the piece, augmenting the orchestration with parts for two flutes, two clarinets, and two bassoons, in addition to touching up the solo line and writing his own cadenzas for it.

The first movement has an initial theme that is unusually Mozartean. It has been pointed out that its tune is strongly reminiscent of Leporello's "Catalogue Song" in *Don Giovanni*. The fly in the ointment, however, is the fact that Mozart wrote *Don Giovanni* three years later.

The slow movement is pure Haydn, it has been fervently declared, and here the solo cello soars out on sequences of "pure song."

The finale is unaffected, a light rondo typical of Haydn's end movements. Some tune sleuths have noticed a similarity between its chief melody and the song "Here We Go Gathering Nuts in May."

R. C. B.

Bernard Herrmann

BORN: NEW YORK CITY, JUNE 29, 1911.

*As a composer I might class myself as a Neo-Romantic, inasmuch as
I have always regarded music as a highly personal and emotional form
of expression. I like to write music which takes its inspiration from
poetry, art, and Nature. I do not care for purely decorative music.
Although I am in sympathy with modern idioms, I abhor music
which attempts nothing more than the illustration of a stylistic fad;
and in using modern techniques, I have tried at all times to subju-
gate them to a larger idea or grander human feeling.*—BERNARD
HERRMANN.

Symphony No. 1

I. Maestoso: Allegro pesante. II. Scherzo. III. Andante sostenuto.
IV. Rondo: Epilogue, 'à la processional.'

WHILE STILL a high school student, Bernard Herrmann won a one-hundred
dollar prize for a symphonic composition. It was not the money but the gaining
of top honors in the competition that decided him on a composer's career. He
studied with Bernard Wagenaar, Albert Stoessel, and Philip James at the
Juilliard Graduate School. At the age of twenty he made his professional debut
as a conductor when he led a pit orchestra through a ballet score of his own
contriving in the Shuberts' *Americana Revue.*

Later he was cofounder of the New Chamber Orchestra, which gave several
concerts in New York City and at the Library of Congress in Washington,
D. C. In 1934, he joined the Columbia Broadcasting System, as composer and
conductor. There he provided scores for the productions of the Columbia
Workshop. In due time he became adviser to the CBS American School of the
Air and, to cap the climax, was appointed a staff conductor. In this last capacity
he has presented over the radio many programs of music by unfamiliar composers, as well as the little known works of the familiars.

Mr. Herrmann's compositions include, besides the Symphony and the afore-
said radio pieces, much music for motion pictures, a Violin Concerto, a String
Quartet, various orchestral suites, a ballet, and other music, not to omit his
cantata, *Moby Dick,* which was given its premiere by the Philharmonic-
Symphony Society under the direction of John Barbirolli at Carnegie Hall on
Thursday, Apr. 11, 1940.

335

The present work is dedicated to the composer's wife, the former Lucille Fletcher. Mr. Herrmann's analysis of the composition follows:

The Symphony is in four movements, each in one of the traditional forms. Its orchestration closely adheres to that of the standard nineteenth-century symphonic orchestra with percussion instruments introduced only in the last movement, and then very sparingly.

The first movement of the Symphony is in sonata form, although not rigidly so. It opens Maestoso, with the main theme given out boldly in unison by the French horns. The tempo then abruptly changes to Allegro pesante, when the strings and wood winds introduce a fast-moving figure which is used contrapuntally against the development of the main theme. A marked contrast is afforded by the second theme, which is introduced in the wood winds, and is pastoral in quality. This theme is then combined with the main theme, and the two are developed at some length and brought to a climax which subsides, until once again we hear in the horns the main theme given out as in the beginning, except in a far-away manner. After this, the development section begins. It may be interesting to note that this development section also includes a kind of "false recapitulation" in which the secondary themes of the first part are heard. This subsides and the true recapitulation is soon heard, with the main themes rising to an impassioned climax. The movement concludes with a short coda, during which the principal theme of the movement is given out once more, emphatically, by the brass.

The second movement is a Scherzo. It might be called a hunt scherzo. After a five-bar introduction, the horns give out a sort of fast hunting call. This theme is of paramount importance, as it keeps recurring throughout the movement as a kind of background to the main theme of the Scherzo proper. At no time does this hunt figure ever really cease. Sometimes we hear it in the woodwinds, as though coming from a great distance. At other times it rises and overpowers the real themes. And again it is presented gloomily in the basses. The trio of the Scherzo is in the nature of a melancholy allegretto, performed mainly by the woodwinds. Its character was inspired to some extent by Milton's line from "Arcades"—"Nymphs and shepherds, dance no more." There is then a return to the Scherzo proper, which is repeated in different instrumentation and with many of the themes inverted. But once again, throughout, the hunt calls are always present. A five-bar coda featuring the tympani brings the movement to a close.

The third movement is marked Andante sostenuto, and is in the nature of an elegy. The clarinet gives out the main theme, a quiet, brooding melody. It is immediately followed by the secondary theme in the flutes. After a due course of development the tempo becomes slower, as the solo trombone proclaims a new theme. This new theme and all the other themes of the movement are then developed to a climax. Finally the clarinet concludes the movement by stating the main theme once more.

The last movement is in rondo form with an epilogue. The trumpet announces the main theme, and with an abrupt change of tempo the entire orchestra gaily picks it up. The contrasting material used includes not only new themes, but one hears again the main theme of the trio of the Scherzo, this time transformed from a melancholy piping to a gay and exuberant tune. Also the hunt call, which figured so prominently in the Scherzo proper reappears, but it is now more of a triumphant fanfare. The vigorous tempo of the Rondo is broken only once, when a new motive is introduced. This theme, a tranquil allegretto, is introduced on the solo flute, accompanied by ancient cymbals in E. The main theme soon returns, and the Rondo continues on its way, leading to a climax in which all the themes of the movement are combined. Then, suddenly, with an abrupt change of tempo, the epilogue begins. This is marked *à la processional*. The clarinets give out still another version of the main rondo theme, now transformed into a slow march, accompanied by a rhythmical pattern on the kettledrums. This seems to draw nearer and nearer and finally rises to a triumphal climax, which brings the Symphony to a close.

R. C. B.

Paul Hindemith

BORN: HANAU, GERMANY, NOV. 16, 1895.

*He is unwilling to exploit his feelings publicly, and he keeps his two
feet squarely on the ground. He merely writes music, the best that he
can produce.*—ALFRED EINSTEIN.

Symphony in E flat

I. Sehr lebhaft. II. Sehr langsam. III. Lebhaft. IV. Mässig schnell halbe.

THE PREMIERE of this work was given by the Minneapolis Symphony Orchestra,
Dimitri Mitropoulos conducting, Nov. 21, 1941. Mr. Mitropoulos again conducted when the Philharmonic-Symphony Society first presented the Symphony
at Carnegie Hall, Dec. 25, 1941.

There are no key signatures in the score, despite the fact that the composer
has entitled his work Symphony in E flat. The music is tonal, although the
play of voices is free.

Hindemith has scarcely been a fervent disciple of atonality. In this composition, as often before, he has not veered sharply away from classical form; the
themes are meant to be themes, they are developed, the construction, in respect
of movements, takes matters of proper contrast fully into consideration. Concentration is the real keynote. There is no wasting time with immaterial details.
There is a beginning and there is also an objective, the shortest line between
those two points being the Symphony.

The horns announce the principal theme of the first movement. It is a
rhythmic theme, which soon undergoes expansion. Further on, other rhythmic
figures derive from the earlier one and together with additional figures they
provide a foil for the principal theme, again played by the horns. The music is
forceful and resounding. An inversion of the first theme introduces a second
of a more lyrical nature. This, after some manipulation, leads to a development,
ending in a climactic announcement of the main theme. The second subject
reappears against a pizzicato in the strings. In the next sequence, probably best
called a coda, the second theme is prominent, for it is presented boldly in the
English horn, bassoons, contra-bassoon, tuba, and basses against a solid string
counterpoint.

The English horn, clarinet, and trumpet give out the theme of the second
movement. As it is continued, the tympani beat out a series of quarter notes,
creating an insistent pattern of rhythm against it. This pattern, with shorter
notes, is heard often in the movement. There is a brief conversation between

strings and flute, whereupon the main theme returns in the violins, the bass supplying a surging counterpoint. The oboe introduces the second subject to an accompaniment of violin chords. The whole orchestra takes up the idea, while the rhythmic pattern becomes much more emphatic. The movement goes on with a reappearance of the main theme in canon (first violins and violas), while the cellos accompany, also in canon. The coda of this section gives the rhythmic pattern an important play.

The third movement has characteristics of a scherzo. The violins offer a tremulous phrase, which is juxtaposed to a hearty theme by English horn, clarinet, and bassoon. There is development of all this material. A trio presents two themes, one by the oboe and the other—which soon replaces it—by English horn and oboe. After a while, the scherzo reappears, this time with a different treatment of the original tremulous phrase.

The Finale follows without pause, and its main theme—resembling its prototype in the first movement—is announced by violins to an accompaniment in the lower strings. After some repetition of the theme, with a consequent development of it in the strings, a *deciso* episode comes through in the brass. Both themes appear, one after the other, now, and the music leads into an intermezzo, whose subject is stated by flute and piccolo, later by the oboe. This subject ends on a descending triplet which itself obtains considerable development. The music reverts to that of the first part of the movement. Gradually the sound intensifies, reaching climactic proportions, while all through it dart a great variety of rhythmic figures. With the slowing up of the tempo, the trombones play the principal theme of the movement in augmentation; the trumpets take it up. The Symphony ends with a sonorous and intense peroration.

The Symphony in E flat is scored for three flutes, piccolo, two oboes, English horn, two clarinets, bass clarinet, two bassoons, contra-bassoon, four horns, three trumpets, three trombones, tuba, snare drum, bass drum, cymbals, glockenspiel, triangle, tympani, and strings.

R. C. B.

Symphony, "Mathis der Maler" ("Matthias the Painter")

I. Angelic Concert. II. Entombment. III. Temptation of Saint Anthony.

THIS SO-CALLED "symphony" is a synthesis of three stylistically related excerpts from Hindemith's opera, *Mathis der Maler*. As such it was first performed at a Berlin Philharmonic concert, Wilhelm Furtwängler conducting, on Mar. 12, 1934. Its American premiere occurred on Oct. 6, 1934, at a New York Philharmonic-Symphony concert led by Otto Klemperer.

The radical modernism of Hindemith so nettled German officialdom that his music was made a political issue and subsequently banned from the concert halls. The opera from which the "symphony" derives was finally performed at the Stadttheater in Zurich on May 28, 1938, and later, in concert form, by the BBC Orchestra in London.

German officials could not have found Hindemith's libretto to their taste, either, since it is based on the life of the early sixteenth-century Matthias Grünewald. In the great peasant uprising against tyranny, Grünewald is reputed to have supported, or at least, sympathized with, the struggle to end serfdom. As a painter he ranks with the best in the Altdorfer-Dürer tradition, combining fierce Gothic imagination and masterly Renaissance technic. Embedded in his finest work is a blunt frankness foreshadowing modern realism.

The three movements of Hindemith's "symphony" were inspired by three panels of Grünewald's masterpiece—the widely known polyptych painted for the Isenheim altar at Colmar, in Alsace. They comprise I. Angelic Concert; II. Entombment; III. Temptation of Saint Anthony. After the Berlin premiere Heinrich Strobel, a German critic and essayist, published an elaborate analysis of the "symphony," from which the following is extracted:

When Paul Hindemith combined three excerpts from his opera *Mathis der Maler* and called the result a "symphony," the term did not imply a symphonic construction as understood by the nineteenth century. These tone pieces do not embody a definite "symphonic idea." They are not related in theme. Their spiritual relationship is derived from a plastic conception: the three movements are based on "themes" suggested by the Isenheim Altar of Grünewald.

But, one may ask, has Hindemith become a composer of romantic program music? Let us dismiss entirely in this connection the word "romantic," which is subject to misinterpretation, and let us simply state that this symphony has nothing whatever in common with program music of the customary descriptive sort. Hindemith has endeavored to approximate by musical means that emotional state which is aroused in the onlooker by Grünewald's famous work.

Hindemith, that is to say, uses here methods which he had previously employed in his instrumental music. He excludes any pictorial intention; also, he abstains from the psychological interpretation and conversion of his themes. He dispenses with dramatizing color effects, changing the sound material in accordance with purely musical laws. The technique of the symphony is the technique of Hindemith's instrumental concertos. The transformation of the emotional tension into purely musical effects is accomplished by the same logical processes that we find elsewhere in his work.

Hindemith's style has gained in tonal plasticity to the same degree that he has simplified his art technically. The few themes of the symphony are tonal symbols of extraordinary vitality and perceptibility, but at the same time they obey a logic that is subject to wholly personal laws. The effect is further increased by the circumstance that in the first part "Angelic Concert" (based on the picture of the Nativity painted by Grünewald for the Isenheim Altar), and in the third part, the "Vision of the Temptation of Saint Anthony," old church melodies are used. These ancient melodies constitute the true germ cell of music; they determine its melodic and harmonic tissue.

But this is nothing new in Hindemith's case. The liturgical modes have exercised a deep influence on his music. This influence is evident in his *Marienleben* and in *Das Unaufhörliche;* it breaks through again with all its force in *Mathis der Maler.* It seems as though Hindemith, after many digressions, were recurring to his works of a decade ago. The pathos, the subdued lyricism, the plasticity of the musical vision—all these appear to establish a connection between his most recent art and its earlier expressions. . . .

The simplicity of *Mathis der Maler* does not mean, however, that Hindemith is renouncing his principle of polyphonic development. Polyphony, counterpoint inspired by Bach, remains the basis of his musical thinking and feeling. In the course of the last few years, however, he has abandoned more and more all dispensable contrapuntal ballast and has lightened his linear style. . . .

This polyphonic style gains, in the *Mathis Symphony,* a symbolic force which is something entirely new for Hindemith. Without, as we have said, employing descriptive music in the ordinary sense, effects are obtained here which could not have been realized by means of dramatic expressiveness. In this connection, we must mention especially the last movement, the pictorial subject of which (the Saint tortured by fantastic beasts) stimulated the tonal imagination of the composer to an exceptional degree.

The development of the three movements is singularly clear. The dynamic curve descends from the festive and happy Angelic Concert of the beginning to the quiet elegy of the Entombment, and then proceeds, after the music of the Saint's ordeal, to the concluding Hallelujah Hymn of the final visionary exaltation.

L. B.

"Nobilissima Visione" (Suite from the Ballet, Also Called "St. Francis")

Hindemith's *Nobilissima Visione* was contrived in collaboration with Leonide Massine of the Monte-Carlo Ballet Russe, the latter supplying the visual allegory and choreography. The ballet entered the troupe's repertory in London in July, 1938, and the following Oct. 14, the company appeared in its American premiere at the Metropolitan Opera House. Mr. Hindemith conducted both times.

The ballet was variously received, some viewing it as a perfect blend of austere medieval piety in musical and choreographic imagery, others singling out the Hindemith music for sole praise. The effort was a notable departure from the usual balletic subjects, and scholars compared notes on the allegorical meaning of Massine's symbolism. The action hinges on St. Francis's gradual conversion to the ideal of poverty, much of the inspiration coming from *The Little Flowers of St. Francis*.

The music, typically spare in outline and color, evokes a kind of liturgical archaism through its austere unity of mood and idiom. Hindemith's polyphonic skill is throughout manifest, and by cannily counterposing themes the rise and fall of dramatic intensity is steadily maintained. Reviewing the American premiere of the ballet, Oscar Thompson analyzed the music as follows:

Taking as its thematic basis what is said to be a troubadour song "Ce fut en Mai," it builds upon a naïve melody many variations, these being interwoven with other material of kindred feeling and suggestion. There is nothing of the consciously archaic. But in spite of twentieth-century harmonization, the music has an aura of old times. For the most part it is . . . rather primitive in color, avoiding the lush and the sensuous in its sonorities. The wood winds have important roles to play in etching the lines of unadorned counterpoint. The music is not curt or satiric; to the contrary it has considerable exploitations and is always in earnest. Whether, in some condensed form, it has before it a separate existence in the concert halls is not an issue of the moment, but conceivably segments of it would have a measure of independent appeal.

L. B.

Gustav Holst

BORN: CHELTENHAM, ENGLAND, SEPT. 21, 1874. DIED: LONDON: MAY 25, 1934.

He was a gifted artist, a gifted teacher; a man of flexible and capacious imagination, a wit, a poet, a mystic. He was on familiar terms with the cosmos.—LAWRENCE GILMAN.

"The Planets," Op. 32

A MAN OF multiple interests and fabulous learning, Gustav Holst found inspiration for his music in the vast realm of nature and history. He mastered the language and background of the great Sanskrit hymns, the better to set them to music. He found stimulus in the rich resources of folk poetry and music, and one day he looked into the skies and felt music surge in him as he sought the meaning of the stars.

He gave the following explanation after the first London performance of the Suite on Feb. 27, 1919:

These pieces were suggested by the astrological significance of the planets. There is no program music in them, neither have they any connection with the deities of classical mythology bearing the same names. If any guide to the music is required, the subtitle to each piece will be found sufficient, especially if it be used in a broad sense. For instance, Jupiter brings jollity in the ordinary sense, and also the more ceremonial kind of rejoicing associated with religious or national festivities. Saturn brings not only physical decay, but also a vision of fulfilment. Mercury is the symbol of mind.

Encouraged by the composer's own remarks, Edward Evans delved further into the contents of Mr. Holst's cosmic studies:

One may be skeptical concerning horoscopes, but one will nevertheless be carried away with the aggressive rhythm of "Mars, the Bringer of War"; and any schoolboy pictures Mercury as the "Winged Messenger." The very word "joviality" connotes Jupiter, and the sandglass and scythe connect Saturn with old age. It may be new to some of us to regard Venus as the "Bringer of Peace"—as she is, astrologically speaking—for many have held her responsible for strife in worldly affairs. It is also unfamiliar to hail Neptune, the sea god, as a mystic, and Uranus as a magician; but once these relations are established in the titles, it is easy to fall into the mood of the respective movements.

The seven movements follow in this order: I. "Mars, The Bringer of War" (Allegro, C major, 5/4); II. "Venus, The Bringer of Peace" (Adagio, E flat major, 4/4); III. "Mercury, The Winged Messenger" (Vivace, 6/8); IV. "Jupiter, The Bringer of Jollity" (Allegro giocoso, C major, 2/4); V. "Saturn, The Bringer of Old Age" (Adagio, C major, 4/4); VI. "Uranus, The Magician" (Vivace, C major, 6/4), and VII. "Neptune, The Mystic" (Andante, 5/4).

L. B.

"St. Paul's Suite for Stringed Orchestra"

ALONG WITH his loftier researches in matters mystical and cosmic, Gustav Holst cultivated a rewarding passion for folk music, particularly that of his native England. In 1905, Holst became head of the music department of St. Paul's School for Girls in London. While there, he occupied a studio in the music wing of the school building. It was in that studio that he wrote the Suite, appropriately entitled *St. Paul's,* besides numerous other works, including the composition which made him famous—*The Planets* (1915).

The Suite consists of four movements: Jig, Ostinato, Intermezzo, Finale. Two English folk tunes are woven into the Finale: the "Dargason" and "Greensleeves." Holst also employed "Dargason" in a suite for military band called *On English Folk Tunes.* Ralph Vaughan Williams, another keen student and exploiter of English folk music, once wrote as follows of Holst's constant recourse to this native material:

The subject of English folk song is a thorny one and has been much misunderstood. It would be out of place to discuss it at length here; but this much may be said, that, to those who have understanding, the folk song is a liberating and not a fettering influence. The contact with new types of melody bound by purely melodic considerations, with rhythms not tied by the convention of bars and time signatures, the expressiveness of short and simple tunes—all this cannot fail to suggest to anyone who is naturally sympathetic new vistas of musical thought which may, indeed, have nothing to do superficially with the curves and cadences of folk song, but are suggested by its spirit if not by its letter. Holst's first introduction to his traditional melodies was a collection of songs from Hampshire which he harmonized at the request of the late Dr. Gardiner.

L. B.

Arthur Honegger

BORN: LE HAVRE, FRANCE, MAR. 10, 1892.

He has a large vision and goes his own way without bothering about passing infatuations or the fashions of the day.—HENRY PRUNIÈRES.

Symphony No. 3 for Large Orchestra ("Liturgique")

I. Allegro marcato—"Dies Irae." II. Adagio—"De profundis clamavi." III. Andante con moto—"Dona nobis pacem."

COMPOSED IN the summer of 1946, with Charles Münch expressly designated to introduce it, the Third Symphony obtained its premiere at Zurich by the Tonhalle Orchestra. Under his direction it was also given its first performances at Paris and London, in November and December, respectively. On Jan. 23, 1947, Mr. Münch conducted the American premiere at a concert of the New York Philharmonic-Symphony.

The Symphony is scored for three flutes, piccolo, two oboes, English horn, two clarinets, bass clarinet, two bassoons, contra-bassoon, four horns, three trumpets, three trombones, tuba, bass drum, snare drum, cymbals, tam-tam, triangle, piano, and strings.

There is no program to this Symphony other than that indicated by its *Liturgique* characterization and the subtitles of the three movements— I. Allegro marcato, "Dies Irae"; II. Adagio, "De profundis clamavi"; and III. Andante con moto, "Dona nobis pacem."

According to Mr. Münch—who made it clear this was a personal viewpoint —"The *Liturgique Symphony* of Honegger poses the problem of humanity vis-à-vis God."

The work is classical in form—exposition, development of the material, and all the other devices involved. There is no scherzo, although the opening movement has sequences of a quasi-prankful sort, not unlike music suitable for a scherzo, yet *Liturgique* would seem to rule out the jocose from the work.

The Symphony is dissonant, although not excessively, and a good deal of its structure is polyphonic. It is quite rhythmical in the two end movements, impressively so in the first, with its vigorously syncopated phrases, the marked accents and the swift give and take, while in the third the rhythm subsides after the excitement. The second movement is songful, perhaps, prayerful. This Symphony strikes Mr. Münch as being an expression of man's revolt against the Higher Will, with a gradual sweetening of disposition and a final, voluntary submission to It.

Arthur Honegger, whose best known work, probably, is his impressionistic *Pacific 231*, is considered a composer of the modern French school, although he is of Swiss parentage. He began his musical studies when he was thirteen in his native city with the organist R. C. Martin. Later he became enrolled at the Zurich Conservatory, remaining there for two years, and subsequently he attended the Paris Conservatory, while still living in Le Havre. At the latter school he took counterpoint lessons from André Géldalge and violin from Lucien Capet. When he settled in Paris, in 1913, he continued his lessons with Géldalge, receiving instruction in composition from Widor and in orchestration from d'Indy.

His compositions date from 1914, when he became interested in the writing of songs. In 1916 he composed his first instrumental work, a Toccata and Variations for Piano. For orchestra he first wrote a Prelude to Maeterlinck's *Aglavaine et Selysette,* this in 1917. Chamber music works followed, a "Rhapsodie" for two flutes, clarinet, and piano reflecting, more or less, his admiration of the style of Debussy.

Gilbert Chase remarks that Honegger, in his search for a style of his own, arrived at a

repudiation of the methods, though not necessarily the materials, of impressionism. That is, he did not seek, like some anti-impressionistic composers, a return to harmonic simplicity, but instead endeavored to employ the complex harmonic vocabulary of the impressionists in a quite different way, as material for essentially rhythmic and linear constructions.

In 1916, with his fellow-pupil Milhaud and other young composers, he formed the group called "Les Nouveaux Jeunes," under the leadership of Erik Satie, with Jean Cocteau as literary spokesman. The group gave its concerts in the Théâtre du Vieux-Colombier, where on Dec. 2, 1918, Honegger's first large-scale work, the masque *Le Dit des jeux du monde* was performed. In 1920 this group, comprising Honegger, Milhaud, Poulenc, Auric, Durey and Germaine Tailleferre, became known as "Les Six," or "The French Group of Six," and as such obtained world-wide notoriety. But Honegger's powerful personality soon asserted its independence of any group.

Dedicated to chamber and symphonic music in "their most serious and austere aspects," it was in this vein that he composed the oratorio or "dramatic psalm" *Le Roi David,* which made an instantaneous success. His classical leanings are mirrored in such compositions as the "mimed symphony" *Horace Victorieux, Antigone,* and *Amphion.* And his interest in the more "modern aspects of living," as subject matter, is recognizable in both *Rugby* and *Pacific* 231.

Other works, besides three symphonies, include *Mouvement Symphonique, No. 3,* incidental music for Paul Claudel's mystery play *Jeanne d'Arc au bûcher*

(*Joan of Arc at the Stake*), the ballet *Sémiramis,* the "dramatic legend" for mixed voices and orchestra *Nicolas la Flue,* numerous items of chamber music for varied combinations, pieces for organ and several songs.

R. C. B.

"Pacific 231," Orchestral Movement

THOUGH A prolific composer in many mediums, including opera, oratorio, and symphony, Arthur Honegger won world renown—or notoriety—through two compositions—*Rugby,* which was an attempt to glorify the excitement of sport, and *Pacific* 231, a realistic expression of the composer's passion for locomotives. When the latter piece was given its premiere in Paris on May 8, 1924, at one of Serge Koussevitzky's concerts, Honegger gave out the following statement:

I have always had a passionate love for locomotives. To me they—and I love them passionately as others are passionate in their love for horses or women—are like living creatures. What I wanted to express in the *Pacific* is not the noise of an engine, but the visual impression and the physical sensation of it. These I strove to express by means of a musical composition. Its point of departure is an objective contemplation: quiet respiration of an engine in a state of immobility; effort for moving; progressive increase of speed, in order to pass from the "lyric" to the pathetic state of an engine of 300 tons driven in the night at a speed of 120 miles per hour. As a subject I have taken an engine of the "Pacific" type, known as "231," an engine for heavy trains of high speed. On a sort of rhythmic pedal sustained by the violins is built the impressive image of an intelligent monster, a joyous giant.

Despite Honegger's own disclaimer of imitation, fault has been found with his descriptive realism. Henry Prunières confessed being shocked by the "locomotive theme with its whistlings and puffings," and preferred the picture of "men struggling, fighting, playing" in *Rugby*. He heard the abrupt, relentless throb of a machine in *Pacific* 231, and it depressed him by its inhumanity. Emile Vuillermoz, on the other hand, was entranced by this same machine "tearing full steam ahead through the night." To him Honegger had achieved a *tour de force* by "evoking in sound that special drunkenness which is the lyric quality of speed." And this internal dynamism, he felt, Honegger had translated into purely musical terms.

No other composer has attempted to present a locomotive in such vivid symphonic guise. One senses the giant puffing into stride, working up speed, whistling through the dark night, panting along at full speed, and suddenly pulling up short in a burst of screeching brakes and whining wheels. This involves a crescendo mounting to terrific pitch, and finally a majestic blare from the brasses, sounding, as one critic phrased it, "a veritable hymn to the glory of speed!"

The scoring of *Pacific* 231 calls for two flutes, piccolo, two oboes, English horn, two clarinets, bass clarinet, two bassoons, double bassoon, four horns, three trumpets, three trombones, bass tuba, snare drum, bass drum, cymbals, tam-tam, and strings.

L. B.

Engelbert Humperdinck

BORN: SIEGBURG, GERMANY, SEPT. 1, 1854. DIED: NEUSTRELITZ, SEPT. 27, 1921.

"Hänsel und Gretel" took the German people back once more into the beloved land of their national stories; and it was the work of a composer with a wholly German idiom and a masterly German technique.—ERNEST NEWMAN.

Prelude to "Hänsel und Gretel"

THE INGRATIATING charm of Humperdinck's *Hänsel und Gretel* has won it a faithful following the world over. The young of all ages have fallen under the spell of its sustained mood of childlike enchantment. There is a homespun simplicity about its melodies, and an aura of folk music lingers about. But the "simplicity" should not be misleading. Humperdinck was a supreme craftsman and an orchestrator of great resource. He had learned much from its creator about the brave new world of Wagnerism. And the master had recognized the idolatrous disciple by engaging him as chief assistant in the giant task of preparing *Parsifal* for its world premiere at Bayreuth. Mingled in the prelude to *Hänsel und Gretel* are these two major traits of Humperdinck: the tender feeling for simple folklike themes and the contrapuntal power colored by the rich glow of Wagnerism.

Destined first for home performance, *Hänsel und Gretel* was composed in 1893 to a libretto by Humperdinck's sister Adelheid Wette, who of course found the woodland fable in the famous collection of the Brothers Grimm. The work was warmly acclaimed at its premiere in the Court Theater of Weimar on Dec. 23, 1893. The opera reached America in an English version on Oct. 8, 1895, when it was produced at Daly's Theater in New York. In its German original it entered the repertory of the Metropolitan Opera House on Nov. 25, 1905.

The familiar nursery tale centers in the forest adventures of Hansel and Gretel, children of the broommaker Peter. The pair are lost one day while picking berries. Night finds them deep in the forest. The Sandman comes and puts them to sleep. Awakened by the Fairy of the Dawn, they continue their wanderings. Hungry and frightened, they finally reach the gingerbread house occupied by a Witch who feeds on children lost in the woods. The children's joy at the sight of the toothsome dwelling promptly turns to terror as the Witch reveals the horrible secret of her diet. They are to be made into gingerbread for her teeming cupboard! But the shrewd little captives outwit their jailor by thrusting her into the oven waiting for them. As the Witch is properly baked, the children free all the other little victims from their gingerbread spell. Peter and his wife Gertrude arrive to join in the happy celebration.

In its compact and colorful scheme the prelude mirrors the course of the fable. The shifting moods of infant frolicking and wide-eyed terror are readily sensed in the richly colored fabric. Most of the material is drawn from the opera and woven freely into a clearly integrated scheme. The prelude opens tranquilly with a Prayer uttered by horns and bassoons. This is then developed, and the pace sharpens. Soon a trumpet intones a ringing call over a web of wood winds and pizzicato strings. A new theme enters among the strings and wood winds, and we are admitted into a fearful world of sorcery. The trumpet call sounds again, and a jubilant, dancelike mood comes over the orchestra. The music sinks back to rest as the Prayer motive of the beginning returns.

L. B.

Jacques Ibert

BORN: PARIS, APR. 15, 1890.

*There is always about his music, as about his person, an air of good
fellowship and delicate amiability that shows the artist of breeding.
He pleases without trifling.*—ANDRÉ GEORGE.

"Escales" ("Ports of Call")

WRITTEN IN 1922, *Escales* was heard for the first time at a Lamoureux concert
in Paris on Jan. 6, 1924. Allegedly, the work grew out of a Mediterranean
cruise. In reviewing the premiere the critic of *Courrier Musical* even gave the
three ports at which the composer's vessel stopped. These Escales were Palermo,
Tunis-Nefta, and Valencia. The three sections of Ibert's composition are
supposed to translate impressions of these ports: I. Palermo (Calme); II. Tunis-
Nefta (Modéré, très rythmé); III. Valencia (Animé). Although the score does
not offer this explanation of the title, Ibert has never disavowed it. André
George, writing in *The Chesterian* in 1926, went even further in detailing the
origin of *Escales*. Whether Ibert authorized it is not known. He writes:

It was a tour in the Mediterranean that produced the *Escales*. The composer
allows his musical sensibility to express itself around three popular themes heard in
the course of the voyage. A calm Italian melody, sung very gently by the flute, from
the second bar, throws various lights on the first piece, which bears the evocative
names of "Rome-Palermo." [*Rome is not mentioned in the score.*] The second
movement takes us to the opposite shore, "Tunis-Nefta"; over an oriental rhythm
given to the divided strings, and supported by the kettledrum, a melancholy phrase
unfolds its chromaticism slowly in the oboe. The third piece, "Valencia," derives its
inspiration from a Hispano-Moorish refrain and is very freely developed in the
manner of a Spanish rhapsody.

Escales is scored for piccolo, two flutes (the second interchangeable with
piccolo), two oboes, English horn, two clarinets, three bassoons, four horns,
three trumpets, three trombones, tuba, four kettledrums, side drum, tambourine, bass drum, cymbals, triangle, xylophone, castanets, gong, celesta, harp,
and strings.

Though known to American audiences mainly as the composer of *Escales*,
Jacques Ibert has written copiously for stage and concert hall. In 1939, Sigurd
Rascher appeared with John Barbirolli and the Philharmonic-Symphony in a
Chamber Concertino for Saxophone and Orchestra, expressly composed by
Ibert for the noted saxophonist. In 1935, Ibert collaborated with Arthur

351

Honegger in an operatic version of Rostand's famous drama *L'Aiglon*. Brought out first at Monte Carlo this ambitious work opened the 1937-1938 season of the Paris Opéra. An earlier light opera *Le Roi d'Yvetot* was produced in 1930 at the Opéra Comique. *Angelique, Persée et Andromède, Le Jardinier de Sames,* and *Les Petites Cardinals* (also written with Honegger) are among Ibert's other stage works. Included, too, are several ballets, *viz., L'Eventail de Jeanne, Diane de Poitiers, Gold Standard,* and *Les Rencontres.* Other important scores include a symphonic poem inspired by Oscar Wilde's "Ballad of Reading Gaol," *Chant de folie* (for chorus and orchestra), and a cello concerto. In 1919 Ibert won the Prix de Rome, having studied with André Gegalde, Roger-Ducasse, and Gabriel Fauré at the Paris Conservatory.

In appraising Ibert's music, M. George contends that any composition bearing his name is certain to have two qualities—clarity and clean workmanship. "Generously gifted as he is in many directions, his musical temperament expands with singular felicity in the orchestra, where he revels in the subtlest management of exquisite sound values. . . . His music is always found to reflect his apt sense of color and his gifts of contriving those iridescent effects which are so striking a feature of his work."

L. B.

Vincent d'Indy

BORN: PARIS, MAR. 27, 1851. DIED: PARIS, DEC. 2, 1931.

The creative flame finds its true nourishment only in love and in a fervent enthusiasm for beauty, truth, and the pure ideal.—D'INDY.

Symphony for Orchestra and Piano on a French Mountain Song, Op. 25

I. Assez lent, modérément animé, un peu plus vite. II. Assez modéré, mais sans lenteur. III. Animé.

LIKE AZUCENA's, Vincent d'Indy's heart was in the highlands. When he could, he spent his summers in a lovely mountain retreat. His letters teem with tributes to the mountains of the Cévennes. "Here is true repose, here one feels at the true source of all art," he once wrote. In 1881 he composed a suite for piano *Poème des montagnes.* Five years later he gave further expression to his feelings in the *Symphony on a French Mountain Song,* and in 1905 he crowned the series with the symphonic triptych *A Summer Day on the Mountain.* One might compile similar nature studies about forests and seas from d'Indy's voluminous writings. He loved the outdoors, and one feels the clean air in his music.

Intensely French, d'Indy was early drawn to his country's folklore. The songs of peasants and mountaineers stirred him. Accordingly, as pivotal theme of a cyclic symphony with piano, he chose a folk song, and, quite naturally, one that was mountain bred. Julien Tiersot, who later included the tune in his collection of popular French songs, sensed a special quality in mountain melodies. They bore "something of the purity of their atmosphere . . . something fluid, ethereal, a gentleness that is not found in folk songs of the plains."

Whatever it was that attracted d'Indy's alert mind to this tune of the Cévennes, he had found the key to an elaborate structure built on a revolving plan and continually returning to the source of its strength. Scholars had long affixed the label of "cyclism" to this form, and César Franck was regarded as its foremost exponent. Cyclical form was nothing new, but in the hands of certain French composers of the time it became virtually a cult. Symphonies and symphonic poems by Lalo, Saint-Saëns, Duparc, Chausson, and Dukas show the cyclic pattern to greater or lesser degree. Franck's D minor Symphony stands as archetype, though d'Indy's own Second Symphony is a close rival.

In his book on Wagner, d'Indy clarified matters by defining "cyclic form" as the use of a "well-chosen theme as nourishment for all the pieces forming the complete work." He pointed out that Liszt and Schumann had worked in this form "with little success," being outdistanced in 1841 by a nineteen-year-old youth named César Franck. "Cyclism" even became a byword, and anticyclist identified it with "formalism." At length Guy Ropartz, in an apologia, pointed out that "one had only to listen to this music for a moment to grasp all its trembling sensuousness under an apparent reserve." Cyclism was nothing more than a form, he insisted, and, like all forms, was valid only in proportion to the good music poured into it. "If such a form suits such and such an artist, can you prevent his using it?" he asked. "It would be equally absurd to deny an artist the use of a particular tonality."

Briefly, all means are legitimate so long as they remain means and not ends in themselves. D'Indy recognized this strongly. In fact, the one logic he professed to obey was the logic of emotion and mood. The unity of the cyclic form was the unity of its emotional heartbeat. Out of the shifting nuances of feeling grew the changing shapes and branchings of the central idea. D'Indy steadily insisted on feeling as the motivating base. Saint-Saëns, more wedded to pure form, could write: "M. d'Indy, like Tolstoy and Barrès and many other thinkers, seem to see nothing in art but expression and passion. I cannot share this opinion. To me art is form above all else."

To d'Indy all musical devices were mere aids to expression. Harmony, melody, rhythm, modulation were good only insofar as they mirrored the true flux of feeling. "Expression is the sole excuse for modulation," he affirms in his *Cours de composition musicale*. About the music of Ducasse he wrote: "I am sure that when M. Ducasse is more willing to trust the impulses of his heart than his researches in sonorities, he will be able to make very beautiful music." As Daniel Gregory Mason remarked, d'Indy's esthetic creed could be boiled down to two dicta: "Emotion is the queen and science the servant" and "In art only the heart can engender beauty."

D'Indy's *Symphony on a French Mountain Song* inspired René Dumesnil to pen a glowing tribute in his *Portraits de musiciens français,* published in 1938:

Nothing gives us such direct and confidential evidence about the composer. Not that he pours out his heart in lyric and grandiloquent phrases. On the contrary, the qualities of spirit, the tastes and aspirations of Vincent d'Indy are all revealed in the choice of themes—so simple, expressively, and clearly arranged—in the exquisite polyphonic treatment setting them off in the classic shape and harmony of the proportions. Everything is directly inspired by his native soil.

The piano plays an essential role, but by no means preponderant. Its use shows a similar care for balance and measure. And what freshness in this mountain theme which engenders the three parts of the symphony!

Here we perceive one of Vincent d'Indy's essential qualities: he seeks inspiration in folklore. It is at the refreshing sources of popular art that he draws his musical ideas. Of course, he is not content to note down songs culled on mountaintop or plain. It is not the exterior aspect of the music the artist reproduces, but the substance itself that he assimilates. The material is preserved, marked by his personality, his free rhythms, his hardy melodic lines, and his supple inflections.

To simple accompaniment the English horn announces the mountain air, followed by the flute. In ascending arpeggios the piano comes in as bassoon, double basses, and cello give out the second theme, capped by a fortissimo outburst, after which the piano discourses it. The original tune returns in bassoon, clarinet, and horn, with the piano skirting about playfully. A livelier theme in B major comes in the wake of tremolo strings and suave chords on harp and piano and undergoes interesting modulations following the entrance of a minor subsidiary theme. Violins and piano take it up in succession.

At length the trumpet gives out the chief theme, which now rises to a great outcry and promptly fades away. After violins and piano toy with the subsidiary theme, the bass clarinet passes the mountain tune back to the trumpet, and a tutti rises on it, with the piano and harp engaged in brisk bravura. With the return of the tune in its original guise, a brief coda begins.

A variant on piano of the mountain air opens the second movement. The piano and bassoons enlarge on a subsidiary theme. The tune is back, first as a horn fanfare over a drum roll, and then in a solemn version for muted horn. Other instruments take it up before the horn recovers it against an accompaniment of strings, piano, and flutes. The piano weaves figures around the clarinet as the movement ends.

The third movement opens with piano and harp giving fresh aspect to the mountain tune. The wood winds take it up as the simple folk song it is. As the tune spreads over the orchestra, piano and harp embroider on it. The clarinet sings out tenderly over a murmur of piano and strings, and the whole orchestra comments excitedly. A dance character has come over the movement. Soon the piano takes up the mountain melody alone, with strings joining in, and the symphony ends in a resounding tutti.

The symphony is scored for three flutes (one interchangeable with piccolo), two oboes, English horn, two clarinets, bass clarinet, three bassoons, four horns, two trumpets, two cornets-à-pistons, three trombones, tuba, kettledrums, big drum, cymbals, triangle, harp, piano, and strings. It was first performed at a Lamoureux Concert, Paris, on Mar. 20, 1887, a year after Saint-Saëns' own symphony with piano was first heard at a London Philharmonic concert. At the time it was something of an innovation to employ the piano as an integral part of a symphony. Phillip Goepp's defence of the practice is ingenious: "An obvious view of such a symphony as the present is in analogy to a sonata for piano and violin. If the symphony is a sonata set for orchestra, the latter can be used in dual with a solo instrument. But it is well to observe that in such a scheme the orchestra has the primary role." In short, d'Indy's *Symphony for Orchestra on a French Mountain Song* is not a "thinly disguised concerto."

L. B.

Leos Janacek

BORN: HUKVALDY, MORAVIA, JULY 3, 1854. DIED: MOHR-OSTRAU, AUG. 12, 1928.

His art at its most typical is rooted in the soil, in the sources of a national consciousness and the psychology of a folk. He has been compared with Moussorgsky; and it is significant of his power and salience as an artist that the comparison does not strike us as preposterous.—LAWRENCE GILMAN.

Sinfonietta

I. Allegretto. II. Andante. III. Moderato. IV. Allegretto. V. Allegro.

THIS COMPOSITION was written early in 1926. Its first performance, by the Czech Philharmonic Orchestra, took place at Prague in May of the same year. Its initial performance in America was given by the New York Symphony Society, Otto Klemperer conducting, on Mar. 4, 1927. Herbert Peyser, then program annotator for the Symphony Society, wrote of it (in part) as follows:

There are five short movements . . . the structural basis of the various movements is short sections (some of them only three bars in length), marked with repeats. The first movement is virtually a prelude to the second (the most elaborately organized division of the work). . . . The tempo at the outset is allegretto, the time, 2/4. The tonality oscillates between E flat minor with D flat major and C sharp minor. . . . The bass trumpet and kettledrums in unison have a persistent motive forming part of the first theme. The theme itself—as well as the second one, in D flat (maestoso), reached by a transitional passage in triple time—is of folklike character and resembles a carillon figure.

An andante (4/8), in which clarinets set up an arpeggio movement in thirty-second notes that plays an insistent part through the following pages of this division, ushers in an allegretto. Two oboes give out a lively subject of popular cut over an ostinato of trombones. There are three other themes, the most prominent of them making its first appearance in horns and lower strings against the arpeggios of the clarinets and reappearing at once in the first violins and violas. Another ostinato—a scale form with whole-tone elements—enters in the strings. A short subject of more warmth is uttered against it by trombones and trumpets. Near the close, the theme of the oboes returns.

The third movement (moderato) contains three themes, the first a songlike melody for muted violins and cellos against arpeggios of harp and violas; the second, measures of solemn brass chords with answering piccolo scales; the third, another trombone phrase. An animated dance theme in 2/4 time given out leggiero by three trumpets in unison opens the fourth movement (allegretto) which consists prin-

cipally of reiterations of it. Near the close, measures of presto and adagio alternate
A subject for three flutes forms the chief thematic backbone of the final allegro, and
the work concludes with a return of the opening movement more elaborately
instrumented.

Although Leos Janacek is best known here through his operas and particu
larly *Jenufa* (produced at the Metropolitan with Maria Jeritza as the peasant
heroine, 1924-1925), he wrote a considerable amount of music in all other forms
Especially notable, among his nonoperatic works, is the *Festival Mass,* which
was performed by the Society of the Friends in Music in 1930.

Seventh child of a village schoolmaster, Janacek was a student at the Organ
School in Prague. Later he attended the Leipzig Conservatory, studying both
conducting and theory under Reinecke. Most of his life was spent in his own
country, where he devoted himself chiefly to teaching, composing, and doing
research in folklore. To supplement these activities, he took on additional duties
for a time, involving conductorship of the Philharmonic Society of Brno
besides accepting the post of director of the Conservatory there.

Like Dvorak and Smetana, Bartók and Kodály, Villa-Lobos, Chávez, Enesco
and Roy Harris, Janacek worked without end investigating his country's folk
music. Further he developed interesting theories about the effects of national
speech rhythms on music, applying his discoveries to the music he wrote.

R. C. B.

Werner Josten

BORN: ELBERFELD, GERMANY, JUNE 12, 1888.

He achieves a subtle blending of the old and the new by tempering his acerbities with exquisite lyricism, with long-breathed, sustained melodic lines, and striking and imaginative harmonic and contrapuntal structure.—JOHN TASKER HOWARD.

"Concerto Sacro No. 1"

LIKE HINDEMITH'S *Mathis der Maler,* Mr. Josten's *Concerto Sacro* was inspired by the powerful and mysterious sixteenth-century triptych painted for the Isenheim altar at Colmar, in Alsace, by the Rhenish master Matthias Grünewald. Mr. Josten first designed the work as a single *Concerto* in four movements. Later he saw the feasibility of dividing the work into two complete units, each capable of being performed alone. These were then called *Concerto Sacro No. 1* and *Concerto Sacro No. 2.*

The two movements of *Concerto Sacro No. 1* are entitled "Annunciation" and "The Miracle." In *Concerto Sacro No. 2* they are entitled "Lament" and "Sepulcher and Resurrection." The scoring is for string orchestra and piano. The Concertos were composed in 1925 and revised in 1927. They were played for the first time anywhere by the Graduate School Orchestra at the Juilliard Musical Foundation in New York, in March, 1929. When *Concerto Sacro No. 1* was performed by the Philadelphia Orchestra in October, 1933, Mr. Josten supplied Lawrence Gilman, the annotator, with the following program:

(a) *The Annunciation:* Mary's dream—Dialogue between Mary and the Angel—O Sanctissima—The Passion—The Angel proclaims victory over death—Mary's ecstasy—The Angel departs—Mary sinks again to sleep.

(b) *The Miracle:* Mary's fear and anguish—Voice of comfort from above—Mary remembers the prophecy—The Miracle is preparing—The Miracle is wrought.

L. B.

Dmitri Kabalevsky

BORN: ST. PETERSBURG, DEC. 30, 1904.

You possess the gift of dramatic development, which is absent in so many good composers.—ROMAIN ROLLAND, *in a letter to Dmitri Kabalevsky.*

Symphony No. 2, Op. 19

I. Allegro quasi presto. II. Andante non troppo. III. Prestissimo. Scherzando; Molto agitato; Allegro.

ACCORDING TO a Soviet source, Kabalevsky was playing the piano by ear at the age of six. Systematic study of music did not begin till 1918, when he was fourteen. The family had moved to Moscow from Leningrad and young Kabalevsky soon enrolled in the Scriabin Music School. For a time he studied composition with Vassilenko and Katuar. Later he was admitted to the Moscow Conservatory. There Miaskovsky was his teacher in composition and Goldenweiser in piano. When Kabalevsky completed his studies at the Conservatory, his name was inscribed on the Golden Panel of Honor. After teaching piano at the Scriabin Music School, he joined the faculty of the Moscow Conservatory as professor of composition. Kabalevsky has served for several years on the editorial board of *Sovietskaya Muzika,* Russia's leading music magazine. Many of its historical and analytical articles have carried his by-line. For a while he even wrote music reviews for the Soviet press. In 1939 Kabalevsky was elected member of the Presidium of the Organizing Committee of the Union of Soviet Composers. A year later he was awarded the Order of Merit.

Like Khatchatourian and Khrennikoff, Kabalevsky is a relatively new name on American concert programs. A small sheaf of his symphonic compositions, including the *Colas Breugnon* overture and a piano concerto, has emerged here in the past few years. Americans interested in the Soviet screen have also heard three of Kabalevsky's film scores: the tautly dramatic music for *Petersburg Night,* the bluntly insurgent music of *Shchors* (a hero of the October Revolution), and the gay operetta score of *Spring Song* (*Vesennaya Pyesnya*). In the Soviet Union, Kabalevsky's music has been before the public since the appearance of a Piano Sonatina in 1930, shortly after he left the Moscow Conservatory. Soon Kabalevsky, like Shostakovich, Khatchatourian, and Prokofieff, was gaining prominence in many fields. Besides writing extensively for the cinema, he composed incidental music for the radio and stage. But very early he disclosed a taste for larger forms, like the concerto, the symphony, and the choral symphony.

In many of his scores, Kabalevsky shows the same preoccupation with Soviet life and tradition as Shaporin, Knipper, Shebalin, Khatchatourian, and Shostakovich. For example, in 1931 he wrote a *Poem of Struggle* for chorus and orchestra. Like Maiskovsky's Twelfth Symphony, Kabalevsky's First—written in 1932—celebrated the fifteenth anniversary of the Revolution. A *Requiem for Lenin* followed in 1933. On a smaller plane were the sketches *From Pioneer Life,* a tribute to Russia's own boy- and girl-scout movements. Kabalevsky's compositions to date include four symphonies, two piano concertos, chamber music, and numerous songs. In 1938 he wrote an opera, *The Master of Clamency,* based on Romain Rolland's *Colas Breugnon,* which Soviet critics regard as his masterpiece. This helped to silence those who had singled out lack of dramatic force as Kabalevsky's main shortcoming. Three years ago Kabalevsky composed a second opera, *Before Moscow.* This work served the double purpose of celebrating the twenty-fifth anniversary of the October Revolution and of commemorating the epic struggle at the gates of Moscow in the autumn of 1941. Shortly after Germany invaded Russia, Kabalevsky published a group of war songs. Later came a cantata for choir, soloists, and orchestra *Our Great Fatherland.* A suite *The People's Avengers*—for chorus and orchestra—was composed at the front with the young Soviet poet Eugene Dolmatovsky, who supplied the text. Moussorgsky, Borodin, Tschaikowsky, Rachmaninoff, Prokofieff, and to a smaller extent Scriabin are traceable influences in the music of Kabalevsky. Another influence is folk music. The ballet *The Golden Spikes* shows interwoven fragments of native White Russian themes, while *The People's Avengers* reveals a marked Ukrainian flavor.

Early criticism of Kabalevsky's music in the Soviet press emphasized its spirit of "academic romanticism," its eclecticism, its "technical primitivism," its hurried facility. It was pointed out that both Kabalevsky and Shostakovich in their earlier symphonic works showed faulty method because they had failed to substitute valid new principles for the classical principles they had discarded. Kabalevsky's Second and Shostakovich's Fifth both revealed a marked swing of the pendulum back to older symphonic forms. Greater warmth and intensity were noted in Kabalevsky's Second Symphony along with compacter classic design. The same is true of the piano concertos. Danilevitch, writing in *Sovietskaya Muzika* in October, 1936, stressed the superiority of Kabalevsky's Second over the "immature, studentlike, utterly eclectic" First Concerto. In his *Eight Soviet Composers* (Oxford), Gerald Abraham speaks of Kabalevsky's Second Piano Concerto as "the only serious rival to Khatchatourian's in the race to surpass Prokofieff."

The world premiere of Kabalevsky's Second Symphony occurred at a concert in the Moscow Conservatory on Dec. 25, 1934, with the British conductor

Albert Coates directing. Arturo Toscanini led the American premiere of the work on a broadcast of the NBC Symphony Orchestra on Nov. 8, 1942, and later, on Feb. 26, 1943, conducted the first American concert performance of the score at a concert of the Philadelphia Orchestra in Philadelphia. The following is an analysis of the Second Symphony which appeared in the February, 1935 issue of *Sovietskaya Muzika* (*Soviet Music*):

In this Symphony, Kabalevsky frees himself from that whole group of influences characteristic of the music of his earlier period, which is distinguished by a certain reticence and a psychological subjectivity in style.

Whereas Kabalevsky's First Symphony shows man finding his "road to life," but only after a severe internal struggle, the Second Symphony depicts another type of man, one who finds his place in life and takes an active part in its reconstruction. In overcoming hardships he gains consciousness of the joy of struggle and labor. The musical structure of the Symphony develops the idea of the growth of man through his daily activities, through work.

The first part is an episode of difficult struggle, in the process of which the forces of the obstacles placed before man threaten to break him in time. In this section of the Symphony we feel that the energy expressed in the first impetuous, fervent theme continually checks itself, throttles and paralyzes itself with a whole group of elements preventing it from asserting itself. In this way there is a dramatic sharpness of rhythm which makes us think of the symphonies of Tschaikowsky and Miaskovsky, and there is an original, in places a gloomily depressed, in places a joyfully light, tonal coloring and a contrast in instrumentation.

The second part of Kabalevsky's Symphony is a slow singing movement, creating a mood of lyric meditation. The very dry and severe prelude, over which still lies the shadow of the dramatic episodes of the storm which has just passed, serves as an introduction into the bright and affable sounding world of clear, peaceful melodies, reaching in places a great lyric height. In the middle portion of the Andante the disciplined firm rhythm of the lyrical march and the broadly drawn out phrase of a singing character speak of an imminent struggle to lead to new victories.

The finale is full of fervor, of temperamental, impetuous movement, sparkling with laughter, gaiety, and pleasantries, but at the same time is shot through with a serious and businesslike attitude. This music has been invoked to tell us that the joy of victory and the jubilant life associated with it have nothing in common with complacent egotistical self-assuagement.

L. B.

Concerto for Piano and Orchestra in G minor, No. 2, Op. 23

I. Allegro. II. Andante. III. Allegro molto: alla breve.

LARGELY CLASSICAL in structure, the G minor Concerto consists of three move-ments. The first and third movements are thematically linked, the rollicking main theme of the Allegro reappearing in altered guise in the finale. In its harmonic structure this theme contains a favorite device of Kabalevsky's: the use of the major subdominant chord in a minor key. Danilevitch suggests it may be intended by Kabalevsky as a kind of musical signature. However, it is not an uncommon device in other Soviet music.

The first movement is almost severely classical in structure. Passages of "schematic squareness" occur frequently. The second movement is woven out of the lyric expressiveness of its two main themes, the first wistful and nostalgic, the second, bolder and more passionate in mood. The finale is in the nature of a toccata or perpetuum mobile, moving with headlong drive.

"The musical language of the concerto is clear and relatively simple," writes Danilevitch. "It is easy to gain a complete picture of it from a single hearing." The piano writing is typically lucid and transparent, at times starkly incisive and percussive. All this is true, too, of the simply patterned accompaniment. Polyphonic intricacy is not a habit of Kabalevsky's. Yet, the orchestra rarely serves purely as background or accompaniment to the piano. Piano and orchestra integrate in one organic scheme.

Danilevitch writes (in *Sovietskaya Muzika,* from which I translate):

The main theme of the first movement—of strong-willed, manly character—contrasts sharply with the softly colored, lyrical subsidiary theme.

The latter's melodic nucleus is related—intervallically—to the second half of the main theme. In the short concluding section—exceptionally simple and clear in structure—elements of the main and subsidiary themes are cleverly synthesized. The development is constructed on the principle of "large, broad breathing." It follows a gradual ascent, leading to an orchestral climax. This is woven out of material of the second theme. There follows a cadenza for piano solo. Like the working-out section, it embodies a gradual dynamic drive culminating in a second, still more striking climax. Dramatic excitement, expressive content, strong pathos, sharp, fresh harmonies, plus clarity of piano writing—all combine to make the cadenza of the first movement one of the best episodes of the Concerto.

In the Andante movement the main themes are first announced in soft aquarelle tones among the solo wood winds and the piano. A melancholy song alternates with a clearer, more challenging melody. The sonorities gradually become full-blooded and solid. A turbulent song of the strings is accompanied by whimsical and fantastic patterns in the solo instrument. The Andante ends with the aquarelle tones of the

beginning, soft and wistful. Despite some dragging and superfluous detail in th
development, the second movement is the best part of the Concerto.

The finale leaves the impression of precipitate movement. In the main them
it is not hard to catch the basic melodic and harmonic elements of the chief them
of the first movement. The development is along lines of a broadly dynami
crescendo, ending in an orchestral climax—built, as in the first movement, o
material from the subsidiary subject. The reprise is laconic, but gives an impressio
of maximum tension. Amid bright, metallically ringing chords, piano and orchestr
engage in a sharp rhythmic exchange of "roll calls." The tempo steadily sharpens
An effective coda ends the concerto."

Kabalevsky's Second Piano Concerto was first performed in America o
May 9, 1943, on the weekly Sunday broadcast of the NBC Symphony Orchestra
Frank Black conducted. Leo Smit was the piano soloist. On May 6, 1945
Bernard Weiser performed the work at a Boston "Pops" Concert, with Arthu
Fiedler conducting. Nadia Reisenberg was the soloist when Artur Rodzinsk
led the New York Philharmonic-Symphony in the first New York concer
performance of the work on Oct. 11, 1945. Besides piano, the scoring calls fo
two flutes, piccolo, two oboes, English horn, two clarinets, two bassoons, fou
horns, three trumpets, three trombones, tuba, tympani, bass drum, snare drum
cymbals, xylophone, triangle, and strings.

L. B.

Overture to the Opera "Colas Breugnon"

THE MUSIC of *Colas Breugnon: The Master of Clamency* is set to a libretto b
V. Bragin, which, in turn, is derived from Romain Rolland's work of the sam
name. The opera was given its premiere performance at Leningrad in 1938.

Not the most operatic subject in the world, Rolland's *Colas Breugnon* is, i
effect, a day-by-day diary—for one year—of philosophic and humorous reflec
tion by a Burgundian craftsman of the sixteenth century. It is a succession o
anecdotes or incidents without a recognizable story, some of which, absorbin
in themselves, pertain to a siege, a riot, and a fire.

Breugnon turns his gaze on many characters, in the course of his "reportorial"
year, and among these we find his wife, his daughter Martine and her husband
and their daughter Clodie (and, incidentally, his favorite grandchild), and hi
friends Paillard the notary and Chamaille the curé of Brèves, in addition t
quite a few other, less important, personalities.

Colas, of course, is the hero of the book. He possesses a humorous outlook or
life, he is witty, proud, sly, and strong. If, on the face of it, that sort of person ir
that sort of book seems not altogether easy to transfer to the operatic stage, with
out loss to either or both (not omitting to an opera itself), there was no apparen
problem for the librettist Bragin, who, quite ingeniously and full of resources

onverted the material to Communistic purpose, giving it the necessary social
ideology and—in the doing—putting the "story" through quite a few handsprings.

It happens that the opera was not received with too great enthusiasm. It was
criticized severely on account of both libretto and music, the former because
put Colas in an undignified position, according to Soviet standards, and the
latter because it was not "an operatic score," but a group of "tasteful musical
water colors."

Anyway, everybody liked the music for itself, and many went so far as to say
it was the best that Kabalevsky had written up to then. The Overture has
already earned an important place in the favor of American symphony
orchestras.

R. C. B.

Jerome Kern

BORN: NEW YORK, JAN. 27, 1885. DIED: NEW YORK, NOV. 11, 1945.

If Jerome Kern had never written a note of music except for his operetta "Showboat," he would be entitled to a high place in the annals of American popular music (perhaps one might even omit the word "popular"). For "Showboat" is a contemporary classic.—JOHN TASKER HOWARD.

"Scenario for Orchestra" on Themes from "Showboat"

SOME YEARS ago, on Dec. 27, 1927, to be exact, *Showboat,* an operetta based on Edna Ferber's best-selling novel, took a sophisticated New York audience by storm at the Ziegfeld Theater. Jerome Kern, one of America's greatest composers of production music, and Oscar Hammerstein, an equally noted lyricist, were the collaborators who brought the mellow sentiment of the Ferber story to the Broadway stage.

Out of the score teeming with melodious tunes, at least five have become classics of the popular repertory. They include the world-famous "Ol' Man River," "Can't Help Lovin' That Man," "Why Do I Love You?," "Can't We Make Believe?" and "My Bill."

At a time when America's folk music is still in the process of formation, it may not be premature to judge these efforts as being strongly contributing elements to what will one day be a great literature. We have "Ol' Man River," for instance, as an index of what may come; for in a relatively few years of life it has attained an enviable position. Distinguished artists of the concert stage have not been unaware of its power and intensity, and noted observers of the musical scene have found in it the true qualities of sincerity and simplicity that one might expect of a noble piece of folk expression.

Kern, encouraged by Artur Rodzinski's desire to bring the music to a fuller realization through the resources of the modern orchestra, set about the task of preparing the *Scenario* in July, 1941. In August the sketches were completed, and in September the finishing touches were added to the orchestration. Dedicated "to Artur Rodzinski with the grateful regards of Jerome Kern," the score carries, further, a quotation from a world-wide broadcast by Winston Churchill: "The British Empire and the United States . . . together . . . I do not view the process with any misgiving. No one can stop it. Like the Mississippi, it just keeps rolling along. Let it roll . . . inexorable, irresistible, to broader lands and better days."

Scenario for Orchestra was given its first performance by the Cleveland Orchestra under the direction of Mr. Rodzinski in Cleveland, in the fall of 1941. The Philharmonic-Symphony introduced it to New York on Nov. 19, 1941.

The *Scenario* begins slowly with a phrase by the cellos, which Kern referred to as "The Mississippi River (Natchez) in the late 1880's." The melancholy measures of "Misery's Done Come" is given out by the English horn, and "Ol' Man River," to all intents and purposes the theme of the piece, is heard softly in the violas and bass clarinet. With the sudden change of the tempo to allegro, there are references to the Negroes giving way, while working, to song. "Can't Help Lovin' That Man" comes forth via a muted trumpet, and, in turn, this ushers in a Tempo di Blues sequence where a quartet of saxophones lords it over the pizzicato strings.

The foregoing material is given a slight development. There follows a take-off on a calliope, presumably the one in use on the showboat *Cotton Blossom,* of the Edna Ferber story. After this "Only Make Believe" rises out of the score, followed by "Why Do I Love You?" Some phrases of a liturgical character correspond to Kim's convent days. The opening "Mississippi River" motive returns, and with considerable employment of the "Ol' Man River" theme, the piece ends. The words, "He jes' keeps rollin' alon,'" in Jerome Kern's hand, are written on the last page of the manuscript.

Jerome Kern studied with Paolo Gallico at the New York Musical College, besides working with Alexander Lambert and others. He composed the scores for a considerable number of musicals, among them *Sally, Sunny, Oh Boy, Sweet Adeline, The Cat and the Fiddle, Very Warm for May* (which contained the lovely song "All the Things You Are"), and *Showboat.* The last named has been revived several times on the stage and for the screen.

R. C. B.

Aram Khatchatourian

BORN: TIFLIS, GEORGIA, JUNE 6, 1903.

*The country which produced Michael Arlen and William Saroyan
has now also a composer who is attracting the attention of the
musical world.*—JOHN N. BURK.

Concerto for Piano and Orchestra

> I. Allegro ma non troppo e maestoso. II. Andante con anima. III. Allegro
> brillante.

COMPOSED IN 1935 and premiered in Moscow the same year, Khatchatourian's
Piano Concerto speedily became a concert favorite throughout the Soviet
Union. Writers hailed it as an "event in Soviet music," and many greeted it as
marking the rehabilitation of the piano concerto in Soviet composition. Something of a stigma had fastened to the form since the A.C.M. (Association of
Contemporary Music) had branded music for the piano as a form of "bourgeois drawing room music making." In any case, only four Soviet piano
concertos had succeeded in gaining wide currency—those of Shekhter, Kabalevsky, Khrennikoff, and Makarov-Rakitin. As one writer expressed it,
"Khatchatourian brought out his Concerto when Soviet music was in danger
of ignoring completely the pianistic traditions of Franz Liszt. Khatchatourian
reinstated them at one stroke."

Along with the frank, untrammeled bravura reverting to an older style,
there was noted the presence of fresh, exotic material in the Concerto, deriving
from Armenian folk sources. This was woven into a throbbing symphonic
scheme hurtling to recurring dramatic climaxes. One writer described the work
as a piece of "virtuoso rivalry between piano and orchestra." As for the
"national" element in the music, Khatchatourian disavowed any intent to quote
literally from Armenian folk material. Rather has he devised themes and color
in the spirit of these folk tunes. Echoes of native Armenian instruments filter
through the score, but never in slavish imitation. Khatchatourian has said that
he "is not and does not wish to be considered a 'national composer' in the
narrow sense of the term." He goes on to say:

Of course, any music worth the name will inevitably have its national characteristics. That applies to the music of Beethoven, Schumann, Rimsky-Korsakoff,
Tschaikowsky. The "Big Five" of Russian music of the last century were first and
foremost Russian composers. But through sincere expression of national feeling, by

means of sound technic and purity of style, they have become representatives of universal art. Looked at from this point of view, folk music for me is not an end in itself, but a means to an end.

In a recent article on Khatchatourian, Nicolas Slonimsky discussed this point. After noting how Russian composers had always been attracted by the folk music of the Russian Orient, he added, "It was only after the Revolution that the minority nations brought forth native composers who made use of melodic and rhythmic resources of their countries *not in the form of exotic stylization, but as creative reconstruction.*"

In reviewing the Concerto, Soviet critics were especially enthusiastic about the slow movement, a poetic reverie in romanza style. Georgi Khubov, writing in *Sovietskaya Musika* in September, 1939, regarded it as an epitome of modern lyricism, with its "perfect inner harmony, its vitality, and its folk character." Throughout, the Orientalism is easily recognized in the structure of melodies used, with the stress on small intervals in eight-note and nine-note scales. Another feature evocative of the Orient is the contrast and novelty of color applied in the scoring for wood winds.

Suggestive of Borodin—and Liszt for that matter—are not only the sweep and surge of theme, but the thematic unity of structure. Material first expounded in the opening movement returns with redoubled force in the finale. In fact, the rather festive, animated theme, with the typically Armenian cadence, introduced in the opening allegro, dominates the concerto like a cyclic motif. The exotic, romanzalike effect of the andante is achieved through a combination of fresh harmonies, folk mood, and laconic expression, the whole giving an impression of severe simplicity. The andante contrasts sharply with the often theatrical brilliance of the end movements.

Of Khatchatourian as orchestrator, Mr. Slonimsky writes that he follows the traditions of Borodin and Glazounoff in contrasting instrumental solos with full orchestral passages. "The effect is secured by means of sonorous accumulation," he writes, "reaching a maximum brilliance, and then subsiding to another period of calm. Khatchatourian's First Symphony he called a "succession of sonorous waves, mounting and receding, in conformity with the larger lines of the formal design."

The son of an Armenian bookbinder, Khatchatourian was nineteen before he began to study music. Then he rapidly made up for lost time. Enrolling in a school in Moscow, he studied cello, but soon turned to composition, his first instructor being Michael Gnessin. Later Miaskowsky and Vassilenko became his teachers at the Moscow Conservatory. Early in his studies he was attracted to Armenian, Georgian, Azerbaijan, and Uzbeck folk music. At the same time Gnessin and Miakowsky opened up the wide field of Russian and classical music to him. In 1926 he began to compose, and his music soon drew attention because of its strange Oriental flavor and gusto. Although the folk note has remained a fixed trait of his music, Khatchatourian for a while toyed with modernistic experiment in dissonance. However, he was soon back at his true métier, "the recreation of his native Caucasian folk music within the bounds of new harmony," to quote Mr. Slonimsky. Success came fast with audiences and critics alike. His First Symphony, written in 1934, and commemorating the Sovietization of Armenia, gave him added prestige.

Khatchatourian already has some '20 compositions to his credit, among them two symphonies, several ballet suites, piano and violin concertos, chamber music (including a trio), songs, marches, overtures, film music, and incidental music for a production of *Macbeth* staged by the Armenia State Theater. In 1938 he wrote a *Poem about Stalin* for the annual October Festival, using a text by the Azerbaijan poet Ashug Mirza. Later he received the highest award of the Soviet Union, the Order of Lenin, for "outstanding services in the development of the music of his native Armenia." Early in 1943 it was decided to have Khatchatourian's name inscribed on a marble tablet in the hall of the Moscow Conservatory, beside the names of other celebrated alumni like Rachmaninoff and Taneieff. Khatchatourian turned down the offer of a professorial post at the Conservatory, preferring to give all his time to composition. His wife and daughter still remain pupils of his, however. Under the name of Nina Makarova, Mrs. Khatchatourian is known to the Soviet public through a cycle of songs based on the verses of the Great Georgian poet Shota Rustaveli and a cantata dedicated to Molotov, the Soviet Foreign Minister.

Besides being widely known in the Soviet Union as a composer, Khatchatourian is a recognized authority on Oriental music and instruments. The autonomous Republics of Uzbekistan and Tadzijkistan have "borrowed" him on occasion for special research in national music.

According to one writer, Khatchatourian "lives enmeshed in the harmonies and rhythms of his native Armenia. He is adding more songs to a lore already rich in material. And when he does become attracted to a four-bar melody of original music, he turns it inside out, making it a richer and more colorful song." (It is interesting to note that when his music to a film was being recorded the directors were at variance as to which was original folk music and which was the Armenian composer's own creation.)

The American premiere of Khatchatourian's Piano Concerto occurred in the concert hall of the Juilliard School of Music on Mar. 14, 1942. The late Albert Stoessel led the Juilliard Graduate School Orchestra, and the talented soloist was, appropriately, a young Armenian girl Maro Ajemian, member of the student personnel. A second performance, by the same forces, took place at a Russian Relief Concert in the Cosmopolitan Opera House on May 17, 1942 when a huge audience drawn largely from New York's Armenian colony greeted the work with cheers. The work was introduced at the Lewisohn

adium at a Philharmonic-Symphony concert led by Efrem Kurtz. William
apell, who was the soloist, reappeared in the work with the Boston Symphony
rchestra in Carnegie Hall on Nov. 20, 1943. Artur Rubinstein was the soloist
hen the New York Philharmonic-Symphony introduced it to its subscribers on
ec. 12, 1943. Artur Rodzinski conducted.

Besides solo piano, the concerto is scored for two flutes, two oboes, two
arinets, bass clarinet, two bassoons, four horns, two trumpets, three trombones,
ba, small drum, bass drum, cymbals, and strings.

L. B.

"Dance with the Sabers" from the Ballet "Gayaneh"

OR "OUTSTANDING merit in promoting the development of Armenian art,"
ram Khatchatourian was awarded the Order of Lenin in 1939. Four years
ter came a further token of recognition for creative effort on behalf of his
ative Soviet republic—the First Degree Stalin Prize. This Khatchatourian
on with his music to *Gayaneh,* a patriotic folk ballet, steeped in native folk-
re and idiom, about cotton pickers on a collective farm (Kolkhoz) in Soviet
rmenia. The libretto was by K. N. Derzhavin. The premiere of *Gayaneh*
ccurred in the city of Molotov on Dec. 9, 1942, during a visit of the Kirov
heater for Opera and Ballet of the Leningrad State Academy. N. A. Anisi-
aova, a noted Soviet ballerina, directed the production and danced the title role.

The story of *Gayaneh* centers in a conflict between a patriotic Armenian girl
ayaneh and her brutal husband Giko. Tragedy arises when Giko turns traitor
 the Soviet regime, joins a band of smugglers, and sets fire to the Kolkhoz.
 a mounting frenzy of hate, Giko almost kills his wife and daughter. They
e saved by Kazakov, commander of a Red Army border patrol, who is in
ve with Gayaneh and marries her when Giko is disposed of. The tale unfolds
gainst a background of workaday life and play on a Soviet plantation.
ussian and Armenian elements dominate the dance. Occasional curtsies are
ade to other Soviet areas. In mood the music ranges from the soft hushed
npressionism of Gayaneh's "Lullaby" to the slashing, explosive drive of the
urdish "Saber Dance." There are simple peasant dances, folkish and colorful;
epherd dances; fiery dramatic dances, exotic in rhythm and verve; even a
Fire Dance." In the final whirlwind of dancing at Gayaneh's engagement
arty, there follow in brisk sequence an Armenian "Shelakho," the Kurdish
Saber Dance," a Gruzian (Georgian) "Lezghinka," and a Ukrainian "Hopak."

The orchestral suite from *Gayaneh* contains thirteen separate dances. Three
f them—"Dance of the Rose Maidens," "Lullaby," and "Dance with the
abers" (Nos. 2, 6, and 11 of the Suite)—were given their American premiere
y Efrem Kurtz and the Kansas City Philharmonic during the season of 1944-
945. The New York concert premiere occurred at the Lewisohn Stadium on

an all-Soviet program of the Philharmonic-Symphony orchestra conducted by Alexander Smallens. In response to prolonged applause, Mr. Smallens repeated "The Dance of the Sabers." Marked Presto, this dance is in bold and spirited vein, with syncopated rhythms and reminiscent flashes of the last movement of Khatchatourian's Piano Concerto. Abrupt changes of tempo add to the wild excited upsurge of rhythms.

L. B.

Tikhon Khrennikoff

BORN: ELETZ, RUSSIA, JUNE 10, 1913.

Khrennikoff's sobriety has the naïveté of youth, but it is often touching, and it yields an occasional page in which familiar things are said with freshness.—LAWRENCE GILMAN.

Symphony No. 1, Op. 4

I. Allegro non troppo. II. Adagio: Molto espressivo. III. Allegro molto.

THIS WORK is dedicated to Dmitri Shostakovich. It was first performed in the Soviet Union in 1935 by the Moscow Radio Orchestra. In America it was given its initial performance by Leopold Stokowski and the Philadelphia Orchestra on Nov. 20, 1936.

The composer, who was still a student at the Moscow Conservatory when he penned this Symphony, has also written incidental music to Shakespeare's comedy *Much Ado about Nothing,* a Piano Concerto, a set of "Five Pieces for the Piano" and another of "Three Pieces for the Piano," the music for a play *Mick,* a number of songs to texts of Pushkin, an opera *The Brothers,* and music for the film "The Pigs and the Shepherd," which won, in 1942, the Stalin prize.

Although Khrennikoff's First Symphony is in four movements, the absent scherzo is present spiritually, at least, in the vigor and pace of certain measures found in the opening and closing of the finale. The two main and contrasting themes are vivid ones and are quite deftly handled in the development.

The second movement, a broad and sustained Adagio, is elegiac in mood and utterance. Its harmonies, not like those of the other sections, are mainly conventional, yet are made to order for a melancholy song delivered by the strings. The orchestration is clear and full, without heaviness, though, as the movement goes on, the melancholy grows deeper.

The solo clarinet and the strings, in turn, bring out a sprightly theme, which is developed at some length. A smooth cantilena follows, involving several subjects. It grows in intensity until it reaches a great sonority, and a mighty crashing tutti closes the Symphony.

R. C. B.

Zoltán Kodály

BORN: RECSKMÉT, HUNGARY, DEC. 16, 1882.

Kodály's music . . . is not "modern" in the current sense of the word. It has nothing in common with atonal, bitonal, polytonal tendencies . . . yet his musical language is entirely new and expresses musical ideas never heard before.—BÉLA BARTÓK.

Suite from "Háry János"

I. The Fairy Tale Begins. II. Viennese Musical Clock. III. Song. IV. The Battle and Defeat of Napoleon. V. Intermezzo. VI. Entrance of the Emperor and His Court.

HÁRY JÁNOS is the swashbuckling hero of comic Hungarian folk legend. In superhuman valor he rivals Baron Munchausen. In amorous exploits, Casanova and Don Juan are adolescent bumpkins beside him. The sly roguery of Till Eulenspiegel is part of his nature, and for prodigious fantasy he is unique. We have his own unimpeachable word for it that Napoleon declared war on Austria to get rid of Háry János. His singlehanded defeat of the Grand Army is still common talk around Magyar campfires. Reportedly, the Empress Marie Louise's infatuation for Háry was Napoleon's *casus belli*. The spectacle of the Emperor begging the Magyar Ajax to spare his life alone deserves a Homeric epic—or at any rate a comic opera.

Zoltán Kodály's *buffo* folk opera was first staged at the Budapest Royal Opera on Oct. 16, 1926. The libretto was by Bela Paulini and Szolt Harsanyi. Later Kodály arranged a symphonic suite from his opera, and in this form *Háry János* was premiered by the New York Philharmonic Orchestra on Dec. 15, 1927. Willem Mengelberg conducted. Kodály supplied the Philharmonic with the following narrative gist of the six movements:

According to a Hungarian superstition, if a statement is followed by a sneeze of one of the hearers, it is regarded as confirmation of the truth of the assertion. The *Háry Suite* begins with a sneeze of this kind. One of Háry's group of faithful listeners, who sneezes at the wildest assertions of the old tale spinner, is equal to the occasion even when Háry declares that he once had occasion to subdue Napoleon himself! With a suggestion of this sneeze "the tale begins" (No. 1 of the Suite). The other movements may be described as follows:

No. II. The scene is laid in the imperial palace in Vienna, where the ingenious Hungarian peasant is amazed and enraptured by the famous Musical Clock with its little soldier figures in their brave uniforms appearing and disappearing at every rotation of the marvelous machinery.

No. III. Háry and his sweetheart are longing for their village home, its quiet evenings, musical with love songs (an ancient Hungarian melody is used).

No. IV. Háry, as general in command of his hussars, confronts the French army. He brandishes his sword, and lo! the French begin to fall before him like tin soldiers! First, two at a time, then four—eight—ten, and so on. Finally there are no more soldiers left, and Napoleon is forced to engage in person the invincible Háry. Háry's fantasy pictures a Napoleon made in the image of his own burly peasant imagination—an immensely tall and formidable Napoleon who, shaking in every limb, kneels before his conqueror and pleads for mercy. The ironical French Victory March is transformed into a dirge.

No. V is an intermezzo without special significance.

No. VI. An ironical march of triumph, in which Háry pictures the entrance of the emperor and the imperial court at Vienna; but it is not the Austrian reality— only a Hungarian peasant's way of imagining the rich happiness of the celebrated Wiener Burg.

The composition of *Háry János* sprang naturally from Kodály's long interest in Hungarian folklore and music. Together with Béla Bártok he is responsible for salvaging, through phonograph recordings and dictation, some thirty-five hundred native Hungarian melodies. Like Bártok, Kodály felt the vital need of preserving this peasant material as a source of inspiration for Hungarian composers. It was believed that only from a thorough assimilation of the spirit of this folk music could a truly national music arise. Neither Bártok nor Kodály endorsed the practice of using folk tunes bodily. They were more concerned with recapturing mood and atmosphere.

Kodály has pointed out that since 1910 most Hungarian music shows traces of this recovered *materia hungarica*. Up to that time the field had long been neglected largely because alluring music parading under the assumed name of "Hungarian" had been flooding European cafés and concert halls for decades. Gypsy bands and Budapest dinner ensembles were mainly responsible for the false harmonies and melodic intervals foisted upon original folk melodies. The prestige of Liszt, Brahms, and Joachim, much of whose music was flavored with this tampered material, was to be reckoned with, too.

There was no quarrel with the frank appeal of this "gypsy-Hungarian" music. The danger, as Kodály and Bártok saw it, was that the authentic Hungarian folk note would be lost forever in the growing acceptance of a spurious substitute.

In a biography of his collaborator, Bártok points out that his style "owes much of its character to the individual musical idiom that Kodály has created for himself out of the Hungarian peasant music he has collected."

L. B.

"Dances from Galanta"

THE FOLLOWING note prefaces the score of this composition:

Galanta is a small Hungarian market town known to travelers between Vienna and Budapest. The composer passed there seven years of his childhood. There existed at that time a gypsy band which has since disappeared. Their music was the first "orchestral sonority" which came to the ear of the child. The forbears of these gypsies were known more than a hundred years ago. About 1800, some books of Hungarian dances were published in Vienna, one of which contained music "after several gypsies from Galanta." They have preserved the old Hungarian tradition. In order to continue it, the composer took his principal subjects from these ancient editions.

Composed in 1934 for the eightieth anniversary of the Philharmonic Society of Budapest, the *Dances from Galanta* are, in fact, separate items, but they are strung together in a chain through the use of recurring material.

The composition opens with a solo cello theme both characteristic and marked. Wood winds and strings offer a speedy passage, and soon the horns repeat the theme. It is then elaborated upon, going to a cadenza for the clarinet and from there to an erratic sort of tune, andante maestoso, which is also played by the clarinet to a string accompaniment. During the course of the piece this little tune comes through quite frequently. Now there is a contrasting melody, vivacious and positive, announced by flutes and taken up by clarinets and violins, whereupon the erratic melody returns, this time in a different form, among the wood winds and strings, with the horns and tympani providing the accompaniment. A short allegro section is given mainly to oboes and flutes, and, following a short, more animated sequence, there appears another andante maestoso. A syncopated idea filters through the orchestral web, gradually increasing to a fortissimo of almost rowdy energy. Against a solid rhythm another melody is begun by the clarinet and picked up by the flute. It gets some treatment and then gives way to an allegro vivace. A sprightly theme springs up in flutes and first violins. It becomes stronger and more positive, and with several references to other themes, especially the syncopated one, the music gets more sonorous and excited, and suddenly everything breaks off. There is a brief pause of silence. Then the wayward melody is heard again, played softly and tenderly, now, played by the wood winds, in turn, while the strings supply the accompaniment. There is a cadenza for the clarinet, leading to an allegro molto vivace, and this brings the movement to a close.

R. C. B.

Ernst Krenek

BORN: VIENNA, AUG. 23, 1900.

Speaking very concretely from the standpoint of the everyday experi-
ence of a twelve-tone composer, the predicament is exactly this:
working along the lines of the "classical" technique, we find ourselves
every now and then embarrassed by the necessity of locating remain-
ing tones of the series, even when we would not "feel like that." The
meaning of this plight is simply that the series pattern suited us well
in the beginning of a certain musical complex, but that our "intui-
tion" took us, during the process of composing, some other way.
—ERNST KRENEK, *in a letter to George Perle.*

Variations on a North Carolina Folk Song
"I Wonder As I Wander," Op. 94

THE COMPOSITION was inspired by a recording of John Jacob Niles's rendering of the folk song "I Wonder As I Wander." Mr. Krenek has given the authors the following information:

My attention was aroused not only by the unique intensity with which Mr. Niles performed this song, which he had discovered in North Carolina, but also by the very unusual modal pattern of the simple and moving tune. Some time later Mr. Mitropoulos let me know that he was interested in my recent work in composition, and this fact prompted me to use the folk song, which had impressed me so deeply, as a symphonic piece. Mr. Niles and the publishing house G. Schirmer were good enough to grant their permission for doing so. The composition was finished on July 1, 1942, in Madison, Wis.

It is a set of seven variations arranged to follow in broad lines the structure of a first movement of a symphony (exposition, development, etc.). I have attempted to unfold the feelings of tragic loneliness and passionate devotion by which the solitary wanderer "under the sky" of the old song is animated.

The words of the song "I Wonder As I Wander" are:

> I wonder as I wander out under the sky,
> How Jesus the Saviour did come to die
> For poor on'ry people like you and I.
> I wonder as I wander out under the sky.
>
> When Mary birthed Jesus 'twas in a cow's stall,
> With wise men and farmers and shepherds and all.
> But high from the heavens a star's light did fall,
> And the promise of ages it then did recall.

If Jesus had wanted for any wee thing,
A star in the sky or a bird on the wing
Or all of God's angels in heaven to sing,
He surely could have had it, 'cause He was the King.

Ernst Krenek has gone through the process of "evolution of style" through experimentation with many styles. In that respect he probably stands alone in his mercurial glory. A pupil of Franz Schreker's, Krenek wrote his earliest works in the late-romantic idiom, in which, of course, he had been industriously schooled by Schreker. He was not long in turning to atonality, which was the modish thing to do, what with the great number of French and German composers who had taken it up. Besides, it represented a welcome change from the heavy mysticism of Schreker's music.

His investigations soon brought him to American jazz, and it was in this field that he wrote his greatest success, the opera *Jonny spielt auf!* The piece, at first rejected by several German companies, finally was introduced at Leipzig, in 1927, and in no time at all it made sensational headway in that it was produced in over a hundred cities (in New York at the Metropolitan Opera House) and translated into eighteen languages. He became famous practically overnight. The young darling of the intellectuals was now a world figure.

He had written five operas before *Jonny,* but that was the one destined to bring his name almost into every household. Still other operas followed. There came an imposing array of works in every conceivable form. Then in 1932, or thereabouts, he suddenly took up the twelve-tone technique, first advanced by Arnold Schönberg. He has since been unswervingly devoted to that. When his *Karl V,* an opera on the subject of the Roman Church vs. the Reformation, was first given in Prague, June 22, 1938, H. H. Stuckenschmidt, covering the event for *Musical America,* reported:

Technically he [the composer] follows the dogma of twelve-tone music as used in Berg's *Lulu,* Schönberg's *Von haute auf Morgen,* Winifred Zillig's *Das Opfer,* Paul von Klenau's *Rembrandt van Rijn,* and other operas of the last decade. But his music is by far the most radical of them all.

The question has been put: Which Krenek ought we to believe, the youth of premature radicalism, the manager of jazz opera and fake classicism, or the new Krenek of the twelve-tone-espressivo music? Without answering that, one may retort that it is to the honor of any artist when he works back from cheap success to the sphere of pure and intellectually refined art.

R. C. B.

Édouard Lalo

BORN: LILLE, FRANCE, JAN. 27, 1823. DIED: PARIS, APR. 22, 1892.

Lalo entered into the very soul of this elemental music and in every case revealed only its noblest essence without any external over-elaboration.—LEOPOLD AUER.

"Symphonie Espagnole," for Violin and Orchestra, Op. 21

I. Allegro non troppo. II. Scherzando: Allegro molto. III. Intermezzo (usually omitted). IV. Andante. V. Rondo.

LALO'S SPANISH ancestry is often brought up in connection with the *Symphonie Espagnole,* though the use of Spanish titles, themes, and locales has been a recurring practice with French composers, whether of Spanish extraction or not. One thinks offhand of Chabrier, Bizet, Debussy, Ravel. The list can be lengthened. In Lalo's day the Parisian ambient was flooded with Spanish art, and musical rhythms and sequences easily found their way into his second extended work for violin and orchestra.

A further exotic angle is observable in the dedication. Lalo wrote the *Symphonie* for that phenomenal Spanish violinist Pablo de Sarasate, who played the solo part at the premiere on Feb. 7, 1875, at a Concert Colonne at the Châtelet, Paris. In short, a combination of Spanish family origins, Spanish fadism, and Spanish soloist prompted Lalo to write a *Spanish Symphony.* Lalo had spent most of the year 1874 composing it. Possibly still another stimulus had come from the success of his Violin Concerto, Op. 20, also dedicated to Sarasate. The performance of the earlier work, with the Spanish violinist also the soloist, at a Châtelet concert in 1874, had extended Lalo's following. Almost overnight he had become a concert favorite, having previously enjoyed the dubious honor of being styled "a musicians' composer."

Incidentally, Sarasate's bow was something of a magic wand. Several other repertory stand-bys received its premiere touch and went into a long life, Bruch's Second Concerto and *Scottish Fantasy* and Saint-Saëns' B minor Concerto among them.

The *Symphonie Espagnole,* as written, is in five movements, though the third, entitled "Intermezzo," is generally omitted. In the opening movement (Allegro non troppo, D minor, 2/2) fragments of the first theme are bandied about by orchestra and solo violin before the orchestra takes up its full development and passes the theme on to the solo voice, which embroiders it along its own lines. Presently the violin announces the second theme, in B flat major.

In the Scherzando movement (Allegro molto, G major, 3/8) brisk orchestral preluding, with the strings pizzicato, leads to a lyrical waltz theme on the solo violin, the wind instruments offering a triplet figure soon echoed by the violin. After a sprightly middle section, involving quick changes of tempo and tonality, the opening section is repeated. The usually omitted Intermezzo movement (Allegretto non troppo, A minor, 2/4) enshrines a beautiful melody for solo violin in E minor. In the fourth movement (Andante, D minor, 3/4) the wind instruments enter first, chanting a cantabile theme promptly taken up by the violins, after which the solo voice sings a plain-spun melody, followed by a florid one. There is a return of the first solo subject and then a peaceful coda. A saltarello-like theme for solo violin, entering after a lively orchestral preface, dominates the Rondo finale (Allegro, D major, 6/8).

The orchestral scoring is for two flutes, piccolo, two oboes, two clarinets, two bassoons, four horns, two trumpets, three trombones, kettledrums, snare drum, triangle, harp, and strings.

Lalo studied both violin and cello at the conservatory in his native Lille before enrolling in Habeneck's violin class at the Paris Conservatory in 1839. He also took private lessons in composition. Later he broadened his acquaintance with the string family by playing viola in the Armingaud-Jacquard Quartet. Cool public response to his music long tempted him to give up composing. In fact, for seven years—1858 to 1865—he wrote practically nothing. Then he fell in love with and married the beautiful contralto Julie Marie Victoire de Maligny, a pupil of his, and with love and marriage came renewed inspiration and ambition.

Yet, Lalo went on suffering neglect and disappointment as a composer, until in 1872, an orchestral divertissement on a Concert Populaire program was warmly received. Two years later the violin concerto brought him his first real success, followed by the still greater triumph of the *Symphonie Espagnole*. In 1882 Lalo's ballet *Namouna* served to confirm his rare skill as orchestrator. His crowning achievement, though, the opera, *Le Roi d'Ys,* was not produced till 1888. The overture, long a popular concert item, had already been premiered eleven years before.

Lalo's fearless and independent character was discussed some years ago by Philip Hale. He pointed out that Lalo, unwaveringly opposed to making concessions or compromises and never mastering the art of fawning and scheming, "was not the man to be welcomed by managers of opera houses." Hale goes on to say:

He was not in the habit of writing salon music, so his name was not known to amateurs. When a ballet master of the Opera urged him to study Adolphe Adam as a model, Lalo replied: "Do you think I am going to make music like that of *Giselle* for you?" . . . Disappointment followed Lalo to the end. He was not chosen a member of the Institute, for he would not pull wires for an election. He did not finish his last opera. His death during the commotion excited by dynamiters at Paris awakened little attention, and there were no funeral eulogies in the journals; but nearly all the French musicians of renown were present at his burial and thus paid tribute to a composer of the highest character and talent. . . .

Lalo's personality during his later years has been described as follows: Slight in stature, he limped a little as the result of paralysis, which attacked him during the rehearsals of *Namouna*. He was otherwise of distinguished appearance, fastidious in dress, with a good deal of color in his cheeks, bright-eyed, with snow-white hair and a white beard and moustache, "which gave him the appearance of an Austrian diplomat." . . . He thought unfavorably of much of the music that was heard in the opera house, but he was not in sympathy with German radical theories concerning the music drama. His temperament was French; he was honest, and he insisted on clearness in art.

L. B.

Concerto for Violoncello and Orchestra in D minor

I. Prelude: Lento. Allegro maestoso. II. Intermezzo: Andante con moto. III. Rondo: Andante. Allegro vivace.

LALO DEDICATED his Cello Concerto to Adolphe Fischer, who played it for the first time at the Cirque d'Hiver, Paris, Jules Etienne Pasdeloup conducting, on Dec. 9, 1877.

A Lento introduction lasting twenty-two bars leads into the main section of the first movement (Allegro maestoso in D minor, 12/8), in strict sonata form. Both the main theme and the second are first given out by the cello.

In the second movement—Intermezzo—the first theme (Andante con moto, G minor, 9/8) is discoursed by the cello after a few prefatory bars. With a shift to the major key, the cello subsequently offers a new melody, Allegro presto, in 6/8 time. Both themes undergo varied treatment.

A short Andante prefaces the finale (Allegro vivace, 6/8) which shapes up to a brilliant rondo.

Lalo also wrote a sonata for piano and cello, premiered in Paris the same year, besides a few shorter pieces for cello, among them a *Chanson villageoise* and a *Sérénade,* dating from an earlier period.

L. B.

Overture to the Opera "Le Roi d'Ys"

FROM AN old Breton legend of the submerged city of Ys, Édouard Blau fashioned the libretto for Lalo's three-act opera *Le Roi d'Ys* (The King of Ys). The same story inspired Debussy's celebrated piano piece *La Cathédrale engloutie* (*The Engulfed Cathedral*).

Although Lalo had begun work on the best known of his three operas in 1876, it was not till 1881 that he had sketched out the whole work, and not till May 7, 1888, that it was produced by the Paris Opéra Comique. As early as 1876, however, Lalo entrusted Adolphe Theophile Manoury, one of the chief baritones of the Paris Opéra, with an aria from *Le Roi d'Ys* for a concert of the Société Nationale. And, several years before the premiere of the opera, the Overture had already begun its popular career in the concert halls.

Though the American premiere of *Le Roi d'Ys* occurred in New Orleans on Jan. 23, 1890, New York waited till 1922 for a hearing. Early that year the Metropolitan Opera Company produced it with a cast headed by Frances Alda (Rozenn), Rosa Ponselle (Margared), Beniamino Gigli (Mylio), Giuseppe Danise (Karnac), and Léon Rothier (the King). In a sense, the production was a long-deferred fulfillment of a promise made by the management thirty-two years earlier. The prospectus of the German season of 1889-1890 had included Lalo's *Le Roi d'Ys* among its plans. Despite the brilliant cast, the opera aroused small response. After the five performances of the 1921-1922 season, *Le Roi d'Ys* returned to its slumbers.

Today, the opera is remembered largely because of the Overture and Mylio's aria "Vainement, ma bien-aimée"—a beautiful aubade, the melody of which Lalo borrowed from a Breton folk song. As for Lalo himself, he is best known to concertgoers as the composer of the *Symphonie Espagnole*. Most critics would agree that his orchestral writing far excels his operatic in grasp of style and imaginative force.

The story of *Le Roi d'Ys* centers in a court triangle. Margared and Rozenn, daughters of the King of Ys—or Is as it is sometimes spelled—both love the young knight Mylio. Of the two, the warrior prefers Rozenn for her gentle disposition, Margared being the domineering type. During Karnac's absence, Margared has been promised as bride to Karnac, a neighboring prince long at war with the city of Ys. All are assured the marriage will bring hostilities to an end. Margared, however, changes her mind when Mylio returns from the wars. Thus rebuffed Prince Karnac challenges his foe to fresh battle, and Mylio accepts. In the ensuing fight, Karnac is defeated. But all is not lost, for Margared, a prey now to jealousy because of her sister's approaching marriage to Mylio, shows him how to turn the tables on his foes. All he need do is to open the floodgates, for the city is protected by a dyke. The prince eagerly accepts her plan, and soon, as Rozenn and Mylio are being wed, Margared gives a wild shout: the sea is pouring into the doomed city! Remorseful now, she cries out that the flood will rise "till it reaches its prey." At length, as the people run for safety to the hills, Margared confesses her guilt and, climbing to the highest peak, plunges into the swirling waters. Thereupon Saint Corentin appears on the surface of the sea and the flood waters miraculously ebb away.

In the overture to *Le Roi d'Ys* Lalo quite plainly sought to epitomize the dominant moods and action of his opera, as well as to introduce the three central characters in their most revealing moments. In the introductory section of the Overture a clarinet solo presents the valiant Mylio by way of a melody borrowed from the knight's defiant aria "Si le ciel est plein de flammes" ("If the sky is full of flames"), which appears in the first act. This introductory passage is divided by a flourish of trumpets from the Overture proper, which begins with an Allegro in D minor, largely depicting the conflicting emotions of Margared —her love for Mylio, her hatred of the suitor forced upon her, and her jealousy of her sister Rozenn. The trumpet figure reappears in a new guise, and we presently made the acquaintance of the gentle Rozenn herself through an Andantino in B flat major built around the girl's tender query, "En silence pourquoi souffrir?" ("Why do you suffer in silence?"). Earlier material is then reviewed briefly, and the Overture ends brilliantly on the theme of Mylio's forceful aria.

L. B.

Anatol Liadoff

BORN: ST. PETERSBURG, MAY 10, 1855. DIED: NOVGOROD, AUG. 28, 1914.

He has neither the power and glow of Borodin and Balakireff, nor the exuberant fancy of Rimsky-Korsakoff at his best, nor the energy and abundance of Glazounoff; but of the minor poets of music—not only Russian—he remains one of the most lovable.—M. D. CALVOCORESSI.

"Le Lac Enchanté" ("The Enchanted Lake"), Legend for Orchestra, Op. 62

LIADOFF EARNED the dubious reputation of being the laziest man of Russian music. Rimsky-Korsakoff often chided him on his indolence. This failing once cost him the chance to write the music for *The Firebird* ballet. The prospect of large-scale composition appalled him. Dozens of projects were abandoned from sheer lack of will power. And Liadoff was hounded by another evil—ruthless self-criticism. He was shy, modest to a fault, and he loathed publicity. He wrote slowly and painfully. The facility of Rimsky, Glazounoff, and Tschaikowsky often filled him with despair. He was sensitive and retiring. So this lone, timid man, fearful of life and reality, retreated into a world of his own—a place of magic spells, and dragons and mermaids . . . and enchanted lakes. "The world," he explained, "is tedious, disappointing, trying, purposeless, terrible." Anatol Constantinovich Liadoff escaped into fairyland.

Liadoff's lethargic temperament is reflected in the way *Le Lac Enchanté* came to be written. In 1905, after much coaxing and cajoling by colleagues, he began work on a ballet. "May his artistic conscience continue to stimulate and sustain him!" was the fervent prayer of one friend. The prayer went unanswered. The ballet remained unfinished. At this point, Rimsky stepped in with a suggestion that his slothful friend write an opera. To strengthen the appeal, he even suggested "a legendary opera." Liadoff was enthusiastic. This time he firmly resolved to shake off his lethargy long enough to keep his promise to Rimsky. But indolence, or weak will, or modesty, again set in. The plan remained a plan. All that survived were some musical sketches. And these later found their way into the tone poems *Kikimora* and *The Enchanted Lake*.

Like other symphonic works of Liadoff—notably *Baba Yaga* and *Kikimora*—*Le Lac Enchanté* weaves a spell of eerie legendry. Liadoff supplied no clue to its program beyond the title. Knowing Liadoff's tastes and temperament, we readily sense a tale of unearthly doings. The gleam of magic moods is on this music. One seems to glimpse the bewitched lake, ringed by towering pines mirrored in its surface. Somewhere, doubtless, are the phantoms and nymphs who peopled Liadoff's imaginative world. "My ideal," he once said, "is to find the unearthly in art. Art is the realm of the nonexisting. Art is a figment, a fairy tale, a phantom. Give me a fairy tale, a dragon, a water sprite, a wood demon—give me something that is unreal, and I am happy."

Recurring through Liadoff's tone picture is the gently shimmering theme of the lake, first heard among muted strings in D flat major. The score calls for three flutes, two oboes, three clarinets, two bassoons, four horns, tympani, bass drum, celesta, harp, and strings. *Le Lac Enchanté,* together with its companion piece *Kikimora,* was dedicated to Nicolai Tcherepnin. The two tone poems were first performed in America at a New York concert by the Russian Symphony Orchestra on Nov. 16, 1910.

L. B.

"Kikimora," Legend for Full Orchestra, Op. 63

THE WORD Kikimora, or Shishimora (cognate with or borrowed from the French *cauchemar*) is associated with "nightmare." On the flyleaf of the published score of Liadoff's *Legend* appears a résumé of the folk tale by Sakharoff from which its program is derived.

Kikimora [the phantom] is brought up by a sorceress in the mountains. In his youth he is beguiled, from early morn to late at night, by the tales of foreign lands told by the sorceress' Magic Cat. From night to dawn Kikimora is rocked in a crystal cradle.

In seven years the phantom grows up. Shiny and black, its head is as small as a thimble, and its body as thin as a straw. Kikimora makes all manner of noises from morning to night and whistles and hisses from early evening to midnight.

Then the phantom spins till daylight; spins and stores up evil in its mind against all mankind.

"Eight Russian Folk Songs," Op. 58

A COMMITTEE MADE up of Liadoff, Liapounoff, and Balakireff was once delegated by the Russian Imperial Geographical Society to make a survey of folk music in certain Russian localities. The incident indicates the recognition Liadoff had won in this field. His settings are regarded as unique in the way they preserve the genuine spirit of the originals. The rich allegory and what has been described as the "pagan and even prehistoric ritual" characterizing Russian folk songs inspired some of Liadoff's best work.

According to the scholar Swan, writing in *The Chesterian,* Liadoff's harmonizations are distinguished by certain peculiar traits that fit the songs to an almost incredible degree.

Such are his universal use of the major and natural minor only, the absence of modulations within one song, the gradual blossoming out of the accompaniment into exquisite figuring, graceful contrapuntal phrases.

Applied with an elegance, taste, and economy, which is yet exuberant, they make Liadoff's settings unique from a purely musical point of view.

Dedicated to J. Bilibin, *Eight Russian Folk Songs* appeared in 1906. The sequence is marked as follows: I. "Religious Song" (Moderato, G major, 2/2); II. "Christmas Song" (Allegretto, E minor, 2/4); III. "Plaintive Melody" (Andante, A minor, 4/4); IV. "Scherzo" (Chant Comique), "I Danced with the Gnat" (Allegretto, A major, 2/4); V. "Legend of the Birds" (Allegretto, D minor, 2/4); VI. "Lullaby" (Moderato, A minor, 3/4); VII. "Dance Song" (Allegro, G major, 2/4), and VIII. "Village Dance" (Vivo, C major, 2/4).

L. B.

Franz Liszt

BORN: RAIDING, NEAR OEDENBURG, HUNGARY, OCT. 22, 1811. DIED: BAYREUTH, GERMANY, JULY 31, 1886.

Then came the thing I had longed for—his playing. I sat near him so that I could see both his hands and face. For the first time in my life I beheld real inspiration—for the first time I heard the true tones of the piano. . . . There was nothing strange or excessive about his manner. His manipulation of the instrument was quiet and easy, and his face was simply grand—the lips compressed and the head thrown backward. When the music expressed quiet rapture or devotion a smile flitted over his features; when it was triumphant the nostrils dilated. There was nothing petty or egotistic to mar the picture.
—GEORGE ELIOT.

Concerto for Piano and Orchestra in E flat major, No. 1

To EDUARD HANSLICK goes the doubtful honor of having silenced this concerto for twelve years with a phrase. When Dionys Pruckner, a Liszt pupil, first played the work in Vienna in 1857, the caustic critic of the *Wiener Presse* promptly dubbed it "The Triangle Concerto." Liszt, emboldened by the examples of Haydn, Beethoven, and Schumann, had dared pontifical wrath by bringing the lowly accessory into a symphonic score. To round off phrases of the scherzo theme he calls for tiny rhythmic strokes on the triangle.

The tag stuck. Not until 1869 did any pianist work up courage enough to defy Vienna's high priest of criticism and the stigma laid upon the concerto. The challenger was a twenty-five-year-old girl from Munich named Sophie Menter. Sophie's friends and colleagues uttered dire warnings. Anton Rubinstein sharply reprimanded her: "You can't be so crazy as to play this concerto!" He told her there was a twelve-year curse on it. Sophie's reply has come down to us in her native patois: *"Wenn I dös nit spielen kann, spiel i goar nit—i muss ja nit in Wien spielen"* ("If I can't play it, I don't play at all—I must not play in Vienna.") Given such determination, it is not surprising to learn the performance was a huge success. If Hanslick coined a fresh phrase for the occasion, it has been lost.

In structure the E flat major Concerto is closer to the symphonic poem than the standard concerto. The form is free, with several themes announced, developed, and modified in time and rhythm. There are four major sections, roughly corresponding to four symphonic movements. But they merge freely and lack the customary development.

The first of the four principal themes is stated by the strings, broken into by wood winds and brasses (Allegro maestoso, tempo giusto, 4/4). Liszt supposedly sang words to this theme, given in one version as *"Das versteht ihr nicht!"* and in another as *"Ihr könnt alle nichts!"* In either case far from a compliment to the listening world! There follows an elaborate cadenza.

Muted cellos and double basses announce the second theme (Quasi adagio, 12/8) and give it to the piano to enlarge on. The third theme (Allegretto vivace, 3/4)—announced scherzolike by the strings with the triangle effects—is preceded by a long trill on the piano. As for the triangle strokes, Liszt cautions that they are to be made with great precision. The piano develops the theme, capriccioso scherzando, and a cadenza ends the section.

The fourth theme, described as "an answer to the chief phrase of the second rather than a separate theme," recurs throughout the work, given first to the orchestra, then to the piano. A rhapsodic Allegro animato leads into the finale, with a return of the chief subject. The finale (Allegro marziale animato, 4/4) recapitulates earlier material at brisker rhythms and quickens to a presto.

Liszt himself wrote at some length about this concerto in a letter to his uncle Eduard Liszt, dated Mar. 26, 1857, from Weimar:

The fourth movement of the Concerto from the Allegro marziale corresponds with the second movement, Adagio. It is only an urgent recapitulation of the earlier subject matter with quickened, livelier rhythm, and contains no new motive, as will be clear to you by a glance through the score. This kind of *binding together* and rounding off of a whole piece at its close is somewhat my own, but it is quite maintained and justified from the standpoint of musical form.

The trombones and basses take up the second part of the motive of the Adagio (B major). The pianoforte figure which follows is no other than the reproduction of the motive which was given in the Adagio by flute and clarinet, just as the concluding passage is a Variante and working up in the major of the motive of the scherzo until finally the first motive on the dominant pedal B flat, with a shake accompaniment, comes in and concludes the whole.

The scherzo in E flat minor, from the point where the triangle begins, I employed for the effect of contrast.

As regards the triangle, I do not deny that it may give offence, especially if struck too strong and not precisely. A preconceived disinclination and objection to instruments of percussion prevails, somewhat justified by the frequent misuse of them. And few conductors are circumspect enough to bring out the rhythmic element in them, without the raw addition of a coarse noisiness, in works in which they are deliberately employed according to the intention of the composer.

The dynamic and rhythmic spicing and enhancement, which are affected by the instruments of percussion, would in more cases be much more effectually produced by the careful trying and proportioning of insertions and additions of that kind. But musicians who wish to appear serious and solid prefer to treat the instruments of percussion *en canaille*, which must not make their appearance in the seemly company of the symphony. They also bitterly deplore, inwardly, that Beethoven allowed himself to be seduced into using the big drum and triangle in the Finale of the Ninth Symphony.

Of Berlioz, Wagner, and my humble self it is no wonder that "like draws to like," and, as we are treated as impotent *canaille* among musicians, it is quite natural that we should be on good terms with the *canaille* among the instruments. Certainly here, as in all else, it is the right thing to seize upon and hold fast [the] mass of harmony. In face of the most wise proscription of the learned critics I shall, however, continue to employ instruments of percussion and think I shall yet win for them some effects little known.

Specific dates of composition are lacking for this concerto. The likeliest years are 1848 and 1849. A revision was made sometime in 1853, and the work was published by Haslinger of Vienna in 1857, the year of its Viennese premiere by Pruckner at a so-called Spirituelle Konzert. The world premiere had occurred on Feb. 17, 1855, during part of a "Berlioz Week" at Weimar, the concerto being the single non-Berlioz work programed. Berlioz conducted and Liszt was soloist.

The record reveals its American premiere as occurring on Apr. 20, 1867, at a concert of the New York Philharmonic Society. The well-buttressed name of Sebastian Bach Mills is given as that of the soloist.

L. B.

Concerto for Piano and Orchestra in A major, No. 2

THE WORLD premiere of Liszt's Second Piano Concerto occurred in the Grand Ducal Theater at Weimar on Jan. 7, 1857, at a concert sponsored by Hans von Bronsart for the benefit of the Weimar Orchestra's pension fund.

Bronsart, a Berlin pianist, composer, and conductor, who had studied with Liszt in Weimar, was the soloist. The composer conducted. Billed on the same program was the first performance anywhere of Liszt's symphonic poem *Ce qu'on entend sur la montagne*. Bronsart was himself represented by a piano trio.

The first sketch of the A major Concerto dates back to September, 1839, and is preserved in manuscript in the Liszt Museum at Weimar. There is some uncertainty about just when Liszt completed the work, though by August, 1849, we find him informing the composer Raff that the orchestral scores of both the A major and E flat major Concertos had just been copied.

However, Liszt revised the Concerto shortly before the Weimar premiere, when Bronsart played it from manuscript. Further revision was made in 1861. A two-piano arrangement appeared the following year, and the Concerto was finally published in 1863. Labeled a *Concert Symphonique* in the manuscript, the work is dedicated to Bronsart.

Like the First Concerto, the A major is in one movement and built along similar lines of free thematic change. A glowing romanticism runs rampant through it. The dreamy, plaintive melody, first announced by the wood winds (Adagio sostenuto assai, A major, 3/4), alters repeatedly in mood, color, and shape, finally thundering out like a victory chant.

It was William Foster Apthorp's opinion that if Liszt had seen fit to give the Concerto a poetic or dramatic title, he would have devised something like "The Life and Adventures of a Melody." Following up this idea, Apthorp, usually a strictly objective analyst, wrote a brilliant biography of the chief theme that deserves being quoted:

The melody or hero of this poem in tones is announced at once on the wooden wind instruments. Both its melodic cut and its harmonization are such as no one but Liszt ever imagined. It is a sort of wild musical moan and wail, accompanied by harmonies ever shifting in tonality. Soon the pianoforte throws over it a network of sonorous arpeggi, adorns it with the richest embroidery. A cadenzalike passage leads to a more brilliant, fitful motive which is developed with great energy by both pianoforte and orchestra, until a third allegro motive is introduced. Of any distinct musical form here it is impossible to speak, all is so fitful, kaleidoscopic, and stormy.

When the hurricane has blown over, a brief reminiscence of the wailing principal theme on the pianoforte leads to the announcement of a new melody in the strings: it is as if a second movement were begun. But no, the pianoforte takes up once more the old moan, the melody emphasized by the cello intersperses its phrases with snatches of the new theme that has just been given out by the strings, until it at last develops the latter with ever-growing passionateness, then with magical effects of light and color.

From this point onward the Concerto is one unbroken series of kaleidoscopic effects of the most brilliant and ever-changing description; of musical form, of musical coherence even, there is less and less. It is as if some magician in some huge cave, the walls of which were covered with glistening stalactites and flashing jewels, were reveling his fill of all the wonders of color, brilliancy, and dazzling light his wand could command. Never has even Liszt rioted more unreservedly in fitful orgies of flashing color. It is monstrous, formless, whimsical, and fantastic, if you will; but it is also magical and gorgeous as anything in the *Arabian Nights*. It is its very daring and audacity that save it.

And ever and anon the first wailing melody, with unearthly chromatic harmony, returns in one shape or another, as if it were the dazzled neophyte to whom the magician Liszt were showing all these splendors, while initiating it into the mysteries of the world of magic, until it, too, becomes magical and possessed of the power of working wonders by black art.

L. B.

"Mephisto Waltz"

KNOWN ALSO as *Der Tanz in der Dorfschenke,* this is the second of two pieces grouped under the title *Two Episodes from Lenau's "Faust."* The present work was begun in 1858 and finished in January, 1861, at Weimar, where it got its first performance in the Grand Ducal castle under Liszt's direction. Several other compositions of Liszt's were inspired by Lenau's *Faust.* He produced a second *Mephisto Waltz* for piano in 1880, later arranging it for orchestra. A third was written for piano in 1881 and *A Mephisto Polka* for the same instrument in 1883. The composer even began a fourth *Mephisto Waltz,* again for piano, but never completed it.

The score of this *Mephisto Waltz* carries a long quotation from Lenau's poem. Following is its essence:

A peasant wedding is being celebrated with song and dance in a village tavern. Mephistopheles, disguised as a hunter, and Faust peer through the window, and Mephistopheles beckons to his companion to enter the room with him. Faust is captivated by a black-eyed damsel, but is not daring enough to greet her. Mephistopheles laughs at him "who has just had it out with hell, and is now abashed before a woman." Suddenly he addresses the musicians. "Dear fellows," he cries, "you draw your bows much too sleepily. Sick pleasure may dance on lame toes to your waltz, but not youth, filled with blood and fire! Give me the fiddle; in my hands it will sound differently, and there will be another kind of springing in the tavern!" Mephistopheles plays. The dancing becomes wild; the souls of the dancers are filled with strange emotions; Faust presses the hand of the dark-eyed girl, and stammers oaths of love. Together they dance through the open door, through the meadows and garden paths, and with the strains of the violin floating to their ears, dance on until they reach the forest. Fainter and fainter becomes the sound of the music as it is heard through the singing of nightingales.

Liszt scored this *Mephisto Waltz* for an orchestra consisting of three flutes (third interchangeable with piccolo), two oboes, two clarinets, two bassoons, four horns, two trumpets, three trombones, bass tuba, kettledrums, cymbals, triangle, harp, and strings. The composer dedicated the music to Karl Tausig.

R. C. B.

Symphonic Poem, "Les Préludes" (after Lamartine)

APART FROM his other claims to fame, Franz Liszt was the father of the "symphonic poem." Following the example of Berlioz, Liszt sought to amplify the "program" possibilities of symphonic music, and with Berlioz he broke away from the strict dictates of sonata form. In the symphonic poem Liszt achieved a new kind of musical and poetic unity. There was freedom here, but at the same time there was the nuclear idea of the program that imparted a new coherence. Liszt composed thirteen such symphonic poems. Of these *Les Préludes* is the third and perhaps the one best typifying the thematic and cyclical structure used. Certainly it is the best known. Here the fabric is woven out of two basic motives, varied and developed according to the shifting moods of Lamartine's romantic verses, from pastoral peace to stormy crisis and ultimate triumph. The lines from the *Méditations Poétiques* prefacing Liszt's score have been translated as follows:

What is our life but a series of preludes to that unknown song, the first solemn note of which is sounded by death? Love forms the enchanted daybreak of every life; but what is the destiny where the first delights of happiness are not interrupted by storm, whose fatal breath dissipates its fair illusions, whose fell lightning consumes its altar.

And what wounded spirit, when one of its tempests is over, does not seek to rest its memories in the sweet calm of country life? Yet man does not resign himself long to enjoy the beneficent tepidity which first charmed him on Nature's bosom.

And when the "trumpet's loud clangor has called him to arms," he rushes to the post of danger, whatever may be the war that calls him to the ranks, to find in battle the full consciousness of himself and the complete possession of his strength.

Les Préludes is scored for three flutes, piccolo, two oboes, two clarinets, two bassoons, four horns, two trumpets, three trombones, bass tuba, kettledrums, snare drum, bass drum, cymbals, harp, and strings.

Les Préludes was written in 1854 and first performed at a Pension Fund Concert of the Court Orchestra at Weimar on Feb. 23, 1854. The genesis of this symphonic poem, however, reaches as far back as 1844, when Liszt contemplated writing a cantata, using a second-rate poem by Aubray as text. The wretched verses discouraged Liszt, and he appealed to Victor Hugo for advice, hoping that Titan would propose writing a substitute text for him. The idea left Hugo cold, so Liszt turned to Lamartine's *Méditations poétiques* (second series) and wrote his third *Symphonic Poem,* instead. Hugo was not altogether excluded from the collaboration, for Lamartine had dedicated the poem to him.

L. B.

Charles Martin Loeffler

BORN: MULHOUSE, ALSACE, JAN. 30, 1861. DIED: MEDFIELD, MASS., MAY 19, 1935.

The soul of a supersensitive child, suddenly brought to maturity by a precocious shock and emotion of a powerful nature, might well be imagined to lie at the bottom of the exquisite sensitivity, the penumbral delicateness, which one is ever aware of in Loeffler the man and musician.—CARL ENGEL.

Symphonic Poem, "Memories of My Childhood"

THREE YEARS of Charles Martin Loeffler's boyhood were spent in a Russian village near the town of Smjela in the Government of Kiev. More than a half century later, during the fall of 1923, Loeffler put down in music what still lingered "in his heart and memory of those happy days." When finished, the composition was entitled *Memories of My Childhood*. Among these memories were strains of Russian peasant songs, the famous litany prayer "God Have Mercy on Us," moods out of fairy tales of long ago, and songs that were danced to. In the closing section of the Symphonic Poem, Loeffler commemorated the death of Vasinka. He was an elderly peasant—*Bayan* or storyteller—a singer, a maker of willow pipes, "upon which he played tunes of weird intervals," and the companion and friend of the boy "who now, later in life, notes down what he hopes these pages will tell," as a prefatory note in the score explains.

Memories of My Childhood was submitted in a contest held by the Chicago North Shore Festival Association and won the prize of $1,000. The judges who heard it at a public rehearsal in Evanston, Ill., as one of four scores picked from eighty-three entries were Adolf Weidig, Ernest Schelling, and Deems Taylor. The date of this hearing was May 29, 1924. The following day, Frederick Stock conducted the Chicago Symphony Orchestra in the official premiere of the score at one of the Festival concerts in the Northwestern University Gymnasium, at Evanston. Loeffler's own analysis of the music, made at the request of Felix Borowski, program annotator of the Chicago Symphony, follows:

Accompanying the distant sound of church bells, the cellos and double basses give out the first theme—a Russian peasant song, this, in its turn, being taken up by the violas and violins. A short melodic and rhythmical diversion leads to a short ecclesiastical section, in which the litany "God have Mercy upon Us" prepares the way for the exultant mood of childhood happiness—an episode in E major, 5/4 time. A Fairy Tale, which follows, is succeeded by a Dance, whose theme is sustained by four harmonicas. The Dance subject, which is of Russian origin, is introduced by the clarinet and piccolo alternately, the violas then taking up the subject, molto tranquillo. The trombones twice repeat the opening theme, its mood being one of sorrow for the death of a beloved friend—the peasant Vasinka. The conclusion of the work has for its basic motive the same opening subject, given to the cellos and double basses. Fifteen measures later there is heard distant music of cheerful character, such as may bring sunshine to those who sit in the darkness of grief, and it is in this mood of hope and consolation that the work is brought to a conclusion.

The extensive scoring calls for three flutes (the third interchangeable with piccolo), two oboes, English horn, two clarinets, bass clarinet, two bassoons, double bassoon, four horns, three trumpets, three trombones, tuba, three tympani, four bells, xylophone, four harmonicas, tambourine, bass drum, cymbals, gong, celesta, piano, two harps, and strings.

R. C. B.

"A Pagan Poem" (after Virgil), for Orchestra with Piano, English Horn, and Three Trumpets Obbligati, Op. 14

THE VERSES that suggested this *Poem* are contained in the Eighth Eclogue of Virgil, often referred to as "Pharmaceutria" ("The Sorceress"). This particular Eclogue was dedicated to Pollio. It consists of two love songs, the one of Damon and the other of Alphesibeus, and it is with the latter that the composer was especially concerned. Alphesibeus sings of a Thessalian girl and of her yearning for her errant friend Daphnis. She raises aloft a love chant and weaves a magic spell in the hope that it will all bring him back to her.

Dedicated to the memory of Gustave Schirmer, the *Poem* was originally composed (1901) as chamber music. During 1905 and 1906 it was revised and augmented for symphonic presentation. Its first performance, in the larger version, was by the Boston Symphony in Boston, Nov. 23, 1927.

The score calls for three flutes (and piccolo), two oboes, English horn, two clarinets, bass clarinet, two bassoons, four horns, six trumpets (three of them off stage), three trombones, bass tuba, kettledrums, glockenspiel, tam-tam, harp, piano, and strings.

The opening of the *Pagan Poem* is Adagio, presenting a short subject, which —together with its inversion—is extensively employed throughout the piece. First of the main themes comes through, mezzoforte, by way of a viola and three flutes. This is a kind of invocation, whose latter half may be regarded as consisting of still two other themes, the first a figure in descending whole tones, the second "a rising and falling wail." Both are used quite often and with a good deal of variety.

Following an exposition of the first main theme, the piano makes its entrance, fortissimo, with an inversion of the introductory subject. The piano plays a glissando, leading to an Allegro where the material already advanced is put through its paces. Soon a second theme appears in the first violins, harp, and piano. There is development, and a piano cadenza brings on a Lento assai, featuring a doleful theme by the English horn.

Off stage the three trumpets intone the ensorcelling phrase of the young girl. The piano supplies a fourth theme, and after a generous use of the second chief theme the three trumpets rather give the impression that Daphnis has been lifted right out of his wanderings and put on the straight path leading to his deserted love. The conclusion of the work is a mass of frenetic joy.

However, be it noted that Loeffler had no intention to set down a literal description of the idyll. His music is a fantasy, no more, no less, which merely took inspiration from Virgil's verses.

R. C. B.

Jean-Baptiste Lully

BORN: FLORENCE, NOV. 29, 1632. DIED: PARIS, MAR. 22, 1687.

With all his vices, this crafty person, this arch-knave, this miser, this glutton, this rake, this cur—whatever name his companions were pleased to call him—with all his vices he was a great artist and a master of music in France.—ROMAIN ROLLAND.

Ballet Suite, "Noce Villageoise"
[*Arranged by Manuel Rosenthal*]

THIS ORCHESTRAL Suite is based on excerpts from the music which Lully wrote for the wedding of the Marquis and the Marquise of Crequi. The title *Noce Villageoise* was derived from the fact that the ceremony was held in the country home of the Marquis. Among the invited guests were the peasants of the vicinity and the numerous servants, chambermaids, and workmen in the employ of the titled bridegroom.

In the general dance which ends the choreographic divertissement, Lully took full cognizance of the nature of the gathering. One notes, for example, *une entrée des paysans* (an entrance—or sequence—for peasants). Another *entrée* is reserved for the appearance of the *vielleurs* (players of a species of bagpipe, a rustic instrument still used in the Auvergne). A final place in the household ensemble is given to the *patissier* (pastry cook).

The six sections of the suite which Mr. Rosenthal has fashioned from Lully's bucolic ballet appear in the following order (the quoted comments are by the arranger) :—

1. *Pavane*—"representing perfectly the emphatic style of the age."

2. *Gigue*—"the verve of which recalls the Italian origin of Lully."

3. *Two Minuets*—"gracious and ceremonial."

4. *Chaconne*—"that is to say, a slow dance, which may be numbered among Lully's loveliest pages alike for its broad expression and melodic line as for the charm and daring of its harmonies."

5. *Two Passepieds* (Breton dances)—"lively dances in 3/8 time."

6. *General Dance*—"ruggedly or fiercely jovial in the style of a *gaillarde*" (originally a brisk Spanish dance, *gallarda;* English, *galliard*).

In preparing the suite for concert use Mr. Rosenthal "adapted, arranged, and orchestrated." In doing so, he adhered with model restraint to the instrumentation usually employed by Lully. This consisted of two flutes, two oboes, two bassoons, tympani, and strings. One small liberty Mr. Rosenthal permitted himself: he added "two instrumental elements not yet employed by the composer of *Noce Villageoise.*" These were two piccolos and two clarinets. In his own arrangement of ballet music by Lully, Felix Mottl added trumpets, horns, and triangle, besides clarinets.

"The melodic, harmonic, and rhythmical writing of this work," Mr. Rosenthal remarks about *Noce Villageoise,* "cannot but suggest to the mind of the listener a definite *rapprochement* between the genius of Lully and that of Ravel, both eminent representatives of the French spirit." Mr. Rosenthal introduced the Suite to America at a concert of the Philharmonic-Symphony in Carnegie Hall, on Dec. 5, 1946.

Though an Italian by birth, Lully became the father of French opera, introducing a style featured by the accompanied recitative as distinct from the "recitativo secco" of Italian opera. Moreover, Lully strengthened the role of ballet and chorus in opera. The so-called "French overture," wherein the use of wind instruments was first stressed, was also an innovation of Lully's.

As court composer, friend, and secretarial factotum of Louis XIV, this naturalized Frenchman ruled with an iron hand over all matters musical. He was feared, envied, and hated by many in the King's entourage. Lully composed court ballets, about thirty in all, besides some twenty operas, most of them rather stiff and stilted to modern ears. Prologues were usually affixed in which gods and goddesses hymned the virtues of *Le Roi Soleil* (The Sun King) whose boast it was that the state and he were one.

Before gaining the King's favor. Lully long collaborated with Molière on a series of ballet comedies, in which the vehement style of dancing once prompted the word "epileptic" from a French commentator. When Lully finally obtained the exclusive right to produce "lyric tragedies" in Paris, French opera was born at the Académie de Musique with *Les Fêtes de L'Amour et de Bacchus.* The epochal date was Nov. 15, 1672.

For Lully—the Florentine turned Frenchman—this was progress indeed. His first job in France had been as kitchen scullion! Melodic gifts of a high order and mastery of ensemble effects were among Lully's distinguishing traits as composer. He was a sound violinist and early formed a group Les Petits Violons, which was long rated the best orchestra in Europe. His ballets were an advance in complexity and variety over the stereotyped products of the time. Himself a trained dancer, Lully took part in many of the court ballets. Often the man standing next to him was none other than his doting royal patron.

Lully's mastery of the supple accents and rhythms of the French language, so marked an influence on his melodic line and declamation, grew out of a close study of the declaiming style of stars of the Theâtre Français. *"Si vous voulez bien chanter ma musique,"* he once counseled a singer, *"allez entendre La Champmeslé"* ("If you wish to sing my music well, go to hear La Champmeslé").

L. B.

Edward MacDowell

BORN: NEW YORK, DEC. 18, 1861. DIED: NEW YORK, JAN. 23, 1908.

*From all that I hear of your husband, his qualities as a man are as
remarkable as his qualities as an artist. He is a complete personality,
with an unusually sympathetic and sensitive nervous system. Such a
temperament gives one the capacity not only for moods of the highest
transport, but for an unspeakable sorrow tenfold more profound.*
—EDVARD GRIEG, *in a letter to Mrs. Edward MacDowell.*

Concerto for Piano and Orchestra in D minor, No. 2, Op. 23

I. Larghetto calmato; Poco più mosso e con passione. II. Presto giocoso.
III. Largo; Molto allegro.

IN 1884, while in London, MacDowell and his wife went to see Henry Irving
and Ellen Terry at the Lyceum Theater in their famous production of Shakespeare's *Much Ado about Nothing.* MacDowell was so stirred that he came
away determined to write a symphonic poem about Beatrice and Benedict.
However, though he set promptly to work on it, he never carried out his plan.
Instead, he incorporated some of the material in the second movement of his
D minor Concerto.

This new work was composed in Germany during 1884 and 1885 and performed for the first time in Chickering Hall, New York, on Mar. 5, 1889.
Theodore Thomas conducted. MacDowell himself was the soloist.

The first movement is marked Larghetto calmato, D minor, 6/8; Poco più
mosso e con passione, D minor and D major, 6/8 and 3/4. The suavely
nostalgic chief theme returns in the introductory passage to the last movement,
which is marked Largo, D minor, 3/4. The middle movement is a brisk rondo
on three themes, marked Presto giocoso, B flat major, 2/4. The main section
of the finale (Molto allegro, D major, 3/4) is built on three contrasting themes.
Elie Seigmeister writes:

MacDowell was important not only for the quality of the compositions he produced, but in a broader sense because he was the first to show that, given the
background and opportunity, an American *could* write serious music of distinction
in the larger forms—this, in spite of the fact that he himself detested chauvinism
in any form, and did not want to be recognized simply because he was an American.
Much of his music was more popular twenty years ago than it is today. But,
whether a large proportion of his compositions survives or not, he gave confidence

398

and a certain standing to his successors. In a more tangible way, his country home—
now the MacDowell Colony—provided a summer haven for composers in none too
affluent circumstances.

L. B.

Suite No. 2 in E minor ("Indian"), Op. 48

I. Legend. II. Love Song. III. In War Time. IV. Dirge. V. Village Festival.

COMPOSED BETWEEN 1891 and 1892, this Suite made its public bow at a concert
of the Boston Symphony Orchestra in the Metropolitan Opera House, New
York, on Jan. 23, 1896. Becoming interested in the music of the American
Indian, MacDowell asked Henry F. Gilbert, a pupil of his, to spend some time
on research and to return with his findings. Gilbert, aiming to please, seems to
have restricted his investigations to one particular book, Theodore Baker's
Die Musik der Nordamerikanischen Wilden, which he brought back triumphantly to the composer.

According to Gilbert, MacDowell gazed on the volume and remarked, "I
knew of this book, but had forgotten about it." And Gilbert further attests that
from this collection the main themes of the *Indian Suite* are taken; that
"although all have been changed, more or less, the changes have been in the
direction of musical beauty, and enough of the original tune has been retained
to leave no doubt as to its barbaric flavor."

The thematic pieces utilized in the *Suite* consist of (1) an Iroquois and a
Chippewa theme; (2) an Iowa love song; (3) a song found among tribes of
the Atlantic coast, combining features common to the Dakotans and also certain aspects of the Iroquois scalp dance; (4) Kiowa, which is a woman's
mourning song; and (5) a women's dance and a war song, both of Iroquois
origin.

The *Indian Suite* is scored for piccolo, two flutes, two oboes, two clarinets,
two bassoons, four horns, two trumpets, three trombones, bass tuba, three
kettledrums, bass drum, cymbals, and strings. Its separate movements and their
description follow:

I. "Legend." (Not fast; with much dignity and character, E minor, 2/2.)
Allegedly inspired by Thomas Bailey Aldrich's Indian legend *Miantowona,*
this section must not be construed as a tonal parallel of the poem, but rather as
an expression of its character in musical terms.

II. "Love Song." (Not fast; tenderly, A major, 6/8.) The wood winds
announce the principal theme at once. This is developed in a pattern involving
two subsidiary phrases, one of which appears as a response in the strings and
the other as a tune of more definite character.

III. "In War Time." (With rough vigor, almost savagely, D minor, 2/4.)
Two flutes in unison, unaccompanied, give out the main theme, whereupon a

subsidiary theme comes answering back through two clarinets, also in unison, also unaccompanied. There is an elaborate working out of this material in a sort of rondo scheme. A feature of the section's latter portion is the frequent change of rhythm, which alternates between 2/4 and 6/8.

IV. "Dirge." (Dirgelike, mournfully, in G minor, 4/4.) Unison violins, muted, supply the chief subject. They are soon joined by the violas, and these strings perform their assignment against an iterated tonic G in the piccolo and two muted horns, one of which is on the stage and the other in the wings—at least, that is the specified arrangement. "The intimate relation between this theme and that of the first movement is not to be overlooked. It is answered by the horn behind the scenes over full harmony in the lower strings, the passage closing with a quaint concluding phrase of the oboe."

V. "Village Festival." (Swift and light, in E major, 2/4.) The material is mostly derived from the first movement and the various themes are developed in a generally sprightly survey of dance rhythms. As in the first movement, MacDowell is concerned with the depiction of a mood, in this case a festal mood. "The composer has been at no pains to suggest any of the specific concomitants of Indian festivities."

Disconsolately, Gilbert reports that after the *Suite's* first performance critical opinion ranged from such pronunciamentos as "Indian, but not beautiful" to "Beautiful, but not Indian," the whole art—or science, if you will—of esthetic criticism flourishing fiercely between. MacDowell had nurtured high hopes concerning his music, and when they were not realized he is supposed to have said, "You can't cram this Indian music down people's throats; they don't want it, and they won't have it." That, of course, was back in 1896.

R. C. B.

Gustav Mahler

BORN: KALISCHT, BOHEMIA, JULY 7, 1860. DIED: VIENNA, MAY 18, 1911.

I must not speak as a musician to a musician if I am to give any idea of the incredible impression your symphony made on me: I can speak only as one human being to another. For I saw your soul, naked, stark naked. It was revealed to me as a stretch of wild and secret country, with eerie chasms and abysses neighbored by sunlit, smiling meadows, haunts of idyllic repose. I felt it as an event of nature, which after scouring us with its terrors puts a rainbow in the sky. . . . I believed in your symphony. I shared in the battling for illusion; I suffered the pangs of disillusionment; I saw the forces of evil and good wrestling with each other; I saw a man in torment struggling toward inward harmony; I divined a personality, a drama, and truthfulness, the most uncompromising truthfulness.—ARNOLD SCHÖNBERG, *in a letter to Gustav Mahler, Dec.* 12, 1904.

Symphony in D major, No. 1

I. Langsam, schleppend wie ein Naturlaut (Slowly, drawn out like a sound of nature). II. Kräftig bewegt, doch nicht zu schnell (Strongly agitated, but not too fast). III. Feierlich und gemessen, ohne zu schleppen (Solemn and measured, without dragging). IV. Stürmisch bewegt (Stormily agitated).

AS AMPLY borne out in letters and biographical memoirs, Gustav Mahler was a sworn foe of "program notes." There is the story of Mahler's violent outburst at a supper party in Munich following a performance of his Second Symphony by the Hugo Wolf Society. Someone inadvertently broached the subject of program notes. Mahler jumped to his feet excitedly, according to Ludwig Schiedermair, who gives the episode in his biographical sketch. "Down with program books! They propagate false ideas!" he shouted. With his eyes flashing fiercely, the effect on the party, says Schiedermair, was like lightning on a sunny landscape.

"The audience should be left to its own thoughts about the work that is being played," Mahler went on. "It should not be forced to read during the performance. It should not be prejudiced in any manner." Growing calmer, Mahler explained that the composer's goal was reached only if, through the sheer power of the music, the listeners somehow grasped the sensations that had coursed through his mind. Given this meeting of minds between artist and audience, "the speech of tones approached that of language," he maintained, though music was "far more capable of expression and illumination" than words. He then lifted his glass, gulped down its contents, and rounded off his tirade with the words, "Damn all programs!"

Mahler subsequently pointed out that in early performances of his symphonies program notes had tended to take people's minds off the music itself. Well-meant guides to the narrative or poetic content often misrepresented his aims, and he felt that verbal résumés risked narrowing the esthetic and emotional scope of the music in the listener's mind. He once stated that if language could tell the whole story, there was no need to write music.

Mahler had reason to complain, for titles and programs had plagued him from the start. For example, the First Symphony underwent constant rechristening. In Budapest, where he first conducted the work on Nov. 20, 1889, it was billed as a "Symphonic Poem in Two Parts." When first played at Weimar on June 3, 1894, it was programmed as the "Titan Symphony," after a novel by Jean Paul Richter. The first section now carried the words, "From the Days of Youth," and the label "Commedia umana" was affixed to the second. That was only the beginning. Each of the movements was pictorially analyzed. For the first the description ran: "Spring and no end. The introduction represents the awakening of nature in the early morning." The second movement, an Andante omitted after the Weimar rendering, was termed "Mosaic, or A Chapter of Flowers." The "meaning" of the third or scherzo movement was presumably conveyed in the words, "Under Full Sail." The then fourth and fifth movements, comprising the "Commedia umana" division, were elaborately set forth as follows:

The hunter's funeral procession; a dead march in the manner of Callot [Jacques Callot, a French engraver of the seventeenth century]. The composer found the external source of inspiration in the burlesque picture of the hunter's funeral procession in an old book of fairy tales known to all children in South Germany. The animals of the forest escort the dead forester's coffin to the grave. Hares carry flags; a band of gypsy musicians, accompanied by cats, frogs, crows, all making music, and deer, foxes, and other four-footed and feathered creatures of the woods, leads the procession in farcical postures.

This movement, expressing moods now ironically merry, now gloomily meditative, is followed immediately by [the fifth] "Dall' Inferno al Paradiso" (allegro furioso), the abrupt outburst of doubt from a deeply wounded heart.

The result was contrary to expectation. If Mahler and his annotator hoped to sharpen interest in the music through an alluring table of contents, they failed. The usual misunderstanding resulted, and protests were heard that some of the episodes did not come off as scheduled in the program. Mahler omitted the descriptive aids when he finally published the work three years later. However, because of the controversy stirred up after the Weimar performance, he felt called upon to clarify his intentions. Centering his analysis in the words *wie ein Naturlaut* ("like a sound of nature"), which occur in the title of the first movement, he wrote to an inquiring music critic:

That nature embraces everything that is at once awesome, magnificent, and lovable, nobody seems to grasp. It seems so strange to me that most people, when they mention the word Nature in connection with art, imply only flowers, birds, the fragrance of the woods, etc. No one seems to think of the mighty underlying mystery, the god Dionysos, the great Pan; and just that mystery is the burden of my phrase *wie ein Naturlaut*. That, if anything, is my "program," or the secret of my composition. My music is always the voice of Nature sounding in tone, an idea in reality synonymous with the concept so aptly described by Bülow as "the symphonic problem." The validity of any other sort of "program" I do not recognize, at any rate, not for my work. If I have now and then affixed titles to some movements of my symphonies, I intended them only to assist the listener along some general path of fruitful reaction. But if the clarity of the impression I desire to create seems impossible of attainment without the aid of an actual text, I do not hesitate to use the human voice in my symphonies, for music and poetry together are a combination capable of realizing the most mystic conception. Through them the world, Nature as a whole, is released from its profound silence and opens its lips in song.

Adolf Weissmann once put the whole problem of Mahler's esthetics in a nutshell when he described it as "program music without a program."

Despite Mahler's injunction against reading "programs" into his music, disciples and associates have been at great pains to interpret his music along mystical and philosophical lines. The first four symphonies have been commonly regarded as a unit in the sense that they complete an emotional and intellectual cycle in Mahler's outlook. To Bruno Walter they reflect "an important part of the history of Mahler's soul." The First is the prelude, "a tempest of emotions," Mahler's "Werther," representing an escape from a "heart-rending experience," according to Mr. Walter. In the Second, Mahler "asks the reason for the tragedy of human existence and is sure its justification is to be found in immortality." In the Third, Mahler looks out upon nature and concludes that "Almighty love forms all things and preserves all things." In the Fourth, Mahler "assures himself and us of a sheltered security in the sublimely serene dream of a heavenly life." Gabriel Engel speaks of the four symphonies as a tetralogical cosmos, the First depicting the "hero" in search of faith, the Second outlining Death and Resurrection, the Third chanting the glories of "universal love and the wonders of nature," the Fourth picturing the "joys of heavenly existence." Mahler's closest associates have generally agreed that the Fifth, Sixth, and Seventh Symphonies are "purely musical," *i.e.,* without philosophical or religious content, and that *Das Lied von der Erde* and the Tenth Symphony are Mahler's "farewells to life," supposedly foreshadowing his death.

The introductory part of the first movement (D major, 4/4) has long been regarded as a tone picture of nature stirring slowly to life at dawn. The strings sound a long-held A against descending fourths in oboe and bassoon, with clarinets and trumpets chiming in at a distance. A clarinet chants a cuckoo call then the basses, in an ascending passage, lead into the main section.

In hushed tones cellos and double basses give out the main theme, deriving from Mahler's song cycle *Lieder eines fahrender Gesellen*. Listeners may detect a resemblance between part of this theme and a passage in Franz Lehar's *The Merry Widow*. In similarly soft mood, the horns announce another subject, promptly taken up by the cellos. After full development, the movement ends briskly.

A Ländler-like tune, suggesting Schubert and Bruckner, ushered in by the wood winds after a short passage for strings, is the chief feature of the scherzo second movement (A major, 3/4), with the trio subject (F major, 3/4) allotted to the violins, which unfold it pianissimo.

The macabre fantasy and ironic burlesque so strong in Mahler's early work reveal through the third movement (D minor, 4/4), where the old French canon "Frère Jacques" is rendered with somber satire in the minor mode. Against the G major second subject, sung soothingly by the violins, the parodied "Frère Jacques" returns in solemn mockery. It was this "Funeral March in the manner of Callot," as billed at Weimar in 1894, that whipped up sharp feeling against Mahler's alleged "triviality and accumulation of extravagances" and that so keenly interested a young aspirant named Bruno Walter. "I admired the daring author of so strange a Funeral March and felt a burning desire to know this extravagant man and his extravagant work," the conductor relates in his monograph on Mahler.

The turbulent finale (F minor, 2/2) draws on the first movement for themes. Here the "raging vehemence" of Mahler's nature breaks forth, according to Mr. Walter. The seven horns heard over the heaving orchestra toward the close have been likened to a "chorale of salvation from paradise after the waves of hell." Mr. Walter views that exultant outcry as a "triumphant victory over life."

In a letter written to Mr. Walter late in December, 1909, shortly after leading the Philharmonic in a New York premiere of the First Symphony, Mahler admitted being "quite satisfied with this youthful sketch." What is psychologically interesting is the way Mahler felt while conducting this early score:

"A burning and painful sensation is crystallized. What a world this is that casts up such reflections of sounds and figures! Things like the Funeral March and the bursting of the storm which follows it seem to me a flaming indictment of the Creator. . . ."

L. B.

Symphony in C minor, No. 2, for Orchestra, Soprano and Alto Solos, and Mixed Chorus

> I. Allegro maestoso. Mit durchaus ernstem und feierlichem Ausdruck (With serious and solemn expression throughout). II. Andante moderato. Sehr gemächlich (Very leisurely). III. In ruhig fliessender Bewegung (In quietly flowing movement). IV. "Urlicht" (Primal Light)—Contralto solo. Sehr feierlich, aber schlicht; Choralmässig (Very solemn, but simple; like a chorale). V. Finale (Chorus. Soprano and contralto solos).

Mahler's Second Symphony dates from the period when he conducted opera at Hamburg. The engagement began in 1891 and lasted till 1897, the year he became conductor, later, general director, of the Imperial Opera in Vienna. In Hamburg he soon found a close friend in Hans von Bülow, then directing the Hamburg Symphony concerts. Mahler attended the Bülow series regularly and Bülow the Mahler performances at the opera. Mutual admiration was freely expressed. So highly did Bülow regard Mahler's vitalizing presence at the opera that he spoke of him as the "Pygmalion of the Hamburg Opera." Yet, he was far from enthusiastic over Mahler's own music. "When I played my 'Totenfeier' [(Death celebration) the first movement of the Second Symphony] for him," Mahler once wrote, "he fell into a state of extreme nervous terror, carrying on like a lunatic, and exclaimed, 'Beside your music *Tristan* sounds as simple as a Haydn symphony!' Indeed, I'm beginning to believe it myself; my symphonies are either maudlin ravings or . . . well, choose your own alternative."

In 1893, when Bülow's declining health obliged him to give up the concert series and seek a warmer climate, Mahler succeeded him. Beginning that year, Mahler spent four summer vacations at Steinbach on the lovely Austrian lake, the Attersee. Free from the cares, annoyances, and intrigues of the Hamburg opera and concert world, which he loathed, he set to work on his Second Symphony. However, Paul Stefan is authority for the statement that early sketches were made during Mahler's Leipzig period (1886-1888). Apparently all but the choral finale were completed during that first summer in his country retreat. The last movement troubled him. Mahler wanted it to convey the idea of Resurrection as a fitting conclusion to the life-and-death scheme and awaited the stimulus that would set off his train of musical thought. It came unexpectedly with the death of Bülow in Cairo, Egypt, in February, 1894. When his friend's body arrived in Hamburg for burial, Mahler was among the mourners. As part of the funeral services the church choir sang the "Resurrection" ("Aufsteh'n") ode of the German poet Klopstock. Mahler's problem was solved. These were the very words for the Finale of his Second Symphony! He wrote:

When I conceive a great musical picture, I always arrive at the point where I must employ the "word" as the bearer of my musical idea. . . . My experience with the last movement of my Second Symphony is such that I literally ransacked the literature of the world up to the Bible to find the releasing [*erlösend*] "word." Deeply significant of the nature of artistic creation is the manner in which I received the prompting to it. I had had for a long time the thought of using the chorus in the last movement, and only the fear that this might be considered an imitation of Beethoven made me hesitate.

About this time Bülow died, and I attended his funeral in Hamburg. The mood in which I sat and thought of the dead man was exactly in the spirit of the work that I was carrying about in my mind. Then the chorus intoned Klopstock's ode "Resurrection." This struck me like a flash of lightning. Everything was revealed clear and plain to my soul. The creative artist was waiting for this flash. What I then experienced I had to create in tones. And yet, if I had not had this work already in me, how could I have had this experience?

Richard Strauss, who early took up the Mahler cause, conducted a partial premiere of the work on Mar. 4, 1895, at a Berlin Philharmonic concert. Only the first three movements, the strictly instrumental ones, were played. Of these the second and third were stormily received, Mahler being called out five times after the scherzo. Yet the Berlin reviewers unanimously attacked the symphony, wilfully misrepresenting the premiere as a fiasco. As for Richard Strauss, there were those among the anti-Mahlerites who insisted that Mahler, despite his colleague's ready championship, looked upon him as a rival in symphonic composition. Curiously, Mahler even wrote a letter to one of the reviewers refuting the charge. He stated:

I shall never cease to be grateful to Strauss, who has so magnanimously given the impetus to public hearings of my works. Nobody should say that I regard myself as his rival, although I'm sorry to say the stupid implication has often been made. Aside from the fact that my music would be looked upon as a monstrosity had not the orchestral achievements of Strauss paved the way for it, I regard it as my greatest joy to have met with a companion fighter and creative artist of his caliber among my contemporaries.

Mahler himself conducted all five movements of the symphony in Berlin with the Philharmonic orchestra, on Dec. 13. The critics, still in high dudgeon, stayed away from the first three movements this time and dropped in only for the unfamiliar remaining two, according to Ernst Otto Nodnagel, who described their behavior as "indecent." One of the reviewers fumed over what he termed "the cynical impudence of this brutal and very latest music maker." On the other hand, the audience again acclaimed the Symphony wildly, and great enthusiasm was expressed by Arthur Nikisch and Felix Weingartner, who were present. During rehearsals Mahler had found everybody highly cooperative. Three days before the performance, in a letter to Anna Bahr-

Mildenburg, a singer at the Hamburg Stadttheater, he referred excitedly to the fine spirit of his coworkers. "They far exceeded all my expectations," he remarked. "Enthusiastic and engrossed, by themselves they found the right expression for everything. If only you had heard it! It was grand and powerful!"

Mahler's Second Symphony was first performed in America by the Symphony Society of New York on Dec. 8, 1908, under the composer's direction. The Philharmonic Society added it to its repertory on Mar. 28, 1925, when Willem Mengelberg conducted, and Marie Sundelius and Mme. Charles Cahier were the soloists.

In writing to Max Marschalk, who had made an "analysis" of the Second Symphony, Mahler himself avowed the link with the First Symphony:

I have called the first movement "Celebration of the Dead" ("Totenfeier"), and if you wish to know, it is the Hero of my First Symphony whom I bear to the grave. Immediately arise the great questions: Why have you lived? Why have you suffered? Has it all been only a huge, frightful joke? We must all somehow answer these questions, if we are to continue living, yes, even if we are only to continue dying. Whoever hears this call must give a reply. And this reply I give in my last movement.

The second and third movements he described as "interludes." The second purported to be a memory, "a sunbeam, pure and cloudless," from the life of this Hero, the sort of recollection coming upon one on returning from a burial, as "of a distant hour of happiness resting, like unobscured sunlight, in the soul." Then, awaking from the nostalgic spell, "to return anew to this confused life," it often happens, Mahler suggested, that this "endlessly troubled, inexplicable, and restless turmoil of life suddenly strikes us as frightful." Life then resembles the surge of dancing figures in a brightly illuminated hall, into which you peer out of the dark night—"from such far-off detachment that you no longer hear the music." Life becomes "senseless to you, a gruesome specter, which you perchance flee with a cry of disgust." That is how Mahler viewed the third movement, considered by Bruno Walter the best of Mahler's scherzos, with its flashes of buffoonery playing on the sinister flow of fantasy. "It was born," Mr. Walter says, "out of a mood of sorrow and grew into a masterpiece of symphonic music."

Actually, the movement is a free fantasy on one of Mahler's songs "St. Anthony of Padua's Sermon to the Fishes" ("Des Antonius von Padua Fischpredigt") from Mahler's favorite German folk-song collection Arnim and Brentano's *Des Knaben Wunderhorn*. The text of the fourth movement "Urlicht" ("Primal Light") also is derived from the anthology. The latter—a song for alto and small orchestra expressing man's trust "that the dear Lord may vouchsafe him a little light to show the way into the blessed life beyond"

—is generally regarded as one of Mahler's supreme inspirations in its delicate weaving of a visionary mood.

The words of the Finale, which Mahler conceived as a "colossal musical fresco of the Day of Judgment," are from Klopstock's ode and the composer's own pen. In the analysis of Paul Stefan, one of Mahler's best biographers and interpreters,

the verses are a summons to faith; nothing is in vain; loving, struggling, suffering are not in vain; on pinions gained through life's feverish struggle the soul will soar to the Light that no eye has ever beheld. In a long preluding to this movement, brass instruments sound the Great Summons. A bird's trilling, falling gradually into silence, is heard before the chorus begins its solemn intonations.

The Symphony ends with the pealing of organ and bells "amid the jubilation of the orchestra."

L. B.

Symphony in G major, No. 4 (with Soprano Solo)

> I. Bedächtig (Deliberately). II. In gemächlicher Bewegung; Ohne Hast (In easy motion; without haste). III. Ruhevoll (Peacefully). IV. Sehr behaglich (Very leisurely). Soprano solo.

MAHLER BEGAN work on his Fourth Symphony at Ausee during the summer of 1899, completing it the following summer at the same place. He found little time for composition during the remainder of the year. In 1897 he had been invited to replace Wilhelm Jahns as first conductor of the Vienna Opera and was soon appointed music director. During the opera season he worked unsparingly. He instituted reforms in staging works by Mozart, Gluck, and Wagner. He fought tirelessly for fresh *mises en scène* and equipment. He sought absolute perfection of ensemble. In short, he gave his beloved Vienna probably its most brilliant decade (1897-1907) of operatic performance. Besides that, he conducted the Philharmonic concerts from 1898 to 1901 and the Gesellschaft concerts from 1898 to 1900. His whole-souled devotion to art made him staunch friends and coworkers among the opera's personnel, despite his insistence on grueling, unremitting rehearsal and revision. Naturally his autocratic rule brought him some enemies, too, and the press was not always unanimous in hailing his operatic innovations.

Necessarily, Mahler was a "holiday" composer, as he once styled himself in a letter to Max Marschalk. Chained to the theater most of the year, he apologized for not composing as much music as the "concert matadors of today." Yet, considering the difficulties, the Mahler output is staggering in extent. During those brief holiday periods between opera seasons he composed his Fourth, Fifth, Sixth, Seventh, and Eighth Symphonies, besides a sheaf of songs with orchestral accompaniment. In a sense the creative work was both a relief and an escape from the terrific hardships of running an opera house and much of Vienna's remaining musical life. And yet, Bruno Walter, who knew him intimately, found him invariably "brisk, inspired, and charged with energy."

Mahler himself conducted the Fourth Symphony at its premiere on a program of the Kaim Orchestra in Munich, in November, 1901. The reaction was largely hostile, the opposition even resorting to vicious and irrelevant jibes at the Viennese composer. Walter speaks of the work's "ungracious reception," and the critic of the *Allgemeine Musik Zeitung* elaborately noted that "amid the applause of a few hearers there was plainly audible the manifestation of disapproval of others." At the Viennese premiere of the following year, opinions clashed so sharply that Mahlerites and anti-Mahlerites almost came to blows. The absence of a "program" giving descriptive clues to the symphony is said to have been partly responsible for the work's failure in both Munich and Vienna, though the song text of the last movement ought to be sufficient key—for those desiring one—to at least the mood of the work. Mahler had become a sworn foe of "programs." In earlier performances of his works, program books had often carried detailed guides to the pictorial or poetic content of his symphonies. However, he finally saw that the practice made for misrepresentation and took people's minds off the music itself. So he disavowed descriptive analyses with the cry, "Damn programs, anyway!" He found verbal summaries restrictive and regarded his music as "pure," however it might freely mirror spiritual and emotional states.

In 1907, Mahler came to New York as conductor of the Metropolitan Opera House, making his first appearance at a performance of *Tristan und Isolde* on Jan. 1, 1908. His American debut as concert conductor occurred on Nov. 29 of that year, the orchestra being that of the Symphony Society. He also directed two Philharmonic concerts, on Mar. 31 and Apr. 6, 1909, and was promptly engaged as regular conductor of that orchestra, serving for almost two seasons. In the course of his second season, 1910-1911, a serious heart condition forced him to cancel the remaining concerts and return to Europe for rest and treatment. Knowing that he was doomed, after some weeks in Paris under the care of a heart specialist, he insisted on going on to Vienna, where he died in the spring of 1911. Later that year the Philharmonic Society played, in his memory, the Funeral March from his Fifth Symphony.

Mahler's attitude toward "programs" may be gathered from a rather apologetic note in the program book of the Philharmonic Society of Jan. 17 and 20, 1910, when the composer conducted his Fourth Symphony (with Bella Alten the soprano soloist), on an "All-modern Program" including Pfitzner's *Das Kätchen von Heilbronn* overture and Richard Strauss's *Ein Heldenleben*. "In deference to Mr. Mahler's wishes, there shall be no attempt at an analysis or description here of his symphony." The New York premiere of the work had taken place five years earlier, on Nov. 6, 1904, at a concert of the Symphony Society, directed by Walter Damrosch.

Although each of Mahler's ten symphonies (including *Das Lied von der Erde*) poses its own special problems of performance—the Eighth, for example, requires almost a thousand vocal and instrumental performers—the Fourth is relatively modest in scope. The scoring calls for four flutes, three oboes, three clarinets, three bassoons, four horns, three trumpets, percussion, one harp, and strings. Trombones and bass tuba are conspicuously absent, and the included trumpets are only moderately used. The number of horns is normal, compared with the six called for in the Second Symphony and the eight required for the Third. The instrumentation shows Mahler's typical mastery of color and combination, though within a somewhat narrower frame than his other symphonies.

A neoclassical label has been affixed to the symphony probably because of the suggestions of Mozart and Haydn embedded in the modern setting. Then, too, it is the only one of Mahler's symphonies containing a movement—the Andante —built on a set of variations. The finale is a thematic link with the Third Symphony. Mahler had planned still another movement for the earlier work, to the latter part of which had originally been fastened a series of titles, "What the Flowers of the Field Tell Me," "What the Animals of the Forest Tell Me," "What Man Tells Me," "What the Angels Tell Me." The section that became the finale of the Fourth Symphony was to be called "What the Child Tells Me." Thematically, the finale recalls the "angel" section of the previous symphony, and in general tone "follows its spiritual direction."

Mr. Walter once asked Mahler what lay behind the "profound quiet and clear beauty" of the andante. The composer explained that the movement had originated in a vision of a church sepulcher, in which recumbent stone images of the dead were shown "with their arms closed in eternal peace." Thus, the setting of the naïve verses from *Des Knaben Wunderhorn,* employed in the finale, would appear to serve as a key to the whole work—"the childlike peace symbolic of heavenly bliss."

In later life, Mahler was gloomily obsessed with the whys and wherefores of life and death, as volumes of reminiscences by friends abundantly attest. An abiding *Weltschmerz* was his, rooted in a conviction that horror gaped on all sides of life. The thought of death and disease haunted him, and he loved life the more eagerly and passionately. Affirmation, laughter, gaiety were mere makeshifts in his outlook; beyond bulked the terror of decay and mortality. His humanity was all-embracing, and many have construed the exultant finales of some of his symphonies as similar to the *Seid umschlungen Millionen* of Schiller and Beethoven. To some, the ten symphonies are rooted in these two impulses—an immense love of life in all its forms and a horror of death and obliteration. The symphonic cycle appears to alternate the double theme, a symphony strikes one as affirming life, and the next as evoking death.

In his music, at least, Mahler found comfort in two refuges, childhood and the outdoors. A childlike simplicity runs through his symphonies, notably the Fourth, sometimes contrasting violently with a grim vein of satanic irony and a strain of Olympian nobility. The traits recur again and again and even manifest themselves in Mahler's literary preferences. All his life he worshipped Goethe. He read him religiously and sought solace in his preachments. (The Eighth Symphony is partly a setting of a scene from the second part of *Faust* and partly a setting of a medieval hymn.) Then, Mahler had early come upon Arnim and Brentano's collection of German folk poetry *Des Knaben Wunderhorn,* which breathed a simple, naïve, childlike quality that strongly appealed to him. It, too, dominated his thoughts. From it Mahler drew the words of some twenty-five of his songs, besides texts for three of his symphonies, including the Fourth. The engaging naïveté of much of Mahler's music owes something to the spirit of the early nineteenth-century collection. One critic goes so far as to trace the melodic design of Mahler's music to the quality of *Des Knaben Wunderhorn,* while ascribing its contrapuntal and harmonic texture to Goethe's mysticism. The Second, Third, and Fourth Symphonies not only drew upon *Des Knaben Wunderhorn* textually, but some of the themes employed in all three are almost identical with Mahler's song settings of other poems from the collection.

L. B.

Symphony No. 5, in C sharp minor

> Part I. I. Trauermarsch (Funeral march). II. Stürmisch bewegt; mit grosser Vehemenz (Stormily agitated; with great vehemence). Part II. III. Scherzo: Kräftig, nicht zu schnell (Vigorously, not too fast). Part III. IV. Adagietto: Sehr langsam (Very slowly). V. Rondo Finale: Allegro commodo.

Because of its unusual dimensions, Mahler's Fifth Symphony was promptly called the "Giant Symphony" when the composer conducted the world premiere at a Gurzenich Concert in Cologne on Oct. 18, 1904. " 'Giant' at the time," Pitts Sanborn once remarked, "but Mahler had not yet written his Eighth Symphony." The spectacular proportions of the Eighth in turn earned it the title of "Symphony of the Thousand."

Why the term "Giant" was applied to the Fifth may be gathered from the enormous assortment of instruments called for in the scoring. Included are four flutes (the third and fourth interchangeable with piccolos), three oboes, three clarinets (the third interchangeable with bass clarinet), two bassoons, one double-bassoon, six horns (in the third movement a horn obbligato), four trumpets, three trombones, one bass tuba, kettledrums, snare drum, bass drum, cymbals, triangle, glockenspiel, gong, harp, and strings.

The scoring would perhaps have been even more formidable had it not been for a convincing outburst of tears on the part of Mahler's wife Alma. She tells in a book about Mahler:

Early in the year there had been a reading rehearsal with the Philharmonic, to which I listened unseen from the gallery. I had heard each theme in my head while copying the score, but now I could not hear them at all! Mahler had over-scored the percussion instruments and kettledrums so madly and persistently that little beyond the rhythm was recognizable. I hurried home sobbing aloud. He followed. For a long time I refused to speak. At last I said between my sobs: "You've written it for percussion and nothing else!" He laughed and then produced the score. He crossed out all the kettledrums in red chalk and half the percussion instruments too. He had felt the same thing himself, but my passionate protest turned the scale.

It is significant to note that Mahler went on revising this taxing score till the end of his life. Having finished the first version in the summer of 1902 at his villa in Maiernigg on the Woerthersee, it was not till 1911 that he was able to write: "The Fifth is finished. I have been compelled to reorchestrate it completely. I cannot understand how at that time (1902) I could have written so much like a beginner. Clearly the routine I had acquired in the first four symphonies deserted me altogether, as if a totally new message demanded a new technique."

After the premiere in Cologne, a critic from Munich reported that the first movement was followed by "a breathless silence which proved more effectively than tremendous applause that the public was conscious of the presence of genius." Actually, there was hardly any applause to speak of after the lengthy performance, and a few anti-Mahlerites relieved their harassed feelings by hissing. Mahler's injunction against program notes was scrupulously observed at that performance and the performances which followed in Dresden and Berlin. No analysis was offered and no clue given to any narrative or dramatic content. Mahler's principle was that the music should speak for itself; that, if words could tell the story, why bother to write the music. "Damn all program books!" he once exclaimed at a supper party.

Still, there was no deterring the program-minded Mahlerites. Shortly after the premiere of the Fifth Symphony an intrepid devotee, Ernst Otto Nodnagel of Darmstadt, filled twenty-three pages of the magazine *Die Musik* with a musico-metaphysical analysis of the score. A quotation by the poet Schiller was used as a motto to the learned disquisition. Later the article was reprinted and sold as a pamphlet for thirty pfennigs.

Herr Nodnagel must have shadowed Mahler in fawning adoration, for he once earned a dubiously complimentary reference to himself in a letter of Mahler's to his wife: "I gave a look around during the first rehearsal yesterday and caught sight of someone standing at the back like a worshipper. It was

Herr Nodnagel! At first I was enraged, and then touched. But what an eccentric!" Obviously the worthy analyst was merely gathering first-hand material for his twenty-three page epic.

Nor did Mahler's blast at program notes hinder Herr Nodnagel's American colleagues from venturing dramatic excursions of their own. The first American performance of the Fifth Symphony occurred in Cincinnati at a concert of the Cincinnati Symphony Orchestra on Mar. 25, 1905. To the gracious lady annotator of that orchestra we owe the following sermon on moral uplift drawn from the music:

Without constructing a program for the work it may be regarded as (1) the plaint of one who has not realized his aspirations, and (2) in his disillusionment stands at the verge of desperation. (3) The harmless play and life of nature reconcile him to his lot, and (4) he returns to his life work, which he resumes (5), with willingness, insight, and renewed strength, finally reaching heights before unattainable. Further than this, it would be useless to attempt to catalogue its meanings.

To which Philip Hale blandly rejoined: "We do not know whether this argument is original with Miss Roedter, or whether she borrowed it from some deep German thinker." Still, the urbane sage of Boston could not resist a poetic flight of his own in a subsequent review of the Fifth: "This symphony is like unto the great image that stood before Nebuchadnezzar in a vision. . . ." Hale, incidentally, was among the first to notice a resemblance between a passage in the Rondo Finale and the sublime theme in D major of the Adagio movement of Beethoven's Ninth Symphony. In the Adagietto he also glimpsed the ghost of Wagner hovering about. Though a Mahler sceptic in some respects, he admitted that everything this tragic genius had written bore the stamp of a rich imagination and a "vital, passionate, well-nigh fanatical enthusiasm that always kindles my sympathy."

The arrangement of the movements of the C sharp minor Symphony is without precedent or subsequent parallel. Under Part I are grouped the first two movements, comprising a funeral march, in C sharp minor, 2/2, and a movement in A minor, 4/4, marked "with stormy emotion; with the utmost vehemence." The vigorous third movement, or Scherzo (D major, 3/4) constitutes Part II. The celebrated Adagietto (F major, 4/4) is the first of the two sections making up Part III, the other and final movement being a Rondo (Allegro commodo) in D major, 2/2. The delicate and tranquilly tender Adagietto once prompted the Viennese playwright Hermann Bahr to remark to Mahler that it reflected a serene cheerfulness which, paradoxically, contained within itself all the world's sorrow. The movement is marked *Sehr langsam* (very slowly) and is scored for strings and harp, with the first violins announcing the haunting melody in F major, and a middle section, of contrasting mood, appearing later in G flat major. Also notable is the new contrapuntal grasp revealed in the massive triple fugue of the Rondo Finale. Both Gabriel Engel and Bruno Walter are agreed that the Fifth represents a high point of Mahler's achievement as symphonist. "In the Fifth," Mr. Walter wrote, "the world has now a masterpiece which shows its creator at the summit of his life, of his power, and of his ability." For Mr. Engel, Mahler's Fifth marked a significant stage in the composer's development much as the Fifth Symphony had in the case of Beethoven and Bruckner.

Among Mahler specialists who have bracketed the Fifth, Sixth, and Seventh Symphonies in a kind of unified "trilogy" are Richard Specht and Hans Tischler. Specht felt that a new symphonic style, partly traceable to Mahler's profounder study of Bach, was initiated here; that a strikingly new polyphony and polyrhythmic style had developed out of the earlier "orchestrophony." More dramatically, Dr. Tischler was convinced that the three symphonies "abandon the idea of the next world" and place the action in this world only, "with its grim reality." What he termed the "dramatic action" of the Fifth would accordingly be broken down as follows:

Mourning and pain (first movement). Fighting and wounds (second movement). Irony and shadowy insecurity, coupled with a forced gaiety (third movement); relieved by the Interlude (fourth movement). The fifth movement concludes the work more cheerfully, describing daily work and haste, still the best phases of ordinary human existence.

At this point it may be instructive to read Mr. Walter's statement about the variously assumed "program" content of Mahler's Fifth Symphony. The devoted friend and associate of the composer wrote:

Nothing in any of my conversations with Mahler and not a single note point to the influence of extramusical thoughts or emotions upon the composition of the Fifth. It is music—passionate, wild, pathetic, buoyant, solemn, tender, full of all the sentiments of which the human heart is capable—but still "only" music, and no metaphysical questioning, not even from very far off, interferes with its purely musical course.

One wonders if, after all, Mahler did not deserve our sympathy when he cried out in all seriousness, *"Pereant die Programme!"*

L. B.

Symphony No. 9

I. Andante commodo. II. Im Tempo eines gemächlichen Ländlers. III. Rondo Burleske. IV. Adagio.

This work was composed during the summer of 1909. It was given its first performance at Vienna in June, 1912, under the direction of Bruno Walter, thirteen months after the composer's death. The scoring, economical in Mahler's case, calls for wood winds in threes (with the exception of four flutes), four horns, three trumpets, three trombones, tuba, two kettledrums, triangle, glockenspiel, and strings. There are four movements to the composition, none of which is in sonata form, although in each of the preceding eight symphonies Mahler had adhered pretty closely to that form, for all the structural experimentation involved.

In the first movement of the Ninth he presents the "duality of themes" basically found in sonata form. However, after the statement of the themes, he subjects them to a development that is improvisatory and rather free. The first theme, in D major, may be found in the sixth measure of the piece, and it has been described as calm, resigned, and dreamlike. The second does not appear until some twenty measures later, in D minor. This is "intense with passion."

The second movement, "an enormously expanded Ländler," is grotesque "with more than a suggestion of bitterness typical of Mahler." The old Austrian country-dance form is first its simple and rather gay self; then it is "dislocated and forced to serve Mahler's expressive intentions."

In the third movement, Mahler employs another dance form, putting it through a fiery and energetic treatment. Of almost any other composer than Mahler it might be said that there is here an exhibitionistic display of contrapuntal skill.

The fourth movement is in two sections, each separately used. The harmony in the initial section is full, and the parts, both inner and outer, cross over and become related in a remarkably smooth fashion. In the second section of the movement there is a gradual rise in the development to heights of intensity. Then comes as gradual a decline in the general sonority until, with instruments successively dropping out, the cellos are alone in a pianissimo passage which fades away into silence. A coda is based on material advanced earlier in the movement, and the music "reaches the most profound and heart-searching degree of poignance."

Henry Boys has this to say of Mahler and his work:

If the Ninth Symphony is not "classical," neither can it be understood by comparing it with any postclassical symphony; in some ways it reaches further, or at least in different directions. Between the classical composers and Mahler the symphony had really become a form of secondary importance; music drama and the symphonic poem were the chief nineteenth-century forms; pure drama had given place to epic. Nevertheless, epic provides ample scope for dramatic as well as for lyric episode. It is here that we come up against the problem of program music, the most important problem of nineteenth-century music, and to know how Mahler tackled it is essential for the proper understanding of his music. "All music since Beethoven," said Mahler, "has been program music."

R. C. B.

"Das Lied von der Erde" ("The Song of the Earth")

I. "Das Trinklied vom Jammer der Erde" ("The Drinking Song of Earthly Woe") (Tenor). II. "Der Einsame im Herbst" ("The Lonely One in Autumn") (Contralto). III. "Von der Jugend" ("Of Youth") (Tenor). IV. "Von der Schönheit" ("Of Beauty") (Contralto). V. "Der Trunkene im Frühling" ("The Drunken One in Springtime") (Tenor). VI. "Der Abschied" ("The Farewell") (Contralto).

THE COMPOSER called this cycle of six songs a "symphony for tenor and alto (or baritone) soli and orchestra." He wrote it in the summer of 1908, but died before he could hear its first performance, which was given in Munich, on Nov. 10, 1911, under the direction of his disciple, friend, and biographer Bruno Walter.

The work was introduced to this country by Leopold Stokowski at a concert of the Philadelphia Orchestra in Philadelphia, on Dec. 15, 1916. It was first heard in New York under the auspices of the Society of the Friends of Music, in Carnegie Hall, on Feb. 1, 1922. On that occasion Artur Bodanzky conducted, and the soloists were Orville Harrold, tenor, and Mme. Charles Cahier, contralto. The Philharmonic-Symphony Society first presented it on Jan. 3, 1929, when Willem Mengelberg conducted. His soloists were Richard Crooks and Margaret Matzenauer. It was given again by the Society with the same conductor and soloists on Jan. 16 and 17, 1930; on Dec. 20 and 21, 1934 (Bruno Walter; Frederick Jagel and Maria Olszewska); and on Jan. 23 and 24, 1941 (Mr. Walter; Charles Kullman and Kerstin Thorborg).

Das Lied von der Erde has been called "one of Mahler's surest claims to immortality as a composer." It consists of six pieces "for tenor or contralto in alternation, the texts being taken from six Chinese poems." These are derived from *Die Chinesische Flöte* (*The Chinese Flute*) by Hans Bethge, the German poet who paraphrased eighth-century Chinese verses. The sixth section of the work consists of two parts separated by an orchestral interlude.

I

[TENOR SOLO]

DAS TRINKLIED VON JAMMER DER ERDE	THE DRINKING SONG OF EARTHLY WOE
Schon winkt der Wein im gold'nen Pokale,	Wine in the golden goblet is beckoning,
Doch trinkt noch nicht, erst sing' ich euch ein Lied!	But drink not yet, first I will sing you a song!
Das Lied vom Kummer soll auflachend in die Seele euch klingen.	The Song of Sorrow, let its mockery laugh itself into your soul.
Wenn der Kummer naht,	When sorrow approaches, the soul's gardens lie
Liegen wüst die Gärten der Seele.	desolate,

Welkt hin und stirbt die Freude, der Gesang.	Joy and song wither and die.
Dunkel ist das Leben, ist der Tod.	Dark is life, is death.
Herr dieses Hauses! Dein Keller birgt die Fülle des goldenen Weins!	Lord of this house! Thy cellar holds the fullness of golden wine!
Hier diese Laute nenn' ich mein!	Here, this lute, I call mine own!
Die Laute schlagen und die Gläser leeren,	To play upon the lute, to empty glasses,
Das sind die Dinge, die zusammen passen.	These are things that fit each other,
Ein voller Becher Weins zur rechten Zeit	At the proper time a goblet full of wine
Ist mehr wert als alle Reiche dieser Erde!	Is worth more than all the kingdoms of this earth!
Dunkel ist das Leben, ist der Tod!	Dark is life, is death!
Das Firmament blaut ewig, und die Erde	The firmament in its eternal blue, and the earth.
Wird lange fest steh'n und aufblüh'n im Lenz.	These will long endure, will blossom in spring-time.
Du, aber, Mensch, wie lang lebst denn du?	But thou, O man, what is the span of thy life?
Nicht hundert Jahre darfst du dich ergötzen	Not a hundred years are you permitted to enjoy
An all dem morschen Tande dieser Erde!	The idle vanities of this earth!
Seht dort hinab! Im Mondschein auf den Gräbern	Look there below! In the moonlight upon the graves
Hockt eine wild gespenstiche Gestalt.	There crouches a wild, ghostly figure—
Ein Aff' ist's! Hört ihr, wie sein Heulen	An ape it is! Hark how his howling
Hinausgellt in den süssen Duft des Lebens!	Shrills out into the sweet airs of this our life!
Jetzt nehmt den Wein! Jetzt ist es Zeit genossen!	Bring on the wine! The time has come, my comrades!
Leert eure gold'nen Becher zu Grund!	Drain your golden goblets to the dregs!
Dunkel ist das Leben, ist der Tod!	Dark is life, is death!

II

[Contralto Solo]

DER EINSAME IM HERBST	THE LONELY ONE IN AUTUMN
Herbstnebel wallen bläulich überm See;	The mists of autumn build their blue wall over the sea;
Vom Reif bezogen stehen alle Gräser;	With hoarfrost covered, stands the grass;
Man meint, ein Künstler habe Staub von Jade	It seems as if an artist had strewn the dust of jade over delicate blossoms.
Über die feinen Blüten ausgestreut.	
Der süsse Duft der Blumen ist verflogen;	The flowers' fragrance has spent itself;
Ein kalter Wind beugt ihre Stengel nieder.	A cold wind bows them to earth.
Bald werden die Verwelkten, gold'nen Blätter	Soon the withered, golden leaves
Der Lotusblüten auf dem Wasser zieh'n.	Of lotus flowers will be scattered upon the waters.
Mein Herz ist müde. Meine kleine Lampe	My heart is weary. My little lamp
Erlosch mit Knistern, es gemahnt mich an def Schlaf.	Has gone out, a-crackling, minding me of need for sleep,
Ich komm' zu dir, traute Ruhestätte!	I come to you, blest resting-place!
Ja, gib mir Ruh, ich hab' Erquickung Not!	Yea, give me rest; for I need quickening!
Ich weine viel in meinen Einsamkeiten,	I weep and weep in all my solitude.
Der Herbst in meinem Herzen währt zu lange.	Autumn in my heart too long is lasting.
Sonne der Liebe, willst du nie mehr scheinen,	O Sun of Love, never again wilt thou shine,
Um meine bittern Tränen mild aufzutrocknen?	Gently to dry my bitter tears?

III

[Tenor Solo]

VON DER JUGEND	OF YOUTH
Mitten in dem kleinen Teiche	Midway in the little pool
Steht ein Pavillon aus grünem	Stands a pavilion of green
Und aus weissem Porzellan.	And of gray porcelain.
Wie der Rücken eines Tigers	Like the back of a tiger
Wölbt die Brücke sich aus Jade	The bridge of jade arches
Zu dem Pavillon hinüber.	Across to the pavilion.
In dem Häuschen sitzen Freunde,	In the little house friends are seated,
Schön gekleidet, trinken, plaudern,	Beautifully gowned, drinking, gossiping;
Manche schreiben Verse nieder.	Some are writing verses.
Ihre seidnen Ärmel gleiten	Their silken sleeves glide
Rückwärts, ihre seidnen Mützen	Backwards, their silken caps
Hocken lustig tief im Nacken.	Hang from the back of their necks.
Auf des kleinen Teiches stiller	On the smooth surface of the quiet pool
Wasserfläche zeigt sich alles	All is mirrored
Wunderlich im Spiegelbilde.	Wondrously.
Alles auf dem Kopfe stehend	All stands upon its head
In dem Pavillon aus grünem	In the pavilion of green
Und aus weissen Porzellan;	And of white porcelain.
Wie ein Halbmond steht die Brücke,	Like a half-moon stands the bridge,
Umgekehrt der Bogen. Freunde,	Reversed is its bow. Friends,
Schön gekleidet, trinken, plaudern.	Beautifully gowned, are drinking, gossiping.

IV

[Contralto Solo]

VON DER SCHÖNHEIT	OF BEAUTY
Junge Mädchen pflücken Blumen,	Youthful maidens are plucking flowers,
Pflücken Lotos blumen an dem Uferrande.	Plucking lotus flowers at the edge of the shore.
Zwischen Büchen und Blättern sitzen sie,	Between bushes and leaves are they sitting,
Sammeln Blüten in den Schoss und rufen	Gathering blossoms in their laps and calling
Sich einander Neckereien zu.	To each other in jest.
Gold'ne Sonne webt um die Gestalten,	The golden sun plays about their forms,
Spiegelt sich im blanken Wasser wider,	Reflected in the quiet water.
Sonne spiegelt ihre schlanken Glieder,	The sun mirrors their slender limbs,
Ihre süssen Augen wider,	Their sweet eyes,
Und der Zephir hebt mit Schmeichelkosen das Gewebe	And a zephir with gentlest caress raises the fabric
Ihrer Ärmel, auf, führt den Zauber	Of their selves, wafts the magic
Ihrer Wohlgerüche durch die Luft.	Of their perfume through the air,
O sieh, was tummeln sich für schöne Knaben	O see, beautiful youths at play
Dort an dem Uferrand auf mut'gen Rossen?	On fiery horses, over there at the edge of the shore.
Weit hin glänzend wie die Sonnenstrahlen;	Glistening from afar like rays of the sun;
Schon zwischen dem Geäst der grünen Weiden	Between the green branches of the willows
Trabt das jungfrische Volk einher!	Fresh youth is making its way!
Das Ross des einen wiehert fröhlich auf	The steed of one whinnies for joy
Und scheut und saust dahin,	And shies and rushes past.
Über Blumen, Gräser, Wanken hin die Hufe,	Over flowers, grasses, gallop his hoofs,

Sie zerstampfen jäh im Sturm die hingesunknen Blüten	Whose stormy stamping crushes the fallen blossoms.
Hei! Wie flattern im Taumel seine Mähnen,	Heigh! How his mane flies in the breeze,
Dampfen heiss die Nüstern!	How his nostrils dilate!
Gold'ne Sonne webt um die Gestalten,	The golden sun plays about the forms,
Spiegelt sie im blanken Wasser wider.	Reflecting them in the quiet water.
Und die schönste von den Jungfrau'n sendet	And the loveliest of the maidens
Lange Blicke ihm der Sehnsucht nach,	Sends the rider glances of yearning.
Ihre stolze Haltung ist nur Verstellung.	Her haughty bearing is no more than feigned.
In dem Funkeln ihrer grossen Augen,	In the sparkle of her wide eyes,
In dem Dunkel ihres heissen Blicks	In the darkening of the eager glance,
Schwingt kagend noch die Erregung ihres Herzens nach.	Ascends the plaint of the passion of her heart.

V

[TENOR SOLO]

DER TRUNKENE IM FRÜHLING

THE DRUNKEN ONE IN SPRINGTIME

Wenn nur ein Traum das Leben ist,	If life is no more than a dream,
Warum denn Müh' und Plag'?	Why bother?
Ich trinke, bis ich nicht mehr kann,	I'll drink, till drink no more I can,
Den ganzen, lieben Tag!	The whole live-long day!
Und wenn ich nicht mehr trinken kann,	And when no longer I can drink,
Weil Kehl' und Seele voll,	When throat and soul are full,
So tauml' ich bis zu meiner Tür	I'll tumble down before my door,—
Und schlafe wundervoll!	And sleep, and sleep and sleep.
Was hör ich beim Erwachen? Horch!	What hear I, awakening? List!
Ein Vogel singt im Baum.	A bird sings in a tree.
Ich frag' ihn, ob schon Frühling sei,	I ask him whether Spring has come,
Mir ist also wie im Traum.	I feel as in a dream.
Der Vogel zwitschert: Ja!	The birdling twitters. Yes! the Spring
Der Lenz ist da, sei kommen über Nacht!	Overnight has come!
Aus tiefstem Schauen lauscht' ich auf,	In contemplation deep I brood,
Der Vogel singt und lacht!	While birdling sings and laughs!
Ich fülle mir den Becher neu	Anew I fill my goblet
Und leer' ihn bis zum Grund	And drain it to the dregs
Und singe, bis der Mond erglänzt	And sing until the moon shines bright
Am schwarzen Firmament!	In the dark'ning firmament!
Und wenn ich nicht mehr singen kann,	And when no longer I can sing
So schlaf' ich wieder ein.	Again to sleep I'll go.
Was geht mich denn der Frühling an?	For what matters Spring to me?
Lasst mich betrunken sein!	Drunk only let me be!

VI

[CONTRALTO SOLO]

DER ABSCHIED

THE FAREWELL

Die Sonne scheidet hinter dem Gebirge.	The sun is sinking 'neath the hills.
In alle Thäler steigt der Abend nieder	Evening descends into the vales
Mit seinen Schatten, die voll Kühlung sind.	With its cool, quiet shadows.
O sieh! Wie eine Silberbarke schwebt	Behold! As a bark of silver
Der Mond am blauen Himmelssee herauf	The moon rises into the blue heaven.
Ich spüre eines feinen Windes Wah'n	I feel the motion of a gentle wind

Hinter den dunklen Fichten!	Behind the dark pines.
Der Bach singt voller Wohllaut durch das Dunkel.	The brook sings its music through the dark.
Die Blumen blassen im Dämmerschein.	The flowers grow pale in the twilight.
Die Erde atmet voll von Ruh' und Schlaf.	The earth breathes the quiet of rest and sleep.
Alle Sehnsucht will nun träumen,	All longing goes a-dreaming.
Die müden Menschen geh'n heimwärts,	Weary humanity is homeward bound,
Um im Schlaf vergess'nes Glück	To seek anew in sleep
Und Jugend neu zu lernen!	Forgotten fortune, youth.
Die Vögel hocken still in ihren Zweigen.	Birds are perched upon their branches.
Die Welt schläft ein!	The world falls into sleep.
Es wehet kühl im Schatten meiner Fichten.	The cool wind is in the shadow of my pines.
Ich stehe hier und harre meines Freundes;	I stand here and await my friend, for a last
Ich harre sein zum letzten Lebewohl.	farewell.
Ich sehne mich, O Freund, an deiner Seite	I long, O friend, at thy side
Die Schönheit dieses Abends zu geniessen.	To drink in the beauty of this evening.
Wo bleibst du? Du lässt mich lang allein!	Where are you? You leave me long in solitude!
Ich wandle auf und nieder mit meiner Laute	I wander to and fro with my lute
Auf Wegen, die von weichem Grase schwellen.	On paths thick with soft grass.
O Schönheit! O ewigen Liebens—Lebens—trunk'ne Welt!	O Beauty! O World, drunk with love eternal—life!

[ORCHESTRAL INTERLUDE]

Er stieg vom Pferd und reichte ihm den Trunk	He climbed from his horse and gave his friend
Des Abschieds dar. Er fragte ihn, wohin	a farewell cup; asked him
Er führe und auch warum es müsste sein.	Whither he was going, and why it needs must be.
Er sprach, seine Stimme war umflort. Du, mein Freund.	He spoke, his voice choking: O my friend, Fate
Mir war auf dieser Welt das Glück nicht hold!	in this world has not been kind to me!
Wohin ich geh'? Ich geh', ich wand're in die Berge.	Whither am I bound! I go, I wander into the mountains.
Ich suche Ruhe für mein einsam Herz.	I seek rest for my lonely heart.
Ich wandle nach der Heimat, meiner Stätte.	I am wand'ring toward my native place, my home,
Ich werde niemals in die Ferne schweifen.	I shall never roam in foreign lands.
Still ist mein Herz und harret seiner Stunde!	My heart is at rest and waits its hour!
Die liebe Erde allüberall blüht auf im Lenz und grünt	The dear Earth blossoms in the Spring and buds anew.
Aufs neu! Allüberall und ewig blauen licht die Fernen!	Everywhere and forever the luminous blue of distant space!
Ewig . . . ewig. . . .	Forever . . . forever. . . .
	(*English version based on that of A. H. Meyer*)

R. C. B.

Bohuslav Martinu

BORN: POLICKA, CZECHOSLOVAKIA, DEC. 8, 1890.

*There are so many who jealously keep their secrets, for fear of losing
them. But the mind of Martinů is so inventive that he does not care.
Besides, is not the proclaiming of a secret the surest means of
keeping it?*—PIERRE OCTAVE FERROUD.

Symphony No. 2

I. Allegro moderato. II. Andante moderato. III. Poco allegro. IV. Allegro.

COMMISSIONED BY a group of Czechoslovaks in Cleveland, this work is dedicated
"To My Fellow Countrymen in Cleveland." It was given its first performance
by the Cleveland Orchestra on Oct. 28, 1943. The score calls for two flutes,
piccolo, three oboes, three clarinets, two bassoons, four horns, three trumpets,
three trombones, tuba, kettledrums, side drum, bass drum, cymbals, triangle,
tam-tam, harp, piano, and strings.

Of the Second Symphony, Mr. Martinu has written:

In contemporary hands the symphony has returned to older, more reasonable
proportions, but the form and the content are always thought of as the expression
of something grandiose, tragic, or pathetic, in a certain sense dependent upon a
"program"; in other words, the idea remains literary rather than musical. . . .
Difficulties and complications present themselves when a composer is trying to
express elevated thoughts . . . simple events and simple things may appear
"grandiose" to the artist. In themselves they may not seem so spectacular, but in
music they may become quite as spectacular and just as inspiring.

Of course, I don't mean to rule out the dramatic conception of a musical work.
My Second Symphony, the case in point, is calm and lyric. It seems to me that we
have no need of a professional and technical expression of torture; rather do we need
orderly thought, expressed calmly.

Artur Rodzinski introduced the Symphony to New York at a Philharmonic-
Symphony concert on Dec. 30, 1943.

Bohuslav Martinu took up the violin when he was six years of age, two years
later appearing before the public. When he was twenty-three he completed the
violin course at the Prague Conservatory, and not long after that he became a
member of the Czech Philharmonic Orchestra's violin section where he remained for ten years. He is almost entirely self-taught as a composer, his formal
instruction consisting of a partial attendance of the Josef Suk course at the

Conservatory. Later, while in Paris, he met Albert Roussel, whose influence over him, however, was that of the admiring adviser.

Mr. Martinu has written an impressive array of works. He began at the age of ten with a piece for string quartet, steadily adding to his store with compositions in practically all the forms, including operas, symphonies, and other orchestral numbers, concertos, items of chamber music, operas for the radio, and scores for ballets.

In *The Musical Quarterly* for July, 1943, Milos Safranek, in an informative and interesting article on Bohuslav Martinu, declares:

We think of many composers who first came into prominence after the last war as *avant-gardistes,* and identify them with certain "advanced" fashions in poetry and painting. Martinu is one of the few contemporary composers of note who never was and never will be an *avant-gardiste.* Does the term, in actual fact, used in connection with artistic creation, mean anything definite? Does it not too frequently indicate the presence of a superficial, often vanishing newness, rather than any truly substantial qualities? To define what is new in the contribution of a contemporary artist is difficult if not impossible for the artist himself as well as for those who scrutinize his work. Mozart's greatness became evident only after his entire work was reviewed from a distance. Contemporary critics found in Cézanne's work many details that were interestingly new, but later generations have completely forgotten these details and have seen the substance of his originality in something quite different.

All this, however, does not mean that Martinu's work contains no new elements, that it is not original, or that in some respects he did not anticipate the current modern music by several years. Still, Martinu, with his close familiarity with the music of all ages and his high respect for all that has been perfect and great in world music through the centuries, could never have been a mere *avant-gardiste* and nothing more.

R. C. B.

Daniel Gregory Mason

BORN: BROOKLINE, MASS., NOV. 20, 1873.

This is writing of a sort which has, for the most part, disappeared from the music that is characteristic of our time. It is music of brain and sinew; it is clear-eyed; it is surefooted.—LAWRENCE GILMAN.

"A Lincoln Symphony," Op. 35

I. "The Candidate from Springfield." II. "Massa Linkum." III. "Old Abe's Yarns." IV. "1865."

THIS SYMPHONY, the composer's third, was written at "Little Cedars," New Canaan, Conn., in the summers of 1935 and 1936. The score bears a dedication "To the memory of Ossip Gabrilowitsch." Its first performance was given by the Philharmonic-Symphony Society under John Barbirolli on Nov. 17, 1937.

To a request for information from Lawrence Gilman, at that time annotating the Philharmonic programs, the composer replied:

The subject of Lincoln is tempting to American composers because by his ideals and measurably by his realities he was so great an American. He was magnanimous and tender; his sadness came from a just and pitiful view of human weakness, his great-hearted sympathy from a wish to help all strivers and sufferers; his humor was the good, realistic, tolerant, earthy kind. Deeply patriotic, he hated chauvinism and rebuked patrioteers. He had the aspiration for peace, with the sad sense of reality that saw how distant it was. His great heart made him one of his own people, his clear head made him a leader for the world as well as the nation. If any of our public men have embodied our ideals it was he. He stands in our pantheon beside Thoreau and Emerson.

Dr. Mason also supplied the following program note:

I. THE CANDIDATE FROM SPRINGFIELD

The brief introduction suggests the basic character of Lincoln—magnanimous and tender-hearted. A livelier theme, an actual quickstep of the 1860 period, "The Quabog Quickstep," then calls up the crowd, thoughtless, restlessly active, trivial. Another tune, for clarinet over plucked strings, suggests the people in their easygoing sentimental mood.

Lincoln's sincerity, however (more sustained melody, strings alone), begins to chasten and ennoble the popular temper, so that the quickstep itself loses its jerkiness and becomes almost wistful (oboe; later flute, answered by horn).

The double fugue and march that end the movement suggest the young leader's triumphal entry into Washington.

II. MASSA LINKUM

The slaves' view of their friend. The English horn, in a sort of spiritual, voices their grief. Lincoln's understanding and pity speak in the solo cello, later in lower strings. Throughout this movement the Negroes' part in the drama is enacted by the wood-wind instruments, particularly the English horn, Lincoln's by the strings, especially the cellos.

III. OLD ABE'S YARNS

In Lincoln's eyes one could read a spirit almost crushed by its load of responsibility. But in the easy stride of his long legs, in his slouching gait as he swung into the corner grocery store, in his wry smile and hoarse laugh as he told stories to his pals, one could sense all the relief he found in his grotesque, half-demoniacal humor.

IV. 1865

The introduction to the first movement recurs, solemnized now by all that America and Lincoln have suffered together. He lies dead. Never shall pity gaze again from his sorrowful, world-old eyes, never again can his friendly voice beseech from us "malice toward none, charity for all." The quickstep we once marched with him in triumph has turned to a funeral march in our tragic hearts. . . .

But now that his love for us can look no more from his eyes nor sound again ever in his voice, it seems for the first time to surround us in the very air, to speak comfort to our inmost hearts, as it could never do until all we had left of him was a memory.

Daniel Gregory Mason, for many years associated with the music department at Columbia University, studied with Ethelbert Nevin before going to Harvard. When he was graduated, he worked in Boston with Chadwick and in New York with Goetschius. In Paris he studied with d'Indy. He has been composing actively since 1900, despite his many duties as pedagogue, lecturer, and writer on music. He was appointed to Columbia University's music faculty in 1909. Twenty years later he was given the post of MacDowell Professor of Music. He retired from the chairmanship of the University's music department in 1940.

R. C. B.

Harl McDonald

BORN: NEAR BOULDER, COLO., JULY 27, 1899.

With all this tumult of accomplishment and frustration, I am always conscious of the fact that I am living in an age that has an almost insatiable appetite for gaiety and entertainment.—HARL McDONALD.

Symphonic Poem, "Bataan"

THIS WORK is the second in a cycle of three concerned with the Second World War. In October, 1941, Mr. McDonald wrote the initial composition of the cycle *October-1941*. It was given its first performance by the Indianapolis Symphony Orchestra under the direction of Fabien Sevitzky. Since then it has been heard in a number of Western cities.

Bataan was introduced by the National Symphony Orchestra July 3, 1942, at one of the Watergate concerts in Washington, D. C. The composer conducted. The following statement by Mr. McDonald was included in the program notes of that occasion:

During the weeks of late March and early Apr., 1942, the attention of all America was focused on Bataan Peninsula. There must have been a wide variety of feeling about the tragic drama that was unfolding there, for in many homes the picture was not simply the heroic stand of the American and Philippine armed forces—in many families it involved the battle for survival against overwhelming odds of a son or father or brother.

It is natural for a composer to translate his most compelling emotional experiences into music, and, as a result, during that three-week period, working late at night or whenever I could find an hour of freedom from other duties, I composed the tone poem I have called *Bataan*.

Against a fluctuating, agitated background appears a melody, slightly Oriental in character, which hints of the tragic ending of the piece. Suddenly the plucked strings introduce the rhythm of marching men, and above the sound of marching, the song continues in a variety of forms. Throughout this development, and with each reappearance of the theme, the music becomes more martial until at the climax the whole orchestra, with drums and trumpets, sings the song of the defenders. Suddenly the sound of drums and bugles recedes—there are a few faint echoes of the bugles, and the tragic song is heard again over the rhythm of the march, faintly, as from a distance. There is a repetition of the agitated opening measures before the music ends, pianissimo.

The composition bears a dedication to General MacArthur and the American and Philippine troops whose monumental courage and heroism will remain a bright spot in our history.

Harl McDonald was brought up in Southern California. Displaying early in life a keen interest in music, he began to compose at the age of seven, and a number of his first pieces have been published. Some years later he served as piano accompanist for well-known concert artists. In 1921, his First Piano Concerto was premiered by the San Francisco Symphony Orchestra.

A period of study in Germany followed, during which time his symphonic fantasy *Mojave* was played in Berlin and London. He has taught at the Academie Tournefort, Paris, the Philadelphia Academy of Music, and in 1927 came an appointment to the faculty of the University of Pennsylvania. He held that post until 1939, when he became the manager of the Philadelphia Orchestra.

Mr. McDonald has written a long list of works, consisting of four symphonies, some suites, a Concerto for Two Pianos and Orchestra, choral compositions, chamber music, and songs, besides the war cycle.

R. C. B.

Felix Mendelssohn

BORN: HAMBURG, FEB. 3, 1809. DIED: LEIPZIG, NOV. 4, 1847.

*To the Noble Artist, who, surrounded by the Baal-like worship of
debased art, has been able, by his genius and science, to preserve
faithfully, like another Elijah, the worship of true art, and once more
accustom our ear, amid the whirl of empty, frivolous sounds, to the
pure tones of sympathetic feeling and legitimate harmony: to the
Great Master, who makes us conscious of the unity of his conception,
through the whole maze of his creation, from the soft whispering to
the mighty raging of the elements.—Inscribed in grateful remembrance by* ALBERT (*Prince Consort*)

Buckingham Palace, 24th April, 1847.

Symphony in A minor, No. 3 ("Scotch"), Op. 56

I. Andante con moto; Allegro un poco agitato. II. Vivace non troppo.
III. Adagio. IV. Allegro vivacissimo; Allegro maestoso assai.
(Played without pause.)

WHILE SEEMINGLY far-fetched, Mendelssohn's *Scotch Symphony* is indirectly
linked with the murder of David Rizzio at Holyrood, on the night of Mar. 9,
1566, in the supper chamber of Queen Mary of Scotland.

Rizzio, an Italian musician who came to Scotland as a member of the
Piedmontese ambassador's entourage, was engaged by the ill-fated queen as
lute player, singer, and *valet de chambre*. Shortly before Mary married Darnley,
Rizzio was elevated to the post of "private foreign secretary." His growing
influence on Mary aroused the envy and hatred of Scottish nobles. A whispering campaign pictured him as Mary's lover. At any event, a band of nobles
broke into Mary's room one night, seized the Italian, and after hacking him to
death, flung his body out the window.

Rizzio's death inspired dramatists, poets, painters, and composers to an
imaginative reconstruction of the episode, often in the lurid light of Mary's
later imbroglios. Though historians still clash over the actual happenings,
romantic writers long ago accepted Rizzio's intimacy with the queen as a fact.

So, apparently, did a romantic-minded youth of twenty named Felix Mendelssohn, who toured Scotland in 1829. From Edinburgh, after a visit to the
rugged ruins of Holyrood, he writes on July 30:

We went, in the deep twilight, to the palace of Holyrood, where Queen Mary lived and loved. There is a little room to be seen there, with a winding staircase leading up to it. This the murderers ascended, and finding Rizzio drew him out. Three chambers away is a small corner where they killed him. . . . Everything around is broken and mouldering, and the bright sky shines in. I believe I found today in the old chapel the beginning of my *Scotch Symphony*.

Though Mendelssohn did not write finis to his Symphony till thirteen years later, he did jot down the first ten bars of the opening Andante section the day of his visit to Holyrood. It is not certain whether they were written in Edinburgh or on the actual site of the bloody deed of 263 years before. Anyway the few measures contained the seeds of his future A minor Symphony.

The intention to give the title of "Scotch" to the work does not appear in Mendelssohn's correspondence until 1832, when he so labeled the symphony to be in letters from Rome. Curiously enough, Mendelssohn omitted the title from the score, possibly fearing to impose too limiting a "program" on the music. The question of how much national rhythm and color went into the symphony has long troubled scholars. On one side are those convinced that Mendelssohn intended to convey the "solemn, pathetic, gay, and warlike" features of Scottish national music. They cite the fact that Mendelssohn attended a contest of Highland Pipers while in Edinburgh and was deeply stirred by the war tunes of the Scottish clans. Reminiscences of those themes are said to be embedded in the scherzo movement.

However, Mendelssohn made it a point never to "explain his music." If there is a "program" to his *Scotch Symphony,* the secret died with him. The pastoral, idyllic, elegiac, and bardic moods of the Symphony may readily suggest romantic Scotland, but just how far the Rizzio story and the border legends of feuding clans colored the musical web is futile speculation. No doubt they helped kindle Mendelssohn's imagination, as did the mingled brooding and vigor of Scottish folk music.

A good test of the Symphony's power to evoke "national" origins is to play it, without the "Scotch" label, before concertgoers hearing it for the first time. Robert Schumann once fell into such a trap. While the *Scotch Symphony* was being performed, a friend assured him he was listening to Mendelssohn's *Italian Symphony*. Schumann was accordingly entranced by visions of the Italian landscape awakened by the music. "It is so beautiful as to compensate a hearer who had never been to Italy," he remarked of a symphony whose last movement allegedly pictures "The Gathering of the Clans"!

As a matter of fact, Mendelssohn was a bit chary of certain brands of "national music." After visiting Scotland in July, 1829, he journeyed down to Wales before returning to London. "No national music for me!" he write from Llangollen on Aug. 25. "Ten thousands devils take all nationality! Now I am in Wales, and, dear me, a harper sits in the hall of every inn of repute playing incessantly so-called national melodies; that is to say, most infamous, vulgar, out-of-tune trash, with a hurdy-gurdy going at the same time!"

Listed as Mendelssohn's third, the *Scotch Symphony* was actually composed last and is thus rightly the fifth. Of the others the C minor dates from 1824, the *Reformation* from 1832, the *Italian* from 1833, and the *Lobgesang* (*Song of Praise*) from 1840. Among Mendelssohn manuscript *juvenilia* were twelve other symphonies, eleven scored for strings and one for full orchestra, all composed in his early teens. The *Scotch Symphony* was completed in Berlin on Jan. 20, 1842. The conductor led it from manuscript in Leipzig on Mar. 3.

After presenting the work the following June at a concert of the Philharmonic Society in London, Mendelssohn was granted the privilege of dedicating it to Queen Victoria. It is odd, to say the least, to find the name of England's rigorously proper Queen affixed to a symphony owing even partial origin to scarlet Mary Stuart. There is no record of Queen Victoria's ever having learnt of Mendelssohn's visit to the scene of an early mishap in Mary's amorous career. And she certainly never heard an account of how the opening bars of a symphony dedicated to her were composed not far from the site of a palace murder. Perhaps it is just as well that Mendelssohn did not divulge the "program" of his *Scotch Symphony*.

Like Mendelssohn's Violin Concerto, the *Scotch Symphony* should be played continuously, *i.e.,* without the usual pauses between movements. Though battles and bagpipes are excluded from Mendelssohn's scheme, except by implication, the first, scherzo (second), and finale movements would surely seem to justify the title given the symphony. In the scherzo there are opening calls in the wood winds and brasses which evoke Scottish moods. Later the clarinet chants a brisk theme reminiscent of Highland dance tunes, then developed in brilliant and rollicking style.

To Apthorp the breezy theme opening the finale Allegro was of "recognizably Scotch character." The movement's impetuous drive and heraldic vigor, together with the sturdy march motives, have suggested heroic Scottish legend and "the gathering of the clans." One analyst even drew from the finale a picture of "the wild Highlander, claymore in hand, sweeping down from his rugged hills joyously to do battle." And poor Schumann heard it as a symphonic trip to Italy!

Of course, Mendelssohn's habit of giving picturesque titles to compositions caused them to be literally viewed as "program music" by many. There is the story of how Schubring told Mendelssohn a certain passage of the *Sea Calm and Prosperous Voyage Overture* suggested to him "the tones of love entranced at approaching nearer the goal of its desires."

Mendelssohn, obviously joking, corrected his good friend Schubring by divulging what he really had in mind while writing that passage: "A good-natured old man sitting in the stern of the vessel and blowing vigorously into the sails, so as to contribute his part to the prosperous voyage."

Apart from the *Scotch Symphony,* Mendelssohn's trip to Scotland resulted in at least three other compositions, the *Fingal's Cave Overture,* the two-part song "O wert thou in the Cauld, Cauld Blast," and the *Sonate Ecossaise* for the piano, later called the F sharp minor Fantasy.

L. B.

Symphony in A major, No. 4 ("Italian"), Op. 90

> I. Allegro vivace. II. Andante con moto. III. Con moto moderato. IV. Saltarello, Presto.

THIS SYMPHONY, by the composer's own order, was not published during his lifetime. He was not satisfied with it. He related that it had caused him considerable pain. He toyed for a time with the idea of revising the last movement, but he never got around to it.

Ironically enough, the Symphony has been called a "perfect work," and the experts, past and present, who consider its last movement a gem are not few. Parry discovers not the least trace of bitterness in any of the Symphony's music, which may or may not be an argument against the idea that a composition reflects the author's physical and spiritual state at the time of its creation.

Mendelssohn visited Italy, and in a letter from Rome, dated February, 1831, he wrote, "I am making great progress with the *Italian Symphony*. It will be the most mature thing I have ever done, especially the last movement, Presto agitato." However, quite some time passed before he completed his work. In November, 1832, he was commissioned by the London Philharmonic Society to write "a symphony, an overture, and a vocal piece." The Symphony turned in was the *Italian,* and it was given its premiere performance in London, on May 13, 1833, under Mendelssohn's direction.

There is evidence that the brilliant Saltarello finale was inspired by the carnival in Rome. We have Mendelssohn's charming account of his participation in the festivities in a letter dated Feb. 8, 1831:

I arrived in the Corso and was driving along, thinking no evil, when I was suddenly assailed by a shower of sugar comfits. I looked up. They had been flung by some young ladies whom I had seen occasionally at balls, but scarcely knew. When in my embarrassment I took off my hat to bow to them, the pelting began in right earnest.

Their carriage drove on, and in the next was Miss T., a delicate young Englishwoman. I tried to bow to her, but she pelted me, too; so I became quite desperate, and clutching the confetti I flung them back bravely. There were swarms of my acquaintances, and my blue coat was soon as white as that of a miller.

My friends, the B's, were standing on a balcony, flinging confetti like hail at my head. Thus pelting and pelted, amid a thousand jests and jeers and the most extravagant masks, the day ended with races.

The *Italian Symphony* is scored for flutes, oboes, clarinets, bassoons, horns, and trumpets in pairs, besides kettledrums and the usual strings. The first movement (Allegro vivace, A major, 6/8) opens brilliantly with a dashing theme in the violins. The second subject, in E major allotted to the clarinets, is of a more leisurely nature. A third theme, treated fugally, introduces the development section.

The second movement (Andante con moto, D minor, 4/4) has been called a Pilgrims' March. Doubtless it was suggested by a religious procession in the streets of Naples. But why Grove heard in the introductory measures the "cry of a muezzin from his minaret" is hard to understand.

The ingratiating third movement (Con moto moderato, A major, 3/4) is virtually a minuet. Especially beautiful is the trio, in E major, with its hint of profundities below the rippling surface.

The finale (Presto, A minor, 4/4) is the famous Saltarello, based on three themes, of which the third, with its series of uninterrupted triplets, the invariably accurate Rockstro declares is not a saltarello theme at all but a tarantella!

R. C. B.

Symphony in D, No. 5 ("Reformation"), Op. 107

I. Andante; Allegro con fuoco. II. Allegro vivace. III. Andante; Andante con moto (Chorale: "Ein feste Burg ist unser Gott"); Allegro vivace; Allegro maestoso.

MENDELSSOHN COMPOSED this Symphony for the tercentenary festival of the Augsburg Confession, which fell on June 25, 1830. The work began to "take shape" in his mind the previous September, while he was being royally feted in London. In fact, several other compositions were also taking shape when, according to the publication *Harmonicum,* "He was thrown from a cabriolet and very severely wounded in the leg, in consequence of the carriage first falling on him, then being dragged over his limb." The injuries were serious enough to keep him on the inactive list, creatively speaking, for a couple of months, but he found considerable recompense in the concern and hospitality of his English friends. As he wrote home, in October, "You cannot know how kind the English people are to me. As I cannot do justice to books and am not allowed to eat meat, they stuff me with fruit and all sorts of sweets."

By Nov. 29, Mendelssohn was well on the way to recovery and home to Berlin. During the following winter he completed the Symphony (though some authorities dispute the date). With the composer off again on his interminable journeying, the work was performed on the appointed day in Berlin.

We hear of it again early in 1832, when François Antoine Habeneck, founder and conductor of the Société des Concerts du Conservatoire of Paris, scheduled it for performance. The piece was rehearsed, and Mendelssohn wrote ecstatic letters about the coming event. His joy was premature, however, for the orchestra disliked the Symphony. "Too learned, too much *fugato,* too little melody," was the verdict. Mendelssohn did not refer to his disappointment in his correspondence.

In November and December, 1832, and January, 1833, he gave three public concerts at the room of the Singakademie, Berlin. Among the works he offered were his *Walpurgisnacht;* three Overtures, *Meerstille, Hebrides,* and *Midsummer Night's Dream;* the G minor Piano Concerto; the Capriccio in B minor; and the *Reformation Symphony.* The Berliners of the time were hard to please, however, and particularly were they so in the case of Mendelssohn, to whom they casually referred as a musician "who had talent as a boy."

The *Reformation Symphony* is not universally considered one of Mendelssohn's most vital works. "Certainly," wrote one observer, "it hardly marches beside the Church revolution which it celebrates. It bustles at times and meanders at others, but nevertheless it has good pages in which the music becomes bold and even lusty."

Some commentators have suggested that the first movement was inspired by "the reformers' joy in combat, their firmness of belief and trust in God." The composer utilizes the *Dresden Amen* in the first movement. (Oddly enough this same *Dresden Amen* is heard in Wagner's *Parsifal* music.) There was a time when devoted admirers of Mendelssohn hurled the charge of "plagiarist" against Wagner for the apparent theft. The musical phrase in question, however, may be found in the Saxon liturgy and, according to prewar advices, has always been in use at the "Court" Church of Dresden. The *Amen* is of unknown origin, though Silvani has been mentioned as its inventor. Very likely, it belongs to the seventeenth century, yet we have knowledge of similar progressions of sixths in the Masses of Palestrina.

The second movement has been described as "typically Mendelssohn, very correct as to form and development and, of course, written long before certain turns of phrase and harmonic sequences became overworked clichés of his style."

The Chorale of the last movement introduces Martin Luther's religious war cry *Ein feste Burg ist unser Gott,* of which effective use is made, particularly in its final quotation where the brass bring it to a compelling climax.

R. C. B.

Concerto for Violin and Orchestra in E minor, Op. 64

I. Allegro molto appassionato. II. Andante. III. Allegretto non troppo; Allegro molto vivace.

(Played without pause.)

LIKE OTHER standard concertos, Mendelssohn's in E minor is the record of a friendship and consultation between composer and soloist. Perhaps the closest parallel is that between Brahms and Joseph Joachim. In Mendelssohn's case the confidant and consultant was Ferdinand David.

The two had been friends since their early youth. The composer was eleven months older than the violinist. Though they were not to meet till they were fifteen and sixteen, by a coincidence they were born in the same house in Hamburg. David become Mendelssohn's concertmaster when the composer was appointed director of the Leipzig Gewandhaus concerts in Leipzig in 1835, remaining there for thirty-seven years, long after his friend's death. Mendelssohn's feeble health often obliged him to delegate much of the Gewandhaus routine to David. When Mendelssohn was stricken during a measles epidemic in Leipzig, it was David who took over the scheduled premiere of the *St. Paul Oratorio*.

Mention of the Violin Concerto does not occur in Mendelssohn's correspondence till July 30, 1838, about the time the great *Elijah Oratorio* was beginning to take shape in his mind. "I should like to write a violin concerto for you next winter," he writes to his first violinist. "One in E minor runs in my head, the beginning of which gives me no peace." Yet, almost a year passed before further reference was made to the project. Why he delayed is hard to say. Pressure of work was an old story with Mendelssohn. It did not interfere with his voluminous writings in other forms. Moreover, the friendship of a great virtuoso like David would normally have sufficed to hasten composition. Then, Mendelssohn had himself studied the violin, though he later preferred the viola when he took part in ensemble playing. Finally, as a boy of fourteen he had already evinced practical interest in the form by writing a violin concerto with string accompaniment. It belongs with a staggering mass of manuscript juvenilia, among which is still another concerto for violin and piano, with similar accompaniment.

In any case, David must have urged him repeatedly to take up the Concerto after the first announcement of the plan. But the winter went by without so much as a hint that the projected Concerto was still "running in his head." Early in July, 1839, Mendelssohn wrote to David from Hochheim, near Coblenz:

Now that is very nice of you to press me for a violin concerto! I have the liveliest desire to write one for you, and if I have a few propitious days here I shall bring you something of the sort. But it is not an easy task. You want it to be brilliant, and how is such a one as I to manage that? The whole first solo is to consist of the high E!

The work was not completed till Sept. 16, 1844. In the interim letters and conferences between composer and violinist were devoted to the detail and structure of the Concerto. David supplied practical counsel for the solo writing, as well as devising most of the cadenza as it now stands. Naturally there were occasional differences of opinion. Mendelssohn would yield where David's craftsmanship was the best guide. Elsewhere his own faultless instinct for form and expression prevailed. Before publication the work underwent further revision by Mendelssohn in the solo and orchestral parts.

As in similar instances of musical collaboration, it is futile to speculate on just what is David's in the E minor Concerto as we know it. Comparison of the final form with the sixty-six folio page manuscript has shown substantial alterations more in keeping with Mendelssohn's fastidious sense of design and polish. Mendelssohn always acknowledged his indebtedness to David. Certainly without his friendly prodding and advice, the world may never have had what many consider the most agreeable violin concerto ever written.

As expected, David was the soloist at the world premiere which occurred at a Gewandhaus concert on Mar. 13, 1845. Mendelssohn, then resting at Frankfort, was unable to conduct the Leipzig premiere, his place being taken by the Danish composer Niels Gade. The great success of the new work no doubt largely accounts for the ovation given Mendelssohn when he returned to Leipzig for his first concert on Oct. 5. Besides the stormy acclaim of the audience, the orchestra gave him a welcoming flourish.

Although the E minor Concerto has already rounded out a century of active life, the music still bears what one biographer rightly calls "the charm of eternal youth." One might go a step further than Stephen S. Stratton, who observed that the Mendelssohn Concerto "has no rival in popular favor save those by Beethoven and Brahms." In sheer popularity the Concerto probably stands first, or, at any rate, has stood first for long periods.

The work is typical of Mendelssohn's polished art. "As perfect as can be" is the way a biographer describes it. In classical poise, melodic suavity, and refined romantic feeling, it is an epitome of Mendelssohn's style. For emotional breadth and daring one naturally goes to Mendelssohn's more ebullient contemporaries. Finesse, cultivated taste, and an unerring sense of the appropriate were among his chief attributes. Romanticism in Mendelssohn took mellow, often elegiac, expression. Rugged strength and depth may be missing from his music, but the gallant *savoir-faire* and humanity remain a needed counterpoise to recurring slovenliness and insincerity. Mendelssohn is the gentleman par excellence of music. Since there was no room for gentlemen in the Nazi hierarchy of art, he came under the early ban of the "Aryan" supermen, and whole nations were soon denied the steadying, refreshing solace of his message. A speculative remark in Stratton's biography, first issued over forty years ago, takes on grim prophecy when viewed in the light of subsequent events.

"If the productions of Mendelssohn could be completely blotted out, would there be no blank in the world of art? Assuredly there would. Take away *Elijah,* the Violin Concerto, and the *Hebrides Overture*—to name only three typical works—and the machinery of the concert giver would be thrown out of gear. The world has not done with these yet." Emphatically not!

"The three movements of the concerto should be played without pause. The first (Allegro molto appassionato, E minor, 2/2) offers in the solo instrument, after one prefatory measure, the broad, patternlike chief subject. A transition theme is announced by the orchestra and taken over by the solo violin. The second subject, quiet and yearning, is given out softly in G major by flutes and clarinets in harmony above a long-held organ point in the solo instrument—its lowest note, G. In the development section the first subject is worked over and the cadenza is introduced before the recapitulation instead of after it.

"From the tempestuous ending of the coda a dramatic transitional passage leads to the second movement (Andante, C major, 6/8). Here an irruption of untimely applause is fatal to the effect intended by the composer. The solo instrument sings the broad, pellucid chief theme of the Andante. There is a middle section, restless and impassioned in mood. The first part is repeated, with an altered accompaniment for the solo violin.

"A short connecting movement (Allegretto non troppo, E minor, 4/4) introduces the finale (Allegro molto vivace, E major, 4/4). This brilliant rondo, beginning with calls of trumpets, horns, bassoons, and drums, to which the solo instrument replies with garlands of arpeggios before giving out the spirited first subject, typifies Mendelssohn in the joyous and elfin vein, but with an undercurrent of a deeper and more serene contentment."

L. B.

Overture, "The Hebrides" ("Fingal's Cave"), Op. 26

As THE result of Mendelssohn's visit to Scotland in August, 1829, two compositions were born, *The Hebrides Overture* and the *Scotch Symphony*. The composer, then twenty years old, made detailed sketches, musical, as well as pictorial, of the interesting things and places he saw and, of course, the two afore-mentioned works are represented frequently enough in his notes.

The Overture, also known as *Fingal's Cave,* has let loose the torrents of Elise Polko's fancy in her *Social and Artistic Biography of Mendelssohn,* and she sees in the music "amid all its sportive strains Mary Stuart's enticing, alluring eyes as they looked forth in bygone days from the ivy-mantled windows of the palace of Holyrood, when listening to the tones of her faithful minstrel Rizzio's lute."

Others have followed the composer's own program, sensing a musical picturization of Fingal's Cave, that and nothing more.

On his return to Berlin, Mendelssohn was assailed by questions concerning the Hebrides. Whereupon the composer is alleged to have answered, "It cannot be told, only played." He then sat at the piano and played the theme and as much else as he had sketched until then.

He took all the material he had collected to Italy, and in a letter to his sister from Rome, dated December, 1830, he announced the completion of the piece. Yet two years later the number was not "quite right," he wrote from Paris. "The middle portion in E is too stupid, and the whole working out smells more of counterpoint than of train oil, seagulls, and salt fish, and must be altered," he continued.

Finally the Overture was given its initial performance by the Philharmonic Society of London, at Covent Garden, on May 14, 1832. It was an immediate success.

The score calls for wood winds in two's, two horns, two trumpets, tympani, and strings.

R. C. B.

Overture, "Zum Märchen von der schönen Melusina" ("To the Legend of Fair Melusina"), Op. 32

THOUGH APPEARING first in the medieval Chronicles of Poitou, the legend of the Fair Melusina early crossed the French borders and became the common property of all lands. The romantic German writer Tieck confected a highly imaginative version, and in time the tale found its way into opera, symphonic poems, and even piano literature. Tieck's version is regarded as one of Mendelssohn's sources of inspiration.

Briefly, Melusina, for an act of sorcery against her own father, was condemned to a hard fate by her mother. Every Saturday she became a mermaid. Soon Melusina met and married Count of Lusignan, who agreed not to see her on Saturdays. But one day he took a peek and the secret was out. Melusina was promptly banished. In revenge, she haunted Lusignan castle ever after whenever death impended. The superstition long lingered in certain parts of France where ominous sounds heard at night were regarded as *les cris de Mélusine*.

Mendelssohn is said to have become interested in the legend after seeing a picture of Melusina "as a mermaid" at Düsseldorf. But it was from that city that he wrote to his sister Fanny on Apr. 7, 1834, explaining that he had written the overture for Konradin Kreutzer's opera *Melusine,* produced in Berlin on Feb. 27, 1833. What attracted him, it seems, was not so much Kreutzer's score as the lady singing the title role—Amalie Hähnel. Mendelssohn found her "charming" and "lovely." According to Sir George Grove, the first performance was at Düsseldorf in July, 1834; according to others, at a Philharmonic Concert in London, on Apr. 7 of the same year.

Schumann, writing after a Leipzig performance of the overture, warned listeners against attempting to follow the tale too literally in Mendelssohn's music. "One must not here, any more than in the overture to Shakespeare's *Midsummer Night's Dream,* wish to trace so coarse a historical thread all through," he pointed out. "Mendelssohn here portrays only the characters of the man and the woman, of the proud, knightly Lusignan and the enticing, yielding Melusina. But it is as if the watery waves came up amid their embraces and overwhelmed and parted them again." The music also reminded Schumann of "those fables of life deep down beneath the watery abyss, full of shooting fishes with golden scales, of pearls in open shells, of buried treasure, which the sea has snatched from men, of emerald castles. . . ." That Mendelssohn himself thought of his overture along the same lines may be gathered from the letter to his sister dated Jan. 30, 1836. He speaks of the music as dealing with "red corals, green sea monsters, fairy palaces, and deep seas."

Three chief themes can be distinguished in the Overture: Melusina's, appearing first with rippling arpeggio figures and then in more sustained lyric guise; the Count's theme, introduced by the first violins, and of robuster spirit, and an easily identified "love" theme, also announced by the first violins and then developed over the undulating support of second violins and violas. The arpeggio figure in the Melusina theme is used by Wagner in the Rhine-daughter music of both *Das Rheingold* and *Götterdämmerung.*

L. B.

Overture, "Ruy Blas," Op. 95

IN FEBRUARY, 1839, representatives of the Theatrical Pension Fund at Leipzig asked Mendelssohn to write "an overture and a romance" for a charity performance of Victor Hugo's play *Ruy Blas,* which was scheduled to be given on the following Mar. 11. Although he was loaded down with work, he was ready to comply with their wishes, for he felt the cause to be a worthy one. When he read the play, he pronounced it "detestable and beneath contempt," so, as a sort of compromise, he wrote only the "romance"—in actuality a chorus, which was delivered some weeks later.

In a letter thanking him for his kind contribution, the directors of the Pension Fund performance also mentioned that apparently they had not given him enough time to compose an overture. Later Mendelssohn said:

This put me on my mettle. I reflected on the matter the same evening, and began my score. On Wednesday there was a concert rehearsal, which occupied the whole forenoon. Thursday, the concert itself, yet the Overture was in the hands of the copyist early on Friday; played three times on Monday in the concert room, tried over once in the theater, and given in the evening as an introduction to the odious play. Few of my works have caused me more amusing excitement.

R. C. B.

Overture to the Opera "The Wedding of Camacho"

COMPLETED IN August, 1825, *Die Hochzeit des Camacho* (*The Wedding of Camacho*) is an opera in two acts with a libretto by Mendelssohn's young friend Karl Klingemann. The subject is taken from an episode in *Don Quixote*.

Klingemann, a member of the very exclusive coterie of friends surrounding the composer, used to write little verses of all kinds which Mendelssohn proceeded to set to music. It was sport for the two young men, and they used to indulge in a great deal of horseplay over their silly collaborations.

An attaché of the Hanoverian legation in London, Klingemann somehow hit on the fragment from *Don Quixote* and managed to make a two-act libretto of it. As blithely as you please and with a bluntness that was characteristic of him, he made Don Quixote a serious hero in full possession of all his faculties.

This transformation, of course, could scarcely stop Mendelssohn from setting the libretto, particularly since in those days he might even have musicated an almanac. Anyway, a performance of the work was given at the Mendelssohn family's home in Berlin. Eduard Devrient was one of the interpreters, but his heart was scarcely in his work. Mendelssohn, as a matter of fact, had rejected a libretto of Devrient's based on Torquato Tasso's *Gerusalemme Liberata* (*Jerusalem Delivered*), and the composer's acceptance of what the singer considered a greatly inferior work made the disappointment all the keener. Klingemann, it can be imagined, was ecstatic.

But though the opera was liked by the group of friendly listeners, it was an entirely different matter when the Royal Opera gave it two years later. The piece was submitted to Spontini, then general music director of the Royal Opera, by Mendelssohn himself. The Italian composer, a rather tart and jealous individual, if the say-so of his contemporaries is to be taken literally, found many faults with it. There were delays and complications of all kinds. Finally, a date was set and the work was given (again with Devrient) in the chamber theater, instead of the large auditorium, on Apr. 29, 1827.

The loyal adherents of the composer were all present. They all applauded mightily. But Mendelssohn knew it was their friendship for him that made them do so. He was sitting a little away from the others. He wanted to listen to the opera objectively, critically. What he heard was not encouraging. He left the hall in great haste before the final curtain.

At the end, the audience called for the composer. The clamor increased, but no Mendelssohn. Finally Devrient, making a guess at what had happened, went before the gathering and apologized for the absence of his friend.

The next day, Mendelssohn saw the newspaper reports. The line "for a rich man's son it was a fair endeavor" practically drove him mad with its smugness. Another wrote, "This has in no way enhanced the greatly overrated reputation of Herr Mendelssohn-Bartholdy. Let him return seriously to his studies and think of composition as a serious profession."

There was talk, for a time, of a repetition, but nothing came of it, much to the composer's satisfaction. In fact, the opera was not given again during his lifetime, and, oddly enough, the next complete stage performance occurred in Boston, on Mar. 19, 1885.

R. C. B.

Excerpts from the Music to "A Midsummer Night's Dream"

(a) Overture. (b) Nocturne. (c) Intermezzo. (d) Scherzo. (e) Wedding March.

In 1826, when Mendelssohn was barely seventeen, he read, together with his sister Fanny, translations by Schlegel and Tieck of Shakespeare's plays. As a direct result of those sessions, Mendelssohn wrote the Overture *A Midsummer Night's Dream*. Hiller remarks on the composer's devotion to that music and of "How in his spare time between lectures at the Berlin University he had gone on extemporizing at it on the piano of a beautiful woman who lived close by; 'for a whole year, I hardly did anything else,' he said; and certainly he had not wasted his time."

Written first as a piano duet, the Overture was performed for Moscheles by the composer and his sister on Nov. 19, 1826. Later it was done by an orchestra in the garden house of the Mendelssohn estate. Publicly it was first played at Stettin in February, 1827, when Karl Löwe conducted it from manuscript. (It is interesting to note that a critic who reviewed the work in the publication *Harmonicum* of the following December could find little of use in it.) A London audience first heard the piece, at the Argyll Rooms, on June 24 (Midsummer Day), 1829, with Louis Drouet to conduct. It was given its initial performance in conjunction with the Shakespeare play at Covent Garden in 1840.

When in 1843 King Frederick William the Fourth of Prussia commissioned Mendelssohn to write incidental music for the plays *Antigone, A Midsummer*

Night's Dream, and *Athalie*—which were to be produced in September of that year—Mendelssohn composed the rest of the score, which now, together with the Overture, comprises the music to *A Midsummer Night's Dream.*

The production complete with this incidental music was given in the theater of the New Palace at Potsdam, on Oct. 14, 1843. The first concert performance took place under Mendelssohn's own conducting in London, on May 27, 1844. The score was published in June, 1848.

Altogether the music to *A Midsummer Night's Dream* consists of thirteen numbers: I. Overture; II. Scherzo; III. Melodrama and March of the Elves; IV. Song for two solo sopranos and choruses of women's voices; V. Melodrama; VI. Intermezzo; VII. Melodrama; VIII. Nocturne; IX. Melodrama; X. Wedding March; XI. Melodrama and Funeral March; XII. Bergomask Dance; XIII. Melodrama and Finale.

Of the various sections of incidental music to *A Midsummer Night's Dream* only five, as a rule, are played in the concert hall, although there have been performances of the score as a whole. The five include the Overture, the Nocturne, the Intermezzo, the Scherzo, and the Wedding March. Of these the Overture and the Scherzo are the most frequently performed.

The Overture (Allegro di molto, E major 2/2) for all its grace and lightness is a very compactly made work. It establishes its thematic material almost at the beginning, develops it, introduces other themes pertinent to the subject matter of the Shakespeare play, and concludes with a charming coda. Of this perennially youthful music Sir George Grove said that Mendelssohn had "brought the fairies into the orchestra and fixed them there." And, coming right down to it, none may deny the piece its bristling imagery, gaiety, and romance. Yet it is possible that Grove, on making the statement, overlooked completely the fact that Weber had "brought fairies into the orchestra" some time before Mendelssohn turned the trick; in January, 1826, to be exact, when he first put pen to paper on behalf of *Oberon.* Furthermore, the opera was completed in April of that year, several months before Mendelssohn's Overture.

The Scherzo (Allegro vivace, G minor, 3/8) comes between the first and second acts of the play. It is scored for two flutes, two oboes, two clarinets, two bassoons, two horns, two trumpets, kettledrums, and strings. The section has two main subjects, the first—carrying a subsidiary one—is announced by the wood winds at the beginning, and the second by the strings in unison.

R. C. B.

Gian-Carlo Menotti

BORN: MILAN, ITALY, JULY 7, 1911.

*Menotti represents something of a phenomenon in American music;
before he was twenty-six he had completed, and seen produced, an
opera ("Amelia Goes to the Ball") of such sparkling gaiety and
charm that it disarmed all criticism.*—JOHN TASKER HOWARD.

Overture to the Opera "The Old Maid and the Thief"

MR. MENOTTI composed his first opera—a "childhood venture"—when he was
eleven, in Italy. The second was *Amelia Goes to the Ball. The Old Maid and
the Thief* was his third. A fourth was *The Island God* and a fifth, *The Medium*.
For all these he provided his own librettos. *Amelia Goes to the Ball* was
produced under the aegis of the Curtis Institute of Music, in Philadelphia, and
produced in New York at the New Amsterdam Theater on Apr. 11, 1937.
The Island God was commissioned by the Metropolitan Opera Association,
which produced it on Feb. 20, 1942. His latest opera *The Medium,* the result
of a commission from the Alice M. Ditson Fund, was given its premiere at the
Brander Matthews Hall on May 8, 1946.

The story of *The Old Maid and the Thief* revolves about three main characters, Miss Todd, an old maid; Laetitia, her servant; and Bob, a handsome
young tramp. There is also Miss Pinkerton, another old maid, who is the town
gossip.

Bob, seeking a handout at Miss Todd's house, makes a very favorable impression, first on the servant and then on Miss Todd. Pity and a variety of
other reasons—deeper rooted—prompt the women to shelter him. He is explained off to Miss Pinkerton as a cousin, and this is satisfactory to Bob, who
just does not seem to care.

Miss Pinkerton rushes in with the information that a desperado has broken
jail in a near-by county and is believed to be hiding in the town. Of course,
the two women who harbor him think Bob is the man, but they like having
him around, so they say nothing to him about the escape. They dance attendance on him, even to providing him with what has always been a tabu in
Miss Todd's house, liquor. What is more, they steal it, because they just could
not be seen walking into a liquor store, you know. Of course, everyone in the
audience is certain that Bob is not the desperado, even though he later proves
his innocence to the maid, anyway.

After a night of solitary tippling, he resolutely announces his departure.
Miss Todd—with romance fleeing—threatens, she storms, she will call·the

police and rushes out to do so. And Bob, realist that he is, picks the house clean of all valuables and, with Laetitia as companion, strikes out for other parts.

The score contains two particularly good arias, Laetitia's "Steal Me, Sweet Thief" and Bob's "I Must Wander Again." The music is melodious and effervescent, generally of the opera-buffa persuasion, not without, however, some incursions into a more modern idiom.

The Old Maid and the Thief was commissioned by the National Broadcasting Company as a "radio opera." It was first performed on the air on Apr. 24, 1939, and made an immediate success. However, the Overture was not written until later, and it obtained its premiere when the Philadelphia Opera Company gave the opera its initial stage presentation.

Gian-Carlo Menotti comes of a family of musicians. As a child he took part in many chamber-music sessions with his brothers and sisters—ten of them. His mother was his first teacher, and his early training stressed the classical; he recalls that his mother used to teach the old Gregorian chants to the local peasants. Mr. Menotti has reversed a usual procedure in that he came to this country to complete his musical education. In 1928, he enrolled at the Curtis Institute of Music, where he studied composition with Rosario Scalero. He has lived in this country ever since.

A Guggenheim Fellowship, recently awarded, will enable him to compose another comic opera *The Last Superman,* about a girl who seeks a primitive hero, finds him in India, and brings the prize with her to New York.

R. C. B.

Suite from the Ballet "Sebastian"

THIS SUITE stems from the score Mr. Menotti wrote for the ballet *Sebastian,* produced by the Ballet International at the International Theater, in November, 1944. The composer was also responsible for the scenario of the Ballet, a tale of magic rites, superstition, and witchcraft in fourteenth-century Venice. Edward Caton composed the choreography; Oliver Smith designed the settings; and the costumes were done by Milena.

The Suite consists of five sections, "Introduction," "Barcarolle," "Street Fight," "Cortège," and "Pavane." Expertly combining elements of both traditional and modern styles, the score is especially tuneful and vividly orchestrated.

Mr. Menotti's mastery of such a time-honored device as a fugato is convincingly illustrated in the section "Street Fight," where he converts it to a sparkling and rhythmically energetic prototype of the stage action. For all its present-day pace and style the music, in general, does not lack a graceful, one might say, medieval atmosphere. Nor does it want emotional intensity.

The *Sebastian* Suite received its first concert performance by the Philharmonic-Symphony at the Lewisohn Stadium on Aug. 8, 1945, Alexander Smallens conducting.

R. C. B.

Nikolai Miaskowsky

BORN: NOVOGEORGIEVSKY, APR. 20, 1881.

The power and action of this music come from its dynamic idiom, which one could ascribe to a state of anxiety of various degrees and colorings: from timorous apprehension to dread of the immobility of nature, of its terrifying silence and menace.—IGOR GLEBOV.

Symphony No. 21

THE MOST prolific of Soviet composers, Miaskowsky baffles attempts to classify him as symphonist. His early compositions moved a Russian critic to label him "the natural and only successor of Moussorgsky and Tschaikowsky." Then the lack of sharp individuality in color or technic served to shift attention to Miaskowsky's grasp of form. He was grouped with the "absolutists." The prevalence of macabre moods in the Sixth Symphony seemed to indicate a trend toward the "symbolism of death." Miaskowsky was now dubbed a "modern musical Dostoevsky." The Eighth Symphony dispersed the gloom with its rollicking folk themes, and the Ninth and Tenth, in light, unaffected vein, confirmed the change.

It is said that with his Twelfth Symphony Miaskowsky frankly attested faith in the October Revolution through an avowed tribute to "the Soviet village." The formerly somber and aloof composer had been swept into the whirling current of the new society. Still, Nicolas Slonimsky associated him with the Moscow, or romantic, school of Soviet music, *i.e.,* with the older generation represented by Ippolitoff-Ivanoff, Gliere, Vasilenko, Gnessin, rather than with the younger and more dynamic set in Leningrad, recognizing, however, that Miaskowsky had discarded his "inherent romanticism" and "switched over to Soviet thematics." As for Miaskowsky's own esthetic credo in symphonic writing, he proclaimed it in 1939 in reply to critics who were hailing his Fifteenth Symphony as a testament of good cheer:

Many commend my Fifteenth Symphony for its cheerfulness and its lyrical feeling. But such things do not constitute the language that I seek to express as a musical creator of our day. I do not know what this language should be, and I hold no formula in the matter of its creation. Neither folk song nor the melodies of cities can be the sole ingredients of the language used by Soviet realism.

Miaskowsky dedicated his Sixteenth Symphony to Soviet fliers, and his Eighteenth to the twentieth anniversary of the October Revolution. In both, the folk feeling is again a dominant feature.

In his Twenty-first Symphony Miaskowsky has evidently resumed the trend first manifested in the Eighth, where he utilized folk themes, though without tossing them bodily into the symphonic fabric. In a communication to *The New York Times* the composer Serge Prokofieff credited Miaskowsky with aiding in the discovery of a hitherto untapped vein of folk music in one of the small Caucasian republics. The Symphony is based in part on fragments of this native material.

Miaskowsky's symphonies vary considerably in length, some being of the standard four-movement duration, others of little more than full-size overture length. The Twenty-first, one of the shortest, is in one movement. Though a central theme unites the symphony, or "Symphony-Fantasy," tempo and feeling shift in clearly defined divisions. The chief theme, readily recognized by its wide-spaced intervals, is built up with dramatic force. An introduction in fugal form precedes the main Allegro theme, followed by a slow episode, then a section in scherzo style, and finally the recapitulation.

The Twenty-first Symphony brought Miaskowsky, who had earlier been made Honored Artist of the Soviet Union, the 1941 Stalin Music Prize. Alexander Hauck had led the world premiere in the Tschaikowsky Concert Hall in Moscow on Nov. 16, 1940. A Leningrad performance followed in the spring of 1941, the occasion being a series of concerts reviewing Soviet Symphonic Music. Prokofieff reported that during the war Miaskowsky devoted himself to composition, "with all the passion of a great artist." Symphonies Nos. 22 and 23, composed partly in Moscow bomb shelters, have been completed, along with two string quartets and a sonatina.

Bernard Herrmann conducted the American premiere of Symphony No. 21 with the Columbia Broadcasting Symphony on Aug. 23, 1942, as part of a Russian-American Festival of Music emphasizing "what the modern Soviet composers are doing in war time."

Howard Barlow conducted the first American concert performance with the New York Philharmonic-Symphony on Nov. 5, 1942.

L. B.

Darius Milhaud

BORN: AIX, PROVENCE, FRANCE, SEPT. 4, 1892.

Springing from a native lyricism, his music always sings. Whether he composes a five-act opera or a two-page song, this singing quality is paramount. The music flows so rationally that it seems to have been improvised rather than composed.—AARON COPLAND.

"Suite Symphonique," No. 2, from Paul Claudel's play "Protée" ("Proteus")

I. Ouverture. II. Prélude et Fugue. III. Pastorale. IV. Nocturne. V. Finale.

CONSISTING OF five pieces drawn from Mr. Milhaud's incidental music to Paul Claudel's mythical fantasy, the *Suite Symphonique,* No. 2, was first performed in Paris on Oct. 24, 1920, at one of the Concerts Colonne directed by Gabriel Pierné. It was introduced to America by Pierre Monteux at a concert of the Boston Symphony Orchestra on Apr. 22, 1921. Of both the play and the music, Mr. Milhaud communicates the following:

Paul Claudel's *Protée* is a satyric drama, a strong mixture of truculent gaiety and poetry. I wrote three different versions for the play, the first in 1913 after a meeting with Claudel at Helleran, Germany, when he had just finished writing *Protée.* This was for chorus and orchestra, consisting merely of pieces necessary to the drama.

In 1916 the actor Gemier planned a performance of *Protée* in a circus, and I rescored the music for small orchestra. When the Théâtre au Vaudeville produced lyric works in 1919, *Protée* was announced for production. I was asked to develop the music, add some preludes, and use a larger orchestra. But the Théâtre did not continue, and it was not till later on that *Protée* was finally produced in certain universities, among them Groningen (Holland), the Sorbonne (Paris), and the University of Geneva.

The Suite is made up of five pieces from my last version. The set consists of an "Ouverture" in a tango habañera rhythm; a "Prélude" (very fast) and "Fugue" (for brasses, with the rest of the orchestra sustaining them), a "Pastorale," using the rhythm 3-3-2; a "Nocturne" in 5/8 time, which has also been used for a piano-and-violin piece called "Le Printemps," and a "Finale," of a strong and bright character.

Claudel's dramatic poem has been described as depicting "with touching pathos and lyric expression the hopeless love of the old man Proteus for a young girl. There is a satiric strain, too, a mockery that assails the unhappy swain from all sides, even from the birds of the air and the seals of the sea." In Greek mythology, Proteus was an old prophet who dwelt in an island cave in the

Aegean Sea and tended the sea god Poseidon's "herd" of seals. He could change himself into any beast or element; hence the adjective "protean."

There is some picturesque background to the *Suite Symphonique,* No. 2, that Mr. Milhaud has modestly refrained from communicating. In fact, its world premiere at the Concerts Colonne was something of a historic occasion, since it involved two phenomena rare in concert-hall annals—an appeal to the police and an attempt to arrest a music critic. M. Pierné had just finished conducting Bach's *Brandenburg Concerto* No. 5. The audience sat through it with model calm and absorption. Nothing suggested an impending upheaval. Then came Mr. Milhaud's innocently entitled novelty. At first there were only indignant mutters. But a chorus of sharp jeers broke out at the end of the "Ouverture." After the "Prélude" and "Fugue" the hissing and whistling were so loud that M. Pierné lowered his baton and appealed for quiet. "Be so good as to authorize us to continue the program as printed," he begged. The plea fell on deaf ears. The hooting only increased, completely drowning out what brave applause came from the Milhaud wing.

Finally, the police were called in. The balcony *fauteuils* were cleared of dissenters, and a dramatic attempt at the forcible removal of a critic was made. His tender feelings affronted by the music, M. Brancour of *Le Ménestrel* was in the vanguard of the rebels. "I was on the point of being delivered to the secular arm charged with the expulsion of the heretics," he related in his column of Oct. 29, "when our eminent colleague, M. Paul Souday, valiantly intervened, attesting the indisputable right of every listener to manifest his opinion, and thus successfully appeasing the guardian of the peace." M. Brancour was not to be cheated of his revenge. "I will not honor this pitiful piece of insanity with an analysis," he affirmed haughtily. "It is low, trivial, and grossly blustering." He gave the number of those applauding as a scant two dozen, describing the rest as "openly expressing their exasperation." He quoted from the program that the music was intended to "illustrate a repast of seals, a kind of nocturnal bacchanale compounded of silence." *Sic!,* M. Brancour commented parenthetically: "Would that the gods had seen fit to replace this unparalleled chaos of noise with silence." M. Brancour could also hiss in print.

At the Concert Colonne of the following Saturday, Oct. 30, M. Pierné saw fit to repeat the *Suite Symphonique.* The hall was jammed. Curiosity seekers flocked to the event, expecting to witness fresh explosions of feeling. This time Pierre de Lapommeraye went as representative of *Le Ménestrel* (it is not known whether M. Brancour again attended—in an unofficial capacity).

"Let me report at once," wrote M. Lapommeraye on November 5, "that there was no demonstration. However, we were now documented by the program on M. Milhaud's polytonality." Of this "confused maze" (*dédale enchevêtré*) the *Ménestrel* reviewer wrote:

The composer had the ironic idea of parodying a classical fugue with the trombones. The opening, frankly amusing in its coarse gaiety, gets complicated with mingled tonalities. Defects arise, as in Beckmesser's song in *Die Meistersinger*. It is then that it crosses the frontiers of the possible and cacophony takes over, prolonged and painful. One leaves all this with a vile headache, scarcely soothed by the oasis freshness of the "Pastorale."

If Mr. Milhaud was at all put out by the reviews of Messrs. Brancour and Lapommeraye, he probably consoled himself with the thought that earlier French critics had used language no less devastating about the First Symphony of another young firebrand of music—Ludwig van Beethoven.

Despite the early blasts against it, the *Suite Symphonique* was widely performed in the early twenties, Mr. Milhaud himself conducting it several times at the Concerts Pasdeloup (Paris), as well as in Brussels, Amsterdam, London, Berlin, and Prague. Both Willem Mengelberg and Serge Koussevitzky directed it in Europe. Shortly after Pierre Monteux brought it into the repertory of the Boston Symphony, Frederick Stock added it to that of the Chicago Symphony Orchestra.

The *Suite Symphonique* is dedicated to Albéric Magnard, a lonely French composer of quiet, peaceful temperament, who was slain by the Germans on Sept. 3, 1914, in a stubborn defence of his country house at Baron (Oise). The work is scored for three flutes (third flute interchangeable with piccolo), two oboes, English horn, two clarinets, bass clarinet, four bassoons, four horns, three trumpets, three trombones, bass tuba, tympani, bass drum, tambourine, cymbals, triangle, *fouet,* celesta, harp, and strings.

Paul Claudel was one of three significant French poets in Milhaud's career. Poet and composer worked together in the French legation in Rio de Janeiro from 1917 to 1919. Between diplomatic assignments they collaborated on works for the theater. From Milhaud's own admission, one gathers that Claudel introduced him to a new outlook on art, one that was "alive and sane." Previously, Milhaud had set verses by Francis Jammes, who apparently exerted a strong influence in drawing him away from the impressionism and symbolism long prevalent in French art. "The verse of Jammes," Milhaud confides, "led me out of the symbolists' fog and revealed to me a new world to be captured, merely by opening one's eyes." Unlike Alexander, Milhaud has always managed to find new worlds "to be captured." His collected works read like a combined Baedeker and seven-arts compendium, with Brazil, ancient Greece, New York night clubs, shimmies, jazz, Russian ballet, Aeschylus, and Christopher Columbus included.

The modernist poet Jean Cocteau enters Milhaud's Parnassian trinity as a sort of publicity agent and patron saint of *Les Six*. Despite Milhaud's repeated efforts to minimize the importance and unity of the group, "The Six" are a cardinal number in the Milhaud register. France's *Les Six* are distantly related to "The Five" of Russian nationalist music. Eric Satie joined Cocteau in offering shrewd counsel to the group of young rebels against Debussy and Franck. The six consisted of Milhaud, Honegger, Tailleferre, Poulenc, Durey, and Auric. They followed no one program, though with varying degrees they stressed simplicity and brevity, recoiled from Debussyan impressionism and Franckian romanticism, and exploited fresh idiomatic material, like jazz. Custom and convention were anathema to this *societé des nouveaux jeunes*. Possibly the numeral originated in the publication of an omnibus album containing a piece of music by each of the six. In any case, Henri Collet, writing in *Comoedia* on Jan. 1, 1920, greeted the composer sextet as the harbingers of a "renaissance of French music." The article bore the title "Les Cinq Russes et les Six Français."

Milhaud told Olin Downes in the course of an interview in July, 1940:

They had no single direction, since each, from the beginning, was a different individuality, strongly distinguished from the others. Each has gone in his logical direction. But as regards public estimate of our position, I can tell you that we have had recently our twentieth anniversary of the *groupe* and ten years ago we had a tenth anniversary. . . . I do not believe that slogans or theories or even very important exterior events ever stem a creative artist's output for a considerable length of time. Creation is his instinctive way of expressing himself. . . .

Thus Honegger perserves in his energetic development. The simplification of his style as he progresses is notable. . . . Poulenc, as you surely know, was a former pupil of Ricardo Viñez, and a virtuoso. He has turned this accomplishment to effective use in former seasons in his very successful concerts with Pierre Barnac, the programs of which, because of their originality and interest, have had wide patronage in France and all Europe. Choral composition has recently engaged Auric. An a cappella Mass is a striking contribution.

Charming Germaine Tailleferre has become Madame Lageat, wife and mother, but has not lost the freshness of feeling in her music, and has written a good deal for the films and also for orchestra. Durey has not come out of his retirement, so far as composition is concerned. But he and the others of the "Six" had parted company, artistically speaking, years ago.

Auric has specialized much in film music, of which Honegger and myself have also composed a great deal.

Discussing the many-sided art of Milhaud—its lofty and poetic vein, its satire and buffoonery—Mr. Downes speculated in his article on which of the many Milhauds expressed in the composer's multifarious works was the "essential Milhaud." He wrote:

For this laconic person who does not pretend to be gay or to be capable of prophecy may well be what Henry Prunières once described him as being: "a follower of the romantic tradition, whose music often expresses a serious and religious feeling which is likewise found in Honegger, but which is entirely foreign to the preoccupations of the other musicians of the so-called "Group of Six."

Milhaud's one-act opera *Médée,* for which his wife wrote the book, enjoys the double distinction of being the Second World War's first new opera and the last opera to be given in a free Paris. The Nazis occupied the capital six days after the first performance on June 8, 1940.

L. B.

"Saudades do Brazil"

MILHAUD'S MUSICAL memories of Brazil grew out of a two-year sojourn in Rio de Janeiro as attaché of the French legation. Paul Claudel, the French poet, was also on the staff. During those years, 1917 and 1918, musician and poet collaborated on works for the theater between their diplomatic assignments. Milhaud also made his stay worth while by a close study and absorption of the musical culture of the country. When he returned to Paris in 1921, he set down his impressions of the Brazilian capital in a dance series called *Saudades do Brazil.*

These *saudades*—or souvenirs—consisted of an overture and twelve short pieces. The premiere occurred later that year at the Théâtre des Champs-Elysées. To Vladimir Golschmann, who conducted, the composer wrote that the dances were "memory echoes" of his musical experiences in Brazil, evocations of mood and atmosphere, not arrangements or syntheses of actual folk themes. It was at Mr. Golschmann's suggestion that the pieces, originally for piano, were orchestrated for the use of the Loie Fuller Ballets.

The composer himself introduced excerpts from his suite to America in 1923 when he appeared as guest conductor of the Philadelphia Orchestra. He then informed Lawrence Gilman, the program annotator, that he "desired that these compositions be regarded not as reproductions of actual dances, but as music suggested by the dance rhythms of Brazil—in the main by tango rhythms." The *Saudades* were to be regarded as a kind of composite portrait of the dances, "to some extent idealized."

Mr. Milhaud also pointed out that composers have always been influenced by the dances of their period and place—Bach by the sarabande and gavotte, Mozart by the minuet, Schubert and Chopin by the waltz, Stravinsky by ragtime. "So the younger men among contemporary composers," he continued, "have logically used the rhythms of the tango and fox trot as suggestive patterns for their music."

As their titles would indicate, the sections of the *Saudades do Brazil* are intended to depict separate districts, or *quartiers,* of Rio de Janeiro. The twelve districts and their respective sections follow in this order: (1) "Sorocabo"; (2) "Botafogo"; (3) "Leme"; (4) "Copacabana"; (5) "Ipanema"; (6) "Gavea";

(7) "Corcovado"; (8) "Tijuca"; (9) "Sumare"; (10) "Paineras"; (11) "Larenjeiras"; and (12) "Paysandu." The score calls for two flutes, two oboes, English horn, two clarinets, two bassoons, two horns, two trumpets, two trombones, tympani, bass drum, cymbals, snare drum, tambourine, triangle, and strings.

L. B.

"Suite provençale"

Animé. Très modéré. Vif. Modéré. Vif. Modéré. Vif. Lent. Vif.

Composed during the summer of 1936, the *Suite provençale* was premiered in September of that year at a concert of the annual Modern Music Festival in Venice. Milhaud directed and was again the conductor when the Boston Symphony Orchestra placed it in its repertory in December, 1940; the San Francisco, Los Angeles, and Illinois orchestras having already added it to theirs. The Suite had earlier made the rounds of the European capitals. Written for two flutes, two oboes, English horn, two clarinets, two bassoons, four horns, three trumpets, three trombones, tuba, tympani, percussion, and strings, the score bears a dedication to "M. D. M." Since Milhaud's wife, the French actress and librettist of his opera *Médée,* is named Madeleine, it is safe to assume the initials are hers.

Much of Milhaud's variegated music stems from the region of his birth. Some have even traced certain lyrical traits to the influence of Provençal folk songs. Before the outbreak of the Second World War Milhaud frequently retired to Aix-en-Provence to work on his latest score. There it was, in November and December, 1939, after two months of inertia following the beginning of hostilities, that he composed his Symphony for the fiftieth anniversary of the Chicago Symphony Orchestra.

In writing the *Suite provençale* Milhaud said he employed "popular folk airs from the Provence of the eighteenth century," some of which he found among the works of the seventeenth- and early eighteenth-century French composer André Campra, who, like himself, was born (1660) in Aix-en-Provence. The tunes, mostly in the markedly song-and-dance spirit of folk music, are briefly treated in a rapid sequence culminating in a broad *vif* section in 3/8 time, where the full orchestra is put to brilliant use.

When Milhaud conducted the Boston Symphony, the program contained three of his compositions, each representing a separate style. This led Grosvenor Cooper in *Modern Music* to speak of "Three Milhauds." One number, *Cortège funèbre,* expressed the Milhaud of somber, tragic vein, the same Milhaud, *i.e.,* who had supplied music for Paul Claudel's translations of Aeschylus. Another piece, the *Fantaisie pastorale,* proclaimed Milhaud "the mature master of intimate lyricism born of a chamber-music attitude." In a totally different category was the *Suite provençale.* This reflected the Milhaud reveling in a "not displeasing boisterousness and a frank acceptance of rhythm, color, and tunefulness, all of a sort sure to have popular appeal." Here was a "certain unsophisticated quality too frequently absent from recent French light music."

L. B.

"Suite française"

ORIGINALLY WRITTEN for band, *Suite française* was given its world premiere on the Mall in Central Park on June 13, 1945, at the opening concert of the Goldman Band's summer season. Edwin Franko Goldman conducted. In a prefatory note to the band score Mr. Milhaud writes:

The parts are not difficult to play either melodically or rhythmically and use only the average ranges for the instruments. For a long time I have had the idea of writing a composition fit for high-school purposes, and this was the result. In the bands, orchestras, and choirs of American high schools, colleges, and universities where the youth of the nation are found, it is obvious that they need music of their time, not too difficult to perform, but nevertheless keeping the characteristic idiom of the composer.

In its subsequent orchestral arrangement, the Suite was heard the following month, on July 29, at the Lewisohn Stadium, on a Philharmonic-Symphony program conducted by Maurice Abravanel. Concerning the material used in his Suite, Mr. Milhaud added the following information:

The five parts of the "Suite" are named after French provinces, the very ones in which the American and Allied armies fought together with the French underground for the liberation of my country: Normandy, Brittany, Île-de-France (of which Paris is the center), Alsace-Lorraine, and Provence.

I used some folk tunes of these provinces. I wanted the young Americans to hear the popular melodies of those parts of France where their fathers and brothers fought to defend the country from the German invaders, who in less than seventy years have brought war, destruction, cruelty, torture, murder three times to the peaceful and democratic people of France.

The Suite was recently performed by the Minneapolis and Chicago Symphony Orchestras (Nov. 18 and 25, 1945, respectively). It lasts about fifteen minutes, and the movements are marked: I. "Normandie": *Animé;* II. "Bretagne": *Lent;* III. "Île-de-France": *Vif;* IV. "Alsace-Lorraine": *Lent,* and V. "Provence": *Animé.* The manuscript bears the closing inscription, "Mills, December, 1944," the allusion being to Mills College, Oakland, California.

L. B.

"Le Bal martiniquais"

I. Chanson créole. II. Biguine.

SHORTLY AFTER the French West Indies were liberated in 1943, Mr. Milhaud received a sheaf of poems from the Governor of Martinique hymning the people's joy over their recovered freedom. Along with the verses came several old folk tunes of the island dependency to which they had been adapted. From this collection Mr. Milhaud made a little suite for piano and voice, calling it *La libération des Antilles*.

The composer has given the authors the following information:

It was the collection of these tunes on which I had just worked that gave me the idea of a two-piano work entitled *Le Bal martiniquais*. I thought these two pieces could be orchestrated. As a matter of fact, following the *Suite Française* which is based on French folk tunes, it makes a normal suite to end my little *fantaisie* on folk tunes of the French Empire.

Douglas Moore

BORN: CUTCHOGUE, LONG ISLAND, N. Y., AUG. 10, 1893.

Moore's music is classical in style—at its best when it is attempting to depict a definite program. Moore's touch is light and deft; his music has sparkle and sting; it is of a wide popular appeal without resorting to cheapness.—DAVID EWEN.

"In Memoriam"

COMPOSED DURING the summer of 1943, this work is in A-B-A form. The first section, a passacaglia, is based on a series of harmonic progressions. There are three variations, in the last of which the music rises to an impressive climax. The middle section is free, a recitative of dramatic intent. The third section is a recapitulation of the first with the exception that the climax, though of greater impact, leads to a concluding passage, subdued and mournful.

Mr. Moore says of his composition, "It is dedicated to those who die young and speaks of the bitterness of youth cut down in its prime, the irreconcilable loss to us and to them. The first and last parts consist of a dirge of mounting intensity. The middle section is a soliloquy in which youth is imagined as speaking with longing for familiar things now lost."

Educated at Hotchkiss School and Yale University, Douglas Moore studied music with Horatio Parker and David Stanley Smith. After serving in the Navy during the First World War, he took instruction from Vincent d'Indy in Paris, Ernest Bloch in Cleveland, and with Nadia Boulanger, again in Paris, as the result of winning a Pulitzer Fellowship.

He joined the music faculty of Columbia University and in 1928 was appointed an associate professor. In 1934 he received a Guggenheim Fellowship, which he enjoyed during a year's sabbatical. Subsequently, he returned to Columbia and in 1940 became head of the music department, succeeding Daniel Gregory Mason.

Mr. Moore has written several orchestral works, notably *Four Museum Pieces* (originally for organ, later transcribed for orchestra), *The Pageant of P. T. Barnum,* the symphonic poem *Moby Dick,* the *Symphony of Autumn,* and *Overture on an American Tune.* He has composed chamber music, the grand opera *White Wings,* the "folk opera" *The Devil and Daniel Webster,* and a considerable number of other pieces.

Invited by the late Lawrence Gilman to explain his *Symphony of Autumn* for the readers of the *New York Herald Tribune* (May 17, 1931), he expressed his artistic credo in the following words:

I feel very strongly that we are all of us overconscious today of the problems of idiom and esthetics. Most of us compose under the deadly fear of being either not modern enough or too modern. Too many of us worry about whether our music is properly a reflection of American, or suitably international, in order to please whatever faction impresses us most. The particular ideal which I have been striving to attain is to write music which will not be self-conscious with regard to idiom, and will reflect the exciting quality of the life, the traditions, and country which I feel all about me.

R. C. B.

Modest Moussorgsky

BORN: KAREVO, UKRAINE, RUSSIA, MAR. 28, 1835. DIED: ST. PETERSBURG, MAR. 28, 1881.

Life, wherever it is shown; truth, however bitter; speaking out boldly, frankly, point-blank to men—that is my aim. . . . I am a realist in the higher sense—that is, my business is to portray the soul of man in all its profundity.—MOUSSORGSKY.

"A Night on Bald Mountain," Fantasy for Orchestra

GEDEONOV, DIRECTOR of the Imperial Theater, hit upon a great plan during the winter of 1871-1872; he invited Cui, Borodin, Rimsky-Korsakoff, and Moussorgsky to compose jointly the score for an opera *Mlada,* a fairy tale. The parts assigned to Moussorgsky consisted of music for several folk scenes, a procession, and another scene of high fantasy "The Sacrifice to the Black Goat on Bald Mountain."

The composer, several years before, had done some sketches for piano and orchestra titled *St. John's Eve,* which it is said he revised for orchestra and chorus. That venture, unhappily for Moussorgsky, fell through. A later opportunity to locate the number came in 1877 with his work on the opera (which he never finished) *The Fair at Sorochintsk.* An intermezzo, "The Dream of the Peasant Lad," was considered the ideal place for it.

Rimsky-Korsakoff, after the death of Moussorgsky, undertook the task of revising the music, retaining the composer's argument:

Subterranean din of supernatural voices. Appearance of Spirits of Darkness, followed by that of the god Tchernobog. Glorification of the Black God, The Black Mass. Witches' Sabbath, interrupted at its height by the sounds of the far-off bell of the little church in a village. It disperses the Spirits of Darkness. Daybreak.

The Bald Mountain referred to is Mt. Triglav, near Kiev, Russia. The legendary Witches' Sabbath is there held annually on St. John's Night, June 24, the Feast of St. John the Baptist. The Black God, Tchernobog, as a black goat, presides over the revelry in this peculiar association of witchcraft and religion. Devils, witches, sorcerers, sorceresses, and all other evil spirits join in the festivities on this night of nights when they are all "especially malignant."

Dedicated to Vladimir Stassov, the piece is scored for piccolo, two flutes, two oboes, two clarinets, two bassoons, four horns, two trumpets, three trombones, bass tuba, kettledrums, bass drum, cymbals, tam-tam, bell in D, and the usual strings.

R. C. B.

"Pictures at an Exhibition"

[Transcribed for orchestra by Maurice Ravel]

Promenade. The Gnome. Old Castle. Tuileries. Bydlo—Polish Oxcart. Ballet of Chicks in Their Shells. Samuel Goldenberg and Schmuyle. Limoges: The Market Place. Catacombs (Con mortuis in lingua mortua). The Hut on Fowl's Legs (Baba Jaga)—Witches' Revelry. The Great Gate at Kiev.

VICTOR HARTMANN, prominent Russian painter and architect who was an intimate friend of Moussorgsky's, died in 1873, at the age of thirty-nine. The composer visited an exhibition of the artist's water colors and drawings, held at the Academy of Arts, St. Petersburg, shortly after Hartmann's death. From that visit grew a resolve to set to music, as it were, ten of the pictures in the form of a piano suite, as a memorial tribute to his friend.

Moussorgsky, not the type to enthuse about his own labors, bubbled and brimmed with excitement in the creating of this composition, and it is not difficult to understand why. In the first place, he was deeply affected by the demise of the painter, a fact that would of itself call the sum total of his resources into play. Then, Moussorgsky could do surprisingly good work under pressure, particularly when not fettered, so to speak, with matters of development, orchestration, and so on.

In a lengthy letter to another member of what was in reality a *cercle intime,* the writer Stassoff, who was in Wiesbaden at the time of Hartmann's death, Moussorgsky covered the curiously bracketed fields of rebellion, self-reproach, and resignation in bitterly emotional phrases. He wrote:

My very dear friend, what a terrible blow! "Why should a dog, a horse, a rat have life"—and creatures like Hartmann must die! . . . This is how the wise usually console us blockheads, in such cases: "He is no more, but what he has done lives and will live!" True—but how many men have the luck to be remembered? That is just another way of serving up our complacency (with a dash of onion, to bring out the tears). Away with such wisdom! When "he" has not lived in vain, but has created—one must be a rascal to revel in the thought that "he" can create no more. No, one cannot and must not be comforted, there can be and must be no consolation —it is a rotten mortality! If Nature is only coquetting with men, I shall have the honor of treating her like a coquette—that is, trusting her as little as possible, keeping all my sense about me, when she tries to cheat me into taking the sky for a fiddlestick—or ought one, rather like a brave soldier, to charge into the thick of life, have one's fling, and go under? What does it all mean? In any case the dull old earth is no coquette, but takes every "King of Nature" straight into her loathsome embrace, whoever he is—like an old worn-out hag, for anyone is good enough, since she has no choice.

There again—what a fool I am! Why be angry when you cannot change anything? Enough then—the rest is silence. . . .

Moussorgsky's original score of the *Pictures at an Exhibition* comprised ten actual program pieces, each connoting a different subject. For preface there is "Promenade," which is also repeated four times between sections as a connecting link.

"Promenade." "The composer here portrays himself walking now right, now left, now as an idle person, now urged to go near a picture; at times his joyous appearance is dampened, he thinks in sadness of his dead friend," according to Stassoff, to whom the suite is dedicated. The "Promenade" appears between sections up to the fifth.

"The Gnome." Stassoff's interpretation of this subject conceives of it as a "child's plaything, fashioned, after Hartmann's design in wood, for the Christmas tree at the Artist's Club (1869). It is something in the style of the fabled Nutcracker, the nuts being inserted in the gnome's mouth. The gnome accompanies his droll movements with savage shrieks." Riesemann, for his part, describes it as "the drawing of a dwarf who waddles with awkward steps on his short, bandy legs; the grotesque jumps of the music, and the clumsy, crawling movements with which these are interspersed, are forcibly suggestive." Authority, however, would seem to rest with Stassoff.

"Old Castle." A medieval castle, before whose ancient tower a troubadour lifts a doleful song. The length of this section reflects Moussorgsky's admiration of the picture.

"Tuileries." The picture shows an alley in the Tuileries Gardens where a group of children are having a dispute after their play. Ravel makes interesting use of the high wood winds here, aiming at a kind of imitation of the children's voices.

"Bydlo—Polish Oxcart." In Polish *bydlo* means "cattle." Here a Polish oxcart, lumbering on giant wheels, draws near, the driver singing a "folksong in the Aeolian mode."

"Ballet of Chicks in Their Shells." With reference to this section, Stassoff says, "In 1870, Hartmann designed the costumes for the staging of the ballet *Trilby* at the Maryinsky Theater, St. Petersburg. In the cast were a number of boy and girl pupils of the theater school, arrayed as canaries. Others were dressed up as eggs."

"Samuel Goldenberg and Schmuyle." A picture of two Polish Jews, one rich, one poor, drawn from life (1868) by Hartmann. Moussorgsky liked it so well that the artist made him a present of it. Riesemann considers this "one of the most amusing caricatures in all music. . . . These two types of the Warsaw Ghetto stand plainly before you—you seem to hear the caftan of one of them blown out by the wind, and the flap of the other's ragged fur coat. Moussorgsky's musical power of observation scores a triumph with this unique musical joke; he proves that he can reproduce the "intonations of human speech" not only for the voice, "but also on the piano."

"Limoges: The Market Place." Another dispute, this time among market women. In order to give an account of his intentions in this section, Moussorgsky wrote the following words in the margin of his score, "Great news! Monsieur de Puissangeout has just recovered his cow, The Fugitive. But the good gossips of Limoges are not totally agreed about this, because Mme. de Remboursac has just acquired a beautiful new set of teeth, whereas Monsieur de Panta-Pantaleon's nose, which is in the way, remains the color of a peony." All this, of course, is meant to be peasant chit-chat.

"Catacombs (*Con mortuis in lingua mortua*)." The drawing portrays Hartmann studying the Paris catacombs by lantern light.

"The Hut on Fowl's Legs (Baba Jaga)—Witches' Revelry." A clock appearing in the fantastic guise of the hut of the witch Baba Jaga. It stands on the legs of fowls.

"The Great Gate at Kiev." Hartmann's drawing of a proposed gate for the city of Kiev. The design "conceived in the massive old Russian style had a cupola in the shape of a Slavonic helmet."

R. C. B.

Prelude to the Opera "Khovanstchina"

CALLED "a musical drama" by its composer, *Khovanstchina* is another work whose hero is the Russian people, just as in *Boris*. Moussorgsky could be very passionate about the oppressed state of the Russian people, as witness,

The past in the present—that is my theme. We have made progress! That is a lie! We are still at the same point. On paper, in books, we have progressed, but really we are still just where we were. So long as the people itself cannot make out what is being done with it, so long as it does not itself will what is to happen to it—it is still just where it was. Public benefactors play their part magnificently, win glory, and record it, but the people still groans, and drinks to stifle its groans, and groans all the louder—and is exactly where it was before.

Moussorgsky, with his strong sense of theater, fell easy prey to the dramatic possibilities in the revolt of the Streltsi, the imperial bodyguards. Their leader in the uprising was the Prince Ivan Khovansky (a king maker at heart), who wished to put his own son André on the throne. The uprising, gathering momentum, the struggle of the Raskolniki (a schismatic group), who chose self-destruction in preference to bowing before dictated reforms in the Greek Church, the defeat of the Streltsi and the ignominious end of the Khovanskys these comprised only the essence of the opera Moussorgsky envisioned.

Stassoff, Moussorgsky's friend, outlined all this and so much more that the composer feared one opera could not hold it all.

But he retained only what he specifically required, excising considerable material, in addition to several important characters, among them young Czar Peter, his brother Ivan, and his sister, the much older Czarevna Sophia, who served as regent during the reign of the two youths.

In effect, *Khovanstchina* is a series of operatic pictures. The work was left unfinished when Moussorgsky died, and it was Rimsky-Korsakoff who did what was necessary to complete the finale, besides orchestrating the whole piece. The first performance was given by the Petersburg Musical and Dramatic Society, in Kononov Hall, St. Petersburg, February, 1886.

The Prelude, to which Moussorgsky gave the title "Dawn on the Moskva River," has as its basis "five melodic variations," so called by Riesemann, who explains them as being,

A method of musical expression long familiar to the Russian people, through their popular songs. When a song is sung in a Russian village—especially by several singers in succession—no two stanzas are usually sung alike. Each singer tries to introduce individual variations in the melody to suit his or her own voice and mood, and in accordance with the meaning of the particular verse. Thus the song loses all rigidity and seems to be a living, breathing organism, capable of varying with every moment. This peculiarity of Russian folk song becomes in Moussorgsky's hands a most effective means of musical expression, which he employs in many of his works, and nowhere more successfully than in this prelude; it is always the same landscape, constantly to change its appearance, in accordance with the changing light.

R. C. B.

Wolfgang Amadeus Mozart

BORN: SALZBURG, JAN. 27, 1756. DIED: VIENNA, DEC. 5, 1791.

*I declare to you before God, and as an honest man, that your son is
the greatest composer I know, either personally or by name.*—JOSEPH
HAYDN *to Leopold Mozart.*

Symphony in G minor, No. 25 (Köchel 183)

I. Allegro con brio. II. Andante. III. Menuetto. IV. Allegro.

OFTEN CALLED the "little G minor symphony," to distinguish it from the
masterpiece in the same key written in the summer of 1788, this work dates
from Mozart's seventeenth year and marks an important development in style
and emotional power. It is usually assigned to the year 1773 and belongs with
a group of five symphonies bearing many traits in common, which the young
master composed in Salzburg between his visits to Vienna and Munich. Of the
five only the D major (K. 202) is dated, May 5, 1774, being specified.

As Abert points out, the five symphonies in question differ radically from
Mozart's previous efforts in this form. Outwardly, they show greater logic and
necessity of development. The themes are more significant and more fully and
broadly expounded. The goal is kept steadily in mind, and there is a maturer
striving toward an ideal of unity through all four movements, especially notable
in the G minor and A major (K. 201). Inwardly they clearly reveal a new
spirit of romantic fervor and passionate energy, a deeper poetry, and a higher
capacity for tragic expression. This fresh vein of romantic utterance has caused
scholars like Wyzewa and St. Foix to regard the early G minor as a prototype,
even an early draft, at least stylistically, of the later work.

The new development proclaimed by the G minor sprang from many sources.
In the first place, Mozart had broken away from his Italian models in composition and come more directly under the influence of the Viennese school,
where a robuster romanticism had begun to flourish. During his visit to Vienna,
he had heard symphonies by Joseph Haydn, and one in particular, the so-called
"Funeral" or "Mourning" Symphony, in E minor, probably deeply impressed
him. Very possibly the Haydn work not only suggested the mood and romantic
character of the G minor, but prompted Mozart to make his first symphonic
essay in the minor mode. Then, too, the literary *Sturm und Drang* of romanticism was getting under way, and Goethe was launching its first fiery mani-
festos. Viennese music was already feeling the crisis in art and beginning to
echo the new currents.

According to Wyzewa and St. Foix, who have a passion for hunting sources, the Haydn symphony, with its marked romantic character as a single factor, best explains the G minor Symphony. "It is the same tragic pain," they say, "full of nobility, to be sure; the same consuming fire . . . the same tendency to make the symphony nothing but a great song of feverish anguish, interrupted by the sweet repose of the Andante." As further resemblances the French collaborators point to the dramatic and double exposition of the opening subject, the alternation of unison and counterpoint, the same large conception of codas. Consciously or unconsciously, they conclude, Mozart was influenced by this Haydn symphony.

Wyzewa and St. Foix also attach great importance to another symphony, that in D major, of Vanhall, belonging, like the Haydn work, to the year 1772. The "romantic ardor" of Vanhall's music had drawn warm praise from Dr. Burney. If the G minor Symphony bears "the general line and spirit of Haydn," say the French sleuths, "it resembles Vanhall in its language, the trembling allure of its song, its syncopated rhythms and whole instrumental fabric." However, they admit that the strangest thing of all about this work is that, while clearly deriving from other sources, it remains one of Mozart's most personal expressions, bearing the "stamp of his heart and genius."

Apthorp detected further derivations from Bach and Gluck. In the style and thematic material of the Andante, he discerned traces of the Leipzig master, whose works Mozart studied eagerly whenever the chance offered. The American analyst directed special attention to the F minor Prelude in the second book of *The Well-tempered Clavier* as a probable source. In the Menuetto he found "unmistakable tokens" of the influence of Gluck.

Of course, apart from all these outside influences, there was Mozart's own inner urge to express his feelings of the moment. That these were not feelings of passionate joy the Symphony makes clear. Despondency over the increasingly oppressive atmosphere in the Archbishop of Salzburg's palace, where he was employed, may be reflected in its pages. Then, too, the letters hint of a romantic attachment which came to nothing. As Eric Blom points out, Mozart's rare use of the minor mode is like "the sudden shedding of a repression," and agrees that the first and last movements "express an unhappy restlessness." Even the minuet has astonished many because of its "gloomy discontent and agitation." In short, Mozart, at seventeen, was quite normally experiencing the stresses and strains of adolescence.

One of the remarkable features of this Symphony is the unison announcement of chief themes in the first and last movements. Another is the fact that Mozart employs four horns, a rarity in the eighteenth century. Haydn seldom uses more than two, and Beethoven employs four only once in his symphonies, in the Ninth. The number is unusual even with Mozart, who employs four horns only in four of his symphonies, and never in the operas. The scoring of the G minor is for two oboes, two bassoons, four horns, and strings.

L. B.

Symphony in C major, No. 34 (K. 338)

I. Allegro vivace. II. Andante di molto. III. Allegro vivace.

THE YEAR 1780 marks a fresh stage in the development of Mozart's genius. Within a few months of each other he composed the C major Symphony (K. 338) and the opera *Idomeneo,* each in its own way representing a brisk stride forward in creative power and expression. Moreover, the C major is the earliest of Mozart's symphonies to achieve "any degree of permanence, as far as concert practice goes," as Eric Blom puts it.

The work belongs to the Salzburg period of 1779-1781, following his return from Paris and Mannheim. The final break with his employer, the Archbishop of Salzburg, a stern and irascible taskmaster, came a few months later in the spring of 1781. The episode is worth recounting as an example of Mozart's independent spirit. He had tired of playing flunky to the Austrian dignitary, had disobeyed a command to return instantly from Vienna, and was called a "knave," "a scoundrel," and a "scurvy fellow" for his rebuff. The doughty twenty-five-year-old composer finally braved the storm. He brought his formal resignation in person to the archbishop's palace. Hot words were exchanged. A well-aimed pontifical kick cut short the interview. "Except as a visitor, Salzburg was to know him no more," says Mr. Blom.

Shortly before the humiliating clash with the Salzburg potentate, we find Mozart writing from Vienna to his father about the performance of one of his symphonies: "I forgot to tell you the other day that at the concert the symphony went *magnifique* and had the greatest *succès*—40 violins played—the wind instruments all doubled—10 violas—10 double-basses, 8 violoncellos, and 6 bassoons." It has been long assumed that the symphony in question was the C major (K. 338). The late Sir Donald Francis Tovey warned against making any such facile identification. "Apart from the bassoons," he pointed out, "the symphony has no wind to double except the oboes and horns, for nobody could suppose that the trumpets wanted doubling. Mozart may have been writing of a revival of the *Paris Symphony,* which has full wind, including clarinets."

The symphony is scored for two oboes, two bassoons, two horns, two trumpets, kettledrums, and strings. Tovey refers specifically to the omission of flutes and clarinets as proof enough that the symphony mentioned in Mozart's letter was not the C major. Yet, the omission need not clash with the loose reference to wind instruments. The word "all" is inconclusive. Tovey also was convinced that what he termed "the substance of the first movement" had caused the oversight on the part of Otto Jahn, Mozart's biographer. It was Jahn who first made the identification.

Of course the striking thing about the symphony is its three-movement division, a departure from contemporary usage. Mozart began sketching a minuet movement, but never completed it. Oddly enough, it was intended for second place in the symphonic scheme, right after the opening Allegro, rather than as the usual third movement. Fourteen measures (Allegro, C major) of the discarded minuet exist, typically Mozartean in their natural beauty. They are shown crossed out in the surviving autograph. Mozart nowhere explains why he decided to omit it, though in masterly unity and compact texture the tripartite plan sufficiently explains itself. Mozart left a record of the date of completion on the score reading: *"Di Wolfgango Amadeo Mozart li 29 d'Agosto, Salisburgo,* 1780."

Three Mozart operas have been mentioned as bearing family resemblances to the C major Symphony. Eduard Hanslick heard unmistakable birth cries of motives used in *The Marriage of Figaro* and *Così fan tutte* overtures. In fact, he thought either of the end Allegros could serve intact as overture to an opera buffa by Mozart. Then, Eric Blom discerns foreshadowings of the music allotted a chief character in *The Escape from the Seraglio,* written two years after the C major Symphony. "Osmin already peeps out of it," writes Mozart's English biographer.

L. B.

Symphony in D major, No. 35 ("Haffner") (K. 385)

I. Allegro con spirito. II. Andante. III. Menuetto. IV. Finale: Presto.

A FESTIVITY IN the home of Burgomaster Sigmund Haffner of Salzburg occasioned the writing of Mozart's D major Symphony, No. 35, in the summer of 1782. Hence the title. The worthy Burgomaster wanted music to go with his party. He so apprised Mozart's father, Leopold, who was still in Salzburg. Leopold relayed the request to Vienna, where Mozart had been rooming with his bride-to-be's family, the Webers.

The request only added to Mozart's mounting woes. Life was growing complicated for the young genius. He was writing voluminously for Vienna's garden fetes and concerts. Orders arrived almost daily for more music. Intrigues and alterations were holding up a planned premiere of his opera *The Escape from the Seraglio.* Then, Papa Leopold was against his marriage to Constanze Weber and long withheld his consent. The Webers, on their side, did not make life any brighter for Mozart. Frau Weber was becoming, to quote Eric Blom, "alcoholically abusive." She expected the couple, when wedded, to come to live with her and pay board. To cap it all, the lovers had a stormy clash, over a trifle. During a game of "forfeits" Constanze allowed a young gallant to measure her leg—a quaint Viennese parlor practice of the time. Mozart, ordinarily a good sport, was furious. The lovers exchanged outbursts of temper, wept, and patched up. Mozart, a bit wiser and sadder for the episode, went back to his music. Constanze and he were finally married on Aug. 4, 1782. On Aug. 5, Leopold's belated consent arrived from Salzburg.

Early in July, while still tangled up with private and professional commitments, Mozart received his father's note conveying the Burgomaster's request for a "Serenade." Herr Haffner, it seemed, was in a frightful hurry. Mozart at first thought of refusing. "How is such a thing possible?" he wrote back. "You have no idea of the difficulty of arranging a work of this kind for an orchestra. Well, all that I can do is to devote the night to the task, for it cannot be managed otherwise. You may count on having something from me by every post, and I will write as quickly as I can, and as well as haste will permit." Six years before, Mozart, while in Salzburg, had composed a March and a D major Serenade for the wedding of Haffner's daughter. The Salzburg merchant and official had paid well. There is also evidence of a loan from him.

Leopold received the Serenade piecemeal, the opening Allegro arriving in Salzburg seven days after Mozart's reply. Between sections Mozart dashed off a new C minor Serenade for Wind Instruments (K. 388). In a final communication, Mozart, pleading lack of time, suggests that the Burgomaster's Serenade be submitted minus a March. The March from the earlier wedding music of 1776 might easily do as a substitute, he adds. Later, however, we find him writing to Leopold: "I sent you a short March yesterday. I only hope that it will arrive in time and be to your taste." He also emphasizes that the first Allegro "must go in a fiery manner and the last as fast as possible."

When the Serenade came back from Salzburg, Mozart added parts for flute and clarinet, dropped one of the two minuets, as well as the March, and launched it afresh as the D major Symphony. Its premiere occurred in Vienna on Mar. 3, 1783. The concert was part of the all-Mozart series, with the Emperor himself present. "What gratified me most was the presence of the Emperor," Mozart writes to his father six days later. "He gave me great applause. It is his usual custom to send the money to the box office of the theater before going there; otherwise I might justly have hoped for a larger sum, for his delight was beyond all bounds." The imperial tightwad sent twenty-five ducats. Mozart appeared as soloist in a piano concerto and also played a short fugue and a set of variations alone. Among the works on the program he mentions "my new symphony for the Haffner festival."

Blom writes in the Master Musicians Series:

The serenade character of the work comes out in the slow movement and in the minuet with its lovely pastoral trio. In the final rondo, which Mozart said ought to go as fast as possible, he sent the Haffners a little personal message by using as his subject what is as nearly as makes no odds a quotation from Osmin's great aria of malicious triumph in *The Elopement,* the opera he had finished just before this serenade symphony.

All the spirited frolic of comic opera is here blended with the grace of the two women in the stage work he wrote so lovingly in the year of his wedding (one feels that he was more deeply attached to Belmonte's Constanze than to his own), and he fell so much in love with the enchanting first episode of his rondo that he could not let it go, but developed and restated it until it became a second sonata subject.

Another striking feature of the Symphony is the use of a single theme as basis for the entire first movement. While frequent in Haydn's music, none of Mozart's other opening movements shows this monothematic pattern. The manuscript score of the D major Symphony carries the words: *"Synfonia di Amadeo Wolfgango Mozart a Vienna nel mese di Luglio,* 1782."

L. B.

Symphony in E flat major, No. 39 (K. 543)

I. Adagio; allegro. II. Andante. III. Minuetto; trio. IV. Finale: Allegro.

THE SUMMER of 1788 shows, in Mozart's personal catalogue, a weighty number of works completed. There were all sorts of odds and ends, arias, trios, piano sonatas, and still more, besides his three greatest symphonies. Earlier in the year he had composed the Piano Concerto in D major. With the exception of the symphonies and the concerto, his output amounted to little more than pot-boilers. But there is something awesome in the mere thought that these three symphonies—the present one, dated June 26; the G minor, July 25, and the C major, Aug. 10—could have been created, even by a Mozart, in less than six weeks!

When Gluck, composer to the Emperor Joseph II, died on Nov. 15, of the previous year, Mozart was appointed his successor. A salary of 2,000 florins was what Gluck earned, but for Mozart the income was cut to 800 florins. In return he was expected to furnish his royal employer with minuets, waltzes, country dances, and that was about all. To which Mozart is said to have observed that the money he received was "too much for what I do—not enough for what I can do."

Nevertheless, he was in desperate financial straits. He wrote several letters to one Puchberg, a merchant whom he had met at a Masonic lodge, asking for loans. In one of them he pleaded, "lend me a couple of hundred gulden, because my landlord in the Landstrasse was so pressing that I was obliged to pay him on the spot (in order to avoid any unpleasantness) which caused me great embarrassment."

The sum was forthcoming, and Mozart, seeking still more money, but evidently trying to acquaint Puchberg with his industrious activity, wrote back, "I have worked more during the ten days I have lived here than in two months in my former apartment; and if dismal thoughts did not so often intrude (which I strive forcibly to dismiss), I should be very well off here, for I live agreeably, comfortably, and, above all, cheaply."

Joseph II, a self-indulgent man, liked to rise at five o'clock every morning; he made it a habit to dine on boiled bacon at 3:15 in the afternoon; he was forever putting little chocolate drops into his mouth; he hated to sit for his portrait; he cared not one whit for flattery and fuss; he was a teetotaler, save for an occasional glass of Tokay, and he gave willingly to the poor.

Michael Kelly, who sang in the premiere of *Le Nozze di Figaro* in 1786, says in his memoirs (which, incidentally, were written by Theodore Hook):

The ridotto rooms, where the masquerades took place, were in the palace; and, spacious and commodious as they were, they were actually crammed with masqueraders. I never saw or indeed heard of any suite of rooms where elegance and convenience were more considered, for the propensity of the Vienna ladies for dancing and going to carnival masquerades was so determined that nothing was permitted to interfere with their enjoyment of their favorite amusement. . . . The ladies of Vienna are particularly celebrated for their grace and movements in waltzing, of which they never tire. For my own part, I thought waltzing from ten at night until seven in the morning a continual whirligig, most tiresome to the eye and ear, to say nothing of any worse consequences.

The E flat Symphony has not wanted for descriptive rhapsodies from commentators. Otto Jahn, for instance, refers to it as a "triumph of euphony—full of charm." Another, A. Apel, was so ecstatic about it that he attempted to "translate the music into poetry" which purported to express the character of each movement. E. T. A. Hoffmann rhapsodized, "Love and melancholy are breathed forth in purest spirit tones; we feel ourselves drawn with inexpressible longing toward the forms which beckon us to join them in their move with the spheres in the eternal circles of the solemn dance."

Richard Wagner, a verbal rhapsodist of verbal rhapsodists, allowed that

The longing sigh of the great human voice, drawn to him by the loving power of his genius, breathes from his instruments. He leads the irresistible stream of richest harmony into the heart of his melody, as though with anxious care he sought to give it, by way of compensation for its delivery by mere instruments, the depth of feeling and ardor which lies at the source of the human voice as the expression of the unfathomable depths of the heart.

The Symphony is scored for one flute, two clarinets, two bassoons, two horns, two trumpets, kettledrums, and strings.

R. C. F

Symphony in G minor, No. 40 (K. 550)

I. Allegro molto. II. Andante. III. Minuetto; Trio. IV. Finale: allegro assai.

THIS WORK has been called the "greatest *little* symphony in existence." It was written during the summer of 1788, when Mozart's inventive powers were, perhaps, at their most prolific, for in two months of that summer he composed three incomparable symphonies, the E flat major (K. 543), dated June 26; the present one, dated July 25; and the *Jupiter Symphony,* dated Aug. 10. That he could write at all was astounding, because his wife was ill, for one thing, and his finances were at a particularly low ebb, for another.

During those trying days he once sought from Puchberg a loan of 200 florins, describing himself, according to that authority, as "a prey to gloomy thoughts which he must repel with all his might." It has been said that the G minor Symphony "reflects something of the composer's troubles." And Mozart's biographer, Otto Jahn, discovers in the first movement "a piercing cry of anguish."

In commenting on the work, Pitts Sanborn noted that:

Though all of us might not go so far, there is no doubt that this Symphony is touched with the ineffable sadness that sometimes crosses like a summer cloud the radiance of Mozart's sun-god temperament. And along with this there are moments of a celestial tenderness. Yet, at the same time, this Symphony has its capricious and spritelike quality, which comes out in the ascending and descending pairs of thirty-second notes in the Andante, echoed distantly in the whimsicality and waywardness of certain measures of the Finale.

There is an amusing and pat little anecdote related by Apthorp, which evolves around a pianistic performance by Liszt. Says Apthorp:

He had just played his own matchless transcription of Beethoven's *Pastoral Symphony* as only he could play it. It should be remembered that the *Pastoral,* though homely enough in its thematic material and generally simple in its development and working out, is, as a piece of orchestration, one of Beethoven's most complicated scores; it thus presents quite peculiar difficulties to the pianoforte transcriber, difficulties which Liszt has conquered in a way that can only be called marvellous.

After Liszt had played it at the concert in question, Franz Lachner stepped up to him in the green room and said, "You are a perfect magician! Think of playing literally everything in the second movement and with only ten fingers! But I can tell you one thing even you can't play with all your magicianship." "What's that?" asked Liszt. "The first sixteen measures of Mozart's little G minor Symphony, simple as they are." Liszt thought a moment and then said with a laugh: "I think you are right; I should need a third hand. I should need both my hands for the accompaniment alone, with that viola figure in it!"

The Symphony is scored for one flute, two oboes, two clarinets (added for the second edition), two bassoons, two horns, and strings.

The first movement (Allegro molto, G minor, 4/4) opens with the first theme given out in octaves by the first and second violins accompanied by the other strings. There is a forceful subsidiary theme before the second theme, wistful in mood, enters in B flat major.

The second movement (Andante, E flat major, 6/8) reminded Reimann of a passage in a letter from Mozart to his father written in 1787: "As death, rightly considered, is the true purpose of our life, I have for a year or two made myself so thoroughly acquainted with this true and best friend of man that his picture no longer frightens me; it brings much that is reassuring and comforting." Unlike most symphonic slow movements, this Andante is in sonata form. The elegiac first subject emerges from the rhythmic figure of the opening measures to be sung by the first violins. The second subject, largely passage work, is in B flat major.

The Minuetto (Allegretto, G minor, 3/4) is vigorous and animated in character and is graced with a trio of an adorable simplicity in the serene tonality of G major.

The Finale (Allegro assai, G minor, 4/4) in its turn adheres to the sonata form. It opens with a theme identical as to the first eight notes with the first eight notes of the theme that starts the Scherzo of Beethoven's Fifth Symphony, but of course in another key. It has been pointed out, though, that the rhythm is so different that detection of any similarity is not easy for the ear. The strings and then the wood winds play the lyric second theme, again in B flat major.

A votary of this Symphony once wrote: "There are few things in art that are perfect. The G minor Symphony is one of them."

R. C. B.

Symphony in C major ("Jupiter") (K. 551)

I. Allegro vivace. II. Andante cantabile. III. Minuetto; Allegretto; Trio. IV. Finale: Allegro molto.

TITLE-MONGERING is an ancient, if not noble, pastime. Mozart wrote this symphony, but someone else gave it the sobriquet *Jupiter*. Why, no one knows. We have had many other delicious labelings. For instance, there are the *Emperor Concerto* and the *Moonlight Sonata*. Neither of these "designations" were of Beethoven inspiration, just as *Jupiter* was no Mozartean brain child. However, there is some good to the thing, especially where a composer has written more than one work in a certain key. It is then obviously much simpler for the layman to say the *Jupiter Symphony* than to go through a mathematical dissertation, such as C major (K. 551). Beyond that there is no justification for the custom.

What is really ludicrous, though, is the habit some commentators have had of "reasoning" up to a title, of inventing, even, a connection between title and work. Thus, *Jupiter* connotes the "calm, godlike beauty" of the music, according to one enthusiast. Another offered the theory that the triplets in the first bar of the symphony are the "thunderbolts of Jove." J. B. Cramer, a London music publisher, is alleged to have originated the expression because of the work's "loftiness of ideas and nobility of treatment." Whatever be the true history of the coinage, we now know the symphony as the *Jupiter*.

It took Mozart less than seven weeks of the summer of 1788 to produce his three greatest symphonies, *viz.*, the E Flat (K. 543), dated June 26; the G Minor (K. 550), July 25; and the present one, Aug. 10. He had three and one-half more years to live, but he had done with symphonies, though his fertile brain did create in that time three operas, *Così fan tutte, La Clemenza di Tito,* and *The Magic Flute,* and several important pieces of chamber music, as well as the last composition of his career, the Requiem in D minor.

Whether or not Mozart intended these super symphonies as a trilogy is not known to us. They are not related, except in supreme mastery of orchestral style. These three works represent Mozart the symphonist at his zenith; they bespeak the facility of the supercraftsman who has never lost the passion for experimentation. With a long string of symphonies already to his credit, he endeavors in these last creations to probe deeper mysteries, to span greater distances.

The *Jupiter Symphony* is scored for flute, two oboes, two bassoons, two horns, two trumpets, kettledrums, and strings. There is an auxiliary theme in the first movement, a tripping melody in G major that Mozart borrowed from himself, a practice that composers have not always followed to the letter. This theme stems from an aria buffa of his, "Un bacio di mano," which he had penned some time previously for interpolation in an opera by Anfossi, *Le Gelosie Fortunate.* The words of that aria are *"Voi siet un po' tondo, mio caro Pompeo, le usanze del mondo andate a studiar"* ("You are a bit dense, my dear Pompeo, go and study the ways of the world").

The second movement has earned the distinction of being called "perhaps the finest of all Mozart's slow movements." Of the Finale, Eric Blom has written:

There is a mystery in this music not to be solved by analysis or criticism, and perhaps only just to be apprehended by the imagination. We can understand the utter simplicity; we can also, with an effort, comprehend the immense technical skill with which its elaborate fabric is woven; what remains forever a riddle is how any human being could manage to combine these two opposites into such a perfectly balanced work of art.

R. C. B.

Concerto for Piano and Orchestra in C major (K. 415)

I. Allegro. II. Andante. III. Allegro.

THIS COMPOSITION belongs to a group of three piano concertos written by Mozart in Vienna during the autumn and winter months of 1782-1783. All three largely reflect a happy period in the composer's life, a period ushered in by his marriage to Constanze Weber in August, 1782. Of the F major Concerto (K. 413), the earliest in the set, Wanda Landowska has written that "it breathes pure joy from beginning to end" and may be described as one long Minuet: "We know how much Mozart loved to dance and what a good dancer he was!"

Mme. Landowska also reminds us that the three concertos have long suffered from the unjust designation of "small." This misconception, she feels, stems partly from Mozart's own reference to the concertos in a letter to his father Leopold dated Dec. 28, 1782:

These concertos are a happy medium between what is too easy and too difficult; they are very brilliant, pleasing to the ear, and natural, without being vapid. There are passages here and there from which connoisseurs alone can derive satisfaction; but these passages are written in such a way that the less learned cannot fail to be pleased, though without knowing why.

Concerning this amazingly candid statement, Mme. Landowska has this to say:

It has been concluded from this letter that Mozart attributed little importance to these concertos and consequently they have been underestimated. The irony of Mozart's "modest" remarks is too apparent to require further explanation, although we might still ask why these concertos have been relegated to oblivion. *Probably because they—and the K. 415 in particular—require more extensive extemporization on the performer's part than any other concerto.*

Continuing, Mme. Landowska makes the following remarks about the C major Concerto:

The first movement of this Concerto is a type of alla marcia which advances in canonic imitations. Tranquil at first, it augments little by little and overflows into the same triplet motif which marks the opening of the *Jupiter Symphony*. Thus, this Concerto, which has so long been neglected and ignored, contains from its first notes the elements of grandeur and dramatic power.

The Andante is a tender and lyrical dialogue between the soloist and strings, the latter supported from time to time by oboes, bassoons, and horns.

But it is, above all, the finale, a frolicsome dance in 6/8, which merits our fullest attention. While so much importance has been attached to the letter quoted above, another letter to his father (Vienna, Jan. 22, 1783) throws a much more penetrating and informative light on the subject:

"I shall send the cadenzas and *Eingange*—(short introductory passages announcing the approach of new moods and extemporized like the cadenzas and organ points, although they are three utterly different aspects of improvisation) to my dear sister at the first opportunity. I have not yet altered the *Eingange* in the rondo, for whenever I play this Concerto, I always play whatever occurs to me at the moment. . . ."

The use of cadenzas at the end of each movement is still common today, while the small organ points, which we come upon expectedly here and there, and, most significantly the *Eingange,* which twice announce the approach of the sublime adagio in C minor, have been virtually ignored since the performance of Mozart himself and the musicians of his time.

At the end of the rondo Mozart introduces, against the murmuring of the strings, a popular folk song, ingratiating and fresh in mood.

When this Concerto entered the New York Philharmonic-Symphony repertory on Oct. 24, 1946, Mme. Landowska, the soloist, improvised the cadenzas, organ points, and *Eingange,* or entrance passages. Artur Rodzinski conducted.

In connection with the C minor episode which appears twice in the Allegro finale, it is interesting to learn that Mozart originally planned the whole second movement in the minor key. Alfred Einstein, in his study of Mozart's music, suggests Mozart gave up the idea when he realized that a slow movement in C minor "would have made it much too serious for the character of these works."

Of the three concertos, the C major is the amplest in scoring, calling for two oboes, two bassoons, two horns, two trumpets, and two tympani. Both the F major (K. 413) and the A major (K. 414) lack trumpets and tympani. Slightest of the three in this respect is the A major, which also omits bassoons. All three concertos were played by Mozart at concerts for his own benefit in the National Theater of Vienna. These events were called "academies." Two of the three concertos—there is no way of determining which two—were rendered at the "academy" of Mar. 22, 1783, quaintly reported by *Cramers Magazin* (as quoted in Mr. Einstein's *Mozart*):

Today the celebrated Chevalier Mozart gave a music academy for his own benefit at the National Theater in which pieces of his own composition, which was already very popular, were performed. The academy was honored by the presence of an extraordinarily large audience, and the *two new concertos* and other fantasies which Mr. Mozart played on the Forte Piano were received with the loudest approval.

Our Monarch, who contrary to his custom honored the whole academy with his presence, joined in the applause of the public so heartily that one can think of no similar example. The proceeds of the academy are estimated at 600 gulden.

L. B.

Concerto for Piano and Orchestra in D minor (K. 466)

I. Allegro. II. Romanze. III. Allegro assai.

Stories of Mozart's feats of memory and technique at the piano are so plenteous that we are scarcely surprised to learn that the little man performed the premiere of the D minor Concerto not only without a rehearsal but without having played the rondo finale through once. This was in Vienna on Feb. 11, 1785. We have Leopold Mozart's word for it that his son was busy at the copyist's before rushing off to the concert hall. "Wolfgang played an excellent new concerto," wrote Leopold to his daughter Marianne in Salzburg. Mozart repeated the performance on Feb. 15. *"Magnifique!"* exclaims Leopold in a second letter to Marianne. Generations of music lovers have echoed the proud father's outburst.

The premiere of the D minor occurred in the Mehlgrube at one of Mozart's subscription concerts held during Lent, a lucrative season for such events in the Vienna of his time. Later to become the Hotel Muench, the Mehlgrube was a popular hall for concerts and balls. It seems flour was stored in the cellar, which accounts for its name, Mehlgrube, literally a "flour pit." We owe what information we have on the proceeds of Mozart's subscription series to his father's famous taste for finance. The series lured 150 subscribers. Wolfgang netted 559 florins, roughly $275. This was a staggering figure to the whole family, specially since Leopold's fabulous son "had often played at other people's concerts for nothing." Only when we compare the figure with the meager sums paid Mozart for the use and publication of some of his scores, can we understand the family's jubilation.

Reverting to Mozart's not having rehearsed the D minor Concerto, it was Edward Holmes who advanced an intriguing theory about the premiere at the Mehlgrube. In the impromptu cadenzas, he suggests, "extempory invention of the fingers of Mozart may have scattered even greater beauties than he has left in that great work." Holmes also makes the pertinent remark: "If the idea of a concerto played without a single rehearsal or trial be surprising, how much more must it appear when we remember the quantity the player wrote, and the little time that his fingers, cramped and contracted by holding the pen, had to recover their wonted freedom and agility."

At the time of the subscription concerts, Leopold Mozart was spending some months in Vienna with his son and daughter-in-law Constanze in their dwelling on the Schulerstrasse. Letters to his daughter contain frequent references to Wolfgang's triumphs. When the Piano Concerto in C major (K. 467) was played at the following concert, Leopold reported that many listeners were moved to tears by its beauty and that the applause was deafening. There was another great thrill in store for Papa Leopold during his Viennese sojourn.

One day, Joseph Haydn came to the house on the Schulerstrasse to play first violin in three new quartets by Mozart dedicated to himself. After the performance Haydn declared to the elder Mozart: "I tell you before God, and as an honest man, that your son is the greatest composer I know, either personally or by name. He has taste and apart from that the greatest science in composition." Haydn was then directing musical evenings in the town residence of Prince Nicholas Esterhazy. On his invitation Mozart often participated in the musical entertainment. A great admirer of Haydn's string quartets, Mozart had earlier planned dedicating six of his own to the senior composer. The last three of the set were completed on Jan. 14, 1785, less than a month before the rush subscription season at the Mehlgrube got under way. Haydn had become a frequent guest of the Mozarts. In the quartet sessions, Mozart himself played the viola.

This was something of an English period in Mozart's social and pedagogical life. Often the string foursome would pack their fiddles and go to Stephen Storace's lodgings for a session. Storace, a twenty-two-year-old English composer, was studying with Mozart. He was in Vienna with his sister Ann Selina (Nancy), who had come to sing Italian opera. Another English youth, Thomas Attwood, two years younger than Storace, was also enrolled as a Mozart pupil. About this time the Irish tenor Michael Kelly came to know Mozart intimately and was vanquished by his seraphic host in a daily game of billiards. Both Nancy Storace and Kelly drew closer to Mozart through *The Marriage of Figaro,* produced on May 1, 1786, with the two friends cast as Susanna and Basilio. Kelly, in his *Reminiscences,* has left a telling close-up of the composer about this time:

He favored the company by performing fantasies and capriccios on the pianoforte. His feeling, the rapidity of his fingers, the great execution and strength of his left hand particularly, and the apparent inspiration of his modulations, astounded me. After this splendid performance we sat down to supper, and I had the pleasure to be placed at table between him and his wife. After supper the young branches of our host had a dance, and Mozart joined them. Madame Mozart told me that, great as his genius was, he was an enthusiast in dancing, and often said that his taste lay in that art, rather than in music.

He was a remarkably small man, very thin and pale, with a profusion of fine fair hair, of which he was rather vain. He gave me a cordial invitation to his house, of which I availed myself, and passed a great part of my time there. He always received me with kindness and hospitality. He was remarkably fond of punch, of which beverage I have seen him take copious draughts. He was also fond of billiards, and had an excellent billiard table in his house. Many and many a game have I played with him, but always came off second best. He gave Sunday concerts, at which I never was missing. He was kind-hearted, and always ready to oblige; but so very particular, when he played, that if the slightest noise was made, he instantly left off.

Mozart felt keenly the necessity of rapport between the artist and his audience. Earlier, in 1778, he had written: "Give me the best clavier in Europe and at the same time listeners who understand nothing or want to understand nothing and who do not feel what I play with me, and all my joy is gone."

His letters give frequent hints of his own style of playing. "That I always remain strictly in time surprises everyone," he remarks in a letter of 1777. "They cannot understand that the left hand should not in the least be concerned in a tempo rubato. When they play, the left hand always follows." The pianist Richter marveled at his effortless ease. "Whenever I played for him," Mozart writes in 1784, "he looked immovably at my fingers, and one day he said, 'My God! how I am obliged to torment myself and sweat and yet without obtaining applause; and for you, my friend, it is mere play!' 'Yes,' said I, 'I had to labor once in order not to show labor now.'" Clementi, probably the most brilliant pianist of his day, always spoke of Mozart's "singing touch and exquisite taste" at the keyboard.

One of the finest analyses of Mozart's keyboard style, reconstructed from the composer's own statements and the testimony of qualified contemporaries, was that written by Philip Hale many years ago for one of Shirmer's collections of Mozart's piano music. After reviewing Mozart's development as pianist, from the time he picked out thirds at the age of three to his last public appearance on Mar. 4, 1791, the year of his death, Hale begins his appraisal:

The fame of the virtuoso is often an unreal thing, magnified or distorted by the testimony of prejudiced contemporaries; in the case of Mozart we not only have the unanimous testimony of skilled musicians of his day, we have also the personal record of his ideas concerning pianoforte playing. His hands were small, and the spectator wondered that they could grasp full chords; his system of fingering, derived from the study of Ph. Em. Bach, cured natural limitations.

The hands were beautiful; they pleased the eye, although they were useless in the cutting of his meat. He avoided all facial and bodily movements that smacked of affectation. According to him the player should have quiet hands; their lightness, suppleness, their unhindered speed should turn difficult passages into "flowing oil." He warned constantly against undue speed and hurrying; for they result only in slovenliness and bungling; and he knew how easy it was to play rapidly and with brilliant inaccuracy.

He insisted on a strict observance of time, and he kept with the beat so strictly that even in the free use of tempo rubato in an adagio the hands preserved unity in rhythm. He laid special stress on accuracy, the sure and easy conquering of technical difficulties, fineness of taste in the delivery, force regulated by the expression. So in reading at sight he demanded the observance of the proper tempo, the careful elaboration of the ornaments, the fitting expression: the player should seem to be the composer.

It is not surprising then that Rochlitz spoke of the "heavenly pleasure given by the elegance and the heart-melting tenderness of his performance"; that Haydn wept at the remembrance of his "incomparable playing."

As a teacher of the pianoforte he was not methodical in his instruction, and he taught rather by playing to his pupils than by listening and correcting. His most celebrated pupil was Hummel, who lived in his house two years and learned there the pure touch, the rounding of the phrase, the finish and the elegance, the facility in improvising that distinguished the performance of his master.

The D minor is one of fifteen piano concertos composed by Mozart between 1782 and 1786. Mozart had now found fresh ways of enlarging the scope of the concerto and enriching its contents. Integrating the solo instrument and orchestra in more vital form was one of them. Through this medium he was achieving a new poetry and individuality. The D minor stands out in impassioned speech. The fervid note of tragic unrest, accentuated by the minor key, is stronger than in the others. The next concerto (C major), with its showy sequences and gay flourishes of trumpets and drums, is a far cry from the gloom and romantic despair that brood fitfully through the pages of the D minor.

I. Allegro (D minor, 4/4). "Begins with a shudder and is full of unhappy commotion," writes Eric Blom of the opening movement of the D minor Concerto. Blom even detects grim design in the way the second theme, announced in the relative major of F, later moves into the tonic D minor: "as though a false promise of relief were mockingly revealing itself as a tragic delusion."

The movement follows the double-exposition pattern common to concertos of Mozart's time. During the orchestral phase, strings announce the first theme in D minor, oboes and bassoons giving out the second in F major. When the Piano takes up its own exposition, it voices the chief theme in lengthier guise. The second subject follows in the relative major, shared with the orchestra. After the material is developed, a review sets in. This time the key of the second subject, at first F major, as at the start, shifts to D minor. The piano now freely discourses the material. The orchestra then builds up a crescendo, pauses, and on the chord of D minor the piano reenters with a cadenza.

II. Romanze (B flat major, 2/2). The limpid, poetic theme recurring in this movement is first chanted by the piano, the orchestra later joining in. Fresh additions to the theme are also echoed by the orchestra, and soon the piano brings in a second subject. This is again dutifully gone over by the orchestra. Piano and orchestra now come back to the earlier theme. What arises at this point Blom has called "a sudden fit of raving despair." It is a "wild episode" in G minor involving piano and wood winds. The first theme returns and all is peace again. Blom sees a prophetic note of romanticism in the very title of this movement, the German word *Romanze*. "He is already in the mood into which Beethoven dropped temporarily and Schumann permanently," he writes. "He got over it again, of course: he had too much traditional artistic breeding and was too much a citizen of the civilized world in his tastes to grow for good into a German of the *Sturm und Drang* direction."

III. Allegro assai (D minor–D major, 2/2). Editions of the D minor Concerto differ in giving the tempo of this movement. Breitkopf and Härtel used a prestissimo marking in their early editions, later substituting Allegro assai. No tempo indications are given in Mozart's autograph score. The form is typically that of the Rondo finale, with the chief theme given out by the piano and orchestra in succession. Blom finds "a kind of unhappy restlessness" here, at the same time noting two striking changes of mood. A cheerier second theme again breaks into the fabric in F major. Later Mozart, as if recanting, brings it back in D minor, but only to have it sally forth afresh—after the cadenza—"in a sunny outburst of happiness" in D major.

"After all," writes Blom, "Mozart remembered this was a concerto, a piece meant to entertain. Feeling that he had done enough to startle his polite hearers with his most impassioned music, he relieved them at the end and let them go away emotionally relaxed."

Mozart was soon to experience the same change of heart in writing his operatic masterpiece *Don Giovanni,* which is in D minor but finally, cheerfully, "clears into D major."

Besides the solo piano, the D minor Concerto is scored for flute, two oboes, two bassoons, two horns, two trumpets, tympani, and strings. The cadenzas usually employed were written by Beethoven. The autograph of the second is now in the British Museum.

L. B.

Concerto for Piano and Orchestra in C major (K. 467)

I. Allegro maestoso. II. Andante. III. Allegro vivace assai.

COMPLETED ON Mar. 9, 1785, the C major Concerto was first played three days later at a concert given by Mozart in Vienna. Leopold Mozart was then spending some months with his son and daughter-in-law Constanze in their dwelling on the Schulerstrasse. Writing to his daughter Nannerl, he described the warm reception accorded the new work. Many listeners were moved to tears by its beauty, according to the proud father, and the applause was deafening. Such behavior spoke well for the audience because, as Eric Blom points out, the Andante "must have made Mozart's hearers sit up by its daring modernities." Among such audacities were "a diminished seventh and a sweeping skip in the first bar, an unexpected transition to the tonic minor in the second, discordant suspensions in the next three, and a grinding false relation (B flat against B natural) in the last."

Whether goaded by debts and efforts to meet the high rent and expenses of the Schulerstrasse residence or merely by a feverish creative urge, the period of the C major Concerto hummed with composition, particularly for piano. Six concertos, two sonatas, and two sets of variations, all for piano, were the count by the end of 1784. Three more piano concertos followed in 1785, besides the C minor Fantasy and the sonata for violin and piano in the same key. By then the concerto form in Mozart's hands had become a "medium in which . . . he succeeded in combining perfect aptness to its special requirements with inexhaustible poetry and originality," according to Mr. Blom.

With its showy sequences and gay flourishes of trumpets and drums, the C major Concerto contrasts sharply with its predecessor, the D minor Concerto (K. 466). Gloom and romantic despair brood fitfully through the pages of the latter, accentuated by the minor key. The change in mood is as from night to day. After glimpsing the romantic future and flinging off hints of Beethoven and Schumann to come, Mozart again slips back into the period groove of a "normal display concerto."

L. B.

Concerto for Piano and Orchestra in E flat (K. 482)

I. Allegro. II. Andante. III. Allegro.

THOUGH COMPOSED in December, 1785, and premiered the same month with Mozart as soloist, the E flat Concerto was one of a group of three intended for subscription concerts during Lent. Its companions the A flat (K. 488) and the C minor (K. 491) were completed in March, 1786.

The advance premiere of the E flat went to a worthy cause. Vienna, then housing some 400 orchestral players, had a welfare organization that contributed to the support of musicians' widows. Like similar societies of today, it kept up a Pension Fund, and concerts were held regularly to add to it. Although it was a time of small ensembles, the orchestras at these concerts often consisted of Vienna's entire instrumental colony. When Dittersdorf's oratorio *Esther* was presented at an earlier Pension Fund concert, the personnel was 200 strong. Kisbeck reported that all 400 players frequently got together and played "as precisely and clearly as if they were only twenty or thirty." He observed proudly, "Surely this is the only concert of the kind in the world." When Mozart appeared in his E flat Concerto, the society's orchestra numbered 108 men. The announcement of the benefit concert merely stated that "During the entr'acte, a newly composed clavier concerto will be played by W. A. Mozart."

The three concertos belong to a period of feverish activity in Mozart's life.

Not that there was ever a letup in his crowded career. But the winter of 1785-1786 is fairly staggering in sheer work. Besides the concertos, he was "up to his ears," as his father put it, in *The Marriage of Figaro,* produced the following May. That alone makes a dismal tale of worry, conflict, and frantic last-minute changes. He wrote a violin sonata, completed Dec. 12, the E flat Piano Concerto coming four days later. He devised a cantata *Davidde penitente* from the earlier unfinished Mass in C minor. On the Emperor's commission, he completed a one-act comedy *Der Schauspieldirektor* (*The Impresario*) for the reception of the Netherlands governors held in the orangery at Schönbrunn on Feb. 7. There were revisions and additions to make for a performance of *Idomeneo* in March. And when he could, he worked at smaller instrumental pieces.

But the composing was only one small part of Mozart's routine. He had pupils at all hours of the day, though for a time he limited the lessons to a strict afternoon schedule, so that he could give his mornings to *The Marriage of Figaro*. Since there was no hope of defraying household expenses from royalties and teaching fees alone, he made frequent appearances as soloist at public and private concerts. Yet, we have Michael Kelly's word for it that in spite of the hectic daily rounds, Mozart found time for dancing and a good game of billiards.

Eric Blom says about the E flat Concerto:

This work is many people's favorite among the piano concertos, until they hear one of the others. For it is with these works as with all serial artistic products that shine as much by variety as by quality: the one you happen to be confronted with at the moment always seems to be the best. . . . However, the Mozart concertos are great art, and they became more and more surprisingly varied as they accumulated year by year.

Regarding her treatment of repeated passages in the Mozart Concerto, Wanda Landowska has supplied the authors with the following note:

"These days, modification in reiterated passages is absolutely essential. It is expected of every performer," said P. E. Bach in the Preface to his Sonatas, composed in 1779 (autograph Berlin).

The truth of this axiom becomes evident in the slow section of the finale in which the orchestra proposes a theme that the soloist repeats and has to embellish according to the custom of the era. What today would be described as the taking of "peculiar liberties" was a *sine qua non* part of the knowledge of every performer. A virtuoso of the time would never have dared play such a passage as it was written, and those performances which we respect today for their literal devotion would have been called ignorant and barbaric by Mozart's contemporaries, for it was in his modification of the reprise that the eighteenth-century performer submitted himself to his audience to be judged an artist of good or poor taste.

L. B.

Concerto for Piano and Orchestra in A major (K. 488)

I. Allegro. II. Andante. III. Presto.

SEVERAL OF Mozart's piano concertos were composed for subscription concerts given in Vienna in Lent and Advent. These were lucrative seasons for a composer of Mozart's gifts—and, it might be added, a composer of Mozart's habitual financial straits. The A major was one of a trilogy of such piano concertos written for the Lenten season of 1786. The others were the E flat major (K. 482) and the C minor (K. 491). The manuscripts give March as the month of composition for both the A major and the C minor—a feat in speed and genius surpassed only by Mozart himself when he later wrote his three greatest symphonies in the space of six weeks! Mozart, of course, was his own soloist at the premiere of the A major Concerto. It may have been that concert, or some similar event, that Ambros Rieder recalled in his memoirs many years after Mozart's death:

I cannot describe my astonishment when I happened to be so fortunate as to hear the immortal W. A. Mozart. . . . I had never been accustomed to hear anything so great or so wonderful. Such bold flights of fancy, that seem to attain the highest regions, were alike a marvel and a delight to the most experienced of musicians. Even to this day, although a very old man, I can still hear those heavenly harmonies, and die in the firm conviction that there has only been one Mozart.

Rossini's own conviction was even more sweeping: "There is *only* Mozart." The A major Concerto is one of fifteen such works composed by Mozart between 1782 and 1786. Constantly experimenting and developing, he had achieved a new synthesis in this medium. The solo piano had moved toward closer intimacy and teamwork with the orchestra. Solo instrument and orchestra were now more firmly integrated in a scheme of common endeavor. And with this new fusion appeared a fresh fund of expressive power. The emotional range had widened, and a brooding poetry often filled the slow movements. There was a new depth and a new sense of stress and conflict in these concertos. One has only to read Mozart's letters—the grim record of mounting bills, the drab chronicles of intrigue and chill reception, the growing domestic turmoil, the sharpening sense of fatalism—to surmise what lies behind this deepening vein. The piano concerto had become, perhaps, the favored medium for expressing his innermost feelings.

Whatever personal secret lies embedded in the Andante of the A major Concerto, there is no escaping its troubled mood. There is subdued passion here and a haunting pathos. Mozart seems preoccupied with some tragic line of thought. Abraham Veinus calls this movement "a passionate siciliana totally plunged into the most heart-gripping melancholy." Alfred Einstein, declaring that the Andante contains the soul of the Concerto, finds in "veiled form" the passion that bursts out openly in the Andante of the previous E flat major Concerto. For him "the resignation and hopelessness are the same."

The mood recurs in the C minor Concerto which followed later that month, recurs with heightened vehemence, for, as Mr. Einstein points out, Mozart at the time "evidently needed to indulge in an explosion of the dark, tragic, passionate emotions."

There is naturally a sunnier side to the A major Concerto, though even in the end movements one glimpses shadows, poignant hints, what Mr. Einstein has called "concealed intensities." After the mauve mood of the Andante, the Presto finale comes like a shout of joy. The piano gives out the sprightly theme, and the rondo is on its irresistible way.

Trumpets and tympani are absent from the scoring of the A major Concerto, which calls for flute, two clarinets, two bassoons, two horns, and strings. The movements are marked as follows: Allegro, A major, 4/4; Andante, F sharp minor, 6/8; Presto, A major, 2/2. Mozart's manuscript gives Mar. 2, 1786, as the date of completion.

L. B.

Concerto for Piano and Orchestra in C minor (K. 491)

I. Allegro. II. Larghetto. III. Allegretto.

THOUGH composing was as natural to Mozart as breathing and, as has been said, "inspiration burned ever brightly within him," there was a utilitarian side to his vast output of piano concertos, because he was constantly in need of new material for his own public performances. (Nor did he look with disfavor on the possibility that others might play these works.)

Nageli tells us that Mozart "broke new ground for orchestral compositions with his pianoforte concertos." How true! What Mozart did was to enlarge the scope of the form to something like that of a symphony with piano. The orchestra became no mere accompanying medium. There was the integration of all the separate elements existing in the two instrumental bodies—the piano and the orchestra.

Speaking of the piano concertos, Otto Jahn says:

The prominence given to the orchestra (which, it must be remembered, owed to Mozart its richer composition, both of wind and stringed instruments) in those larger portions of a work where it is heard independently of the piano, as in the *tutti* of the *ritornelli,* gives a symphonic character to the concertos. . . . Mozart's art of blending the tone coloring of the orchestra, which drew tears from his old father at the hearing of one of his new pianoforte concertos, shows his delicate sense of euphony and accurate knowledge of instrumental effects.

In fact, Mozart was extremely sensitive to the imperfections of the pianos of his time. And in his works for piano and orchestra he attempted to steer the listener away from shortcomings by means of novel—and in his day, radical— devices. Along these lines, too, his ingenuity was remarkable. For instance, he would give the entering piano a brilliant passage, following a simple one for the orchestra, thus drawing attention to the excitement produced by the contrast and holding it through a clever manipulation of his material.

In the construction of his piano concertos Mozart distributed his themes equally between piano and orchestra. When the orchestra takes the theme it is often fully exploited, and its later acceptance by the piano, in contrast, may be in the nature of a subdued, almost opposing, utterance. Says Jahn, "Thus the charm of the concertos . . . depends upon active cooperation of the contrasting elements, by means of which the whole work is richly and brilliantly grouped, as a picture is grouped by a judicious disposition of light and shade."

The present work was written in March, 1786. The orchestral part of the score calls for flute, two oboes, two clarinets, two bassoons, two horns, two trumpets, tympani, and strings.

Eric Blom, whose biography of Mozart is one of the high lights of the Master Musicians Series, writes:

That he [Mozart] can be quite gloomy, though without ever sacrificing the most limpid euphony, is shown by the next Concerto, in C minor (K. 491), the work immediately preceding *Figaro* and as different from it as a rainy day from a cloudless one. However, it is almost equally unlike the only other concerto in a minor key Mozart ever wrote. Less dramatic than the D minor, it is more declamatory. It has a more classical repose of gesture, more poise and shape, more unity of atmosphere. There is nothing like the unexpected ending of the earlier work: it closes, as it began, in the dark key of C minor. The one resemblance is the rondo form of the slow movement, with rather too frequent recurrences of a subject of very much the same type. There is no dramatic episode here, however, for Mozart again takes to a serenading tone with concertizing wind instruments, and there is another *Così fan tutti*-ish episode in A flat major. The finale is a set of very original variations on a shapely and sorrowfully elegant C minor allegretto theme. If tunes really can be portraits, as Couperin wished them to be, this would be one of a well-dressed and perfectly mannered widow who lets the world guess her grief without consciously showing it. There are two beautiful incidents in major keys, but the final variation in 6/8 not only keeps to the minor to the end, but has Neapolitan depressions.

R. C. B.

Concerto for Piano and Orchestra in C major (K. 503)

I. Allegro maestoso. II. Andante. III. Allegretto.

CHRONOLOGICALLY, THE C major Concerto nestles midway between Mozart's two operatic masterpieces *The Marriage of Figaro,* produced in May, 1786, and *Don Giovanni,* produced late in 1787. Mozart's autograph gives Dec. 4, 1786, as the date of completion. Like many of the other fourteen piano concertos Mozart had composed in Vienna since 1782, the C major was written for a concert series given by him during Advent, a season rivaling Lent in lucrative returns for a pianist composer in Vienna who was also a genius. As usual, Mozart was heavily in debt. The dwelling on the Schulerstrasse was expensive. Medical bills were mounting. The *Figaro* opera proved a disappointment as an immediate revenue raiser. To add to the emotional stress, Mozart's latest son, Johann Thomas Leopold, born on Oct. 18, died less than a month later. The concert series was a sure way to raise quick funds—and, possibly, to forget. Composition came easily; performance even more easily. On Dec. 6, only two days after finishing the C major Concerto, we find the busy little man inscribing a fresh date of completion on the manuscript of the D major Symphony (K. 504)! "As soon as he set pen to paper, the usual miracle happened," writes Eric Blom; "trouble forsook him." Could anyone begrudge Mozart this avenue of escape?

The ill luck that hounded Mozart during those bleak December days of 1786 did not stop there. Something of a curse has lain on the C major Concerto. Despite the ardent espousal of specialists, the public, until recently scarcely knew this work. When Artur Schnabel and George Szell first collaborated in the Concerto with the Vienna Symphony at the Grosser Konzerthaussaal in May, 1934, they made an astounding discovery. There was no record of a previous performance in Vienna since Mozart's time!

As for America, research among the program files for major orchestras in the Music Room of the New York Public Library revealed one definite listing— a pair of performances by Webster Aitken with Eugene Goossens and the Cincinnati Symphony on Jan. 30 and 31, 1942. In recent years Nadia Reisenberg, in a WOR broadcast series, and Clarence Adler, on WQXR and at the Town Hall, have included it in their Mozart surveys. The rest is silence—always barring, of course, possible private and unlisted renderings.

Just why the C major has been a dark horse among Mozart's twenty-seven piano concertos it is hard to say. No less an authority than Professor Tovey ranked it with the *Jupiter Symphony* in "triumphant majesty and contrapuntal display." Perhaps one reason may be found in the treacherous rondo finale. There Mozart, exceeding himself, demands the utmost dexterity in what amounts to an endurance test for the right hand. But, then, whoever heard of fright in these days of intrepid virtuosity?

Almost alone among Mozart specialists, Blom has refused to grant the C major's claims to first rank. Ordinarily writing in highly laudatory vein about Mozart's music, the British scholar reserves some of his harshest judgments for the C major. He agrees that its technical problems make it "on the whole" the most difficult of the Mozart piano concertos. "But the performer is not sufficiently repaid by the effort of overcoming them," he insists. "For it is all rather frigid and comparatively unoriginal." Compare Professor Tovey's words about the concerto's "breadth" and "boldness and richness of style." To Blom, the C major was the one work of this period betraying "a certain laxity of spirits." To Tovey it represented Mozart at the highest maturity of his powers. Of the first movement he wrote: "The music carries us out with its tide, and we realize that we have indeed begun a grand voyage of discovery."

The few earlier references in Mozart literature to the C major would seem to uphold Professor Tovey rather than his learned colleague. Carl Reinicke speaks of its "lively brilliance and dramatic excitement" (*"lebhafter Glanz und dramatische Erregung"*). Abert, in his revised and amplified edition of Jahn's biography, noted a quality common to all three of the late C major Concertos (K. 415, K. 467, and K. 503): "A powerful, at times taut dignity, which in the last of the three is constantly struggling with all kinds of dark undercurrents, thanks to the characteristic changes of major and minor." Jahn himself described the concerto as *glänzend und prächtig*—another reference to its brilliance and splendor. Abraham Veinus's phrase for the score is suggestive: "A bit impersonal in a towering sort of way"—on the whole, though, "an inscrutable work."

What strikes one particularly is the amazing polyphonic wealth of the score, its myriad-hued texture, yielding, on closer scrutiny, ever-growing design in its intricacy of detail. The orchestration is typical of Mozart's maturest style in the imagination and resource with which he utilizes every instrument. In these later scores of Mozart, integration of piano and orchestra in a fresh and vital unity had become an established fact in concerto writing. The accompaniment is no longer merely a prop. A new reciprocal play of themes, novel coloring, and rich counterpoint serve to heighten the effect of the whole fabric, besides setting off the solo voice more vividly. In short, a new teamwork between piano and orchestra had been found.

Another remarkable feature is the way the three movements are strongly differentiated. Despite its tender second subject, a majestic spirit sweeps through the opening Allegro maestoso. Contrastingly, the second movement (Andante) is of a "celestial placidity" rarely equalled even by Mozart himself. Special vigilance is needed in the sustained song of the Andante since the performer "must express very much with very few notes." The finale (Allegretto) again leaps to a sharply divergent mood, being witty, joyous, and exuberant. Here a *perpetuum mobile* is suggested in an almost continuous span of sixteenth-note triplets. While the writing is difficult for both hands, the right is subjected to a sharper test of staying power. Special note has been taken of the development section of the opening Allegro maestoso, built on a march theme in E minor. Of it Professor Tovey writes:

The Concerto has been grand and surprising, leaving us continually mystified as to what is to happen, and now it takes shape. This theme that so happily pulls the whole design together all the way back from its single appearance in the ritornello, now moves calmly through a long series of very straightforward sequences through various keys.

But though the sequences are simple in their steps, they are infinitely varied in coloring, and they rapidly increase in complexity until, to the surprise of any one who still believes that Mozart is a childishly simple composer, they move in eight real parts. These eight parts are in triple, or, if we count added thirds, quadruple canon, two in the strings, four in the wind with the added thirds, and two of light antiphonal scales in the pianoforte. *"No such polyphony has occurred since in any concerto, except one passage in the middle of the finale of Brahms' D minor* [author's italics]."

In the Andante the big moment comes when the piano builds up the second subject and returns "by a really colossal passage on a dominant pedal to the main theme in the tonic." In the rondo finale Mozart achieves a breadth of style in the free-rhythmed connecting passages between the main sections "that was never approached until surpassed by Beethoven," according to Professor Tovey. Besides the piano, the Concerto is scored for one flute, two oboes, two bassoons, two horns, two trumpets, tympani, and strings. Trumpets and tympani are omitted from the second movement.

The work was first published by Mozart's widow Constanze at her own expense in 1798. This is indicated in an Italian inscription found in that edition: *"Nr. l del retaggio del defunto publicato alle spese della vedova."* The *retaggio*, or legacy, alluded to was the huge mass of manuscript scores left by Mozart. The subsequent story of these posthumous publications is involved and at times dismal. There was the expected bargaining and bickering. Even Constanze's new husband, the Danish diplomat George N. Nissen, felt called upon to play a part in the transactions. He suspected chicanery on the part of the first publisher to buy up the priceless bequest. "Don't attach too much importance to his fussiness and preciseness," Constanze mollifies Johann A. André, the buyer, after casually mentioning her husband's suspicions. "See that you preserve your present good will, which, indeed, I merit in return for what I feel as your most devoted friend and servant." It seems Nissen, who kept a careful tally of successive opus issues, thought he had detected a sinister discrepancy in André's numbering.

While one of the world's greatest artistic legacies was making its way into profitable circulation, what still remained of the legator lay buried in a pauper's grave.

L. B.

Concerto for Piano and Orchestra in B flat major (K. 595)

I. Allegro. II. Larghetto. III. Allegro.

THE LAST of Mozart's piano concertos is dated Jan. 5, 1791. It was first performed on Mar. 4 of the same year. The piece is in the traditional three movements, and its orchestral score calls for one flute, two oboes, two bassoons, two horns, and strings.

Eric Blom, in the Master Musicians Series, describes it as a "truly valedictory work, with a kind of chastened mood occasionally verging on a feeling of oppressive foreboding."

Abert, in turn, defines it as the best among the last group of piano concertos. He discovers a relationship between it and its predecessors in form and structure, but that it departs considerably from them in character and compass. He says:

One gets the impression that Mozart had composed it for himself rather than for the general public, for the joyous brilliance of the old yields here to a highly personal and remarkably resigned tone, which distinguishes it sharply, for one thing, from the passionate fervor of both earlier concertos in the minor.

Mozart here makes more reserved use of his contrapuntal art than is his wont in this form, though in this respect the working out of the first movement, for example, does not disown its period of origin. The striving for unity and inwardness of the whole idiom emerges so much the clearer.

Though even this work demands a brilliant technic, more so than before technic is brought to the service of musical thought development, and even the concerto idea is more sharply grasped.

Nine days after the completion of the B flat major Concerto Mozart wrote a song entitled "Sehnsucht nach dem Frühlinge," which bears an unmistakable resemblance to the rondo theme of the concluding Allegro.

R. C. B.

Concerto for Violin and Orchestra in D major (K. 218)

I. Allegro. II. Andante cantabile. III. Rondeau: Andante grazioso; Allegro ma non troppo.

MOZART COMPOSED five violin concertos between the months of April and December, 1775. This was during his Salzburg appointment and, doubtless, they were for his own use, as well as for the court Kappellmeister Brunetti. Three of these are considered the most important of the set, *viz.,* the G major (K. 216), the present work, and the A major (K. 219). Dyneley Hussey considers them

magnificent examples of his [Mozart's] work of the period. They are not free from the faults of style, notably the routinier working out, full of "bare runs and un-meaning passages" [a quotation from Edward MacDowell] of the first movements, the subjects of which are always enchanting.

On the other hand, the delicate grace of the slow movements and the delightful inventions of the Rondeaux (he uses always the French spelling, which indicates also the French form and style of the music) fully compensate us for the rather banal decorations of the solo parts. His prodigality of ideas finds full scope in these final movements, where one delightful melody follows another and nothing comes amiss.

However, emphasis on the French characteristics of form and style need not obscure the fact that "the young Mozart of these concertos," as the late Pitts Sanborn once wrote, "was an accomplished cosmopolitan." And he substantiated his theory with the suggestion that they are "German in melody, Italian in the violin technic—Tartini and Nardini come first to mind—and to a lesser degree in the melody also." Eric Blom adds an international fillip of his own with the discovery that Hungarian gypsy influences may be found in the A major (K. 219).

Mozart's own nickname for the D major was "the Strassburg Concerto." That information comes from a letter he wrote to his father on Oct. 19, 1777. Mozart had had lunch at the Heiligkreuz Monastery, it seems, and he spoke of the occasion as follows:

During the meal we had some music. In spite of their poor fiddling, I prefer the monastery players to the Augsburg orchestra. I performed a symphony and played Vanhall's Violin Concerto in B flat, which was unanimously applauded. The Dean, who is a cousin of Eberlin, by name Zschinger, is a fine, jolly fellow and knows Papa quite well. In the evening at supper I played my Strassburg Concerto, which went like oil. Everyone praised my beautiful, pure tone.

The Strassburg epithet is not entirely inapropos, for a theme over the drone bass in the finale is remindful of a Strassburg dance tune.

As is customary with all the concertos in the series, the accompanying orchestra consists only of the strings, two oboes, and two horns.

In the first movement (Allegro, D major, 4/4) the main subject appears immediately with the notes of the common chord in D used in natural sequence, as in a military call. A melodious second subject is brought in by the solo violin, which is given two cadenzas, one in this movement and another in the next.

The slow movement (Andante cantabile, A major, 3/4) is very lyrical and flowing.

The Rondeau (Andante grazioso, D major, 2/4) offers hints of sonata as well as rondo form. Its second section is an Allegro ma non troppo (6/8).

R. C. B.

Concerto for Violin and Orchestra in A major, No. 5 (K. 219)

I. Allegro aperto. II. Adagio. III. Rondo: Tempo di menuetto.

ERIC BLOM joined in the international hunt for stylistic origins by tracing Hungarian gypsy influences in the A major Concerto, a theory later sustained by Abraham Veinus, who dubbed the trio middle section of the finale an "uninhibited Hungarian rhapsody—the kind of wonderful folkish outburst one expects to find in Haydn rather than in Mozart." One passage in the Rondo finale even admits Turkey to the conference table of this polyglot concerto, as we shall see.

I. Allegro aperto (A major, 4/4). The first and second themes are heard in a *tutti* typical of the period (the first theme only partially foreshadowed). The solo violin now enters surprisingly, in almost improvisational fashion. "Instead of introducing the first theme full blown," wrote Sanborn, "it enters with a melodious Adagio, the running accompaniment of which has been likened to the figure that accompanies Agathe's 'Leise, leise' in Weber's *Der Freischütz*." As the impromptu-like episode ends, the Allegro aperto (*aperto,* meaning "open," designates a broadly and clearly phrased Allegro) returns and the violin expounds the first theme fully. A second subject follows in E major, while a third theme, in C sharp minor, is discoursed by the solo voice before the brief development begins.

II. Adagio (E major, 2/4). The material of both themes of this movement again first appears in an orchestral announcement. The haunting first melody is then heard in the upper octave of the violin. Later the key shifts to B major as the strings chant the second theme. The solo violin then takes it up. There is again a short development section. A year after composing the Concerto, Mozart wrote a substitute movement for this Adagio. Kapellmeister Brunetti, we learn from a letter of Leopold's to his son dated Oct. 9, 1777, "found the other one too artificial." [*Sic!*] The alternate movement appears in the Mozart catalogue as K. 261. Of it Alfred Einstein ventures to say that "despite its tenderness and its enchanted, shimmering sonority, it cannot match the simplicity and innocence of the original Adagio."

III. Rondo: Tempo di menuetto (A major, 3/4). Though not strictly a minuet the final movement of this Concerto "has something of its character." The contrasting two themes are in A major and E major. The trio suggesting Hungarian folk music is in F sharp minor. At one place the movement is interrupted by a contredanse in A minor (2/2), "a take-off of the dance music favored at the public balls of the period in Vienna." This episode, often compared to the Turkish rondo of Mozart's A major Piano Sonata, Einstein describes as "a humorous outbreak of sound and fury in 'Turkish' style." Moreover, he points out, "Mozart borrowed the noisy *tutti* in A minor of this 'Turkish' intermezzo from himself. It had originally occurred in the ballet *Le Gelosie del serraglio,* which he wrote in 1773 in Milan for his *Lucio Silla.*" The contrast of this passage with the "menuetto" proper is striking. The themes undergo tricky embroidery in the recapitulation section of the finale.

Joseph Joachim, who wrote excellent cadenzas for this work, numbered it among his favorite concertos. So did the great English scholar Donald Francis Tovey, who spoke of its "special vein of epigrammatic comedy" and its "fantastic kind of childlike beauty." Of his own performance of one of these concertos Mozart said that "it went like oil"—which is, perhaps, a good rule to lay down regarding the way they should all be played.

L. B.

"Sinfonia Concertante" for Violin, Viola, and Orchestra in E flat major (K. 364)

I. Allegro maestoso. II. Andante. III. Presto.

A shroud of silence and mystery covers the origin of this composition. That it dates from the summer or late summer of 1779, while Mozart was still in the service of the Archbishop of Salzburg, seems fairly certain. There is no surviving manuscript to give us the precise date and no reference in Mozart's voluminous correspondence to indicate the occasion of the premiere. Sketches of the few final bars of the first movement are extant, with fragments of cadenza writing on the other side. Johann André brought out the first edition of this "double concerto" in 1801. Subsequent editions include arrangements for piano (four hands), and for violin, viola, and piano (Breitkopf and Härtel). There is a strong possibility that Mozart wrote the viola part with himself in mind as soloist. Although he was a facile violinist, he began to favor the viola during the Salzburg period, a switch in allegiance that infuriated his father Leopold. Later, when Joseph Haydn used to visit him in Vienna, Mozart would play the viola in the frequent quartet sessions. Haydn would be first violinist, his friend Karl Dittersdorf second violinist, and Johann Wanhal cellist. Dittersdorf, a brilliant virtuoso, is assumed to have trained Haydn in the violin, though Haydn's first love, of course, like Mozart's, was the keyboard.

Mozart's special feeling for the viola may be noted in the writing for the solo part of the *Sinfonia Concertante*. The part for viola is written a half-tone lower, *i.e.*, in D, instead of E flat. There was good reason for this. By tuning the viola a half-tone up, the soloist would achieve greater brightness and clarity against the supporting violas of the orchestra. Mozart probably wanted the friendly rivalry of the solo instruments to run on an evener plane. One notes this impartiality throughout the work in the treatment of the solo voices. The solo instruments move in chatty emulation, almost the precise way they do in Mozart's Concerto for Two Pianos (K. 365), which is in the same key and dates from the same period. In the allotment of melodies the basis is also one of strict equality. Shortly after composing the *Sinfonia Concertante,* Mozart tackled another for violin, viola, and cello, but never finished it. Alfred Einstein refers to this second *Concertante* as a "mighty torso" and lists it in an appendix of his monumental edition of the Köchel catalogue as No. 104.

Despite the scant hearings accorded the *Sinfonia Concertante* for violin and viola, the Mozart scholars all hail it as a creative summit of Mozart's Salzburg period. Alfred Einstein goes so far as to call it Mozart's "crowning achievement in the field of the violin concerto." Another keen Mozart student, Noel Straus, frankly affirmed in a recent review that the *Sinfonia Concertante* excelled Beethoven's triple concerto and Brahms's double concerto in its "unification and fusion of the symphonic and concertolike factors involved," Abert speaks of its "proud, dark splendor," and Eric Blom returns to this theme of dim luster by sensing still darker things:

"A beautiful, dark-colored work in which a passion not at all suited to an archiepiscopal court, and perhaps disclosing active revolt against it, seems to smolder under a perfectly decorous style and exquisite proportions."

Mr. Blom's suspicion that the *Sinfonia Concertante* hides a secret aim under its suave mantle is not so far-fetched. Mozart was not happy in the oppressive atmosphere of the Salzburg court. He had returned from triumphs in Paris and Mannheim a maturer artist with a new sense of freedom and independence. There had been stormy sessions with his employer over the court rules and regulations that bound down the young genius. Requests for leaves of absence and even complete release led to fresh unpleasantness. The final break with the Archbishop of Salzburg was to come in the spring of 1781, when Mozart appeared one day with a formal resignation. Employer and employee exchanged some candid thoughts, and the interview came to an abrupt end with the celebrated episcopal kick. The revolt that was smoldering in the *Sinfonia Concertante* of two years before had finally come to a furious and perhaps inglorious climax.

The fresh power that Mozart brought back with him from his tours throbs through all three movements of the *Sinfonia Concertante*. The work seems an epitome of Mozart's resources during those summer months of 1779. The style is broader, the feeling richer. The orchestra is no mere support, but a highly articulate participant in this symposium of theme and development. Though the solo instruments have right of way, the other instruments insist on rights of their own. There is a closer rapport between the violin and viola and the orchestra, and the emotional focus is stronger. As Einstein points out, the *Sinfonia Concertante* has broken away from the diverting gallantries of "entertainment" music. Something deeper and graver has replaced the light chatter and rippling laughter of earlier serenades. Each of the movements reveals a firmer unity of structure, the orchestra is continuously alive with fresh details, and wind instruments are assigned major thematic roles in the orchestral scheme. Mozart seems to have concentrated his strongest feelings in the first two movements, but the finale has a driving power of its own. As Abert puts it, "the dark spirits have vanished, but the strength remains."

Notable in the first movement, too, is the use of the "Mannheim crescendo," another souvenir of Mozart's recent travels. The effect of orchestral unity is also enhanced by the single tonality. Both end movements are in E flat, the Andante being in the relative key of C minor. Even the side theme brought in by the winds in the first movement is in E flat. The three movements of the *Sinfonia Concertante* are: I. Allegro maestoso, 4/4, E flat major; II. Andante, 3/4, C minor; III. Presto, 2/4, E flat major. The original scoring calls for two violins, two violas, bass, two oboes, and two horns, besides the solo violin and viola. Mozart wrote out the cadenzas for the *Sinfonia Concertante*. The story is that the copy used by André for the first edition contained the cadenzas in Mozart's handwriting. This edition was used at the Mozart Festival in Salzburg in 1856, which Otto Jahn refers to in his biography of Mozart.

L. B.

Overture to "The Marriage of Figaro" ("Le Nozze di Figaro")

Mozart's bubbling opera buffa was first produced at the Burgtheater, Vienna, on May 1, 1786. Lorenzo da Ponte had provided the libretto, based, of course, on Beaumarchais' satiric comedy of manners *Le Mariage de Figaro, ou la Folle journée*. There is a tradition that the opera was first heard in America in 1799, when it was supposedly presented in New York with the title *The Follies of a Day*. Yet, a performance in English at the Park Theater, New York, on May 10, 1824, was billed as the "first time in America." English versions of

Mozart's comic masterpiece were popular in both England and America throughout the first half of the nineteenth century.

The Metropolitan Opera House first brought the work into its repertory on Jan. 31, 1894, when the original Italian was used. In the cast were Emma Eames as the Countess Almaviva, Lillian Nordica as Susanna, Sigrid Arnoldson as Cherubino, Edouard de Reszke as Almaviva, and Mario Ancona as Figaro. Emilio Bevignani conducted. A historic Metropolitan revival of the opera was that of Jan. 13, 1909, with Gustav Mahler conducting and Emma Eames, Marcella Sembrich, Geraldine Farrar, Antonio Scotti, and Adamo Didur heading the cast. Mahler had earlier acquired great prestige as a Mozart interpreter in Vienna.

In his lively *Memoirs,* librettist da Ponte gives an account of how the opera buffa came to be written and produced.

Talking one day with Mozart, he asked me if I could turn Beaumarchais' *Noces de Figaro* into an opera. The idea was to my taste, and its success was immediate and universal.

For some time this play had been forbidden by the Emperor because of its immorality. How then to propose it anew . . . I awaited the opportune moment to propose the poem either to the Intendent or, if I had the courage, to the Emperor himself.

As fast as I wrote the words, Mozart wrote the music, and it was all finished in six weeks. The lucky star of Mozart willed an opportune moment and permitted me to carry my manuscript directly to the Emperor.

"What's this?" said Joseph to me. "You know that Mozart, while remarkable for his instrumental music, has with one exception never written for song, and the exception is not much good."

I answered timidly, "Without the kindness of the Emperor, I should have written only one drama in Vienna."

"True. But I have already forbidden the German company to give this play, *Figaro.*"

"I know it; but in turning it into an opera, I have cut out whole scenes, shortened others, and been careful everywhere to omit anything that might shock the conventionalities and good taste. In a word, I have made a work worthy of the theater honored by His Majesty's protection.

"As for the music, as far as I can judge, it seems to me a masterpiece."

Da Ponte's persuasive eloquence worked. "Very well," said the Emperor, according to the ebullient factotum, "I trust to your taste and prudence. Send the score to the copyists."

Mozart personally coached the whole cast for the Burgtheater premiere of 1786. There were repeated meetings. The Irish tenor Michael Kelly, who took part in that performance, has left a vivid glimpse of Mozart during one such session with the company: "I shall never forget his little animated countenance, when lighted up with the glowing rays of genius; it is as impossible to describe as it would be to paint sunbeams."

Lacking a development section, the Overture (D major, 4/4) is in condensed sonata form. A fleet passage in eighth notes presents the gay first theme. A subsidiary subject is brought in, and then the second theme, in A major, flashes brightly from the violins. The customary free fantasia is lacking in this Overture, which ends, however, in a longer coda than usual. The score calls for flute, two oboes, two clarinets, two bassoons, two horns, two trumpets, kettledrums, and strings.

L. B.

Overture to "Don Giovanni"

Of the two versions employed in concert halls, Leopold Stokowski has observed:

In concert performances Mozart's Overture to *Don Giovanni* is usually played with a Finale composed by Johann André, published by Breitkopf and Härtel. André's Finale is scholarly, but conventional and uninspired. It would be far better for the Finale to be Mozart's own music. The end of the great scene between the Commendatore and Don Giovanni is musically perfect for this Finale. Not only is this inspired music, but it is appropriate in character and design, because the Overture will then begin and end in the same mood of dramatic intensity, thus unifying the whole composition.

The moral play *El Burlador de Sevilla, y Convidado de Piedra* (*The Mocker of Seville and the Stone Guest*) by the Spanish monk Gabriel Tellez, who used the pen name of Tirso de Molina, is, according to Ernest Newman, "the ultimate origin of the story of *Don Giovanni*." The Tirso play, dated 1630, is believed to be a compact of old legends about a rakehelly Spanish nobleman and certain festivities interrupted by the appearance of a statue.

Lorenzo da Ponte's libretto, it has been pointed out, is not entirely unrelated to that of one Bertati, who did the libretto for the opera *Il Convitato di Pietra* (*The Stone Guest*), music by the Italian Gazzaniga, a work given in Venice, 1787, some time before the premiere, in Prague, Oct. 28, 1787, of Mozart's.

In any case, the celebrated tale has had numerous interpretations from a great variety of authors, among them Molière, whose *Don Juan, ou le Festin de pierre* was produced in Paris in 1665. Another is Thomas Shadwell's play *The Libertine,* given in 1676. There was a drama by one Giliberti (Naples, 1652) and another by a Cigogni around the same time. Still other Italian versions exist, as well as French, German, and Spanish ones.

The composers have by no means neglected it; for, in addition to the Mozart and Gazzaniga works, there is the unfinished opera *The Stone Guest* by Dargomyjsky, besides a Gluck ballet score, and so on.

A provocative legend about the composition of the Overture to *Don Giovanni* is that Mozart wrote it during one night—the night before the premiere, naturally—handing the manuscript to the copyists the following morning. His wife Constanze is supposed to have sat up with him, telling him stories to keep him awake. The story tells also that the piece was read at sight by the orchestra on the all-important evening.

Some hold that all this took place the night before the eve of the performance —before the final rehearsal, that is.

Newman observes:

Mozart's own dating of his score makes this a matter of certainty. Nor is the feat of writing the Overture in a single night quite as remarkable as it sounds. Mozart had not only extraordinary facility in composition; he had marvelous memory. "Composition," for him, meant developing the work in his head; he found the business of writing it out rather tiresome, and he would often postpone it as long as he could.

There can be little doubt that the Overture to *Don Giovanni* had been worked out in his head long before the final rehearsal and that all he had to do on that historic night was to put the notes on paper.

R. C. B.

Overture to "The Magic Flute"

Two DAYS before the premiere of his opera *The Magic Flute* Mozart wrote the Overture. A product of his last months, when the composer was worn by illness and abject poverty, *The Magic Flute* is considered the forerunner of German opera.

The libretto, by Emmanuel Schikaneder, head of a traveling company of players, is extravagant, as well as allegorical. It is Masonic in its symbolism.

The action is laid in a mythical Egypt. Sarastro, high priest of Isis, has abducted Pamina, daughter of the malefic Queen of the Night, in order to impart wisdom to her. Saved from the toils of a huge serpent by the Queen's attendant ladies, Prince Tamino, the hero, sets out to "rescue" Pamina. He is accompanied by Papageno, the bird catcher. However, in trying to effect Pamina's release he himself becomes taken up with the high ideals and aims of Sarastro and his followers. He serves his novitiate and, finally, he is married to Pamina, who has by now absorbed all the wisdom to which she has been exposed.

The libretto has been unmercifully ridiculed by many, but it has not been without its staunch defenders. Goethe, for one, averred that "the author understood perfectly the art of producing great theatrical effects by contrasts." Hegel praised it inordinately, perhaps, for its admixture of the real and the supernatural and for the series of tests the hero is put through.

Philip Hale, writing of Schikaneder, said he was a "wandering theater director, poet, composer, and play actor. Vain, improvident, shrewd, a bore, he nevertheless had good qualities that won for him the friendship of Mozart." Dynely Hussey, on the other hand, wrote:

Born at Regensburg (Ratisbon) in 1751 of the poorest imaginable parents, he spent his early years as a vagabond fiddler. He became an actor and was sufficiently successful to achieve the management of a company of his own by the time he was twenty-seven. He had no education whatever, yet he was not devoid of taste, as will be seen from the fact that his repertory included plays by Shakespeare (*Macbeth, Hamlet,* and *King Lear*), Schiller, and Lessing, and Gluck's *Orfeo.* Indeed he contributed a great deal towards the creation of a German national drama in the last years of the century. But his chief activity was the production of popular comic pieces, in which the spectacle played an important part.

The Overture (E flat major, 4/4) opens with three great chords for the full orchestra. In the subsequent Allegro a brilliant fugue emerges. It is interrupted, however, by the return of the three great chords of the opening. There is supposed to be some Masonic meaning attached to those chords, and it is interesting to note that they represent the only part of the Overture that reappears in the music of the opera itself.

The score calls for two flutes, two oboes, two clarinets, two bassoons, two horns, two trumpets, three trombones, and strings.

R. C. B.

Overture to "Die Entführung aus dem Serail"

[*Arranged by Ferruccio Busoni*]

In 1781, Mozart, then living with the Weber family in Vienna, took up the matter of writing a German opera. The libretto was supplied him by Gottlieb Stephanie, an actor and inspector at the Burgtheater. The *Singspiel* type of German opera had there received considerable support from the Emperor and it had already met with popular favor. Umlauf's *Die Bergknappen* had been the first of such works to be produced there, in 1778, but the repertory was scarcely teeming with examples of the kind, and the impresarios were constrained to put on translations of foreign pieces, especially French ones.

Stephanie's libretto of *Die Entführung aus dem Serail* (*The Abduction or Elopement from the Seraglio or Harem*)—which translation covers just about all the possibilities—is based on a comedy by Christoph Bretzner. Mozart's pleasure in the subject was unbounded, though he did find many little faults of construction with it, as letters written to his father attest. However, he took his own good time about completing it, particularly because of his superior critical faculties and because the desire to accomplish a worthy job with a type of work new to him was strong, indeed. Perhaps, other reasons had their influence in delaying it. These had to do with situations surrounding him in the Weber household. Frau Weber, ever on the *qui vive* for a likely husband for her daughters (though she had not done too well for one of them), played a neat little game for the benefit of uniting her daughter Constanze to Mozart.

Meanwhile, Mozart *père* had been sending fulminating letters to his son, and in one of them ordered him to leave the Weber household. But he was already engaged to Constanze by that time. The opera, after many huddles between composer and librettist, finally was finished, and now came further delays owing to all sorts of jealous interferences and other complications. The Emperor Joseph II, at long last, stepped in and ordered its production for July 16, 1782. It was given before a capacity crowd, which enthused over it, in spite of a minority group's attempts to wreck it. Each of the numbers received great applause, bringing about many encores. Much was made of the music's originality and daring, and even the conservative Emperor informed Mozart that it was better than Viennese ears deserved. He also said that there were too many notes in it, but Mozart gently retorted that he had written down only as many as were required. The work was given frequently during the season, and it always drew large audiences.

The Overture ties in immediately with the first aria of the opera, Belmonte's "Hier soll ich dich denn sehen," and it is suffused with an idiom, known then in Vienna as "Turkish music." Mozart in discussing the Overture has written, "It alternates between forte and piano, the Turkish music being always forte, modulated by changes of key, and I do not think anyone can go to sleep over it."

R. C. B.

Overture to "Idomeneo"
[*Arranged by Ferruccio Busoni*]

THE FULL title of Mozart's opera, which dates from his twenty-fifth year, is *Idomeneo, Rè di Creta, ossia: Ilia ed Idamante.* An *"opera seria"* in three acts, it was composed for the Munich Carnival of 1781 and produced there on Jan. 29, 1781. Mozart's father, Leopold, regarded the work as a strictly community affair for the city of Salzburg: "It is remarkable," he wrote, "that every part of the work is by persons residing in Salzburg—the poetry by the Court Chaplain (Varesco), the music by my son, and the German translation by Schachtner." The Abbé G. B. Varesco had derived the libretto from a French text of Danchet, to which Campra had written an opera some seventy years earlier. In setting it to music Mozart, according to Edward J. Dent, was "French by deliberate intention, but Italian by natural instinct." Dent also speaks of the "monumental strength and white heat of passion that we find in this work and shall never find again." On Jan. 18, eleven days before the premiere, we discover Mozart, who had been struggling with what he termed "the cursed dances" for a divertissement, sighing with relief: "Praised be God, at last I have come to the end of it!"

Besides the Overture, Busoni also arranged the Festal March of the second act and the Sacrifice Scene of the third act for concert use, dedicating the set to Othmar Schoeck when it was published in 1919.

L. B.

Overture to "Der Schauspieldirektor" ("The Impresario") (K. 486)

THOUGH OFTEN included among Mozart's operas, *Der Schauspieldirektor* (*The Impresario*) is a slight one-act farce with incidental music consisting, in all, of five numbers, the bright and bustling Overture included. Gottlieb Stephanie, actor, librettist, and Burgtheater inspector, wrote the winding and witless text, which Mozart adorned with four vocal gems: two arias and two trios.

The comedy was commissioned by the Emperor Joseph II and produced at the orangery in Schönbrunn on Feb. 7, 1786, less than two months before the premiere in Vienna of Mozart's comic masterpiece *Le Nozze di Figaro*. The occasion was a reception in honor of visiting Netherlands officials. Both the German and Italian troupes earlier organized by the Emperor took part in the festivities, the Italians concentrating on Salieri's *Prima la Musica e Poi le Parole* (*First the Music and Then the Words*). The Germans apparently did most of the talking, since the rambling dialogue between the Mozart arias runs to absurd lengths.

Eric Blom maintains that the vocal music, meager though it be, ranks with Mozart's maturest dramatic and psychological style. The arias are full of tenderness and delineative power, besides demanding great technical skill. The real marvel is the trio, in which the buffo tenor (the Impresario) tries to mollify two claimants for a prima-donna role. In the finale—actually a somewhat modified rondo—all three agree that singers should forget their petty squabbles and jealousies and serve only art, or, as freely adapted by Blom:

> Artists, it is true, must ever
> Hold in high esteem their fame;
> But that each alone is clever
> Is a thought that must forever
> Be redounding to the shame
> Of an artist with a name.

Der Schauspieldirektor has been revived from time to time, though seldom in its original form. The plot has undergone drastic change, and Mozart and his librettist Schickaneder have been brought into the cast as key figures in a theatrical tangle. By introducing Mozart himself, adapters naturally did not overlook the chances for romantic intrigue in the plot. In the comedy the Impresario settles the issue by giving the top role to both prima donnas. Each is to depict one aspect of the character. When the singers protest that the hero cannot be in love with two heroines, the wily Impresario meets the objection with the query: "Do *I* not love you both?"

Naturally, none of the versions employing Mozart as a character was staged while Frau Constanze Mozart was still alive. Whatever the seraphic qualities of his music, Mozart was of course no saint in his private life. The stories of his amours with singers, while no doubt exaggerated, have been handed down by fairly reliable colleagues and associates of Mozart. It was rumored that while *Don Giovanni* was in rehearsal Mozart carried on love affairs with his Zerlina, Donna Anna, and Donna Elvira—"perhaps," sardonically remarks Blom, "with a view to still greater realism." It is even possible that a similar situation arose during the *Schauspieldirektor* rehearsals. The arias were such as to require arduous coaching. At any rate, Mozart in the role of romantic *intrigant* in a modified version of *The Impresario* is not far-fetched. In later revivals of the little work, arias culled from other Mozart sources have been interpolated to fill out the scant allotment of music.

What Blom, following Abert, detects as a note of "deliberate, tongue-in-the-cheek parody" in the Overture may be traceable to the presence on the Schönbrunn program of a work by Mozart's rival, Salieri. As an exponent of the Italian school, Salieri was the Emperor Joseph's favorite composer. Now, the Overture is Italian in form almost to mock imitation. If Mozart intended it as such, the parody was certainly lost on the Emperor. Salieri, however, probably got it. Did not Mozart's friend Michael Kelly speak of the Emperor's Maestro di Capella as "a clever, shrewd man possessed of crooked wisdom"?

L. B.

"Eine Kleine Nachtmusik," Serenade for String Orchestra (K. 525)

I. Allegro. II. Romanze. III. Menuetto; Allegretto. IV. Rondo: Allegro.

THE MOST widely played and popular of Mozart's works for orchestra, *Eine Kleine Nachtmusik* dates from 1787. It was a crucial period for Mozart. *Don Giovanni* was composed that year, along with two of his finest string quintets, in C major and G minor (K. 515-516), and the brilliant A major Violin Sonata (K. 526). In February his little Viennese circle of friends broke up, with the Storaces, Kelly, and Attwood all returning home to England.

Mozart almost went along. On May 28 his father died. Then one day a rough-looking lad of seventeen, with a heavy Rhenish accent, came in for an audition. Mozart listened, at first politely, then sharply. The visitor showed startling gifts at the piano. Later Mozart remarked to others present in the room: "This young man should be watched. He will soon make a noise in the world." The boy's name was Ludwig van Beethoven.

The manuscript score of *Eine Kleine Nachtmusik* carries Aug. 10, 1787, as the date of completion. It is a compact and faultlessly balanced work, with beautiful melodies woven into a highly polished fabric. The opening Allegro (G major, 4/4) is a perfect sonatina. Its mood is frankly romantic in places. The vigorous chief theme contrasts neatly with the suave theme following it. In the slow movement (Romanze, Andante, C major, 2/2) four themes are used, the form being that of a rondo. Mystery and romance are suggested in the murmurous middle section. The Menuetto (Allegretto, G major, 3/4) has a whispery trio in D major.

The theme of the bright and chattery Rondo finale (Allegro, 2/2) is "the naïve Viennese popular song to the very life of Schikaneder's Papageno in *The Magic Flute*," to quote Eric Blom.

L. B.

"Six German Dances" (K. 571)

When Gluck died on Nov. 15, 1787, Emperor Joseph II cast about for a successor to the court composer. The choice fell on Mozart. Thus, on Dec. 7 of that year the Salzburg genius became "court chamber musician" at a salary of 800 florins a year, a saving of 1,200 florins for the economical Joseph, who had paid Gluck 2,000. But, then, Joseph II never professed to like Mozart's music, despite Michael Kelly's statement that he was "passionately fond of music and a most excellent and accurate judge of it." Still, the money came in handy, what with Mozart's haphazard budgeting, an increasing family, and mounting doctor's bills. This was the period of the repeated borrowings from the merchant Puchberg.

Mozart's imperial duties boiled down to writing dance music for the masked balls held in the Redoutensaale, located in a wing of the Hofburg on the right side of the Josephplatz in Vienna. Quite philosophically he regarded the pay as "too high for what he did."

"What he did" in the next few years reads like a ballroom dance catalogue. The Emperor ordered no operas or symphonies, only dance music for the gay celebrants of the Redoutensaale. The year 1788 brought six *Deutsche* (or *Teutsche*) and twelve minuets. Twelve *Deutsche* and a fresh dozen of minuets followed the next year. The year 1790 yielded none. In respectful observance of Joseph II's death (Feb. 20), the Redoutensaale festivities were suspended.

Leopold II ascended the throne on Mar. 13. When the masquerades were resumed the following year, Mozart's pen again got busy, and dances poured out afresh. First came six additional minuets, then six more *Deutsche*, followed by four minuets, two country dances, two more minuets, and three more *Deutsche*. The record also includes six Ländler and later that year a half dozen more country dances, besides *Ein Deutscher mit Leirer-Trio*, the *Leirer* being the hurdy-gurdy man.

Viennese from all classes were invited to the Redoutensaale "masked balls," the Emperor delighting in the spectacle of democratic mingling. They usually took place on Sundays during the Carnival season, on Shrove Tuesday, and on the last three days of the carnival. As may be gathered from the Mozart inventory, minuets, waltzes (*Deutsche*), and country dances were alternately played. Hence the waltz—the *Deutscher Tanz*—was already the rage of Vienna. Because of the huge crowds drawn to the affairs, it is said only the "lower classes danced the waltz." After the Emperor's death the director of the Court Theater went on purchasing dances from local composers. Hummel, Haydn, and Beethoven all earned a few ducats filling the director's orders.

In Mozart's time the Viennese waltz, the *Deutscher*, was a lilting, gliding dance, "a more popular Ländler," with the beat sharply marked and the dance divided into two parts, each generally eight measures long. A *Deutscher* figures in Weber's *Der Freischütz*. In the elaborate finale of the first act of Mozart's *Don Giovanni*, the stage directions call on Leporello and Masetto to dance a *Teutscher*, one of the three dances running simultaneously in the contrapuntal web. The spirit of the "German dance" was strongly folkish, alike in its sentimental strains as in its brusker aspects. The minuet, of course, was more elegant. Thus, in the opera the Don assigns the minuet to his more distinguished guests. He himself dances a country dance with Zerlina, and Leporello drags the duped Masetto into the whirl of a *Deutscher Tanz*.

Abert, in his monumental revision of Jahn's biography of Mozart, observes that the most striking thing about these Mozart dances is their "inexhaustible inventiveness," despite the fact that the simple pattern offers little scope for marked individuality. A trio section, often containing snatches of folk music, is usually in the minor key, and Abert speaks of the delightful little touches of orchestral wit often occurring in the codas, giving as an instance the "Mannheim crescendo and finale of the K. 571 group." He mentions, too, the curiously tart chromatics of the concluding dance. In the K. 568 to 586 sets he detects Hungarian and Spanish echoes.

The Mozart *Verzeichnis* gives 1789 as the year of composition of the K. 571 group, and the place Vienna. A manuscript containing only the parts for wind instruments in pairs reposes in the Malherbe Collection in the library of the Paris Conservatory. The autograph reads "6 *teutsches*." The corresponding manuscript of the string parts (two violins and bass) has been in the Vienna

National Library since 1927. It bears the words "6 *teutsche di Wolfgango Amadeo Mozart.*" The catalogue points out that the autograph was "previously in the possession of the Emperor Maximilian in the Miramar Castle." On another copy of the score appear the words "6 *Deutsche Tänze aus dem k. k.* [*königlichenkaiserlichen*] *kleinen Redoutensaale* 1790."

Michael Kelly, in his *Reminiscences* published in London in 1826, describes the Viennese as "in my time dancing mad." The ladies of Vienna who attended the Redoutensaale masquerades were "particularly celebrated for their grace and movements in waltzing, of which they never tire." He confessed that for his part he found waltzing from ten at night until seven in the morning "a continual whirligig most tiresome to the eye and ear, to say nothing of any worse consequences."

Kelly, who was Mozart's first Basilio in Vienna, speaks of his friend and patron as "an enthusiast in dancing." Mozart's wife went even further. "His taste," she maintained, "lay in that art rather than in music."

L. B.

"Serenata Notturna" (Serenade No. 6) in D major for Two Small Orchestras (K. 239)

I. March. II. Menuetto. III. Rondo.

Title and music alike would establish this Serenade, which dates from January, 1776, as an "occasional" offering, though no clue to the occasion inspiring it is available. The possibilities are many. Mozart, at the time, was in the employ of the Archbishop of Salzburg. Divertimentos and Cassations flowed from the young genius's pen for the amusement of the Archbishop's entourage during repasts and celebrations. As a rule the Archbishop encouraged only the composition of religious music. There were exceptions. The *Serenata Notturna* could have been written for a gala occasion in the reception hall of the palace, though it is unlikely. The time of the year would dismiss its having been designed for outdoor use at a garden party. Other Serenades of Mozart were so destined.

If the *Serenata* was composed during the last days of December, 1775, it might possibly have been intended as a New Year's Day surprise. In that case his sister Nannerl should be numbered among the likely beneficiaries. Later, in July, 1776, Nannerl received the Divertimento in D as a birthday gift from her brother. Again, Mozart's own birthday occurred on Jan. 17. Could he have impishly intended the Serenade as a self-bestowed memento? Perhaps the likeliest theory of all is to ascribe the Serenade to the request of a Salzburg merchant or titled aristocrat. Mozart rarely turned down a commission. He was soon to compose his Serenade in D for the marriage of Elisabeth Haffner, daughter of Salzburg's burgomaster, and later the larger scale *Notturno* for the Countess Lodron. Music's marvellous boy could shake "occasional" tunes from his coat sleeve at a moment's notice. Accordingly, the "occasion" may have been a ball in sumptuous surroundings, with the division of the playing personnel into two detached units imparting a special note of swank.

There have been two ways of regarding this music. One was typically Eduard Hanslick's: that its charm vanished with the occasion it served and that its courtly fragrance evaporates in a concert hall. The other has been to welcome sunshine even when it beams from a *Night Serenade*. The *Serenata* is scored for two orchestras, one consisting of two violins, viola and contrabass, the other of a string quartet and tympani (later Mozart went himself two better by composing the *Notturno* (K. 286) for four orchestras, as if sketching out plans for the ballroom scene in *Don Giovanni*). Fascinating effects of light and shade abound, and the obvious possibilities of contrast are fully exploited. Often orchestra No. 1 acts as soloist against orchestra No. 2, with a resulting richness in tonal coloring. The percussion heightens the contrast, and pizzicati are worked in deftly to extend the color scheme.

L. B.

Otto Nicolai

BORN: KÖNIGSBERG, JUNE 9, 1810. DIED: BERLIN, MAY 11, 1849.

After the fourth performance of his "Merry Wives of Windsor"
Nicolai died suddenly, prematurely. Yet his opera lives on, and even
that masterpiece of Verdi's old age—"Falstaff"—has not displaced it.
—GEORG RICHARD KRUSE.

Overture to "The Merry Wives of Windsor"

THE WORLD premiere of Nicolai's *Die Lustigen Weiber von Windsor* (*The Merry Wives of Windsor*) took place at the Berlin Hofoper on Mar. 9, 1849, two months before the composer's sudden death. It obtained a sensational success. Vienna first heard it on Feb. 12, 1852, and in this country it had its initial performance at the Philadelphia Academy of Music on Mar. 16, 1863. The following April the work had its first New York production at the Academy of Music, given in the original German. An English translation by Henry Edward Krehbiel was given also at the Academy of Music, New York, as one of the presentations of the American Opera Company.

Nicolai's opera has had but one Metropolitan performance, that, in German, on Mar. 9, 1900, the reason for its appearance in the repertory of that season being the presence in the company of Fritz Friedrichs, a baritone who had abandoned the spoken drama for opera. This artist knew three parts, in all, Beckmesser, Alberich, and the Falstaff of Nicolai. He was highly regarded in Germany, but his voice won for him no encomiums here, so that *The Merry Wives of Windsor* was dropped from the Metropolitan repertory after that one hearing. This despite the rest of the personnel in that cast, *viz.,* Sembrich, Schumann-Heink, Theodor Bertram, Olga Pevny, Lemprière Pringle, and Andreas Dippel.

Another New York performance of *The Merry Wives of Windsor* was given at the Lexington Theater by a German opera company that had promised a "Wagnerian Opera Festival." How the Nicolai work got mixed up with Wagner and festivals is something of a mystery. In any case, the cast of that production offered Theodor Latterman, Maria Ivogün, Emma Bassth, Benno Ziegler, and Desidor Zador. And in April, 1936, the Juilliard School of Music's Opera Department presented the work four times in an English translation.

The Overture to the opera has been a consistent favorite of concert-hall audiences, one of its earliest performances in this country being that given it by the Philharmonic Society at the Academy of Music, New York, on Jan. 9, 1858.

The Overture has an introduction (Andante moderato, F major, 4/4), which begins with a sustained high C in the violins. Against that the basses and then the other instruments play a flowing melody that is developed in contrapuntal imitation. There follows a transitory passage of light and graceful character in the tonality of F minor. It modulates to A flat, bringing in the main body of the Overture (Allegro vivace, F major, 2/4). "A sprightly first subject and a nimble subsidiary one lead to the second subject, announced by the violins in octaves, which is to the life that dainty rogue, Anne Page. There is a jocund conclusion theme. Falstaff himself does not come into the picture till the working out, where he makes a blustering entrance in F minor. Thereafter he and Anne, in an access of jest and jollity, romp in their merry game of tag the length and breadth of the orchestra."

The Overture to *The Merry Wives of Windsor* is scored for two flutes (one interchangeable with piccolo), two oboes, two clarinets, two bassoons, four horns, two trumpets, three trombones, kettledrums, bass drum, cymbals, and strings.

R. C. B.

Niccolò Paganini

BORN: GENOA, OCT. 27, 1782. DIED: NICE, MAY 27, 1840.

His melody is the great Italian melody, but alive with an ardor generally more passionate than that which one finds in the most beautiful pages of the dramatic composers of his country. His harmony is always clear, simple, and of an extraordinary sonority.—
HECTOR BERLIOZ.

Concerto for Violin and Orchestra in D major, Op. 6

I. Allegro mastoso. II. Adagio. III. Rondo: Allegro spiritoso.

COMPOSED PROBABLY in 1820 (rather than 1811, as some allege) and published in 1851, this Concerto has had a curious history, dating from August Wilhelmj's arrangement of the first movement as a separate piece. This arrangement found favor with violinists and they played it with such persistence that for a long time the second and third movements were all but forgotten. In December, 1938, Fritz Kreisler gave those two sections a securer place in limbo with his transcription of the first movement, which he entitled simply *Concertstück* and introduced at a Carnegie Hall concert of the Philadelphia Orchestra. Zino Francescatti, on the other hand, abides exclusively by the original with a devotion equally distributed over all three movements.

The first movement (Allegro maestoso, D major, 4/4), in the usual sonata form, gives the solo violinist every opportunity to play the dazzling virtuoso.

The second movement (Adagio, B minor, 4/4) owes its existence to an especially moving performance by the Italian tragedian Demarini, according to Paganini's biographer Stephen S. Stratton. Paganini attended the performance, was overwhelmed, and returned home to spend a sleepless night. In the attempt to express his tortured feelings, it is said, he wrote this movement, and Stratton is of the opinion that this is the music in which William Gardiner heard "tones more than human, which seemed to be wrung from the deepest anguish of a broken heart."

The third movement, a Rondo (Allegro spiritoso, D major, 2/4), is lengthy, as originally written, and teeming with technical difficulties.

The score of the Concerto calls for flutes, oboes, and clarinets in pairs, bassoon, double bassoon, two horns, two trumpets, three trombones, kettledrums, bass drum, cymbals, and strings.

It was Hector Berlioz who wrote:

A man of much wit, Choron said in speaking of Weber: "He's a meteor!" With equal justice one could say of Paganini: "He's a comet!" For never did a flaming star burst more abruptly on the firmament of art or excite in the course of its immense ellipse more astonishment mixed with a sort of terror before vanishing forever. The comets of the physical world, if poets and popular ideas are to be believed, only appear in times prophetic of terrible storms which overwhelm the human ocean.

Certainly it is not our epoch or the apparition of Paganini which will give the lie to tradition. This exceptional genius, unique in his kind, grew up in Italy at the beginning of the greatest events mentioned in history. He began to emerge at the court of one of Napoleon's sisters at the most solemn hour of the Empire; he triumphantly toured Germany at the moment when the giant was lying in his tomb; he came forward in France to the sound of the crumbling of a dynasty, and it was together with cholera that he entered Paris.

Truly a fabulous individual, Paganini excited the curiosity of all who saw him, because of his strange exterior, and the mingled amazement and admiration of all who heard him play. The spectacular virtuoso, in fact, exercised a magical influence over everyone who came in slightest contact with him, whether minor dilettante or prince of the musical art. Rossini, ever scornful of unrestrained enthusiasm, is said to have looked upon Paganini with devotion and, at the same time, something akin to fear. And Meyerbeer followed the fantastic creature through all his travels in northern Europe, dogging him, drinking in his every performance, in the vain attempt to penetrate the mystery of his powers.

Suspicion, innuendo, jealousy, and the idle machinations of the superstitious whirred madly in the wake of this pitifully thin and gaunt man of music. "His bony fingers seemed to stretch from one end of the violin fingerboard to the other without an effort; and it has been asserted that without such a length of finger he never could have played the passages he is known to have executed." They said the "devil was at his elbow." Someone swore that he saw him directing Paganini's arm and guiding the bow! And Paganini, who knew how to capitalize on a situation, once had the "bizarre inspiration to publish a letter from his mother, disproving the rumor that he was the devil's son!"

As a composer Paganini has had his detractors, both during and after his time. Yet as astute a musician as Berlioz could declare,

One would have to write a volume to indicate all the finds Paganini has made in his works in respect of novel effects, ingenious procedures, noble and imposing forms, orchestral combinations not even suspected before him.

His melody is the great Italian melody, but alive with an ardor generally more passionate than that which one finds in the most beautiful pages of the dramatic composers of his country. His harmony is always clear, simple, and of an extraordinary sonority.

And with regard to Paganini's technique, Berlioz comes to the conclusion, "Paganini is one of those artists of whom it must be said, 'They are because they are and not because others were before them.'"

R. C. B.

John Knowles Paine

BORN: PORTLAND, ME., JAN. 9, 1839. DIED: CAMBRIDGE, MASS., APR. 25, 1906.

*It is an error to consider me bound to the past. I believe thoroughly
in the future of music.*—JOHN KNOWLES PAINE.

Prelude to Sophocles' Tragedy "Oedipus Tyrannus," Op. 35

STUDENTS AND faculty members of the Greek Department at Harvard University
produced Sophocles' tragedy *Oedipus Tyrannus* in the original tongue, in
Sanders Theater, Cambridge, on May 17, 1881. "The academic enterprise," to
quote an observer, "covered Harvard with glory at the time." For that performance John Knowles Paine, then full Professor of Music at Harvard, wrote
the incidental music for orchestra and male chorus. This consisted of a Prelude,
choral and orchestral interludes, and a Postlude. Something of a Greek scholar
himself, Paine had given brilliant lectures on Greek poetry and music. A
prelude to Aristophanes' comedy *The Birds* further attests his interest. Paine
made no attempt to recapture any supposed antiquarian spirit in his music.
He drew freely on the resources of contemporary choral and orchestral writing,
trying to convey the tragic and fatalistic mood of Greek drama in the idiom of
his own day.

The following year, on Mar. 11, the Prelude figured on the twentieth and
last program of the Boston Symphony Orchestra's first season in the Boston
Music Hall. Paine was invited to conduct his own work. Georg Herschel,
whose own setting of Psalm CXXX was part of the program, directed the rest
of the concert. The Wedding March from Mendelssohn's *Midsummer Night's
Dream* music and Beethoven's Ninth Symphony were the other numbers.
When the Prelude was revived in 1894 it moved a local critic to put Paine's
music "side by side with the works of Beethoven and Schumann." After a
subsequent hearing many years later, H. T. Parker, of the *Boston Transcript,*
took a more sober view: "The composer was no genius. Rather he followed the
best models and the orthodox procedures of his tonal time, and in a commissioned piece for an occasion devised, designed, knitted, and rounded music of
substance and skill."

Paine was once dubbed "The Patriarch of American Music." With Edward
MacDowell, Horatio Parker, and George W. Chadwick, he founded an
American school of symphonic music, frankly influenced, to be sure, by domi-

nant European styles. Despite earlier claimants, his oratorio *St. Peter* is the first full-scale composition in that form by an American. Similarly, his C minor Symphony, led by Theodore Thomas in Boston in 1876, and viewed by Paine as "the turning point in my career," is generally accepted as the first real symphony written on American soil. That same year he wrote the *Centennial Hymn* for the Philadelphia exposition.

Paine had joined the Harvard staff as music teacher in 1862, being elevated to a full professorship in 1876. He was largely responsible for putting music on an equal credit footing with other branches of study in the A.B. and M.A. curricula. Thoroughly American and democratic in conviction, he long planned a symphonic poem on his great idol, Abraham Lincoln. He was working on the score when he died. On the last page of the manuscript appear the words, *"Orchestra tacet"* ("the orchestra is silent"). Though repeatedly charged with a conservative outlook, particularly because of his early distaste for Wagner and the first French impressionists, he retained an open mind to the end. In later years he admitted to the critic and Wagnerian standard-bearer Henry T. Finck, who had been a Paine pupil, that he now agreed with him. Moreover, Paine used Wagner as a model when writing his opera *Azara,* which he regarded as his masterpiece.

The New York Telegram of Apr. 26, 1906, carried a tribute to Paine in which it predicted that the death of "the head and founder of American music" would leave "a wide, sad void in the musical life of this country, in the little band of mental pioneers in Cambridge and in many a human heart throughout the musical world." Time and changing taste, however, have dealt harshly with Paine's music. But his ideals of workmanship and education left their permanent mark on American music.

Rossini, Moussorgsky, and Stravinsky are a few of the numerous composers who have used the Sophocles play, as well as the other two tragedies in the trilogy *Oedipus in Colonos* and *Antigone* for symphonic and choral treatment. Mendelssohn wrote incidental music for the last two plays when performances in Donner's German translation were given at the New Palace in Potsdam in the winter of 1841. In 1887, six years after the Harvard production, Cambridge University in England staged similar performances in Greek. The incidental music was by Charles Villiers Stanford, who occupied in British music an academic place in many ways similar to Paine's in American music.

L. B.

Hans Pfitzner

BORN: MOSCOW, MAY 5, 1869.

*His art seeks depth rather than extent and endeavors to represent
spiritual experiences alone.*—RUDOLF FELBER.

Three Preludes from "Palestrina"

ALTHOUGH KNOWN as an opera, *Palestrina* was given the label "musical legend,"
according to Bruno Walter, by the composer himself. The work is in three acts,
each preceded by a prelude which carries the sense and describes the atmosphere of its particular act. Mr. Walter further declares that in this composition
Pfitzner pits the world of the creative musician, the thinker, and the spiritual
man (Acts I and III) against that of bustle and politics and disunity and
what not in all the levels of thought and action (Act II).

The underlying theme is not one of struggle, but of contrast philosophically
noted and commented upon. Palestrina is the central figure, appearing only in
the first and third acts, and what plot there is involves his composition of the
Missa Papae Marcelli as a bulwark against a threatening abolition of music.

We also learn from Mr. Walter that Pfitzner's music touches on old church
modes and that it possesses, therefore, a certain archaic or medieval quality,
although the plan is not imitation at all. It calls for a large orchestra, "but not
an oppressive one."

Palestrina was first performed at Munich, under Bruno Walter's direction,
June 12, 1917. Pfitzner was his own librettist. It has been said that following
a precedent "set by Wagner (and adopted once by Richard Strauss in
Feuersnot) the composer identified his hero with himself and made Palestrina's
inspiration in the composition of the *Missa Papae Marcelli* a symbol of his own
spiritual condition."

At any rate, the premiere of *Palestrina* proved such a success that it was sent
out on tour (in a war year) to Basle, Zurich, and Berne. It has been given many
times in Germany—Stuttgart, Berlin, and other cities—and also in Vienna.

Although he was born in Moscow, Hans Pfitzner came of German stock.
His father was a violinist who gave Hans his first lessons. When seventeen
years old Pfitzner entered Hoch's Conservatory in Frankfort, where he studied
piano with James Kwart and composition with Ivan Knorr. After graduation
he was appointed to the faculty of the Coblenz Conservatory, not long after
that giving a concert of his own compositions.

He became conductor of the Strassburg Opera, being, at the same time, a member of the local Conservatory's faculty. Later, Strassburg University presented him with a doctorate. In the meantime, he wrote a good many compositions, consisting of several operas, works for orchestra and for orchestra and voices, chorals, songs, and chamber music pieces, all of which have made him an established musical figure in Germany. Along literary lines he has penned numerous critical pieces on musical trends, doing a considerable amount of inveighing against "modernism."

The Three Preludes from *Palestrina* were given their first New York performance by the Philharmonic Society under Willem Mengelberg on Nov. 11, 1926.

R. C. B.

Walter Piston

BORN: ROCKLAND, ME., JAN. 20, 1894.

He is an American composer speaking the international idiom of absolute music.—NICOLAS SLONIMSKY.

Symphony No. 2

I. Moderato. II. Adagio. III. Finale: Allegro.

COMMISSIONED BY the Alice M. Ditson Fund of Columbia University, this work was written in 1943 at Belmont, Mass., the composer's home. The premiere occurred on Mar. 5, 1944, in Washington, D. C., at a concert of the National Symphony Orchestra conducted by Hans Kindler. A month later the Boston Symphony Orchestra, led by G. Wallace Woodworth, played it for the first time in Boston on a program broadcast by the Blue Network.

The symphony reached New York on May 12, 1945, in a performance at the McMillin Theater, Columbia University, by the NBC Symphony, with Howard Hanson conducting. The occasion was the First Annual Festival of American Music. Admission to the concert was by invitation only. On the strength of the New York premiere, Mr. Piston's new work won the Music Critics' Circle Award of 1944-1945.

Artur Rodzinski introduced it to New York Philharmonic-Symphony subscribers on Nov. 15, 1945. The composer has disavowed any "descriptive or other programmatic intent" in his Symphony, the three movements of which he has analyzed as follows:

The first movement (Moderato) is based on two themes, one given out at the opening of the movement by violas and cellos, legato and flowing, the other first played by the oboe, accompanied by clarinets and bassoons, staccato and rhythmic. The first of these themes receives the principal development, and the movement ends with a canonic statement of the melody by the brass choir (pianissimo).

The second movement (Adagio) is a quiet, lyrical development of the motive announced at the beginning by the bassoon, and the melody played by the clarinet, accompanied by muted strings. The movement is continuous rather than sectional in form.

The Finale (Allegro) is composed of three themes: the first vigorous and rhythmic, played by cellos and horns; the second marchlike, by clarinets and bassoons; and the third, of more songful character, first heard in English horn and clarinet. Recurrence of the first theme gives an impression of rondo form to the movement.

The symphony is scored for two flutes, piccolo, two oboes, English horn, two clarinets, bass clarinet, two bassoons, contra-bassoon, four horns, three trumpets, three trombones, tuba, tympani, snare drum, triangle, tambourine, cymbals, bass drum, and strings.

Walter Piston's interest in music was a mild one during his early youth. He was graduated from the Massachusetts School of Art in 1914, apparently headed for a painter's career. However, when he entered Harvard, music became a major concern of his, and on his graduation, in 1924, he went abroad to study with Nadia Boulanger. When he returned, he joined the music faculty at the University.

He has written many works, including piano pieces, chamber music, orchestral suites, two symphonies, a concerto for orchestra, a piano concerto, a violin concerto, music for ballets, and compositions for organ. Among his other accomplishments, Mr. Piston has published a book on musical theory, *Principles of Harmonic Analysis.*

On Oct. 22, 1944, Artur Rodzinski led the Philharmonic-Symphony in a premiere of Mr. Piston's *Fugue on a Victory Tune,* submitted in the "war series" jointly sponsored by the Society, the League of Composers, and the Columbia Broadcasting System.

R. C. B.

Suite from the Ballet "The Incredible Flutist"

THE BALLET *The Incredible Flutist,* with choreography by Hans Wiener, music by Walter Piston, and setting and costumes by Marco Montedoro, was composed for performances by Hans Wiener's dancers at the "Pops" concerts in Symphony Hall, Boston, of May 30 and 31, 1938, under the direction of Arthur Fiedler. The work was given again in May of the following year under the same auspices.

The Suite, which is about one-half the length of the original score, was first played in concert by Fritz Reiner and the Pittsburgh Symphony in Pittsburgh, Nov. 22, 1940. It consists of the following episodes:

Introduction (Lento)
Siesta Hour in the Market Place; Entrance of the Vendors
Dance of the Vendors (Allegretto moderato)
Entrance of the Customers (short transition)
Tango of the Four Daughters (Moderato, espressivo)
Arrival of the Circus, and Circus March
Solo of the Flutist (Lento)
Minuet (short)—Dance of the Widow and the Merchant
Spanish Waltz
Eight O'clock Strikes

Siciliano (Andante)—Dance of the Flutist and the Merchant's Daughter
Polka finale

In an issue of *Dance* magazine, August, 1938, the following summary of the
action was printed:

The siesta hour is over. With a hearty yawn and wide stretch the village shakes
off its drowsiness. First to wake up, the apprentice opens the shop and life begins
its uneventful flow. The merchant's daughters demonstrate their father's wares to
the shoppers. The busybody and the crank have their argument. But what is this?
A march is heard! The band, the circus band, marches in, followed by the people
of the circus. They're all here; the barker, the jugglers, the snake dancer, the
monkey trainer with her monkeys, the crystal gazer, and, of course, the main
attraction, the Flutist. The Flutist is a remarkable fellow, an incredible fellow.
He not only charms snakes; believe it or not, also the snake dancer. He is so
romantic, the Incredible Flutist, and, perhaps, just a bit promiscuous, for he also
charms the merchant's daughter, for they meet at eight o'clock that very evening.
When the clock strikes eight, young couples are all over the place, and love is in
the air. Even the prudish, rich widow, cannot resist the charged atmosphere and
grants the merchant that kiss he's been begging for well nigh two years. But they
don't fare so well. Their sustained embrace is discovered, and the poor rich widow
faints right into the arms of her bewhiskered boy friend. But the Incredible Flutist
hies to the rescue. A little dancing, a little fluting and the widow comes out of her
swoon, none the worse for wear. And then—the band strikes up; the spell is broken;
the circus, Incredible Flutist and all, leaves the village.

R. C. B.

Francis Poulenc

BORN: PARIS, JAN. 7, 1889.

*There is in Poulenc's music an ingenuity, a gaiety, and a freshness
that seem always to have an undercurrent of folklore at the base.
This art delights in plunging its roots into the popular soil of
marching songs and nursery tunes.*—EMILE VUILLERMOZ.

Concerto in D minor for Two Pianos and Orchestra

I. Allegro ma non troppo. II. Larghetto. III. Finale.

WHEN THE group of French musical and esthetic rebels known as *Les Six* was
organized in Paris in 1920, Francis Poulenc was one of them. The others were
Milhaud, Honegger, Tailleferre, Durey, and Auric. Their guides and mentors
were Jean Cocteau the poet and Erik Satie the composer. Their program was
simplicity and succinctness. Their chief enemies were the inheritors of
Debussyan impressionism and Franckian romanticism. To *Les Six* the composer was no longer the erratic long-haired individual who lived apart and
toiled, in hunger, in some obscure attic. He was to be a regular fellow "who
liked to go to night clubs like everybody else," in the words of Aaron Copland.

Whatever the accomplishments of this group, it succeeded in one thing:
public and press took immediate notice of their claims and pontifications. Many
critics lampooned the rebellious sextet, but only added to the publicity campaign. As for their individual qualities, Mr. Copland has written as follows:

As for the composers themselves, they turned out to be a variegated set of new
talents. Francis Poulenc hewed closest to the Satie line, particularly in his first works;
Auric wrote a pungent and witty music, somewhat dry and ascetic in quality;
Tailleferre could not quite pull herself away from the attractions of impressionism;
and Durey shortly dropped out of sight altogether. It was clear from the start that
the two leading members of the group were to be Arthur Honegger and Darius
Milhaud.

Besides their other artistic bonds, "The Six" were united by a practical
interest in the modern ballet. "It was a sort of cult with them," writes Verna
Arvey. "Often, the flavor of lusty music-hall tunes has crept into their ballet
music, but it has served only to define more clearly the moods of the moment."
It was Muriel Draper who once declared that the greatest distinction of this
"half-dozen of intelligent musical investigators and compilers of rhythm and
sound," was its contribution to Diaghileff's Russian Ballet repertory.

514

Among Poulenc's ballets are *Les Mariés de la Tour Eiffel* (given in New York by the Swedish Ballet), *Cocardes, Diana, Football,* and the satirical one-act fantasy, *Les Biches,* using popular *chansonettes,* besides *Aubade*—a choreographic concerto for piano and eighteen instruments. The flair for melodic naturalness and dancelike animation is felt in much of Poulenc's other music, too. A light vein of parody and burlesque also appears, and at times one hesitates to say whether he is showing fondness or ridicule for a "hit tune," a tango, or a military march.

Besides the Concerto for Two Pianos, Poulenc has written considerable chamber music, a *Rhapsodie Nègre,* a sonata for four hands, numerous songs, and a large sheaf of delicately wrought piano pieces.

Composed in 1932, the Concerto in D minor for Two Pianos and Orchestra was first performed on Sept. 5, 1932, at a concert of the International Music Festival in Venice. Poulenc and Jacques Febrier were the soloists, and Desiré Defauw conducted the orchestra of La Scala, Milan. Notable in the scoring is the modest array of strings called for: eight first and eight second violins, four violas, four cellos, and four double-basses, two flutes, two oboes, two clarinets, two bassoons, two horns, two trumpets, two trombones, one tuba, and percussion.

Woven into the web of the first movement (Allegro ma non troppo, D minor, 4/4) are fragments of so-called "Parisian folklore," *i.e.,* popular tunes, dating back several years, from the *café-concert* circuit. A pert and lively melody serves as main theme and opens the way to a host of similar *chansonettes.* These are brought together at one place in a clever web of counterpoint. A reverielike passage sets in as the first piano begins the coda (*trés calme*), and the movement ends tranquilly.

The second movement is a Larghetto, built largely from two ingratiating themes, the first of which is announced by one piano in B flat major, 2/2. At a point where the tempo quickens the two pianos join in voicing the second subject, in A flat major.

Poulenc's melodic gifts are perhaps best shown in the Finale, which opens Allegro molto (2/2, 3/4), with a passage for two pianos very much in the style of a toccata. The dominant theme of the movement then appears in a march announced by both pianos and violins. There is a peaceful interlude, and Poulenc returns to his favored *café-concert* mood with a sheaf of gay new strains. The march theme is back (*Agité*), now worked up to a fierce climax. Finally, one of the "hit-tune" motives is reviewed and raised to a sharp fortissimo, and the Two-piano Concerto ends on a note of brilliance.

L. B.

Serge Prokofieff

BORN: EKATERINOSLAV, RUSSIA, APR. 23, 1891.

If we wished to establish Prokofieff's genealogy as a composer, we would probably have to betake ourselves to the eighteenth century, to Scarlatti and other composers of the good old times, who have inner simplicity and naïveté of creative art in common with him. Prokofieff is a classicist, not a romantic, and his appearance must be considered as a belated relapse of classicism in Russia.—LEONID SABANEYEFF.

"Classical" Symphony in D major, Op. 25

I. Allegro. II. Larghetto. III. Gavotte: Non troppo allegro. IV. Finale: Molto vivace.

THE COMPOSER'S purpose in this work was simply to write a symphony as Mozart might have written it had he been a contemporary of his. The piece is scored for two flutes, two oboes, two clarinets, two bassoons, two horns, two trumpets, kettledrums, and strings, but the four movements run about thirteen minutes. Dedicated to Boris Assafieff, the Symphony was played for the first time at Leningrad on Apr. 21, 1918, Prokofieff conducting. He again conducted when it was premiered in this country at a concert of the Russian Symphony Society in Carnegie Hall on Dec. 11, 1918.

Prokofieff's mother was his first music teacher, and she later turned her charge over to Glière and Taneieff. He began to compose at the age of five, and by the time he was nine he had already written two works for the stage. *The Giant,* composed at the age of seven, and *The Deserted Islands* at the age of nine. A third, *The Feast,* was completed when he was thirteen. The first two were written in piano score, but the third was orchestrated by Prokofieff himself. Another stage work, *Undina,* was a product of his thirteenth year. Two years earlier he had already composed a symphony.

He became a student at the St. Petersburg Conservatory in 1903, where he was graduated with highest honors in 1910. All through his Conservatory years, under the tutelage of such masters as Rimsky-Korsakoff and Tcherepnine, he composed, putting to his credit a fantastic number of works—no less than 100, it has been said. Prokofieff, his own best critic, as well as best friend, probably, has permitted none of these early essays to be published.

The compositions of his maturer years again reach an incredible figure and, what is extremely revealing, he has written in practically all the forms. Commentators have remarked on the mischievous quality of his music, the tongue-in-cheek mockery, satire and irony that are either implicative or out-and-out obvious. His later works show less of such affairs, yet it has not been impossible to connect these creations with a strong political credo.

The *Classical Symphony,* with its acknowledgments to some sort of "modern Mozart," reflects little of the haranguery, subtle or otherwise, of his other works. Here, the radical Prokofieff has prescribed conditions for himself that involve melodic mimicry, structural parallels, and such matters.

The symphony is in the regular four movements, a gavotte supplanting the usual minuet. The dance known as the gavotte, whose name is allegedly derived from the Gavots, or people of the Pays de Gap, was originally a *danse grave,* which departed from the usual type in that the dancers lifted their feet from the ground, instead of shuffling about flat-footed. Grove explains the gavotte as being in common time and in two parts, each repeated, as is customary with the older dances. "In the original form of the dance," he says, "the first part consisted of four and the second of eight bars; when introduced as one of the movements of a suite, it has no fixed number of bars."

In the sixteenth century the gavotte was introduced at the French court by native provincial dancers. It later reached the stage where it became, "the dignified, pompous, and chaste dance of the eighteenth century, with slow and measured postures and low bows and curtsies."

The music Mozart wrote for the ballet pantomime *Les Petites Riens* contained a "Gavotte joyeuse" (Allegro vivo, 2/4), a "Gavotte gracieuse" (Andante non troppo, 6/8), and a "Gavotte sentimentale" (Andante, 4/4). The different time markings indicate that Grove may have been mistaken concerning "common time." (Prokofieff's *Gavotte,* of course, would have to be in common time!)

R. C. B.

Symphony No. 5, Op. 100

I. Andante. II. Allegro marcato. III. Adagio. IV. Allegro giocoso.

THIS WORK was composed during the summer of 1944 and was given its premiere in Moscow on Jan. 13, 1945, Prokofieff conducting. Its first performance in this country occurred at a concert of the Boston Symphony Orchestra, the same band introducing it to New York in Carnegie Hall on Wednesday, Nov. 14, 1945.

In an interview with Robert Magidoff, Moscow correspondent of *The New York Times* (Mar. 25, 1945), Prokofieff declared that he had worked on the Fifth Symphony "for several years," and that he had been "gathering themes for it in a special notebook. I always work that way," he said, "and probably that is why I write so fast. The entire score of the Fifth was written in one month in the summer of 1944. It took another month to orchestrate it, and in between I wrote the score for Eisenstein's film 'Ivan the Terrible.' "

Magidoff, commenting on the work, said, "The Fifth Symphony, unlike Prokofieff's first four, makes one recall Mahler's words: 'To write a symphony means for me to create a whole world.' Although the Fifth is pure music and— Prokofieff insists it is without a program, he himself said, 'It is a symphony about the spirit of man.' "

In the traditional four movements, the Fifth Symphony begins with an Andante which brings forward a pair of themes in triple and duple time, respectively. Prokofieff develops the material quite fully, making much use of rhythmic contrast, and the movement closes with a longish coda.

The second movement (Allegro marcato) has been likened to the classical scherzo. A steady, marcato 4/4 beat serves as accompaniment to the theme, which travels from wood wind to wood wind. There is a middle section resembling a trio. Here the rhythm is again emphasized, although it is now in 3/4 time. After this the first section reappears in a new treatment, thus ending the movement.

The third movement (Adagio) starts with a melody in the wood winds (espressivo), which is then taken by the strings. This movement, something like a passacaglia, is eerie and tragic in quality, impressions enhanced by the sounds of descending scales. A livelier section relieves the tension, following which the previous music returns.

The finale, an Allegro giocoso, opens with the divided cellos and basses in a passage brief and serene, whereupon the entire theme appears. The second theme is initiated by the flute. There is development of the two, as the music rises in brilliance to its end.

R. C. B.

Concerto for Piano and Orchestra in D flat major, Op. 10

DEDICATED TO Nicolai Tcherepnine, the D flat major Concerto was completed in 1911. It was given its first performance at Moscow in 1912, with the composer himself playing the solo part. America's introduction to this work occurred at a concert of the Chicago Symphony, Dec. 11, 1918, Prokofieff again appearing as soloist and Eric De Lamarter conducting.

The score requires two flutes, piccolo, two oboes, two clarinets, two bassoons, contra-bassoon, four horns, two trumpets, three trombones, tuba, tympani, bells, and strings.

Prokofieff views this Concerto, which is in one movement, as an allegro movement in sonata form. The key, at the opening and closing, is D flat major, although the work embraces a variety of tonalities and episodes between the two ends. There is an Andante section and another marked Allegro scherzando, which give an impression of three-movement form, though only in passing.

The Allegro scherzando develops not its own but material heard earlier in the piece; and in the conclusion there is an amplified restatement of the introduction, all of which leans somewhat toward the cyclical scheme.

A tutti introduction (allegro brioso), in which the piano joins, leads to a solo statement of subject material, comprising an upward C major scale (poco piu mosso) and a downward scale in D flat major (tempo primo). Prokofieff adopts a Beethoven idea in repeating the introductory music after the exposition (*Pathetique Sonata*).

The Andante assai comes between exposition and development, and the melody is like a cantilena in its long and sinuous phrases. First the strings play it, then a solo clarinet, then the piano and, finally, the whole orchestra. The music rises to a climax and gradually subsides, at which point the Allegro scherzando begins, developing, as previously noted, the main ideas. The piece ends brilliantly.

R. C. B.

Concerto for Piano and Orchestra in C major, No. 3, Op. 26

I. Andante; Allegro. II. Theme. Andantino. III. Allegro ma non troppo.

WORK WAS begun on this Concerto at Leningrad, in 1917. However, the composer's visit to America held up proceedings and the piece was not completed until October, 1921. The composer himself played the piano part for the first time at a concert of the Chicago Symphony Orchestra on Dec. 17 of that year.

The following is the composer's own analysis of his score:

The first movement opens quietly with a short introduction (Andante, 4/4). The theme is announced by an unaccompanied clarinet and is continued by the violins for a few bars. Soon the tempo changes to Allegro, the strings having a passage in sixteenths, which leads to the statement of the principal subject by the piano. Discussion of this theme is carried on in a lively manner, both the piano and the orchestra having a good deal to say on the matter. A passage in chords for the piano alone leads to the more expressive second subject, heard in the oboe with a pizzicato accompaniment. This is taken up by the piano and developed at some length, eventually giving way to a bravura passage in triplets. At the climax of this section, the tempo reverts to Andante, and the orchestra gives out the first theme, *ff*. The piano joins in, and the theme is subjected to an impressively broad treatment. In resuming the Allegro, the chief theme and the second subject are developed with increased brilliance, and the movement ends with an exciting crescendo.

The second movement consists of a theme with five variations. The theme is announced by the orchestra alone, Andantino.

In the first variation, the piano treats the opening of the theme in quasi-sentimental fashion, and resolves into a chain of trills, as the orchestra repeats the closing phrase. The tempo changes to Allegro for the second and the third variations, and the piano has brilliant figures, while snatches of the theme are introduced here and there in the orchestra. In Variation Four the tempo is once again Andante, and the piano and orchestra discourse on the theme in a quiet and meditative fashion. Variation Five is energetic (Allegro giusto). It leads without pause into a restatement of the theme by the orchestra, with delicate chordal embroidery in the piano.

The Finale begins (Allegro ma non troppo, 3/4) with a staccato theme for bassoons and pizzicato strings, which is interrupted by the blustering entry of the piano. The orchestra holds its own with the opening theme, however, and there is a good deal of argument, with frequent differences of opinion as regards key. Eventually the piano takes up the first theme and develops it to a climax.

With a reduction of tone and slackening of tempo, an alternative theme is introduced in the wood winds. The piano replies with a theme that is more in keeping with the caustic humor of the work. This material is developed, and there is a brilliant coda.

R. C. B.

Concerto for Violin and Orchestra in D major, No. 1, Op. 19

I. Andantino. II. Scherzo vivacissimo. III. Moderato.

Said to reflect "very strongly the influence of the Russian national school, particularly Rimsky-Korsakoff and Glazounoff," the D major Concerto was begun in 1913, completed, it is believed, in 1917, and given one of its early performances at the Prague International Festival, in 1924, with Joseph Szigeti as the soloist. Its American premiere occurred at a concert of the Boston Symphony Orchestra on Apr. 24, 1925, when Richard Burgin played the solo part.

The work is not a virtuoso piece in the general sense, being singularly free from cadenzas and preoccupations with out-and-out bravura. Nor may the orchestral writing be considered an accompaniment, but rather an integral part of the whole, symphonic and devoid of echoes between solo and tutti.

A gentle melody appears in the solo violin, for which the strings and clarinet provide a thin background. The mood changes, and the sustained melody is followed by some rhythmic passage work over a marked bass. Toward the end of the first movement the initial melody returns, this time in a slower tempo, and as it is being played by the flute, the solo instrument weaves over it a close texture of notes.

In the second movement the solo violin runs a mercurial course through accented rhythms, leaps of long intervals, slides on double stops resulting in double harmonics, down-bow strokes, and the rest of the business, none of which, however, may be construed as display music.

The bassoon brings a brief but definite theme into the third movement. This is followed by the principal theme in the solo instrument, a combination of staccato and sustained phrases. Development and recurrence are shot through with sharp orchestral comments. After the climax there is a return to the gentle melody of the first movement. The orchestral violins play that softly, while the solo line trills the identical notes an octave above, ending on high D.

The orchestral score calls for wood winds in pairs (with piccolo), four horns, two trumpets, tuba, tympani, snare drum, tambourine, harp, and strings.

Prokofieff, who has written two violin concertos (the second, in G major) analyzed, in his autobiography, the development of his creative style:

The principal lines which I followed in my creative work are these: The first is classical, whose origin lies in my early infancy when I heard my mother play Beethoven sonatas. It assumes a neoclassical aspect in the sonatas and the concertos, or imitates the classical style of the eighteenth century, as in the Gavottes, the *Classical Symphony,* and, in some respects, in the *Sinfonietta.* The second is innovation, whose inception I trace to my meeting with Taneieff, when he taunted me for my rather "elementary harmony." At first, this innovation consisted in the search for an individual harmonic language, but later was transformed into a desire to find a medium for the expression of strong emotions, as in *Sarcasms, Scythian Suite,* the opera *The Gambler, They Are Seven,* the Second Symphony, etc. This innovating strain has affected not only the harmonic idiom, but also the melodic inflection, orchestration, and stage technique. The third is the element of the toccata, or motor element, probably influenced by Schumann's Toccata, which impressed me greatly at one time. In this category are the Etudes Op. 2, Toccata, Op. 11, Scherzo, Op. 12, the Scherzo of the Second Piano Concerto, the Toccata in the Fifth Piano Concerto, the persistent figurations in the *Scythian Suite, Le Pas d'acier,* and some passages in the Third Piano Concerto. This element is probably the least important. The fourth element is lyrical. It appears at first as lyric meditation, sometimes unconnected with melos, as in *Fairy Tale,* Op. 3, *Rêves, Esquisse automnale,* Legend, Op. 21, etc., but sometimes is found in long melodic phrases, as in the opening of the First Violin Concerto, the songs, etc. This lyric strain has for long remained in obscurity, or, if it was noticed at all, then only in retrospection. And since my lyricism has for a long time been denied appreciation, it has grown but slowly. But at later stages I paid more and more attention to lyrical expression.

I should like to limit myself to these four expressions, and to regard the fifth element, that of the grotesque, with which some critics are trying to label me, as merely a variation of the other characteristics. In application to my music, I should like to replace the word grotesque by "Scherzoness," or by the three words giving its gradations: "Jest," "laughter," "mockery."

R. C. B.

Concerto for Violin and Orchestra in G minor, No. 2, Op. 63

I. Allegro moderato. II. Andante assai. III. Allegro ben marcato.

COMPOSED DURING the summer and autumn of 1935, Prokofieff's Second Violin Concerto was premiered in Madrid on Dec. 1, of that year. Enrique Arbos conducted the Madrid Symphony Orchestra, with the Belgian violinist Robert Soetens playing the solo part. Prokofieff himself was present and later directed the same orchestra in his *Classical Symphony*. Jascha Heifetz was the soloist when Serge Koussevitzky and the Boston Symphony Orchestra first performed the new Concerto in America.

Twenty-two years had elapsed since Prokofieff had composed his first Violin Concerto in D, so comparisons were promptly made between the styles and idioms manifested by the two scores. Apart from the normal development and change expected over so long a period, another factor was emphasized by many. The G minor Concerto marked Prokofieff's return to his home land after a long Odyssey abroad. He was now a Soviet citizen and once more a participant in the social and cultural life of his country.

The new Concerto revealed a warmth and lyricism, even a romantic spirit that contrasted with the witty glitter and grotesquerie of the early Concerto. The old terseness, rigorous logic, and clear-cut form were still observable though less pronounced. There were even flashes of the "familiar Prokofieffian naughtiness," as Gerald Abraham pointed out. But the new mood was inescapable. "So far as the violin concerto form is concerned," wrote the English musicologist, "Prokofieff's formula for turning himself into a Soviet composer has been to emphasize the lyrical side of his nature at the expense of the witty and grotesque and brilliant sides."

The daring thrusts, the crisp waggishness, the fiendish virtuosity and steely glitter seemed now to be giving way to warmer, deeper preoccupations, at least in the first two movements. "The renascence of lyricism, warm melody, and simple emotionality is the essence of the second violin concerto," writes Abraham Veinus in his book, *The Concerto*. The earlier spirit of mockery and tart irreverence was almost lost in the new surge of romantic melody.

Besides solo violin, the score calls for two flutes, two oboes, two clarinets, two bassoons, two trumpets, two horns, bass drum, snare drum, triangle, cymbals, castanets, and strings. In the first movement (Allegro moderato, G minor, 4/4) the solo instrument, unaccompanied, gives out a readily remembered first theme which forms the basis of the subsequent development and the coda. The appealing second theme is also announced by the violin, this time against soft

hythmic figures in the string section. Abraham finds a "distant affinity" be-
ween this second theme and the Gavotte of Prokofieff's *Classical Symphony*.
The shift to frank melodic appeal is especially noticeable in the slow movement
Andante assai, E flat major, 12/8). Here the mood is almost steadily lyrical
and romantic from the moment the violin sings the theme which forms the
basic material of the movement. There is varied treatment and some shifting in
onality before the chief melody returns to the key of E flat. In the finale
Allegro ben marcato, G minor, 3/4) the old Prokofieff is back in a brilliant
ondo of incisive rhythms and flashing melodic fragments. There are bold
taccato effects, tricky shifts in rhythm, and brisk repartee between violin and
orchestra. If there is any obvious link with the earlier Concerto in D it is here
n this virtuoso's playground.

L. B.

"Summer Day," Children's Suite for Little Symphony, Op. 65B

I. "Morning." II. "Tag." III. "Waltz." IV. "Regrets." V. "March."
VI. "Evening." VII. "Moonlit Meadows."

IN 1935, Prokofieff composed a set of "twelve easy pieces for piano," to which
he gave the collective title *Music for Children*. Recently he transcribed seven of
them for orchestra, and these now comprise the Suite *Summer Day*. The score
calls for two flutes, two oboes, two clarinets, two bassoons, two horns, two
trumpets, percussion, and strings.

Some brief instructions in the manuscript read:

All transposing instruments in this score are written in C—*i.e.,* just as they sound.
In the parts the clarinets must be written in A, trumpets in B flat, and horns in F.

Three performers are needed for the percussion, in accordance with which the
instruments are divided into three groups—I. Tympani; II. Triangle, cymbals, and
bass drum; and III. Tambourine, drum, and castanets.

The separate sections of the Suite are:

I. "Morning" (Andante tranquillo, C major, 4/4). An odd little phrase is
played by the first flute with occasional reinforcement from the second, while
the other wood winds engage in a mild counterpoint and the strings and bass
drum supply the rhythmic anchorage. In a middle part the bassoons, horns,
cellos and (later) the violas and bass sing a rather serious melody, as violins
and flutes offer accompanying figures.

II. "Tag" (Vivo, F major, 6/8). A bright, tripping melody begins in the
violins and flutes and is soon shared by bassoons. It is repeated, this time leading

to the key of E flat where the oboes play it in a modified form. There follows a short intermediary passage in the same tripping spirit, although the rhythm i stressed more. After some additional modulations the section ends with the opening strain.

III. "Waltz" (Allegretto, A major, 3/4). A tart and tangy waltz theme introduced by the violins, has an unusual feel about it because of the unex pected intervals in the melody. In a more subdued manner the violins usher in a second theme, which, however, is given a Prokofieffian touch by the inter spersed wood-wind chords in octave skips. As before, the opening idea serves a the section's close.

IV. "Regrets" (Moderato, F major, 4/4). An expressive, straight-forward melody starts in the cellos. Oboes pick it up in a slightly revised form, and they and the first violins conclude it. Next the violins and clarinets give it a simple variation. In the meantime, there are some subsidiary figures in the other instruments. All ends in just the slightest kind of finale.

V. "March" (Tempo di marcia, C major, 4/4). Clarinets and oboes each take half of the chief melody. The horns then play it and, following a brief middle sequence with unusual leaps, the tune ends in a harmonic combination o flutes, oboes, horns, and trumpets.

VI. "Evening" (Andante teneroso, F major, 3/8). Prokofieff's knack o making unusual melodic intervals sound perfectly natural is here well illus trated. A solo flute intones the opening bars of a pleasant songlike tune, the rest of which is given to the solo clarinet. Still in the same reflective mood, the music continues with a passage of orchestral arpeggios, while the first violin take their turn with the melody. A middle portion in A flat major present some measures of syncopation. With a change of key to C major and again to F major, the section ends tranquilly with a snatch of the opening tune.

VII. "Moonlit Meadows" (Andantino, D major, 2/4). The solo flute open this section with a smooth-flowing melody which rather makes the rounds though in more or less altered form. The section ends quite simply with three chords.

This transcription departs but slightly from the piano originals, and when i does so it is because the composer has obviously felt the need of a stronger accent here or some figure there, unimportant in themselves, which might serve to bolster up the Suite.

Artur Rodzinski led the American premiere at a New York Philharmonic Symphony concert on Oct. 25, 1945.

R. C. B.

Four Excerpts from the Ballet "Romeo and Juliet," Op. 64

I. "Montagues and Capulets." II. "Friar Laurence." III. "Masks."
IV. "Death of Tybalt."

As a ballet in four acts and nine tableaux, Prokofieff's *Romeo and Juliet* was first produced by the Bolshoi Theater in Moscow in 1935. Like many standard Russian ballets, the performance took a whole evening. Prokofieff assembled two Suites from the music, the First premiered in Moscow on Nov. 24, 1936, under the direction of Nicolas Semjonowitsch Golowanow. The premiere of the Second Suite followed less than a month later.

Prokofieff himself directed the American premieres of both Suites, of Suite No. 1 as guest of the Chicago Symphony Orchestra on Jan. 21, 1937, and of Suite No. 2 as guest of the Boston Symphony Orchestra on Mar. 25, 1938. Serge Koussevitzky and the Boston unit introduced the Suite to New York on Mar. 31 following.

After a trial performance of the ballet in Moscow, V. V. Konin reported to the *Musical Courier* that Soviet critics present were "left in dismay at the awkward incongruity between the realistic idiom of the musical language, a language which successfully characterizes the individualism of the Shakespearean images, and the blind submission to the worst traditions of the old form, as revealed in the libretto."

Fault was also found because "the social atmosphere of the period and the natural evolution of its tragic elements had been robbed of their logical culmination and brought to the ridiculously dissonant 'happy end' of the conventional ballet. This inconsistency in the development of the libretto has had an unfortunate effect, not only upon the general structure, but even upon the otherwise excellent musical score."

Critical reaction to both Suites has varied, some reviewers finding the music dry and insipid for such a romantic theme, others' hailing its pungency and color. Prokofieff's classicism was compared with his romanticism. If we are prepared to accept the *Classical Symphony* as truly classical, said one critic, then we must accept the *Romeo and Juliet* music as truly romantic. The cold, cheerless, dreary music "is certainly not love music," ran the verdict. Prokofieff was taken to task for describing a love story "as if it were an algebraic problem."

Said Olin Downes of *The New York Times* in his review of the Boston Symphony concert of Mar. 31, 1938: "The music is predominantly satirical. . . . There is the partial suggestion of that which is poignant and tragic, but there is little of the sensuous or emotional, and in the main the music could bear almost any title and still serve the ballet evolutions and have nothing to do with Romeo and Juliet."

Others extolled Prokofieff for the "fundamental simplicity and buoyancy" of the music, finding it typically rooted in the "plane, tangible realities of tone design, and color." Prokofieff himself answered the repeated charge that his score lacked feeling and melody:

Every now and then somebody or other starts urging me to put more feeling, more emotion, more melody in my music. My own conviction is that there is plenty of all that in it. I have never shunned the expression of feeling and have always been intent on creating melody—but new melody, which perhaps certain listeners do not recognize as such simply because it does not resemble closely enough the kind of melody to which they are accustomed.

In *Romeo and Juliet* I have taken special pains to achieve a simplicity which will I hope, reach the hearts of all listeners. If people find no melody and no emotion in this work, I shall be very sorry. But I feel sure that sooner or later they will.

Of the four excerpts listed here the first two "Montagues and Capulets" and "Friar Laurence" are from Suite No. 2. The other two "Masks" and "The Death of Tybalt" are taken from Suite No. 1.

I. "Montagues and Capulets" (Allegro pesante). Intended to portray satirically the proud, haughty characters of the noblemen. There is a trio in which Juliet and Paris are pictured as dancing.

II. "Friar Laurence" (Andante espressivo). Two themes are used to depict the Friar. Bassoons, tuba, and harps announce the first; cellos, the second.

III. "Masks" (Andante marciale). The music accompanies the action at the Capulet ball and features the unobserved entrance into the palace of Romeo and two friends, wearing masks.

IV. "The Death of Tybalt" (Precipitato). Both street duels are depicted in this section, the first in which Tybalt slays Mercutio; the other in which Romeo in revenge, slays Tybalt. Capulet's denunciation follows.

L. B.

"Lieutenant Kije," Orchestral Suite, Op. 60

THE BELGOSKING film studios of Leningrad produced a motion picture "Lieutenant Kije," in 1933, which boasted incidental music by Serge Prokofieff From that music the composer contrived a Suite, which was completed and published the following year. The score calls for two flutes, piccolo, two oboes two clarinets, two bassoons, tenor saxophone, cornet, two trumpets, four horns three trombones, tuba, tympani, bass drum, military drum, triangle, cymbals, tambourine, sleigh bells, harp, celesta, piano, and strings.

An amusing anecdote about the Czar Nicholas I forms the subject of the film. In misreading the report of a military aide the Czar inadvertently coined a new name for a Russian officer by combining the last syllable *ki* of the name involved with the Russian intensive expletive *je*. Thus did *Kije* come about

Naturally, the courtiers were loath to inform their ruler of his mistake, so much so that they went to the expedient of inventing a Lieutenant Kije. Out of this idea in the film arise numerous comical situations and adventures.

The five sections comprising the Suites and their explanation follow:

I. "The Birth of Kije" (Allegro). An off-stage cornet fanfare, the tattoo of a military drum and some high fife passages announce the birth of the officer in the Czar's brain. Other instruments join the parade. There is a brief andante with a consequent return to the original tempo, fanfare, tattoo, fife music, and all.

II. "Romance" (Andante). A song, intended for baritone solo, is incorporated in this section, though its music, according to alternative versions, is given to the tenor saxophone and, sometimes, other instruments. In translation the song goes:

Heart, be calm, do not flutter;	My grey dove is full of sorrow—
Don't keep flying like a butterfly.	Moaning is she day and night.
Well, what has my heart decided?	For her dear companion left her,
Where will we in summer rest?	Having vanished out of sight,
But my heart could answer nothing,	Sad and dull has gotten my grey dove.
Beating fast in my poor breast.	

III. "Kije's Wedding" (Allegro). The Lieutenant is a soldier, but, as the melodic quality of this section reveals, he is also a gallant and sentimental lover.

IV. "Troika" (Moderato). Another song appears, this time a Russian tavern song. Again the melody is given an instrumental alternative, and its accompaniment suggests the motion of a three-horse sleigh. The translated words are:

A Woman's heart is like an inn:	Be you bachelor or not,
All those who wish go in,	Be you shy or be you bold,
And they who roam about	I call you all to come here.
Day and night go in and out.	So all those who are about,
Come here, I say; come here, I say.	Keep going in and coming out,
And have no fear with me.	Night and day they roam about.

V. "Burial of Kije" (Andante assai). The Lieutenant's career is briefly reviewed in this section. The off-stage fanfare, the love and the wedding themes come through anew. The Suite ends with the muted cornet's phrase fading into silence.

First performance of this Suite took place in Moscow in 1934. At a Lamoureux concert, Paris (Feb. 20, 1937), which was conducted by the composer, the piece "made a stunning impression," according to an English reviewer. Its American premiere occurred at a concert of the Boston Symphony Orchestra in Boston, on Oct. 15, 1937.

R. C. B.

"Peter and the Wolf," Orchestral Fairy Tale for Children, Op. 67

COMPLETED IN Moscow on Apr. 24, 1936, *Peter and the Wolf* was given its first performance at a children's concert of the Moscow Philharmonic on May 2 of that year. America was introduced to the work at a concert of the Boston Symphony Orchestra, Boston, Mar. 25, 1938, when it was given the first performance it had had outside Russia.

The score carries the following explanation:

Each character of this Tale is represented by a corresponding instrument in the orchestra: the bird by a flute, the duck by an oboe, the cat by a clarinet in a low register, the grandfather by a bassoon, the wolf by three horns, Peter by the string quartet, the shooting of the hunters by the kettledrums and the bass drum. Before an orchestral performance it is desirable to show these instruments to the children and to play on them the corresponding *leitmotives*. Thereby the children learn to distinguish the sonorities of the instruments during the performance of this Tale.

Henry Purcell

BORN: LONDON(?), BETWEEN JUNE AND NOVEMBER 20, 1659. DIED: LONDON, NOV. 21, 1695.

What no one will fail to find in Purcell at his best is a spring of life, a vitality that glows with the effort of the whole man. To listen is to share an experience, to catch some of his glancing fire and to have a part in his aching regret. He was a man of changing moods and sympathies, ready to boast, to worship, to sigh, and to lament. He could bid the trumpets sound for majesty, or seeking flight from love's sickness find the fever in himself.—J. A. WESTRUP.

"Prelude and Death of Dido" from "Dido and Aeneas"
[*Arranged by Dimitri Mitropoulos*]

REGARDED AS a chamber opera for amateurs, Purcell's tragic little drama about the Queen of Carthage and her Trojan lover was written about 1689 for a "school for young ladies in Chelsea" run by Josias Priest, a dancing teacher and occasional *maître de ballet* of the London theaters. The text was that of Nahum Tate, the poet laureate, who drew it largely from his earlier play *Brutus of Alba*. The story derives, of course, from the fourth book of Virgil's *Aeneid*. Having fled devastated Troy, Aeneas, on his way to Latium, is forced ashore at Carthage, where he and his men are fêted by its widowed queen. Dido promptly falls in love with Aeneas and he with her. But the gods have destined Aeneas to found a new nation in Italy and order his departure from Carthage. Sorrowfully he sails away and Dido, after voicing her own threnody, commits suicide. In Purcell's opera the final recitative would seem to indicate death from a broken heart, rather than suicide, a compromise evidently dictated by the tender feelings of audience and performers alike at the girls' school in Chelsea.

Though prevailingly a work of marked individual genius, many influences went into Purcell's score, among them the Italian cantata style, the tradition of the English masque, Lully's technic of dance music. Then, too, Lully's pattern of the miniature overture, "a slow introduction followed by a quasi-fugal allegro," was also followed by Purcell in devising his own little prelude to the opera, as pointed out by J. A. Westrup. In the deeply moving "Lament" (Death of Dido), where expressive sublimity is achieved through the simplest means, the first four lines are used as a recitative, the last three, beginning with the words, "When I am laid in earth," being the area, one of Purcell's supreme lyric flights, in which "technique and passion are miraculously fused in one."

With an eye on the Prelude and Love Death from Wagner's *Tristan und Isolde,* Mr. Mitropoulos decided to affix a somewhat similar title and sequence to the two selections from *Dido and Aeneas* arranged by him for large orchestra.

                                                                                                            L. B.

Sergei Rachmaninoff

BORN: NOVGOROD, APR. 1, 1873. DIED: BEVERLY HILLS, CALIF., MAR. 28, 1943.

*Rachmaninoff will take his place in history as a great and original
personality, not only as a pianist of genius, in which capacity he has
already become a part of history, but also as a prominent composer
with flashes of true genius. . . . He stands side by side with
Tschaikowsky, not only as disciple and follower, but also in musical
personality. Rachmaninoff is the extreme expression of turbulent Russian Bohemianism, a passive and heroic soul.*—LEONID SABANEYEFF.

Symphony in E minor, No. 2, Op. 27

I. Largo; Allegro moderato. II. Allegro molto. III. Adagio. IV. Allegro
vivace.

A PROLIFIC COMPOSER in many forms, Rachmaninoff wrote only three symphonies. (*The Bells,* based on Poe's poem, is a "choral symphony.") Of the three
only two remained in circulation after their world premieres. The first, composed in 1895, had one luckless hearing in St. Petersburg and remained forever
silent. The second, composed in 1906-1907, was first heard in Moscow in
February, 1909. Almost thirty years elapsed before Rachmaninoff completed the
Third Symphony during the summer of 1936 in a Swiss chalet overlooking
Lake Lucerne. Its world premiere occurred at a concert of the Philadelphia
Orchestra on Nov. 6, 1936.

The black sheep of Rachmaninoff's symphonies—the First—precipitated a
sharp mental crisis in the gloomy young composer. Critics and friends excori-
ated it freely. The composer, morbidly self-critical, seemed only too eager to
join in the dismal chorus of reproof. "I found the orchestration abominable,
and I knew that the music did not amount to much, either," he admitted.
"There are serious illnesses and deadly blows from fate which entirely change
a man's character. This was the effect of my own symphony upon myself."

Turning to the twenty-two-year-old composer, Rimsky-Korsakoff remarked
blandly, "Forgive me, but I do not find this music at all agreeable." César Cui
was beside himself with rage. "If there was a Conservatory in Hell," fulminated
the spokesman of the big "Five" of Russia's national school, "Rachmaninoff
would gain the first prize for his symphony."

A period of acute despondency and inertia set in for Rachmaninoff. Convinced that the creative muse was not for him to woo, he very nearly called it

a day as composer. In bleaker moments there were even hints of darker plans. "When the indescribable torture of this performance had at last come to an end, I was a different man," he recounted later. A combination of Count Tolstoy, Dr. Dahl, and Natalie Satin seems to have rescued him from his tragic state. Count Tolstoy lectured the gifted youth for three days. Inferiority complexes, he pointed out, assailed even the gods. "Young man," he asked, "do you suppose I have no troubles, never hesitate, never lose confidence in myself?" Dr. Dahl prescribed exercises in self-assertion, which were scrupulously carried out. Mlle. Satin became Mrs. Rachmaninoff. The First Symphony was permanently retired from public life.

Thereafter, composition quickened in pace and vitality. By 1906, Rachmaninoff, his work obstructed by widening social and professional commitments, felt compelled to take a long sabbatical in a foreign land. Accompanied by his wife and baby daughter he left Moscow for Dresden. For three years the family occupied a smart little house with a garden. There, in virtual seclusion, Rachmaninoff composed two of his best symphonic works—the tone poem *The Isle of the Dead* and the Second Symphony. Several songs, a piano sonata and an unfinished opera *Mona Vanna* were also composed in the Dresden retreat. While he was there, America beckoned with a lucrative offer. Twenty concerts during the winter of 1909 in the double role of pianist and conductor! Rachmaninoff was excited. Yet he hesitated. The prospect was tempting, but the tour would mean a long separation from wife and child. Since his marriage he had not left his wife's side for more than a few days. At length he accepted "though with a heavy heart."

Before leaving for his American trip, Rachmaninoff directed the world premiere of his E minor Symphony with the Russian Musical Society, Moscow on Feb. 15, 1909. Its success was immediate and emphatic. Moreover, two months earlier the score had brought the composer the Glinka Prize of 1,000 rubles. This award was established through a bequest made by Mitrosar Petrovitch Belaieff (1836-1904), the noted patron of the arts. Belaieff had sponsored the work of the famous "Five" and in 1885 founded a publishing house in Leipzig for Russian music. Rachmaninoff's Second Piano Concerto earlier won him a Glinka Prize of 500 rubles.

Like the Third Symphony that was to come almost three decades later, the Second was introduced to America by the Philadelphia Orchestra. The date was Nov. 26, 1909. Rachmaninoff conducted the concert, besides playing three of his piano preludes, including the famous one in C sharp minor. Three weeks earlier, on Nov. 4, the distinguished visitor had made his American debut, as pianist, with a recital at Smith College, Northampton. Critics and public alike had welcomed the chance to appraise him at his full worth. An inadequate and misleading reputation had preceded Rachmaninoff based largely on the C sharp minor Prelude. This captivating piece was already widely known here. Piano teachers solemnly spoke of it as a "necessary number in the repertory of every young lady amateur." The tour corrected many false impressions of Rachmaninoff as a pianist who also happened to write music. If the visit made Americans aware of an astonishing keyboard personality, it also acquainted them with a symphonist of striking power.

One critic wrote:

If Tschaikowsky voices the passionate, the somber, the tragic, the swift ecstasy of beauty, and if Rimsky-Korsakoff reflects the sunny, the legendary, and the fanciful, Rachmaninoff prefigures the brooding, the somber reflective state of soul. He endures the sight of the dark aspects of Russian life, of all life, but rather as the seer than as the rebel. There is almost a Tolstoyan resistance to evil in his attitude. The world that he looks out upon is a somber world of dim distances, of golden lights and shadows, of fateful and steady motion. His attitude toward it is impersonal and dispassionate. His creed is moderation.

At a time when "ultra-modernity" was being freely lampooned, Rachmaninoff's frank conservatism and traditionalism were hailed as salutary correctives. A few, however, flailed this music as artistic reaction. The shrewdest agreed that Rachmaninoff was steering a strictly personal course between the extreme left and the extreme right. Avowedly he had no patience with "experimental" music. Expressive appeal through melodic warmth was his avowed goal. In the world of music, he felt, there was one supreme ruler—Melody. Melody, bearing the imprint of a warm temperament, implied, gave rise to, and developed the harmonic treatment natural and best suited to it. Embedded in the melodic and harmonic fabric was the composer's whole personality. This was and remained Rachmaninoff's creed. "I compose music because I must give expression to my feelings," he said, "just as I talk because I must give utterance to my thoughts."

In a personal statement to David Ewen, Rachmaninoff declared that a composer's music should express the country of his birth, his romantic life, his religion, the books that have influenced him, the pictures he loves. "It should be the product of the sum total of a composer's experiences," he declared. During an interview in the early twenties Rachmaninoff revealed that "a poem, a picture, something concrete," usually touched off the creative processes of his imagination. Such avowals of method have prompted attempts to read "programs" into Rachmaninoff's music. In some cases, of course, the title alone suffices as an index to narrative or pictorial content. In others a "program" was given, presumably with Rachmaninoff's authority. The First Symphony admittedly followed a program. Hence, Riesemann cannot be blamed for venturing one for the Second. Rachmaninoff himself remained noncommittal. Riesemann suspected that Tschaikowsky's Fourth Symphony and Liszt's B minor Sonata had served Rachmaninoff as models for the Second Symphony, *i.e.,* programatically. Tschaikowsky's theme, of course, is Fate, just as it was in Beethoven's C minor. Says Riesemann:

Rachmaninoff replaces the fanfare of Fate in Tschaikowsky's symphony by threatening, heavily oppressive chords pregnant with a premonition of death, trumpets and violins swelling to a desperate groan that collapses and dies away. The words *Memento mori* (remember death) would make a suitable motto for the symphony. Whenever the work succeeds for a moment in reaching a carefree, exuberant mood, the dull inflexible chorus cuts in with its gloomy warning of death even in the most ecstatic moments of the lover's surrender. This is most effective at the conclusion of the scherzo, which is almost unique in the musical literature of the last decade. In grandeur of design it can hardly find an equal, the possible exception being the Scherzo of Bruckner's Ninth Symphony.

I. An introductory Largo section (E minor, 4/4) offers material to be expounded in the first movement proper, besides themes that will return later in the Symphony. Chief of these is a subject first broached by the violins over sustained chords in the wood winds. The main body of the movement (Allegro moderato, E minor, 2/2), really begins when the violins chant a theme, molto espressivo, first hinted at by cellos and double basses in the extended Largo prelude. Wood winds and strings later share the second theme between them, in G major (moderato). The solo violin opens the development section with the first theme in augmentation. The remaining strings soon join the wood winds in the working out process. The first violins bring back the chief theme in the review, while the second theme returns, somewhat modified, in E major. A brilliant coda ends the movement.

II. (Allegro molto, A minor, 2/2). First sung by the horns, the opening theme of this scherzo movement is picked up midway by the violins. This material supplies the basis for the whole first section of the movement. A bright new melody appears in the violins in C major (Moderato), and the opening section returns, soon fading away (diminuendo). After a vigorous chord, the trio (meno mosso) sets in by way of the second violins, echoed presently by the first violins. A striking passage for brasses, strengthened by cymbals and tambourine, follows. The earlier scherzo section is freely recalled, and as the movement ends an allusion is heard to the Largo opening of the symphony. Some of Rachmaninoff's best fugal writing appears in this movement, which Philip H. Goepp called "a complete change from introspection and passion to an abandon as of primitive dance."

III. First violins give out the main theme of the majestic third movement (Adagio, A major, 4/4). The clarinet joins in with a second theme, followed by oboes and violins, which share a third subject. In the middle of the movement the first theme of the Adagio combines with the central idea of the Symphony first heard in the violins in the first movement Largo. After the previous material is reviewed, a reminiscence of the Largo theme is again heard.

IV. A brief fortissimo passage for full orchestra opens the restless, energetic finale (Allegro vivace, E major, 2/2). The orchestra builds its main theme into a brisk development, after an announcement among the strings and winds. A diminuendo follows, and the wood winds introduce a subject in march rhythms. The main theme returns, followed now by a lyric theme in D major, sung in octaves by the strings. Discoursed at some length, the new theme leads to a brief Adagio. There the orchestra recalls material from the first and third movements and seems to take a full breath before starting on an elaborate journey of development and recapitulation toward the resounding coda. A marked cyclic unity is given the symphony by the brisk interweaving of themes of the opening Largo and closing Allegro.

Dedicated to Rachmaninoff's teacher, Sergei Taneieff, who in 1878 followed Tschaikowsky as teacher of composition at the Moscow Conservatory, the Symphony is scored for three flutes (one interchangeable with piccolo), three oboes, English horn, two clarinets, bass clarinet, two bassoons, four horns, three trumpets, three trombones, bass tuba, tympani, snare drum, bass drum, cymbals, tambourine, glockenspiel, and strings.

For all its Slavic color and frequent resemblances to other Russian composers, Rachmaninoff's music stands in a class by itself. He has followed the dictates of his own individuality, and although he early tended toward the so-called "Westerners" or "Eclectics" of Russian music, *i.e.*, those consciously influenced by non-Russian currents, Rachmaninoff cannot be given a "school" label.

In its first stage the division between the "Nationalists" and "Eclectics," or "Orientalists" and "Occidentalists," resulted in bitter verbal clashes. On one side were the "Five" (Moussorgsky, Balakireff, Rimsky-Korsakoff, Borodin, and Cui), also styled "The Invincible Band," whose art was rooted in folk song and legend, in brief, in the "unspoiled genius of the Russian people." Their slogan was "Freedom, the Picturesque, Nationalism."

In the other camp were grouped men like Tschaikowsky, Taneieff, the Rubinsteins, Liadoff, Glazounoff, and Arensky, who frankly sought and accepted European technic and discipline. The sharp lines of demarcation gradually faded, and heated factionalism lapsed into friendly interchange. Rachmaninoff has been regarded as something of a link between both schools. Because of his technical equipment and grasp of French and German symphonic methods and procedures he belongs, in a sense, with the "Eclectics"; while "his thematic material, the whole color and feeling of his music is unmistakably Russian," as one writer puts it.

The name most often associated with Rachmaninoff is Tschaikowsky. Taneieff, his teacher at the Moscow Conservatory, had been Tschaikowsky's pupil, and many have tried to trace a direct line of symphonic descent in their works. As a young man Rachmaninoff met Tschaikowsky and was deeply stirred by the older man's sympathy and interest in his work. In fact, Rachmaninoff has regarded the meeting as a crucial turn in his career. He writes:

To him I owe the first and possibly the deciding success in my life. It was my teacher Zvierew who took me to him. Tschaikowsky at that time was already world famous and honored by everybody, but he remained unspoiled. He was one of the most charming artists and men I ever met. He had an unequaled delicacy of mind. He was modest, as all really great people are, and simple, as very few are.

Tschaikowsky was about fifty-five at that time, that is to say, more than twice my age, but he talked to me, a young beginner, as if I were his equal. He listened to my first opera *Aleko* and arranged for it to be performed at the Imperial Theater. . . . Tschaikowsky did even more. Timidly and modestly, as if he were afraid I might refuse, he asked me if I would consent to have my work produced with one of his operas. To be on a poster with Tschaikowsky was about the greatest honor that could be paid to a composer, and I would not have dared to suggest such a thing. Tschaikowsy knew this. He wanted to help me, but was anxious also not to offend or humiliate me.

I soon felt the result of Tschaikowsky's kindness. I began to be known, and some years later I became leader of the Imperial Opera orchestra. Having once reached this important position, the rest came easy.

Rachmaninoff remained active in all three capacities, as conductor, pianist, and composer, though his appearances on the podium were too few to give him the widely recognized status that his music and piano playing have brought him. As a rule, such appearances in his last years were restricted to concerts of his own music. He has often filled a triple role on one program. To Frederick H. Martens he once explained how, in his manifold pursuits, he tried to restrict himself to one field at the time:

When I am concertizing I cannot compose. When I feel like writing music I have to concentrate on that—I cannot touch the piano. When I am conducting I can neither compose nor play concerts. Other musicians may be more fortunate in this respect; but I have to concentrate on any one thing I am doing to such a degree that it does not seem to allow me to take up anything else.

When composing I am a slave. Beginning at nine in the morning I allow myself no respite until after eleven at night. A poem, a picture, something concrete, helps me immensely.

L. B.

Symphony in A minor, No. 3, Op. 44

I. Allegro moderato. II. Adagio ma non troppo. III. Allegro

ALMOST THIRTY years intervene between the composition of Rachmaninoff's Second and Third Symphonies, the former dating from 1906-1907, the latter from 1935-1936. The earlier Symphony was one of many important works written by Rachmaninoff in Dresden during a three-year retreat from Moscow. Social and professional routine had interfered with his composing in the Russian capital and he found virtual seclusion in a suburban house with his wife and baby daughter. The tone poem *The Isle of the Dead,* a piano sonata, several songs, and an unfinished opera *Mona Vanna* were further products of the Dresden period. Moreover, it was while sojourning in the German city that America beckoned with an offer to do twenty concerts during the winter of 1909. The Second Symphony, though first heard in Moscow, shortly before he sailed, accompanied him for an American premiere in Philadelphia on Nov. 26, with himself conducting the Philadelphia Orchestra.

The Third Symphony runs parallel with the Second in one or two surrounding circumstances. It was begun in the spring of 1935 during a similarly placid and retired period in the composer's life and completed during the summer of 1936 in a Swiss chalet overlooking Lake Lucerne. Then, the Philadelphia Orchestra was again involved in its American premiere—this time its world premiere as well—and the concert again occurred in November (the 6th, 1936). Both symphonies were warmly received. The second speedily became a repertory staple, and the third is by way of following suite. Critics have commended the later work for its "sincerity and personal accent," its "technic and skill in orchestration," and "its impassioned stress."

Lawrence Gilman has emphasized the score's profusion of those sweeping cantabile phrases, darkened by moods of melancholy brooding. . . . "Sombre, lyrical, defiant, it is a work wholly representative of the Slavic genius and of Mr. Rachmaninoff in particular, by reason of certain unmistakable turns of phrase and orchestral rhythm and diction."

Instead of the usual four movements, the Third Symphony is divided into three. However, the middle section of the second movement, which is rather unorthodox in form, might be considered a subdivision. The main body of the opening movement, Allegro moderato, is prefaced by a slow passage, four bars in length, marked Lento. An Allegro vivace of some length nestles in the long slow movement, Adagio ma non troppo. This intermediary section ends with the return of the Adagio mood and structure. There is brilliant fugal writing in the finale, based on the major theme.

L. B.

Concerto for Piano and Orchestra in F sharp minor, No. 1, Op. 1

I. Vivace. II. Andante. III. Finale: Allegro vivace.

THE LEAST played of Rachmaninoff's piano concertos, the F sharp minor dates from the composer's student days in Moscow. Rachmaninoff was only eighteen when he wrote it. Safonoff, then director of the Moscow Conservatory, where Rachmaninoff was awarded the highest honors as pianist in 1891, conducted its premiere that year. The response was far from encouraging. Rachmaninoff himself at first thought so little of the Concerto he decided not to take it with him when the London Philharmonic invited him over for a series of appearances. However, before leaving Russia in 1917, he subjected the score to drastic revision. Though no fresh material was employed, structure and instrumentation were thoroughly modified. By then Rachmaninoff had composed his phenomenally successful Second Concerto. What mature technic and style were now his, reflected back on the earlier work.

Rachmaninoff was soloist in the First Concerto when the new version was introduced to New York by the Russian Symphony Orchestra on Jan. 28, 1919. On Dec. 26 of that year the New Symphony Orchestra—later to become the National Symphony Orchestra—played the work in Carnegie Hall with the composer as soloist and Artur Bodanzky as conductor. Rachmaninoff was again the soloist when the Philharmonic-Symphony brought the Concerto into its repertory at the concerts of Dec. 29 and 30, 1938. The work is dedicated to Alexander Siloti, with whom he had studied piano at the Moscow Conservatory. Lawrence Gilman analyzed the Concerto as follows for the Philharmonic-Symphony performances of 1938:

The Concerto begins (Vivace, 4/4) with the material of the first theme: a reiterated F sharp, fortissimo, for clarinets, bassoons and horns and an impetuous descending passage in octaves for the piano. A brief cadenza for the solo instrument introduces a contrasting subject, a songlike theme for the first and second violins in unison (Moderato, espressivo). The principal cadenza occurs toward the end of the movement.

In the Andante (D major, 4/4) a phrase for the horn, answered by strings, wood winds, and trombones, and a short cadenza for the piano, introduce a meditative song for the solo instrument. This is unaccompanied until the eighteenth measure, when a solo bassoon, with an air of somewhat bashful uneasiness, intrudes upon the piano's cloistral contemplation; but it withdraws after four measures, with its finger on its lips, and the piano is again momentarily alone in its romantic solitude. The strings are bolder, but even they dare enter only on tiptoe, *ppp*. Later, a solo horn and wood winds add their voices, and the orchestra regains its rights.

The Finale (beginning Allegro vivace, 9/8) is capricious in mood, restless and complex in its rhythmical transformations. A contrasting middle section (Andante ma non troppo, 3/4) proffers a sentimental interlude, wherein the strings, adorned by the piano, soon give place to the solo instrument, which, left to itself, becomes for a time the mouthpiece of the poet's lyric fervor. The resumption of the first tempo leads to a tumultuous close, in F sharp major.

L. B.

Concerto for Piano and Orchestra in C minor, No. 2, Op. 18

I. Moderato. II. Adagio sostenuto. III. Allegro scherzando.

In 1900-1901, ten years after the fiasco of his First Concerto, Rachmaninoff completed the present work, which has done much to spread his fame as both composer and pianist. The introductory performance of the Second Piano Concerto was given by the Philharmonic Society of Moscow on Oct. 14, 1901, Rachmaninoff appearing as soloist.

In his memoirs he discloses the curious circumstances surrounding the composition of this Concerto. He had become the victim, so to speak, of an all-possessing apathy. His friends and relations became alarmed. They proposed a hundred possible methods of attacking it. Several of those attempted proved of meager therapeutic value, but a series of sessions with one of the pioneers in the field of autosuggestion, Dr. N. Dahl, brought about the desired end, so the composer himself admits. In fact, the Concerto is dedicated to Dr. Dahl, who had been importuned to cure him of the apathy and to bring him again into a creative frame of mind. The good doctor, quite seriously, inquired what type of composition they desired of Rachmaninoff and, just as seriously, they suggested a piano concerto.

The moods and manners of the healer's approach might be introduced at this point, since such a glistening success was obtained. The composer would lie half asleep in a chair in Dr. Dahl's sanctum, while the mesmeric and curative formula, "You will begin to write your Concerto. . . . You will work with great facility. . . . The Concerto will be of excellent quality . . ." was repeated endlessly. Rachmaninoff says of this, "Although it may sound incredible, this cure really helped me. Already at the beginning of the summer I began again to compose. The material grew in bulk, and new musical ideas began to stir within me—far more than I needed for my Concerto."

Two movements were completed by autumn, the Adagio and the finale, besides a sketch for a two-piano Suite (Op. 17). The first movement of the Concerto was finished later, which is the reason for the Op. 18 numbering. Rachmaninoff played the second and third sections at a benefit concert under the direction of Siloti, and they were received with tremendous enthusiasm, which was just the incentive required for the completion of the whole work.

Rachmaninoff, reviewing trials and tribulations of his youth, has said, "Although I had to fight for recognition, as most young men have to, although I have experienced all the troubles and sorrow which precede success, and although I know how important it is for an artist to be spared such troubles,

I realize, when I look back on my early life, that it was enjoyable, in spite of all its vexations and bitterness."

The concerto falls into the customary three movements:

I. The first (Moderato, C minor, 2/2) begins with a series of chords for the piano. The chief subject is presently announced by the strings against an arpeggio figure in the solo instrument. After a brief orchestral interlude the piano gives out the second subject in E flat major.

II. The slow movement (Adagio sostenuto, E major, 4/4) is introduced by sustained harmonies in the muted strings, to which wind instruments soon are added. Over a figure for the piano a flute and then a clarinet intone the melody from which the movement is constructed. New thematic material is heard in the coda.

III. In the finale (Allegro scherzando, C minor, 4/4) prefatory measures are followed by the first theme, allotted to the piano. Oboe and cellos have the second theme, the piano taking it up later. The first theme is developed further in a section marked "Allegro scherzando, moto primo." In a fugato the first violins are answered by the piano and the lower strings. After elaborate working out the concerto ends with a brilliant coda.

The instruments employed in the orchestral part are two flutes, two oboes, two clarinets, two bassoons, four horns, two trumpets, three trombones, bass tuba, a set of three kettledrums, bass drum, cymbals, and the usual strings.

R. C. B.

Concerto for Piano and Orchestra in D minor, No. 3, Op. 30

I. Allegro ma non tanto. II. Intermezzo. III. Finale.

RACHMANINOFF WROTE his Third Piano Concerto for his American tour of 1909. On his journey over he used a practice keyboard to prepare himself for the fall premiere of the new work with the New York Symphony Society. In his memoirs, Rachmaninoff declares that he never employed a "dumb piano" again. With the composer as soloist, the performance took place on Nov. 28. Walter Damrosch conducted. Gustav Mahler directed the second performance. Of Mahler's behavior at rehearsal Rachmaninoff later wrote:

At that time Mahler was the only conductor whom I considered worthy to be classed with Nikisch. He touched my composer's heart straight away by devoting himself to my Concerto until the accompaniment, which is rather complicated, had been practiced to the point of perfection, although he had already gone through another long rehearsal. According to Mahler, every detail of the score was important —an attitude which is unfortunately rare among conductors.

Otto Kinkleday, who wrote the notes for the New York performances, described the new Concerto as "Russian throughout, Russian in its melodic conception, in its rhythms, and in the robust, virile qualities even of its gentler passages." Kinkleday also strongly stressed "the composer's place in the lineage of Tschaikowsky."

Typically Slavic in mood, the first theme of the opening movement (Allegro ma non tanto) is stated simply by the piano against a rhythmic accompaniment of muted strings and pizzicato basses. It is then taken up by the horns and violas. The atmosphere here is soft and mysterious. The second theme is briefly foreshadowed by horns and trumpets. Brief but striking, it is then given out by soft strings, staccato. The piano answers, and out of the second theme is fashioned a gorgeous episode. This theme is used to give a cyclic semblance to the concerto, for it recurs in the second and last movements.

The Intermezzo movement opens with a theme again markedly Russian in flavor. "Tender and melancholy, yet not tearful," was Otto Kinkleday's description of it. A contrasting passage in 3/8 time follows, against pizzicato support from the strings. The opening theme of the Concerto, now altered, returns for a dreamy reminiscence among the wood winds. There is no break between the last two movements. Throbbing, forward motion fills the Finale (alla breve), with the first theme imparting a challenging note. One or two passages grow out of echoes of the first movement. There is a momentary interruption in the pulsing drive of rhythm as a Lento intervenes, and the race is on again.

The Concerto is dedicated to Josef Hofmann.

L. B.

Rhapsody on a Theme of Paganini for Piano and Orchestra, Op. 43

THE THEME on which this Rhapsody is based is taken from the last of the Paganini Caprices for solo violin. Not only did Paganini himself do a set of variations on this theme, but Brahms did, too. The Rhapsody was composed between July 3 and Aug. 24, 1934, while Rachmaninoff was living on Lake Lucerne in Switzerland. It was given its first performance by the Philadelphia Orchestra under the direction of Leopold Stokowski in Baltimore, on Nov. 7, 1934. The composer was the soloist.

The full theme of the piece is not fully announced until the first variation, *Precedente,* when it is played by the violins and later taken up by the piano. Prior to that it appears sketchily in a nine-measure prelude. Most of the variations are brief. An unusual feature of the composition is the introduction of the liturgical melody *Dies Irae* in the seventh, tenth, and final variations. It appears in the piano in No. 7, while the thematic measures are played against it in the bass. The *Dies Irae,* a part of the Catholic Mass for the Dead, describes forcefully the happenings to come on the Day of Judgment. Its opening line has been employed frequently by composers of the nineteenth century for a variety of reasons, dramatic, symbolic, or purely humorous. It may be found in works of Berlioz, Liszt, Saint-Saëns, and Tschaikowsky.

In the Rachmaninoff Rhapsody it is heard in the tenth variation again by way of the piano. In the twenty-fourth the whole orchestra thunders it out in a brilliant climax. Many of the composer's works are said to contain some esoteric meaning, which he is loath to reveal. It has been suggested that the inclusion of the *Dies Irae* in this composition is a case in point.

Besides the piano, the score calls for piccolo, two flutes, two oboes, English horn, two clarinets, two bassoons, four horns, two trumpets, three trombones, tuba, kettledrums, tambourine, triangle, cymbals, drum, bells, harp, and strings.

R. C. B.

"Symphonic Dances for Orchestra," Op. 45

I. Non allegro. II. Andante con moto, tempo di valse. III. Lento assai; Allegro vivace.

INTENDED AS a set of idealized dance motives in free symphonic treatment, this work was written in 1940 while the composer was vacationing from a crowded concert schedule at his home in Huntington, Long Island. The *Symphonic Dances* were begun early that summer and completed late in October. They were premiered in Philadelphia on Jan. 4, 1941, by the Philadelphia Orchestra, Eugene Ormandy conducting. The score is dedicated to both orchestra and conductor.

For a time Mr. Rachmaninoff considered giving the three movements the titles of "Midday," "Twilight," and "Midnight," later abandoning the idea as likely to give misleading impressions of content and mood. Even as "dances" only the second in the set bears any clear designation as such in the phrase "tempo di valse." What dance content there is moves on a boldly executed plane of romantic idealization. As a rule, conventional dance patterns are only sporadically suggested. To emphasize the "symphonic" rather than the "dance" in the titles, Mr. Rachmaninoff decided on largely musical indications for the set: I. Non allegro; II. Andante con moto—tempo di valse; III. Lento assai; Allegro vivace. He has offered no hint, other than that afforded by the discarded and adopted titles, as to any possible "program." Mr. Rachmaninoff's *Paganini Rhapsody for Piano and Orchestra* has proved so effective as a ballet score that it was first thought the *Symphonic Dances* were similarly destined for choreographic use. The composer disavowed any such intention.

In reviewing the New York premiere of the *Dances* by the Philadelphia Orchestra in Carnegie Hall on Jan. 7, Olin Downes rightly noted that they bore the "unmistakable stamp of Rachmaninoff's creative personality." The idiom and moods he found so strictly Rachmaninoff's that "none other could have written the music." Without attempting to ferret out a program, he felt that the *Symphonic Dances* "could easily reflect a series of moods, presented in a certain loose sequence—of Nature, and memories, and reveries, with some Dead Sea fruit in them—all unpretentious, melodic, sensuously colored, and admirably composed music." In the third Dance the plain chant *Dies Irae,* which recurringly haunts Rachmaninoff's music, makes a grisly appearance amid a brilliant fantasy in strong rhythms.

L. B.

"Die Toteninsel" ("The Isle of the Dead"), Symphonic Poem for Full Orchestra, after a Painting by A. Böcklin, Op. 29

RACHMANINOFF HIMSELF conducted the first performance of his Symphonic Poem in 1909 at a concert of the Moscow Philharmonic. Its American premiere occurred at a concert of the Theodore Thomas Orchestra in Chicago on Dec. 3, 1909.

Böcklin's famous picture was painted in 1880, though it was not till the summer of 1909 that Rachmaninoff saw it in Paris and resolved on the spot to suggest its macabre moods and implications in music. Of the painting itself, Böcklin had earlier written to a friend that "it must produce such an effect of stillness that any one would be frightened to hear a knock on the door." Several other composers, among them Anders Hallen and Prince Joachim Albrecht of Prussia, have also attempted to translate the Swiss master's picture into music.

Böcklin's *Toteninsel* was not wholly a creation of his imagination. There is evidence that the sight of the brooding Ponza Islands, which lie north of the Gulf of Naples, impressed him deeply, one in particular—the remaining half of what had once been a volcanic peak. Philip Hale has written of the island as follows:

The waves in the course of centuries shaped a little haven. Birds brought the seeds of cypress trees. The trees in time shot up in the ledges. At last man came and made paths and hollowed chambers and threw up a rough wall as a protection against the waves.

The island even then was as solemn as a pyramid. It was a hidden nook for the dead that wished to lie undisturbed. Böcklin expressed this rest of the dead in a place remote and forgotten by the world. The sea is still, there is no cry of bird, no fluttering, no voice.

The boat approaching the little harbor of the island with its towering blue-green cypresses and awful rocks is rowed noiselessly by the ferryman. The white and quiet figure near the coffin—is it some mourner or is it a priest?

Dedicated to Nicholas von Struve, Rachmaninoff's Symphonic Poem is scored for three flutes, piccolo, two oboes, English horn, two clarinets, bass clarinet, two bassoons, double bassoon, six horns, three trumpets, three trombones, tuba, kettledrums, bass drum, cymbals, harp, and strings.

Beginning slowly (Lento, A minor, 5/8), the music promptly evokes a somber mood through muted strings and low, plaintive phrases in the harp. Soon an undulating motive appears among the cellos, descriptive of the water murmuring lugubriously along the shores of the island. Both this figure and a theme first announced by horn recur throughout the work, giving the composition a kind of cyclic unity.

As the music gains momentum we hear flurries among the cellos, brasses and wood winds suggesting the *Die Irae,* which is almost a leitmotif of all Rachmaninoff's music. Later a string passage shows further traces of the old hymn. Presently the lapping theme of the cellos is back, as the sea again closes mournfully about the Island of the Dead.

L. B.

Maurice Ravel

BORN: CIBOURE, BASSES-PYRÉNÉES, MAR. 7, 1875. DIED: PARIS, DEC. 28, 1937.

Ravel's music has been compared to those formal French gardens in which the trees and shrubs are trimmed to precise shapes and the flowers laid out in well-ordered patterns. . . . Within the forms that he chose to cultivate, his inspiration seldom waned, his artistry never lost its consummate skill. Even those who hold that there is too much artifice in his art must admit that he conceals this artifice with infinite grace.—GILBERT CHASE.

"La Valse," A Choreographic Poem

A CRAFTSMAN AMONG craftsmen, a fastidious and tireless worker, a consummate scholar, Maurice Ravel found eloquent supporters early in his career. As the years went on, he also found—and, very likely, not to his surprise—as many detractors. The latter coterie frothed and fulminated, as coteries will, along the various sectors of the drawing-room front: Ravel was a dilute Debussy, they averred; he was an imitator, rather than an originator; he was clever (at least, they granted him that) but not profound. In the meantime his music made splendid headway.

Ravel confessed his debt to Debussy rather archly, one must say, "And if I have been influenced by Debussy, it has been deliberately, knowing that I could leave him whenever I chose. In any event, never have I completely accepted his principles, and I believe that this should be plain to all." However, he did pay supreme homage to Chabrier, as a source of Ravellian inspiration and style. Chabrier, he felt, was the origin from which all modern French music springs. Furthermore, he claimed Edgar Allan Poe as his mentor on musical technic, by way of the essay on the genesis of a poem.

Ravel recognized only one art, not several, in that music, painting, and literature differ from one another only as regards means of expression. Developing the thought further, he envisioned not various kinds of artists, only various kinds of specialists. One of his excelling talents was his understanding of styles, and he delighted in transferring into his own idiom the essence of another. This is amply demonstrated in many of his works, the *Sonatine,* for instance, and *Le Tombeau de Couperin,* reflecting the eighteenth-century moods and musical manners; the *Rapsodie espagnole,* the *Bolero, L'Heure espagnole, Alborada del Gracioso,* all pointing to his extraordinary interest in the idiom of Spain; and, last but not least, *La Valse,* which runs its mercurial course through the humors and graces of Viennese music.

La Valse, dedicated to the painter Misia Sert, was given its premiere at a Lamoureux Concert in Paris, on Dec. 12, 1920. That performance suggested to Raymond Schwab, "the atmosphere of a Court ball of the Second Empire, at first a frenzy indistinctly sketched by the pizzicati of double basses, then transports sounding forth the full hysteria of an epoch."

According to the celebrated composer and pianist Alfredo Casella, Ravel had some thought of a dance production in mind when he wrote *La Valse,* although no actual choreographic scheme had occurred to him. He further explains that the composition is in the form of a triptych, offering an opening movement, "The Birth of the Waltz," which "begins with dull rumors—as in *Rheingold* and from this chaos gradually takes form the development."

A second movement is simply dubbed "The Waltz," and the concluding one, "The Apotheosis of the Waltz."

The actual "argument," printed on the score, gives this information, "Whirling clouds give glimpses, through rifts, of couples waltzing. The clouds scatter little by little. One sees an immense hall peopled with a twirling crowd. The scene is gradually illuminated. The light of chandeliers bursts forth fortissimo. An Imperial Court, about 1885."

La Valse is scored for three flutes (one interchangeable with piccolo), two oboes, English horn, two clarinets, bass clarinet, two bassoons, double bassoon, four horns, three trumpets, three trombones, bass tuba, tympani, side drum, bass drum, tambourine, cymbals, castanets, tam-tam, triangle, crotales (as employed in this work the crotales may be described as small cymbals slightly thicker than the ones known as antique), two harps, and strings.

R. C. B.

"Rapsodie Espagnole"

I. Prélude à la nuit. II. "Malagueña." III. Habanera. IV. Fería.

LIKE DEBUSSY's *Iberia,* Ravel's symphonic tribute to Spain is a set of impressions evoked by Spanish themes and customs, rather than an album of picture postcards reproducing landmarks in detail. In the Bergsonian sense, Ravel and Debussy both expected their music to be grasped solely through feeling. Sympathy and intuition, rather than analysis, were sought, the same channels pursued by Henri Bergson in his quest for reality.

When the "Malagueña" was encored by Ravel devotees at the Parisian premiere of Mar. 15, 1908, a gallery enthusiast, troubled by the crass coolness of the parterre, shouted down to the conductor: "Play it again for the people below! They have not understood it!" They have not *felt* it, Ravel would have amended. "To understand it right," points out Mrs. Franz Liebich, an authority on French music, "the listener must be able to put himself into the same *emotional mood* as that which inspired the composer."

No doubt Ravel's *emotional mood* stemmed in part from his having been born near the Spanish border and from his having a mother of Basque origin. The music of Spain and that of the Orient, to which it owed much, always fascinated this facile cosmopolite coolly scrutinizing all musical mediums and cultivating them at leisure.

In the first of the *Rapsodie's* four movements—"Prélude à la nuit"—an atmosphere of warm languor and quiet is evoked through the use of an undulating figure first assigned to muted violins and violas and dominating the whole section. Clarinets and bassoons have a brilliant flurry at one place.

Though the famous folk dance song of Malaga is nominally in 3/8 time, Ravel's "Malagueña" is written in 3/4. The major theme, first given out by double basses, recurs for twenty-nine measures. Later the violins softly chant a theme in octaves; and after the whole orchestra asserts itself brilliantly, the English horn discourses a plaintive theme, supported by harp and viola figures. There is an echo of the undulating motive of the "Prélude." Then the double basses are back with the "Malagueña" theme.

"The Malagueña may be heard to perfection in the Chinitas, the little popular cafés where the people congregate to listen to these sad and almost sullen folk tunes," writes Mrs. Liebich. "They are extraordinarily impressive by reason of their uncommon rhythm and startling alterations of fierce emotion and profound melancholy."

In 2/4 time, the next section is an enlargement of a Habanera for two pianos written by the French composer in 1895. Ravel's rare delicacy and originality as orchestrator are evident throughout this movement, which grows largely out of a sheaf of thematic fragments. As a popular dance, the Habanera is often supposed to have reached Spain by a roundabout route taking in Africa and Cuba.

"The dancers stand opposite to each other and accompany their singing with indolent and alluring gestures," explains Mrs. Liebich. "The feet are scarcely lifted from the ground. The graceful movements of the dancers, the swaying of the arms and hips, the switch of the skirts and gliding of the feet are subtly evoked by Ravel's daintily picturesque music."

The "Feria" movement, intended to evoke the wildly joyous commotion of a Spanish fair, is marked *assez animé* (very lively), 6/8. Between the opening and closing sections, which are built on identical themes and patterns in resounding style, comes a slower section featuring a theme discoursed in turn by English horn and clarinet. An imposing fortissimo caps the finale.

The ample scoring calls for two piccolos, two flutes, two oboes, English horn, two clarinets, bass clarinet, three bassoons, one sarrusophone, four horns, three trumpets, three trombones, tuba, kettledrums, bass drum, cymbals, side drum, triangle, tambourine, gong, xylophone, celesta, and two harps.

L. B.

"Ma Mère l'oye" ("Mother Goose"), Five Children's Pieces

I. "Pavane of the Sleeping Beauty." II. "Tom Thumb." III. "Little Ugly One, Empress of the Pagodas." IV. "The Conversations of Beauty and the Beast." V. "The Fairy Garden."

Ravel originally wrote *Ma Mère l'oye* in 1908 as a set of piano pieces for four hands, intending them for the pleasure of Mimi and Jean, the gifted young children of his friends the Godebskis. When first performed in public, at the Salle Gaveau, Paris, on Apr. 20, 1910, the performers were again children, Christine Verger, six, and Germaine Duramy, ten.

An orchestral version, prepared the following year for a ballet production, was first heard at the Théâtre des Arts, Paris, on Jan. 28, 1912. Ravel devised a special introduction, *Danse rouet, et scène,* for that performance. On Nov. 8 of that year, the ballet suite first figured on an American program at a New York Symphony concert in Aeolian Hall.

Among Ravel's other compositions first written for piano and then arranged for orchestra are *Pavane pour une Infante defunte, Alborada del Gracioso,* and *Le Tombeau de Couperin.* When the four-hand piano version of *Ma Mère l'Oye* was printed in 1910, it carried a dedication to the Godebski children.

The orchestral scoring calls for piccolo, two flutes, two oboes, English horn, two clarinets, two bassoons, double bassoon, two horns, kettledrums, bass drum, cymbals, triangle, tam-tam, *jeu de timbres* (*à clavier*), xylophone, celesta, harp, and strings. The five pieces are as follows:

I. "Pavane de la belle au bois dormant" ("Pavane of the Sleeping Beauty"). The second flute gives out the theme, with a counter-melody brought in by muted horn and violas. The movement, only twenty measures long, is marked *Lent,* A minor, 4/4, and suggests the solemn, ceremonial style of Ravel's better known *Pavane.*

II. "Petit Poucet" ("Tom Thumb"). Ravel introduces this section with a quotation from one of the famous *Contes de fée* of Charles Perrault: "He believed he would easily find his way back by means of his bread crumbs, which he had scattered as he passed along; but to his surprise he could not find a single crumb, for the birds had come and eaten them up."

The scene is cleverly pictured in the music, with a solo oboe chanting above wavering muted strings, meant to convey the winding path followed by Tom

Thumb. Further realism is added in the middle section with suggestions of birds chirping and chattering.

III. "Laideronnette, Imperatrice des pagodas" ("Little Ugly One, Empress of the Pagodas") derives from Marie Catherine d'Aulnoy's story *Le Serpentin vert* (*The Green Serpent*), from which the following quotation is given: "She undressed and entered the bath. Immediately the pagodas, male and female, began to sing and to play on various instruments. Some had *theorbos,* or lutes, made of walnut shells, others viols made of almond shells. For they were obliged to use instruments proportionate to their shapes and sizes."

Laideronnette, formerly a princess, had been rendered ugly by a wicked witch. Ashamed to show herself, she hid in a faraway castle. While walking in the forest one day, she met a huge green serpent, who consoled her by divulging that he too had been handsome once. The same evil witch had cursed him with ugliness. Later the spell was broken and the two were married. On one of their adventures, Laideronnette and the green serpent come to a country of living pagodas, made of porcelain, crystal, diamonds, and emeralds.

The movement is in march time and full of iridescent effects of magic and fantasy, especially in the section depicting the pagodas. A vast battery of pulsatiles goes into action in the eerie sequences.

IV. "Les Entretiens de la belle et de la bête" ("The Conversations of Beauty and the Beast"). The prefatory quotations used for this section come from a story by Jeanne Marie Leprince de Beaumont:

"When I think how kind-hearted you are, you don't seem so ugly."
"Yes, it is true, I have a kind heart. Still, I am a beast."
"Many men are more beastly than you."
"If I were witty I would think up a fine compliment by way of thanks, but I am only a beast."
"Beauty, will you be my wife?"
"No, Beast!"
"I die happy because I have had the pleasure of seeing you again."
"No, my dear Beast, you shall not die. You shall live to be my husband!"

The Beast vanished and at her feet she saw a prince as beautiful as the God of Love. The Prince thanked her for breaking the spell laid upon him.

This section (F major, 3/4) is marked *mouvement de valse très modéré.* At the beginning a solo clarinet conveys Beauty's part of the conversation, a double bassoon being spokesman for the Beast. Beauty's voice later shifts to solo flute and solo oboe. After the transformation back to normal guise, Beauty becomes a solo violin and the Beast a solo cello. A clash of cymbals announces the end of the wicked witch's spell.

V. "Le Jardin féerique" ("The Fairy Garden"). Marked *Lent et grave,* C major, 3/4, this section tells of Sleeping Beauty's awakening by Prince

Charming. The celesta is assigned the role of depicting the enchanted princess as she slowly opens her eyes in the sun-flooded room. A joyous fanfare sounds at the end as other storybook characters gather about her and the Good Fairy gives the happy pair her blessings.

L. B.

Suite for Orchestra, "Le Tombeau de Couperin" ("The Grave of Couperin")

I. Prélude. II. Forlane. III. Menuet. IV. Rigaudon.

THIS SUITE is a kind of memorial wreath placed by a modern French classicist on the tomb of a revered predecessor. Clearly Ravel shared with Couperin the passion for grace and lucidity, so long a mark of the French tradition. Without slavish imitation, he sought here to evoke the courtly world of Couperin. Perhaps his aim, too, was to show that Couperin, after all, was the first of the moderns. In any case, the title should not mislead us. As Philip Hale remarked, "the fantastical title was probably invented to give the idea that the Suite was in the ancient manner, after the manner of the great writer for the clavecin, whose exquisite music is still modern."

Like so many other orchestral scores, *Le Tombeau de Couperin* began as a Suite for piano. Ravel set to work on it in July, 1914, but soon the call to arms forced him to abandon music for service in the First World War. For three years Ravel drove motor lorries, till his health gave out and he returned to civilian life. Resuming work on his Suite, he completed the piano version in November, 1917. With the shattering experiences of the war fresh in his mind, he now dedicated each of the original six sections to comrades who had fallen in battle. The various sections were marked and dedicated as follows:

I. Prélude (Vif, 12/16)—"To the memory of Lieut. Jacques Charlot."
II. Fugue (Allegro moderato, 4/4)—"To the memory of Second Lieut. Jean Cruppi."
III. Forlane (Allegretto, 6/8)—"To the memory of Lieut. Gabriel Deluc."
IV. Rigaudon (Assez vif, 2/4)—"To the memory of Pierre and Pascal Gaudin."
V. Menuet (Allegro moderato, 3/4)—"To the memory of Jean Dreyfus."
VI. Toccato (Vif, 2/4)—"To the memory of Capt. Joseph de Marliave."

Shortly after publication of the piano suite, Ravel scored four of these sections for small orchestra, omitting the Fugue and Toccata. The new orchestral version calls for two flutes, two oboes (one interchangeable with English horn), two clarinets, two bassoons, two horns, one trumpet, harp, and string. Thus arranged, *Le Tombeau de Couperin* was first performed at a Pasdeloup concert in Paris on Feb. 28, 1920. Rhené-Baton conducted. Pierre Monteux led the

American premiere of the Suite at a concert of the Boston Symphony Orchestra the following Nov. 20.

The "Forlane" which constitutes the second section of the orchestral suite draws its name from an old Italian dance highly popular with the Venetian gondoliers, who were said to dance it in pairs, using arm motions involved in rowing. Together with numerous other Italian dances, the forlane found its way into France toward the end of the sixteenth century. Rameau and Bach both used it in their works, and a forlane occurs at the end of the first act of Ponchielli's opera, *La Gioconda*. Spelled "forlana" or "furlana" in Italian, the dance was once thought to have originated in Friula, probably because the people of that region were known as *Furlani*.

The "Rigaudon" section is based on a dance widely regarded as Provençal in origin, though this has been disputed. In his Dictionary of Music, Rousseau advanced the theory, on the word of a dancing master whom he knew, that the word derived from the name of Rigaud, the alleged inventor of the dance who supposedly held forth at Marseilles. Among French variants of "rigaudon" are "rigadon," "rigodoun," and "rigaud." English composers of the seventeenth and eighteenth centuries adopted it as "rigadoon."

L. B.

"Daphnis et Chloé": Ballet in One Act—Orchestral Excerpts

Suite No. 1: "Nocturne," "Interlude," "Warlike Dance." Suite No. 2: "Daybreak," "Pantomime," "General Dance."

AFTER FOUNDING the Ballets Russes in 1909, Serge Diaghileff went about collecting some of the greatest talents in the many-mansioned world of art. Painters like Bakst, Picasso, Derain, and Matisse were enrolled for scenery and costumes. Stravinsky, Debussy, de Falla, Ravel, Prokofieff, Poulenc, and Milhaud in time all joined the composers' wing. Of course in the dazzling array of dancers were fabulous creatures like Nijinsky and Pavlova, and at the choreographic end was Michel Fokine, who doubled at authorship and dancing. Through the Ballets Russes vital new ideas were to find vivid expression and gain wider currency.

During the troupe's first season in Paris, Diaghileff heard music by the young composer Maurice Ravel and, being struck by its strong rhythmic basis and brilliant colors, kept the name for future reference. Early in 1910, Fokine prepared a scenario founded on the early Greek romance of Longus, *Daphnis and Chloë*. Diaghileff at once approached Ravel as the composer best equipped to handle the legendary theme. Ravel accepted eagerly. Subject, period, and mood appealed strongly to him, though both Fokine's revision of the Longus fable and Bakst's Oriental scenic plans made him wince. In the words of Madeleine

Goss, Ravel "saw the Greek legend of Daphnis and Chloë in a typically eighteenth-century atmosphere of Watteau shepherdesses . . . while Bakst planned the stage settings in a complete antithesis of bold and gorgeous Oriental coloring." The disputants somehow compromised, though the stage was set for future discord in the Diaghileff community.

In March, 1910, his friends the Godebskis invited him to their villa at Valvins. Ravel went. Undisturbed by the visits of friends and colleagues, he promptly set to work. The surroundings were ideal for composing music to accompany a pastoral legend. How much of the bracing outdoor freshness found its way into his music is idle speculation. Certainly a modern Longus would not have to go far into the Fontainebleau forest to find material for a new legend. In her book on Ravel, Miss Goss tells how the Seine overflowed its banks one day while Ravel was composing in his room. The water rose to the door of the Godebski villa. Unaware of the flood, Ravel quietly went on working. Finally, some friends, fearing that he might be marooned or worse, hastened to his rescue. They found him at the piano, serenely oblivious of the outer world. The flood waters were already buckling the floor of the living room.

Always a meticulous workman, Ravel toiled unsparingly over every detail of the score. Nothing short of supreme finish and absolute perfection of design and detail would satisfy him. He revised, edited, and modified repeatedly. The "Bacchanale" section alone is said to have taken almost a year. At length, the music was published and ready for Diaghileff. The premiere was set for June. Trouble was soon brewing again in the Diaghileff company. Complaints were made that not enough time was being allowed for rehearsals of the new ballet. Friction sharpened between Nijinsky and Fokine, said to have been mischievously incited by Diaghileff himself. Fokine even quit the troupe for a time. Nijinsky's own ideas about the role of Daphnis apparently clashed with Fokine's. Then Diaghileff and Bakst found cause for quarreling in the scenic preparations. The chorus, called for by the score, struggled over Ravel's wordless music. To add to the catalogue of headaches, the tricky 5/4 rhythm of the concluding section ruffled the tempers of the *corps de ballet*. It is not surprising to read that the world premiere of *Daphnis et Chloé* as a ballet was not a howling success.

The score of each suite contains a synopsis of the corresponding action of the ballet. The following is Philip Hale's translation of the words accompanying both Suites:

First Suite: A little flame suddenly burns on the head of one of the statues. The nymph comes to life and leaves her pedestal. Others descend, come together, and begin a slow and mysterious dance. They see Daphnis, bend over him and dry his tears. Reanimating him and leading him to the rock, they invoke the god Pan. Little by little the form of the god assumes definite shape.

Daphnis kneels in supplication. All is dark. Behind the scenes voices are heard, far off at first. And now there is a dim light. The pirates' camp is disclosed. There is a bold cast; the sea is in the background, with rocks to the right and left. A trireme is near the shore. Cypresses are here and there.

The pirates, laden with booty, run to and fro. Torches are brought, which at last throw a strong light on the stage.

Second Suite: No sound but the murmur of rivulets fed by the dew that trickles from the rocks. Daphnis lies stretched before the grotto of the nymphs. Little by little the day dawns. The songs of birds are heard. Afar off a shepherd leads his flock. Another shepherd crosses the back of the stage. Herdsmen enter, seeking Daphnis and Chloë. They find Daphnis and awaken him. In anguish he looks about for Chloë. She at last appears, encircled by shepherdesses. The two rush into each other's arms. Daphnis observes Chloë's crown. His dream was a prophetic vision: the intervention of Pan is manifest. The old shepherd Lammon explains that Pan saved Chloë, in remembrance of the nymph, Syrinx, whom the god loved.

Daphnis and Chloë mime the story of Pan and Syrinx. Chloë impersonates the young nymph wandering over the meadow. Daphnis as Pan appears and declares his love for her. The nymph repulses him; the god becomes more insistent. She disappears among the reeds. In desperation he plucks some stalks, fashions a flute, and on it plays a melancholy tune. Chloë comes out and imitates by her dance the accents of the flute.

The dance grows more and more animated. In mad whirlings, Chloë falls into the arms of Daphnis. Before the altar of the nymphs he swears on two sheep his fidelity. Young girls enter; they are dressed as Bacchantes and shake their tambourines. Daphnis and Chloë embrace tenderly. A group of young men come on the stage.

Joyous tumult. A general dance. Daphnis and Chloë.

L. B.

"Bolero"

IDA RUBINSTEIN, the noted mime, dancer, and actress, commissioned Ravel to write a piece of music for a dance pantomime with a Spanish setting. The outcome was Ravel's most spectacular work: *Bolero*.

With Mme. Rubinstein as the tantalizing dancer who enacts the bolero on a table top in a Spanish inn, the novelty was produced at the Paris Opéra on Nov. 22, 1928. The action of the dance involved a relentlessly worked up crescendo of passion. The men gathered in the public room of the inn eye the dancer fixedly. As her movements grow more animated, their excitement mounts. They beat out an obbligato with their hands and pound their heels. At the peak of the crescendo, where the key abruptly shifts from C major to E major, the sharpening tension snaps. Knives are drawn, and there is a wild tavern brawl.

Ravel said to the critic M. D. Calvocoressi:

I am particularly desirous that there should be no misunderstanding about this work. It constitutes an experiment in a very special and limited direction and should not be suspected of aiming at achieving anything different from or anything more than it actually does achieve.

Before its first performance I issued a warning to the effect that what I had written was a piece lasting seventeen minutes and consisting wholly of "orchestral tissue without music"—of one long, very gradual crescendo. There are no contrasts, there is practically no invention except the plan and the manner of the execution. . . . I have carried out exactly what I intended, and it is for listeners to take it or leave it.

Staged widely in Europe and America, *Bolero* was first performed in this country as a concert number at a concert in Carnegie Hall of the Philharmonic-Symphony. Arturo Toscanini conducted. The date was Nov. 14, 1929. The audience was scarcely prepared for the sensation. Few of the musicians suspected at rehearsal that they were working on a bombshell. The effect on the Carnegie Hall audience was almost unprecedented. Even critics joined in the frantic storm of applause. "If it had been the American custom to repeat a number at a symphonic concert," said Pitts Sanborn, "*Bolero* would surely have been encored, even at the risk of mass wreckage of the nerves!" Sanborn, ordinarily a sedate observer, himself joined the cheering throng. He wrote:

For the prime object of *Bolero* musically is the creation of nervous tension. A two-limbed melody of Spanish character, uttered first by the flute, after the drum has given out the rhythm, is reiterated by solo instruments and instruments in groups while the volume of sound increases steadily, inexorably. When it seems that human nerves can endure no more, the key shift comes with the impact of dynamite. This Philharmonic-Symphony debut made *Bolero* an American craze.

L. B.

"Piano Concerto for the Left Hand"

ALTHOUGH THE Parisian premieres of Ravel's two piano concertos were separated by a year—one occurring on Jan. 14, 1932, the other on Jan. 17, 1933—the works were "conceived and realized simultaneously," according to the composer's own admission. Actually, the world premiere of the two-hand concerto came only eight days after the first performance on Jan. 6 of its one-hand twin in Vienna.

Apparently Ravel's original idea was to write a concerto for a second tour of America, the first visit having proved triumphant. He planned the work for leading American orchestras, with himself as soloist. In the midst of his plans he was approached one day by Paul Wittgenstein, an Austrian pianist. Mr. Wittgenstein had only a left arm, having lost the right in the First World War. He asked Ravel to write a concerto for him, with obvious concessions.

Already Richard Strauss, Erich Korngold, Franz Schmidt, and Serge Prokofieff had armed Mr. Wittgenstein with special scores. Ravel agreed and promptly set to work on both concertos.

A slightly different version of the twin birth is that Ravel concentrated first on his original plans. Then ideas and thoughts began to take shape which somehow did not quite fit into the scheme. Recalling Mr. Wittgenstein's request, he found the place for them in the Concerto for Left Hand alone. When published in 1931, the Concerto was virtually deeded to the one-armed pianist as his "exclusive property." It is said conflict arose between pianist and composer when the former repeatedly altered passages to suit his style. Previously they had debated long and anxiously over the score, Mr. Wittgenstein complaining about difficulties, Ravel "steadfastly refusing to alter a single note." According to Madeleine Goss, in her book on Ravel, the composer, in despair over the "unpardonable liberties" Mr. Wittgenstein was taking in performing the work, "looked about for someone to play the Concerto as he himself wished it performed." He evidently found "an able and sympathetic interpreter" in Jacques Février, the son of a Conservatory colleague of his student days. Ravel proceeded to coach the younger Février. When the work was introduced to America at concerts of the Boston Symphony Orchestra on Nov. 9 and 10, 1934, Mr. Wittgenstein was the soloist, as he had been in Paris, London, Vienna, and Berlin.

On the subject of his composing the concertos jointly Ravel expressed himself as follows:

It was an interesting experiment to conceive and to realize simultaneously the two concertos. The first . . . is a concerto in the most exact sense of the term and is written in the spirit of Mozart and Saint-Saëns. . . . It includes some elements borrowed from jazz, but only in moderation. The Concerto for the Left Hand alone is of a rather different character and in one movement only, with many jazz effects, and the writing is not so simple. In a work of this kind it is essential to create the effect not of light, delicate texture, but of a score written for both hands.

According to Henry Prunières, who hailed the Concerto as "an authentic work destined to live," the Concerto discloses "what Ravel had implacably banished from the other"—sentiment. "And sentiment," he asserts, "has taken its revenge for this long exile; it lights up the work magnificently and sometimes almost romantically. Those who have never understood that sentiment is always in abeyance in Ravel . . . were astounded to see him, for once, baring his soul." He observed that in certain places in the Concerto "there seem to be at least two hands at work, and sometimes it sounds like four."

The work is scored for three flutes, piccolo, two oboes, English horn, two clarinets, E flat clarinet, bass clarinet, two bassoons, contrabassoon, four horns, three trumpets, three trombones, tuba, triangle, tambourin, cymbals, large drum, wood block, tam-tam, tympani, harp, piano, and strings.

The Concerto entered the Philharmonic-Symphony repertory on Mar. 17, 1938, when Robert Casadesus, a close friend and associate of Ravel, was also the soloist.

L. B.

"Tzigane," Rhapsody for Violin and Orchestra

AT THE time of its premiere in London in 1924, Ravel's dazzling virtuoso piece in frank gypsy rhythms was suspected by the *London Times* critic of being a "parody of the Liszt-Hubay-Brahms-Joachim school of Hungarian violin music." Of course no such satire was intended or, at least, never avowed by Ravel, though a vein of sardonic sophistication runs through a great deal of his music. *La Valse* has been interpreted by some as a clever thrust at the lush Viennese waltz, and even *Bolero* is supposed to mask a mocking grin. Yet, the freely rhapsodic style of *Tzigane,* its broad melody, its unabashed virtuoso glitter, besides what Herbert Antcliffe called its "lack of self-consciousness," rule out any satiric angle.

Tzigane was part of a program devoted to Ravel's works presented in London on Apr. 26, 1924. Ravel was still working on it less than a week before the concert. The soloist was to be Yelly d'Aranyi, the Hungarian violinist and grandniece of Joseph Joachim. The composition is dedicated to her. It seems that Miss d'Aranyi had no more than two or three days in which to master the work's technical hazards. After her brilliant rendering of the music, Ravel paid her a highly flattering compliment: "If I had known, I should have made the music still more difficult. I thought I had written something very difficult, but you have proved the contrary."

Ravel appears to have first designed the accompaniment for the *luthéal,* described as "rather an attachment to a piano than a musical instrument." The luthéal, adjusted inside the piano, can be regulated to furnish harp, celesta, and "overtone" effects. Later Ravel scored the accompaniment for small orchestra.

Samuel Dushkin played the work in Paris on Oct. 15, 1924, at a concert of the Société Musicale Independante, and on Dec. 7, the Dutch violinist, André Pollah, was the soloist at the American premiere, which took place in Aeolian Hall, New York, at a concert of the International Composers' Guild.

Pollah, who had studied *Tzigane* with the composer, later communicated his impressions of the music along with Ravel's alleged intentions: "Ravel's idea was to represent a gypsy serenading—with all the extravagance of his fiery temperament and all the good and bad taste at his command—some real or imaginary beauty. . . . In the solo part, not only has every known technical effect been used, but Ravel has invented new ones."

The French critic and musicologist Henry Prunières cautioned listeners against attaching "greater importance to the work than the composer himself had done," conceding, however, that "admiration for the superhuman ingenuity of the skill displayed in contriving it was quite in order."

L. B.

Ottorino Respighi

BORN: BOLOGNA, JULY 9, 1879. DIED: ROME, APR. 18, 1936.

*Here is an elegant way of writing, in the sense of the rhetoric of another day; a beautiful harmonizing; a splendid method of orchestration; and with these is a desire to be agreeable, well-mannered, and respectable at all costs.—*GUIDO M. GATTI.

Symphonic Poem, "The Fountains of Rome"

COMPOSED IN 1916, Respighi's tribute to Rome's fountains was first performed in Rome on Feb. 10, 1918, under the direction of Arturo Toscanini. The concert was part of a series organized for the benefit of artists disabled in the First World War. The audience received it warmly, and critics hailed Respighi's mastery of orchestral color. After the performance Mr. Toscanini was recalled several times.

The American premiere occurred at a concert of the New York Philharmonic Society on Feb. 13, 1919. The score calls for two flutes, piccolo, two oboes, English horn, two clarinets, bass clarinet, two bassoons, four horns, three trumpets, three trombones, tuba, kettledrums, triangle, cymbals, bells, harps, celesta, piano, organ (*ad libitum*), and strings.

The fountains are specified as follows: (1) The Fountain of Valle Giulia at dawn; (2) The Triton Fountain in the morning; (3) The Fountain of Trevi at midday; and (4) The Villa Medici Fountain at sunset. An analysis of the music, appearing in the score in Italian, French, and English, runs as follows:

In this symphonic poem the composer has endeavored to give expression to the sentiments and vision suggested to him by four of Rome's fountains, contemplated at the hour in which their character is most in harmony with the surrounding landscape, or in which their beauty appears most impressive to the observer.

The first part of the poem, inspired by the Fountain of Valle Giulia, depicts a pastoral landscape; droves of cattle pass and disappear in the fresh, damp mists of the Roman dawn.

A sudden loud and insistent blast of horns above the trills of the whole orchestra introduces the second part, "The Triton Fountain." It is like a joyous call, summoning troops of naiads and tritons, who come running up pursuing each other and mingling in a frenzied dance between the jets of water.

Next there appears a solemn theme, borne on the undulations of the orchestra. It is Fountain of Trevi at midday. The solemn theme, passing from the wood to the brass instruments, assumes a triumphal character. Trumpets peal; across the radiant surface of the water there passes Neptune's chariot, drawn by sea horses and followed by a train of sirens and tritons. The procession then vanishes, while faint trumpet blasts resound in the distance.

The fourth part, the Villa Medici Fountain, is announced by a sad theme, which rises above a subdued warbling. It is the nostalgic hour of sunset, the air is full of the sound of tolling bells, birds twittering, leaves rustling. Then all dies peacefully into the silence of the night.

L. B.

Symphonic Poem, "The Pines of Rome"

THIS IS the second of three works comprising a Roman series. Each celebrates some aspect of the Eternal City. The first was *The Fountains of Rome,* dated 1916, and the third, *Roman Festivals,* dated 1928. The present composition was written in 1924, obtaining its premiere at the Augusteo, Rome, Dec. 14, of the same year, under the direction of Bernardino Molinari. Its first performance in America occurred at a concert of the New York Philharmonic Society in Carnegie Hall on Jan. 14, 1926, with Arturo Toscanini to conduct.

On the day after its American premiere Respighi himself conducted the piece in Philadelphia at a concert of the Philadelphia Orchestra. The program on that occasion carried the following explanation, written by the composer:

While in his preceding work, *The Fountains of Rome,* the composer sought to reproduce by means of tone an impression of nature, in *The Pines of Rome* he uses nature as a point of departure, in order to recall memories and visions. The century-old trees which dominate so characteristically the Roman landscape become testimony for the principal events in Roman life.

The Pines of Rome consists of four connected sections, whose description is printed as a preface to the score:

1. "The Pines of Villa Borghese" (Allegretto vivace, 2/8). Children are at play in the pine grove of the Villa Borghese, dancing the Italian equivalent of "Ring around a Rosy"; mimicking marching soldiers and battles; twittering and shrieking like swallows at evening; and they disappear. Suddenly the scene changes to—

2. "The Pines near a Catacomb" (Lento, 4/4; beginning with muted and divided strings, muted horns, *p*). We see the shadows of the pines, which overhang the entrance of a catacomb. From the depths rises a chant which reechoes solemnly, like a hymn, and is then mysteriously silenced.

3. "The Pines of the Janiculum" (Lento, 4/4; piano cadenza; clarinet solo). There is a thrill in the air. The full moon reveals the profile of the pines of Gianicolo's Hill. A nightingale sings (represented by a gramophone record of a nightingale song, heard from the orchestra).

4. "The Pines of the Appian Way" (Tempo di marcia). Misty dawn on the Appian Way. The tragic country is guarded by solitary pines. Indistinctly, incessantly, the rhythm of innumerable steps. To the poet's phantasy appears a vision of past glories; trumpets blare, and the army of the Consul advances brilliantly in the grandeur of a newly risen sun toward the Sacred Way, mounting in triumph the Capitoline Hill.

R. C. B.

Silvestre Revueltas

BORN: SANTIAGO, PAPASQUIAR, STATE OF DURANGO, MEXICO, DEC. 31, 1899. DIED: MEXICO CITY, OCT. 5, 1940.

Revueltas was the spontaneously inspired type of composer, whose music was colorful, picturesque, and gay.—Aaron Copland.

"Janitzio"

ONE OF the most promising of Western Hemisphere composers was Silvestre Revueltas whose career was cut short by death in 1940. A thoroughly grounded musician, he had studied violin at Colima, later continuing his musical training at the Institute of Juarez de Durango; with Rocabruna at Mexico City; at Saint Edward College, Austin, Tex., and with Sametini and Borowski in Chicago.

After a number of violin recitals in his native Mexico, he returned to Chicago to take up further work with Kochanski and Sevcik. He made some appearances in joint recitals with Carlos Chavez, whose assistant he subsequently became in the conductorship of the Orquesta Sinfonia de Mexico, at the same time holding the post of professor in violin and chamber music at the Conservatorio de Musica. In 1938 he traveled through Europe, returning to take up his permanent abode in Mexico City, where he devoted himself exclusively to composing.

His music, it has been said, is close to the soil. He has employed native dance rhythms wherever possible and, while he has never committed himself to the use of actual folk melodies, his tunes have been described as being unmistakably Mexican. The composer has preferred giving his works titles, instead of the usual opus numbers, explaining, however, that his pieces "have no program, merely literary themes," the titles having "little significance in the music itself."

Janitzio was inspired by the simple beauties of an island on Lake Patzcuaro, whose sole inhabitants are fisher folk. He has written many orchestral compositions, ballets, music for films, several string quartets, items for violin and piano, songs, and other numbers. *Janitzio* received its first performance in this country by the Pittsburgh Symphony under Fritz Reiner.

R. C. B.

Wallingford Riegger

BORN: ALBANY, GA., APR. 29, 1885.

*Dancers, not having studied harmony, are not prejudiced against the "modern" idiom, so from that standpoint I have enjoyed working with them, and have developed a great versatility of style. The recent change of outlook on the part of American dancers—originating with Martha Graham, about 1930—is extremely important for the composer. . . . Inasmuch as the Modern Dance is not stylized but much more organic than the ballet, no set piece of music will do. The composer watches the dance, endeavors to catch the mood, and notes down the rhythmic design. To create within such a straitjacket taxes one's ingenuity. Fortunately, the dancer is willing to make a concession now and then.—*WALLINGFORD RIEGGER.

Finale from "New Dance"

AWARE OF the special importance of rhythm in modern music, Mr. Riegger, borrowing a leaf from the Latin Americans, has made considerable use of the Conga beats in his composition. *New Dance* was originally written as accompaniment music for a dance creation of Doris Humphrey's—in a four-hand piano arrangement. Later the composer recast his work for two pianos, in which form it was introduced at a Carnegie Hall recital by Pierre Luboshotz and Genia Nemenoff. He then orchestrated the Finale of the piece, and it was introduced by Mr. Reiner and the Pittsburgh Symphony at a concert given in the Syria Mosque, Pittsburgh, on Jan. 30, 1942. It has been performed by several orchestras since then.

Wallingford Riegger studied at the Institute of Musical Art in New York City and at the Hochschule in Berlin. Possessor of a Doctor of Music degree from the Cincinnati Conservatory of Music, he has taught at Drake University, the Ithaca Conservatory, and the Institute of Musical Art, besides privately. Among his orchestral works are an *American Polonaise* in triple jazz, a Rhapsody, a Fantasy and Fugue, and a Lyric Suite. His chamber orchestra pieces include a *Study in Sonority* and *Dichotomy,* while other chamber music of his embraces several quartets, trios, and further works.

The modern dance has been a fertile source and medium of Riegger's inspiration. Besides Doris Humphrey, he has written provocative scores for Martha Graham, Hanya Holm, and Tamiris.

R. C. B.

Nicholas Rimsky-Korsakoff

BORN: TIKHVIN, GOVERNMENT OF NOVGOROD, MAR. 18, 1844. DIED: ST. PETERSBURG, JUNE 21, 1908.

The folk song, the Orient, and the sea were the three influences or inspirations which pursued Rimsky-Korsakoff throughout his career, and he never got very far away from any of them. . . . He turned everything in his life to artistic account: his early life at sea, his trips to the Crimea, his summer vacations, when he noted down folk and bird songs. He was always seduced by the picturesque and the exotic. He might be called, indeed, a musical Eurasian.—CARL VAN VECHTEN.

"Capriccio Espagnole," Op. 34

FIRST PLANNED as "a virtuoso violin fantasy on Spanish themes," this work was revised and given final shape as the *Capriccio Espagnole* early in 1887, the premiere occurring in St. Petersburg on Oct. 31, with Rimsky-Korsakoff conducting. The *Capriccio* was "to glitter with dazzling orchestral color, and, manifestly, I had not been wrong," writes the composer, with engaging candor, in his memoirs. Few composers, in fact, have written with such frank self-appraisal as shown by Rimsky-Korsakoff in the pages devoted to his *Capriccio*. To quote him:

The opinion formed by both critics and the public, that the *Capriccio* is a *magnificently orchestrated piece,* is wrong. The *Capriccio* is a brilliant *composition for the orchestra*. The change of timbres, the felicitous choice of melodic designs and figuration patterns, exactly suiting each kind of instrument, brief virtuoso cadenzas for instruments solo, the rhythm of the percussion instruments, etc., constitute here the very *essence* of the composition and not its garb or orchestration.

The Spanish themes, of dance character, furnished me with rich material for putting in use multiform orchestral effects. All in all, the *Capriccio* is undoubtedly a purely external piece, but vividly brilliant for all that. I was a little less successful in its third section ("Alborada," in B flat major), where the brasses somewhat drown the melodic designs of the wood winds; but this is very easy to remedy, if the conductor will pay attention to it and moderate the indications of the shades of force in the brass instruments by replacing the fortissimo with a simple forte.

The composer also dwells on the great ovation given the premiere, not only by the public, but by the members of the Russian Symphony, which he directed. He writes:

At the first rehearsal, the first movement had hardly been finished when the whole orchestra began to applaud.

Similar applause followed all the other parts wherever the pauses permitted. I asked the orchestra for the privilege of dedicating the composition to them. General delight was the answer. The *Capriccio* went without difficulties and sounded brilliant.

At the concert itself it was played with a perfection and enthusiasm the like of which it never possessed subsequently, even when led by Nikisch himself. Despite its length the composition called forth an insistent encore.

The *Capriccio* is in five movements, played, as directed by the composer, without interruption: I. "Alborada" (Vivo e strepitoso, A major, 2/4); II. Variations (Andante con moto, F major, 3/8); III. "Alborada" (Vivo e strepitoso, B flat major, 2/4): a repetition of the first section with changes in key and orchestration; IV. "Scene and Gypsy Song" (Allegretto, D minor, 6/8); and V. "Fandango of the Asturias" (A major, 3/4). As coda Rimsky-Korsakoff brings back the "Alborada" theme.

L. B.

"Scheherazade," Symphonic Suite after "The Thousand Nights and One Night," Op. 35

BOTH THIS work and the *Easter Overture* were composed by Rimsky-Korsakoff in 1888, during a summer spent on Lake Cheryemenyetskoye. It had its world premiere in St. Petersburg during the following musical season. The Suite is dedicated to Vladimir Stassoff. It calls for the following instruments: piccolo, two flutes, two oboes (one interchangeable with English horn), two clarinets, two bassoons, four horns, two trumpets, three trombones, tuba, kettledrums, snare drum, bass drum, tambourine, cymbals, triangle, tam-tam, harp, and strings. On the score of the composition is printed this program:

The Sultan of Schahriar, persuaded of the falseness and faithlessness of women, has sworn to put to death each one of his wives after the first night. But the Sultana Scheherazade saved her life by interesting him in tales which she told him during the thousand and one nights. Pricked by curiosity, the Sultan puts off his wife's execution from day to day, and at last gave up his bloody plan.

Many marvels were told Schahriar by the Sultana Scheherazade. For her stories the Sultana borrowed from the poets their verses, from folk songs the words; and he strung together tales and adventures.

In Rimsky-Korsakoff's autobiography, *My Musical Life,* he has this to say about the *Scheherazade Suite* (translation by J. A. Joffe):

The program I had been guided by in composing *Scheherazade* consisted of separate, unconnected episodes and pictures from *The Arabian Nights:* the fantastic narrative of the Prince Kalandar, the Prince and the Princess, the Baghdad festival, and the ship dashing against the rock with the bronze rider upon it. The unifying thread consisted of the brief introductions to Movements I, II, and IV and the intermezzo in Movement III, written for violin solo, and delineating Scheherazade herself as telling her wondrous tales to the stern Sultan. The conclusion of Movement IV serves the same artistic purpose.

In vain do people seek in my suite leading motives linked always and unvaryingly with the same poetic ideas and conceptions. On the contrary, in the majority of cases, all these seeming leitmotives are nothing but purely musical material or the given motives for symphonic development. These given motives thread and spread over all the movements of the suite, alternating and intertwining each with the other. Appearing as they do each time under different moods, the self-same motives and themes correspond each time to different images, actions, and pictures.

Thus, for instance, the sharply outlined fanfare motive of the muted trombone and trumpet, which first appears in the Kalandar's Narrative (Movement II) appears afresh in Movement IV, in the delineation of the doomed ship, though this episode has no connection with the Kalandar's Narrative. The principal theme of the Kalandar's Narrative (B minor, 3/4) and the theme of the Princess in Movement III (B flat major, 6/8, clarinet) in altered guise and quick tempo appear as the secondary themes of the Baghdad festival; yet nothing is said in *The Arabian Nights* about these persons taking part in the festivities. The unison phrase, as though depicting Scheherazade's stern spouse, at the beginning of the Suite appears in the Kalandar's Narrative, where there cannot, however, be any thought of Sultan Schahriar.

In this manner, developing quite freely the musical data taken as a basis of the composition, I had in view the creation of an orchestral suite in four movements, closely knit by the community of its themes and motives, yet presenting, as it were, a kaleidoscope of fairy-tale images and designs of Oriental character—a method that I had to a certain degree made use of in my *Skazka* (*Fairy tale*), the musical data of which are as little distinguishable from the poetic as they are in *Scheherazade*. Originally I had even intended to label the movements of *Scheherazade*: No. I.— "Prelude"; No. II.—"Ballade"; No. III.—"Adagio"; No. IV.—"Finale"; but on the advice of Liadoff and others I did not do so. My aversion for the seeking of a too definite program in my composition led me subsequently (in the new edition) to do away with even those hints of it which had lain in the headings of each movement, such as: "The Sea," and "Sindbad's Ship," the "Kalandar's Narrative," etc.

In composing *Scheherazade* I meant these hints to direct but slightly the hearer's fancy on the path which my own fancy had traveled, and to leave more minute and particular conceptions to the will and mood of each listener. All I had desired was that the hearer, if he liked my piece as *symphonic music,* should carry away the impression that it is beyond doubt an Oriental narrative of some numerous and varied fairy-tale wonders and not merely four pieces played one after the other and composed on the basis of themes common to all four movements. Why, then, if that be the case, does my Suite bear the name, precisely, *Scheherazade?* Because this name and subtitle After *The Thousand and One Nights* connote in everybody's mind the East and fairy-tale wonders; besides, certain details of the musical exposition hint at the fact that all of these are various tales of some one person (which happens to be Scheherazade) entertaining therewith her stern husband.

Overture, "The Russian Easter," Op. 36

IN THE summer of 1888, Rimsky-Korsakoff completed two works, for which he had done merely sketches earlier in the year. These works were "an orchestra composition on the subject of certain episodes from *Scheherazade*," and the present Overture which is based on themes of the "Obikhod"—a collection of the best-known canticles of the Orthodox Church. The composer himself felt that these two pieces, plus the *Capriccio Espagnole,* exposed "a considerable degree of virtuosity and bright sonority without Wagner's influence, within the limits of the usual make-up of Glinka's orchestra."

The score of *The Russian Easter* employs the following instruments: three flutes (third interchangeable with piccolo), two oboes, two clarinets, two bassoons, four horns, two trumpets, three trombones, tuba, three kettledrums, glockenspiel, triangle, cymbals, bass drum, tam-tam, harp, and strings.

In his book *My Musical Life* (translation by J. A. Joffe) Rimsky-Korsakoff writes of the Overture as follows:

The rather lengthy, slow introduction of the *Easter Sunday Overture,* on the theme of "Let God Arise!" alternating with the ecclesiastical theme "An angel wailed," appeared to me, in its beginning, as it were, the ancient Isaiah's prophecy concerning the resurrection of Christ. The gloomy colors of the Andante lugubre seemed to depict the Holy Sepulcher that had shone with ineffable light at the moment of the Resurrection—in the transition to the Allegro of the Overture. The beginning of the Allegro, "Let them also that hate Him flee before Him," led to the holiday mood of the Greek Orthodox church service on Christ's matins; the solemn trumpet voice of the Archangel was replaced by a tonal reproduction of the joyous, almost dancelike bell tolling, alternating now with the sexton's rapid reading and now with the conventional chant of the priest's reading the glad tidings of the Evangel. The "Obikhod" theme "Christ Is Arisen," which forms a sort of subsidiary part of the Overture, appears amid the trumpet blasts and the bell tolling, constituting also a triumphant coda. In this Overture there were thus combined reminiscences of the ancient prophecy, of the Gospel Narrative and also a general picture of the Easter Service with its "pagan merrymaking." The capering and leaping of the Biblical King David before the Ark, do they not give expression to a mood of the same order as the mood of the idol-worshippers' dance? Surely the Russian Orthodox "Obikhod" is instrumental dance music of the Church, is it not? And do not the waving beards of the priests and sextons clad in white vestments and surplices, and intoning "Beautiful Easter" in the tempo Allegro vivo, etc., transport the imagination to pagan times? And all these Easter loaves and twists and the glowing tapers. . . . How far a cry from the philosophic and socialistic teaching of Christ! This legendary and heathen side of the Holiday, this transition from the gloomy and mysterious evening of Passion Saturday to the unbridled pagan-religious merry-making on the morn of Easter Sunday is what I was eager to reproduce in my Overture. Accordingly, I requested Count Golyenischeff-Kootoozoff to write a program in verse—which he did for me. But I was not satisfied with his poem and wrote in prose my own program, which same is appended to the published score. Of course in that program I did not explain my views and my conception of the "Bright Holiday" [the popular Russian name for Easter], leaving it to tones to speak for me. Evidently these tones do, within certain limits, speak of my feelings and thoughts, for my Overture raises doubts in the minds of some hearers, despite the considerable clarity of the music. In any event, in order to appreciate my Overture even ever so slightly, it is necessary that the hearer should have attended Easter morning service at least once and, at that, not in a domestic chapel, but in a cathedral thronged with people from every walk of life, with several priests conducting the cathedral service—something that many intellectual Russian hearers, let alone hearers of other confessions, quite lack nowadays. As for myself, I had gained my impressions in my childhood passed near the Tikhvin monastery itself.

Printed in the score—which is dedicated "to the memory of Moussorgsky and Borodin"—is a program compact of two verses from Psalm LXVIII, six verses from the Gospel according to St. Mark (Chapter XVI), and some other words by the composer himself.

R. C. B.

Suite from the Opera "Tsar Saltan"

I. Allegretto alla marcia. II. Introduction to Act II. III. The Flight of the Bumblebee. IV. The Three Wonders (Introduction to the last scene).

THE COMPLETE title of Rimsky-Korsakoff's opera is *The Fairy Tale of the Tsar Saltan, his son the Renowned and Mighty Paladin, the Prince Gvidon Saltanovich, and the Beautiful Tsarevna Lebed*. It was composed between 1899 and 1900, and it was given its first performance (privately) at Moscow in the latter year. From the score a suite of "musical pictures" obtained its premiere at a concert sponsored by the Imperial Russian Musical Society shortly thereafter, although it did not then contain the second-act scherzo, later incorporated, "The Flight of the Bumblebee."

This Suite is scored for two flutes, piccolo, two oboes, English horn, three clarinets, bass clarinet, two bassoons, double bassoon, four horns, three trumpets, three trombones, bass tuba, tympani, side drum, bass drum, cymbals, triangle, small bells, xylophone, celesta, harp, and strings. Before each section of the Suite there is a quotation from the poem of Pushkin, which inspired the four-act opera.

Ernest J. Simmons remarks that Pushkin borrowed the plot of the *Tsar Saltan* from some source or other, much as Shakespeare himself did. He continued:

But the finished product becomes an original work of beauty. Pushkin had learned to move easily and surely in this world of complete fantasy. The artlessness of the folk is never subordinated to the sophisticated rules of art. Meaning and understanding, or logic, is not allowed to obtrude upon the natural laws of folk-tale narration. The story moves on, as it were, by its own volition. And Pushkin's recognition of this inherent artlessness and his complete acceptance of it serve to make these folk tales his most perfect creations.

The folkish narrative poems of Pushkin were ever fascinating to Rimsky-Korsakoff, as witness his early work *Fairy Tales*, based on the prologue to Pushkin's *Russlan and Ludmilla*. In later years he set music to librettos by Vladimir Bielsky for the opera *Le Coq d'or* and, of course, *Tsar Saltan*.

Commenting on the *Tsar Saltan,* Rimsky-Korsakoff says, "In the spring [of 1889] V. I. Bielsky began to write his splendid libretto, making use of Pushkin as much as was possible, and artistically as well as skillfully, imitating his style. He would hand me the scenes, one by one, as they were finished, and I set to work on the opera. . . . The libretto came to me piecemeal continuously from Bielsky." He goes on to say that he attempted to abide by the fairy-tale character of the lines, and also that he had in mind a Suite, to be made from the "longish orchestral preludes to Acts I, II, and IV," with the title "Little Pictures to the Fairy Tale of Tsar Saltan."

The plot of *Tsar Saltan* is fantastic and elaborate, like all fairy tales. There is the Tsar himself, who has the habit of wandering about his kingdom incognito. This, naturally, makes it easy for him to hear gossip about himself. One day he listens, as each of three sisters tells how she would treat his majesty, were she his bride. The first would bake for him a magnificent bread; the second would like nothing better than to weave fine linens for him; and the third would bear him a beautiful heir.

As things go in fairy tales, the Tsar weds the youngest, but the mistake he makes is to invite the other sisters to live in the palace. In the course of time a son is born to him, while he is away at the wars. The plotting sisters send their royal brother-in-law all sorts of vicious messages, lurid stories about the monstrosity that is his heir. When he responds that he will come to see for himself, they retaliate with another sensational feat by deliberately changing his message, so that it becomes an order to cast the mother and her child, inclosed in a barrel, into the sea.

The cask, after days of aimless floating, reaches an alien shore, the island of Buyan. And there the boy, Prince Gvidon, growing daily in spiritual and bodily beauty and vigor, happens, one day, to save the life of a swan, which—you might expect—possesses the most magical powers and, in gratitude, endows the island with three wonders. The first of these is a whistling squirrel, which extracts kernels of pure emerald from nuts with golden shells. The second is a tidal wave, which, overwhelming the shore, disgorges thirty-three armed warriors. The third is a princess of incomparable beauty, whose hair is as the light of moonbeams and upon whose brow there glistens a star.

Prince Gvidon, expressing a longing to see his father, is transformed, through the good offices of the swan, into a bumblebee, whereupon he flies straight to his father's land and, after a series of adventures on the side of the right, is joined by the Tsar on the island of Buyan, where he has married in the meantime, the princess of incomparable beauty, who all along was the swan.

R. C. B.

Manuel Rosenthal

BORN: PARIS, JUNE 18, 1904.

*As a master of the orchestra he is in the line and of the quality of
Berlioz. There is not to my knowledge another living composer who
orchestrates with comparable precision, freedom, and joy. There are
force, originality, and life in every measure.*—VIRGIL THOMSON.

"La Fête du vin" ("The Festival of Wine")

THIS WORK was written in 1937 on commission from the French government
for the "Fêtes de la Lumière" of the International Exposition. Mr. Rosenthal
says:

There is no real program but a kind of connecting thread, which is, in sum, the
dream of the man who loves the juice of the vine; that is to say, all good Frenchmen.
In the course of the dream there are evoked successively the various activities concerning the care of the vine and of the vintages, as also the libations which follow.

The principal episode consists of a great bacchanale, a homage, if one chooses, to
champagne and its beneficial effects; but the dream and the work come to a conclusion evocative of a melancholy awakening.

The composer has utilized in this piece a Bacchic song of French folk origin, as
well as some popular Canadian airs, whose frank and joyful allure seem to him to
belong to the program.

The score calls for three flutes (all three interchangeable with piccolo), three
oboes, three clarinets (third interchangeable with bass clarinet), three bassoons,
three horns, four trumpets, three trombones, bass tuba, harp, piano, celesta,
glockenspiel, kettledrums, bass drum, two cymbals, suspended cymbal, snare
drum, long drum, tambourine, vibraphone, four Chinese blocks, wood block,
triangle, gong, castanets, chimes, xylophone, and strings. Mr. Rosenthal conducted the American premiere of *La Fête du vin* as guest of the Philharmonic-
Symphony Orchestra in Carnegie Hall on Dec. 5, 1946.

Well does Virgil Thomson observe, in his article on "Musical Gastronomy"
(*New York Herald Tribune,* Oct. 10, 1946) that "An American composer,
designing for musical depiction his ideal dinner, would certainly either have
left out half of this abundance or topped it off with a finale about bicarbonate."
Mr. Thomson was writing about *Musique de table,* then, and he bemoaned the
omission, from the program of that score, of the explicit mention of suitable
wines. For, as he remarked, "Wine . . . is essential to the ingestion of any

reasonably good French meal, not to mention the majestic menu dreamed up in 1942 by Mr. Rosenthal."

Yet he sensed,

in the delicious scoring of this memorable work plenty of the appropriate grape. The characteristic blood flavor of roast beef and the darkly outdoor taste of venison, rendered in the scoring by trumpets and trombones in the one case and by hunting horns in the other, were so aptly set off by contrasting instrumental timbres that the richness of the whole effect could only have been conceived with something more on the imaginary palate than meat alone. The salad, on the other hand, with which one does not drink wine, because it tastes already of vinegar, had no such third dimension. It was all light and high and clear and clean and pale, fresh to the taste and quite without perspective.

In any case, two works of Mr. Rosenthal's, the present one and *Musique de table,* comprise for the record, at least, a concert repast of food and drink in the grand manner, a "compleat" feast for the most discerning (and capacious) tastes. This is true, even if not all the delights gastronomic and potational may be enjoyed by some of us at one sitting, unless that could be a simultaneous rendering of *Musique de table* and *La Fête du vin.*

Manuel Rosenthal, a pupil in violin of Jules Boucherit at the Paris Conservatory, made his debut as a composer in 1923 with his Sonatine for Two Violins and Piano. The piece came to the attention of Maurice Ravel, whose friend and "favorite disciple" he became. In 1928 he won the prize of the "Fondation americaine pour la pensée et l'art française (Foundation Florence Blumenthal)."

On Sept. 3, 1939, the first day of the war, he was mobilized as a corporal in the infantry. Later, after being awarded the Croix de Guerre, he was taken prisoner of war in Germany, not being released until March, 1941, when he returned to France. There he was hunted by the Gestapo, as a member of the French Resistance movement and of the "Comité des musiciens du front national."

Since the liberation of Paris, Rosenthal has been director and chief conductor of the "Orchestre national de la radio diffusion française," one of Europe's best known orchestras. As head of this organization, he brought before French audiences many new works, domestic and foreign, in addition to reviving unfamiliar ones by old masters.

Mr. Rosenthal has composed a large number of works in all forms, and the list shows such representative ones as *Rayons de soieries,* an *opéra bouffe; La Poule noire,* a musical comedy; *Un Baiser pour rien,* a ballet; a Serenade for Orchestra; the orchestral suite *Les Petits métiers;* the symphonic suite *Jeanne d'Arc;* the oratorio *St. Francis of Assisi;* the *Cantate pour le temps de la nativité;* the string quartet *Les Soirées du petit Juas;* the six prayers for four voices, string orchestra and trumpet solo entitled *La Pietà d'Avignon*—all these and many others, in addition to the present composition and numerous songs and piano pieces.

Other American premieres of works by Manuel Rosenthal comprise *Les Petits métiers*—Vladimir Golschmann and the St. Louis Symphony, Mar. 6, 1936; *Jeanne d'Arc; Musique de table*—Artur Rodzinski and the Philharmonic-Symphony, Oct. 10, 1946; and *St. Francis of Assisi*—Eugene Ormandy and the Philadelphia Orchestra, Carnegie Hall, Oct. 29, 1946.

R. C. B.

Gioacchino Rossini

BORN: PESARO, ITALY, FEB. 29, 1792. DIED: PASSY, NEAR PARIS, NOV. 13, 1868.

*At the age of thirty-seven Rossini had written thirty-seven operas,
and thirty-four of these had been produced within the space of
fourteen years—not a bad record for a man who was regarded as
constitutionally one of the laziest of mankind.*—ERNEST NEWMAN.

Overture to "The Barber of Seville," Opera Buffa in Two Acts

THIS OVERTURE was written originally not for *The Barber of Seville,* but for
an earlier opera of Rossini's, *Aurelian in Palmyra* (1813). It was later transferred to his *Elizabeth, Queen of England* and, finally, made its way to the
position it occupies now—one and indissoluble with *The Barber of Seville.* The
original *Barber* overture, a piece based, it is said, on Spanish themes, was lost,
hence, the shifts and shuffles.

Observers have remarked on the complete kinship between the present work
and the opera it has so long prefaced. They have marveled that it is so much
closer to the mercurial Figaro than to the subjects or dramatic circumstances
advanced in *Aurelian* and "his splendid foe Zenobia." In this respect the situation has been likened to the curious and, perhaps, psychic transference cited by
George Moore, who maintained that the character Bunthorne, in *Patience,* was
meant by Gilbert to be a parody of Oscar Wilde, yet what he did do was "draw
William Butler Yeats from the womb of time."

The most enduring, most popular, and—considered in some quarters—the
master work of Gioacchino Rossini, *The Barber of Seville* was first performed
at the Teatro di Torre Argentina, Rome, on Feb. 20, 1816. Yet, despite a cast
that held such reputedly brilliant singing actors as Manuel Garcia (Almaviva),
Luigi Zamboni (Figaro), and Geltrude Giorgi-Righetti (Rosina), it was, to say
the least, not a success. Chief of the criticisms hurled at Rossini was the fact that
he had dared to compose an opera on the subject utilized by the revered
Paisiello some twelve years before Rossini was born. Further, he had consented
to Garcia's singing a serenade of his own, accompanying himself on the guitar.
This matter found little favor with the audience, in addition to which a string
on the guitar broke, bringing down a torrent of laughs. There were other
expressions of derision when a cat, as composed as you please, walked across the
stage during a tense vocal moment. These and more contretemps were certainly
not beneficial either to Rossini or his opera.

On the following evening, however, the work was received with a respectful silence, excepting applause and other evidences of appreciation at proper intervals. The third performance was an unqualified success.

Rossini's *Barber of Seville* was the first opera to be produced in Italian in this country, at New York's Park Theater, Nov. 29, 1825. The same Manuel Garcia, heading the company, again sang the Almaviva, and the occasion was truly a Garcia family affair. Mme. Garcia was the duenna Berta; the son Manuel, Jr., the Figaro, and the daughter—later to become the celebrated Maria Malibran— took on the duties of Rosina.

The role of Rosina, incidentally, was originally written for contralto, although it has now found what seems to be a permanent abode in the hearts—and vocal cords—of sopranos.

The Overture is itself a masterpiece of imagination and workmanship. None of its themes may be found in the opera, since—as we have seen—it was not composed expressly for it. Yet its light and bubbling gaiety, the sprightly and sometimes ironic charm of the material, the music's general (and accidental!) resemblance to the ideal of Figaro are wholly expressive of what transpires in the entire work, both musically and dramatically.

R. C. B.

Overture to "L'Italiana in Algeri" ("The Italian Woman in Algiers")

AT TWENTY-ONE Rossini was the most talked of composer in Italy. A serious opera *Tancredi* followed in two months by a comic opera *L'Italiana in Algeri* spread his fame far beyond the confines of Venice, where both were produced. Just as the Venetians, tiring of the solemn *opere serie* of other writers, flocked to Rossini's melodrama, so they packed the Teatro San Benedetto to hear the gay and rippling comedy about a harem mix-up on the Barbary Coast. Noted foreign tourists like Stendahl wrote reams about *L'Italiana's* popularity. "Never has a public enjoyed a spectacle more harmonious with its character," said the French novelist. Not long after its premiere in 1813, *L'Italiana* was being simultaneously staged in Brescia, Verona, Venice, Vicenza, and Treviso.

Along with Rossini's fame as composer grew his repute as wit and gallant. Social Italy buzzed with stories of his latest conquests. His *mots*—Rossini was always a nimble pundit—were already making the rounds. Like Byron, after publishing two cantos of *Childe Harold* in 1812, the Italian could truly boast: "I woke up one morning and found myself famous." The parallel did not stop there. Rossini, free, handsome, and twenty-one, was fast becoming the Don Juan of Italy, and he was four years the English lord's junior. It is said the aria "Di tanti palpiti" from *Tancredi* proved so popular with the Venetians that a court edict was issued to stop people from humming and whistling it publicly morning, noon, and night. For a change, the Venetian public stopped eating cakes and ices during the recitatives. Rossini's operas claimed undivided attention. To young Rossini, therefore, goes the credit of having reformed the audience as well as *opera buffa* and *opera seria*. In the serious vein, *Tancredi* was the forerunner of Rossini's *Otello* and *Semiramide,* while *L'Italiana* began a series of comedies capped by *Cenerentola* and that gem of gems, *The Barber of Seville.*

As might be guessed, the plot of *L'Italiana in Algeri* shows little resembling Italy or Algiers. Its pseudo-Oriental intrigue suggests Mozart's *Escape from the Seraglio.* Basically it derives from the legend of Roxelana, the favorite slave of Solomon II. Anelli's libretto had already been used by Luigi Mosca in an opera produced in Milan in 1808. Still another precursor of Rossini, Cimarosa, had begun the operatic cycle of wandering Italian women in 1779 with a work entitled *L'Italiana in Londra.*

The heroine of *L'Italiana in Algeri* is a young Italian girl named Isabella. Her sweetheart Lindoro has fallen into the hands of Mustafa, the Bey of Algiers. The Bey, wearied of Elvira, his favorite wife, plans to marry her off to Lindoro, now a slave. Elvira rages, and Lindoro pines for Isabella. Conveniently, Isabella is shipwrecked along the Barbary Coast and brought before Mustafa, who promptly appoints her Elvira's successor. Lindoro and Isabella of course recognize one another. They plot to escape with the help of the ex-favorite. Isabella is ordered to the Bey's chambers. Before going, she and Elvira arrange to have several accomplices concealed in various parts of the room. The Bey enters and is speedily "hazed" by the conspirators. Elvira and Isabella explain they are members of a secret organization, the "Papatacci," who believe in gluttony and riotous living. Naturally the Bey wants to belong, too. So the wily ladies "initiate" him in a series of mock ceremonies, including some weighty banqueting. As the Bey grumbles in discomfort, Lindoro and Isabella make their escape. Mustafa, grown wise and magnanimous, takes back Elvira.

Though the main note of *L'Italiana in Algeri* is frank and lively gaiety, there are at least two striking instances of a suaver mood, the duet "Se inclinassi a prender moglie" and the tender cavatina "Languir per una bella." The trio "Papatacci" is a fine sample of Italian buffoonery; and for fetching verve the ensemble "Va sossopra il mio cervello" ranks with Rossini's best comic sallies. Rossinian elegance and bubbling comedy blend in the overture, which is in the style of a symphonic allegro: an introductory andante, 3/4, followed by the main section, Allegro, 4/4; then a development section and reprise, reinforced by two themes. Rossini's flair for sweeping crescendos shows itself twice, in the middle section and in the finale. One agrees, however, with Francis Toye, who said of the overture that he felt loath "to dissect even momentarily such a delightful butterfly."

L'Italiana in Algeri was first performed in America on Nov. 5, 1832, at New York's Richmond Hill Theater, once the home of Aaron Burr. There is a record of the overture having been played even earlier, at a concert of the New York Sacred Music Society, on Feb. 21, 1829. The Metropolitan Opera House first staged the opera on Dec. 5, 1919. In the cast were Gabriela Besanzoni (Isabella), Marie Sundelius (Elvira), Charles Hackett, (Lindoro), Giuseppe de Luca (Taddeo), and Adamo Didur (the Bey). There were four performances in all that season and none since. The late Conchita Supervia appeared in subsequent stagings of *L'Italiana* in London and Paris.

Coincidentally, the opera was first performed anywhere on the day of Wagner's birth, May 22, 1813, and Venice, the scene of the premiere, was also the place of Wagner's death.

L. B.

Overture to "Semiramide," Melodramma tragico in Two Acts

QUEEN SEMIRAMIS reigned over Assyria and Babylonia about 800 B.C. Her real name, according to Professor Lehmann-Haupt, a recent apologist of the royal murderess, was Sammurpamat. In either case, she was a byword in history, another name for perfidy and evil enchantment, till the good professor set about rehabilitating her as an able ruler.

Few historical figures have inspired as many plays and operas as the Assyrian regicide. At least thirty-five full-length operas have sung her violent story. Of the plays, Voltaire's tragedy *Semiramis* (1748) is probably the most famous. At any rate, Gaetano Rossi used it as a source book in preparing the libretto for Rossini's opera.

In the opera, Semiramis, having slain her husband King Ninus with the help of her lover Prince Assurus, now occupies the throne. But for her conscience, all goes well until the warrior chieftain Arsaces arrives. Now Arsaces is really the queen's son, but neither of them knows it. When Arsaces presents himself to be decorated for his victories, Semiramis promptly falls in love with him. Arsaces, however, is in love with Azema. In the midst of the victory celebration the tomb of the slain king opens. As the court looks on in horror, the ghost of Ninus stalks through the palace. Solemnly he declares that Arsaces will be king. Mother and son quickly grasp the king's meaning. But their joy is short-lived. Prince Assurus aims a dagger thrust at Arsaces, but kills Semiramis instead. Arsaces, in turn, slays the Prince. The ghost's prophecy is fulfilled, and Azema becomes the new king's bride.

Radiciotti, author of the monumental three-volume study of the composer, has adjudged the *Semiramide* Overture the finest Rossini wrote in Italy. "Like the opera to which it is prefixed," he says, "it dazzles with its trills, its variations, its fioriture, and the incredible flexibility of its intertwining sonorities." Francis Toye—Radiciotti's British counterpart—speaks of the overture as "a splendid composition alike as regards thematic material, form, treatment, and scoring."

The overture is in the key of D major. A short Allegro vivace (6/8), which starts pianissimo and ends fortissimo, leads to an Andantino (6/8) which enshrines the opera's most famous melody in a passage for four horns. In the first act of the opera this theme is woven into the quintet of the oath. There the voice of Semiramis is heard in an obbligato of roulades once compared to the "flowers adorning a solemn altar." The Andantino section leads in turn to an Allegro (4/4), which soon gathers momentum for one of the most stirring crescendos in music. The late Pitts Sanborn likened its flashing sweep to "an onrushing river beneath an Asiatic sun." The main theme of this passage returns in Act II in the orchestral prelude to the male chorus "Un traditor con empio ardir." Writing a month after the premiere of the opera, Prividali discerned in this theme a marked similarity to the German folk song "Freut euch des Lebens." In the first eight measures, he pointed out, "there is no other difference than one of tempo: that of the song being sextuple, that of the chorus triple."

Semiramide was the last opera Rossini wrote for the Italian stage. Radiciotti, incidentally, exploded the theory that the premiere at the Teatro Fenice on Feb. 3, 1823, was greeted by the Venetians with cold disdain, if not worse. It now seems that the overture and Act II were quite cordially received. Act I was less fortunate, and no wonder! It lasted two hours and a half! Rossini later made cuts, and after the third performance the Venetian papers could report "the unanimous approval of the numerous listeners from beginning to end."

Apparently the initial presentation of *Semiramide* in the United States took place at New Orleans on May 1, 1837. The New York premiere occurred at Palmo's Opera House on Jan. 3, 1845. The most recent performances in this country were given at the Metropolitan Opera House, New York, and elsewhere in 1894 and 1895, with Nellie Melba as Semiramis, Sofia Scalchi as Arsaces, and Edouard de Reszké as Assurus.

Pitts Sanborn, an ardent American Rossinian, wrote as follows:

In the first cast of *Semiramide* Rossini's wife, Isabella Colbran, sang the title role. Arsaces, composed not for a man but for a deep contralto, was assigned to Signora Mariani, her basso husband being the Assurus. The tenor part of Idrenus (in most subsequent performances reduced to comprimario rank through the omission of his two arias) went to the Scottish tenor John Sinclair, who had had lessons and good counsel from Rossini at Naples in 1821.

The extreme floridity of the solo parts has been largely responsible for the desuetude of *Semiramide* in a period when vocal virtuosity has been on the decline. However, there were rumors of an impending revival of *Semiramide* at the Metropolitan when Tullio Serafin was chief Italian conductor there. Rosa Ponselle was spoken of for Semiramis and Ezio Pinza for Assurus, but the difficulty of deciding on an Arsaces proved effectively discouraging.

L. B.

Overture to the Opera "William Tell"

THE LAST opera Rossini composed was *William Tell*. He was thirty-seven when he completed it, and he had written, up to that time, thirty-seven operas. Though he lived to be seventy-six, Rossini did not again put pen to an opera, although in the thirty-nine years remaining to him he did compose the *Stabat Mater* and the *Messe Solennelle,* together with a trifling handful of vocal and piano pieces.

Much has been said about Rossini's change of heart. Some maintain that he feared Meyerbeer's growing powers, others that he had "written himself out," and Chorley makes the suggestion that Rossini's viewpoint may have taken a sadistic turn in a desire to keep the world waiting breathlessly—and unavailingly—for another opera to spring forth from him.

It happens that just prior to *William Tell,* a new form of opera was taking hold. The mythological librettos had had their day, and now the public looked toward more realistic ones. Rossini, keenly aware of the "shape of things to come" and mindful of the success attained recently by Auber's *Masaniello,* with its theme of Neapolitan revolt against Spanish oppression, sought a subject of contemporary interest, something on a larger, more universal scale than he had heretofore employed.

Schiller's German play *Wilhelm Tell* seemed ideal, since it offered, as timely bait, a people's conflict against tyranny, besides many excellent theater potentials. The play had arrived in Paris in a translation, and it had caused a good deal of talk. Rossini, then musical director of the Théâtre Italien, decided on *William Tell,* and he confided his choice to a minor dramatist, one M. de Jouy, who had enjoyed some success with the librettos he devised for several Spontini operas.

Jouy, a complete egotist, handed in a poem no less than 700 verses long, and this without so much as a "by your leave." But just as promptly as he turned in his faulty chef-d'oeuvre, so promptly did Rossini find the text next to be impossible. He called in a script doctor in the person of a M. Bis. What his literary contribution amounted to exactly history does not say, though he is credited with most of the second—and best—act. For the rest, what with

Rossini's insistence on having the verses comply with his musical plan and his general worrying tactics, plus the entrance of another person, Armand Marrast, into textual matters, it was finally put into fairly presentable shape, though as we look on such things today, it is certainly one of the poorest jobs in libretto annals.

Anyway, *William Tell,* the first opera Rossini wrote exclusively for the French stage, was given its premiere at the Opéra on Aug. 3, 1829. In spite of a considerable success, it gradually lost ground in public esteem. Astute critics all agreed on its manifold excellences, sounding a unanimous opinion as to its musical greatness. It was positively Rossini's magnum opus, they said, but even so it failed to make the grade with the public.

A rather curious side light to all this is Hector Berlioz' change of attitude regarding *William Tell.* Eighteen days after its premiere he could write to his friend Humbert Ferrand, *"William Tell?* I think all the newspapers are distinctly mad: it is a work that has some beautiful pieces, which is not absurdly written, where there is no crescendo and a little less bass drum; that's all. For the rest, not a bit of real sentiment, always art, habit, workmanship, handling of the public."

Five years later came the turnabout. An article by him published in the *Revue musicale* said, among other rhapsodic things:

Rossini, tired of hearing fault forever found with his works in respect of dramatic expression and still more tired perhaps of the blind admiration of fanatical partisans, employed a very simple method to silence the one and get rid of the others: that was to write a score seriously thought out, pondered at leisure, and conscientiously executed from one end to the other in accordance with the conditions demanded at all times by good sense and taste. He wrote *William Tell.*

This beautiful work must therefore be considered as the application of the author's new theories, as the awakening of greater and nobler faculties, the development of which had been rendered impossible by the requirements of the sensual people for whom he had written hitherto.

The Overture to *William Tell* has been called "a complete symphonic poem in miniature." Its introduction opens with the cellos and basses depicting, supposedly, sunrise in the mountains. A second section is devoted to the gathering fury of an Alpine storm, and, as it subsides, an Andante comes through with the shepherds' thanksgiving, the English horn intoning the *ranz des vaches.* Soon a trumpet announces the approach of Swiss soldiers, who go on the march, following which a coda, brilliant and rapid, brings the music to its close.

R. C. B.

Albert Roussel

BORN: TURCOING, FRANCE, APR. 5, 1869. DIED: ROYAN (NEAR BORDEAUX), AUG. 23, 1937.

*The whole world has recognized the value of Roussel's art, an art essentially youthful, which retains all the sympathies of the young because his spirit and heart remained perpetually open to everything new. In him there was not a trace of conservatism. He renewed himself incessantly and followed with a generous sympathy the most audacious attempts of his juniors.—*PAUL LANDORMY.

Symphony in G minor, No. 3, Op. 42

I. Allegro vivo. II. Adagio. III. Vivace. IV. Allegro con spirito.

SOMETHING OF a standard-bearer of the reaction against Debussyism, Roussel was regarded both as antiromantic and anti-impressionist in his outlook. Delicacy, discretion, balance were key words in his esthetic vocabulary. There were finesse, subtlety, and serenity in his music, placing it in the long line of French classicism. "Like that extraordinary mandarin face of his," wrote Lazare Saminsky, "it makes us dream of the soberly delicate lines of early Chinese painting and the taciturn soul of the Mongol."

To G. Jean-Aubry, Roussel's music was the perfect mirror of the man's "love of life without loudness, restrained but lively ardor, exquisite sense of pleasure, a thousand refinements without affectation, and, beneath this delicacy and this smiling nature, a gentle and firm power, with occasional melancholy."

Together with music, literature and nature dominated the thoughts and feelings of this professor of counterpoint at the Paris Schola Cantorum. Created in his own image, his music seems far from the madding crowd. Yet this same retired esthete stepped down from his tower of ivory to write a symphonic poem based on Tolstoy's "Resurrection," which by no stretch of the imagination can be termed a woodland idyl.

"Roussel realized himself without stir," said Jean-Aubry, "without attempting to attract anyone's curiosity, relying solely on his works." To the French writer this music brought dreams of ponds reflecting "the beauty of the trees and a glimpse of the sky," ponds, moreover, which "from the bosom of their meditative beauty bring forth the unsullied calices of water lilies to germinate slowly and blossom upon their surface like a durable ecstasy."

As a finishing touch to his pastoral portrait, Jean-Aubry wrote of his friend: "He tarries, reads a poem, listens to a spring, observes a smiling nymph, sings of his dreams, and, like a dream, plunges into the heart of the forest." It is not surprising to learn that to this Gallic Endymion of the woods "the disputes of theorists did not seem desirable."

As part of its fiftieth anniversary observance the Boston Symphony invited Roussel over in the autumn of 1930. The composer responded not only with his presence, but with a G minor Symphony which he had completed in Paris on Mar. 29 of that year. On Oct. 23, Serge Koussevitzky led the world premiere in Symphony Hall, Boston. Conforming to principles expounded by César Franck and Vincent d'Indy, whom Roussel revered as masters, the symphony revolves in cyclic form around a five-note theme in three of the four movements. Though the opening Allegro is broadly in sonata form, the Adagio follows unusual patterns of form. The Vivace is in the nature of a "valse scherzo" and the finale a rondo, ending in a majestically broad statement of the nuclear theme of the Symphony.

L. B.

"Bacchus et Ariane," Ballet Suite No. 2, Op. 43

CHARLES MUENCH conducted the Second Suite from Roussel's ballet, *Bacchus et Ariane* in Boston at a concert of the Boston Symphony Orchestra on Dec. 27, 1946. Ten years before, on Nov. 26, 1936, he had directed the concert premiere of this music on a program of the Société Philharmonique de Paris. The Suite was published in 1932 with a dedication to Hélène Tony-Jourdan. A year before that, in May, 1931, the two-act ballet from which the concert suite was drawn had been performed at the Paris Opéra with choreography by Abel Hermant and a cast headed by Serge Lifar, Leonide Massine, and Spessitzewa. Alfred Cortot conducted. Writing of that performance in *The New York Times* of June 14, 1931, Henry Prunières declared that "the ballet gripped us with the opening measures and did not cease to hold us until the very end." The music, M. Prunières found "spiritual and forceful," adding that a "characteristic French verve filled every moment of the two acts, never allowing the auditor to be bored for even a single instant." According to the French critic and musicologist, the infinite variety of rhythm could best be described as exhibiting "the resiliency of elastic springs."

Printed in the score of Suite No. 2, which is drawn from the second act of the ballet, is the following description, quoted from the Boston Symphony program note of John N. Burk:

Introduction (Andante). Awakening of Ariane. She looks around her surprised. She rises and runs about looking for Thésée and his companions. She realizes that she has been abandoned. She climbs with difficulty to the top of a rock. She is about to throw herself into the stream. She falls into the arms of Bacchus, who has appeared from behind the boulders. Bacchus resumes with the awakened Ariane the dance of her dreaming. Bacchus dances alone (Allegro; Andante; Andantino) the

Dionysiac spell. A group marches past (Allegro deciso). A faun and a Bacchante present to Ariane the golden cup into which a cluster of grapes has been pressed. Dance of Ariane (Andante). Dance of Ariane and Bacchus (Moderato e pesante). Bacchanale (Allegro brilliante).

In Greek mythology, Ariadne was the daughter of King Minos of Crete. Theseus was the son of King Aegeus of Athens. The two met when the Greek hero came to Crete to slay the frightful monster, the Minotaur, which claimed periodic human sacrifice from the Athenians. Ariadne gave Theseus a thread which he used to find his way out of the labyrinth where the Minotaur lived. Later Theseus and Ariadne fled to the island of Naxos, and it was there that the Greek hero abandoned her. According to legend, Theseus conquered the Amazons and married their warrior queen. As for the Greek god of wine, he is early identified with Dionysus, though the Romans knew him best as Bacchus.

L. B.

Anton Rubinstein

BORN: WECHWOTYNEZ, NEAR JASSY, RUSSIA, NOV. 28, 1829. DIED: PETERHOF, NOV. 20, 1894.

> *Can I compare myself to him? He is the first pianist of our time.*
> *In Rubinstein great virtuosity is united with great talent for compo-*
> *sition, and the first carries the second. I shall never in my life achieve*
> *a tenth of what Rubinstein has achieved, because he begins by being*
> *the greatest virtuoso of our time.*—TSCHAIKOWSKY.

Concerto for Piano and Orchestra in G major, No. 3, Op. 45

I. Moderato assai. II. Moderato. III. Allegro non troppo.

WHEN Adele Aus der Ohe played the solo part of this Concerto at a concert of the Philharmonic Society on Nov. 16, 1889, Arthur Mees, then program annotator for the Society, included this amusing commentary in his notes:

Rubinstein, while in America, was playing this Concerto at an orchestral rehearsal during which the close of the last movement gave considerable trouble. In explanation of its unusual difficulty, Rubinstein gave the following account as to the purport of the composition: "In the first movement, the piano repeatedly requests admittance into the temple of the orchestra. The orchestra takes the matter into consideration and decides to test the capabilities of the piano. After frequent consultations and trials, the orchestra concludes that the piano is not worthy to enter into its sanctuary. In the second movement, the piano bemoans its fate, but soon recovers its equanimity and asserts its dignity. The beginning of the last movement represents the piano as repeating its requests to be admitted. Again consultations are held, during which single instruments express their opinions. The decision of the orchestra is again adverse to the appeals of the piano. Now the piano loses its temper and challenges the orchestra to imitate what the piano can do, and in the tumult of this attempt the Concerto closes."

The first movement of the Concerto (Moderato assai, G major, 6/8) opens with a melodic subject for violins, accompanied by a figure in the violas. At the fifth measure the piano makes its entrance with a cadenza, following which the opening subject is taken up by the wood winds. The piano plays still another cadenza, and again the first subject is heard in the orchestra. The piano now brings out the subject, and this is repeated with orchestral accompaniment. Soon a clarinet announces a new theme (con espressione), which presently is taken up by the piano alone in the key of the dominant. Out of one of the phrases in this second subject evolves a melody which obtains

582

development in the orchestra, while the solo instrument runs arabesques around it.

The second movement (Moderato, 6/4) begins with a phrase for muted strings and wood winds, whereupon the piano enters upon a sort of monologue in the key of E minor, the strings making occasional and brief comments. The tempo becomes Adagio, the key changes to E major, the time to 12/8, and the piano introduces the section with an up-and-down melody, which first increases in ardor, then diminishes when the original tempo of the movement returns. Here the first subject is assigned to the orchestra, while the piano—reversing the process—makes occasional and brief comments. The movement closes with the reappearance of the Adagio melody.

The third movement (Allegro non troppo, 2/4) is in binary form, its two subjects following the usual procedure of entrance and recurrence. However, the section contains also material from the previous movements. The Concerto closes with a lively coda (Prestissimo).

R. C. B.

Charles Camille Saint-Saëns

BORN: PARIS, OCT. 9, 1835. DIED: ALGIERS, DEC. 16, 1921.

Without consideration of his many admirable compositions, one should bear this in mind: in the face of difficulties, discouragement, misunderstanding, sneers, he worked steadily from his youth up, and always to the best of his ability, for righteousness in absolute music; he endeavored to introduce into French music thoughtfulness and sincerity for the advantage and the glory of the country that he dearly loved.—PHILIP HALE.

Symphony in C minor, No. 3, Op. 78

I. Adagio; Allegro moderato; Poco adagio. II. Allegro moderato; Presto; Maestoso; Allegro.

THIS SYMPHONY was composed on commission from the Philharmonic Society of London for the concerts of its seventy-third season. Begun early in 1886, it was soon completed, and it obtained its first performance in St. James' Hall, London, on May 19, of that year. The occasion was indeed a gala one for Saint-Saëns; he not only conducted his own work, but he appeared as soloist in the Beethoven Piano Concerto in G major. It is worth mentioning the remainder of the program at that concert, which was conducted, except for the Saint-Saëns Symphony, by Sir Arthur Sullivan—obviously in one of his less satiric moods. The list contained Haydn's E flat Symphony (No. 8 of the *Salomon* series), Mozart's *Quando Miro,* delivered by Antoinette Sterling; the song "Couplets du Mysoli" from Felicien David's *La Perle du Brésil,* sung by Agnes Larkcom; and the Prelude to Wagner's *Die Meistersinger.*

The usual pro and con took place concerning the merits of the work. Most of the professional critics, however, commended it as a piece of music, fuming, at the same time, against the composer's departure from established ideas of construction. One of them wrote, "Those advanced in the new school as far as M. Saint-Saëns professes to be should invent new titles for their works. As we have said, there is a great deal to admire in this glowing orchestral rhapsody, but we distinctly decline to term it a 'symphony'"—which about explains the general to-do.

The C minor Symphony was given its first hearing in France at a Conservatoire concert, Paris, on Jan. 9, 1887. (Charles Gounod, who was present, is alleged to have said to a friend, as he pointed to Saint-Saëns, "There is the

French Beethoven.") The Philharmonic Society of New York played it for the first time in this country on Feb. 19, 1887, under the direction of Theodore Thomas.

Philip Hale has said:

Saint-Saëns's Symphony in C minor has the finest and most characteristic qualities of the best French music: logical construction, lucidity, frankness, euphony. The workmanship is masterly. There is no hesitation. The composer knew exactly what he wanted and how to express himself. A few of the themes, that when first exposed might seem to some insignificant, assume importance and even grandeur in the development. The chief theme of the adagio, the theme for strings, is very French in its sustained suavity, in a gentle, emotional quality that never loses elegance, and the preparation for the entrance of this adagio is worthy of the greatest masters.

Because he felt it was high time for the symphonic form to take cognizance of advancement in instrumentation, Saint-Saëns scored his composition for three flutes, two oboes, English horn, two clarinets, bass clarinet, two bassoons, double bassoon, four horns, three trumpets, three trombones, tuba, three kettle-drums, organ, piano ("now for two hands, now for four"), triangle, a pair of cymbals, bass drum, and strings.

The composer, eminently aware that much might be made of the piece's nonconformance with stricter precepts, prepared an analysis of it for the world premiere. In that he pointed out that the Symphony

is divided into two parts, after the manner of Saint-Saëns's Fourth Concerto for Piano and Orchestra and Sonata for Piano and Violin. Nevertheless, it includes practically the traditional four movements: the first, checked in development, serves as an introduction to the adagio, and the scherzo (presto) is connected, after the same manner, with the finale. The composer has thus sought to shun in a certain measure the interminable repetitions which are more and more disappearing from instrumental music.

The score of the C minor Symphony carries the inscription, "To the memory of Franz Liszt." The Abbé died a good two months after the premiere, so that those observers who read into certain pages the grief of Saint-Saëns at the passing of his celebrated friend were entirely in the wrong. Besides, the program at the introductory performance stated simply that the Symphony was composed expressly for the Philharmonic Society of London, implying, of course, dedication.

R. C. B.

Concerto for Piano and Orchestra in G minor, No. 2, Op. 22

I. Andante sostenuto. II. Allegretto scherzando. III. Presto.

A BRILLIANT TECHNICIAN at the keyboard, Saint-Saëns was the soloist in the premieres of all five of his piano concertos. We have the testimony of qualified observers like Anton Rubinstein, Wagner, Isidor Philipp, and Romain Rolland of his phenomenal fluency and mastery of style. He began to study the piano before he was three. At five he played a Grétry opera from score. At ten he astonished a gathering of musicians in Paris with precocious feats of memory and technique. Wagner recalls being "simply amazed" in 1860 at Saint-Saëns's "skill and talent" in playing lengthy sections of *Tristan und Isolde* at the piano from memory. Philipp, who studied with him, spoke of the unique blend of *esprit*, rhythm, naturalness, and vitality in his master's playing. "Pure, chiseled pianistic marvels," he called Saint-Saëns's readings, whether they were of Mozart or Liszt.

It was Anton Rubinstein, the great Russian pianist and composer, who prompted the writing of Saint-Saëns's G minor Concerto in April, 1868. Rubinstein, who was planning to conduct a concert at the Salle Pleyel, in Paris, invited the French composer to take part in it. The Salle was booked up for three weeks. There was still time for a fast writer to meet the deadline.

"Very well," said Saint-Saëns, "I will write a concerto for the occasion." Actually, it took him seventeen days to complete the work. Of course, ideas for a second piano concerto had already been buzzing in his head. Rubinstein's invitation helped crystallize them.

The new Concerto was premiered at the Salle Pleyel on May 13, 1868, with Rubinstein conducting, and the composer appearing as soloist. The following year Saint-Saëns sent the G minor Concerto to Liszt for criticism and advice. In July, 1869, the celebrated virtuoso's reply arrived. The reaction was favorable, with some minor reservations about technic and development. Liszt wrote from Rome:

The form of it is new and very happy. The interest of the three portions goes on increasing, and you take into just account the effect of the pianist without sacrificing anything of the ideas of the composer, which is an essential rule in this class of work. At the very outset the prelude on the pedal G is striking and imposing; after a very happy inspiration you do wisely to reproduce it at the end of the first movement and to accompany it this time with some chords.

Among the things which particularly please me I note: The chromatic progression (last line of the prelude) and that which alternates between the piano and orchestra (from the last measure of page 5—repeated then by the piano alone, page 15); the arrangement of thirds and sixths in thirty-second notes, charmingly sonorous, pages

8 and 9, which opens superbly on the entry off the subject fortissimo; the piquant rhythm of the second subject of the Allegro scherzando, page 25.

Possibly this would have gained somewhat by more combination and development, either of the principal subject or of some secondary subject . . . I should like there to be some incidence and polyphonic entanglement, as the German Polyphemuses say. Pardon me this detailed remark, dear Monsieur Saint-Saëns, which I venture to make only while assuring you in all sincerity that the totality of your work pleases me singularly.

Liszt went on to say that he had twice played the Concerto to Sgambati, "of whom Planté will speak to you as an artist above the common run, and even more than ordinarily *distingué.*" Sgambati apparently responded warmly to the Concerto, for Liszt announced that the Roman pianist would play it the following winter. "It ought to meet with success in every country," he added.

The Concerto was first played in America at a concert of the Harvard Musical Association in Boston on Feb. 3, 1876.

L. B.

Concerto for Piano and Orchestra in C minor, No. 4, Op. 44

I. Allegro moderato. II. Andante. III. Allegro vivace; allegro.

THE C minor Concerto was played for the first time on Oct. 31, 1875, at a Châtelet concert in Paris, the performance being from manuscript. Saint-Saëns published the work two years later with a dedication to Anton Door, the Viennese pianist and pedagogue who toured extensively for many years before teaching piano at the Imperial Institute in Moscow and the Vienna Conservatory. The score of the C minor Concerto calls for two flutes, two oboes, two clarinets, two bassoons, two horns, two trumpets, three trombones, kettledrums, and strings, besides the solo piano.

Like Saint-Saëns's Third Symphony (and the Sonata for Piano and Violin as well), the C minor Concerto falls into two broad divisions, each consisting of two continuous movements. It was Charles Malherbe who first pointed out that, while the four movements of the classical symphony are present—Allegro moderato, Andante, Allegro vivace, Allegro—they lead not to four but two conclusions. To the noted French editor and scholar this represented "an economy of formulas more in accordance with the musical habits of our time." Others have found fault with both the Third Symphony and the C minor Concerto for this very "economy of formulas," condemning both works as departures from classical form. To quote Malherbe further:

The themes are distinct, peculiar to each movement, but they intermingle at times in the developments, and the return establishes a sort of natural bond between the different portions of the work. Thus the Andante in 4/4 of the first section is transformed to triple time in the second, and the first Allegro reappears with a different measure in the Finale.

The work begins with a sort of free prelude (Allegro moderato, C minor, 4/4). A theme of eight measures is given out alternately by the orchestra and the pianoforte; it is treated now contrapuntally, now in free preluding fashion, somewhat after the manner of a cadenza. This species of introduction leads to the main body of the movement, an Andante in A flat major, 4/4. There are soft and mysterious harmonies for orchestra with flowing arpeggios for the pianoforte. The chief theme, a simple melody, is developed at some length and enriched with varied ornamental work.

The second movement (Allegro vivace, C minor, 2/4, 6/8) begins with a lively scherzando. The theme of the prelude to the first movement reappears in a faster tempo. There is a short Andante (C minor, 4/4) with reminiscences of the first movement. This leads to the finale (Allegro, C major, 3/4). A theme that has the character of a folk song is developed energetically and brilliantly somewhat after the manner of the rondo.

L. B.

Concerto for Violin and Orchestra in B minor, No. 3, Op. 61

I. Allegro non troppo. II. Andantino quasi allegretto. III. Molto moderato e maestoso; Allegro non troppo.

Of Saint-Saëns's three violin concertos, the third is the most liked and most played. Violinists favor it because it offers wide scope for varied technical display besides abounding in melodic and poetic charm. The same qualities probably explain its abiding appeal to concertgoers. In popularity the B minor holds almost the same position in relation to the other two violin concertos that Saint-Saëns's Second Piano Concerto holds in relation to the other four concertos in that form. In his book on Saint-Saëns, Watson Lyle attributes this to the B minor's "perpetual aliveness." Also included among Saint-Saëns's works for violin and orchestra are the *Introduction and Rondo Capriccioso* (Op. 28), written in 1863; a *Havanaise* (Op. 83); and a *Caprice andalous* (Op. 122); besides a *Morceau de concert* (Op. 62), composed in 1880, shortly after Saint-Saëns had completed his Third Violin Concerto.

The work was introduced at a Châtelet concert in Paris on Jan. 2, 1881, with Pablo de Sarasate as soloist. Sarasate was also the soloist at the second performance on the following Feb. 20, when some of his Spanish Dance arrangements and the French premiere of Max Bruch's *Scottish Fantasy,* written especially for him, were also featured. The Concerto was published the following year with a dedication to the great Spanish violinist. Lalo composed his first violin concerto and the *Symphonie Espagnole* for Sarasate; Bruch his second concerto, as well as the *Scottish Fantasy;* and A. C. Mackenzie the *Pibroch Suite.*

The Concerto inspired some highly imaginative writing among students of Saint-Saëns. Otto Neitzel, for example, in his biography of 1899, speaks of the first and third movements as characterized by "somber determination," which in the finale rises to "intensified passion." Over the slow movement "the spring sun smiles." And in the finale "a hymn serves as an appeasing episode in the stormy play of passion," though "warring strings try to drive it away."

To the English biographer Lyle, the *Andantino quasi allegretto,* which of course is a barcarolle, was "like the echo of a song wafted across the expanse of a peaceful lake from a little boat drifting idly, with its freight of youth, toward the setting sun." Lyle found the movement "languorous in its happiness." As for the thirteen-bar cadenza of broken chords sounded in harmonics, it gave him a clear picture of a "most gradual evaporation of sound as the little boat drifts out of sight."

Continuing the Lyle analysis:

The third movement is full of life and virile force and the warmth of Southern skies. The solo instrument enters with a passionate throb that is like a smoldering fire, ready to burst into a fierce flame at the slightest encouragement.

Soon we have a motive that will not be denied the happiness of life and is alternately assertive and cajoling. Then victory, victory that is intoxicated with the ecstasy of reciprocated passion; victory that sweeps onward in arrogant indifference, to whatever life may still hold, because it believes it has found love.

Despite Watson Lyle's panoramic prose, the Concerto is scored quite conventionally for solo violin, two flutes (one interchangeable with piccolo), two oboes, two clarinets, two bassoons, two horns, two trumpets, three trombones, kettledrums, and strings.

Two strongly contrasting themes form the substance of the opening movement. The first, announced forte and appassionato by the solo violin, is of a vigorous and challenging character. The second, appearing in B major, is of more tranquil mood. The French biographer Georges Servières regards it as "one of the most tender melodic inspirations from Saint-Saëns's pen." Servières had heard Sarasate play the Concerto for the first time in Saint-Saëns's home and was especially struck by the Spaniard's style in differentiating the opposing themes.

In the Andantino quasi allegretto (B flat major, 6/8) the solo violin chants the languid and graceful barcarolle, with the last figure of each phrase taken up by other instruments and the oboe presently repeating the theme. The finale opens (Molto moderato e maestoso, B minor, 4/4) with a violin recitative to orchestral accompaniment. The solo voice then launches into a brisk Allegro, with support from bassoons and horns. A second theme, cantabile, is sung by the violin. A brusque third theme, in D major, also stated by the violin, appears, and after it a melody (theme No. 4) in G major of a religious suavity, given out pianissimo by muted violins and violas. In its serenely sustained mood the theme suggests Wagner's *Lohengrin* prelude. There is elaborate development before the coda, built mainly on the third theme, sets in.

L. B.

Concerto for Cello and Orchestra in A minor, Op. 33

I. Allegro non troppo. II. Allegretto con moto. III. Comme prima, un peu moins vite.

[*Played without pause*]

THIS, THE first of two cello concertos by Saint-Saëns, was composed in 1872. It was first played at a Paris Conservatory concert on Jan. 19, 1873, August Tolbecque, first cellist of the orchestra, doing the solo honors. The Concerto is dedicated to Tolbecque.

The orchestration calls for two flutes, two oboes, two clarinets, two bassoons, two horns, two trumpets, kettledrums, and strings. The work does not follow the orthodox form such as is found in the concertos of Mozart, Beethoven, Schumann, Brahms, and the others. Rather is it in one continuous movement with a principal theme running through each of what are in effect three sections.

The Concerto begins (Allegro non troppo, A minor, 2/2) with the announcement of the main theme by the solo instrument against a quivering figure in the violins and violas. The cello develops the theme, and later it is taken over by the orchestra. Following that a new subject appears through the solo cello. This is in F major, and it is given the benefit of a brief development, after which the former theme is reintroduced and developed at length by the solo instrument and the orchestra. At the conclusion of this a new theme comes through in a sort of episode (Allegro molto, F major). Soon the music glides into what might be termed a new section (Allegretto con moto, B flat major, 3/4), which is a minuet. The muted strings utter the theme and the cello ushers in still another dance theme. There is a development of this material, with the minuet going to the orchestra, the slow waltz to the solo cello. Presently the strings return to the original subject. Then the cello enters a new phase, playing runs of sixteenth notes against a forte sequence by the orchestra. There is a melody in F major, offered by the cello, while the second violins and violas supply a syncopated background. A good deal of solo passage work occurs. The first theme reappears, the tempo accelerates, and the Concerto closes in a brilliant climax.

R. C. B.

Symphonic Poem, "Danse Macabre," Op. 40

Saint-Saëns's graveyard concert holds an honorable place in the realm of symphonic spooks. Composers turn to the theme of death a-dancing recurringly, and the annals of music creep with *Danses macabres* and *Totentänze*. A Viennese ballet opera by Titl is called *Der Totentanz,* Liszt's *Totentanz* paraphrases the *Dies Irae,* and our own Charles Martin Loeffler once penned a *Carnaval des morts,* with a grisly danse finale. In short, when Death takes a holiday he goes tripping the light fantastic.

Saint-Saëns drew inspiration for his symphonic poem from a set of macabre verses bearing the same title by Henri Cazalis. In fact he first wrote music for the words, publishing the song and then discarding it as unsingable in favor of an orchestral piece. As such it was completed in 1874 and premiered at a Châtelet concert conducted by Colonne on Jan. 24, 1875, when it was promptly encored.

Cazalis's poem runs as follows:

> Zig et Zig et Zig, la Mort en cadence
> Frappant une tombe avec son talon,
> La Mort à minuit joue un air de danse
> Zig et Zig et Zig, sur son violon.
>
> Le vent d'Hiver souffle, et la nuit est sombre;
> Des gémissements sortent des tilleuls;
> Les squellettes blancs vont à travers l'ombre,
> Courant et sautant sous leurs grands linceuls.
>
> Zig et Zig et Zig, chacun se trémousse,
> On entend claquer les os des danseurs. . . .
>
> Mais psit! tout à coup on quitte la ronde,
> On se pousse, on fuit, le coq a chanté! . . .

(Zig, zig, zig, Death is striking a tomb with his heel in cadence. Death is playing a dance tune on his violin at midnight. The winter wind blows, and the night is dark. From the linden-trees come moans. White skeletons move across the shadows, running and leaping in their shrouds. Zig, zig, zig, each one gives a tremor, and the dancers' bones rattle. Hush! they suddenly leave off dancing, they jostle one another, they flee—the cock has crowed.)

The poem ends mockingly with the words *"Vive la Mort et l'Égalité"*— "Long Live Death and Equality!"

In the Symphonic Poem, Death begins to tune his fiddle after midnight strikes on the harp. With the flute taking up a theme, the weird dance gets under way in a *mouvement modéré de valse*. Death unreels a melody (Larga-mente), as the whirling grows in intensity and the xylophone rattles ·bonily. The scarcely recognizable *Dies Irae* is brought in. The themes merge as the pace quickens feverishly. The horns suddenly announce dawn. The cock crows via the oboe, and the grisly crew disbands to the vanishing strains of Death's tune.

When first heard in London, the *Danse Macabre* was greeted by one critic as "one of the many signs of the· intense and coarse realism that is entering into much of the musical composition—so-called—of the day."

L. B.

Symphonic Poem, "La Jeunesse d'Hercule" ("The Youth of Hercules"), Op. 50

THE ACTION depicted in *La Jeunesse d'Hercule* is summarized in the score:

The fable relates that Hercules on his entrance upon life saw two roads lie open before him—that of pleasure and that of virtue. Insensible to the seductions of nymphs and bacchantes, the hero chooses the paths of struggle and combats, at the end of which he catches a glimpse of the reward of immortality, through the flames of the funeral pyre.

Muted violins, against other strings and wood winds, open the symphonic poem. After a roll of kettledrums the first subject is announced by the strings, followed by a development section for strings, wood winds, and horns. The violins discourse a subsidiary theme, with wood-wind support. Flute and clarinet take up a second subject, followed by the first violins, then the harp and the horn, softly. An allegro theme for flute enters over shimmering violas and is taken up by the second violins. The first subject is back, richly worked out and mounting to a powerful tutti. Woodwinds, harp, and horns recall the second subject by way of contrast, and in the ensuing clash the first theme rises in full force, triumphantly.

L. B.

Pedro Sanjuan

BORN: SAN SEBASTIAN, SPAIN, NOV. 15, 1886.

*This music, which blends an orgy of sonorities with delirious frenzy,
accomplishes what all great music does, that is, it satisfies the experts
as much as it does the amateurs.*—ANDRÉ COEROY.

Cuban Dance Suite, "Liturgia Negra"

THE LITURGIA NEGRA (*Negro Liturgy*), described in the score as an "Afro-Cuban Suite," is divided into five parts, of which the second, "Iniciación," represents a chant accompanying the medicine-man's initiation ritual. The opening section of the *Liturgia*—entitled "Chango"—is an invocation of the deity presiding at sessions of African magic and empowered to ban evil spirits. "Babaluayé," the third part, invokes the god of resurrection and "the eternal fusion of spirit and matter." The fourth section "Canto a Oggun" is a hymn to Oggun, the god of moonbeams, in which he is made a kindred spirit of Chango by the officiating sorcerer. "Comparsa Lucumi," the final section, represents "the parade of gay and noisy chieftains (*lucumi*)" in the streets of Havana on Kings' Day in colonial times.

Mr. Sanjuan explains the origin and ceremony of the Afro-Cuban rite in a prefatory note in the score:

The slaves of the colonial period, who originally came from the west coast of Africa, continued to practice their ancient rites in Cuba, father transmitting them to son. Even today all this is preserved with the same rigors as formerly, and although gay and noisy parades of revelers are no longer seen in the streets of Havana, as on the Kings' Day in the colonial period, one can still, though not without some difficulty, be present at the festive rituals in certain districts where the real "Cabildos" of Afro-Cuban origin hold their meetings. The religious practices of the "initiated" are countless, but practically all of them include the same ancestral invocation to their deities, manifested in the form of ritual dances and magic tricks, a very complex and exotic cult.

During the Cabildo ceremonies the drumming grows in frenzied insistence. The "initiated," maddened by the ceaseless throb of sacred drums, dances on feverishly, until, possessed of the "god," he lapses into "a sort of epileptic fit" to the accompaniment of primitive chants. Mr. Sanjuan's suite is built around some of the actual chants and rhythms employed in the initiation services, though as a whole the work is a reflection of the composer's personal impressions.

"It would be difficult to define the exact source and circumstances which give rise to these chants and rhythms," Mr. Sanjuan writes. "The listener may imagine himself in any part or section of Buanabacoa or Regla in Havana, always mindful, however, of the fact that this *Liturgia Negra* is not intended as a literal note-for-note reproduction of the ritual music."

On the percussion side the score calls for Cuban tympani (resembling *caisses claires,* one larger than the other and producing hard, indefinite sounds), the Guiro, the Maracas, the Clave (consisting of two pieces of wood, one rapped against the other), and the Cencerro (resembling a cow bell without the clapper and struck with a short metal rod).

Mr. Sanjuan left his native Basque province early to study music in Madrid. He was the pupil of Perez Casas and Joaquin Turina before he served as violinist in the Madrid Symphony Orchestra (1906-1914). In 1924 he began conducting the Orquestra Sinfonica of Havana; and as founder of Havana's Philharmonic helped to give vital impetus to musical activity in his adopted country. His orchestral works include an overture *El Dragon de Fuego,* a piano concerto, and several tone poems, among them *Afrodita,* besides a large number of songs and piano pieces. His *Liturgia Negra* won the National Music Prize of Spain in 1934. The American premiere of "Iniciación" occurred at a Philharmonic-Symphony concert in the Lewisohn Stadium, New York, on June 24, 1941.

L. B.

Ernest Schelling

BORN: BELVIDERE, NEW JERSEY, JULY 26, 1876. DIED: NEW YORK CITY, DEC. 8, 1939.

The seeds he sowed in awakening a love and understanding of great music in the minds and hearts of thousands of our younger generation will in time yield a rich harvest.—HOWARD BARLOW.

"A Victory Ball": Fantasy for Orchestra

THE POEM of Alfred Noyes *A Victory Ball* was the inspiration for this composition. Ernest Schelling had been a major in the United States troops during the First World War. He had seen service in France and later, as he explained:

I had come back from Europe, still very much under the impression of the cataclysm, much troubled for the future, and was amazed to find that so few seemed to remember what the war had really meant with its sacrifice of life and youth. I wondered, when watching the seething mass of humanity at some cabaret, what our boys would think of it all, and I had a sinister vision. . . . I came across Alfred Noyes's poem, while in this mood, and was impelled to use it as the basis of an orchestral fantasy.

Alfred Noyes pulled no punches when he wrote lines like these:

> The cymbals crash and the dancers walk,
> With long black stockings and arms of chalk,
> Butterfly skirts and white breasts bare,
> And shadows of dead men watching 'em there.
>
> Shadows of dead men stand by the wall,
> Watching the fun of the Victory Ball.
> They do not reproach, because they know
> If they're forgotten, it's better so.
>
> Under the dancing feet are the graves
> Dazzled and motley, in long bright waves.
> Brushed by the palm-fronds, grapple and whirl
> Ox-eyed matron and slim white girl. . . .
>
> "What did you think we should find?" said a shade,
> "When the last shot echoed and peace was made?"
> "Christ," laughed the fleshless jaws of his friend,
> "I thought they'd be praying for worlds to mend."
>
> "Pish," said a statesman standing near,
> "I'm glad they can busy their thoughts elsewhere!

We mustn't reproach 'em. They're young, you see!"
"Ah," said the dead men, "so were we!"

Victory! Victory! On with the dance!
Back to the jungle the new beasts prance!
God! How the dead men grin by the wall,
Watching the fun at the Victory Ball.

In describing his work, the composer wrote, "I have used two Army bugle calls—the 'Call to Arms' and 'Charge,' which ominously usher in the War Vision—and at the very end of the piece I have used 'Taps.' The work is a perfectly free fantasy, with, however, a certain amount of thematic development."

Music for the ballroom is heard at the beginning of the piece, a polonaise, hints of the foxtrot, and the tango. This is followed by trumpet calls, and the music evokes a vision of the hosts of war. The brasses suddenly intone the *Dies Irae*. With that the dance begins again. It is a waltz, which soon gives way to the tempo of marching feet, as the Scotch pipers tread over the joyful proceedings. There is a resounding climax and, as the music subsides—"Taps."

Ernest Schelling, distinguished pianist, pedagogue, lecturer, and composer, began the study of music with his father, Dr. Felix Schelling. He made his debut in Philadelphia at the age of five, and at nine he became a student at the Paris Conservatory. He achieved fame as a child recitalist, making several tours of Europe. In later years he circled the globe many times in his concert travels. In New York City he is remembered not only for his eminence as pianist and composer, but also as the founder of the Philharmonic-Symphony Society's Young People's Concerts, which he conducted until his death.

Schelling's *A Victory Ball* is inscribed "To the Memory of an American Soldier." The composition has been performed frequently by the leading orchestras in this country and abroad. It may not be generally known that Schelling arranged it for the band of the late John Philip Sousa, who played it some 300 times.

R. C. B.

Arnold Schönberg

BORN: VIENNA, SEPT. 13, 1874. NOW LIVING NEAR LOS ANGELES.

It is possible, of course, that Schönberg is another Cézanne, an artist misunderstood and despised during his lifetime, only to be canonized after his death. But at present it would seem that his influence, not his work, is to cast the longer shadow.—RICHARD ANTHONY LEONARD.

"Verklärte Nacht" ("Transfigured Night"), Op. 4 (Arranged for String Orchestra)

THE PRESENT composition was written originally for a string sextet. However, the composer, aware of the work's rather wide scope, added a double-bass part to it, besides making some revisions for the sake of orchestral balance and unity. In this form it has been frequently performed by orchestras.

Verklärte Nacht was written in 1899, when Schönberg was a mere twenty-five, and a pupil of Alexander von Zemlinsky. In all, it took the young Schönberg three weeks to create this music, which is today the most often played of his works. It was born in a definitely preatonal period in the composer's life and during a time when the Wagnerian influence—emotionalism, chromatics, and the rest of the magic—was at its strongest.

The inspiration for *Verklärte Nacht* came from Richard Dehmel's poem *Weib und die Welt,* a fragment of which is printed on the flyleaf of the score. Henry Krehbiel thus paraphrased that excerpt:

Two mortals walk through a cold, barren grove. The moon sails over the tall oaks, which send their scrawny branches up through the unclouded moonlight. A woman speaks. She confesses a sin to the man at her side: she is with child, and he is not its father. She had lost belief in happiness, and, longing for life's fullness, for motherhood and mother's duty, she had surrendered herself, shuddering, to the embraces of a man she knew not. She had thought herself blessed, but now life had avenged itself upon her, by giving her the love of him she walked with. She staggers onward, gazing with lack-luster eye at the moon which follows her. A man speaks. Let her not burden her soul with thoughts of guilt. See, the moon's sheen enwraps the universe. Together they are driving over chill waters, but a flame from each warms the other. It, too, will transfigure the little stranger, and she will bear the child to him. For she has inspired the brilliant glow within him and made him too a child. They sink into each other's arms. Their breaths meet in kisses in the air. Two mortals wander through the wondrous moonlight.

Philip Hale, remarking on this composition, once wrote:

Schönberg's music, to be enjoyed, does not need either the original verse or the paraphrase. Indeed, it would be better if the argument were not printed for the concertgoer. As it is, he may be too anxious to discover the emancipated woman and the good, easy-going, complaisant man in the music, and be oblivious of the strains of beauty and passion. For this music, on the whole prolix, has beautiful and passionate pages of compelling eloquence. Other pages are a sandy, dreary waste. The impression would be still stronger, the music still more significant, if the composition were much shorter. Whether the music itself gains by the revision and enlargement is a question that admits of discussion.

That particular question, insofar as Egon Wellesz, Schönberg's biographer, is concerned, is closed, to judge from the following declaration:

As might be expected, the setting of a program to music, and especially in a youthful work full of the zest of life, has made the music of *Verklärte Nacht* something unusually dramatic; so much so that one could wish in many places for greater fulness and strength of tone. Hence, when this work is played in large halls it is a good idea to increase the number of performers. This certainly reduces the intimate effect of certain passages, but, on the other hand, it gives to the whole a far greater intensity, bringing out more clearly the flight and *élan* of the composition.

Verklärte Nacht consists of five sections. The second refers to the "passionate plaint of the woman, the fourth the sustained answer of the man." The first, third, and fifth sections are of "more epic nature and so portray the deep feelings of the people wandering about in the cold, moonlit night."

The listener, of course, will either consider this as abstract music or attempt to trace in its measures the progress and implications of the poem's "argument." He is welcome to whichever choice he makes, Dehmel, Schönberg, Krehbiel, Hale, Wellecz having made theirs.

R. C. B.

"Theme and Variations for Orchestra," in G minor, Op. 43B

COMPOSED IN October, 1943, this work was first scored for band. Schönberg intended it primarily for school use and gave it the opus number 43A. Later, on a suggestion of his friend the late Carl Engel, he rescored it for symphony orchestra. The new opus number was 43B. In this version the composition was premiered by the Boston Symphony Orchestra on Oct. 20, 1944.

First among the score's surprising features is the use of a key signature. The tonality of G minor is fixed and definite. With Arnold Schönberg this is real news. Key signatures have been so rare in the output of this "atonal" innovator that, except for the G major Suite of 1934, the student must search back to 1907 for another—the F sharp minor of the String Quartet.

A partial explanation has been given for Schönberg's two lapses from atonality. John N. Burk, in his Boston Symphony program note, suggests that the G major Suite of 1934 was designed for "amateur uses," basing his theory on Schönberg's own reference to it as a "school suite." This also applies to the *Theme and Variations,* written first as "Variations for Band," with students in mind. The composer evidently realized that youngsters uninitiated in the mysteries of his twelve-tone system, might perform the music. So, the surmise that Schönberg had given up the twelve-tone technic and "returned remorsefully to normal composing" was perhaps wishful thinking.

Largely because of the use of orthodox tonality, *Theme and Variations* is relatively simple beside other works of Schönberg. Yet there is rich polyphony throughout, and the finale is an elaborately worked out contrapuntal web. A lyric and introspective mood marks some of the variations. The theme itself, of rather bold march character, is given out by the winds, thus retaining the decided band flavor of the original. Mr. Burk has quoted the composer's own statement regarding the variations:

In general, the variations proceed in the traditional manner, using motival and harmonic features of the theme, thus producing new themes of contrasting character and mood. In the first two variations the tempo increases considerably. Variation III is an adagio of a more songful character. Variation IV is a stylized waltz. Variation V, molto moderato cantabile, is a canon in inversion. Variation VI is very fast (alla breve) and violent in character, while the texture is contrapuntal. Variation VII approaches the style of a chorale prelude. The finale, as usual in classical music, adds a number of ideas, which vary only part of the theme. The treatment is mostly contrapuntal, and the aim towards a final climax is predominant.

The sections are marked as follows: Theme, Poco allegro; Variation I, Poco allegro; Variation II, Allegro molto; Variation III, Poco adagio; Variation IV, Tempo di valse; Variation V, Molto moderato cantabile; Variation VI, Allegro; Variation VII, Moderato; Finale, Moderato. The scoring calls for two flutes, piccolo, two oboes, English horn, two clarinets, bass clarinet, two bassoons, contra-bassoon, four horns, three trumpets, two trombones, tuba, tympani, bass drum, cymbals, triangle, snare drum, glockenspiel, tambourine, xylophone, gong, chimes, and strings.

To return to the question of atonality in Schönberg's music: it is curious that, though the composer abandoned tonality in 1907 and shortly began experimenting in the twelve-tone scale, he has never himself spoken of his music as atonal. He has even denied that any of his compositions is "at variance with the principles taught by the old masters." He does not consider his twelve-tone scale as a credo, merely as a technic. Thus, the occasional switch to another technic or idiom is natural on the principle that the content and purpose of a composition dictate its language. Mr. Schönberg has felt that the particular things he had to say could be said best in his twelve-tone scale. But he disavows any predetermined theory or formula. He maintains:

If the composer does not write from the heart, he simply cannot produce good music. I have never had a theory in my life. I get a musical idea for a composition, I try to develop a certain logical and beautiful conception, and I try to clothe it in a type of music which exudes from me naturally and inevitably. I do not consciously create a tonal or a polytonal or a polyplanal music. I write what I feel in my heart—and what finally comes on paper is what first coursed through every fiber of my body. It is for this reason I cannot tell anyone what the style of my next composition will be. For its style will be whatever I feel when I develop and elaborate my ideas.

L. B.

Franz Schubert

BORN: LICHTENTHAL, SUBURB OF VIENNA, JAN. 31, 1797. DIED: VIENNA, NOV. 19, 1828.

My music is the production of my genius and my misery.—SCHUBERT.

Symphony No. 2 in B flat major

> I. Largo; Allegro vivace. II. Andante. III. Menuetto: Allegro vivace.
> IV. Presto vivace.

IT HAS been said of Franz Schubert that he has no superior and few equals in the spontaneity of melodic invention. Lacking the thorough training of the cultured composer, he could, nevertheless, envision whole worlds of song, according to the dictates of a very individual urge to express himself. The influence of Mozart and Beethoven is strongly marked in many of his works, an influence that he did not try to escape, by the way. Philip Hale once emphasized the peculiarly personal quality of Schubert's gifts. He said, "His voice was his own; his melody was unmistakable, and as the boy developed and wrote, not merely because he wished to write, but because for him there were no other ways of expression, his harmonic schemes, his surpassing merits, his weaknesses, his failures, were equally individual." This Symphony was begun when Schubert was not yet eighteen, on Dec. 10, 1814, and finished on Mar. 24, the following year, seven weeks after his eighteenth birthday.

An introduction of ten measures (Largo 4/4) ushers in the first movement proper (Allegro vivace, B flat major, 2/2). The development is of no great consequence and, after some experimental touches here and there, a second idea is presented and the movement is then taken up with repetitions of thematic matters, more development, and so on.

The second movement is an Andante in E flat, 2/4 (theme and variations). The variations have a Mozartean flavor, and they are well balanced and agreeable.

The Menuetto (Allegro vivace, in C minor, 3/4) is likewise charming and well constructed.

The finale (Presto vivace, B flat, 2/4) is perhaps the most interestingly made of the four movements. The initial measure of the first theme of this section is later given a development of excellent effect. Also worthy of mention is the fact that the second theme in E flat appears at the end in G minor, showing that even early in his career Schubert liked to depart from classical restraints.

R. C. B.

Symphony in C minor, No. 4 ("Tragic")

I. Adagio molto; Allegro vivace. II. Andante. III. Menuetto: Allegro vivace. IV. Finale: Allegro.

By the time Schubert was nineteen years old he had already composed four symphonies. His first, D Major, was completed in 1813; the second, B flat major, in 1814-1815; his third, D Major, 1815; and the present work on Apr. 27, 1816. The *Tragic Symphony,* it was observed by Henry Edward Krehbiel, had remained unpublished, "as a whole," for sixty-eight years. In 1870 the Andante was given separate publication and in the same year was published also a four-hand piano version of the entire symphony. In 1884, however, Breitkopf and Härtel's Complete Edition of Schubert's works brought forward the full score.

The title of the work, *Tragic,* has posed a particular problem for a number of years. Sir George Grove could find no reason for such a description, hazarding a guess that Schubert's poverty may have been the inspiration. Percy Goetschius, on the other hand, tells us that the title is

inaccurate, pompous, and a bit pretentious. For no youth of nineteen summers really knows what tragedy signifies—at least Schubert did not; he bases his conception of it upon what he has read or heard, but not upon what he has *felt* and known. Therefore, there is to be found in this Symphony no more than a general, artificially emphasized dramatic strain (in the first and last movements only), and a few pathetic touches, but no genuine tragic outbursts.

Another observer, Hermann Grabner, says in his preface to the Eulenberg edition of the score that there was some reason for the title. "After the first three joyful symphonies," he opines, "the opening movement of the fourth breathes a spirit of sorrow and resignation, though [he admits] it is not long maintained."

The score of the Fourth Symphony calls for two flutes, two oboes, two clarinets, two bassoons, two horns, two trumpets, kettledrums, and strings. The first movement opens with a slow introduction, launched by a unison C, fortissimo for full orchestra. The first violins enter with a plaintive melody and, after a while, the chief subject of the movement is played softly by the strings. A second subject is taken up by the strings in the key of A flat, instead of the expected E flat, with the recapitulation taking place, surprisingly, in G minor, rather than in the dominant. A coda in C major follows.

The second movement is in sonatina form, starting with a melody for the strings, which are joined in bar 10 by an oboe. All is played dolce and pianissimo. A contrasting sequence, of agitated character, is juxtaposed against the tranquil music, with the latter finally prevailing.

The third movement is more of a Beethovenish scherzo than a Menuetto, its title. There is some very interesting chromatic writing in it, and a trio is especially effective.

The sonata-form final movement boasts a particularly beautiful second subject and the astonishingly pat handling of the orchestra by a nineteen-year-old. A long coda in C major concludes the Symphony.

Again with respect to this Symphony Grove has said that in the Andante and the Finale "we have exceedingly happy examples, in which, without absolutely breaking away from the old world, Schubert revealed an amount of original feeling and an extraordinary beauty of treatment which already stamp him as a great orchestral composer."

Speaking of the early symphonies, Grove continues:

But whether always original or not in their subjects, no one can listen to these first six symphonies without being impressed with their *individuality*. Single phrases may remind us of other composers, the treatment may often be traditional, but there is a fluency and continuity, a happy cheerfulness, an earnestness and want of triviality, and an absence of labor, which proclaim a new composer. The writer is evidently writing because what he has to say must come out, even though he may occasionally couch it in the phrases of his predecessors.

Beauty and profusion of melody reign throughout. The tone is often plaintive, but never obscure, and there is always the irrepressible gaiety of youth and of Schubert's own Viennese nature, ready and willing to burst forth.

R. C. B.

Symphony in B flat major; No. 5

> I. Allegro. II. Andante con molto. III. Menuetto: Allegro molto; Trio.
> IV. Finale: Allegro vivace.

It took Schubert four weeks to compose this Symphony, which was completed by Oct. 3, 1816. It was first performed at a semiprivate session in the same year. It is generally supposed that the Symphony, together with the Third in D major, the Fourth (*Tragic*) in C minor, and the *Little Symphony* in C major, was written for a small orchestra—which had grown up from a string quartet that used to perform at the house of Schubert *père*. The work is also known as the "symphony without trumpets and drums."

The score of the present Symphony was believed lost for a great number of years. George Grove and Arthur Sullivan came upon the orchestral parts, which were in the possession of Johann Herbeck in Vienna, in 1867. Herbeck, by the way, had discovered the *Unfinished* among some musty old papers in the house of Anselm Hüttenbrenner two years previously. In any case, the score of the Fifth was eventually found at the Royal Library of Berlin. A four-hand piano version was published in 1872 and the complete score in 1882.

Perhaps, it's to be expected that the composer's early essays in the symphonic form should have been influenced by a galaxy of celebrities, including Mozart, Haydn, Beethoven, Weber and even Rossini. (One might play a neat little game of tracing interinfluences among these, too.) And it is not altogether in matters of construction and development that this holds true. Parenthetically, there is a bit of melody in the first movement of Schubert's Second that flirts outrageously with Beethoven, and another bit in the following Andante that pays slavish homage to Mozart. However, we should be doing an injustice to Schubert were we to assume that anything but pure coincidence had to do with the similarity. He was, in fact, melodically too prolific to be bothered with borrowing.

It is common knowledge, by now, that Schubert's symphonies of this particular period are decent models of form. The B Flat is devoid of long developments, rather giving the impression that its composer, as Donald Tovey says, "relished the prospect of having nothing to do but recapitulate."

Tovey flays those authorities who charge Schubert's "later defects to his lack of sound early training." And he declares further, "Schubert's early forms are stiff. And, as the upholders of musical orthodoxy were in the 'eighties (and are still) painfully puzzled by any forms that were not stiff, they were in no position to criticize Schubert's early education or its early and later results."

As for Schubert's "later defects," he suggests they weren't so much that as attempts at new forms, all of which makes, apparently, a pretty strong case against the musical pontiffs.

Be that as it may, the Symphony has known its share of neglect. The first performance in this country was apparently given it by the Boston Symphony Orchestra under the direction of George Henschel, in Boston, on Feb. 10, 1883. It was played in New York by Sam Franko and the American Symphony Orchestra on Feb. 4, 1902. Henry E. Krehbiel's program notes informed all and sundry that he had not been able to find any record of previous performance in New York, singular or plural. The Symphony was first played under the auspices of the Symphony Society of New York on Nov. 3, 1927, with Fritz Busch conducting, and the Philharmonic Symphony Society's initial experience with it came under the guest-directorship of Georges Enesco on Jan. 20, 1928.

The first movement (Allegro, B flat major, 4/4) opens with four enchanting measures for wood winds and violins, after which the playful first theme enters pianissimo in the strings, the lower strings answering the higher. After due working over of this theme the strings give out the second, and even more Mozartean, theme piano. The development section is short, followed by the unorthodox beginning of the recapitulation in E flat.

The second movement (Andante con moto, E flat major, 6/8) has the melodic and harmonic richness of a Schubert Lied. The chief subject, given out softly at the beginning by the strings, is, however, tinctured with Mozart, as a comparison with the rondo of his F major Sonata for Violin (K. 377) will prove. The movement is in sonatina form, without a development section.

The third movement (Allegro molto, G minor, 3/4), though marked Menuetto by Schubert, is really a scherzo because of the tempo. In spite of important differences, it inevitably recalls the minuet of Mozart's G minor Symphony. The Trio in G major has been called by Tovey a regular rustic dance, with more than a suspicion of a drone bass. In the first part of the Trio the hearer can detect a resemblance to the popular song "Ach, du lieber Augustin," and in the second part, to the song generally known as "Schubert's Serenade."

In sonata form the Finale (Allegro vivace, B flat major, 2/4) runs a blithe early-Schubertian course, punctuated by episodes of deeper significance. The two principal themes, the first wholly frolicsome, the second tinged with wistfulness, both given to the strings piano, are deliciously Mozartean. A codetta in triplets, which rounds off the exposition, concludes the symphony in a rush of merriment.

The work is scored for one flute, two oboes, two bassoons, two horns, and two strings.

R. C. B.

Symphony in C major, No. 7

> I. Andante; Allegro ma non troppo. II. Andante con molto. III. Scherzo: Allegro vivace; Trio. IV. Finale: Allegro vivace.

THOUGH NOT performed till after Schubert's death, the C major Symphony was completed in March, 1828, according to an inscription on the manuscript. It would thus seem that Schubert never heard a note of the Symphony, except on his own piano while composing it. However, it is generally believed that Schubert was present while the work was in rehearsal at the hall of the Musikverein of Vienna. After making corrections, Schubert supposedly sent the society the score, at its request. Apparently the men had difficulty with the lengthy work. On the composer's advice, it was withdrawn, and his earlier C major Symphony, written in 1817, substituted. When submitting the score to the Musikverein, Schubert remarked that he was through with song writing and now planned to "confine himself to opera and symphony."

A month after Schubert's death the Viennese Gesellschaft der Musikfreunde performed a "C major Symphony" by Schubert in the Redoutensaal, repeating the work the following Mar. 12. While most biographers and annotators assume the symphony to have been the earlier one in that key, one or two hold out for the later symphony.

In any case, the score gathered dust for ten years amid a pile of manuscript in the possession of Schubert's brother Ferdinand. Then one day Robert Schumann paid the brother a visit in Vienna. In a letter to the Leipzig publishers, Breitkopf and Härtel, Schumann describes Ferdinand Schubert as "a poor schoolmaster, entirely without means." There were eight children to support, and all that remained as a legacy of the gifted Franz was this heap of musty manuscripts. Rummaging through it, Schumann "discovered" the great C major Symphony and promptly announced his find to the Leipzig house. So warmly was the work recommended by him that Mendelssohn was persuaded to conduct what is widely accepted as its premiere at a Gewandhaus concert in Leipzig on Mar. 21, 1839.

Though himself in dire straits at the time, Schumann used all his powers of persuasion to get Schubert's needy brother a handsome price for the precious hoard of manuscript. Schumann's devotion to the memory of Schubert is further shown in a little episode connected with his visit to the graves of Beethoven and Schubert. Near the tombstone over Beethoven's grave he found a steel pen. Stirred by romantic associations, he treasured it. With it he composed his B flat major Symphony. And with it he penned the rhapsodic review of the Schubert C major, following the Leipzig premiere. In that review reappears the famous reference to the work's "heavenly" length, without which no account of the Symphony is complete. Schumann wrote:

In Schubert's symphony, in the transparent, glowing, romantic life therein reflected, I see Vienna more clearly mirrored than ever, and understand more perfectly than before why such works are native to the scene around me. I will not try to extol and interpret the symphony; men in the different stages of life take such different views of the impressions they derive from artistic fancies, and the youth of eighteen often discovers in a symphony the echo of some world-wide event, where the mature man sees but a local matter, whereas the musician has never thought of either the one or the other, and has merely poured forth from his heart the very best music he could give.

But grant that we believe that its outer world, today fair, tomorrow dark, may appeal deeply to the inmost heart of the poet and musician, and that more than merely lovely melody, something above and beyond sorrow and joy, as these emotions have been portrayed a hundred times in music, lies concealed in this symphony— nay, more, that we are by the music transported to a region where we can never remember to have been before—to experience all this we must listen to symphonies such as this.

Here we have, besides masterly power over the musical technicalities of composition, life in all its phases, color in exquisite gradations, the minutest accuracy and fitness of expression, and, permeating the whole work, a spirit of romance such as we recognize in other works of Franz Schubert. And this heavenly, long-drawn-out symphony is like some thick romance of Jean Paul's in four volumes, which can never end—and, indeed, for the very best reasons, in order that it may draw along the reader with it up to the last moment. How refreshing this feeling of satisfaction of being deceived by the large wealth of melody, whereas with other composers one always fears the end, and feels often saddened by the feeble conclusion!

Schubert's easy and brilliant mastery over the resources of an orchestra would be unintelligible, if one did not know that six other symphonies had preceded his last effort, and that he wrote it in the full maturity of his powers. Those gifts must be pronounced extraordinary in a man who, having during his lifetime heard so little of his own instrumental works, succeeded in so masterly a handling of the general body of instruments which converse with one another like human voices and chorus.

The Andante introduction (C major, 4/4) of the first movement opens with a nobly tender theme announced by the horns in unison and destined to play an important part in the Allegro section. Later the wood winds take it up, and cellos and violas continue it. There is a resounding crescendo, and the main theme of the movement, a kind of hunting motive, is given out in sturdy rhythm by the strings (Allegro ma non troppo, C major, 2/2). A second theme of contrastingly idyllic mood soon enters by way of oboes and bassoons in thirds, with string support. Wood winds join in, and the whole orchestra reaches a stirring fortissimo. During the development the trumpets, in unison, solemnly recall part of the opening horn theme, while the rest of the orchestra discourses fragments of the second theme. An elaborate working out of this material follows, the themes are brought back, and the horn theme of the introduction returns with redoubled vigor, given out first by wind instruments, then by the strings.

The second movement (Andante con moto, A minor, 2/2) is constructed on two subjects. The first, a plaintive, haunting melody chanted by the oboe to string accompaniment, suggests a gypsy tune. The second subject appears pianissimo in the violins, closing with a beautiful horn passage. "All is hushed," said Schumann, "as if a celestial host were moving about the orchestra." With the return of the first theme in the oboe, there enters a famous passage for solo cello, in tender vein. After the second theme is freshly treated, the horn passage is repeated and the movement trails off with the main march theme.

The Scherzo movement (Allegro vivace, C major, 4/4) has been called a game of "hide-and-seek of two rhythms through the orchestra: six headlong eighths and three headlong fourths." Exuberant humor and wistful romance combine in this movement. The strings in octaves announce the subject. Phrases are added by wood winds and horns. A lighter theme for strings is brought in, with bassoons and clarinets accompanying. The Trio (A major), in sharp contrast with the rollicking rhythms of the main section, is "the perfect romantic song," typically Schubertian in its inimitable tenderness. It is introduced by horns and clarinets. "Expressively played," wrote Edmoundstone Duncan, "the Trio might easily draw tears."

The brilliant Finale (Allegro vivace) has been compared to a variety of exciting phenomena. The mythical Phaeton's ride in the sun chariot was supposedly pictured there. One commentator likened the movement to the approach of the Stone Guest in Mozart's *Don Giovanni*. Others have called it an "orgy" and "ferment" of giant rhythms. "A vertiginous whirl of aspiration," was one critic's phrase for it. Another viewed it as belonging "in the country of the gods." Felix Weingartner confessed that the music produced on him "the effect as of flight through a bright ether."

An impetuous, headlong drive, sharpened by a blunt motive of four drum beats heard earlier in the Symphony, characterizes the movement. Everything is swept forward on a heaving surge of rhythm, mounting steadily in fiery strength. According to Ralph Bates:

It is as if we were borne up on that pulsating atom of rhythm, above the world and out from its limits over the cold purity of universal space, as if we beheld the circling of worlds and the laws they manifest. Again and again we are lifted with such excitement that we do not notice it is the means of changing tonality which is being used. The pealing joy of the wood winds after every upsoaring flight only serves to exhilarate us more.

The great C major Symphony was the work of a man living in abject poverty and recurring pain. Its sweep and grandeur contrast ironically with the bleak struggle of Schubert's last months. Publishers' prices were ridiculously low. Plans to escape Vienna's stifling summer were dropped because of lack of funds. He worked feverishly. Fatigue and despair increased. The mounting gloom is mirrored in his *Winterreise* cycle of songs. Then the dizzy spells and growing illness. Finally typhus. "I am ill," he writes his friend Schober; "for eleven days I have eaten nothing and drunk nothing. I wander wearily and wobble from chair to bed and back again." He asks Schober to leave some novels by J. Fenimore Cooper "with Frau von Bogner at the coffee house," for his brother Ferdinand to pick up for him. The letter is dated Nov. 12. Seven days later Franz Schubert was dead. In his final agony he is reported to have cried out: "It is not Beethoven who lies here!" He was buried beside the Bonn master. His earthly possessions were assessed at fifty-three gulden. Many years later a single letter of Schubert's brought 1,450 gold marks at an auction. Who would dare put a price on the C major Symphony?

L. B.

Symphony in B minor, No. 8 ("Unfinished")

I. Allegro moderato. II. Andante con moto.

Schubert wrote the following words to the Musikverein of Graz, in Styria, an organization which had deemed fit to bestow an honorary membership upon him. "In order to express my liveliest thanks in music, I will make so bold as to present your honored Society at the earliest date with the score of one of my symphonies." He set to work on the Symphony in 1822. After completing two movements and some measures of a third, he gave it to Anselm Hüttenbrenner, president of the Society, for delivery to the Musikverein. Anselm, a friend of the composer's, who had been a hearty spreader of the Schubertian gospel, never delivered it. The manuscript took on the dust of years among other yellowing papers, and had it not been for a chance query by Johann Herbeck, conductor of the concerts of the Vienna Gesellschaft der Musikfreunde, it might never have been restored to the world.

Herbeck visited Graz, in May, 1865, escorting his sister-in-law, ostensibly, to a health resort. He had earlier been apprised by Joseph Hüttenbrenner of a Schubert Symphony in B minor, which was in the possession of his brother Anselm. Joseph's information about the work had issued quite casually, almost at the same time as he suggested that Herbeck play one of Anselm's compositions at a Musikfreunde concert. Obviously, Herbeck was not passing through Graz for his sister-in-law's health. He wished to speak to Anselm about that Symphony. He wanted it, because it had been highly recommended to him by Joseph, and he was even willing to play some number of Anselm's as a bribe.

He was having breakfast at an inn at Ober-Andritz, one eventful morning, pondering on the various problems facing him. He looked up suddenly and saw Anselm himself entering the room. Following the usual amenities, the conductor worked up the courage to ask, tactfully, for a work of his. Anselm became most cordial. He invited Herbeck to his house, whither they soon repaired. There, in a study literally crammed with yellowing manuscripts, Anselm discussed this and that composition of his. He took out several unpublished ones, pointing out their various merits, no doubt. But still no mention of Schubert.

After playing the game a bit with his host, selecting one of the latter's overtures for possible performance, Herbeck gently, very gently, remarked that he would be glad to look at some unproduced creation of Schubert's, if such there were in his possession. Anselm, in the full flush of victory, with an overture in line for a premiere, pulled out a drawer and took out an armful of scores. One of them carried the inscription in Schubert's own hand, "Symphonie in H moll." Herbeck looked it over without undue show of excitement. He finally said that it would do, offering to have it copied at his own expense. But Anselm could afford, now, to be magnanimous, so he told his guest that he might take it away with him.

In Vienna, on Dec. 17, 1865, the *Unfinished Symphony* had its first performance. In the same program appeared an Overture in C minor by one Anselm Hüttenbrenner. Also noteworthy was the fact that Herbeck had "completed" the *Unfinished* by augmenting its two movements with the Finale from Schubert's Third, a Presto vivace in the key of D major.

The theories and hypotheses advanced for Schubert's unfinishing of the *Unfinished,* so to speak, have been legion. The fancies of certain watchers of the musical skies have known no bounds. Without any basis in fact, one of these offered the idea that Schubert wrote his work as a "tribute to the Glory of the Incomplete." How wrong this peremptory summation is may be proved by the fact that Schubert not only sketched portions of a third movement, but he also orchestrated some nine measures of it! Incidentally, we have the widely diverging opinions of two eminent authorities on the quality of the fragmentary third movement. Tovey remarks that the first subject will please anyone who knows a good theme when he sees it. Philip Hale, however, has this to say:

Let us be thankful that Schubert never finished his work. Possibly the lost arms of the Venus of Milo might disappoint if they were found and restored. The few measures of the Scherzo that are in the manuscript furnish but a slight hope that here, at last, Schubert would not, as in so many of his works of long breath, maintain a steady decrescendo.

There have been attempts to finish the Symphony, you may be sure, one of them by a certain August Ludwig of Berlin. He added the two requisite movements, entitling the "third" *Philosophen-Scherzo,* in which "a ring is put through the nose of the bear Learning, *i.e.,* counterpoint, that he might dance to the amusement of all." A second theme, a tender one, mind, "conjures from the fairyland of poetry (Invention) a fay which tames and frees the bear, who pines in constraint." To the "finale" he gave the title *March of Fate,* and shuddery, indeed, is its description. For motto he submits, "Brazen stalks Fate, yet she is crowned with roses and love!" He explains, "Truly, Fate has stalked with brazen steps over our ancient masters. A new age has awakened a new music era." The foregoing is merely a sample of the purple rhetoric. Unbelievable as it may seem, the Ludwig-finished *Unfinished* of Schubert was performed in Berlin on Dec. 8, 1892. To which may be added the observation —with due apologies—the Unglory of the Complete!

The symphony is scored for flutes, oboes, clarinets, bassoons, horns, and trumpets in pairs, three trombones, kettledrums, and the usual strings.

R. C. B.

Concerto in A for Cello and Orchestra

[*Freely transcribed by Gaspar Cassadó from the Arpeggione Sonata*]

I. Allegro moderato. II. Adagio. III. Allegretto.

THE APPENDIX to Kreissle von Hellborn's *Life of Franz Schubert* carries Sir George Grove's story of his Schubert researches at Vienna in 1867. At one place he reports: "At the Library of the Musik-Verein, besides the autograph of the great Symphony in C, I saw the copy of a Sonata by Schubert for Piano and Arpeggione (whatever that may have been), which, being dated as late as 1824, ought to possess some value. The themes of the movements are as follows": and here Sir George cited three themes from the Sonata.

One assumes that Sir George's mystification over the arpeggione was short-lived. At any rate, it was something of a cross between a guitar and a cello, invented by Johann Georg Staufer, a Viennese, in 1823. It had the shape of a guitar, the size of a viola da gamba, and its six strings were tuned—in rising order—to E, A, D, G, B, and E. Furthermore, it was played with a bow. Though the arpeggione has outlived its usefulness, Schubert considered it important enough to write a Sonata for it. But then, he may have done that out of friendship for Vincent Schuster, who was the best known arpeggione player of his time.

Sir George Grove, the researcher, and Gaspar Cassadó, merely the browser, came upon this work in the Musik-Verein library seventy years apart. It is the browser who is responsible for its revival, albeit in transcription.

R. C. B.

Music from "Rosamunde"

ELEVEN SEPARATE pieces, in all, comprise the incidental music for the drama *Rosamunde, Fürstin von Cypern* by Wilhelmine de Chézy, which was produced at the Theater an der Wien on Dec. 20, 1823. The play had exactly two showings, and the music was put away and not discovered until 1867, "by two English travelers in Vienna," says Sir George Grove. The travelers were Grove himself and Arthur Sullivan.

All the numbers, save the Overture, were written in five days by Schubert. The Overture had been composed three years previously for a melodrama entitled *Die Zauberharfe,* according to one story. Newman Flower, however, declares that it had belonged to another work, *Alfonso and Estrella.*

Countess de Chézy's creation went the way of all immateria at that opening performance, but the public was stirred by the beauty of Schubert's music. The Overture, in particular, was so well received that it had to be repeated.

A persistent soul, the Countess de Chézy decided to revise her libretto, a task completed the following summer. In August, Schubert wrote to her:

Convinced of the value of *Rosamunde* from the moment I read it, I am very pleased that your honor has undertaken to correct, surely to the greatest advantage, a few shortcomings which only a spiteful public would censure. I should consider it a particular honor if you would let me have a copy of the manuscript when you have worked over it.

As regards the price of the music, I do not think I can put it at less than 100 florins without depreciating the music itself. In case that price should be too high, I beg your honor to fix the price yourself, but at not much below the above-named figure, and to forward it to the subjoined address, as I am absent from Vienna.

Nothing of value came to Schubert from that adventure in letter writing. The whole thing was done with, and that was that. Could he have had a glimpse into the future reception of his music, however, he might have found greater compensation for the woeful lack of florins in his own time.

Besides the Overture, the *Rosamunde* music comprises three entr'actes, two ballets, a number for clarinets, horns, and bassoons, known as "Shepherd's Melody," a soprano solo, and three choruses.

R. C. B.

William Schuman

BORN: NEW YORK CITY, AUG. 4, 1910.

I feel that I have to write music, so I write it.—WILLIAM SCHUMAN.

Symphony No. 3
[*In Two Parts, and Four Movements*]

I. (a) Passacaglia. (b) Fugue. II. (c) Chorale. (d) Toccata.

BEARING THE dedication, "This work is for Serge Koussevitzky," the Symphony No. 3 calls for the following orchestration: two flutes, piccolo, three oboes, English horn, E flat clarinet, two B flat clarinets, bass clarinet, two bassoons, four horns, four trumpets, four trombones, tuba, tympani, snare drum, bass drum, cymbals, xylophone, and strings. The composer lists other instruments, whose use is optional. They consist of a third flute and second piccolo, a third oboe, a third bassoon and contra-bassoon, a quartet of horns, and a piano. The composer suggests that "to obtain the best results, they are most desirable."

This Symphony received the initial award made by the Music Critics' Circle of New York City for the best new orchestral work played locally during the season 1941-1942. Its first performance was given in Boston by the Boston Symphony Orchestra, under the direction of Serge Koussevitzky, on Oct. 18, 1941. Under the same auspices it obtained its New York premiere on Nov. 22, 1941.

Composed in January, 1941, the work is in two parts, each having two connected movements. The first movement contains a Passacaglia, followed by a Fugue; the second a Chorale and a Toccata.

Part I. The theme of the Passacaglia appears in the violas, with a subsequent upward surge in semitones by the string sections and the wood winds. The development is in four-part canon. Trumpets and trombones paraphrase the theme in one variation. After a transitional passage the wood winds take the initiative in melodic figures against a harmonic and rhythmic web in the next variation. Another transitional passage brings on the last two variations. Of these the first gives play to a long melodic version of the theme. There is a crescendo and a quickening of the pace to a climax, after which the last variation appears. Strings provide the harmony and rhythm, as a trombone quartet gives the Passacaglia theme a concluding flourish.

The Fugue, whose subject is related to the theme of the Passacaglia, is in a different rhythm. Further relationships occur between Fugue and Passacaglia in the upward rises on semitones and a canonic development, which, however, extends to seven parts. The first variation of the Fugue subject is stated by the English horn (solo), and the following developments are confined exclusively to wood winds and strings. The second variation is brought in on the wave of a rhythm which is put into motion by the tympani and swelled by the strings. There is a development, now leading into the final section. This consists of three main parts: (a) an organ point around E flat, (b) a third variation (dialogue between wood winds and strings), and (c) a melodic dialogue between trombones and horns. In the coda the subject of the Fugue appears in altered augmentation against the first variation. Other material heard previously in the section reappears, as Part I comes to a close.

Part II. The Chorale has an introductory passage by divided violas and cellos. A variant of the Passacaglia theme becomes the Chorale melody, which appears by way of the solo trumpet. The melody is given several different treatments, and the section flows right into the Toccata.

The Toccata theme is established by the snare drum, and its first developments are in canonic form, as in Part I. There is a transition, and the strings enter into a passage resembling a cadenza. The concluding part of the composition gives emphasis to a rhythmic version of the Chorale, further development of the Toccata theme and the introduction of entirely new material.

William Schuman was educated in the public schools of New York City, receiving Bachelor of Science and Master of Arts degrees from Columbia University. He studied harmony with Max Persin, counterpoint with Charles Haubiel, and composition with Roy Harris.

After a period of further study (at the Mozarteum in Salzburg) he was appointed, on his return, to the faculty of Sarah Lawrence College, Bronxville, where he both taught and conducted. He held two Guggenheim Fellowships, from 1939 to 1941, and in 1943 he received the grant in Music from the American Academy of Arts and The National Institute of Arts and Letters.

Mr. Schuman is a prolific composer. He has written, thus far, five symphonies (the Fifth, *Symphony for Strings*); two cantatas, *This Is Our Time,* text by Genevieve Taggard, and *A Free Song,* text by Walt Whitman (this was awarded the Pulitzer Prize in Music in 1943); *the American Festival Overture;* the Concerto for Piano and Orchestra, *Newsreel* (band); *Prayer,* 1943 (orchestra); three string quartets, and numerous short instrumental and choral works.

On Oct. 1, 1945, William Schuman was appointed to the office of President of the Juilliard School of Music.

R. C. B.

"American Festival Overture"

THE COMPOSER's own description of his Overture follows:

The first three notes of this piece will be recognized by some listeners as the "call to play" of boyhood days. In New York City it is yelled on the syllables "Wee-Awk-Eee" to get the gang together for a game or a festive occasion of some sort. This call very naturally suggested itself for a piece of music being composed for a very festive occasion. From this it should not be inferred that the Overture is program music. In fact, the idea for the music came to my mind before the origin in the theme was recalled. The development of this bit of "folk material," then, is along purely musical lines.

The first section of the work is concerned with the material discussed above and the ideas growing out of it. This music leads to a transition section and the subsequent announcement by the violas of a fugue subject. The entire middle section is given over to this fugue. The orchestration is at first for strings alone, later for wood wind alone and, finally, as the fugue is brought to fruition, by the strings and wood winds in combination. This climax leads to the final section of the work, which consists of opening materials paraphrased and the introduction of new subsidiary ideas. The tempo of the work is fast.

American Festival Overture is scored for two flutes, piccolo, two oboes, English horn, two clarinets, bass clarinet, four horns, two trumpets, three trombones, tuba, tympani, bass drum, cymbals, snare drum, xylophone, and strings.

"William Billings Overture"

THE THEMES of this Overture are from three choral works by America's first professional composer William Billings (1746-1800). To an increasing number of musicians and laymen alike, Billings has become more than a mere reference listing in a history book. For some who perform his music he remains, for all his shortcomings, a composer of great strength, with a deep religiosity and rugged individuality. Mr. Schuman has written about his Overture as follows:

The opening section uses material from one of Billings' *Fuguing Tunes*. The first theme is set to the words: "Be Glad, Then, America, Shout and Rejoice." (Incidentally the theme is like that used in the Third Pianoforte Concerto of Beethoven, composed the year of Billings' death.) At bar 40 a development in brass of the Rejoice theme leads to the transition (bars 76 through 107) on the first theme. In this first section two other fragments are used: (bars 108 through 129) on the words: "Yea, the Lord will answer and say unto His people: 'Behold! I will send you corn and wine and oil,'" and (bars 130 through 192) on the words: "And ye shall be satisfied therewith." The opening section comes to a climax with the combination of the first theme with the third, and then with the second (bars 193 through 241). A slow transition (bars 242 through 259) leads to the middle section, (bars 260 through 324) based on Billings' round:

> When Jesus wept, the falling tear
> In mercy flowed beyond all bound;
> When Jesus groaned, a trembling fear
> Seized all the guilty world around.

The final section of the Overture is on Chester. This music was composed as a church hymn but was later taken up as a marching song by the Continental Army and enjoyed great popularity. In the Overture it is stated at first as a hymn with the original harmonies. Following a sharp interruption by percussive chords in the fast tempo of the opening, the tune is developed alone and in combination with materials from the first section. The original words with one of the verses written for its subsequent use as a fighting song follow:

> Let tyrants shake their iron rods,
> And slavery clank her galling chains.
> We fear them not, we trust in God.
> New England's God forever reigns.
> The foe comes on with haughty stride,
> Our troops advance with martial noise;
> Their vet'rans flee before our youth,
> And gen'rals yield to beardless boys.

Robert Schumann

BORN: ZWICKAU, SAXONY, JUNE 8, 1810. DIED: ENDENICH, NEAR BONN, JULY 29, 1856.

> *More than to the intelligence, it is to the heart that this soul unveils*
> *itself. Those of others, it is true, are grander, and more loftily dominate*
> *the centuries. None, not even that of Beethoven, is more winged with*
> *love, more human, more rare, and more like Tancred's enchanted*
> *forest where, from every tree, there escape sighs, laughs, or groans.*
> —ROBERT DE LAUNAY.

Symphony in B flat major, No. 1, Op. 38

I. Andante un poco maestoso; Allegro molto vivace. II. Larghetto.
III. Scherzo: Molto vivace. IV. Allegro animato grazioso.

[Played without pause]

BY COMMON consent, including the composer's, Schumann's First Symphony may be safely termed a "Spring Symphony." We have Schumann's own word for it that it grew out of a mood of springtime rapture. Lacking it, we would still sense the vernal note in its sunny cheer and buoyance. If we assume that music can mirror seasonal moods, this symphony could never be mistaken for an autumnal lament. "During the last few days I have finished a task which filled me with happiness, and almost exhausted me," Schumann wrote early in 1841; "Think of it, a whole symphony, and, what is more, *a spring symphony!*"

Later he confided to the composer Spohr: "I wrote the Symphony in the vernal passion that sways men until they are very old, and still surprises them again with each coming year. I have not wished to portray or to paint. But I believe firmly that the period in which the Symphony was produced influenced its form and character and shaped it as it is."

Schumann was emphatic about the seasonal content of his symphony on several other occasions. In writing to the conductor Wilhelm Taubert, then rehearsing the Symphony for Berlin, he pleaded: "Could you infuse into your orchestra, while playing it, a sort of *longing for the spring,* which I had chiefly in mind when I wrote it?" The excited composer specified just what he had "in mind." The first entrance of the trumpets should sound "as though it were from high above, like a call to awakening." For the introduction the men should "read between the lines." Thus they would see "how everywhere it begins to grow green, how a butterfly takes wing, how little by little everything appears that in any way belongs to spring." Schumann conceived the finale as "the good-by of spring."

If any further clue were needed, we have it in the words and music Schumann later inscribed on Kriehuber's portrait of himself which he sent to the German poet, Adolph Böttger. There he quoted the first three bars of his "Spring Symphony," explaining that the work had been "inspired" by one of Böttger's poems, the last line of which reads, *"Im Thale blüht der Frühling auf!"* ("Spring is blooming in the valley"). After reading the poem and hearing the music, a friend of Böttger's remarked: "This symphony is the apotheosis of spring and all that it symbolizes in philosophy and life."

For a while Schumann played with the idea of using descriptive titles for the movements of his Symphony. He wrote them down tentatively: I. "Spring Beginning"; II. "Evening"; III. "Merry Companions"; IV. "Spring at the Full." At the last moment he abandoned them, probably because of their restrictive literalness. Schumann, the romanticist, was mainly interested in conveying subjective states induced by nature. As he implied to Spohr, he was not trying to be a landscape artist in tone. All he could mirror was his own ecstasy before the miracle of spring.

Early American criticism of Schumann's First Symphony showed remarkable discernment and sympathy, compared with the sharp blasts of the English critics. William Mason, who heard the work in the early 1840's in Leipzig, wrote: "I was so wrought up by it, that I hummed passages from it as I walked home. I sat down at the piano when I got there, and played as much of it as I could remember. I hardly slept that night for the excitement of it." After the first performance in Boston late in 1852, John S. Dwight, in his *Journal of Music,* called the Symphony "a grand, consistent, original, inspired whole," which "moved" him "to respect and to desire deeper acquaintance with the new symphonist."

Per contra, British critics ridiculed the work as another product of the so-called "Broken Crockery School." One reviewer called Schumann's work "the ugliest possible music." Another spoke of "delirium tremens." The London weekly *Musical World* pronounced its doom with the words: "Herr Schumann's Symphony in B flat made a dead failure, and deserved it." In brief, the Symphony represented "the convulsive efforts of one who has never properly studied his art to hide the deficiencies of early education under a mist of pompous swagger." Today we know all about Schumann's "deficiencies"— those of form and orchestration, for instance. But we would think twice before speaking of the Symphony's bubbling spirits and ringing vitality as "convulsive efforts." Nor would the severest critic of Schumann's imperfect workmanship now dream of dismissing its romantic freedom and joyous lyric warmth as "a mist of pompous swagger."

L. B.

Symphony in C major, No. 2, Op. 61

I. Sostenuto assai: Allegro, ma non troppo. II. Scherzo: Allegro vivace: Trio I and II. III. Adagio espressivo. IV. Allegro molto vivace.

Work on this Symphony began in December, 1845. It was finished the following year, and on Nov. 5, 1846, it was given its first performance at a Gewandhaus concert. Mendelssohn conducted. Schumann's ailment, be it duly noted, had been undermining his health for some twelve years. The distress and pain he suffered were alleviated somewhat by his concentrated labors on this work. He could forget aches in his devotion to the task of completing the Symphony. He had found, at least, a palliative, if not a panacea, for some ills. In later years Schumann remarked that the piece reminded him "of a dark time." He even went so far as to proffer a kind of program for the Symphony with his statement, "I sketched it when I was still in a state of physical suffering; nay, I may say it was, so to speak, the resistance of the spirit which exercised a visible influence here, and through which I sought to contend with my bodily state. The first movement is full of this struggle and is very capricious and refractory."

He made reference, on another occasion, to the "melancholy bassoon," in the Adagio. But in another view of the work, not in keeping with the foregoing, he opined, "I think it's a regular Jupiter!" It has been said by experts, exclusive of Schumann, that the Symphony tells of a great struggle; that the ideal of conquest over mighty foes is its ultimate aim; that the will and the soul are in conflict with dark powers that would destroy them. And when aren't they? The listener occasionally likes to create his own program. Here he might wish to joust with quadratic equations or, perhaps, thread Cleopatra's Needle, depending on his inventive capacities.

The idea of struggle, nevertheless, is the predominant one, and we have also the words of Frederick Niecks, one of Schumann's biographers, to guide us in this respect. He says, going Schumann one or two better, "In the first movement the composer seems to be wrestling actively with evil powers; the feverish Scherzo reveals indecision, more passivity; the sweet Adagio is an outpouring of prayer, resignation, hope, and thankfulness; and in the last movement he gathers up his whole strength and triumphantly begins the battle of life again." After the battle just finished a new one with life would seem to be a good deal to ask of any self-respecting contestant. But biographers have a way of putting their subjects through Herculean paces.

Niecks goes on, "The youthful bloom and sprightliness of the earlier symphonies [incorrect numbering of the symphonies, though now generally accepted, being responsible for that plural] must not be sought in this work; but in place of these qualities we find a noble independence and greater depth of thought—in short, while there is a loss in sensuous beauty, there is a gain in intellectual intensity." Apparently Niecks shows little affection for the lovely measures of the Adagio. If this section represents "loss in sensuous beauty," then would that Schumann had been as melodically unfruitful elsewhere in his writings!

The C major Symphony, to get back to realistic matters, is his longest and most impressive. The lengthy introduction (Sostenuto assai, C major, 6/4) offers "bugle calls" in the brass. These phrases and still others in the Introduction serve a mottolike purpose in their reoccurrence in the subsequent movements. Now comes the music indicative of "struggle" (Allegro, ma non troppo, C major, 3/4). This is followed by the Scherzo (Allegro vivace, C major, 2/4) which is brilliantly hurtling, thanks to the flood of sixteenth notes in the first violins. Two Trios enter the scheme. The first one, G major, 2/4 (actually 6/8), brings forward two themes, a vivacious one chiefly for horns and wood winds, and another that is more serene, for strings. The second Trio is mainly lyrical.

The Adagio espressivo is constructed of beautiful melody's own essence. A fugal subject, which some authorities consider an intrusion on the "mood of exalted lyricism," serves the structural purpose of combination with the restated chief theme. The finale runs a mercurial course. The "bugle calls" of the Introduction to the first movement reappear. The Symphony ends exultantly.

The score calls for two flutes, two oboes, two clarinets, two bassoons, two horns, two trumpets, three trombones, kettledrums, and strings. The Symphony is dedicated to "Oscar I, King of Sweden and Norway."

R. C. B.

Symphony in E flat major, No. 3 ("Rhenish"), Op. 97

I. Lebhaft (Lively). II. Scherzo: Sehr mässig (Very moderate). III. Nicht schnell (Not fast). IV. Feierlich (Solemnly). V. Lebhaft (Lively).

DETERMINING THE numerical order of a composer's overtures or symphonies is often an involved sport. The Haydn symphonies are still subject to scholarly scrutiny in this respect. Schubert's symphonies have posed one or two problems. and the intricate matter of Beethoven's *Fidelio* and *Leonore* Overtures was only satisfactorily worked out in recent years. One may call either of Chopin's two piano concertos "No. 1" and still be correct, depending on the perspective adopted.

Schumann's four symphonies also offer the strict chronologist some puzzling moments. The numbering of the *Rhenish Symphony* is misleading, for example. Actually it is the fourth, not the third, symphony. But precedent prevails, the precedent of date of publication. Nine years before he composed the

Rhenish Symphony, Schumann had written and released a Symphony in D minor. This was No. 2. As so often happened, Schumann was unhappy about this Symphony in its first estate. So No. 2 was retired from circulation for ten years. Meanwhile Schumann composed two more symphonies: the C major and the E flat major, called the *Rhenish.* Then he returned to No. 2 and reorchestrated it. The new version proved highly successful and was promptly published. But Symphony No. 2 now became Symphony No. 4. It is a comfort to know that one, at any rate, of Schumann's four symphonies is its true numerical self. That is Symphony No. 1, in B flat.

As for the "Rhenish" character of the Symphony, we have Schumann's own remarks to guide us. Shortly after the work was first performed in Düsseldorf in February, 1851, he wrote to Simrock the publisher, modestly stating that he would have been happy to see a greater composition about the Rhine brought out. His Symphony, he notes, "perhaps mirrors here and there something of Rhenish life." In writing the fourth movement, Schumann dwelt reminiscently on a ceremony he himself had witnessed in the Cologne Cathedral when the Archbishop of Geissel was installed as Cardinal.

Later he was more explicit. His plan, he divulged, had been to picture the Rhine valley in the joyous simplicity and fresh naturalness of its folk life. But Schumann wisely refrained from labeling the movements with descriptive mottos. One such title—"An Accompaniment to a Solemn Ceremony"—he affixed to the fourth movement, but speedily discarded it. "One ought not to show one's heart to people," he explained. "For a general impression of an art work is more effective; the listener then will not institute any absurd comparisons. Schumann himself thought especially well of this Symphony despite the cool response of public and critics to its first performance. His wife Clara evidently joined him in his predilection. After the Düsseldorf premiere of Feb. 6, 1851, at which Schumann conducted from manuscript, we find the devoted chronicler noting:

> The creative power of Robert was again ever new in melody, harmony, and form. I cannot say which one of the five movements is my favorite. The fourth is the one that at present is the least clear to me; it is most artistically made—that I hear—but I cannot follow it so well, while there is scarcely a measure in the other movements that remains unclear to me. And indeed to the layman this Symphony, especially in its second and third movements, is easily intelligible.

"The Symphony's first movement (*Lebhaft,* E flat major, 3/4) begins with the principal subject, proclaimed by the full orchestra. Flutes, oboes, and clarinets, answered by other wood winds and violins, give out the mournful second subject.

"The second movement (*Sehr mässig,* C major, 3/4) is a Scherzo, whose chief theme, announced by cellos and bassoons, is likened by William Foster Apthorp to 'a modified version of the so-called "Rheinweinlied." ' The theme, 'of a rather ponderous joviality,' well expresses 'the drinkers' "Uns ist ganz cannibalisch wohl, als wie fünf hundert Säuen!" ("As 'twere five hundred hogs, we feel so cannibalic jolly!") in the scene in Auerbach's cellar in Goethe's *Faust*.' In the trio the horns and other wind instruments play an A minor cantilena over a pedal C.

"The third movement (*Nicht schnell,* A flat major, 4/4) has for its chief subject, allotted to the clarinets and bassoons against an undulating viola accompaniment and pizzicati in the cellos, a melody that has reminded some of Mendelssohn and others of Edgardo's dying song, 'O tu che a Dio spiegasti l'ali,' in the last act of *Lucia di Lammermoor.*

"The fourth movement (*Feierlich,* E flat minor, 4/4) is usually called 'Cathedral Scene,' for obvious reasons. Here, for ecclesiastical effect, three trombones are added to the orchestra. The principal theme appears immediately in the horns and trombones.

"The jubilant finale (*Lebhaft,* E flat major, 2/2) is supposed to portray a festival in the Rhineland. Toward the end, music from the 'Cathedral Scene' emerges. There is a brilliant coda."

Besides the customary strings and the three trombones, the score calls for two flutes, two oboes, two clarinets, two bassoons, four horns, two trumpets, and kettledrums.

L. B.

Symphony in D minor, No. 4, Op. 120

I. Ziemlich langsam; Lebhaft (Un poco lento; Vivace). II. Romanze: Ziemlich langsam (Un poco lento). III. Scherzo: Lebhaft; Trio (Vivace). IV. Finale: Langsam; Lebhaft (Lento; Vivace).

[*Played without pause*]

THROUGH REVISION and delayed publication, Schumann's D minor is listed as Symphony No. 4. Actually it was Schumann's second. Written and premiered in 1841, the work remained in manuscript for ten years. Dissatisfied with it, largely because of the instrumentation, Schumann refused to have it published. Then in December, 1851, he took up the manuscript again. Drastic revision resulted. By March, 1853, the Symphony was ready for a second premiere. Publication followed that December. But meanwhile Schumann had written and published the symphonies in C and E flat. Thus, the D minor Symphony is No. 4 only in point of revision and date of publication.

Entries in Clara Schumann's diary, if accurate, show the Symphony to have been started late in May, 1841. "Robert," reads the notation under May 31, "began yesterday another symphony, which will be in one movement, and yet contain an adagio and a finale. I have heard nothing about it, yet I see Robert's activity and I hear the D minor sounding wildly from a distance, so that I know in advance that another work will be fashioned in the depths of his soul."

The devoted diarist evidently slipped in her chronology, or else her husband had been secretly at work on the Symphony for some time. For, three days later, she records the completion of three movements and expresses the hope that the Symphony will be ready by Schumann's birthday, which fell on June 8. Something must have gone wrong, for three full months went by before the ink dried on the final note. The Symphony still served to mark a birthday, however, if not Schumann's. Clara's came on Sept. 13, which was also the baptismal date of their first child Marie. Accordingly, on Sept. 13 Schumann tendered the finished score as a birthday gift. His words, "which I have quietly finished," would seem to indicate that he had planned it as a surprise. Wagner, it will be remembered, carried a similar surprise one step further by having the *Siegfried Idyl* presented on the morning of his wife's birthday through an actual performance on the staircase leading to her bedroom.

December 6, 1841, was the date of the D minor's premiere at the Gewandhaus in Leipzig. Featured on the program, however, was Liszt's *Hexameron* for two pianos, with the Schumanns appearing as soloists. The now forgotten work caused a sensation, utterly eclipsing the new *Symphony*. Clara writes grudgingly of the Liszt novelty: "It made a furore, as far as the audience was concerned, and we were obliged to repeat a part of it." The couple went home thoroughly unhappy that night. Robert kept reminding Clara of her bad playing in the *Hexameron,* and Clara could not get over Ferdinand David's poor conducting of the Symphony. For ten long years no more was heard of the D minor. Incidentally, the work was called a "Symphonistische Phantasie" in this early form.

When the Symphony again saw the light, in its altered version, Schumann himself conducted from manuscript. The concert occurred on Mar. 3, 1853, in Düsseldorf. Included, too, were excerpts from a Schumann Mass, and of course Clara Schumann was on hand to play the solo part of a Beethoven Concerto. The unbroken plan of the symphony was conveyed in the listing: *"Einleitung* [Introduction], Allegro, Romanze, Scherzo, and Finale *in einem Satz* [in one movement]." Schumann insisted that there be no pauses between movements. Mendelssohn was equally firm about having the *Scotch Symphony* played without interruption. The linking up of movements through certain recurring themes in part accounts for Schumann's wish to have it performed "without pause." By so relating the movements, Schumann to some extent foreshadowed the later cyclic form of symphony, in which reiterated themes are used to knit the work together.

Long after Schumann's death, a theory gained ground that the original version of the D minor Symphony was in many ways superior to the later.

Brahms, who owned the manuscript, was induced to have it published in an edition prepared by Franz Wüllner. So in October, 1889, forty-eight years after its sole hearing, the D minor cropped up again in its early form at a concert in Cologne. Performances followed in Boston and New York (Philharmonic Society) in 1892. Naturally comparisons were made of the two versions. Skillful cutting and condensing had obviously been made by Schumann, but many gave the 1841 version their vote for superior clarity of orchestration. On that point Schumann, however, had thought just the contrary. To Verhulst he wrote in May, 1853, that he had "thoroughly reinstrumented the symphony, and truly in a better and more effective way than it was scored at first." Of course, the consensus of opinion has long been that Schumann was no great judge of good or bad orchestration.

A somewhat somber introduction (Un poco lento, D minor, 3/4), opens the first movement, with violas and cellos stating the theme. The chief subject of this opening section is heard later as a theme of the Romanze movement. The main body of the first movement is a Vivace in D minor (2/4), built chiefly on an ascending figure brought in by the first violins at the end of the introduction. A second theme, in F major, is also announced by the first violins after the first section is repeated. Schumann's break with orthodox symphonic form may be noted in the free fantasia style of the second part, where wholly fresh material is introduced. Similarity has been found between a trombone figure here and a passage in Schumann's E flat Piano Quartet.

The plaintive chief theme of the Romanze slow movement (Un poco lento, D minor), given out by oboes and cellos against string pizzicati, is said to derive from a Provençal tune. For a time Schumann toyed with the idea of adding guitar accompaniment as well. The theme heard in the introduction returns at this point. Later the solo violin is featured in a web of counterpoint in D major. The Romanze ends with a return of the exquisite chief melody.

A rising and falling scale passage serves as base for the robust and energetic Scherzo (Vivace, D minor, 3/4). Wood winds give out the theme of the dreamy Trio, with its fascinating rhythms. The main Scherzo section returns, with the Trio then acting as coda.

After the winds chant a melodious phrase, the Finale gets under way with a brief introduction (Lento, B flat major, then D minor, 4/4), bringing back earlier material. The brisk, marchlike theme used as chief subject of the Finale proper (Vivace, D major, 4/4) recalls the first movement. A frolicsome second theme follows, first in B minor, the key of the ensuing free fantasia. There is elaborate development, after which the second theme returns and is worked over until the Coda brings in still another theme. The fast-moving scheme closes presto in D major.

Schumann dedicated the revised symphony to the Hungarian violinist Joseph Joachim, the inscription on the manuscript reading: "When the first tones of this symphony were awakened, Joseph Joachim was still a little fellow [ten years old]; since then the symphony and still more the boy have grown bigger, wherefore I dedicate it to him, although only in private. Düsseldorf, Dec. 23, 1853. Robert Schumann."

L. B.

Concerto for Piano and Orchestra in A minor, Op. 54

I. Allegro affettuoso. II. Intermezzo: Andantino grazioso. III. Allegro vivace.

ALTHOUGH WORK on this Concerto was begun in Leipzig in May, 1841, it was not till July 31, 1845, in Dresden, that Clara Schumann was able to record in her diary: "Robert has finished his Concerto and given it to the copyists." The intervening period was one of hectic activity for Schumann. During those three years he composed endlessly, in every form. Despite frail health, he traveled widely and even accompanied his wife on a Russian tour. A professorship in composition came to him from the newly founded Leipzig Conservatory. Until June, 1844, he was still editor of the *Neue Zeitschrift für Musik*. Twice his health broke under the strain, and once the overwork and feverish pace brought him to the verge of insanity, though it was not till a decade later that his mind finally snapped beyond repair.

On the other hand, they were years of great personal happiness. After ceaseless, at times slanderous, opposition from her father, Clara Wieck had become his wife. To the end it remained an ideal marriage, with unbounded love and devotion on both sides. Perhaps this new-found happiness was the incentive behind Schumann's extended efforts during those first three years as composer, editor, and teacher. Certainly his wife's alert understanding and encouragement were an unfailing stimulus to artistic activity. And in those first years of their marriage Clara had borne him two daughters, Marie and Elise.

Much of the Piano Concerto's romantic glow and exuberance are doubtless directly traceable to this happy home life. The same is true of Grieg's Piano Concerto, also written in the first years of his marriage. Neither composer, of course, believed in art as self-concealment. But the Concerto boasts a firmness of structure, a melodic inventiveness, a disciplined rhythmic force and richness of color, geared to high expressive purpose, indicating that Schumann's technical and artistic faculties were all at their prime during this period. Some critics regard it as Schumann's highest achievement, alike for form as for poetic content.

Yet the Concerto came into shape piecemeal, and all three movements in time were to have as many titles as a royal family. When the first movement was completed during the summer of 1841, Schumann had no thought of incorporating it into a Concerto. It bore the title "Phantasie in A minor" when Clara Schumann played it, rather informally, at a "private rehearsal" in the Gewandhaus, in Leipzig, on Aug. 13, 1841, held chiefly for revisions in her husband's first symphony. Two years later Schumann made several attempts to publish the piece separately, first as an "Allegro affettuoso," then as a "Concert Allegro," with the opus number "48." Nobody wanted it. The other two movements were finished in Dresden during the early summer months of 1845. They were then apparently labeled "Intermezzo" and "Finale." The three movements were listed as "Allegro affettuoso," "Andantino," and "Rondo" at the world premiere occurring in the Hall of the Hôtel de Saxe in Desden, on Dec. 4, 1845, when Clara Schumann was the soloist, and their devoted friend, Ferdinand Hiller, to whom the Concerto is dedicated, the conductor. The work was played from manuscript. (The orchestral parts were not published until July, 1846, while the full score had to wait another sixteen years for publication.)

Clara was again the soloist when Mendelssohn directed a second performance, in Leipzig, where the first movement had been composed. Schumann himself conducted the first Viennese performance on Jan. 1, 1847, with his wife at the keyboard for the third time. On that occasion the movements were listed as "Allegro affettuoso," "Intermezzo," and "Rondo vivace." S. B. Mills was the piano soloist when the Concerto was brought into the repertory of the New York Philharmonic Society on Mar. 26, 1859. Three years earlier Clara Schumann, on her first visit to England, had introduced the work to London at a concert of the New Philharmonic Society. That was on May 14. On the following June 30 she gave a recital that inspired the critic of the *Musical World* to write: "The reception accorded to this accomplished lady on her first coming to England will no doubt encourage her to repeat her visit. Need we say, to make use of a homely phrase, that she will be as 'welcome as the flowers in May'?"

Speaking of this Concerto, in his volume on the romantic composers, Daniel Gregory Mason observes:

The sincerity, tenderness, grace, and impetuous enthusiasm of the youthful romanticist are not in the least abated. What could be more contagious than the exuberant first movement, in which one hardly knows what to admire the more, the felicity of such details as the clarinet cantabile, the Andante espressivo for solo piano, and the nobly polyphonic cadenza, or the broadly climactic plan of the whole?

What could appeal more simply and directly to the heart than the delicate and yet ecstatic Andante grazioso, with its winding intermeshed melodies, clustering about the violoncello phrases as a grapevine festoons itself upon a tree? Yet perfectly wedded with all this feminine suavity and grace is a more masculine quality, a fine poise, restraint, reservation of force, which counteracts all tendency to feverishness, and gives the work a sort of impersonal dignity and beauty. . . .

One feels that the composer, no longer the victim of his moods, is shaping his work with the serene detachment of the artist. Particularly manifest is this new mastery in the rhythmical treatment of the finale. The rhythms here are as salient, as seizing, as ever, but they are far more various.

The orchestral part of the concerto calls for flutes, oboes, clarinets, bassoons, horns, trumpets in pairs, kettledrums, and the usual strings.

"While the first movement (Allegro affettuoso, A minor, 4/4) shows, naturally enough, the characteristics rather of a fantasia for piano and orchestra than of the authentic first movement of a concerto, it nevertheless demands through its own bigness supplementary movements. If the orchestra does not play here the orthodox role of a concerto's orchestra, it still is employed with more than Schumann's ordinary feeling for orchestral tone. This movement abounds in thematic material and changes of time and key. The principal theme, familiar as a household word, is first given out by wind instruments. From it is derived the second theme.

"For the second movement (Intermezzo: Andantino grazioso, F major, 2/4) Schumann has provided a romanze in at once his tenderest and most playful vein. It begins with a dialogue between piano and orchestra. A broadly lyrical second theme is introduced by the cellos. The first part of the movement is heard again. The principal theme of the first movement is hinted at before the Intermezzo passes without pause into the final Allegro vivace (A major, 4/4).

"Here again is a wealth of thematic material. The form of the movement is the sonata, and the development is elaborate and often brilliant. The coda runs to great length. Conspicuous in this movement are the chief subject, given out by the solo instrument, and the syncopated second subject, which the orchestra announces in E major."

L. B.

Concerto for Cello and Orchestra in A minor, Op. 129

I. Nicht zu schnell (Not too fast). II. Langsam (Slowly). III. Sehr lebhaft (Very lively).

[*Played without pause*]

EARLY IN September, 1850, Schumann, though already a sick man in mind and body, took up arduous new duties as music director at Düsseldorf. Clashes soon arose between him on one side and the orchestra personnel and governing committee on the other. A whispering campaign started, and charges were made that he was mentally unstable. As time went on orchestra and choir grew increasingly unruly. Finally, the committee sought to remove him. Schumann complained to his wife Clara that he was being cruelly persecuted. Clara agreed, though she doubtless sensed what was happening. Her husband was already on the downhill path to madness.

The gloom deepened. Schumann grew lax in his duties as Düsseldorf's director. The city's musical prestige began to suffer. The man was now hearing things and becoming suddenly terrified by spectral happenings. He suspected intrigues and conspiracies against him. Then one day he wrote down a theme given him by the angels in a dream, and once during an acute crisis he dashed out in the rain half-dressed and plunged into the Rhine. Rescued, he asked to be taken to a private asylum at Endenich, where, after some flashes of lucid thought and recognition, he went hopelessly insane and died one night in his sleep.

Overwork no doubt speeded Schumann's mental decline, especially during the Düsseldorf period. In the early months of his regime we find him working at the *Rhenish Symphony,* numerous songs, "Scenes from Goethe's 'Faust,'" the overture to Schiller's *The Bride of Messina,* and orchestrating Ruckert's "New Year Song." As music director, he conducted the subscription concert series, rehearsed the choir, and led performances of church music. Pupils came for lessons, among them Albert Dietrich. Schumann even organized a Düsseldorf chamber-music society. The pace was too sharp for his feeble health and nerves. For a time things went smoothly. Then the strain began to tell, and trouble started.

With such a record of feverish activity, it is perhaps not surprising to learn that Schumann completed the A minor Cello Concerto in a fortnight, from Oct. 10 to Oct. 24, 1850. References to the Concerto occur in Clara Schumann's diary. One, made on Nov. 16, reads: "Robert is now at work on something, I do not know what, for he has said nothing to me about it. The month before he composed a concerto for violoncello that pleased me very much. It appears to me to be written in true violoncello style."

Another entry is dated Oct. 11, 1851: "I have played Robert's Violoncello Concerto again and thus procured for myself a truly musical and happy hour. The romantic quality, the flight, the freshness, and the humor, and also the highly interesting interweaving of cello and orchestra are, indeed, wholly ravishing, and what euphony and deep sentiment are in all the melodic passages!"

There is evidence that Schumann was dissatisfied with the Concerto in its early version. As late as Nov. 1, 1852, he remarks in a letter to Härtel that the Concerto is at last ready for publication. However, Schumann was still busy correcting proofs in February, 1854, the month, incidentally, of his attempted suicide by drowning. The Concerto was finally published in Leipzig in August, 1854, a few months after Schumann was confined, at his own request, in the Endenich asylum. There is no record of a performance in his lifetime. The honor of a world premiere would seem to go to a performance at the Leipzig Conservatory on June 9, 1860, with Ludwig Ebert the soloist. The occasion was the fiftieth anniversary of Schumann's birth. Fifty years later, on Oct. 7, 1910, the Concerto was part of a centenary Schumann program played by the Boston Symphony Orchestra under the direction of Max Fiedler. Alwin Schroeder was the soloist.

Wood winds and pizzicato strings open the first movement [*Nicht zu schnell* (not too fast) A minor, 4/4] with a brief introductory passage. The cello then announces the main theme, with string support. This is developed. A tutti passage, given forte, leads to the second theme, given out in C major by the solo cello, which is then kept busy with passage work. After more development, the first theme returns in A minor. The second theme reappears in A major, the movement's final key. After the coda, the cello links the first with the second movement in a transition phrase.

A soothing cantabile theme serves as base for the second movement [*Langsam* (slow) F major, 4/4], which is largely a romanza for solo cello. The support is mostly in the strings, with occasional wood-wind entrances. A double-note passage for cello occurs immediately after the announcement of the theme. Toward the end of the movement the *Langsam* marking changes to *etwas lebhafter* (somewhat livelier) and a quick passage for the solo instrument ushers in the last movement without a break.

In the finale [*Sehr lebhaft* (very lively), A minor, 2/4] orchestra and cello begin with a brisk exchange of phrases. There is a tutti crescendo, and the cello brings in the first theme, starting in C major and modulating to A minor. After a flurry of passage work, the cello ushers in the second theme. Meanwhile fragments of the first theme crop up in the accompaniment. The material is worked out, the first theme then returning in the orchestra. At the end there is a brilliant cadenza for solo cello.

The orchestral scoring calls for two flutes, two oboes, two clarinets, two bassoons, two horns, two trumpets, kettledrums, and strings.

L. B.

Overture to Byron's "Manfred," Op. 115

IN HIS early biography of the composer, Joseph von Wasielewski tells how one day in Düsseldorf Schumann read Byron's poem aloud to a group of friends. As he read he became more and more excited, until at a particularly fervid passage, his voice broke. He burst into tears and stopped reading. Clara Schumann's diary is further testimony of Schumann's strange passion for Byron's so-called "witch drama." An entry of 1848 records the fact that her husband had set to work "on a new work, a sort of melodrama, Byron's *Manfred,* which stirred him to an extraordinary degree." When Robert read the poem to her—this time without interruption—she confesses being "deeply moved." On Nov. 14 she notes that Robert had come home the previous night with a bottle of champagne, the occasion being the "birthday festival" of the first section of the *Manfred* music.

The Overture is only part of Schumann's music for the dramatic poem. The composer projected the work for dramatic performance, supplying entr'actes, monologue accompaniment, and other incidental music. This, despite Byron's own avowal in a letter to his publisher Murray that he had rendered the poem *"quite impossible* for the stage, for which my intercourse with Drury Lane has given me the greatest contempt." Byron's suggested terms for the work were *Poem in Dialogue* or *Pantomime*—"anything but a green-room synonym."

When completed, the score was sent to Franz Liszt for a planned premiere at Weimar. After revising and rearranging it, Schumann felt convinced it could be "risked on the stage." Byron's *personae dramatis* of "spirits," Schumann suggested, should come on the stage not as "apparitions" but as "real people." In forwarding the manuscript to Liszt he expressed the pious hope that the great man would like the Overture, "one of the finest of my brain children," adding humbly, "I wish you may agree with me." Liszt did agree. "I count it among your greatest successes," he wrote back, after two performances in Weimar, which Schumann was unable to attend. "I believe that you would not have been dissatisfied with the musical preparation and performance of the work. The whole impression was a thoroughly noble, deep, elevating one, in accordance with my expectations."

One would suppose that Mrs. Schumann, in gratitude, would at least allow Liszt to keep the autograph score, as requested. Yet, the favor was refused, and we find the adroit Liszt addressing an oddly phrased letter with the returned manuscript.

I confess that I had flattered myself a little *in petto* that Robert would leave it with me in virtue of *possession* in a friendly manner. Our theater possesses an exact copy, which will serve us for subsequent performances of *Manfred*.

I was tempted to send you this copy, which for revision of proofs, would be sufficient, but I know not what scruple of honor kept me from doing so. Perhaps you will find that it is possible generously to encourage my slightly wavering virtue, and in that case you will have no trouble in guessing what would be to me a precious reward.

Later Clara waged bitter, unrelenting war on Liszt and his campfollowers. There was no restraint now, since her husband was dead. How she felt may be gathered from the fact that she removed the dedication to Liszt from the Fantasie, Op. 17.

Schumann was drawn to Byron's grandiloquent poem for many reasons. The hero was involved in some wild, impetuous struggle for human freedom. Romantic ardor surges through the poem, as well as Manfred's frantic anguish over a mysterious, inexpiable crime. Untrammeled remorse, expressed in rhapsodic laments, mingles with a kind of Promethean intensity. In the poem, Manfred's nobler side grapples with the forces of evil. The gnawing sense of guilt runs like a leitmotif through the drama. The spirit of Astarte, Manfred's dead sister, comes to console and guide him in the great spiritual bout. The struggle grows fiercer. Unlike Faust, Manfred rejects the compact with evil, remains the master of his fate, and dies liberated and redeemed.

No doubt William Hazlitt was right in regarding Manfred as Byron in fancy clothes. But it is a Byron far ahead of the earlier Byronic images of *Childe Harold* and the Oriental tales. The spiritual anguish is more genuine and the poet of freedom more resolute in his fight against dogma and tyranny. While Byron may have intended the poem as a tribute to his half-sister Augusta, to whom he was deeply attached, and as a gesture of self-pity over the undivulged "crime," the immediate inspiration came from a reading of Goethe's *Faust* and a tour of the Bernese Alps. The drama unfolds "amongst the Higher Alps— partly in the Castle of Manfred and partly in the Mountains." A typical romantic touch is found in Byron's directions for the opening scene—"A Gothic Gallery."

Goethe not only regarded *Manfred* as a "wonderful phenomenon," but declared that "Hamlet's soliloquy appears improved on here." When Byron, who knew only a few oaths in German, was shown the German newspaper containing Goethe's remarks, he concluded from the one word *hypocondrisch* that the review was unfavorable. His friend Hoppner, however, translated the whole review and Byron was elated that "the greatest man of Germany, perhaps of Europe" had praised his poem in such glowing terms. Some of the tonic grandeur of *Manfred* doubtless stems from Byron's view of the famous Staub- bach peak, where he "heard the avalanches falling every five minutes—as if God was pelting the Devil down from Heaven with snowballs." In another letter he describes the glacier at Grindelwald as a "frozen hurricane."

Byron's dramatic poem is closely followed in the plan of Schumann's Over- ture. The mysterious "crime" haunting Manfred is immediately suggested in the three quick syncopated chords given out by full orchestra. The slow intro- duction that follows conveys Manfred's brooding, troubled nature. The pace quickens, leading to the main section of the overture, marked *In leidenschaft- lichem Tempo* (in a passionate tempo). Manfred's struggle appears in the chief theme, assigned to the first violins. This is enlarged upon, with the syncopated motive of Manfred's guilt, reappearing. Then a contrasting second theme enters —pathetic, plaintive—Astarte's melody. Brisk development follows, intended to mirror the growing fierceness of Manfred's struggle, leading to a free fan- tasia section. The theme of guilt returns in an ominous chord for trumpets. Finally the unrest simmers down, part of the Astarte theme is heard in the wood winds, the violins give a brief echo of the first theme, and the Overture sighs out the death of Manfred.

L. B.

Alexander Scriabin

BORN: MOSCOW, JAN. 6, 1872. DIED: MOSCOW, APR. 27, 1915.

Scriabin has given us synthetic music, "musicine," a product which bears much the same relation to music as margarine to butter, and saccharine to sugar.—CECIL GRAY.

"Prometheus: The Poem of Fire," Op. 60

SCRIABIN'S SYMPHONIC ode to the mythical fire bearer was his last work for orchestra. Composed in 1909-1911, it was performed in Moscow on Mar. 15, 1911, and published later that year. Two preceding works, *The Divine Poem* and *The Poem of Ecstasy,* were parts of a planned cosmic cycle. *Prometheus* was to be followed by *Mysterium,* which the so-called "Muscovite seer" envisioned as a gigantic ritual of the senses blending music, color, word, mimicry, and smell. The rebirth of man was to be its theme. Its premiere was reserved for India, the home of Karma and strange mysticism. In the midst of this vast creation, death stepped in. Thus the cycle ended with *Prometheus.*

From all reports Scriabin's *Mysterium* would have made *Prometheus* sound puny by comparison. Yet, *The Poem of Fire* is no small-scale phenomenon in program and project. Scriabin planned it as "a symphony of sounds" to be accompanied by "a symphony of color rays." For the purpose he invented a special color keyboard, called a *tastiera per luce* or *clavier à lumière.* With it, colored lights were projected on a screen. Light and music were thus to be synchronized in symbolic union. Scriabin apparently saw special significance in that as "a perfect rite." It is not known exactly why the *clavier à lumière* did not figure in the Moscow performance. One story is that the instrument was not ready. Another is that at the last moment it failed to function.

At any rate, the contraption was used when Modest Altschuler and the Russian Symphony Orchestra played the *Poem* in New York in 1915. Scriabin's wishes were carried out to the letter. Colors flashed on a screen in shifting nuance with the music. The audience was distracted by the novelty. Few paid any attention to the music. Those who did, found little parallel between the lighting and the music. The result was described as "not encouraging." Possibly it was not time for Walt Disney "Fantasias." Although the score calls for piano, organ, chorus of mixed voices, *clavier à lumière,* besides a huge array of instruments, Scriabin considerately authorized performances of *The*

Poem of Fire without chorus or color. In the score the part for the *clavier à lumière* appears with notes on the top staff.

At this point a few definitions may be helpful in understanding Scriabin's Promethean aims. Theosophy, which he professed, involves a knowledge of the Divine Being through "spiritual ecstasy, direct intuition, or special individual relations." Karma, the Sanskrit word for fate, is used by theosophists to mean the quality of an action which imposes on the subject an obligation or condition in a future state. Mysticism, of course, involves communication between Man and his Maker. The Mystic also solves mysteries through "internal revelation." As for Prometheus, the "forethinker," he was the Titan who stole fire from heaven and gave it to mortals. According to Scriabin's program, mankind lived in a crude Karma-less state before Prometheus came along. The gift of fire awakened good men to creative activity. But it also turned grosser natures to evil purpose. Fire was thus a boon and a curse to Man. The conflict between both forces is imaged in Scriabin's *Poem* in two contrasting themes, ending in the triumph of High Purpose. Rosa Newmarch boldly set forth the program as follows:

We have here the elements of a fairly definite and infinitely varied psychological program: the crepuscular, invertebrate state of Karma-less humanity; the awakening of the will to create, in both its aspects; the strange moods of bliss and anguish which follow the acquisition of consciousness; probably, also, the last, fierce rebellion of the lower self preceding final ecstasy of union, when the human mingles with the divine—with *Agni*, the fire which receives unto itself all other sparks in the ultimate phase of development.

Of course this Prometheus sounds like a very distant cousin indeed of the Prometheus of Aeschylus and Shelley.

It was this sort of thing that made *illuminati* worship at Scriabin's shrine for years. Even in 1925 it was said that "among European modernists his ghost disputes with the living Stravinsky the distinction of being the musical idol of the younger set." His later works were hailed as "mystical rites" by votaries. "Music," they said, "was merely the language Scriabin used to foretell the future." Art and religion were regarded as one by the starry-eyed Russian. Music was a medium of "religious ecstasy." The world was expected to go to Scriabin's symphonic creations as to High Mass. If Wagner had devised the perfect drama, Scriabin had discovered the perfect rite. "As Byrd brings pathos," the epigram ran, "Bach brings drama, Beethoven heroism, so Scriabin brings ecstasy into music." Cognoscenti insisted that a knowledge of theosophy was needed to grasp Scriabin's music. To which D. C. Parker retorted: "Few musicians are theosophists and few theosophists musicians." When we listen to Scriabin, said Siegfried Lavoie-Herz, in a pronouncement worthy of the master, "the human body ceases to be felt as body."

Karma works mysteriously. The composer who felt destined to play a great part in Man's salvation, the Mystic of Mystics who at times thought himself God, this prophet of universal uplift and cosmic design, while confecting a giant amalgam of the senses in art died ironically from a common boil.

L. B.

Dmitri Shostakovich

BORN: ST. PETERSBURG, SEPT. 25, 1906.

I consider that every artist who isolates himself from the world is doomed. I find it incredible that an artist should want to shut himself away from the people, who, in the end, form his audience. I think an artist should serve the greatest possible number of people. I always try to make myself as widely understood as possible, and, if I don't succeed, I consider it my own fault.—DMITRI SHOSTAKOVICH.

Symphony No. 1, Op. 10

I. Allegretto; Allegro non troppo. II. Allegro. III. Lento: Largo. IV. Allegro molto.

DMITRI SHOSTAKOVICH's music is unique in having been written about almost as if it were a chapter in Karl Marx's *Das Kapital*. Political and social theory has played a dominant role in appraising his work, and Shostakovich's own statements on Soviet institutions and the role of music in a classless society have stimulated analysts to keener research into symphonic polemics. For a time many outside Russia regarded his work as a kind of regimented materialism stated in symphonic terms, and the shadow of the Kremlin was held to bulk large over his esthetics.

From the time the outer world began to take notice, Shostakovich never hesitated to outline his aims and purposes, and of course they coincided so closely with the dialectical teachings of Marx, Engels, and Lenin, not to overlook Stalin, that many jumped to the conclusion that the dictates of propaganda were straitjacketing an exciting new talent. Others did not care and heard only music. The fact that some of Shostakovich's symphonies celebrated the October Revolution and a May Day vision of world socialism only made matters worse. This startling young genius, many felt, was assuredly working in a groove. They pounced on statements like the following as admission of doctrinaire rigidity and submission to authority:

I am a Soviet composer, and I see our epoch as something heroic, spirited, and joyous. . . . Music cannot help having a political basis—an idea that the bourgeoisie are slow to comprehend. There can be no music without ideology. The old composers, whether they knew it or not, were upholding a political theory. Most of them, of course, were bolstering the rule of the upper classes.

We revolutionists have a different conception of music. Lenin himself said that "music is a means of unifying broad masses of people." Not a leader of masses, perhaps, but certainly an organizing force! It is no longer an end in itself, but a vital weapon in the struggle.

The plain, irrefutable fact of the matter, according to a later verdict, is that Shostakovich is the typical Soviet youth, nurtured during a revolutionary upheaval, knowing no other social order, and trained to view all phenomena, including art, as rooted in and reflecting political and economic reality. To what extent the Marxist method, as pure theory, works side by side with native genius in his creative processes is indeterminate. Deciding how much of Shostakovich's output is the direct result of dialectics carried consciously into practice and how much the normal artistic reaction of genius to external stimuli is futile speculation. Yet, Shostakovich cannot be considered apart from his milieu. But, then, that also applies to Palestrina, Beethoven, and Wagner. It is merely a shift in focus and emphasis.

Many critics alleged that Shostakovich was taking his creed too literally and regarded the politics as irrelevant. Marxists accepted it as exemplifying the doctrine of art as struggle toward a new synthesis. At any rate, Shostakovich is an active cog in the Soviet machine. Its heroes are his and its criteria of heroic deeds evidently his pride and guide. He worships the memory of Lenin, and his bookshelves are said to be laden with the writings of the founding Marxist fathers. In the bomb cellars of Lenin's city he completed his Seventh Symphony and helped defend his own birthplace as a fire warden. The actual and the abstract, the real and the ideal, the immediate and the ultimate merge remarkably in his work. He admitted frankly in 1936:

I cannot think of my further progress apart from our socialist structure, and the end which I set to my work is to contribute at every point toward the growth of our country. There can be no greater joy for a composer than the inner assurance of having assisted by his works in the elevation of Soviet musical culture, of having been called upon to play a leading role in the recasting of human perception.

Shostakovich has for many years been considered a kind of "composer laureate to the Soviet State." His *October Symphony,* composed when he was twenty-one for the tenth anniversary of the Bolshevik Revolution, was presented simultaneously in Moscow, Leningrad, Kiev, and Karkoff as part of the nationwide celebration. It has since been repeated annually at similar festivities. His *May Day Symphony,* written two years later, in 1929, is also an annual rite, reportedly "stirring Russian audiences on each succeeding May Day."

Shostakovich suffered a temporary but significant eclipse early in 1936 when his opera *Lady Macbeth of Mzensk* was denounced by Soviet critics as "un-Soviet, unwholesome, cheap, eccentric, tuneless, and leftist." Others flouted its "bourgeois formalistic tendencies" and "vulgar realism," and the issue was raised of "folk consciousness" versus "an indulgence in fruitless devices to enrapture the art gourmands." The composer whom the outside world feared too deeply enmeshed in theories of proletarian culture, was now charged with failing to talk to the people "in a new, powerful, and intelligible language." As an "advanced" Soviet composer, he had failed to "plunge into the social currents swirling around him." His Fifth Symphony reestablished him at home and gave him greater prestige abroad.

The First Symphony was completed in 1925, "the product," Shostakovich tells, "of my culminating studies at the Conservatory." He had entered the Leningrad academy in 1919, after studying music for four years, and won his diploma in 1925. After taking courses in piano and composition with L. Nikolaiev, counterpoint with M. Sokolov, and harmony and orchestra with Maximilian Steinberg, he attended post-graduate lectures in composition given by Steinberg. He writes:

I was then absorbing with enthusiasm and quite uncritically all the knowledge and fine points being taught me. But once my studies were completed, the necessity of assorting a large part of the musical baggage which I had acquired arose. I sensed that music was not merely combinations of sounds, arranged in a particular order, but an art capable of expressing through its own means the most varied ideas and feelings. This conviction I did not reach without difficulty. During the whole of 1926 I did not write a single note, but from 1927 I have never stopped composing.

According to the American writer Nicolas Slonimsky and the Leningrad critic I. I. Sollertinsky, Shostakovich's earliest music reflected the Rimsky-Korsakoff and Glazounoff tradition still flourishing at the Leningrad Conservatory. Mr. Slonimsky writes:

Yet his first symphony shows some definite departure from traditionalism. Thus, the recapitulation in the first movement reverses the order of the subjects (he uses the same method in his Cello Sonata of 1934, which shows that it is no youthful whim). The harmony of the Symphony is far more acrid than any academic training would justify, and the linear writing is hardly counterpoint conscious. There are such strange interludes as a kettledrum solo. The melody structure is angular, chromatic at times, and then again broad, suggesting a folk song rather than a subject for a symphony. Yet, there is enough symphonic academism in this first important work of Shostakovich to connect it with his academic training.

The Symphony was first heard in Leningrad on May 12, 1926, at a concert directed by Nicolas Malko. By the following year it had carried the name of Shostakovich to other parts of Europe. Bruno Walter conducted it in Berlin in November, 1927, and on Nov. 2, 1928, Leopold Stokowski introduced it to America at a concert of the Philadelphia Orchestra. The New York Philharmonic-Symphony brought the work into its repertory on Apr. 8, 1931, when Arturo Toscanini directed. The score fails to number the symphony, merely labeling it "Symphony for Orchestra, Op. 10."

Unlike the *May Day* and *October* Symphonies, as well as the Fifth, composed in 1937 for the Soviet Republic's twentieth anniversary, and the Seventh, inspired by the siege of Leningrad, Shostakovich's First Symphony is not avowedly an utterance of urgent political and social faith. Lawrence Gilman termed it "primarily an esthetic expression rather than a tonal tract," pointing out that if the music is a vehicle of economic doctrine, "Shostakovich has kept the fact to himself."

"There is an Allegretto introduction to the first movement (4/4) in which the first theme, in three sections, is heard. The theme is heard again, in F minor, when the movement proper begins (Allegro non troppo). The flute gives out the second theme in C minor against a background of strings played pizzicato. It passes to the clarinet and thence to the basses. After impassioned development the movement closes softly.

"A scherzo (Allegro, 4/4; 5/4) follows. The chief theme, in A minor, is announced by the violins to a pizzicato accompaniment. The trio (Meno mosso, E minor, 3/4) has a subject assigned to two flutes under an inverted pedal E which persists in the second violins for fifty measures.

"The slow movement (Lento, D flat major, 4/4) opens lyrically with a mournful oboe solo chromatic in character. Eventually the melancholy song dies away, and after a hushed passage in the divided strings a crescendo drum roll leads into the finale, marked by sharp contrasts in pace and mood.

"One measure of Allegro molto prefaces twenty-nine measures of Lento which constitute an introduction to the main body of the movement. Beginning Allegro molto in F minor, this movement presents its chief theme in the clarinet. A new theme in A major is given out by strings and wood winds. Still another theme is heard from a solo violin (Meno mosso) and then from a solo horn. The Allegro molto comes back, and the movement proceeds through an Adagio and a Largo to a Presto close in F major."

                                                                        L. B.

Symphony No. 5, Op. 47

I. Moderato. II. Allegretto. III. Largo. IV. Allegro non troppo.

At its first performance, Leningrad, Nov. 21, 1937, The Fifth Symphony was received with tremendous enthusiasm, press and public alike going virtually into hysterical raptures over the work. It was said that Shostakovich —just previously rather at odds with the powers that be—had, at last, freed himself from "individualistic chaos and formalistic experimentation." Even the late Alexei Tolstoy, writing about the piece in *Izvestia,* remarked on the

composer's "emancipation." "Glory be to our people which procreates such
talents," he declared. "Today we have ten masters, tomorrow there will be
hundreds. Soviet art is world art, it must be world art!"

Another said:

Shostakovich's Fifth Symphony is a work of great importance, as a milestone in
the composer's development. The fetters of formalism, which held the composer so
long and prevented him from creating works profound in conception, have been
torn off. He must follow up this new trend in his work. He must turn more boldly
toward Soviet reality. He must understand it more profoundly and find in it a new
stimulus for his work.

The first American performance of the Symphony was at a concert of the
NBC Symphony, Artur Rodzinski conducting, on Apr. 9, 1938. It entered
the Philharmonic-Symphony's repertoire during the Society's Centennial Season on Feb. 19, 1942, Serge Koussevitzky appearing as guest conductor.

It is scored for two flutes, piccolo, two oboes, clarinets in A, B flat, and
E flat, two bassoons, contra-bassoon, four horns, three trumpets, three trombones, tuba, tympani, bass drum, cymbals, triangle, tambour militaire, tam-
tam, xylophone, bells, celesta, piano, two harps, and strings.

The first movement presents two themes; the first, made of wide intervals,
is given antiphonal treatment by low and high strings, the second, a long
melody. The movement is developed mostly by means of melodic accumulation, and there is an interplay of rhythms, by turns mild and vigorous, each
successive change serving to alter the quality (and occasionally the mood)
of the material.

The second movement has themes that resemble the Ländler waltz, and
their manipulation is much in the form of a scherzo.

The Largo again presents a development based on melodic rise and
change, with the theme passing from string to wind choirs. An especial
feature is the fortissimo at the end, contrived without brass.

The fourth movement, a rondo in design, high lights a march rhythm,
plus a tune of Russian origin, or, perhaps, resemblance. A slower part presents once more material from the first movement, a particular fragment of
which gets new development. The tempo speeds up, as the Symphony ends.

R. C. B.

Symphony No. 6, Op. 53

I. Largo. II. Allegro. III. Presto.

THE Leningrad premiere of the Fifth Symphony occurred on Nov. 21, 1937.
Almost exactly a year later Shostakovich announced plans for a new symphony

in the *Sovietskoyo Iskusstvo* (*Soviet Art*) of Nov. 20, 1938. A great admirer and student of Lenin, he had long projected a musical memorial to the Soviet's founding father. Lenin, he now revealed, was to be the theme of his Sixth Symphony. He was going to express "through the medium of sound the immortal image of Lenin as a great son of the Russian people and a great leader and teacher of the masses." Shostakovich also disclosed that his decision had been prompted by letters received by him from every corner of the Soviet Union. They contained advice about his next symphony. What especially impressed him was the recurring suggestion "to make ample use of musical folklore." As Slonimsky observes, Shostakovich probably intended to link Russian folklore and the Revolution through "the symbolic figure of Lenin." Chorus and soloists were included in the new plans. The verses were to be by peasant poets.

For some reason, Shostakovich abandoned the project. Lenin's name was not on the Symphony when it was first performed on Dec. 3, 1939, during the two-month Festival of Soviet Music held in Moscow. As a matter of fact, the Symphony stirred up little interest at the time. The festival audience received it without excitement. The biggest ovations went, insead, to cantatas by Prokofieff (*Alexander Nevsky*), Shaporin (*On Kulikov Field*), and Koval (*Emelian Pugatchov*), all based on heroic exploits in early Russian history. The following month the magazine *Sovietskaya Musica* was far from adulatory in its objective analysis. "The lesson was made fairly clear," says Mr. Slonimsky. "What was needed in the year 1940 was the romanticization of Russia circa 1240, while Shostakovich devoted his talent principally to satirizing Russia circa 1840." However, the Soviet public responded more cordially at subsequent hearings, which have been numerous.

The American premiere of the Sixth Symphony—also announced as "the first performance outside Russia"—occurred in Philadelphia on Nov. 29, 1940, at a concert of the Philadelphia Orchestra. Leopold Stokowski conducted. The work entered the Boston Symphony repertory on Mar. 20, 1942. At the Philadelphia premiere the program book carried a statement by Mr. Stokowski about the differences in aim and style between Shostakovich's Fifth and Sixth Symphonies. Mr. Stokowski stated:

In his Fifth Symphony, Shostakovich painted in tone the inner and outer experiences of an artist's life—sometimes expressing the boisterous humor of crowds in the street, as in the fourth part—sometimes painting with ironic splashes of color a gaminlike humor, as in the second part—and sometimes telling by the simplest orchestral means the innermost reveries of his spirit in dark and melancholy coloring, or rising to sublime heights of ecstasy, as in the third part.

In his Fifth Symphony, Shostakovich has composed music in the usual sequence of symphonic form, but in his Sixth Symphony he has become more individualistic. It is in three parts, instead of four, and the first part is the slow movement, the second the scherzo, the third is based on dance rhythms and later has themes inspired by the popular folklore of Russia. These three parts are strongly contrasted and are remarkable for the firmness of their melodic outline, rhythm, and musical character.

In each symphony Shostakovich shows himself to be more of a master, to be ever growing, ever expanding in his imagination and musical consciousness. In his Sixth Symphony he has reached new depths, especially in the first part. Here are harmonic sequences, and several melodies sounding at the same time, making modern counterpoint, which are of great originality and intensity of expression. At the first hearing they sound strange and even obscure, as if the meaning was concealed and hidden. But after hearing this music three or four times it suddenly becomes clear and has great depth of expression.

The three-movement scheme is unusual for Shostakovich. It is as if the Symphony had shed an opening Allegro movement and begun with its slow movement, Largo—Shostakovich's "favorite indication for a slow tempo," as Mr. Slonimsky points out. An unusual feature of the second, or scherzo, movement is the first appearance of the E flat clarinet in a symphonic score by Shostakovich. The extensive array of instruments also includes, besides strings, two flutes, piccolo, two oboes, English horn, three clarinets in B, bass clarinet, two bassoons, contra-bassoon, three trumpets, four horns, three trombones, tuba, tympani, tambourine, military drum, bass drum, cymbals, triangle, tam-tam, xylophone, celesta, and harp.

The Largo exceeds in length the combined second and third movements. Cellos, violas, and wood winds state the lyric first subject of the movement, with the high strings carrying it upward. The strings then take up a somber second theme. This is broadly expanded. As the development subsides, expressive solos are assigned to English horn and flute. At one point the strings repeat the main theme, lifting it to quivering heights as the brasses apply sonorous phrases against it. A four-note figure, heard earlier, recurs prominently toward the end, uttered in succession by winds and strings, and with its melodic intervals somewhat altered. The movement dies down gradually.

The scherzolike second movement—with its skirling runs, bouncing rhythms, weird percussive effects, and sudden shifts to pastoral moods—contrasts sharply with the somber intensity and broad lyricism of the Largo. The E flat clarinet and piccolo have vital roles in scherzo scheme, and the xylophone rattles out in slightly macabre or sardonic vein. In one of the abrupt transitions a flute chants a quaintly bucolic passage. From a fairly amiable start, the movement climbs to a shattering climax toward the end, with brasses and battery going strong, and finally returns to normal.

In the rondolike Presto finale (in common time, like the Largo movement) folklike march and dance motives mingle in a brash and swaggering whirl of rhythms. One of the themes bears a saucy, Offenbachian flavor. The second part of it seems to twist itself sardonically out of shape. At one place there is that sudden intrusion of a village-band motive which comes up repeatedly in Shostakovich's music for humorous or satiric effect. A certain quick phrase will remind many of the opening of the Mexican folk song "Cielito Lindo." The xylophone even tosses in a rhythmic suggestion of the "Anvil Chorus" from Verdi's *Il Trovatore*. A brisk marching song bursts into the scheme, and the dominant impression is of some outdoor holiday frolic.

L. B.

Symphony No. 7, Op. 60

> Allegretto. II. Moderato poco allegretto. III. Adagio. IV. Allegro non troppo.

It is now known that Shostakovich had planned a Seventh Symphony some time before the sudden rupture of the Russo-German entente. As early as December, 1940, he had said, "In 1941, I hope to complete my Seventh Symphony, which I shall dedicate to the great genius of mankind—Vladimir Ilyitch Lenin." Then came the bombshell before the bombs. But let Shostakovich himself tell it:

On that peaceful summer morning of June 22, 1941, I was on my way to the Leningrad Stadium to see my favorite Sunday soccer game. Molotoff's radio address found me hurrying down the street. . . . Our fruitful, constructive existence was rudely shattered! At the Leningrad Conservatory, where I was head of the pianoforte department, vacations begin on July 1. But this was not the usual vacation time. Professors and students remained to form a local air-raid defense unit. I served as a fire fighter. I had already applied as a volunteer in the army, but, although my application was already accepted, I was not called for duty. Instead, I was asked to join the theater section of the People's Volunteer Army. . . . Meanwhile, in the first hot July days, I started on my Seventh Symphony, conceived as a musical embodiment of the supreme ideal of patriotic war. The work engrossed me completely. Neither the savage air raids nor the grim atmosphere of a beleaguered city could hinder the flow of musical ideas. . . . I worked with an inhuman intensity. I continued to compose marches, songs, and film music, and attended to my organizational duties as chairman of the Leningrad Composers' Union, and then would return to my symphony, as though I had never left it.

One can visualize the difficulties under which the Symphony was written. The composer's duties during the period of the Symphony's development included, besides those of fire warden, occasional visits to the front lines where he played for the Russian heroes. He consorted with the men who had "halted the fascist hordes at the very gates of Leningrad—airmen, artillerymen, sailors and infantry, tankmen and snipers."

His hatred of the enemy was enough to destroy all fear of him. And that Symphony which had been intended as a monument to Lenin, now came into being in a dedication to "the ordinary Soviet people, the heroes of this patriotic war."

Shostakovich began on the actual composition toward the end of July, 1941. The first movement was ready by Sept. 3, the second by Sept. 17, and the third at the end of that month. The Government moved to Kuibyshev and the composer followed, putting the finishing touches to the Symphony at that city in December.

In a broadcast Shostakovich explained his work. He said:

The first and longest movement bears a dramatic and, I would say, tragic character. Our peaceful life has been broken up by a threatening event, war, and everything has to be subordinated to its laws. The music also has another theme; a requiem expressing the people's sorrow over their dead heroes.

The next two movements were intended as an intermezzo. They confirm life in opposition to war. I tried to express the thought that art, literature, and science must advance in spite of war. It is, if you like, a polemic against the statement that "when the cannons roar the muse is silent."

The fourth movement is dedicated to our victory. It is an immediate continuation of the second and third movements; their logical outcome. It is the victory of light over darkness, wisdom over frenzy, lofty humanism over monstrous tyranny.

Francis D. Perkins, reviewing the American premiere of the Seventh Symphony for the *New York Herald Tribune,* wrote:

The work, as a whole, has been described as a symphony about the men and women of the Soviet Union. The first movement's programmatic course is easily understood in the light of an interpretation furnished by the composer, or, indeed, without any advance information. The opening theme, straightforward and vigorous, and the pastoral episodes which follow, represent ordinary people going about their daily lives. A long crescendo, in which an initially light tapping on a drum and a persistent marching figure wax for twelve minutes to an overwhelming sonority, portrays the onset of war, and elegiac measures follow.

The programmatic intent of the second and third movements is less apparent. The second is dominated by a pleasing, fluent melody of rather rural character; the third movement is episodic and varied in mood. The finale signifies victory. Here a rushing, martial theme gives way to weighty measures whose rhythms recall a theme in Beethoven's *Egmont Overture,* and the mood and character of the music then herald a waxing triumph.

This huge Symphony, with its lengthy first movement, "virtually a tone poem in itself," said Mr. Perkins, requires a giant orchestra. The composer's orchestration has been praised for its lightness and transparency, despite the many instruments.

The Seventh Symphony's premiere performance occurred at Kuibyshev on Mar. 1, 1942. It was played by the orchestra of Moscow's Bolshoi Theater under the direction of Samuel Samosud. The large audience, containing many high diplomats and Red Army dignitaries, rose to the occasion with sensational enthusiasm. The composer, called many times to the stage, accepted his accolade politely. Politely, too, he declined to speak.

In keeping with the superdrama of the work's composition is the romantic tale of its arrival on microfilm to this country. Packed safely in a little tin box, the photographed score traveled by plane from Kuibyshev to Teheran, by automobile from Teheran to Cairo, and by plane from Cairo to New York. In something over a week a corps of photographers printed from those films 252 pages of music, a healthy four volumes of symphonic score. On July 19, 1942, Arturo Toscanini and the NBC Symphony Orchestra played it over the National Broadcasting Company's network in the first performance to be given it in this country.

The Symphony had by then already wild fired its way through the major cities of the Soviet Union, and the gathering at the Moscow premiere, on Mar. 19, was so absorbed in it that all present remained glued to their seats throughout its considerable length, despite the shrill sounds of an air-raid alarm. To complete the record, the initial performance of the Symphony outside Russia took place at Albert Hall in London, on June 29, 1942, three weeks before the NBC broadcast. The following August Serge Koussevitzky led the Berkshire Music School Orchestra in two performances. Artur Rodzinski brought the Symphony into the Philharmonic-Symphony's repertoire on Oct. 14, 1942.

R. C. B.

Symphony No. 8, Op. 65

I. Adagio. II. Allegretto. III. Allegro non troppo. IV. Largo. V. Allegretto.

[*Last three movements played without pause*]

THIS SYMPHONY was given its official premiere in Moscow on Nov. 4, 1943, during the holiday period celebrating the twenty-fifth anniversary of the birth of the Soviet Union (the actual anniversary date was Nov. 7, 1943). The piece was previewed the evening before at a concert in the Bolshoi Zal of the Moscow Conservatorium before an audience of artists, musicians, actors, opera singers, critics, and journalists. Its first performance in the Western Hemisphere was given by the Philharmonic-Symphony under Arturo Toscanini's direction on Apr. 2, 1944.

William Downs, Moscow correspondent of the Columbia Broadcasting System and the magazine *Newsweek* said of that preview:

This was the acid test. The opinions of those people make or break a work of art in the Soviet Union. They will return to their artists', actors', writers', and singers' clubs to discuss the new work. Out of those discussions will come the final decision

—and the only recourse from their opinion is the acceptance of the general public, which overrules expert decisions in any country in the world.

Before the performance, Shostakovich wandered nervously around the hall, shaking hands and greeting friends. He was exceedingly nervous. He still manages to look like a twelve-year-old schoolboy caught playing hookey. He kept brushing the forelock of his hair from his forehead.

Eugene Mravinsky [to whom the Symphony is dedicated], conductor of the Leningrad Symphony, an old friend of the composer and one of the best music brains in the Soviet Union, had been imported from Novosibersk to conduct the State Symphony Orchestra for the event. . . .

Whatever the world's verdict, the all-important critics' audience applauded with more than polite enthusiasm (Prokofieff was most enthusiastic), and the public premiere the next night was a repetition of success.

Of course, the premiere of any new work by Shostakovich is an event of prime importance in the Soviet Union. The newspapers carry endless stories about it, heaping praise—if that be the order of things—or, on the other hand, doing as extensive and complete a job of fulminating. From a perusal of critiques in the Soviet press, following the premiere of the Eighth Symphony, one would judge the work to have been received with acclaim, to say the least. However, neither *Izvestia* nor *Pravda,* Russia's leading publications, had so much as a word of evaluation to say concerning this latest essay of Shostakovich. If there is significance in their silence, none of it has been interpreted officially, as yet. At any rate, the score of the Symphony carries the bold stamp "permission granted for export," which is significant enough in itself.

Grigori Shneerson, writing in *Moscow News,* the only English language newspaper in the Soviet Union, delivered himself of the following review:

It is extremely difficult, and often inadvisable, to try to give an exhaustive analysis of this truly great work after hearing it for the first time. A composition of this kind should be heard several times so that it may be digested and assimilated.

In his new Symphony, the composer himself has given a key for understanding it. According to Shostakovich, the Eighth Symphony is "an attempt to look into the future, into the postwar epoch." He spoke of its ideological and philosophical conception being expressed in the words "All that is evil and ugly will disappear and beauty will triumph."

If we regard the Symphony from this aspect, we will see how Shostakovich by his very nature sets off in its own pure light the "beautiful" from the "heavy, somber shadows of the ugly and the evil" until he achieves out of the blackness of Dante's *Inferno* the radiant glory of the future. Shostakovich gives a stirringly tragic picture from the present grim and majestic drama of peoples suffering from "blood, sweat and tears."

The composer's thoughts and emotions of the war and of the future are contained in his war diary written not in the storm days of Autumn 1941 but in the present time of rejoicing, when final victory and peace are no longer mere slogans but are within the reach of all mankind. This diary is written with his heart's blood. That is why it is so powerful.

The Eighth Symphony is not easy to understand. It has few "catchy" passages. Its first movement, an Adagio, takes twenty-eight minutes, and its two marches have little in common with what we are generally accustomed to expect from this form. In the Passacaglia there are no broad melodies, and the finale lacks the traditional triumphant march. Nevertheless, the Symphony makes a profound impression.

The five movements of the Eighth Symphony comprise an Adagio; an Allegretto (March); an Allegro non troppo (March); a Largo (Passacaglia), and a concluding Allegretto (Pastorale). The last three movements are played without pause.

The score calls for four flutes (one interchangeable with piccolo), two oboes, English horn, two clarinets, E flat clarinet, bass clarinet, two bassoons, contra-bassoon, four horns, three trumpets, three trombones, tuba, tympani, percussion, and strings.

R. C. B.

Symphony No. 9, Op. 70

I. Allegro. II. Moderato. III. Presto. IV. Largo. V. Allegretto.

[*Last three movements played without pause*]

COMPLETED on Aug. 30, 1945, at a Composers' Rest Home near Ivanovo, the Ninth Symphony was given its world premiere on the following Nov. 3 by the Leningrad Philharmonic Orchestra, at the inaugural concert of its twenty-fifth season. Eugene Mravinsky conducted. Performances followed in other parts of Russia and on the Soviet radio. A year later the inaugural note was repeated here when Serge Koussevitzky and the Boston Symphony featured the American premiere of the symphony at the opening concert of the Berkshire Festival at Tanglewood, Mass., on July 25, 1946. Artur Rodzinski and the New York Philharmonic-Symphony introduced the work to New York on Nov. 7, 1946.

A few days after its completion, a private performance of the Ninth Symphony was given on the piano by the composer at the home of Vladimir Vlasov, director of the Moscow Philharmonic. Four listeners were present on that occasion, among them Robert Magidoff, correspondent of *The New York Times,* and Grigori Schneerson, correspondent of *The Moscow News* published in New York. All four listeners were evidently surprised by the light quality and unusual brevity of the new Symphony. After the huge spans of the Seventh and Eighth Symphonies, the twenty-five-minute score, with its relatively simple and frolicsome character, caught them off their guard. In a dispatch to his paper, printed on Dec. 2, 1946, Mr. Magidoff described Shostakovich as he appeared that day in Mr. Vlasov's study: "Looking pale and tired but nervously alive, he came into the house . . . hardly said hello, rushed to the piano, paused as if remembering that etiquette demanded that he be asked to play, and when he was asked, started without any preliminary explanations." The Symphony then struck Mr. Magidoff as "the gayest, most youthful, and most melodious" Shostakovich had ever written. The correspondent was also impressed by its classicism, even its hints of Haydn, and it became clear to him why Shostakovich had been playing the classics at the piano daily the entire six weeks it took to compose the new Symphony. During that time Shostakovich and Dimitri Kabalevsky had played piano scores of Haydn's symphonies every evening from six to eight, as well as music by Mozart and some of the earlier works of Beethoven.

Mr. Magidoff's was only one voice in a chorus of jubilation over Shostakovich's change of mood from the tragic and weighty themes of the two previous symphonies. Mr. Schneerson spoke of the opening movement as "transporting us at once to a bright and pleasant world." In its whimsical dance themes and rhythms he heard "joyous abandon, the warm pulsation of life, and the exuberance of youth." Nor were the eighteenth-century associations lost on him either. Apparently the public was equally stirred by the Symphony, for at the first two performances every movement but the opening Allegro was encored.

Then, one year after its Leningrad premiere, a sharp note of dissension shattered the Soviet chorus of praise. Writing in the newspaper *Culture and Life,* I. Nestiev now flailed the Ninth Symphony for its "ideological weaknesses" and its failure "to reflect the true spirit of the Soviet people." Since the paper is published by the Agitation and Propaganda Committee of the Central Committee of the Communist Party, it was felt that the tirade carried the ominous weight of official disfavor. Mr. Nestiev was unsparing. While others delighted in the breezy, jocund character of the music, Mr. Nestiev now angrily rebuked the composer for writing "a playful and fanciful trifle." Was this a time, he asked scornfully, for the composer whose Leningrad Symphony was a triumph of Soviet art, "to take a vacation, to rest from modern problems"? As reported in *The New York Times,* Mr. Nestiev also noted in the Symphony "a cynical and evil grotesquerie, a tone of merciless joking and ridicule, a cold irony of stylization."

A possible culprit was named in the indictment as exerting an alien influence on Shostakovich's score, none other than the *émigré* Igor Stavinsky— "an artist without a fatherland, without confidence in the leadership of high ideals, and without ethical principles." As for the first movement of the Symphony, the movement which had transported Mr. Schneerson to "a bright and pleasant world," Mr. Nestiev found it nothing but a sorry hodgepodge of "tiny, archaic, simplified forms, joyful, traditional, classical rhythms, toylike instrumentation, with an abundance of high whistling and screaming timbres."

Perhaps Shostakovich knew what was coming when he remarked after the informal premiere on the keyboard, "It is a merry little piece. Musicians will love to play it, and critics will delight in blasting it." After a year's wait the blast, official or not, had finally come. But such manifestations of disfavor were nothing new in the career of this Soviet composer. In 1936, his opera *Lady Macbeth of Mzensk* was denounced as "un-Soviet, unwholesome, cheap, eccentric, tuneless." Bourgeois formalism was another stern charge hurled at the offending composer. To make matters worse, Shostakovich's ballet *The Limpid Stream* was withdrawn because the composer had allegedly "merely painted peasants, the kind you see on the covers of candy boxes." When Artur Rodzinski learned of the attack on Shostakovich's Ninth Symphony in the Soviet periodical, he observed: "I prefer to present the Shostakovich Ninth to the music lovers of New York and the radio listeners. History alone can sit in final judgment on any artistic effort; only through familiarity can humanity weigh its value."

Almost purely classical in form, the Ninth Symphony takes twenty-four to twenty-five minutes. There are five short movements, the last three played without a break. Classical, too, is the orchestra employed, with many instruments paired, and piccolo added. The score calls for two flutes, piccolo, two oboes, two clarinets, two bassoons, two trumpets, four horns, three trombones, tuba, tympani, triangle, bass drum, cymbals, military drum, tambourine, and strings.

Daniel Zhitomirsky, who stayed at the Ivanovo country house while Shostakovich was there, was in a position to observe the daily growth of the Symphony during the six summer weeks it took to complete it. Shostakovich worked three hours a day at it, usually in the morning, composing without piano. Quoted below is Mr. Zhitomirsky's first-hand analysis of the Symphony. Emendations have been made in many places by the author.

The Ninth Symphony opens with an Allegro of Haydn-like simplicity, in which one senses a subtle note of sly irony. In essence, the music seeks to recapture the spirit of bubbling, unrestrained mirth typical of the early Allegro up to the time of Rossini's overtures. Yet a mood of ultramodernism inheres in this classical form. As in many early classics, the first theme glides in effortlessly, almost imperceptibly, not so much as an individual melody, but as a kind of pure, abstract motion. By contrast, an element of buffoonery now appears in the subsidiary theme which follows. A simple, naïve pattern of accompaniment is set up, and against this emerges a pert yet not ungraceful lyrical theme. The headlong drive of the movement continues unbroken through the development section. The material is exposed to varied comic treatment, and at one point the subsidiary theme returns in a variation of frank drollery.

In the second movement (Moderato) Shostakovich shifts to a mood of romantic lyricism. The main theme unreels like a romanza, distantly reminiscent of an aria of Katherine's in the composer's opera *Lady Macbeth of Mzensk,* yet curiously whimsical in outline. A striking lucidity marks the texture of the entire movement, as if patterned on glass.

A scherzo of precipitous pace now follows. The music swishes by like a gust of wind, whistling piercingly in its upward and downward sweep. This ceaseless Presto drive grows and develops out of the first bars of the central theme of the scherzo. The contrasting middle section enfolds a theme of "sharp theatrical pathos" with hints of irony and "impassioned romantic stress."

The Fourth movement (Largo) intervenes between the scherzo and finale as a contrasting intermezzo. It consists almost entirely of an extended bassoon solo of improvisational character, heard against a background of sustained chords. One senses here a thoughtful concentration, a sort of lyrical and philosophical meditation on the whole work, perhaps a reminder of the "precious human sources" of this light, unhampered flow of music.

The Allegretto finale returns largely to the dominant mood of the first movement, though the keynote now is rather open buffoonery than spontaneous gaiety. The principal theme suggests an attempt to blend classical naïveté and a spirit of vaudeville-like dance extravaganza. The material undergoes vigorous development, with frequent flashes of frank farce, and a brief coda accelerates this "merry theatrical run" to top speed.

L. B.

Concerto for Piano and Orchestra, Op. 35

I. Allegretto; Allegro vivace. II. Lento. III. Moderato. IV. Allegro con brio; Presto.

This Concerto was composed in 1933 and given its first performance with the composer as soloist. Eugene List was the soloist when it was first played in this country at a concert of the Philadelphia Orchestra in the Academy of Music, Dec. 12, 1934. Its unusual scoring is for an orchestra of strings and a single trumpet, plus, of course, the solo piano. In view of the general pattern of the work it would not be entirely mistaken to call it a Concerto for piano and string orchestra, with a comical trumpet obbligato.

The first movement opens with a trumpet call, accompanied by figures in the piano, which soon presents the first theme. A disarming, rather simple melody, it is taken up by the violins which play it against a variant in the basses. With the changing of the tempo to an Allegro vivace, a second theme is ushered in by the piano, while the strings give out a series of staccato chords, with the trumpet joining in. After an animated development of the material the movement leads, in a crescendo, to the next section.

The second movement is modal in feeling. The muted strings bring on the main theme, which becomes a cantilena for the first violins, the piano coming into the picture with a countertheme. The movement grows in sonority and suddenly launches into a quicker tempo, as a dialogue takes place between piano and strings. The solo instrument is heard in a forceful passage of scales in octaves, coming to a Largo, *ffff*. Its voice diminishes, as the strings enter again, and the trumpet softly intones the main theme over them. The piano reappears, takes up its song, and the movement presently ends on a sustained chord by the solo instrument and orchestra.

The third movement is a brief intermezzo, offering two cadenzas for the piano, the one unaccompanied, the other with accompaniment.

The fourth movement opens with the piano, accompanied by bass strings, in a short prelude, following which the orchestra sounds the main theme, a figure in repeated notes with a grouppetto in sixteenths. Some moments later the piano reenters, and the trumpet joins the proceedings with a more significant part. There is a long cadenza for the piano, and this is followed by a coda, which is brilliant and lively, with the trumpet keeping pace all the way.

R. C. B.

Polka and Dance from the Ballet "The Golden Age," Op. 22

SHOSTAKOVICH HAS written three ballets, the first of them being *The Golden Age*. Called an "athletic ballet," it dates from 1930, when it was presented in Leningrad. The score had been winner in 1929 in a contest for the best ballet on a Soviet subject. "An industrial ballet" is Shostakovich's own subtitle for his second ballet *The Bolt,* brought out in Leningrad in 1931. Contrastingly, his third ballet *The Limpid Stream,* produced in Moscow in 1936, might be called an "agricultural ballet," since its theme is a collective farm harvest in the Kuban.

The libretto of *The Golden Age* (in Russian, *Zolotoy Vyek*) is by A. V. Invanovsky. Its title derives from the name given a trade exhibit in a non-Soviet city where the action unfolds. An athletic meet has been arranged as part of the entertainment. The soccer team of a Soviet factory has been invited to participate. Boxing, fencing, tennis, javelin throwing are also included in the program. Romance enters the picture when the captain of the visiting team, the hero of the ballet, gets involved with a sinister beauty named Diva. Conflict arises when it develops that Diva has Fascist leanings.

Shostakovich drew the material for his Suite from the last section of the ballet, which is largely a sequence of divertissements. There are four parts to the Suite: an Introduction, featuring a waltz; an Adagio, enshrining an extended cantabile theme, for saxophone solo; the Polka; and the finale Dance. The Polka, incidentally, is intended to burlesque the Geneva Disarmament Conference and carries the title "Once in Geneva." In his article on Shostakovich in *The Musical Quarterly* of October, 1942, Mr. Slonimsky quoted the full program of the ballet, as given below. Of course by "football" is meant "soccer," not the American game.

ACT I: INDUSTRIAL EXPOSITION

Procession of Guests of Honor. Review of Window Displays. Demonstration of Exhibits. Barker. Prestidigitator. Prize Fighting for Publicity. Riot at the Boxing Match. Dance of Flaming Youth. Director's Appearance with Diva. Adagio Dance. Arrival of the Soviet Football Team. Diva's Variations. Soviet Dance. Soviet Worker Invites Diva to a Dance. Diva Dances with the Fascist. Dance of the Negro and Two Soviet Football Players. Waltz: Alleged Bomb Plotters ("The Hand of Moscow"). Confusion Among the Fascists. A Rare Case of Mass Hysteria. Fox Trot.

ACT II

Pantomime: Sleuthing by an *Agent Provocateur,* and an Arrest. Workers' Procession to the Stadium. Pioneers' Dance. Reception of the Soviet Football Team. The Football Game. Interlude.

ACT III: MUSIC HALL

Tap Dance: Shoe Shine of the Best Quality. Polka: "Once in Geneva" (Angel of Peace). Touching Coalition of Classes, Slightly Fraudulent. Cancan. Liberation of Prisoners. General Exposure. Finale: Solidarity Dance of Western Workers and the Soviet Team.

In the satiric Polka the jocund chief theme is given out by the xylophone. The saxophone takes up the second tune, also of gay character. A village band seems to break into the scheme, with tuba and trumpets combining. Soon the whole orchestra joins in the ground swell of merriment. The freely joyous mood continues through the finale Dance. Percussive instruments are strikingly featured here in a boisterous rhythmic whirl mounting to a fierce climax.

In the vast assortment of instruments are piccolo, flute, oboe, English horn, E flat clarinet, B flat clarinet, bass clarinet, soprano saxophone, bassoon, contra-bassoon, three trumpets, three horns, three trombones, tuba, baritone horn in B flat, harmonium, kettledrums, xylophone, triangle, tambourine, snare drum, wood block, gong, cymbals, bass drum, and strings.

L. B.

Jean Sibelius

BORN: TAVASTEHUS, FINLAND, DEC. 8, 1865.

The roots of his art remain deep in his soil, and its origins stretch far back into the past of his people. In one sense he is a singular anachronism; in another, he is as modern as tomorrow.—OLIN DOWNES.

Symphony in E minor, No. 1, Op. 39

I. Andante ma non troppo; Allegro energico. II. Andante ma non troppo lento. III. Allegro. IV. Finale (quasi una fantasia): Andante; Allegro molto.

LIKE THE Fourth Symphony of Brahms and the Fifth of Tschaikowsky this work is in the "symphonically unpopular" key of E minor. And just as Brahms' Fourth had aroused some early resentments, because of the choice of key, so this Symphony, on its westward trek, found more than passing opposition. However, it was not long before the surge and sweep of this music could surmount all superstitious objections and majestically show that a new and arresting voice had suddenly made itself known.

Cecil Gray sees the E minor Symphony as "the last of an old line, rather than the first of a new," explaining his views with the statement that "the Symphony has distinctive affinities, both formal and coloristic, with . . . the romantic symphonies of various predecessors." That this composition has the power to evoke images, whole heroic sagas in the minds of listeners, is attested by some of the word portraits penned early in its career by imaginative hearers. For instance, certain chromatic scales running in contrary motion in the first movement earned this from Arthur Shepherd, "scudding clouds in a windswept sky, with screaming gulls rudely tossed from their course." Rosa Newmarch, considering the whole work, compares it with the "melancholy grandeur of some masterpiece by Ruysdael."

From Bengt de Törne, orchestration pupil of Sibelius, we get a sort of apologio pro construction in his claim that "the first movements of Sibelius' first two symphonies are built up like the corresponding parts of Mozart's symphonic works." And, having thus silenced the pedantic snipers, he points out, "In the long series of Sibelius' compositions it is the first two symphonies which evoke the magic spell of the North with a particular power and intensity. Their monumental style and heroic romanticism, adding new and unknown words to the idiom of the preceding masters, are unique in the history of music."

Some reference to orchestration would naturally be expected of a pupil of Sibelius in that subject, so that we find him elaborating the above with:

One day I mentioned [to Sibelius] the impression which always takes hold of me when returning to Finland across the Baltic, the first forebodings of our country being given us by low reddish granite rocks emerging from the pale blue sea, solitary islands of a hard, archaic beauty, inhabited by hundreds of sea gulls. And I concluded by saying that this landscape many years ago was the cradle of the vikings. "Yes," Sibelius answered eagerly, and his eyes flashed, "and when we see those granite rocks we know why we are able to treat the orchestra as we do!"

The E minor Symphony was written in 1899, when Sibelius was thirty-four years old. He himself conducted the world premiere at Helsingfors, on Apr. 26 of that year. The work abounds in contrasts. Herein is represented the unfettered, mercurial thinking of a young symphonist who is scarcely learned in the ways of practical economy. He has many things to say, many different and startling manners of saying them. Everything is of the utmost importance, nothing that comes springing to his mind must be omitted. So he writes with a feverish enthusiasm, not in the least concerned with the formalities of strict symphonic logic. Restraint is something to be cultivated later, but now the thing, it would appear, is to express these ideas, these powerful teeming urges, and they leap into miraculous strings of notes.

They must be developed, these ideas and urges. They must be made to tell their tales in countless emphatic ways, each more impressive than the preceding one. The young composer pours great melodies into his work, melodies that sing with an exultant joy, melodies that rise and fall with tremendous intensity, and also melodies that are nostalgic and mellow and suffused with a tender pathos.

There are grace and lightness in the music as it comes rushing to the creator's pen. There are also wild, barbaric shouts, outbursts of tremendous passion, raging unbridled utterances that hurl themselves forward like the roar of giant winds.

At last the Symphony is finished, the first essay (in the form) of a composer whose style was later to court the soberer symphonic muses.

"And so this Symphony is more than conventionally interesting," says Philip Hale. "It is dramatic, as if Sibelius had had a drama in his mind, perhaps one of his own life. The music is free, outspoken. It is without fear of the learned professor at the conservatory. One might say of the Symphony, one hears this music and is in the mighty presence of a man."

The first movement (Allegro energico, E minor, 6/4) begins with a short introduction distinguished by a striking clarinet solo, after which the first violins give out the chief subject. The second subject (Piano ma marcato) is assigned to the flutes.

The second movement (Andante ma non troppo lento, E flat major, 2/2) starts off with a motive in the first violins and cellos. The bassoons, against an accompaniment of other wood winds, offer a contrasting theme. Supported by harp arpeggios, the horns announce a third subject.

A scherzo (Allegro, C major, 3/4) follows. The humor of this "joke" as represented in the principal theme (announced by the kettledrums and then the first violins) seems wild and harsh. The second theme is more ingratiating, and the trio (Lento ma non troppo, E major), with its theme in the horns, is gentler.

The Finale (quasi una fantasia) opens (Andante, E minor, 2/2) with a return of the melody intoned by the clarinet at the beginning of the symphony, now proclaimed by all the strings. The main body of the movement (Allegro molto, 2/4) presents its first subject in the wood winds. The second subject (Andante assai, C major, 4/4) is announced broadly by the violins. The initial theme of the slow movement is heard again in the first violins and cellos. Then the Allegro molto returns, its first subject serving as basis for an impassioned fugato. The second subject returns in the clarinet. There is stormy development. The Symphony ends, however, in what has been described as a "broad hymn of sadness."

The scoring calls for two flutes, two oboes, two clarinets, two bassoons, four horns, three trumpets, three trombones, tuba, kettledrums, bass drum, cymbals, triangle, harp, and strings as usual.

R. C. B.

Symphony in D major, No. 2, Op. 43

I. Allegretto. II. Tempo andante ma rubato. III. Vivacissimo. IV. Finale: Allegretto moderato.

DESPITE ITS adherence to certain nineteenth-century norms, the Second Symphony marks a bold forward stride in compact idiom and firm concentration—a stride that is bringing Sibelius closer to the wondrous economy of the later symphonies. Strength and simplicity are here, and a fierce eloquence, the more fascinating because laconic. Still, there is romantic nostalgia, and at times Tschaikowsky broods over the span—a reminder that Russia is close at hand.

It was Georg Schneevoigt, Sibelius' friend and colleague, who interpreted this tightly passionate score as the expression of Finnish revolt against oppression and the final triumph. Schneevoigt, a pioneer conductor of Sibelius' music, sensed a huge patriotic plan in the score. For him the first movement depicted the calm pastoral life of the Finns, untroubled by fear of oppression. The second movement teemed with nationalist fervor, "but the thought of a brutal rule over the people brings with it a timidity of soul." The third movement—roughly a scherzo—pictured to Schneevoigt the awakening of rebellious feelings, the people's growing determination to defend their rights. The Finale, in this scheme, mirrors the promise of deliverance. Reviewing the Armistice Day program of the Boston Symphony, Philip Hale was ready to agree with the Schneevoigt thesis: "Is it fantastic to think that the Symphony, with its wails and groans of anguish, its sullen gloom alternating with shouts of triumph, was singularly appropriate on Armistice Day? Is it not at all probable that the composer had war or rumors of war in mind when he composed this music?"

Outwardly, the Second Symphony appears to follow the standard sequence of four movements, allegro, andante, scherzo, and finale. But even a casual hearing reveals a method of reversed synthesis that prompted Cecil Gray to term it "a veritable revolution . . . the introduction of an entirely new principle into symphonic form." For in handling his material Sibelius would seem to have worked backward, as compared with orthodox procedure. Instead of introducing full themes and then pulling them apart for separate development, Sibelius gives out fragments of themes, juggles them adroitly, and then pieces them together in a final integration. The method at times involves, as in the Finale, a constantly postponed climax that is steadily building, but never quite ready, that is interrupted by other material, yet is so much the more overpowering when at last it arrives.

The four movements are marked as follows: I. Allegretto, D major, mainly 6/4; II. Tempo andante ma rufato, D minor, 4/4, 3/8, 4/4; III. Vivacissimo, B flat major, 6/8; and IV. Finale: Allegro moderato, D major, 3/2. Dedicated to Axel Carpelan, the symphony is scored conventionally for two flutes, two oboes, two clarinets, two bassoons, four horns, three trumpets, three trombones, tuba, tympani, and strings.

The work was composed in 1901-1902 and performed for the first time at Helsingfors on Mar. 8, 1902. Sibelius himself conducted. Theodore Thomas introduced it to America at one of his Chicago concerts on Jan. 2, 1904. Josef Stransky brought it into the New York Philharmonic repertory during the season of 1916-1917.

At first derisively reviewed as beneath serious notice, the Symphony has gradually come into its own in recent years. In fact, no symphony since Tschaikowsky's *Pathétique*—with the possible exception of Shostakovich's Fifth—has won such popularity in America. "It has entered the household-word class," remarked Pitts Sanborn in 1940, "and its most conspicuous theme is as familiar as 'Home, Sweet Home.' Indeed, it is now far oftener whistled and hummed." Sanborn was referring, of course, to the jubilant, long-delayed lyric theme of the Finale.

L. B.

Symphony in C major, No. 3, Op. 52

I. Allegro moderato. II. Andantino con moto, quasi allegretto. III. Allegro.

THE FIRST performance of this Symphony was conducted by the composer himself at Helsingfors, Sept. 25, 1907. On that occasion two other works by Sibelius were also given their world premieres, *Pohjola's Daughter* and the Suite *Belshazzar's Feast.*

By the year 1907, Sibelius had already attracted considerable attention in countries other than his own. As a matter of fact, he conducted his Second Symphony in Berlin, in 1905, a year in which Arturo Toscanini brought to audiences in Milan the *Swan of Tuonela* and *Finlandia,* both of which made their Parisian bows under the direction of Chevillard. In the meantime, Hans Richter labored for the cause with performances of the First and Second Symphonies in Manchester, England. The composer visited England and France, pleased no end with the enthusiastic receptions accorded him. On his return to Finland, in January, 1906, Sibelius took with him the first sketches of a third symphony.

However, it was over a year and one half before the piece was completed. He had been invited to conduct it in London, at a concert scheduled for March, 1907, which, by the way, would have provided him with his debut in that city. Yet his slow progress—not an unusual thing for him—put an end to that plan. Sibelius did accept the London invitation, but not until February, 1908, when the Third Symphony was played there for the first time.

The Third Symphony is in three movements, consisting of two allegros sandwiching between them a section, which derives from the scherzo and andante types without specifically being either. The movements in this work are all shorter than those of the previous symphonies, and here Sibelius seems to have aimed at simplicity, especially in the first two movements. They contain little of the formal complication evidenced in their preceding counterparts. The third movement, however, does not altogether forsake complexity, although this exists for a space in only the earlier pages.

In this Symphony, too, the composer has given a less important role than formerly to the wind choirs. The strings appear to have taken over, instead, and the trumpets and trombones, it is to be noted, are given no more than an occasional prominence. The whole piece, in fact, is of a lighter, suppler structure; the writing is economical almost in the extreme. The first movement has two principal themes, which are manipulated in the traditional classical manner, and the second is still more direct and to the point, with its one subject a series of announcements in different degrees of the scale.

The third movement, whose first part consists of phrase fragments later fused into a unified pattern, is like the preceding one in its later stages, where again there are melodic and harmonic changes of a single idea, this time a rhythmical one. The entire effect of this Third Symphony is of brightness and geniality, parting company, as it does, with the dark and brooding quality of the First and the passionate outcry of the Second.

R. C. B.

Symphony in A minor, No. 4, Op. 63

I. Tempo molto moderato quasi adagio. II. Allegro molto vivace. III. Il tempo largo. IV. Allegro.

COMPOSED IN 1911, the Fourth Symphony was first played at Helsingfors on Apr. 3, 1911, at a concert of works by Toivo Tuula and Sibelius. It was given its American premier by the New York Symphony Society, Walter Damrosch conducting, on Mar. 2, 1913. The Symphony is dedicated to Eero Jarnefelt, and the score calls for two flutes, two oboes, two clarinets, two bassoons, four horns, two trumpets, three trombones, kettledrums, bells, and strings.

If this Symphony is skeletal in construction, *i.e.,* pared right down to the bone of anything superfluous like, as it seems here, flesh, it is also closely knit, concentrated, yet utterly complete. In this work Sibelius was experimenting, perhaps, with the thought of eliminating all that was possible, in order to say his piece as starkly straight as he could—and, as we know now—he did. Having reduced his orchestra to little more than the essentials in the Third Symphony, he became even more economical here, tossing out the third trumpet, and generally calling upon few instruments in mass at any time during its course.

The thematic material is of a solitary quality, almost distant and, as one astute listener put it, sometimes "uncouth." While it has the ability to spring surprises on its hearers, it is not an effect per se that it flaunts, because some of the surprises grow naturally out of the pattern Sibelius set down for it. There is, in other words, always for the listener the expectation of the unusual, so that when it comes it is both unexpected and unusual, a provocative device not mastered by every composer. In the year 1911, it occasioned much discussion, controversy even. Today, with the intellectual strivings, the search for new forms, and the constant experiment with method in musical creation, it may not be so striking as it must have been then. However, the Sibelius of the first three symphonies is virtually nowhere present in this work, save in the abrupt vigor of his speech.

R. C. B.

Symphony in E flat major, No. 5, Op. 82

I. Tempo molto moderato. II. Allegro moderato, ma poco a poco stretto.
III. Andante mosso, quasi allegretto. IV. Allegro molto.

THE FOLLOWING words appear as an entry in a diary: "God opens his door
for a moment, and his orchestra plays the Fifth Symphony." One might be
excused for suspecting them to be an allusion to Beethoven's C minor Symphony. The reference, however, is to Sibelius' work of the same number,
and the words are his. He penned them one day in September, 1914, when
the horror of Europe's First World War was already two months old. Three
years had elapsed since the completion of his Fourth Symphony. The interval
teemed with minor program music and salon odds and ends. Sibelius was
again feeling symphonic stirrings within him and had resolutely turned down
an offer to write music for a ballet, explaining, "I cannot become a prolific
writer; it would mean killing all my reputation and my art." (Yet, how
much of Sibelius' output was frankly ephemeral, forced from him by sheer
budgetary need!)

Besides, writing a symphony offered the best escape from bleak reality.
Perhaps as a recoil, the terror raging in Europe even sharpened his thirst for
life. "This life that I love so infinitely!" he exclaimed. Seemingly the grim
and somber brooding of the Fourth Symphony had left him. One day he
finds himself in a deep dell. "I begin already dimly to see the mountain that
I shall certainly ascend," he records in his diary; "God opens his door for a
moment and his orchestra plays the Fifth Symphony."

Despite Sibelius' habit of never giving subtitles or clues to the poetic or
dramatic content of his symphonies, anyone can readily grasp the surge of
energy and exuberance setting the Fifth apart from the gloomily subjective
Fourth. Cecil Gray goes so far as to discribe it as a "sunny, genial work
throughout." Bengt de Törne, a close friend and pupil, though repeatedly
rebuffed when querying Sibelius about the Symphony's personal message,
speaks of it as the composer's "return to life," and as embodying "an intimate
contact with the world of men." To the worshipping disciple the work constituted "an impressive ode to the courage and perseverance of man."

De Törne even hazarded a guess that some secret relation existed between
Sibelius' bold finale and "the gigantic drama enacted on the battlefields of
Europe." If so, Sibelius has sedulously guarded the secret. His one allusion to
a possibly nonabsolute aim in the Symphony is contained in a letter written
in 1918 while revising the work a second time. In elliptical language he notes
the extent of revision in each movement: "Movement IV the old motive, but

stronger in revision," he concludes. "The whole, if I may say so, a vital climax to the end." To which he appends the single word, "Triumphal."

Perhaps to prevent followers from reading irrelevances into his music, Sibelius once stated: "I do not wish to give a reasoned exposition of the essence of the Symphony. I have expressed my opinion in my works." However he did make clear that the Symphony marked an important stylistic departure from earlier efforts: "I should like . . . to emphasize a point that I consider essential: the directly symphonic is the compelling vein that goes through the whole. This in contrast to the depicting." The program book of the London premiere, with Sibelius conducting, on Feb. 12, 1921, contained this significant announcement: "The composer desires his work to be regarded as absolute music, having no direct poetic basis."

The Fifth is Sibelius' birthday symphony. To celebrate his fiftieth birthday the work was premiered at a special concert in Helsingfors on Dec. 8 with Robert Kajanus conducting. Kajanus remained something of a custodian of correct Sibelian style. About him the composer once remarked to de Törne: "You see how Kajanus builds up my Symphony. He actually makes you feel the construction of the work like a huge building." This early version of the Symphony was never printed. A second version was played in Helsingfors a year later, and the third and final on Nov. 24, 1919. In the course of its last reshaping the words, "The V Symphony in a new form, practically composed anew," appear in a letter of Sibelius' dated May 20, 1918.

De Törne was intrigued by that early version that never reached publication. He speculated on the interesting comparison it might offer in view of a significant statement made by Sibelius. About six months after finishing the Fifth Symphony in its first form the two were discussing instrumentation. "Do you know whom I consider the two greatest geniuses of the orchestra?" asked Sibelius. "You will be surprised to hear it: Mozart and Mendelssohn."

In his valuable brochure on Sibelius' symphonies, Cecil Gray speaks of the "comparative accessibility" of the Fifth, explaining it in part as follows:

The terseness, economy, and extreme concentration of thought, the reticence and sobriety of style which characterizes the former are not to be found in the Fifth. The form, too, of all its movements is comparatively straightforward, the thematic material more definitely melodic, the harmony diatonic and consonant, the instrumentation rich and sonorous, despite the fact that the orchestra employed in it is precisely the same as that of the two preceding symphonies, except for the addition of a third trumpet.

There is still no bass tuba, no harp, no "extra" instrument of any kind, and no percussion save the ordinary kettledrums, but the volume and opulence of tone which the composer here elicits from the modest forces at his disposal are truly remarkable.

Sibelius' omission of the tuba from his later scores has been frequently commented upon. "Personally I feel convinced that a composer can do without the tuba," he told de Törne. "I do not like this instrument. To my mind it is far too heavy—what the Germans call *schwerfällig.* . . . There is always a way of building up a fortissimo without a tuba."

Though divided into three parts by two pauses, the Fifth Symphony is actually in four movements, for the opening section is made up of two distinct movements varying in mood and structure. However, these are linked, cycle fashion, by a common theme, the terse, four-note motto announced at the opening of the Symphony by the first horn over a tympani roll.

The first movement moves in a kind of pastoral calm, dreamily at times. Gradually a change comes over the music; it grows darker, passionate. There is then an abrupt transition—without break—to what is really the second movement (Allegro moderato), a dancelike scherzo building to a fierce crisis. The Andante grows with miraculous spareness out of a seemingly trivial theme, and the finale, noble and spacious, leads to a final fortissimo, "savage and grand as the sunrise," according to Olin Downes.

L. B.

Symphony No. 6, Op. 104

I. Allegro molto moderato. II. Allegro moderato. III. Poco vivace. IV. Allegro molto.

IN THE Sixth Symphony Sibelius employs an orchestra that is not the austere one of his other symphonies, nor does he take advantage of all that modern orchestration could supply. True, he does include a harp in his instrumentation, a novelty for him, except for the First, and a bass clarinet, which here makes its first and only appearance among his works in this form. The complete scoring is for two flutes, two oboes, two clarinets, bass clarinet, two bassoons, four horns, three trumpets, three trombones, tympani, harp, and strings. Dedicated to Dr. Wilhelm Stenhammer (a pianist and conductor of Stockholm), the Sixth Symphony, finished in January, 1923, was first performed at Helsingfors, Feb. 19, of the same year.

The first movement opens with the strings (no basses) in a brief introduction based on a melodic phrase moving in diatonic steps. The flutes, in thirds, present the theme. It is followed, in due course, by still other themes, also in thirds and diatonically. There is a subject in eighth notes, which is heard in the first violins (divided in three lines) spiccato. This subject resembles, somewhat, the previous one of the flutes. All through this movement one hears the familiar device of thirds. Soon some bright figures appear in the wood winds, thus ushering in a subject given to second violins and cellos (later also the violas), and it proceeds upward and downward against octaves for bassoons and flutes, going in opposite direction always. The development continues, along these lines, and finally, after some measures of a modal quality, the movement ends.

The scale passages again appear in the second movement, whose chief theme is given out by the first violins, divided, against wood-wind chords. As the music progresses the sonority increases, and the scale idea rises in importance. Soon a lyrical theme emerges in the first violins and cellos, an octave apart, while chords support it in the accompaniment. Following a particularly clever handling of the materials and devices set forth, the movement again leans toward the modal in a passage for harp, strings, and oboes.

A rhythmical chief subject brings on the scherzo, and this makes a sharp contrast with the softer and more melodic second theme heard in the wood winds, first, then in the violins, where it takes on the importance of a flowing melody. These two themes are juxtaposed and played alternately, with the gentler one taking possession abruptly and fortissimo at the end.

Heroic in character, the first subject of the final movement is played by violins, wood winds, and two horns, forte. It is answered, by way of contrast, in a lyrical phrase for the lower strings, after which development ensues. The music grows increasingly restless and, oddly enough, chromatic for the first time in the work. A crescendo leads to a powerful climax for the entire orchestra, after some hints of previous material in the movement. The coda, in a rather impressive manner, epitomizes the whole foundation of the Symphony—the diatonic scale and the interval of the third. After all this, the music closes serenely, in a lingering fade-out of the strings and the tympani.

R. C. B.

Symphony in C major, No. 7 (In One Movement), Op. 105

SIBELIUS ONCE said, "The greatest labor I have expended, perhaps, was on works that have never been completed." As prelude to that observation he remarked, "The thing that pleased me most is that I have been able to reject."

The proof of that is implicit in the fact that his last three symphonies have taken greater time to compose. Creation has waited on technique, on an expert's ability to gaze objectively on his work and to retain what he approved of, to "reject," as he put it, the rest.

Sibelius began work on his Fifth Symphony during the chaotic beginnings of the First World War and completed it in 1915, while the conflict still raged —or could there have been in the past such a thing as a raging conflict considering more recent global happenings?

In any case, the Fifth was revised in 1916. It was performed, and the composer thought best to rewrite the piece from start to finish, so that it came through as a completed product in 1919. He was more careful with his Sixth and Seventh Symphonies. These he would not release to the world until he was utterly satisfied with them. The Fifth and its premature birth had been the object lesson.

Sibelius refers to the present work as "joy of life and vitality with appassionato passages." He added, "By all this I see how my innermost self has changed since the days of the Fourth Symphony. And these Symphonies of mine [the Fifth, Sixth, and Seventh] are more in the nature of professions of faith than my other works."

To the Sixth Symphony he wrote finis in January, 1923; and to the Seventh in March, 1925. The Seventh he calls a *fantasia sinfonica*.

This Seventh Symphony in one huge movement follows, more or less, a pattern he chose in writing the first movement of the Sixth. There is only a single subject important enough to be called the dominating one, and the numerous others, as they crop up quite naturally out of the music, are just the merest fragments of ideas, a handful of which—more prominent—combine and intertwine, make contrast, and vary and develop in a continuous design, which is a mosaic of the most intricate inner relationships.

The Seventh has been showered with praise for the remarkable construction, as well as for its nobility and dignity of expression.

R. C. B.

Concerto for Violin and Orchestra in D minor, Op. 47

I. Allegro moderato. II. Adagio di molto. III. Allegro ma non tanto.

Two EVER-PRESENT strains in Sibelius' biography are his love of nature and his fondness for epic literature. He has styled himself a "dreamer and poet of nature." Friends have asserted that he can quote Homer and Virgil by the canto; and the *Kalevala,* Finland's great epic, is his second Bible. It is only natural that his music should to some degree stem from both impulses. And the two seem closely linked in his case. Sibelius' symphonies and tone poems frequently strike one as great canvases of Finland's landscape and heroic past. Geography and legend appear to march side by side in his bold spans of tone. Even the Violin Concerto has evoked visions of topography and a bardic lay of long ago. For Sibelius' music appears somehow to combine the qualities of picture and story. Scenery and deed alternate in the shifting blends of tone. Sibelius' own remarks lend color to the practice of viewing his music as a second *Kalevala* and Finnish travelogue combined.

"I love the mysterious sounds of the fields and forests, water and mountains," he says. "It pleases me greatly to be called an artist of nature, for nature has truly been the book of books for me."

Accordingly, it is not surprising to find imaginative Sibelians sensing vast patterns of nature study and saga even in the works presumably free from programmatic content. Sibelius never tacked a narrative to his D minor Violin Concerto, but that did not prevent one commentator from envisioning the Allegro moderato as an ancient rite of "bardic songs heard against a background of torches or pagan fires in some wild Northern night." To another, the music conveyed "the settled melancholy of a Finland of Northern darkness, where the sea heaves blindly to the shore and human lives blossom only briefly and precariously to the joy of melody."

From the second-movement romanza, with its strange tinge of melancholy, some have gleaned reminiscent glimpses of Sibelius' boyhood, when he would mount a huge rock beside a lake and play his violin. It had been the young Sibelius' habit to play out of doors in the country and away from people, surely an early sign of his regarding music as a medium of communion between himself and nature. The fact is that he has always spoken of this Concerto with feeling, and perhaps it is a kind of testament of nature and departed youth. In the last movement a reviewer even heard "an ancient folk song in which the old careless bravery had been replaced by a kind of contemplative fear of death." Possibly the clairvoyant gentleman was not so wide of the mark, since Sibelius, some time later, reportedly dubbed the movement a "Danse Macabre."

Though finished in 1903, the Concerto underwent thorough revision and was published in 1905. Finnish critics, in a position to make comparisons, regarded the later version as highly superior to the earlier. At the time, Sibelius was rewriting much of his music to bring it into closer conformity with certain accepted norms, according to Rosa Newmarch. "With the advance of years he has shown an increasing respect for the requirements of conventional form," she stated in an early monograph, "without, however, becoming conventional in the contemptible sense of the word. The sign of this reaction has been the revision of many of his early works. The Violin Concerto, Op. 47, is a case in point." Mrs. Newmarch went on to say that Sibelius' Violin Concerto, "like that of Tschaikowsky, has been pronounced impossibly difficult; but it has not had to wait so long for its interpreter as the Russian concerto waited for a Brodsky."

The Tschaikowsky Concerto waited precisely three years for a performance. Sibelius' was played by Carl Halir in Berlin on Oct. 19, 1905, the year it was revised and published. On Nov. 30 of the following year the American violinist Maud Powell introduced it to this country at a concert of the New York Philharmonic Society in Carnegie Hall, repeating the work with the Theodore Thomas Orchestra in Chicago the following Jan. 25 and with the Boston Symphony Orchestra on Apr. 20.

The American poet Walter Conrad Arensberg, reviewing the Concerto for a New York paper, commented on the powerful contrast of orchestra and solo instrument that has struck so many listeners: "The violin expresses, now in passages of angular abruptness, now in slow, laboring phrases, convulsively ended, the labor and the love of a sensitive, almost morbidly modern, personality among the crude and prehistoric conditions of an unprotected land and ancient myths."

Despite its strongly modern character and modified sonata form, Sibelius' score belongs to the romantic tradition of the nineteenth-century concerto. The so-called "bardic" moods and exotic folkish strains give it a special salience of its own. The opposition of violin and orchestra is almost unique in its brooding contrasts, and the rhapsodic note of remote minstrelsy is strong, especially in the first movement. But the technic, the mounting climaxes, the surging drama of tone and theme, the high-register flutterings all give it a marked kinship with other repertory classics of the later romantic period. The ruggedly rhapsodic mood of the first movement is promptly set in the melodic sweep of the first theme, chanted by the solo violin against a somber background of divided and muted violins (Allegro moderato, D minor, 2/2). The second theme, of more lyrical repose, is also given out by the violin (Largamente, D flat major). The second movement (Adagio di molto, B flat, 4/4) is in the nature of a romanza. Wood winds sound a brief preface in thirds, and the solo violin begins a tender melodic discourse, tinged with melancholy. This is heard against chords in the horns and bassoons. A sharply contrasting middle section soon intervenes. The finale is an impetuous rondo on two themes (Allegro ma non tanto, D major, 3/4). The sturdy rhythmic base of the movement is promptly set by the tympani and string basses, and soon the violin plunges into its alleged "Danse Macabre." Violins and cellos introduce the second theme. Besides the solo instrument, the scoring calls for two flutes, two oboes, two clarinets, two bassoons, four horns, two trumpets, three trombones, tympani, and strings.

L. B.

"En Saga," Tone Poem for Orchestra, Op. 9

THE COMPOSITION which later became the orchestral *En Saga* was first envisioned as an octet for strings, flute, and clarinet. Sibelius had jotted down the themes for such a work during a visit to Vienna in 1890. Subsequently, he accepted the suggestion of Robert Kajanus that he compose a piece of music "for the general public and not making too great demands upon their powers of concentration and comprehension." *En Saga* was the result.

It was given its initial performance in Helsinki, on Feb. 16, 1893, under the composer's direction. He revised it in 1901, and it was finally published in 1903. Thus, all told, it required over a decade to bring it to its present form. Sibelius believed powerfully in the worth of youthful impressions. He once told his pupil Bengt de Törne, "Be careful not to be spendthrift with the themes and musical ideas of your youth. They are the richest and best you will ever invent, and if you cannot give them at once their definite shape, they will later on form the basis of some of your happiest conceptions." Whereupon he recounted in detail one specific experience of his own along such lines, the very first draft of *En Saga* for the projected octet, besides others in passing.

"In your old age," he continued, "you will look back on the ideas of your youth, and you will, perhaps, be fortunate enough to find some of them in your sketchbooks quite forgotten amongst many other notes, and never used. Then you will take them up, and the ardor of your youth expressed in the themes themselves will be combined with the knowledge and experience acquired during a long musical career."

Ferruccio Busoni, one of Sibelius' earliest champions, introduced the work on the continent. It soon spread like wild fire, preaching the gospel, as it were, of a new composer. For some years following that, in fact, Sibelius was known in Europe chiefly through *En Saga, Finlandia,* and the *Valse Triste.*

The orchestration calls for two flutes, piccolo, two oboes, two clarinets, two bassoons, four horns, three trumpets, three trombones, tuba, bass drum, cymbals, triangle, and strings.

R. C. B.

"The Swan of Tuonela," Legend from the "Kalevala," Op. 22

LIKE so much of Sibelius' other music, *The Swan of Tuonela* was inspired by the great Finnish epic *Kalevala*. The composition forms part of a symphonic tetralogy devoted to Lemminkäinen, one of the leading heroes of the poem. In the four-part cycle *The Swan of Tuonela* comes third, followed by *Lemminkäinen's Homecoming*. The first two sections are entitled *Lemminkäinen and the Maidens* and *Lemminkäinen's Sojourn in Tuonela*.

Since most of Sibelius' writing for the stage consists of incidental music for plays, it is surprising to learn that he first planned to use this epic material in an opera. During the summer of 1893, Sibelius discussed the possibilities of turning some episodes in the *Kalevala* into lyric drama with his friend the writer J. H. Erkko. This was to be called "Veneen Luominen" ("The Creation of the Boat"). Sibelius later related what happened to his biographer Karl Ekman.

It was originally intended that Erkko should write the book of the opera, but somehow or other I did so myself, while Erkko helped me as literary adviser. During the summer I completed the prologue to the opera and the book. When I returned to Helsingfors in the autumn, I called on Kaarlo Bergbom, the creator of the Finnish operatic stage, to ask for his opinion of the book. He said that it was effective, but too lyrical. In this he was indeed right; I realized this at once.

This sealed the doom of the opera. But the labor I had devoted to carrying out the idea was not entirely wasted, for my fresh absorption in the world of the *Kalevala* gave me the idea for the Lemminkäinen Suite. In the prologue to the opera I really had one movement of the suite ready made: *The Swan of Tuonela.*

The pictorial content of the tone poem is briefly given in a preface to the score: "Tuonela, The Kingdom of Death, the Hades of Finnish mythology, is surrounded by a broad river of black water and rapid current, in which the Swan of Tuonela glides in majestic fashion and sings."

Supported by muted strings and soft drum rolls, the broad, exotic theme of the swan floats in broodingly in a solo for English horn. Sad, fitful comments are soon heard in the lower strings. These Rosa Newmarch ventured to interpret as the farewell sighs "of some soul passing to Tuonela." A muted horn presently adds to the lugubrious mood by chanting part of the swan song. "Gradually," wrote Mrs. Newmarch, "the music works up to a great climax, indicated con gran suono, followed by a treble pianissimo, the strings playing with the back of the bow.

"To this accompaniment, which suggests the faint flapping of pinions, the swan's final phrases are sung. The strings return to the natural bowing, and the work ends in one of the characteristic, sighing phrases for violoncello."

The omission of flutes and high clarinets further deepens the somber color of the tone poem. Called for in the scoring are oboe, English horn, bass clarinet, two bassoons, four horns, three trombones, kettledrums, bass drum, and strings.

Sibelius himself conducted the world premiere of *The Swan of Tuonela* on Apr. 13, 1896, at Helsingfors. The work was introduced to America at a concert of the Chicago Orchestra in Chicago on Dec. 6, 1901. Philip Hale asked:

Suppose the hearer had no knowledge of the legend, had never read of Lemminkäinen's adventures; how, to win the maid Pohjola, he set out to accomplish certain tasks, among them to shoot a swan on this River of Death. How would the hearer then be impressed?

Surely he would be moved by the strangeness of the music, by the mysterious first measures, by the unearthly melancholy of the song, by the quiet intensity of it all. He would find in the music a tragic mood, simply but unmistakably expressed.

L. B.

"Finlandia," Tone Poem for Orchestra, Op. 26, No. 7

Both the title and the thematic substance of this work gave rise to the false assumption that Sibelius had employed actual folk melodies. Many regarded it as a fantasia on Finnish folk music. Sibelius himself has flatly denied this.

"There is a mistaken impression among the press abroad that my themes are often folk melodies," he told his English biographer, Rosa Newmarch. "So far I have never used a theme that was not of my own invention. Thus the thematic material of *Finlandia* and *En Saga* is entirely my own."

Olin Downes, among the first Americans to hail the genius of Sibelius, was equally emphatic in one of his many articles on the Finnish composer. "Sibelius does not make his scores of Finnish folk music. He does not employ folk songs in his symphonies at all and has never done so. But his musical speech is naturally tinged with idioms of his country, and his writing is so often in the vein of Finnish melody that it is mistaken for it."

Composed in 1894, *Finlandia* was first heard in America on Dec. 24, 1905, at the Metropolitan Opera House on a special Sunday night program conducted by Arturo Vigna. The following Saturday night, Modest Altschuler led the work in Carnegie Hall at a concert of the Russian Symphony Society. An analysis of its contents, which appeared in the program book, ran as follows:

An agitated, almost angry theme for the brass choir, short and trenchant, begins the introduction, Andante sostenuto (alla breve). This theme is answered by an organlike response in the wood winds, and then a prayerful passage for strings, as though to reveal the essential earnestness and reasonableness of the Finnish people, even under the stress of national sorrow. This leads to an Allegro moderato episode, in which the restless opening theme is proclaimed by the strings against a very characteristic rhythmic figure, a succession of eight beats, the first strongly accented.

With a change to Allegro, the movement, looked at as an example of the sonata form, may be said to begin. A broad, cheerful theme by the strings, in A flat, against the persistent rhythm in the brass, is followed by a second subject, introduced by the wood winds and taken up by the strings, then by the cello and first violin. This is peaceful and elevated in character, and might be looked upon as prophetic of ultimate rest and happiness. The development of these musical ideas carries the tone poem to an eloquent conclusion.

The tone poem is scored for two flutes, two oboes, two clarinets, two bassoons, four horns, three trumpets, three trombones, bass tuba, kettledrums, bass drum, cymbals, triangle, and the customary strings.

For a time during the struggle for Finnish independence from Russia, performances of *Finlandia* were prohibited by the Czarist authorities. In its forceful utterance they shrewdly sensed a rallying cry for revolution. The rumbling defiance of the opening measures brought an answering throb in the heart of every Finnish patriot. "Hot with the spirit of revolt," were Philip Hale's words for this symphonic manifesto from the brooding North.

Significantly, *Finlandia* was one of the works directed by Sibelius during his visit to America in the crucial summer of 1914. As guest of Carl Stoeckel, the Finnish composer conducted one of the concerts of the Litchfield County Choral Union in the Music Shed at Norfolk, Conn. *The Swan of Tuonela, Pohjola's Daughter,* and *Valse Triste* were also listed, besides *Aalottaret,* written especially for that occasion.

L. B.

Elie Siegmeister

BORN: NEW YORK, JAN. 15, 1909.

*The value of a man's work resides in the music itself, and not in how
frequently it is played, how many honors its composer has won, or
how much critical acclaim he has received.*—ELIE SIEGMEISTER.

"Prairie Legend," A Midwestern Set

1. Bullwhacker's Dance. 2. Harvest Evening. 3. County Fair.

THE COMPOSER has submitted the following, concerning his work:

This is one of a series of orchestral compositions inspired by the people, stories,
songs, landscapes of various parts of this country. *Prairie Legend* is a short work in
three movements: 1. "Bullwhacker's Dance"; 2. "Harvest Evening"; 3. "County
Fair."

It was in the spring of 1944, while touring through Ohio, Indiana, Illinois,
Michigan, Iowa, and Kansas with my American Ballad Singers, that I was struck
with the strength and poetic sweep of these states, and it seemed to me that this
could be expressed in music.

The opportunity came in the summer of 1944, when I was commissioned to write
a work for symphonic band. *Prairie Legend* was sketched in ten days in July, scored
for band, then scored for orchestra the following spring.

1. "Bullwhacker's Dance" suggests the boisterous, raw-boned ox drivers of
pioneer days . . . the men who carted the early settlers over the mountains and to
the legendary Promised Land that was then the Midwest.

2. "Harvest Evening"—the quietness and simple beauty of endless fields and the
black earth.

3. "County Fair"—the tumult, gaiety, hog callers, side shows, prize bulls, good-
natured crowds, races, games, and contests. Fragments of old tunes are heard,
especially a phrase of "Camptown Races."

The score calls for two flutes (second interchangeable with piccolo), two oboes
(second interchangeable with English horn), two clarinets (second interchangeable with bass clarinet), two bassoons, four horns, three trumpets, three trombones, tuba, tympani, bass drum, snare drum, triangle, tambourine, cymbals,
wood block, cow bell, xylophone, glockenspiel, and strings. The Suite was
introduced in its entirety by the Philharmonic-Symphony, Leopold Stokowski
conducting, in Carnegie Hall on Jan. 18, 1947.

Elie Siegmeister is widely known for his many orchestral and stage works on
native American themes. His music has been performed by leading American

symphony orchestras and has also won wide attention abroad. Outstanding among his works are *Ozark Set, Sunday in Brooklyn, Prairie Legend, American Sonata,* and *Abraham Lincoln Walks at Midnight.* Most of them reflect the legendary or real life of Americans of today or of the past. Among his works for the theater are the Broadway hit *Sing Out, Sweet Land, Doodle Dandy,* and others.

In addition to composing, Mr. Siegmeister has distinguished himself as a collector and arranger of American folk music. In 1939 he founded the American Ballad Singers. He has traveled throughout the country conducting these singers in their concerts, pausing here and there to listen to the songs of the people. In collaboration with Olin Downes he wrote *A Treasury of American Song.* Two other volumes of his are *A Music Lover's Handbook* and *Work and Sing.*

Earning his Phi Beta Kappa key at Columbia University in 1927, he won a three-year fellowship in conducting at the Juilliard School. He studied composition with Wallingford Riegger and Nadia Boulanger.

Mr. Siegmeister's most recent compositions include *Sunday in Brooklyn* (Efrem Kurtz and the NBC Symphony, July 21, 1946); *Funny Bone Alley* (Saratoga Music Festival, Sept. 9, 1946); and *A Tooth for Paul Revere* (High School of Music and Art, Nov. 9, 1946).

R. C. B.

Bedrich Smetana

BORN: LEITOMISCHL, BOHEMIA, MAR. 2, 1824. DIED: PRAGUE, MAY 12, 1884.

His music sings to us today of the Bohemia of old—its woods and cultivated plains, its villages, its romantic hills and old legends, its great past and even its future. It is all one great pageant of song and dance—dancing to native rhythms of astounding variety, singing to melodies of a unique beauty.—PAUL STEFAN.

Symphonic Poem, "Vltava" ("The Moldau") from the Cycle "Ma Vlast" ("My Fatherland")

AN ARDENT Bohemian patriot and nationalist, Bedrich Smetana enshrined his love and loyalty in a cycle of six symphonic poems collectively entitled *Ma Vlast* (*My Fatherland*). Of these, *Vltava* (*The Moldau*) is the second. Few artists in any medium have set forth the glory and beauty of their land with such fiery eloquence. History, tradition, and legend sweep through the cycle, and the gay laughter and healthy vigor of the Bohemian countryside pulse in its folkish interludes.

In the surging power and lyricism of *Ma Vlast,* Smetana wanted Bohemians to treasure their glorious history and envision a still nobler future. Through its vivid tapestry of tone he wanted outsiders to see his brave little land and learn to love it, too. No artistic manifesto could be as relevant to the recent plight of Smetana's imprisoned fatherland and to its heroic liberation. In this cycle a staunch lover of freedom voices his sadness, his hope—and his prophecy.

The story of *Ma Vlast* is not without its personal note of ironic pathos. Smetana never heard a single note of his series! He went deaf the very day the heroic theme of the opening *Vysehrad* section came to him. Smetana himself relates how he woke up that morning in a soundless world. "One night I listened with great pleasure to Leo Delibes' opera *Le Roi l'a dit,*" he writes. "When I returned home after the last act, I sat at the piano and improvised for an hour on whatever came into my head. *The following morning I was stone deaf.*" That was late in 1874. For almost ten years, up to his tragic death in an insane asylum, Smetana lived in absolute deafness, withdrawn from the world, and like Beethoven surmounting his affliction to give that world the maturest utterances of his genius. To the end he suffered great physical pain. Shortly before his mind finally snapped Smetana noted on the margin of a page of his D minor Quartet: "Composed in a state of disordered nerves—*the outcome of my deafness.*"

In 1882 a performance in Prague of the whole *Ma Vlast* cycle was turned into a patriotic rally. After each section the public, waving hats and handkerchiefs, repeatedly shouted Smetana's name . . . and Bohemia's. Feeling mounted steadily, until after *Blanik,* the final section—an irresistible battle cry to all true Czechs—it swelled into fiery jubilation. Nationally colored wreaths were showered on the composer. Hundreds shook his hand. Many kissed him. Smetana, stone deaf, physically and mentally a broken man, stood there, according to his friend Zeleny, "happy in the knowledge that he had made others happy." Prefacing the score of *Vltava* is the following descriptive analysis:

Two springs pour forth in the shade of the Bohemian Forest, one warm and gushing, the other cold and peaceful. Their waves, gayly flowing over rocky beds, join and glisten in the rays of the morning sun. The forest brook, hastening on, becomes the river Vltava (Moldau). Coursing through Bohemia's valleys, it grows into a mighty stream. Through thick woods it flows, as the gay sounds of the hunt and the notes of the hunter's horn are heard ever nearer. It flows through grass-grown pastures and lowlands where a wedding feast is being celebrated with song and dance. At night wood and water nymphs revel in its sparkling waves. Reflected on its surface are fortresses and castles—witnesses of bygone days of knightly splendor and the vanished glory of fighting times. At the St. John Rapids the stream races ahead, winding through the cataracts, hewing out a path with its foaming waves through the rocky chasm into the broad river bed—finally, flowing on in majestic peace toward Prague and welcomed by time-honored Vysehrad. Then it vanishes far beyond the poet's gaze.

The Symphonic Poem opens with an undulating flute passage (E minor, 6/8), heard against pizzicato chords in the violins and harp. The strings then carry the rippling figure as first violins, oboes, and bassoon chant the warm, rich melody in E minor which Smetana borrowed from a Czech folk song. Horns and harp enter the harmonic scheme, picturing the stream coursing through the Bohemian forest. Hunting calls, given out by the horns in C major, are soon heard over the river theme. Vltava swells in volume as the hunting episode gains force. Then, as the calls recede, a brisk wedding dance (G major, 2/4)—part march and part polka—sets in, working up to a fortissimo outburst of gaiety. The rustic dance subsides. Soft wood-wind harmonies now depict the moon rising over Vltava's glistening span. Accompanied by strings, clarinets, and horns, the flutes weave into the fabric an elfin dance of legendary water nymphs. Next, the horns, trumpets, and tuba join in a solemn, subdued passage. Then the strings bring back the "wave" figure, against which the first violins, oboes, and bassoon repeat the river theme. After some development, the pace sharpens; Vltava, swirling and foaming, is approaching the St. John Rapids. The whole orchestra rages as the river forces its way through. Cymbals and bass drum join in picturing the whirling din of the cataracts. Then, as Vltava.

clearing the rapids, streams majestically toward Prague, the theme modulates to E major, gradually fading in the distance.

The scoring is for piccolo, two flutes, two oboes, two clarinets, two bassoons, four horns, two trumpets, three trombones, bass tuba, tympani, bass drum, cymbals, triangle, harp, and strings.

If Smetana's *Vltava* causes fervid stirrings in the breast of every patriotic Czech, it also carries a special throb for Zionist Jews. For the melody used in the Jewish National Anthem "Hatikvah" ("Hope") stems from the same Czech folk song used by Smetana for his haunting river theme. The Hebrew poet Naphtali Herz Imber wrote the ardent verses of aspiration in 1878, and Samuel Cohen, a pioneer settler in Rishon Le Zion, Palestine, later adapted the song to them. Nowhere could this early Zionist have found a better theme for singing warmth and yearning prophecy than in this brave, unquenchable melody of another freedom-loving people.

L. B.

Symphonic Poem, "Blanik" from "Ma Vlast"

This symphonic hymn of patriotic hope rounds out Smetana's national cycle *Ma Vlast (My Fatherland)*. *Blanik* pictures the spectral Knights of the Hussite wars of independence in their mountain retreat, awaiting the day of reckoning when they will fall on Bohemia's oppressors and drive them out. Over them looms majestic Mount Blanik. As misery and terror spread through the land, the Hussite warriors prepare to heed the call for help. Magically the mountain opens and out stream Bohemia's saviors. Soon the enemy is crushed, and peace and freedom reign again. In exultant symphonic speech, Smetana, a staunch nationalist, voiced his hope and prophecy.

To the true Czech, *Blanik* has long been a battle cry. Implicit in this heroic synthesis of Czech glory and legend is the tradition of John Huss, the fourteenth-century Czech heretic and rebel who died at the stake. Fragments of the Hussite battle choral burst out fervently in both *Blanik* and the preceding section *Tabor,* to which it is closely linked in Hussite background. The whole orchestra seems to intone the words, "With God on your side you will triumph over the foe." Finally, in mounting jubilation, the main theme of the first section of *Ma Vlast*—the *Vysehrad*—returns. The unity of Czech history and legend, the cycle of Liberty, is complete.

L. B.

Overture to the Opera "The Bartered Bride"

To begin with, the title of Smetana's comic opera is *Prodana nevesta* in the original Czech, and the standard German version of the work offers the label *Die verkaufte Braut,* both of which may be literally Englished to *The Sold*

Bride. However, for possible reasons of euphony or cadence or just plain accident, the piece is known in English as *The Bartered Bride,* which does seem an improvement on the ultralaconic definitiveness of the other. In any case, the opera with a libretto by Karl Sabina, was given its world premiere in Prague, May 30, 1866. Forty-three years later Giulio Gatti-Casazza produced it at the Metropolitan Opera House in the German version. On that occasion Gustav Mahler conducted and the leading soprano role of Marie was entrusted to Emmy Destinn, both of whom were of Bohemian birth. The opera took, as the saying goes, and it fluctuated slightly in popularity for the next three seasons.

In January, 1926, it was revived at the Metropolitan, remaining on the active list for three seasons more. A later revival, in February, 1933, brought its sum total of performances for that season to two. All the afore-mentioned productions were given in the German translation. In the meantime there had been considerable bustle all along concerning a presentation in English, but not until the "popular" spring season of 1936 did it crystallize into fact. A number of writers, grouped collectively under the name of Graham Jones, were responsible for it, and it had a remarkable success, so much so that the opera in that English adaptation entered the Metropolitan's repertory of the following winter season.

The Overture, however, has ever been a favorite with American concert audiences, antedating the staging of the opera by more than twenty years. Hanslick, who made some declarations in his time, notably the anti-Wagnerian tirades, delivered himself of a curious thought when he said that the Overture might serve admirably as a prelude to a comedy by Shakespeare, as if its natural and original function in preluding a compellingly amusing opera were not service enough! True, it has occasionally carried the title *Comedy Overture* in concert performances, but that, too, would seem to be of a piece with Hanslick's odd juxtaposing.

It been said that Smetana was driven to the composition of "national" music by a chance utterance of Herbeck's to the effect that Czechs "were simply reproductive artists," and initial steps in that "nationalistic" direction were taken with the founding of the Czechic Interims Theater in Prague, Nov. 18, 1862. Smetana's first operatic contribution to that venture, *Branibori v Cecach,* came a little over three years after the establishing of the Theater. (The libretto for that first essay has been described as "undramatic," "improbable," and "ridiculous.") The composer began work on *The Bartered Bride* in May, 1863, and completed it in March, 1866. At its one hundredth performance in Prague, May 5, 1882, Smetana said, "I did not compose it from any ambitious desire, but rather as a scornful defiance, for they accused me after my first opera of being a Wagnerite, one that could do nothing in a light and popular style."

In its original form the opera was in two acts without change of scene, and it consisted of twenty lyric parts connected by spoken dialogue. For a projected performance at the Opéra Comique in Paris, Smetana augmented his score with a male chorus in praise of beer, an air for Marenka, and a dance. He divided the first act into two scenes, later ending the first scene with a polka and opening the second with a furiant (peasant dance), which made three acts of the original two. For the St. Petersburg production, given in January, 1871, the composer changed the spoken dialogue into recitative, bringing the opera to its present form.

Philip Hale has lucidly summed up Smetana's aims in opera with the following words:

He believed in the ever-flowing melody in the operatic orchestra; this melody should never interrupt, never disturb, the dramatic sense; the music should have a consistent physiognomy; it should characterize the dramatic; the leitmotive should individualize; but Smetana knew the folly of imitation, nor was he the kind of man to play the sedulous ape. He once said, "We cannot compose as Wagner composes," and therefore he sought to place in the frame of Wagnerian reform his own musical style, his musical individuality, which had grown up in closest intimacy with his love of the soil, with the life, songs, legends of his countrymen.

R. C. B.

String Quartet in E minor, No. 1 ("From My Life")

I. Romantic longing, and foreboding of misfortune (Allegro vivo appassionato). II. The merriment of youth; my love of dancing and dance music (Alla polka). III. Memories of the happiness of my first love (Largo sostenuto). IV. Joy in discovering how to treat Bohemian national elements in music; the catastrophe of deafness, reminiscences of happier days, and resignation (Vivace, meno mosso).

[*Transcribed for orchestra by George Szell*]

PREMIERED ON the air on Mar. 8, 1941, by the NBC Symphony Orchestra, the present orchestral version was performed the following Jan. 29 and 30 by the Boston Symphony Orchestra in Boston. Mr. Szell conducted on all three occasions. In rescoring Smetana's first string quartet, the arranger calls for a huge instrumental array consisting of two flutes, piccolo, two oboes, two clarinets, two bassoons, four horns, two trumpets, three trombones, tuba, tympani, triangle, tambourine, side drum, bass drum, cymbals, tam-tam, harp, and strings.

Fully aware of the risks in making such an arrangement and knowing all the arguments against the practice, Mr. Szell hesitated long before setting to work on the great quartet. He wrote his publisher:

In general I am in entire sympathy with such arguments. But in this case I reached the opposite conclusion. Smetana himself had doubts as to the reception of this composition. In a letter of Oct. 12, 1878, to his friend Joseph Srb-Debrnov, he wrote that others would have to judge the style of the quartet; that he would not be surprised to find they did not like it, since it was contrary to the usual familiar form of the string quartet.

Mr. Szell pointed out that the great quantity of arpeggios in the quartet were in themselves proof enough that Smetana found the four string instruments inadequate for expressing his musical ideas. A further clue may be found in the indication *quasi tromba*—as if with a trumpet—in the polka of the second movement. Then Mr. Szell felt the "many tremolos sustaining the full melodies" show an orchestral quality. He wrote, in 1941:

All these considerations made me decide last autumn to arrange this Czech masterpiece for the orchestra. It deserves wider musical horizons in orchestral form than are possible, or have been possible up to the present, for the string quartet.

As for my conscience, I have not changed a note or made any alteration of the harmony which would disturb it. In choosing the symphonic form familiar to Smetana in his compositions, I have simply underlined the musical thought of the original Smetana expression.

Smetana's own statements about the quartet are worth quoting as indicative of his personal, subjective approach to art. The *alla polka* movement, he wrote, "recalls memories of my gay life in youth when I used to write dance music and give it away right and left to other young folk, being known myself as an enthusiastic dancer." He weighed charges made by performers that the middle section of this movement was "impossible" to play, the "purity of the chords" being unattainable. "I remind you," replied the composer, "that in this movement I paint in tones my recollections of the aristocratic circles in which I moved for years. I think the difficulty of this movement is the real reason why musicians refuse to play it, and not the 'orchestral style' to which they refer."

According to Smetana, the Largo sostenuto "recalls the bliss of my first love for the girl who afterwards became my faithful wife." The finale he described as "My joy in discovering how to treat Bohemian national elements in music; my successes in this direction until the interruption of the terrible catastrophe, the beginning of deafness; a glimpse at the gloomy future, a slight ray of hope for betterment; painful impressions aroused by the thought of my first artistic beginnings."

Summarizing his aims, Smetana referred to the quartet as "a work which in a sense is private and therefore written for four instruments, which should converse together in an intimate circle about the things which so deeply trouble me. Nothing more."

L. B.

David Stanley Smith

BORN: TOLEDO, OHIO, JULY 6, 1877.

He is greatly interested in the architecture of music; he considers it no less important than melodic invention and feeling. And he strives to avoid equally sentimentality on the one hand and harsh impersonality on the other.—JOHN TASKER HOWARD.

"Credo": Poem for Orchestra

THE COMPOSER of this work has been associated during his entire professional career with Yale University, as student, professor of composition, Dean of the Yale School of Music—1920 to 1940—besides his duties as conductor of the New Haven Symphony Orchestra. Several of his compositions have been performed by leading orchestras, two of them by the Philharmonic-Symphony Society, *viz.,* his Second Symphony, performed in 1918, with Mr. Smith conducting, and 1929—*A Satire,* conducted by Bruno Walter on Nov. 15, 1933.

Mr. Smith's First, Third, and Fourth Symphonies have obtained hearings by major organizations, as have his *Prince Hal—An Overture, Fête Galante,* for Flute and Orchestra, and other works. He has also composed nine string quartets and a number of sonatas, choral compositions, and songs.

Mr. Smith has kindly supplied the following analysis of his work:

The theme from which this work takes its title is the most famous of the medieval intonations of the Creed, the one used by Bach in the B minor Mass. It dates from the eleventh century or earlier. As it is here displayed by flutes and clarinets in octaves over a sustained C major chord, it is easily recognized. Later on chimes intone it against other melodies and again at the end. Though the Credo theme serves to give a hint as to the meaning of the work, it can hardly be called the "first subject." In point of time the leading motive is a calm, severely diatonic melody for four horns in unison. There are several other melodies of almost equal importance. The pattern woven out of these various ideas is intricate, but free from scholastic treatment. The music is intended to be an affirmation of faith in abiding spiritual values at a time when these are subject to forces of upheaval and discouraging doubt.

Bruno Walter conducted the world premiere of this score at a New York Philharmonic-Symphony concert on Nov. 8, 1941.

R. C. B.

Leo Sowerby

BORN: GRAND RAPIDS, MICH., MAY 1, 1895.

I try to be myself, not thinking about my style or idiom; trying constantly to improve my technic, so that when I shall have something to say, I shall be able to say it clearly and directly, and—God willing —simply.—LEO SOWERBY.

Symphonic Poem, "Prairie"

As WITH so many other modern American composers, the native soil has been a fertile source of inspiration for Leo Sowerby. Among his compositions rooted in the good American earth is the Symphonic Poem *Prairie,* based on the well-known poem of Carl Sandburg which was later to serve Lukas Foss as text for his brilliant cantata of the same name. Mr. Sowerby completed the score during the spring of 1929 and conducted its world premiere with the National High School Orchestra at Interlochen, Mich., on Aug. 11, 1929.

Two excerpts from Mr. Sandburg's poem are printed in the score to indicate the kind of imagery and mood the composer sought to evoke in the music. They run as follows:

Have you seen a red sunset drip over one of my cornfields, the shore of night stars, the wave lines of dawn up a wheat valley?

Have you heard my threshing crews yelling in the chaff of a strawpile and the running wheat of the wagon boards, my cornhuskers, my harvest hands hauling crops, singing dreams of women, worlds, horizons?

The structure of Mr. Sowerby's Symphonic Poem is such that the poet's imagery follows in an unbroken sequence in the delineation of mood. The hush of the "red sunset drip" returns at the end of the composition, and one is again made to glimpse the huge, unrelieved uniformity of Middle-Western farmland. Mr. Sowerby, however, disclaimed any effort to write to strict "program music." When the work was performed by the Chicago Symphony Orchestra, the composer wrote Felix Borowski, the annotator, disclosing his aims:

The composer asks only of the listener that he imagine himself alone in an Illinois cornfield, far enough away from railways, motor cars, telephones, and radios to feel himself at peace and at one with the beauty that is about him. If the situation has something of the "homely" about it, so much the better for the situation.

The score calls for two flutes, piccolo, two oboes, English horn, two clarinets, bass clarinet, two bassoons, double bassoon, four horns, three trumpets, three trombones, tuba, tympani, side drum, bass drum, cymbals, triangle, bells, celesta, and strings.

Born in Grand Rapids, Michigan, of an English father and Canadian mother, Leo Sowerby early studied music in Chicago. He was appointed organist at the St. James Episcopal Church there and teacher of composition at the American Conservatory of Music. In 1917 he enlisted and played clarinet in an army band, later becoming bandmaster with American Expeditionary Forces in England and France. He was the first American composer to be awarded the Prix de Rome in 1921. After three years of study in Italy he returned home and was appointed organist of the St. James church.

A composition of his, the orchestral suite *A Set of Four* was performed as early as 1918 by the Chicago Symphony Orchestra. Later that year the New York Symphony played his first concert overture, *Comes Autumn Time.* Among his other works are a cantata *The Vision of Sir Launfall,* a symphony for organ, and a *Mediaeval Poem* for organ and orchestra, besides considerable chamber music, an organ concerto, and two piano concertos. A *Concert Overture,* composed in the summer of 1941, has proved popular with high-school and college orchestras in the Middle West. Mr. Sowerby's music has been praised for the fresh vigor and directness of style evidenced in this work.

Rejecting "labels, tags, groups, and schools," he points out that in late years he has been drifting away from the "consciously national" trend of his earlier work. However, critics still aver that his works are "the sort that could have been written only by an American." The stylistic variety of Mr. Sowerby's music has elicited such contrasting responses from reviewers that he once remarked: "I have been accused by right-wingers of being too dissonant and cacaphonous, and by the leftists of being old-fashioned and derivative."

L. B.

Louis Spohr

BORN: BRUNSWICK, GERMANY, APR. 5, 1784. DIED: KASSEL, OCT. 22, 1859.

There is nothing eternal about the Spohr concertos. They represent him in the parliament of composers as a local conservative who knew a few set speeches and delivered them well.—ABRAHAM VEINUS.

Concerto for Violin and Orchestra in D minor, No. 9, Op. 55

I. Allegro. II. Adagio. III. Rondo.

THOUGH INFLUENTIAL for decades as composer, conductor, violinist, and general musical arbiter, Louis Spohr is only a name to average concertgoers today. In his time he was known from one end of Europe to the other, and his name spelled magic across the sea. He toured widely and often, virtually founded the first great German music festival, and for thirty-seven years directed the ducal opera at Kassel. He had his likes and dislikes, abhorred the Fifth and Ninth Symphonies of Beethoven, yet championed Wagner. In 1811, Spohr gave a recital in Berlin, the accompanying pianist being a youth named Giacomo Meyerbeer. Four years later he played his own Concertante for Two Violins in Rome. The other soloist was Nicolo Paganini, for whose "lighter and freer" style of bowing he had no taste.

Despite the constant traveling, conducting, and playing, he found time to compose. His output is stupendous in the mere listing, the last opus number being 154, not counting some fifteen other compositions outside the series and a vast quantity of manuscripts. His violin concertos alone number seventeen, his symphonies nine, his oratorios four. Thirty-three string quartets came from his pen, and he even composed ten operas, including a *Faust,* regarded as his best.

Of the concertos the Ninth, considered the best of the seventeen, still holds the concert stage, though as far back as 1888 a Boston reviewer could write: "The Spohr concerto sounds very old now." The Seventh and Eighth were also in currency at the time, though already lagging behind. Still, long after Spohr's death, the violinist Paul David, writing in *Grove's Dictionary,* maintained that the concertos were "surpassed only by those of Beethoven and Mendelssohn." He thought they would live "longer than any other of his works" and praised their "noble and elevated ideas" and "masterly thematic treatment," as well as the "supreme fitness of every note in the solo part to the nature of the violin."

In Spohr's own lifetime, Henry F. Chorley, the English critic, praised their "verve, brightness, and contrast," calling them "of their kind the first of the first." To Chorley they constituted "a blessed thing for the great and noble school of violin players in Germany . . . a fact no more to be denied than that Mozart helped opera a step forward, Beethoven the orchestra, and Clementi the pianoforte."

The Ninth Concerto entered the New York Philharmonic repertory during its thirty-second season, on Nov. 15, 1873. The soloist was Ernst Schiever, the conductor Carl Bergmann. A symphony of Spohr's—*The Consecration of Tone* —figured in the programs of the fifth, sixth, eighth, and tenth seasons, almost as a "request" number.

The work dates from the autumn of 1820. Earlier that year Spohr made his first visit to London, conducted the Philharmonic, and brought on a storm by doing something—for London—unprecedented: he used a baton! On his return home he set immediately to work on the Concerto and brought it out himself on Oct. 14 at a festival in Quedlinburg. Wild enthusiasm greeted it. A similar reception was in store of it at Frankfurt. Paris, on the other hand, responded tepidly, and Spohr's letters home bristle with sharp strictures on French taste.

Spohr's *Violin School*—long a standard manual—bears his own comments on the Concerto. The Allegro is "serious but impassioned"; the Adagio, "mild and serene"; the Rondo "agitated and imperious." A prefatory section, following the then accepted practice, gives out the main themes. The solo violin then tackles two subjects, the first in brisk chromatics, the second a song in F major, leading to a flurry of typical bravura and a development section with returning themes. In the Adagio two "mild and serene" melodies are announced and, amid more florid writing, brought back in new guise. The Rondo, full of double stops and decorative brilliance, used to be avoided by many violinists.

L. B.

William Grant Still

BORN: WOODVILLE, MISS., MAY 11, 1895.

By far the most widely recognized Negro composer today is William Grant Still. . . . About 1925, Still decided definitely to devote himself to the development of the Negro idiom and the treatment of Negro subjects in his programmatic works.—JOHN TASKER HOWARD.

"And They Lynched Him on a Tree," Ballad Poem by Katharine Garrison Chapin

THE POEM on which this music is based was brought to the attention of William Grant Still by Dr. Alain Locke, of Howard University. Impressed by the dramatic quality of its theme, he saw in its words a subject eminently suited to the talents of the well-known Negro composer. Mr. Still, then toiling industriously during the one-year term of a Rosenwald Fellowship, found the idea entirely agreeable to him and he began to work on it at once.

Miss Chapin's poem, briefly, tells of the lynching of a Negro. She draws pictures of the surrounding circumstances—the mob, enjoying its gruesome work, the raw ecstasy of sadistic song after the deed, the coming of darkness and with it the appearance of Negroes, friends of the victim, who seek his body in the black night. Then the mother, a broken, distraught figure, emerges out of the group and, as if by some psychic relationship, all launch into a lament. The song grows into an apotheosis, white voices joining those of the Negroes in a protest against the rule of the mob, against lawlessness, and together they sing of the hope for an understanding and a tolerance that will remove forever every trace of such hate and prejudice and injustice from the hearts of men.

And They Lynched Him on a Tree was given its initial hearing on June 24, 1940, at a Philharmonic-Symphony Concert in the Lewisohn Stadium.

R. C. B.

"Plain-Chant for America," Based on a Poem by Katharine Garrison Chapin

THIS WORK represents the second collaboration with Miss Chapin. *Plain-Chant for America,* the leading poem in a book of poems by Miss Chapin, first appeared in a national magazine in August, 1939, a few weeks before the beginning of hostilities in the Second World War, when international sneers and muscular gestures had not yet given way to actual warfare.

Concerning the origin of her verses, Miss Chapin says,

An American poem had been germinating in my mind for a long time, but the final circumstances that helped to thrust it into being was the fact that I had spent a few days in the company of some persons who are sympathetic to the Fascists, charming people, whose talk enraged me in inverse proportion to their charm, and showed me vividly the gap between totalitarianism and the American democracy in which I believed. The emotion of the poem began there; I found completion when we stood beside President Roosevelt in the sunshine at Key West, Fla., while he made a fine radio broadcast, opening the San Francisco World's Fair in February, 1939.

The poem follows:

> For the dream unfinished
> Out of which we came,
> We stand together,
> While a hemisphere darkens
> And the nations flame.
>
> Our earth has been hallowed
> With death for freedom;
> Our walls have been hallowed
> With freedom's thought.
>
> Concord, Valley Forge, Harper's Ferry
> Light up with their flares
> Our sky of doubt.
>
> We fear tyranny as our hidden enemy;
> The black-shirt cruelty, the goose-step mind.
> No dark signs close the doors of our speaking,
> No bayonets bar the door to our prayers,
> No gun butts shadow our children's eyes.
>
> If we have failed—lynchings in Georgia,
> Justice in Massachusetts undone,
> The bloody fields of South Chicago—
> Still a voice from the bruised and the battered
> Speaks out in the light of a free sun,
>
> Saying, "Tell them again, say it, America:
> Say it again till it splits their ears:
> Freedom is salt in our blood and its bone shape;
> If freedom fails, we'll fight for more freedom—

This is the land, and these are the years!
When freedom's a whisper above their ashes
An obsolete word cut on their graves,
When the mind has yielded its last resistance,
And the last free flag is under the waves—

"Let them remember that here on the western
Horizon a star, once acclaimed, has not set;
And the strength of a hope, and the shape of a vision
Died for and sung for and fought for,
And worked for,
Is living yet."

Mr. Still's music is in the form of an accompanied oration. It teems with dramatic recitative, and it offers two melodic themes. The first comes immediately at the opening of the piece, and the second enters with the line, "Our earth has been hallowed." This latter subject obtains a brief development during the course of the number, then it swells into a great postlude. Mr. Still followed a suggestion of John Barbirolli's in the inclusion of the two purely orchestral sequences.

The music endeavors to parallel the message of the text in a simple and direct manner. Complicated formal devices have been put aside in the interest of a straightforward declaration, whose appeal is aimed at the widest possible audience.

Mr. Still dedicated his composition to President and Mrs. Franklin Delano Roosevelt. It was first performed at a New York Philharmonic-Symphony concert, John Barbirolli conducting, on Oct. 23, 1941.

R. C. B.

Symphonic Poem, "Old California"

SUGGESTED BY Werner Janssen, this work was written in commemoration of the one hundred and sixtieth anniversary of the city of Los Angeles. It was given its first performance in a program of the Mutual Broadcasting System, *Standard Symphony Hour,* under Mr. Janssen's direction on Sept. 4, 1941. Since then it has been revised and lengthened, in which form it has obtained performances by various orchestras. Mr. Still himself writes of the composition:

The symphonic poem *Old California* does not pretend to be anything more than program music. The short introduction indicates that, before the coming of the red man, California's destiny was established. Then the composition depicts, in turn, the Indian and his tribal dances (the thematic material suggested by an authentic American Indian melody); the Spaniard with his religious life and colorful fiestas; a time of struggle when the American appeared on the scene; and finally a merging of all these groups to bring an era of peace and plenty. The composer has dedicated the work to the memory of his friend George Fischer, who worked tirelessly on behalf of American composers and their music.

The score calls for three flutes, two oboes, English horn, two clarinets, bass clarinet, two bassoons, four horns, three trumpets, three trombones, tuba, tympani, two percussion, harp, and strings.

R. C. B.

"Poem for Orchestra"

THE FOLLOWING explanation of the *Poem for Orchestra* is by the composer:

In 1944, Erich Leinsdorf, then conductor of the Cleveland Orchestra, wrote to commission a new orchestral work from me. He placed no limitations on the kind of work I should write, nor was there any specification as to time limit. The commission was made possible by the Fynette H. Kulas Original American Composers Fund, created by Mr. and Mrs. E. J. Kulas, who are both trustees of the Cleveland Orchestra.

At the time, my mind had already been turning toward a new orchestral work, so the commission came at an opportune moment. I determined to express in music to the best of my ability the spiritual rebirth of mankind through a drawing closer to God. Accordingly I wrote the *Poem for Orchestra,* and after it was finished I asked my wife to write a short poem which would express in words what I tried to express in music. This is the poem which now appears in the printed score:

> Soul-sick and weary,
> Man stands on the rim of a desolate world.
> Then from the embers of a dying past
> Springs an immortal hope.
> Resolutely evil is uprooted and thrust aside;
> A shining new temple stands
> Where once greed and lust for power flourished.
> Earth is young again and on the wings of its rebirth
> Man draws closer to God.
>
> Verna Arvey

The *Poem for Orchestra* is in three sections. The first, expressing the desolation of the world, is dissonant. The second section, a development of material that may be found in the opening section, is more like an energetic scherzo, signifying the building for a new world. The third section has in it completely new musical material—and this time the harmonies are consonant—signifying a spiritual rebirth and an exaltation in the approach to the Divine Force. At the very end of the work, there are some remainders of the opening thematic material, but these do not come with the same desolate feeling that they had in their first appearance.

The *Poem for Orchestra* was given its first performance by the Cleveland Orchestra under the direction of Rudolph Ringwall on Dec. 7, 1944. It is dedicated, Mr. Still adds, "to Arthur Judson, not only because I am personally grateful to him for many things, but also because I feel that he has been a constructive force in shaping and propagandizing American culture in various forms."

R. C. B.

"In Memoriam: The Colored Soldiers Who Died for Democracy"

In 1943 the League of Composers invited each of seventeen well-known composers to write a short work for orchestra commemorative of the Second World War, the series to be introduced by the New York Philharmonic-Symphony, under the direction of Artur Rodzinski, and broadcast by the Columbia Broadcasting System.

Besides Mr. Still, the composers concerned were Nicolai Berezowsky, John Alden Carpenter, Henry Cowell, Norman Dello Joio, Howard Hanson, Roy Harris, Bernard Herrmann, Charles Ives, Werner Josten, Bohuslav Martinu, Darius Milhaud, Douglas Moore, Walter Piston, Quincy Porter, Bernard Rogers, and Roger Sessions.

Mr. Rodzinski wrote of the project,

In my opinion this series of commissions will serve three excellent purposes: It will serve as a strong and moving reminder to our country that the preservation and furtherance of our cultural resources is a duty and a privilege of the first importance in times as critical as our own. It will create a living musical record of various aspects of this war and its accompanying social manifestations. It will continue to encourage and stimulate composers resident in America, who are given all too rarely an opportunity to be heard.

Of his own composition Mr. Still has written:

When it was suggested to me that I compose something patriotic there immediately flashed through my mind the press release which announced that the first American soldier to be killed in World War II was a Negro soldier. Then my thoughts turned to the colored soldiers all over the world, fighting under our flag and under the flags of the countries allied with us.

Our civilization has known no greater patriotism, no greater loyalty than that shown by the colored men who fight and die for democracy. Those who return will, I hope, come back to a better world.

I also hope that our tribute to those who died will be to make the democracy for which they fought greater and broader than it has ever been before.

Mr. Rodzinski led the world premiere of this work on Jan. 5, 1944.

Johann Strauss

BORN: VIENNA, OCT. 25, 1825. DIED: VIENNA, JUNE 3, 1899.

One of Strauss's waltzes as far surpasses in charm, finish, and real musical worth hundreds of the artificial compositions of his contemporaries, as the tower of St. Stephen's surpasses the advertising columns on the Paris Boulevards.—RICHARD WAGNER.

Waltz, "Wiener Blut" ("Vienna Blood"), Op. 354

DEDICATED TO King Christian IV of Denmark, the *Wiener Blut* waltz was composed early in 1873 and first performed at a Viennese spring festival held that year in the Volksgarten. Oddly enough, it left the Viennese public cold at first. Later, when the popular folk singer Ulke set words to it and featured it in his repertory, it became one of Vienna's great favorites from the "Waltz King's" pen. In discussing resemblances among the Strauss waltzes, H. E. Jacob points to thematic parallels in *Wiener Blut* and the *Künstlerleben* (*Artists' Life*) of five years earlier. "But nobody could mistake one for the other," he adds. "In the earlier work we have the grace and light-heartedness of the artists' lives, while in *Wiener Blut* we have a dreamy, heavy-lidded sensuality. . . ." There is even a hint in its pages of the *Rosenkavalier* waltzes of a later Strauss. The *Wiener Blut* is one of almost 400 waltzes credited to Johann Strauss, who was already writing in three-quarter time at the age of six.

In a way the Viennese waltz was at once the clue to the Viennese temper and the city's history. In its lush flow the Viennese was mirrored. Melancholy, sparkle, a ripe, voluptuous love of life combine in its entrancing spell. Vienna, the brilliant and festive and pleasure loving, chants through it. From the Ländler and folk dances of Bavaria and Bohemia, from city and countryside, from café and wine shop came the elements coalescing in the city's great anthem—The Waltz. In a city of carnivals and café life it blossomed richly. As a revolt against the stiff elegances of minuet and gavotte it made its triumphant way. This was the dance of bourgeois democracy, of the citizenry. Some even see a distant kinship with the round dance of the French Revolution, the Carmagnole. But the waltz as such was born and baptized in this "Falstaff of Cities." Vienna that had known plagues, floods, invasions, and wars, and lay wrapped in Catholic mysticism in the shadow of St. Stephen's and brooding Alpine vistas, this same Vienna had cradled the waltz as a "flight from death." The Viennese was and remains obsessed with the brevity of life. Some saw a narcotic in this spinning frenzy, and Richard Wagner called its then king, Johann I, a "nerve demon." In the 1830's an observer, stunned by the sight of forty-thousand waltz fanatics whirling around in the Brigittenau during the Festival of St. Bridget, thought of a "Red Indian Festival."

Weber and Schubert and Beethoven belong in the waltz genealogy, and Haydn and Mozart as well. In dance forms and rhythms they borrowed, perfected, and laid down new patterns. Nameless minstrels of town and country gifted with rhythmic improvisation contributed. At first a simple tune of a few bars, it branched out. Several themes were strung together. Trios and codas were added, and with Joseph Lanner and the Strausses the waltz reached full, pulsating maturity. Nineteenth-century Vienna waltzed, and the sport spread like wildfire. Feverishly, the populace succumbed. Other dances were brusquely banished from the capital. As the rage grew and intensified, the waltz grew with it, until in the hands of an arch-magician, the younger Johann Strauss, it became a wizardly compound of sentiment, brilliance, abandon, glitter, and nostalgia—the perfect expression of a romantic city athirst for gay life and seeking escape from a gnawing conviction of emptiness. The waltz invaded cafés, theaters, homes. The Mondscheinsaal, the Neue Welt, the Sperlsaal, the Apollopalast hummed nightly with it. "Lanner flattered the Viennese heart," it is said; "Strauss commanded their feet." Later in the century Eduard Hanslick in horror harked back to this flood tide of waltzing frenzy as a sign that the Viennese were "incapable of intellectual exertion." Wagner, visiting Vienna in his youth, found the waltz "a stronger narcotic than alcohol," and later described the "passions bordering on mad fury" when the great Johann conducted. What a change from the courtly minuet and gavotte of the old order, when finger tips met in refined restraint! Vienna was now a mad whirl of enlaced figures.

And Vienna knew how to honor her waltz-makers. Arduous testimonials and celebrations were the younger Strauss's lot in later life. On the fortieth anniversary of his first appearance at the Dommayer Casino, Vienna feted him till he sagged. An endless chain of wordy, bowing, hand-shaking deputations besieged him. The burgomaster of the City and an adulatory retinue paid their respects. Delegates from the chief theaters and musical societies followed suit. Telegrams and poems were read pompously. Speeches droned on ceaselessly. Medals and diplomas came in showers. From morning to night Vienna worshipped. At a banquet, fish from the beautiful blue Danube was served. The Golden Jubilee was even more staggering in scope and endurance. Flowers, letters, gifts came in carloads. Composers—Goldmark, Rubinstein, Nikisch, Leoncavallo—paid their respects. Conservatory pupils sang in Strauss's honor. Deputations again. Performances all over town of Strauss works. America despatched a silver laurel wreath, each leaf bearing the title of a Strauss waltz. From Honolulu came a photograph of the members of the Hawaii Orchestra. The city pulsed and throbbed to the name of Johann Strauss, and all Vienna waltzed. "If it be true that I have some talent I owe its development to my beloved native city, Vienna," he said. "Vienna! I drink to her! May she grow and prosper!"

When he died in 1899, something of Vienna died with him. The whole city mourned him. As the elaborate cortege passed along the streets, the Viennese bowed their heads in silence and wept. He was buried at the side of Brahms and Schubert. Adoration had come to him from the lowest to the highest in Vienna's social scale. In return, Strauss had adored his Vienna. While *The Beautiful Blue Danube* lives, Vienna must linger in the hearts of men. The Queen of Waltzes is her song of perpetual youth and romance. Faces brighten involuntarily with the opening bar. At its premiere in 1867 it drove the Diana-saal gathering into a delirium of joy unequaled in the annals of Viennese music. Truly it became Vienna's anthem. What Strauss had received from this throbbing, intoxicating city he gave back with lavish interest. In *Wiener Blut,* in the *Emperor Waltz,* in *Tales from the Vienna Woods,* in *Artists' Life*—actually in all his music—he hymned the enchantments of his immortal city for all time.

L. B.

Overture to the Operetta, "Die Fledermaus" ("The Bat")

HAVING COMPOSED a vast number of widely acclaimed waltzes and garnered heaps of laurels as conductor, Johann Strauss turned to the theater in 1871 with his first operetta *Indigo und die vierzig Rauber.* In spite of a poor libretto, the work succeeded, thanks to the fetching score. But it was not until 1874 that Strauss produced a highly popular operetta, *Die Fledermaus,* owing its success to both libretto and music, and "Operetta King" was appended to "Waltz King" in his string of honorary titles. Haffner and Genée had based the book on Meilhac and Halévy's *Le Réveillon.* George P. Upton's synopsis of the plot follows:

The scene opens with Adèle, maid of the Baroness Rosalind, seeking permission to visit her sister Ida, a ballet dancer, who is to be at a masked ball given by Prince Orlofsky, a Russian millionaire. She receives permission, and after she is gone, Dr. Falke, a notary, who has arranged the ball, calls at the house of the Baron Eisenstein, and induces him to go to it before going to jail, to which he has been sentenced for contempt of court.

The purpose of the doctor is to seek revenge for his shabby treatment by the Baron some time before at a masquerade which they had attended—Eisenstein dressed as a butterfly, and Falke as a bat. The doctor then notifies the Baroness that her husband will be at the ball. She thereupon decides that she will also be present.

An amusing scene occurs when the Baron seeks to pass himself off as a French marquis, and pays his devotions to the ladies, but is quite astonished to find his wife there, flirting with an old lover. There are further complications caused by Falke, who manages to have Alfred, the singing master, in the Baroness' apartments when the sheriff comes to arrest the Baron, and arrests Alfred, supposing him to be Eisenstein. In the last act, however, all the complications are disentagled, and everything ends happily.

Waltzes and polkas mingle in this bright medley of ravishing tunes, with sparkling drinking songs, romanzas, and czardas interspersed, the whole being virtually an apotheosis of song and dance and a rare compound of "Viennese gaiety and French drollery."

In his *Johann Strauss, Father and Son,* H. E. Jacob indicates the sonatalike structure of the Overture—the exposition—"the main theme with the short transition to the subdominant, to the subsidiary movement," and then admits that Strauss had no intention of writing a sonata.

"The *Fledermaus Overture,*" he writes, "is a potpourri and makes no pretense to being anything else. Only his [Strauss's] unerring taste (the most unerring since Rossini) was capable of welding so much wild beauty into the likeness of a sonata."

L. B.

"Treasure" Waltz from "Der Zigeunerbaron" ("The Gypsy Baron")

BRILLIANT SOLOS and duets, smart marches, and lively Magyar-gypsy dance rhythms pepper the score of *Der Zigeunerbaron* (*The Gypsy Baron*), not to mention a full quota of gay waltzes reaching fine flower in the *Schatz* ("Treasure") number. This waltz, lodged snugly in a situation centering in buried treasure, almost became literally buried treasure—in a wastepaper basket. One day, while at work on the new score, Strauss played the waltz on the harmonium to the Viennese critic Max Kalbeck, who sang along with him. Suddenly Kalbeck leaped several bars ahead. Strauss, surprised, and stung by the thought of plagiarism, coiled the sheet up and flung it angrily into the basket, shouting, "Ach, someone has beaten me to it!" Assuring Strauss of his originality and that he had heard him play the waltz the summer before, Kalbeck rescued the "treasure" for posterity.

When in 1883 Strauss made a trip to Budapest to conduct his comic opera *Der lustige Krieg* (*The Merry War*), he was accompanied by his young bride, the former Adele Deutsch. Shortly after the death of his first wife Jetty Strauss, he had married the ravishing Angelica Dietrich, age twenty, blonde, and easy of virtue. Five years of unnerving deceit led to a divorce, and then a fresh start with the widow Deutsch, who was everything Angelica Diabolica—as a Strauss biographer dubs her—was not. Adele was later known to the Viennese as

"Frau Cosima in three-quarter time." Thus, *Der Zigeunerbaron*, with its medley of flashing czardas, bright waltzes, and romantic duets, was the first fruit of a new happiness.

In Budapest, Adele urged him to seek out the Hungarian novelist Maurus Jokai for a book. Strauss did, and later Jokai sent him the novel *Saffi*, a swash-buckling fantasy of Magyar-gypsy life teeming with Turkish Pashas, buried treasures, ennobled nomads, dashing gypsies—even a fiddling skeleton. Jokai recommended the Viennese journalist Ignaz Schnitzer for the job of confecting a plausible libretto, and Schnitzer devised words that melted sunnily into Strauss's music.

The Austro-Hungarian bond found vivid expression in this blend of *Puszta* wildness and Viennese sparkle, of nomad wandering and city soldiery, of fiery gypsy dances and velvety Viennese paces. And the *Schatzwalzer* showed that the Viennese heart of this young man of sixty still beat fervidly in three-quarter time.

L. B.

"Perpetuum Mobile," Musical Joke, Op. 257

THE "musical joke" involved in Strauss's rollicking piece of orchestral fun comes off at the end, consisting of an abrupt stop in mid air. Being a "perpetual motion," the piece could not properly end at a natural resting place, so Strauss snaps off the current in the middle of a phrase, "with one foot in the air," as Apthorp put it. Logically it was the only way to keep the thing from going on forever. Otherwise the title would be a misnomer.

An Allegro in E flat major, 2/4, the piece flows on continuously, with a recurring theme. Variations in galop time follow in quick succession, and the "Schnell Polka" accompaniment furnishes the "perpetual" rhythmic motion.

L. B.

Richard Strauss

BORN: MUNICH, JUNE 11, 1864.

Thirty years ago I was regarded a rebel. I have lived long enough to find myself a classic.—RICHARD STRAUSS.

Tone Poem, "Don Juan," Op. 20

FEW CHARACTERS of fact or fiction have filled library shelves with as many poems, plays, and stories as the legendary Spanish libertine brought into literature by Tirso de Molina in 1630 in his play *El Burlador de Seville*. The Don's exploits in love and duelling went through ceaseless variations. A whole mythology of love and lechery grew around him. His conquests were as known as the deeds of Spain's actual conquistadors.

Zorilla, Molière, de Musset, Dumas, and G. B. Shaw enshrined him in drama. Byron hymned the heartbreaker at epic length. Operas by Le Tellier, Righini, Tritto, Gardi, and Gazzaniga glorified him long before Mozart's *Don Giovanni* pushed them all into the dustbin of history. Out of it all grew the composite portrait of a swashbuckling sensualist with a single goal, cunning and ruthless in reaching it, but, withal, a fearless cavalier who took life in grand stride and superbly mocked at death.

This was the Don Juan of legend and art. In Byron's poem, the sullen and railing outlook of an exiled *bon vivant* already colors the last of the Don's intrigues. In the poem of Nicolaus Lenau, a philosophical and mystic German poet of the early nineteenth century, we find a new Don. He is an idealist, even a thinker, on a gallant hunt for womanly perfection. To Lenau, Don Juan is not "hot-blooded man eternally pursuing women." He is pathetic and pitiful in his futile quest for the woman who will incarnate all womanhood. Disillusioned by his failure, disgusted with himself and the world, Lenau's rake repents in virtual suicide. In a duel with Don Pedro, the slain commander's son and sworn avenger, the brooding Don drops his sword and receives the fatal thrust. "My deadly foe is in my power," are his last words, "and this, too, bores me, as does life itself."

Lenau's poem dates from the early part of 1844. Later that year he went mad and was confined to an insane asylum at Oberdöbling, near Vienna, where he died on Aug. 22, 1850. His full name was Nicolaus Franz Niembsch von Strehlenau. Some years before the "Don Juan" poem he had written his own version of the "Faust" legend. About both he once stated: "Goethe's great poem will not hurt me in the matter of 'Faust,' and Byron's *Don Juan* will do me no harm. Each poet, as every human being, is an individual self."

Strauss was only twenty-four when the Lenau verses struck him as excellent material for symphonic treatment. Though published as the first of his tone poems, he had already completed *Macbeth* the year before. His purpose was not to itemize and catalogue a series of amatory episodes, but to present a unified picture of the Don's unavailing search through a set of interlocking themes and moods. What attracted him, too, was the pattern of "emotional phases" outlined in the poem—the pursuit of an Ideal; the beauty and appeal of Woman; the disillusionment and "partial atonement by death." The score bears extracts from Lenau's poem, two from the opening scene and one from the final scene, in which Don Juan tells his friend Marcello of his dead desires and blighted hopes, adding resignedly, "Exhausted is the fuel, and on the hearth the cold is fiercely cruel." The basic theme of Lenau's poem is clue enough to Strauss's general plan. The composer furnished no guideposts to the unfolding drama other than the quoted fragments and his own delineative apparatus. Structurally, the work falls into a freely adapted fantasia form.

Of course Strauss's failure to give stage direction for entrances and exits of the supposed dramatis personae in his tone play did not stop his followers from doing the job for him. In fact the Master's omission only stimulated disciples to keener research. Promptly they set about fingerprinting every phrase, theme, modulation for narrative reference. They put their ears to the score and heard a wondrous tale of multiple seduction, told as plainly as the morning's news. Wilhelm Mauke even gave names to the Don's victims as their doleful stories cropped up. Each was neatly indexed in the symphonic filing cabinet, with all the particular nuances. Yet the Lenau poem offered too few trophies, so Zerlina was borrowed from Mozart's opera and permitted to bow into Strauss's sighing sisterhood. In fact Mozart's coquettish minx became the first and easiest of the fair sacrifices, her theme appearing in a contrapuntal tangle with the alleged themes of the Don's gallantry and the Don's longing.

Still, granted Strauss's intention to depict Lenau's libertine in his true colors and given his ability to turn the trick, the Tone Poem undoubtedly pictures a sequence of acute emotional states. These range from fierce longing and high exultation to fits of dejection and raw disgust. No one can take the last notes as anything but a final helpless sigh of bleak resignation.

L. B.

Tone Poem, "Tod und Verklärung" ("Death and Transfiguration"), Op. 24

THIS IS the third of Richard Strauss's compositions in the form of a tone poem. Begun in Munich in 1888, it was finished the following year. The composer himself conducted the world premiere, which took place on June 21, 1890, in

Eisenach at the fifth concert of the Twenty-seventh Musicians' Convention of the Allgemeiner Deutscher Musikverein.

A year before the premiere in Eisenach, Strauss played the whole tone poem on the piano for Hans von Bülow, who became an early admirer and champion of the daring young innovator. Bülow and Strauss were then living in Weimar. From there Bülow wrote his wife on Nov. 13, 1889:

Strauss is enormously beloved here. His *Don Juan* the evening before last had a wholly unheard-of success. Yesterday morning Spitzweg [the Munich music publisher] and I were at his house to hear his new symphonic poem *Tod und Verklärung*—which has again inspired me with great confidence in his development. It is a very important work in spite of sundry poor passages, and it is also refreshing.

At the Einsenach premiere the program book carried an anonymous poem suggesting the emotional and narrative content of Strauss's music. The poet's identity was later revealed—Alexander Ritter, a kind of intellectual coach of the young Strauss. "Ritter," said Strauss, "was exceptionally well read in all the philosophers, ancient and modern, and a man of the highest culture. His influence was in the nature of a storm wind. He urged me to the development of the poetic, the expressive, in music, as exemplified in the works of Liszt, Wagner, and Berlioz."

Rightly regarded as the aptest description of the tone poem, the poem was later amplified by Ritter and printed on a flyleaf of the score. For those who prefer a step-by-step guide to "program music," Ritter's verses offer the likeliest clues. The poem runs as follows in the sensitive prose translation of William Foster Apthorp which is now standard:

In the necessitous little room, dimly lighted by only a candle end, lies the sick man on his bed. But just now he has wrestled despairingly with Death. Now he has sunk exhausted into sleep, and thou hearest only the soft ticking of the clock on the wall in the room, whose awful silence gives a foreboding of the nearness of Death. Over the sick man's pale features plays a sad smile. Dreams he, on the boundary of life, of the golden time of childhood?

But Death does not long grant sleep and dreams to his victim. Cruelly he shakes him awake, and the fight begins afresh. Will to live and power of Death! What frightful westling! Neither bears off the victory, and all is silent once more!

Sunk back tired of battle, sleepless, as in fever frenzy the sick man now sees his life pass before his inner eye, trait by trait and scene by scene. First the morning red of childhood, shining bright in pure innocence! Then the youth's saucier play— exerting and trying his strength—till he ripens to the man's fight, and now burns with hot lust after the higher prizes of life. The one high purpose that has led him through life was to shape all he saw transfigured into a still more transfigured form. Cold and sneering, the world sets barrier upon barrier in the way of his achievement. If he thinks himself near his goal, a "Halt!" thunders in his ear. "Make the barrier thy stirrup! Ever higher and onward go!" And so he pushes forward, so he climbs, desists not from his sacred purpose. What he has ever sought with his heart's deepest yearning, he still seeks in his death sweat. Seeks—alas! and finds it never. Whether he comprehends it more clearly or that it grows upon him gradually, he can yet never exhaust it, cannot complete it in his spirit. Then clangs the last stroke of Death's iron hammer, breaks the earthly body in twain, covers the eye with the night of death.

But from the heavenly spaces sounds mightily to greet him what he yearningly sought for here: deliverance from the world, transfiguration of the world.

The Tone Poem, dedicated to Friedrich Rösch, composer and author, is scored for three flutes, two oboes, English horn, two clarinets, bass clarinet, two bassoons, double-bassoon, four horns, three trumpets, three trombones, tuba, a set of three kettledrums, two harps, gong, and the usual strings.

So discerning an enthusiast of Strauss's music as the late Romain Rolland found *Tod und Verklärung* not only one of the "most moving works of Strauss, but the one constructed with the noblest unity." The tone poem falls into four snugly linked sections: I. Largo (Sleep, Illness, and Reverie); II. Allegro molto agitato (Fever and Struggle with Death); III. Meno mosso, ma sempre alla breve (Dreams, Childhood Memories, and Death); IV. Moderato (Transfiguration).

Strauss's inimitable powers of characterization have inspired reams of eulogy from musicians and musicologists. Daniel Gregory Mason wrote, in 1916:

Superlatives are dangerous, but probably no other musician has ever carried to such a point the power of music to depict, or at least, to suggest, varieties of character, both in human beings and in inanimate objects. Strauss's reported remark that music was becoming so definite that we should soon be able to portray a tablespoon so unmistakably that it could be told from the rest of the silverware is probably an instance of his sardonic delight in hoaxing the public.

But if anyone is going to subject the art of tones to this curious test, we are all agreed, doubtless, that it should be Strauss himself. Meanwhile, failing a tablespoon, we have a sufficiently varied collection of portraits in his gallery, each sketched with a Sargent-like penetration.

L. B.

Tone Poem, "Also Sprach Zarathustra" ("Thus Spake Zarathustra"), Op. 30

THE IDEA was current for a time, following the first performance of this work, that Strauss had set Friedrich Nietzsche's philosophical prose poem to music. That, as we might imagine, was the contention of a group unalterably opposed to program music. However, we have the word of the composer himself that such were not his intentions. When the work had its premiere at Frankfort-am-Main, on Nov. 27, 1896, Strauss made the statement, "I did not intend to write philosophical music or to portray ·Nietzsche's great work musically. I meant to convey by means of music an idea of the development of the human race from its origin, through the various phases of development, religious as well as scientific, up to Nietzsche's idea of the Superman."

Even such a program-music-maker as Strauss could find the story of the human race a trifle outside of symphonic scope.

Be that as it may, a quotation from Zarathustra's introductory speech in Nietzsche's book is utilized by the composer as a preface to his subject, rather than to the music:

Having attained the age of thirty, Zarathustra left his home and went into the mountains. There he rejoiced in his spirit and his loneliness, and for ten years did not grow weary of it. But at last his heart turned—one morning he got up with the dawn, stepped into the presence of the Sun and thus spake unto him: "Thou great star! What could be thy happiness, were it not for those for whom thou shinest?

"For ten years thou hast come up here to my cave. Thou wouldst have got sick of thy light and thy journey, but for me, mine eagle and my serpent. But we waited for thee every morning, and, receiving from thee thine abundance, bless thee for it! Lo! I am weary of my wisdom, like the bee that hath collected too much honey; I need hands reaching out for it. I would fain grant and distribute until the wise among men could once more enjoy their folly, and the poor once more their riches. For that end I must descend to the depth; as thou dost at even, when, sinking behind the sea, thou givest light to the lower regions, thou resplendent star! I must, like thee, go down, as men say—men to whom I would descend. Then bless me, thou impassive eye, that canst look without envy even upon over-much happiness. Bless the cup which is about to overflow, so that the water, golden flowing out of it, may carry everywhere the reflection of thy rapture. Lo! this cup is about to empty itself again, and Zarathustra will once more become a man."—Thus Zarathustra's going down began.

After a simple introduction, which brings forward a trumpet call, there is an impressive orchestral climax. On the score, immediately following this, is the title, "Von den Hinterweltern" ("Of the Dwellers in the Rear World"). These would be seekers after consolation in religion, as Zarathustra himself had once been.

"Von der grossen Sehnsucht" ("Of the Great Yearning") is the next title. There is an ascending passage in B minor for cellos and bassoons (tremolo in the double basses).

With "Von den Freuden und Leidenschaften" ("Of Joys and Passions") there comes a doleful cantilena for second violins, oboes, and horn.

"Grablied" ("Grave Song") is a section in which the oboe intones an air derived from the preceding motive.

"Von der Wissenschaft" ("Of Science") introduces a fugal sequence, (related to the very first theme) which is played by the cellos and double basses.

"Der Genesende" ("The Convalescent") comprises a section for strings.

"Tanzlied" ("Dance Song") is indicative of "the song sung by Zarathustra when Cupid and the girls danced together." It begins with trill passages in the wood winds.

"Nachtwanderlied" ("Song of the Night Wanderer," which Nietzsche later changed to "The Drunken Song"). A fortissimo clap of the bell, which then sounds twelve times.

The work's conclusion mystified many in the early days of polytonality, for Strauss has the higher wood winds and violins playing in B minor, while the basses go on imperturbably in C. The composer has given no explanation of this ending, though some have suggested that here Zarathustra discovers life to be as much a mystery as it had ever been. This, however, is merely conjecture.

Also Sprach Zarathustra is scored for piccolo, three flutes (one interchangeable with a second piccolo), three oboes, English horn, two clarinets in B flat, clarinet in E flat, bass clarinet, three bassoons, double bassoon, six horns, four trumpets, three trombones, two tubas, tympani, bass drum, cymbals, triangle, glockenspiel, low bell in E, two harps, organ, sixteen first violins, sixteen second violins, twelve violas, twelve cellos, eight basses.

R. C. B.

Tone Poem, "Ein Heldenleben" ("A Hero's Life"), Op. 40

Begun in Munich, in August, 1898, this work was completed at Charlottenburg in December of the same year. It was given its first performance at the eleventh concert of the Museumsgesellschaft, Frankfurt-am-Main, on Mar. 3, 1899, the composer conducting from manuscript, and Alfred Hess playing the violin solo. *Ein Heldenleben* was first heard in this country in Chicago, when the Chicago Symphony performed it under the direction of Theodore Thomas on Mar. 10, 1900. And it was the Philharmonic Society which gave the work its initial New York hearing, Emil Paur conducting, on Dec. 8, 1900, when the orchestra numbered 125 players.

Strauss himself has declared that *Ein Heldenleben* was written as a companion work to his *Don Quixote,* Op. 34. In that work he had "sketched the tragi-comic figure of the Spanish Knight whose vain search after heroism leads him to insanity." In *A Hero's Life* he presents:

Not a single poetical or historical figure, but rather a more general and free ideal of great and manly heroism—not the heroism to which one can apply an everyday standard of valor, with its material and exterior rewards, but that heroism which describes the inward battle of life, and which aspires through effort and renunciation towards the elevation of the soul.

Probably Friedrich Rösch's is the longest of the composition's numerous "amplifications by sympathetic" analysts. It contains, all told, seventy thematic illustrations, in addition to a descriptive poem by Eberhard König. Yet Romain Rolland quotes Strauss, "There is no need of a program. It is enough to know there is a hero fighting his enemies." In any case, *Ein Heldenleben* is in six sections, played without pause.

I. The Hero
II. The Hero's Adversaries
III. The Hero's Helpmate
IV. The Hero's Battlefield
V. The Hero's Works of Peace
VI. The Hero's Release from the World—Conclusion

Rösch's explanation is in two parts; the first concerned with the sequence of poetic ideas, the second with the purely technical aspects.

The poetic ideas he groups as follows:

I. The Hero (first section)
II. The World that enters in opposition to the Hero (second section)
    (a) The Foes of the Hero (second section)
    (b) The Helpmate of the Hero (third section)
III. The Life-Work of the Hero
    (a) The Battlefield of the Hero (fourth section)
    (b) The Hero's Works of Peace (fifth section)
IV. The Hero's Escape from the World, and the Completion, the Conclusion of the whole matter (sixth section).

The technical division is:

I. Introductory clause (introduction of themes).
    (a) Group of chief themes of the whole work (section I)
    (b) Group of chief contrasting themes (sections II and III)
II. Intermediate sentence (thematic development). Working up of the themes from the preceding introduction; and there is a subordinate clause with themes which are new in part (sections IV and V).
III. Concluding clause (coda). Short development and repetition of earlier themes.

I. "The Hero." Typifying the Hero is the chief theme, "the whole and noble man," as it is announced by the horns, violas and cellos, with the violins soon participating in the exposition. The theme allegedly contains four submotives which illustrate his will power and self-confidence. With the entrance of further thematic material, showing his emotional side, his pride, etc., the portrait is completed. The section closes brilliantly, as the main theme roars out of the brass. "A pause is made on a dominant seventh: 'What has the world in store for the young dreamer?'"

II. "The Hero's Adversaries." Here the composer is said to depict the ever-present sneerers, the jealous, petty critics who "mock and snarl," through the flute and oboe. Some half-dozen themes represent the belittlers. Again the Hero's theme enters, this time in the minor, and his surprise and confusion at the onset of derision are shown by a "timid, writhing figure." However, the music indicates that his enemies are temporarily, at least, shaken off.

III. "The Hero's Helpmate." The solo violin speaks for the loved one, who seems to be coy, at first, and not altogether favorable to the Hero's suit. She displays still other characteristics, whose import may be gathered from the score's expression markings, such as, "hypocritically gushingly," "gaily," "frivolously," "tenderly," "somewhat sentimentally," "very sharply," "playfully," "amiably," "furiously," "suddenly quiet again and very feelingly," "in a rage," "quickly scolding," "tenderly and lovingly." All lead, however, to a rhapsodic love duet, though toward its conclusions there are echoings of the contemptuous phrases. From behind the scenes comes a fanfare by three trumpets—the call to battle.

IV. "The Hero's Battlefield." The section begins with a loud battery of side drums. The theme of the adversaries is flung out by a blaring trumpet, and this music soon becomes pitted against the themes of the Hero and the Heroine. The raging contention has been described by Romain Rolland as "the most splendid battle that has ever been painted in music." At last, triumph and a song of victory. But the world looks upon the Hero "with indifferent eyes."

V. "The Hero's Works of Peace." The development of the Hero's soul is the subject of this section. Revealingly, Strauss incorporates fragments from well-known compositions of his to illustrate the point. There are quotations from *Don Juan, Also Sprach Zarathustra, Tod und Verklärung, Don Quixote, Till Eulenspiegel,* and *Guntram,* besides an excerpt from his Lied *Traum durch die Dämmerung.* But the scoffers are by no means stilled, as citations of their themes show.

VI. "The Hero's Release from the World—Conclusion." After some minutes of raging opposition against the stupid pedantry, the Hero finds an inner repose. Now he has truly conquered, for in the struggle he has also conquered his own contradictions. The theme of the loved one is heard again and, finally, with one more utterance of his theme—sonorous and impressive—he breathes his last. The end is peaceful, solemn, as might be the music of funeral rites.

R. C. B.

Rondo, "Till Eulenspiegel's Merry Pranks," Op. 28

COMPLETED IN May 1895, published in September of the same year and performed for the first time on Nov. 5, this work is based on the mad career of Till Eulenspiegel, hero of an old *Volksbuch* attributed to Dr. Thomas Murner (1475-1530). The composer slyly refrained from giving any explanation of his music other than to say:

It is impossible for me to furnish a program to *Eulenspiegel;* were I to put into words the thoughts which its several incidents suggest to me, they would seldom suffice, and might give rise to offense. Let me leave it, therefore, to my hearers to crack the hard nut which the Rogue has prepared for them. By way of helping them to a better understanding, it seems sufficient to point out the two "Eulenspiegel" motives, which, in the most manifold disguises, moods, and situations, pervade the whole up to the catastrophe, when, after he has been condemned to death, Till is strung to the gibbet. For the rest, let them guess at the musical joke which a Rogue has offered them.

The Till of Dr. Murner's *Volksbuch* is an itinerant mechanic of Brunswick, who is, at the same time, a clownish imp of the perverse. His practical—and impractical—jokes run all the way from medieval "hot foots" to who knows what else, and the most perverse thing about it all is that he always "prevails." In the book, Till even escapes the gallows and breathes his peaceful last in bed, having first worked another of his tricks on his heirs.

If Strauss, studiedly or waggishly, avoided supplying a program, there has been no lack of volunteers to do it for him. An exhaustive—and, possibly, exhausting—one is credited to Wilhelm Klatte, who delivered himself of a detailed explanation of the story behind the music in an article which appeared in the *Allgemeine Musik-Zeitung* three days after the world premiere of the piece. A translation by C. A. Barry follows:

A strong sense of German folk feeling pervades the whole work; the source from which the tone poet drew his inspiration is clearly indicated in the introductory bars. . . . To some extent this stands for the "once upon a time" of the storybooks. That what follows is not to be treated in the pleasant and agreeable manner of narrative poetry, but in a more sturdy fashion, is at once made apparent by a characteristic bassoon figure which breaks in sforzato upon the piano of the strings. Of equal importance for the development of the piece is the immediately following humorous horn theme. . . . Beginning quietly and gradually becoming more lively, it is at first heard against a tremolo of the "divided" violins and then again in the tempo primo. . . .

Here he [Till] is (clarinet phrase followed by chord for wind instruments). He wanders through the land as a thoroughgoing adventurer. His clothes are tattered and torn: a queer, fragmentary version of the Eulenspiegel motive resounds from the horns. Following a merry play with this important leading motive, which directly leads to a short but brilliant tutti, in which it again asserts itself, first in the flutes, and then finally merges into a softly murmuring and extended tremolo for the violas, this same motive, gracefully phrased, reappears in succession in the basses, flute, first violins, and again in the basses. The rogue, putting on his best manners, slyly passes through the gate, and enters a certain city. It is market day; the women sit at their stalls and prattle (flutes, oboes, and clarinets). Hop! Eulenspiegel springs on his horse (indicated by rapid triplets extending through three measures, from the low D of the bass clarinet to the highest A of the D clarinet), gives a smack of his whip, and rides into the midst of the crowd. Clink, clash, clatter! A confused sound of broken pots and pans, and the market women are put to flight. In haste the rascal rides away (as is admirably illustrated by a fortissimo passage for the trombones) and secures a safe retreat.

This was his first merry prank; a second follows immediately. . . . Eulenspiegel has put on the vestments of a priest and assumes a very unctuous mien. Though posing as a preacher of morals, the rogue peeps out from the folds of his mantle (the Eulenspiegel motive on the clarinet points to the imposture). He fears for the success of his scheme. A figure played by muted violins, horns, and trumpets makes it plain that he does not feel comfortable in his borrowed plumes.

But soon he makes up his mind. Away with all scruples! He tears them off (solo, violin, glissando).

Again the Eulenspiegel theme is brought forward in the previous lively tempo, 6/8, but is now subtly metamorphosed and chivalrously colored. Eulenspiegel has become a Don Juan, and he waylays pretty women. And one has bewitched him: Eulenspiegel is in love. Hear how now, glowing with love, the violins, clarinets, and flutes sing. But in vain. His advances are received with derision, and he goes away in a rage. How can one treat him so slightingly? Is he not a splendid fellow? Vengeance on the whole human race!

He gives vent to his rage (in a fortissimo of horns in unison followed by a pause), and strange personages suddenly draw near (cellos). A troop of honest, worthy Philistines!

In an instant all his anger is forgotten. But it is still his chief joy to make fun of these lords and protectors of blameless decorum, to mock them, as is apparent from the lively and accentuated fragments of the theme, sounded at the beginning by the horn, which are now heard first from horns, violins, cellos, and then from trumpets, oboes, and flutes. Now that Eulenspiegel has had his joke, he goes away and leaves the professors and doctors behind in thoughtful meditation. Fragments of the typical theme of the Philistines are here treated canonically. . . .

If we take a formal view, we have now reached the repetition of the chief theme. A merry jester, a born liar, Eulenspiegel goes wherever he can succeed with a hoax. His insolence knows no bounds. Alas! there is a sudden jolt to his wanton humor. The drum rolls a hollow roll; the jailer drags the rascally prisoner into the criminal court. The verdict "guilty" is thundered against the brazen-faced knave.

The Eulenspiegel theme replies calmly to the threatening chords of wind and lower strings. Eulenspiegel lies. Again the threatening tones resound; but Eulenspiegel does not confess his guilt. On the contrary, he lies for the third time. His jig is up. Fear seizes him. The hypocrisy motive is sounded piteously; the fatal moment draws near; his hour has struck! The descending leap of a minor seventh in bassoons, horns, trombones, tuba, betokens his death. He has danced in air. A last struggle (flutes), and his soul takes flight.

After sad, tremulous pizzicato of the strings the epilogue begins. At first it is almost identical with the introductory measures, which are repeated in full; then the most essential parts of the second and third chief-theme passages appear, and finally merge into the soft chord of the sixth on A flat, while wood winds and violins sustain. Eulenspiegel has become a legendary character. The people tell their tales about him: "Once upon a time. . . ." But that he was a merry rogue and a real devil of a fellow seems to be expressed by the final eight measures, full orchestra, fortissimo.

R. C. B.

"Don Quixote" (Introduction, Theme with Variations and Finale), Fantastic Variations on a Theme of Knightly Character, Op. 35

THE CELEBRATED hero of Cervantes has had his share of musical interpretation. Operas, both serious and comic, have been written about him, and the symphonic literature has been enriched—Philip Hale thought not altogether—by this "virtuoso tone poem" of Richard Strauss.

Composed at Munich in 1897, *Don Quixote* was given its first performance at a Gürzenich Concert, Cologne, on Mar. 8, 1898. On that occasion it was played from manuscript. Franz Wüllner was the conductor. The composer conducted the work at a concert of the Frankfort Museumgesellschaft ten days later.

The composition, dedicated to Joseph Dupont, calls for piccolo, two flutes, two oboes, English horn, two clarinets, bass clarinet, three bassoons, double bassoon, six horns, three trumpets, three trombones, tenor tuba, bass tuba, kettledrums, snare drum, bass drum, cymbals, triangle, tambourine, wind machine, harp, sixteen first violins, sixteen second violins, twelve violas, ten cellos, and eight double basses. In addition, Don Quixote is represented by a solo cello, and his squire, Sancho Panza, mostly by a solo viola, after brief mentions in the bass clarinet and the tenor tuba.

Don Quixote, which came between two other tone poems, *Also Sprach Zarathustra,* Op. 30 (1896), and *Ein Heldenleben,* Op. 40 (1898), is a program piece without an actual program supplied by the composer. At least, the score itself is not provided with one. Yet the work has had explanations without end, among them being one by Arthur Hahn which is remarkable both for its length—twenty-seven printed pages—and its fancifulness. He declares, for instance, that certain curious harmonies found in what is in reality a simple passage of the introduction "characterize admirably the well-known tendency of Don Quixote toward false conclusions."

On the other hand, Max Steinitzer, in his biography of Richard Strauss, reports that the piece is quite acceptable as absolute music, with the exception of several unimportant details. And he says, further:

The introduction begins immediately with the hero's motive and pictures with constantly increasing liveliness by other themes of knightly and gallant character life as it is mirrored in writings from the beginning of the seventeenth century. "Don Quixote, busied in reading romances of chivalry, loses his reason—and determines to go through the world as a wandering knight."

The following program of *Don Quixote* is derived from an explanation accompanying the two-piano arrangement. The Introduction, ten Variations, and Finale are played without pause.

Introduction (Moderato, D major, 4/4). The elderly hero's fancy teems with the "impossible follies" of the romantic works he has been reading. He goes mad (as exemplified in the music by a piercing discord, on the heels of a harp glissando) and in his madness he vows that he will become a knight-errant.

Theme: Don Quixote, the Knight of the Rueful Countenance; Sancho Panza (Moderato, D minor, 4/4). Here the theme of the hero is announced by the solo cello. Sancho Panza's theme emerges first in the bass clarinet, then in the tenor tuba; later, however, it is always given to the solo viola.

VARIATION I

"The Knight and His Squire Start on Their Journey." (In a leisurely manner, D minor, 12/8). Inspired by the beautiful Dulcinea of Toboso, the Knight attacks some "monstrous giants," who are nothing more than windmills revolving in the breeze. The sails knock him down, and he is in a "very evil plight."

VARIATION II

"The Victorious Battle against the Host of the Great Emperor Alifanfaron" (Warlike, D major, 4/4). A huge army approaches in a swirling cloud of dust. It is a great herd of sheep, but the Knight's tottering mind perceives the flashing weapons of soldiery. He rushes in to the charge, unmindful of Sancho's warnings, and the muted brass depicts the pitiful bleating of the animals. The Knight is stoned by the shepherds, and he falls to the ground.

VARIATION III

"Colloquies of Knight and Squire" (Moderato, D major, 4/4). Honor, glory, the Ideal Woman, these are the things Don Quixote speaks on. Sancho, the realist, holds forth for a more comfortable life, but he is ordered to hold his tongue.

VARIATION IV

"The Adventure with the Penitents" (Somewhat broader, D minor, 4/4). Mistaking a band of pilgrims for robbers and villains, Don Quixote attacks, only to receive a sound drubbing from them. The pilgrims depart, intoning their churchly theme, and the senseless Knight revives to the great delight of Sancho, who soon falls asleep.

VARIATION V

"The Knight's Vigil" (Very slow, D minor, 4/4). Don Quixote spurns sleep. He will watch by his armor, instead. Dulcinea, in answer to his prayers, comes to him in a vision, as the theme of the Ideal Woman is heard in the horn. There is a cadenza for harp and violins followed by a rhapsodic passage.

VARIATION VI

"The Meeting with Dulcinea" (G major, 2/4, 3/4). Jestingly, Sancho points to a country wench as Dulcinea. There are words between Knight and Squire; the former will not believe it, the latter swears it is so. Don Quixote then vows vengeance against the wicked magician who has wrought the transformation.

VARIATION VII

"The Ride through the Air" (A little quieter than before, D minor, 8/4). Blindfolded, Knight and Squire sit astride a wooden horse, which—they have been informed—will carry them aloft. Their themes surge upward and one hears the whistling of the wind about them through the chromatic flute passages, the music for the harp, a drum roll, and the whine of the wind machine. However, the persistent tremolo on D in the double basses and kettledrums tells the listener that the wooden horse has never left the ground.

VARIATION VIII

"The Journey in the Enchanted Park." An oarless boat lying idle on a bank of the Ebro is the conveyance by which Don Quixote may speed to the rescue of some important dignitary. He and Sancho embark, as the typical theme of the Knight comes through in a barcarolle. Though the boat capsizes, the two finally reach shore and give thanks for their safety.

VARIATION IX

"The Combat with Two Magicians" (Quickly and stormily, D minor, 4/4). Back on his horse and eager as ever for adventure, Don Quixote violently charges into a peaceable pair of monks, who are going by on their mules. In his maddened brain the monks are mighty magicians, and the Don is elated beyond measure with their utter rout.

VARIATION X

(Much broader, D minor, 4/4). The greatest setback of his knightly career is suffered by the Don at the hands of the Knight of the White Moon, who is, after all, a true friend. He explains that he hoped to cure Don Quixote of his madness and, having won the duel, orders him to retire peacefully to his home for a year, "so nothing more were required of him in prejudice of his fair Dulcinea."

FINALE

"The Death of Don Quixote" (Very peacefully, D major, 4/4). The worn and harried Knight is no longer bemused. The solo cello expresses his new understanding of the state of things, as he recalls his useless aims and empty maneuvers. It was all vanity, he reflects, and he is prepared, now, for the peace that is death.

R. C. B.

"Symphonia Domestica," Op. 53

Introduction. Scherzo. Cradle Song and Adagio. Finale: Double Fugue.

THIS WORK obtained its premiere in Carnegie Hall on Mar. 21, 1904, the composer conducting. The event was the fourth and last concert of a Richard Strauss Festival (the orchestra was Hans Hermann Wetzler's) which did not prove to be too successful a venture, either artistically or financially. In fact, the press was hostile enough to unruffle Strauss himself, though none of the critics' vitriol was particularly hurled at him. It seems that Wetzler's orchestra broke down on a previous evening during a performance of *Don Quixote,* not an inspiring memory for a conductor, especially one about to premiere a new composition of his.

As always with Strauss, he rejected all suggestions about supplying a program for the piece. In an article by Richard Aldrich, which appeared in the *New York Times* of Mar. 6, 1904, the composer's idea about literary programs were set down. Aldrich said:

He wishes it to be taken as music, for what it is, and not as the elaboration of the specific details of a scheme of things. The Symphony, he declares, is sufficiently explained by its title and is to be listened to as the symphonic development of its themes. It is of interest to quote the title as he wishes it to stand. It is *Symphonia Domestica* (*"meiner lieben Frau und unserm Jungen gewidmet"*), Op. 53, which is, interpreted, *Domestic Symphony dedicated to my dear Wife and our Boy,* Op. 53. It bears the descriptive subtitle *In einen Satze und drei Unterabteilungen:* (a) Einleitung und Scherzo; (b) Adagio; (c) Doppelfuge und Finale. [In one movement and three subdivisions: (a) Introduction and Scherzo; (b) Adagio; (c) Double Fugue and Finale.]

It is highly significant that the composer desires these movements to be listened to as the three movements of a composition, substantially, as he declares, in the old symphonic form. He believes, and has expressed his belief, that the anxious search on the part of the public for the exactly corresponding passages in the music and the program, the guessing as to the significance of this or that, the distraction following a train of thought exterior to the music, are destructive to the musical enjoyment. Hence he has forbidden the publication of any description of what he sought to express till after the concert.

"This time," says Dr. Strauss, "I wish my music to be listened to purely as music."

If literary programs were taboo at the premieres of Strauss's works, they certainly were not at later performances. Usually they turn out to be extensive ones, as witness that of *Till Eulenspiegel*. This is not less true of the *Symphonia Domestica,* which has been accorded such honors generously.

Two days before the English premiere (Feb. 25, 1905) the *London Daily News* had this about the Symphony:

In accordance with his custom the composer has not put forward a definite program of his own, but, with some inconsistency, he has allowed a description to be made public, with some inconsistency, because he has declared that he wishes his music to be listened to as if it meant nothing in particular if the hearer feels more comfortable in ignoring the program. The only indications given are in the sub-headings to the separate sections of the Symphony.

The official description of the Symphony (an analysis was prepared by Alfred Kalisch and Percy Pitt) runs as follows:

The Symphony continues without a break, but has four well-defined sections:

1. Introduction
2. Scherzo
3. Cradle Song and Adagio
4. Finale: Double Fugue

The Symphony is concerned with three main themes, that of the husband, that of the wife, and that of the child. The "husband" theme is divided into three sections, the first of which is marked *gemachlich* (easygoing or deliberate), the second *sinnend* (meditative), and the third *feurig* (fiery). The first section of the Symphony, the introduction, is devoted to an exposition and treatment of the chief themes, or groups of themes, its most striking feature being the introduction of the "child" theme on the oboe d'amore, an instrument which has practically fallen out of use. The composer himself has spoken of this theme as being of "almost Haydnesque simplicity."

On this follows a very characteristic passage, which has been interpreted as representing the child in his bath. The scherzo bears the headings: "Elterngluck—Kindliche Spiele" ("Parents' Happiness—The Child at Play"). Its chief theme is the "child" theme in a new rhythm. At its end the music suggestive of the bath recurs, and the clock strikes seven. We then come to the lullaby, where we have another version of the "child" theme.

The subheadings of the Adagio are "Schaffen und Schauen—Liebesscene!—Traume und Sorgen" ("Doing and Thinking—Love Scene—Dreams and Cares"). This elaborate section introduces no new themes of any importance and is really a symphonic slow movement of great polyphonic elaboration and superlatively rich orchestral color. The gradual awakening of the family is next depicted by a change in the character of the music, which becomes more and more restless, the use of rhythmical variants being very ingenious; and then there is another reference to the bath music, and the glockenspiel indicates that it is 7 A.M.

In this way we reach the final Fugue. The principal subject of this is also a new variation of the "child" theme. Its subtitle is "Lustiger Streit—Frohlicher Beschluss" ("Merry Argument—Happy Conclusion"), the subject of the dispute between father and mother being the future of the son. The Fugue (the chief subject of which is another variant of the "child" theme) is carried on with unflagging spirit and humor and great variety of orchestration, the introduction of the four saxophones adding fresh colors to the score.

As the Fugue proceeds, the "child" theme gradually becomes more and more prominent and finally seems to dominate the whole score. Some new themes, all more or less akin to it, and all in the nature of folk tunes, are introduced. The father and mother, however, soon assume their former importance, and the whole ends with great spirit and in the highest good humor, with an emphatic reassertion of the "husband" theme with which it began, suggesting that the father had the last word in the argument.

It must be pointed out that in the published score the "husband" theme (its second section) is marked *traümerisch,* instead of *sinnend,* as explained above. Furthermore, following the *traümerisch* excerpt, is a short phrase for three clarinets and bass clarinet marked by the composer *mürrisch* (morose, ill-tempered).

The *Symphonia Domestica* is scored for piccolo, three flutes, two oboes, oboe d'amore, English horn, clarinet in D, clarinet in A, two clarinets in B flat, bass clarinet, four bassoons, double-bassoon, eight horns, four trumpets, three trombones, bass tuba, four saxophones (*ad libitum*), four kettledrums, bass drum, cymbals, triangle, tambourine, glockenspiel, two harps, sixteen first violins, sixteen second violins, twelve violas, ten cellos, eight double basses.

The oboe d'amore, invented circa 1720 and much employed by Bach, is pitched a minor third below the oboe. In quality its tone lies between the oboe and the English horn. Regarding the four saxophones mentioned in the orchestration, Strauss suggests that they be used "only in cases of extreme necessity."

R. C. B.

"Burleske" for Piano and Orchestra in D minor

In 1885, Strauss took a position as assistant to Hans von Bülow, who was then the conductor of the orchestra at Meiningen. It has been observed that Bülow's extraordinary admiration of Brahms's works had its collateral effect on the impressionable young Strauss. In fact, certain Brahmsian influences are not to be denied the music of *Burleske*.

Be that as it may, the piece, presented to Bülow in the winter of 1886 for appraisal, naturally with the hope that he might find some opportunity to perform it, was rejected by him with the terse declaration "it is unplayable!" Oddly, Strauss himself had some misgivings about it, for, after giving it a rehearsal reading or two, he slipped it into a portfolio, accompanying the deed with the comment, "sheer nonsense."

Four years later, though, it was fished out of its hiding place and played for the first time at a concert in the town theater of Eisenach (June 21, 1890). The solo pianist was Eugen d'Albert, to whom the piece is dedicated; the conductor, Strauss. The occasion was the twenty-seventh annual musical festival of the Allgemeiner Deutscher Musikverein.

The publisher Hainauer, who attended the premiere, manifested a great interest in the number, and he made its composer a flattering offer for it. But Strauss, still doubtful of its worth, wrote to his friend Alexander Ritter, "I really need the money. What shall I do? It goes against me to permit publication of a work which I have left far behind, and to which I cannot give my approval."

Strauss did know what to do, however, for he did not accede to Hainauer's request, at least, not until four years had passed, in all, eight years after the composition of *Burleske*.

Bülow's later devotion to Strauss's compositions contrasted curiously with an early judgment made before their association at Meiningen. A publisher named Spitzweg, who had brought out several pieces of the youthful Strauss, sent Bülow a few more. The latter wrote back, "Piano pieces by R. Str. have thoroughly displeased me. Immature and precocious. Compared with him Lachner had the imagination of a Chopin. I miss all the youthfulness in the invention. Not a genius, I am thoroughly convinced, but at most a talent that requires sixty to make a bushel."

R. C. B.

Igor Stravinsky

BORN: ORANIENBAUM, RUSSIA, JUNE 17, 1882.

The critics have always misunderstood me. They say that I revived in "Oedipus" the old-time oratorio. As a matter of fact, I never look backward. "Oedipus" was no deviation in my forward path, but another step on the way I began with "Petrouchka." In everyday life we choose our garments to fit the occasion, though our personality is the same whether we wear a dress suit or pajamas. The same applies to art. I garb my ideas in robes to fit the subject, but do not change my personality.—IGOR STRAVINSKY.

"Feu d'Artifice" ("Fireworks"), A Fantasy for Orchestra, Op. 4

TWO RUSSIANS—each a genius and innovator in his field—played a significant role in the early career of Igor Stravinsky. One was Serge Diaghileff, the other Nikolas Rimsky-Korsakoff. To Diaghileff, Stravinsky owed his initiation into the world of modern art and ballet. From that patron of the arts and apostle of the dance came the incentive for such scores as *The Firebird, Petrouchka,* and *Le Sacre du Printemps,* the incentive that helped the young Stravinsky find himself as a composer with something of his own to say.

The influence of Rimsky-Korsakoff was perhaps even more crucial, because it came earlier. Stravinsky first met him in 1902 at a time of indecision. As a student he was wavering between law and music. Rimsky heard the ebullient youth play some of his piano music—callow, eclectic, irresolute music, to be sure, but music that threw off hints of power and originality. Rimsky's verdict, though cautious, was all the twenty-year-old Stravinsky needed to make up his mind. Later he brought Rimsky a piano sonata. The master's comments were scathing, unsparing. There were defects on every page, but again the older man caught the tell-tale note of something new and genuine. There followed two fruitful years of study in orchestration with Rimsky. Tasks such as transcribing a Beethoven sonata or a Schubert quartet were assigned. Gradually master and disciple saw their hopes being fulfilled. By 1908, Rimsky frankly envisioned a bright future for the law student turned composer.

Thus, it was a very grateful young man of twenty-six, who sat down to sketch out a symphonic piece one summer day in 1908. The project was daring, quite unprecedented, in fact—the depiction in tone of the mad, dazzling, and explosive action of fireworks. Rimsky's daughter was shortly to marry Maximilian Steinberg. The *Feu d'Artifice* would be young Stravinsky's wedding gift, to be played at the festivities. The gesture would please the aging master for another reason. In the bold splash of pyrotechnics he would grasp a disciple's tribute to the founder of a new orchestral realism. The score was finished in six weeks and promptly despatched to Rimsky's country place. A few days later the package came back—unopened. Stamped on it were the words "Not delivered on account of death of addressee." Stravinsky was stunned by the loss. He put aside the *Feu d'Artifice*. The symphonic tribute seemed ironic now, in its jubilant, festive spirit. To express his grief, he wrote a *Chant funèbre*.

Some months later Alexander Siloti featured two of Stravinsky's compositions at one of his orchestral concerts in St. Petersburg. One of them was *Fireworks*. Oddly enough this little "fantasy for orchestra" became a link between Rimsky-Korsakoff and the patron who was to replace him in Stravinsky's career. Diaghileff was present at that concert. Intrigued by the young composer's vivid handling of visual phenomena, he approached him with an offer. Would Stravinsky orchestrate some Chopin pieces for a ballet to be called *Sylphides?* Stravinsky would, and did. The second great turning point in Igor Stravinsky's life had come.

Every listener is his own pyrotechnist in following Stravinsky's firework display. The crackle and splutter of violins and piccolo are suggestive. Sparks seem to fly from the harp. A picture of Catherine wheels may be gleaned from the wriggling wood-wind figures. Rockets seem to shoot up on the ascending path of high violins and burst among the muted brasses. Lawrence Gilman suggested "pinwheels in the swirling wood-wind figures of the opening" and "a joyously triumphant bomb at the end." Arthur Brock, an English fireworks expert, noted "the successive crescendos which we always strive to obtain through firework displays, leading up to the grand melee and impressive 'final bouquet.'" Whenever he heard the piece, Michel Fokine swore he saw flames sweeping across the skies. Yet, despite the explosive content and the great upheavals to come, Stravinsky's harmony here, as one annotator phrased is, "is not yet subversive."

L. B.

Suite from "L'Oiseau de feu" ("The Firebird")

I. Introduction and Dance of the Firebird. **II.** Adagio (Pas de deux). **III.** Scherzo. **IV.** Rondo (Khorovod). **V.** Infernal Dance. **VI.** Lullaby and Final Hymn.

(New Version)

WE OWE Stravinsky's *Firebird* music partly to the dilatory habits of Anatol Liadoff. It seems Michel Fokine had the "Music Box" composer in mind when he confected his new scenario for Serge Diaghileff's Ballets Russes.

Liadoff accepted the assignment, but never carried it out. He delayed and delayed. Finally, in despair, Fokine and Diaghileff turned to the twenty-seven-year-old Igor Stravinsky. That was late in 1909. By May of the following year the score was ready. Thus began an association that brought glory to both composer and impresario. Stravinsky's genius flourished in the ballet setting. Think of *Petrouchka* and *Le Sacre du Printemps,* of that succession of pulsing, throbbing scores bound vitally to choreographic imagery. One speculates on whether Stravinsky's gifts would have turned into other channels had not Diaghileff and ballet beckoned, and if Liadoff, say, had turned in the job on schedule. What suggested Stravinsky to the ballet men was the fact that the year before the daring young man had literally skyrocketed to fame with a piece called *Fireworks,* written for the wedding of Rimsky-Korsakoff's daughter Nadeshda. Again, the association of ideas through the "fire" elements in both titles may have unconsciously swayed the two ballet minds.

The Diaghileff troupe presented the new ballet at the Paris Opéra on June 25, 1910, one month after the completion of the score. Mr. Fokine, already the scenarist and choreographer, danced the role of Ivan Tsarevitch. Tamara Karsavina was the Firebird, Vera Fokina the Tsarevna, and Enrico Cecchetti, Kastchei the Immortal. Golovine and Bakst were responsible for the stage settings. Gabriel Pierné conducted. To fill out an evening's program two further numbers were presented—*Les Orientales* and the dances from the second act of Borodin's opera *Prince Igor.* The new ballet was first seen in New York when the Diaghileff organization presented it at the Century Theater, on Jan. 17, 1916. The cast was the same, but the conductor was Ernest Ansermet. As a concert suite the Stravinsky score was first rendered by the New York Symphony Orchestra on Dec. 31, 1916.

In working out the scenario, Fokine drew on various Russian fairy tales. The Firebird appears in many of them, and Ivan Tsarevitch often figures as hero. Balakireff planned an opera based on the Firebird legends, but never got beyond a few sketches. Kastchei, a legendary monster, was used by Rimsky-Korsakoff as the central character of the opera *Kastchei the Immortal: An Autumn Legend,* produced in 1902 at the Private Opera, Moscow. In an earlier work by the same composer, the fairy ballet *Mlada,* produced in St. Petersburg, in 1893, Kastchei appears as "the man skeleton." Of course in the Fokine-Stravinsky ballet, the ogre is only an "accessory character so far as concerns the dramatic action," to quote Montagu-Nathan, "but his presence in the scheme is nevertheless vital to it."

The story follows the familiar fairy-tale formula of the broken spell. While out hunting Ivan Tsarevitch strays into an enchanted wood surrounding the castle of the wizard Kastchei. Near him is a magic tree, gleaming with golden fruit. There is a sound of wings, and a bird of dazzling plumage lights on the tree. It is the Firebird. As it plucks an apple Ivan aims an arrow and misses. The frightened bird flies off. Soon it returns and Ivan springs from his hiding place and seizes it. The Firebird begs for its life. Ivan sets it free and is rewarded with a golden feather.

A wistful melody comes from afar as twelve maidens appear through the woods. Ivan conceals himself. He watches them shake apples from the tree and toss them to one another. They draw back startled as Ivan reveals himself. The leader urges him to flee, lest he fall into Kastchei's power and be turned into stone. Ivan is determined to remain and match his prowess with the demon's.

Suddenly there is a menacing outcry, and the terrified maidens dash back to the castle. Ivan is alone again. As the dark deepens fear begins to grip him. A lurid light now floods the forest, and a band of demons swoops down on Ivan. The dread Kastchei himself appears. He scowls malignly. Ivan fights off the spell by waving the golden feather. The Firebird helps by leading Kastchei's demons into a frenzied dance. Dazed and powerless, they fall asleep. The Firebird directs Ivan to a buried casket. In it Ivan finds a huge egg. Contained in the egg is the soul of Kastchei—the source of his evil. Kastchei watches frantically as Ivan tosses the egg into the air and catches it. Finally Ivan drops it. There is a sudden black-out and a shattering turmoil. Kastchei and his cohorts are swept away. The castle vanishes, and youths and maidens, freed from the spell, rush out joyously and acclaim Ivan their savior and ruler. Ivan marries the loveliest of the liberated maidens.

As in the earlier *Fireworks,* Stravinsky here is still the partial disciple of Rimsky-Korsakoff. There are brilliant flashes of the new realism, of a mastery of evocative imagery. The ties with Russian nationalism are still strong, and the folk note recurs. But there is something more—a frank assertion of independence in the application of color and rhythm. True, it is not yet the new world of *Petrouchka* and polytonality. Stravinsky has not yet broken completely with tradition. There is still eclecticism perhaps—hints of Glazounoff and the shadow of "The Five." It is only with *Petrouchka* that these ties are severed and Stravinsky creates the style that is all his, the style that is still Russian, but stamped indelibly with a new power.

In *Petrouchka* Stravinsky becomes his own master. Yet the new orientation is already clear in *Firebird*. One senses it in the thematic compactness, the keen visual images, the power to seize and fix a mood. To be sure, it is music bound to kinetic and narrative enactment, possibly not always self-sustaining, but still a many-hued web of orchestral enchantment. The themes are brief, but supple, the rhythms are protean. The patterns are lucid, possibly decorative. Stravinsky seems always to keep the *Firebird* legend in mind—the richness of story and raiment, the riot of outdoor color, the brightness of plumage, the grisly hues of sorcery. There are panting rhythms of tragic dance and splashing colors of broken spells. Over it broods a mood of exotic fantasy, part tender, part barbaric, drawn from far-off Russian legend. *Firebird* helped shape Stravinsky's career and chart his future. By setting a new fashion in ballet music, it directed modern ballet toward new goals.

Certain changes will be noted in this "new augmented version" of *The Firebird* music. Mr. Stravinsky refers to it as Suite No. 3. It is necessary to recall that Suite No. 1 retained the huge instrumentation of the original ballet score. Later, when Mr. Stravinsky reduced the size of the orchestra for Suite No. 2, the Adagio and Scherzo (sections II and III of the augmented version) were not included. These sections now appear for the first time in the smaller orchestration of Suite No. 2.

A second change is the use of what Mr. Stravinsky describes as "short pantomimic episodes." These serve to link the sections in an unbroken sequence. The latest version of *The Firebird* music was first performed in 1945 during the regular fall season of Ballet Theater at the Metropolitan Opera House, New York. The company staged a new version of the ballet on Oct. 24, with sets by the distinguished surrealist painter Marc Chagall and altered choreography by Adolph Bolm. The scoring of Suites No. 2 and 3 calls for three flutes, two oboes, two clarinets, two bassoons, four horns, two trumpets, three trombones, tuba, tympani, percussion, piano, harp, and strings. In the new titles supplied by Mr. Stravinsky the Rondo section is subtitled "Khorovod." This is the Russian term for dancing in rings with singing accompaniment.

L. B.

Fair Scenes from the Ballet "Petrouchka"

In 1910 when Diaghileff produced *The Firebird* ballet in Paris, the fresh orchestral colors and ingenious effects of the score had made Stravinsky famous almost overnight. The noted patron and impresario was soon after the daring young man for another score. The association that had begun two years earlier in St. Petersburg with a commissioned arrangement of some Chopin pieces was to continue for two decades. Igor Stravinsky was to remain a leading tenant in Diaghileff's many-mansioned temple of ballet. Stravinsky now toyed with the project of a choreographic tribal rite, centering in an act of pagan sacrifice. This was to become *Le Sacre du Printemps*.

But meanwhile another idea was teasing the young composer—an idea of a concert piece for orchestra and piano. The thought had first come to him back in St. Petersburg. In this *Konzertstück* the piano was to perform all kinds of mischief in a game of sly dodging with the orchestra. The exasperating piano solo suddenly took shape in Stravinsky's mind as a rascally little puppet miraculously endowed with life. With "diabolical cascades of arpeggios" the puppet went on trying the patience of the orchestra. "Menacing trumpet blasts" would come in response. In Stravinsky's own words, the outcome of the bout between piano and orchestra was "a terrific noise ending in the sorrowful and querulous collapse of the poor puppet." Stravinsky was hunting a title for his *Konzertstück* when Diaghileff came to visit him at Clarens on Lake Geneva. Diaghileff, who was waiting to be shown the sketches of the projected *Rite of Spring,* was surprised to learn that Stravinsky had been working on a concert piece instead. The composer sat down at the piano and played the sketch for him.

Diaghileff was so delighted that he urged Stravinsky to make a ballet out of the piece. Stravinsky proposed a general outline, and together they worked out the sequence and scheme of the new ballet. It would be called *Petrouchka.* The scene would be a fair. There would be crowds, booths, a marionette show. The action would grow out of a magician's tricks with three lifelike dolls. There would be Petrouchka, a rival, and the dancing charmer. The ballet would end with Petrouchka's death, and a ghastly surprise for the magician. Stravinsky now set to work on the expanded project. Months of unremitting toil followed. Finally on May 26, 1911, a few weeks before his twenty-ninth birthday, he completed the score in Rome. The following June 13, Diaghileff's Ballets Russes produced the new ballet at the Théâtre du Châtelet in Paris, its full title being *Petrouchka, Scènes burlesques en 4 tableaux.* Pierre Monteux conducted, and the cast included Vaslav Nijinsky in the title role, Tamara Karsavina as the Ballerina, Orloff as the Moor, and Enrico Cecchetti as the Magician-Charlatan. Michel Fokine was the choreographer. Alexander Benois designed the scenery and costumes. The scenario for *Petrouchka* was officially the joint product of Stravinsky and Benois, to whom the score is dedicated. But Stravinsky's own account of the genesis of the ballet would seem to admit a third collaborator—Serge Diaghileff himself.

The setting of *Petrouchka* is the weirdly exotic Admiralty Square of St. Petersburg on a winter day in 1830. It is carnival time. Coachmen, nursemaids, Cossacks, merchants, and children move about briskly, laughing and chatting gayly. Standing before a marionette booth is an old Magician, clad in rich Oriental robes. There is something sinister in his expression. He draws attention to himself by playing a flute. As the merrymakers approach, he invites them to watch a puppet show. When the curtain rises, the Magician solemnly introduces three animated dolls: the chalk-faced clown Petrouchka, a uniformed Moor, a Ballerina in red pantalets. The crowd gapes as the three puppets do a lively dance.

Behind this marionette display, however, there is drama, human drama—and pathos, for the wizard has breathed life into his dolls, not just mechanical life, but a semblance of real life, with its fateful passions. Petrouchka is endowed with even more—a sensitive human soul. This makes him rebellious, and tragic and romantic, too. The pathetic puppet is in love with the Ballerina. But she spurns his clumsy love-making and mocks his twisted, doleful features. The Moor is more successful—perhaps because he uses caveman tactics. He is wild, uncouth, and spiteful, but he also wears sumptuous clothes which dazzle the Ballerina.

In his cell Petrouchka nurses his bitterness. He rages at thoughts of his captivity. He loathes the Magician, and the Moor, too, for jealousy is rising in his marionette soul. He waves his arms wildly as he thinks of the Ballerina and the Moor in the adjoining chamber. Petrouchka leaves his cell and breaks in on their love-making. The Moor seizes him savagely and throws him out. The Ballerina returns to her place on the Moor's knees.

Outside the carnival spirit is mounting. The excitement is spreading, the dancing is brisker, the revelry grows rowdy. Coachmen and nursemaids join in a round of Russian folk dance. An animal trainer leads in a dancing bear. A tipsy merchant, accompanied by two gypsy girls, breaks through the crowd, flinging banknotes into the air. The commotion reaches its height as masked revelers dash in and begin a frenzied dance. Suddenly the merrymaking stops. Agitated cries reach the crowd from behind the curtain of the puppet booth. Petrouchka rushes out frantically, pursued by an infuriated Moor. The Moor catches Petrouchka and kills him with a blow of his scimitar. The crowd, gasping with horror, surrounds the squirming body of the puppet. Someone calls for the police. The Magician appears. Sardonically he chides the by-standers as he picks up the limp form and shows that it is only so much wood and sawdust. The crowd, with mixed feelings of relief and disappoint-ment, leaves the scene. The Magician angrily seizes the crumpled doll. Sud-denly he looks up, puzzled, then terrified. There on the roof of the puppet booth waving his arms eerily about is the mocking and menacing ghost of Petrouchka.

Into the ballet *Petrouchka* went many traditional elements of the European carnival theater. The Petrouchka-Moor-Ballerina triangle is, of course, pat-terned on the Pierrot-Harlequin-Columbine formula. Through the lineaments of native Russian puppetry may be seen features of the old Commedia dell'Arte. Over it, too, broods the ghastly fantasy of Hoffmann's animated doll world. Some have even glimpsed in Petrouchka a close cousin of the pathetic misfit immortalized by Charlie Chaplin. Stravinsky himself referred to Petrouchka as "the eternal and unhappy hero of all fairgrounds and all countries." Others have sensed deeper connotations: *Petrouchka* as a parable of vast political import. The puppet is the downtrodden masses of old Russia, fondling hopes of rebellion. The Magician is the symbol of a ruthless despotism. Petrouchka's ghostly emergence becomes a derisive warning—a last laugh—of the end of oppression. Arnold L. Haskell saw three possible interpretations of *Petrouch-ka's* symbolism: "The dawn of intelligence and the struggle for self-expression of the underdog—the *moujik;* the triumph and final resurrection of the soul; the birth of the imagination stimulated by love." Such implications will always be read into *Petrouchka,* which because of its very silence, "becomes universal drama, the tragedy of every man."

The music of *Petrouchka* showed a vitality and self-sufficiency assuring it an inevitable place in the concert repertory. Its importance—apart from its ballet efficacy—quickly dawned on the music world. The vivacious wit, sardonic comments, the bustle and turmoil of flashing rhythms revealed bold invention and master craftsmanship. There was a new musical irony here, a fresh humor in the use of certain brasses. And Stravinsky was proving that street tunes could be woven into a serious musical fabric without cheapening it. This was an advance in musical realism from the descriptive imagery of *Fireworks.* The pictures were sharp and forceful, without being photographically slavish. Characterization was critical and probing. There was also form, organic form, in this heaving carnival of color and rhythm. Stravinsky himself compared the score to a sonata, "with its succession of movements, allegro, adagio, scherzo." Whether by accident or intent, the score contains a device that was a startling innovation in 1911: the "Petrouchka chord"—the merging of the white keys of the C major chord and the black keys of the F sharp major chord. Polytonality had crept into music under the mantle of Russian ballet. The heresy of combining two keys would in time become an orthodoxy of modernism.

The score calls for four flutes, two piccolos, four oboes, English horn, four clarinets, bass clarinet, four bassoons, double bassoon, four horns, two trumpets, two cornets-à-piston, three trombones, bass tuba, tympani, snare drum, tambour de provence, bass drum, tambourine, cymbals, triangle, glockenspiel, xylophone, gong, celesta, piano, two harps, and strings.

L. B.

"Le Sacre du Printemps" ("The Consecration of the Spring"), Pictures of Pagan Russia, in Two Parts

I. The Adoration of the Earth. Introduction. Harbingers of Spring. Dance of the Adolescents. Abduction. Spring Rounds. Games of the Rival Cities. The Procession of the Wise Men. The Adoration of the Earth (The Wise Man). Dance of the Earth. II. The Sacrifice. Introduction. Mysterious Circles of the Adolescents. Glorification of the Chosen One. Evocation of the Ancestors. Ritual of the Ancestors. The Sacrificial Dance of the Chosen One.

IN VIOLENT response, few events in the history of music have rivaled the Paris premiere of Stravinsky's ritualistic ballet, *Le Sacre du Printemps* at the Théâtre des Champs-Elysées on May 29, 1913. One observer said that the reaction scarcely stopped short of massacre. Battlelines formed sharply, with vehement cheering from one camp and lusty howling and hooting from the other. The wild turmoil set off by the starkly barbaric spectacle prompted Serge Diaghileff, the impresario, to rise in his box and shout to the crowd: *"Je vous prie, laissez achever le spectacle!"* ("I beg you, let the show go on!") Backstage the bewildered dancers were on the verge of tears. At one point where the crescendo of jeering completely drowned out the music Nijinsky was obliged to stand in the wings and pound out the rhythms with his fists. As Nicholas Slonimsky later wrote: "From the initial bassoon solo to the final frenzy of the sacred dance, *Le Sacre du printemps* relentlessly moves on, creating musical values so new that the world was faced with the alternative either to reject this music as a freakish exhibition of an unbalanced young man, or to accept it as a revolutionary innovation."

From the pen of Carl Van Vechten, who attended the sensational premiere of the "anarchistic" ballet, we have the following report, incorporated later in the book *Music after the Great War:*

A certain part of the audience, thrilled by what it considered to be a blasphemous attempt to destroy music as an art, and swept away with wrath, began very soon after the rise of the curtain to whistle, to make catcalls, and to offer audible suggestions as to how the performance should proceed. Others of us, who liked the music and felt that the principles of free speech were at stake, bellowed defiance. It was war over art for the rest of the evening, and the orchestra played on unheard, except occasionally when a slight lull occurred. The figures on the stage danced in time to music that they had to imagine they heard, and beautifully out of rhythm with the uproar in the auditorium. I was sitting in a box, in which I had rented one seat. Three ladies sat in front of me, and a young man occupied the place behind me. He stood up during the course of the ballet to enable himself to see more clearly. The intense excitement under which he was laboring, thanks to the potent force of the music, betrayed itself presently when he began to beat rhythmically on the top of my head with his fists. My emotion was so great that I did not feel the blows for some time. They were perfectly synchronized with the beat of the music. When I did, I turned around. His apology was sincere. We had both been carried beyond ourselves.

The opposition found its most vitriolic manifesto in the review of Alfred Capu which appeared in *Le Figaro.* As rendered by the late Philip Hale, it ran as follows:

Bluffing the idle rich of Paris through appeals to their snobbery is a delightfully simple matter. The process works out as follows: Take the best society possible, composed of rich, simple-minded, idle people. Then submit them to an intense regime of publicity. By pamphlets, newspaper articles, lectures, personal visits, and all other appeals to their snobbery, persuade them that hitherto they have seen only vulgar spectacles and are at last to know what is art and beauty. Impress them with cabalistic formulas. They have not the slightest notion of music, literature, painting, and dancing; still, they have heretofore seen under these names only a rude imitation of the real thing. Finally assure them that they are about to see real dancing and hear real music. It will then be necessary to double the prices at the theater, so great will be the rush of shallow worshippers at this false shrine.

The historic performance had occurred during the brilliant season of the Diaghileff Ballets Russes. Pierre Monteux directed. The choreography was by Vaslav Nijinsky, who was also one of the two leading dancers in the performance, the other being Marie Piltz. Scenery and costumes were designed by the noted Russian painter Nicolas Roerich, who had collaborated with the composer on the preparation of the book. The music was introduced to America at a concert of the Philadelphia Orchestra in Philadelphia, under the direction of Leopold Stokowski, on Mar. 3, 1922. Two years later, on Jan. 25, 1924, Mr. Monteux led the Boston Symphony Orchestra in the Boston premiere of the score, bringing it to New York on Jan. 31 for its local premiere in Carnegie Hall. It was not till Apr. 11, 1930, however, that the controversial ballet was staged for the first time in this country. On that night, it was produced in Philadelphia under the auspices of the League of Composers, with Mr. Stokowski conducting the Philadelphia Orchestra and Martha Graham dancing the role of The Chosen Maiden. The production reached New York at the Metropolitan Opera House the following Apr. 22.

The vision of this rugged picture of pagan Russia first came to Stravinsky in St. Petersburg while he was finishing the last pages of the *Firebird*. In his autobiography he recounts how surprised he was in the midst of other thoughts to find his mind suddenly flooded with images of a remote act of pagan ritualism. In the vision he beheld a solemn group of elders, seated in a circle, watching a young girl dance herself to death.

They were sacrificing her to propitiate the god of spring. Such was the theme of the *Sacre du printemps*. I must confess that this vision made a deep impression on me, and I at once described it to my friend Nicolas Roerich, he being a painter who had specialized in pagan subjects. He welcomed my inspiration with enthusiasm and became my collaborator in this creation. In Paris I told Diaghileff about it, and he was at once carried away by the idea.

For years after the Paris premiere, discussion of Stravinsky's most provocative score grew deep and learned. While dissenters continued to scream in print over its heresies, embattled champions of the rebellious score grew lyrical and philosophical in its defense. Edith Sitwell found that it gave us "the beginning of energy, the enormous and terrible shaping of the visible and invisible world through movement." The music's giant pulsations prompted the grave prophecy that "life is energy, and the very fact of that life will eventually push us over the abyss into the waiting and intolerable darkness." To Lazare Saminsky the imagination of Stravinsky perceived things and presented them musically "in terms of noises immanent to those things, eternally present in them." The Russian composer was found "curiously and characteristically deaf to the *inner* music of things—to their spiritual pulse." Stravinsky, in short, was "the father of rebarbarization in music," the composer who had "reduced melody to the primitive, inarticulate refrain of a Zulu" and converted the orchestra into "a gigantic rattle, the toy and mouthpiece of the new savage."

Yet, Erik Satie found "transparency of sound" amid this primitive throb of earth.

This is a quality that one always finds in the purists, who never leave any "residuum" in their sonority, that residuum which you will always encounter in the musical fabric of impressionistic composers and also, alas!, in that of the Romantics. Palestrina makes us "hear" this sonorous "transparency"; he was an expert manipulator of it and seems to have been the first to import this phenomenon into music. The exquisite Mozart used it in a way that defies analysis. One stands confounded before such mastery, such a subtle "clairvoyance" of sound, a phonic lucidity so calm and so perfect. Any one of Igor Stravinsky's works will cause you to perceive with extraordinary clearness this vibratory "transparency" of which I speak. *Le Sacre du Printemps* is full of it; and it is perhaps in this work that it will appear to you with the most persuasiveness: you will be prodigiously bathed in it, deeply saturated.

At a revival of the ballet in Paris, some years after the premiere, the Nijinsky choreography was discarded in favor of a new scenario by Leonide Massine. According to Stravinsky:

Massine never knew the original setting for *Le Sacre*—he was still at school in Moscow. Upon his first hearing of it, he perceived that my music, far from being descriptive, was of an "objective" construction. All musical works begin as impressions, which crystallize themselves in the brain, in the ear, and little by little, but mathematically, become concretely realized as notes and rhythm. The choreographer ought, in his turn, to crystallize his impression, and realize it, not for the ear, but for the eye.

It is generally accepted that the subject of Stravinsky's ballet deals with the worship of the forces of Nature by primitive man. Superficially it is a work evocative of a prehistoric religious ritual, in which the season of Spring and its fertility are venerated, all leading to a propitiatory sacrifice.

The score calls for a large orchestra, which consists of the following instruments: two piccolos, two flutes, flute in G, four oboes (one interchangeable with a second bass clarinet), clarinet in E flat, bass clarinet, four bassoons (one interchangeable with a second double bassoon), double bassoon, eight

horns (two interchangeable with Bayreuth tubas), four trumpets, trumpet
in D, bass trumpet, three trombones, two tubas, four kettledrums, small
kettledrums, bass drum, tambourine, cymbals, antique cymbals, triangle, *rape
guero* (scratcher), and strings.

                                                                    L. B.

Symphonic Poem, "Le Chant du rossignol" ("The Nightingale's Song")

THE SUBJECT of Stravinsky's three-act opera *Le Rossignol* (*The Nightingale*)
stems like that of *Le Baiser de la fée,* from one of Hans Christian Andersen's
stories. The composer and his friend Stepan Mitoussoff collaborated on the
libretto.

A summarized version of the opera's plot follows:

The Emperor of China, fallen into a state of utter dejection, is finally
aroused by the singing of a nightingale given to him as a gift. He is so
elated over his "cure" that he promises to grant the bird any favor it desires.
The nightingale answers that his recovery is favor enough, or words to that
effect.

Soon the Emperor receives another gift, a mechanical nightingale "made
in Japan." He is very pleased with its song, whereupon the real nightingale
becomes offended and flies away. The Emperor makes it all legal by banishing
the bird officially.

Of course, the Emperor's illness returns. Death is about to claim his victim
when the real nightingale hears of it and, out of compassion for its friend,
sings so eloquently that Death, this time, does the disappearing act. All the
courtiers, thinking their ruler dead, find him, instead, fully recovered and
happy.

The composer completed the first act of the work in 1908 and he wished
to continue, but other matters interfered with its progress. In 1909 he again
thought of finishing the opera, but again conditions were unfavorable. In
his autobiography he relates, "By the end of summer the orchestration of
the first act was finished . . . and I meant to go on with the rest. But a telegram then arrived for *L'Oiseau de feu* for the Russian Ballet season at the Paris
Opéra in the spring of 1910."

However, Stravinsky did not return to *Le Rossignol* until May, 1913, at
the request of the then new organization, the Théâtre Libre of Moscow.
Whereupon a problem in genres suddenly came. He explains, "Only the
Prologue—that is to say, Act I—was in existence. It had been written four
years earlier and my musical language had been appreciably modified since
then. I feared that in view of my new manner the subsequent scenes would

clash with the Prologue." He suggested that the Théâtre Libre utilize the Prologue alone, but they insisted on a three-act work.

Nevertheless the composer hit on a plan which, he thought, might cover all sides of the situation. He says:

As there is no action until the second act, I told myself that it would not be unreasonable if the music of the Prologue bore a somewhat different character from that of the rest. And, indeed, the forest, with its nightingale, the pure soul of the child who falls in love with its song, all this gentle poetry of Hans Andersen's could not be expressed in the same way as the baroque luxury of the Chinese court, with its bizarre etiquette, its palace fetes, its thousands of little bells and lanterns, and the grotesque humming of the Japanese nightingale, in short, all this exotic fantasy obviously demanded a different musical idiom.

As Stravinsky was putting the last touches on the piece, the Théâtre Libre bowed out of existence. At this point, Serge Diaghileff jumped in with an offer to produce it at the Paris Opéra the following season. On May 26, 1914, therefore, the work was given its first performance. About that premiere Stravinsky says, "Benois created sumptuous scenery and costumes and, conducted by Monteux, the opera was performed with the utmost perfection."

A couple of years later, Diaghileff proposed a ballet version of the opera. The composer countered with another suggestion. He declares:

I had been thinking of making a symphonic poem for orchestra by combining the music of the second and third acts of Le Rossignol, which were homogeneous, and I told Diaghileff that I would place that at his disposal if he cared to make a ballet of it. He warmly welcomed the suggestion, and I adapted a scenario from Andersen's fairy story to serve the purpose.

The present Symphonic Poem was completed in 1919. It was introduced to a New York audience by Walter Damrosch and the Symphony Society in Carnegie Hall on Nov. 1, 1923. Several days before that the Philadelphia Orchestra under the direction of Leopold Stokowski had given it its American premiere in Philadelphia.

The opera was first produced in this country at the Metropolitan on Mar. 6, 1926, appearing in a double bill with Manuel de Falla's La Vida breve, which was also performed for the first time in America on that date.

R. C. B.

Concerto for Piano and Wind Orchestra (with Double Basses and Tympani)

I. Lento; Allegro; Lento. II. Largo. III. Finale: Allegro.

The PRESENT work was given its first performance at a Koussevitzky concert in Paris, on May 22, 1924, the composer appearing as piano soloist. On that occasion the program listed the work as *Concerto pour piano avec l'orchestre d'harmonie.* Besides piano, it is scored for the following instruments: piccolo, two flutes, two oboes, two clarinets, English horn, two bassoons (one interchangeable with contra-bassoon), four horns, four trumpets, three trombones, bass tuba, tympani, and double basses.

The following analysis of the Concerto appeared in the program book of the Paris concert:

The Concerto is in three movements; and these movements are themselves divided as follows: The first movement consists of (a) Lento; (b) Allegro; (c) Maestoso. The second movement, after the opening Largo, introduces a cadenza (Poco rubato), which is linked with a melodic section, followed by a second melody, the last two being stated in a very compact manner. The cadenza then returns, and the movement ends with a variant of the Largo passage at the beginning of the movement, which in this place represents rather a continuation of the cadenza.

The concluding measure of the second movement serves also as the subject of the Fugato with which the Finale begins (Allegro, 2/4). The subject, assuming several forms, is heard sometimes in the piano part, sometimes in the orchestra, in a slower movement (doubled), although the time value of the metronomic base does not vary. A short melodic episode follows, giving place to another, in imitation. This is succeeded by a brief, rhythmic period (tutti), with a counterpoint for the piano, ending in a kind of stretto. This last is brusquely interrupted by a reminiscence (Lento, 2/4) of the slow movement and, further on, of the music with which the Concerto began. A pause separates this return of the opening martial movement from the eight measures which conclude the Concerto—a stringendo passage (forte, marcatissimo) for the piano, over a syncopated accompaniment in the orchestra.

Mr. Stravinsky has described this Concerto as "a sort of passacaglia or toccata. It is quite in the style of the seventeenth century—that is, the seventeenth century viewed from the standpoint of today."

By *orchestre d'harmonie* Mr. Stravinsky means a "type of orchestra separate and distinct from the symphony orchestra." He admits of three kinds of orchestras: the symphonic, the harmonic, and the fanfare (brass and percussion). A Parisian critic who heard the premiere of the Concerto spoke of the *orchestre d'harmonie* as "a symphony orchestra minus strings" (violins, violas and cellos). That, according to the composer, was a contradiction.

In a note contributed to the program book of a Concertgebouw Orchestra concert, Willem Mengelberg conducting (Amsterdam, Nov. 20, 1924), Mr. Stravinsky explained further:

It is six months since I played this Concerto before the Paris public for the first time. The work had just been completed. I remember that in one of the reviews of the performance which I read the next day, I was reproached on the subject of the constitution of the orchestra, which was said to be "incomplete," because of the absence of strings (except for the double basses). The unfortunate critic did not know at the time that there is such a thing, aside from the regular symphonic orchestra, as *un orchestre d'harmonie*. It is this *orchestre d'harmonie* which I have chosen for my Piano Concerto, and not the symphonic orchestra, as an instrumental body more appropriate to the tone of the piano. This instrumental ensemble had its definite design; for it, as well as the part for the piano, has been conceived contrapuntally.

However, these conceptions of tonal relationships—or the lack of them— between "scraped" and "struck" sounds underwent many changes in the composer's mind, for, as he told the annotator, "I worked more with strings and learned things about their nature of which I had not been aware." His many compositions for piano in combination with strings, following this Concerto, he avers, amply illustrate the application of his later knowledge.

The Concerto, begun in August, 1923, and finished at Biarritz in April, 1924, is dedicated to the late Nathalie Koussevitzky. Its first performance in this country was given by the Boston Symphony Orchestra on Jan. 23, 1925, Mr. Koussevitzky conducting and the composer appearing as pianist. The composer was again the soloist at the work's first New York performance, by the Philharmonic Society, on Feb. 5, 1925, under Willem Mengelberg.

R. C. B.

Divertimento from "Le Baiser de la fée" ("The Fairy's Kiss")

AN ALLEGORICAL ballet in four tableaux, *Le Baiser de la fée* was composed for Ida Rubinstein and first performed under the composer's direction at the Paris Opéra on Nov. 28, 1928. It was shown during the same season at the Théâtre de la Monnaie, Brussels, in Monte Carlo, and at La Scala, Milan.

Subsequently, Stravinsky arranged this orchestral suite from the ballet's score and found that he could do it "without difficulty, on account of straightforward plan."

The ballet, according to the composer's manuscript, was "Inspired by the Muse of Tschaikowsky," and melody after melody from the latter's pen weaves its way through the pattern of Stravinsky's score. The main theme, for instance, is the "Wiegenlied im Sturm," and among the others are "Humoresque," "Natha," and "A Peasant Plays the Harmonica."

Stravinsky wrote on his score, "I dedicate this ballet to the memory of Peter Tschaikowsky, identifying his muse with the Fairy, and it is from this fact that the ballet becomes an allegory. His genius has in like degree marked the score with a destined kiss—a mystic influence which bespeaks the whole work of this great artist."

Herbert Fleischer, further, discovers that Stravinsky "removes the often too sweet and rather feminine meltingness of Tschaikowsky's melos. He recasts the tones of the master, so reverenced by him, in his own rigid tonal language. Yet the lyrical tenderness of Tschaikowsky's melos is not lost."

The movements of the Divertimento are as follows: I. Sinfonia: Andante—Allegro sostenuto; II. Danse suisse: Tempo giusto—Valse; III. Scherzo: Moderato—Allegretto; IV. Pas de deux: (a) Adagio, (b) Variation (Allegretto grazioso), (c) Coda (Presto).

R. C. B.

"Four Norwegian Moods"

I. "Intrada." II. "Song." III. "Wedding Dance." IV. "Cortège."

Composed in Hollywood, in 1942, *Four Norwegian Moods* is based on Norwegian folk tunes "although," as the composer explains, "the title *Moods* must not be interpreted as *impression* or *frame of mind*. It is purely a mode, a form of manner of style without any assumption of ethnological authenticity." (It occurred to John N. Burk, program annotator of the Boston Symphony Orchestra, that "Mr. Stravinsky evidently uses the title *Moods* in a certain generic sense of the word which survives as a term in grammar.")

Mr. Stravinsky further declares that he "has no more than followed the tradition of folklore treatment used by Joseph Haydn in his time" and that he "approaches the given problems in formal order to reach the solution, using the folklore thematic only as a rhythmic and melodic basis."

The "Intrada" combines, as essentials, an introduction, featuring wood winds and horns, and a Scherzando grazioso. The section has also a trio for clarinets and bassoons and a brief conclusion.

The "Song" gives a melody chiefly to the wood winds; first the English horn, then oboe and bassoon, then flutes and, finally, English horn.

"Wedding Dance," lively and in 2/4 rhythm, offers a principal theme of "peasant suggestion."

"Cortège" is of a marchlike rhythm. It brings the composition to a quiet conclusion.

The piece is scored for two flutes, piccolo, two oboes, English horn, two clarinets, two bassoons, two trumpets, four horns, two trombones, tuba, tympani, and strings.

R. C. B.

"Circus Polka"

THIS MUSIC was originally written for band, as the score for a ballet commissioned by the Ringling Bros. and Barnum and Bailey Circus. George Balanchine was the choreographer. The ballet was a sensation of the Circus season at its first performance, in Madison Square Garden, New York, during the spring of 1942. Vera Zorina led the dancing in the center ring, surrounded by both elephant and human ballerinas.

The composer rescored his piece for orchestra in October of that year, the orchestration calling for flute, piccolo, two oboes, two clarinets, two bassoons, four horns, two trumpets, three trombones, tuba, tympani, snare drum, brass drum, cymbals, and strings. The piece was given its premiere in orchestral form by the Boston Symphony in January, 1944.

R. C. B.

"Ode" in Three Parts, for Orchestra

COMPLETED IN 1943, the *Ode* was composed for the Koussevitzky Musical Foundation, Inc., and dedicated to the memory of Mme. Nathalie Koussevitzky. It was given its first performance by the Boston Symphony Orchestra on Oct. 8, 1943. The score calls for two flutes, piccolo, two oboes, two clarinets, two bassoons, four horns, two trumpets, tympani, and strings.

The following explanation is by the composer:

The *Ode* is a chant in three parts for orchestra. It is in appreciation of Nathalie Koussevitzky's spiritual contribution to the art of the eminent conductor, her husband, Dr. Serge Koussevitzky.

I. "Eulogy," praise, a song in sustained melody with accompaniment, the whole in fugal treatment.

II. "Eclogue," a piece in lively mood, a kind of *concert champêtre,* suggesting out-of-door music, an idea cherished by Nathalie Koussevitzky and brilliantly materialized at Tanglewood by her husband.

III. "Epitaph," an inscription, *air serein,* closes this memorial triptych.

R. C. B.

"Scènes de Ballet"

MR. STRAVINSKY describes this work as:

A classical ballet which I composed the summer of 1944. This music is patterned after the forms of the classical dance, free of any given literary or dramatic argument. The parts follow each other as in a sonata or in a symphony in contrasts or similarities.

"This music was composed by request of Mr. Billy Rose. Portions of this work were used as a ballet number in his *Seven Lively Arts*.

The eleven parts of the score, played without pause, are as follows:

1. Introduction
2. Corps de Ballet Dances (Moderato, più mosso moderato)
3. Variation of the Ballerina (Allegretto)
4. Pantomime (Lento)
5. Pas de Deux (Adagio, Allegretto, Adagio)
6. Pantomime (Agitato)
7. Variation of the Dancer (Risoluto)
8. Variation of the Ballerina (Andantino)
9. Pantomime (Andantino)
10. Corps de Ballet Dances (Con moto)
11. Apotheosis

Mr. Stravinsky conducted the first concert performance of the *Scènes de Ballet* by the Philharmonic-Symphony Orchestra in Carnegie Hall on Feb. 3, 1945.

Franz von Suppé

BORN: SPALATO, DALMATIA, APR. 18, 1819. DIED: VIENNA, MAY 21, 1895.

Von Suppé has often been compared with Offenbach because of his fecundity and wide popularity in his own country. Each is a force to be reckoned with in the development of light opera, although most of their work is now tradition.—J. WALKER McSPADDEN.

Overture to "Die Schöne Galathea" ("The Beautiful Galathea")

IF SUPPÉ was the Viennese counterpart of the French Offenbach, as some aver, his comic opera *The Beautiful Galathea* (1865) was even more the Viennese counterpart of the French Victor Massé's *Galatée,* produced more than a decade earlier in Paris. Suppé's librettists, Zell and Genée, borrowed the modern setting of the Greek myth lock, stock, and barrel from the Parisian book Jules Barbier and Michel Carré wrote for Massé. Suppé's work, bubbling over with bright melody, became a Viennese favorite. The engaging Overture sets the pace for the two-act blend of lighthearted gaiety and lush sentiment.

The Greek fable is worked cleverly into a bantering and mildly risqué modern version. According to legend, Galathea was a statue wrought by the Greek sculptor Pygmalion. The artist fell hopelessly in love with his marble creation. The gods took pity and breathed life into the stone image. In Suppé's operetta, a rich man called Midas admires Galathea in her pre-life state and offers to buy her. Pygmalion is naturally affronted. In a rage he prepares to smash the statue, for having been violated by another's gaze. Venus intervenes with the gift of life. Galathea's first look falls on Pygmalion. Love blossoms.

But Galathea proves anything but constant. Life has made her fickle. During Pygmalion's absence she flirts with the servant Ganymede. Midas appears laden with jewels, which she accepts as Pygmalion spies on the coquette. In despair he calls on Venus to turn his wife back into a statue. Venus does so. Galathea is stone again, and Pygmalion turns to Midas: "How much do you offer? She's yours!"

Die Schöne Galathea belongs with *Fatinitza, Franz Schubert, Donna Juanita, Boccaccio,* and *Pique Dame* as one of Von Suppé's best contributions to the light-opera repertory. The Overture is one of four or five from his pen recurringly played in popular symphonic series. The best known of them, of course, is *The Poet and Peasant.* The comic opera *Boccaccio* has figured in the repertory of New York's Metropolitan Opera House.

L. B.

Karol Szymanowski

BORN: TIMOSHOVKA, UKRAINE, SEPT. 21, 1883. DIED: NEAR LAUSANNE, MAR. 29, 1937.

*He stands alone, a belated romanticist who longs for great peace.
. . . He carries the death dream of romanticism to the border of
awakening.*—ERWIN FELBER.

Concerto for Violin and Orchestra, Op. 35

THE COMPOSER began work on this Concerto in 1917 and completed the job in 1918. Its first performance was given at Warsaw, in 1922, when Mlynarski was the soloist and Gregor Fitelberg the conductor. It had its American premiere by Paul Kochanski at a concert of the Philadelphia Orchestra in Philadelphia, Nov. 28, 1924. The piece is dedicated "To my friend Paul Kochanski."

Although the Concerto is in one movement, it shows clearly a subdivision into three sections. The first (Vivace, 4/4) opens with an orchestral introduction, in which the oboe leads off with a sinuous figure closely surrounded by dissonances in the strings and other instruments. This idea is repeated in different forms several times, after which the solo violin offers a broad cantilena type of melody that is not unrelated to the opening figure. The oboe comes along to give the melody some variation. The violins present a new theme (which is important later) after the solo instrument has disported itself in a florid passage, to the accompaniment of wind, brass, and the pizzicato strings. This figure, it will be seen, has also an important function in the finale.

The second section (Andantino, 3/4) brings forward a main theme, which is in two parts, an upward and a descending figure, possibly representative of the question and answer technique. An accompanied cadenza follows (solo violin against string tremolos, harps, and cymbals). Another subject is ushered in, rather episodic in nature, and all the material is closely woven together in the development.

The third section (Vivace assai, 2/4) is truly sprightly, for a time, in the manner of a prefinale scherzo. This leads, more or less, into a second subject, tranquil and expressive. Later the two are brought together contrapuntally. Subsequently there is a reminiscence of earlier material, then a lilting 6/8 dance rhythm takes the initiative in the whole orchestra (con passione). After some moments a fermata makes way for the cadenza, composed by Kochanski. It is based on previous themes of the piece. When it is completed the music rises and rises in sonority and complication to a great climax. Then the whole subsides down to a whisper. The solo violin echoes briefly the reply part of the second section's first theme, and soon all is over quietly.

Karol Szymanowski, born into an aristocratic family, took his first theory lessons from Gustav Neuhaus. His creative talents showed themselves early during this association, resulting in a set of piano preludes, composed in 1900 (and published in 1905, as Op. 1). In 1903 he went to Warsaw to study there with Noskowski, and in 1905 his C minor Piano Sonata won first prize at the Chopin Festival in Lemberg.

In Berlin, two years later, he joined forces with some other musicians of Polish birth to form a group known as "Young Poland in Music." On his return to Poland he devoted most of his time to composing, and he wrote in six years, or so, a considerable number of works for piano, violin, voice, and orchestra (a concert overture and two symphonies), in addition to the opera *Hagith.*

During the First World War Szymanowski was interned in Russia by the Bolsheviks, but he managed to escape to Warsaw. After the war he traveled far and wide, coming to this country in 1921, where he was already known, thanks to performances of his music by Leopold Stokowski and the Philadelphia Orchestra. The following year he accepted an appointment as professor of composition and director of the Warsaw State Conservatory. In 1926 Szymanowski was appointed director of the Warsaw Conservatory, in which capacity he reorganized the institution thoroughly, substituting for the old and conventional system one in accordance with modern views. All along he kept composing, his works betraying more and more a nationalistic spirit which had been strong in him from the start. One of the compositions expressing that most powerfully is the ballet *Harnasie.* The *Stabat Mater,* produced at Warsaw in 1928, proved to be his most successful work.

R. C. B.

Alexandre Tansman

BORN: LODZ, POLAND, JUNE 12, 1897.

All that the folklore of his country can suggest is a melodic curve, a natural harmony; all that it contains is the very emotion of his race, which he has learned to capture and give expression to.—IRVING SCHWERKÉ.

"Polish Rhapsody"

LIKE Dmitri Shostakovich's Seventh Symphony and Harl MacDonald's *Bataan,* the *Polish Rhapsody* of Alexandre Tansman grew out of the Second World War.

When the work was premiered on Nov. 14, 1941, in St. Louis, at a concert of the St. Louis Symphony Orchestra, Vladimir Golschmann conducting, the composer stated that he was inspired to write the *Rhapsody* by the invasion of Poland. The score carries a dedication, above the title: "To the Defenders of Warsaw." Besides the polonaise and mazurka rhythms pulsing through sections of the *Rhapsody,* phrases from the Polish and English anthems are worked into the scheme toward the end to clarify and enrich the content.

In the introductory section a melody is given out by the oboe that serves as link between sections of the *Rhapsody.* A polonaise then sets in, strongly rhythmed and in stately mood. The first theme now returns, leading to a brighter mazurka section. Once more the bridge theme, and then the central episode, a processional device, gets under way. At first faint, it grows to a shattering fortissimo before fading away again. The brasses intone echoes of the Polish and English anthems. As if forecasting victory, the music grows gradually more brilliant and confident as the mazurka tempo returns.

The *Polish Rhapsody* is scored for piccolo, two flutes, two oboes, English horn, two clarinets, two bassoons, four horns, three trumpets, three trombones, tuba, piano, celesta, xylophone, tympani, snare drum, triangle, and strings. It was written in Nice in November and December, 1940.

Alexandre Tansman first studied piano and composition in his native Lodz, having begun to jot down original ideas at the age of nine. His teachers were Gavronski and Vas. Later he went to Warsaw, to study law, but soon switched back to music. At twenty-two, while a volunteer in the Polish army, he won first and second prizes in a musical contest by the simple device of entering compositions under two pseudonyms. The works were a Romance for Violin and Piano and a Suite for Piano, winning in that order.

Like other Polish composers before him, notably Chopin, Tansman was drawn to Paris. There Vladimir Golschmann, who became a close friend, led premieres of *Impressions* and *Intermezzo Sinfonico* at his Concerts Golschmann. With Paris as center, Tansman toured widely, coming to America four times before finally making it his home. Often he appeared at concerts in the triple role of conductor, composer, pianist.

Chopin's influence is strong in Tansman's early music. Traces of the styles of Richard Strauss and Scriabin are noticeable, too. Later influences have been Ravel, Stravinsky, and jazz, which flavors some of his music in highly original fashion.

Melodic breadth and inventiveness mark much of his music. The bold modernism of certain compositions contrasts sharply with others couched in moods of lyric delicacy. Fragments of Polish folk music recur in his works, though without literal treatment.

A writer in *Pro Musica* observed that Tansman believes music to be an absolute and pure art, which has power to act on the sensibilities as well as on the intelligence.

"The Tansman technic," he goes on, "prefers a long, broad melodic line. Thematic subjects are of a considerable length. It is through melodic development, Tansman believes, that the classic forms in music can be rejuvenated."

L. B.

Giuseppe Tartini

BORN: PIRANO, ISTRIA, ITALY, APR. 8, 1692. DIED: PADUA, FEB. 26, 1770.

Tartini was a bit of a mystic. The "Devil's Trill Sonata" came to him in a dream, and if it really was inspired by the devil, proves that whatever his other faults, His Satanic Majesty is a musician of the first order.—LEOPOLD AUER.

Concerto for Violin and String Orchestra in D minor

I. Allegro. II. Grave. III. Presto.

TARTINI'S FAME rests mainly on the *Devil's Trill Sonata,* which grew out of a dream, or perhaps a nightmare. According to the composer, the devil seized his violin and conjured unearthly sounds from it. Like Coleridge and his vision of *Kubla Khan,* Tartini woke up and wrote down the dream, using notes instead of words. But the Padua master's claim to a place in music history has broader and securer grounds. The Padua school of violin playing founded by him was long influential. Tartini's improvements in bowing became standard equipment in violin technic. In his heyday he was widely feted as the virtuoso of virtuosos, and many courts vied for his services. The beauty and passion of his style of playing are glowingly recorded by contemporaries. Moreover, he was a theorist of marked originality. At least two treatises of his became indispensable guide books. Tartini was the discoverer of the so-called "combination tone," also known as the "difference tone," the "differential tone," and the "Tartini harmonic." This was a device first used by him to secure pure intonation. The "differential" is heard when two notes are played with sustained intensity. The vibrations of this third note were found to equal the difference between the original two. Tartini often told his pupils that if they could hear this third note their double-stopping was in tune.

An early estimate of Tartini's vast musical output included 200 violin concertos. There is a story that 127 concertos by Tartini were offered for sale in Venice not long after his death. Many of Tartini's concertos are probably lost; some may still be in private hands, and a good number may be scattered—unindexed—in small European libraries. To date, 125 have been accounted for. Fifty-nine of them repose in manuscript in the Biblioteca Antoniana at Padua. Several others are in the Berlin State Library and the Paris Conservatory.

A thorough study of the extant collection was made some years ago by a Greek student at the Berlin University named Minos Dounias. The researches were published as his doctor's thesis. In compiling a thematic index of the Tartini concertos Dounias grouped them according to keys. Chronological order was out of the question, though valid speculation is possible about three definite periods in Tartini's style of composition. Three of the concertos are in D minor—Nos. 43, 44, and 45 in Dounias's tabulation. The third of these is the one in which we are interested in the edition made by Joseph Szigeti in 1937. It consists of an Allegro (D minor, 3/4), a Grave (A minor, 4/4), and a Presto (D minor, 2/4). Mr. Szigeti's alterations consisted of (1) a short cadenza in the first movement; (2) omission of the cadenzas of the second movement, for which he substituted a concluding passage based on material taken from the first movement; and (3) a cadenza of more normal length in the third movement. Except where he altered the ending of the second movement, Mr. Szigeti made very slight changes in the string accompaniment.

An unusual feature of the D minor Concerto is the 3/4 time of the opening movement. The more orthodox marking is 4/4. "Another striking quality," says Mr. Szigeti, "is its departure from the brittle and formalistic plane of the typical concerto of Tartini's day. There is poignancy in the thematic material, not quite sad, but poignancy with a smile."

Scholars were long baffled by the mottos in cipher appearing over movements of Tartini's violin concertos. The signs included short lines, crosses, angles of all kinds, full and half circles, and other geometric figures. When this odd script was deciphered, the mottos proved to be poetic quotations, most of them bitter and ironic comments on love. Some are pleas for mercy, one or two express bleak despair. Whatever it was Tartini was hiding beneath a cipher, it assuredly was more than just an impish flair for mystification. Over the Largo of the A major Concerto (No. 97) is the following motto, in cipher: *"A rivi, a fonti, a fiumi correte, amare lagrime, sin che consumi l'acerbo mio dolor"* ("O bitter tears, flowing like streams, fountains, and rivers, without drowning this bitter pain of mine"). The good man is even more explicit in the G major Concerto (No. 82). *"So che pietà non hai!"* ("I know you have no pity!") he cries out in cipher over the opening page of the Largo. Of course, the reference may have been to Signora Tartini. Then, again, it may not have been.

L. B.

Deems Taylor

BORN: NEW YORK, DEC. 22, 1885.

*It is a pleasure to find an American composer of talent who is willing
to write music that is cheerful, not portentous; whose fancy is delicate;
who uses a large orchestra discreetly, not chiefly to make a thunderous
noise.*—PHILIP HALE.

Suite, "Through the Looking Glass"

WRITTEN IN 1917-1919, the Suite, *Through the Looking Glass* was originally
scored for small chamber orchestra consisting of flute, oboe, clarinet, bassoon,
horn, piano, and strings. In this version it was first played by the New York
Chamber Music Society on Feb. 18, 1921.

Late that year Mr. Taylor set to work amplifying the score. Two years later,
it was ready for full symphonic performance. There was also an additional
movement, "The Garden of Wild Flowers." Thus altered and extended, the
Suite was performed by the New York Symphony Orchestra in Brooklyn on
Mar. 10, 1923, and repeated in Aeolian Hall, New York, the next day. Walter
Damrosch conducted. Based on Lewis Carroll's humorous classic, the Suite
falls into four sections, the first being subdivided into two connected parts,
I. (a) Dedication; and I. (b) "The Garden of Wild Flowers," which was added
to the later version.

"The Suite needs no extended analysis," wrote the composer for the program
book of the New York Symphony premiere. "It is based on Lewis Carroll's
immortal nonsense fairy tale, *Through the Looking Glass and What Alice
Found There,* and the five pictures it presents will, if all goes well, be readily
recognizable to lovers of the book." Printed in the program—and later in the
published score—were the relevant passages from the book, interlarded with
Mr. Taylor's comments. They are as follows:

I. (a) "Dedication"—Carroll precedes the tale with a charming poetical foreword,
the first stanza of which the music aims to express. It runs:

> "Child of the pure unclouded brow
>   And dreaming eyes of wonder!
> Though time be fleet, and I and thou
>   Are half a life asunder,
> Thy loving smile will surely hail
>   The love-gift of a fairy-tale.

> "And, though the shadow of a sigh
> May tremble through the story,
> For happy summer days gone by,
> And vanished summer glory—
> It shall not touch, with breath of bale,
> The pleasance of our fairy-tale."

A simple song theme, briefly developed, leads without pause to—

I. (b) "The Garden of Live Flowers"—"O Tiger-Lily," said Alice, addressing herself to one that was waving gracefully about in the wind, "I *wish* you could talk."

"We *can* talk," said the Tiger-Lily; "when there's anybody worth talking to."

"And can *all* the flowers talk?"

"As well as you can," said the Tiger-Lily, "and a great deal louder."

Shortly after Alice had entered the looking-glass country she came to a lovely garden in which the flowers were talking—in the words of the Tiger-Lily, "as well as you can, and a great deal louder." The music, therefore, reflects the brisk chatter of the swaying, bright-colored denizens of the garden.

II. "Jabberwocky"—The theme of that frightful beast, the Jabberwock, is first announced by the full orchestra. The clarinet then begins the tale, recounting how, on a "brillig" afternoon, the "slithy toves did gyre and gimble in the wabe." Muttered imprecations by the bassoon warn us to "beware the Jabberwock, my son." A miniature march signalizes the approach of our hero, taking "his vorpal sword in hand." Trouble starts among the trombones—the Jabberwock is upon us! The battle with the monster is recounted in a short and rather repellent fugue, the double basses bringing up the subject and the hero fighting back in the interludes. Finally his vorpal blade (really a xylophone) goes "snicker-snack," and the monster impersonated by the solo bassoon, dies a lingering and convulsive death. The hero returns, to the victorious strains of his own theme—"O frabjous day! Callooh! Callay!" The whole orchestra rejoices—the church bells are rung—alarms and excursions.

Conclusion. Once more the slithy toves perform their pleasing evolutions, undisturbed by the uneasy ghost of the late Jabberwock.

III. "Looking-Glass Insects"—Here we find the vociferous *diptera* that made such an impression upon Alice . . . the Bee-elephant, the Gnat, the Rocking-horse-fly, the Snap-dragon-fly, and the Bread-and-butter-fly. There are several themes, but there is no use trying to decide which insect any one of them stands for.

IV. "The White Knight"—He was a toy Don Quixote, mild, chivalrous, ridiculous, and rather touching. He carried a mouse-trap on his saddle-bow, "because, if they *do* come, I don't choose to have them running about." He couldn't ride very well, but he was a gentle soul, with good intentions. There are two themes: the first, a sort of instrumental prance, being the Knight's own conception of himself as a slashing, dare-devil fellow. The second is bland, mellifluous, a little sentimental—much more like the Knight as he really was. The first theme starts off bravely, but falls out of the saddle before very long, and has to give way to the second. The two alternate, in various guises, until the end, when the Knight rides off, with Alice waving her handkerchief—he thought it would encourage him if she did.

The score of *Through the Looking Glass* carries a dedication to Katherine Moore Taylor—"from a difficult son."

L. B.

Fantasy, "Circus Day," Op. 18

In 1925, Paul Whiteman commissioned Deems Taylor to write something for his band. The result was *Circus Day*. When the composition was premiered by the bandmaster in Carnegie Hall in November, 1925, it was heard with Ferde Grofe's instrumentation for jazz orchestra. In 1933, Mr. Taylor rescored his *Fantasy* for symphonic orchestra. This later version was first performed at a Children's Concert of the Philharmonic-Symphony Society. Mr. Taylor then supplied the following analysis of the piece, which is subtitled "Eight Pictures from Memory":

As the title indicates, the music attempts to convey one's early impressions of a day at the circus. You must not, however, think of one of the huge three-ring affairs that divide their time among the big cities and go into winter quarters at the first sign of frost. Our particular circus is a much more humble entertainment than that. It travels about the country in trucks and busses, plays under its own tent, and seldom remains in any town longer than a day or two. Its menagerie, while satis-factorily ferocious, is a small one; its performers, while intrepid, are few; and its canvasmen are not above playing in the band when their other duties permit.

I. "Street Parade." The whole town is out, crowding the main street and buzzling with excitement. Presently we hear the circus parade approaching. It draws nearer, to the further excitement of the spectators. As it passes, the band playing lustily, we hear, as well, the steam calliope, playing the tune that steam calliopes always play. This, needless to say, has nothing in common with the tune the band is playing. The parade passes on down the street; the playing of the band grows fainter and dies away in the distance.

II. "The Big Top." Peanuts, popcorn, pink lemonade, bawling side-show barkers, sights, sounds, smells, excitement, bliss—here we are, at last, under the main tent, the "big top"!

III. "Bareback Riders." Into the ring lumber the huge, broad-backed cream-colored horses; and as the ringmaster cracks his whip, their riders perform the miraculous feats—handstands, headstands, hoop jumping, somersaults—that make bareback riders the objects of such awe and admiration.

IV. (a) "The Lion Cage." Now the lion tamer brings on his cage full of ferocious felines. Their roars are blood curdling, but they go through their tricks with no damage to any of us.

(b) "The Dog and Monkey Circus." The lions having temporarily retired, into the ring dash a whole kennel full of small dogs disguised as race horses, ridden by monkeys who are dressed as jockeys. They race madly around the ring, the steeds barking at the top of their lungs, the riders chattering madly. In the excitement no one notices which entry wins; but it hardly matters.

(c) "The Waltzing Elephants." The great beasts come into the ring and solemnly waltz to a tune that is a pachydermous version of the theme of the bareback riders.

V. "Tight-rope Walker." He balances his parasol; he pirouettes, and slips and slides as he makes his perilous way along the taut wire; but he never quite falls off.

VI. "Jugglers." They juggle little balls and big ones, knives, dishes, hats, lighted candles—what you will. Even the orchestra is seized by the contagion and finally juggles its main theme, keeping three versions of it in the air at once.

VII. "Clowns." Two of the clowns come out to play us a tune. They begin with a great flourish, but are laughed down by their companions. Clown number one begins a long speech, is heckled, and gets into a quarrel with the others. Two other clowns try to play the tune. They fail. Two others try it, with no better success. Finally, after a furious argument, the entire clown band manages to play the tune through, amid loud applause.

VIII. "Finale." This might better be called "Looking Back." For the circus is over, and we are back at home, trying to tell a slightly inattentive family what we saw and heard. The helpful orchestra evokes recollections of jugglers, clowns, bareback riders, tight-rope walkers, trained animals—all the wonders that went to make up an unforgettable day.

Randall Thompson

BORN: NEW YORK, APR. 21, 1899.

Thompson is one of the finest craftsmen among American composers. Whatever he does is beautifully constructed. . . . His style, less dissonant than that of Copland and Harris, is more melodious, but the music is nonetheless American in spirit.—DOUGLAS MOORE.

Symphony in E minor, No. 2

I. Allegro. II. Largo. III. Vivace. IV. Andante moderato; Allegro con spirito; Largamento.

THE FIRST of Mr. Thompson's two symphonies dates from 1929, the second, in E minor, from 1931, completed at Gstaad, Switzerland, in September of that year. The work did not wait long for a hearing. Howard Hanson placed it on a program of American music in Rochester on Mar. 24, 1932. New York was introduced to the work under the auspices of Bruno Walter and the Philharmonic-Symphony on Nov. 2, 1933, when it enjoyed a tremendous success.

According to the composer, the Second Symphony is without literary or spiritual program. Mr. Thompson's aim was to write four contrasting movements, "separate and distinct," evolving a sense of balance and completeness in the mass, without cyclical unity and development. As regards the scoring, he says:

I have used the ordinary full orchestra by threes. I have not used all the instruments in every movement. Limiting the percussion to cymbals and kettledrums may seem to be a curious twist for a contemporary composer. I have been sparing in my use of percussive punctuation in an attempt to make the music itself intrinsically rhythmic. The kettledrums are used only in the first two movements; the cymbals only in the last two. The orchestra is greatly reduced in the second movement. The brass in the scherzo is limited to horns and one trumpet. The trombones and tuba are employed only in the last movement.

Mr. Thompson's own analysis of his music follows:

I. Allegro, E minor; two-four time. The movement runs from beginning to end without change in tempo. The principal theme is announced immediately by the horns, forte, and answered by the trumpets. From this motive is derived a series of rhythmic figures which form the toccata-like background of the entire movement. The subsidiary theme (G minor, oboes, English horn, and bassoon) is of a more reticent nature, but the cellos accompany it in a persistent rhythm.

The development section begins quietly, and forms a gradual crescendo, at the apex of which the first theme returns in an ominous fortissimo against a counter-rhythm on the kettledrums. A more extended transition leads to a sinister presentation of the second theme (C minor, muted trumpets answered by bassoon and clarinets antiphonally). At the close, a major version of the second theme in augmentation is sounded fortissimo by the horns and trumpets against the continuous pulse of the strings. The movement subsides, apparently to end the major. An abrupt minor chord brings it to a close.

II. Largo, C major; four-four time. The violins play a warm, quiet melody against pizzicato chords in the cellos. A contrasting melody is sung by the oboe. The movement is not long, but its mood is concentrated. It ends simply, on a C major chord with lowered seventh.

III. Vivace; seven-four time. Scherzo with trio. The first section begins in G minor and ends in D minor. The trio (Capriccioso, six-eight and nine-eight time) progresses from B major to G major. The first section returns transposed. Now beginning in C minor and ending in G minor, it serves as a kind of extended "subdominant answer" to its former presentation. There is a short coda making an intensified use of material from the trio.

IV. Andante moderato—Allegro con spirito—Largamente, E major. The slow sections which begin and end this movement serve to frame the Allegro, a modified rondo.

The theme of the Allegro is a diminution of the theme of the first and last sections. The Largamente employs for the first time the full sonorities of the orchestra in a sustained assertion of the principal melody.

The symphony is dedicated to Mr. Thompson's wife.

Virgil Thomson

BORN: KANSAS CITY, NOV. 25, 1896.

He is our musical satirist, our Erik Satie.—JOHN TASKER HOWARD.

"Symphony on a Hymn Tune"

I. Introduction and Allegro. II. Andante cantabile. III. Allegretto. IV. Alla breve.

THE FIRST three movements of this Symphony were written in Paris in 1926. Two years later Mr. Thomson completed and orchestrated the work, returning to it again in 1944 for some slight revision.

The Symphony is based on the old Scotch melody that is sung in the South to many texts but most commonly to "How Firm a Foundation." The property of no one denomination, the hymn has long been used to close the meetings of the Southern Baptist Convention. In 1939 it appeared as "The Christian's Farewell" in a reprint by the W.P.A. Writers Project of Kentucky of the 1854 edition of William Walker's *Southern Harmony*. Another familiar tune, "Yes, Jesus Loves Me," appears as a secondary theme.

Mr. Thomson's work is in four movements, each a variation or development of the pentatonic melody used as chief theme. It has been described as "simple, straightford, and folklorish in style, evoking nineteenth-century rural America by its dignity, its sweetness, and its naïve religious gaiety." Paul Rosenfeld once compared it to a Currier and Ives print.

Mr. Thomson has supplied the authors with the following terse analysis of his Symphony:

Introduction and Allegro. The Introduction is a conversational passage for solo instruments and pairs of instruments, followed by a statement of the hymn tune (in half-in and half-out-of-focus harmonization). The Allegro is a succession (and superposition) of dancelike passages derived from the main theme. Only the introduction gets recapitulated. The movement ends with a cadenza for trombone, piccolo, solo cello, and solo violin.

The Andante Cantabile is songlike and contemplative, a series of variations on a melody derived from the hymn tune, ending with the suggestion of a distant railway train.

The Allegretto is a passacaglia of marked rhythmic character on the hymn-tune bass.

The finale (Alla breve), a canzona on a part of the main theme, reintroduces all the chief material of the Symphony, including the hymn in full, and ends with a coda that recalls the introduction.

This movement was used by Mr. Thomson in a slightly altered version as the finale of Pare Lorentz's film "The River," for which he composed the musical score.

The Symphony is scored for two flutes (one playing also piccolo), two oboes, two clarinets, two bassoons, one contra-bassoon, four horns, two trumpets, three trombones, tuba, kettledrums, snare drums, rattle, tambourine, triangle, cymbals, tam-tam, bass drum, and the usual strings.

Mr. Thomson conducted the premiere of his symphony on Feb. 22, 1945, at a New York Philharmonic-Symphony concert directed by Artur Rodzinski. He gives the following information about himself:

I was born in Kansas City, grew up there, and went to war from there. That was the other war. Then I was educated some more in Boston and Paris. In composition I was a pupil of Nadia Boulanger. While I was still young I taught music at Harvard and played the organ at King's Chapel, Boston. Then I returned to Paris and lived there for many years, till the Germans came, in fact. Now I live in New York, where I am music critic of the *Herald Tribune*.

My best-known works are the opera *Four Saints in Three Acts* (libretto by Gertrude Stein), "The Plow That Broke the Plains" and "The River" (films by Pare Lorentz), though there are also symphonies and string quartets and many other works in many forms. I have made over a hundred musical portraits, too, all of them drawn from life, the sitter posing for me as he would for an artist's portrait.

Mr. Thomson is the author of two books: *The State of Music* and *The Musical Scene,* as well as of numerous magazine articles on subjects ranging from esthetics to new trends in world music.

Mr. Thomson made his Carnegie Hall debut as conductor in 1923, when he led a concert of the Harvard Glee Club in a program of ancient and modern choral works. Among the compositions listed was a Latin motet of his own, entitled *Tribulations*.

L. B.

Suite from the Ballet "Filling Station"

THE BALLET *Filling Station* was first produced by the Ballet Caravan, Lincoln Kirstein, director, in Hartford, Jan. 6, 1938. Lew Christensen did the choreography, and Paul Cadmus designed the costumes. The following synopsis of the action in *Filling Station* was carried in the program of the Ballet Caravan:

America has so many kinds of people in so many parts of the country, with so many different local stories, that it is difficult to find a fable to fit a modern Hero. But everyone who has ridden in an automobile recognizes the typical self-reliant, resourceful, and courteous Filling Station mechanic as Friend indeed. We call him Mac. He keeps his washroom spick and span. The chromium on his pumps gleams. His road maps are neatly stacked to be given away on request. His friends are two truck drivers, Roy and Ray, chased by a State Trooper, who warns them against speeding and overloading. A distressed Motorist inquires the route he has lost. His wife and child burden him down with demonstrations of domestic bliss. A rich young couple from the Country Club stagger and turn the Filling Station into a dance hall. A nervous Gangster finds himself involved in murder. Mac summons the State Trooper. The station is emptied, and Mac, finding himself alone again, spreads his tabloid and turns on his radio, waiting for whatever will turn up next.

Mr. Kirstein, in his book *Blast at Ballet* thus explains the problems facing the creation and production of the piece and the manner in which they were solved:

When we were planning to mount a ballet on an everyday subject, which finally turned out to be *Filling Station,* we first of all searched for a basic fable that would be already familiar to most of our prospective audiences, on which we could make our own comment. We couldn't find one ready made. We looked into Aesop and La Fontaine, trying to reclaim an old fable with modern implications. No use. We had to make the whole thing up ourselves. It wasn't as if we didn't know what our ballet was about. We did. It was about work, today. It couldn't be put in a factory, on an open road or on a farm, because we didn't have enough dancers to suggest a mass of workers. . . .

We chose as locale a gasoline Filling Station. It was both crossroads and way station. It would be a logical place in which work could be done and where different kinds of people could meet. . . .

So, lacking a modern myth, we made one up, and discovered that it was already in existence since everyone immediately recognized it. Any success we may have had was due as much to our method as to our material. The handling of both was by a complete collaboration of painter, choreographer, and musician.

Mr. Thomson, discussing the score of *Filling Station,* has written:

Musically it is in the vernacular. It sounds like all the familiar American tunes, though there is no direct quotation from any of these, excepting in the case of the tune known in England as "For he's a jolly good fellow" and here as "We won't go home until morning," which among English-speaking white peoples is the ceremonial hymn to male fellowship. . . . The whole musical material of the work is, as we say in the Middle West, "Common as Dick's hatband"; and its relation to the incidents of the story is, I hope, obvious.

Artur Rodzinski conducted the concert premiere of the Ballet Suite at a New York Philharmonic-Symphony on Dec. 14, 1941.

R. C. B.

Ernst Toch

BORN: VIENNA, DEC. 7, 1887.

*There must be form—the outer shape dictated by a work's inner
organic life. That form will present, in some aspect, a struggle between
differing concepts. There must be a curve as inevitable as the trajectory
of a shell.*—ERNST TOCH.

"Big Ben": Variation Fantasy on the Westminster Chimes

WRITTEN IN New York during the fall of 1934, while the composer was on the
staff of the New School for Social Research, this work was given its first
performance by the Boston Symphony Orchestra on Dec. 20, of that year.

Dr. Toch visited England in 1933 and 1934. On one of those fog-enshrouded
evenings, he was walking across the Westminster Bridge in London. As he did
so he heard the deep-toned chimes of Big Ben announcing the hour. Though
he had listened to them on many other occasions, they seemed now to be
especially strange and moving, muffled, as they were, in the mist that blanketed
the river Thames. There and then he hit on the idea to compose a fantasy in
variation form, basing it on the memorable song of Big Ben.

Dr. Toch has described the impressions he received on that foggy midnight
and, discussing the genesis of his work, he has said: "The familiar theme
lingered in my imagination for a long while, and evolved into other forms,
somehow still connected with the original one, until, finally, like the chimes
themselves, it seemed to disappear in the fog from which it emerged. I have
sought to fix the impression in my Variation Fantasy."

The score calls for two flutes, piccolo, two oboes, English horn, two clarinets
in B flat, clarinet in E flat, two bassoons, four horns, four trumpets, three
trombones, bass tuba, tympani, low chimes (E-D-C-G), small chimes, large
drum, side drum, cymbals, xylophone, triangle, castanets, two small Chinese
wood drums, tam-tam, celesta, harp, and strings.

The piece begins and ends with the statement of the Westminster chimes,
played against figures in the violins and, later, against a roll of the tympani
and small drums. Variations are suggested, here and there, through the juxtaposition of different tempi.

Ernst Toch came of a family of merchants. He seems to have been the only
one of the line to turn to music for a career. He attended the Vienna Conservatory of Music and subsequently, by way of a scholarship, the Conservatory at
Frankfurt-am-Main. He taught at the Mannheim Hochschule für Musik until

the beginning of the First World War when he enlisted in the Austrian army, serving in the infantry on both the Italian and Russian fronts.

On his return to civilian life he took up composing and soon earned wide renown. He has written a number of operas, orchestral music, chamber music, and pieces incidental to stage productions. Latterly he has written several scores for films.

R. C. B.

"Pinocchio, A Merry Overture"

WHILE VISITING Alvin Johnson, director of the New School for Social Research in New York in 1935, Ernst Toch became acquainted with Carlo Collodi's famous story of the puppet Pinocchio. Mr. Toch had been teaching at the New School. He promptly decided to write an overture on the subject of Pinocchio. The "merry" result of his decision is dedicated to Mr. and Mrs. Johnson.

On the title page of the score is printed the following stanza:

> Italian lore would have us know
> That gay marionette Pinocchio!
> With deviltry and gamin grace
> He led them all a merry chase.

Readers of *Pinocchio* will wonder at the interpretation of the pathetic little misfit who is its subject as a "gay" marionette instinct "with deviltry and gamin grace."

The score also carries this description of the animated puppet:

Pinocchio is a legendary figure in Italian folklore created by Carlo Collodi. According to the story, he was fashioned by old Gepetto, a wood carver, from a curiously animated piece of wood. His rascally demeanor and mischievous escapades gave his creator many an anxious moment. His particular failing was fibbing, each lie prompting his already long nose to grow longer. He is a sort of brother-in-mischief to the German Till Eulenspiegel. To this day Italian children are warned by their elders that their noses will grow as long as Pinocchio's if they do not tell the truth.

The work is scored for two flutes, piccolo, two oboes, two clarinets, two bassoons, two trumpets, two horns, three trombones, kettledrums, triangle, side drum, cymbals, xylophone, and the usual strings.

Peter Ilyitch Tschaikowsky

BORN: VOTKINSK, MAY 7, 1840. DIED: ST. PETERSBURG, NOV. 6, 1893.

Because of its opportunities for soul expansion, music has ever attracted the strong, free sons of earth. The most profound truths, the most blasphemous things, the most terrible ideas, may be incorporated within the walls of a symphony, and the police be none the wiser. Supposing that some Russian professional supervisor of artistic anarchy really knew what arrant doctrines Tschaikowsky preached! It is its freedom from the meddlesome hand of the censor that makes of music a playground for great brave souls.—JAMES GIBBONS HUNEKER.

Symphony in C minor, No. 2, Op. 17

I. Andante sostenuto; Allegro vivo. II. Andantino marziale, quasi moderato. III. Scherzo: Allegro molto vivace. IV. Finale: Moderato assai.

EMBEDDED IN Tschaikowsky's Second Symphony is one of the little ironies of Russian music. Though at one time close to it, Tschaikowsky was never identified with the school of Russian nationalism launched by "The Five"—Balakireff, Rimsky-Korsakoff, Cui, Borodin, and Moussorgsky. In fact, critical spokesmen of the group later denounced Tschaikowsky's music as eclectic, Western, non-Russian. They taunted him with being drawn to German and Italian models, rather than to native sources for inspiration. Much of their criticism reads like a patriotic tirade against some dangerous renegade. Yet, Tschaikowsky's Second Symphony is drenched in Russian color. The themes of the first and last movement are based on "Little Russian" (*Malorusski*) folk melodies, whence the term "Little Russian Symphony," often used as a descriptive subtitle for the C minor. For a time "The Five," the self-styled *Koochka* (literally, "little heap or huddle") of Russian nationalism, hailed the Symphony as a token of Tschaikowsky's conversion. But not for long. The cleavage widened again, relations became strained, and Tschaikowsky resolved to continue along his own path. How sharp the divergence grew may be gathered from a passage in a letter to his brother written only one year after the Moscow premiere of the Second Symphony. There he speaks of Moussorgsky's music as "the lowest, commonest parody of music; it may go to the devil for all I care." In retrospect, the controversy between the "Westerns" and the "Nationals" of nineteenth-century Russian music seems futile and regrettable. The concert repertory, indifferent to the claims of "schools," has found room for their best compositions. And both Russian and non-Russian audiences would now probably agree in finding Tschaikowsky's music no less "national" in feeling and content than that of "The Five." As a matter of fact, for many he is the Russian composer par excellence, though others would insist on Moussorgsky, whose strong, rugged music is said to reflect best the sturdy, irrepressible spirit of Russia.

As in the case of the poet Homer, several cities might lay claim to having had the Second Symphony cradled there. The process of composing and revising the work is a tale of five cities. Even Rome is included. Tschaikowsky began the Symphony at Kamenka, in June, 1872. Work on it continued at Ussovo while Tschaikowsky was visiting a sick friend. Back in Moscow in November, we find him apologizing to his brother for a long delay in writing: "What can I do when the Symphony, which is nearing completion, occupies me so entirely that I can think of nothing else? . . . It seems to me to be my best work, at least as regards correctness of form, a quality for which I have not so far distinguished myself." Early in January, Tschaikowsky showed the manuscript to Rimsky-Korsakoff in St. Petersburg. Some alterations followed. On Feb. 7, 1873, Nicholas Rubinstein led the Imperial Musical Society in the world premiere of the C minor. "My Symphony met with great success," writes Tschaikowsky to V. Stassoff the following day. "So great in fact, that N. Rubinstein is repeating it at the tenth concert, 'by general request.'" He then confesses he is not quite satisfied with the first two movements. Yet, the Finale, based partly on "The Crane," a "Little Russian" folk song, "has turned out admirably." On Mar. 9, Napravnik conducted the new score in St. Petersburg. Most of the "Koochka" received it warmly. Not Cesar Cui, however. This dread paladin of the pen, something of a Hanslick of Russia, pounced ruthlessly on the new Symphony:

The Introduction and first Allegro are very weak; the poverty of Tschaikowsky's invention displays itself every moment. The March in the second movement is rough and commonplace. The Scherzo is neither good nor bad; the Trio is so innocent that it would be almost too infantile for a *Sniegourotchka*. The best movement is the Finale, and even then the opening is as pompously trivial as the introduction to a *pas de deux,* and the end is beneath all criticism.

Whether goaded by Cui's strictures or by his own powers of self-criticism, Tschaikowsky revised the Symphony. Six years later, he writes to Mme. von Meck, from Rome: "Today I set out to remodel my Second Symphony. How much seven years can mean when a man is striving for progress in his work! Is it possible that seven years hence I shall look upon what I write today as I look now at my music written in 1872? I know it is possible because perfection —the ideal—is boundless."

One of the earliest American appraisals of Tschaikowsky's Second Symphony, first rendered here by the New York Symphony Society in 1883, was that of the noted critic and essayist, James Gibbons Huneker. He wrote:

In it Tschaikowsky begins to reveal his skill in orchestration, and the themes of the first movement are all strong; at least two of its movements are not symphonic in character. The first Allegro, the strongest, is very Russian in thematic quality. The entire movement is characterized by a bizarre freedom, even recklessness. But there can be no doubt about the skill of its maker. The fantastic *Durchführungsatz* and the melancholy beauty of the opening—and very Slavic theme—are intimations of the greater Tschaikowsky who came later. He omits the slow movement and marches us to the lilting rhythms of Raff and Gounod. The harmonies are more piquant, for the Russian wields a marvelous color brush. It is a clever episode, yet hardly weighty enough for symphonic treatment. For that matter neither is the banal march in Raff's *Lenore Symphony*. The Scherzo that follows is in the Saint-Saëns style. It reveals plenty of spirit and there is the diabolic, riotous energy that pricks the nerves, yet never strikes fire in our souls. . . . The Finale is very charming, and the variation-making genius of the composer peeps out. The movement has the whirl and glow of some wild dance mood, and over all Tschaikowsky has cast the spell of his wondrous orchestration. In the work are potentialities that are realized in his later symphonic works. It is our beloved Tschaikowsky, but as yet in precipitation. In style immature, there is much groping after effects—effects which he used with such a sure touch in *Hamlet* and *Francesca*. Those piano staccato chords for the brass choir, a genuine mannerism, are already here, and his fondness for chromatic scales, contrapuntally used, may be noted. An interesting symphony!

I. A long introduction (Andante sostenuto, C minor, 4/4) built partly on a typical Slavic theme, elegiac in mood, precedes the main section (Allegro vivo) of the first movement. Violins announce the principal subject, with other strings accompanying. The orchestra develops the material before the oboe brings in a second theme, of lyric and mellow character, supported by clarinets and bassoons. Violas and cellos pick up the theme, as the violins counter with one of their own. Fragments of the folk-line melody first used in the Introduction are heard again in the coda, which dwindles back to an Andante sostenuto.

II. The second movement (Andantino marziale, quasi moderato, E flat major, 4/4) opens and closes to a roll of tympani rhythms. Clarinets and bassoon join in the opening march theme, taken from Tschaikowsky's unpublished opera *Undine,* which the St. Petersburg Opera turned down in 1869. First violins give out the second theme, *espressivo,* repeated by bassoons and cellos. Then the march theme is back. Both subjects are developed fully. The march is stated again brilliantly by the orchestra, and the movement fades out to the returning beat of the kettledrums.

III. Brimming with rollicking rhythms and sharp changes of mood, the Scherzo (Allegro molto vivace, C minor, 3/8) opens with the first theme in the violins. Descending chromatics in the second violins and violas lead to the second subject, also assigned to the first violins. There is a repetition of the first theme and the trio begins (L'istesso tempo, E flat major, 2/8). This is based on a simple song of Slavic flavor, first chanted by horns and wood winds. There is some whimsical bandying about of the material, ending in a crisp exchange between wood winds and strings. The Scherzo section returns, leading to a coda containing echoes of the trio theme.

IV. After an introductory passage (Moderato assai), the Finale gets under way with the first violins announcing the chief theme (Allegro vivo, C major, 2/4). This is the little tune "The Crane," which, more than anything else, prompted Nicholas Kashkin to christen the C minor the "Little Russian Symphony." A plain, eight-bar melody, it undergoes varied, shifting treatment, before the strings introduce a second theme, more expressive and Tschaikowsky's own this time. This, too, is subjected to interesting variation. Both themes are heard again in succession, finally combined. The material is worked up with furious verve in a brilliant Presto, where the first theme has the last word.

L. B.

Symphony in F minor, No. 4, Op. 36

I. Andante sostenuto; Moderato con anima in movimento di valse. II. Andantino in modo di canzona. III. Scherzo: Pizzicato ostinato; Allegro. IV. Finale: Allegro con fuoco.

At first sight, this Symphony arouses no *cherchez-la-femme* mystery. Seemingly, the lady is not far to seek. In fact, Tschaikowsky throws off the search in his dedication. The lady is Madame Nadia Filaretovna von Meck. She was his loyal confidante and benefactress. The least Tschaikowsky could do was to dedicate a symphony to her. Comfort and encouragement in the form of checks and adulatory letters from Mme. von Meck saw the sorrowing Slav through many bleak periods.

The association has been called "the most amazing romance in musical history." That the "romance" was purely platonic does not make it any the less "amazing." Whatever Mme. von Meck's secret hopes and longings, Tschaikowsky shrank from carrying the liaison beyond an epistolary scope. Mme. von Meck resigned herself to an advisory role of patroness friend, and played it nobly. The world reveres her for it. *"Our* symphony," Tschaikowsky wrote to her, communicating his intention to dedicate the Fourth to her. "I believe you will find it in echoes of your deepest thoughts and feelings."

What Tschaikowsky meant, of course, was *"my* deepest thoughts and feelings." The plural possessive *"ours"* is gallant rather than collaborative. Even so, he could with more truth than courtesy have written to another woman, Antonina Ivanovna Miliukov, in similar style. Antonina was Tschaikowsky's wife in a domestic farce lasting two weeks. The whole episode—spanning a wild sequence of engagement, marriage, flight in the night, attempted suicide, separation—nestles snugly in the period of the Symphony's origin. Antonina would have understood the words *"our* symphony." Only fate and brother Anatol saved it from becoming Tschaikowsky's obituary. Not that it was Antonina's fault. Far from it. But no psychological analysis of the Fourth can be complete without her.

The girl was a conservatory pupil. Tschaikowsky's music had begun to act like a potion upon her, and through it she had come to a slavish, fanatic worship of the composer. Next followed written avowals of passion which at first amused Tschaikowsky, then alarmed him, and finally, as they became frantic, haunted him. The girl was persistent, and as her pleas became more frequent, they grew more piteous and despairing. To make matters worse, the sensitive Tschaikowsky was immersed at the time in his romantic opera *Eugene Onegin*. He had just composed music for Tatiana's impassioned love letter to Onegin. Antonina's own plight was too much like the spurned Tatiana's to be lost on Tschaikowsky's susceptible nature. Onegin's cold disdain had virtually wrecked the girl's life, and it suddenly dawned on the composer that Antonina might even kill herself. In a moment of dramatic self-analysis, he probably saw himself as another and more heartless Onegin. The situation was not unflattering to his vanity.

At length, he made a courteous offer of friendship, but the gesture only stirred up more trouble. After studious delay, Tschaikowsky finally granted the long-sought meeting. Antonina was convinced she had won. Tschaikowsky depicted himself to her as a morose, ill-tempered neurotic who would assuredly drive her mad. But the girl was not to be balked of her prey: there was only one way out—marriage. With a sigh of helplessness, Tschaikowsky gave in, and they were soon engaged. Attempts to break the engagement proved futile, for Antonina was bent on becoming Mrs. Tschaikowsky at all costs. They were married, and in a few lurid days Tschaikowsky had already fled for his sanity. Then came a reconciliation, and now followed two dreadful weeks of tragico-farcical life together in Moscow. One night, in a wild daze, Tschaikowsky fled again, wandering about wildly till he reached the Moscow River. He had made up his mind. He waded in till he stood waist deep in the cold water, hoping to freeze to death. Luckily, he was seen standing there and rescued in time.

Though for long he bordered on insanity, somehow the bewildered composer came through the crisis with his reason intact. His brother Anatol took him to Switzerland, and slowly Tschaikowsky returned to his normal self. He never saw Antonina Ivanovna again. The clinical aspects of this curious mesalliance have been thoroughly aired in recent years. Through the publication of long-withheld letters, fresh light was thrown on Tschaikowsky's temperament. It is obvious, and should have been obvious to all who knew Tschaikowsky well, that Antonina and he were mentally and physically incompatible. The gentleman to the end, Tschaikowsky never made a harsh reference to his wife. And Antonina, for her part, graciously cleared him in her memoirs. Reviewing the whole episode in temperate tones, she observed, "Peter was in no way to blame."

During this period, which extends from May to September, 1877, Tschaikowsky worked on his Fourth Symphony. Just how much of his private woes was transmuted into symphonic speech cannot be determined, even from Tschaikowsky's own written confidences. Possibly, the Symphony was an avenue of escape from his mounting anxieties. Anyway his completion of the sketch coincides with his engagement to Antonina in May. The orchestration of the first movement took up a month, from Aug. 11 to Sept. 12—the breathing spell between his two flights from Antonina. Then followed the nerve-racking fortnight in Moscow. The other three movements were completed in the Swiss Alps, where, thanks to his brother, he regained his full sanity and working tempo. A passage in a letter to Mme. von Meck, during the Antonina regime, suggests an explanation of Tschaikowsky's abstract talk of Fate in connection with his Fourth: "We cannot escape our fate, and there was something fatalistic about my meeting with this girl." In January, 1878, when the whole dismal affair was safely locked away in the past, he wrote to Mme. von Meck that he could only recall his marriage as a bad dream:

Something remote, a weird nightmare in which a man bearing my name, my likeness, and my consciousness acted as one acts in dreams: in a meaningless, disconnected, paradoxical way. That was not my sane self, in possession of logical and reasonable will powers. Everything I then did bore the character of an unhealthy conflict between will and intelligence, which is nothing less than insanity.

Tschaikowsky wrote to the composer Tanieff that there was not a single bar in his Fourth Symphony which he had not truly felt and which was not an echo of his "most intimate self." He frankly avowed the Symphony's "programmatic" character, but declared that it was "impossible to give the program in words." Yet, to Mme. von Meck, who insisted on knowing the full spiritual and emotional content of the Symphony, he wrote out a detailed analysis which has long been familiar to concert audiences. In reading it the listener usually does one of three things: takes it literally; regards it as irrelevant to the music as such; relates it to Tschaikowsky's private life. There is the fourth choice of combining all three. In that choice lies the synthesis of mind, emotion, and external stimuli which is regarded as the very essence of art.

Our Symphony has a program. That is to say, it is possible to express its contents in words, and I will tell you—and you alone—the meaning of the entire work and its separate movements. Naturally I can only do so as regards its general features.

The Introduction is the kernel, the quintessence, the chief thought of the whole Symphony. This is Fate, the fatal power which hinders one in the pursuit of happiness from gaining the goal, which jealously provides that peace and comfort do not prevail, that the sky is not free from clouds—a might that swings, like the sword of Damocles, constantly over the head, that poisons continually the soul. This might is overpowering and invincible. There is nothing to do but to submit and vainly to complain.

The second movement shows another phase of sadness. Here is that melancholy feeling which enwraps one when he sits at night alone in the house exhausted by work; the book which he had taken to read has slipped from his hand; a swarm of reminiscences has arisen. How sad it is that so much has already *been* and *gone!* And yet it is a pleasure to think of the early years. One mourns the past and has neither the courage nor the will to begin a new life. One is rather tired of life.

There is no determined feeling, no exact expression in the third movement. Here are capricious arabesques, vague figures which slip into the imagination when one has taken wine and is slightly intoxicated. The mood is now gay, now mournful. One thinks about nothing; one gives the fancy loose rein, and there is pleasure in drawings of marvellous lines. Suddenly rush into the imagination the picture of a drunken peasant and a gutter song. Military music is heard passing by in the distance. These are disconnected pictures which come and go in the brain of the sleeper. They have nothing to do with reality; they are unintelligible, bizarre, out at the elbows.

Fourth movement. If you had no pleasure in yourself, look about you. Go to the people. See how they can enjoy life and give themselves up entirely to festivity. The picture of a folk holiday. Hardly have we had time to forget ourselves in the happiness of others when indefatigable Fate reminds us once more of its presence. The other children of men are not concerned with us. They do not spare us a glance nor stop to observe that we are lonely and sad. How merry and glad they all are. All their feelings are so inconsequent, so simple. And you will still say that all the world is immersed in sorrow? There still *is* happiness, simple, native happiness. Rejoice in the happiness of others—and you can still live.

L. B.

Symphony in E minor, No. 5, Op. 64

I. Andante: Allegro con anima. II. Andante cantabile, con alcuna licenza. III. Valse: Allegro moderato. IV. Finale: Andante maestoso; Allegro vivace.

IF SURROUNDINGS alone determined the mood of a piece of music, Tschaikowsky's Fifth Symphony, composed one summer in a country villa near Klin, would be a sunlit idyl. Of course it is nothing of the sort, for though Tschaikowsky responded keenly to outdoor beauty, he was a prey to gloomy thoughts and visions that constantly found their way into his music. His own inner world crowded out the other. Frolovskoe, where he wrote his Symphony in 1888, was a charming spot, fringed by a forest. Between spurts of composing he took long walks in the woods and puttered around the villa garden.

On his return from Italy two years later he found that the forest had been cut down. "All those dear shady spots that were there last year are now a bare wilderness," he grieved to his brother Modeste. This is nothing to what he would say if he saw the vandalized Tschaikowsky museum at Klin, completely wrecked by Hitler's retreating hordes and subsequently restored by the Soviet government. Ironically, Tschaikowsky also composed his *Hamlet Overture* in the sylvan retreat at Frolovskoe, though from his own and others' description, the place was a better setting for an "As You Like It" symphonic fantasy, say.

The first intimation that Tschaikowsky was considering a new symphony appears in a letter to his brother Modeste dated May 27, 1888. A dread that he had written himself out as composer had been steadily gaining a grip on Tschaikowsky's mind. He had complained about his imagination being "dried up." He felt no urge to write. Finally he resolved to shake off the mood and convince the world and himself there were still a few good tunes in him.

"I am hoping to collect, little by little, material for a symphony," he writes to his brother on May 27. The following month we find him inquiring of his lady bountiful, Nadia von Meck, "Have I told you that I intended to write a symphony? The beginning has been difficult; but now inspiration seems to have come. However, we shall see." In the same letter he makes no bones about his intention to prove that he is not "played out as a composer."

On Aug. 6 he reported progress on the new work. "I have orchestrated half the symphony," he writes. "My age, although I am not very old, begins to tell on me. I become very tired, and I can no longer play the piano or read at night as I used to do." Ill health troubled him during the summer months, but by Aug. 26 he was able to announce the completion of the Symphony. At first he was dissatisfied with it. Even the favorable verdict of a group of musical friends, among them Taneieff, did no good.

Early performances of the Symphony only strengthened Tschaikowsky's misgivings. The work was premiered in St. Petersburg on Nov. 17, 1888, with Tschaikowsky conducting. A second performance followed on Nov. 24, at a concert of the Musical Society, with the composer again conducting. Then came a performance in Prague. The public was enthusiastic. The critics, on the other hand, almost unanimously attacked it as unworthy of Tschaikowsky's powers. In a letter to Mme. von Meck in December he expressed frank disgust with the Symphony:

Having played my Symphony twice in Petersburg and once in Prague, I have come to the conclusion that it is a failure. There is something repellent in it, some over-exaggerated color, some insincerity of fabrication which the public instinctively recognizes. It was clear to me that the applause and ovations referred not to this but to other works of mine, and that the Symphony itself will never please the public. All this causes a deep dissatisfaction with myself.

It is possible that I have, as people say, written myself out, and that nothing remains but for me to repeat and imitate myself. Yesterday evening I glanced over the Fourth Symphony, *our* symphony. How superior to this one, how much better it is! Yes, this is a very, very sad fact.

A composer who was still to write the *Hamlet* overture fantasy, the *Sleeping Beauty* and *Nutcracker* ballets, the opera *Pique Dame,* and the *Pathetic Symphony* was anything but "written out," as Tschaikowsky feared!

After the Symphony triumphed in both Moscow and Hamburg, Tschaikowsky speedily changed him mind and wrote to his publisher Davidoff: "I like it far better now, after having held a bad opinion of it for some time." He speaks of the Hamburg performance as "magnificent," but expresses his old complaint about the Russian press, that it "continues to ignore me," and bemoans the fact that "with the exception of those nearest and dearest to me, no one will ever hear of my successes." Modeste Tschaikowsky attributed the work's early failure in Petersburg (*i.e.,* with the critics) to his brother's poor conducting.

The assumed programmatic content of the Fifth Symphony has aroused much speculation. Most analysts are convinced that Tschaikowsky had a definite autobiographical plan in mind. Yet he left no descriptive analysis such as we have of the Fourth Symphony. There he had set out to depict the "inexorableness of fate." One Russian writer discerned "some dark spiritual experience" in the Fifth. "Only at the close," he observed, "the clouds lift, the sky clears, and we see the blue stretching pure and clear beyond."

Ernest Newman spoke of the sinister motto theme first announced in the opening movement as "the leaden, deliberate tread of fate." Many have agreed with Newman in classing the Fifth with the Fourth as another "fate" symphony.

"The Symphony begins with a bodeful phrase, announced by the clarinets against chords in the strings. The phrase is reiterated in the course of the first three movements, now with imperious emphasis, now like a veiled but ominous threat. It might be likened to the greeting of the Trappist monks: 'Brother, remember death!'

"In the Finale the motto phrase, which has appeared like a sinister intruder, an unwelcome guest at the musical feast, emerges as the chief thematic factor, not only of the introduction to the Finale, but of the whole movement. Here, however, it is expanded in form and presented not in the minor but in the major.

"After the prefatory Andante (E minor, 4/4) the first movement proper follows (Allegro con anima, 6/8). The principal subject, given out by clarinet and bassoon in octaves, is said to stem from a Polish folk song.

"The second movement (Andante cantabile, con alcuna licenza, D major, 12/8) is a lyrical romanza. The songlike chief subject is allotted first to a horn, then to a cello, and afterward to a body of strings. Twice the flow of the music is interrupted by the Symphony's menacing motto.

"Instead of a scherzo the third movement offers a graceful waltz (Allegro moderato, A major, 3/4). But before it has danced its course, clarinets and bassoons intone the theme of 'fate' as from a distance.

"The Finale (Andante maestoso, E major, 4/4; Allegro vivace, E minor, 2/2), in which the 'fate' theme appears in the major, is traditionally supposed to depict a psychological reversal—defeat turning into triumph. Yet others, less optimistic, whatever Tschaikowsky himself may have intended, hear the pomp and frenzy as of a madman who imagines himself king."

The Symphony is scored for three flutes (one interchangeable with piccolo), two oboes, two clarinets, two bassoons, four horns, two trumpets, three trombones, tuba, three kettledrums, and the strings as usual.

L. B.

Symphony in B minor, No. 6 ("Pathetic"), Op. 74

I. Adagio; Allegro non troppo. II. Allegro con grazia. III. Allegro molto vivace. IV. Finale: Adagio lamentoso.

SOMETIME BEFORE he wrote the *Pathetic,* Tschaikowsky had partially composed a Sixth Symphony. First drafts were done on his return voyage from America in the spring of 1891. However, the unpredictable Tschaikowsky tore up the manuscript in one of his frequent moods of depression and doubt over his alleged inability to create. In December, 1882, he wrote to his nephew Davidow, "The symphony is only a work written by dint of sheer will on the part of the composer; it contains nothing that is interesting or sympathetic. It should be cast aside and forgotten. This determination on my part is admirable and irrevocable."

We first hear of the *Pathetic Symphony*—which, by the way, had not yet been given that name—in another of Tschaikowsky's letters, this time to his brother Anatol (February, 1893). He says:

I am now wholly occupied with the new work . . . and it is hard for me to tear myself away from it. I believe it comes into being as the best of my works. I must finish it as soon as possible, for I have to wind up a lot of affairs and I must soon go to London. I told you that I had completed a Symphony which suddenly displeased me, and I tore it up. Now I have composed a new symphony *which I certainly shall not tear up.*

He more fully explains his intentions regarding this new work in a letter to Davidow written the following day. He describes his joy with the projected Symphony; he tells of a mysterious program associated with it—"let them guess it who can." He relates how speedily he composes, how novel is the form, how persuaded he is that "his day is not yet over," and so on. Yet, as it turned out, later progress on the Symphony proved scarcely as rapid as he had envisioned, for in August, 1893, we find him "sitting all day over two pages."

The Symphony was composed in a little two-story house at Klin. He found contentment in the secluded surroundings, for the dwelling and its pretty garden were situated in a wood not far from the high road to Moscow. On Oct. 19, he left Klin forever (though he did not know it then). He went to Moscow to attend a funeral where he met his friend Kashkin. They talked of life and death, Tschaikowsky, oddly enough, being in particularly lively spirits. "I told Peter," said Kashkin, "that he would outlive us all. He disputed the likelihood, yet he added that never had he felt so well and happy." The conversation took another turn when the composer asserted his strong belief in the first three movements of the Symphony, adding, however, that he was doubtful about the last. He even suggested that after the premiere he might destroy the Finale and write a new one.

When he arrived in St. Petersburg he was still in excellent spirits, looking forward eagerly to the day of the first performance. Mercurial soul that he was, though, he soon became morose when it seemed that the musicians did not respond to the Symphony at rehearsals. Tschaikowsky had always held great stock in the reactions of orchestra men, conducting well when he felt they admired his music. We are told, "A cool facial expression, an indifferent glance, a yawn—these tied his hands; he lost his readiness of mind, he went over the work carelessly, and cut short the rehearsal, that the players might be freed from their boresome work." And all the time Tschaikowsky knew that he had never composed and never would compose a greater symphony than this.

The introductory performance took place, finally, on Oct. 28, Tschaikowsky conducting. "There was applause and the composer was recalled," says Modeste Tschaikowsky, "but with more enthusiasm than on previous occasions. There was not the mighty, overpowering impression made by the work when it was conducted by Napravnik, on Nov. 18, 1893 [twelve days after Tschaikowsky's death] and later, wherever it was played."

After the world premiere the composer sat at a tea table in a thoughtful mood. He told Modeste that the Symphony was shortly to go to the publisher and that he regretted not having coined a title for it. "No. 6" seemed too lonely by itself and "Program Symphony" appealed to him not at all. He asked, "What does 'Program Symphony' mean when I will give it no program?" Modeste, in a helpful spirit, suggested the title "Tragic," which Peter turned down. "I left the room before he had come to a decision," Modeste tells us.

"Suddenly I thought, 'Pathetic,' I went back to the room—I remember it as though it were yesterday—and I said the word to Peter. 'Splendid, Modi, bravo, *Pathetic*,' and he wrote in my presence the title that will forever remain."

On Nov. 1, Tschaikowsky went to a performance of *A Warm Heart,* a play by Ostrowsky. He visited the actor Warlamov's dressing room later and, somehow or other, the talk turned to spiritualism. Warlamov protested laughingly against "those abominations which remind one of death."

"There is plenty of time," interposed Tschaikowsky, "before we have to reckon with this snub-nosed horror; it will not come to snatch us off just yet! I feel that I shall live a long time." Five days later he was dead, a victim of the dread cholera.

The mystery of the Symphony's program, of course, will never be solved, though some have sensed in it the composer's presentiment of death. Kashkin deems it logical

to interpret the overwhelming energy of the third movement and the abysmal sorrow of the Finale in the broader light of a national or historical significance, rather than to narrow them to the expression of an individual experience. If the last movement is intended to be predictive, it is surely of things vaster and issues more fatal than are contained in a mere personal apprehension of death. It speaks, rather, of a *lamentation large et souffrance inconnue,* and seems to set the seal of finality on all human hopes. Even if we eliminate the purely subjective interest, this autumnal inspiration of Tschaikowsky's, in which we hear "the ground whirl of the perished leaves of hope, still remains the most profoundly stirring of his works."

R. C. B.

Concerto for Piano and Orchestra in B flat minor, No. 1, Op. 23

I. Allegro non troppo e molto maestoso; Allegro con spirito. II. Andantino semplice; Allegro vivace assai. III. Allegro con fuoco.

It took something like a month for Tschaikowsky to compose this exceedingly popular work of his. He began seriously on it in November, 1874. The next month it was finished. Eager and excited over his accomplishment, he yet deemed it important to get a professional opinion, so he asked his friend and patron Nicholas Rubinstein and another colleague at the Moscow Conservatory, Nicolai Albertovich Hubert, to listen to it. This private performance was given in one of the classrooms of the Conservatory on Christmas Eve.

Tschaikowsky played through the whole work, expecting an occasional word of approval or otherwise from his noted guests. None was forthcoming. Impatient, he turned to Rubinstein and urged him to express his thoughts. They came—all too vehemently. Rubinstein, in a fiery tirade, piled abuse after abuse upon it. He called it unpianistic, tawdry, mostly derivative, and the like. He sat at the piano and cavorted through a good bit of it, burlesque fashion.

Tschaikowsky thus described the following scene:

I left the room without a word and went upstairs. I could not have spoken for anger and agitation. Presently Rubinstein came to me and, seeing how upset I was, called me into another room. There he repeated that my Concerto was impossible, pointed out many places where it needed to be completely revised, and said that if I would suit the Concerto to his requirements, he would bring it out at his concert. "I shall not alter a single note," I replied, "I shall publish the work precisely as it stands." This intention I actually carried out.

Actually Tschaikowsky did make alterations, a number of them proposed, it is alleged, by Edward Dannreuther, who first played it in London.

What the composer did after that historical private session any resourceful man would have done. He cast about for some other pianistic luminary, someone important enough to give the required prestige to his work. Hans von Bülow, who had labored much for the cause of Tschaikowsky in Germany, was suggested to him, and he acted upon that suggestion immediately.

Bülow, in a letter of thanks, went completely rhapsodic over the Concerto. He wrote:

The ideas are so original, so noble, so powerful; the details are so interesting, and though there are many of them, they do not impair the clearness and the unity of the work. The form is so mature, ripe, distinguished in style, for intention and labor are everywhere concealed. I should weary you if I were to enumerate all the characteristics of your work—characteristics which compel me to congratulate equally the composer, as well as all those who shall enjoy actively or passively (respectively) the work.

The pendulum had swung to the other end of its arc. Bülow played it in Boston, the world premiere, on Oct. 25, 1875. American audiences waxed enthusiastic, and Tschaikowsky was no end delighted by the reports from overseas. He also found amusement in some of the reviews of the performance. He quoted, perhaps with cruel pleasure, some of the statements made. He said:

The Americans think that the first movement of my Concerto "suffers in consequence of the absence of a central idea"—and in the finale this reviewer has found "syncopation in trills, spasmodic pauses in the theme, and disturbing octave passages"! Think what healthy appetites these Americans must have: each time Bülow was obliged to repeat the whole finale of my Concerto! Nothing like this happens in our country!

However, there were further victories in store for Tschaikowsky. A most impressive one was Rubinstein's thorough disavowal of his earlier opinions and his capitulation to the Concerto's charms. He played it in public, thereafter, and made a huge success with it.

It may have been Tschaikowsky's star to have such things happen to him, for we come upon almost the same circumstances with respect to a work of later vintage, the Violin Concerto. The composer had dedicated it to Leopold Auer, but the celebrated violinist did Tschaikowsky the small service of pronouncing it unplayable when he first saw it. Later, though, he not only performed it many times himself—eating his own words with gusto—but he taught it to his many pupils, showing that as a verbal trencherman he had few equals.

An interesting side light on the Piano Concerto's first performance is the circus-barker announcement printed in the program on that eventful occasion:

The above grand composition of Tschaikowsky, the most eminent Russian maestro of the present day, completed last April [*sic*] and dedicated by its author to Hans von Bülow, *has never been performed,* the composer himself never having enjoyed an audition of his masterpiece. To Boston is reserved the honor of its initial representation and the opportunity to impress the first verdict on a work of surpassing musical interest.

Besides the Concerto, Bülow played Liszt's arrangement of the C major Fantasie by Schubert and Beethoven's Sonata, Op. 27, No. 2. The other numbers on that program consisted of the Overture to Spohr's *Jessonda,* the Beethoven *Prometheus* Overture and the Wedding March from Mendelssohn's *Midsummer Night's Dream* music.

"The Concerto begins with a long introduction (Allegro non troppo e molto maestoso, D flat major, 3/4). The imposing theme of this introduction is one of the most deservedly renowned of all Tschaikowsky's melodies. After a few prefatory measures the strings announce it. Then, somewhat altered rhythmically, the solo instrument repeats it. After a cadenza for the piano, all the strings, except the double basses, give it out for a third time, while the piano provides an obbligato of ascending chords. To the regret of most listeners, Tschaikowsky never reverts to this theme.

"The main body of the movement (Allegro con spirito, B flat minor, 4/4) has as chief subject, introduced by the piano, a melody that is commonly known as the 'blind-beggar tune.' It is called so because the first part of it Tschaikowsky heard sung at Kamenko by a blind beggar. To Mme. von Meck the composer wrote: 'It is curious that in Little Russia every blind beggar sings exactly the same tune with the same refrain. I have used part of this refrain in my pianoforte concerto.' The second subject (Poco meno mosso, A flat major) is given to the horns and wood winds, the piano picking it up.

"In the second movement (Andantino semplice, D flat major, 6/8) the flute utters the lyrical first theme. A second theme is given to oboe and clarinets over a drone bass in the bassoons. There is a scherzolike middle section (Prestissimo, F major). Presently violas and cellos interject a waltz. Modeste Tschaikowsky is authority for this tune being the refrain of a French song that his brother Anatol and he had sung and whistled in their youth.

"The Finale (Allegro con fuoco, B flat minor, 3/4) is a rondo based on three themes. The first, announced by the piano, has been likened to a wild Cossack dance. The national flavor is also pronounced in the second subject. The violins give out the third subject, completing the thematic material. The Cossack theme dominates the spirited coda."

R. C. B.

Concerto for Violin and Orchestra in D major, Op. 35

I. Allegro moderato. II. Canzonetta: Andante. III. Finale: Allegro vivacissimo.

Before occupying its permanent niche in the repertory, Tschaikowsky's Violin Concerto had to run a fierce gauntlet of fault-finding. Friend and foe alike took pokes at it. The wonder is that it survived at all. Even Mme. von Meck, Tschaikowsky's patroness-saint, picked serious flaws in the work, and the lady was known for her unwavering faith in Tschaikowsky's genius.

As a matter of fact, Tschaikowsky, often an unsparing critic of his own music, started the trend by finding objection with the Andante and rewriting it whole. That was in April, 1878. He was spending the spring at Clarens, Switzerland. Joseph Kotek, a Russian violinist and composer, was staying with him. Tschaikowsky and Kotek went over the work several times, and evidently saw eye to eye on its merits.

Then came the first outside rebuff. Mme. von Meck was frankly dissatisfied and showed why in detail. Tschaikowsky meekly wrote back pleading guilty on some counts but advancing the hope that in time his Lady Bountiful might come to like the Concerto. He stood pat on the first movement, which Mme. von Meck particularly assailed. He writes:

Your frank judgment on my Violin Concerto pleased me very much. It would have been very disagreeable to me if you, from any fear of wounding the petty pride of a composer, had kept back your opinion. However, I must defend a little the first movement of the Concerto.

Of course, it houses, as does every piece that serves virtuoso purposes, much that appeals chiefly to the mind; nevertheless, the themes are not painfully evolved: the plan of this movement sprang suddenly in my head and quickly ran into its mold. I shall not give up the hope that in time the piece will give you greater pleasure.

Next came a more serious setback from Leopold Auer, the widely respected St. Petersburg virtuoso. Auer was then professor of violin at the Imperial Conservatory and the Czar's court violinist. Tschaikowsky, hoping to induce Auer to launch the Concerto on its career, originally dedicated the work to him. But Auer glanced through the score and promptly decided against it. It was "impossible to play."

Tschaikowsky later made a quaintly worded entry in his diary to the effect that Auer's pronouncement cast "this unfortunate child of my imagination for many years to come into the limbo of hopelessly forgotten things." Justly or unjustly, he even suspected Auer of having prevailed on the violinist Emile Sauret to abstain from playing it in St. Petersburg.

The ice finally broke when Adolf Brodsky, after two years of admitted laziness and indecision, took it up and succeeded in performing it with the Vienna Philharmonic on Dec. 4, 1881. Yet, even Brodsky, despite his wholehearted espousal of the work, complained to Tschaikowsky that he had "crammed too many difficulties into it." Previously, in Paris, Brodsky had experimented with the Concerto by playing it to Laroche, who, whether because of Brodsky's rendering or the Concerto's inherent character, confessed "he could gain no true idea of the work."

Even the premiere went against the new Concerto. In the first place Brodsky had to do some strong propagandizing to get Hans Richter to include the work on a Philharmonic program. Then, only one rehearsal was granted. The orchestral parts, according to Brodsky, "swarmed with errors." At the rehearsal nobody liked the new work. Besides, Richter wanted to make cuts, but Brodsky promptly scotched the idea. Finally, during the performance, the musicians, still far from having mastered the music, accompanied everything pianissimo, "not to go smash."

Of course, Brodsky outlines the chain of contretemps in a letter to Tschaikowsky, partly to assuage the composer's pained feelings on receiving news of the Vienna fiasco. For the premiere ended with a broadside of hisses, completely obliterating the polite applause coming from some friendly quarters. As the *coup de grâce* Eduard Hanslick, Europe's uncrowned ruler of musical destinies, wrote a scathing notice, which has been rendered as follows:

For a while the Concerto has proportion, is musical, and is not without genius, but soon savagery gains the upper hand and lords it to the end of the first movement. The violin is no longer played. It is yanked about. It is torn asunder. It is beaten black and blue. I do not know whether it is possible for any one to conquer these hair-raising difficulties, but I do know that Mr. Brodsky martyrized his hearers as well as himself. The Adagio, with its tender national melody, almost conciliates, almost wins us. But it breaks off abruptly to make way for a Finale that puts us in the midst of the brutal and wretched jollity of a Russian kermess. We see wild and vulgar faces, we hear curses, we smell bad brandy. Friedrich Vischer once asserted in reference to lascivious paintings that there are pictures which "stink in the eye." Tschaikowsky's Violin Concerto brings to us for the first time the horrid idea that there may be music that stinks in the ear.

The jarring echoes of the Hanslick blasts further embittered Tschaikowsky's already gloomy disposition, and it is not surprising to learn that the review haunted him till the day he died. But Brodsky's unflagging devotion to the Concerto, together with his practical missionary zeal in acquainting the European public with it, finally started the Concerto on its path of glory.

"Nor was that the end of time's revenges," wrote Pitts Sanborn. "Hanslick was to write glowingly of the *Pathétique Symphony,* and in due course Leopold Auer not only played the unplayable Concerto himself, but made a specialty of teaching it to his pupils, who have carried its gospel the world over: But while the belated triumphs were accruing Tschaikowsky died."

The dedication is to Brodsky, who certainly earned it.

The first movement (Allegro moderato, D major, 4/4) opens with a melody for strings and wood winds. Then the solo violin is heard in a cadenzalike sequence followed by the first theme (Moderato assai). A second theme, Molto espressivo, is next discoursed by the violin in A major. Instead of the usual development there is an intricate cadenza without accompaniment. A long and brilliant coda concludes the movement.

The second movement (Canzonetta: Andante, 3/4) starts with the muted solo violin chanting, after a brief preface, a nostalgic theme in G minor. The flute and clarinet then offer the first phrase of this theme, and later the solo violin unreels a Chopinesque second subject, in E flat major, con anima. The clarinet is heard in an obbligato of arpeggios when the first theme returns. The rousing Finale in an Allegro vivacissimo in D major, 2/4.

The rondolike last movement, typically Russian in theme and rhythm, develops from two folklike melodies. Listeners will be reminded of the well-known Russian dance, the Trepak, in this movement. The music builds up at a brisk pace to a crashing climax.

L. B.

Theme and Variations from Suite No. 3, in G, Op. 55

Tschaikowsky was seized with the idea of the Suite, of which this Theme and Variations is the fourth and final section, on Apr. 28, 1884. As recorded in his diary, he spent a good part of the day in fruitless attempts to lay the plan for a new symphony. From that day to shortly before the premiere of the work in St. Petersburg, on Jan. 24, of the following year (Hans von Bülow was the conductor), the diary fairly groans under the weight of the composer's lamentations. Inspiration lagged, he complained about the banality of his ideas, about the slow progress of the Suite, about the precious little he had accomplished (he was then 44, and he had already written four symphonies, two piano concertos, a violin concerto, two suites for orchestra, several operas, several quartets, and many songs).

Yet through all this spiritual turmoil, Tschaikowsky could find occasion to admire his own handiwork. On July 12, in a letter to his publisher, he wrote, "A work of greater genius than the new Suite never existed! My opinion of the new-born composition is so optimistic. God knows what I shall say about it next year." (Again a complicated mind at work.)

The Suite met with enormous success at its first hearing. It was given its initial New York performance at a Thomas Popular Concert on Nov. 24, 1885. Tschaikowsky conducted it himself at the Music Festival in the then new Carnegie Hall on May 7, 1891.

The "Theme and Variations" section of the Suite is in G major, 2/4. Its theme is a simple one, given to the first violins, accompanied by chords in the other choirs.

Variation 1. The strings again take the theme here pizzicato, with the flute and clarinet lines running contrapuntally above them.

Variation 2. Fleet passages of thirty-second notes by the first and second violins in unison, accompanied by flutes, oboes, clarinets, bassoons, and horns.

Variation 3. Three flutes, two clarinets, and two bassoons are concerned here, first the subject is announced by a single flute with the clarinet heard subsequently in the continuation of the theme. Polyphonic elaboration is assigned to the other instruments.

Variation 4. The full orchestra launches into the chief thematic material. The key is B minor, pochissimo meno animato. Cellos, clarinets, and English horn supply a special tonal richness.

Variation 5. Allegro vivace, G major, 3/4, for flutes, oboes, clarinets, bassoons, and strings. The first and second portions of the theme act as chief theme, in turn, for a fugato.

Variation 6. The instruments involved in this variation are the same as in the preceding one with the addition of the snare drum. A sonorous tarantella is abruptly ended by the chorallike mood of the next variation.

Variation 7. This is the choral mentioned above, played by the wood winds in 2/4 tempo.

Variation 8. A combination of modal harmony and folkish melody, or the suggestion of that. The violins, divided, play a tremolo, and the English horn is entrusted with a melody sequence.

Variation 9. The violins give out the melody in this variation, which is in A major, allegro molto vivace, 2/4. There is an insistent repetition of two bars of rhythmic import. The tempo speeds up, and the solo violin plays a cadenza which ushers in the next variation.

Variation 10. The solo violin once more is featured, assisted by a chord accompaniment.

Variation 11. A tonic pedal is the foundation for this variation, the basses arriving at a low F sharp, which foreshadows the finale's pedal point.

Variation 12. The finale is a Polacca, moderato maestoso e brillante, 3/4. A festival atmosphere pervades the section. After a short introduction growing out of the low F sharp, there is a crescendo and the Polacca begins. It proceeds with great ceremony and the huge flourish of drum and cymbal crashes. The trumpets and trombones offer fragments of the main theme, and the contrasting melody is supplied by the violins and the violas. A good portion of the introduction, as well as the dance, is repeated. The Variation concludes with a poco più mosso.

R. C. B.

Suite No. 4, "Mozartiana," Op. 61

IN THE temple of music Tschaikowsky worshipped one god above all others —Mozart. Before this god he knelt in lifelong homage. "It is thanks to Mozart that I have devoted my life to music," he wrote. In later years he confessed to a friend: "Do you know that when I play Mozart I feel brighter and younger, almost a youth." A diary entry of May 17, 1884, gives the first mention of what was eventually to become the Russian composer's graceful little offering at the Salzburg shrine: "Played Mozart with great enjoyment. *Idea for a suite from Mozart.*" But the idea incubated slowly. For it was not till three years later, on Aug. 10, 1887, that Tschaikowsky applied the final touches to the *Mozartiana Suite,* at, of all places, Aachen—an odd footnote to the grimmer annals of that historic site. Tschaikowsky had hastened there to be with his friend Kondratiev, who was gravely ill. When the score was published in Moscow later that year, it carried some words of explanation in Russian, French, and German.

"For some incomprehensible reason, several excellent compositions by Mozart are little known not only to the general public but to many musicians," ran Tschaikowsky's preface, dated October 5. "The arranger of this Suite, which is entitled *Mozartiana,* hoped to give a fresh impulse to the playing of these little masterpieces. Though simple in form, they are full of inimitable beauties." (Tschaikowsky's adjective is *nyedosyagayetikh,* literally "beyond reach," "unattainable.") The basic scoring of the Suite is for two flutes, two oboes, two clarinets, two bassoons, four horns, two trumpets, tympani, and strings. In the "Menuet" the horns are reduced to two and the tympani omitted. The "Preghiera" adds a harp. Glockenspiel and cymbals are added in the "Thème et Variations."

I. "Gigue" (Allegro, G minor, 6/8). Tschaikowsky found this music in a collection of twelve piano pieces published in Leipzig by Breitkopf and Härtel. It is No. 11 of the set. Alfred Einstein lists it as Op. 574 in his edition of Köchel's *Chronological Thematic Catalogue* of Mozart's music, where it is called *Eine kleine Gigue für Klavier*. Mozart composed it in Leipzig on May 16, 1789, jotting it down in an album kept by the court organist Engel. This was evidently Mozart's way of paying his respects to Bach, Leipzig's *genius loci,* as Einstein points out. No effort was made to flatter Bach by a strict imitation of style. Divided into two sections, each of which is repeated, the "Gigue" at first follows the patterns of a four-voice fugue, soon loses its strict form and goes its blithe, unhampered way.

II. "Menuet" (Moderato, D major). This is the twelfth in the Breitkopf and Härtel set of piano pieces. Einstein gives it an opus listing of 355, placing its composition in Vienna in 1790. Köchel had dated the minuet ten years earlier. Marked evidence of Mozart's "highest maturity" prompted the later revision of date. The "Menuet" follows the same sequence as the "Gigue": it is in two parts, each being repeated. Omitting repetitions, the minuet takes up only forty-four measures. The usual trio is conspicuous by its absence—an omission gallantly repaired in the early nineteenth century by the Abbé Stadler.

III. "Preghiera" (Andante non tanto). Here Tschaikowsky reaches Mozart through an intermediary—Franz Liszt, for the "Preghiera" ("Prayer") is based on Liszt's transcription of Mozart's motet "Ave, verum corpus (K. 618). The piano version, in typically rhapsodic vein, is entitled, "A la Chapelle Sistine." Mozart's motet, calling for four voices, two violins, viola, bass, and organ, was completed on June 18, 1791, at Baden, where he had gone to visit his wife, who was to bear him his last son, Franz Xavier Wolfgang, the following month. Einstein's conjecture is that the motet was written as a Corpus Christi Day service for Anton Stoll, a school teacher and choirmaster who had befriended Mozart in time of need and performed many of his church works. The medieval Latin hymn used in the motet is given below with a line-for-line prose translation:

Ave verum corpus natum	Hail, true body born
De Maria Virgine;	of the Virgin Mary;
Vere passum, immolatum	truly suffering One, sacrificed
In cruce pro homine;	on the cross for man;
Cujus latus perforatum	whose pierced side
Unda fluxit, sanguine,	ran with water and blood,
Esto nobis adoratum.	be thou worshipped by us
In mortis exanime.	in dread of death.

IV. "Thème et Variations" (Allegro giusto). In the Mozart piano original these are ten variations on the Kalendar Monk's buffo aria "Unser dummer Pöbel meint" from Gluck's best *opéra comique, Die Pilger von Mecca.* The comedy was produced in Vienna in 1764 in its French version *La Rencontre imprévue* (*The Unexpected Meeting*) based on a risqué comedy by Lesage and D'Orneval, first staged in Paris in 1726. After a European tour, it came back to Vienna in 1776 as a German Singspiel. In the French version, the Kalendar Monk's aria begins with the words "Les hommes pieusement." Gluck came to hear Mozart play at one of Mme. Lange's concerts on Mar. 11, 1783. Two weeks later he also attended Mozart's own concert. By way of tribute to the older man, Mozart then improvized the variations on the comic monologue. Mozart's own Singspiel, *The Abduction from the Seraglio*, produced a year earlier, is very similar in plot to *Die Pilger von Mecca*. Both revolve around a far-fetched tale of divided and reunited lovers against a mock Oriental background of harem intrigue and Sultanic mercy. In Osmin, Mozart has his own version of Gluck's Kalendar Monk, and he was not above pilfering some ideas from Rézia's music for the first-act aria of his hero Belmonte. For more reasons than one he owed the venerable Gluck the graceful obeisance of a set of variations on a theme from a comic opera so utterly overshadowed by his own. Gluck's aria, if not the opera, lives today largely because Mozart let his nimble fancy and fingers wander over it in 1783 and perhaps because Tschaikowsky, a century later, carried the process a step further.

L. B.

"Overture, 1812," Op. 49

Although clearly a *pièce d'occasion* prompted by the commemoration of a crucial page in Russian history, the *Overture, 1812* is a minor mystery in the Tschaikowsky catalogue. Supposedly, Nicholas Rubinstein commissioned Tschaikowsky in 1880 to write a festival overture for the Moscow Exhibition. At least the composer admits as much in letters to Nadia von Meck and the conductor Napravnik.

But his friend Kashkin insisted that the piece was requested for the ceremonies consecrating the Moscow Cathedral of the Saviour, intended to symbolize Russia's part in the Napoleonic struggle. The Overture, accordingly, pictured the great events beginning with the Battle of Borodino (Sept. 7, 1812) and ending with Napoleon's flight from Moscow, after the city was set aflame. To make it more effective, the work was to be performed in the public square before the cathedral. An electric connection on the conductor's desk would set off salvos of real artillery, and all Moscow would thrill with thoughts of its heroic past. In any case Tschaikowsky finished the Overture at Kamenka in 1880, and though the cathedral was dedicated in the summer of 1881, there is no record of the planned street scene having come off.

Instead, we find Tschaikowsky offering the Overture to Eduard Napravnik, then directing the Imperial Musical Society of St. Petersburg: "Last winter, at Nicholas Rubinstein's request, I composed a Festival Overture for the concerts of the exhibition, entitled '1812.'" Tschaikowsky then makes a statement that possibly suggests an earlier rebuff: "Could you possibly manage to have this played? It is not of great value, and I shall not be at all surprised or hurt if you consider the style of the music unsuitable to a symphony concert." Apparently Napravnik turned down the Overture, and its premiere was postponed to Aug. 20, 1882, when it figured on an all-Tschaikowsky concert in the Art and Industrial Exhibition at Moscow.

Tschaikowsky's attitude to the work is further expressed in the letter to his benefactress Mme. von Meck. There he speaks of the overture as "very noisy" and having "no great artistic value" because it was written "without much warmth of enthusiasm." In a diary entry of the time he refers to it as having "only local and patriotic significance."

The "patriotic significance," of course, is what gives the Overture its *raison d'être* as a motion picture of historical events. Tschaikowsky's brushstrokes are bold and obvious. The French and Russians are clearly depicted through the use of the Czarist National Anthem and the "Marseillaise." Fragments of Cossack and Novgorod folk songs enter the scheme, and the battle and fire scenes are as plain as pictures. As the Overture develops, one envisions the clash of arms at Borodino, with the Russians stiffly disputing every step and the "Marseillaise" finally rising dominant. The Russians are hurled back; the French are in Moscow. Finally the city is ablaze and the dismal rout begins, as cathedral bells mingle with the roll of drums and the hymn "God Preserve Thy People" surges out in a paean of victory.

L. B.

Overture Fantasy, "Romeo and Juliet"

Shortly before the overture fantasy on Shakespeare's tragedy took shape in Tschaikowsky's mind, he had been jilted by the French soprano Desirée Artôt, then enjoying a prodigious vogue as opera singer in St. Petersburg. The twenty-eight-year-old composer and Mlle. Artôt had become engaged in 1868, but the lady promptly left him and married the Spanish baritone Padilla y Ramos. The theory is that Tschaikowsky's composition grew out of the resulting emotional upset, or at least that his frame of mind conduced to tragic expression on a romantic theme.

The Artôt episode may have acted as stimulus, but the concrete suggestion for using Shakespeare's tragedy in a symphonic work came from Balakireff during a walk with Tschaikowsky and their friend Kashkin "on a lovely day in May." Balakireff, head of the group of five young Russian composers (Tschaikowsky was not one of them) bent on achieving a pure national idiom, went so far as to outline the scheme to Tschaikowsky, unfolding the possibilities of dramatic and musical coordination so vividly that the young composer took eagerly to the project. Balakireff even furnished the keys and hints for themes and development.

However, four months went by before Tschaikowsky plunged into the actual composition of the overture fantasy. Balakireff kept in close touch with him and virtually supervised the process. His dogmatism and narrowness often bored and irritated the young composer. Balakireff accepted this and rejected that, was pitilessly graphic in his comments, and yet somehow egged on the hypersensitive Tschaikowsky to completion of a taxing assignment. Finally, in January of the following year, Balakireff and Rimsky-Korsakoff came to visit him and he could write: "My Overture pleased them very much and it also pleases me." Still, the Moscow public responded coolly, and Tschaikowsky felt obliged to revise much of the score that summer. Further rewriting was done for the definitive edition brought out in 1881.

The thematic scheme is easy to follow. Friar Laurence takes his bow in a solemn andante introduction for clarinets and bassoons in F sharp minor. The feud of the Montagues and Capulets rages in a B minor allegro. Romeo and Juliet enter via muted violins and English horn in a famous theme in D flat major suggesting Tschaikowsky's song, "Wer nur die Sehnsucht kennt" ("None But the Lonely Heart"). The strife-torn Montagues and Capulets return for another bout. Chords of muted violins and violas hinting at mystery and secrecy bring back the love music. The themes of Romeo and Juliet, the embattled families, and Friar Laurence are heard in succession, followed by a fierce orchestral crash, and the storm subsides to a roll of kettledrums.

L. B.

Francesca da Rimini, Fantasia for Orchestra (after Dante), Op. 32

WRITTEN IN 1876, Tschaikowsky's symphonic treatment of the celebrated love story of Paolo and Francesca grew out of an original project for an opera on the same subject. He abandoned the idea of an opera when the libretto submitted to him proved impossible. Later, Tschaikowsky again read through the fifth canto of Dante's *Inferno,* in which the tragedy is related. Stirred by the verses and also by Gustave Doré's illustrations, he resolved to write an orchestral fantasy on the subject.

Prefacing the score are the following lines from Dante's great poem:

Dante arrives in the second circle of hell. He sees that here the incontinent are punished, and their punishment is to be continually tormented by the cruelest winds under a dark and gloomy air. Among these tortured ones he recognizes Francesca da Rimini, who tells her story.

"There is no greater pain than to recall a happy time in wretchedness; and this thy teacher knows. But if thou hast such desire to learn the first root of our love, I will do like one who weeps and tells.

"One day, for pastime, we read of Lancelot, how love constrained him. We were alone, and without all suspicion. Several times reading urged our eyes to meet, and changed the color of our faces. But one moment alone it was that overcame us. When we read of how the fond smile was kissed by such a lover, he, who shall never be divided from me, kissed my mouth all trembling. The book, and he who wrote it, was a Galeotto. That day we read in it no farther."

While the one spirit thus spake, the other wept so that I fainted with pity, as if I had been dying; and fell, as a dead body falls.

Tschaikowsky used to insist that the following titles be given in the program book at performances of his Fantasia:

I. Introduction: The gateway to the Inferno ("Leave all hope behind, all ye who enter here"). Tortures and agonies of the condemned.
II. Francesca tells the story of her tragic love for Paolo.
III. The turmoil of Hades. Conclusion.

The composition starts with a descriptive setting, in which a sinister, gruesome picture is painted of the second circle of Dante's *Inferno*. The awesome scene, with its haunting, driving winds, desolate moans, and dread terror, is repeated at the end. In the middle occurs a section featuring a clarinet in a plaintive and tender melody heard against string pizzicati. This instantly evokes the image of Francesca telling her tragic tale, which mounts in fervor and reaches its shattering crisis before the wailing winds of Dante's nether world close in again.

L. B.

"Marche Slave," Op. 31

Composed in Moscow in September, 1876, for a benefit concert, the *Marche Slave* stands foremost among Tschaikowsky's marches, of which he wrote a number, including several incorporated in his operas and suites. Most of them were composed for special purposes or occasions. There is the *Marche solennelle,* written "for the law students," which figured on the housewarming program at the opening of Carnegie Hall in May, 1891, besides a *Marche militaire,* which he wrote for the band of the Czar's 98th Infantry Regiment. In 1883, the city of Moscow requisitioned a *Coronation March* from him. Earlier, Tschaikowsky had written a march in honor of the famous General Sokobelev. But he held it in such low esteem that he allowed it to circulate as the work of a nonexistent composer named Sinopov.

The *Marche slave* is based chiefly on folk music from the south of Russia and from Serbia. Its main theme, in fact, is taken almost directly from the Serbian folk song "Sunce varko ne fijas jednako" ("Come, my dearest, why so sad this morning?")

The work is scored for two flutes, two piccolos, two oboes, two clarinets, two bassoons, four horns, two cornets, two trumpets, three trombones, tuba, kettledrums, bass drum, side drum, cymbals, gong, and strings. Made into three sections, the work incorporates in the middle portion fragments of the erstwhile Russian national hymn, "God Save the Emperor." There is an interesting story in connection with the composition of the hymn, which was written by Alexis Feodorovich Lvov. He himself thus tells the tale of its birth.

In 1833, I accompanied the Emperor Nicholas during his travels in Prussia and Austria. When we had returned to Russia I was informed by Count von Benkendorf that the sovereign regretted that we Russians had no national anthem of our own, and that, as he was tired of the English tune which had filled the gap for many years, he wished me to see whether I could not compose a Russian hymn.

The problem appeared to me to be an extremely difficult and serious one. When I recalled the imposing British national anthem "God Save the King," the very original French one, and the really touching Austrian hymn, I felt and appreciated the necessity of writing something big, strong, and moving; something national that should resound through a church as well as through the ranks of an army; something that could be taken up by a huge multitude and be within the reach of every man, from the dunce to the scholar. The idea absorbed me, but I was worried by the conditions thus imposed on the work with which I had been commissioned.

One evening as I was returning home very late, I thought out and wrote down in a few minutes the tune of the hymn. The next day I called on Shoukovsky to ask him to write the words; but he was no musician and had much trouble to adapt them to the phrases of the first section of the melody.

At last I was able to announce the completion of the hymn to Count von Benkendorf. The Emperor wished to hear it, and came on Nov. 23 to the chapel of the Imperial Choir, accompanied by the Empress and the Grand Duke Michael. I had collected the whole body of choristers and reenforced them by two orchestras. The sovereign asked for the hymn to be repeated several times, expressed a wish to hear it sung without accompaniment, and then had it played first of all by each orchestra separately and then finally by all the executants together. His Majesty turned to me and said in French: "Why, it's superb!" and then and there gave orders to Count von Benkendorf to inform the Minister of War that the hymn was to be adopted for the army. The order to this effect was issued Dec. 4, 1833. The first public performance of the hymn was on Dec. 11, 1833, at the Grand Theater in Moscow. The Emperor seemed to want to submit my work to the judgment of the Moscow public. On Dec. 25 the hymn resounded through the rooms of the Winter Palace on the occasion of the blessing of the colors.

As proof of his satisfaction the Emperor graciously presented me with a gold snuff box studded with diamonds, and in addition gave orders that the words "God Save the Tsar" should be placed on the armorial bearings of the Lvov family.

R. C. B.

"Capriccio Italien," Op. 45

DESCRIBED BY Edwin Evans as a "bundle of Italian folk tunes," the *Capriccio Italien* draws partly on published collections of such melodies and partly on popular airs heard by Tschaikowsky in 1880 while touring Italy. "I am working on a sketch of an 'Italian Fantasia' based on folk songs," he notifies his patroness-confidante, Nadia von Meck, from Rome on Feb. 17, 1880. "Thanks to the charming themes, some of which I have heard in the streets, the work will be effective."

Tschaikowsky's room at the Hotel Constanzi overlooked the barracks of the Royal Cuirassiers. Apparently the bugle call sounded nightly in the barrack yards contributed another theme "heard in the streets," for it may be heard in the trumpet passage of the introduction. The "Italian Fantasia" was fully sketched out in Rome and the orchestration begun. With the title now changed to *Capriccio Italien,* the work was completed that summer on Tschaikowsky's return to Russia. Nicolas Rubinstein directed the premiere at Moscow on Dec. 18, 1880. Six years later Walter Damrosch introduced it to America at a concert in the Metropolitan Opera House, the precise date being Nov. 6, 1886.

After the introduction section, the strings chant a lyric theme of slightly melancholy hue, which the orchestra then develops. Later the oboes announce, in thirds, a simple folk melody of less somber character. This, too, is elaborately worked out, before the tempo changes and violins and flutes bring in another tune. This promptly subsides as a brisk march section sets in, followed by a return of the opening theme. There is a transition to a lively tarantella, then another bright theme in triple rhythm, and finally the Presto section, with a second tarantella motive leading to a brilliant close.

L. B.

Suite from the Ballet "Le Lac des Cygnes" ("Swan Lake")

I. Scene. II. Waltz. III. Dance of the Swans. IV. Scene. V. Hungarian Dance (Czardas).

ALL TOLD, Tschaikowsky wrote three ballets, plus a scattering of incidental dances for operas, beginning with the surviving *Voyevode* fragments. The composition of *Swan Lake,* first of the trio—the others being *The Sleeping Beauty* and *The Nutcracker*—originated in a twofold impulse, the need for

ready cash and a fondness for French ballet music, especially the works of
Delibes and the *Giselle* of Adolphe Adam, which Tschaikowsky regarded as
archetype.

He evidently thought little of his initial effort, for shortly after the Moscow
production of *Swan Lake* he recorded in his diary: "Lately I have heard
Delibes' very clever music. *Swan Lake* is poor stuff compared to it. Nothing
during the last few years has charmed me so greatly as this ballet of Delibes'
and *Carmen.*" Per contra, the same entry bemoans the "deterioration" of
German music, the immediate offender being the "cold, obscure and pretentious" C minor Symphony of Brahms!

Tschaikowsky was probably sincere when he described his own ballet as
"poor stuff" compared with Delibes'. That was in 1877. Performances of *Swan
Lake* at the Bolshoi Theater had been flat, shabby, and badly costumed. A
conductor inexperienced with elaborate ballet scores had directed. Modeste
Tschaikowsky in the biography of his brother, testifies to this. Numbers were
omitted as "undanceable," and pieces from other ballets substituted. At length
only a third of the original remained, and not the best. The ballet dropped
out of the Moscow repertory, and it was not until 1894 that the enterprising
Marius Petipa wrote to Moscow for the full score and produced *Swan Lake*
with brilliant success at the Maryinsky Theater in St. Petersburg, on Jan. 15,
1895. It has since remained a repertory staple, both the current Ballets Russes
and the Ballet Theater having staged it successfully. Pavlova, Karsavina, and
Markova, among others, have interpreted the heroine Odette, and Prince
Siegfried has been embodied by Nijinsky, Lifar, Mordkin, and Dolin. *Swan
Lake* was one of the first ballets witnessed in his youth by Serge Diaghileff,
founder of the famous Ballets Russes.

Tschaikowsky first refers to *Swan Lake* in a letter to Rimsky-Korsakoff,
dated Sept. 10, 1875: "I accepted the work partly because I need the money
and because I have long cherished a desire to try my hand at this type of
music." V. P. Begitchev, stage manager of the Bolshoi, offered 800 roubles
(less than $500) and in turn granted Tschaikowsky's request for a story from
the age of chivalry, making the sketch himself. Tschaikowsky set to work in
August, 1875, and had the first two acts planned out in a fortnight, but the
score was not completed till the following March and for some reason held
up for performance until February, 1877.

The story, possibly of Rhenish origin, tells how Prince Siegfried woos and
wins Odette, the Swan Queen. At a celebration the prince is told he must
soon choose a bride. A flight of swans overhead distracts him and a hunt is
proposed. Siegfried and the hunters are at the lakeside. It is evening. Odette
appears surrounded by a bevy of swan maidens. She begs the hunters to
spare the swans. They are maidens under the spell of the enchanter Rotbart.
Swans by day, they return briefly to human form at midnight. The prince

and Odette fall in love. Siegfried swears she will be his wife. Odette cautions him about Rotbart's evil power. Breach of promise will mean her death. Rotbart brings his own daughter to the court ball, disguised as Odette. Siegfried makes the false choice of bride, and the pledge is broken. Discovering Rotbart's ruse, he hastens to Odette, who at first rebuffs him. Siegfried blames Rotbart, and Odette relents. At length Rotbart whips up a storm which floods the forest. When Siegfried vows he will die with Odette, Rotbart's spell is shattered and all ends happily.

Tschaikowsky's close friend and collaborator Kashkin is authority for the statement that an adagio section in *Swan Lake* was a love duet in the opera *Undine* before it found new lodgings. Conversely, a Danse Russe in the group of piano pieces, Op. 40, was written for *Swan Lake,* thus balancing matters. Like *The Sleeping Beauty* and *The Nutcracker, Swan Lake* is famed for its waltz. The score brims with typical Tschaikowskyan melody, and probably for the first time in ballet music a scheme of leitmotives is used, two of the principal subjects being the tremulous theme of the swans in flight and the hauntingly wistful theme of Odette herself, assigned to the oboe against soft strings and harp arpeggios. The music adjusts itself snugly to the technic of pure classical ballet, and solos and ensembles are contrasted adroitly.

L. B.

Suite from the Ballet "The Nutcracker," Op. 71a

(a) Miniature Overture. (b) March. (c) Dance of the Sugarplum Fairy. (d) Russian Dance: Trepak. (e) Arabian Dance. (f) Chinese Dance. (g) Dance of the Mirlitons. (h) Waltz of the Flowers.

THE ST. PETERSBURG Opera honored Tschaikowsky with two commissions early in 1891. The first for an opera in one act, entitled *Iolanthe,* which was based on *King René's Daughter,* a play by the Danish poet Hendrik Herz. The second was a ballet, whose subject was drawn from the E. T. A. Hoffmann story *Nussknacker und Mausekönig* (*Nutcracker and Mouse King*) as represented in Dumas' French version, known as *Histoire d'un casse-noisette* (*History of a Nutcracker*). Tschaikowsky did not respond with his usual alacrity to the ballet subject, but, good trouper that he was, he set to work.

The composer started out on a tour in March, which was eventually to bring him to America. During a Parisian stopover, he conducted a Colonne Concert. As he was about to sail for the United States however, he was notified of his sister's death, his beloved Alexandra Davidova. He was all for canceling the tour and heading right home for Russia, but he finally decided to go through with the original plans. On his return he wrote (June 25) that he had finished sketches for the proposed ballet. Nevertheless, in a typical fit of depression, he added that what he could have accomplished in five days he had scarcely been able to do in a fortnight. He says:

No, the old man is breaking up. Not only does his hair drop out, or turn as white as snow; not only does he lose his teeth, which refuse their service; not only do his eyes weaken and tire easily; not only do his feet walk badly, or drag themselves along, but he loses bit by bit the capacity to do anything at all. The ballet is infinitely worse than *The Sleeping Beauty*—so much is certain; let's see how the opera will turn out.

Both opera and the ballet were produced at the Imperial Opera House, St. Petersburg, on Dec. 18, 1892. They were received apathetically by the audience. In the case of the ballet this was strange, on the face of it, for a concert version of the music, played previously in St. Petersburg, had earned for it unqualified praise.

However, there was reason for its nonfurore, so to speak, chiefly owing to the illness of Marius Petipa, who had been entrusted with the stage production. A substitute, chosen by Petipa himself, proved an inferior creator. Furthermore, the sophisticated ballet audience could see no good in having a host of children scurry through the first act. It was accustomed, if you please, to a bona fide corps de ballet. To make matters worse, the girl who danced the Sugarplum Fairy was a fine enough technician, but all that could not compensate for her plainness.

Act I treats of a Christmas Tree party. Children and mechanical dolls people the scene. Marie, daughter of the host, is fascinated by a German nutcracker, which is fashioned in the figure of an old man with massive jaws. The nutcracker is broken by several boys during rough play, and at night Marie lies sleepless in pity for the utensil. She gets out of her bed, in order to take another look at her broken darling. She hears strange sounds and, presently, the Christmas Tree grows, the toys come to life, as do the cakes and fancy tidbits, and, of course, the nutcracker.

The strange sounds had been caused by the rustling of mice. The mice now wage a war against the toys, and the nutcracker, siding with the toys, challenges the king of the mice in single combat. The No. 1 mouse appears to be having the best of it when Marie lets him have a well-aimed shoe. He is killed. At this point the nutcracker is transformed into a handsome young prince, who thanks Marie profusely for saving his life and then takes her with him to his enchanted kingdom.

In the second act the scene is a jam mountain, the realm of the Sugarplum Fairy. Together with her court she eagerly awaits Marie and the Prince. There is great jubilation when the two arrive, and there follows a series of dances of the sweetmeats. The numbers are eight:

"Miniature Overture" (Allegro giusto, B flat Major, 2/4). Two contrasting themes are the features of this introduction, which is scored for the high-register instruments.

"March" (Tempo di marcia vivo, G major, 4/4). The children enter to the accompaniments of this music. The main subject is given to the clarinets, horns, and trumpets.

"Dance of the Sugarplum Fairy" (Andante con moto, E minor, 2/4). The charming melody is assigned to the celesta, against a pizzicato string accompaniment.

"Russian Dance: Trepak" (Tempo di trepak, molto vivace, G major, 2/4). A rhythmic figure heard in the opening measure is the basis for the whole movement.

"Arabian Dance" (Allegretto, G minor, 3/8). Entrusted first to the clarinet, an oriental-style melody, is soon transferred to the violins, while a double pedal point of G's and D's is carried through the entire section. This number represents Coffee.

"Chinese Dance" (Allegretto moderato, B flat Major, 4/4). Here Tea is the idea. There is a persistent pizzicato figure in the bassoons and double basses, while the flute sings the theme.

"Dance of the Mirlitons" (Moderato assai, D major, 2/4). Three flutes give out the main subject, followed by a contrasting subject in F sharp minor for trumpets. The first subject returns.

"Waltz of the Flowers" (Tempo di valse, D major, 3/4). After an introductory passage for wood winds and horns and a cadenza for harp, the horns announce the principal theme, which is soon taken up by the clarinet. Other tunes are given to the flute, oboe, and strings. The section ends with a brilliant coda.

R. C. B.

Suite from the Ballet "The Sleeping Beauty," Op. 66

BASED ON Perrault's famous fairy tale, Tschaikowsky's *Sleeping Beauty* ballet dates from the summer of 1889. Its music is generally regarded as superior to that of the *Swan Lake* ballet and inferior to that of the *Nutcracker Suite*. Few ballet scores are so suitable in mood and style for the action they accompany. The music is truly melodious in Tschaikowsky's lighter vein. The fantasy is conveyed in bright, glittering colors, and, as Mrs. Newmarch pointed out, the music "never descends to the commonplace level of the ordinary ballet music." There are thirty numbers in all, many of them, especially the waltz, endearing in their lilting and haunting grace. The work was first produced in St. Petersburg on Jan. 2, 1890. In the early twenties, Diaghileff, the great ballet producer, revived the work in London and elsewhere with immense artistic éclat. Fragments of the ballet have been gathered in the Monte Carlo Ballet Russe's production of *Aurora's Wedding*.

L. B.

Polonaise from the Opera "Eugene Onegin"

THE CELEBRATED Russian poet Alexander Pushkin wrote a verse novel, bearing the title *Eugene Onegin,* which served as inspiration for the Tschaikowsky opera. The first cantos of the poem were written during Pushkin's exile in the Caucasus, and he later said of the piece, "I have begun a poem in the style of *Don Juan.*" Years afterward, however, he could declare, "I see nothing in common between *Eugene Onegin* and *Don Juan.*"

Tschaikowsky, drawn powerfully to this romantic story, chose to call his work "lyric scenes," rather than an opera. One of the most forceful reasons for Tschiakowsky's admiration of the Pushkin poem was its complete lack of pomp and spectacle. He wrote to his brother:

How delightful to avoid the commonplace Pharaohs, Ethiopian Princesses, poisoned cups and all the rest of these dolls' tales. *Eugene Onegin* is full of poetry. I am not blind to its defects. I know well enough the work gives little scope for treatment and will be deficient in stage effects; but the wealth of poetry, the human quality and simplicity of the subject, joined to Pushkin's inspired verses, will compensate for what it wants in other respects.

The opera is in three acts. Briefly, the story goes: Eugene Onegin, a young sophisticate, world traveler, wise and bored, unwittingly arouses feelings of love for himself in Tatiana, a young country girl of gentle breeding. She, in her simple innocence, writes him a letter revealing her love, and the best that Onegin can do is tell her that he can only be a brother to her.

In the meantime, Onegin deliberately arouses the jealousy of Lensky, his friend and the suitor of Tatiana's sister Olga. There is a duel, and Lensky is slain.

The victor, after a lapse of some years, meets Tatiana again. She is now the Princess Gremina, a glittering woman of the world in the glittering capital of St. Petersburg. Onegin, who could not find love in his heart for the simple country girl, is completely bowled over by the Princess. However, Tatiana is more human than he had been; she admits that she still loves him, but makes no bones about the fact that she will be forever true to the Prince, a luckier man than most. Obviously everything is finished, and on a rich note of disappointment.

The Polonaise is played in scene I of Act III, showing the hall in the palace of the Princess Gremina. A gathering of fashionable guests dances to its strains.

R. C. B.

Suite for Strings, "Souvenir de Florence," Op. 70

I. Allegro con spirito. II. Adagio cantabile e con moto. III. Allegretto moderato. IV. Allegro vivace.

COMPARED WITH his output in other forms, Tschaikowsky's chamber music is small, consisting of an early quartet, of which only the first movement survives, three complete string quartets, a trio, and the *Souvenir de Florence*, written for violins, violas, and cellos in pairs.

As the title implies, the work grew out of a visit to Italy early in 1890, though as a clue to the mood and manner of the music, *Souvenir de Florence* is a better title for the first two movements than for the others. The remaining Allegretto moderato and Allegro vivace bear an Italian "memory" only insofar as much other music by Tschaikowsky and other composers may share the same quality. Even a marked Slavic character is evident in places, which is only natural. As is well known, Tschaikowsky's Overture Fantasy *Romeo and Juliet* is often dubbed "Romeo and Juliet of the Steppes."

A first mention of the *Souvenir* occurs in a letter to Ippolitoff-Ivanoff dated May 5, 1890, written shortly after Tschaikowsky's return from abroad. It is quoted by his brother Modeste: "My visit brought forth good fruit. I composed an opera, *Pique Dame,* which seems a success to me. . . . My plans for the future are to finish the orchestration of the opera, sketch out a string sextet [the *Souvenir*], go to my sister at Kamenka for the end of the summer, and spend the whole autumn with you at Tiflis."

On the following June 30 he communicated news of the sextet to his patroness-saint Mme. von Meck, hoping that she would be "pleased to hear" about it. "I know your love of chamber music," he writes, "and I hope the work will please you. I wrote it with the greatest enthusiasm and without the least exertion."

In November, Tschaikowsky went to St. Petersburg for a rehearsal of *Pique Dame.* While there he arranged for a private hearing of the sextet by friends. The performance left him cold, and he resolved to rewrite the scherzo and finale. By the following May the work was thoroughly remodeled. It was not till June, 1892, while in Paris, that he actually completed the revision to his satisfaction.

The four movements comprise an Allegro con spirito (D minor, 4/4), an Adagio cantabile e con moto (D major, 3/4), an Allegretto moderato (A minor, 2/4), and an Allegro vivace (D minor–D major, 2/4). The form is largely that of the classical string quartet, though, characteristically, bold and novel devices of color and structure abound. Often the strings are ingeniously treated to suggest wind instruments, and one senses Tschaikowsky's frequent striving for orchestral effects.

Research has failed to unearth the "opprobrious epithets" Tschaikowsky is alleged to have heaped upon this slight but appealing work.

L. B.

Elegy and Waltz from the "Serenade for Strings" in C major, Op. 48

WRITTEN SOMETIME in 1881, the *Serenade for Strings* has been called, and with reason, "one of the most charming works he [Tschaikowsky] has bequeathed to the musical world." The piece obtained its first performance at Moscow, on Jan. 16, 1882, where it made a very favorable impression. Revealing, too, is the fact that the music won plaudits from laymen and professionals alike. It is not too difficult to understand why the latter group would find the work interesting, particularly since Tschaikowsky achieved some telling color effects without recourse to wind instruments.

The "Elegy" is a piece of writing "that belongs to the composer's inspired moments. It strikes the one note of melancholy in an otherwise cheerful and even joyous work, but it is subdued melancholy expressed in phrases of haunting beauty." The "Waltz," of engaging thematic material, is, as usual, treated with that exquisite craftsmanship practically always associated with Tschaikowsky's work.

R. C. B.

Joaquin Turina

BORN: SEVILLE, SPAIN, DEC. 9, 1882.

Viewed as a whole, the general character of his work is subjective and impressionistic and has a certain flavor of romanticism.—LEIGH HENRY.

"Sinfonia Sevillana"

IN A competition sponsored by the Gran Casino of San Sebastian, Spain, the *Sinfonia Sevillana* took first prize. This was in 1920. The work was not published until five years later. An American audience heard the work for the first time at a concert in the Hollywood Bowl, California, in 1928. A subsequent performance in this country took place in Chicago, on Jan. 29, 1933. The work is dedicated to José Mas.

Joaquin Turina studied first with Evaristo Garcia Torres in his own native city of Seville. Later the youth went to Madrid where he became a piano pupil of José Trago, eminent Spanish pedagogue. The next few years saw Turina at work with Moszkowski in Paris, and later with d'Indy. In 1914, the First World War broke out and the young composer hurried back to Madrid, understandably. Turina's compositions are numerous and varied. He has written works for the stage, for orchestra, for chamber groups and for the piano, besides several songs.

The *Sinfonia Sevillana* is scored for three flutes (third interchangeable with piccolo), two oboes, English horn, two clarinets, bass clarinet, two bassoons, double bassoon, four horns, three trumpets, three trombones, bass tuba, tympani, bass drum, cymbals, side drum, triangle, tambourine, castanets, celesta, harp, and the usual strings.

It is divided into three sections, first, an Andante, 3/4, which leads into an Allegro molto moderato, 2/4; second, an Andante, 6/8, succeeded by an Allegretto, which is then followed by a Vivo; and third, an Allegro vivo, 3/8, with a transition into an Allegretto (tempo di Garrotin lento) in the middle of the movement and a return of the faster tempo toward the end.

R. C. B.

Ralph Vaughan Williams

BORN: DOWN AMPNEY, GLOUCESTERSHIRE, ENGLAND, OCT. 12, 1872.

He flounders about in the sea of his ideas like a vast and ungainly porpoise, with great puffing and blowing; yet in the, end, after tremendous efforts and an almost heroic tenacity, there emerges, dripping and exhausted from the struggle, a real and lovable personality, unassuming, modest, and almost apologetic. His personality is wholly and without admixture English, and this is at once his virtue and his defect.—CECIL GRAY.

"A London Symphony"

I. Lento; Allegro risoluto. II. Lento. III. Scherzo. IV. Andante; Allegro; Epilogue.

THE FIRST performance of this Symphony took place at Queens Hall, London, on Mar. 27, 1914, under the direction of Geoffrey Toye. The British Music Society was responsible for a subsequent performance, allegedly the fourth, wherein a revised version of the work was employed. This was conducted by Albert Coates. The Symphony, according to some advices, had been "shortened a good deal, particularly at the closes of the movements."

Albert Coates directed the premiere in America at a concert of the Symphony Society in New York, on Dec. 30, 1920, when the conductor also made his American bow.

It is to Albert Coates that an imaginative exposition of the work's program is due:

The first movement opens at daybreak by the river. Old Father Thames flows calm and silent under the heavy gray dawn, deep and thoughtful, shrouded in mystery. London sleeps, and in the hushed stillness of early morning one hears Big Ben (the Westminster chimes) solemnly strike the half-hour.

Suddenly the scene changes (Allegro). One is on the Strand in the midst of the bustle and turmoil of morning traffic. This is London street life of the early hours— a steady stream of foot passengers hurrying, newspaper boys shouting, messengers whistling, and that most typical sight of London streets, the costermonger (Coster 'Arry), resplendent in pearl buttons, and shouting some coster song refrain at the top of a raucous voice, returning from Covent Garden Market, seated on his vegetable barrow drawn by the inevitable little donkey.

Then for a few moments one turns off the Strand into one of the quiet little streets that lead down to the river, and suddenly the noise ceases, shut off as though by

779

magic. We are in the part of London known as the Adelphi. Formerly the haunt of fashionable bucks and dandies about town, now merely old-fashioned houses and shabby old streets, haunted principally by beggars and ragged street urchins.

We return to the Strand and are once again caught up by the bustle and life of London—gay, careless, noisy, with every now and then a touch of something fiercer, something inexorable—as though one felt for a moment the iron hand of the great city—yet, nevertheless, full of that mixture of good humor, animal spirits, and sentimentality that is so characteristic of London.

In the second movement the composer paints us a picture of that region of London which lies between Holborn and the Euston Road, known as Bloomsbury. Dusk is falling. It is the damp and foggy twilight of a late November day. Those who know their London know this region of melancholy streets over which seems to brood an air of shabby gentility—a sad dignity of having seen better days. In the gathering gloom there is something ghostlike. A silence hangs over the neighborhood broken only by the policeman on his beat.

There is tragedy, too, in Bloomsbury, for among the many streets between Holborn and Euston there are alleys of acute poverty and worse.

In front of a "pub," whose lights flare through the murky twilight, stands an old musician playing a fiddle. His tune is played in the orchestra by the viola. In the distance the "lavender cry" is heard: "Sweet lavender; who'll buy my sweet lavender?" Up and down the street the cry goes, now nearer, now farther away.

The gloom deepens, and the movement ends with the old musician still playing his pathetic little tune.

In this [the third] movement one must imagine one's self sitting late on a Saturday night on one of the benches of the Temple Embankment (that part of the Thames Embankment lying between the Houses of Parliament and Waterloo Bridge). On our side of the river all is quiet, and in the silence one hears from a distance coming from the other side of the river all the noises of Saturday night in the slums. (The "other" side, the south side of the River Thames, is a vast network of very poor quarters and slums.) On a Saturday night these slums resemble a fair; the streets are lined with barrows, lit up by flaming torches, selling cheap fruit, vegetables, produce of all kinds; the streets and alleys are crowded with people. At street corners coster girls in large feather hats dance their beloved "double-shuffle jig" to the accompaniment of a mouth organ. We seem to hear distant laughter also, every now and then, what sounds like cries of suffering. Suddenly a concertina breaks out above the rest; then we hear a few bars on a hurdy-gurdy organ. All this softened by distance, melted into one vast hum, floats across the river to us as we sit meditating on the Temple Embankment.

The music changes suddenly, and one feels the Thames flowing silent, mysterious, with a touch of tragedy. One of London's sudden fogs comes down, making Slumland and its noises seem remote. Again, for a few bars, we feel the Thames flowing through the night, and the picture fades into fog and silence.

The last movement deals almost entirely with the crueler aspects of London, the London of the "unemployed" and unfortunate. After the opening bars we hear the

'Hunger March"—a ghostly march of those whom the city grinds and crushes, the great army of those who are cold and hungry and unable to work.

We hear again the noise and bustle of the streets (reminiscences of the first movement), but these now also take on a crueler aspect. There are sharp discords in the music. This is London as seen by the man who is "out and under." The man "out of a job" who watches the other man go whistling to his work, the man who is starving watching the other man eat—and the cheerful, bustling picture of gay street life becomes distorted, a nightmare seen by the eyes of suffering.

The music ends abruptly, and in the short silence that follows one again hears Big Ben chiming from Westminster Tower.

There follows the Epilogue, in which we seem to feel the great deep soul of London—London as a whole, vast and unfathomable—and the symphony ends as it began, with the river—Old Father Thames—flowing calm and silent, as he has flowed through the ages, the keeper of many secrets, shrouded in mystery.

In the meantime the composer has been quoted to the following effect:

The title might run "A Symphony by a Londoner," that is to say, various sights and sounds of London may have influenced the composer, but it would not be helpful to describe these. The work must succeed or fail as music, and in no other way. Therefore, if the hearers recognize a few suggestions of such things as the Westminster chimes, or the lavender cry, these must be treated as accidents and not essentials of the music.

The symphony is scored for three flutes (one interchangeable with piccolo), two oboes, English horn, two clarinets, bass clarinet, two bassoons, double bassoon, four horns, two trumpets, two cornets-à-piston, three trombones, bass tuba, three kettledrums, snare drum, bass drum, cymbals, triangle, jingles, tam-tam, glockenspiel, two harps and strings.

R. C. B.

"Pastoral" Symphony

I. Molto moderato. II. Lento moderato. III. Moderato pesante; Presto.
IV. Finale: Lento; Moderato maestoso; Molto largamente; Lento.

ONE ENGLISH critic said of this work: "There is nothing in the *Pastoral Symphony* but music." The composer himself remarked on the absence of a program for the Symphony, "though some British commentators have concocted one." It was his idea to "let the music suggest whatever images come to the individual mind."

The Symphony was given its premiere performance by the Royal Philharmonic Society under the direction of Adrian Boult on Jan. 26, 1922. On June 7 of the same year it was introduced to an American audience at the Festival of the Litchfield County Choral Union, Norfolk, Conn., with the composer conducting. The Philharmonic Society gave its initial New York performance on Nov. 24, 1922, under Josef Stransky.

The *Pastoral Symphony* is Vaughan Williams' third. The two preceding ones also bear quasi-programmatic titles, the first being the *Sea Symphony* for solo, chorus and orchestra (text by Walt Whitman), and the second the *London Symphony*.

Perhaps there was some justification for the "concocted" program of this Symphony, whatever it may have been. After all, those "British commentators" were not unaware of another *Pastoral* Symphony, whose subtitles do a good job of telling a programmatic story which the hearer does not find too complicated to follow.

On the other hand, a composer who disavows any programmatic intent is to be given consideration, too. After all—and this time, very emphatically after all—he knew what ideas he was or was not writing about. In any case, the piece is neither program nor absolutely absolute music, but it may not be amiss, at this point, to introduce a statement by Lawrence Gilman to the effect that "there is plenty of food for the fancy and the imagination to feed upon if the sensitive hearer is content, as he should be, with a profoundly poetic utterance, in musical terms, of the moods, the atmosphere, the spirit evoked by the title of the work."

Vaughan Williams has devoted a good part of his life to the affectionate study of English folk music. In this Symphony there is to be noted a melodic and harmonic resemblance to certain modal characteristics in such music.

"No foreign musicians," we have been told, "will ever understand why Vaughan Williams moves us so, until an essay is written beginning with 'Bushes and Briars' and other modal folk songs, and continuing with Vaughan Williams' arrangements of them, down to the stuff out of which he made the *Pastoral Symphony*."

In company with many others of its type, "Bushes and Briars" shows an intervallic structure not unlike the kind found in the music of the medieval church. The melody of "Bushes and Briars," whose "sweet, quaint, homespun ghost . . . hovers behind the curtain of lovely sound woven by Vaughan Williams," was published in the *Journal of the Folk Song Society* in 1906, in special section devoted to *Songs Collected from Sussex*.

A shepherd named Pottipher sang this tune to the composer at Ingrave near Brentwood, on Dec. 4, 1903. Asked if he knew anything of the origin of this or other songs in his repertoire, Pottipher replied, "If you can get the words, the Almighty will send you the tune." The words he sang to the tune in question went:

> Through bushes and briars of late I took my way,
> All for to hear the small birds sing and the lambs to skip and play;

> I overheard my own true love, her voice it was so clear,
> Long time I have been waiting for the coming of my dear.

Oddly enough, Pottipher amazed the composer by singing the same tune to an altogether different text, entitled "Willy on the Wagon Train." Not unmindful of his musicological duties, Vaughan Williams noted that the tune is in the Aeolian mode (the ninth of the ecclesiastical modes, fifth Authentic).

The composer has referred to the musical folklore from which he drew his collection as

that precious heritage of beautiful melody which is being allowed to slip through out hands through mere ignorance and apathy. . . . I could imagine a much less propitious way of spending a long winter evening than in the parlor of a country inn taking one's turn at the mug of "four-ale" (surely the most innocuous of all beverages), in the rare company of minds imbued with that fine sense which comes from advancing years and a life-long communion with Nature—and with the ever-present chance of picking up some rare old ballad or an exquisitely beautiful melody.

In the Lento of the last movement of this Symphony the composer has written a vocalise for either soprano or tenor voice. It is in the nature of a song heard from a great distance, a melancholy song.

R. C. B.

Symphony in F minor, No. 4

> I. Allegro. II. Andante moderato. III. Scherzo (allegretto molto). IV. Finale con epilogo fugato (allegro molto).

First sketches for this Symphony were struck during 1931 and 1932. It was given its first performance in 1935, in which year it was also published. This symphony by the dean of British composers carries no programmatic connotations, no title that might give rise to such ideas. As a matter of fact, neither the *London* nor the *Pastoral* Symphonies are to be conceived as *program* works.

Yet when Albert Coates introduced the *London* in New York he supplied an elaborate *program* description of it. That has had a wide circulation since then, and it is generally believed that it was done with at least the partial consent of the composer.

The *Pastoral Symphony* carries no subtitles, differing radically from another *Pastoral* Symphony. There are no so-called bucolic episodes in it and, as an English critic has remarked, "there is nothing in the *Pastoral Symphony* but music," in which, doubtless, he is seconded by the composer.

The Fourth Symphony, it may be interesting to note, has earned this expression from its creator: "I don't know whether I like it, but this is what

I meant." The listener, one supposes, may be permitted to go on from there.

We are told that this is a work of great logic and emotional power. The subject, whatever it may be, is contained within it. Further, "it is a subject of a logical nature." The essence of the Symphony is a sort of "disputation on two themes, which run right through all four movements." One of these themes (both appear early in the first movement) is what might be termed "horizontal," its melodic line possessing the merest semblance of intervallic structure. The other is, in contrast, a "vertical" theme.

The final movement, a combination of symphonic and fugal writing, makes important use of the themes, which, because of their contrasting natures, fit the composer's plan admirably.

The Symphony's opening measures are of enormous power, and the power, generated by full and heavy scoring, continues almost undiminished to the end. There are few light moments in the music. The closing movement is reserved for the "weightiest matter." As Frank Howes points out in his essay, *The Later Works of R. Vaughan Williams,* Brahms did likewise in three of his four symphonies. He shows that Mozart started the vogue in his *Jupiter Symphony* and that Beethoven proceeded at his most significant pace in the concluding section of the *Choral Symphony.*

The Finale of the Vaughan Williams Fourth is tied to the preceding movement. The linkage point is not readily evident. The fact is that the chief subject of the Finale is related to a minor one in the second movement.

As in the *London Symphony* and the Piano Concerto, the composer has written an Epilogue, which corresponds to some Beethoven super-coda. It is a summary, in other words, of the separate movements, though of much wider scope and of a more complex form than a coda. He aims, therefore, at a conclusion which must be the logical outgrowth of the arguments presented. Moreover, his purpose is to achieve an "emotional peroration."

From Vaughan Williams' book *Music and Nationalism* comes the following statement:

Every composer cannot expect to have a world-wide message, but he may reasonably expect to have a special message for his own people, and many young composers make the mistake of imagining they can be universal without at first having been local. Is it not reasonable to suppose that those who share our life, our history, our customs, our climate, even our food, should have some secret to impart to us which the foreign composer, though he be perhaps more imaginative, more powerful, more technically equipped, is not able to give us? This is the secret of the national composer, the secret to which he only has the key, which no foreigner can share with him, and which he alone is able to tell his fellow countrymen. But is he prepared with his secret? Must he not limit himself to a certain extent so as to give his message its full force? For after all it is the millstream forcing its way through narrow channels which gathers strength to turn the water wheel. As long as composers persist in serving up at second hand the externals of the music of other nations, they must not be surprised if audiences prefer the real Brahms, the real Wagner, the real Debussy, or the real Stravinsky to their pale reflections.

R. C. B.

Symphony in D major, No. 5

I. Preludio. II. Scherzo. III. Romanza. IV. Passacaglia.

Inscribed on the score of the Fifth Symphony are the words, "Dedicated without permission to Jean Sibelius," whom Vaughan Williams numbers among the greatest geniuses of our time. The composer further notes that "some of the themes of this Symphony are taken from an unfinished opera *The Pilgrim's Progress,* but except in the slow movement the Symphony has no dramatic connection with Bunyan's allegory."

The composer led the London Philharmonic in the world premiere of this Symphony on June 24, 1943, in Albert Hall, at a Promenade concert given under the auspices of the British Broadcasting Corporation (B.B.C.). Stimulated by the work of the Society for Cultural Relations with Russia in bringing new Soviet scores to the attention of the English public, the B.B.C. joined other groups in a similar hunt for novelties.

Two and three new compositions were offered weekly in the Promenade series. Among the first few featured was the Vaughan Williams symphony: "by far the most notable of all the new music heard from orchestras and chamber-music players," according to F. Bonavia, London correspondent of *The New York Times.* The rest Mr. Bonavia had found "rather bewildering." To what he described as "this unsteady, restless, perplexing world of music," the new symphony of Vaughan Williams had come "to restore faith and confidence." Continuing his appraisal, Mr. Bonavia reported as follows:

Here at least there is no faltering, no adapting of one's thoughts to the fashion of the day, no experimenting with new, untried tools. Modal harmony there is but modal harmony is the very breath of life to Vaughan Williams and always has been. In others—including some of the pupils—it has become an affectation; it is perfectly natural to him.

It is significant that in this Symphony Vaughan Williams reverts to his earlier style, the style that gave us the *Fantasia on a Theme of Tallis.* And although divided in four movements it is all pervaded by the same spirit. The orchestra is comparatively small, having but two horns in place of the usual four, and there is nowhere anything like a climax of great sonority; yet nowhere does one feel the slightest need for greater variety either in tone or texture. The reason is not far to seek.

The motive power is given not by an academic trick but by a spiritual impulse which guides the hand of the artist and leads him to express himself in the simplest manner. What he has to say does not need the addition of questionable ornament, and his thought is averse to rhetoric. The charm of the work is in the ideas it presents rather than in the manner of presentation, although anyone who has dabbled in musical composition must know that it is far more difficult to present an idea without than with elaborations.

How we shall come to regard this Symphony when we know it well it is impossible to surmise at present. Its simplicity and its sincerity may well create a new fashion, based not on imitation but on those elemental principles of artistic honesty and integrity which give it its true strength and character. It may in time be regarded as Vaughan Williams' best achievement, even though during the first performance the first section, in which the composer lingers and plays with one of his favorite harmonic combinations, seemed slightly overlong.

But it is obviously the work of a man whose faith is entire and whose courage rises above conventions. It needed courage of a rare kind to return to the earlier style, after the experiments of the Piano Concerto, of the Fourth Symphony and the String Sextet. Only a profound faith could have suggested ideas so remote from the torment and turmoil of today.

This is the work of one who has attained what he had long labored to find—peace and serenity of mind and soul, as well as a perfect balance between thought and medium.

The scoring of the D major Symphony is for two flutes, one oboe, one English horn, two clarinets, two bassoons, two horns, two trumpets, three trombones, tympani, and strings.

The four movements are marked as follows: I. Preludio (4/4, Moderato Allegro; Moderato), enclosed within statements by two horns of a theme which strikingly sets the whole mood of the Symphony; II. Scherzo (Presto 3/4), the main motive of which is given out by the strings; III. Romanza (Lento, 3/4), which the composer admits has "dramatic connection" with John Bunyan's allegorical classic, from which the score quotes these words: "Upon that place there stood a cross, and a little below, a sepulchre. Then he said: 'He hath given me rest by His sorrow, and life by His death'"; and IV. Passacaglia (3/4, Moderato), in which the cellos expound the ground bass, the movement ending in a coda with a return to the tempo of the Preludio.

Writing for the B.B.C. publication *The Listener,* A. E. F. Dickinson tersely analyzed the Symphony as follows:

In the Preludio (I) the Allegro, although covering by harmonic means a wide area in a short space, is only an interlude in a series of wayward variants on the notes GCD/AGA, essentially a plainsong phrase.

After this Moderato a scherzo (II) follows naturally; its refrain (muted strings) forces the rising fourth of the "plainsong" into *two* fourths (and back), in varied rhythmic detail, with a plain auxiliary theme announced by flute and bassoon; but two episodes show more sprightly material, the second a phrase from the wood in unison with trenchant falling thirds.

The slow Romanza (III) treats in characteristic rhapsodic manner two themes, first associated with the alto oboe and divided strings, and introductory chords prove useful and for one moment lively companions.

In the final Passacaglia (IV), secure at last in D major, the introductory mood is maintained, but the grand ground bass (one bar *under* the usual eight) gathers increasing dignity, like Bach's *Dona nobis pacem,* and although striking variations of meter appear in the clarinet and elsewhere, the note of quiet confidence is continued in a second major tune.

This acquires a rare exultation and finally, after a recollection of the preluding plainsong, seems to fill the whole world with its song of goodwill. In the comparatively smooth melodic texture of the Symphony this simple but suggestive melody is able to summarize in its "objective" eight bars all that has preceded.

Dickinson noted the curious fact that the persistent opening chord of the Preludio echoed the final tranquil interlude of Vaughan Williams' previous symphony, in F minor, a work whose dominant mood is one of grim, jarring, almost satanic force. Like Bonavia he viewed the Fifth Symphony as "a patent reaction toward tranquillity."

Vaughan Williams' serene lyricism, even "sweetness" in this score contrasts oddly with the stark, at times brutally harsh, character of the Symphony in F minor, which Eric Blom described as "among the most strident things in modern music." As Mr. Bonavia pointed out, in the Fifth Symphony the English composer returns to an earlier idiom—a style more tranquilly personal and at the same time flavored with the folk tradition of English song and poetry. So sharp is the swing from preceding scores, that W. H. Haddon Squire, writing for *The Christian Science Monitor,* even predicted its simplicity, in these piping days of dissonance, would shock "young ears attuned to harsh discords."

As another possible source of shock to "young ears" Mr. Squire notes the "pentatonic flavor—which like the faint, indefinable odor of a room in an old English country house pervades the Symphony from end to end."

Artur Rodzinski conducted the American premiere of the Fifth Symphony on an all-British program of the New York Philharmonic-Symphony in Carnegie Hall on Nov. 30, 1944.

L. B.

Overture to the Comedy "The Wasps" of Aristophanes

VAUGHAN WILLIAMS wrote this Overture, as well as several pieces of incidental music, for a performance of the Greek comedy at Cambridge in November, 1909. Included in the set were vocal solos, choruses, and orchestral interludes. In 1925 the composer published a Suite drawn from the music. This contained the Overture, which was first heard here at a concert in the Lewisohn Stadium, New York, on July 26, 1932. Albert Coates was the conductor.

Of the witty and sprightly overture to Aristophanes' comedy, the critic and biographer, Edwin Evans, a close friend of the English composer, has written:

> Though quite unpretentious, and unaffected by Hellenistic or any other kind of learning, it is possible that this playful music really does reflect something of the mental attitude of an average Athenian citizen when stimulated by the witty irreverence of the father of comedy.
>
> The music has even a touch of innuendo. . . . That it is an outrageous anachronism is entirely in its favor. Imagine how dull the same subject could have been made by certain musicians possessing views or theories upon what is authentically Greek!

Produced in 422 B.C., *The Wasps* was Aristophanes' satiric thrust at the Athenian passion for litigation. In an earlier comedy *The Clouds,* the Greek playwright had flouted the philosophical trend typified by the Socratic schools. In *The Wasps* he turned the whiplash of deadly parody on the law courts. Athenians loved to serve on juries. They idolized abstract and abstruse "justice." Day after day the older men flocked to the trials, neglecting their private affairs. Aristophanes saw defects in the whole court system of Athens.

Besides, he hated the Assembly leader Cleon, who had prosecuted him earlier. So-called Greek "democracy" was anathema to him, an affluent aristocrat and landowner. He traced all Greece's woes to the "liberal" spirit. In short, Aristophanes belonged in the camp of "reaction." Still, he battled fearlessly against incompetence and dogma. He spared no one, not even the gods. He caricatured Euripedes and chided the sophists. He exposed the meanest of human foibles and slashed at sanctimonious smugness.

Aristophanes could stoop to the vilest buffoonery in picturing the poor and his language often smacks of the gutter. But at his best he combines the comic verve of Molière, the flaying irony of Juvenal, the satiric sharpness of Swift. In fantasy he is wilder than Lewis Carroll and Gilbert, and no less an authority than Gilbert Murray credits him with writing poetry of the "most exquisite beauty."

In *The Wasps* Aristophanes' feud with the popular self-made statesman is evidenced by the names allotted to the two main characters—Philocleon (meaning "Love-Cleon") and his son Bdelycleon ("Loathe-Cleon"). Of course "Love-Cleon" is the villain of the piece, the jury addict, and "Loathe-Cleon" the sane and sagacious hero.

Philocleon leaves home every day to serve as "dicast" or juryman. His son implores him to mend his wasteful ways, to no avail. At length Bdelycleon locks him in the house. Philocleon makes futile attempts to escape. He turns himself into smoke and tries to leave through the chimney. A stone is placed over the chimney. Through a hole in the tile he makes his way to the roof and perches there as a sparrow. He is caught in a net. Finally, a group of fellow jurymen come to his rescue. This is the famous "Chorus of Wasps" from which the play's title derives. They storm their colleague's prison and put their wasp sting to good use. But they are hurled back.

Bdelycleon then makes a concession to his father's weakness. He will stage a trial at home. The house dog Labes is arraigned for stealing cheese. Witnesses are summoned and examined. Philocleon indulges his judicial flair to the full. Through a fluke the dog is acquitted. It is Philocleon's first acquittal, and the old man nearly dies of mortification. The mock trial resolves into a parody of alleged Athenian court practice, with the judge's feelings cannily played upon by the defense. The whole machinery of trial by jury is travestied, and we are not surprised to learn that the dog Labes represents the general Laches who had been condemned by Cleon for extortion.

In the second scene of the comedy the jurymen come to liberate Philocleon dressed up grotesquely as wasps, "whose acrimonious, stinging, exasperated temper is meant to typify the character fostered among Athenian citizens by excessive addiction to forensic business." Apparently they wore wasplike masks, black-and-yellow gowns, and carried weapons looking like magnified wasp stings. At one point the chorus chants:

> If any of this good company should note our strange array—
> The wasplike waists and cross-barred suits that we have donned today—
> And if he asks what means this sting we brandish, as you see,
> Him will we undertake to teach, dull scholar though he be.

Philocleon urges them to the attack: "Come, my dear companions, wasps with relentless hearts, fly against him, animated with your fury. Sting him in the back, in his eyes, and on his fingers."

Racine, the great French dramatist, famed for his tragedies, wrote a single comedy, *Les Plaideurs,* which is largely a translation (with the locale and the characters' names changed) of Aristophanes' comedy. In his preface the polished and cultivated Frenchman confesses, apologetically, that naturally the refined art of Menander and Terence appealed to him more strongly than the blunter speech and drolleries of Plautus and Aristophanes.

L. B.

"Fantasia on a Theme by Thomas Tallis" for Double String Orchestra

THE FIRST performance of the *Fantasia* took place in Gloucester Cathedral, on Sept. 6, 1910, on the occasion of the Three Choirs Festival (including the choirs of Gloucester, Worcester, and Hereford) of that year. It was not published, however, until 1921. The work was introduced to this country at a concert of the Symphony Society of New York in Carnegie Hall on Mar. 9, 1922, Walter Damrosch conducting.

The composer wrote the following instruction in his score:

The second orchestra: two first-violin players, two second-violin players, two viola players, two violoncello players, and one contra-bass player—these should be taken from the third desk of each group (or in the case of the contra-bass by the first player of the second desk) and should if possible be placed apart from the orchestra. If this is not practicable, they should play sitting in their normal places. The solo parts are to be played by the leader in each group.

Thomas Tallis, insofar as is known, was born about 1505. Conjecture has it that he was a chorister at either St. Paul's Cathedral or the Chapel Royal. It has been established that he held some sort of official position at the Abbey of the Holy Cross at Waltham, in Essex, when the Abbey came to the end of its days in 1540. It may be, also, that Henry VIII nominated him even before that a Gentleman of the Chapel Royal, which office he held, possibly, until his death, on Nov. 23, 1585, in the reign of Elizabeth. Since the period includes the reigns of Edward VI and Mary I, it is then quite plausible to believe that Tallis took each of the successive religious changes in stride, conforming, as it were, readily, if not devotedly.

Be that as it may, he was a Protestant in 1567, when he penned eight tunes, each founded on one of the eight ecclesiastical modes, for the Metrical Psalter of Matthew Parker, Archbishop of Canterbury. Because the *cantus firmus* in the original volume is in the tenor part, the following explanation appears: "The tenor of these partes be for the people when they will sing alone, the other partes for greater queers [choirs] or to such as will play or sing them privately."

One of the customs of Tallis' time was to ascribe special characteristics to the eight ecclesiastical modes, as witness their unusually quaint description in verse:

The first is meeke: deuout to see.
The second sad: in maiesty.
The third doth rage: and roughly brayth.
The fourth doth fawne: and flattry playth.
The fyfth delight: and laugheth the more.
The sixth bewaileth: it weepth full sore.
The seuenth tredeth stoute: in froward race.
The eyghth goeth mild: in modest pace.

The tune on which the *Fantasia* is based is the third. It is not likely that it will rage or bray, as it once did, but anyway Tallis considered it excellent for the second Psalm:

> Why fumeth in sight: the Gentile spite
> In fury raging stout?

Vaughan Williams, wishing to retain all the tune's ecclesiastical character, has utilized its authentic harmonies.

In passing, Thomas Tallis and William Byrd (his godson) obtained from Queen Elizabeth in 1575 the exclusive privilege to print music and ruled music paper. The little monopoly lasted for twenty-one years, Byrd taking over when Tallis died. Thomas Tallis was buried in the parish church at Greenwich. A brass plate carrying his epitaph was removed when the church underwent alterations early in the eighteenth century. The inscription ran:

> Enterred here doth ly a worthy Wyght
> Who for long Tyme in Musick bore the Bell:
> His Name to shew, was Thomas Tallys hyght,
> In honest vertuous Lyff he dyd excell.
> He serv'd long Tyme in Chapell with grete prayse
> Fower Sovereygnes (a thing not often seen)
> I mean Kyng Henry and Prynce Edward's dayes,
> Quene Mary, and Elizabeth our Quene.
> He maryd was, though Children he had none,
> And lyv'd in Love full thre and thirty yeres,
> Wyth loyal Spowse, whos name yclyipt was Jone,
> Who here entomb'd him company now bears.
> As he did lyve, so also did he dy,
> In myld and quyet Sort (O happy Man)
> To God ful oft for Mercy did he cry,
> Wherefore he lyves, let Death do what he can.

R. C. B.

Giuseppe Verdi

BORN: LE RONCOLE, NEAR BUSSETO, DUCHY OF PARMA, OCT. 10, 1813. DIED: MILAN, JAN. 27, 1901.

His was a voice from the nether stratum, frank, fierce, lurid, unheard before on the lyric stage; he brought into over-sophisticated opera the popular song . . . and turned its siren warblings to passionate utterance. . . . His volcanic heat fairly singed the boards; people began to wake up, and say: Here verily is a man!—WILLIAM FOSTER APTHORP.

Overture to "Luisa Miller"

SALVATORE CAMMARANO sent his scenario for *Luisa Miller* to Verdi, who was in Paris, on May 3, 1846. Almost immediately an exchange of letters began between the collaborators. Their content is interesting in many respects, but chiefly because of the detailed instructions and suggestions on the work that sallied back and forth. The libretto was completed in August of that year, though Verdi had already started on the music in July. In the first week of September he notified Cammarano that the music would be finished—outside of the orchestration—by early October, and that the opera could be put on at the end of that month. (Orchestration, apparently, was the least of his worries!)

However, the world premiere of the opera was not to take place until Dec. 8, at the Teatro San Carlo, a quarantine and still other matters seeing to that. Verdi had not wanted to go to Naples at all, relenting only after urgent appeals from Cammarano and the impresario Flauto. Some of the circumstances leading to the first performance add up to a comedy of errors, as seen in the cold light of today, but they must have given all concerned many a pretty headache at the time.

The impresario's financial status was something on the order of nil. Verdi, taking a cue from Cammarano, threatened to make a sudden exit, unless 3,000 ducats were turned over in advance, as promised. A would-be trouble-maker by the name of the Duke of Ventignano, Superintendent of the Royal Theaters, tried to checkmate the composer, invoking a ridiculous law which prohibited any artist from leaving Naples without sanction from the former's august office. Characteristically, Verdi responded that he would board a French frigate, then in the port, and depart, bag, baggage, and opera. History tells us that Verdi won the little joust.

In addition, Verdi's friends went to all sorts of devices to keep one Capecelatro, a minor composer, from seeing him. Capecelatro, the word went, was cursed with the *mal'occhio* (evil eye), and it just would not do to have him cast an awful optic or two on the hard-working Verdi. Had he not been responsible for the failure, four years before, of Verdi's *Alzira* and in the very same city? So the well-meaning coterie kept their charge far away from such dangers. When *Luisa Miller* finally was produced the audience liked least the last act, which is considered the best in certain informed circles. It happens that in the intermission period just before it Capecelatro met Verdi face to face and, in an adorational fervor, threw his arms around him.

The libretto of *Luisa Miller* is an adaptation of Schiller's *Kabale und Liebe* (*Intrigue and Love*). Some Verdian students have fulminated against it, others have rallied nobly to its defense. Francis Toye, in fact, goes so far as to call it "an excellent piece of work which carries conviction even today." Cammarano made some changes in several of the characters, eliminated two of them entirely. For musico-dramatic purposes he removed all political and social significance from the Schiller play, being content to "concentrate exclusively on the individual poignancy of the situations."

The Overture is one of the best the composer has written, offering only one theme, which is cleverly put through a variety of moods and paces. Toye says of it, "The polyphonic treatment is admirable, the orchestration adequate; its rediscovery by some enterprising conductor seems overdue." One may add, the time has come.

R. C. B.

Tomás Luis de Victoria

BORN: AVILA, CIRCA 1535-1540. DIED: MADRID, AUG. 27, 1611.

*One seems to behold this Christian rising from prayer, his heart
flooded with a profound joy and an infinite gratitude.*—LOUIS LALOY.

"Jesu, dulcis memoria," Motet

[*Symphonic transcription by Leopold Stokowski*]

IN ITS original form this composition is a four-voice motet on the famous hymn
of St. Bernard of Clairvaux (1091-1113). Entitled merely "Hymnus," it appears
as the second entry in Volume VIII of the monumental edition of Victoria's
works edited for Breitkopf and Härtel by the distinguished Spanish musicologist Philippe (or Felipe) Pedrell. This volume appeared in 1913 as a supplement
to the previous seven. Besides many short pieces, among them the "Hymnus" in
question, it included Victoria's long-lost mass *Missa Domenicalis,* which Pedrell
had recently found in the Cathedral of Tortosa. In the index the short motet
on St. Bernard's hymn is grouped under "Cantiones Sacrae" ("Sacred Songs").
The four-line stanza used by Victoria runs as follows:

> Jesu, dulcis memoria,
> Dans vera cordi gaudia;
> Sed super mel et omnia
> Eijus dulcis praesentia.

Some years ago Winfred Douglas made a free rendering of the Latin words
for a collection of *Spanish Sacred Motets* which Kurt Schindler edited for the
Oliver Ditson Company of Boston. The singable adaptation was as follows:

> Jesu, only to think of thee,
> Doth give heart's dearest joy to me;
> But more than all things honey-sweet
> Would be thy very self to meet.

Schindler's arrangement for mixed voices was No. 8 in the collection, which
included a few other specimens by Victoria as well as several motets of the
composer's great contemporaries, Francisco Guerrero and Cristobal Morales.

The motet form has a long and honorable history in the development of
Renaissance music. It acquired marked importance during the sixteenth century
as a universal form in liturgical polyphony. Strictly speaking, it was a composition for voices to a sacred Latin text used in Roman Catholic worship and
usually divided into two sections running continuously.

The motet was freer in form than the fixed parts of the Mass, and, as Tovey pointed out, it never formed a permanent section of the ritual. He wrote:

The most important kind of motet is that which is written for a particular holy day. Such motets are sung between the *Credo* and the *Sanctus* of the Mass. They are often founded on the Gregorian tones of their texts, and the Mass is founded on the same themes, thus giving the whole service a musical unity which has never since been approached in any Church music even under Bach.

The term motet has also been freely used to designate secular compositions, Tovey offering as an instance the dedicatory motet at the beginning of Palestrina's Fifth Book. The history of this form is closely paralleled by the growth of its nonliturgical counterpart—the unaccompanied madrigal, which also flourished at the height of the Renaissance and rivaled it in beauty and wealth of output.

As for Victoria himself, it is assumed he was born at Avila, Spain, though the frequent references to him as "Presbyter Abulensis" would seem to point merely to his having been priest of that parish. Because of his name, many have assumed the town of Victoria was his birthplace. In 1573, Victoria was made Maestro di Cappella at the Collegium Germanicum of Rome, which he left in 1589 to become vice-choirmaster of the Royal Chapel at Madrid, a post he retained till 1602.

Victoria was one of the great triumvirate that ruled sixteenth-century music, the others being Orlando di Lasso and Palestrina. His music is marked by a lofty mysticism as well as an impulsive fervor of speech. Some of his vehement flights of imagery have prompted charges of "morbid sensualism" and "sensational effects of ecstasy." Of Victoria, Tovey once wrote:

His mastery is unfailing, but his methods are those of direct emotional effect; and the intellectual qualities that strengthen and deepen this emotion are themselves innate and not sought out. The emotion is reasonable and lofty, not because he has trained himself to think correctly, but because he does not know that anyone can think otherwise.

While the note of kinship to Palestrina and di Lasso is strong in Victoria's music, one or two telltale traits of Spanish origin may be discerned, especially the intense mystical ardor and fierce sensuous imagery, which in Spanish painting find their fullest expression in the impassioned style of El Greco.

As if to confound lexicographers and annotators, Victoria's name is equally acceptable in three forms: Tommasus Ludovicus Victoria (Latin), Tomaso Ludovico da Vittoria (Italian), and Tomás Luis de Victoria (Spanish).

L. B.

Henri Vieuxtemps

BORN: VERVIERS, BELGIUM, FEB. 20, 1820. DIED: MUSTAPHA-LES ALGERS, ALGIERS, JUNE 6, 1881.

When we speak of Vieuxtemps, we are apt to think of Paganini.
—ROBERT SCHUMANN.

Concerto for Violin and Orchestra in D minor, No. 4, Op. 31

I. Andante; Moderato. II. Adagio religioso. III. Scherzo: Vivace. IV. Finale marziale: Andante; Allegro.

MORE THAN one hundred years ago, the Philharmonic Society of New York extended its hospitality to Henri Vieuxtemps, a young Belgian violinist, who, though only twenty-four, was widely regarded in Europe as one of the reigning virtuosi of the day. Vieuxtemps appeared as guest at the concert of May 18, 1844, held in the Society's first meeting place, the Apollo Rooms, located at 410 Broadway, between Walker and Lispenard Streets. For "the first time in America" he played his own *Fantasia pour le violin sur la quatrième corde,* Op. 18. An extended tour of America followed Vieuxtemps' New York appearance, and he later revisited this country in 1857 and again in 1870, when he toured with a company that included the singer Christine Nilsson.

A musician of prodigious resource, Vieuxtemps brought gasps of astonishment with his facile sight reading. After the death of Paganini, many of his contemporaries ranked him first among the technicians of the magic bow. Testimonials of his fabulous beauty and purity of tone were left by trustworthy witnesses like Wieniawski, and even a formidable critic like Berlioz once called him "a remarkable composer, no less than an incomparable virtuoso." In 1873, this great artist suffered a stroke that paralyzed his entire left side, thus ending one of the most brilliant concert careers in music. Making a partial recovery, Vieuxtemps continued teaching for a time at the Brussels Conservatory.

Of the seven concertos written by Vieuxtemps, the Fourth was evidently his favorite. Certainly it aroused the greatest acclaim wherever he played it, besides which it has shown the sturdiest survival value of the group. It was Vieuxtemps' playing of this Concerto that prompted Berlioz, in his review in the *Journal des Débats* of the Paris premiere of 1851, to remark, "There are some talents that disarm envy." Vieuxtemps had composed the Concerto in 1849-1850 in St. Petersburg, where he served in the double capacity of professor at the Conservatory and court violinist to the Czar. As an added imperial note the score carries a dedication "To His Majesty Friedrich Wilhelm IV of Prussia." All of which led the late Lawrence Gilman to observe aptly that the Concerto "was born to the purple."

An unusual feature of the D minor Concerto is the presence of four movements, instead of the customary three. Included in the scheme is a Scherzo vivace in D minor 3/4, which is usually omitted—a practice authorized by the composer's own statement on the flyleaf of the violin part. "This concerto," wrote Vieuxtemps, "can be played without the Scherzo. In this case, the performer will pass immediately from the Adagio to the final Allegro, omitting the fourteen measures of Andante which serve as Introduction to it."

The Concerto opens with an orchestral introduction in D minor, 4/4, after which the voice of the solo violin is heard in an extended recitative, broad and dramatic in places. There is a brief excursion into the key of F major, but soon the violin is back in D minor with a sustained cantabile theme, against which the orchestra pits a melody of its own. A cadenza of sweeping brilliance follows for the solo violin. Then the orchestra returns, in dramatic mood, and the music bridges over to the next movement.

A few orchestral phrases promptly set the devotional mood of the Adagio religioso (E flat major, 12/8) through a chantlike theme. The violin is first heard in a series of arpeggios and then in a suavely lyric theme against a return of the orchestral chant. A second theme is now subjected to lengthy and varied treatment by the violin. In one graceful passage the violin is heard in serene discourse with the cellos and harp. The solo instrument then takes up the hymnlike motive of the orchestra, lifting it to its highest expression. The movement ends with a brief coda. Of this Adagio religioso Leopold Auer observed that it "must be interpreted in a spirit of the greatest reverence and with inner conviction."

A lively, piquant theme, richly developed by the violin, forms the center of the Scherzo vivace which is rarely performed. In places the movement (D minor, 3/4) swings along brightly with a verve and rhythm reminiscent of the Viennese waltz. For the solo theme of the trio (Meno mosso, D major), Vieuxtemps uses a kind of hunting motive, which is picked up by the orchestra before the main body of the Scherzo returns.

Marked Finale marziale, the last movement starts with an orchestral prelude (Andante, D minor, 4/4) which reverts to the opening of the Concerto. The martial mood of the movement begins with the Allegro in D major (2/2) that follows—a mood presently imitated by the solo violin, which performs some acrobatics and then launches into a broad melody that becomes the most active theme of the movement. A third theme of warm, romantic character is later brought in by the violin. Orchestra and solo instrument now review the earlier themes, and presently, with the violin engaged in brisk passage work, the coda sets in, ending the freest and most impassioned of the four movements.

                                                                   L. B.

Heitor Villa-Lobos

BORN: RIO DE JANEIRO, MAR. 5, 1881.

He is a Rabelais of the new music with a laughter that is generous, rude, and gusty. And yet, beneath his colorful phrases, his lawless rhythms . . . there is a profound and glowing feeling.—IRVING SCHWERKÉ.

"Choros": No. 8, for Two Pianos and Orchestra; No. 9, for Orchestra

As USED by Villa-Lobos, the term *Choros* has specific reference to a musical composition of his own invention. The word itself derives from the Brazilian *choro,* a type of sentimental serenade sung by itinerant musicians. In an authorized statement, Villa-Lobos has described his *Choros* as "a serious music of this sort, with all the elements of my country welded together—the birds, the forests, the mountains, the Indians, the cries, the people, and the gay, boisterous carnivals." The preface to the composer's *Choros* No. 10 further clarifies the *Choros* as a composition "in which are synthesized the different modalities of Brazilian, Indian, and popular music, having for principal elements Rhythm and any typical melody of popular character. The word 'serenade' gives an approximate idea of the significance of the *Choros.*"

Fourteen such *Choros* were written by Villa-Lobos between 1920 and 1929. In numbering them the composer has followed a plan of progressive complexity, rather than chronology; *i.e.,* if a later *Choros* proved of simpler structure, he gave it an earlier, rather than a later number. No. 11, for example, was composed in 1928, whereas No. 9 dates from 1929. How flexible a term "Choros" is may be seen in the scoring of the successive numbers. No. 1 is for guitar solo. No. 2 is a duet for flute and clarinet. No. 3 is for male chorus and winds, including saxophone. No. 4 calls for three horns and a trombone. No. 5 is for piano. No. 6 is for clarinet, trumpet, *bombardine,* and guitar. No. 7 is for a chamber orchestra. No. 8 calls for two pianos and orchestra. No. 9 is scored for large orchestra. No. 10 is for chorus and orchestra. No. 11 returns to the piano-and-orchestra combination, and so does No. 13. No. 12 is for orchestra. No. 14 calls for large orchestra, military band, and mixed chorus.

According to the composer, the series is completed by an *Introduçao aos Choros* for Orchestra, and a *Choros Bis* for violin and cello. The latter Nicolas Slonimsky has described as "a tour de force of instrumental writing, in which double-stops, harmonics, and a simultaneous use of pizzicato and arco produce the effect of a complete four-part ensemble." Mr. Slonimsky's own contribution to the definition of "Choros" is that they contain the rhythms, melos, and rhapsodic fervor of Brazilian music. The composer told the present writer that one might call the "Choros" a kind of "Brasilofonia."

Choros No. 8 was composed in Rio de Janeiro in 1925 and bears a dedication to Tomás Téran. The work was heard here at the World's Fair on May 4, 1939, when Burle Marx conducted the Philharmonic-Symphony in a concert sponsored by the Brazilian Government. Mr. Marx then wrote of the work:

It would not be easy to analyze this singularly original score in detail—its rhythmic combinations, often primitive, yet highly complex; its exotic scheme and novelty of instrumentation. A long introduction propounds several short themes. Later on a new mood is established by violas and celli over an accompaniment of bassoons and harp. A passage in dark and tragic vein, beginning as a heavy lament, mounts to an orgiastic pitch of excitement. A *mouvement de marche modérée* develops essentially as a dance movement. Toward the end, *un peu moderé,* rhythms of 5/16 and 6/16 are utilized, with further audacities of instrumentation. An important part is played by the two pianos, requiring virtuoso capacities.

Villa-Lobos himself conducted the first North American performance of *Choros* No. 9 at a New York Philharmonic-Symphony concert on Feb. 8, 1945.

In a talk with the author, Mr. Villa-Lobos, who spoke in French, singled out some features of his *Choros* No. 8 which he thought worth noting.

My main esthetic intention was to create an atmosphere of the primitive feeling of music projected into our own epoch.

The dominant note I would call *sentiment.* This may appear singular, for against it you will find the paradox of the highest instrumental brutality. In the introduction I evoke a serious mood with popular and typical instruments [*des instruments vulgaires et typiques.*] Later comes an agitated passage which I would call "the battle of the rhythms." It was my friend Florent Schmitt who once called the march section, *la marche funèbre des éléphants.*

You ask me about *development*—how I would define my method? I can only reply I worship liberty! Imagine for yourself what a composer who worships liberty will do with *development!*

Mr. Villa-Lobos remarked, smiling, that a Parisian colleague had started the practice of referring to *Choros* No. 8 as *le fou huitième*—the mad eighth.

In comparing the two *Choros,* the dynamic Brazilian spoke of a "diversity of sonorous material." What he termed the "level of instrumental situation," was the same in both. He said:

There is, however, no paradox in No. 9. Instrumentation and *sentiment* do not seem to contradict one another as in the No. 8. My *Choros* No. 9 is perhaps closer to classicism. No. 8 is freer in structure. In No. 9 there are no interruptions—it advances directly. No. 8 is more like a rhapsodic suite, while No. 9 is more suggestive of the symphony and the symphonic poem.

On the subject of themes, Mr. Villa-Lobos said he followed the same procedure in No. 8 and No. 9. He explained:

In fact, in all my *Choros* I have no fixed formula for the use of themes. I use them for development or atmosphere, as I feel the need. I never repeat themes purely for the pleasure of repetition or to create "cyclic" music. I bring a theme back only as its return grows out of necessity. I do not use ready-made folk songs and dances. My themes often *suggest* folk themes, that is they have the *aspect* of folk themes. I do not believe in quoting anyone else's music.

In my music there are no so-called influences. It is thoroughly American—of our continent—belonging to no school or special trend. To follow a fashion in art is to become a prisoner of one's models. Naturally I draw on elements of classical technic. Let me express it thus: I have made my own form on the basis of elements of the symphony, the rhapsody, the classical suite, the symphonic poem, and the sonata. What results is mine alone. I am an American composer—American in the inclusive sense—who has evolved a new American form.

He was asked about his sources of *inspiration*. Mention of the word prompted a warm outburst from Mr. Villa-Lobos.

How do I know what inspired *Choros* No. 8 and *Choros* No. 9? My answer is that I do not know what the word *inspiration* means. I create music out of necessity, biological necessity. I write because I cannot help it. I follow no style or fashion. My artistic creed is *la liberté absolue*. When I write, it is according to the style of Villa-Lobos.

Mr. Villa-Lobos has also written a Fantasia for Cello and Orchestra, dedicated to Serge Koussevitzky; a *Bachiana* No. 9, dedicated to Aaron Copland; and a Concerto for Harmonica and Orchestra. For a time he gathered photographic material for a composite picture of the mountains of the United States. From it was to grow his Symphony No. 7. An earlier symphony brought the mountains of his native Brazil into similar focus. He is a phenomenally prolific composer in all forms.

In an interview with Olin Downes, critic of *The New York Times,* the Brazilian composer declared he did not believe in music as "culture, or education, or even as a device for amusement or for quieting the nerves, but as something more potent, mystical, and profound in its effect. Music has this power to communicate, to heal, and to ennoble, when it is made a part of man's life and consciousness."

Although he has collected several thousand Brazilian folk melodies and thoroughly absorbed the spirit of native music, Mr. Villa-Lobos told Mr. Downes that he never used this material in any literal or imitative way. He said:

I compose in the folk style. I utilize thematic idioms in my own way, and subject to my own development. An artist must do this. He must select and transmit the material given him by his people. . . . I study the history, the country, the speech, the customs, the background of the people. I have always done this, and it is from these sources, spiritual as well as practical, that I have drawn my art.

Choros Nos. 8 and 9 call for a huge assortment of native percussion instruments. Among them are the *reco-reco* (notched stick); the *chocalho* (a rattle made by natives either with gourd seeds inside, or with strung and netted gourd seeds on the outside); the *pios* (used only in No. 9), a thin wooden stick producing a whistling sound when rubbed with a piece of folded cloth; the *puita* ("small animal roar"), described by John N. Burk, Boston Symphony annotator, as "a tin cylinder about 15 inches deep and 10 inches in diameter with a drumhead on one end and a gut string rubbed with rosin which extends from the center of the drumhead through the cylinder"—it is played by tightly pulling the hand over the strings; the *matraca* (ratchet), the *caxambu,* a glass bottle filled with gravel; and the *camisao grande* and *camisao pequeno* (literally "large shirt" and "little shirt," terms used for boxlike drums struck with the hand). A big snare drum may be used to replace the *caxambu,* as well as the *camisao grande* and *camisao pequeno,* which are used only in *Choros* No. 9. Three additional native drums are called for in *Choros* No. 9—the *tartaruga,* the *tambor surdo* (muted drum), and the *tambourine de samba.* The snare drum may be substituted for the first two, and a tambourine without jingles for the third.

Choros No. 9, composed in 1929, is dedicated to Arminda Neves d'Almeida, who later became the composer's wife.

In music circles the name of Heitor Villa-Lobos is almost synonymous with Brazil. Indo-Brazilian lore and the country's colorful history find concrete expression in his art through a rhythmic and melodic medium of marked national character. In the minds of most concertgoers he is associated with Brazil the way Jan Sibelius is with Finland, Carlos Chavez with Mexico, and Georges Enesco with Rumania—perhaps even more closely. Certainly, no other composer of that fascinating tropical land has so thoroughly absorbed its popular and cultural heritage and so richly communicated it in terms of his own personality.

Largely self-taught, Villa-Lobos admits that he did not find himself as creative artist till the day he decided to join a jungle expedition. Out of that trip grew extensive studies in tribal musical habits. In 1922 he went to Paris, not with the idea of "imitating what others had done," but "to show what he had accomplished," as Robert Sabin wrote in *Musical America.* Villa-Lobos had been composing "revolutionary" music of his own for years before he came into contact with the Parisian vanguard. Some early compositions date as far back as 1900. Invited by the government to organize musical education in

Brazil, Villa-Lobos gave up creative work almost entirely for ten years, during which he founded schools and built huge choruses that now perform in the chief cities of Brazil, especially on Sept. 7, which is the country's Independence Day. Mr. Sabin writes:

Today music is a vital part of the training of all Brazilian school children and more than a million people have been trained in the system which Villa-Lobos has worked out. Music to him is a socially collective force and experience. At first the piano and all other instruments are forbidden. Children learn the basic elements of music through singing, sometimes in unison and sometimes in parts. They are trained to think of and to feel music as a part of all life. The geographical, biological, and psychological aspects of music, and all of the other fields of human experience in which music exists are part of Villa-Lobos' conception of musical education.

L. B.

"Descobrimento do Brasil," Suite No. 1

COMPLETED IN Rio de Janeiro in 1939, the *Descobrimento do Brasil* was a logical outgrowth of Villa-Lobos' interest in native folklore and legend. The work was planned as a patriotic gesture centering in a great historical fact. The style is largely rhapsodic and typifies the composer's remarkable grasp of exotic color and rhythms.

The researches leading to the composition of the *Descobrimento* and the course of events descriptively surveyed are outlined in a prefatory text in Portuguese by Villa-Lobos himself, which may be translated and condensed as follows:

The material for the symphonic series came from historical documents dating from the period of Brazil's discovery. Almost no typical Portuguese music of that time is extant. Portugal was then dominated by the artistic and religious outlook of Spain and France. This, with popular religious singing and Moorish, Italian, and modern Greek songs, exerted a great influence on European centers.

I tried to absorb the spirit of the letters of Pero Vaz Caminha to King D. Manoel. These letters lend themselves perfectly to a variety of artistic reconstructions. They evoked for me the moods and "states of soul" characteristic of that period.

The work is divided into two main parts, the first describing the voyage of outcasts and slaves in a galleon commanded by Pedro Alvares Cabral and bound for Brazil. The second recounts what occurred in Brazil after their arrival.

From the narrative left by Pedro Alvares Cabral I took material suggesting several musical episodes. The piece called *Alegria* is one. It evokes the outcasts and crew thinking back to their native celebrations.

Villa-Lobos then describes his *Cançao Moura (Moorish Song)*, assuming the presence of Moors in the crew, then an *Adagio sentimental,* picturing the feelings of the nobleman aboard. Later he assigns a section to the slaves and their dreams of tribal feats and dancing. He continues:

During the uncertain crossing of the Atlantic, there arise in the musical pieces already cited, suggestions of doubt, revolt, hallucination, sadness, hope, false confidence; moods of pity for lost ships, of mirages of land; of prayers and counsels. These "states of soul" intertwine with the storm at sea and are represented by vividly characteristic themes.

Then comes a section, "Flores ta Virgem," conveying the thrill of sighting land, followed by a meditative passage.

Pre-Columbian themes collected by Jean de Lary and other historians enter the orchestral fabric of the Second Part, besides melodic strands of Villa-Lobos' own invention in the same indigenous spirit. Primitive songs and dances based on material gathered by himself and on available recordings are introduced into the scheme.

For the transporting of the Cross used in celebrating the first Mass in Brazil, I composed a religious piece entitled "Procissao da Cruz," contrasting two themes of different character, one authentically native, of a droning melancholy suggesting the vanishing trees of the forest where the sacred birds no longer sing; the other based on the "Creator alma siderum," attributed to St. Ambrose, Bishop of Milan, author of popular Christian hymns.

For the celebration of the Mass I wrote a great double chorus, a capella, the first part, for men's voices, based on a theme from the classical Kyrie of the Gregorian missal, for women's voices, being a combination of primitive themes set to a text in the Tupi-Guarini dialect.

Thus I tried to bring to life the mood of this unforgettable picture which was the first Mass in Brazil.

The "Symphonic Series"—thus subtitled—is divided into three suites, consisting of the Introduçao (Introduction) and "Alegrias na Horta" ("Gay Dances in the Orchard"). The key of C minor prevails in both.

The folkish character of the music is unmistakable, and dancelike episodes of the same flavor crop up at every turn. The opening movement starts with a broad Largo, followed by the first of the lively dance themes. An intriguing passage for flute, against an accompaniment of bassoon and solo viola, evokes an exotic setting. There is a slow section for saxophone solo, promptly repeated by the full orchestra.

Soon the song previously allotted to the flute is taken up by the strings, and after a brisk passage the English horn, a solo horn, and a solo cello discourse a new subject. In a short Allegro section a set of trumpet calls sound, accompanied by one trombone, with the contrasting effects of nearness and distance. After the contra-bassoon intones a slow solo passage, the movement merges into the "Alegrias na Horta." This is much simpler in structure, consisting mainly of a set of dances with two distinct themes, one broader and statelier, the other quick and sprightly.

The orchestration calls for two flutes, one piccolo, two oboes, English horn, two clarinets, bass clarinet, alto saxophone, two bassoons, one contra-bassoon, four horns, three trumpets, three trombones, tuba, celesta, xylophone, piano, harp, and the usual percussion and strings.

The *Descobrimento* was first performed in America at the Philharmonic-Symphony concerts of Mar. 12 and 14, 1941, with John Barbirolli directing.

L. B.

Toccata, "O Trenzinho do Caipira" ("The Little Train of the Caipira"), from "Bachianas Brasileiras," No. 2

VILLA-LOBOS has completed eight so-called *Bachianas Brasileiras,* described as "fusions of Bach style and folk style." To the Brazilian composer, Bach is the universal spirit as expressed in music—a source and end in itself. The Suites are a form of homage to the Leipzig master, whom he speaks of as "a mediator among all races." This homage Villa-Lobos has tried to express through a synthesis of the Bach spirit, Brazilian folklore, and his own individual style. To Villa-Lobos what Bach represents is "deeply rooted in the folk music of every country in the world." Some have suspected a slightly different motive in the choice of title. "Probably a desire to tweak solemn noses," is Paul Rosenfeld's conjecture.

A blithe little piece of program music—the Toccata is the last movement of Villa-Lobos' *Bachiana Brasileira* No. 2. Its title, "O Trenzinho do Caipira," is a reference to the bumpy little steam train used by berry pickers and farm workers between villages in São Paulo province. Villa-Lobos took a trip on it one day in 1931. As the train chugged along the composer found himself weaving phrases around the theme of the rotating wheels. In an hour the Toccata—or toccatina—was complete. That night Villa-Lobos and his wife, a brilliant cellist, played it in its first version for cello and piano. Later, in 1938, at the suggestion of the Brazilian conductor Burle Marx, the composer arranged the piece for chamber orchestra, plus a group of native percussion instruments. Thus, it became the final section of the *Bachiana Brasileira* No. 2. *Caipira,* meaning "yokel" or "rustic," derives from *curupira,* a word in the language of the Tupi Indians, one of the two major native tribes of Brazil.

Marked un poco moderato, 2/4, the piece is scored for one flute, one oboe, one clarinet, saxophone, bassoon, two horns, one trombone, tympani, triangle, celesta, piano, and strings. Among native percussion instruments used are the *reco-reco* (a "notched stick"), the *chocalho* (a rattle made by natives either with gourd seeds inside, or with strung and netted gourd seeds on the outside), and the *ganza* (a metal tube filled with gravel). Also included are a *caixa* and *caixa surda* (snare drum and muted snare drum), the *matraca* (ratchet), and *bombo* (large bass drum).

This work was included on the first program of Brazilian music at the World's Fair on May 4, 1939, when Burle Marx led the Philharmonic-Symphony Orchestra.

"Bachianas Brasileiras," No. 5, for Eight Cellos and Soprano

In the *Bachianas Brasileiras* No. 5 the air is first intoned by the soprano on an open vowel (vocalise), then with the Portuguese text given below, and finally hummed.

Tarde . . . Côr de rósa e ouro;	Afternoon . . . pink and gold;
O crepusculo desce,	Dusk falls,
Vai tingindo a superficie do mar . . .	Tingeing the surface of the sea . . .
Sem saber porque a gente se entristece,	Without knowing why people sadden,
Sem querer, os olhos se poem a chorar . . .	Without wanting, eyes begin to weep . . .
Sem sentir minh'alma se desvanece,	Unaware, my soul grows faint . . .
E'a serena hora em que os jardins do cèu	It is the serene hour in which heaven's gardens
Abremse em flores de luz sobre o universo.	Open in flowers of light upon the universe.
Êmudecem as aves, trilan tristes insetos . . .	The birds are silent; insects are chirping sadly . . .
E'um poêma do mar, cada onda é um verso.	A poem of the sea, each wave a verse . . .
Vem chegando a noite suave e lenta	Night approaches, suave and slow . . .
E' saudade bôa que me atormenta . . .	A bitter-sweet longing troubles me.
Tarde côr de rósa e ouro,	Afternoon . . . pink and gold,
O crepusculo desce,	Dusk falls,
Vai tingindo a superficie do mar.	Tingeing the surface of the sea.

Like the preceding work, *Bachianas Brasileiras* No. 5 was featured on the first program of Brazilian music at the World's Fair on May 4, 1939, when Burle Marx led the Philharmonic-Symphony Orchestra. Bidu Sayao was the soprano soloist.

L B.

Giovanni Battista Viotti

BORN: FONTANETTO, ITALY, MAY 23, 1753. DIED: LONDON, MAR. 3, 1824.

He has been called "the father of modern violin playing," and while the modern violinist would rather fancy his performances a reincarnation of Paganini's flaming virtuosities, he still turns first to Viotti's cooler and easier concertos for a substantial part of his basic training.
—ABRAHAM VEINUS.

Concerto for Violin and Orchestra in A minor, No. 22

I. Moderato. II. Adago. III. Agitato assai.

THE SON of a village blacksmith, Giovanni Battista Viotti learned to play on a small fiddle which he received as a present. He became so proficient that when he was a mere eight years of age he was recommended by the Bishop of Strambino to a patron of the arts, the Prince della Cisterna, of Turin, who placed the youngster in the care of Gaetano Pugnani, one of Piedmont's foremost violinists.

He was appointed to the violin section of the royal orchestra while he was still a student and presently went with his master on a tour which took them through Germany, Poland, and Russia. He made many public appearances, receiving encomiums everywhere. One day in 1783, however, his pride was given a serious blow when a minor violinist of his time drew a packed house, whereas he had been able to lure only a few scant listeners at one of his own events some days previously. He decided to give up public appearances forever.

In any case, he was later appointed accompanist to Marie Antoinette and *maître de chapelle* to the Princess Soubise. In the meantime, he strongly refused to play in public. After some experiences as a manager at the Théâtre Italien and later the Théâtre Feydeau he went to London where he finally succumbed to pressure and took up again the career of the violin virtuoso.

In 1793, suspected of being in league with emissaries of the French Revolution, he fled to Hamburg where he remained for two years. He then returned to London and bought a partnership in a wine house. A short stay in Paris in 1802 brought him immense gratification, for at a recital in the Salle du Conservatoire he astonished everyone with his extraordinary powers.

He visited Paris in 1814. Five years later he settled there, having accepted the directorship of the Académie de Musique. Viotti held the position until 1822, when he resigned. While on a trip to London, two years later, he died.

Viotti is regarded as the founder of the so-called modern school of violin playing. His compositions, among which are numbered many classics for the violin, include the published twenty-nine concertos (the first in "modern sonata form, supported by a broadened orchestration").

Concerning this Concerto, Brahms once wrote to Clara Schumann, "It is my very special enthusiasm. It is a splendid work, of remarkable fineness of invention. Everything is thought out and worked out in masterly fashion and with imaginative power."

R. C. B.

Tommaso Antonio Vitali

BORN: BOLOGNA, CIRCA 1665. DIED: MODENA(?), CIRCA 1735.

The "Ciacona" in G minor is a forerunner of Bach's great work in the same form for violin solo. It is a "Ciacona" with variations, in which a clean-cut rhythmic theme is developed in a number of contrasting variations whose ornamentation is no mere external virtuoso embellishment. . . . A special charm of these variations is the change of tonality which occurs in certain ones among them—something unusual in seventeenth-century compositions—and some decidedly inspired modulations. I know of no other work of its period which compares with the Vitali "Ciacona" as regards wealth of harmonic development.—LEOPOLD AUER.

"Chaconne"

[*Transcribed for Strings and Organ by Alfonso Gibilaro*]

OF THE many Vitali's flourishing in the history of music, the first, Filippo, was a Florentine priest, singer, and composer; the second, Giovanni Battista, a violinist and composer of ballet music; the third, Tommaso Antonio. Little is known about Tommaso. He was the son of Giovanni Battista. Probably like all great sons of still greater fathers, he was overshadowed by the greater Vitali. The year of a man's birth is often lost to history. In Tommaso's case not even the decade of his birth is known. Grove dates his birth from "about the middle of the seventeenth century at Bologna." By a conjectural sequence of vital statistics, the Italian encyclopedists have decided on 1664 (Vitali *père* having been born in 1644, for one thing). Some of the German chroniclers, even more practical minded, have added a year.

Anyway, Giovanni and Tommaso both migrated to Modena in 1674. There Tommaso joined the court cappella and in due time became its director. That was during the reigns of the Dukes Francesco II and Rinaldi I. In the humble dedicatory style of the time, Tommaso, inscribing his initial work to his ducal superior, speaks of himself as the *"servitore attuale della medesima altezza."*

Tommaso's association with the Accademia de' filarmonici of Bologna dates from 1706. Grove lists a sonata of his for two violins and bass as included in a Bologna publication of that year. The album—the combined effort of a dozen composers—bore a fancy botanical title beginning with the words, *"Corona di dodici fiori armonici"* ("A Garland of Twelve Harmonic Flowers"). Later Tommaso wrote several works for solo violin and string ensembles. Earlier, in

1692, as an act of filial piety, he had brought out an edition of the elder Vitali's violin sonatas. Supposedly, he was a brilliant virtuoso of the fiddle, and among his famous pupils he numbered Girolamo Nicolo Laurenti.

Today, Tommaso Vitali is remembered almost solely as the composer of a sturdy violin solo, with figured bass, the *Ciaconna,* or *Chaconne.* Violinists regard it as a "worthy predecessor" of Bach's more famous *Chaconne* in its inventive power and masterly sequence of variations. The *Ciaconna* was first edited by Ferdinand David in 1867 for "Die Hohe Schule" collection of violin studies. Shortly thereafter, Hermann arranged it for viola and piano. Later the Italian Anzoletti and the Belgian Charlier made fresh versions for violin. Ottorino Respighi was apparently the first composer to expand the *Ciaconna* to fuller scoring, his rendering calling for string quartet and organ, besides solo violin.

As in the case of the Bach *Chaconne,* many musicians consider the solo violin incapable of conveying the full breadth and cumulative massiveness of the original *Ciaconna.* Material and implications both seem to invite broader development. In making his transcription, Mr. Gibilaro assigned the "great moments" of the Vitali work to the massed strings, reserving the more delicate variations for the solo violin. In places the theme is used contrapuntally against the variations, the whole mounting to a resounding close, in which strings and organ combine in full force.

Mr. Gibilaro, a pianist, composer, and opera coach, was born in Porto Empedocle, Sicily. In 1897, at the age of nine, he entered the Palermo Conservatory, where he was later a fellow pupil of Gino Marinuzzi. He came to London in 1911 and has since resided there. In 1916, he married John Barbirolli's sister Rosa. Mr. Gibilaro has several published compositions to his credit.

The transcription was written in London during the frightful "air blitz" days of 1940. To quote Mr. Gibilaro, "it helped pass the time between periods of fire-watching on the roof." John Barbirolli led the New York Philharmonic-Symphony in the premiere of the arrangement on Mar. 19, 1942.

L. B.

Antonio Vivaldi

BORN: VENICE(?), CIRCA 1675. DIED: VIENNA, JULY, 1741.

The compositions chosen for the festival confronted us with a Vivaldi who can be compared without hesitation to J. S. Bach. Every day it is more evident that the influence exerted by Vivaldi on the Cantor was considerable and perhaps even decisive in his molding.—ALFREDO CASELLA, *writing of the Vivaldi Festival in Siena, in* 1939.

Concerto in D minor, Op. 3, No. 11

[*Transcribed for Orchestra, with Organ, by Alexander Siloti*]

I. Maestoso. II. Largo. III. Allegro.

AWAITING PUBLICATION in the Biblioteca Nazionale of Turin is a vast store of musical manuscripts dating from the eighteenth century. The gift of a Dr. Foa, it consists of 300 concertos and twenty-two operas. Dr. Foa inherited the collection from descendants of the man who wrote them, and this man was Antonio Vivaldi, in his time a composer far more celebrated than his German contemporary, Johann Sebastian Bach. It would have been one more ironic footnote in history if Vivaldi's music, to which the Leipzig master owed so much, should have fallen prey to the roving incendiaries of Bach's country.

And perhaps the more ironic because Vivaldi's fame for years survived largely through Bach's admiration for his music, partly manifested in several organ and harpsichord transcriptions. Yet, this humble Venetian violinist and priest, director of a foundling asylum, pioneer in organizing and directing an all girls' orchestra and choir, found time between his pedagogical and priestly tasks to compose 40 operas, 100 religious works, and at least 400 concertos. Two of these concertos, found in the Turin state library, were polished up for performance at a Vivaldi festival held in Siena in 1939 at the Accademia Musicale Chigiana, a school founded by the well-known patron of the arts, Count Guido Chigi-Saracini. One of these concertos, calling for mute all through, was called *Il riposo,* the other, *Alla rustica.*

Vivaldi's biography is almost all in his music. Few other facts about him have come down. Like himself, his father was a violinist in the service of St. Mark's Church. History has given the younger Vivaldi the soubriquet of "red priest" (*il prete rosso*), an allusion either to the color of his hair or to the loud semiclerical suit often worn by him; in any event, not a reference to political radicalism, as in the case of Britain's famous "red Dean." Vivaldi's rigorous

810

piety yielded only to the urge to write music. Only then would he drop the rosary for the pen. There is a story that when an old man he was once summoned before the Inquisition on the charge that while conducting Mass he suddenly stopped, rushed off to the sacristy to jot down a musical idea, and promptly returned to his duties. The Inquisition is said to have dismissed him as mentally unfit for celebrating Mass. Doubtless Vivaldi, as creative artist and priest, would have traced his dereliction to divine fire.

It is not surprising to find the D minor Concerto entangled in a mesh of mystery and confusion. Appearing as the eleventh of twelve *concerti grossi* published in Amsterdam circa 1714, it was transcribed for organ by Bach. Until 1840 this transcription, together with Bach's copy of Vivaldi's score, gathered dust in the Berlin State Library. Then the Leipzig publishing house of Peters brought out the transcription. But with each fresh copy issued went two gratuitous blunders. Vivaldi's name was nowhere on the score, and the Bach whose name it carried was not Johann Sebastian but Wilhelm Friedemann Bach, his son. This was corrected some time later, and Vivaldi's modest share in the work's history was finally established in 1911.

The scoring of the original pre-Bach and pre-Siloti Concerto is for four violins, two violas, cello, and organ bass. Siloti's arrangement calls for double wood-wind choir (with double bassoon), string orchestra, and organ. Sam Franko also made a transcription of the same work.

Covering the Siena festival in 1939, Alfredo Casella was moved to pen a glowing appraisal of the music of this "red priest" of Venice:

The compositions chosen for the festival confronted us with a Vivaldi who can be compared without hesitation to J. S. Bach. Every day it is more evident that the influence exerted by Vivaldi on the Cantor was considerable and perhaps even decisive in his molding.

The prodigious wealth of musical invention; the dramatic force, which recalls so imperatively the brilliance and fire of the great Venetian painters; the mastery of choral polyphony; the marvelous dynamism of the instrumental part, the incessant movement of which, independent of the voices and chorus, plainly forecasts the Wagnerian style and finally, the high quality of the emotion which animates his works. All these put Vivaldi in a wholly new light.

L. B.

Richard Wagner

BORN: LEIPZIG, MAY 22, 1813. DIED: VENICE, FEB. 13, 1883.

He had one mistress to whom he was faithful to the day of his death: Music. Not for a single moment did he ever compromise with what he believed, with what he dreamed. There is not a line of his music that could have been conceived by a little mind. Even when he is dull, or downright bad, he is dull in the grand manner. There is greatness about his worst mistakes. Listening to his music, one does not forgive him for what he may or may not have been. It is not a matter of forgiveness. It is a matter of being dumb with wonder that his poor brain and body didn't burst under the torment of the demon of creative energy that lived inside him, struggling, clawing, scratching to be released; tearing, shrieking at him to write the music that was in him. The miracle is that what he did in the little space of seventy years could have been done at all, even by a great genius. Is it any wonder that he had no time to be a man?—DEEMS TAYLOR.

Overture to the Opera "The Flying Dutchman"

WAGNER'S OPERA *The Flying Dutchman* is based on an old legend, which he came upon in Heine's *Memoires of Herr Schnabelewopski*. It is the story of the mariner, who prevented by adverse winds from "doubling the Cape," vows to do so, should Hell itself say no. Hell, as it happens, does; whereupon the mariner, for his audacity, is sentenced to a life of aimless and stormy wanderings over the oceans of the world, until he "finds a woman who will be faithful to him unto death." Senta is that woman, and so strong is her devotion that she flings herself into the sea to prove it. With that comes release for Erik, the mariner, and an ecstatic reunion with his beloved in the empyrean.

In the construction of his Overture, Wagner utilizes several of the motives heard later in the opera, although, as John F. Runciman remarks, "It is the atmosphere of the sea that counts." He continues, "The sea, indeed, is the background, the foreground, the whole environment of the drama. . . . The smell and atmosphere of the sea maintained with extraordinary vividness to the last bar." In any case, the Overture presents the theme of the Dutchman, which appears in the opening measures by way of horns and bassoons; the up-and-down motive of Senta (the Angel of Mercy) is given to the English horn, horns, and bassoons.

The instruments called for are piccolo, two flutes, two oboes, English horn, two clarinets, four horns, two bassoons, two trumpets, three trombones, bass tuba, kettledrums, harp, and strings.

Richard Wagner himself conducted the world premiere, which took place at the Dresden Court Opera, Jan. 2, 1843. Beside the obvious problems posed by the staging of the work—how to navigate two ships on one stage—there was the usual business of finding the right singers for the parts. The composer was fortunate in obtaining for Senta the services of Wilhemine Schröder-Devrient, an artist, it is said, of considerable equipment, vocal and mental. But to cast the role of the Dutchman was something else again. Wagner had, among the elements of the company then functioning, a baritone, one Wächter, who "had the requisite, a voice, described as sonorous, with a metallic ring, and of such compass that both bass and baritone parts lay within his range."

This Wächter, though, was a fat fellow, and a very poor actor. About him Sincerus, writing of the Dresden Theater, some years later, declared that he had "outlived himself." So it fell to Schröder-Devrient to carry the main load, which she did quite handsomely, not having avoided, however, a few upsetting experiences during rehearsals. One of these came at the point where Senta implores heaven that she might be Erik's redeemer. She stopped her plea suddenly to whisper in despair to the composer, "How can I say it when I look into those beady eyes? Good God, Wagner what a mess you have made!"

C. B.

Preludes to Act I and Act III of "Lohengrin"

IN THE summer of 1845, while Wagner was at Marienbad, he worked out the plan for *Lohengrin*. The libretto he wrote during the following winter. Then came a topsy-turvy scheme of creation. In composing the music he began with the hero's Narrative in the last act, "because the monologue contained the most significant musical germs in the whole score." He finished the third act on Mar. 25, 1847; the first act on June 8, of that year; the second act on Aug. 2; and the Prelude on Aug. 28. The orchestration was done during the following winter and spring. Franz Liszt conducted the premiere of the opera at Weimar, on Aug. 28, 1850.

In discussing his libretto for *Lohengrin* Wagner explained that the hero, Lohengrin, awaited the woman who believed in him,

who should ask not who he was, nor whence he came, but should love him for what he was and because of what he was. He sought not admiration or adoration, but the one and only thing that could deliver him from his loneliness and appease his longing, and that was love—to be loved, to be encompassed by love. With every fiber of his being he yearned to become fully and completely a man, giving and receiving impressions and sensations with equal ardor, but a man above all, that is to say, a perfect artist, yet not a god. And so he yearned for woman; and so he came down from the solitary, sun-smitten heights, when there fell upon his ear, from the crowded haunts of humanity, the cry of that tortured heart.

Yet "that tortured heart" (Elsa) was regarded by Wagner as the very antithesis of Lohengrin, the other half of his nature in whom the hero seeks release. She is all woman "and so rooted in her jealousy that she rushes freely to her death," thus exposing a major motivation of most of Wagner's librettos—the renunciation of love. He once said:

It was written that I should slay her, in order to follow the traces of the true feminine which shall bring salvation to the world and to me, by annihilating the egoism of man, how pure soever it may be. Elsa, woman, the ultimate expression of fatality, has made me a whole-hearted revolutionary. She was the spirit of the masses from whom, as an artist, I looked for my redemption.

The Prelude to Act I, is, according to William Apthorp:

Like the hero's career in the opera. It begins, as it were, in the clouds, then gradually descends farther and farther until it embraces all the lower tones of the orchestra, and then returns to the clouds again. Its single theme is developed in free polyphony by various successive groups of instruments, each of which groups proceeds with free counterthematic work as the next group enters with the theme. First we have the violins piano in the higher registers; then come the flutes, oboes, and clarinets; then the violas, cellos, horns, bassoons, and double basses; lastly the trumpets, trombones, and tuba fortissimo; then comes the decrescendo, ending pianissimo in the high violins and flutes.

The Prelude to Act III is a very animated and, at the same time, rather pompous Allegro in 4/4 time. It has a middle section which is related to the music sung by Elsa in her dramatic scene with Ortrud in Act II.

R. C. B.

Overture to the Opera "Tannhäuser"

FOLLOWING A tradition established by Weber, the Overture to *Tannhäuser*, through its unreeling of themes that appear in the opera, represents a sort of condensed account of the whole work. It begins with the "churchly harmonies" of the "Pilgrims' Chorus." The melody running its course along with them is variously known as the "religious motive," the "motive of faith, salvation by grace." The next definite theme we hear is that called the "motive of contrition" or, perhaps, the "motive of repentance." After a Wagnerian workout, involving, among other things, a crescendo, comes a series of broken triplets in the violins. This has become familiar as the "motive of rejoicing" and also as the "pulse of life."

Following a long diminuendo, the "churchly harmonies" return, and with the sustaining of the last chord pianissimo a figure in the violas brings on the main section of the Overture, and presently the orchestra crashes out its Hörselberg, or Venusberg, revelries. The knight Tannhäuser passes in review by way of his ode to the goddess Venus. The musical scene changes back and forth, and now the seductive measures of Venus' appeal are heard. The revelry continues. Once again the knight's song in praise of Venus makes its way forward. The music describing the orgy becomes intensified. There are a few downward phrases and the "pulse of life" beats passionately in the violins. At a later point the Pilgrims' chant breaks into the scheme, and soon "Salvation," as expressed in a triumphal theme, takes over.

In the opera the Bacchanalian pages of the Overture lead right into the riotous scene in the Venusberg. Wagner connected the two sections, omitting the "salvation" coda for the Paris production of the work given at the Opéra on Mar. 13, 1861. Incidentally, the Overture is heard in the theater only when the opera is given in the last of the three Dresden versions.

The Overture is scored for piccolo, two flutes, two oboes, two clarinets, two bassoons, four horns, three trumpets, three trombones, bass tuba, kettledrums, triangle, cymbals, tambourine, and strings.

                                                                        R. C. B.

Bacchanale from "Tannhäuser"

THIS OPERA, in three acts, was first produced at the Royal Opera House, Dresden, on Oct. 19, 1845. Some sixteen years later, due to the interest and influence of Princess Metternich, wife of the Austrian Ambassador to France, the work was introduced to Paris. For that production Wagner extended his first scene to include a Bacchanale, the reasons for this being as amusing to us as they must have been tragic to Wagner. The Princess revealed, in an article written for the *Pall Mall Magazine* (London, 1894), some of the reasons for the failure of the opera there, and it was a complete failure. The Princess says:

The day of the performance drew nigh, and in most circles little good will was confessed. It was stated generally that a protest should be made against the abominable futurist music, and it was rumored that stormy scenes might be expected at the Opéra. In the clubs men were annoyed because Wagner would not have a regular ballet, but only a few poses of the ballerinas in the Venusberg. The club subscribers to the Opera expected a ballet at nine-thirty sharp, no matter what the opera. This, at least, was the custom of the time. No one who knew anything of art could conceive where a ballet could be introduced into the midst of *Tannhäuser*. Wagner declared that he would not accede to the silly wishes of the subscribers, because he could not. And he was perfectly right, but his refusal was to be paid for dearly.

The Bacchanale music is that part of the opera's first scene which precedes the duet between Venus and Tannhäuser. It is wild and sensual music, teeming with measures that are swift and passionate.

Wagner had entertained great hopes for this Parisian production of *Tannhäuser*. To mount his work at the justly famed Opéra was reason enough, what with that organization's habit of ignoring expense. He labored industriously at making revisions, which included a complete rewriting of the bacchanalian scene, as well as of the music for Venus and Tannhäuser in Act I.

When he had completed his revisions he played the music for several friends. Charles Nuitter, one of these, reported on that private hearing as follows:

When we arrived the composer sat down to the piano. He played with indescribable animation and fury. His hands pounded the keys, and at the same time he strove to acquaint me with the action of the scene, crying out the entrance of the various groups. "Arrival of the fauns and satyrs; all are put to flight; the confusion mounts to its climax," he flung at me, and his hands continued to bang the keys, the musical delirium always augmenting. When he was piling on a succession of quivering chords Wagner suddenly cried, "Now a crash of thunder. We are all dead!" At that moment a wagon of paving stones discharged its load into the street, thus producing a prolonged and terrible noise. Wagner turned round and regarded us with stupefaction, his eyes staring wildly. It took us some moments to recover from this stirring of our feelings. Thus it was that I was initiated into the new music.

The first Paris performance of *Tannhäuser* took place on Mar. 13, 1861. That was the first of three fiascos in the French capital. The second occurred on Mar. 18. Napoleon III and the Empress both attended, but their presence had no effect on the rest of the audience, whose catcalls, howls, and kindred strange noises were even louder, if not funnier, than the first time.

The work was given for the third time on Mar. 24. This was not a regular subscription performance, and it seemed to all and sundry that, finally, a Parisian audience would be honest and unprejudiced in its attitude toward the opera. However, the composer's enemies had bought out the house and the result was the same. Whereupon Wagner withdrew his score. *Tannhäuser* was not given again in Paris until thirty-four years later.

R. C. B.

Prelude to "Die Meistersinger"

At precisely 8 p. m., on Oct. 24, 1867, Richard Wagner breathed a deep, long-due sigh of relief. He had just scrawled an inscription over a final score sheet: "The completion of *Die Meistersinger,* Triebschen, Thursday, Oct. 24, 1867, 8 o'clock in the evening, R. W." What Ignace Paderewski once called "the greatest work of genius ever achieved by any artist in any field of human activity" lay on his desk, a finished product.

Twenty-two stormy years had elapsed since that summer of 1845 in Marienbad when the first rough sketch of his comedy was made. *Tannhäuser* was finished, and the idea of writing a humorous companion piece intrigued him. Moreover, his doctor had then ordered complete relaxation. He could relax best over a comedy. "Something thoroughly light and popular," he felt, too, would be just the thing to get him popularly launched in the German theaters. He planned it, avowedly, for "rapid circulation through the European opera houses." The idea grew. Intermittent researches in German history and legend followed. The idea would slumber, then be revived. All kinds of obstacles intervened. Wagner was a slave of mood. The composition of *Lohengrin* first diverted his attention. Maybe Ernest Newman is right in believing that Wagner's instinct told him he was not quite ready to woo the comic muse. Anyway, he turned to other matters, among them a first sketch of *Der Ring des Nibelungen* and *Tristan und Isolde*.

What with these recurring new projects, Wagner's frequent domestic snarls, his revolutionary activities and exile, the staggering efforts to get his operas produced, *l'affaire* Wesendonck, and his recurring financial troubles, the wonder is the idea of writing a comedy—of all things—did not die of slow strangulation. Ironically, it was in the midst of the gloomy seizure caused by the humiliating *Tannhäuser* fiasco in Paris of 1861 and the nerve-racking confusions of a Viennese production of *Tristan* that he returned to his gay music drama—possibly as comic relief. Possibly, too, because in that same year he again met the arch enemy of Wagnerism, Eduard Hanslick. Vienna's dreaded critical oracle was to be immortally pilloried in *Die Meistersinger* as the scoundrelly pedant Beckmesser. There is even evidence that Wagner's "Lady Bountiful" of inspiration—Mathilde Wesendonck—threw some gentle reminders to the dejected composer during his brief spell of recuperation in Venice. Why did not Richard take up *Die Meistersinger* to show the world that he could laugh in the teeth of hostility? Thus, it may not be so "curious," as Mr. Newman says, that Wagner should have found "the humor and the serenity of soul to create his comedy."

"I suddenly conceived the idea of a comic play that might serve as a pendant to the tragedy of *Tannhäuser*," he had written in 1845. "This was *Die Meistersinger von Nürnberg*, with Hans Sachs at their head." The sixteenth-century cobbler poet long exerted a "vital charm" on his imagination. In Sachs's work the medieval institution of "mastersingers" reached its finest development. The broad humanity and homespun wisdom of Sachs, as delineated by Wagner, can be read in his own extant poems and tales. For the customs and manners of the period Wagner consulted a book in Latin brought out in 1697 by Johann Christoph Wagenseil, a professor of Oriental languages at the University of

Altdorf. He even copied out some of the names for his *dramatis personae:* Veit Pogner, Fritz Kothner, Conrad Nachtigall, Balthasar Zorn, Sixtus Beckmesser. Beckmesser, oddly enough, was a perfectly harmless and respectable custodian of the old guild order, no fit model, apparently, for the maliciously portrayed villain of Wagner's opera. In one of the early sketches Wagner made no bones about naming the derided philistine "Hanslich." Of course, the character of Sachs is altered in the transition to the stage. It is his hopeless and self-sacrificing love for Eva that accounts for the work's being called a "tragicomedy."

Armed with Wagenseil's old chronicle, Wagner began serious work on the final libretto in Paris during the winter of 1861-1862. Then came more trouble. The money borrowed in Vienna from the publisher Schott as an advance on the *Meistersinger* score was used up. The old specter of poverty haunted his tiny room on the Quai Voltaire. In February, 1862, Wagner moved on to Biberich on the Rhine, where he began to compose the music. The process was slow. Wagner's Viennese creditors grew insistent. Budgetary prospects were getting blacker and blacker. Then, like a Greek *deus ex machina,* the "mad" King Ludwig II of Bavaria, stepped into the picture and Wagner was rescued from his financial quicksands. After more wandering, he settled in Switzerland in the spring of 1866. There, in Triebchen, on Oct. 24, 1867, he completed the "great universal comedy of manners that hymns the liberation of the artistic spirit and its emancipation from bigoted tradition."

Briefly, the plot of *Die Meistersinger* centers in an impending song contest to be held in Nuremberg on St. John's Day. The winner is to marry Eva, the beautiful daughter of the goldsmith Veit Pogner. Walther Stolzing, a Franconian Knight passing through the city, sees Eva in St. Catherine's Church one day and falls in love with her. Permission is granted him to compete with the town's mastersingers for her hand. Beckmesser, the town clerk, is also a contestant. As the "marker" he does his best to discredit Walther at a trial hearing. Eva and Walther communicate their love for each other to the poetical shoemaker Hans Sachs, who remains their best friend and adviser, despite his own love for the girl. Sachs is delighted with a song Walther has contrived after hearing it in a dream. As the knight sings it, the cobbler notes it down. Later Beckmesser slips into the shop unobserved and pockets the manuscript. At the scheduled singing contest, the old pedant makes a laughing stock of himself through a lame effort to palm the song off as his own. Walther is duly acclaimed the victor when his turn comes, and Sachs hangs the collar of the guild around his neck. Of course the goldsmith Pogner awards him his daughter. As for the kindly cobbler, the populace shouts: "Hail, Hans Sachs! Hail, Nuremberg's beloved Sachs!"

In the prelude, Wagner works the chief motives of *Die Meistersinger* into a masterly epitome of the mood and action of the ensuing comedy, the themes of the mastersingers and the Walther-Eva romance weaving ultimately into a rich polyphonic fabric of imposing power.

L. B.

Selections from "Der Ring des Nibelungen"

IN DEVELOPING the plan and continuity of the *Ring* cycle, Wagner worked backward. After casting about in history and mythology, he had chosen the Volsung hero's exploits for his next project after *Lohengrin* and outlined a poem, "Siegfried's Tod" ("Siegfried's Death"), completed late in 1848. This was later renamed *Götterdämmerung* (*The Twilight of the Gods*). But that left much unexplained in the tragic sequence of legend. So he wrote a second poem, "Der Junge Siegfried" ("The Young Siegfried"), later shortened to *Siegfried,* which set the stage more fully for the final catastrophe. This in turn opened new prefatory vistas, and two further segments, *Die Walküre* (*The Valkyr*) and *Das Rheingold,* came into being in the same reverse order. Having achieved clarity and unity of narrative, he published the poems in 1853.

Normal chronological order was reserved for the music. In 1854 he put the finishing touches to *Das Rheingold,* and by 1856 *Die Walküre* had reached final form. One act of *Siegfried* was finished by the middle of 1857. While at work on the second act he flung down his pen, and a pause of twelve years ensued. Wagner had resolved to renew contact with the stage through a less staggering production than the *Ring.* Accordingly *Tristan und Isolde* and *Die Meistersinger* intervened before he resumed work on the tetralogy, completing *Siegfried* in 1869 and *Götterdämmerung* in 1874. Two years later, in August, at the Bayreuth Festspielhaus built for the purpose, *Der Ring des Nibelungen* was given to the world in a cyclic performance spread out over four days.

A four-part drama spanning the whole range of human passion from hate and greed to love and ardent self-sacrifice, the *Ring* hinges on the twofold theme of the Norse god Wotan's thirst for power and the moral idea of redemption. Wotan, having built Valhalla for himself and his godly retinue, wrests from the Nibelung Alberich a power-giving ring made of gold stolen from the Rhine daughters. Alberich lays a curse upon it, which only a valiant hero, acting as a free agent, can remove. Such a savior is Siegfried, son of the Volsung Siegmund and his sister Sieglinde, who must redeem their sin in death. For attempting to defend Siegmund, Brünnhilde, Wotan's Valkyr daughter, is condemned to sleep within a fence of fire until awakened by a fearless hero. Wotan watches the Volsung grow to bold manhood in the forest. Siegfried slays the dragon guarding the accursed ring and rescues the goddess from her fire-girt slumbers. They fall in love. Siegfried gives Brünnhilde the ring as token of his love, and Brünnhilde gives him her battle steed Grane.

Urged by Brünnhilde, Siegfried departs for fresh adventures down the Rhine and arrives at the court of King Gunther and his sister Gutrune. Hagen, Gunther's half-brother and Alberich's son, plots to marry the King to Brünnhilde and Gutrune to Siegfried and steal the ring. Through a magic potion, Siegfried forgets Brünnhilde and is attracted to Gutrune. Still drugged, he returns to Brünnhilde, snatches the ring from her, and forces her to accompany him back to the Gibichung king. During a hunt Hagen plunges a spear into Siegfried's back. In the ensuing quarrel in the hall he also slays his half-brother. By way of redemption, Brünnhilde, taking the ring from the dead Siegfried's finger, mounts her steed and plunges into Siegfried's funeral pyre.

ENTRANCE OF THE GODS INTO VALHALLA FROM "DAS RHEINGOLD"

Ernest Newman has compared the *Ring* to a symphony. *Das Rheingold,* he suggested, resembled the first or expository section: "The main motives, psychological and musical, are here set forth, to be worked out in detail in the later movements, blended, contrasted, and at last brought triumphantly to their logical conclusion." In this scheme *Die Walküre* would be the slow movement—by reason of its rich emotions, according to the English musicologist. *Siegfried* would be the scherzo of this *Ring* symphony, *Götterdämmerung* the shattering finale. We have Wagner's own record of his feelings on completion of the first movement of this monumental "symphony":

"Well, *Rheingold* is done," he writes to Franz Liszt in a letter dated Jan. 15, 1854. "With what faith, with what joy I began this music! In a real frenzy of despair I have at last completed it. Alas, how I too was walled in by the need of gold! Believe me, no one has ever composed like this. I fancy my music is fearful—a pit of terrors and grandeurs."

The story of the *Ring* begins at the bottom of a river, the Rhine. There a deposit of gold is being guarded by a bevy of waternymphs, the Rhine daughters. The crafty Nibelung dwarf Alberich steals this precious hoard and fashions a ring from it, a magic ring of boundless power. Meanwhile, Wotan has commissioned the brother giants, Fafner and Fasolt, to build a sumptuous home for the gods, a palace towering amid the clouds. As a reward for their work Wotan has promised them Freia, goddess of youth and love. When the giants come to claim their pay, Wotan demurs. There is a sharp quarrel. Loge, the god of fire, now returns with a report of Alberich's theft of the Rhine gold. The giants gloat over the story of the magic booty. They will accept that in place of Freia. By trickery Wotan obtains the ring from Alberich. In a rage over his loss the dwarf lays a curse upon it—the curse of fear and suffering and death for its possessors. Soon the ring's malign force begins to work. In a struggle for the ownership of the ring, Fafner strikes his brother dead. The gods look on horrified.

Wotan's thoughts turn to Valhalla, the new citadel of the gods, now shrouded in storm clouds. Donner, the storm god, mounts a huge rock and begins to swing his hammer. Lightning flashes and thunder roars from his blows. As the cloudburst ends, the sky clears and a rainbow is seen, arching its brilliant span like a bridge to the very portals of Valhalla, looming radiantly in the distance. With mingled awe and jubilation, the gods begin their stately march over the rainbow to their new home. From below comes the mournful song of the Rhine daughters, bemoaning the loss of their glittering hoard.

This awesome scene, beginning with the cloud-gathering summons of Donner, is vividly pictured in the concert excerpt. Appearing in the glowing fabric are the "rainbow" motive and the surging theme of Valhalla, which bursts forth in massive challenge as the gods make their majestic way over the span.

ACT III FROM "DIE WALKÜRE"

This act involves a tragic conflict between father and daughter, rising to a powerful climax of poignant farewell. Brünnhilde has flouted divine law on two counts. She has shielded the Volsung twins, Sieglinde and Siegmund, in their illicit union. And, defying Wotan's will, she has interceded on Siegmund's side in the duel with Hunding, Sieglinde's husband. In that combat Wotan, forced to side with Hunding at his wife Fricka's behest, had helped him slay Siegmund. Then, with a look of divine wrath, he had struck the hateful Hunding dead. Goaded by Fricka in her role as protectress of marriage, Wotan plans dire punishment for his Valkyr daughter. First, she will be shorn of godliness. Then she will be plunged into an enchanted sleep and left at the roadside a prey to the first passer-by's will. Meanwhile, the duel ended, Brünnhilde has fled in panic from her father's fury. Accompanying her in her wild flight is Sieglinde, bereaved and terrified. Wotan wrathfully pursues his rebel daughter.

"THE RIDE OF THE VALKYRIES"

The third act of *Die Walküre* opens dramatically with the famous "Ride of the Valkyries." (The concert excerpt prepared by Wagner himself was first heard in America on a program led by Theodore Thomas at the Central Park Garden in New York on Sept. 17, 1872, or five years before the American premiere of the whole opera at the New York Academy of Music.) The scene is the rugged mountain retreat of the Valkyries, the warrior daughters of Wotan and Fricka. Wind-driven storm clouds sweep over the mountaintop. Arrayed in gleaming mail, armed with spears and shields, the Valkyries spur their battle steeds on through the raging tempest. Hanging from their saddles are the bodies of heroes fallen in battle. Through the tumult of dashing steeds and clanging armor may be heard the wild cry of the Valkyries. Giant rhythms and hurtling tone surge through the orchestra as the flight of the Valkyr daughters mounts in power.

As they appear on the scene, the sisters exchange tumultous greetings. Finally, Brünnhilde dashes in with Sieglinde. Frantic with terror, she implores her sisters' protection against Wotan's ire. They promise, but there is little they can do. In despair, Brünnhilde entrusts Siegmund's shattered sword to Sieglinde. She predicts that she will bear a glorious son and urges her to flee for safety into the forest. "He that brandishes the sword, newly welded," Brünnhilde tells the Volsung girl, "let him be named Siegfried, winner of victory." Sieglinde exultantly replies: "For his sake will I live!" and hurries off.

Thunderclouds now wrap the rocky peak. A storm rages fiercely. Amid the roar of thunder is now heard the angry voice of Wotan. As he approaches, the Valkyrs hide their rebel sister. The god stalks furiously on the scene. "Where is Brünnhilde?" he demands. He vows like punishment for all of them if their sister fails to appear. Brünnhilde now steps forward and meekly faces the irate god. "Here I am, father. Pronounce your sentence upon me." Wotan retorts that she has sentenced herself with her mad rebellion. She had violated his command. What can she expect? Brünnhilde counters with a proud defence: that actually she had carried out his secret wish. But Wotan is not to be swayed from his dread resolve. He names the penalty. She will be rendered mortal and left asleep in the open for any stranger to violate.

Brünnhilde is horrified. Losing immortality is severe punishment indeed! But the second indignity is too much. She pleads fervidly to be spared such dishonor. Wotan is adamant. Then let him at least build a wall of fire about her, she begs, a formidable barrier so that only a real hero may break through and find her.

"If not," she cries, "then crush out my life—let me not suffer such shame!" This time Wotan listens. The father is at last moved by the daughter's plea. He is no longer Wotan, the stern and unrelenting god bent on retribution. He is now only the girl's father, wretched in the grip of iron law. Love and grief surge in his breast. He turns tenderly to Brünnhilde, and in a long farewell full of noble pathos and beauty he expresses a father's feelings.

"MAGIC FIRE MUSIC"

Wotan commands Loge to appear, and now subtle flames begin to weave and gleam through Wagner's orchestral web. They crawl and flicker in wood-wind passages of vivid evocation. Against the leap and crackle of the growing blaze is heard the swaying theme of Brünnhilde's enchanted slumbers. Like a brooding undercurrent the theme of fate moves through the spreading flames, and then the brasses intone an exultant prophecy—the awakening of Brünnhilde by the hero Siegfried. The orchestra sinks to a hushed reminder of the slumber theme as Wotan the father takes a last, loving look at his daughter and leaves the scene a desolate deity.

"WALDWEBEN" ("FOREST MURMURS") FROM "SIEGFRIED"

The title of this excerpt is usually rendered "Forest Murmurs" on concert programs. Literally "Waldweben" means "Forest Weavings." Wagner used the title in preparing the fascinating tone picture from the second act of *Siegfried* for concert use. The music is descriptive of the scene at the entrance to the dragon's cave. The dwarf Mime has just left Siegfried.

As the Volsung hero meditates on the strange web of adventure he is being drawn into, we hear the rustling of the leaves in the woodland imagery of Wagner's orchestra. The murmuring begins in D minor, then changes to B major. Siegfried is deep in thought and wonder. Who is he? Who was his father? Certainly not Mime. Soon the theme of the Volsung race, chanted softly in 6/8 time, appears among the clarinets, then the bassoons and horns.

Siegfried's thoughts turn to his mother. And now from the cellos, violas, and double basses rises the motive known as the "love life." The entire string body takes up the theme. Horns and bassoons follow suit. Then an ingenious touch of deification comes over the music. Siegfried's mother (Sieglinde), though mortal, is now pictured in a violin passage in C major woven from the motive associated with Freia, goddess of youth and love. As muted strings play arpeggios against the theme, we glimpse Sieglinde's borrowed glory.

The "forest weavings" spread and intensify. Through the murmurous fabric emerges the elusive theme of the forest bird in E major (3/4, 9/8), sung chiefly by oboe, flute, and clarinet. The music ends with a Vivace, in which are incorporated the themes of fire, Siegfried, slumber, and the forest bird.

RHINE JOURNEY FROM "GÖTTERDÄMMERUNG"

Often called a "scherzo," Siegfried's "Rhine Journey" serves as transition from the Prologue to Act I. The rapturous duet over between Siegfried and Brünnhilde, the Volsung hero starts on his journey. As he recedes down the slope Brünnhilde waves a lingering farewell. The Prologue ends. The orchestra, in a rich web of Leitmotive, now paints a vivid picture of the voyaging Siegfried. His past exploits come up in retrospect as the themes unfold, combine, change and take on fresh emotional coloring. Siegfried's horn-call sounds brilliantly and part of the Fire-motive joins in. Presently, against undulating strings, the brass and woodwind proclaim the Rhine-motive. Amid the swaying motion, the winds give out a version of the theme known as the Renunciation of Love. There is a resounding outburst as the Rhine-Daughters' theme rises in triumph. Bassoons, bass trumpet, and trombones offer a fragment of the horn-call. A more solemn reference to the Rhine-Daughters leads to a variant of the Rhine-motive, and a subdued mood soon spreads over the orchestra. The Rhinegold theme passes in review from the horns to the bass trumpet, and finally the theme of the Nibelungs' Servitude batters ominously through the fabric.

FUNERAL MUSIC FROM "GÖTTERDÄMMERUNG"

During the hunt in the third act, Hagen gives the hero a drug restoring his memory. Siegfried recalls the flame-encircled rock and his bride Brünnhilde as the others listen in stunned silence. Hagen, intent on treachery from the start, asks Siegfried to translate the speech of two ravens passing overhead. As Siegfried's eyes turn upward, Hagen drives a spear into his back. Gunther and his vassals are horrified, but Hagen, charging Siegfried with breaking a grave vow, walks off remorseless.

A last cry of greeting to his *heilige Braut* and the wounded hero falls back lifeless. Gunther's followers lift the body and carry it solemnly to the hall of the Gibichungs. Meanwhile the orchestra pronounces a funeral oration on the Volsung hero and his race. A mighty lament fit for a god's demise, it is not strictly a funeral march. In the thematic scheme motives of race, murder, and sword appear in sequence and mingle with the motive of Siegfried and echoes of the Siegmund-Sieglinde love music in *Die Walküre*. At one point the Volsung motives combine in a great crescendo over an iterative bass brooding on the race's tragic destiny. Toward the close horns and bass trumpet shout the hero's theme, and as the rest of the orchestra harks back mightily to the "murder" theme, the brasses intone a rhythmic variant of the horn call. There is a reminiscence of Brünnhilde as the music fades away.

BRÜNNHILDE'S IMMOLATION FROM "GÖTTERDÄMMERUNG"

Brünnhilde's great monologue occurs in the hall of the Gibichungs in the concluding scene. Hagen has just slain Gunther over possession of the ring of the dead Siegfried's finger. As Hagen stoops to claim the booty, the corpse lifts a warning hand and the Gibichung falls back. Brünnhilde enters and scornfully silences the loud lamenting as ill-befitting a hero's death. In the course of her apostrophe she orders a funeral pyre erected and Siegfried's body placed upon it. Removing the ring, she puts it on her own finger, and after applying a torch to the pyre, she dashes with Grane into the flames.

L. B.

"A Siegfried Idyl"

AT PRECISELY 7:30 on Christmas morning, 1870, Cosima Wagner was astonished to hear some strangely familiar music flooding the interior of her villa at Triebschen, near Lucerne. She promptly recognized it as themes from her husband's music drama *Siegfried* woven into fascinating new patterns with the folk song "Schlaf' mein Kind, schlaf' ein." Those were pre-radio and pre-phonograph days. She knew no magic dial had been turned. The musicians were right there in the house. She opened the door and beheld an odd huddle of men and instruments on the staircase leading to her bed chamber. There stood her husband Richard, conducting from the landing as the musicians toiled away at their violins and cellos and clarinets from the carpeted stair treads. It was Cosima's birthday. The serenade was Richard's surprise birthday gift. So cleverly had arrangements and rehearsals been maneuvred that no suspicion had entered Cosima's mind of what was going on. The kitchen was used for the early-morning tuning up. The musicians were from Zürich, and a final rehearsal had taken place on Christmas Eve in the hall of the Hôtel du Lac at Lucerne.

Naturally, the household premiere of the *Siegfried Idyl* was a great success. We have Hans Richter's word for it that the performance was faultless. The work was repeated several times that day at the Wagner Villa.

The music was a birthday token in still another sense. The year before, Cosima had borne Wagner a son, quite understandably named Siegfried. In writing the *Idyl,* Wagner admittedly sought to express his feelings as father and husband both. Siegfried was born at Triebschen, near Lucerne, on June 6, 1869, before Cosima obtained her divorce from her first husband, Hans von Bülow. She married Wagner at Lucerne on Aug. 25, 1870. Concerning Cosima, who had thus flouted convention, Wagner wrote to his friend, Frau Wille:

She has defied every disapprobation and has taken upon herself every condemnation. She has borne to me a wonderfully beautiful boy, whom I can boldly call Siegfried; he is now growing, together with my work; he gives me a new long life, which has at last attained a meaning. Thus we get along without the world, from which we have wholly withdrawn.

The *Siegfried Idyl,* scored for flute, oboe, two clarinets, bassoon, trumpet, two horns, and strings, was originally entitled "Triebschener Idyll," which is a better title circumstantially, if not musically.

L. B.

Prelude and "Love Death" from "Tristan und Isolde"

IN 1854, when Wagner was in the midst of composing the *Ring* the idea for an opera on the Tristan theme came to him. Not till three years later, however, did he begin actual work on it, and the music drama was finished in August, 1859. Complications of various kinds interfered with the production of the opera, but it finally obtained its premiere at the Royal Court Theater in Munich, on June 10, 1865, under the direction of Hans von Bülow.

Wagner's version of the tale combines features from numerous legends. Very likely of Celtic origin, the story, as the German composer utilized it, makes room for myriad delvings into psychology and metaphysics, some of which are not easy to follow. We must assume, as Ernest Newman suggests, that the characters and their motivations were perfectly clear to the composer, if they seem not to be altogether to the listener. The essence of the music drama's plot, extracted from Wagner's own description, follows:

We are told of Tristan and Isolde in an ancient love poem, which is "constantly fashioning itself anew, and has been adopted by every European language of the Middle Ages." Tristan, a faithful vassal of King Marke, woos Isolde for his king, yet not daring to reveal to her his own love.

Isolde, powerless to do otherwise, follows him as bride to his lord. The love potion, which has been intended for the king, in order to ensure the marriage, is given to Tristan and Isolde to drink, a circumstance which . . . opens their eyes to the truth and leads to the avowal that for the future they belong only to each other. . . . The world, power, fame, splendor, honor, knighthood, fidelity, friendship, all are dissipated like an empty dream. One thing only remains: longing, longing, insatiable longing, forever springing up anew, pining and thirsting. Death, which means passing away, perishing, never awakening, their only deliverance. . . . Shall we call it death? Or is it the hidden wonder world from out of which an ivy and vine, entwined with each other, grew upon Tristan's and Isolde's grave, as the legend tells us?

The Prelude (A minor, 6/8) makes a very gradual and long crescendo to a mighty fortissimo, followed by a briefer descrescendo, which leads to a whispered pianissimo. Free as to form, and ever widening in scope of development, it offers two chief themes, a phrase, uttered by the cellos, is united to another, given to the oboes, to form a subject called the "love potion" theme, or the theme of "longing." Another theme, again announced by the cellos, "Tristan's love glance," is sensuous, even voluptuous in character.

After the Prelude, the orchestra enters into the "Liebestod" or "Love Death," that passionate flow of phrases, taken mostly from the material in the second act love duet. Isolde (in the opera) sings her songs of sublimated desire. Franz Liszt is responsible for the application of the term "Liebestod" to that part of the music which originally had been named "Verklärung" by Wagner himself.

R. C. B.

Transformation Scene; Klingsor's Magic and Flower Maidens' Scene; Good Friday Spell, from "Parsifal"

MOST OF the *Ring,* all of *Tristan,* and a considerable portion of *Die Meistersinger* had been written by Wagner before he started actual work on the "consecrational festival stage play," *Parsifal,* in 1865. He made a first outline of the libretto in August of that year, some two decades after he had become acquainted with the Parsifal poem of Wolfram von Eschenbach, the Minnesinger. Not till 1877, however, did the text attain its final shape, and it was published in December. Some time previously Wagner had turned to the task of composing the music and completed it in 1879. The orchestration was finished in Jan. 1882. The opera was given for the first time at Bayreuth on July 26, 1882. The Prelude, written in December, 1878, obtained its premiere performance at Wagner's house, Wahnfried, on Christmas Day, with the composer conducting, the occasion, his wife Cosima's birthday.

The ethical essence of *Parsifal* has thus been expressed: "Enlightenment coming through conscious pity brings salvation." Wagner, whose earlier music dramas each revolved about some *idée fixe* of philosophical or moral implication, brought to *Parsifal,* besides, religious elements derived from the twin sources of Christian doctrine and Buddhism. Some years before he had done the sketch for a play on the subject of Jesus of Nazareth, and, parenthetically, it is quite likely that he had no intention to write music for it. Nevertheless, here is shown the composer's religious urge, mingled with other aspects of his creative bent. During that period Wagner drafted another play, which he titled *Die Sieger* (*The Victors*), one of Buddhistic import, whose story centers on the dictum that Prakriti, the hero, may not become one with Amanda, the heroine, unless he "shares the latter's vow of chastity." In these two works may be found qualities and tones of thought also incorporated in *Parsifal.*

Parsifal's locale is Monsalvat in the Spanish Pyrenees. The castle of the Holy Grail is tenanted by a company of Knights, guardians of the Spear which pierced Jesus' side as He hung on the Cross, and of the Cup He drank from at the Last Supper and which received His precious blood from the Spear wound. This brotherhood of Knights of the Grail refuses membership to all, save the pure in heart, and the Knights go about the world doing good through the high powers given them by the Grail.

A certain other knight, Klingsor, sinful and scheming, enraged against the Knights for having been denied admission to the Brotherhood has built a magic garden, whose many charms have proved strong enough to tempt several of the weaker willed Knights. Amfortas, king of the Grail, is one of these. He had fallen victim to the wiles of Kundry, a creature of Klingsor. The latter has seized the Spear from Amfortas and has humiliated him further by

wounding him with it. The wound may be cured only by being touched
with the point of the Spear held by a Guileless Fool, a youth who can with-
stand all temptation. This youth, of course, is Parsifal, a forest lad who enters into the picture through having killed a swan sacred to the Grail. Parsifal
is made to go through the rituals prescribed by the libretto, *viz.,* he is present
at the ceremony of the Eucharist, or the Lord's Supper, without grasping
anything of its meaning; he resists the lures thriving in Klingsor's garden
(Kundry and the Flower maidens), then he seizes the Spear, flung at him by
Klingsor, and, as he makes the sign of the cross, the garden is destroyed. He
wanders about the world, for a time, and returns on Good Friday. He meets
the aged Knight Gurnemanz. Kundry, now a repentant woman dedicated
to the Grail's service, washes Parsifal's feet and dries them with her hair.
Next Parsifal goes to the temple where he restores Amfortas to health and,
as the latter bends before him in homage, Kundry dies. Having thus attained
"Enlightenment . . . through conscious pity," Parsifal has become the saviour
of Monsalvat.

R. C. B.

"A Faust Overture"

In the autumn of 1839 the twenty-six-year-old Wagner was fighting off star-
vation and creditors in a Paris attic on the Rue de la Tonnellerie. For company he had his first wife, Minna Planer, and a big Newfoundland dog named
Robber. He had come to Paris full of hopes and projects. But each day brought
fresh disappointment and defeat. In the midst of mounting misery, which included an agonizing toothache, he summoned the will power to write *A Faust
Overture.* He reveals in his autobiography:

> In order to gain the graces of the Parisian salon world through its favorite singers,
> I composed several French romances, which, after all my efforts to the contrary,
> were considered too out of the way and difficult to be actually sung. Out of the depth
> of my inner discontent, I armed myself against the crushing reaction of this out-
> ward art activity by the hasty sketches and as hasty composition of an orchestral
> piece which I called an *Overture to Goethe's Faust,* but which was in reality intended
> for the first section of a grand *Faust* symphony.

The startling contrast of "several French romances" and a grim *Faust* Overture is borne out sharply by the manuscript of the earliest sketch of the Overture. On the other side of the sheet is scrawled a fragment of a French chanson-
ette! Several years later Liszt and Wagner exchanged some interesting correspondence regarding this Overture. Writing from Weimar in 1852, Liszt
remarks: "Your *Faust Overture* made a sensation and went well." Then,
encouraged by Wagner's avowed intention to alter the score, he suggests a slight

revision: why not add "a soft, tender, melodious part, modulated *à la Gretchen.*"
Wagner's reply is revealing:

You spotted the lie beautifully when I tried to make myself believe that I had
written an overture to *Faust.* You have felt quite justly what is wanting: the woman
is wanting. Perhaps you would at once understand my tone poem if I called it
"Faust in Solitude." At this time I intended to write an entire "Faust" Symphony.
The first movement, that which is ready, was this "Solitary Faust," longing, despairing, cursing. The "feminine" floats around him as an object of his longing,
but not in its divine reality; and it is just this insufficient image of his longing which
he destroys in his despair. The second movement was to introduce Gretchen, the
woman. I had a theme for her, but it was only a theme. The whole remains unfinished. I wrote my *Flying Dutchman* instead. This is the whole explanation.

If now, from a last remnant of weakness and vanity, I hesitate to abandon this
"Faust" work altogether, I shall certainly have to remodel it, but only as regards
instrumental modulation. The theme you desire I cannot introduce. This would
naturally involve an entirely new composition, for which I have no inclination.
If I publish it, I shall give it its proper title, "Faust in Solitude," or "The Solitary
Faust: A Tone Poem for Orchestra."

Classical in form, *A Faust Overture* begins with a slow introduction (*Sehr
gehalten*—assai sostenuto; D minor, 4/4) in which the themes to be used are
first propounded. Against a soft drum roll double basses and tuba give out
the opening phrase, to which the cellos respond more briskly. The violins
vary the phrase soon to grow into the main theme of the Overture. The
material is then gone over by the orchestra before a staccato chord rings out
and the Overture proper begins. This is marked *Sehr bewegt* (assai con moto,
D minor, 2/2). The main theme is now discoursed by violins over harmonies
from the bassoons and horns. A flurry of wood winds, first heard in the introduction, returns, ushering in a development section. Then the flute brings in
a second theme in F major, followed by a free fantasia passage of some length.
The main theme returns as a review of the earlier material begins. Some
further elaboration of the themes occurs before the extended coda gets under
way.

Wagner's scoring calls for piccolo, two flutes, two oboes, two clarinets,
three bassoons, four horns, two trumpets, three trombones, bass tuba, kettledrums, and strings. *A Faust Overture* was first played at a charity concert
in the pavilion of the Grosser Garten at Dresden on July 22, 1844, with
Wagner himself directing. Carl Zerrahn conducted the American premiere in
Boston on Jan. 3, 1857, with a "Philharmonic" orchestra consisting of thirty-
five men.

L. B.

William Walton

BORN: OLDHAM, LANCASHIRE, ENGLAND, MAR. 29, 1902.

After an earlier revelation of cleverness and wit, William Walton has consolidated the ground and proved himself a composer endowed with more solid gifts. Having displayed in some instrumental works a delicate lyricism as well as a brilliant incisiveness, he startled the musical world, in 1931, with one of the most beautiful choral works ever written.—DYNELEY HUSSEY.

Overture, "Portsmouth Point"

WALTON WAS only twenty-four when the International Society for Contemporary Music performed his *Portsmouth Point* Overture in the Tonhall at Zürich on June 22, 1926. Since then, of course, he has added prolifically to his symphonic and choral output, and, incidentally, revised the Overture.

Portsmouth, opposite the Isle of Wight, has been England's chief naval arsenal. In name and theme, however, the Overture was inspired by a print made by Thomas Rowlandson, the great English caricaturist and social satirist. This was published in 1817. At that time Portsmouth Point was little more than a row of taverns along the shore. Officers and men were continually passing through for embarkation. Charles G. Harper gives a vivid glimpse of the place in "The Portsmouth Road: The Sailor's Highway":

It was a place throbbing with life and excitement—the sailors going out and returning home; the leave takings, the greetings, the boozing and the fighting are all shown in Rowlandson's drawing as on a stage, while the tall ships form an appropriate background like the backcloth of a theatrical scene.

It is a scene full of humor. Sailors are leaning on their arms out of a window; a gold-laced officer bids goodby to his girl while his trunks are being carried down the stairs; a drunken sailor and his equally drunken woman are belaboring one another with all the good will in the world; and a wooden-legged sailor is scraping away for very life on a fiddle, and dancing grotesquely to get a living.

This settles the pictorial possibilities of Walton's suggestive Overture. Constant Lambert, British composer and writer, has made an acute analysis of its musical web. He writes:

Melodically speaking, the work derives to a certain extent from traditional nautical tunes and from the more breezy English eighteenth-century composers. It is interesting to note a similarity in certain passages to the symphonies of Boyce, although at the time the composer was completely ignorant of these works.

Another melodic influence has been the sardañas of Catalonia. These folk dances have nothing in common with the rest of Spanish music and are distinguished by their clear-cut form and vigorous melodic line; the tunes are often curiously English in atmosphere, and therefore their influence has in no way caused an inconsistency of style in Walton's music. (With the possible exception of Déodat de Sévérac, I know of no other composer who has been swayed by this delightful popular tradition.)

From the harmonic point of view the work raises no problems. The style is broadly diatonic, with a free use of diatonic discords, but with nothing approaching atonality or polytonality; we are presented with neither clichés nor innovations.

"Scapino," A Comedy Overture

PREMIERED BY the Chicago Symphony Orchestra, Frederick Stock conducting, on Apr. 3 and 4, 1941, Walton's "comedy overture" bears a dedication to the Chicago organization and its leader "in commemoration of the fiftieth Anniversary of its foundation." Mr. Stock directed two further performances on Apr. 17 and 18. The Philharmonic-Symphony orchestra played it at the Lewisohn Stadium the following July 21. Efrem Kurtz conducted.

Composition of the Overture was begun in 1940 when Walton was already serving in the British army, and interruptions were naturally frequent before he penned the final note. The full title reads "Scapino, A Comedy Overture for Full Orchestra, After an Etching from Jc. Callot's 'Balli Sfessania,' 1622."

Scapino was a member of the great family of stage characters belonging to the Commedia dell'Arte, Pantaloon, Harlequin, and Columbine being some of the others. The French Callot, who had lived and worked in the Florence of Cosimo de Medici, left something like 1,500 etchings, a set of them, the "Balli Sfessania," published in 1622, inspired by the Commedia dell'Arte clowns. Reproductions of two of Callot's etchings were pasted by Walton on the manuscript score of his Overture. One, belonging to the "Sfessania" set, is entitled, "Le Zani, ou Scapin." In his book on Jacques Callot, J. Lieure gives the following description of the etching (quoted by Felix Borowski, Chicago Symphony annotator):

Scapin is standing upright, his body half turned to the right, his right hand resting on the handle of his broadsword which projects behind him. His face is in profile, with a mask on the upper part, which permits the malicious eyes to be seen. Under his upturned moustache his tongue is protruding impudently. His broad-brimmed felt hat has at the right two thin feathers, which stick up vertically.

The background represents some spectators at the rear, looking at a scene, in which Scapin himself figures at the right. With an obsequious curtsy he is presenting to a lady a letter from his master, who waits standing at the left.

Scapin's cocky and rascally character is mirrored vividly in Walton's brisk Overture, especially in the opening section (molto vivace), which gives a kind of full-length portrait of the clown. Midway in the composition the cellos take up a mock-sentimental theme (come una serenata), against guitar-like pizzicato chords. A scherzevole section recalls earlier material and hustles the work jauntily to the end.

L. B.

"Peter Warlock"

(Philip Heseltine)

BORN: LONDON, OCT. 30, 1894. DIED: LONDON, OCT. 9, 1930.

Tragedy is a much-abused word. But the death of Philip Heseltine (whom an even wider public knew as Peter Warlock) was a tragedy. An exceptionally gifted artist, in the full vigor of healthy manhood, suddenly silenced. Incalculable potentialities unfulfilled. Such a loss must ever be mourned. There is nothing here in which one can find consolation.—BERNARD VAN DIEREN.

"Capriol Suite for Strings"

A TIRELESS STUDENT of the songs and dances of all periods and a balladeer of no mean merit himself, Peter Warlock was naturally drawn to Thoinot Arbeau's famous *Orchesographie,* a collection of dances, with instructions, first published in 1588, selecting six of the illustrations for string arrangement. When the classic dance manual was first translated into English by Cyril W. Beaumont in 1925, Peter Warlock did the preface. In a foreword Mr. Beaumont states that Warlock "transposed the airs into modern musical notation, and a system of numbering was employed to show clearly the distribution of steps to the notes."

The name "Arbeau" was an anagram for Jehan Tabouret, a Catholic priest, later canon at Langres, born in Dijon in 1519. The *Orchesographie* was thus published when the august dignitary was sixty-nine years old. To it we owe "all the exact knowledge that we have of the dances of the fifteenth and sixteenth centuries," according to Cecil Sharp. Although the best work on the dance of that period, the *Orchesographie* was by no means the only one, as Mr. Beaumont points out. Robert Copland's *The Maner of Dauncynge of Bace Daunces after the Use of Fraunce* had appeared in 1521. Fabrito Sermonetta's *Il Ballarino* dates from 1581, and a work by Cesari Negri, *Nuove inventioni di balli,* was published in 1604. Arbeau's treatise is in the form of a dialogue and gives detailed descriptions of the social dances in vogue throughout the sixteenth century—"whereby all manner of persons may easily acquire and practice the honorable exercise of dancing." Practical lessons are included for mastering the Basse danse, the Pavane, the Gaillarde, the Volte, the Courante, the Allemande, the Gavotte, the Bouffons, the Morisque, the Pavane d'Espagne, and twenty-three varieties of the Branle.

Like "Thoinot Arbeau," "Peter Warlock" was only a pen name, the actual name being Philip Heseltine, composer, scholar, and critic, best known as author of an excellent biography of Frederick Delius, the English composer. His compositions include a large number of songs, choral works, part songs, instrumental pieces, and arrangements. The English Singers have helped keep his name alive in past seasons by including his *Corpus Christi* on their annual Yuletide programs. Peter Warlock was self-taught. In his thirty-seventh year he cut short a brilliant career by committing suicide.

L. B.

Carl Maria von Weber

BORN: EUTIN, GRAND DUCHY OF OLDENBURG, DEC. 18, 1786. DIED: LONDON, JUNE 5, 1826.

*There never was a more German composer than you; in whatever
distant fathomless realms of fancy your genius bore you, it remained
bound by a thousand tender links to the heart of your German people,
with whom it wept or smiled like a believing child listening to the
legends and tales of its country. Yes, it was your childlike simplicity
which guided your manly spirit, like a guardian angel, keeping it
pure and chaste, and that purity was your chief characteristic. . . .
Till death did you preserve that supreme virtue. You could never
sacrifice it or alienate this beautiful inheritance of your German origin;
you could never betray us. Behold, the Briton does you justice, the
Frenchman admires you, but only the German can love you. You are
his own, a bright day in his life, a drop of his blood, a particle of his
heart.*—RICHARD WAGNER, *from a funeral oration over the body of
Weber.*

Overture, "Jubel" ("Jubilee")

OFFICIAL DUTIES in the form of pieces written for special events occupied
most of Weber's time at Dresden in 1818. He once remarked about such items:

These compositions for special occasions, which are mere ephemera in the artistic
world, belong to the dark side of an official position, and from their transitory nature
are always dreary work, however devoted and loving and loyal one may feel towards
the person for whom they are written.

One of these commissioned "ephemera" was a cantata to celebrate the
fiftieth anniversary of the King of Saxony's accession to the throne. He called
it the *Jubilee Cantata,* a work written in eleven days. However, thanks to the
fine Italian intrigues of one Francesco Morlacchi, Weber's batonistic colleague
at the Dresden Opera, the number was eased out of the ceremonial proceedings.
To replace it Weber wrote the *Jubilee Overture.* Cantata and Overture are
separate and distinct works.

The Overture begins with an arresting Adagio, one of whose parts—a
passage for the basses—leads to the main movement. The first theme arrives
and it is developed, following which an episode brings on a second theme—
of a light and dancy character. That Weber particularly favored this second
theme is attested by its considerable development. After the inevitable free
fantasia the concluding section of the piece brings forward anew the original

835

themes and, finally, the violins lead the way to a rousing intonation of the then national anthem "Heil dir im Siegerkranz," with the wind instruments playing fortissimo against a string accompaniment.

R.C.B.

Overture to the Opera "Der Freischütz"

THE GERMAN romantic opera movement began considerably before Weber's time, but it fell to that composer's *Der Freischütz* to become the first internationally known representative of that type of lyric drama. The work is fantasial in character, "evoking the forest with its mystery, its haunted recesses and its supernatural terror as a living entity." Demons dwell there, and man enters at his own peril. However, Weber supplies man (the hero, Max) liberally with protective influences against the powers of darkness, as witness the angelic purity of the heroine Agatha and the holiness of the Hermit.

The Overture is concerned with the clashing opposing forces—good and evil. It opens serenely. A hymnlike tune is given to the horns. Soon the powers of evil appear and are about to convert the music to their own ends, when a rhapsodic melody, which is connected with Agatha (from the finale of her scene in Act II, "All' meine Pulse schlagen"), wins the day, and all ends in jubilation.

The initial performance of *Der Freischütz* took place in Berlin on June 18, 1821. English was the language used for the American premiere, at the Park Theater, New York, Mar. 2, 1825. Oddly enough, on that occasion the opera was provided with a subtitle, "The Wild Huntsman of Bohemia." And that brings up the question of a proper translation of the term *Der Freischütz,* which is not explained by "Freeshooter" or "Sharpshooter," but rather by the idea of a man who shoots with magic bullets.

When the opera was given at Palmo's Opera House, New York, Dec. 8, 1845, the original German text was employed. New York, meanwhile, had heard a French version in 1827, and in 1850 it was given in an Italian translation. From Mar. 23, 1924, on, whenever it has been given at the Metropolitan Opera House, recitatives by Artur Bodanzky replaced the spoken dialogue of the original.

R.C.B.

Overture to the Opera "Oberon"

COVENT GARDEN, in 1824, was under the management of Charles Kemble, a member of a famous theater family. Struck with the enormous popularity of *Der Freischütz,* he considered the possibilities of another opera by Weber, which was to be done specifically for British audiences. Armed with that idea and boundless enthusiasm, he visited Weber at Ems, where the composer, then in the advanced stages of consumption, was taking the waters, as they say.

During his talk with Weber, Planché, the librettist, suggested two possible subjects for the proposed opera; the one based on Goethe's *Faust,* the other on Wieland's poem *Oberon,* in turn derived from the *chanson de geste,* "Huon de Bordeau." As we now know, Weber selected *Oberon,* the Goethe work being summarily rejected.

Not one to do things by halves, he believed that he could write an operatic score to an English libretto, only after he had mastered the language. Whereupon he busied himself with lessons, taking a good hundred and fifty of them from an Englishman named Carey. His progress was amazing, as can be proved by the well-ordered letters he wrote to Planché. In January, 1825, the librettist sent him the first two acts, and on the twenty-third of that month, musical sketches were begun. Weber set out for London on Feb. 7 of the next year with a score that was still incomplete. The dampness and the fog which greeted him on his arrival were anything but salutary, but he took up his work almost immediately. On Mar. 9, rehearsals started, Weber putting in an appearance at fifteen of them, all told. The Overture was the last section to be written, being completed on Apr. 9, its autograph score bearing this expression, "Finished April 9, 1826, in the morning at a quarter of twelve, and with it the whole opera. *Soli Deo Gloria!!!* C. M. Weber."

Oberon was given its first performance at Covent Garden, London, on Apr. 12, 1826, with the composer conducting. It made a tremendous success. The Overture, in particular, won such an ovation that it had to be repeated. Benedict, Weber's biographer, tells us, "When the curtain fell the entire audience, who had shown the composer their attention and regard by remaining in their places till all was over, rose simultaneously with frantic and unceasing calls for Weber, who at last appeared, trembling with emotion, exhausted, but happy."

The Overture begins with an Introduction (Adagio sostenuto ed il tutto pianissimo possibile, D major, 4/4) after the sounding of Oberon's magic horn. Flutes and clarinets reply to the call in light passage work. A brief marchlike section is barely audible, and the strings carry on in dreamy whispers. With the utterance of a chord for the full orchestra the listener is suddenly ushered into a "world of chivalric legend and romance."

A phrase from the quartet in Act II, "Over the Dark Blue Waters," brings in the main section of the Overture (Allegro con fuoco, D major, 4/4). A second subject, in A major, announced by the clarinet, comes from the tenor aria, "From Boyhood Trained." Following that, the melody accompanying the soprano's words, "My husband, my love, we are saved, we are saved!" from her big scena "Ocean! Thou Mighty Monster," comes in as another quotation from the score. There is a development of the material presented, and this last theme dominates the brilliant coda.

R. C. B.

Overture to the Opera "Euryanthe"

AN ECCENTRIC bluestocking, Wilhelmine de Chézy, German wife of the French Orientalist and Sanskrit savant, was responsible for the gnarled libretto of Weber's *Euryanthe*. Largely because of this handicap, the opera is rarely revived, and the Overture alone persists as a repertory staple. *Rosamunde* was another of Frau de Chézy's dramatic confections. Of that magnum opus the title alone survives as a label for Franz Schubert's incidental music. Weber's pupil Julius Benedict described her as a "stout, elderly lady, with all the qualities of a real bluestocking, careless and slovenly in her appearance, not blessed with any earthly goods, but with a great deal of self-sufficiency."

We owe the Chézy libretto to an emergency and its quality probably to the scholarly atmosphere of the Chézy household. After the tumultuous success of *Der Freischütz* in Berlin and Vienna, Barbaja, the impresario of Vienna's Kärntnerthor Theater, commissioned Weber to write another opera. Weber had already sketched out a comic opera *The Three Pintos,* based on Seidel's novel *Der Brautkampf.* This was brushed aside as unsuitable, and composer and impresario cast about for a librettist. At the time, Frau de Chézy had chanced, in her erudite pursuits, upon the thirteenth-century French romance *L'Histoire de Gérard de Nevers et de la belle et vertueuse Euryanthe de Savoye, sa mie,* which had almost certainly been the source of Boccaccio's tale of the merchant Bernabo's wife (*Decameron,* second day, ninth novella). Her proposal of a libretto based on the legend was promptly accepted, and in due course she submitted the two acts to Weber. The score was ready in August, 1823, and the production came off at the Kärntnerthor on Oct. 25. Weber's music was generally praised, but the libretto stood in the way of the opera's ever occupying a steady place in the repertory.

Besides, the Viennese public had been enjoying a run of Rossini operas, and *Euryanthe* contrasted heavily with them. Complaints were made about its length, its puzzling story, its lack of dramatic impact. Even the music found dissidents. Schubert, who had been deeply stirred by *Der Freischütz,* was anything but won over by its successor. "This is no music," he objected. "There is no finale; no concerted piece according to the rules of art. It is all striving after effect. And he [Weber] finds fault with Rossini! It is utterly dry and dismal." In spite of which the hugely handicapped opera ran up a total of twenty performances that season, though it was many years before Vienna heard it again. Despite its difficulties, *Euryanthe* has been revived from time to time, especially in the German-speaking countries, and some outstanding names in the annals of singing and conducting have been associated with it. The eminent soprano Henriette Sontag created the role at the Kärntner-thor, when Weber himself conducted. Lilli Lehmann was the Euryanthe and Anton Seidl the conductor when the Metropolitan Opera Company first presented the work on Dec. 23, 1887. When the company last gave *Euryanthe,* during the season of 1914-1915, Arturo Toscanini led and Frieda Hempel had the title part.

In the Overture the first subject, announced after a fiery exordium, derives from Adolar's phrase in Act I, "Ich bau' auf Gott und meine Euryanth'." Adolar's "O Seligkeit, dich fass' ich kaum," in the second act, accounts for the lyric second theme, brought in by the first violins. The Largo passage offers an interlude in ghostly mystery before the brilliant development and coda.

The central idea in *Euryanthe* of betting on a wife's fidelity and then subjecting her to a severe test of virtue apparently goes back to early Greek balladry. The theme underwent multiple variations, in prose and poetry, in medieval literature, and after appearing in Boccaccio and ballad versions in many languages, it lapsed into disuse, only to reemerge in full Elizabethan splendor in the Posthumous-Iachimo wager in Shakespeare's *Cymbeline.*

L. B.

"Concertstück" for Piano and Orchestra in F minor, Op. 79

WEBER'S INITIAL sketches for this work were begun in 1815. For some unknown reason, however, he did not return to them until February, 1821, at Dresden. During the eventful days preceding the production of his opera *Der Freischütz* he labored feverishly to complete the *Concertstück* and, as it happened, he put the finishing touches to it on the very day of the opera's premiere in Berlin.

Before returning to Dresden, with the rhapsodic praise of *Der Freischütz* still ringing in his ears, he conceived the idea of playing the piano and orchestra piece at a farewell concert. Arrangements were made for the event, and it took place in the auditorium of the new theater on June 25, 1821. The *Concertstück,* according to an entry in Weber's diary, made an "enormous success." He played it again, four days later, at another concert, and the number was received (again referring to the diary) "with unbelievable applause."

The piece was published in 1823, with a dedication to Princess Marie Augusta of Saxony. Sir Julius Benedict, Weber's friend and pupil, is authority for the statement that the *Concertstück* is not abstract, but program music. In substantiation he submitted a plan alleged to have been followed by the composer:

The Châtelaine sits all alone on her balcony, gazing far away into the distance. Her knight has gone to the Holy Land. Years have passed by; battles have been fought. Is he still alive? Will she ever see him again? Her excited imagination calls up a vision of her husband lying wounded and forsaken on the battlefield. Can she not fly to him and die by his side. She falls back unconscious. But, Hark! What notes are those in the distance? Over there in the forest something flashes in the sunlight nearer and nearer. Knights and squires with the cross of the Crusaders, banners waving, acclamations of the people; and there—it is he. She sinks into his arms. Love is triumphant. Happiness without end. The very woods and waves sing the song of love; a thousand voices proclaim his victory.   R. C. B.

Jaromir Weinberger

BORN: PRAGUE, JAN. 8, 1896.

His music, which frequently employs folk song and folk-song idiom, carries on the tradition of Dvorak and Smetana.—Egon Wellesz.

Polka and Fugue from the Opera "Schwanda"

Coolly received at its world premiere in the Czech National Theater, Prague, Apr. 27, 1927, *Schwanda, the Bagpipe Player* later achieved a sensational popularity. Over 1,000 performances of the work have been given on more than one hundred stages, in fourteen languages. America first became acquainted with music from the opera when Albert Coates conducted the Overture, the Polka, and the Fugue at a Lewisohn Stadium concert in New York, on Aug. 4, 1930. The initial showing of the opera itself in this country took place at the Metropolitan Opera House, Nov. 7, 1931.

Schwanda, der Dudelsackpfeifer, in two acts and five tableaux, has a text in the Czech language by Milos Kares. Max Brod is responsible for the German version. The story, based on a Bohemian legend, may be outlined as follows:

The bold and, of course, notorious bandit Babinsky has eluded capture by hiding in the farmyard of Schwanda, the bagpiper. While there, he sees and falls in love with Schwanda's wife Dorota. But the bagpiper must be gotten out of the way, so Babinsky regales him with fantastic stories about Queen Ice-Heart's court, where Schwanda can earn fame and riches. Convinced, the bagpiper agrees to go with Babinsky to this fabulous place.

When they arrive, Schwanda begins to play and his music is of such potency that it immediately breaks the gloom which a sorcerer had wreaked on the entire court. The Queen is elated. She kisses Schwanda and, before he knows it, they are about to be married. However, Dorota appears on the scene and claims her man. Whereupon she orders Schwanda put to death.

Through Babinsky's maneuverings, though, Schwanda is saved, and the whole court again plunges into merrymaking on hearing his magical music. But Babinsky, a persevering villain, is still after Dorota. Comes a moment in the dialogue when, in answer to a question by Dorota, he works Schwanda into saying, "May the devil take me to hell on the spot, if the Queen kissed me." Thunder, lightning, the yawning earth, and Schwanda is swallowed up. When Babinsky is convinced that Dorota will never be his, he promises to reform and somehow bring Schwanda back to her.

So Babinsky has a game of cards with the devil, and he is lucky enough to win half the infernal kingdom from him. This brings about Schwanda's release from the lower regions and, as he is reunited with his wife, Babinsky fades out of the picture slowly and sadly.

Mr. Weinberger settled in New York City in 1939. Since that time he has composed also the *Variations and Fugue on Under the Spreading Chestnut Tree; The Legend of Sleepy Hollow; Two Poems by Edgar Allan Poe, The Devil in the Belfry* and *The Raven; Song of the High Seas,* and *Prelude and Fugue on "Dixie,"* and a *Lincoln Symphony.*

The composer has two operas to his credit, a pantomime, incidental music for Shakespeare's *The Tempest, A Winter's Tale, Romeo and Juliet,* and *Hamlet.* He had written, prior to taking up residence here, several other concert works.

Mr. Weinberger studied music first at Prague, with Kricka and Hoffmeister. He later joined Max Reger's Master Class at the Leipzig Conservatory. He first came to this country in 1922, when he took up duties as a teacher of composition and theory at Ithaca, N. Y. On his return to Czechoslovakia he became the Director of the Music School at Eger.

R. C. B.

Emerson Whithorne

BORN: CLEVELAND, OHIO, SEPT. 6, 1884.

He is rarely the realist, and while he uses polytonality on occasion, and never hesitates at invoking acrid dissonance to gain the effects he wants, he always seems more interested in an impressionism designed to produce atmosphere, rather than in any devices advanced for their own sake alone.—JOHN TASKER HOWARD.

Symphonic Poem, "The Dream Pedlar," Op. 50

SOME YEARS ago Mr. Whithorne was strolling along the left bank of the Seine in Paris. He walked up to a small huddle of people gathered around a pedlar. The man seemed to be offering an article for sale. The price was only a few sous. Suddenly, a quarrel arose. Sharp words of anger were flung at the little vendor. Abruptly the pedlar retorted: "I am only selling you blind ones a glorious sunset; look at it and be grateful that you have bought beauty at so small a price!"

It was this incident that inspired Mr. Whithorne to write his symphonic poem, *The Dream Pedlar*. The work was composed in 1930 and performed for the first time anywhere on Jan. 15, 1931, at a concert of the Los Angeles Philharmonic Orchestra, under the direction of Artur Rodzinski. A note in the score reveals that *The Dream Pedlar* was sketched in New York City between Mar. 13 and Apr. 12, 1930, and orchestrated in Dark Canyon, Hollywood, Calif., between July 9 and Aug. 7 of the following summer.

The composer has prefaced the score with the following statement:

The little pedlar of dreams plods along the highway of life. With a small bell in his cap, tinkling to the rhythm of his weary tread, he cries his wares as he goes. To you he sells the dream of beauty; to you, the dream of love; to you, the dream of conquest; and to you, the dream of vast power. So when you hear his tinkling bell and meet him on the highroad, stop and buy. For he is *The Dream Pedlar*— and what he sells may be of greater value than gold and precious stones.

He has also divulged a literary source of his symphonic score—the poem *Dream-Pedlary* of Thomas Lovell Beddoes (1803-1849):

> If there were dreams to sell,
>   What would you buy?
> Some cost a passing bell;
>   Some a light sigh,
> That shakes from Life's fresh crown

Only a rose-leaf down.
If there were dreams to sell,
Merry and sad to tell,
And the crier rang the bell,
　What would you buy?

A cottage lone and still,
　With bowers nigh,
Shadowy, my woes to still,
　Until I die.
Such pearl from Life's fresh crown
Fain would I shake me down.
Were dreams to have at will,
This would best heal my ill,
　This would I buy.

The music shows few formal patterns, being, rather, a fantasy in impressionistic imagery, richly suggestive in its symbolic coloring. Lawrence Gilman called it "luminous, full of pleasant sounds and fairy evocations."

Among Mr. Whithorne's scores are three symphonies, a *Poem* for piano and orchestra—showing a recurring interest in syncopated rhythms—a *Fata Morgana* for orchestra, chamber music, and music for ballets and plays.

Living in London between 1907 and 1915, Mr. Whithorne wrote music reviews for the *Pall Mall Gazette*. On his return to America he became associated with publishing houses, before deciding, in 1922, to turn all his energies to composing.

L. B.

Henri Wieniawski

BORN: LUBLIN, JULY 10, 1835. DIED: MOSCOW, APR. 2, 1880.

Impetuous, warm-hearted, witty, an excellent storyteller—such was the man and such were the qualities that shone through his performances. He has been accused of now and then overstepping the bounds of good music taste, and indeed his fiery temperament led him sometimes to a certain exaggeration, especially in quick movements, or to such errors as the introduction of an enlarged cadenza in Mendelssohn's concerto. But who would not forgive such pecadilloes to so rare and genuine a talent?—PAUL DAVID.

Concerto for Violin and Orchestra in D minor, No. 2, Op. 22

I. Allegro moderato. II. Romance: Andante non troppo. III. Allegro moderato—à la Zingara (in gypsy style).

IN CATALOGUING the benefactions of Nadejda von Meck, the name of Peter Ilyitch Tschaikowsky inevitably stands out. There were others, however, who benefited from the practical interest of this generous woman. One of them was Henri Wieniawski, the fiery Polish violinist, whose wondrous tone, prodigious skill, and warm temperament had placed him among the reigning virtuosos of his time. But that time had passed. Wieniawski's health was broken. In his last months, sick and helpless, he was stranded in Moscow; helpless, but for the comfort and aid of Mme. von Meck's charity. It was Tschaikowsky who penned the record of her good deed—the same Tschaikowsky who was to render her name immortal. "Your benevolence to poor, dying Henri Wieniawski touches me deeply," he wrote to her on Mar. 22, 1880. "I pity him greatly. In him we shall lose an incomparable violinist and a gifted composer." On Apr. 2—eleven days later—the "poor, dying Henri Wieniawski" was dead.

At the zenith of his power, Henri Wieniawski was one of the two most dazzling personalities of the magic bow. The other was Joseph Joachim. There is a touching story of friendship and fellowship related of these two virtuosos. Despite ill health, Wieniawski once gave a recital in Berlin. In the middle of a concerto the ailing violinist was stricken with a sudden spasm. Paralyzed by the pain, he stopped playing. Joachim, who was present, leaped from his seat and rushed to the side of his colleague. Assured that he was not in danger, he took up Wieniawski's violin and finished the program—"amid the enthusiastic applause of an audience delighted by so spontaneous an act of good fellowship."

Wieniawski wrote two violin concertos. The first, in F sharp minor, Op. 14, is a virtuoso's paradise, the work of a young paladin of the bow who glories in his stupendous skill. The second belongs to a later and emotionally richer period. The virtuosity remains, but there is more. "It shows the composer intended to write not merely a virtuoso composition for the violin, but to produce as well an interesting musical creation." Such was the verdict of Leopold Auer, who also suggested that the Concerto had been written under the influence of Gounod, Saint-Saëns, and even Lalo. When he made his statement, in the early 1920's, Auer felt that the success of the D minor Concerto could be compared only with that of Saint-Saëns' B minor and Lalo's *Symphonie Espagnole*—always excepting "the three violin super-concertos" of Beethoven, Mendelssohn, and Brahms.

The first two movements of the D minor Concerto are played without pause, the link being a twelve-bar clarinet solo. The first movement is marked Allegro moderato in D minor, 4/4, though Auer states that Wieniawski himself played it "more moderato than allegro." The main theme appears first in the orchestral passage that opens the movement. There a foreshadowing of the second subject may also be heard in a passage for horn. The solo violin then makes its first encounter with the main theme before turning to the second, in F major, against a background of cellos.

The second movement, a Romance marked Andante non troppo, B flat major, 12/8 grows out of the lyric subject given out by the solo violin. "It is a song to be sung in a way to make us forget the instrument," said Auer of this movement.

The finale returns to the Allegro moderato of the first movement—with a difference. The words *à la Zingara* (in gypsy style) are added, and the emphasis this time should be on the allegro rather than on the moderato, again according to Auer. The key is D minor, the time 2/4.

The movement opens with a cadenza for violin. Then the orchestra sounds a few measures and the violin is back with the chief theme of the movement. The orchestra reviews the theme before the violin again returns, this time with a restatement of the second melody of the first movement, now given in E flat major. Later the real second theme of the movement—a vigorous subject in G major—is given out by the violin in double notes, returning the same way toward the very end, where its key is now D major.

L. B.

Ermanno Wolf-Ferrari

BORN: VENICE, ITALY, JAN. 12, 1876.

As his name suggests, the composer is half German, half Italian. He is similarly divided in artistic loyalties: roughly, his heart is with the Italians, his head with the Germans—Italian melody and sparkle, German soundness and technique.—WALLACE BROCKWAY and HERBERT WEINSTOCK.

Overture to the Opera "The Secret of Suzanne"

WOLF-FERRARI's one-act opera *The Secret of Suzanne* follows the tradition of the operatic "intermezzo," which was a work given unfailingly with some other opera. In this respect it might be considered a contemporary *Serva Padrona.* Enrico Golisciani's libretto presents only three characters. Count Gil, baritone; Countess Gil or Suzanne, soprano; and an elderly servant, Sante. Of the trio only the Count and Countess have voice parts.

The story has to do with the Count's jealousy of his lovely wife. She has a secret—she smokes. Returning home unexpectedly, one day, he detects the odor of tobacco about the house and, naturally, suspects a lover. He berates Suzanne, who—after much excitement—quiets him down and persuades him to go to his club. The Count, however, is not to be turned aside so easily. He feigns departure, but in reality takes a position outside the window and spies. What he sees—Suzanne doing her very own smoking—is proof enough of her fidelity. So overjoyed is he that he reenters immediately and joins his wife in a few puffs of peace.

The Secret of Suzanne was first given at the Hofoper, Munich, on Nov. 4, 1909, in a German translation by Max Kalbeck. It was produced in Italian at the Metropolitan on Mar. 14, 1911, by the visiting Philadelphia-Chicago troupe, Mario Sammarco impersonating the Count, Caroline White the Countess, and Francesco Daddi the servant. The Metropolitan Opera Association gave it first on Nov. 27, 1912, with Antonio Scotti, Geraldine Farrar, and Angelo Bada. Later performances by the company offered either Frances Alda or Lucrezia Bori as the Countess, with Scotti again to supply the Count.

The brief Overture (Vivacissimo, D major, 4/4) presents the chief subject in the first violins and the wood winds. There is some development and a second subject appears by way of the flute and clarinet to string accompaniment. Both themes are joined in a contrapuntal exposition, which brings the Overture to a close.

R. C. B.

847

BIBLIOGRAPHY

The following books are listed both as sources of material quoted in this volume and as works recommended for consultation by the music-lover with the time to pursue his interest further. In almost all cases the quoted extracts had appeared regularly in the program-books of the New York Philharmonic-Symphony Society; and for their use there and in *The Concert Companion* the authors wish to express their deep-felt thanks to the publishers and authors concerned. This bibliography is in no sense complete as a list of recommended reading. Such a list would be endless, and Beethoven alone would easily occupy the space now allotted to this catalogue of indebtedness. For more extensive biographical and historical listings it is suggested that reference be made to *Grove's Dictionary* (Supplementary volume of 1940 included) and the late Oscar Thompson's *International Cyclopedia of Music and Musicians* (New York: Dodd, Mead & Co., 1943).

BIOGRAPHY

The Master Musicians, the new series of twenty volumes revised and edited by Eric Blom, London, J. M. Dent & Sons, Ltd.; New York, E. P. Dutton & Co., Inc., from 1934 on.

Lives of the Great Composers, edited by A. L. Bacharach, New York, E. P. Dutton & Co., Inc., 1936.

BACH

SCHWEITZER, ALBERT, *J. S. Bach,* translated by Ernest Newman, 2nd edition, London, A. & C. Black, Ltd., 1935.

SPITTA, PHILIPP, *Johann Sebastian Bach,* translated by Clara Bell and J. A. Fuller Maitland, London, Novello, 1898.

TERRY, C. SANDFORD, *Bach; a Biography,* Oxford University Press, 1928.

BEETHOVEN

BEKKER, PAUL, *Beethoven,* translated by M. M. Bozman, London, J. M. Dent & Sons, Ltd., 1925.

THAYER, A. W., *The Life of Ludwig van Beethoven,* Beethoven Association, New York, 1920.

BRAHMS

MAITLAND, J. A. FULLER, *Brahms,* London, Methuen & Co., 1911.

MAY, FLORENCE, *Life of Johannes Brahms,* London, Edward Arnold & Co., 1905.

DELIUS

FENBY, ERIC, *Delius as I Knew Him,* London, George Bell & Sons, Ltd., 1936.

DVǑRÁK

STEFAN, PAUL, *Dvořák,* translated by Y. W. Vance, New York, The Greystone Press, 1941.

HANDEL

FLOWER, NEWMAN, *Handel,* Cassell & Co., Ltd., London, 1922.

849

ROLLAND, ROMAIN, *Handel*, translated by A. Eaglefield Hull, Kegan Paul, Trench, Trubner & Co., London, 1916.

MAHLER

MAHLER, ALMA, *Memories and Letters*, New York, The Viking Press, Inc., 1946.

MOUSSORGSKY

RIESEMANN, OSKAR VON, *Moussorgsky*, translated by Paul England, Alfred A. Knopf, Inc., 1929.

MOZART

EINSTEIN, ALFRED, *Mozart: His Life and His Character*, New York, Oxford University Press, 1945.

HUSSEY, DYNELEY, *Mozart*, London, Kegan Paul, Trench, Trubner & Co., 1928.

JAHN, OTTO, *Mozart* (in German), revised by Hermann Abert, Leipzig, 1922.

WYZEMA, T. DE, and G. DE SAINT-FOIX, *W. A. Mozart*, Vols. I and II, Paris, 1912; Volume III, by de Wyzema alone, Paris, 1937.

RAVEL

GOSS, MADELEINE, *Bolero; The Life of Ravel*, Henry Holt and Co., 1940.

RIMSKY-KORSAKOFF

RIMSKY-KORSAKOFF, NIKOLAI ANDREYEVICH, *My Musical Life*, translated by Judah A. Joffe, New York, Alfred A. Knopf, Inc., 1923; revised edition, 1942.

ROSSINI

RADICIOTTI, GIUSEPPE, *Gioacchino Rossini*, Trivoli, 1923.

TOYE, FRANCIS, *Rossini; a Study in Tragi-Comedy*, London, William Heinemann Ltd., 1934.

SAINT-SAËNS

WATSON, LYLE, *Camille Saint-Saëns*, London, Kegan Paul, Trench, Trubner & Co., Ltd., 1923.

SCHUMANN

SCHAUFFLER, ROBERT HAVEN, *Florestan: The Life and Work of Robert Schumann*, New York, Henry Holt and Co., 1945.

STRAUSS

JACOB, H. E., *Johann Strauss, Father and Son*, translated by Marguerite Wolff, New York, The Greystone Press, 1940.

STRAVINSKY

STRAVINSKY, IGOR, *Chroniques de ma Vie*, Paris, 1935.

TSCHAIKOWSKY

NEWMARCH, ROSA, *Tschaikowsky*, New York, J. Lane, 1900.

TSCHAIKOWSKY, MODEST, *The Life and Letters of Peter Ilyitch Tschaikowsky*, edited by Rosa Newmarch, London, New York, J. Lane, 1906.

WEINSTOCK, HERBERT, *Tschaikowsky*, Alfred A. Knopf, Inc., 1943.

VERDI

TOYE, FRANCIS, *Giuseppe Verdi: His Life and Works*, London, 1931.

WAGNER

WAGNER, RICHARD, *My Life*, translated from the German, New York, Dodd, Mead & Co., 1911.

GENERAL

AUER, LEOPOLD, *Violin Masterworks and Their Interpretation*, New York, Carl Fischer, 1925.

BROCKWAY, WALLACE, and HERBERT WEIN-STOCK, *The Opera*, New York, Simon and Schuster, Inc., 1941.

CALVOCORESSI, M. D., and GERALD ABRAHAM, *Masters of Russian Music*, New York, Alfred A. Knopf, Inc., 1936.

CAMPOS, RUBEN M., *El Folklore y la Musica Mexicana*, Mexico, 1928.

COPLAND, AARON, *Our New Music*, New York, Whittlesey House (McGraw-Hill Book Co., Inc.), 1941.

CORTOT, ALFRED, *French Piano Music*, translated by Hilda Andrew, Oxford University Press, 1932.

EWEN, DAVID, *The Book of Modern Composers*, New York, Alfred A. Knopf, Inc., 1942.

EWEN, DAVID, *Composers of Today*, New York, The H. W. Wilson Co., 1934.

HOWARD, JOHN TASKER, *Our American Music*, New York, The Thomas Y. Crowell Co., 1946.

KELLY, MICHAEL, *Reminiscences*, London, 1826.

KIRSTEIN, LINCOLN, *Blast at Ballet*, New York, Kamin Publishers, 1939.

KOLODIN, IRVING, *The Metropolitan Opera —1883-1935*, New York, Oxford University Press, 1936.

MASON, DANIEL GREGORY, *From Grieg to Brahms*, New York, The Macmillan Co., 1902.

NEWMAN, ERNEST, *Stories of the Great Operas*, New York, Alfred A. Knopf, Inc., 1928-30.

Oxford History of Music: Volume III, *The Music of the 17th Century*, Oxford University Press, 1902.

PARRY, SIR CHARLES HUBERT, *The Evolution of the Art of Music*, New York, D. Appleton & Co., Inc., 1930.

TAYLOR, DEEMS, *Of Men and Music*, New York, Simon and Schuster, Inc., 1937.

TAYLOR, DEEMS, *The Well-Tempered Listener*, New York, Simon and Schuster, Inc., 1940.

THOMSON, VIRGIL, *The State of Music*, New York, William Morrow and Co., 1939.

TOOR, FRANCES, Editor, *Cancionero Mexicano*, Mexico, 1931.

TOVEY, DONALD FRANCIS, *Essays in Musical Analysis*, Volumes I to VI, Oxford University Press, 1935-1939.

UPTON, GEORGE P. and FELIX BOROWSKI, *Standard Opera and Concert Guide*, New York, Halcyon House.

VAN VECHTEN, CARL, *Music After the Great War*, New York, G. Schirmer, Inc., 1915.

VEINUS, ABRAHAM, *The Concerto*, New York, Doubleday & Co., Inc., 1944.

PROGRAM NOTES

PERIODICALS, CATALOGUES, SCORES, ETC.

Among the many magazines and newspapers from which useful information was extracted are *Musical America, Musical Courier, The Musical Quarterly, Modern Music, The Chesterian, The New York Times, The New York Herald-Tribune, The New York Sun,* and the *New York World-Telegram.* Magazines in French, Italian, German, Spanish, and Russian to which indebtedness is due are far too numerous to mention; but a special word of appreciation must be rendered to *Sovyetskaya Musika,* the Soviet periodical which in many cases has been the sole source of detailed information about living Russian composers. Alfred Einstein's monumental edition (1937) of the Mozart Catalogue has been invaluable, and so have been the various publications of Nicholas Slonimsky. The authors have already signified their debt to many early American annotators whose pioneer work has been a constant guide and inspiration to all subsequent workers in this field. A final offering of thanks is made to the combined staffs of the Music Division of the New York Public Library and the 58th Street Music Library for their indispensable help in providing music scores and books. To these must be added special mention of Howard Keresy, librarian of the New York Philharmonic-Symphony Society and the many members of the Philharmonic-Symphony office staff.

INDEX

A

ALBÉNIZ, ISAAC, [1-2]
"Fête-Dieu à Séville" from the Suite
Iberia, [1]

ARENSKY, ANTON STEPANOVICH, [3-4]
"Variations on a Theme by Tschai-
kowsky" (for String Orchestra),
Op. 35 A, [3]

B

BACH, CARL PHILIPP EMANUEL, [5-6]
Concerto for Stringed Instruments
in D major, [5]

BACH, JOHANN SEBASTIAN, [7-17]
Brandenburg Concerto in F major,
No. 2, for Solo Flute, Oboe,
Trumpet, Violin, and Orchestra,
[13]

"Chaconne," [8]

Chorale-Prelude, "Credo" ("Wir
glauben all' an einen Gott"),
[11]

Three Chorale-Preludes: "Nun
komm', der Heiden Heiland,"
"Meine Seele erhebt den Herren,"
"Wachet auf, ruft uns die
Stimme," [12]

"Passacaglia in C minor," [7]

Prelude and Fugue in B minor for
Organ, [11]

Suite No. 3, in D major, [15]

Toccata and Fugue in C major,
[16]

Toccata and Fugue in D minor,
[17]

BALAKIREFF, MILY ALEXEIEVITCH, [18]
"Islamey," Oriental Fantasy, [18]

BARBER, SAMUEL, [19-21]
"Symphony in One Movement,"
[19]

Adagio for String Orchestra, Op.
11, [20]

"Second Essay," [20]

BARTÓK, BÉLA, [22-25]
Concerto for Orchestra, [24]
Concerto for Two Pianos with Or-
chestral Accompaniment, [22]

BEETHOVEN, LUDWIG VAN, [26-73]
Symphonies
No. 1, C major, Op. 21, [26]
No. 2, D major, Op. 36, [29]
No. 3, E flat major, Op. 55
("Eroica"), [31]
No. 4, B flat major, Op. 60, [33]
No. 5, C minor, Op. 67, [36]
No. 6, F major, Op. 68 ("Pasto-
ral"), [39]
No. 7, A major, Op. 92, [41]
No. 8, F major, Op. 93, [44]
No. 9, D minor, Op. 125, [46]
Concertos
For Piano and Orchestra, C
major, No. 1, Op. 15, [52]
For Piano and Orchestra, C
minor, No. 3, Op. 37, [53]
For Piano and Orchestra, G
major, No. 4, Op. 58, [55]
For Piano and Orchestra, E flat
major, No. 5 ("Emperor"),
Op. 73, [57]

H

W

WAGNER, RICHARD, [812-829]

Overtures

"A Faust Overture," [828]

"The Flying Dutchman," [812]

"Tannhäuser," [814]

Selections from "Der Ring des Nibelungen," [819]

Entrance of the Gods into Valhalla from "Das Rheingold," [820]

Act III from "Die Walküre," [821]

"The Ride of the Valkyries," [821]

"Magic Fire Music," [822]

"Waldweben" ("Forest Murmurs") from "Siegfried," [823]

Funeral Music from "Götterdämmerung," [823]

Brünnhilde's Immolation from Götterdämmerung," [824]

Prelude to "Die Meistersinger," [816]

Preludes to Act I and III of "Lohengrin," [813]

Transformation Scene; Klingsor's Magic and Flower Maidens' Scene; Good Friday Spell, from "Parsifal," [826]

"A Siegfried Idyl," [824]

WAGNER, RICHARD (Cont.)

Bacchanale from "Tannhäuser," [815]

Prelude and "Love Death" from "Tristan und Isolde," [825]

WALTON, WILLIAM, [830-832]

Overture, "Portsmouth Point," [830]

"Scapino," A Comedy Overture, [831]

"WARLOCK, PETER" (Philip Heseltine), [833-834]

"Capriol Suite for Strings," [833]

WEBER, CARL MARIA VON, [835-840]

Overtures

"Der Freischütz," [836]

"Euryanthe," [838]

"Jubel" ("Jubilee"), [835]

"Oberon," [836]

"Concertstück" for Piano and Orchestra in F minor, Op. 79, [839]

WEINBERGER, JAROMIR, [841-842]

Polka and Fugue from the Opera "Schwanda," [841]

WHITHORNE, EMERSON, [843-844]

Symphonic Poem, "The Dream Pedlar," Op. 50, [843]

WIENIAWSKI, HENRI, [845-846]

Concerto for Violin and Orchestra in D minor, No. 2, Op. 22, [845]

WOLF-FERRARI, ERMANNO, [847]

Overture to the Opera "The Secret of Suzanne," [847]

333 7226